REGNUM EDINBURGH CENTENARY SERIES
Volume 35

# Ecumenical Missiology: Changing Landscapes and New Conceptions of Mission

Oxford: Regnum
and
Geneva: World Council of Churches

REGNUM EDINBURGH CENTENARY SERIES

The centenary of the World Missionary Conference of 1910, held in Edinburgh, was a suggestive moment for many people seeking direction for Christian mission in the 21st century. Several different constituencies within world Christianity held significant events around 2010. From 2005, an international group worked collaboratively to develop an intercontinental and multi-denominational project, known as Edinburgh 2010, based at New College, University of Edinburgh. This initiative brought together representatives of twenty different global Christian bodies, representing all major Christian denominations and confessions, and many different strands of mission and church life, to mark the centenary.

Essential to the work of the Edinburgh 1910 Conference, and of abiding value, were the findings of the eight think-tanks or 'commissions'. These inspired the idea of a new round of collaborative reflection on Christian mission – but now focused on nine themes identified as being key to mission in the 21st century. The study process was polycentric, open-ended, and as inclusive as possible of the different genders, regions of the world, and theological and confessional perspectives in today's church. It was overseen by the Study Process Monitoring Group: Miss Maria Aranzazu Aguado (Spain, The Vatican), Dr Daryl Balia (South Africa, Edinburgh 2010), Mrs Rosemary Dowsett (UK, World Evangelical Alliance), Dr Knud Jørgensen (Norway, Areopagos), Rev John Kafwanka (Zambia, Anglican Communion), Rev Dr Jooseop Keum (Korea, World Council of Churches), Dr Wonsuk Ma (Korea, Oxford Centre for Mission Studies), Rev Dr Kenneth R. Ross (UK, Church of Scotland), Dr Petros Vassiliadis (Greece, Aristotle University of Thessalonikki), and co-ordinated by Dr Kirsteen Kim (UK, Edinburgh 2010).

These publications reflect the ethos of Edinburgh 2010 and will make a significant contribution to ongoing studies in mission. It should be clear that material published in this series will inevitably reflect a diverse range of views and positions. These will not necessarily represent those of the series' editors or of the Edinburgh 2010 General Council, but in publishing them the leadership of Edinburgh 2010 hopes to encourage conversation between Christians and collaboration in mission. All the series' volumes are commended for study and reflection in both church and academy.

## Series Editors

| | |
|---|---|
| Knud Jørgensen | Areopagos, Norway, MF Norwegian School of Theology & the Lutheran School of Theology, Hong Kong. Former Chair of Edinburgh 2010 Study Process Monitoring Group |
| Kirsteen Kim | Leeds Trinity University and former Edinburgh 2010 Research Co-ordinator, UK |
| Wonsuk Ma | Oxford Centre for Mission Studies, Oxford, UK |
| Tony Gray | Words by Design, Bicester, UK |

REGNUM EDINBURGH CENTENARY SERIES
Volume 35

# Ecumenical Missiology: Changing Landscapes and New Conceptions of Mission

Edited by
Kenneth R. Ross, Jooseop Keum,
Kyriaki Avtzi and Roderick R. Hewitt

Oxford: Regnum
and
Geneva: World Council of Churches

First published 2016 by Regnum Books and the World Council of Churches
Regnum is an imprint of the Oxford Centre for Mission Studies
St Philip and St James Church
Woodstock Road
Oxford OX2 6HR, UK
www.ocms.ac.uk/regnum

WCC Publications, World Council of Churches
150 route de Ferney, P.O. Box 2100, 1211 Geneva 2, Switzerland
http://www.wcc-coe.org
09 08 07 06 05 04 03 7 6 5 4 3 2 1



**British Library Cataloguing in Publication Data**
A catalogue record for this book is available from the British Library

ISBN: 978-1-911372-02-8

Typeset by Words by Design
Printed and bound in Great Britain for Regnum Books International
by TJ International Ltd, Padstow, Cornwall

Front cover photo from World Council of Churches Photo Archive shows Filipino dancers at the WCC CWME Manila Conference in 2012
Back cover photo shows a scene from the Edinburgh 2010 conference.

The publication of this volume is made possible through the generous financial assistance of the World Council of Churches Commission on World Mission and Evangelism.

# CONTENTS

SECTION 2: CORE THEMES ACROSS A CENTURY

# ACKNOWLEDGEMENTS

A volume like this does not come into being without incurring many debts of gratitude. First of all, the book is the child of the World Council of Churches Commission on World Mission and Evangelism and profound thanks are due to its Commissioners and staff for their unstinting support and encouragement. It also forms part of the Regnum 'Edinburgh 2010' Series and it is fitting to record what a great pleasure it has been to work with the series editors Knud Jørgensen, Kirsteen Kim, Wonsuk Ma and Tony Gray as well as all the staff at Regnum. Likewise we are grateful to WCC Publications for co-publishing the volume, particularly for all the help and advice received from Michael West, WCC publisher.

We are, of course, hugely indebted to all the contributors to the book. Given the importance of timeously providing a textbook to support the study of *Together towards Life* throughout the world and the fact that the Edinburgh 2010 series draws to completion in 2016, we had to ask our contributors to do their work on unusually short deadlines. The spirit in which they accepted this challenge is one that helped us to understand that we are also part of the mission that is the subject of the book. We express particular appreciation also to Allie Schwaar, doctoral candidate at New College, University of Edinburgh, for her excellent work on the preparation of the bibliography.

From the beginning, the story told in this book has been a matter of people coming together for the sake of the mission of God. How grateful we are that this dynamic continues to unfold today in ways that are full of promise and fruitfulness. Our prayer is that this movement of mission will be served and strengthened by the present volume.

Kenneth R. Ross
Jooseop Keum
Kyriaki Avtzi
Roderick R. Hewitt

Pentecost 2016

# List of Abbreviations

| | |
|---|---|
| *AG* | *Ad Gentes* |
| *AIC* | African Independent Churches |
| *AD* | *Aparecida Document* |
| *CA* | *Centesimus Annus* |
| CELAM | Latin American Episcopal Conference |
| CWME | Commission on World Mission and Evangelism of the World Council of Churches |
| *DN* | *Doctrinal Note on Some Aspects of Evangelization* |
| *EA* | *Mission and Evangelism: An Ecumenical Affirmation* |
| *EN* | *Evangelii Nuntiandi* |
| *EG* | *Evangelii Gaudium* |
| *GS* | *Gaudium et Spes* |
| IMC | International Missionary Council |
| *LS* | *Laudato Si'* |
| *MEUT* | *Mission and Evangelism in Unity Today* |
| *RM* | *Redemptoris Missio* |
| *SC* | *Sacrosanctum Concilium* |
| *TTL* | *Together Towards Life: Mission and Evangelism in Changing Landscapes* |
| WCC | World Council of Churches |

# PREFACE

The Edinburgh 2010 Common Call emerged from the Edinburgh 2010 study process and conference marking the centenary of the World Missionary Conference, Edinburgh 1910. The Common Call, cited below, was affirmed in the Church of Scotland Assembly Hall in Edinburgh on 6 June 2010, by representatives of world Christianity, including Catholic, Orthodox, Evangelical, Pentecostal, and other major Protestant churches.

As we gather for the centenary of the World Missionary Conference of Edinburgh 1910, we believe the church, as a sign and symbol of the reign of God, is called to witness to Christ today by sharing in God's mission of love through the transforming power of the Holy Spirit.

*1. Trusting in the Triune God and with a renewed sense of urgency, we are called to incarnate and proclaim the good news of salvation, of forgiveness of sin, of life in abundance, and of liberation for all poor and oppressed. We are challenged to witness and evangelism in such a way that we are a living demonstration of the love, righteousness and justice that God intends for the whole world.*

*2. Remembering Christ's sacrifice on the Cross and his resurrection for the world's salvation, and empowered by the Holy Spirit, we are called to authentic dialogue, respectful engagement and humble witness among people of other faiths – and no faith – to the uniqueness of Christ. Our approach is marked with bold confidence in the gospel message; it builds friendship, seeks reconciliation and practises hospitality.*

*3. Knowing the Holy Spirit who blows over the world at will, reconnecting creation and bringing authentic life, we are called to become communities of compassion and healing, where young people are actively participating in mission, and women and men share power and responsibilities fairly, where there is a new zeal for justice, peace and the protection of the environment, and renewed liturgy reflecting the beauties of the Creator and creation.*

*4. Disturbed by the asymmetries and imbalances of power that divide and trouble us in church and world, we are called to repentance, to critical reflection on systems of power, and to accountable use of power structures. We are called to find practical ways to live as members of One Body in full awareness that God resists the proud, Christ welcomes and empowers the poor and afflicted, and the power of the Holy Spirit is manifested in our vulnerability.*

*5. Affirming the importance of the biblical foundations of our missional engagement and valuing the witness of the Apostles and martyrs, we are called to rejoice in the expressions of the gospel in many nations all over the world. We celebrate the renewal experienced through movements of migration and mission in all directions, the way all are equipped for mission by the gifts of the Holy Spirit, and God's continual calling of children and young people to further the gospel.*

*6. Recognising the need to shape a new generation of leaders with authenticity for mission in a world of diversities in the twenty-first century, we are called to work together in new forms of theological education. Because we are all made in the image of God, these will draw on one another's unique charisms, challenge each other to grow in faith and understanding, share resources equitably worldwide, involve the entire human being and the whole family of God, and respect the wisdom of our elders while also fostering the participation of children.*

*7. Hearing the call of Jesus to make disciples of all people – poor, wealthy, marginalised, ignored, powerful, living with disability, young, and old – we are called as communities of faith to mission from everywhere to everywhere. In joy we hear the call to receive from one another in our witness by word and action, in streets, fields, offices, homes, and schools, offering reconciliation, showing love, demonstrating grace and speaking out truth.*

*8. Recalling Christ, the host at the banquet, and committed to that unity for which he lived and prayed, we are called to ongoing co-operation, to deal with controversial issues and to work towards a common vision. We are challenged to welcome one another in our diversity, affirm our membership through baptism in the One Body of Christ, and recognise our need for mutuality, partnership, collaboration and networking in mission, so that the world might believe.*

*9. Remembering Jesus' way of witness and service, we believe we are called by God to follow this way joyfully, inspired, anointed, sent and empowered by the Holy Spirit, and nurtured by Christian disciplines in community. As we look to Christ's coming in glory and judgment, we experience his presence with us in the Holy Spirit, and we invite all to join with us as we participate in God's transforming and reconciling mission of love to the whole creation.*

## Themes Explored

The 2010 conference was shaped around the following nine study themes:

1. Foundations for mission
2. Christian mission among other faiths
3. Mission and post-modernities
4. Mission and power
5. Forms of missionary engagement
6. Theological education and formation
7. Christian communities in contemporary contexts
8. Mission and unity – ecclesiology and mission
9. Mission spirituality and authentic discipleship

### The Regnum Edinburgh Centenary Series to Date

Against this background a series of books was commissioned, with the intention of making a significant contribution to ongoing studies of mission. This series currently includes: [1]

*Edinburgh 2010: Mission Then and Now*, David A. Kerr and Kenneth R. Ross (eds).

*Edinburgh 2010 Volume II: Witnessing to Christ Today*, Daryl Balia and Kirsteen Kim (eds).

*Mission Continues: Global Impulses for the 21st Century*, Claudia Wahrisch-Oblau and Fidon Mwombeki (eds).

*Holistic Mission: God's Plan for God's People*, Brian Woolnough and Wonsuk Ma (eds).

*Mission Today and Tomorrow*, Kirsteen Kim and Andrew Anderson (eds).

*The Church Going Local: Mission and Globalization*, Tormod Engelsviken, Erling Lundeby and Dagfinn Solheim (eds).

*Evangelical and Frontier Mission: Perspectives on the Global Progress of the Gospel*, A. Scott Moreau and Beth Snodderly (eds).

*Interfaith Relations after One Hundred Years: Christian Mission among Other Faiths*, Marina Ngursangzeli Behera (ed).

*Witnessing to Christ in a Pluralistic Age: Christian Mission among Other Faiths*, Lalsangkima Pachuau and Knud Jørgensen (eds).

*Mission and Post Modernities*, Rolv Olsen (ed).

*A Learning Missional Church: Reflections from Young Missiologists*, Beate Fagerli, Knud Jørgensen, Rolv Olsen, Kari Storstein Haug and Knut Tveitereid (eds).

*Life-Widening Mission: Global Anglican Perspectives*, Cathy Ross (ed).

*Foundations for Mission*, Emma Wild-Wood and Peniel Rajkumar (eds).

*Mission Spirituality and Authentic Discipleship*, Wonsuk Ma and Kenneth R. Ross (eds).

*A Century of Catholic Missions*, Stephen Bevans (ed).

*Mission as Ministry of Reconciliation*, Robert Schreiter and Knud Jørgensen (eds).

*Orthodox Perspectives on Mission*, Petros Vassiliadis (ed).

*Bible in Mission,* Pauline Hoggarth, Fergus Macdonald, Knud Jørgensen and Bill Mitchell (eds).

*Pentecostal Mission and Global Christianity*, Wonsuk Ma, Veli-Matti Karkkainen and J. Kwabena Asamoah-Gyadu (eds).

*Engaging the World: Christian Communities in Contemporary Global Society*, Afe Adogame, Janice McLean and Anderson Jeremiah (eds).

*Mission At and From the Margins: Patterns, Protagonists and Perspectives*, Peniel Rajkumar, Joseph Dayam, I.P. Asheervadham (eds).

*The Lausanne Movement: A Range of Perspectives*, Margunn Serigstad Dahle, Lars Dahle and Knud Jørgensen (eds).

---

[1] For an up-to-date list and full publication details, see www.ocms.ac.uk/regnum/

*Global Diasporas and Mission*, Chandler H Im & Amos Yong (eds).
*Theology, Mission and Child: Global Perspectives*, B Prevette, K White, CR Velloso Ewell & DJ Konz (eds).
*Called to Unity for the Sake of Mission*, John Gibaut and Knud Jørgensen (eds).
*Korean Church, God's Mission, Global Christianity*, Wonsuk Ma and Kyo Seong Ahn (eds).
*Reflecting on and Equipping for Christian Mission*, Stephen Bevans, Teresa Chai, J. Nelson Jennings, Knud Jørgensen and Dietrich Werner (eds).
*Freedom of Belief and Christian Mission*, Hans Aage Gravaas, Christof Sauer, Tormod Engelsviken, Maqsood Kamil and Knud Jørgensen (eds).
*Creation Care in Christian Mission*, Kapya J Kaoma (ed).
*The Reschaping of Mission in Latin America*, Miguel Alvarez (ed).
*Witnessing to Christ in North East India*, Behera Marina (ed).
*Evangelism and Diakonia in Context*, R Dowsett, I Phiri, D Birdsall, DO Terfassa, H Yung and K Jørgensen (eds).
*Mission and Power: History, Relevance and Perils*, Atola Longkumer, Michael Biehl and Jorgen Skov-Sorenson (eds).
*Mission in Central and Eastern Europe*: Realities, Perspectives, Trends, Corneliu Constantineanu, Marcel V. Măcelaru, Anne-Marie Kool and Mihai Himcinschi (eds).

# FOREWORD

**Mission** and Ecumenism are the life lines of Church. As such, ecumenical missiology is an expression of these life lines in conceptual terms. It is no wonder, then, that ecumenical missiology today has become 'life'-centric. For instance, the World Council of Churches 2013 Busan Assembly focused on 'God of **Life**' and the new WCC Mission Statement is entitled 'Together Towards **Life**'. Ecumenical missiology has travelled quite far since Edinburgh 1910. It has undergone sweeping changes ever since. The accent on missiology has shifted away from colonial models to post-colonial paradigms; from classical modes to contextual modes; from monolithic, Eurocentric ways of thinking and doing mission to polyphonic expressions of missiology; from confessional slants to truly ecumenical perspectives; and from human centredness to life centric missiologies. The new Commission on World Mission and Evangelism book *Ecumenical Missiology: Changing Landscapes and New Conceptions of Mission*, among other things, provides a succinct yet comprehensive account of the history of ecumenical missiology since 1910, tracing various landscape shifts and missiological reflections during the last century.

There have been a wide range of themes within the broad spectrum of ecumenical missiology that the last century has addressed and pondered over through various world mission conferences and mission events. Section 2 of the book is a theological survey of the 'core themes across a century', the most significant missiological themes such as 'evangelism', 'church, mission and unity', 'worship', 'healing', 'culture', 'other faiths', 'formation', 'discipleship', 'partnership', 'contextualization', 'transformation', 'justice', 'margins', 'environment ', 'gender' and 'migration'. The thematic articulations have been efforts of the ecumenical movement to address mission concerns in ever-changing global landscapes.

The final section of the book concentrates specifically on the new WCC/CWME Mission Statement: *Together Towards Life: Mission and Evangelism in Changing Landscapes* (*TTL*). An edifying and enlightening discussion on *TTL* from various confessional, contextual and regional perspectives is provided in this section. The wide reception that *TTL* has received is indicative of the huge influence it has had on ecumenical mission thinking and praxis. The pneumatological mission paradigm, the Mission of the Holy Spirit, that *TTL* articulates within a comprehensive Trinitarian framework, provides fresh insights on transformative spirituality that is feminine/womanist, inter religious and earthly. The accent on mission as quest for justice and sharing in a world of gross injustice makes *TTL* one of the most prophetic texts ever on mission and evangelism. The ecological perspective where creation is treated as an agent of creation is not only ground breaking but also strikes chords with indigenous worldviews on creation. Perhaps what makes *TTL* most popular and controversial at the same time is its new concept of 'Mission from the Margins'. This indeed is a paradigm shift. After *Missio Dei* (Willingen, 1952), no other mission paradigm, in my view, has received such recognition and enjoyed such wide currency. 'Mission from the Margins' goes beyond the classical liberation theology on behalf of the marginalized in that the marginalized here assume agency and subjecthood of liberative mission. The 'epistemological privilege' of the marginalized provides them with a particular viewpoint that those at the centre are not able to see. In this sense 'Mission from the Margins' is a subaltern version of liberation missiology. 'Margins' here refers to the marginalized all over and also to the perspective of the Global South. *TTL* in general and 'Mission from the Margins' in particular will surely have wide and lasting influence on ecumenical missiology for a long time to come. Therefore, the final section where *TTL* is the focus, is of great relevance.

The new CWME anthology on mission entitled *Ecumenical Missiology: Changing Landscapes and New Conceptions of Mission* is a significant contribution in the arena of ecumenical missiology. Not only does it provide a historical overview of the theology of world mission since Edinburgh 1910 but also throws much light on various themes that the ecumenical mission movement has dealt with over a century. The book assumes great importance also because of it's last section which functions effectively as a commentary on *TTL*.

CWME is proud to present this new volume to the ecumenical movement. On behalf of the Commission, it is my privilege to thank Prof. Dr Kenneth R. Ross, the Rev. Dr Jooseop Keum, Ms Kyriaki Avtzi and Prof. Dr Roderick R. Hewitt for having edited this volume in an impressive manner. The Commission is particularly grateful to Dr Jooseop Keum, Director of CWME, for his excellent leadership and passionate commitment to the cause of world mission and evangelism. My hope and prayer is that the book will receive wide readership and exert great influence on churches, mission agencies and mission minded people across the globe.

*Metropolitan Geevarghese Coorilos*
*Moderator, Commission on World Mission and Evangelism,*
*World Council of Churches*

# EDITORIAL INTRODUCTION

The World Council of Churches 2012 mission affirmation is entitled *Together towards Life*. These three simple words capture the meaning of ecumenical missiology. It is a matter of coming *together*, across the fault-lines of geography, race, gender, politics, theology, ecclesiology and anything else that might divide those who confess Jesus as Lord. It is a matter of movement – '*towards*' – being on a journey rather than being static or complacent. It is a matter of *life* – reaching out to the reality of the world in the conviction that the last word is not one of death but rather of life. *Together towards Life* is the title of a 2012 document but it is also an apt description of a century-long quest by churches and mission agencies around the world to understand what is involved in their calling to bear witness to Christ.

This book has been prepared with acute awareness of how challenging it can be to comprehend the meaning of mission and to find direction for our own engagement in it – as individuals, churches, agencies or institutions. This is all the more so today as the managerial approach which prevailed at the height of the modern missionary movement has been found wanting. Mission today is conducted along lines that are 'unmanageable' and yet the challenge remains to understand its genius and meaning. As we wrestle in the early decades of the 21st century with the missional challenges of our time and situation, we have much to learn from those who met the challenges of their time and context in earlier years. By recalling how mission thinking responded to changing circumstances in the past, we can be better equipped to develop the fresh thinking about mission that will be required in the future.

Two milestone events in the history of Christian mission frame this volume. The first is the Edinburgh 1910 World Missionary Conference to which has been traced both the beginning of the modern ecumenical movement and the start of the systematic study of mission known as 'missiology'. The second is the adoption in 2012 of the World Council of Churches mission affirmation *Together towards Life*, a comprehensive statement on the meaning of mission that has been well received by a broad cross-section of world Christianity. Between the two lie one hundred years of constant engagement with the quest to understand the missionary impetus and the call to unity found at the heart of the Christian faith. The purpose of this book is to clarify the main lines along which this quest has been pursued and to assess the result of the one hundred years of reflection as it finds expression in *Together towards Life*.

The century-long process of reflection has unfolded against a backdrop of changing landscapes. Just four years after the epochal Edinburgh 1910 World Missionary Conference, the First World War broke out with the result that many of the presuppositions on which Edinburgh 1910 had worked were called into question. This proved to be a recurrent pattern as events such as the Second World War, the collapse of western colonial rule in much of Asia, Latin America and the Caribbean and Africa, the arms race, the Cold War, the advance of economic globalisation, the rise of China, and the increase in worldwide migration, provoked fundamental rethinking of the meaning of mission. Indeed, the post-war period has seen an acceleration in the speed with which the global landscape is being transformed. As a changing global context has challenged the churches to rethink their understanding of mission, so the 'landscape' of ecumenical missiology has also changed. As the practice of mission changed, so missiology was reshaped accordingly. Features that were prominent one hundred years ago have faded into the background while new features, unknown in 1910, have taken centre stage. It is this 'changing landscape' that the present volume seeks to survey.

The first section of the book allows those who shaped the understanding of mission across the century to speak for themselves. Assembled on its pages are extracts from the vast body of documents generated by the periodic global mission conference held under the auspices first of the International Missionary Council and then of the Commission on World Mission and Evangelism of the World Council of Churches (the form in which the life of the IMC continued after integration with the WCC in 1961). Brief explanatory introductions set these extracts in context and allow the reader to engage with the issues which gripped the imagination at the time and, in particular, to discern the changes in the landscape as these were brought into focus by the successive conferences.

The second section of the book surveys the same terrain as the first but uses a different frame of analysis. It identifies the key issues with which ecumenical missiology has been concerned across the century and examines them on a thematic basis. Scholars of mission seek to trace the decisive developments that have shaped the ecumenical understanding of each particular theme. They appraise the state of our understanding today and seek to discern where key challenges may lie for the future.

The third section is focused particularly on *Together towards Life* (*TTL*), the mission statement produced at the end of the 100-year span of ecumenical missiology. This section sets out the immediate background to the creation of the document and analyses it from a variety of confessional and geographical perspectives. This critical engagement with the text will be invaluable to anyone seeking to study *TTL*. More broadly, it draws together the threads of ecumenical mission thinking that have run through the century into consideration of a single comprehensive statement. Not that this is the end of the story – critical consideration of *TTL* reveals areas where further work is required, and a concluding chapter suggests where the challenges for ecumenical missiology might lie in the future.

Besides making a contribution to the comprehensive analysis of Christian mission attempted by the Regnum Edinburgh 2010 series, this book has the particular purpose of missional formation. It aims to be a tool that can be used at personal, congregational or institutional levels. Churches and church-related agencies for mission and development are invited to evaluate and rethink their mission policy in the light of the ecumenical journey that has led to *Together towards Life.* This will help to chart the new directions for mission required in changed landscapes. The book also aims to be a resource for education and formation. Engaging at depth with *Together towards Life*, and the century of ecumenical engagement that lies behind it, is an exercise that will immeasurably strengthen the leadership formation urgently required in many contexts today.

# SECTION ONE

# TRACING CHANGING LANDSCAPES AND NEW CONCEPTIONS OF MISSION

Compiled and introduced by Kenneth R. Ross

## Introduction

The 'ecumenical century' is widely acknowledged to have begun with the World Missionary Conference held at Edinburgh in 1910. However, scarcely had its Continuation Committee begun the task of implementing its vision when the First World War broke out. It soon became apparent that this shattering event had permanently altered the way the world was understood. Mission too would need a new interpretation. This turned out to be but the first of a series of episodes which changed the landscape in which people were living. Each called for a new conception of Christian mission.

This section will trace the changing landscapes across the century and discern the outlines of the new conceptions of mission which were formed in response. A primary frame of reference for this exercise will be the conferences which were held approximately every ten years by the International Missionary Council and, after that body's integration with the World Council of Churches in 1961, by the WCC Commission on World Mission and Evangelism. These conferences will be allowed to speak for themselves through extracts from their findings. Introduction and commentary will set them in context and make reference to leading figures and publications by which they were influenced. '(These primary texts are reproduced exactly as they originally appeared including, especially in the earlier years, expressions that display attitudes to such matters as race and gender that would not be acceptable today. Part of the observation of changing landscapes is to see how such attitudes changed in the course of the century.)

The purpose and importance of these world mission conferences is captured in a statement made by the first of them at Edinburgh in 1910: 'Assuredly, then, we are called to make new discoveries of the grace and power of God, for ourselves, for the Church, and for the world; and, in the strength of that firmer and bolder faith in Him, to face the new age and the new task with a new consecration.'[1] This is what succeeding generations have sought to do. As the landscape has changed, so understanding of mission has deepened and broadened. New discoveries of the grace and power of God have indeed been made. From these there is much to be learned as mission theologians and practitioners meet the challenges posed by the world of the 21st century.

---

[1] 'Message to Members of the Church in Christian Lands', World Missionary Conference, 1910, *The History and Records of the Conference* (Edinburgh and London: Oliphant, Anderson & Ferrier; New York, Chicago and Toronto: Fleming H. Revell, 1910), 109; cit. Wolfgang Günther, 'The History and Significance of World Mission Conferences in the 20th Century', in *International Review of Mission*, 92.367 (October 2003), 521-37, at 521.

# THE WORLD MISSIONARY CONFERENCE, EDINBURGH 1910 – A FOUNTAIN-HEAD

- Representative gathering of the entire Protestant missionary movement
- Christendom framework of the 'Christian World' and the 'Non-Christian World'
- Sense of opportunity and obligation to take the gospel to the whole world
- In-depth research, study and reflection informed the conference
- Divisive doctrinal and ecclesial issues excluded
- Greater co-operation and collaboration needed for the sake of effectiveness in mission
- Birth of the modern ecumenical movement

**The Nature and Purpose of 'Edinburgh 1910'**

From the mid-19th century the western Protestant missionary movement adopted the practice of holding a major international conference on a decennial basis. The World Missionary Conference, usually remembered as 'Edinburgh 1910', stood in this succession. It was distinguished, however, by the range of its participants, the breadth and depth of its enquiry, the scale of its ambition, the sense of urgency and opportunity with which it was imbued, and the magnitude of its historical legacy in mission and ecumenism. Its leaders were united in the conviction that they stood at a moment of unprecedented opportunity in terms of fulfilling the Church's task of taking the Christian message to the whole world. They were convinced that they had arrived at a moment when political, economic and religious factors had combined to create opportunities for worldwide missionary advance which, if not grasped now, might never recur. The conference therefore convened with a strong sense that it had a role to play in world evangelisation which would prove to be historic.

An informal alliance of British and American missionary societies, with support also from continental Europe, provided the leadership and organisation for the conference. The American Methodist layman, John R. Mott, well known as a leader of the Student Volunteer Movement and the Young Men's Christian Association, chaired the organising committee and the conference itself.[1] The secretary was a young man from Scotland, J.H.

---

[1] See C. Howard Hopkins, *John R. Mott 1865-1955: A Biography* (Geneva: WCC and Grand Rapids, MI: Eerdmans, 1979).

Oldham, a masterful thinker and organiser who would later become a major figure in the twentieth-century ecumenical movement.[2] The participants were drawn from the missionary societies and church mission boards of the western Protestant churches. Only agencies having missionaries in the foreign field and with foreign missions expenditure of at least £2,000 annually were invited to be represented, and they were entitled to an additional delegate for every additional £4,000 of foreign missionary expenditure.[3] On this basis 176 missionary societies and boards sent delegations – 59 from North America, 58 from continental Europe, 47 from the United Kingdom and 12 from South Africa and Australia. The delegates were overwhelmingly British and American – 509 from Britain, 491 from North America, 169 from continental Europe, 27 from the white colonies of South Africa and Australasia, and 19 from 'the younger churches' of India, China and Japan. Only one African attended and there were no delegates from Latin America, the Caribbean or the Pacific.

Complex ecclesiastical diplomacy lay behind the composition of the conference and the framing of its enquiry. A major objective of the organising committee was to secure the participation of the Anglo-Catholic or 'High Church' Anglican missionary societies – the Society for the Propagation of the Gospel and the Universities' Mission to Central Africa.[4] In order to do so, they had to concede that territories where Eastern Orthodox or Roman Catholic churches predominated should be regarded as already evangelised, not a view usually taken at that time by Evangelical Protestant missions. Hence Latin America, much of the Middle East and eastern Europe were effectively excluded from the consideration of the conference. Its discussion was framed around the 'Christian world' of western Europe and North America, and the 'Non-Christian world' of Africa, Asia and the Pacific. The question was how to take the gospel of Christ from the former to the latter. To further allay apprehensions among the societies and boards invited to participate, the International Committee agreed 'to confine the purview of the Conference to work of the kind in which all were united... No expression of opinion should be sought from the conference on any matter involving any ecclesiastical or doctrinal question on which those taking part in the conference differed among themselves'.[5] This meant that the conference was necessarily oriented to practical issues of method, administration and co-operation in missionary work.

---

[2] See Keith Clements, *Faith on the Frontier: A Life of J.H. Oldham* (Edinburgh: T. & T. Clark and Geneva: WCC, 1999).

[3] World Missionary Conference, 1910, *The History and Records of the Conference* (Edinburgh and London: Oliphant, Anderson & Ferrier; New York, Chicago and Toronto: Fleming H. Revell, 1910), 7.

[4] See Clements, *Faith on the Frontier*, 81-88.

[5] *History and Records*, 8.

A distinctive feature of Edinburgh 1910 was that it did not aim to be a rallying of the faithful supporters of the missionary movement. Whereas earlier gatherings had concentrated on a demonstration of enthusiasm, Edinburgh aimed to be a working conference, its subtitle being 'To consider Missionary Problems in relation to the Non-Christian World'. It was distinguished by its attempt to achieve a more unified strategy and greater co-ordination within the worldwide engagement of Christian mission. The aim of the organising committee was that it should be 'a united effort to subject the plans and methods of the whole missionary enterprise to searching investigation and to co-ordinate missionary experience from all parts of the world'.[6] It was driven by the belief that the missionary movement had arrived at a unique moment of opportunity. There was a great sense of urgency to the conference, prompted by a conviction that the opportunity could be lost if the right strategy were not formed and implemented. 'Never before,' stated its flagship text, 'has there been such a conjunction of crises and of opening of doors in all parts of the world as that which characterises the present decade.'[7] In the words with which Mott entitled the book he published soon after the conference, it appeared to be 'the decisive hour of Christian missions'.[8]

Much of the drive and inspiration of the conference derived from the delegates' realisation that their goal of world evangelisation was much more likely to be achieved if there were a greater degree of co-operation and collaboration among the western missionary agencies. The only formal resolution of the conference came on the report of its Commission on 'Cooperation and the Promotion of Unity'. The conference unanimously resolved that a Continuation Committee be formed, 'international and representative in character... to maintain in prominence the idea of the World Missionary Conference as means of co-ordinating missionary work, of laying sound lines for future development, and of evoking and claiming by corporate action fresh stores of spiritual force for the evangelisation of the world'.[9] The conference resulted in structures quite quickly being put in place to facilitate co-operation between missionary agencies.

Its significance, however, went much further. Though its terms of reference explicitly excluded consideration of divisive doctrinal and ecclesiastical questions, the Edinburgh Conference spawned an epoch-making vision of church unity. The Asian delegates, though few in number, were particularly influential in voicing an aspiration for greater church unity, drawing on movements in this direction which were already

---

[6] Cit. Clements, *Faith on the Frontier*, 77.

[7] World Missionary Conference, 1910, *Report of Commission I: Carrying the Gospel to all the Non-Christian World* (Edinburgh and London: Oliphant, Anderson & Ferrier; New York, Chicago and Toronto: Fleming H. Revell, 1910), 1.

[8] John R. Mott, *The Decisive Hour of Christian Missions* (New York: Student Volunteer Movement for Foreign Missions, 1912); cf *Carrying the Gospel*, 363.

[9] 'Minutes of the Conference', in *History and Records*, 95-96.

underway in their contexts. They in turn took fresh impetus from the dynamic of the conference. A direct line of continuity runs from the Edinburgh Conference to the formation of the Church of South India (1947), the Church of North India (1970), a single non-denominational Protestant Church in China (1951), and the United Church of Christ in Japan (1941).[10] Though the conference was an exclusively Protestant affair, there were moments when it looked to a wider church unity. Silas McBee, editor of The Churchman, read a letter from Bishop Bonomelli, the Roman Catholic Bishop of Cremona, in which the Bishop wrote that he recognised amongst the Edinburgh delegates elements of faith 'more than sufficient to constitute a common ground of agreement, and to afford a sound basis for further discussion, tending to promote the union of all believers in Christ'.[11]

Dr R. Wardlaw Thompson of the London Missionary Society told the conference: 'I long for the time when we shall see another Conference, and when men of the Greek Church and the Roman Church shall talk things over with us in the service of Christ.'[12] Thus the conference proved to be the widely acclaimed starting point of the twentieth-century ecumenical movement, with a direct line of continuity running through to the formation of the World Council of Churches in 1948. 'Edinburgh 1910,' wrote Hugh Martin, 'was in fact a fountain-head of international and inter-church co-operation on a depth and scale never before known.'[13]

Nonetheless, in many respects the expectations of Edinburgh 1910 were disappointed. The world was not evangelised in that generation. The gospel was not carried to the entire non-Christian world. Within a few years of the conference, the energies of the 'Christian world' would be consumed by a war more destructive than any experienced hitherto and a great deal of the worldwide evangelistic effort would be put on hold. Nor would this prove to be a temporary interruption. Edinburgh 1910, which understood itself to be on the brink of a great new surge of missionary advance, in fact proved to be the high point of the movement. Never again would the western Protestant missionary movement occupy centre-stage in the way that it felt it did at Edinburgh. For most of the mission boards and societies represented, the twentieth century would be one of remorseless decline in their operations. Today, moreover, the limitations of the conference's conceptual landscape are plain to see. The framework of thought, the categories of analysis and the forms of language are clearly outdated.

---

[10] See Brian Stanley, *The World Missionary Conference, Edinburgh 1910* (Grand Rapids, MI, and Cambridge, UK: Eerdmans, 2009), 310-12.

[11] World Missionary Conference, 1910, *Cooperation and the Promotion of Unity*, Report of Commission VIII (Edinburgh and London: Oliphant, Anderson & Ferrier; New York, Chicago and Toronto: Fleming H. Revell, 1910), 220-21.

[12] *Cooperation and the Promotion of Unity*, 216.

[13] Hugh Martin, *Beginning at Edinburgh: A Jubilee Assessment of the World Missionary Conference 1910* (London: Edinburgh House Press, 1960), 3.

However, the twentieth century has witnessed a vindication of a fundamental conviction of Edinburgh 1910: that the good news of Jesus Christ can take root in every culture across the world and produce fruit in Church and society everywhere. Edinburgh 1910 proved to be the first glimpse of what Archbishop of Canterbury William Temple would describe as 'the great new fact of our time' – a truly worldwide Christian Church.[14] The great drama of the coming century, in terms of church history, would be the growth of Christian faith in Asia, Africa, Oceania and Latin America. In some respects, this has surpassed even the most sanguine expectations of the 1910 conference. Since this epoch-making vision of the church as a truly global missionary community found its first concentrated expression at Edinburgh in 1910, the unique place of the conference in the history of Christianity is assured. However imperfect its conceptual equipment, the Edinburgh Conference, like no other, anticipated the transformation through which Christianity would become a truly worldwide faith. As Andrew Walls has written: 'The World Missionary Conference, Edinburgh 1910, has passed into Christian legend. It was a landmark in the history of mission; the starting point of the modern theology of mission; the high point of the modern western missionary movement and the point from which it declined; the launch-pad of the modern ecumenical movement; the point at which Christians first began to glimpse something of what a world church would be like.'[15]

This volume will follow the story of the International Missionary Council, the direct institutional outcome of Edinburgh 1910. It is important, however, to recognise that the conference also spawned two other strands of the modern ecumenical movement. The first is the Faith and Order movement which deliberately concentrated on the doctrinal and ecclesiological aspects of unity that had been excluded from the discussions of Edinburgh 1910.[16] The moving spirit in the inception of Faith and Order was Bishop Charles H. Brent who had been a delegate at the Edinburgh Conference and was profoundly affected by the experience. In his own words, he 'was converted. I learned that something was working that was not of man in that conference; that the Spirit of God... was preparing a new era in the history of Christianity'.[17] This new era, for Brent, would involve

---

[14] William Temple, *The Church Looks Forward* (London: Macmillan, 1944), 2-3.

[15] Andrew F. Walls, *The Cross-Cultural Process in Christian History: Studies in the Transmission and Appropriation of Faith* (Maryknoll, NY: Orbis Books, and Edinburgh: T. & T. Clark, 2002), 53.

[16] See Günther Gassmann, 'Faith and Order', in Nicholas Lossky, José Miguez Bonino, John S. Pobee, Tom F. Stransky, Geoffrey Wainwright and Pauline Webb, *Dictionary of the Ecumenical Movement* (Geneva: WCC and Grand Rapids, MI: Eerdmans, 1991), 411-13.

[17] Charles H. Brent, cit. W. Richey Hogg, *Ecumenical Foundations: A History of the International Missionary Council and its Nineteenth Century Background* (New York: Harper & Brothers, 1952), 134.

the pursuit of doctrinal unity and the bridging of the gulf between Protestant and Catholic Christianity. The second strand of modern ecumenism with roots in Edinburgh 1910 was the Life and Work movement which was concerned with the diaconal dimension of Christian witness.[18] It was inspired by the idea that 'doctrine divides while service unites'. J.H. Oldham, the secretary of Edinburgh 1910, also played a highly influential role in the emergence of the Life and Work movement in the 1920s and 1930s. The formation of the World Council of Churches in the mid-twentieth century was a matter of bringing together these three streams of ecumenical life that had flowed from Edinburgh 1910.

One feature which distinguished Edinburgh 1910 from earlier missionary conferences was the depth of the studies undertaken to prepare for it. Eight Commissions were established in July 1908, each focused on a topic deemed to be of great significance to the missionary movement. Each Commission was composed of a roughly equal number of British and Americans, with a sprinkling of continental Europeans. The membership struck a balance between leaders of the missionary movement and sympathetic scholars. Most of the Commissions used a questionnaire method to consult widely with missionaries in the field. Through a communication effort unprecedented in its scale and ambition, they gathered the accumulated wisdom of the missionary movement in relation to their assigned topics. In the course of this exercise, the Commissions carried out a vast amount of original research which brought unusual authority to their conclusions. Each Commission was given a day to present its report, and delegates had the opportunity to respond with what were then considered very short speeches – maximum seven minutes. The final published versions of the Commission reports include the speeches made by way of response at the conference itself. It is these eight volumes that constitute the documentary outcome of Edinburgh 1910 and from which the following extracts have been culled.

## Commission One: Carrying the Gospel to all the Non-Christian World

This was the flagship Commission of the Edinburgh 1910 Conference. Its title, 'Carrying the Gospel to all the Non-Christian World', represented the primary focus of the conference. The missionary task was conceived as the 'occupation' of the vast regions of the world from which Christianity was, at the beginning of the twentieth century, still absent. [19] The Commission's Report was to be read in conjunction with the *Statistical Atlas of Christian Mission*, prepared in New York and New Haven. This included a directory

---

[18] Paul Abrecht, 'Life and Work', in Lossky et al., *Dictionary of the Ecumenical Movement,* 612-14.

[19] *Carrying the Gospel*, 58.

of Protestant missionary societies, statistics on the history of the missionary movement, maps of the distribution of Protestant mission throughout the world, and an index of mission stations 'occupied' by foreign missionaries.[20] Information about Roman Catholic and Orthodox missions was also included in a separate section of the Atlas.

The entire document exudes an optimistic sense of momentous opportunity. Communications, railway lines, treaties and trade made the non-Christian world accessible to the 'carrying of the Gospel' as never before. Though the phrase was studiously avoided, much of the tenor of the report reflects a passion for 'the evangelisation of the world in this generation'.[21] This was the watchword which Mott had popularised in his capacity as General Secretary of the World Student Christian Federation. It was, however, not unchallenged in the work of the Commission. An alternative view was stated most succinctly, not in the Report itself, but in an appended letter from Gustav Warneck, the pioneer of mission studies in Germany, who was not present at the conference itself. Addressing himself to Mott, he argued that 'a predilection for the watchword "the occupation of the whole world in this present generation"... can easily miss the most hopeful opportunities'.[22] These lay, in his view, in strengthening local churches. He argued: 'The great lesson which the foreign missionary enterprise of our time has to learn from the history of the expansion of Christianity during the first three centuries is that the principal strength of missions lies in the native congregations... We are at present in that stage of modern missions when the watchword must be the self-propagation of Christianity.[23] The relationship of foreign missions and native churches, and the relative value of each in the missionary enterprise was an issue held in tension throughout the work of Commission One. Another tension revolved around the question of whether it was preferable to aim for the conversion of individuals or communities.

## Commission One Report

### *The Present Possibility of Carrying the Gospel to all the Non-Christian World*

When in the history of our religion has the Christian Church been confronted with such a wide opportunity as the one now before her in the non-Christian world as a whole? As always, opportunity spells

---

[20] World Missionary Conference, 1910, *Statistical Atlas of Christian Missions* (Edinburgh: World Missionary Conference, 1910).

[21] See John R. Mott, *The Evangelization of the World in This Generation* (London: Student Volunteer Missionary Union, 1900).

[22] *Carrying the Gospel*, 435.

[23] *Carrying the Gospel*, 434.

responsibility, and this unparalleled openness comes to us as a great test and trial of the reality and living strength of our faith, and of our capacity for comprehensive Christian statesmanship and generalship.

It is possible today as never before to have a campaign adequate to carry the Gospel to all the Non-Christian world *so far as the Christian Church is concerned.* Its resources are more than adequate. There are tens of millions of communicant members. The money power in the hands of believing Christians of our generation is enormous. There are many strong missionary societies and boards in Europe, America, Australasia and South Africa, and they have accumulated a vast fund of experience, and have developed a great variety of helpful methods and facilities through generations of activity throughout the world. Surely they possess directive energy amply sufficient to conceive, plan and execute a campaign literally worldwide in its scope? The extent, character and promise of the native Christian Church make it by no means an inefficient part of the Body of Christ.

Attention should be called to the abounding energy and tremendous possibilities of the inspiring movements recently called into being to facilitate the realisation of the aims of the missionary propaganda; for example, the Student Volunteer Movement; the more comprehensive World Student Christian Federation; the Foreign Departments of the Young Men's and Young Women's Christian Associations; the Young People's Missionary Movement; the Laymen's Missionary Movement; and the efficient women's missionary societies; the various Forward Movements within different Christian communions; the army of youth in the Sunday Schools, and various young people's societies and guilds. The Holy Spirit has certainly been preparing and marshalling the forces for a campaign commensurate with the missionary responsibility of the Church. Above all these are the superhuman resources: the dynamic power of the Gospel of Christ; the unrealised possibilities of intercession; the triumphant power of holy lives – lives unreservedly yielded to the sway of the risen Christ; and the presence of Christ Himself in His Church by His Spirit, the One who is able to subdue all things unto Himself. Thus, as the followers of Christ look outward over the great areas of the non-Christian world, and then turn to survey the resources of Christendom, and to gaze by faith upon their superhuman resources, can they question the possibility today of making Christ known to all people?[24]

### *The Urgency in View of Present Tendencies and Movements in the Non-Christian Religions*

The non-Christian religions are losing their hold on certain classes. Missionaries who have been on the field from twenty to forty years bear

---

[24] *Carrying the Gospel*, 10-11.

testimony that the influence of the non-Christian religions, especially over the educated classes, is waning, whether they contrast the power of these religions today with what it was a generation ago, or whether they contrast the place and influence of these religions with that of Christianity.[25]

### *The Urgency in View of the Plastic Condition of Non-Christian Nations*

The Asiatic peoples, following the leadership of Japan, have awakened from their long sleep. Through the whole of Asia a ferment is in process which has spread from the intellectual leaders and is fast taking possession of the masses of the people themselves. It affects over three-fourths of the human race, including peoples of high intelligence and ancient civilisation. The leaders are concerned with the question of enlightenment, of intellectual and social freedom, of economic development, and of national efficiency. In all history there has not been a period when such multitudes of people were in the midst of such stupendous changes, social, commercial, industrial, educational and religious.[26]

### *Making Christ Known: Fundamental Requirements*

There must be united planning and concerted effort on the part of the missionary forces of the Church. We fall back frankly in front of this task if it must be faced by a divided Christendom. We approach it with calmness and confidence if the true disciples of Jesus Christ stand together as members of a common family. It is our deep conviction that a well considered plan of co-operation in the missionary work of the Societies represented in this hall, entered into and carried out with a sense of our oneness in Christ, would be more than equivalent to doubling the present missionary staff.

The great task of making Christ known to all mankind will not be achieved without a great enlargement of the evangelistic forces of the Churches on the mission fields themselves. The evangelisation of the world as we have come to see it increasingly, is not chiefly a European and American enterprise, but an Asiatic and African enterprise. Whatever can be done should be done which will result in still further developing the power of initiative, of aggressive evangelism, and of self-denying missionary outreach on the part of the Christians of Asia and Africa, and in raising up an army of well qualified native evangelists and leaders.

The most crucial problem in relation to evangelising the world is the state of the Church in the Christian countries. The missionary enterprise after all is the projection abroad of the Church at home. At this time of the shrinkage of the world, the closeness of that relationship is startlingly close.

---

[25] *Carrying the Gospel*, 11.

[26] *Carrying the Gospel*, 25.

We are frank to concede that it is futile to talk about making Christ known to the world in this generation or any generation unless there be a great expansion of vitality in the members of the Churches of Christendom.[27]

Beyond doubt the most fundamental requirement of the missionary enterprise is a greater appropriation of the power of the Spirit of God. Important as are those aspects of the undertaking which deal with the statistics, the machinery and the strategy of missions, the leaders of the movement should concern themselves far more with the spiritual dynamics of missions. All workers in foreign missions should seek a fresh and constant realisation of the truth that they are fellow-workers with God.[28]

## Commission Two: The Church on the Mission Field

As was already apparent from passing allusion in Commission One, the question of 'the Church on the mission field' was both an energising and a challenging theme for the conference. On the one hand, it was a measure of the achievement of the missionary movement that indigenous churches were emerging throughout Asia and Africa in areas where Christianity had been unknown until the arrival of western missionaries during the nineteenth century. On the other hand, the vitality and growing confidence of these emergent churches posed the question as to what would be their relationship to the 'mother' churches to whose missionary work they owed their origins. To critics, both at the conference itself and subsequently, the celebration of the emergence of 'the Church on the mission field' was not combined with trust and confidence in its capacity to take the initiative in the organisation of church life and witness. Despite giving recognition to the missionary initiative and potential of 'the Church on the mission field', the Report does not examine this in any detail. It concentrates instead on ecclesial issues of constitution and membership, on the edification and education of its members, the training and employment of workers, the character and spiritual fruitfulness of Christian life, and the need for Christian literature and theology that will support the development of these 'younger churches' into full maturity.

The Commission chairman, John Campbell Gibson, had an intimate knowledge of the Church in China, having served in southern China since 1874 under the auspices of the English Presbyterian Mission. It was, however, the representatives of 'the Church on the mission field' who offered the most telling remarks. Taking up the Commission's metaphor of choice which likened the relationship of missions and churches to that of parent and child, V.S. Azariah of India trenchantly observed that 'we have

---

[27] *Carrying the Gospel*, 404-05.

[28] *Carrying the Gospel*, 370.

a new generation of Christians who do not wish to be treated as children'.[29] The Chinese delegate, Cheng Ching Yi, looked to a day when the tensions evident at the conference would be transcended and it would be recognised that 'all Churches of Christ are dependent first upon God and then upon each other'.[30] Such a vision was little developed in the Commission's Report. Nonetheless, it proved to be a suggestive document as it looked to the day when a framework of 'mission' and 'church' would be obsolete.

## Commission Two Report

### *Significance of the Church on the Mission Field*

It is perhaps one of the most encouraging signs, both of the progress of mission work itself, and of the advance which has been made in the thought of the Church at home with regard to it, that 'The Church on the Mission Field' now occupies so prominent a position in the discussion of mission questions and methods.[31]

What we desire to concentrate the mind of the Conference upon is this view, not details of polity and organisation, but the fact that questions of polity and organisation are impressing themselves upon the minds of Christian folk all over the world in the mission field, and that is an epoch-making fact. That is to say, you recognise that the Church on the Mission Field is a sphere of labour in which you are no longer dealing with little scattered companies of unimportant people, converts under the wing and under the charge of a missionary; it is now a complex body, which has in some countries already attained, and in others is fast attaining, a high degree of organisation and corporate life. The point on which we desire to fix your attention is this great view of the corporate life of the young Church in the Mission Field, because the recognition of this fact we consider to be of vital importance in the conduct of all foreign mission work. You have now what we begin to call not a little but a great Church in the Mission Field.

We have now to think of the Church on the mission field not as a by-product of mission work, but as itself by far the most efficient element in the Christian propaganda. The words of Christian people, spoken to their own countrymen in all lands, are the most efficient, as well as the most

---

29 V.S. Azariah, 'The Problem of Cooperation between Foreign and Native Workers', *History and Records*, 306-15.

30 World Missionary Conference, 1910, *The Church in the Mission Field*, Report of Commission II (Edinburgh and London: Oliphant, Anderson & Ferrier; New York, Chicago and Toronto: Fleming H. Revell, 1910), 352.

31 *The Church in the Mission Field*, 2.

extensive, preaching of the Gospel, and their lives are everywhere the most conspicuous and conclusive evidence of its truth.[32]

It should be remembered, however, that that our use of the phrase 'mission field' is inexact. The whole world is the mission field, and there is no Church that is not a Church in the mission field. Some Christian communities are younger and some are older, but that is all the difference. The Commission has perforce accepted the popular but inexact usage of calling only those regions 'the mission field' where the Church has been more recently planted, and where its history falls, roughly speaking, within the last two centuries.[33]

The Church on which we report presents itself no longer as an inspiring but distant ideal, nor even as a tender plant or a young child, appealing to our compassion and nurturing care. We see it now as an actual Church in being, strongly rooted, and fruitful in many lands. The child has, in many places, reached, and in others is fast reaching, maturity; and is now both fitted and willing, perhaps in a few cases too eager, to take upon itself its full burden of responsibility and service.

For these reasons we lay emphasis on the questions of organisation, Church membership, discipline and edification, the training and employment of workers, the development of the new life within the Church in character and spiritual fruitfulness, and its deepening and strengthening by means of an adequate Christian literature in all its departments.[34]

### *The Extent of the Church on the Mission Field*

Perhaps the simplest and yet most impressive way of realising the wide fellowship in worship and service of the Church of God, is to take into account what happens week by week in the course of the Lord's Day. The day first dawns about sunset on our Saturday, in longitude 180 degrees east of Greenwich, and the first inhabited country where the day's call to worship is heard and answered is in the Fiji Islands, in the heart of the Pacific. The period is not very remote when these islands were typical of the darkest depths of heathenism; now the Fijian Church leads the world in worship on the Lord's Day.

It is followed in New Zealand by the Christian section of the remnant of the Maori race, and next come the worshipping thousands of the aborigines of Australia, in Christian fellowship with as many Polynesian labourers from their island homes, and Christian immigrants from the ancient seats of their race. Close upon these follow the Christians of New Guinea, gathered out of a wild and savage race, and won at a heavy cost of precious life by Europeans and Polynesian fellow-labourers.

---

[32] *The Church in the Mission Field,* 2.
[33] *The Church in the Mission Field,* 4.
[34] *The Church in the Mission Field,* 3.

From New Guinea the day passes with hardly an interval to Japan, where a vivid contrast is presented. Here the Christian Church is found, not amongst barbarous tribes, but in the midst of an ancient civilisation. In Japan too, the opposition to the entrance of the Gospel was fierce and long continued, being unhappily intensified, in the time of the earlier Roman missions, by the political complications into which the missions were drawn. Now we can rejoice over hundreds of thousands of Christian worshippers, who have made the name of Christ to be known and honoured throughout this reconstructed Empire, and are bearing a worthy part in working out the great future of their race.

One hour later the Church of Manchuria begins its worship; and here we find a Christian community which has passed through fire and water, repeatedly scattered and broken up by war and persecution, and coming out of these sufferings to enter almost at once into a movement of spiritual revival of strange power. Almost contemporaneous with the worship, of Manchuria is that of the Korean Churches. It has been gathered in a field long closed against the Gospel and its whole history falls within the lifetime of one generation. Next in order of time come the worshippers of the Philippine Islands, and with these is associated an old and interesting Christian community in the Moluccas and the Celebes Islands.

In close succession to the Philippines comes Borneo, with its contingents of Christian Dyaks, Malays and Chinese; and the rich island of Java, where, too, a worshipping Church is found, though feeble as yet, amid the millions not yet evangelised.

Long before the day has traversed the length of Java it has begun in China and Formosa,[35] and over a vast territory are scattered congregations which – to speak only of those represented at the Shanghai Conference – number at least 200,000 communicant members and a Christian community of one million souls. A little earlier than Java, the day has begun in Mongolia, but although evangelistic journeys have been made in its wide territory, Mongolia is still silent, and its scattered population takes no part in the day's service of Christian worship.

With China may be associated Siam,[36] the Malay Peninsula and Sumatra, closely followed by Burma and Assam, where multitudes of souls continue the strains of Christian worship.

But in these longitudes, too, occur the great blank spaces of Tibet and Turkestan, in which as yet scarcely a single voice of Christian worship is found. Immediately on Burma follows the great Christian Church of India and Ceylon, whose yearly increase is more than four times as rapid as that of the total population, and which is rapidly gathering into Christian fellowship even the long despised pariahs of the South.

---

[35] Now Taiwan.

[36] Now Thailand.

As the day passes over the western frontier of India, it enters the small but solid blocks of untouched ground in Baluchistan and Afghanistan. For them apparently the time of evangelistic effort and triumph has not yet begun.

Immediately in their rear comes the old kingdom of Persia, with its great history of literary and political glory, where only a small proportion of its interesting people acknowledge Christ as Lord; while in Arabia also another name has usurped the place due to His alone, and a few of the 'desert rangers' yet bow the knee to Him.

Passing over Arabia, the day almost immediately enters upon Africa, one of the wildest and most varied of all the mission fields. The old tradition that Africa was the home of wonders has been fully maintained in the history of the Church, both in the islands of its eastern coast, and within the borders of the continent itself.

First on the eastern threshold the martyr Church of Madagascar hails the return of the Lord's Day. But the Church, planted at many points with untold labour and sacrifice, maintains across the intervals, through Livingstonia[37] and Uganda to Congoland and Old Calabar,[38] the far-reaching succession of Christian worship, and hands on the day of rest from the Indian Ocean to the Atlantic, its day of worship coinciding with that of the old Mother Churches of Europe.

Greenland in the far north, with its Christian Church, fills up the interval between Africa and Europe on the east of the Atlantic, and the Americas on the west. So by Eskimos and Aleutians and American Indians, by Christian negroes in the West Indies and the United States, and by Patagonians in the farthest south, joining with all the American Churches, the strain of worship is continued unbroken, till finally, when the day has completed its long circuit, it ends, as it began, in the Pacific Ocean, and the last lingering worshippers in the worldwide House of God are the Christian people of Samoa and the Friendly Islands.[39] It is these simple people of the Islands – savages a century ago – who first greet the Lord's Day with their songs of praise, and it is they who close it with their lingering prayers.

It is inspiring to reflect how the younger Christian communities make good the lack of service of the older, and the older join with the younger, so that throughout the Lord's Day, from the rising of the sun to the going down of it, incense and a pure offering ascends unceasingly to God, land answering to land as each in turn takes up the chorus.[40]

---

[37] A mission station of the United Free Church of Scotland in northern Malawi.

[38] A town and mission centre of the United Free Church of Scotland in eastern Nigeria.

[39] Now Tonga.

[40] *The Church in the Mission Field,* 6-9.

## Commission Three: Education in Relation to the Christianisation of National Life

Almost universally, education was seen as integral to the missionary task. The particular line of enquiry assigned to Commission Three was based on a broad view of the purpose of missionary education which saw it as leavening, like yeast, the entire life of each nation with Christian beliefs and values. In tension with such a view was a more church-centred approach which put the priority on the formation of leadership for the emerging indigenous churches. Both perspectives were accommodated within the Report with the balance of emphasis falling more to the latter. The Report also acknowledged the directly evangelistic role of education which was emphasised by many of the missionary correspondents.

Framed by an Introduction and Conclusion, the Report consists of nine chapters: the initial five are regional surveys, summarising the responses of missionaries in India, China, Japan, Africa and 'Muhammedan lands in the Near East' to the Commission's questionnaire; the final three chapters deal with thematic issues centring upon on training – both industrial and educational – and literature. Between the two parts of the Report, Chapter Seven, entitled 'The Relating of Christian Truth to Indigenous Thought and Feeling', comprised the heart of the enquiry. The Report is inspired by a vision of indigenous Christianity, coming to expression under the guidance of national leaders, educated and trained in their own vernacular. The catholicity of the Church could come to full expression, argued the Report, only when the faith was appropriated by each nation in terms which were true to its own particular character.

The veteran Scottish educational missionary, William Miller, Principal of Madras Christian College from 1877 to 1907, was unable to attend the conference on account of old age and infirmity but he circulated a paper which robustly defended the diffusionist strategy which had marked the contribution of Scottish Colleges of higher education in India since their beginnings under the influence of Alexander Duff from the 1830s.[41] While Commission Chairman Charles Gore accorded great respect to the argument advanced by Miller, he made it clear that it was not one which the Commission could accept. The education and formation of leaders for the emerging indigenous churches took priority, in the estimation of the Commission, over the diffusion of Christian values and principles throughout the wider society.

---

[41]'Extracts from Pamphlet by Dr Miller of Madras, circulated among delegates attending the Conference', World Missionary Conference, 1910, *Education in Relation to the Christianisation of National Life,* Report of Commission III (Edinburgh and London: Oliphant, Anderson and Ferrier; New York, Chicago and Toronto: Fleming H. Revell, 1910), 441-46.

## Commission Three Report

The subject of education in missionary work is of special and far-reaching importance. No one, who knows the history of missions, can doubt that missionaries were pioneers of education wherever they went, and it is hardly possible to exaggerate the debt of gratitude which is due to them for their labours in education, nor can it be doubted how important a part education has played in the process of evangelisation. At the same time, education, as pursued under missionary auspices, has exhibited certain weaknesses in its methods, and is exposed to certain perils.[42]

1. There has been a tendency, especially in certain lands and districts, to denationalise converts, that is, to alienate them from the life and sympathies of their fellow-countrymen, so as to make it possible to suggest that Christianity is a foreign influence, tending to alienate its converts from the national life.

2. Missionary education, as carried out during the last fifty years under the influence of English-speaking missionaries, naturally shared the weakness of their educational methods at home. It has become a commonplace that much of our education in the home-lands has been futile, because it is not sufficiently been a training for life. It is coming to be recognised among us that education needs to be directed far more consciously and deliberately towards preparing boys and girls for domestic and social life and service; that it ought to be a training and stimulating of the whole nature of the child, and not merely or chiefly the imparting of information, or an appeal to the memory.

3. There has been an astonishing awakening of national consciousness among the peoples of all the regions we are specially considering. In some countries, as in Japan and China, this national consciousness has shown itself in the development of national systems of education under Government auspices. In other countries, those under English Government, the English authority has thrown itself vigorously into the development of educational policy, and there has resulted an immense extension of educational effort under Government control with the resources of Government behind it. There has arisen hence a peril that missionary education, having much smaller resources at its command, should come to be of an inferior character, and should fall out of the main stream of educational progress.

4. If the native Churches are to become independent, self-governing Churches, it is a matter of chief importance that leaders should be provided and trained.

5. It is necessary to reconsider the question of the whole training of missionaries, and to enquire whether the missionary staff should not be enriched in every country, and for every denomination of Christians, with a much larger supply of properly equipped and trained teachers.

---

[42] *Education in Relation to the Christianisation of National Life,* 6.

6. If missionary education is not, in its plant and equipment, to fall behind the education conducted under Government auspices, there is need of much fuller co-operation between the different Christian bodies.[43]

### *The Importance of Seeking to Develop an Indigenous Christianity*

Though the original home of Christianity is, as it were, the half-way house between East and West, the modern missionaries have represented strongly defined or intensely western forms of Christianity. There has thus been a gulf, very difficult to bridge, between the whole mental equipment of the modern – especially the Anglo-Saxon – missionary and the people of the East. And on the whole it must be said that, though there have been among the missionaries men of great genius, as well as great zeal, yet singularly little attention was paid by the pioneers, and even until today, on the whole, singularly little attention has been paid to presenting Christianity in the form best suited to the Oriental spirit.[44]

The aim of Christian missionaries should be not to transplant to the country in which they labour that form or type of Christianity which is prevalent in the lands from which they have come, but to lodge in the hearts of the people the fundamental truths of Christianity, in the confidence that these are fitted for all nations and classes, and will bear their own appropriate and beneficent fruits in a type of Christian life and institution consonant with the genius of each of the several nations.

The modern missionary enterprise is wholly right in its increasing tendency to avoid attacking needlessly the ethical systems current amongst the people for whom it labours, and instead to commend and conserve all that is good in their thought and practice. It is thus best prepared to add to this good the higher and larger truths which Christianity has to present. If in some respects the practice of the non-Christian peoples is better than that which is common among Christian nations, this also should be freely, even if sadly, confessed.[45]

We are convinced that, though foreign evangelists should study to present Christianity in the form best suited to its appropriation by orientals, yet the work of 'acclimatising' will be done in the main by native teachers; and from this point of view we desire to urge not only, as we have already done in other connections, that the training of native pastors and teachers is the pre-eminently important work of Christian missions, but also that profound study and attention should be given to the point of how they are to be trained, so that their training may not tend to denationalise them or to

[43] *Education in Relation to the Christianisation of National Life,* 6-8.
[44] *Education in Relation to the Christianisation of National Life,* 245.
[45] *Education in Relation to the Christianisation of National Life,* 264.

occupy their minds with distinctively western elements and controversies of religion.[46]

In particular, we desire to lay the greatest emphasis on the importance of giving religious teaching, not only of the elementary kind, but as far as possible throughout, in the vernacular. We feel certain that those of our witnesses are right who believe that religion can only really be acclimatised in the heart of the natives of any country if it finds expression in their native language – the language of their homes. And we feel sure that a theology, which is really indigenous as well as properly Christian and Biblical, must develop a native terminology, an end which is only likely to be attained where the vernacular is used for the expression of religious ideas. Again, we are sure that the greatest pains must be taken as far as possible to use all that is available in the literature of the nation to provide preparation for a distinctively Christian learning and literature, and it must never be left out of sight that an indigenous Christian Church means a native Christian literature by competent native writers. We cannot conceal from ourselves that a quite fresh effort seems to be required in this, the primary task of the evangelist, namely, the raising up of properly equipped and instructed native Churches and of native leaders who shall have not temptation to feel that they are alienated from the life and aspiration of their nation in becoming Christians.'[47]

### *A Vision of Truly National Churches*

A universal religion, a catholic religion, needs a common message such as is contained in the Apostles' Creed, and as is recorded in the Bible, but a common message comprehended by very different and various peoples and individuals, each with very different gifts, so that each in receiving the one message, brings out some different or special aspect of the universal truth or character which lies in the common religion. So it is, and only so, that the glory and honour of all nations are brought within the light and circle of the Holy City; so it is alone that the real breadth and catholicity of life is brought out.

We look around, we see the profound and wonderful qualities of the Indian and the Chinese, and the Japanese and the Africans, and we are sure that when the whole witness of Christianity is borne, when Christ is fulfilled in all men, each of these races and nations must have brought out into the world a Christianity with its own indigenous colour and character, and that the rising up of any really national Church will be to us, who remain, who were there before, life from the dead. We regard this question as central. We start from this. Are we by means of education, training truly national Churches to stand each on its own basis, and bring out that aspect

---

[46] *Education in Relation to the Christianisation of National Life,* 265-66.
[47] *Education in Relation to the Christianisation of National Life,* 373.

of Christian truth and grace which it is the special province of each separate race to bring out?'[48]

**Commission Four:**
**The Missionary Message in relation to Non-Christian Religions**

This was the most strikingly original of all the Commission Reports and the one which attracts the greatest interest today, described by Kenneth Cracknell as 'one of the great turning points in the Christian theology of religion'.[49] It is remarkable for the degree to which it scotches the idea that western missionaries were iconoclasts bent on the eradication of existing religions in order to impose their own understanding of Christianity. On the contrary, the Report consistently argues that the appropriate attitude of the Christian missionary to the non-Christian religions is one of sympathetic understanding. Decisive for the innovative and ground-breaking work of the Commission was the choice of the Chairman. Mott and Oldham opted not for a recognised missionary leader but for the Professor of Systematic Theology at the United Free Church College in Aberdeen, David Cairns. As Cracknell observes: 'The choice of a theologian suggests already that Mott and Oldham were looking for something more than a competent survey of the world's religions.'[50]

The guiding theology of the Report is attributable primarily to the work of two missionaries of the London Missionary Society: T.E. Slater and J.N. Farquhar, the latter described by Andrew Walls as 'the most considerable Indologist produced by the missionary movement'.[51] Anticipating his soon-to-be-published and highly influential work, The Crown of Hinduism,[52] Farquhar's extensive response to the questionnaire developed the idea of fulfilment which saw Hinduism as India's Old Testament which prepared the way for the coming of Christ and found its fulfilment in Him. This allowed him both to engage Hinduism with deep understanding and profound sympathy, and to regard it as being fulfilled and therefore superseded by the coming of Christ. As he would conclude his magnum opus: 'In [Jesus Christ] is focused every ray of light that shines in Hinduism. He is the Crown of the faith in India.'[53] The Commission applied the paradigm of fulfilment to other non-Christian religions also. This allowed it to recognise their positive features, such as the civic and moral order of Confucianism, or Buddhism's detachment from material

---

[48] *Education in Relation to the Christianisation of National Life,* 406-07.
[49] Kenneth Cracknell, *Justice, Courtesy and Love: Theologians and Missionaries Encountering World Religions 1846-1914* (London: Epworth Press, 1995), xi.
[50] *Justice, Courtesy and Love,* 187.
[51] A.F. Walls, 'Farquhar, John Nicol', in Nigel M. de S. Cameron (ed), *Dictionary of Scottish Church History and Theology* (Edinburgh: T. & T. Clark, 1993), 315.
[52] J.N. Farquhar, *The Crown of Hinduism* (London: OUP, 1913).
[53] Farquhar, *The Crown of Hinduism*, 458.

desire. Islam was the religion which was hardest to accommodate in this paradigm. The Commission made the case for an irenic Christian encounter with non-Christian religions which would present the gospel as the fulfilment of their own inner hopes and yearnings. The 'schoolmaster to Christ' replaced the 'soldier of the cross' as the guiding metaphor for the missionary in the theology of Commission Four. Nonetheless, particularly through the influence of the Madras-based Scottish missionary A.G. Hogg, the supremacy of the Christian revelation and its unique redemptive power were unambiguously stated in its conclusions.[54]

## Commission Four Report

### *Main Conclusions*

1) We are all agreed that Christianity is the final and absolute religion. We believe this on what we were convinced were adequate grounds before we compared Christianity with the other religions of the world. The effect of that comparison has been to confirm and solidify this conviction. And it is precisely because we hold this conviction that we believe we dare take the most generous and fearless attitude towards all the other religions. We thought it best to compare the best in each pagan religion with the best in Christianity. Just because we hold so firmly to the finality and absoluteness of the Christian faith, we dare go further than any other religion dare go, in laying down our goods for comparison with any other goods in the world.

2) After all, the question that is before us is not whether we believe that Christianity is the final and absolute religion, but how are we going to get the world to believe it. The question is not whether we are prepared to call Christianity supreme, but how we are really going to make it supreme, and how get it accepted as such by all the world. That is the second conviction, not on what ground do we believe that Christianity is the final and absolute religion, but how may we induce religious men on the other side of the world to share our conviction?

3) The third point is the point of the reaction of the contact of Christianity with the non-Christian religions and peoples, not upon Christianity, but upon our apprehension and conceptions of Christianity. No one of us believes that we have the whole of Christian truth. If we believed that we had the whole of this truth, that would be the surrender of our conviction that Christianity is the final and absolute religion. How is it possible for us in a small fragment of the long corporate experience of humanity, a few races in a mere generation of time, to claim that we have gathered all the truth of the inexhaustible religion into our own personal comprehension and experience? We know that we have not, by reason of

[54] See further, Stanley, *The World Missionary Conference*, 222-27.

the primary and fundamental conviction we hold of the value of Christianity. We see this also as we lay Christianity over against the non-Christian religions of the world. We discover, as we do so, truths in Christianity which we had not discerned before, or truths in a glory, in a magnitude, that we had not before imagined. We begin to see that only a Christianity understood by universal application to known life can avail to meet the needs of human life in any community or nation. Only a Gospel that is laid down upon all the life of man will enable it to deal with any of the problems of mankind. These problems are in their sense universal problems, and they can never be dealt with until we deal with them with a Gospel understood from its world application and known as a comprehensive world power.

4) Not only is it necessary that we should have a world-conquering gospel, a gospel understood by applying it to all the life of man in order to deal with our problems in the world anywhere, but we need an immense deepening and quickening of the Christian life at home. We can carry no message save the message that we have and we come here upon the great need of the missionary enterprise today. Our appeal has been not that we should seek in the non-Christian religions for truths which are not in Christianity, but that we should seek in Christ the truth which we have not yet known, and the power which we have not yet experienced, but which is there for the Church in all the fullness of God in the day of her faith and obedience.[55]

### *The Attitude of the Missionary*

Does the evidence not disclose that we are face to face today with a new and formidable situation which is too great for our traditional thoughts of God? We seem to be looking into the great workshop of history. We discern the forces at work which make nations and make religions. We see the clash of the great historic religions; we see the forming of a new world. Something very vast, something very formidable, something very full of promise and wonder is there if we have the eyes to see it. But inevitably the question arises, Whether the Church has within itself, resident within it, the forces to meet this great emergency? Is it equal to the providential calling? Here is the very heart of the whole matter, the one great question of destiny.

Do we not need the broadening and deepening of all our conceptions of the living God, the deepening and liberating of all our thoughts of what He has done for us in Christ, of what by His Providence and His Spirit He is ready to do for us in this day of destiny and of trial? Do we not above all other things need the intensifying of the sense of the living God? For us this can only mean a new discovery of God in Christ. It is this motive which has

---

[55] *The Missionary Message,* 324-26.

set us on our quest, this search for the hidden riches of God in Him. We are persuaded that in the religions of the world we have the utterance of human need and that the answer to that long need and prayer of humanity is found in the Lord Jesus Christ and His Spirit.[56]

The true attitude of the Christian missionary to the non-Christian religions should be one of true understanding and, as far as possible, of sympathy. That there are elements in all these religions which lie outside the possibility of sympathy is, of course, recognised, and that in some forms of religion the evil is appalling is also clear. But nothing is more remarkable than the agreement that the true method is that of knowledge and charity, that the missionary should seek for the nobler elements in the non-Christian religions and use them as steps to higher things, that in fact all these religions without exception disclose elemental needs of the human soul which Christianity alone can satisfy, and that in their higher forms they plainly manifest the working of the Spirit of God. On all hands, the merely iconoclastic attitude is condemned as radically unwise and unjust.

But along with this generous recognition of all that is true and good in these religions, there goes also the universal and emphatic witness to the absoluteness of the Christian faith. Superficial criticism might say that these two attitudes are incompatible, that if Christianity alone is true and final, all other religions must be false, and that as falsehoods they should be denounced as such. Deeper consideration of the facts leads us to the conviction that it is precisely because of the strength of their conviction as to the absoluteness of Christianity that our correspondents find it possible to take this more generous view of the non-Christian religions. They know that in Christ they have what meets the whole range of human need, and therefore they value all that reveals that need, however imperfect the revelation may be. One massive conviction animates the whole evidence that Jesus Christ fulfils and supersedes all other religions, and that the day is approaching when to Him every knee shall bow and every tongue confess that He is Lord to the glory of God the Father.[57]

The spectacle of the advance of the Christian Church along many lines of action to the conquest of the five great religions of the modern world is one of singular interest and grandeur. But at least as remarkable as that spectacle of the outward advance of the Church is that which has also been revealed to us of the inward transformations that are in process in the mind of the missionary, the changes of perspective, the softening of wrong antagonisms, the centralising and deepening of faith in the Lord Jesus Christ, the growth of the spirit of love to the brethren and to the world. Once again the Church is facing its duty, and therefore once more the ancient guiding fires begin to burn and shine.[58]

---

[56] *The Missionary Message,* 294.
[57] *The Missionary Message,* 267-68.
[58] *The Missionary Message,* 273-74.

## Commission Five:
## The Preparation of Missionaries

Training for missionary service is the subject with which Commission Five was concerned. Chairman of the Commission was Professor Douglas Mackenzie – born of Scottish missionary parents in South Africa, Edinburgh-educated, Professor of Systematic Theology in Chicago, and from 1904 the President of Hartford Seminary Foundation which was already pioneering the professional training of missionaries in the United States, combining theological and regional studies with character formation. The Commission gathered evidence from the United States, Britain, Germany and Scandinavia, and from a wide cross-section of missionaries. It brought to the conference the conviction that the quality of the missionary was the decisive factor in the achievement of world evangelisation. As Douglas Mackenzie expressed it: 'The whole matter on the human side of it hinges on the quality of the missionary... The quality of the missionary will triumph over the absence of money. The quality of the missionary therefore becomes a supreme question for this Conference.'[59]

Like the conference as a whole, the Commission was deeply impressed by the fact that the financial and human resources urgently needed on the mission field were available within 'the home church'. It sought to make the case that these resources needed to be mobilised for world mission as never before. Another recurrent theme was the observation that the level of co-operation which was being achieved on the mission field was often eluding missionary societies in their home countries. Missionary training was seen as an area which cried out for a higher degree of co-operation. The Commission is notable for the attention which it paid to the training of women missionaries. Their role was understood to extend far beyond 'women's work for women' towards the fulfilment of a vision of women building up the entire fabric of national life. In terms of training inspired by this wide-ranging vision, the example cited was the Women's Missionary College in Edinburgh whose Principal, Annie Small, was one of the four women Commissioners. An Appendix to the Report describes the philosophy of the College.[60]

---

[59] World Missionary Conference, 1910, *The Preparation of Missionaries*, Report of Commission V (Edinburgh and London: Oliphant, Anderson & Ferrier; New York, Chicago and Toronto: Fleming H. Revell, 1910), 300.

[60] *The Preparation of Missionaries*, 250-52.

## Commission Five Report

### *General Features of All Missionary Training*

The spiritual or essentially Christian part is that by which the soul, drawn out of itself, lives in God – in the first place, by love for Him, which is its central principle; secondly, by faith in Him which is the basis of all Christian work; thirdly, by hope in Him, as the End of all activity. All these are ways in which God rather than self becomes the actual centre of life. For that very reason they are purely the gift of God. No act of the self can win them, and it follows that no training can give them, though it may remove some obstacles in the way of their development.

There are, besides, special considerations which have to be taken into account in the spiritual training of a missionary. He has to be ready in case of necessity to face the tremendous spiritual dangers of isolation among heathen surroundings. He must know how to face great strain and heavy responsibility without the support of visible Christian fellowship, and to maintain a high level of spiritual life without the continual renewing which is supplied under normal conditions by the ordinances of common worship.[61]

A missionary more than most men has the need and opportunity of cherishing all his life long the peculiar grace that belongs to a teachable spirit. Any course of preparation which fails to produce in the missionary candidate the humility and the hopefulness of the patient learner, has failed at the foundation. It has failed to impart the right personal attitude.[62]

The question of manner presents peculiar difficulties. The white man so instinctively feels that he is the lord of creation, that it is hard for him, no matter how Christian he may be, to get over the idea that men of a different colour are his inferiors. He is apt to be brusque and peremptory. He is always in a hurry and impatient of delays. His very kindness is apt to have an element of condescension, of which he may not be conscious but which the native is quick to detect. Blunders of tact may be almost as serious as want of sympathy. It is difficult, but at the same time most important, always to remember that no man who cannot control his temper can hope to exert spiritual influence in the mission field.[63]

A missionary is powerless to help a people whom he cannot love. All preparation, therefore, which has for its aim the development of a power of mutual understanding between ourselves and all with whom we come in contact, the quickening of our perception of the good points in our neighbours and associates which comes from the determination to look always for the Christ in every man, is directly missionary preparation. It

---

[61] *The Preparation of Missionaries*, 100.
[62] *The Preparation of Missionaries*, 101-02.
[63] *The Preparation of Missionaries*, 103.

must tend to build up a habit of generous appreciation both of the glories of ancient civilisation and of the childlike and, therefore, Christ-like elements in the character of the backward races. It will deepen reverence for all things reverent and honour for all things honourable, without blinding the eyes to the evil that must be eradicated. It will make it possible, when the time comes for a genuine identification of interests, to exhibit a love even for a strange people which shall be over-mastering, unfeigned and personal.[64]

### *Women's Share in Christian Missions*

No thoughtful student of the missions of the Christian Church will deny the supreme importance of women's share in them. Women must be missionaries if it were only that they may testify to gracious uplifting love of their Lord, if it were only that the long chain of courageous, patient, loving missionaries may be unbroken. But there is far more than the historic call. A vast proportion of any population would have to be left without the message, if there were no women to present it. The Christian life would be very partially manifested if the womanly characteristics were absent from a missionary settlement. The Christian Church, the Christian nation, might indeed be organised but could not be built up apart from the education and training of the womanhood of each community into Christian ideals of wifehood, motherhood, leadership; and this only Christian women can supply. And if it be remembered that the wives and mothers of one generation are the true moral founders of the whole community of the next, it must be acknowledged that the character and preparation of the women who are to be commissioned to train them are matters of the gravest consideration.[65]

### *Proposals for the Establishment of Central Institutions*

The evidence laid before the Commission has shown that there is a practically unanimous recognition of the need for more specialised preparation of missionaries for their work and for their particular mission field. The preparation is taken to include (1) a literary and scientific study of languages, (2) a knowledge of the religious history and sociology of special races, (3) acquaintance with the general principles and laws of missionary enterprise and method. It is equally clear that the necessity cannot be adequately met by existing institutions, or by Societies separately. The co-operation of Missionary Societies is essential, and it is a hopeful and guiding sign that while the necessity of which we speak is recognised on every hand, there have been very numerous and spontaneous

---

[64] *The Preparation of Missionaries*, 104.
[65] *The Preparation of Missionaries*, 147.

indications of a desire for co-operation on the part of experienced representatives of many Societies and Churches.[66]

## Commission Six: The Home Base

Fundamental to the conceptual framework of the conference was the understanding that there was a 'home base' in western Europe and North America and a 'mission field' in Asia and Africa. The task of Commission Six was to examine the means by which the 'church at home' might adequately discharge its responsibility for the evangelisation of the world. It thus addressed one of the primary concerns of the conference: that the churches of the western world might step up their commitment to foreign mission in order to exploit the unique moment of opportunity which now presented itself. James Levi Barton, from the United States, chaired Commission Six. The Commission's espousal of a highly managerial approach makes it a very American report in its provenance, principles and prognoses. As David Dawson has commented, 'pragmatism reigned'.[67] Nonetheless, the Commission is marked by an acute awareness of the spiritual dimension of the missionary movement and the need for renewed vigour at the spiritual level.

The titles of its eighteen chapters indicate that the subject was understood as 'scientific'. not merely practical: 'missionary intelligence' and 'the science of missionary societies' are the terms that define the opening and concluding chapters of the Report, setting out the conceptual framework in which issues of missionary recruitment, funding, home leadership and administration are discussed. 'The science of the home base' and 'the science of the operation of Missionary Societies' were to be understood as essential to the science of missions as a whole – a science yet in its infancy, to which the Report aspired to make a formative contribution, as demonstrated by the inclusion of an extensive bibliography of missionary publications.[68] The hope of the Commission was that a more sophisticated and comprehensive understanding of mission would translate into increased active support among the 'home churches'. The Report recognised the growing contribution of women to mission, both in the home churches and overseas. However, its influential recommendation that, in the interests of efficiency, separate women's missionary organisations should be integrated into the mainstream (male-run) organisations has been

[66] *The Preparation of Missionaries*, 181.

[67] David G. Dawson, 'The Church and the Edinburgh Missionary Conference', in *Missiology: An International Review*, Vol. XXXIX No. 2 (April 2011), 168.

[68] See World Missionary Conference, *The Home Base of Missions*, Report of Commission VI (Edinburgh and London: Oliphant, Anderson & Ferrier; New York, Chicago and Toronto: Fleming H. Revell, 1910), 333-558.

criticised for stifling women's initiative and leadership in overseas mission.[69]

## Commission Six Report

### *The Spiritual Resources of the Church*

In dealing with the Home Base of Missions, the Commission is concerned with the whole subject of the means by which the Church at home may adequately discharge its responsibility for the evangelisation of the world. It is evident that this problem is not one of machinery, but of life. The mere multiplication of machinery does not necessarily increase power. The subject which has been entrusted to the Commission to investigate drives us back at every turn to the question of the spiritual condition of the home Church. Has that Church sufficient vitality for the tremendous task to which it is called? Wherever a belief is intensely and passionately held, it naturally and inevitably propagates itself. It does not need wealth or numbers to cause it to spread. Repeatedly in history one man with a conviction has been more powerful than a mighty host. The Christian Church, if it were possessed, mastered, and dominated by the faith which it professes, could easily evangelise the world. When, therefore, we direct our attention to the Home Base of Missions, we realise that the fundamental problem is that of the depth and sincerity of the religious experience of the Church, the quality of its obedience, the intensity and daring of its faith.[70]

Any view of the conduct of the work of the Church that does not place supreme reliance upon prayer is at variance with the entire teaching of the New Testament. No thoughtful reader of the Gospels can fail to recognise the pre-eminent place which Jesus Christ gave to prayer both in His teaching and in the practice of His own life. The greatest leaders of the missionary enterprise have been men of prayer. 'Prayer is power; the place of prayer is the place of power; the man of prayer is the man of power.'[71]

### *The Science of Missionary Societies*

A general desire has been expressed by eminent missionary leaders on both sides of the Atlantic that some arrangement may be made which will result not only in a continuous systematic study of missionary questions and problems, but which will draw together the active missionary forces of the world in the consideration of questions of common interest. The hope is

---

[69] See Stanley, *The World Missionary Conference*, 312-16; Dana L. Robert, *American Women in Mission: A Social History of Their Thought and Practice* (Macon, GA: Mercer University Press, 1996), 303-07.
[70] *The Home Base of Missions*, 6.
[71] *The Home Base of Missions*, 7-8.

freely expressed that provision may be made for embodying the conclusions reached in this Conference, in some form that will make them permanently valuable, and thus present to the Christian world the spectacle of systematic and scientific co-operation in the work of Missionary Societies in all communions such as will command the confidence of all, raise to the maximum the efficiency of the great missionary enterprise, and present to the non-Christian world the spectacle of the united advancing forces of Christendom. They will even go further than this and say that it would seem to be a mistake if, out of this Conference, there should not emerge some form of organisation or organisations that will be competent to deal with this matter and produce some general and permanent Committee, international and interdenominational in character, to which the Missionary Societies of the world shall look, to whose work all will contribute, and from which all will receive direct benefit.[72]

### *The Fundamental Value of Missions to the Church*

The value of missions to the remote nations of the earth can never be computed in human figures. It can be expressed only in terms of eternity. But however valuable this is in the new and renewed intellectual, social and moral life imparted to peoples who were sitting in ignorance and moral darkness, and however much the mission work of last century has cost in the expenditure of life and money for the advance of the Kingdom of God in the regions beyond, the reflex influence upon the Churches engaging in this work, and upon individuals who have given themselves in whole or in part to it, is well worth the cost. We may go even farther and say that, but for the new life that has come to the Church of Christ through the effort it has put forth to evangelise the world, the very life of the Church itself would have been imperilled. Foreign missions are saving the Church to itself and to the world.[73]

We have come to the conclusion in our investigations that the Church of Christ here at home is dependent for its continuance upon the part it has in missionary work. We can never understand our own Holy Scriptures until they are interpreted to us through the language of every nation under heaven. We can never know our Lord Jesus Christ in fullness and in the length and breadth of His love until He is revealed to the world in the redeemed life and character of men out of every race for which He died.[74]

---

[72] *The Home Base of Missions*, 252.
[73] *The Home Base of Missions*, 267.
[74] *The Home Base of Missions*, 296.

## Commission Seven: Missions and Governments

An original theme for a missionary conference was taken up by Commission Seven which examined the interrelation of missions and governments. The 21-member Commission predominantly consisted of distinguished laymen of wide experience in public and foreign affairs: ten British, six US-American, three German, one Norwegian and one Canadian. Chairman of the Commission was Lord Balfour of Burleigh – Scottish Tory grandee, cabinet minister and Presbyterian elder – who also served as president of the conference as a whole. The Commission adopted the conceptual framework of a hierarchy of civilisation, with Europe and North America setting the benchmark for high civilisation and other nations being assessed on how close they were to meeting this standard. Japan was considered to have the most civilised of non-Christian governments while at the other end of the scale was 'the absolutely independent savage chief'.[75] In determining how missions should relate to the government in any given context the Commission argued that account must be taken of the degree of civilisation attained both by the people and the government of the territory concerned. The higher on the scale the responsible government, the more missions could reasonably appeal for protection and redress.

Part One, 'A Survey of Existing Conditions in Various Mission Fields', drafted by the British members, was based on an unusually small sample of missionary correspondents – only forty-one. It examined relationships between missions and governments in the various mission fields in what it understood to be a descending order of hierarchy: Japan, China, India, the Dutch East Indies, 'Mohammedan Lands', Mid-Africa and Southern Africa. Part Two, drafted by the American members who had extensive political but little missionary experience, extrapolated 'Principles and Findings', and applied them to a range of problems that recur in mission-government relationships across the regions. No challenge was offered to the colonial system which prevailed in much of Asia and Africa at this time but the Report did offer sharply critical comment on such injustices as the opium trade, liquor traffic and human rights abuses in the Congo.

However varied the contexts, the Report recommended that missions should, as a matter of principle, relate to governments wherever possible in a conciliatory and reasonable manner. It affirmed a consensus that missionaries should have nothing to do with opposition political movements. Governments were regarded as having received their authority from God and therefore as being entitled to respect and co-operation from missions. At the same time, governments were urged to be mindful of the

---

[75] World Missionary Conference,1910, *Missions and Governments*, Report of Commission VII (Edinburgh and London: Oliphant, Anderson & Ferrier; New York, Chicago and Toronto: Fleming H. Revell, 1910), 88-89.

debt they owed to missions and of all that was contributed by missionaries to the elevation of the people.

## Commission Seven Report

### *Varieties of Governments*

We may divide mission lands roughly into five groups: (a) those of low civilisation, but independent; (b) those of higher civilisation, and independent; (c) those of low civilisation, under Christian rule or influence; (d) those of higher civilisation under Christian rule or influence; (e) those of the highest international rank.

The absolutely independent savage chief, representative of group (a), has disappeared; and the ethical and prudential rules governing the dealings of missionaries with such potentates, though intensely interesting as a study of character, need not occupy the attention of this Commission.

Under group (e) we may mention, as a conspicuous instance, Japan. However different in spirit and in detail her civilisation may remain from that of Western nations, she has entered into equal external relations with the leading Powers of the world, and has established such internal order and toleration that problems of mission policy, *in relation to government*, have ceased to exist in any acute form. Christian Missions enjoy a freedom of action greater than that which they possess in some lands under Christian rule, and though doubtless there are laws and regulations which some would like to see changed, Christian Missions find no grievous political obstacles in their way.

There remain group (b) which may be illustrated by Persia and China, group (c) illustrated by the African Protectorates, and group (d) illustrated by India.[76]

In countries like Persia, Missions are conducted under a Government which is not in sympathy with their operations, and where freedom of conscience – the right and duty of the individual in matters of religion – is, generally speaking, an unintelligible term, and toleration (in the Western sense) seems a violation of religious obligation. In China there is more intellectual toleration, but a standing suspicion of the Church itself as an organisation and also as the presumed organ of Foreign Powers. Missionaries cannot and do not under such circumstances expect official countenance of their work, and can only ask for freedom of action. If that freedom is denied, or circumscribed, missionaries must, for the time being, accept the situation, however earnestly they may strive to modify the

---

[76] *Missions and Governments*, 88-89, italics original.

official attitude. They must work under these restrictions or not work at all.[77]

We now take up the case of countries inhabited by races of low civilisation, and ruled or dominated by Christian Powers, as in the African Protectorates and colonies. In this case Missions may fairly expect, not only freedom of action, but even the countenance and encouragement of the civil power on the ground of the proved value of the missionary enterprise to civilisation, peace and humanity. Here there is no independent Government to be respected; there is no sensitive community, united by a great history or a great religion, to be approached with circumspection. Civilisation and religion come to them almost indistinguishably from the one power, and Missions and Governments may work in the closest sympathy. There should be little controversy here as to the duty of mutual support; and there would be none except for the regrettable fact that not all Colonial Governments have made the welfare of the people the ruling principle in their administration.[78]

Some modification of these principles must be made in countries of the last group which come under our consideration, namely, those in which Christian rule has been established over peoples of considerably advanced civilisation. Political independence may be lost, while many institutions and the religion of the people remain intact; and so long as these are left intact, the people may remain comparatively quiescent. In such circumstances, even Governments with the highest ideals must make innovations cautiously; and in Governments with lower ideals, caution may easily degenerate into cowardice and unfaithfulness. Missions may be excluded or severely restricted, because they are controversial in their operations and revolutionary in their effects. In such circumstances, what can missionaries ask as of right? We do not think they can ask for more than freedom of action. Freedom of action we do consider they are entitled to expect, as of moral right, from any Christian Government.[79]

### *Missionaries and Loyalty*

The missionary is usually concerned with two Governments, that of the country from which he has come, and that of the country in which he works. And he must be regardful of his duty to both. The unanimity with which missionaries of all Societies, living under Governments of the most varied kinds, insist upon the paramount duty of respect for government is remarkable. It may, therefore, be assumed that when missionaries, or Mission Boards, or Conferences protest against the act of any Government or its agents, as affecting unfavourably either their own rights or the

---

77 *Missions and Governments*, 89.
78 *Missions and Governments*, 90.
79 *Missions and Governments*, 91.

welfare of the people, their action is not to be attributed to disloyalty or hostility to the administration. Few, indeed, are the cases in which missionaries find themselves out of all sympathy with the general policy of any Government. But claiming, as they do, justice for themselves and for their converts, and having a deep interest in the welfare of all the people, they do, from time to time, fall into difficulties with the civil power or its subordinate agents, when they consider that official actions are in plain violation of justice or humanity.[80]

### *Social and Political Aspirations*

In the evidence before us there is abundant proof of awakened political and social aspirations throughout the world. Movements towards the realisation of national life are found everywhere, and cannot but affect mission work, more especially in the many mission lands where the missionary belongs to a dominant race. The duty of missionaries to the civil authorities, their devotion to the welfare of the people, and their responsibility for the training of the young Christian communities, make the ascertaining of the precise line to be followed in time of political stress a difficult task for them. We have no hesitation in endorsing the missionary opinion, which is practically unanimous on the following points: (1) Missionaries should have nothing to do with political agitation. This is outside their sphere, and engaging in it can only harm their work. (2) It is their duty to teach and practise obedience to settled government. (3) It is at the same time their duty to exercise their influence for the removal of gross oppression and injustice, particularly where the Government is in the hands of men of their own race. It may be added that missionaries have not parted with their intelligence, nor have they lost their rights as citizens of enlightened communities, so that they cannot but form convictions as to the wisdom or unwisdom of the 'colonial policy' they see in operation around them. These convictions it may be their duty on proper occasions to press with all the influence they can command upon the attention of the State officials responsible, provided that in so doing they keep clear of association with any political movement.[81]

### *Some Public Questions*

The Commission believe that they represent the feeling of missionaries and the supporters of Missions in recording: (1) their conviction that the traffic in opium should cease, unless under the restrictions proper for a dangerous drug; (2) their regret that the history of this traffic in China has brought discredit upon Christian Missions by associating them in the Chinese mind,

---

[80] *Missions and Governments*, 93.
[81] *Missions and Governments*, 95.

through the action of some Western Governments, with the spread of opium; (3) their sympathy with the Chinese Government in the steps at present being taken to restrict the use of opium; (4) their hope that the British Government will act in full harmony with the Chinese Government; (5) their hope that the British Imperial and Indian Governments may be able to meet the financial difficulties created by the cessation of the opium revenue, in a way which shall not increase the taxation of the mass of the people in India nor injure the Feudatory States concerned.[82]

We are of the opinion that the claims of humanity and the rights of Missions have been so flagrantly and continuously violated by the Government of the Congo State (now taken over by Belgium), that an appeal for action should be made by the Conference to all the Powers which were signatories to the General Act of Berlin.[83]

## Commission Eight: Co-operation and the Promotion of Unity

The mandate of Commission Eight represented one of the two central aims of the Edinburgh 1910 World Missionary Conference. 'Carrying the Gospel to all the Non-Christian World' (Commission One) necessitated 'Co-operation and the Promotion of Unity' if the goal of 'plant[ing] in every non-Christian nation one united Church of Christ'[84] was to be achieved. Commission Eight addressed this latter concern. It was the most ecumenically focused of the Edinburgh 1910 Commissions – though the word 'ecumenical' does not appear in the Report – and it justified the conference's subsequent reputation as the 'symbolic beginning of the modern ecumenism'.[85] The need for greater co-operation and unity had been laboured in Report after Report to the point where Commission Eight brought to expression an aspiration which energised and united the conference.

An experienced Scottish colonial administrator, Sir Andrew Fraser, formerly governor of Bengal, chaired the Commission. The Commission included four bishops, and church mission boards were as strongly represented as autonomous missionary societies. Although the Commission took evidence from only ninety-five correspondents – considerably fewer than most other Commissions – they included a larger percentage of persons who could speak on behalf of the missionary boards and societies that they represented. While avoiding any semblance of speaking on behalf

---

[82] *Missions and Governments*, 116-17.

[83] *Missions and Governments*, 121.

[84] World Missionary Conference, 1910, *Co-operation and the Promotion of Unity*, Report of Commission VIII (Edinburgh and London: Oliphant, Anderson & Ferrier; New York, Chicago and Toronto: Fleming H. Revell, 1910), 131.

[85] Michael Kinnamon and Brian Cope (eds), *The Ecumenical Movement: an Anthology of Key Texts and Voices* (Geneva: WCC, 1997), 1.

of churches, or of addressing them officially, the Report went beyond recommending greater co-operation for the sake of missionary effectiveness to affirm moves towards the attainment of visible unity by indigenous national churches on the mission field, and to evoke an anticipation of what this might mean for the 'home churches'.

The Report divided its subject into five main chapters: Comity, Conferences, Joint Action, Federation and Union, and Co-operation at the Home Base. The chapters were mainly descriptive in character. However, they were introduced and concluded with two chapters that gave an insightful analysis of the hindrances and horizons of co-operation and unity. Twelve appendices comprise an invaluable archive of documents relating to the promotion of unity among churches, and co-operation between churches and missions in Asia – China, India, the Philippines and Japan. These supported the main argument of the Report: that Christians in these regions were 'the first to recognise the need for concerted action and closer fellowship',[86] and that their pioneering action called for 'hearty sympathy (on the part of western churches) with the movements toward unity in the mission field.'[87]

The recommendation to form a permanent Continuation Committee was unanimously approved by the conference plenary on 21 June 2010. The foundation on which the International Missionary Council would stand had been laid – though on account of the First World War its creation was delayed until 1921. Following the unanimous vote, the delegates joined together in singing the doxology: 'Praise God from whom all blessings flow.'[88]

## Commission Eight Report

It is more than ever incumbent upon the Christian Church to realise its responsibility to carry the Gospel to the lands which are now open to receive it, and to guide the awakening nations to God in Christ. For the accomplishment of this overwhelming task, it seems essential that the Christian Church should present a united front. Its divisions are a source of weakness and impair the effectiveness of its testimony to the one Gospel of the Son of God which it professes. The issues are so great that there can be no trifling in the matter. The evangelisation of nations, the Christianising of empires and kingdoms, is the object before us. The work has to be done now. It is urgent and must be pressed forward at once. The enterprise calls for the highest quality of statesmanship, and for the maximum of efficiency in all departments of the work. It is not surprising that those who are in the front of this great conflict, and on whose minds and souls the gravity of the

---

[86] *Co-operation and the Promotion of Unity,* 133.
[87] *Co-operation and the Promotion of Unity,* 144.
[88] *History and Records*, 98.

issues presses most immediately, should be the first to recognise the need for concerted action and closer fellowship.[89]

### *Federation and Union*

It is natural that the converts of each Mission should be instructed in the doctrines, and organised according to the polity, of the Church to which that Mission owes its origin. As separate Christian communities, however, thus begin to grow up in a non-Christian country, the question presents itself whether these communities shall be allowed to remain isolated and distinct, or whether it is not the aim of all missionary work to plant in each non-Christian nation one undivided Church of Christ.

That the latter is the ideal which is present to the minds of the great majority of missionaries is evident from the movements in the direction of unity, which are taking place in many mission fields, and which find notable expression in the unanimous declaration of the members of the Centenary Missionary Conference at Shanghai in 1907, that in planting the Church of Christ on Chinese soil, it was their desire 'only to plant one Church under the sole control of the Lord Jesus Christ, governed by the Word of the living God, and led by His guiding Spirit'. It is probable that all would not agree as to the form in which the unity referred to in the foregoing declaration should find expression, but that the statement of the goal to be aimed at should be so clear and explicit is a fact of far-reaching significance.

Not only is the ideal of a united Church taking more and more definite shape and colour in the minds of foreign missionaries at work in non-Christian lands, but it is also beginning under the influence of the growing national consciousness in some of these countries to capture the imagination of the indigenous Christian communities, for whom the sense of a common national life and a common Christianity is stronger than the appreciation of differences which had their origin in controversies remote from the circumstances of the Church in mission lands. The influence of this national feeling is most powerful in China.[90]

### *Comity*

In the meantime there is much that we can do of a practical kind to prepare the way for the larger unity that is to come. It is very desirable that Missions working in the same area should agree on a common plan to secure the most effective occupation of the field and to avoid overlapping and waste.[91]

---

[89] *Co-operation and the Promotion of Unity,* 132-33.

[90] *Co-operation and the Promotion of Unity,* 83-84.

[91] *Co-operation and the Promotion of Unity,* 139-40.

*The Possibility of International Co-operation*

These observations cannot be confined to the Societies of any one country. The operations in the foreign field are often carried on in the same country, and even side by side, by agents representing Churches and Societies of different Christian nations. And the movements towards unity and co-operation in the mission field include missionaries of different nationalities. Therefore not only the Missionary Societies in a single country, but Missionary Societies throughout the world, must be in as close communion as possible with one another. Accordingly it appears to us that the adoption in some form of the proposal to create an International Committee that would serve as a medium of communication between all Missionary Societies is absolutely necessary for the carrying out of any statesmanlike and concerted plan for the evangelisation of the world.[92]

We recommend that a Continuation Committee be appointed, such as can deal effectively with any duties that may be relegated to it; that it be international and representative, reflecting in this respect the comprehensive character of the Conference itself; and that it be instructed to deal with the same range of subjects as the Conference, and on the same lines and under the same restrictions.[93]

The value of such a body will, as we believe, be more than the sum of the values of the individual pieces of work which it may accomplish. It will be the standing witness of a great idea, a lasting reminder of a great piece of religious experience, and an abiding monument of our belief in the Divine guidance that has led us already so much further than we dared anticipate in the direction of co-operation and the promotion of unity, and will yet lead us further still if only we continue steadfast in this faith, in this hope, and in this fervent charity.[94]

---

[92] *Co-operation and the Promotion of Unity,* 144.
[93] *Co-operation and the Promotion of Unity,* 145-46.
[94] *Co-operation and the Promotion of Unity,* 148.

# JERUSALEM 1928: MISSION AND THE KINGDOM OF GOD

- The First World War provoked fresh thinking – the idea of mission as conquest now obsolete
- The 'younger churches' of Asia and Africa significantly represented
- Mission distanced from the framework of western colonialism
- Recognition of the advance of secularism in the western context
- New sensitivity to adherents of other faiths balanced with confidence in the gospel
- Social and economic change in tension with evangelism and church growth

The only formal outcome of Edinburgh 1910 was the formation of the Continuation Committee under the leadership of John Mott as Chairman and J.H. Oldham as Secretary. Its responsibility was 'to confer with the Societies and Boards as to the best method of working toward the formation of such a permanent International Missionary Committee as is suggested by the Commissions of the Conference and by various missionary bodies apart from the Conference'.[1] Within two years the Continuation Committee helped form the Conference of British Missionary Societies with its membership of forty missionary societies. The two bodies shared single premises in London, suitably named Edinburgh House. This initiative pointed the way which would be followed in many other countries also. The First World War (1914-1918) retarded the development of international missionary co-operation, but within three years of the war's end, in 1921, the International Missionary Council was constituted at Lake Mohonk in New York State, USA, with Mott as the first Chairman, and Oldham and the American A.L. Warnshuis as its first Secretaries.[2] With headquarters in London (Edinburgh House) and New York, its membership included 14 interdenominational missionary associations and 16 interdenominational field bodies.

The second notable achievement of these years was the launching of the International Review of Missions in 1912. The journal, edited by Oldham, was dedicated to continuing Edinburgh 1910's emphasis on the disciplined study of mission. As Kenneth Scott Latourette commented: 'The Review immediately took its place as the outstanding supra-confessional

---

[1] *History and Records*, 96.

[2] See William Richey Hogg, *Ecumenical Foundations: A History of the International Missionary Council and its Nineteenth Century Background* (New York: Harper & Brothers, 1952), 202-43.

international journal in the field of missions. Its wide range of contributors and reviewers, from many lands and differing ecclesiastical and theological traditions, its extensive bibliographies, and its annual surveys of world mission, covering as they did Roman Catholic as well as Protestant developments, contributed notably to the nourishment of the ecumenical spirit.'[3] It has continued to appear regularly and is unsurpassed as a barometer of thinking about mission over the past century.[4]

The first full meeting of the International Missionary Council took place in Jerusalem in 1928. This gathering saw 'the younger churches' much more widely represented than they had been at Edinburgh, revealing the direction of travel for the coming century. Of the 250 participants, more than fifty were nationals from 'the mission field'. 'Among them,' recalled Richey Hogg, 'one saw a bright yellow Indian sari, the blue silk gown of a Chinese scholar, here a fez, there a turban... here was gathered the first truly representative, global assembly of Christians in the long history of the church.'[5] The voices of 'national' leaders were influential and made it clear that the time had come for the indigenous churches to take responsibility for mission in their contexts. This would mean a change of role for the 'missions', involving the handover of property and mission staff coming under the authority of the churches with which they served. Taking advantage of the Jerusalem venue, the IMC also seized the opportunity to establish fraternal relationships with Orthodox Churches, another initiative which would have far-reaching effects.

It also meant that the division of the world into 'Christian' and 'non-Christian' on geographical, territorial terms had already become obsolete. The vitality and maturity of the churches on the 'mission field' on the one hand, and the growing secularism of the so-called 'Christian world' on the other, made it plain that a Christendom understanding of the world was no longer serviceable. The challenges involved in mission to a secularised western world were registered for the first time at Jerusalem. 'We go to Jerusalem,' stated Rufus Jones in an influential address, 'not as members of a Christian nation to convert other nations which are not Christian, but as Christians within a nation far too largely non-Christian, who face within their own borders the competition of a rival movement as powerful, as dangerous, as insidious as any of the great historic religions.'[6] There was

---

[3] Kenneth Scott Latourette, 'Ecumenical Bearings of the Missionary Movement and the International Missionary Council', in Ruth Rouse and Stephen C. Neill (eds), *A History of the Ecumenical Movement 1517-1948*, 4th edition (Geneva: WCC, 1994), 351-402.

[4] See *International Review of Mission,* 100.393 (November 2011), 'A Century of Ecumenical Missiology'; particularly Brian Stanley, 'Edinburgh 1910 and the Genesis of the *IRM*', 149-59.

[5] Hogg, *Ecumenical Foundations*, 244.

[6] *The Christian Life and Message in Relation to Non-Christian Systems*, Report of the Jerusalem Meeting of the International Missionary Council, 24th March-8th

also a much sharper awareness of the dangers posed to the missionary enterprise by the risk of being complicit in colonialism. Far more than had been the case at Edinburgh, a hermeneutic of suspicion was applied to the relationship between the missionary enterprise and the global domination of the West. This led to greater sensitivity to the pitfalls facing western-based missions and a determination to ground mission on a theological and Christological basis. Rather than thinking of the advance of Christian mission simply in quantitative terms, there was a new attention to the qualitative aspect. This would have far-reaching effects. As Jooseop Keum comments: 'Since Jerusalem, the two different approaches, the quantitative and qualitative concepts of mission, have become a missiological backbone of the division between ecumenical and evangelical perspectives in mission.'[7]

The Jerusalem conference followed the pattern of Edinburgh in commissioning comprehensive preparatory studies. These studies had already started to deconstruct the terms on which the Edinburgh Conference had been held. Whereas Edinburgh 1910 had worked on an assumption of agreement about the content of the Christian message, by the time of Jerusalem 1928 this was an issue which was very much in question. The First World War had badly shaken confidence in western civilisation as the embodiment of the gospel, prompting critical reflection on the substance of the Christian message. Metaphors of warfare and conquest no longer seemed appropriate in relation to other faiths. In fact, delegates such as W.E. Hocking were inclined to think much more in terms of mutual understanding and co-operation between the different faiths, a trend which would soon find more extensive expression in the Laymen's Foreign Mission Enquiry of 1932-33.[8] Others were alarmed by this new direction of thought and feared that the missionary movement was moving towards syncretism. European continental delegates met with John Mott in Cairo two days before the conference to express such misgivings.[9] There was a new sharpness to the challenge of how to be irenic towards people of other faiths without undermining confidence in the gospel of Christ. The Council Statement, drafted by William Temple, at that time Archbishop Designate of York and later Archbishop of Canterbury, and Robert Elliot Speer, long-

---

April 1928, Vol. I (London: OUP, 1928), 273; cit. Hogg, *Ecumenical Foundations*, 247.

[7] Jooseop Keum, 'Beyond Dichotomy: Towards a Convergence Between the Ecumenical and Evangelical Understanding of Mission in Changing Landscapes', in Margunn Serigstad Dahle, Lars Dahle and Knud Jorgensen (eds), *The Lausanne Movement: A Range of Perspectives* (Oxford: Regnum, 2014), 386.

[8] See W.E. Hocking (ed), *Rethinking Missions: a Laymen's Inquiry After One Hundred Years* (New York and London: Harper & Brothers, 1932); *Laymen's Foreign Mission Enquiry, Supplementary Series*, 7 vols. (New York: Harper & Brothers, 1933).

[9] Hogg, *Ecumenical Foundations*, 242.

serving Secretary of the American Presbyterian Mission, sought to reflect a new sensitivity to adherents of other faiths while strongly affirming the core of Christian belief.

Another major point of tension was the question of how far Christian mission should be concerned with effecting change in the social and economic order as opposed to an exclusive concentration on personal conversion and the growth of the church. Again, Anglo-Saxon perspectives on social witness contrasted with continental Europeans' insistence that the focus on eternal salvation must not be compromised. The preparatory studies revealed a broadening scope of enquiry, including such topics as religious education, race conflict, industrialisation and rural problems. This widening of the understanding of mission was energising for some but others feared that this rethinking of Christian mission in terms of its engagement with the political and economic structures of society was moving in the direction of the 'social gospel' and losing its evangelistic edge. Theologically, this found expression in intense debate about the meaning of the 'Kingdom of God'. While some spoke in terms of humans building the Kingdom of God, others insisted that it was God's kingdom. This tension was recognised, though perhaps not resolved, in the reference in the Council's Statement to working 'in preparation for the coming of the Kingdom of God in its fullness'.[10]

## Jerusalem 1928: Statement on the Christian Message

### *Our Message*

Our message is Jesus Christ. He is the revelation of what God is and of what man through Him may become. In Him we come face to face with the ultimate reality of the universe; He makes known to us God our Father, perfect and infinite in love and in righteousness; for in Him we find God incarnate, the final, yet ever-unfolding, revelation of the God in whom we live and move and have our being.

We hold that through all that happens, in light and in darkness, God is working, ruling and over-ruling. Jesus Christ, in His life and through His death and resurrection, has disclosed to us the Father, the Supreme Reality, as almighty Love, reconciling the world to Himself by the Cross, suffering with men in their struggle against sin and evil, forgiving them as they, with forgiveness in their own hearts, turn to Him in repentance and faith, and creating humanity anew for an ever-growing, ever-enlarging, everlasting life.

---

[10] *The Christian Life and Message*, 481; see discussion of this phrase in Timothy Yates, *Christian Mission in the Twentieth Century* (Cambridge: CUP, 1994), 68.

The vision of God in Christ brings and deepens the sense of sin and guilt. We are not worthy of His love; we have by our own fault opposed His holy will. Yet that same vision which brings the sense of guilt brings also the assurance of pardon, if only we yield ourselves in faith to the spirit of Christ so that His redeeming love may avail to reconcile us to God.

We affirm that God, as Jesus Christ has revealed Him, requires all His children, in all circumstances, at all times and in all human relationships, to live in love and righteousness for His glory. By the resurrection of Christ and the gift of the Holy Spirit, God offers His own power to them that they may be fellow-workers with Him, and urges them on to a life of adventure and self-sacrifice in preparation for the coming of His Kingdom in its fullness.[11]

### *The Missionary Motive*

Questions concerning the missionary motive have been widely raised, and such a change in the habits of men's thoughts, as the last generation has witnessed, must call for a re-examination of these questions.

Accordingly we would lay bare the motives that impel us to the missionary enterprise. We recognise that the health of our movement and of our souls demands a self-criticism that is relentless and exacting.

In searching for the motives that impel us, we find ourselves eliminating decisively and at once certain motives that may seem, in the minds of some, to have become mixed up with purer motives in the history of the movement. We repudiate any attempt on the part of trade or of governments, openly or covertly, to use the missionary cause for ulterior purposes. Our Gospel by its very nature, and by its declaration of the sacredness of human personality, stands against all exploitation of man by man, so that we cannot tolerate any desire, conscious or unconscious, to use this movement for purposes of fastening a bondage, economic, political or social, on any people.

Going deeper, on our part we would repudiate any symptoms of a religious imperialism that would desire to impose beliefs and practices on others in order to manage their souls in their supposed interests. We obey a God who respects our wills and we desire to respect those of others.

Nor have we the desire to bind up our Gospel with fixed ecclesiastical forms which derive their meaning from the experience of the western Church. Rather the aim should be to place at the disposal of the younger churches of all lands our collective and historic experience. We believe that much of that heritage has come out of reality and will be worth sharing. But we ardently desire that the younger churches should express the Gospel through their own genius and through forms suited to their racial heritage.

---

[11] *The Christian Life,* Jerusalem, 1928, 480-81.

There must be no desire to lord it over the personal and collective faith of others.

Our true and compelling motive lies in the very nature of the God to whom we have given our hearts. Since He is love, His very nature is to share. Christ is the expression in time of the eternal self-giving of the Father. Coming into fellowship with Christ, we find in ourselves an over-mastering impulse to share Him with others. We are constrained by the love of Christ, and by obedience to His last command. He Himself said, 'I am come that they might have life, and that they may have it more abundantly,' and our experience corroborates it. He has become life to us. We would share that life.[12]

### *The Call to the World*

To non-Christians also we make our call. We rejoice to think that just because in Jesus Christ the light that lighteneth every man shone forth in its full splendour, we find rays of that light where He is unknown or even is rejected. We welcome every noble quality in non-Christian persons or systems as further proof that the Father, who sent His Son into the world, has nowhere left Himself without witness.

Thus, merely to give illustration, and making no attempt to estimate the spiritual value of other religions to their adherents, we recognise as part of the one Truth that sense of the Majesty of God and the consequent reverence in worship, which are conspicuous in Islam; the deep sympathy for the world's sorrow and unselfish search for the way of escape, which are at the heart of Buddhism; the desire for contact with ultimate reality conceived as spiritual, which is prominent in Hinduism; the belief in the moral order of the universe and consequent insistence on moral conduct, which are inculcated by Confucianism; the disinterested pursuit of truth and of human welfare, which are often found in those who stand for secular civilisation but do not accept Christ as their Lord and Saviour.

Especially we make our call to the Jewish people, whose Scriptures have become our own, and 'of whom is Christ as concerning the flesh', that with open heart they turn to that Lord in whom is fulfilled the hope of their nation, its prophetic message and its zeal for holiness. And we call upon our fellow-Christians in all lands to show to Jews that lovingkindness that has too seldom been shown towards them.

We call on the followers of non-Christian religions to join with us in the study of Jesus Christ as He stands before us in the Scriptures, His place in the life of the world, and His power to satisfy the human heart; to hold fast to faith in the unseen and eternal in face of the growing materialism of the world; to co-operate with us against all the evils of secularism; to respect freedom of conscience so that men may confess Christ without separation

---

[12] *The Christian Life,* Jerusalem, 1928, 484-85.

from home and friends; and to discern that all the good of which men have conceived is fulfilled and secured in Christ.

Christianity is not a western religion, nor is it yet effectively accepted by the western world as a whole. Christ belongs to the peoples of Africa and Asia as much as to the European or American. We call all men to equal fellowship in Him. But to come to Him is always self-surrender. We must not come in the pride of national heritage or religious tradition; he who would enter the Kingdom of God must become as a little child, though in that Kingdom are all the treasures of man's aspirations, consecrated and harmonised. Just because Christ is the self-disclosure of the One God, all human aspirations are towards Him, and yet of no human tradition is He merely the continuation. He is the desire of all the nations; but He is always more, and other, than they had desired before they learnt of Him.[13]

---

[13] *The Christian Life,* Jerusalem, 1928, 490-92.

# Tambaram 1938 – The Christian Message in a Non-Christian World

- Responsibility for mission transferring to indigenous churches
- Focus on the church as agent of mission
- Passion for the unity of the church – for the sake of mission
- Dialectical approach to other religions with stress on discontinuity
- Overshadowed by the rise of Nazism and impending Second World War

The IMC held its second major international conference at Tambaram, near Madras (now Chennai) in south India in 1938. By now, representatives of the 'younger churches' were clearly in a majority with almost half of the 471 delegates coming from Asia and significant delegations from Africa and Latin America. An important backdrop to the conference was the speed at which the relationship between western missions and indigenous churches was changing. By now it was fully apparent that responsibility for mission was transferring to the indigenous churches whose leaders set the tone at Tambaram. This dynamic meant that the Church was very much at the centre of attention. As John Mott stated in his opening address: 'It is the Church which is to be at the centre of our thinking… the Divine Society founded by Christ and His apostles to accomplish His will in the world. It is a worshipping Society, a witnessing Society, a transforming Society – the veritable Body of Christ.'[1]

The Asian delegates in particular brought a passion for church unity, arguing powerfully that the divided state of the church was proving a grave impediment to mission in their contexts. 'The real significance of Madras,' in Richey Hogg's assessment, 'lay in what it was rather than in what it did. It was a unifying event in the life of the whole church – an event which revealed to the churches the fellowship of the church universal. No other experience made so deep an impact on those at Madras as that of the church, of a worldwide community united in love.'[2] At the same time, the conference was marked by a concern for indigenisation of the faith – a theme that would preoccupy generations to come. Another significant contribution to the conference was the work led by Merle Davis on the economic basis of the church and the need for the younger churches to become self-supporting. Meanwhile, a group convened by Bishop Stephen

---

[1] John R. Mott, 'The Possibilities of the Tambaram Meeting', in *Addresses and Other Records*, Tambaram Madras Series, Vol. VII (London: Oxford University Press, 1939), 4.
[2] Hogg, *Ecumenical Foundations*, 301.

Neill highlighted the urgency and importance of the development of theological education with a view to the formation of the leaders required by the younger churches.

The question of the Christian understanding of other religions and its implications for missiology remained prominent. An important part of the preparation for Tambaram was a commission to the Dutch missiologist Hendrik Kraemer to 'state the fundamental position of the Christian church as a witness-bearing body in the modern world, relating this to conflicting views of the attitude to be taken by Christians towards other faiths, and dealing in detail with the evangelistic approach to the great non-Christian faiths'.[3] The result was a book entitled The Christian Message in a Non-Christian World.[4] This volume represented a very different approach to the Laymen's Foreign Mission Enquiry of the early 1930s. The church, Kraemer argued, draws its true identity 'from the apostolic urgency of gladly witnessing to God and his saving and redeeming Power through Christ'.[5] He expressed strong suspicion of any notion that the Kingdom of God would come through human effort, stressing instead the divine initiative.

Nor could Christianity, in Kraemer's view, be regarded as the fulfilment of other religions. Rather, a dialectical approach was required in which the presence and action of God in other religious traditions could be affirmed but where this would always be seen in the light of the unexpectedness and 'discontinuity' of God's decisive action in Jesus Christ. If missionaries lacked the confidence that Jesus was 'the Way, the Truth and the Life', how would they be able to call men and women to costly conversion? 'Cast in one piece,' observed Carl Hallencreutz, 'his book was decisive for "Tambaram 1938". It invited a missiological reorientation as regards "the evangelistic approach to the great non-Christian faiths"'.'[6]

The rise of Nazism and the impending Second World War formed an unmistakable background to the conference. China and Japan were already at war, and in this context it was moving to see Chinese and Japanese delegates taking communion together. Kraemer's insistence on the centrality of the apostolic witness was driven, in part, by the need to counter the claims of such false absolutes as fascism, National Socialism and communism. As Timothy Yates comments: 'Neo-pagan darkness was indeed about to descend on Europe: it was a context of sharp polarities, when shades of grey were of little value to embattled Christians. Rather, the need was for the ringing tones of the Barmen Declaration of 1934, for

---

[3] IMC Ad Interim Committee Minutes, Old Jordans, 1936; cit. Yates, *Christian Mission*, 108.

[4] Hendrik Kraemer, *The Christian Message in a Non-Christian World* (London: Edinburgh House Press, 1938).

[5] Kraemer, *The Christian Message*, vi.

[6] Carl F. Hallencreutz, *Kraemer Towards Tambaram: A Study in Hendrik Kraemer's Missionary Approach* (Uppsala, Sweden: Gleerup, 1966), 307.

Barth's outright rejection of nationalist religion rooted in nature and for Kraemer's concentration on Christ as the Light shining with absolute clarity in a world of darkness, darkness made all the more profound by way of the calls for total allegiance by fascist and communist to the state and its purposes, those pseudo-absolutes Kraemer had condemned with such great effect.'[7]

## Tambaram 1938

### *Hendrik Kraemer – Continuity or Discontinuity*

The relation of the world of spiritual realities, spread out before us in biblical realism, towards the world which is manifested in the whole range of religious experience and striving is not that of continuity, but of discontinuity. Theologically speaking, 'nature', 'reason' and 'history' do not, if we want to think stringently, afford preambles, avenues or lines of development towards the realm of grace and truth as manifest in Jesus Christ. There are, to be sure, longings and apperceptions in the religious life of mankind outside the special sphere of the Christian revelation, of which Christ, what He is and has brought, may be termed *in a certain sense* the fulfilment. Yet, it is mistaken and misleading to describe the religious pilgrimage of mankind as a preparation or a leading up to a so-called consummation or fulfilment in Christ. I did not make this statement in my book because the only way to maintain strongly that the Christian religion contains *the* one way of truth is to isolate it entirely from the whole range of human religious life. Nor is this statement inspired by any desire to minimise or despise the value and significance of much that stirs us in the religious quest of various peoples. It simply follows from respect for the facts. These facts clearly teach us two things of crucial importance. First: even when we recognise that Christ may *in a certain sense* be called the fulfilment of some deep and persistent longings and apprehensions that everywhere in history manifest themselves in the race, this fulfilment, when we subject the facts to a close scrutiny, never represents the perfecting of what has been before. In this fulfilment is contained a radical recasting of values, because these longings and apprehensions, when exposed to the searching and revolutionary light of Christ, appear to be blind and misdirected. That does not detract in the least from the fact that these longings and apprehensions, humanly speaking, are heart-stirring and noble, but if we want to be loyal to the divine reality that has come to us in Jesus Christ, this appreciation, which is simply a matter of justice and honesty in the human plane, must not obscure our eyes to the truth that in Christ all things become new, because He is the crisis of all religions. In

---

[7] Yates, *Christian Mission*, 124.

this we recognise that God as He is revealed in Jesus Christ is *contrary* to the sublimest pictures we made of Him before we knew of Him in Jesus Christ. If the word 'reconciliation' has not merely become an edifying term, readily used (or rather, blasphemously abused) because it appears to be a rather successful instrument of arousing a sentiment of numinous awe; if the pronouncement that God was reconciling the world in Jesus Christ to Himself belongs to the core of the Gospel, we cannot escape the conclusion that somehow mankind in its totality is in a state of hostility towards God as He *really is*.

This fundamental discontinuity of the world of spiritual reality, embodied in the revelation in Christ, to the whole range of human religion, *excludes* the possibility and legitimacy of a *theologia naturalis* in the sense of a science of God and man, conceived as an imperfect form of revelation, introductory to the world of divine grace in Christ. The rejection of a *theologia naturalis* as affording the basic religious truths on which the realm of the Christian revelation rises as the fitting superstructure, does not, however, *include* denying that God has been working in the minds of men outside the sphere of the Christian revelation and that there have been, and may be now, acceptable men of faith who live under the sway of non-Christian religions – products, however, not of these non-Christian religions but of the mysterious workings of God's spirit. God forbid that we mortal men should be so irreverent as to dispose of how and where the Sovereign God of grace and love has to act. Yet to represent the religions of the world as *somehow*, however imperfect and crude it may be, a *paidagogos*, a schoolmaster to Christ, is a distorted presentation of these religions and their fundamental structure and tendencies, and a misunderstanding of the Christian revelation. This apprehension of the essential 'otherness' of the world of divine realities revealed in Jesus Christ from the atmosphere of religion as we know it in the history of the race, cannot be grasped merely by way of investigation and reasoning. Only an attentive study of the Bible can open the eyes to the fact of Christ 'the power of God' and 'the wisdom of God' stands in contradiction to the power and wisdom of man. Perhaps in some respects it were proper to speak of contradictive or subversive fulfilment.[8]

### *The Call of the Church*

In this time when brute force stalks the earth, the Church is summoned to bear courageous and unflinching witness to the nations that the base purposes of men, whether of individuals or of groups, cannot prevail against the will of the Holy and Compassionate God. It is commissioned to warn mankind of the judgement which shall assuredly overtake a

---

[8] H. Kraemer, 'Continuity or Discontinuity', in *The Authority of the Faith*, Tambaram Madras Series, Vol. I (London: Oxford University Press, 1939), 3-5.

civilisation which will not turn and repent. It is under obligation to speak fearlessly against aggression, brutality, persecution and all wanton destruction of human life and torturing of human souls.

Recognising that Christ came to open to all the way of life abundant but that the way for millions is blocked by poverty, war, racial hatred, exploitation and cruel injustice, the Church is called to attack social evils at their roots. It must seek to open the eyes of its members to their implication in unchristian practices. Those who suffer from bitter wrong, it is constrained to succour and console, while it strives courageously and persistently for the creation of a more just society.

Above all, it is called to declare the Gospel of the compassion and pardon of God that men may see the Light which is in Christ and surrender themselves to His service. And all this it must do at any cost, in fidelity and gratitude to Him who at so great cost wrought its salvation.

But the further summons to the Church is to become in itself the actualisation among men of its own message. No one so fully knows the failings, the pettiness, the faithlessness which infect the Church's life, as we who are its members. Yet, in all humility and penitence, we are constrained to declare to a baffled and needy world that the Christian Church, under God, is its greatest hope. The decade since we last met has witnessed the progressive rending of the fabric of humanity; it has witnessed an increasing unification of the body of Christ. As we meet here, from over sixty nations out of every continent, we have discovered afresh that unity is not merely an aspiration but also a fact; our meeting is its concrete manifestation. We are one in faith; we are one in our task and commission as the body of Christ; we are resolved to become more fully one in our life and work. Our nations are at war with one another; but we know ourselves brethren in the community of Christ's Church. Our peoples increase in suspicion and fear of one another; but we are learning to trust each other more deeply through common devotion to the one Lord of us all. Our Governments build instruments of mutual destruction; we join in united action for the reconciliation of humanity. Thus in broken and imperfect fashion the Church is even now fulfilling its calling to be within itself a foretaste of the redeemed family of God which He has purposed humanity to be. The Church itself must stand ever under the ideal of the Kingdom of God which alone can guard it against becoming an end in itself and hold it true to God's purpose for it. By faith, but in deep assurance, we declare that this body which God has fashioned through Christ cannot be destroyed.

Meanwhile, in countless obscure places in the world where, through the centuries, disease and darkness, poverty and fear have reigned, the Christian Church to-day is bringing effective healing, enlightenment, alleviation and a true and living faith.

To all who care for the peace and health of mankind we issue a call to lend their aid to the Church which stands undaunted amidst the shattered fragments of humanity and works tirelessly for the healing of the nations. And those who already share in its life, and especially its leaders, we summon to redouble their exertions in its great tasks, to speed practical co-operation and unity, to bear in concrete ways the burdens of fellow-Christians who suffer, and above all to take firm hold again of the faith which gives victory over sin, discouragement and death. Look to Christ, to His Cross, to His triumphant work among men, and take heart. Christ, lifted up, draws all men unto Himself.[9]

### *The Relevance of the Church*

We recognise that both in the East and in the West, especially among the younger generation, there are many who are not convinced of the relevance of the Church to the life of the Christian and the spread of the Gospel. We find in many countries those who desire to follow Jesus Christ as their Lord, but do not join in the fellowship of the organised Church, and even more frequently those who, though baptised, do not accept the privileges nor fulfil the duties of membership of the Church. We are aware that there may be circumstances which make it unwise or even impossible for one to join the Church immediately after conversion, but we would ask all Christians who are unaffiliated or only loosely affiliated to the Church to consider the following affirmations:

1. In spite of all its past and present failure to live up to its divine mission, the Church is and remains the fellowship to which our Lord has given His promises, and through which He carries forward His purpose for mankind.
2. This fellowship is not merely invisible and ideal, but real and concrete, taking a definite form in history. It is therefore the duty of all disciples of Christ to take their place in a given Christian Church, that is, one of those concrete bodies in which and through which the Universal Church of Christ, the worldwide company of His followers, is seeking to find expression.
3. It is part of the obedience and sacrifice which Jesus Christ demands of us that we accept participation in the humiliation and suffering which membership of the Church may often mean in actual practice.
4. It is indeed precisely when we realise deeply that there is a gulf between the Church as it is and the Church as Jesus Christ desires it that we shall devote ourselves to the task of vitalising and reforming it from within.

It is the Church and the Church alone which can carry the responsibility of transmitting the Gospel from one generation to another, of preserving its purity and of proclaiming it to all creatures. It is the Church and the Church

---

[9] *The Authority of the Faith*, 191-93.

alone which can witness to the reality that man belongs to God in Christ with a higher right than that of any earthly institution which may claim his supreme allegiance. It is within the Church and the Church alone that the fellowship of God's people receives together the gifts which He offers to His children in Word and Sacrament.

We may and we should doubt whether the churches as they are do truly express the mind of Christ, but we may never doubt that Christ has a will for His Church, and that His promises to it hold good. If we desire to live according to that will and to become worthy of those promises we shall accept both the joy and the pain of membership in His Body.[10]

### *Statement by Delegates from the Younger Churches*

During the discussion it became abundantly clear that the divisions of Christendom were seen in their worst light in the mission field. Instances were cited by the representatives of younger churches of disgraceful competition, wasteful overlapping, and of groups and individuals turned away from the Church because of divisions within. Disunion is both a stumbling block to the faithful and a mockery to those without. We confess with shame that we ourselves have often been the cause of thus bringing dishonour to the religion of our Master. The representatives of the younger churches in this Section, one and all gave expression to the passionate longing that exists in all countries for visible union of the churches. They are aware of the fact of spiritual unity; they record with great thankfulness all the signs of co-operation and understanding that are increasingly seen in various directions; but they realise that this is not enough. Visible and organic union must be our goal. This, however, will require an honest study of those things in which the churches have differences, a widespread teaching of the common church membership in things that make for union and venturesome sacrifice on the part of all. Such a union alone will remove the evils arising out of our divisions. Union proposals have been put forward in different parts of the world. Loyalty, however, will forbid the younger churches going forward to consummate any union unless it receives the wholehearted support and blessing of those through whom these churches have been planted. We are thus often torn between loyalty to our mother churches and loyalty to our idea of union. We, therefore, appeal with all the fervour we possess, to the missionary societies and boards and the responsible authorities of the older churches, to take this matter seriously to heart, to labour with the churches in the mission field to achieve this union, to support and encourage us in all our efforts to put an end to the scandalous effects of our divisions, and to lead us in the path of union – the union for which our Lord prayed, through which the world

---

[10] *The Growing Church*, Tambaram Madras Series, Vol. II (London: Oxford University Press, 1939), 292-93.

would indeed believe in the Divine Mission of the Son, our Lord Jesus Christ.[11]

[11] *The Life of the Church*, Tambaram Madras Series, Vol. IV (London: Oxford University Press, 1939), 402-03.

# WHITBY 1947 – PARTNERSHIP IN OBEDIENCE

- Expectant evangelism – sensing a time of opportunity after years of warfare
- A new sense of equality and mutuality
- Partners in obedience – working together for the fulfilment of God's will

The Second World War intervened before the IMC could hold what had become by tradition an approximately decennial meeting. Post-war austerity meant a smaller gathering than previously. 'Expectant evangelism' was its theme as it sought to return to core business after the disruptions of the war years. Having come through the chaotic environment of wartime, the delegates were determined to focus afresh on the centrality and urgency of the proclamation of the gospel. The small size of the gathering – just 112 delegates – perhaps fostered the intimacy between representatives of the older and younger churches which led to a sense of equality and mutuality such as had never been known before. As it was expressed by a Chinese delegate: 'At Jerusalem and Madras the relationship between older and younger churches was like that between a father and his children. Here it is like that between an older brother and a younger brother.'[1] The result was a new emphasis on 'partnership in obedience' as the keynote of their working together. They understood themselves to be partners in obedience to the will of God in the fulfilment of a common task. Foreign missionary and indigenous pastor were called to work together, on an equal basis, in the task of evangelism. By this time Latin American leaders had become familiar figures in IMC gatherings, their exclusion from Edinburgh 1910 becoming a distant memory.[2]

### Partners in Obedience

The task which confronts the churches of the world is one. The commission to that task is one, spoken to all who name the name of Christ. The challenge must be met unitedly.

That a united approach to the common task must be – can be – achieved by the younger and older churches of the world was made abundantly clear at Whitby. An equality, a mutuality, a shared partnership between the younger and older churches was there manifest to a marked degree. There was no need to argue the necessity for more understanding between the

---

[1] Cit. Hogg, *Ecumenical Foundations*, 340-41.

[2] See further, J. Samuel Escobar, 'The Missiological Significance of Latin American Protestantism', in *International Review of Mission*, 101.393 (November 2011), 232-43.

two. What had once been discussed and hoped for was now a reality. In the very nature of things, there are and will be differences between the younger and older churches. That fact is inescapable. But whereas in the past the relationship has been as that between parent and child, with the frequent recurrence of unhappy paternalism and undue dependence, now in very truth the relationship is one between brothers who recognise that in their common sonship each has responsibilities to the other, and together, for the world. This new partnership in obedience to God's will is part of the tomorrow which the Whitby delegates knew was here.

It was not always so. Western churches, the so-called 'sending' churches, provided the missionaries, supplied the money and supervised its expenditure. Unfortunately too, some missionaries were imbued with an attitude of 'the white man's burden'. Paternalism and the patriarchal missionary at the head of a small Christian community were the all too common results. These, of course, made difficult the widespread development of first-rate indigenous leadership – nationals who could assume full responsibility for the welfare of the Church in their homeland.

On the other hand, there has been frequently among the younger churches a too easy, complacent acceptance of continued dependency. Even today not more than 15 per cent of the local congregations of the younger churches are totally self-supporting. Some of the reasons for this must be considered later. It has been most difficult, also, to claim the ablest men of the younger churches for leadership in the Church. This, too, issues from glaringly evident causes which must be met realistically before any serious advance can be made. 'Colonial churches' have often resulted, with the difficulties that attend any colonial relationship. When in the past representatives of the younger and older churches met together in conference, the lines were clearly drawn between the two. Both shared responsibility for the resultant friction, but each tended to recognise the other's shortcomings only. Naturally, in conference this produced heated discussions. The contrasting unanimity which marked the Whitby meeting has already been noted.

Today the colonial churches are coming of age. Indeed, some of the so-called younger churches in India are actually older than one of the major denominations in the United States, the Disciples of Christ. In fact, the distinction between the terms 'older' and 'younger' became largely obsolete at Whitby, proof of the coming of age of the younger churches. After a few minutes of a fresh nomenclature, it was decided to retain the familiar terms for convenience only.

The war, with accompanying shifts in the financial status of the churches, the shared burdens, and the suffering together of missionaries with younger churchmen; the growing fellowship of the churches in the ecumenical movement; and the changing world scene in which Communism, secularism, religious imperialism, mechanisation, and depersonalisation of life confront older and younger churches equally – at

Whitby all these combined to create a new unity and urgency. In this changed relationship the whole problem of effecting mutuality disappeared. Instead younger and older together in an accomplished reciprocity undertook to outline a single programme to do no less than carry the Gospel to the whole world. This was the difference between Madras [Tambaram] and Whitby.

Evangelism, the evangelisation of the whole world – expectant evangelism in the face of an unprecedented massing of forces opposed to Christianity – this is the one, immediate, supreme challenge confronting the Church today. This is not the special task of the younger churches, nor of the older churches, but of both. World evangelism – the evangelisation of every area of life by men and women ablaze with the fire of God, torches flaming with the Gospel of Christ – is the task of the Church. The compelling urgency of a world whose agony now may drive it to one blinding flash of atomic death leaves the Church no time for considered alternatives. The Church has but one choice, like it or not, meet it or not. The very desperation of the world – worse now than during the war – gives to the Church its one unexampled opportunity. It is momentary. But in God's grace the moment has been thrust before the Church. The task – urgent, of unimaginable magnitude, thrilling beyond the comprehension of man's mind – is the fulfilment of the Great Commission.

Confronting an unprecedented world challenge, Whitby categorically declared that all churches together must revive and deepen their own life, that the spiritual nurture of each individual Christian may be strengthened. If the Church is to be the Church, it will be so to the extent that it produces within and without a far-reaching revival. With equal emphasis Whitby asserted the necessity for every local church to inculcate within each member a sense of responsibility as a member of the Holy Catholic Church – the Church Universal. The unsurpassed glory of realised kinship in the ecumenical community of world Christianity is the divine intention for all who confess Jesus Christ as Lord. It was never meant to be the exclusive privilege of the leaders of the churches. But the *sine qua non* for the whole of the larger accomplishment is the training by the churches of every member according to his ability for the work of Christian witness. Wherever that is accomplished, each layman will be bearing his own testimony in seeking the sanctification of the life of the home, in winning the younger generation for Christ, and in permeating the whole common life with Christian principles and ideals. When that witnessing is effective, it will instil in every Christian as a son of God a sense of total stewardship for the maintenance of the existing Church and for the great evangelistic task ahead.

Upon younger and older churches alike, the demand of the hour is to establish pioneer work in all those areas of the world where the Gospel has not yet been preached and where the Church has not yet taken root. But within this partnership in obedience to the Divine Commission, one special charge is given to the older churches and one to the younger churches. To the older churches the commission is to make compelling to youth the needs of younger churches and to enlist young people in the world mission in numbers far greater than ever before. It must be admitted with shame that among the older churches there are many which have never yet taken seriously the obligation of the Great Commission and accept grudgingly, if at all, the duty to make available their ablest men and women in the work of the younger churches. There are still instances of church leaders discouraging rather than encouraging recruitment among those best suited for missionary service. This must be set right. For the younger churches there is the call to put away once for all every thwarting sense of dependence upon the older churches, and on the true ground of absolute spiritual equality and under the guidance of the Holy Spirit, 'to bear their own distinctive witness in the world, as the instrument by which God wills to bring to Christ the whole population of the lands in which they dwell'.[3]

[3] Kenneth Scott Latourette and William Richey Hogg, *Tomorrow is Here: A Survey of the worldwide mission and work of the Christian Church* (London: Edinburgh House Press, 1948), 93-102.

## WILLINGEN 1952 – *MISSIO DEI*

- Backdrop of western colonialism in decline and Communist revolution in China
- Mission under question as United Nations signalled era of international co-operation
- Mission reinterpreted as the mission of God rather than an activity of the church
- Church-centred understanding of mission in tension with a broader conception
- Participation, for the first time, of leaders of Pentecostal churches

The global landscape was changing rapidly when the IMC met at Willingen in Germany in 1952. Two world wars had fatally undermined the moral authority of the 'Christian' West. The advent of the United Nations placed a premium on mutual understanding and co-operation among nations and implicitly questioned the role of the Christian missionary enterprise. Colonial rule had come to an end in south Asia and was increasingly under question in Africa. The Communist revolution in China had led to the expulsion of all missionaries from what had been regarded as a premier mission field. Meanwhile the continuing rise of secularism in the West eroded the strength of what had once been the 'home base' of missions. It was a shattering and soul-searching time for missionary leaders. Familiar features were disappearing from the landscape. The outlook was unclear, confusing and threatening. Mission, it appeared, was in crisis. As Max Warren, General Secretary of the Anglican Church Missionary Society, put it: 'We have to be ready to see the day of missions, as we have known them, as having already come to an end.'[1]

The crisis prompted a quest for a deeper theological meaning and justification of mission. The far-reaching result was a new focus on an understanding of mission as the mission of God. Anthropocentric and ecclesiocentric conceptions of mission gave way to theocentric, Christocentric and basileio-centric conceptions. Though the term *missio Dei* was not used at Willingen, it was coined soon afterwards by German missionary leader Karl Hartenstein to describe the main theological emphasis of the conference. This was truly a new departure in the understanding of mission, one which rested on the pioneering theological work of Karl Barth. As David Bosch observed: 'In the new image, mission is not primarily an activity of the church, but an attribute of God. God is a missionary God… Mission is thereby seen as a movement from God to the

---

[1] Cit. Lesslie Newbigin, 'Mission to Six Continents', in Harold E. Fey (ed), *The Ecumenical Advance: A History of the Ecumenical Movement, Volume 2, 1948-1968*, 3rd edition. (Geneva: WCC, 1970), 178.

world; the church is viewed as an instrument for that mission. There is church because there is mission, not vice versa. To participate in mission is to participate in the movement of God's love toward people, since God is a fountain of sending love.'[2]

This new understanding has subsequently been recognised as a decisive paradigm shift for ecumenical missiology and has ever more widely commended itself as a key to understanding the meaning of mission. This led, in turn, to the emergence of consensus about the missionary character of the church. This conviction would soon find its most celebrated expression in the opening words of *Ad Gentes*, the Second Vatican Council's statement on mission: 'The Church on earth is by its very nature missionary since, according to the plan of the Father, it has its origin in the mission of the Son and the Holy Spirit.'[3] Such an understanding of mission was anticipated by the Willingen Conference.

This theological understanding of mission provided an anchor in changing times. However, it also provoked questions which would be unsettling in the missionary movement. *Missio Dei* was an inspiring but also an ambiguous conception. For some it represented a radically new conception of mission in which the world rather than the church was the primary locus of God's activity. The Dutch missiologist J.C. Hoekendijk was an especially strong critic of the church-centric understanding of mission, and urged that the Kingdom of God should be understood on the much broader basis of the totality of the action of God in the life of the world, particularly within political, cultural and scientific movements of the time.[4] This proved to be a fertile line of thought which would have great influence in the ecumenical movement in the 1960s and 1970s. Yet it also provoked a reaction from those who feared that the distinct meaning of Christian mission was being dissolved and who continued to view the planting and growth of churches as the core of the missionary project. The Willingen conference worked hard to hold these emphases in tension, particularly by grounding the missionary calling of the church in the Triune life of God and by its oft-quoted dictum that there is no participation in Christ without participation in his mission to the world.

Once again national Christian leaders from the younger churches spoke eloquently of the urgency and importance of church unity. They were acutely conscious that the integrity of mission depended on the unity of the

---

[2] David J. Bosch, *Transforming Mission: Paradigm Shifts in Theology of Mission* (Maryknoll, NY: Orbis Books, 1991), 390.

[3] *Ad Gentes,* §2, Austin Flannery (ed), *Vatican Council II: The Conciliar and Post Conciliar Documents* (Wilmington: Scholarly Resources, 1975), 814; see further, Stephen B. Bevans, 'Mission at the Second Vatican Council: 1962-1965', in Stephen B. Bevans (ed), *A Century of Catholic Mission: Roman Catholic Missiology 1910 to the Present* (Oxford: Regnum, 2013), 101-11.

[4] See J.C. Hoekendijk, *The Church Inside Out* (Philadelphia, PA: Westminster Press, 1966).

church. The gospel of reconciliation would always sound hollow if it did not give rise to reconciled communities. A significant development at Willingen, in terms of participation, was the presence of Pentecostal leaders. Moreover, they prepared a statement which was submitted by David du Plessis and included in the official record: 'After nearly half a century of misunderstanding and ostracism, for which they recognise they have not been entirely without blame on their own part, the Pentecostal Churches offer their fellowship in Christ to the whole of the Church in this grave hour of her history. They believe they have something to gain by larger fellowship with all who truly belong to Christ. They are greatly encouraged by many worldwide tokens that old prejudices are melting and a new era of mutual appreciation dawning. Brethren, let us receive one another, as Christ also received us to the glory of God.'[5]

## A Statement on the Missionary Calling of the Church

### *1. The Missionary Situation and the Rule of God*

We meet here at Willingen as a fellowship of those who are committed to the carrying out of Christ's commission to preach the Gospel to every creature. Like the great missionary gatherings which have gone before, we face a world largely ignorant of the Gospel. But unlike them, we face a world in which other faiths of revolutionary power confront us in the full tide of victory, faiths which have won swift and sweeping triumphs, and which present to the Christian missionary movement a challenge more searching than any it has faced since the rise of Islam. Amid the world-shaking events of our time, when men's hearts are failing them for fear of the things coming on the earth, what does the Spirit say to the churches about the missionary task?

The answer given to us is this: 'Lift up your heads, because your redemption draweth nigh.' Our word in this dark hour is not one of retreat but one of advance. We have to confess with penitence our share of responsibility for the terrible events of our time. Yet we preach not ourselves but Christ crucified – to human seeming a message of defeat, but to those who know its secret, the very power of God. We who take our stand here can never be cast down by any disaster, for we know that God rules the revolutionary forces of history and works out His purpose by the hidden power of the Cross. The Cross does not answer the world's questions, because they are not the real questions. It confronts the world with the real questions, which are God's questions – casting down all that

---

[5] Norman Goodall (ed), *Missions Under the Cross: Addresses delivered at the enlarged meeting of the Committee of the International Missionary Council at Willingen, Germany, 1952; with statements issued by the meeting* (London: Edinburgh House Press, 1953), 250.

exalts itself in defiance of Him, bringing to nothing the idolatries by which men are deceived, and raising up those who are sunk in disillusionment and despair. Inside the Church and out, men are asking: What is happening to us in our time? We answer this with the word of the Cross, and demand of all men everywhere that they should put their whole trust in Him who was cast out and crucified by men, but was raised by God to the right hand of His power. His rule is hidden but sure, and His word to us is this: 'These good tidings of the Kingdom shall be preached in the whole world for a testimony to all the nations, and then the end shall come.' The battle is set between His hidden Kingdom and those evil spiritual forces which lure men on towards false hopes, or bind them down to apathy, in difference and despair. There is no room for neutrality in this conflict. Every man must choose this day whom he will serve.

### *2. The Missionary Obligation of the Church*

The missionary movement of which we are a part has its source in the Triune God Himself. Out of the depths of His love for us, the Father has sent forth His own beloved Son to reconcile all things to Himself, that we and all men might, through the Spirit, be made one in Him with the Father in that perfect love which is the very nature of God. In the following affirmations we seek to set forth the nature of the duty and authority which are given to the Church to be His witnesses to all men everywhere:

1. God has created all things and all men that in them the glory of His love might be reflected; nothing therefore is excluded from the reach of His redeeming love.
2. All men are involved in a common alienation from God from which none can escape by his own efforts.
3. God has sent forth one Saviour, one Shepherd to seek and save all the lost, one Redeemer who by His death, resurrection and ascension has broken down the barrier between man and God, accomplished a full and perfect atonement, and created in Himself one new humanity, the Body of which Christ is the exalted and regnant Head.
4. On the foundation of this accomplished work God has sent forth His Spirit, the Spirit of Jesus, to gather us together in one Body in Him, to guide us into all truth, to enable us to worship the Father in spirit and in truth, to empower us for the continuance of His mission as His witnesses and ambassadors, the first fruits and earnest of its completion.
5. By the Spirit we are enabled both to press forward as ambassadors of Christ, beseeching all men to be reconciled to God, and also to wait with sure confidence for the final victory of His love, of which He has given us most sure promises.

We who have been chosen in Christ, reconciled to God through Him, made members of His Body, sharers in His Spirit, and heirs through hope of His Kingdom, are by these very facts committed to full participation in His mission to the world. That by which the Church receives its existence is that by which it is also give its world mission. 'As the Father hath sent me, even so send I you.'

### *3. The Total Missionary Task*

God sends forth the Church to carry out His work to the ends of the earth, to all nations, and to the end of time.

1. The Church is sent to every inhabited area of the world. No place is too far or too near. Every group of Christians is sent as God's ambassadors to the people in its immediate neighbourhood. But its responsibility is not limited to its neighbourhood. Because Christ is King of kings and Saviour of the world, each group of Christians is also responsible for the proclamation of His Kingship to the uttermost parts of the earth.
2. The Church is sent to every social, political and religious community of mankind, both to those near at hand and to those far off. It is sent to those who deny or rebel against the reign of Christ; and no weakness, persecution or opposition may be allowed to limit this mission. Such are the conditions which the Church must expect for its warfare. Faithfulness to Christ will require the Church to come to grips with the social, political, economic and cultural life of the people to whom it is sent.
3. The Church is sent to proclaim Christ's reign in every moment and every situation. This means that the mission of the Church forbids it to drift or to flee before the events of our time. At one and the same moment, opportunities for advancing the mission of the Church lie alongside the catastrophic destruction of that mission. Because the Church is sent forth to do its work until the completion of time, and because Christ is the only One sent forth to judge and redeem the life of men, the Church is bidden in its mission to seek out the moments of opportunity and to interpret the catastrophes as the judgements of God which are the other side of His mercy.

The Church is thus compelled by the terms of its charter not merely to build up its life where it is and as it is, but also to go forth to the ends of the earth, to all nations, and to the completion of time. The mission of the Church will always transcend boundaries, but these can no longer be identified with national boundaries and certainly not with any supposed line between the 'Christian West' and the 'non-Christian East'. The mission involves both geographical extension and also intensive penetration of all spheres of life.

The call to missionary service may come to any believer in any church anywhere in the world. If and when that call comes, he is bound to leave land and kindred, and go out to do *that* missionary job. The Church is like an army living in tents. God calls His people to strike their tents and go forward. And Christ's promise holds that He will be with them even to the end of the world.

### *4. Solidarity with the World*

The Church's words and works, its whole life of mission, are to be a witness to what God has done, is doing, and will do in Christ. But this word 'witness' cannot possibly mean that the Church stands over against the world, detached from it and regarding it from a position of superior righteousness or security. The Church is in the world, and as the Lord of the Church identified Himself wholly with mankind, so must the Church also do. The nearer the Church draws to its Lord, the nearer it draws to the world. Christians do not live in an enclave separated from the world; they are God's people in the world.

Therefore the Church is required to identify itself with the world, not only in its perplexity and distress, its guilt and its sorrow, but also in its real acts of love and justice – acts by which it often puts the churches to shame. The churches must confess that they have often passed by on the other side while the unbeliever, moved by compassion, did what the churches ought to have done. Wherever a church denies its solidarity with the world, or divorces its deeds from its words, it destroys the possibility of communicating the Gospel and presents to the world an offence which is not the genuine offence of the Cross.

### *5. Discerning the Signs of the Times*

Our Lord bade His disciples discern the signs of the times. To human sight this may be a time of darkness and confusion. But eyes opened by the Crucified will discern in it sure signs of God's sovereign rule. We bear witness to the mighty works of His Spirit among us in many parts of the Church since we met together at Whitby. We believe that the sovereign rule of Him who is Saviour and Judge of all men is no less to be discerned by eyes of faith in the great events of our day, in the vast enlargements of human knowledge and power which this age is witnessing, in the mighty political and social movements of our time, and in countless personal experiences of which the inner history cannot be revealed until the Last Day. Above all, we are encouraged by our Lord Himself to discern at such a time as this His summons to us to go forward.

When all things are shaken, when familiar landmarks are blotted out, when war and tumult engulf us, when all human pride and pretension are humbled, we proclaim anew the hidden reign of our crucified and ascended

Lord. We summon all Christians to come forth from the securities which are no more secure and from boundaries of accepted duty too narrow for the Lord of all the earth, and to go forth with fresh assurance to the task of bringing all things into captivity to Him, and of preparing the whole earth for the day of His Coming.[6]

[6] Goodall, *Missions Under the Cross*, 188-92.

## ACHIMOTA 1957-58 – CHURCH AND MISSION

- Debate on whether the IMC should integrate with the WCC
- Theological argument that church and mission belong together
- Concern that passion for mission might be swamped by ecclesiastical agendas
- Tension between traditional understanding of evangelism and broader conceptions
- Leadership training paramount – establishment of the Theological Education Fund

When the World Council of Churches was formed in 1948, the International Missionary Council was formally 'in association'. Soon the question was raised as to whether the two global bodies should be integrated. With Tambaram having brought a clear understanding that responsibility for mission lies primarily with the church, there was a strong theological argument in favour of integration. A WCC meeting at Rolle in 1951 had adopted an influential statement on 'The Calling of the Church to Mission and Unity', drafted by Lesslie Newbigin, which argued at a theological level for the indissoluble connection of mission and unity.[1] Others, however, were concerned that a church-centric view of mission was inhibiting missionary initiative. Max Warren, General Secretary of the Anglican Church Missionary Society, argued that, 'Today the gravest embarrassment of the mission societies lies in the actual unwillingness of the younger churches to set them free to perform the tasks for which they properly exist – the pioneering of those new frontiers, not necessarily geographical, which have not yet been marked with a cross.'[2] There were also fears among mission activists that the mission agenda would be swamped by the ecclesial and bureaucratic concerns of a body like the World Council of Churches. This debate came to a head when the IMC met at Achimota, Ghana, at the end of 1957.

As well as wrestling with the question of the best institutional framework in which to advance ecumenical commitment to mission, the Achimota conference was concerned with the very definition of mission. As Mark Laing remarks: 'At one level the debate on integration was about

[1] See Lesslie Newbigin, *Unfinished Agenda: An Updated Autobiography* (Geneva: WCC, 1993), 133-34; Mark T.B. Laing, *From Crisis to Creation: Lesslie Newbigin and the Reinvention of Christian Mission* (Eugene, OR: Pickwick, 2012), 61-69.

[2] Warren, cited by S.C. Graaf van Randwijk, 'Some Reflections of a Mission Board Secretary', in Ronald K. Orchard (ed), *The Ghana Assembly of the International Missionary Council, 28th December to 8th January, 1958* (London: Edinburgh House Press, 1958), 94.

organisational structures. But beyond structural obsessiveness lay more searching theological questions on the relationship between mission and church. By the middle of the twentieth century there was a realisation that the Protestant missionary movement had reached a crisis. Factors within and outwith the movement force those engaged in missions to the realisation that missions not only needed to be reorganised, but the concept of mission itself required rehabilitation.'[3] The *missio Dei* thinking which had emerged at Willingen was again prominent. The German missiologist Walter Freytag spoke of how missions had lost their way and suggested that understanding mission broadly as God's reality in this world was the best basis on which to face the future. While some were ready to embrace this new understanding of mission, others espoused a more traditional evangelistic approach. It was a point of divergence which was to have far-reaching effects.

A far-reaching initiative of the Achimota Conference was the establishment of the generously endowed Theological Education Fund which would play a significant role in enabling the development of theological education in the 'younger churches'. In years to come it would foster and resource the training and formation of many of those who were to provide leadership to the ecumenical movement.

### The Christian Mission at This Hour

The Christian world mission is Christ's, not ours. Prior to all our efforts and activities, prior to all our gifts of service and devotion, God sent His Son into the world. And He came in the form of a servant – a servant who suffered even to the death of the Cross.

This conviction was emphasised by the Chairman in his opening address. We have seen it to be the only true motive of Christian mission and the only standard by which the spirit, method and modes of Christian missionary organisation must be judged. We believe it is urgent that this word of judgement and mercy should be given full freedom to cleanse and redeem our present activities, lest our human pride in our activities hinder the free course of God's mission in the world.

But we are none the less fellow-workers with Christ in His mission. That is ground for humility, not for pride. For He trusts *us* with *His* mission. 'All power is given to *Me* in heaven and on earth. Go *ye* therefore and make disciples of all nations, baptising them into the name of the Father, and of the Son and of the Holy Spirit' – not into your own name, nor the name of your Church or culture. Christ trusts us to discharge His mission in His form, the form of a servant, a servant whose characteristics are humility and suffering.

---

[3] Laing, *From Crisis to Creation*, 33.

So we are responsible. Each of us in his own place, each local company of Christ's people, each church in its organised life, cannot be Christ's without being His missionary servant. A vague and generalised acceptance of the world mission is no substitute for responsible action in the discharge of missionary obedience.

But we are responsible to one another in Christ. We are called in Him to recognise with gladness that our fellow-Christians, our neighbouring congregations, our sister denominations in our own and other lands, are called by the same missionary Lord, and need the same freedom as we ourselves do to respond to His calling.

There is a tension which can easily become a contradiction – the tension between missionary passion and a due regard for the claims of the Christian fellowship. It has shown itself at many points in our discussions, as we have talked together about the place and function of the missionary, the structure and tasks of the Christian Councils, and especially in our discussion of the proposal that the IMC and the WCC should become one body. We have not seen how the contradiction can be removed. It may well be that the tension is one that is inherent in the Christian life. We have, however, we believe, discerned some points at which the tension can be creative within the fellowship.

### *Reasons For and Against the Integration of the Two World Bodies*

The arguments advanced in favour and against integration may be roughly grouped under five heads, though there can be no hard-and-fast divisions between them.

(1) Integration is the appropriate outcome of the trends of development which have brought the two bodies to their present situations. This trend of historic development was referred to by many speakers, both those who favoured and those who were opposed to integration. Reference was made to: (a) The fact that it was the missionary movement which gave rise to the movement towards unity (both internationally and in the lands of the 'younger' Churches). This point was especially emphasised by several speakers from Councils in Asia. (b) The development of the 'association' of the two bodies, especially in their joint activities, the Churches' Commission on International Affairs, the East Asia Secretariat, the Division of Studies, the 'emergency' activities of the Division of Inter-Church Aid, and the Joint Committee. (c) The concern of both bodies with 'mission and unity'. (d) The increase in common planning in response to specific needs. (e) The geographical and functional overlapping, as more Churches in Asia and Africa become members of the WCC, and as the integration of faith and mission takes place locally, especially in Asia, and in world confessional bodies.

This historical trend was diversely interpreted. For some, it was 'the inherent logic of events'. Others saw in it the result of 'the pressure of the

Holy Spirit'. The latter interpretation was questioned by several (both those favouring and those opposing the plan) on the ground that the integration of the two world bodies was a purely organisational question. For two speakers, the trend implied that 'things had gone too far' for the plan to be opposed even by those who regarded it as a mistake.

(2) Integration was commended for theological reasons, such as: that mission and unity belong together; mission is of the *esse* of the Church; the Church needs mission and missions need the Church; 'theological consistency' requires that the two world bodies should become one. Reference was made to the summary of these theological considerations in the introduction to the Plan, p. 29, viz.:

> A basic and long-forgotten truth is being re-discovered in our time, which might be stated thus: the *unity* of the Church and the *mission* of the Church both belong, in equal degree, to the *essence* of the Church. If Christian churches would be in very truth the Church, they must carry the Gospel into all the world. They must also strive to achieve the unity of all those throughout the world for whom Jesus Christ is Lord. This truth has already become manifest in the life of both the world bodies. It has led them into association with each other and now obliges them to go further. They exist to help the churches to witness to the wholeness of the Gospel and must, therefore, seek to express the wholeness in their own life.

The theological arguments were challenged on the grounds that (1) the question is an organisational one, and the real issue is obscured by being taken into the sphere of theology; (2) 'that mission and unity belong together' says something about church and mission relationships, but not about the relationships of the WCC (which is not a church) and the IMC (which is not a mission); it does not necessarily involve the administrative unity of the two organisations. (3) Church history and the contemporary scene provide evidence that mission can be fulfilled without unity; the most active groups in mission today (amongst whom are some whose work is undoubtedly effective) are Pentecostalists and other 'evangelicals' and the Roman Catholics; yet they are not notable for their concern for unity. (4) It was a tenable theological position that only in mission shall we begin to understand what is the unity which God wants for His Church; this view questions presuppositions about organic unity in current ecumenical discussion.

(3) Integration was commended on the ground that it would put mission at the heart of the ecumenical movement. It would mean that the Churches could not possibly meet together without being faced with their responsibility for mission. Several speakers referred to the importance of the 'younger' Churches as they became members of the WCC, finding mission at its centre. Some considered that integration would facilitate the development by the 'younger' Churches of their missionary outreach; one speaker gave this as the reason for his council's approval of integration for which otherwise it felt no enthusiasm. On the other hand, reference was

made to the fear of some lest 'evangelical zeal' should be sacrificed for the sake of a 'nominal unity'.

(4) Integration was held to be necessary by those who considered that there was no justification for the continued existence of two world bodies. They pointed out that Churches, both 'older' and 'younger', especially those in which the mission was an integral part of the Church organisation, were perplexed by having to deal with two separate world bodies. The continued separation of what belongs together leads to tension and embarrassment in the work of the two bodies themselves, which, it was suggested, would increase the longer the separation continued. Several speakers considered that the bringing of the two bodies together would strengthen the response of Christians to the challenge of non-Christians and of the changes in the social and political scene. Several speakers who had been associated with both the WCC and the IMC spoke of the similarity in the outlook and purposes of the two bodies.

On the other hand, there were those who questioned whether the integration of the two world bodies would in fact reflect the reality of the local relationship of Church and mission in the world generally. Two speakers contended that the cause of mission and the cause of unity could best be served by a continuance of the present relationship of 'association'; several others expressed their doubts of this view. One speaker referred to fear that many had that integration would result in the creation of a 'mammoth organisation'.

(5) The 'Draft Plan' was commended because it would conserve in the new body all that was represented by the IMC Assembly, which was virtually unchanged in the proposed integrated body, and is provided with an interim body to implement its decisions. But one speaker thought the plan implied absorption rather than integration.[4]

[4] Orchard, *The Ghana Assembly*, 180-81, 157-60.

# New Delhi 1961 – Integration of International Missionary Council and World Council of Churches

- Integration of IMC and WCC grounded on theological imperative
- WCC constitution amended to reflect the missionary nature of the church
- Growing tensions between 'ecumenicals' and 'evangelicals'
- Interrelation of universal horizon and local congregational expression
- Admission of several Orthodox Churches to membership of the WCC

While there were structural and organisational arguments in favour of the integration of the IMC and the WCC, it was also driven by the theological conviction that church and mission belonged together. For Lesslie Newbigin, IMC General Secretary, the unity of the church was essential to the integrity of mission just as much as its missionary nature was essential to the integrity of the church. There was thus a theological imperative driving the integration process, as well as practical and organisational considerations. This found expression in a change to the 'Basis' of the World Council of Churches at the New Delhi Assembly where integration was formally enacted. Originally, the WCC had identified itself as 'a fellowship of churches which accept our Lord Jesus Christ as God and Saviour'. At New Delhi, the verb 'accept' was replaced by 'confess' and a new phrase was added: 'and therefore seek to fulfil together their common calling to the glory of the one God, Father, Son and Spirit.' This gave the WCC a much more missionary orientation as integration with the IMC was recognised in fundamental constitutional terms.[1]

However, the resistance to integration that had found expression at Achimota had by no means abated. It was viewed with deep suspicion by a growing Evangelical constituency. IMC General Secretary Norman Goodall, estimated that, in 1957, 70% of foreign missionaries were American. Of these only 42% belonged to agencies which related to the National Christian Council of Churches. The other 58% worked with agencies which did not co-operate with the IMC or WCC.[2] This growing Evangelical constituency was forming its own networks which were often

---

[1] *The New Delhi Report: The Third Assembly of the World Council of Churches, 1961* (London: SCM, 1962), 152-59; cit. Laing, *From Crisis to Creation*, 120.
[2] Cit. Laing, *From Crisis to Creation*, 49.

defined by their opposition to the trends evident in the IMC and WCC. The Protestant missionary movement was increasingly marked by a sharp division between 'Ecumenicals' and 'Evangelicals'. As Mark Laing observes: 'The loose, broad-based association the IMC had maintained for decades was fractured, and the relationship between evangelicals and 'ecumenicals' became increasingly polarised and antagonistic.'[3]

Though integration, ironically, was to lead to a fragmentation of the missionary movement, its historic significance cannot be underestimated. As Stephen Neill remarked: 'This was indeed a revolutionary moment in Church history. More than two hundred Church bodies in all parts of the world, assembled in the persons of their official representatives, had solemnly declared themselves in the presence of God to be responsible as Churches for the evangelisation of the whole world. Such an event had never taken place in the history of the Church since Pentecost.'[4] The Assembly gave the following mandate to the Department of World Mission and Evangelism: 'To assist churches, missions and other Christian bodies to recognise and draw the practical conclusions from the fact that:

1. The Christian mission is one throughout the world, for the Gospel is the same and the need of salvation is the same for all men.
2. This world mission has a base which is worldwide and is not confined to the areas once regarded as constituting 'Western Christendom'.
3. The mission implies a reaching out both to one's own neighbourhood and to the ends of the earth.'[5]

This latter point was emphasised in an influential paragraph of the New Delhi report which was drafted by Lesslie Newbigin: 'We believe that the unity which is both God's will and his gift to his Church is being made visible as all in each place who are … reaching out in witness and service to all and who at the same time are united *with the whole Christian fellowship in all places* and all ages in such wise that ministry and members are accepted by all, and that all can act and speak together as occasion requires for the tasks to which God calls his people.'[6] The interrelation of the universal horizon and the local congregational expression of church life were to be a constant preoccupation of ecumenical missiology in the years to come.

Another influential development at New Delhi was the admission of several Orthodox Churches to full membership of the WCC. From this point onwards their perspectives would exercise growing influence on the ecumenical understanding of mission, through such characteristic themes as

---

[3] Mark Laing, 'The Church Is the Mission: Integrating the IMC with the WCC', *International Review of Mission,* 100.393 (November 2011), 218.

[4] Stephen Neill, *The Church and Christian Union* (London: Oxford University Press, 1968), 108-09; cit. Yates, *Christian Mission*, 157.

[5] Newbigin, 'Mission to Six Continents', 188.

[6] *New Delhi Report*, 116; cit. Laing, *From Crisis to Creation*, 202.

the cosmic character of salvation, the eschatological nature of mission and the duty to incarnate the gospel in every culture.[7] Soon the Second Vatican Council would open the way for greatly increased involvement by the Roman Catholic Church in ecumenical missiology. Though it never became a member-church of the WCC,, from the 1960s the Roman Catholic Church became an influential partner in ecumenical missiological endeavour.

## Lesslie Newbigin – The Missionary Dimension of the Ecumenical Movement

The deepest reason for our coming together lies in the nature of the Gospel itself. As the Central Committee said ten years ago at Rolle:

> The obligation to take the Gospel to the whole world, and the obligation to draw all Christ's people together, both rest upon Christ's whole work and are indissolubly connected. Every attempt to separate these tasks violates the wholeness of Christ's ministry to the world.

And the Central Committee was right, therefore, in drawing attention to the danger of a false use of the word *ecumenical*, a use which omits the missionary dimension and therefore parts company wholly with the original meaning of the word. It is time to say again plainly that the words 'ecumenical' and 'interdenominational' are not synonymous. A meeting among churchmen is not, in itself, an ecumenical occasion. This is not a minor matter. The way we use words eventually shapes the way we act. This is a moment, surely, to remember what the word 'ecumenical' really means.

### *The Contribution of the IMC to the Integrated World Council*

I have sought to remind you of the deep interconnection between our two councils from the very beginning of their histories, and of the source of this interconnection in the nature of the Gospel itself. Mission and unity are two sides of the same reality, or rather two ways of describing the same action of the living Lord who wills that all should be drawn to Himself. But it would be a false simplification to suggest that within the whole ecumenical movement, the IMC stands for mission and the WCC for unity. A moment's reflection on the history of the two councils is enough to dispel the idea. From the Edinburgh Conference onwards, the IMC has been profoundly concerned about unity. No stronger call for visible reunion has come from any meeting than those which were given by the IMC conferences at Tambaram in 1938 and at Willingen in 1952. Perhaps the most massive single piece of ecumenically organised inter-church aid at the present time is the Theological Education Fund of the IMC. And on the

[7] Anastasios Yannoulatos, 'The Purpose and Motive of Mission', in *International Review of Mission,* 54 (1965), 281-97.

other hand, the World Council of Churches has from the beginning concerned itself deeply with the missionary task – as witness the work of the 2nd Commission at Amsterdam.

Few things have done more to strengthen the understanding of the missionary task of the Church than the work of the WCC's Department on the Laity. Both Councils have been drawn by the logic of the Gospel itself to concern themselves both with the mission of the Church and with its unity. Their coming together is a wholly natural and proper response to the continuing pressure of that logic.

But human structures are never simply visible embodiments of theological principles. They have particular and individual characteristics that arise from their history, from the obedience and disobedience of the many men and women who have shaped them. The IMC is no exception. Rather than speaking only of mission and unity as theological principles, it will be wise at this moment to look at the concrete character of that which is brought from the side of the IMC into the integrated council. Let me suggest three characteristics which seem to me worthy of special attention at this moment in our common history.

1. The original base of the IMC was in the mission boards and societies of the western churches. Of its 17 original member councils, 13 were missionary councils. Today, of course, the majority of the 38 member councils represent the churches in what were formerly called the mission fields, and a great part of the history of the Council during the past 40 years has been concerned with the shift in the centre of gravity from mission boards to younger churches. Nevertheless, it remains true and important that a very great part of the spiritual substance – if I may put it so – which the IMC will bring into the integrated council, is constituted by the foreign missionary movement. This movement is a concrete historical phenomenon of the past 250 years. It has its own particular characteristics arising from its coincidence in time with the movement of colonial expansion from the West, and from other particular historical circumstances. We are familiar with the criticism that can be directed against it. I am not concerned here either with criticism or with defence. It is enough to say in this Assembly that the ecumenical movement owes its existence largely to the missionary movement, and that millions of those whom we here represent owe their existence as Christians to it. My concern here is to draw attention to elements in it which are of permanent importance, and which – with whatever changes of form – must remain part of the essential spiritual substance of any living ecumenical movement.

Among these elements I would place the presence at the heart of missions of a continuing and costly concern for individual people and places, expressed in sustained intercessory prayer, sacrificial giving and personal commitment. The many thousands of people, often poor and hard-pressed by their own troubles, who give regularly and pray constantly for people and causes known only through an occasional meeting or magazine article, these have given the missionary movement the spiritual force which it has had… New contacts and broad horizons, the vision conjured up by a big international meeting of a worldwide fellowship and a worldwide task – these can be exhilarating and liberating experiences. But for the long haul, for the days and years of routine without which no great enterprise is brought to victory, there can be no substitute for that kind of personal commitment expressed in unremitting intercession, unwearied giving and life-long commitment by which missions have lived for these two hundred years.

2. Secondly, the missionary movement whether in East or West has been above all concerned to reach out beyond the existing frontiers of the Christian fellowship, to *go* to the place where men live without the knowledge of the Gospel, and there to be so identified with those men that they may hear and see, in their own idiom and in the forms of their own life, the grace and power of the Lord Jesus Christ. This impulse to *go* is at the heart of missions and must remain so. It is true that both the starting point of the journey and its end are different now from what they were in the 19th century. The starting point is now everywhere that the Church is, and the end is every place where men are without the knowledge of Christ. Christendom is no longer a geographical area. The very fact that we now bring the affairs of missions right into the heart of the day-to-day life of a World Council of Churches will expose more vividly the impropriety of some ways of thinking and speaking about the missionary journey which still illegitimately survive into the 20th century. The decision that the IMC's studies in the life and growth of the younger churches should now be extended to enable representatives of the younger churches to make parallel studies in the life of the older churches is an example of the kind of changes we must hope for. I hope also that these studies will be followed by real missionary journeys; that the churchmen of Asia and Africa, having studied the spiritual situation of some of the older churches, their conflicts, their victories and their defeats, will be moved to send missionaries to Europe and America to make the Gospel credible to the pagan masses of those continents who remain unmoved by the witness of the churches in their midst. My point is that this impulse to *go*, to reach out beyond the accustomed boundaries for the sake of witness to Him who is Lord of all, has been central to the missionary movement and must remain so in the new circumstances which integration will create. Among the many things which change, this must not change. If we will think for a moment of the multitudes who are out of effective earshot of the Gospel, we shall realise how absurd is the suggestion that the call to go is less urgent than it was when Carey wrote his 'Enquiry' or when St Paul wrote: 'How shall they hear without a preacher, and how shall men preach unless they be sent?'

I emphasise this point because there are those who deprecate this emphasis on the command to go, who point to the very large place taken in the Bible by the centripetal as opposed to the centrifugal understanding of the mission of God's people, to the fact that this mission is a gathering and not just a sending. In certain contexts this reminder is needed: missions are not the whole content of the Church's mission. God's mission is more than the activities called missions. But the activities called missions are an indispensable part (a part, not the whole) of the obedience which the churches must render to God's calling. To quote Walter Freytag, missions have to remind every church 'that it cannot be the Church in limiting itself within its own area, that it is called to take part in the responsibility of God's outgoing into the whole world, that it has the Gospel because it is meant for the nations of the earth'. This remains true in the new situation in which we shall be after integration. The Commission on World Mission and Evangelism, which – God willing – will be established immediately after this Assembly, will exist 'to further the proclamation of the Gospel of the Lord Jesus Christ to all men to the end that they may turn to Him and be saved'. It will be the task of the Commission within the life of the World Council to press upon every church in every part of the world the obligation to take its share in that task, as an indispensable element without which its own confession of the Gospel would lack something of full integrity.

3. The IMC has been from the beginning of its existence deeply concerned with the issues – spiritual and administrative – which have arisen in the development from mission to Church, and in the relation between older and younger churches. These issues have been deep and often perplexing. There have been – on the positive side – the abiding love, knowledge and concern which the sending boards and societies have had, and continue to have, for the churches which are the fruit of their work, and the reciprocal affection and trust which – thank God – bind these younger churches to those from whom their first knowledge of the Gospel came. There have also been – on the negative side – the strains and stresses that that intimate relation has often entailed. The World Council has made possible a series of relationships between churches in which these strains were absent and everything could begin with all the freshness, the surprise and the delight of first love. It is of God's goodness that this has been so and we can all rejoice in it. The coming together of the IMC and the World Council of Churches means that these two kinds of relationships are to be held increasingly within one continuing fellowship. There will be much to learn on both sides. It will be necessary to remember, and sometimes to say sharply, both that paternalism is a sin which (like all sin) tends to blind the sinner to its existence, and also that paternity is a fact with enduring implications.

It is, I think, not out of place to mention these things in this moment, for it is only if we recognise them and face them in a spirit of mutual forgiveness and forbearance that the integration of our two councils will be fruitful, and that, speaking the truth in love, we shall grow up to Him who is Head of the whole body, and in obedience to Him who is the one Father of us all.

My purpose in speaking of these three matters has been to remind you that we have to think at this moment not only of the mission of the Church in general, but of those particular activities that are called missions, and of the issues with which those involved in these activities have sought to wrestle together in the International Missionary Council. The form of these activities must change with the changing human situation. I am convinced that the step which we are proposing to take at this Assembly will in due course lead to fruitful changes in the pattern of missionary action. Many responsibilities which were carried in the past by the International Missionary Council because it was the only world Christian body able to carry them can now be fruitfully shared with or transferred to other divisions of the World Council of Churches. Relations between churches which were formerly linked through the activity of a mission board can now be diversified through the opening of the many other channels of communication now available. Through all of these changes I hope that the effect will be to make the missionary task stand out more clearly. But this will only come about if there is – along with the administrative integration which is now proposed – a deep-going spiritual integration of the concerns which have been central in our two councils. For those who have been traditionally related to the IMC, this means a willingness to acknowledge that the particular forms and relationships characteristic of the missionary activity of the past two centuries must – like all things human – be held constantly open to the new insights that God may have to give us in the wider fellowship into which we now enter. For the churches which constitute the World Council this means the acknowledgement that the missionary task is no less central to the life of the Church that the pursuit of renewal and unity. No movement is entitled to the use of the word 'ecumenical' which is not committed to taking its share in bearing that witness.

### *The Missionary Dimension*

But God forbid that we should talk in such negatives! Our mission is not a duty but a doxology. 'O give thanks to the Lord for he is good… Let the redeemed of the Lord say so, whom he has redeemed and gathered from the lands, from the east and from the west, from the north and from the south' (Ps. 107). How can those whom He has redeemed be silent? They exist only as the first-fruit of His loving purpose for all mankind: how can they pretend otherwise? How can we, who rejoice in this gathering together by the one Lord, think that His plans end with us? How can we think that we are more than mere witnesses of what He is doing? Where is there any light in this dark world – or in our dark minds – except in Him? Where is there any hope of salvation for mankind but in Him? What sort of sense does this world make, if there be not at the heart of it the dying and rising of the Son of God? What are we in this World Council of Churches but a mere global sectarianism unless we are missionary through and through?

Sixty-six years ago a group of graduates of Madras Christian College sent a letter to the General Assembly of the Free Church of Scotland to thank them for what the College had done. The Assembly's reply thanked them for the letter and spoke of the mutual sharing of gifts between East and West that such sharing of gifts made possible. The Assembly then went on: 'But in that spirit we desire affectionately and above all things to commend you, as our missionaries have done, the Lord Jesus Christ… We have no better claim to Him than you have. We possess nothing so precious – we value nothing so much – we have no source of good so full, fruitful and enduring – we have nothing to compare with the Lord Jesus Christ. To Him we must bear witness. And we should gladly consent that you should cease to listen to us if you would be led to give your ear and your heart to him.'

There is the missionary dimension of any movement, any labour, any programme that bears the name of Christ! Over every phase of it there will be written urgently and insistently 'Don't look at us; look at him'.[8]

---

[8] Lesslie Newbigin, 'The Missionary Dimension of the Ecumenical Movement', in *The Ecumenical Review,* 14.2 (1962), 208-15; cit. Kinnamon and Cope, *The Ecumenical Movement*, 343-47.

# MEXICO CITY 1963 – WITNESS IN SIX CONTINENTS

- No longer ‘sending’ and ‘receiving’ countries – now ‘from everywhere to everywhere’
- No longer ‘missions’ – now ‘mission’, understood on a broad canvas
- Need for western churches to develop missionary congregations in their own context
- Tensions regarding the action of God through secular structures and/or the church

The first meeting of the former IMC in its new guise as the World Council of Churches Division for World Mission and Evangelism took place in 1963. The integration of church and mission inspired a vision of the church active in mission in every part of the world. The conference was marked by a new perception that the time had now passed in which one could think of the ‘home base’ and the ‘mission field’ in distinct geographical terms. Indeed, the conference’s focus on the challenges posed by secularism revealed how far the West itself had become a mission field. The question of how western churches shaped by the Christendom model could recover the missionary nature of the church became the focus of a major WCC study on the missionary structure of the congregation.[1] No longer would mission be understood in terms of ‘sending’ and ‘receiving’ countries. Instead, it was suggested that the missionary frontier runs around the world as the line that separates belief from unbelief, the unseen frontier which cuts across all other frontiers and presents the universal church with its primary missionary challenge.

Henceforth it would be a matter of mission ‘from everywhere to everywhere’. This had far-reaching implications, as Lalsangkima Pachuau observes: ‘By eliminating the old religio-geographical boundaries as the norm to define frontiers, the conference also implicitly affirmed cultural plurality and diversity. Since “mission in and to six continents” involves mutuality between Christians of all continents, unity in mission – the enduring theme of ecumenical missiology – came to be understood in a new light, namely, unity in diversity.’[2] A small but significant indication of the changing understanding of mission in this period would come in 1969

---

[1] *The Church for Others and The Church for the World: A Quest for Structures for Missionary Congregations* (Geneva: WCC, 1967).

[2] Lalsangkima Pachuau, ‘Ecumenical Missiology: Three Decades of Historical and Theological Development (1951-1982)’, in Lalsangkima Pachuau, *Ecumenical Missiology: Contemporary Trends, Issues and Themes* (Bangalore: United Theological College, 2002), 29-50.

with the removal of the 's' from the title of the International Review of Missions, so that from that year it appeared as the International Review of Mission.[3] This, as Larsson and Castro explain, 'reflected the change in attitude from "missions", meaning organised missionary work from Western Christendom to what were regarded as non-Christian countries, to "mission" as the task of the one, holy, catholic and apostolic church through its members wherever they are located.'[4]

Tensions which had been building in ecumenical missiology were clearly apparent at Mexico City. The conference's most innovative work was done around the question of how to understand the missionary task in the context of what God is doing in the secular events of our time. It struck a note of dialogue: 'The pattern of Christian mission in the secular world must therefore be one of constant encounter with the real needs of our age. Its form must be that of dialogue, using contemporary language and modes of thought, learning from the scientific and sociological categories, and meeting people in their own situations.'[5] However, while some were adventurous in advocating a view of the mission of God that perceived the action of God primarily through secular structures and agencies, others defended the view that the church is the primary sphere where the mission of God finds expression. A parallel tension was evident around the question of how to understand other religions. While some saw the presence and work of God in other religions, others maintained that other religions were demonic and stressed the continuing need for evangelism. The conference sought to take a middle line, emphasising that the gospel of Christ is for all.

## The Message

We have been concerned with 'God's Mission and Our Task' and with the witness of the whole Church of Jesus Christ to the whole Gospel of Christ to all men, whatever their race or nation, faith or lack of faith. We are constrained by a fresh awareness of the love of God for all men to send this message.

1. Our world is changing faster than it has ever done before. New patterns of life are taking form for the whole of mankind. In this revolutionary change, science and technology play a decisive part. This means two things: it makes possible for masses of people greater freedom,

---

[3] See William H. Crane, 'Dropping the S', in *International Review of Mission,* 58 (1969), 141-44.

[4] Birgitta Larsson and Emilio Castro, 'From Missions to Mission', in John Briggs, Mercy Amba Oduyoye and George Tsetsis, *A History of the Ecumenical Movement, Volume 3, 1968-2000* (Geneva: WCC, 2004), 125.

[5] Ronald K. Orchard (ed), *Witness in Six Continents: Records of the Meeting of the Commission on World Mission and Evangelism of the World Council of Churches held in Mexico City, December 8th to 19th, 1963* (London: Edinburgh House Press, 1964), 121.

greater security, more leisure and a more truly human life; but it poses a great question – is technology to be the servant of man or his master? It is a question of life and death for the world.

2. We who know the God of the Bible know that the growing dominion of man over nature is the gift of God, but also that it is a trust to be exercised in responsibility to him. God's Lordship is the sole security of man's freedom.

3. Knowing this:

a. We affirm that this world is God's world. The very turbulence of contemporary life is a product of man's response, either in obedience or disobedience to the living God. Men may not know this. They may ignore it. But the fact remains that God is Lord not only of creation but also of history. What is happening in the world of our time is under the hand of God, even when men do not acknowledge Him. We are called to a sustained effort to understand the secular world and to discern the will of God in it. This means seeking to know what is in accordance with His purpose and what is under His judgement. Thus we rejoice in all the possibilities for fuller life now open to men, but we affirm that man is only free in God's service, and if he refuses that service he will become the slave of other powers and will end in destroying himself.

b. We affirm that the God whose world this is has revealed Himself in Jesus Christ. He who is head of the Church is Lord of all. His is the name above every name. His love is for all mankind. He has died and risen again for all. Therefore we can go to men of other faiths or to men of one in humility and confidence, for the Gospel we preach is the account of what God has done and still does for all men. All men have the right to know this, and those who do know it are committed to making it known. No one, and least of all Christians, can hold that it does not matter what men believe as long as they believe something. The ultimate issue in human life is precisely who God is, and this we know in Jesus Christ. Christian witness does not rest on any kind of superiority in Christians; it rests wholly on the commission from the Christ, who came for all men, to make Him known to all. Mission is the test of faith.

c. We affirm that all Christians are called to go forward in this task together. We believe that the time has now come when we must move onwards to common planning and joint action. The fact that Christ is not divided must be made unmistakably plain in the very structure of missionary work. Our present forms of missionary organisation do not openly manifest that fact; they often conceal it. The far-reaching consequences for all churches must be faced.

d. We thus affirm that this missionary task is one and demands unity. It is one because the Gospel is one. It is one because in all countries the Churches face the same essential task. It is one because every

Christian congregation in all the world is called to show the love of God in Christ, in witness and service to the world at its doors. It demands unity because it is obedience to one Lord, and because we cannot effectively witness to the secularised or to the non-Christian world if we are isolated from one another. We need the gifts God has given to each Church for the witness of the whole Church.

e. We affirm that inevitably means crossing frontiers. This is true of the Christian missionary, who leaves one culture and one nation to go to people of other cultures to proclaim the Gospel of Christ. Moreover, there is an increasing number of men and women who go to other countries than their own, as Christians, in commerce and industry, or in the professions or government service. This is a two-way traffic, and all such people need the prayerful support of the congregations from which they go out. But there are other frontiers we need to cross: the Christian congregation must recognise that God sends it into the secular world. Christians must take their part in it – in office, factory, school and farm, and in the struggle for peace and a just order in social and racial relationships. In this task they must seek the power of the Holy Spirit to bear witness, by word and by life, to the reality of the living God, in whatever ways are open to them.

We therefore affirm that this missionary movement now involves Christians in all six continents and in all lands. It must be the common witness of the whole Church, bringing the whole Gospel to the whole world. We do not yet see the changes this demands; but we go forward in faith. God's purpose still stands: to sum up all things in Christ. In this hope we dedicate ourselves anew to His mission in the spirit of unity and in humble dependence upon our living Lord.[6]

---

[6] Orchard, *Witness in Six Continents*, 173-75.

# BANGKOK 1972-73 – SALVATION TODAY

- Re-setting relationships of 'older' and 'younger' churches – moratorium proposal
- New appreciation of distinct cultural identities and contextual theologies
- Balancing socio-political concerns with evangelism and personal conversion
- Evangelicals disturbed by socio-economic emphasis at the expense of evangelism
- Formation by Evangelicals in 1974 of Lausanne Committee for World Evangelization

The concerns of the Bangkok CWME conference found expression particularly in the moratorium debate. The 'younger churches' were not so young any more and were determined to assume responsibility for mission in their respective spheres. This would involve the western 'sending' churches in redefining their role. As Wolfgang Günther observes: 'The representatives of the rich Western churches found themselves in the dock as never before.'[1] A provocative proposal was that they should accept for a time a moratorium on missionary appointments so as to provide an opportunity for the indigenous churches to truly assume authority in their own context. This would set the scene for a new era of working in partnership. Soon, for example, the Paris Evangelical Missionary Society would evolve into the Evangelical Community for Apostolic Action (CEVAA) and the London Missionary Society into the Council for World Mission (CWM).

This attempt to re-set the operative relationships in mission was undergirded by a fresh emphasis on contextual theology and a recognition of cultural identities. The conference sought to balance socio-political concerns with a commitment to evangelism and personal conversion. In the judgement of Birgitta Larsson and Emilio Castro, 'To a remarkable extent the Bangkok conference released its participants from the old polarisation between personal and social salvation. A great number of third world participants contributed to this by objecting to being involved in a theological division that had never been their reality… The gospel manifests itself, the Bangkok conference argued, both in the justification of the sinner and in socio-political justice, and thus demands both evangelism

[1] Günther, 'World Mission Conferences', 531.

and active struggle on behalf of the oppressed. Alone, neither does justice to the reign of God which Jesus announced and inaugurated.'[2]

To many Evangelicals, however, the conference appeared to be heavily biased towards the social and political realm and to lack a sufficiently clear theology of salvation. They had been alarmed by the prominence of social and political concerns at the WCC Assembly at Uppsala in 1968. This was an Assembly which met in the aftermath of student riots in Paris, the communist invasion of Prague, the Vietnam War, the Cultural Revolution in China and the confrontation of fascism and communism in Latin America. It viewed such developments through the lens of a report on a study of the missionary structure of the congregation which decisively departed from a church-centric view of mission in favour of an understanding of mission built around the action of God in society at large. It followed through on Hoekendjik's argument that 'God-church-world' must be replaced by 'God-world-church'.

The calling of the church, on this view, is to participate in God's missionary action which is valid for the whole world and embraces both church and society. In an arresting phrase, it was said that the world must be allowed to provide the agenda for the churches.[3] This means, as Dietrich Werner explains, 'The church does not have a mission, it is itself mission. The structure and aim of its missions are legitimate only in so far as they serve God's mission.'[4] This opened the way to a major focus on the social and political witness of the church which appeared to many Evangelicals to be at the expense of the spiritual dimension.

These concerns informed their approach to the Bangkok conference. Donald McGavran spoke for many when he expressed concern that '"Evangelism" ceases to be proclaiming Jesus Christ by word and deed and persuading men to become His disciples and responsible members of His Church and becomes changing the structures of society in the direction of justice, righteousness and peace… Evangelicals should work and pray that this deliberate debasing of Christian currency cease and that the reformation of social order (rightly emphasised) should not be substituted for salvation'.[5] Bangkok marked a fork in the road between 'Ecumenicals' and 'Evangelicals' – something that was clearly expressed when Evangelicals held the Lausanne Congress the following year and established the Lausanne Committee for World Evangelization as

---

[2] Larsson and Castro, 'From Missions to Mission', 126.

[3] See further, Bosch, *Transforming Mission*, 383.

[4] Dietrich Werner, 'Missionary Structure of the Congregation', in Nicholas Lossky et al (ed), *Dictionary of the Ecumenical Movement* (Geneva: WCC and Grand Rapids, MI: Eerdmans, 1991), 699-701.

[5] Donald A. McGavran, 'Salvation Today', in Ralph Winter (ed), *The Evangelical Response to Bangkok* (Pasadena, CA: William Carey Library, 1973), 31; see also Peter Beyerhaus, *Bangkok 73: The Beginning or End of World Mission?* (Grand Rapids, MI: Zondervan, 1974).

something of an Evangelical parallel to the WCC's CWME. Nonetheless, despite disagreement and distrust, the two sides in this debate continued their dialogue. It found expression through participation in each other's conferences and in a lively debate in the International Review of Mission.[6] Leaders such as Lesslie Newbigin, John Stott, David Bosch, Emilio Castro and Mortimer Arias sought to bridge the gulf.[7]

## Report of Section I: Culture and Identity

### *On Conversion and Cultural Change*

1. It is very difficult to describe the existential experience of conversion – whether personal or corporate, as an event or a process – in terms which do justice to rational thinking as well as other levels of consciousness. In order to express this experience, one has to seek other ways of communication than just report language.

Conversion as a phenomenon is not restricted to the Christian community; it finds its place in other religions as well as in certain political and ideological communities; its forms may vary. The content of the experience differs according to the person or to the ideological system within which the person or the group is converted.

Conversion is a comprehensive concept: it changes the person's or the group's thinking, perspectives on reality and action. It relates a person to people who have similar experiences or who are committed to the same person or ideology.

The Christian conversion relates to God and especially to His son Jesus Christ. It introduces people into the Christian community, the structure of which may differ greatly from one culture to another, and which will always include a great variety of persons.

Christian conversion gathers people into the worshipping community, the teaching community and the community of service to all men. Even if Christians are not called out of their culture and separated from the society in which they were born, they still will form cells of worship, or reflection and of service within their original cultures.

Personal conversion always leads to social action, but here again the forms will greatly differ. We heard action reports which gave us some idea how diverse the consequences may be. In the one case, people who had never known an identity of their own formed a very closely-knit group, within which intensive social care for each other developed. When such a group grows, it almost inevitably enters into the full civic life at the local level; if it grows further, it will acquire political power which may align it

---

6 See, e.g. John Stott, 'The Significance of Lausanne', in *International Review of Mission,* 64. 255 (1975), 288-94.

7 See Laing, *From Crisis to Creation*, 132.

to either conservative or progressive political platforms. Where conversion takes place among the destitute and powerless, the sustaining community will tend to begin to empower the poor and oppressed.

But it is also possible that conversion means a calling out of people, away from what is regarded as an oppressive power structure or even away from a type of social action which is regarded as dehumanising or superficial.

It is important that the community of those converted to Christ is so sustained by the study of Scripture and the work of service that renewal of the conversion experience is possible.

Our group was unanimous in thinking that conversion is always related to the place and the circumstances where it occurs; therefore we recommend that detailed study be made of the form and consequences of conversion in different situations.

The relation between conversion and social change may be clear, but the relation between social change and conversion is much less easily described. It may be that secular conversion experiences remind the Christian community of elements in their own life which need to be renewed; it may also be that conversion phenomena within a new cultural situation will force Christians back on their unique identity and make them oppose the cultural development; their conversion in such situations is away from the prevailing cultural situation. To generalise about these various possibilities would hardly be helpful.

2. Everywhere people are seeking for new experiences of community, whatever the name: cultural revolution, sub-culture or counter-culture. The relation of the Christian community to such a search cannot be described without serious consideration of each of these scenes. We have learned in our group that the line between culture, sub-culture and even counter-culture is not as sharp as these groups themselves often proclaim. People move from one to the other without observing strict sociological or theological rules.

It is difficult to describe 'the community in Christ and in the Holy Spirit' in this context. We played with the concept of the Christian community itself as a counter-culture; but we abandoned this idea because it cut us off too definitely from the communities of men of which we are also a part. Only in extreme cases may we be called to shake the dust of the city from our shoes; usually we shall have to live in a somewhat dialectical relationship, participating with a certain hesitation, identifying ourselves while keeping our critical distance. This dialectic should not hinder us from being fully engaged with others in the search for justice and freedom. Our identity is in Christ and with Him we identify ourselves; by Him also we may be withdrawn. The criteria for so tender a relationship are taught us only when we let the Scriptures continuously surprise us and keep our communion with the Lord and His people.

3. The manifestations of God are always surprising. Basically there is no realm of life and no situation where He cannot reveal Himself. We believe that He is present in His whole creation. But we do not want to make this belief an operative principle for pointing out exactly where He is at work, lest we say: here is the Messiah, or there is the Messiah, when He is not there.

Although we expect His presence with men and although we know that the Spirit translates the groaning of all mankind into prayers acceptable to God, we believe that this insight is more a reason to worship His freedom than an invitation to build our theological theories. Our preoccupation is with the revealed Christ and with the proclamation of Him as He has been made known to us. Scripture tells us that Christ identifies Himself with the poor and that the Spirit translates the groaning of men; this may indicate the direction in which we are invited to move but it does not give us power to pinpoint the details of His presence. The observation that Christ-like action and insights which we know from the Gospels are also present among other groups does not give us the right to claim such groups for Christ; it should lead us deeper into the process of our own conversion and bring us to worship Our Lord even more humbly. He asked us to follow Him, not to spy on Him.

## Report of Section II

### *1. The Mission of God*

In the power of the Spirit, Christ is sent from God, the Father, into this divided world 'to preach the Gospel to the poor, to heal the brokenhearted, to preach deliverance to the captives and recovery of sight to the blind, to set at liberty the oppressed, and to proclaim the year of God's favour' (Luke 4:18). Through Christ, men and women are liberated and empowered with all their energies and possibilities to participate in His Messianic work. Through His death on the Cross and His resurrection from the dead, hope of salvation becomes realistic and reality hopeful. He liberates from the prison of guilt. He takes the inevitability out of history. In Him the Kingdom of God and of free people is at hand. Faith in Christ releases in man creative freedom for the salvation of the world. He who separates himself from the mission of God separates himself from salvation.

The salvation which Christ brought, and in which we participate, offers a comprehensive wholeness in this divided life. We understand salvation as newness of life – the unfolding of true humanity in the fullness of God (Col. 2:9). It is salvation of the soul and the body, of the individual and society, mankind and 'the groaning creation' (Rom. 8:19). As evil works both in personal life and in exploitative social structures which humiliate humankind, so God's justice manifests itself both in the justification of the sinner and in social and political justice.

As guilt is both individual and corporate, so God's liberating power changes both persons and structures. We have to overcome the dichotomies in our thinking between soul and body, person and society, human kind and creation. Therefore we see the struggles for economic justice, political freedom and cultural renewal as elements the total liberation of the world through the mission of God. This liberation if finally fulfilled when 'death is swallowed up in victory' (1 Cor. 15:55). This comprehensive notion of salvation demands of the whole of the people of God a matching comprehensive approach to their participation in salvation.

### *2. Salvation and Liberation of Churches and Christians*

Many Christians who for Christ's sake are involved in economic and political struggles against injustice and oppression ask themselves and the churches what it means today to be a Christian and a true church. Without the salvation of the churches from their captivity in the interests of the dominating classes, races and nations, there can be no saving church. Without liberation of the churches and Christians from their complicity with structural injustice and violence, there can be no liberating church for mankind. Every church, all Christians, face the question of whether they serve Christ and His saving work alone, or at the same time also the powers of inhumanity. 'No man can serve two masters, God and Mammon' (Matt. 6:24). We must confess our misuse of the name of Christ by the accommodation of the churches to oppressive powers, by our self-interested apathy, lovelessness and fear. We are seeking the true community of Christ which works and suffers for His Kingdom. We seek the charismatic church which activates energies for salvation (1 Cor. 12). We seek the church which initiates actions for liberation and supports the work of other liberating groups without calculating self-interest. We seek a church which is the catalyst of God's saving work in the world, a church which is not merely the refuge of the saved but a community serving the world in the love of Christ.

### *3. Salvation in Four Dimensions*

Within the comprehensive notion of salvation, we see the saving work in four social dimensions:

a. Salvation works in the struggle for economic justice against the exploitation of people by people.

b. Salvation works in the struggle for human dignity against political oppression of human beings by their fellow men.

c. Salvation works in the struggle for solidarity against the alienation of person from person.

d. Salvation works in the struggle of hope against despair in personal life.

In the process of salvation, we must relate these four dimensions to each other. There is no economic injustice without political freedom, no political freedom without economic justice. There is no social justice without solidarity, no solidarity without social justice. There is no justice, no human dignity, no solidarity without hope, no hope without justice, dignity and solidarity. But there are historical priorities according to which salvation is anticipated in one dimension first, be it the personal, the political or the economic dimension. These points of entry differ from situation to situation in which we work and suffer. We should know that such anticipations are not the whole of salvation, and must keep in mind the other dimensions while we work. Forgetting this denies the wholeness of salvation. Nobody can do in any particular situation everything at the same time. There are various gifts and tasks, but there is one spirit and one goal. In this sense, it can be said, for example, that salvation is the peace of the people in Vietnam, independence in Angola, justice and reconciliation in Northern Ireland, and release from the captivity of power in the North Atlantic community, or personal conversion in the release of a submerged society into hope, or of new lifestyles amidst corporate self-interest and lovelessness.

### *4. Means and Criteria of Saving Work*

Speaking of salvation realistically, we cannot avoid the question of proper means. The means are different in the four dimensions referred to. We will produce no economic justice without participation in, and use of, economic power. We will win no political freedom without participation, and discriminating use of, political power. We cannot overcome cultural alienation without the use of cultural influence. In this framework we discussed the physical use of liberating violence against oppressive violence. The Christian tradition is ambiguous on this question because it provides no justification of violence and no rejection of political power. Jesus' commandment to love one's enemy presupposes enmity. One should not become the enemy of one's enemy, but should liberate him from his enmity (Matt. 5:43-48). This commandment warns against the brutality of violence and reckless disregard of life. But in the cases of institutionalized violence, structural injustice and legalized immorality, love also involves the right of resistance and the duty 'to repress tyranny' (Scottish Confession) with responsible choice among the possibilities we have. One then may become guilty for love's sake, but can trust in the forgiveness of guilt. Realistic work for salvation proceeds through confrontation, but depends, everywhere and always, on reconciliation with God.[8]

[8] *Bangkok Assembly 1973: Minutes and Report of the Assembly of the Commission on World Mission and Evangelism* (Geneva: WCC, 1973), 75-78, 88-90; cit. Kinnamon and Cope, *The Ecumenical Movement*, 354-58.

# MELBOURNE 1980 – GOOD NEWS FOR THE POOR

- Affirmation of the poor – the church's relation to the poor crucial for mission
- New models of mutuality and ecumenical sharing of resources
- Evangelicals critical of social concern weakening evangelism and church growth
- Renewed confidence in the church as the instrument of the mission of God

Emilio Castro opened the Commission for World Mission and Evangelism Conference at Melbourne in 1980 with the words: 'The era of world missions is over; the era of world mission is beginning.'[1] It was a captivating vision, yet there was frustration that older patterns of power and control persisted and progress with the ecumenical sharing of resources was slow. The 1970s had seen the London Missionary Society transformed into the Council for World Mission and the Paris Missionary Society transformed into Cevaa – Communauté d'Eglises en Mission – both seeking to move from a model of mission, 'from the West to the rest', to one of mutuality and mission 'from everywhere to everywhere'. Despite such inspiring initiatives, however, the mainstream of church life in many contexts appeared little concerned by the need to share resources in the interests of the one mission of God. In this context, Melbourne sought to highlight the issue of poverty and the question of what it would mean for the churches to represent good news for the poor. This was the era of Liberation Theology and the conference proved receptive to its emphases. Emilio Castro suggested that its affirmation of the poor was the 'missiological principle par excellence' and the church's relationship with the poor 'the missionary yardstick'.[2]

Whatever the merits of this attempt to retrieve biblical teaching on poverty and to think through the contemporary implications of God's bias to the poor, it created a negative reaction among Evangelicals who were now organized under the Lausanne Committee for World Evangelization, formed in 1974. Melbourne was criticized for having a deep passion for the poor but not for the lost, and for having more concern for the renewal of the church than with the evangelistic mobilization of congregations for mission.[3] Despite the attempts of the conference to balance the

---

[1] Larsson and Castro, 'From Missions to Mission', 127.
[2] Emilio Castro, *Freedom in Mission: The Perspective of the Kingdom of God* (Geneva: WCC, 1985), 151; cit. Bosch, *Transforming Mission*, 435.
[3] Larsson and Castro, 'From Missions to Mission', 138-39.

proclamation of the gospel with social commitment and action, many Evangelicals were unconvinced and continued to feel that Christian witness was being diluted in the ecumenical movement by excessive preoccupation with social and political concerns. Melbourne, however, did see a renewed confidence in the church as the instrument of the mission of God after two decades when the action of God in the world had been at the centre of attention in ecumenical thinking about mission.

## The Record of God's Preference

The Kingdom of God which was inaugurated in Jesus Christ brings justice, love, peace, and joy and freedom from the grasp of principalities and powers, those demonic forces which place human lives and institutions in bondage and infiltrate their very textures. God's judgement overturns the values and structures of this world. In the perspective of the kingdom, God has a preference for the poor.

Jesus announced at the beginning of His ministry, drawing upon the Word given to the prophet Isaiah, 'The Spirit of the Lord is upon me, because he has anointed me to preach good news to the poor…' (Luke 4:18). This announcement was not new; God had shown His preference for the poor throughout the history of Israel. When Israel was a slave in Egypt, God sent Moses to lead the people out to the land which He had promised, where they established a society according to God's revelation given through Moses, a society in which all were to share equally. After they had come into the land, God required them to remember that they had once been slaves. Therefore, they should care for the widow, the fatherless, the sojourner within their gates, their debtors, their children, their servants and even their animals (Deut. 5:13-15; 15:1-18). Time and again the prophets had to remind Israel of the need to stand for the poor and oppressed and to work for God's justice.

God identified with the poor and oppressed by sending His Son to live and serve as a Galilean speaking directly to the common people; promising to bless those who met the needs of the hungry, the thirsty, the stranger, the naked, the sick and the prisoner; and finally meeting death on a cross as a political offender. The good news handed on to the Church is that God's grace was in Jesus Christ, who 'though he was rich, yet for your sake he became poor, so that by his poverty you might become rich' (2 Cor. 8:9).

Poverty in the Scriptures is affliction, deprivation and oppression. But it can also include abundant joy and overflow in liberality (2 Cor. 8:1-2). The Gospel which has been given to the Christian Church must express this continuing concern of God for the poor to whom Jesus has granted the blessing of the kingdom. Jesus' option for the poor shows how the Kingdom of God is to be received. The poor are 'blessed' because of their longing for justice and their hope for liberation and a life of human dignity.

The Good News to the rich affirms what Jesus proclaims as the Gospel for the poor, that is, a calling to trust in God and His abundant mercy. This is a call:

- to renounce the security of wealth and material possessions which is, in fact, idolatry;
- to give up the exploiting power which is the demonic feature of wealth; and
- to turn away from indifference and enmity toward the poor and toward solidarity with the oppressed.

The coming of the kingdom as hope for the poor is thus a time of judgement for the rich. In the light of this judgement and this hope, all human beings are shown to have been made less than human. The very identification of people as either rich or poor is now seen to be a symptom of this dehumanization. The poor who are sinned against are rendered less human by being deprived. The rich are rendered less human by the sinful act of depriving others.

The judgement of God thus comes as a verdict in favour of the poor. This verdict enables the poor to struggle to overthrow the powers that bind them, which then releases the rich from the necessity to dominate. Once this has happened, it is possible for both the humbled rich and the poor to become human, capable of response to the challenge of the kingdom.

To the poor this challenge means the profound assurance that God is with them and for them. To the rich it means a profound repentance and renunciation. To all who yearn for justice and forgiveness Jesus Christ offers discipleship and the demand for service. But He offers this in the assurance of victory and in sharing the power of His risen life. As the kingdom in its fullness is solely the gift of God Himself, any human achievement in history can only be approximate and relative to the final goal – that promised new heaven and new earth in which justice abides. Yet that kingdom is the inspiration and constant challenge in all our struggles.

We wish to recommend the following to the churches:

### ***Become*** *Churches in Solidarity with the Struggles of the Poor*

The poor are already in mission to change their own situation. What is required from the churches is a missionary movement that supports what they have already begun, and that focuses on building evangelizing and witnessing communities of the poor that will discover and live out expressions of faith among the masses of the poor and oppressed.

The churches will have to surrender their attitudes of benevolence and charity which have marked their relations to the poor; in many cases this will mean a radical change in the institutional life of the missionary movement. The churches must be ready to listen to the poor, to hear the Gospel from the poor, to learn about the ways in which they have helped to make them poor.

Ways of expressing this solidarity are several, but each must be fitted to the situation of the poor and respect their leadership in the work of evangelization and mission. There is the call to act in support of the struggles of the poor against oppression. This means support across national boundaries and between continents, without neglecting the struggles within their own societies. There is the call to participate in the struggle themselves. To free others of poverty and oppression is also to release the bonds that entangle the churches in the web of international exploitation. There is the call to become churches of the poor. Although not all will accept the call to strip themselves of riches, the voluntary joining of church members in the community of the poor of the earth could be the most telling witness to the Good News.

### ***Join** the Struggle against the Powers of Exploitation and Impoverishment*

Poverty, injustice and oppression do not voluntarily release their grip on the lives of the poor. Therefore, the struggle against the powers that create and maintain the present situation must be actively entered. These powers include transnational corporations, governments and the churches themselves and their missionary organisations where they have joined in exploitation and impoverishment. In increasing numbers, those who will claim the rewards that Jesus promised to those who are persecuted are those who join the struggle against these powers at the side of the poor.

### ***Establish** a New Relationship with the Poor inside the Churches*

Many of the poor belong to the churches, but only the voices of a few are heard or their influence felt. The New Testament churches were taught not to be respecters of persons but many churches today have built the structures of status, class, sexual and racial division into their fellowship and organization. The churches should be open to the presence and voice of the poor in their own life. The structures of mission and church life still must be changed to patterns of partnership and servanthood. This will require a more unified mission outreach that does not perpetuate the wastefulness and confusion of denominational divisions. The lifestyles of both clergy and lay leaders need to be changed to come closer to the poor. The churches, which now exploit women and youth, will need to create opportunities for them to participate in leadership and decision-making.

### ***Pray** and Work for the Kingdom of God*

When the churches emphasize their own life, their eyes are diverted from the Kingdom of God, the heart of the Lord's message and the hope of the poor. To pray for the kingdom is to concentrate the church's attention on what God is trying to give to His whole creation. To pray for the kingdom will enable the churches to work more earnestly for its development, to look more eagerly for its signs in human history and to await more patiently its final consummation.[4]

[4] 'Melbourne Conference Section Reports – Good News for the Poor', *International Review of Mission* (October 1980-June 1981), 69. 276-77, 388-90, 395-96; see also *Your Kingdom Come: Mission Perspectives – Report on the World Conference on Mission and Evangelism, Melbourne, Australia, 12th-25th May 1980* (Geneva: WCC, 1980).

# 1982 MISSION AND EVANGELISM: AN ECUMENICAL AFFIRMATION

- A convergence document – both social witness and personal conversion
- Trinitarian understanding of mission
- The Kingdom of God a key motif in interpreting mission
- Witness integral to the experience of faith itself
- Church unity urgently needed – for the sake of the credibility of Christian witness

This document emerged from an attempt to build bridges between the Ecumenical Movement and the Evangelicals during the 1970s. It was a conciliatory document designed to encompass the characteristic concerns of each side in what had been a highly divisive debate. How could the justice issues which had been so prominent in the WCC during the 1960s and 1970s be related to the traditional missionary outreach of the churches and the evangelistic task of calling people to personal faith in Jesus Christ? During the preparations for the Melbourne 1980 Conference, CWME, as its Director Emilio Castro explained, 'engaged in a long and fruitful conversation with churches of all confessions and regions, assessing the priorities for our missionary obedience today.'[1] The result was a re-balancing of the understanding of mission to complement prophetic social witness with insistence on the importance of decision and personal conversion, leading to a life of service. After the Melbourne Conference Castro wrote a first draft which was widely circulated and discussed before the draft document was ready for a first reading by the WCC Central Committee in July 1981.[2] Finally, the Affirmation was approved by the Central Committee in July 1982, the only official statement on mission and evangelism to be adopted by the WCC until *Together towards Life* in 2012.

With a Trinitarian basis and Christological concentration it sought to break down false dichotomies between the spiritual gospel and the material gospel. A clear commitment to the proclamation of the gospel was complemented by prophetic engagement with questions of social justice. Concern with social and political issues is balanced with an unequivocal affirmation of the centrality of the church in God's divine economy. 'To appreciate the value and motive of this affirmation,' suggests Lalsangkima

---

1 Emilio Castro, 'Foreword', in *Mission and Evangelism: An Ecumenical Affirmation* (Geneva: WCC, 1983), v.

2 Jean S. Stromberg, 'Ecumenical Affirmation on Mission and Evangelism – A Review', *International Review of Mission,* 90.358 (2001), 243-52, at 244.

Pachuau, 'one needs to recognize the pains of the transition, the longing for a deeper theology of mission that would provide ground for doing mission in the new age, and the efforts and difficulties involved in developing a common perception and comprehensive view of mission.'[3] Yet not all are convinced that it succeeded in its objectives. Pachuau finds it to be: '... a hodgepodge of differing ideas and emphases... While each section appears to be clear in itself, the reading of the entire document leaves the reader unclear of its message.'[4] It has also been criticised for having quite minimal statements on controversial matters, such as relationships with people of other faiths, in order to secure the widest possible agreement. Nonetheless, by incorporating the characteristic emphases of both sides, it did play a significant role in bridging the gulf which had opened up between Ecumenicals and Evangelicals during the 1970s. It has been described by Jacques Matthey as 'a genuine convergence document'.[5]

Jean Stromberg has noted four key emphases of the Affirmation: 1) It is thoroughly Trinitarian in its understanding of mission, something she attributes to the influence of Orthodox Churches but also to liberation and contextual theologies. 2) Jesus' announcement of the kingdom, or reign, of God is central to the text – fertile ground for consideration of how a passion for justice and personal conversion might be integrated. 3) Witness is understood as integral to the experience of faith itself – a mature expression of the aspiration underlying the integration of the WCC and IMC twenty years earlier, that church and mission are two aspects of the one reality. 4) The urgency of the call to conversion is linked with the urgent need for church unity. Precisely for the sake of credibility in an unbelieving world, it is urgently required that the church attain the unity for which Christ prayed.[6]

## Mission and Evangelism: An Ecumenical Affirmation

### *Preface*

The biblical promise of a new earth and a new heaven where love, peace and justice will prevail (Ps. 85:7-13; Isa. 32:17-18, 65:17-25 and Rev. 21:1-2) invites our actions as Christians in history. The contrast of that vision with the reality of today reveals the monstrosity of human sin, the evil unleashed by the rejection of God's liberating will for humankind. Sin, alienating persons from God, neighbour and nature, is found both in individual and corporate forms, both in slavery of the

---

[3] Pachuau, 'Ecumenical Missiology', 44.
[4] Pachuau, 'Ecumenical Missiology', 45.
[5] Jacques Matthey, 'Milestones in Ecumenical Missionary Thinking from the 1970s to the 1990s', in *International Review of Mission,* 88.350 (1999), 291-303, at 296.
[6] Stromberg, 'Ecumenical Affirmation', 245-46.

human will and in social, political and economic structures of domination and dependence.

The Church is sent into the world to call people and nations to repentance, to announce forgiveness of sin and a new beginning in relations with God and with neighbours through Jesus Christ. This evangelistic calling has a new urgency today.

In a world where the number of people who have no opportunity to know the story of Jesus is growing steadily, *how necessary it is to multiply the witnessing vocation of the church!*

In a world where the majority of those who do not know Jesus are the poor of the earth, those to whom He promised the Kingdom of God, *how essential it is to share with them the Good News of that kingdom!*

In a world where people are struggling for justice, freedom and liberation, often without the realization of their hopes, *how important it is to announce that God's kingdom is promised to them!*

In a world where the marginalized and the drop-outs of affluent society search desperately for comfort and identity in drugs or esoteric cults, *how imperative it is to announce that He has come so that all may have life and may have it in all its fullness (John 10:10)!*

In a world where so many find little meaning, except in the relative security of their affluence, *how necessary it is to hear once again Jesus' invitation to discipleship, service and risk!*

In a world where so many Christians are nominal in their commitment to Jesus Christ, *how necessary it is to call them again to the fervour of their first love!*

In a world where wars and rumours of wars jeopardize the present and future of humankind, where an enormous part of natural resources and people are consumed in the arms race, *how crucial it is to call the peacemakers blessed, convinced that God in Christ has broken all barriers and has reconciled the world to himself (Eph. 2:14; 2 Cor. 5:19)!*

This ecumenical affirmation is a challenge which the churches extend to each other to announce that God reigns, and that there is hope for a future when God will 'unite all things in him, things in heaven and things on earth' (Eph. 1:10). Jesus is 'the first and last, and the Living One' (Rev. 1:17-18), who 'is coming soon' (Rev. 22:12), who 'makes all things new' (Rev. 21:5).

## *The Call to Mission*

1. The present ecumenical movement came into being out of the conviction of the churches that the division of Christians is a scandal and an impediment to the witness of the Church. There is a growing awareness among the churches today of the inextricable relationship

between Christian unity and missionary calling, between ecumenism and evangelization. 'Evangelization is the test of our ecumenical vocation.'[7]

As 'a fellowship of churches which confess the Lord Jesus Christ as God and Saviour, according to the Scriptures, and therefore seek to fulfil together their common calling to the glory of the one God, Father, Son and Holy Spirit',[8] the rallying point of the World Council of Churches is the common confession of Jesus Christ. The saving ministry of the Son is understood within the action of the Holy Trinity; it was the Father who in the power of the Spirit sent Jesus Christ the Son of God incarnate, the Saviour of the whole world. The churches of the WCC are on a pilgrimage towards unity under the missionary vision of John 17:21, 'that they may all be one; even as thou, Father, art in me, and I in thee, that they also may be in us, so that the world may believe that thou hast sent me.'[9]

2. Already in the Old Testament the people of Israel were looking forward to the day of peace where God's justice will prevail (Isa. 11:1-9). Jesus came into that tradition announcing that the Kingdom of God was at hand (Mark 1:15), that in Him the reality of the kingdom was present (Luke 4:15-21). God was offering this new justice to the children, to the poor, to all who labour and are heavy laden, to all those who will repent and will follow Jesus. The early Church confessed Jesus as Lord, as the highest authority at whose name every knee shall bow, who in the cross and in the resurrection has liberated in this world the power of sacrificial love.

3. Christ sent the disciples with the words: 'As the Father has sent me, even so I send you' (John 20:21). The disciples of Jesus were personal witnesses of the risen Christ (1 John 1:2-3). As such they were sent — commissioned apostles to the world. Based on their testimony which is preserved in the New Testament and in the life of the Church, the Church has as one constitutive mark its being apostolic, its being sent into the world (Appendix I). God in Christ has equipped the Church with all gifts of the Spirit necessary for its witness. 'You shall receive power when the Holy Spirit has come upon you; and you shall be my witnesses in Jerusalem, and in all Judaea and Samaria, and to the ends of the earth' (Acts 1:8).

4. The book of Acts tells the story of the expansion of the early Church as it fulfils its missionary vocation. The Holy Spirit came upon that small Jerusalem community on the day of Pentecost (Acts 2:1-39), in order that through them and through others who were to believe in Christ through their word (John 17:20), the world may be healed and redeemed.

---

[7] Philip Potter's speech to the Roman Catholic Synod of Bishops. Rome, 1974.
[8] Constitution of the World Council of Churches.
[9] Constitution of the Conference on World Mission and Evangelism.

The early Church witnessed to its Risen Lord in a variety of ways, most specially in the style of life of its members. 'And day by day, attending the temple together and breaking bread in their homes, they partook of food with glad and generous hearts, praising God and having favour with all the people. And the Lord added to their number day by day those who were being saved' (Acts 2:46-47) (Appendix 2). Through the persecutions suffered by the early Christians, the word spread spontaneously: 'Now those who were scattered went about preaching the word' (Acts 8:4). The apostles then came to confirm the faith of those who had accepted the Word of God (Acts 8:14-17). At other times, the word spread through more explicit and purposeful ministries. The church in Antioch organized the first missionary trip. Barnabas and Paul were sent by the church in response to the Holy Spirit (Acts 13:1-4). Time and time again, the church was surprised by God's calling to face entirely new missionary situations (Acts 8:26; 10:17; 16:9-10).

5. Jesus Christ was in Himself the complete revelation of God's love, manifested in justice and forgiveness through all aspects of His earthly life. He completed the work of the Father. 'My food is to do the will of him who sent me and to accomplish his work' (John 4:34). In His obedience to the Father's will, in His love for humanity, He used many ways to reveal God's love to the world: forgiving, healing, casting out demons, teaching, proclaiming, denouncing, testifying in courts, finally surrendering His life. The Church today has the same freedom to develop its mission, to respond to changing situations and circumstances (Appendix 3). It is sent into the world, participating in that flow of love from God the Father. In that mission of love (Matt. 22:37) through all aspects of its life, the Church endeavours to witness to the full realization of God's kingdom in Jesus Christ. The Church is called, like John the Baptist, to point towards the 'Lamb of God who takes away the sin of the world' (John 1:29).

### *The Call to Proclamation and Witness*

6. The mission of the Church ensues from the nature of the Church as the Body of Christ, sharing in the ministry of Christ as Mediator between God and His Creation. This mission of mediation in Christ involves two integrally related movements – one from God to Creation, and the other from Creation to God. The Church manifests God's love for the world in Christ – through word and deed, in identification with all humanity, in loving service and joyful proclamation; the Church, in that same identification with all humanity, lifts up to God its pain and suffering, hope and aspiration, joy and thanksgiving in intercessory prayer and eucharistic worship. Any

imbalance between these two directions of the mediatory movement adversely affects our ministry and mission in the world.

Only a Church fully aware of how people in the world live and feel and think can adequately fulfil either aspect of this mediatory mission. It is at this point that the Church recognizes the validity and significance of the ministry of others to the Church, in order that the Church may better understand and be in closer solidarity with the world, knowing and sharing its pains and yearnings. Only by responding attentively to others can we remove our ignorance and misunderstanding of others, and be better able to minister to them.

At the very heart of the Church's vocation in the world is the proclamation of the Kingdom of God inaugurated in Jesus the Lord, crucified and risen. Through its internal life of eucharistic worship, thanksgiving, intercessory prayer, through planning for mission and evangelism, through a daily lifestyle of solidarity with the poor, through advocacy even to confrontation with the powers that oppress human beings, the churches are trying to fulfil this evangelistic vocation.

7. The starting point of our proclamation is Christ and Christ crucified. 'We preach Christ crucified, a stumbling block to Jews and folly to Gentiles' (1 Cor. 1:23). The Good News handed on to the Church is that God's grace was in Jesus Christ, who 'though he was rich, yet for your sakes he became poor, so that by his poverty you might become rich' (2 Cor. 8:9).

Following human wisdom, the wise men from the Orient who were looking for the child went to the palace of King Herod. They did not know that 'there was no place for Him in the inn' and that He was born in a manger, poor among the poor. He even went so far in His identification with the poverty of humankind that His family was obliged to take the route of political refugee to Egypt. He was raised as a worker, came proclaiming God's caring for the poor, announced blessedness for them, sided with the underprivileged, confronted the powerful and went to the cross to open up a new life for humankind. As His disciples, we announce His solidarity with all the downtrodden and marginalized. Those who are considered to be nothing are precious in God's eyes (1 Cor. 1:26-31). **To believe in Jesus the King is to accept His undeserved grace and enter with Him into the Kingdom, taking sides with the poor struggling to overcome poverty. Both those who announce Jesus as the Servant King and those who accept this announcement and respond to it are invited to enter with Him daily in identification and participation with the poor of the earth.**

With the Apostle Paul and all Christian churches, we confess Christ Jesus, 'who, though he was in the form of God, did not count equality with God a thing to be grasped, but emptied himself, taking the form of a servant, being born in the likeness of men. And being found in human form, he humbled himself and became obedient unto death, even death on a cross. Therefore God has highly exalted him and bestowed on him the name which is above every name, that at the name of Jesus every knee should bow, in heaven and on earth and under the earth, and every tongue confess that Jesus Christ is Lord, to the glory of God the Father' (Phil. 2:6-11).

But Christ's identification with humanity went even more deeply, and while nailed on the cross accused as a political criminal, He took upon Himself the guilt even of those who crucified Him. 'Father, forgive them; for they know not what they do' (Luke 23:34). The Christian confession reads, 'For our sake he made him to be sin who knew no sin, so that in him we might become the righteousness of God' (2 Cor. 5:21). The cross is the place of the decisive battle between the powers of evil and the love of God. It uncovers the lostness of the world, the magnitude of human sinfulness, the tragedy of human alienation. The total self-surrendering of Christ reveals the immeasurable depth of God's love for the world (John 3:16).

On this same cross, Jesus was glorified. Here God the Father glorified the Son of Man, and in so doing confirmed Jesus as the Son of God (John 13:31). 'The early Christians used many analogies to describe what they had experienced and what they believed had happened. The most striking picture is that of a sacrificed lamb, slaughtered but yet living, sharing the throne, which symbolized the heart of all power and sovereignty, with the living God himself.'[10]

It is this Jesus that the Church proclaims as the very life of the world because on the cross He gave His own life for all that all may live. In Him misery, sin and death are defeated once for ever. They cannot be accepted as having final power over human life. In Him there is abundant life, life eternal. **The Church proclaims Jesus, risen from the dead. Through the resurrection, God vindicates Jesus, and opens up a new period of missionary obedience until He comes again** (Acts 1:11). The power of the risen and crucified Christ is now released. It is the new birth to a new life, because as He took our predicament on the cross, He also took us into a new life in His resurrection. 'When anyone is united to Christ, there is a new creation; the old has passed away, behold, the new has come' (2 Cor. 5:17) (Appendix 4).

Evangelism calls people to look towards that Jesus and commit their life to Him, to enter into the kingdom whose king has come in the powerless child of Bethlehem, in the murdered one on the cross.

## Ecumenical Convictions

9. In the ecumenical discussions and experience, churches with their diverse confessions and traditions and in their various expressions as

---

[10] *Your Kingdom Come,* CWME Conference, Melbourne, 1980, 210.

parishes, monastic communities, religious orders, etc., have learned to recognize each other as participants in the one worldwide missionary movement. *Thus, together, they can affirm an ecumenical perception of Christian mission expressed in the following convictions under which they covenant to work for the Kingdom of God.*

### *1. Conversion*

10. The proclamation of the Gospel includes an invitation to recognize and accept in a personal decision the saving lordship of Christ. It is the announcement of a personal encounter, mediated by the Holy Spirit, with the living Christ, receiving His forgiveness and making a personal acceptance of the call to discipleship and a life of service. God addresses Himself specifically to each of His children, as well as to the whole human race. **Each person is entitled to hear the Good News**. Many social forces today press for conformity and passivity. Masses of poor people have been deprived of their right to decide about their lives and the life of their society. While anonymity and marginalization seem to reduce the possibilities for personal decisions to a minimum, God as Father knows each one of His children and calls each of them to make a fundamental personal act of allegiance to Him and His kingdom in the fellowship of His people.

11. While the basic experience of conversion is the same, the awareness of an encounter with God revealed in Christ, the concrete occasion of this experience and the actual shape of the same differs in terms of our personal situation. **The calling is to specific changes, to renounce evidences of the domination of sin in our lives and to accept responsibilities in terms of God's love for our neighbour.** John the Baptist said very specifically to the soldiers what they should do; Jesus did not hesitate to indicate to the young ruler that his wealth was the obstacle to his discipleship.

**Conversion happens in the midst of our historical reality and incorporates the totality of our life, because God's love is concerned with that totality. Jesus' call is an invitation to follow Him joyfully, to participate in His servant body, to share with Him in the struggle to overcome sin, poverty and death.**

12. The importance of this decision is highlighted by the fact that God Himself through His Holy Spirit helps the acceptance of His offering of fellowship. The New Testament calls this a new birth (John 3:3). It is also called conversion, *metanoia,* total transformation of our attitudes and styles of life. Conversion as a dynamic and ongoing process 'involves a turning *from* and a turning *to.* It always demands reconciliation, a new relationship both with God and with others. It involves leaving our old security behind (Matt. 16:24) and putting ourselves at risk in a life of

faith'.[11] It is 'conversion *from* a life characterized by sin, separation from God, submission to evil and the unfulfilled potential of God's image, *to* a new life characterized by the forgiveness of sins, obedience to the commands of God, renewed fellowship with God in Trinity, growth in the restoration of the divine image and the realization... of the love of Christ...'[12]

**The call to conversion, as a call to repentance and obedience, should also be addressed to nations, groups and families.** To proclaim the need to change from war to peace, from injustice to justice, from racism to solidarity, from hate to love, is a witness rendered to Jesus Christ and to His kingdom. The prophets of the Old Testament addressed themselves constantly to the collective conscience of the people of Israel, calling the rulers and the people to repentance and to renewal of the covenant.

13. Many of those who are attracted to Christ are put off by what they see in the life of the churches as well as in individual Christians. How many of the millions of people in the world who are not confessing Jesus Christ have rejected Him because of what they saw in the lives of Christians! **Thus the call to conversion should begin with the repentance of those who do the calling, who issue the invitation.** Baptism in itself is a unique act, the covenant that Christians no longer belong to themselves but have been bought for ever with the blood of Christ and belong to God. But the experience of baptism should be constantly re-enacted by daily dying with Christ to sin, to themselves and to the world and rising again with Him into the servant body of Christ to become a blessing for the surrounding community.

**The experience of conversion gives meaning to people in all stages of life, endurance to resist oppression, and assurance that even death has no final power over human life because God in Christ has already taken our life with him, a life that is 'hidden with Christ in God' (Col. 3:3).**

### *2. The Gospel to all Realms of Life*

14. In the Bible, religious life was never limited to the temple or isolated from daily life (Hos. 6:4-6; Isa. 58:6-7). The teaching of Jesus on the Kingdom of God is a clear reference to God's loving lordship over all human history. We cannot limit our witness to a supposedly private area of life. The lordship of Christ is to be proclaimed to all realms of life. In the Great Commission, Jesus said to His disciples: 'All authority in heaven and on earth has been given to me. Go, therefore,

---

[11] *Your Kingdom Come*, 196.

[12] *Confessing Christ Today*, Reports of Groups at a Consultation of Orthodox Theologians, 8.

and make disciples of all nations, baptizing them in the name of the Father and of the Son and of the Holy Spirit, teaching them to obey all that I have commanded you. And lo, I am with you always, to the close of the age' (Matt. 28:19-20). The Good News of the kingdom is a challenge to the structures of society (Eph. 3:9-10; 6:12) as well as a call to individuals to repent. 'If salvation from sin through divine forgiveness is to be truly and fully personal, it must express itself in the renewal of these relations and structures. Such renewal is not merely a consequence but an essential element of the conversion of whole human beings.'[13]

15. 'The Evangelistic Witness is directed towards all the *ktisis* (creation) which groans and travails in search of adoption and redemption… The transfiguring power of the Holy Trinity is meant to reach into every nook and cranny of our national life… The Evangelistic Witness will also speak to the structures of this world: its economic, political and societal institutions… We must re-learn the patristic lesson that the Church is the mouth and voice of the poor and the oppressed in the presence of the powers-that-be. In our own way we must learn once again "how to speak to the ear of the King", on the people's behalf… Christ was sent for no lesser purpose than bringing the world into the life of God.'[14]

16. In the fulfilment of its vocation, the Church is called *to announce* Good News in Jesus Christ, forgiveness, hope, a new heaven and a new earth; *to denounce* powers and principalities, sin and injustice; *to console* the widows and orphans, healing, restoring the brokenhearted; and *to celebrate* life in the midst of death. In carrying out these tasks, churches may meet limitations, constraints, even persecution from prevailing powers which pretend to have final authority over the life and destiny of people.

17. In some countries there is pressure to limit religion to the private life of the believer – to assert that freedom to believe should be enough. The Christian faith challenges that assumption. The Church claims the right and the duty to exist publicly – visibly – and to address itself openly to issues of human concern. 'Confessing Christ *today* means that the Spirit makes us struggle with… sin and forgiveness, power and powerlessness, exploitation and misery, the universal search for identity, the widespread loss of Christian motivation, and the spiritual longings of those who have not heard Christ's name. It means that we are in communion with the prophets who announced God's will and promise for humankind and society, with the martyrs who sealed their confession with suffering and

[13] *Breaking Barriers*, 233.
[14] *Confessing Christ Today*, 10, 3.

death, and also with the doubtful who can only whisper their confession of the Name.'[15]

18. The realm of science and technology deserves particular attention today. The everyday life of most children, women and men, whether rich or poor, is affected by the avalanche of scientific discoveries. Pharmaceutical science has revolutionized sexual behaviour. Increasingly sophisticated computers solve problems in seconds for which formerly a whole lifetime was needed; at the same time they become a means of invading the privacy of millions of people. Nuclear power threatens the survival of life on this planet, while at the same time it provides a new source of energy. Biological research stands at the awesome frontier of interference with the genetic code which could – for better or for worse – change the whole human species. Scientists are, therefore, seeking ethical guidance. Behind the questions as to right or wrong decisions and attitudes, however, there are ultimate theological questions: what is the meaning of human existence? the goal of history? the true reality within and beyond what can be tested and quantified empirically? The ethical questions arise out of a quest for a new worldview, a faith.

19. The biblical stories and ancient creeds do furnish precious insights for witnessing to the Gospel in the scientific world. Can theologians, however, with these insights, help scientists achieve responsible action in genetic engineering or nuclear physics? It would hardly seem possible so long as the great communication gap between these two groups persists. Those directly involved in and affected by scientific research can best discern and explicate the insights of Christian faith in terms of specific ethical positions.

**Christian witness will point towards Jesus Christ in whom real humanity is revealed and who is, in God's wisdom, the centre of all creation, the 'head over all things'** (Eph. 1:10; 22-23). This witness will show the glory and the humility of human stewardship on this earth.

### *3. The Church and its Unity in God's Mission*

20. To receive the message of the Kingdom of God is to be incorporated into the body of Christ, the Church, the author and sustainer of which is the Holy Spirit (Appendix 5). The churches are to be a sign for the world. They are to intercede as He did, to serve as He did. **Thus Christian mission is the action of the body of Christ in the history of humankind – a continuation of Pentecost. Those who through conversion and baptism accept the Gospel of Jesus partake in the life of the body of Christ and participate in an historical tradition.** Sadly, there are many betrayals of this high calling in the history of the churches. Many who are attracted to the vision of the

[15] *Breaking Barriers*, 48.

kingdom find it difficult to be attracted to the concrete reality of the Church. They are invited to join in a continual process of renewal of the churches. 'The challenge facing the churches is not that the modern world is unconcerned about their evangelistic message, but rather whether they are so renewed in their life and thought that they become a living witness to the integrity of the Gospel. The evangelizing churches need themselves to receive the Good News and to let the Holy Spirit remake their life when and how he wills'[16] (Appendix 6).

21. The celebration of the eucharist is the place for the renewal of the missionary conviction at the heart of every congregation. According to the Apostle Paul, the celebration of the eucharist is in itself a 'proclamation of the death of the Lord until he comes' (1 Cor. 11:26). 'In such ways God feeds His people as they celebrate the mystery of the Eucharist so that they may confess in word and deed that Jesus Christ is Lord, to the glory of God the Father'[17] (Appendix 7).

**The eucharist is bread for a missionary people. We acknowledge with deep sorrow the fact that Christians do not join together at the Lord's table. This contradicts God's will and impoverishes the body of Christ. The credibility of our Christian witness is at stake.**

22. Christians are called to work for the renewal and transformation of the churches. Today there are many signs of the work of the Holy Spirit in such a renewal. *The house gatherings of the Church in China or the Basic Ecclesial Communities in Latin America, the liturgical renewal, biblical renewal, the revival of the monastic vocation, the charismatic movement, are indications of the renewal possibilities of the Church of Jesus Christ.*

23. In the announcement to the world of the reconciliation in Jesus Christ, churches are called to unite. Faced with the challenge and threat of the world, the churches often unite to defend common positions. **But common witness should be the natural consequence of their unity with Christ in His mission.** The ecumenical experience has discovered the reality of a deep spiritual unity. The common recognition of the authority of the Bible and of the creeds of the ancient Church and a growing convergence in doctrinal affirmations should allow the churches not only to affirm together the fundamentals of the Christian faith, but also to proclaim together the Good News of Jesus Christ to the world. In solidarity, churches are helping each other in their respective witness before the world. In the same solidarity, they should share their spiritual and material resources to announce together and clearly their common hope and common calling.

24. 'Often it is socially and politically more difficult to witness together since the powers of this world promote division. In such situations

---

[16] Philip Potter's Speech to the Roman Catholic Synod of Bishops, Rome, 1974.

[17] *Your Kingdom Come*, 206.

common witness is particularly precious and Christ-like. Witness that dares to be common is a powerful sign of unity coming directly and visibly from Christ and a glimpse of His kingdom.'[18]

The impulse for common witness comes from the depth of our faith. 'Its urgency is underlined when we realize the seriousness of the human predicament and the tremendous task waiting for the churches at present.'[19]

25. It is at the heart of Christian mission to foster the multiplication of local congregations in every human community. The planting of the seed of the Gospel will bring forward a people gathered around the Word and sacraments and called to announce God's revealed purpose.

Thanks to the faithful witness of disciples through the ages, churches have sprung up in practically every country. **This task of sowing the seed needs to be continued until there is, in every human community, a cell of the kingdom, a church confessing Jesus Christ and in His name serving His people.** The building up of the Church in every place is essential to the Gospel. The vicarious work of Christ demands the presence of a vicarious people. A vital instrument for the fulfilment of the missionary vocation of the Church is the local congregation.

26. The planting of the Church in different cultures demands a positive attitude towards inculturation of the Gospel. Ancient churches, through centuries of intimate relations with the cultures and aspirations of their people, have proved the powerful witnessing character of this rooting of the churches in the national soil. 'Inculturation has its source and inspiration in the mystery of the Incarnation. The Word was made flesh. Here flesh means the fully concrete, human and created reality that Jesus was. Inculturation, therefore, becomes another way of describing Christian mission. If proclamation sees mission in the perspective of the Word to be proclaimed, inculturation sees mission in the perspective of the flesh, or concrete embodiment, which the Word assumes in a particular individual, community, institution or culture.'[20]

Inculturation should not be understood merely as intellectual research; it occurs when Christians express their faith in the symbols and images of their respective cultures. *The best way to stimulate the process of inculturation is to participate in the struggle of the less privileged for their liberation. Solidarity is the best teacher of common cultural values.*

27. This growing cultural diversity could create some difficulties. In our attempt to express the catholicity of the Church we may lose the sense

---

[18] *Common Witness*, 28.
[19] *Common Witness*, 28.
[20] *SEDOS Bulletin*, 81.7.

of its unity. **But the unity we look for is not uniformity but the multiple expression of a common faith and a common mission.**

'We have found this confession of Christ out of our various cultural contexts to be not only a mutually inspiring, but also a mutually corrective exchange. Without this sharing, our individual affirmations would gradually become poorer and narrower. We need each other to regain the lost dimensions of confessing Christ and to discover dimensions unknown to us before. Sharing in this way, we are all changed and our cultures are transformed.'[21]

The vision of nations coming from the East, the West, the North and the South to sit at the final banquet of the kingdom should always be before us in our missionary endeavour.

### *4. Mission in Christ's Way*

'As the Father has sent me, even so I send you' (John 20: 21). The self-emptying of the servant who lived among the people, sharing in their hopes and sufferings, giving His life on the cross for all humanity – this was Christ's way of proclaiming the Good News, and as disciples we are summoned to follow the same way. 'A servant is not greater than his master; nor is he who is sent greater than he who sent him' (John 13:16).

Our obedience in mission should be patterned on the ministry and teaching of Jesus. He gave His love and His time to all people. He praised the widow who gave her last coin to the temple; He received Nicodemus during the night; He called Matthew to the apostolate; He visited Zacchaeus in his home; He gave Himself in a special way to the poor, consoling, affirming and challenging them. He spent long hours in prayer and lived in dependence on and willing obedience to God's will.

An imperialistic crusader's spirit was foreign to Him. **Churches are free to choose the ways they consider best to announce the Gospel to different people in different circumstances. But these options are never neutral. Every methodology illustrates or betrays the Gospel we announce. In all communications of the Gospel, power must be subordinate to love.**

29. Our societies are undergoing a significant and rapid change under the impact of new communication technologies and their applications. We are entering the age of the information society, characterized by an ever-increasing media presence in all relationships, both interpersonal and intersocial. Christians need to rethink critically their responsibility for all communication processes and redefine the values of Christian communications. In the use of all new media options, the communicating church must ensure that these instruments of

---

[21] *Breaking Barriers*, 46.

communication are not masters, but servants in the proclaiming of the Kingdom of God and its values. As servants, the new media options, kept within their own limits, will help to liberate societies from communication bondage and will place tools in the hands of communities for witnessing to Jesus Christ.

30. Evangelism happens in terms of interpersonal relations when the Holy Spirit quickens to faith. Through sharing the pains and joys of life, identifying with people, the Gospel is understood and communicated.

*Often, the primary confessors are precisely the non-publicized, unsensational people who gather together steadfastly in small caring communities, whose life prompts the question: 'What is the source of the meaning of your life? What is the power of your powerlessness?', giving the occasion to name THE NAME.* Shared experiences reveal how often Christ is confessed in the very silence of a prison cell or of a restricted but serving, waiting, praying church.

Mission calls for a serving church in every land, a church which is willing to be marked with the stigmata (nailmarks) of the crucified and risen Lord. In this way the church will show that it belongs to that movement of God's love shown in Christ who went to the periphery of life. Dying outside the gates of the city (Heb. 13:12), He is the high priest offering Himself for the salvation of the world. Outside the city gates the message of a self-giving, sharing love is truly proclaimed; here the Church renews its vocation to be the body of Christ in joyful fellowship with its risen Lord ( 1 John 3:16).

### *5. Good News to the Poor*

31. There is a new awareness of the growing gap between wealth and poverty among the nations and inside each nation. It is a cruel reality that the number of people who do not reach the material level for a normal human life is growing steadily. An increasing number of people find themselves marginalized, second-class citizens unable to control their own destiny and unable to understand what is happening around them. Racism, powerlessness, solitude, breaking of family and community ties are new evidences of the marginalization that comes under the category of poverty.

32. **There is also a tragic coincidence that most of the world's poor have not heard the Good News of the Gospel of Jesus Christ; or they could not receive it, because it was not recognized as Good News in the way in which it was brought. This is a double injustice: they are victims of the oppression of an unjust economic order or an unjust political distribution of power, and at the same time they are deprived of the knowledge of God's special care for them. To announce the Good News to the poor is to begin to render the justice due to them. The Church of Jesus Christ is called to preach the**

**Good News to the poor following the example of its Lord who was incarnated as poor, who lived as one among them and gave to them the promise of the Kingdom of God. Jesus looked at the multitudes with compassion. He recognized the poor as those who were sinned against, victims of both personal and structural sin.**

Out of this deep awareness came both His solidarity and His calling to them (Matt. 11: 28). His calling was a personalized one. He invited them to come to Him, to receive forgiveness of sins and to assume a task. He called them to follow Him, because His love incorporated His respect for them as people created by God with freedom to respond. He called them to exercise this responsibility towards God, neighbours and their own lives. **The proclamation of the Gospel among the poor is a sign of the Messianic kingdom and a priority criterion by which to judge the validity of our missionary engagement today** (Appendix 8).

33. This new awareness is an invitation to rethink priorities and lifestyles both in the local church and in the worldwide missionary endeavour. Of course, churches and Christians find themselves in very different contexts: some in very wealthy settings where the experience of poverty as it is known to millions in the world today is practically unknown, or in egalitarian societies where the basic needs of life seem to be assured for almost everybody, to situations of extreme poverty. **But the consciousness of the global nature of poverty and exploitation in the world today, the knowledge of the interdependence between nations and the understanding of the international missionary responsibility of the Church – all invite, in fact oblige, every church and every Christian to think of ways and means to share the Good News with the poor of today.** An objective look at the life of every society, even the most affluent and those which are, theoretically, more just, will show the reality of the poor today in the marginalized, the drop-outs who cannot cope with modern society, the prisoners of conscience, the dissidents. All of them are waiting for a cup of cold water or for a visit in the name of Christ. **Churches are learning afresh through the poor of the earth to overcome the old dichotomies between evangelism and social action. The 'spiritual Gospel' and 'material Gospel' were in Jesus one Gospel.**

34. **There is no evangelism without solidarity; there is no Christian solidarity that does not involve sharing the knowledge of the kingdom which is God's promise to the poor of the earth. There is here a double credibility test: a proclamation that does not hold forth the promises of the justice of the kingdom to the poor of the earth is a caricature of the Gospel; but Christian participation in the struggles for justice which does not point towards the promises of the kingdom also makes a caricature of a Christian understanding of justice.**

A growing consensus among Christians today speaks of God's preferential option for the poor.[22] We have there a valid yardstick to apply to our lives as individual Christians, local congregations and as missionary people of God in the world.

35. This concentration point, God's preferential option for the poor, raises the question of the Gospel for all those who objectively are not poor or do not consider themselves as such. It is a clear Christian conviction that God wants all human beings to be saved and to come to the knowledge of the truth, but we know that. while God's purpose is for the salvation of all, He has worked historically through the people of Israel and through the incarnation of His own son Jesus Christ. While His purpose is universal, His action is always particular. What we are learning anew today is that God works through the downtrodden, the persecuted, the poor of the earth. And from there, He is calling all humanity to follow Him. 'If any one would come after me, let him deny himself and take up his cross and follow me' (Matt. 16: 24).

**For all of us, the invitation is clear: to follow Jesus in identification and sharing with the weak, marginalized and poor of the world, because in them we encounter Him. Knowing from the Gospel and from historical experience that to be rich is to risk forfeiting the kingdom, and knowing how close the links are, in today's world, between the abundance of some and the needs of others, Christians are challenged to follow Him, surrendering all they are and have to the kingdom, to a struggle that commits us against all injustice, against all want. The preferential option for the poor, instead of discriminating against all other human beings, is, on the contrary, a guideline for the priorities and behaviour of all Christians everywhere, pointing to the values around which we should organize our lives and the struggle into which we should put our energy.**

36. There is a long experience in the Church of voluntary poverty, people who in obedience to their Christian calling cast aside all their belongings, make their own the fate of the poor of the earth, becoming one of them and living among them. Voluntary poverty has always been recognized as a source of spiritual inspiration, of insight into the heart of the Gospel.

Today we are gratefully surprised, as churches are growing among the poor of the earth, by the insight and perspective of the Gospel coming from the communities of the poor. They are discovering dimensions of the Gospel which have long been forgotten by the Church. The poor of the earth are reading reality from the other side, from the side of those who do not get the attention of the history books written by the conquerors, but who surely get God's attention in the book of life. Living with the poor

[22] Catholic Bishops Conference, Puebla, 1979, para 1134.

and understanding the Bible from their perspective helps to discover the particular caring with which God both in the Old and in the New Testament thinks of the marginalized, the downtrodden and the deprived. We realize that the poor to whom Jesus promised the Kingdom of God are blessed in their longing for justice and in their hope for liberation. They are both subjects and bearers of the Good News; they have the right and the duty to announce the Gospel not only among themselves, but also to all other sectors of the human family.

Churches of the poor are spreading the liberating Gospel of Jesus Christ in almost every corner of the earth. The richness and freshness of their experience is an inspiration and blessing to churches with a centuries-old history. The centres of the missionary expansion of the Church are moving from the North to the South. **God is working through the poor of the earth to awaken the consciousness of humanity to His call for repentance, for justice and for love.**

### *6. Mission in and to Six Continents*

37. **Everywhere the churches are in missionary situations.** Even in countries where the churches have been active for centuries we see life organized today without reference to Christian values, a growth of secularism understood as the absence of any final meaning. The churches have lost vital contact with the workers and the youth and many others. This situation is so urgent that it commands priority attention of the ecumenical movement. The movement of migrants and political refugees brings the missionary frontier to the doorstep of every parish. **The Christian affirmations on the worldwide missionary responsibility of the Church will be credible if they are authenticated by a serious missionary engagement at home.**

As the world becomes smaller, it is possible even for Christians living far away to be aware of and inspired by faithful missionary engagement in a local situation. Of special importance today is the expression of solidarity among the churches crossing political frontiers and the symbolic actions of obedience of one part of the body of Christ that enhance the missionary work of other sectors of the Church. So, for example, while programmes related to the elimination of racism may be seen as problems for some churches, such programmes have become, for other churches, a sign of solidarity, an opportunity for witness and a test of Christian authenticity.

**Every local congregation needs the awareness of its catholicity which comes from its participation in the mission of the Church of Jesus Christ in other parts of the world. Through its witnessing stance in its own situation, its prayers of intercession for churches in other parts of the world, and its sharing of persons and resources, it participates fully in the world mission of the Christian Church.**

38. This concern for mission everywhere has been tested with the call for a moratorium, a halt – at least for a time – to sending and receiving missionaries and resources across national boundaries, in order to encourage the recovery and affirmation of the identity of every church, the concentration on mission in its own place and the freedom to reconsider traditional relations. The *Lausanne Covenant* noted that 'the reduction of foreign missionaries and money in an evangelized country may sometimes be necessary to facilitate the national church's growth and self-reliance and to release resources for unevangelized areas'.[23] Moratorium does not mean the end of the missionary vocation nor of the duty to provide resources for missionary work, but it does mean freedom to reconsider present engagements and to see whether a continuation of what we have been doing for so long is the right style of mission in our day.

Moratorium has to be understood *inside* a concern for world mission. **It is faithfulness of commitment to Christ in each national situation which makes missionary concern in other parts of the world authentic. There can never be a moratorium of mission, but it will always be possible, and sometimes necessary, to have a moratorium for the sake of better mission.**

39. The story of the churches from their earliest years is the story of faithfulness in their respective localities, but also the story of the carrying of the Gospel across national and continental boundaries: first from Jerusalem to Judaea and Samaria, then to Asia Minor, Africa and Europe, and now to the ends of the earth. Christians today are the heirs of a long history of those who left their home countries and churches, apostles, monastics, pilgrims, missionaries, emigrants, to work in the name of Jesus Christ, serving and preaching where the Gospel had not yet been heard or received. With the European colonization of most of the world and later on with the expansion of the colonial and neo-colonial presence of the western powers, the churches which had their bases mainly in the West have expanded their missionary service to all corners of the earth.

Surely, many ambiguities have accompanied this development and are present even today, not least the sin of proselytism among other Christian confessions. Churches and missionary organizations are analysing the experience of these past centuries in order to correct their ways, precisely with the help of the new churches which have come into being in those countries. **The history of the Church, the missionary people of God, needs to continue. Each local parish, each Christian, must be challenged to assume responsibility in the total mission of the Church. There will always be need for those who have the calling and**

---

[23] *Lausanne Covenant*, No. 9.

**the gift to cross frontiers, to share the Gospel of Jesus Christ and to serve in His name** (Appendix 9).

40. Out of this sense of being the whole Church in mission, we recognize the specific calling to individuals or communities to commit themselves full-time to the service of the church, crossing cultural and national frontiers. **The churches should not allow this specialized calling of the few to be an alibi for the whole Church, but rather it should be a symbolic concentration of the missionary vocation of the whole Church.** Looking at the question of people in mission today, 'We perceive a change in the direction of mission, arising from our understanding of the Christ who is the centre and who is always in movement towards the periphery. While not in any way denying the continuing significance and necessity of a mutuality between the churches in the northern and southern hemispheres, we believe that we can discern a development whereby mission in the eighties may increasingly take place within these zones. We feel there will be increasing traffic between the churches of Asia, Africa and Latin America among whose numbers both rich and poor are counted. This development, we expect, will take the form of ever stronger initiatives from the churches of the poor and oppressed at the peripheries. Similarly among the industrialized countries, a new reciprocity, particularly one stemming from the marginalized groups, may lead to sharing at the peripheries of the richer societies. While resources may still flow from financially richer to poorer churches, and while it is not our intention to encourage isolationism, we feel that a benefit of this new reality could well be the loosening of the bond of domination and dependence that still so scandalously characterizes the relationship between many churches of the northern and southern hemispheres respectively.'[24]

### *7. Witness among People of Living Faiths*

41. Christians owe the message of God's salvation in Jesus Christ to every person and to every people. Christians make their witness in the context of neighbours who live by other religious convictions and ideological persuasions. **True witness follows Jesus Christ in respecting and affirming the uniqueness and freedom of others.** We confess as Christians that we have often looked for the worst in others and have passed negative judgement upon other religions. We hope as Christians to be learning to witness to our neighbours in a humble, repentant and joyful spirit (Appendix 10).

42. **The Word is at work in every human life. In Jesus of Nazareth the Word became a human being. The wonder of His**

[24] *Your Kingdom Come*, 220-21.

**ministry of love persuades Christians to testify to people of every religious and non-religious persuasion of this decisive presence of God in Christ. In Him is our salvation. Among Christians there are still differences of understanding as to how this salvation in Christ is available to people of diverse religious persuasions. But all agree that witness should be rendered to all.**

43. Such an attitude springs from the assurance that God is the creator of the whole universe and that He has not left Himself without witness at any time or any place. **The Spirit of God is constantly at work in ways that pass human understanding and in places that to us are least expected. In entering into a relationship of dialogue with others, therefore, Christians seek to discern the unsearchable riches of God and the way He deals with humanity.** For Christians who come from cultures shaped by another faith, an even more intimate interior dialogue takes place as they seek to establish the connection in their lives between their cultural heritage and the deep convictions of their Christian faith.

44. Christians should use every opportunity to join hands with their neighbours, to work together to be communities of freedom, peace and mutual respect. In some places, state legislation hinders the freedom of conscience and the real exercise of religious freedom. Christian churches as well as communities of other faiths cannot be faithful to their vocation without the freedom and right to maintain their institutional form and confessional identity in a society and to transmit their faith from one generation to another. In those difficult situations, Christians should find a way, along with others, to enter into dialogue with the civil authorities in order to reach a common definition of religious freedom. With that freedom comes the responsibility to defend through common actions all human rights in those societies (Appendix 11).

45. **Life with people of other faiths and ideologies is an encounter of commitments. Witness cannot be a one-way process, but of necessity is two-way; in it Christians become aware of some of the deepest convictions of their neighbours. It is also the time in which, within a spirit of openness and trust, Christians are able to bear authentic witness, giving an account of their commitment to the Christ, who calls all persons to Himself.**

## Looking Towards the Future

46. Whether among the secularized masses of industrial societies, the emerging new ideologies around which societies are organized, the resurging religions which people embrace, the movements of workers and political refugees, the people's search for liberation and justice, the

uncertain pilgrimage of the younger generation into a future both full of promise and overshadowed by nuclear confrontation, the Church is called to be present and to articulate the meaning of God's love in Jesus Christ for every person and for every situation.

47. The missionary vocation of the Church and its evangelistic calling will not resist the confrontation with the hard realities of daily life if it is not sustained by faith, *a faith supported by prayer, contemplation and adoration.* 'Gathering and dispersing, receiving and giving, praise and work, prayer and struggle – this is the true rhythm of Christian engagement in the world.'[25] Christians must bring their hearts, minds and wills to the altar of God, knowing that from worship comes wisdom, from prayer comes strength, and from fellowship comes endurance. 'To be incorporated into Christ through the work of the Holy Spirit is the greatest blessing of the kingdom, and the only abiding ground of our missionary activity in the world.'[26] The same Lord who sends His people to cross all frontiers and to enter into the most unknown territories in His name, is the one who assures: 'I am with you always, to the close of the age.'

## Appendices

1. Now, the Gospel was given to the Apostles for us by the Lord Jesus Christ: and Jesus the Christ was sent from God. That is to say, Christ received His commission from God, and the Apostles theirs from Christ. The order of these two events was in accordance with the will of God. So thereafter, when the Apostles had been given their instructions, and all their doubts had been set at rest by the resurrection of our Lord Jesus Christ from the dead, they set out in the full assurance of the Holy Spirit to proclaim the coming of God's kingdom. And as they went through the territories and townships preaching, they appointed their first converts-after testing them by the Spirit – to be bishops and deacons for the believers of the future.

(Clement of Rome, *The First Epistle to the Corinthians*, 42, p. 45)

2. The difference between Christians and the rest of mankind is not a matter of nationality, or language, or customs. Christians do not live apart in separate cities of their own, speak any special dialect, nor practise any eccentric way of life. The doctrine they profess is not the invention of busy human minds and brains, nor are they, like some, adherents of this or that school of human thought. They pass their lives in whatever township – Greek or foreign – each man's lot has determined, and conform to ordinary local usage in their clothing, diet and other habits. Nevertheless, the organization of their community does exhibit some features that are remarkable, and even surprising. For instance, though

[25] *Your Kingdom Come*, 205.
[26] *Your Kingdom Come*, 204.

they are residents at home in their own countries, their behaviour there is more like that of transients: they take their full part as citizens, but they also submit to anything and everything as if they were aliens. For them, any foreign country is a motherland, and any motherland is a foreign country. Like other men, they marry and beget children, though they do not expose their infants. Any Christian is free to share his neighbour's table, but never his marriage bed. Though destiny has placed them here in the flesh, they do not live after the flesh: their days are passed on the earth, but their citizenship is above in the heavens. They obey the prescribed laws, but in their own private lives they transcend the laws. They show love to all men – and all men persecute them. They are misunderstood and condemned; yet by suffering death they are quickened into life. They are poor, yet making many rich; lacking all things, yet having all things in abundance. They are dishonoured, yet made glorious in their very dishonour; slandered, yet vindicated. They repay calumny with blessings, and abuse with courtesy. For the good they do, they suffer stripes as evil-doers: and under the strokes they rejoice like men given new life. Jews assail them as heretics, and Greeks harass them with persecutions: and yet of all their ill-wishers there is not one who can produce good grounds for his hostility.

To put it briefly, the relation of Christians to the world is that of a soul to the body . . .

(*The Epistle to Diognetus*, points 5 and 6)

3. There is no single way to witness to Jesus Christ. The Church has borne witness in different times and places in different ways. This is important. There are occasions when dynamic action in society is called for: there are others when a word must be spoken: others when the behaviour of Christians one to another is the telling witness. On still other occasions the simple presence of a worshipping community or man is the witness. These different dimensions of witness to the one Lord are always a matter of concrete obedience. To take them in isolation from one another is to distort the Gospel. They are inextricably bound together, and together give the true dimensions of evangelism. The important thing is that God's redeeming Word be proclaimed and heard.

(*Theological Reflection on the Work of Evangelism*, 1959)

4. Through Christ, men and women are liberated and empowered with all their energies and possibilities to participate in His Messianic work. Through His death on the Cross and His resurrection from the dead hope of salvation becomes realistic and reality hopeful. He liberates from the prison of guilt. He takes the inevitability out of history. In Him the Kingdom of God and of free people is at hand. Faith in Christ releases in man creative freedom for the salvation of the world. He who separates himself from the mission of God separates himself from salvation.

(*Bangkok Assembly*, 1973, p. 88)

5. Those who take part in the life of Christ and confess Him as Lord and Saviour, Liberator and Unifier, are gathered in a community of which the author and sustainer is the Holy Spirit. This communion of the Spirit finds its primary aim and ultimate purpose in the eucharistic celebration and the glorification of the Triune God. The doxology is the supreme confession which transcends all our divisions.

(*Breaking Barriers*, p. 48)

6. As Monseigneur Etchegaray said to the Synod a few days ago: 'A church which is being renewed in order more effectively to evangelize is a church which is itself willing to be evangelized... We lack not so much the words to say to people as credible persons to say the Word.' ('Une eglise qui se renouvelle pour mieux evangeliser est une eglise qui accepte d'être evangelisée elle-même... Il nous manque moins de paroles à dire aux hommes que d'hommes credibles pour dire la parole.')

(Philip Potter's speech to the Roman Catholic Synod of Bishops, Rome, 1974)

7. There are times and places where the very act of coming together to celebrate the Eucharist can be a public witness. In certain states, Christians may be discouraged from attending such worship or being penalized for it. We hear of those who come together at great risk, and whose courage reveals to those around them how precious is this sacrament. In other situations the Eucharist may be an open-air witness so planned that many may see it. Such a joyful celebration as this may offer fresh hope in cynical, secular societies. There is, at the Lord's table, a vision of God which draws the human heart to the Lord... Each Christian minister and congregation has to seek this understanding, and we can only give some indications: where a people is being harshly oppressed, the Eucharist speaks of the exodus or deliverance from bondage. Where Christians are rejected or imprisoned for their faith, the bread and wine become the life of the Lord who was rejected by men but has become 'the chief stone of the corner'. Where the church sees a diminishing membership and its budgets are depressing, the Eucharist declares that there are no limits to God's giving and no end to hope in Him. Where discrimination by race, sex or class is a danger for the community, the Eucharist enables people of all sorts to partake of the one food and to be made one people. Where people are affluent and at ease with life, the Eucharist says, 'As Christ shares his life, share what you have with the hungry.' Where a congregation is isolated by politics or war or geography, the Eucharist unites us with all God's people in all places and all ages. Where a sister or brother is near death, the Eucharist becomes a doorway into the kingdom of our loving Father.

(*Your Kingdom Come*, pp. 205-06)

8. The proclamation of the Gospel to the poor is a sign of the new age inaugurated by Jesus Christ. As witnessed in the Scriptures, the

situation of the poor, and what the Holy Spirit can do among them, is a wonderful locus for the manifestation of God's love and power. This implies that evangelization to the poor, with the poor, for and by the poor, must be considered one of the churches' highest priorities.

(*Towards a Church in Solidarity with the Poor*, p. 26)

9. The proclamation of the Good News is a continual necessity and all people, believers and unbelievers, are challenged to hear and respond since conversion is never finished. We acknowledge and gladly accept our special obligation to those who have never heard the Good News of the kingdom. New frontiers are continually being discovered. Jesus our Lord is always ahead of us and draws us to follow Him, often in unexpected ways. The Christian community is a community on the way, making its proclamation, both to itself and to those beyond its fellowship, even as it shows forth its other marks 'on the way'.

(*Your Kingdom Come*, p. 195)

10. Christians engaged in faithful 'dialogue in community' with people of other faiths and ideologies cannot avoid asking themselves penetrating questions about the place of these people in the activity of God in history. They ask these questions not in theory, but in terms of what God may be doing in the lives of hundreds of millions of men and women who live in and seek community together with Christians, but along different ways. So dialogue should proceed in terms of people of other faiths and ideologies rather than of theoretical, impersonal systems. This is not to deny the importance of religious traditions and their interrelationships but it is vital to examine how faiths and ideologies have given direction to the daily living of individuals and groups and actually affect dialogue on both sides.

Approaching the theological questions in this spirit Christians should proceed…

- with repentance, because they know how easily they misconstrue God's revelation in Jesus Christ, betraying it in their actions and posturing as the owners of God's truth rather than, as in fact they are, the undeserving recipients of grace;
- with humility, because they so often perceive in people of other faiths and ideologies a spirituality, dedication, compassion and a wisdom which should forbid them making judgements about others as though from a position of superiority; in particular they should avoid using ideas such as 'anonymous Christians', 'the Christian presence', 'the unknown Christ', in ways not intended by those who proposed them for theological purposes or in ways prejudicial to the self-understanding of Christians and others;
- with joy, because it is not themselves they preach; it is Jesus Christ, perceived by many people of living faiths and ideologies as prophet, holy one, teacher, example;

- but confessed by Christians as Lord and Saviour, Himself the faithful witness and the coming one (Rev. 1:5-7);
- with integrity, because they do not enter into dialogue with others except in this penitent and humble joyfulness in the Lord Jesus Christ, making clear to others their own experience and witness, even as they seek to hear from others their expressions of deepest conviction and insight. All these would mean an openness and exposure, the capacity to be wounded which we see in the example of our Lord Jesus Christ and which we sum up in the word 'vulnerability'. (*Guidelines on Dialogue with People of Living Faiths and Ideologies,* pp. 11-12)

11. The attitude of the churches to the ongoing revivals or reassertions of institutional religions will have to vary according to the specific situation. In some countries the situation of the churches has become extremely difficult, particularly where the revival has led to erosion of civil liberties including, in some cases, the freedom of religion.

- The prayer of the worldwide church must be that the Christians in those situations may find strength in the Holy Spirit to witness for the Kingdom of God in humility and endurance, that oppression can be met with love and that God may use their sufferings to bring about a renewal of their own Christian faith.
- We express our solidarity with them as with all oppressed people.
- In all situations of religious conflicts the churches are called upon to help their individual members to re-examine their own basic loyalties and to understand better their neighbours of other faiths. On all accounts, the churches must try to find meeting points in their contexts for dialogue and co-operation with people of other faiths. The above-mentioned criteria as well as the common cultural heritage and a commitment to national unity and development could be the starting points for a mutual witness in dialogue. This presupposes a mind of openness, respect and truthfulness in the churches and among their members towards neighbours of other faiths, but also courage to give an account of the hope we have in Jesus Christ as our Lord.
- As has been pointed out in the Guidelines on Dialogue, received by the Central Committee of the WCC, Jamaica 1979, a dialogical approach to neighbours of other faiths and convictions is not in contradiction with mission. Our mission to witness to Jesus Christ can never be given up. The proclamation of the Gospel to the whole world remains an urgent obligation for all Christians and it should be carried out in the spirit of our Lord, not in a crusading and aggressive spirit.
- 'Let us behave wisely towards those outside our number; let us use the opportunity to the full. Let our conversation be always

full of grace and never insipid; let us study how best to talk with each person we meet' (Col. 4:5-6). (*Your Kingdom Come,* pp. 187-188)

## San Antonio 1989 – Mission in Christ's Way

- God's unconditional will to gather up and renew all things in Christ
- Present pain and struggle of people on the periphery
- The Church as a sign and foretaste of God's purpose for all creation
- Creative tension between confidence in Christ and respect for other faiths
- Attempts to build better relationships with Evangelicals

The CWME conference held at San Antonio in Texas, USA, in 1989 attempted to recognise tensions in the understanding and practice of mission and to take these forward in a way of life and a form of action which were true to the incarnation of Christ. It attempted to bring together the advocates of differing approaches to mission in an active commitment to follow Christ. 'Creative tension' was a key phrase. The conference theme was: 'Your will be done: mission in Christ's way'.

Christopher Duraisingh suggested that three 'concentration points' can be discerned in the proceedings of the conference. 'They are God's unconditional will to gather up and renew all things in Christ, the present pain and struggle of people at the periphery and the provisional experience of the church as a sign and foretaste of God's purpose for all creation.'[1] The conference has also been remembered for its formulation of an understanding of the relationship of Christianity with other faiths, a perennial theme in ecumenical mission conferences. In an oft-quoted sentence it stated: 'We cannot point to any other way of salvation than Jesus Christ; at the same time we cannot set limits to the saving power of God.'[2] It acknowledged that there was a tension built into this understanding but argued that it is a tension to be respected rather than resolved.

At the same time as the WCC conference convened in San Antonio, Evangelicals gathered in Manila for 'Lausanne II'. The division in the Protestant missionary movement was plain to see. However, significant attempts at bridge-building were taking place and there were voices at San Antonio urging that in future parallel conferences on the same site be arranged.[3] A letter to this effect was signed by 160 Evangelical delegates at San Antonio, a harbinger of rapprochement.

---

[1] Christopher Duraisingh, 'Editorial', in *International Review of Mission,* 89.313 (1990), 3.

[2] Frederick R. Wilson (ed), *The San Antonio Report. Your Will be Done: Mission in Christ's Way* (Geneva: WCC, 1990), 32.

[3] See Yates, *Christian Mission*, 226.

**Message of the Conference**

In the name of the Triune God,
Creator of heaven and earth
Saviour and Comforter,
people gathered from all parts of the world
in San Antonio, Texas, USA,
as a Conference on World Mission and Evangelism
of the World Council of Churches,
under the theme: YOUR WILL BE DONE – MISSION IN CHRIST'S WAY.
The two most significant trends of this conference were
the spirit of universality (catholicity) of the gathering,
and its concern for the fullness of the gospel, namely:
to hold in creative tension
spiritual and material needs
prayer and action
evangelism and social responsibility
dialogue and witness
power and vulnerability
local and universal.
Mirror of that diversity,
San Antonio is a multicultural city
where many strands meet, clash and intermingle:
Hispanic, Anglo-Saxon, black, indigenous peoples, others.
In this context, the gathered people looked ahead to 1992,
the five hundredth anniversary of the conquest of the Americas,
a time when the gospel message was brought to these lands
under the auspices of colonial powers,
which often distorted Christian love with violence and oppression.
The heirs and survivors of the indigenous people recall this date with bitterness.
This past cannot be undone, but
reparation must be done to redeem the future,
and the hands of all people must join
to weave a new world community.
Concerned with the discernment of the will of God in today's world,
the representatives of the churches gathered in San Antonio,
and spoke about shared signs of hope and renewal.
They celebrated the new opportunity
for religious expression in many socialist countries.
They realized that the Holy Spirit,
Spirit of truth, freedom, communion and justice,
is at work today in different parts of the world.
Communities, and even entire nations, in unexpected ways,
are involved in self-examination, repentance, renewal

and struggle for justice,
turning to the Living God,
stressing the infinite value of human dignity,
and turning to one another to make peace.
For all this,
we rejoice in the Spirit;
we thank the living God,
and in these signs we hear a new call to faith
And see a new challenge for mission and evangelism.
At the same time,
Christ is still suffering in many parts of the world,
and is waiting for our concrete response:
solidarity and action.
We have heard many voices of anguish and pain:
voices of poor and oppressed peoples,
voices of women who suffer discrimination,
voices of youth challenging injustice in church and society,
voices of children who suffer innocently in body, mind and spirit,
voices of victims of foreign intervention and militarism,
voices of those who are discriminated against and violated because of race,
voices of those who are being destroyed by nuclear abuse,
voices of people suffocating under the burden of external debt,
voices of indigenous peoples yearning for self-determination,
voices of refugees and displaced persons,
voices of hunger for food and for meaning in life,
voices of anger at blatant violation of human rights,
voices of longing for liberation and justice,
voices of solidarity in the quest for a new human community.
We also heard of the voiceless suffering of religious communities
whose right to exist is denied constitutionally, as is the case in Albania.
In the study of Holy Scripture,
in worship and prayer,
in self-examination and penitence,
we have sensed anew
the urgent voice of God calling us to love mercy
to act justly
and to walk humbly with our God.
This is a time for repentance,
to make reparation
to turn to the living God.
Judgement begins in the household of God.
In faithfulness to God's will,
it is time for a new commitment to a Mission in Christ's Way,
and prayer, witness and action,

in the power of the Holy Spirit.
God calls us, Christians everywhere, to join in:
proclaiming the Good News of God's redeeming love in Jesus Christ;
acting in solidarity with those who suffer and struggle for justice and human dignity;
sharing justly the earth's resources;
bearing witness to the gospel through renewed communities in mission.
To those who hear or experience a twisted or partial gospel,
or no gospel at all:
Mission in Christ's Way calls us by deed and word
to share the wholeness of the gospel,
the love of God revealed in the incarnate Word, Jesus Christ.
To churches and nations where divisions, barriers and enmities prevail:
Mission in Christ's Way calls us to strive
for unity with justice as a basis for effective mission.
To peoples of wonderfully diverse cultures across the earth:
Mission in Christ's Way calls us to extend understanding and respect,
relating the gospel of Christ to these cultures with sensitivity.
To persons of other religious faiths of the world:
Mission in Christ's Way calls us to listen to and respect their beliefs,
witness our faith to them in word and deed,
seek with them for peace and justice.
To young people and all those resisting injustice and war,
facing repression and death:
Mission in Christ's Way calls us to solidarity in the struggle for life,
turning hopelessness into strength.
To those whose land and livelihood are taken away, despoiled or polluted:
Mission in Christ's Way calls us to resist all that violates human rights,
that basic justice may extend to all.
To those who suffer and whose life is threatened, exploited, shattered or oppressed:
Mission in Christ's Way calls us to commit all in our power
to defend life in all its fullness
and self-determination for every human being, community and nation.
Proclamation of the kingdom,
of hope for the whole creation
of a Mission in Christ's Way,
is not just an affirmation,
but a way of life.
We are called to concrete acts of faithfulness,
a living expression of the prayer that Christ has taught us:
'YOUR WILL BE DONE'

### *Witness among People of Other Living Faiths*

25. In reaffirming the 'evangelistic mandate' of the ecumenical movement, we would like to emphasize that we may never claim to have a full understanding of God's truth: we are only the recipients of God's grace. Our ministry of witness among people of other faiths presupposes our *presence* with them, *sensitivity* to their deepest faith commitments and experiences, *willingness* to be their servants for Christ's sake, *affirmation* of what God has done and is doing among them, and *love* for them. Since God's mystery in Christ surpasses our understanding and since our knowledge of God's saving power is imperfect, we Christians are called to be *witnesses* to others, not judges of them. We also affirm that it is possible to be non-aggressive and missionary at the same time – that it is, in fact, the only way to be truly missionary.

26. We cannot point to any other way of salvation than Jesus Christ; at the same time we cannot set limits to the saving power of God. At times the debate about salvation focuses itself only on the fate of the individual soul in the hereafter, whereas the will of God is life in its fullness even here and now. We therefore state: (a) that our witness to others concerning salvation in Christ springs from the fact that we have encountered Him as Lord and Saviour and are hence urged to share this with others; and (b) that in calling people to faith in Christ, we are not only offering personal salvation but also calling them to follow Jesus in the service of God's reign.

27. We have paid attention to the complex debate about the relationship between *witness* and *dialogue*. We recognize that both witness and dialogue presuppose two-way relationships. We affirm that witness does not preclude dialogue but invites it, and that dialogue does not preclude witness but extends and deepens it.

28. Dialogue has its own place and integrity and is neither opposed to nor incompatible with witness or proclamation. We do not water down our own commitment if we engage in dialogue; as a matter of fact, dialogue between people of different faiths is spurious unless it proceeds from the acceptance and expression of faith commitment. Indeed, life with people of other faiths and ideologies is by its very nature an encounter of commitments. In dialogue we are invited to listen in openness to the possibility that the God we know in Jesus Christ may encounter us also in the lives of our neighbours of other faiths. On the other hand, we also see that the mutual sharing with people of other faiths in the efforts for justice, peace and service to the environment engages us in dialogue – the dialogue of life. We wish to commend that, in recognition that all humankind is responsible before God and the human family.

29. In affirming the dialogical nature of our witness, we are constrained by grace to affirm that 'salvation is offered to the whole creation through Jesus Christ' (Tambaram II). 'Our mission to witness to Jesus Christ can never be given up' (Melbourne, p. 188). We are well aware that these convictions and the ministry of witness stand in tension with what we have

affirmed about God being present in and at work in people of other faiths; we appreciate this tension, and do not attempt to resolve it.

30. We affirm our unequivocal endorsement of the principle and practice of religious freedom. We are aware that many people are discriminated against, harassed and even persecuted for their faith, often when they have converted from one faith to another; we deplore this and every manifestation of religious or ideological fanaticism. We commend to our Christian communities all those who suffer for their faith, whatever their religious persuasion may be.[4]

---

[4] Wilson, *The San Antonio Report*, 20-24, 32-33.

## SALVADOR DE BAHIA 1996 – GOSPEL AND CULTURE

- Respect for cultural integrity in post-Cold War world
- Need to critique and challenge cultural expression on a gospel basis
- Creative tension between contextuality and catholicity
- Need for responsible relationships in mission; avoidance of proselytism
- Attention to the witness of local congregations
- Participation of indigenous peoples, women and youth

The interrelationship of gospel and culture had been an influential theme at Bangkok in 1973 but it was taken up in the new context of the 1990s at Salvador de Bahia, in Brazil, in 1996. The end of the Cold War and the disintegration of the Soviet Union had ushered in a new world order in which cultural and ethnic factors underlay many conflicts. It was clear by this time that each culture had to discover its own way of expressing the gospel rather than replicating western models. Respect for cultural integrity was a strong emphasis at Salvador de Bahia but it also emphasised the need to critique and challenge cultural expression on the basis of the gospel, and to be open to other identities. 'The special emphasis of Salvador lies,' suggested Jacques Matthey, 'in the affirmation of the ambiguity of each culture… All cultures need to be approached with both love and understanding and with a critical eye and spirit… When encountering a culture, the gospel illuminates parts of it and challenges others, especially when they lead to oppression, in justice and violence. Salvador laid much emphasis on the real danger of exclusivist ethnic politics: in such situations, the gospel becomes captive and alienated by a wrong sense of struggle for identity.'[1] The conference explored the creative tension between contextuality and catholicity. In a global context of violence, fragmentation and the destruction of community, the conference met under the title 'Called to One Hope: The Gospel in Diverse Cultures'.

The conference was marked by a conscious effort to hear the voices of those who had been excluded from earlier gatherings, such as Christians from the global South, indigenous peoples, women and youth. The inclusion of significant numbers of young people was an innovative feature of the conference. Lesslie Newbigin had suggested that, '… the only possible hermeneutic of the gospel is a congregation which believes it',[2] and the Salvador conference gave considerable attention to the life of the

---

[1] Jacques Matthey, 'Salvador among the World Mission Conferences of this Century', in *International Review of Mission,* 86.340-41 (1997), 20-21.

[2] Lesslie Newbigin, *The Gospel in a Pluralist Society* (London: SPCK, 1989), 232.

local congregation. A particular challenge at this level was posed by large-scale migration which was presenting congregations with the challenge of how to be inclusive of people arriving from other contexts and cultures

Structural issues which make for oppression and call for liberation were prominent in the discussions and reinforced by a visit to a quay where slaves taken from Africa disembarked for hundreds of years. The conference was also aware that Christian mission can also be guilty of abuse of power. Attention was given to proselytism as an unwelcome and invalid form of evangelism which jeopardises common Christian witness.[3] A key question, as Christopher Duraisingh suggested, is: 'If the unity of the church and its witness to the gospel of reconciliation are inseparably related and if the hope to which Christians are called is one, how may the churches promote responsible relationships in mission that witness to God's purpose to reconcile all things into unity in Christ?'[4]

## Conference Message

The conference on world mission and evangelism has met in Salvador, Bahia, Brazil, at a significant moment in history – the approach of the end of the century and of a new millennium.

Soon after the start of this century, the first comprehensive ecumenical mission conference took place in Edinburgh. It stated: 'The work [of mission] has to be done now. It is urgent and must be pressed forward at once.' The work of mission, however, did not turn out to be straightforward. Within four years of that conference the world was engulfed in war. Since then, it has known massacres and mass deportations, another World War, the development of new forms of colonialism, life under nuclear threat, the destruction of ecosystems by human greed, the growth and collapse of the Soviet bloc, violent and separatist ethnic struggles, rampant capitalism leading to an ever-greater gap between rich and poor.

We believe that it is still the church's primary calling to pursue the mission of God in God's world through the grace and goodness of Jesus Christ. Yet this mission, history-long, worldwide, cannot be seen in narrow ways – it must be an every-member mission, from everywhere to everywhere, involving every aspect of life in a rapidly changing world of many cultures now interacting and overlapping.

In conference here in Salvador, we have sought to understand better the way in which the gospel challenges all human cultures and how culture can

---

[3] A product of the conference, published the following year, is 'Towards Common Witness: A Call to Adopt Responsible Relationships in Mission and to Renounce Proselytism', in *'You are the Light of the World': Statements on Mission by the World Council of Churches 1980-2005* (Geneva: WCC, 2005), 39-58.

[4] Christopher Duraisingh (ed), *Called to One Hope: The Gospel in Diverse Cultures* (Geneva: WCC, 1998), xiii.

give us a clearer understanding of the gospel. It would be difficult to find a more appropriate venue for such a conference. Brazil has the second largest population of people of African origin of any nation. Salvador is a microcosm of the world's diversity of cultures and spiritualities. Yet this very place made us aware of the pain and fragmentation that comes from the racism and lack of respect for other religions that still exist in sectors of the Christian churches.

The theme of the conference was 'Called to One Hope – The Gospel in Diverse Cultures'.

The hope of the gospel is expressed in the gracious coming of God in Jesus of Nazareth. From the day of Pentecost this hope manifests itself as the fruit of faith and in the struggle of the community of faith. It reaches out to all people everywhere. This conference has been a foretaste and impulse of this hope.

In the conference we have experienced much which has given us such hope:

- the wide diversity of peoples and churches represented (in Edinburgh in 1910 the large majority of the participants were European or North American; in Salvador over 600 Christians of a wide spectrum of cultures from almost 100 nations participated in the life of the conference);
- the genuine attempt which has been made to listen and to share ways and wisdom across cultures;
- the thrill of participating in the life of a community where the voices of young and old, women and men, from Christian churches around the globe have all been speaking out;
- the willingness of the churches and mission agencies to admit past failures and to refuse to engage in stereotyping, and the determination to stay together and work together for the good of our common mission;
- the solidarity of standing at the dockside in Salvador where, for 300 years, the African slaves who were still alive after their capture and deportation were unloaded. By the 'Stone of Tears' together we wept tears of repentance;
- the encouragement of participating in the rhythm of daily worship where the honouring and use of different sounds and languages did not result in a divisive and confusing 'babel', but rather gave a hint of the unity and inspiration of a Pentecost;
- the privilege of sharing for a short time in the life of a continent and people with a rich cultural history and a diversity of religious spirituality, whose churches are responding to the challenges of social change and poverty through the embodiment of gospel hope.

It is our profound hope that this last great mission conference of the twentieth century has clearly illuminated that for the gospel to be most fruitful needs to be both true to itself, and incarnated in the culture of a people. We have had a first-hand experience of seeing and hearing Christians from many diverse cultures expressing their struggles and hopes.

- We have heard the cries of pain from indigenous peoples who have faced the near extermination of their communities and cultures, and we have marvelled at their resilience and their determination to make connections between their indigenous spirituality and their Christian faith so that their identity is not divided.
- We have heard the longing of women around the world for a real partnership in church and society.
- We have listened to the voices of young Christians telling us that they do not wish to be objects of the church's mission but full partners in the work of mission, particularly in relating the faith to the energy and aspirations of youth culture today.
- We have learned from our Latin American hosts the importance of 'doing' theology which seeks to create a 'community called church', which is rooted in the life of the people amongst whom the church is set, and which shows itself, for example, in their response to the plight of the street children in their cities.
- We have heard the voices of Christians in the Pacific who seek mutuality with their Christian partners from the West, insisting that full partnership in mission is reciprocal, not paternalistic.
- We have heard the anger of African people, Afro-Caribbean people, Afro-Latino people and African people of North America at the horror of slavery, and we have heard how the faith, though presented to them in distorted forms, became the hope of liberation. We have admired their determination not to be trapped in a lament over history but to co-operate together in a strengthened partnership between African people and people of the African diaspora.
- We have been moved by the stories of disaster and disease which led one speaker from Africa to say, 'Times are ripe for flirting with hopelessness', and we have been astonished at the strength and determination of African Christians, women in particular, to share the pain of their people, and to combat despair and plant the seeds of both food and hope.
- We have benefitted from hearing of the long-term experience of Asian Christians of living a life of Christian discipleship in multi-faith societies, sometimes as vulnerable and threatened minority groups. We have also heard of a surge of grassroots missionary activity.
- We have been moved by the experiences of Christians in the Middle East living with the privilege and pain of life in a 'holy land' torn apart by division and injustice, and their indignation at the way in which biblical texts are misinterpreted so that their culture is blemished and some are made to feel strangers in their own land.

- We have admired the commitment of those from the Orthodox and other local churches in the former Soviet Union and Eastern Europe now determined, in the new atmosphere of religious freedom, to serve their people in such way that the faith which sustained many through times of persecution might now be an equal blessing in times of new challenge. We have heard their protest at the ways in which rich foreign Christian groups are seeking to proselytize their people.
- We have recognized the caution of Christians in Germany about being too ready to see God's spirit in all human cultures, growing out of their painful memories of how churches risked becoming captive to Nazi ideology in a previous generation.
- We have heard how the churches, against the background of the post-modern background influencing much of western Europe, are studying the phenomenon of secularism and engaging with those turning from traditional faith and seemingly seeking a private 'pick-and-mix' spirituality.
- We have heard reports of the growing localism of North American churches which, while strengthening their commitment to mission and evangelism in their own context, may lead to an isolation and insulation from global realities.
- We have shared the concern of many at how the global free-market economy seems to exercise sovereign power over even strong governments, and how the mass media disseminate worldwide images and messages of every description which influence – and, some believe, undermine – community and faith.
- We have discussed how, perhaps as a reaction to these developments, new fundamentalisms are emerging in all world faiths, adding to the divisions in an already fractured world.
- We have heard how Christians in many places around the globe are engaging in serious dialogue with people of other faiths, telling the Christian story, listening attentively to the stories of others, and thus gaining a clearer and richer understanding of their own faith and helping to build a 'community of communities' to the benefit of all.

In such ways we have recognized how the church engages in mission with cultures around the globe today. What then would we want to emphasise from this conference?

- The church must hold on to two realities: its distinctiveness from, and its commitment to, the culture in which it is set. In such a way the gospel becomes neither captive to a culture nor alienated from it, but each challenges and illuminates the other.
- Perhaps as never before, Christians in mission today need to have a clear understanding of what God has done in history through Jesus Christ. In this we have seen what God requires of individuals, communities and structures. The biblical witness is our starting

point and reference for mission and gives us the sense of our own identity.

- We need constantly to seek the insight of the Holy Spirit in helping us better to discern where the gospel challenges, endorses or transforms a particular culture.
- The catholicity of a church is enhanced by the quality of the relationships it has with churches of other traditions and cultures. This has implications for mission and evangelism, and calls for respect and sensitivity for churches already located in the place concerned. Competitiveness is the surest way to undermine Christian mission. Equally, aggressive evangelism which does not respect the culture of a people is unlikely to reflect effectively the gracious love of God and the challenge of the gospel.
- Local congregations are called to be places of hope, providing spaces of safety and trust wherein different people can be embraced and affirmed, thus manifesting the inclusive love of God. For congregations in increasingly plural societies, inclusion of all cultural groups which make up the community, including those who are uprooted, marginalized and despised, is important. Strengthening congregations through a spirituality which enables them to face the vulnerability involved in this openness is critical.
- Small steps which involve risk and courage can break through barriers and create new relationships. Such steps are available to us all. They can be the 'miracle' which changes a church or community's self-image and enables new God-given life to break forth.

Music at the conference has had a rhythm, a harmony, a beat. In a place with a deep African tradition it is natural that in our worship the beat of the drum has frequently been the vehicle to carry our souls to resonate with the beat of God's love for us and for all people. With hearts set on fire with the beat of mission and a prayer on our lips that many will share with us in being 'Called to One Hope', and take and find 'the Gospel in Diverse Cultures', we commend the fruits of the conference to Christians and churches everywhere. Our profound hope is that they too may be renewed in mission for the sharing of the knowledge of Christ, to the glory of the triune God.[5]

---

[5] Duraisingh, *Called to One Hope*, 20-25.

## ATHENS 2005 – HEALING AND RECONCILIATION

- After 9/11 attack in New York – increasing violence, fragmentation, exclusion
- Calling of church to work for reconciliation, healing and fullness of life in Christ
- First CWME conference to be hosted in a predominantly Orthodox country
- Participation of Evangelical, Pentecostal and independent church movements
- Reconciliation of *missio Dei* approach with *missio Ecclesiae* approach
- Fresh attention to the Holy Spirit, and to the ecological dimension of mission

In May 2005 a WCC conference on World Mission and Evangelism was held in a predominantly Orthodox country for the first time. This not only influenced the style of the conference but demonstrated the influence of Orthodox theology on ecumenical missiology in regard to the Trinity, the Holy Spirit, worship, healing and reconciliation.[1] It was also marked by a diversity of participation and a deliberate move to include representatives of growing parts of world Christianity which had not always been represented at major ecumenical events. As Ruth Bottoms, Moderator of CWME, commented: 'For me, one of the great gifts and joys of the conference was that by the grace of God the Spirit built community amongst the participants over our days together. Given the wide range of people represented, with a Roman Catholic delegation fully participating as well as those from Pentecostal and evangelical churches and movements not necessarily in membership of the World Council of Churches, this in itself was significant.'[2] This prompted the adoption of a different style to earlier Conferences. There were no long reports intended to be received or adopted by the conference plenary. Instead, the emphasis was on 'creating spaces for sharing, dialogue, debate, listening, presenting experiences and case studies or theological reflections.'[3]

---

[1] See Jacques Matthey (ed), *Come Holy Spirit, Heal and Reconcile! Called in Christ to be Reconciling and Healing Communities – Report of the WCC Conference on World Mission and Evangelism, Athens, Greece, May 9-16, 2005* (Geneva: WCC, 2008).
[2] Matthey, *Come Holy Spirit*, 9.
[3] Matthey, *Come Holy Spirit*, 25.

An important development detected by Jacques Matthey, CWME Secretary, was the attempt that was made to reconcile a missio Dei approach with missio Ecclesiae:

> Since the International Missionary Council (IMC) Conference in Willingen in 1952, the wide missio Dei perspective gained in importance in the ecumenical movement, in reaction to narrower or exclusively ecclesiocentric formulations of the missionary task. It was essential indeed to liberate Christian witness from narrow perspectives, as if the Triune God's presence in, and availability to, the world was manifested only inside the visible frontiers of existing church life. The whole 'oikumene' as inhabited world, and ultimately the whole creation, was to become the horizon and space for God's challenging and life-enabling presence. Ecumenical missiology widened its scope to include social, political and religious movements or institutions in its vision of history moving towards the accomplishment of God's promises of peace and justice. It did so in some extreme formulations by neglecting the specific purpose and mission of the church, disregarding the spiritual needs of persons and communities, and uncritically referring to a linear western perspective on time and history, considered as 'progress'.[4]

Without sacrificing the depth and range brought to missiology by the *missio Dei* perspective, the Athens conference saw renewed attention to the centrality of the church in the mission of God.

As the conference title suggests, fresh attention was given to the Holy Spirit – a move which would prove to be significant for ecumenical missiology. The ecological dimension of mission received serious attention as awareness of the issues posed by climate change was rising. Matthey also discerned: 'a more humble approach to what Christians and churches can accomplish in the world today than seemed to have been the approaches in earlier CWME conferences… Humanity cannot "heal the world" nor create "shalom". We have to acknowledge our limitations and thus we call on God: "Come, Holy Spirit, heal and reconcile!"'[5]

A prominent feature on the changing landscape was the 9/11 attack on the Twin Towers in New York in 2001 and the 'war on terror' which followed. A time of globalization with increasing violence, fragmentation and exclusion brought sharper focus and new energy to the calling of the church to receive, celebrate, proclaim and work for reconciliation, healing and fullness of life in Christ. The conference offered a summary overview of the current missiological situation and expressed a missiological response to it in terms of prayer and commitment.

### Summary Overview of Current Missiological Context

After the Cold War era, the world order has moved towards a unified market, which, accompanied by social and cultural phenomena, is usually

---

[4] Matthey, *Come Holy Spirit*, 330.
[5] Matthey, *Come Holy Spirit*, 328-29.

referred to by the term 'globalization'. The bipolar political economic ideology has become a monopolar neo-liberal one, in which the market becomes the main reference all over the world and the measure for judging values, social achievements and even human beings and communities themselves. Partly in reaction to the risk of cultural levelling by the leading market forces and the media, new conflict areas emerged, among and within nations, often with a cultural, ethnic or religious background. These developments modify local and regional political alliances and tend to reinforce the control of the power centres of western societies over the world.

In this context, missiology needs to focus anew intentionally on Christ's life-affirming ministry as an alternative and a means of resistance to political, economic and religious trends and forces leading to oppression, alienation and death. Witnessing to the fullness of life in Christ leads Christians and churches to consider the whole of creation as the horizon of mission. The basis and framework of Christian mission must be consistently Trinitarian, based on and related to the work of God the Father, Son and Holy Spirit, from the beginning of creation to the end of time. There is particular urgency to better understand the role of the Spirit in church and world and to work out the consequences for mission in practice.

Reconciliation appears to be a central term, describing God's forgiveness given in Christ, the intention of God's own presence and action in the world, and the vision of the final aim of God's mission (*missio Dei*). Authentic reconciliation is costly and cannot easily be reached if separated from justice, truth about responsibilities, love for enemies and forgiveness. It has personal, community, social and ecological dimensions. It implies healing from past and present wounds, from injustice and guilt, at personal, community and social levels.[6]

Come, Holy Spirit, heal and reconcile

Calling on the Spirit, we confess that mission is not ours.

Mission is the mission of the triune God, the creator of heaven and earth, whose purpose is that all may have fullness of life.

In Jesus Christ, God laid the basis for real reconciliation and healing, overcoming all enmity and evil.

God the Holy Spirit is continually present and active as healer and reconciler in church and world.

So we believe that God makes it possible to:

Repair broken relationships between

- God and human beings
- People and people
- Churches and churches
- Nations and nations
- Humanity and creation

---

[6] Matthey, *Come Holy Spirit*, 28.

Overcome enmity and violence
We hope to see many signs of:
Health, balance and wholeness of life:
For individuals
For whole communities
For humanity
For creation

We call on God the Spirit: heal and reconcile, empower us, so that as persons and communities, we may receive, become and share signs of forgiveness, peace, justice and unity, and renounce sin, enmity, violence, injustice and divisions.

### *Called in Christ to be Reconciling and Healing Communities*

At this time in a globalized context, God entrusts and commissions us with a message of healing and reconciliation.[7] The crucified and resurrected Christ invites us to participate in God's mission. It is **our mission** to form healing communities in celebration, witness, mutual love, forgiveness and respect, and to intervene in peace-building, reconciliation processes and healing of memories in society, overcoming violence wherever we can.

Our being, and our way of being together, needs to reflect our vision of reconciliation.
We are called
to create and multiply safe spaces, hospitable to those who are stigmatized, lost, searching for meaning, solidarity and community,
and to journey as and with victims of violence and sin towards reconciliation and justice.

Reconciliation and healing need to be experienced within communities (member to member), between communities where brokenness exists, and in humanity's relationship with creation.

By using the term 'communities' (instead of 'Community' as referring to the Church) we want to affirm the plurality and the diverse nature of the communities in which we live.[8]

---

[7] These themes are more fully elaborated in two documents of the Athens Conference: 'Mission as Ministry of Reconciliation', in *'You are the Light of the World': Statements on Mission by the World Council of Churches 1980-2005* (Geneva: WCC, 2005), 90-128; and 'The Healing Mission of the Church', in *'You are the Light of the World'*, 129-62.

[8] Matthey, *Come Holy Spirit*, 23-24.

# EDINBURGH 2010: WITNESSING TOGETHER

- Representatives of all traditions of Christianity share in centenary conference
- A moment of celebration, healing and convergence of the missionary movement
- Extensive study process offering comprehensive analysis of mission themes
- Significant shared understanding reflected in the *Common Call*

The approach of the centenary of Edinburgh 1910 prompted an attempt in Scotland to take account of Christian mission a century after the epoch-making conference.[1] This in turn led to a meeting in mid-2005 to consider what might be done internationally in regard to the Edinburgh 1910 centenary. The twenty people who came together had no formal authority but were broadly representative of world Christianity. The nine themes they identified provided the structure for the Edinburgh 2010 study process and eventually shaped the 'Common Call' issued by the Edinburgh 2010 Conference.[2] A General Council formed in 2007 to take responsibility for this initiative included representatives from every stream of world Christianity including the Orthodox, Catholics, Evangelicals, Pentecostals and Independents as well as the Protestant descendants of the bodies which participated in Edinburgh 1910. Jooseop Keum highlights the significance of this: 'For the first time in mission history, representatives of all traditions of Christianity and global mission actors gathered together to celebrate the centenary.'[3] This new convergence was also apparent in the emergence of the Global Christian Forum, which met for the first time in Nairobi in 2007. Like Edinburgh 2010, it minimized formal commitment and maximized width of participation and the building of relationships.

Not only did the delegates to the Edinburgh 2010 conference enjoy their fellowship but they found that they could join in affirming a shared understanding of Christian mission. Among the notes they struck are the following:

- The missionary mandate is reaffirmed, indeed its urgency is emphasised, but it is recognised that authenticity is paramount and

---

[1] See David A. Kerr and Kenneth R. Ross (eds), *Edinburgh 2010: Mission Then and Now* (Oxford: Regnum, 2009).
[2] See Kenneth R. Ross, 'Edinburgh 2010: The Common Call', in *Forum Mission*, Band 7 (2011), 192-202.
[3] Keum, 'Beyond Dichotomy', 395.

mission must be practised in a way which resonates with people's experience.

- Recognising plurality in regard to religious conviction, a fine balance is struck between affirming the uniqueness of Christ and maintaining an open and hospitable attitude towards those who adhere to other faiths and belief-systems.
- On the basis that God often chooses to work through the young and that many people have their most formative religious experiences in their earliest years, young people are viewed not only as the objects but also as the subjects of mission.
- The natural environment is recognised as a legitimate focus of concern in the practice of mission. Indeed, there is a broadening of the understanding of mission to embrace the renewal of the whole creation and the fulfilment of all things in Jesus Christ.
- Mission is understood as being critically engaged with the prevailing power structures. God's identification with those on the receiving end of unjust exercise of power spurs mission practitioners to work for a transformation of power.
- The spiritual character of mission is emphasised, with the dynamic work of the Holy Spirit finding expression in relation to such areas as mass migration, reconciliation in situations of conflict and the cry for healing at all levels.
- Formation of leaders is a major focus, with concern to move away from the exclusively cerebral approach of the European Enlightenment towards approaches which are more holistic, inclusive and empowering.
- The biblical call to unity is reaffirmed, with a recognition that, while structural unity remains elusive, this is no excuse for failing to develop common witness, to create collaborative models of working and to be healing and reconciling communities.

Edinburgh 2010 brought together probably the widest spectrum of world Christianity ever to engage in a shared global project of mission study. It arrived at a remarkable moment when representatives of so many different sectors of the world church were able to affirm an incisive statement of the meaning of Christian mission for our time. It has a particular significance for ecumenical missiology. Jooseop Keum comments: 'An analysis of the Common Call produced at the Edinburgh Conference shows that positions defended over decades by WCC have now become somewhat common ground: missio Dei, empowerment and humility, creation as the scope of mission, holistic content of the Gospel, mission from everywhere to everywhere, unity and mission… Indeed, Edinburgh 2010 was a moment of celebration, healing and convergence of the missionary movement. At the same time, The Common Call highlighted the evangelical concern for 'the uniqueness of Christ' and for conversion.'[4]

## The *Common Call*

The *Common Call* of Edinburgh 2010 was affirmed in the Church of Scotland Assembly Hall in Edinburgh on 6th June 2010 by representatives of world Christianity, including Catholic, Evangelical, Orthodox, Pentecostal and Protestant churches, in the following terms:

As we gather for the centenary of the World Missionary Conference of Edinburgh 1910, we believe the church, as a sign and symbol of the reign of God, is called to witness to Christ today by sharing in God's mission of love through the transforming power of the Holy Spirit.

1. Trusting in the Triune God and with a renewed sense of urgency, we are called to incarnate and proclaim the good news of salvation, of forgiveness of sin, of life in abundance, and of liberation for all poor and oppressed. We are challenged to witness and evangelism in such a way that we are a living demonstration of the love, righteousness and justice that God intends for the whole world.

2. Remembering Christ's sacrifice on the Cross and his resurrection for the world's salvation, and empowered by the Holy Spirit, we are called to authentic dialogue, respectful engagement and humble witness among people of other faiths – and no faith – to the uniqueness of Christ. Our approach is marked with bold confidence in the gospel message; it builds friendship, seeks reconciliation and practises hospitality.

3. Knowing the Holy Spirit who blows over the world at will, reconnecting creation and bringing authentic life, we are called to become communities of compassion and healing, where young people are actively participating in mission, and women and men share power and responsibilities fairly, where there is a new zeal for justice, peace and the protection of the environment, and renewed liturgy reflecting the beauties of the Creator and creation.

4. Disturbed by the asymmetries and imbalances of power that divide and trouble us in church and world, we are called to repentance, to critical reflection on systems of power, and to accountable use of power structures. We are called to find practical ways to live as members of One Body in full awareness that God resists the proud, Christ welcomes and empowers the poor and afflicted, and the power of the Holy Spirit is manifested in our vulnerability.

5. Affirming the importance of the biblical foundations of our missional engagement, and valuing the witness of the Apostles and martyrs, we are called to rejoice in the expressions of the gospel in many nations all over the world. We celebrate the renewal experienced through movements of

[4] Keum, 'Beyond Dichotomy', 396.

migration and mission in all directions, the way all are equipped for mission by the gifts of the Holy Spirit, and God's continual calling of children and young people to further the gospel.

6. Recognising the need to shape a new generation of leaders with authenticity for mission in a world of diversities in the twenty-first century, we are called to work together in new forms of theological education. Because we are all made in the image of God, these will draw on one another's unique charisms, challenge each other to grow in faith and understanding, share resources equitably worldwide, involve the entire human being and the whole family of God, and respect the wisdom of our elders while also fostering the participation of children.

7. Hearing the call of Jesus to make disciples of all people – poor, wealthy, marginalised, ignored, powerful, living with disability, young and old – we are called as communities of faith to mission from everywhere to everywhere. In joy we hear the call to receive from one another in our witness by word and action, in streets, fields, offices, homes and schools, offering reconciliation, showing love, demonstrating grace and speaking out truth.

8. Recalling Christ, the host at the banquet, and committed to that unity for which he lived and prayed, we are called to ongoing co-operation, to deal with controversial issues and to work towards a common vision. We are challenged to welcome one another in our diversity, affirm our membership through baptism in the One Body of Christ, and recognise our need for mutuality, partnership, collaboration and networking in mission, so that the world might believe.

9. Remembering Jesus' way of witness and service, we believe we are called by God to follow this way joyfully, inspired, anointed, sent and empowered by the Holy Spirit, and nurtured by Christian disciplines in community. As we look to Christ's coming in glory and judgment, we experience his presence with us in the Holy Spirit, and we invite all to join with us as we participate in God's transforming and reconciling mission of love to the whole creation.[5]

[5] Kirsteen Kim and Andrew Anderson (eds), *Edinburgh 2010: Mission Today and Tomorrow* (Oxford: Regnum, 2011), 1-2.

# 2012 Together towards Life

The end of the first decade of the 21st century proved to be a propitious time to offer a re-assessment of Christian mission. Besides the *Common Call* and accompanying study process of Edinburgh 2010, the *Cape Town Commitment* was adopted by the third Lausanne Congress later the same year. Two years later, the World Council of Churches adopted a new mission affirmation *Together towards Life* and Pope Francis issued his encyclical *Evangelii Gaudium*. Section 3 of this book includes the full text of *Together towards Life* (*TTL*), together with extensive analysis, including comparison with the other major mission documents that emerged around the same time.

At this point, for the sake of completeness, it is necessary to recognize that the adoption of *TTL* marked, in institutional terms, the completion of the century of ecumenical missiology that began with Edinburgh 1910. The document was shaped by a major CWME conference held in Manila in March 2012, adopted by the WCC Central Committee later that year and presented to the tenth Assembly of the WCC at Busan, South Korea, in 2013. As a comprehensive statement of the meaning of Christian mission it attempts to draw together all that has been learned in the course of one hundred years of ecumenical missiology. The journey, of course, will continue and the pilgrims who pursue it will always stand to benefit from knowledge of its earlier stages.

# SECTION TWO

# CORE THEMES ACROSS A CENTURY

## Introduction

In Section Two the authors from different social locations within the global South and North seek to interrogate selected missional themes that have emerged from people's engagement with global threats to life. The changing landscape of mission since 1910 has resulted in different epochs, shaped by global political, socio-economic and religio-cultural upheavals. The shift in the population strength of Christianity from the global North to the global South and mapped in Section Three has resulted in Christianity journeying from being a predominantly western religion to becoming a global religion with different contextual expressions. No longer is there any global centre that manages the missional spread of the faith.

People everywhere are setting the agenda and the themes identified in this section reflect that agenda. They are presented in an order that speaks to the era when they became urgent agenda item for ecumenical discussions. The first three articles on 'Evangelism', 'Church, Mission and Unity' and 'Worship' appeared as early agenda items for discussions because they fitted into the inner ecclesial discourse of the ecumenical agenda. Pertinent questions emerged on the ecumenical understanding and practice of these four themes. Ecumenical reflections on *Evangelism* allowed room for different interpretations in some core areas of Christian belief and use of language that is broad and leaves space for further questions and clarifications to be sought. Of major importance is the emphasis on evangelism not becoming proselytism. The focus on *Church, Mission and Unity* gives an insider perspective of the journey made in finding the tensions, challenges and opportunities encountered. The diversity in the theologies that undergird *worship* liturgies is argued to be the result of the missional journey made by churches. Those within the global North exhibited worship that reflected their contextual theological controversies and those in the global South being motivated by questions about inculturation and contextualization in their quest for authentic meaning in their worship experiences.

The next five articles interrogate themes of 'Healing', 'Culture', 'Other Faiths', 'Formation' and 'Discipleship'. The chapter on *Healing* describes the many ways in which churches during the past century have demonstrated the commitment of their ministry and mission to a holistic and comprehensive understanding and practice of health and healing. The question of the relationship between gospel and *Culture* is always a crucial one for the understanding and practice of mission – as demonstrated in an engrossing chapter on this topic. An insightful discourse on *Other Faiths* provides a critical mapping of the complex and multi-layered relationship between mission and other faiths. The ecumenical focus on *Formation* argues for leadership development that embodies life-affirming mission and transformative action in the world that embodies in-depth research, reflection and debate. Christian *Discipleship* is presented as an important ecumenical agenda that concerns what constitutes authentic following of 'mission in Christ's way'.

The rise of new nation-states in the post-colonial era of the late 1950s and early 1960s saw ecumenical themes changing to include: 'Partnership and Resource Sharing', 'Contextualization' and 'Transformation'. An overview of the ecumenical *Partnership and Resource Sharing* is mapped out to illustrate how this important missional stewardship phenomenon is embraced as a justice matter that must be addressed by all churches that wish to participate in *missio Dei*. The focus on contextualization outlines the dynamics that are involved in the inculturation process of the gospel and ecclesial communities in diverse contexts. *Transformation* of people's lives and the context in which they live and work has permeated all ecumenical explorations of key themes.

Finally, the essays on 'Justice', 'Margins', 'Environment', 'Gender' and 'Migration' trace the contemporary challenges facing the ministry and mission of the church and offer some fresh analysis and responses that are needed. However, one could posit that *these final themes* constitute the pivotal undergirding agenda that are informing missiological hermeneutics on the identity, vocation and witness of the ecclesial community in the world.

# EVANGELISM

Claudia Währisch-Oblau

> ‘Evangelism is missionary activity which makes explicit and unambiguous the centrality of the incarnation, suffering and resurrection of Jesus Christ without setting limits to the saving grace of God. It seeks to share this good news with all who have not yet heard it and invites them to an experience of life in Christ.’[1]

This definition of evangelism is found in *Together towards Life,*[2] a 2012 ecumenical affirmation on mission and evangelism drawn up by theologians from all major Christian traditions (Orthodox, Roman Catholic, Protestant, Evangelical and Pentecostal). After a century of often controversial and even acrimonious discussion, it marks a broad consensus in the understanding of what evangelism means. Nevertheless, once one starts to look closer at what is being said here, it becomes obvious that the phrasing allows quite different interpretations depending on theological decisions not mentioned here. What exactly is meant by ‘the centrality of the incarnation, suffering and resurrection of Jesus Christ’? What is ‘the saving grace of God’? How exactly is this ‘good news’? And finally, what is ‘an experience of life in Christ’?

Part of the problem is that the ecumenical discussion has mostly been about ‘mission’, and often used the term ‘evangelism’ to mean the same thing.[3] It is only fairly recently that a tendency can be observed to describe evangelism as one part or aspect of mission, as in *Together towards Life*.

‘Evangelism’ is derived from the Greek word εὐαγγελίζω, bringing or proclaiming good news. In the broadest sense, the term means to make

---

[1] *Together towards Life: Mission and Evangelism in Changing Landscapes* (Geneva: WCC, 2012), §80.

[2] *TTL*, §80.

[3] ‘Confusion about ecumenical evangelism results in part from the interchangeability of key terms in ecumenical documents.’ This is the summary of Priscilla Pope-Levison, ‘Evangelism in the WCC. From New Delhi to Canberra’, in James A. Scherer and Steven B. Bevans (eds), *New Directions in Mission and Evangelization 2: Theological Foundations* (Maryknoll, NY: Orbis Books, 1994). See also David Bosch, ‘Evangelism: Theological Currents and Cross-Currents Today’, in Paul W. Chilcote and Laceye C. Warner (eds), *The Study of Evangelism: Exploring a Missional Practice of the Church* (Grand Rapids, MI: Eerdmans, 2008). A somewhat different assessment can be found in Dietrich Werner, ‘Evangelism from a WCC Perspective: A Recollection of an Important Ecumenical Memory, and the Unfolding of a Holistic Vision’, in *International Review of Mission*, 96.382/383 (2007), 183-203.

known the Gospel (εὐαγγέλιον), the good news of Jesus Christ, with an implication that this is done through language, i.e. proclamation or sharing.

But what is the motivation for evangelism, who actually is the actor, what is the message, what is the aim or goal, and how should it be done? These are the basic questions to be answered in a theology of evangelism.

In reviewing the history of the theological discussion on evangelism, it can be helpful to work with two basic distinctions:[4] is evangelism a distinct practice of the church, or is it a quality of all Christian practice, or possibly both? And if we look at it as a distinct practice, do we understand it first and foremost as a *productive* activity, meaning that it is defined and evaluated by its outcome (i.e. conversions, however those may be understood), or is it understood as a *virtue*, a praxis that is faithful to God's reign and guided by the fruits of the Holy Spirit, such as love, hope, faith, humility, patience and courage, and therefore evaluated by its faithfulness? We should keep these questions in mind as we look at the discussion on evangelism in the last one hundred years.

## Evangelism as Enlarging Christendom

'The present is the time of all times for the Church to undertake with quickened loyalty and sufficient forces to make Christ known to all the non-Christian world.'[5] The first World Missionary Conference in Edinburgh in 1910 believed it possible to evangelize the whole world within one generation, if only churches would mobilize all their resources and follow the best scientific methods.[6] Clearly, this evangelism was the white Christian's burden: Of the 1,215 official delegates at the conference, only 19 came from the global South. [7] And equally clearly, evangelism aimed to enlarge Christendom as it was understood in the global North through the growth of existing and the foundation of new churches. In the report of Commission I, 'Carrying the Gospel to All the Non-Christian World', we find a detailed analysis of the conditions for evangelism in different parts of the world and a technical approach to the work to be done. The urgency of the task comes from the fact that the entire world is now in easy reach and non-Christian cultures are in flux. Non-Christian religions are seen as obstacles to be overcome, different missionary methods evaluated as to their efficiency, and strategies for the future developed.

---

[4] These considerations are based on Bryan P. Stone, *Evangelism After Christendom: The Theology and Practice of Christian Witness* (Grand Rapids, MI: Brazos Press, 2006).

[5] World Missionary Conference, 1910, *Report of Commission I: Carrying the Gospel to all the Non-Christian World* (Edinburgh and London: Oliphant, Anderson & Ferrier; New York, Chicago and Toronto: Fleming H. Revell, 1910), 362.

[6] See Report of Commission I, and also Brian Stanley, *The World Missionary Conference, Edinburgh 1910* (Grand Rapids, MI: Eerdmans, 2009), 3-5.

[7] Stanley, *Edinburgh 1910*, 12.

There is little reflection about the message and the content of the Gospel. The language is one of conquest, military metaphors abound, and there is no clear distinction between the Gospel and western civilization.

## Pragmatic Approaches to Evangelism

In this sense, the Edinburgh World Missionary Conference was the first embodiment of what could be termed a pragmatic approach to evangelism which is still going strong more than one hundred years later and strongly dominated by American organizations.[8] The aim of evangelism is to make as many converts as possible, to 'save souls', to 'win people for Christ'. The motivation for this approach is often, if not always, so clearly expressed, a theology that sees all those who have no 'personal relationship to Christ' as 'lost', facing damnation and eternal suffering in hell.[9] 'Winning people for Christ' usually also means adding them as members to one's own church, denomination or group, and the growth of the church is more or less equated with the strengthening of God's reign over the world. As a productive activity, evangelism is planned and evaluated following an instrumental logic: what methods are effective in bringing about conversions? How can such methods be developed, taught and possibly improved?[10] Evangelism here basically becomes a marketing strategy for a North Atlantic-dominated Evangelical Christendom.

The culmination of this marketing approach is found in the church growth movement inspired by Donald McGavran and C. Peter Wagner, and developed at the Fuller Theological Seminary School for World Mission.[11] Universal 'principles' were determined, each of which, 'when properly interpreted and applied, contributes significantly to the growth of churches and denominations'.[12] Looking at just one of them, the 'homogeneous unit', shows how a marketing approach to evangelism can actually collide with

---

[8] See, for example, the global reach of US-based organizations like Cru (formerly Campus Crusade for Christ: www.cru.org), or Evangelism Explosion (http://evangelismexplosion.org).

[9] So phrased in the faith statement of Evangelism Explosion: http://evangelismexplosion.org/about-us/statement-of-faith. Cru has different wording, but the same theology: www.cru.org/about/statement-of-faith.htm.

[10] To see just two examples of this approach, look at a classic: Robert Coleman, *The Master Plan of Evangelism* (Grand Rapids, MI: Revell Publishing, 1963, 1964, 1993), and a current bestseller: Timothy Keller, *Preaching: Communicating Faith in an Age of Skepticism* (New York: Viking, 2015).

[11] See, among many others, Donald A. McGavran, *Understanding Church Growth,* 3rd edition, revised and edited by C. Peter Wagner (Grand Rapids, MI: Eerdmans, 1990); Donald A. McGavran, *Bridges of God: A Study in the Strategy of Mission* (Eugene, OR: Wipf and Stock, 2005 [1955]); C. Peter Wagner, *Strategies for Church Growth* (Eugene, OR: Wipf & Stock, 1989).

[12] Donald A. McGavran and Win Arn, *Ten Steps for Church Growth* (New York, Harper & Row, 1977), 15.

the content of the Gospel message: McGavran observed that 'people like to become Christians without crossing racial, linguistic or class barriers'[13] and therefore suggested that where 'marked differences of color, stature, income, cleanliness, and education are present', people should be evangelized by 'their own kind of people' and find a church 'whose members look, talk, and act like themselves',[14] completely disregarding the basic experience of the early church that the Gospel message overcomes such separations.[15]

## Early Pentecostal Practice: Evangelism in the Power of the Spirit

But an evangelism driven by the urge to make as many converts as possible does not necessarily have to result in a pragmatic approach, as is shown by early Pentecostal evangelism.[16] From the 1906 revival in Azusa Street,[17] missionaries, convinced that the Holy Spirit had called and given them the gift of foreign languages (*xenolalia*), set out for countries as far apart as Japan, China or Argentina. With little money and basically no preparation, and not discouraged by the eventual discovery that they did not speak the language of the people they wanted to reach, they preached a 'full' Gospel encompassing salvation, healing, and baptism in the Spirit, and expected the power of the Holy Spirit to convince people. Pentecostals shared with the mainline Protestants assembled in Edinburgh the sense of urgency of the missionary task, enhanced in their case by a strong expectation of Christ's imminent return which compelled them to save as many as possible from damnation.[18] Consequently, itinerant preaching and healing became the method of choice. Living simply and with the local people, Pentecostal evangelists expected and experienced signs and wonders to validate their message and saw many people becoming Christians. New

---

[13] McGavran, *Understanding Church Growth,* 46.

[14] McGavran, *Understanding Church Growth,* 167.

[15] See René Padilla, *The Unity of the Church and the Homogeneous Unit Principle*, in Wilbert Shenk (ed), *Exploring Church Growth* (Eugene, OR: Wipf & Stock, 2010). A further critique came from David Bosch, 'Church Growth Missiology', in *Missionalia,* 16.1 (1988), 13-24. For a concise summary of the critical debate on the church growth movement, see Darrell L. Guder, 'Evangelism and the Debate Over Church Growth', in *Interpretation,* 48.2 (April 1994), 145-55; also Gary McIntosh (ed), *Evaluating the Church Growth Movement* (Grand Rapids, MI: Zondervan, 2004).

[16] For background on this paragraph, see Allan Anderson, *Spreading Fires: The Missionary Nature of Early Pentecostalism* (London: SCM, 2007).

[17] For a detailed account of this revival, see Cecil M. Robeck Jr, *The Azusa Street Mission and Revival. The Birth of the Global Pentecostal Movement* (Nashville TN: Thomas Nelson, 2006).

[18] See also L.G. McClung Jr, 'Evangelism', in Stanley M. Burgess (ed.), *International Dictionary of Pentecostal and Charismatic Movements* (revised and expanded edition, Grand Rapids, MI: Zondervan, 2002).

local converts (some of whom had first been evangelized by Protestant missionaries) quickly took charge of developing congregations which in many cases soon developed into independent, indigenous churches.[19]

It is unfortunate that this early Pentecostal practice has been little reflected in ecumenical discussions on evangelism, as a number of issues debated over decades found a paradigmatically different treatment here. Pentecostal missionaries relied on the power of the Holy Spirit rather than on strong organizations or ample financing, they were usually poor, they abstained from hegemonial control of their mission fields, and they brought a holistic Gospel which included physical healing and spiritual empowerment.

## Evangelism and Non-Christian Religions

It was not until the late 1920s that a controversial debate began on the question of evangelism and non-Christian religions. This topic dominated discussions at both the World Mission Conferences in Jerusalem in 1928 and in Tambaram in 1938, and came up time and again later.[20] The basic question was: is Christianity uniquely true and should therefore replace other religions, or is it the fulfilment of the best values of the non-Christian religions? In the first case, evangelism would have to show the uniqueness of Christianity in contrast to other religions, while in the latter, a dialogue approach was seen as appropriate. Or, was there just one universal faith in a supreme being which was simply being expressed in different religious forms, so that all religions should work together to fight secularism, making evangelism obsolete? This radical position was taken by a 1932 report under the title 'Re-Thinking Missions'[21] which stated that Christian missionaries were called to live in co-existence with other faiths and work towards the aim that all religions would eventually grow together in the 'completest [*sic!*] religious truth'.[22]

---

[19] Just two examples: Paul Wei, one of the founders of the True Jesus Church in China, originally worked with the London Mission. (Deng Zhaoming, 'Indigenous Chinese Pentecostal Denominations', in Allan Anderson and Edmond Tang (eds), *Asian and Pentecostal: The Charismatic Face of Asian Christianity* (Oxford: Regnum, and Baguio City: APTS Press, 2005). Joseph Ayodele Babalola, the founder of Christ Apostolic Church in Nigeria, was born into an Anglican family. (David Oyaliwola, 'Joseph Ayodele Babalola', in *Dictionary of African Christian Biography*: www.dacb.org/stories/nigeria/babalola2_joseph.html).

[20] James L. Cox, 'Jerusalem 1928: Its Message for Today', in *Missiology: An International Review,* 9.2 (April 1981), 139-53. See also Harold Netland, *Encountering Religious Pluralism: The Challenge to Christian Faith and Mission* (Downers Grove, IL: IVP, 2001).

[21] William E. Hocking (ed), *Re-Thinking Mission: A Laymen's Enquiry After One Hundred Years* (New York/London: Harper & Brothers, 1932).

[22] Hocking, *Re-Thinking Missions,* 65.

In preparation for the Tambaram conference, Dutch missionary Hendrik Kraemer wrote a statement entitled 'The Christian Message in a non-Christian World',[23] insisting on the 'radical discontinuity' between religions, which are simply human efforts, and 'God's acts of revelation and salvation' presented in the Bible. 'Evangelization, proselytism and conversion… belong to the core of the missionary enterprise.'[24] Rejecting the idea that God was at work in non-Christian religions, Kraemer was at the same time critical of Christianity and imperialistic mission and suggested an approach that combined 'evangelism, adaptation, and service'.[25]

Kraemer's viewpoint was rejected at Tambaram by many[26] and the question was not resolved[27] but in the end, the conference, which for the first time had a majority of delegates from the 'younger churches', defended the continued need for evangelism, though it called for a dialoguing and listening approach.[28]

The question underlying this discussion was, of course, whether God saved only Christians, or whether his salvation extended to other religions. The WCC mission conference at San Antonio in 1989 finally suggested a consensus which can be summarized as follows: 'We cannot point to any other way of salvation than Jesus Christ; at the same time we cannot put any limit to God's saving power. There is a tension between these affirmations which we acknowledge and cannot resolve.'[29] The ongoing study work on this issue shows how the line of reasoning has changed. Rather than discussing absolute truth, a 2006 WCC study paper speaks of

---

[23] Hendrik Kraemer, *The Christian Message in a Non-Christian World* (New York: Harper & Brothers, 1938).

[24] Kraemer, *The Christian Message,* 296.

[25] Kraemer, *The Christian Message,* 302.

[26] Jan van Lin, *Shaking the Fundamentals: Religious Plurality and Ecumenical Movement* (Amsterdam/New York: Editions Rodopi, 2002), 206-08. See also Richard J. Plantinga, 'Missionary Thinking about Religious Plurality at Tambaram 1938: Hendrik Kraemer and His Critics', in Lamin Sanneh and Joel Carpenter (eds), *The Changing Face of Christianity: Africa, the West and the World* (New York: Oxford University Press, 2005).

[27] 'As to whether the non-Christian religions… may be regarded as in some sense or to some degree manifesting God's revelation, Christians are not agreed.' *The World Mission of the Church. Findings and Recommendations of the Meeting of the International Missionary Council, Tambaram, Madras, India, Dec. 12-29, 1938* (London: International Missionary Council, no date), 52.

[28] *The World Mission of the Church*, 31-63.

[29] Quoted from https://www.oikoumene.org/en/what-we-do/cwme/history. The phrasing in the actual document from San Antonio is more complicated: see Frederick R. Wilson (ed), *The San Antonio Report. Your Will be Done: Mission in Christ's Way* (Geneva: WCC, 1990), 31-33.

religious traditions as personal 'journeys' and 'pilgrimages'.[30] The study continues: 'We need to acknowledge that human limitations and limitations of language make it impossible for any community to have exhausted the mystery of the salvation God offers to humankind. … It is this humility that enables us to say that salvation belongs to God, God only. We do not possess salvation; we participate in it. We do not offer salvation; we witness to it. We do not decide who would be saved; we leave it to the providence of God.'[31] Clearly, within the WCC, evangelism is now understood as an activity that can only be evaluated by its faithfulness to the Gospel, and not by numbers of conversions.

### Evangelism and Socio-Political Action – the Evangelical-Ecumenical Divide

From the 1950s to the early 1970s, the term 'evangelism' was rarely found in WCC documents. This may be a consequence of the development of the concept of *missio Dei*, the mission of God, which was first formulated at the 1952 conference of the International Missionary Council in Willingen.[32] *Missio Dei* means that mission is first and foremost God's action, the sending of his son with the aim of establishing the lordship of Christ over the whole redeemed creation. 'Out of the depths of his love for us, the Father has sent forth His own beloved Son to reconcile all things to Himself.'[33] In this mission, the church simply participates – she is an instrument of mission, not its goal. While in general terms this concept was and remains broadly consensual, it quickly turned out that it was possible to interpret it in completely different ways. One could understand the Kingdom of God as an eschatological, discontinuous new creation into which people entered by God's grace through faith in Jesus Christ – in which case the church had the role of proclaiming this, i.e. to evangelize – or see the Kingdom as God's radical transformation of the world to be achieved gradually, not only through the work of the church, but also through political and social action aiming at *shalom*, peace with justice, in

---

[30] *Religious Plurality and Christian Self-Understanding* Geneva: WCC, 2006): https://www.oikoumene.org/en/resources/documents/assembly/2006-porto-alegre/3-preparatory-and-background-documents/religious-plurality-and-christian-self-understanding, Section 44.

[31] *Religious Plurality and Christian Self-Understanding*, Sections 46-7.

[32] The term *missio Dei* to sum up this new concept actually was used only after the conference: see John G. Flett, *The Witness of God: The Trinity, Missio Dei, Karl Barth and the Nature of Christian Community* (Grand Rapids, MI: Eerdmans, 2010).

[33] 'A Statement on the Missionary Calling of the Church', reprinted in *International Review of Mission*, 92.367 (October 2003), 606-09, 607.

which case evangelism was replaced by or redefined as participation in liberating and reconciling action.[34]

The latter position soon dominated WCC discussions. A 1967 WCC report, 'The Church for Others',[35] described evangelism as the church discovering God at work in secular movements working towards *shalom* and joining them. Similarly, the World Mission Conference in Bangkok 1973 under the theme 'Salvation Today' saw salvation at work in the struggles for economic justice against exploitation, human dignity against oppression, solidarity against alienation, and hope against despair in personal life,[36] and hardly ever mentioned the term 'evangelism'.[37]

Evangelicals blamed the WCC as giving up evangelism altogether[38] and came together to formulate their own alternative concept. The 1974 Lausanne Congress for World Evangelization brought together participants from over 150 countries[39] and resulted in the *Lausanne Covenant*[40] which defined evangelism as 'the whole church taking the whole Gospel to the whole world',[41] binding together evangelism as 'the proclamation of the historical, biblical Christ as Saviour and Lord, with a view to persuading people to come to him personally and so be reconciled to God'[42] with action for justice, reconciliation and liberation. 'Evangelism and socio-political involvement are both part of our Christian duty.'[43] But as the ensuing debate among Evangelicals showed very clearly, the inherent logic of the *Lausanne Covenant* was the primacy of evangelism with the goal of

---

[34] There is a plethora of literature on the concept of *missio Dei*, and there is no room in this chapter for even an overview of the debate. Influential representatives of the two alternatives in the 1960s were Georg F. Vicedom, *The Mission of God: An Introduction to a Theology of Mission,* trans. Gilbert A. Thiele and Dennis Hilgendorf (St Louis, MO: Concordia Press, 1965) and Johannes C. Hoekendijk, *The Church Inside Out* (Philadelphia, PA: Westminster Press 1966). See also *International Review of Mission,* 92.367, particularly the summaries of the discussion by Jacques Matthey, 579-87, and by Wilhelm Richebächer, 588-605.

[35] *The Church for Others – Two Reports on the Missionary Structure of the Congregation* (Geneva: WCC, 1967).

[36] *Salvation and Social Justice,* Report of Section II, CWME Assembly, Bangkok, 1973, Chapter 3. Reprinted in Michael Kinnamon and Brian E. Cope (eds), *The Ecumenical Movement. An Anthology of Key Texts and Voices* (Geneva: WCC and Grand Rapids, MI: Eerdmans, 1997). See also David J. Bosch, *Transforming Mission: Paradigm Shifts in Theology of Mission* (Maryknoll, NY: Orbis Books, 1991), 406.

[37] See Pope-Levison, 'Evangelism in the WCC', 129-30.

[38] See Ralph D. Winter (ed), *The Evangelical Response to Bangkok* (South Pasadena, CA: William Carey Library, 1973).

[39] See www.lausanne.org/gatherings/congress/lausanne-1974

[40] *The Lausanne Covenant*, 1974:
www.lausanne.org/content/covenant/lausanne-covenant

[41] *Lausanne Covenant*, Section 6.

[42] *Lausanne Covenant*, Section 4.

[43] *Lausanne Covenant*, Section 5.

saving people from eternal damnation, while socio-political action was seen as dealing with a world that was anyhow going to end with the coming of God's Kingdom.[44]

Following Bangkok and Lausanne, missiologists from evangelical and ecumenical backgrounds worldwide engaged in heated discussions about the relationship between evangelism and socio-political action.[45] The crux of the issue was, of course, how to understand salvation: was it salvation *out of* the world, or the salvation *of* the world? And if the latter, were peace, justice and reconciliation a foretaste of the *shalom* of the Kingdom radically discontinuous with human history, or was history developing towards it?

## 'Good News for the Poor': Evangelism in Holistic Mission

The split between Evangelicals and Ecumenicals notwithstanding, dialogue between the two sides never stopped.[46] A number of Evangelicals also remained active within WCC structures, and the 1975 Nairobi Assembly of the WCC, similarly to Lausanne, spoke about 'the whole Gospel for the whole world by the whole church'.[47]

In ecumenical documents, the discussion in the 1980s and 1990s centred on an understanding the Gospel as 'good news for the poor', tying together the spiritual and political aspects of a holistic evangelism. The 1982 WCC

---

[44] Valdir Steuernagel, *The Theology of Mission in its Relation to Social Responsibility within the Lausanne Movement* (Chicago, IL: Lutheran School of Theology, 1988).

[45] See, for example, Alan J. Bailyes, 'Evangelical and Ecumenical Understandings of Mission', in *International Review of Mission,* 85.339 (1996), 485-503. Al Tizon, 'Evangelism and Social Responsibility: The Making of a Transformational Vision', in Margunn Serigstad Dahle, Lars Dahle and Knud Jørgensen (eds), *The Lausanne Movement: A Range of Perspectives* (Oxford: Regnum, 2014). Erhard Berneburg, *Das Verhältnis von Verkündigung und sozialer Aktion in der evangelikalen Missionstheorie* (Wuppertal: Brockhaus, 1997), lists the following relationship models within evangelical theology: 1. Social action is a watering down of evangelism; 2. Social action is a betrayal of evangelism; 3. Social action is evangelism; 4. Social action is a bridge for evangelism; 5. Social action is an illustration of evangelism; 6. Social action is the result or consequence of evangelism; 7. Social action is a partner of evangelism; 8. Social action and evangelism are equally important and two aspects of the one mission of the church.

[46] Jooseop Keum, 'Beyond Dichotomy: Towards a Convergence between the Ecumenical and Evangelical Understanding of Mission in Changing Landscapes', in Dahle, Dahle and Jørgensen, *The Lausanne Movement.*

[47] Martien E. Brinkman, *Progress in Unity? Fifty Years of Theology in the World Council of Churches: 1945-1995. A Study Guide* (Louvain: Peeters Press and Grand Rapids, MI: Eerdmans 1995), 157ff.

document, 'Mission and Evangelism: An Ecumenical Affirmation',[48] used 'mission' and 'evangelism' more or less interchangeably, and while rejecting 'the old dichotomies between evangelism and social action',[49] spoke of the invitation to faith and discipleship as well as Christian participation in the struggles for justice.[50] Similarly, the term 'conversion' was applied both to a personal acceptance of 'the saving lordship of Christ'[51] and to the 'change from war to peace, from injustice to justice, from racism to solidarity, from hate to love'.[52] How the Kingdom of God and salvation relate to this world was never clearly spelt out. The World Mission Conference in San Antonio confirmed: 'The 'material gospel' and the 'spiritual gospel' have to be one... There is no evangelism without solidarity; there is no Christian solidarity that does not involve sharing the message of God's coming reign.'[53] A document published by the Commission on World Mission and Evangelism in 2000, 'Mission and Evangelism in Unity Today',[54] finally and explicitly differentiated the terms 'mission' and 'evangelism' as follows: 'Mission' is understood in a holistic way as encompassing both sharing the news of the Gospel by word (*kerygma*), deed (*diakonia*), prayer and worship (*leiturgia*), and the everyday witness of the Christian life (*martyria*), and building up and strengthening people in their relationship with God, each other and creation. Evangelism, 'while not excluding the different dimensions of mission, focuses on explicit and intentional voicing of the gospel, including the invitation to personal conversion to a new life in Christ and to discipleship'.[55]

Evangelicals, meanwhile, took up the challenge by theologians from the South not to overlook the state of the world in their zeal to save souls, and developed a theology of 'mission as transformation'[56] which integrates 'proclamation, evangelism, church planting and social transformation in a seamless whole of Christian mission'.[57] Mission as transformation means

---

[48] *Mission and Evangelism: An Ecumenical Affirmation* (Geneva: WCC, 1982), Chapter 5, Sections 31-36. Reprinted in *'You are the Light of the World'. Statements on Mission by the World Council of Churches 1980-2005* (Geneva: WCC 2005), available online at: www.mission2005.org/fileadmin/files/mission_statements_web.pdf

[49] *Ecumenical Affirmation,* Section 33.

[50] *Ecumenical Affirmation,* Sections 34-35.

[51] *Ecumenical Affirmation,* Section 10.

[52] *Ecumenical Affirmation,* Section 11.

[53] *The San Antonio Report, Your Will Be Done: Mission in Christ's Way,* F.R. Wilson (ed) (Geneva, WCC, 1990), 26.

[54] *Mission and Evangelism in Unity Today,* reprinted in *'You Are the Light of the World'.*

[55] *Mission and Evangelism in Unity Today,* Section 7.

[56] Vinay Samuel and Chris Sugden, *Mission as Transformation* (Eugene, OR: Wipf & Stock, 2009).

[57] Samuel and Sugden, *Mission as Transformation*, back cover.

'an integral relation between evangelism and social change'.[58] Here now, Evangelicals also shift from an understanding of evangelism as producing converts to an understanding of evangelism as faithful witness.

Pentecostal voices were not much heard in this debate (or were – in my opinion wrongly – subsumed under 'Evangelical'). This is probably due to the fact that there was, in the 1980s and 1990s, very little written academic Pentecostal mission theology. But, as Miroslav Volf showed, coining the term 'material salvation', Pentecostal and charismatic evangelism built on an understanding of salvation which, while not 'political', encompassed physical healing, deliverance and liberation as an expression of and a contribution to God's ultimate redemption. [59]

## Evangelism and the Church

The ecumenical discussion with its focus on the Kingdom of God in the 1970s and 1980s tended to look at the church very critically. As an instrument witnessing to the Kingdom of God, its shortcomings were glaring. The report of the 1980 World Mission Conference in Melbourne saw the church entangled with capitalism and neo-colonialism and therefore an obstacle to evangelism.[60] But in another section, the report described the church as 'witness to the Kingdom'[61] which had to proclaim the word of God: 'The story of God in Christ is the heart of all evangelism, and this story has to be told, for the life of the present church never fully reveals the love and holiness and power of God in Christ. The telling of the story is an inescapable mandate for the whole church.'[62] This double implication is clear: the church is called to be evangelistic, even though it will always be flawed in conveying the message.

In somewhat similar terms, Pope Paul VI, in his 1976 encyclical *Evangelii Nuntiandi*,[63] confirmed evangelism as the essential mission of the

---

[58] Chris Sugden, *Gospel, Culture and Transformation* (Oxford: Regnum 2000), 23.

[59] Miroslav Volf, 'Materiality of Salvation: An Investigation in the Soteriologies of Liberation and Pentecostal Theologies', in *Journal of Ecumenical Studies*, 26.3 (1989).

[60] E.g. the Report of Section III, 'The Churches and the Poor', *International Review of Mission*, 69.276-77, 539-42. See David Bosch, 'The Melbourne Conference: Between Guilt and Hope', in *International Review of Mission*, 69. 276-77, 394-96.

[61] *Your Kingdom Come: Melbourne, 1980. World Conference on Mission and Evangelism*, reprinted in James A. Scherer and Stephen B. Bevans, *New Directions in Mission and Evangelization 1: Basic Statements* (Maryknoll, NY: Orbis Books, 1992), 27-35, Chapter III. See also James A. Scherer, 'Church, Kingdom and *Missio Dei*: Lutheran and Orthodox Correctives to Recent Ecumenical Mission Theology', in Charles van Engen et al (ed), *The Good News of the Kingdom: Mission Theology for the Third Millenium* (Eugene, OR: Wipf & Stock 1993), 87-88.

[62] *Your Kingdom Come*, III, 2.

[63] *Evangelii Nuntiandi*. Apostolic Exhortation of Pope Paul VI promulgated on 8th December 1975: www.papalencyclicals.net/Paul06/p6evan.htm.

church while declaring, at the same time, the need of the church itself to be re-evangelized so as to become an appropriate witness.[64]

While Catholics and Ecumenicals looked at the shortcomings of the church, Evangelicals focused mainly on the churches' opportunities in evangelism. This became particularly evident at the Lausanne Movement's conference in Pattaya, Thailand, also in 1980. The role of the church in evangelism was that of a herald which had to speak, and little thought was given to a broader understanding of witness by its life. In addition, the church was defined in exclusivist terms, making nominal (and possibly even all) Catholics and Orthodox legitimate objects of evangelism.[65]

Orthodox influences in the 1980 documents of the WCC opened up a new perspective on the evangelistic role of the church. The 1982 Affirmation on Mission and Evangelism spoke of the 'evangelistic vocation of the church' which was fulfilled, first of all, 'through its internal life of Eucharistic worship, thanksgiving, intercessory prayer', and only then through 'planning for mission and evangelism' and 'a daily life-style of solidarity with the poor'.[66] Sharing in the ministry of Christ as mediator between God and his creation, the church also offered up 'the world's pain and suffering to God in the context of its worship, specifically in intercessory prayer and the Eucharist'.[67] Clearly, Orthodox theology helped to shape an ecumenical understanding of evangelism as a quality of all what the church does, however fragmented and imperfect that may be.

In recent years, ecumenical documents have reflected the role of the church in evangelism in more practical ways. The 2012 WCC Affirmation *Together towards Life*[68] has a whole chapter on local congregations, describing their 'crucial role' in contextualizing the Gospel message and 'forming a community marked by the presence of the risen Christ'.[69] And Pope Francis, in *Evangelii Gaudium,*[70] speaks of the church as a pilgrim people which is the 'agent of evangelism', pointing out the 'evangelizing power of popular piety'.[71]

---

[64] See also Paul W. Chilcote and Laceye C. Warner, 'Introduction', in Chilcote and Warner, *The Study of Evangelism*, xxiii.

[65] David Bosch, 'Behind Melbourne and Pattaya – a Typology of Two Movements', in *IAMS Newsletter,* 1980/16-17/21.

[66] *Ecumenical Affirmation,* Section 6.

[67] *Ecumenical Affirmation,* Section 6.

[68] *TTL*.

[69] *TTL,* §72-78.

[70] *Apostolic Exhortation Evangelii Gaudium of the Holy Father Francis* (Rome: Vatican, 2013):
http://w2.vatican.va/content/francesco/en/apost_exhortations/documents/papa-francesco_esortazione-ap_20131124_evangelii-gaudium.html.

[71] *Evangelii Gaudium,* §122-26.

## Evangelism and Culture: The Issue of Contextualization

The question how the Gospel relates to culture is an enormously complex one and, while discussed particularly at the 1996 World Mission Conference in Salvador de Bahia,[72] has not been resolved satisfactorily. The problem here is: what is meant by 'Gospel', and what by 'culture'? A popular misunderstanding sees contextualization as condensing the Gospel message into a few abstract, 'universal' truths to be 'translated' into different cultures which are seen as clearly defined entities. The Gospel may then change the culture, but the culture cannot change the Gospel.

But in fact, the Gospel comes to us in a variety of already contextual testimonies (i.e. the Gospels and letters), writings shaped by certain cultures and a certain time. For Paul, e.g. the underlying paradigm of the Gospel is the salvation of sinners, while for the Gospel of John, the underlying paradigm is that Jesus came to bring life in its fullness. Neither paradigm is exclusive of the other, but each shapes the reading and understanding of the story of Jesus Christ in certain ways. At the same time, cultures are neither clearly delineated nor static, and always consist of both elements which correspond to the Gospel message and elements which contradict it. Evangelism, in consequence, must be a dynamic process of a continuously renewed communal searching of how the story of Christ can be told[73] for a particular people in a particular place at a particular time – a process in which the 'new' understanding of the Gospel by those who are being evangelized will change both the evangelizing church and the cultural context it lives in. The question of 'syncretism'[74] – a mixture of the Gospel with other elements which darken its message – is one that can never be answered once and for all, but needs to be continuously considered and negotiated. *Together towards Life* remains rather vague when seeing the Gospel 'taking root' in different cultures, challenging, endorsing or transforming them 'for the sake of life',[75] while critically

---

[72] The conference documents are published in Christopher Duraisingh (ed), *Called to One Hope: The Gospel in Diverse Cultures* (Geneva: WCC ,1998).

[73] Note that telling a story is very different from presenting a propositional truth! James Smith has written convincingly about the need for narratives in Christian formation, and the same need exists in evangelism: James K.A. Smith, *Desiring the Kingdom: Worship, Worldview and Cultural Formation* (Grand Rapids, MI: Baker Academic, 2009).

[74] There is no room in this short chapter for a deeper discussion on syncretism. In WCC documents, it is often pointed out that the accusation of syncretism is used against churches and movements which deviate from 'Western' forms of Christianity. A good short overview of the ecumenical debate is found in James A. Maxey, *From Orality to Orality: A New Paradigm for Contextual Translation of the Bible* (Eugene, OR: Cascade Books, 2009), 21-28. For an evangelical debate on this issue, see Gailyn Van Rheenen (ed), *Contextualization and Syncretism: Navigating Cultural Currents* (Pasadena, CA: William Carey Library, 1996).

[75] *TTL*, §100.

noting – in view of the connection of evangelism with colonial powers – that 'evangelism by those who enjoy economic power or cultural hegemony risks distorting the gospel'.[76]

It is worth noting here that some widespread practices of contextual evangelism are almost completely ignored within ecumenical documents even though they are hotly debated among Evangelicals and Pentecostals.[77] A case in point is the 'power evangelism'[78] practised by, among others, indigenous West African Pentecostal churches.[79] People who live in constant fear of demons and witchcraft, and blame them for every problem from illness through unemployment to marital problems, are told that Christ can free and protect them, and that the power of the Holy Spirit can change their lives from poverty to fullness.[80]

## Evangelism in the 21st Century: Broad Consensus, New Challenges

Why evangelize, and how, and towards what goal? Ecumenical consensus is that evangelism is a consequence of what God has done, of his love and the renewal and joy he gives.[81] An evangelism so motivated will work 'in

---

[76] *TTL,* §98.

[77] This is even more remarkable when one considers that those practices have been developed at the margins, and *TTL* has a whole chapter on 'Mission from the Margins'.

[78] The actual term 'power evangelism' may go back to American John Wimber; see John Wimber and Kevin Springer, *Power Evangelism* (San Francisco, CA: Harper & Row, 1986); but the practice started among Pentecostals and charismatics in the global South and is strongly influenced by traditional religion. See J. Kwabena Asamoah-Gyadu, 'Pulling Down Strongholds: Evangelism, Principalities and Powers and the African Pentecostal Imagination', in *International Review of Mission,* 96. 382/383, 306-21.

[79] As far as I could ascertain, the practice is not mentioned in any of the official WCC documents. J.K. Asamoah-Gyadu's paper, 'Pulling down Strongholds' seems to be the only case of this topic being discussed at an ecumenical gathering.

[80] For background reading on these issues, see Henning Wrogemann and Claudia Währisch-Oblau (eds), *Witchcraft, Demons and Deliverance – A Global Conversation on an Intercultural Challenge* (Münster, Germany: LIT-Verlag, 2015). For a Pentecostal discussion on this kind of evangelism, see Katherine Attanasi and Amos Yong, *Pentecostalism and Prosperity: The Socio-Economics of the Global Charismatic Movement* (New York: Palgrave Mcmillan, 2012). Evangelicals deal with this in *The Cape Town Commitment: A Confession of Faith and a Call to Action* (Cape Town: The Lausanne Movement, 2011), downloadable from www.lausanne.org/content/ctc/ctcommitment, Section IIE.5.

[81] The Evangelical *Cape Town Commitment* sees mission and evangelism as motivated by love – the love of the Triune God, of the Gospel, of the world, of the people (*The Cape Town Commitment: A Confession of Faith and a Call to Action* (Cape Town: The Lausanne Movement, 2011): www.lausanne.org/content/ctc/ctcommitment). The Apostolic Exhortation *Evangelii Gaudium* of Pope Francis speaks of the joy of the Gospel which

Christ's way';[82] it will be humble, relational, dialogical and respectful of other religions and different cultural practices.[83] Talking about the Christ we love means that we are not introducing a propositional truth, but telling a story about what God has done for the world in Christ and about the Kingdom we hope for, inviting people to follow Christ and letting their lives be changed. How we talk about this is always shaped by our own context, but may be understood differently according to the context of the person listening. The worldwide church, flawed as it is, is the prime witness to the Gospel in what it preaches and what it does, but it also acknowledges that God is at work outside and before it, and gladly identifies the traces of this work. Evangelism is not only an occasional activity, but a constitutive practice of a 'missional' church which is open to change and receptive to newcomers.[84] Evangelism is an expression of discipleship and aims at it, knowing that conversion is the work of the Holy Spirit.[85]

It is unfortunate that these theological considerations often have little to do with what happens on the ground. Evangelism as practised by Protestant or Pentecostal local congregations all over the world far too frequently follows the old American model, introducing the Gospel via the 'Four Spiritual Laws'[86] in personal encounters or via 'evangelism crusades'. Other Pentecostal and charismatic churches engage in power evangelism, proclaiming a message that promises health and wealth to those who believe in Christ.[87] How the ecumenical consensus on evangelism can be translated into practices and materials which will actually be put to use by the majority of Christians at the grassroots remains an open challenge.

Evangelism today is no longer the white Christian's burden but has become truly globalized. Koreans evangelize in Tanzania, Brazilians in the Philippines, and Nigerians in Ukraine. As all of them are active in areas

---

overflows into evangelism (*Apostolic Exhortation Evangelii Gaudium of the Holy Father Francis* (Rome: Vatican, 2013): http://w2.vatican.va/content/francesco/en/apost_exhortations/documents/papa-francesco_esortazione-ap_20131124_evangelii-gaudium.html). And *TTL* sees evangelism flowing from the experience of God's love, redemption and renewal.

82 *TTL,* §86-92.

83 See also *Christian Witness in a Multi-Religious World. Recommendations for Conduct* (2011): https://www.oikoumene.org/en/resources/documents/wcc-programmes/interreligious-dialogue-and-cooperation/christian-identity-in-pluralistic-societies/christian-witness-in-a-multi-religious-world.

84 Acts 10–15 shows paradigmatically that evangelism changes not only those who are evangelized, but the evangelizers as well.

85 See also Paul W. Chilcote and Laceye C. Warner, 'Introduction', in Chilcote and Warner, *The Study of Evangelism.*

86 This little tract has been translated into dozens of languages and has sold many millions of copies. The text can be found at http://crustore.org/four-laws-english.

87 This generalization may be too broad, but builds on my 25 years of experience with local churches in Asia, Africa and Europe.

where churches already exist, the question of 'proselytism', motivating members of one church or denomination to join another one, will become ever more urgent. Can churches with very different theologies and practices live together in one area, accept each other, and even co-operate in evangelism? And are existing churches ready to be re-evangelized by missionaries from a different context and tradition?[88]

At the end, I would like to suggest looking at Luke 10:1-9 as a biblical model for evangelism in the 21st century. Jesus sends his disciples without money or material protection, and asks them to become the guests of those whom they want to evangelize.[89] Twice he tells them to eat what they are offered, a potent image of an outreach that is totally dependent on the addressees and accepts what they have to offer before offering something to them. Such evangelism is vulnerable, trusting in God's power and people's goodwill, but it stands under the promise that God will do great things.

---

[88] This is one of the questions raised by the 'reverse mission' from the global South to the global North: see Claudia Währisch-Oblau, *The Missionary Self-Conception of Pentecostal/Charismatic Church Leaders from the Global South in Europe: Bringing Back the Gospel* (Leiden: Brill, 2008).

[89] This is in marked contrast to common practices and theologies of evangelism as hospitality which aim at inviting people into our community. These theologies are valuable as hospitality is a vanishing virtue in many parts of the world, but could do well to be complemented by a theology of being guests.

# CHURCH, MISSION AND UNITY

Jacques Matthey

The topic will be addressed in three parts which should ideally be read in parallel: co-operation in mission, church and mission, and finally mission and unity. There is overlap between them and inevitably, the reader will also find links with other chapters of this book.[1] The chronological ordering of issues does not imply that these pertain to that period only.

## Co-operation in Mission

With regard to missionary co-operation, the twentieth century was shaped by two partly contradictory dynamics in the Protestant world.[2]

The first leads to more co-operation. This was the clear purpose of the 1910 Edinburgh Conference, in particular of its Commission VIII. Experiences on the 'mission fields' had proved the need for working together in order to avoid duplication and excessive competition, and to enhance efficiency of the Christian testimony among peoples of other or no religion. The need for comity arrangements was particularly urged by the few, but influential, Asian delegates who pointed to the disaster of division for witness in their regions. Edinburgh was a step forward insofar as the organisers had succeeded in calling evangelical Protestants and high church Anglicans to debate on the practicalities of mission, thus enlarging the range of participants in comparison with earlier international mission conferences. Edinburgh however had very few contacts with Roman Catholic or Orthodox churches.[3]

The 1910 event became historic in particular thanks to its decision to create a continuation committee that soon set up the *International Review*

---

[1] For a more detailed study of various perspectives related to mission and unity, one must refer to John Gibaut and Knud Jörgensen (eds), *Called to Unity for the Sake of Mission* (Oxford: Regnum, 2014).

[2] Cf Jacques Matthey, 'Continuités et ruptures entre les deux conférences d'Edimbourg 1910 et 2010', in *Perspectives missionnaires,* No 60 (2010/2), 21-37.

[3] Cf the introduction to the report of Commission VIII: World Missionary Conference 1910, *Report of Commission VIII, Co-operation and the Promotion of Unity, with supplement: presentation and discussion of the report in the Conference on 21st June 1910* (Edinburgh and London: Oliphant, Anderson & Ferrier; New York, Chicago and Toronto: Fleming H. Revell, 1910), 1-11. Recent presentations of Edinburgh 1910 and its preparations include: Keith Clements, *Faith on the Frontier – A Life of J.H. Oldham* (Edinburgh: T. & T. Clark and Geneva: WCC, 1999); Brian Stanley, *The World Missionary Conference, Edinburgh 1910* (Grand Rapids, MI, and Cambridge, UK: Eerdmans, 2009).

*of Missions (IRM)*. Regular meetings plus a theological review were to become essential instruments for dialogue, the exchange of news and reflections on mission theory and practice. The International Missionary Council (IMC), created in 1921, and the national mission councils which made up its membership, strengthened their co-operation, including that with other ecumenical movements, such as Life and Work. Following the creation of the World Council of Churches (WCC) in 1948,[4] there was intensive dialogue and cross-fertilisation with the IMC and mission councils, leading to the integration of both bodies in 1961 and a decisive widening of the scope of co-operation, more and more including Orthodox churches and, after Vatican II, also Roman Catholic mission organisations with whom there were many studies on common witness.[5] Contacts with individual Pentecostals increased from the 1950s on,[6] without yet leading to lasting or real co-operation.

The second dynamic tended to more separation in mission work. After 1910, some of the most conservative movements, influenced by the fundamentalist approach, distanced themselves from the IMC,[7] seen as too liberal and political. The increased links between IMC and WCC after World War II and the widening of the understanding of mission in the 1950s reinforced uneasiness with such developments among Evangelicals. Some IMC member councils disagreed with the plans to merge IMC and WCC, and despite a good majority of councils voting for integration, the debate on the wisdom of closer links with more ecumenical circles never ceased.[8] Theological and socio-political developments in the 1960s

---

[4] IMC and WCC in formation had already created together the Commission of the Churches on International Affairs (CCIA) in 1946.

[5] Cf. among others: Joint Working Group between the WCC and the Roman Catholic Church, 'The Challenge of Proselytism and the Calling to Common Witness', 25th September 1995, in J. Gros, H. Meyer and W.G. Rush (eds), *Growth in Agreement II, Reports and Agreed Statements of Ecumenical Conversations on a World Level, 1982-1998* (Grand Rapids, MI: Eerdmans, and Geneva: WCC, 2000), 891-99; WCC, 'Towards Common Witness: A Call to Adopt Responsible Relationships in Mission and to Renounce Proselytism', document commended by the 1997 WCC Central Committee to all member-churches, in Jacques Matthey (ed), *You are the Light of the World: Statements on Mission by the World Council of Churches 1980-2005* (Geneva: WCC, 2005), 39-58.

[6] Walter Hollenweger described the early contacts between Pentecostals and ecumenical representatives in the chapter on 'ecumenical roots' in his major work on Pentecostalism. Noteworthy are the pages on David J. Du Plessis, who participated in the 1952 Willingen IMC conference, later also in WCC assemblies. See W. J. Hollenweger, *Pentecostalism: Origins and Developments Worldwide* (Peabody, MA: Hendrickson, 1997), 350-56.

[7] Stanley, *The World Missionary Conference*, 320-24.

[8] Mark Laing, *From Crisis to Creation: Lesslie Newbigin and the Reinvention of Christian Mission* (Eugene, OR: Pickwick, 2012). Laing presents in detail the

reinforced Evangelicals' critiques of the WCC. In 1974 the debate reached a peak with the organisation of a worldwide mission event in Lausanne, Switzerland, and the creation of the Lausanne Committee for World Evangelization (Lausanne Committee). Thanks to the strong influence of Latin American Evangelicals and the wisdom of some of Lausanne's leadership, the break was not total. The *Lausanne Covenant*, extremely critical of WCC positions as expressed in the Uppsala Assembly of 1968 and the Bangkok mission conference of 1973, offered nonetheless some points of connection with a recognition of the importance of witness also in the socio-political field.

Indeed, from the mid-1970s on, signs of common understanding re-emerged in the debates. One year after the 1974 *Lausanne Covenant*, Pope Paul VI published the encyclical *Evangelii nuntiandi* that was inspirational, thanks to its holistic approach. In the aftermath of the 1980 Melbourne conference, the WCC and its Commission on World Mission and Evangelism (CWME)[9] faced up to the challenge of Liberation Theology, the Evangelical critique and the Roman Catholic integral approach in a synthetic affirmation that became, like the other mentioned documents, a cornerstone for new approaches to co-operation.[10]

It took many years to build up new trust and deconstruct false images on all sides. One example of this was the letter sent by participants at the CWME San Antonio conference to those attending the Manila Lausanne meeting, pointing to similarities in convictions that should break the barriers. Still, for many years, the two competing mission movements, Lausanne and CWME, have continued to organise mission conferences at regional or world levels, sometimes during the same year.[11] Among the signs of increasing dialogue, one should mention the Stuttgart consultation and declaration on evangelism by representatives of Evangelical mission bodies, such as Lausanne or the World Evangelical Fellowship and of CWME in 1987.[12] Contacts with the Pentecostal-charismatic world

---

debates on integration within IMC, in particular also the position of conservative evangelicals.

[9] In 1961, following integration, there was in the WCC a Division on World Mission and Evangelism with a Divisional Committee. The Commission on World Mission and Evangelism (CWME) was the name for what we would now call the Conference on World Mission and Evangelism. After the 1973 Bangkok mission conference and the 1975 Nairobi Assembly of the WCC, the names were changed in the by-laws. The Divisional Committee became the CWME Commission, and the Commission was renamed Conference.

[10] Cf. Jacques Matthey, 'Mission et évangélisation dans l'optique de Lausanne, Rome et Genève', in *Perspectives Missionnaires*, 10 (1985), 36-50.

[11] Melbourne and Pattaya in 1980, San Antonio and Manila in 1989. In 2010, Lausanne held its third major world meeting (after Lausanne and Manila) despite the holding of the common 2010 Edinburgh conference.

[12] Published in Raymond Fung (ed), *A Monthly Letter on Evangelism*, 10/11, October-November 1987 (Geneva: CWME, 1987).

remained difficult or non-existent for much too long a time. There were exceptions to that, e.g. in 1980 with a study process and a consultation bringing together in Bossey, Switzerland, senior leaders of WCC and of some of the main charismatic churches and movements.[13] Bilateral dialogues by the Roman Catholic Church allowed for theological debates with Pentecostals. At WCC level, it was only from the 1990s onwards that really significant contacts started again, resulting in the creation of a dialogue group between the WCC and individual Pentecostals in the year 2000. CWME had, since its creation, left the door open for delegates from non-WCC member-churches, both at commission and conference levels. Following the debates within WCC on a new common understanding and vision of ecumenism and the changed ecclesial landscape of world Christianity, mission work in WCC opened the door even more to co-operation in its programmatic work also with Evangelicals and Pentecostals, which became particularly visible in the 2005 Athens conference on healing and reconciliation.[14]

The discussions and processes leading to the creation of the Global Christian Forum (GCF) are the latest example of a successful approach to unity through co-operation. The GCF succeeded in bringing together Christians and leaders from nearly all significant traditions, thanks to careful building of trust and a renewed dialogue method.[15] Mission issues feature regularly in GCF meetings. The GCF process also contributed to the possibility of a common planning and organisation of the Edinburgh centenary conference and its study process. Edinburgh 2010 showed a growing willingness to co-operate in mission, based on common convictions expressed in the documents and the message. It did not succeed in bringing to the table all major segments of world Christianity, but a larger part than was possible at earlier meetings. Frontier missions stood aside and other parts of the Christian family, such as many charismatic churches and movements, were not really represented. Unfortunately, too many other church world events took place that same year, including the Lausanne Cape Town conference, so that the witness of Edinburgh 2010 to unity in mission was weakened. Nevertheless, two years later and for the

---

[13] A. Bittlinger (ed), *The Church is Charismatic. The World Council of Churches and the Charismatic Renewal* (Geneva: WCC, Renewal and Congregational Life, 1981).

[14] Jacques Matthey (ed), *Come Holy Spirit, heal and reconcile! Report of the WCC Conference on World Mission and Evangelism, Athens, Greece, May 2005* (Geneva: WCC, 2008). Since 1999, there was also CWME participation in meetings of the Missions Commission of the World Evangelical Alliance (WEA).

[15] Meetings of the GCF emphasise the sharing of personal faith stories by participants. Huibert van Beek (ed), *Revisioning Christian Unity: The Global Christian Forum* (Oxford: Regnum, 2009) contains the records of the first Global Christian Forum gathering in Limuru, Kenya, in 2007, and a brief survey of proceedings leading to that first worldwide GCF gathering.

very first time in history, the World Evangelical Alliance (WEA), the Pontifical Council for Interreligious Dialogue (PCID) and the WCC were able to publish an important document on mission together.[16]

## Mission and Church

It is well known that Edinburgh 1910 could take place only because debates on ecclesiology had been banned from the conference. What people are less aware of, however, was the intensity and wisdom of the debates precisely on ecclesiology in Commission VIII.

Delegates attending its meetings discerned two clearly conflicting views on church matters. One group considered that agreement in faith on matters such as the Trinity, the forgiveness of sins, life everlasting, and Christian scripture as authority and guide, were sufficient as conditions for real unity, while other matters, as important as they might be, were to be classified as secondary and subordinate. In the opinion of a second group of delegates, matters of church order could not be considered secondary, but were a means of grace essential to the understanding of divine revelation and had to be shared in mission to new Christians. The commission agreed to include the discussion in its report to the conference plenary.[17] I refer to it mainly to point to the awareness people had right at the beginning of the ecumenical movement that ecclesiological issues did matter for a proper reflection on mission.

The issue became prominent after 1948 and the intense contacts between IMC and WCC. A milestone was the definition of ecumenism reached at the WCC Central Committee in Rolle, Switzerland, in 1951: 'We would especially draw attention to the recent confusion in the use of the word "ecumenical". It is important to insist that this word… is properly used to describe everything that relates to the whole task of the whole Church to bring the Gospel to the whole world. It therefore covers equally the missionary movement and the movement towards unity, and must not be used to describe the latter in contradistinction to the former… Our concern in this study is the recovery in thought, in action, and in organization, of the true unity between the Church's mission to the world (its Apostolate) and the Church's obligation to be one.'[18] This position became the basis for the negotiations towards integration of IMC and WCC, realised in 1961.

---

[16] 'Christian Witness in a multi-religious World: Recommendations for Conduct', in *Resource Book, WCC Tenth Assembly, Busan, 2013* (Geneva: WCC 2013), 77-81. The document is referred to in *TTL*, §90.

[17] World Missionary Conference 1910, *Report of Commission VIII*, 131-39. See also Samuel Kobia, 'Cooperation and the Promotion of Unity: A World Council of Churches Perspective', in David A. Kerr and Kenneth R. Ross (eds), *Edinburgh 2010. Mission Then and Now* (Oxford: Regnum, 2009), 241-42.

[18] WCC, *Minutes and Reports of the Fourth Meeting of the Central Committee, Rolle (Switzerland), August 4-11, 1951* (Geneva: WCC, 1951), 65.

There were serious debates on the relevance of integration. On one hand, it was understood as the embodiment of theological convictions such as the one reached in Rolle, meaning that the church bears responsibility for mission and that the visible unity of the church matters for mission, as well as mission for the visible unity of the church. Following 1961, several mission bodies ceased to exist as independent organisations and became church departments. It was hoped that such institutional reformation would both strengthen missionary outreach and empower local churches for witness.[19] International mission structures were transformed into bodies of church co-operation. Partnership in mission was to happen between independent churches, acting in full responsibility, and not any more between a church in the South and a mission organisation in the North.

On the other hand, fears were expressed that integration into church structures could limit missionary freedom and jeopardise the interdenominational and international character of some of the main missionary societies. Why should mission work become dependent on church hierarchy priorities? This was a power issue, but also a theological dispute on the balance between two ministries: mission militants tend, in a centrifugal dynamic, to cross barriers and form new communities that lead to new inculturations and interpretations of the gospel. Their witness can contribute to a questioning of the existing understanding of unity and harmony of a particular church or community. Bishops or church presidents often understand the ministry of unity in the sense of keeping existing communion structures and habits. For them, mission work can be experienced as disturbing and counter-productive.

These problems were heavily debated in the years preceding the decision in favour of integration. Mission bodies with strong Evangelical theology and spirituality were hesitant to join the WCC as a church body, and within WCC, mainly Orthodox churches feared that integration would enhance proselytism. Many of these questions remain relevant in the debate between churches and mission departments or para-church structures.[20] In a post-modern and globalised world, however, the issue has moved from strictly structural debates to the consideration of complementary roles and criteria for authentic relationships. 'While para-church movements can find accountability and direction through ecclesial mooring, para-church structures can help churches not to forget their dynamic apostolic character.'[21]

---

[19] The remarkable CWME study on the missionary structure of the congregation was an attempt to empower the witness of local communities as a consequence of integration. It influenced in particular congregations in the Western world.

[20] In 1980 I was of the opinion that Melbourne had reached a maximum of integration. Cf. Jacques Matthey, 'Integration of Church and Mission: the Challenge of Melbourne', in *International Review of Mission* (October 1981), 259-66.

[21] *TTL,* §64. CWME, the main embodiment and champion of integration has *de facto* since 1961 offered a space for dialogue and co-operation between WCC

Integration highlighted the importance of the United/Uniting church movement which always understood itself as a support for mission. Based on an understanding of unity as organic unity, overcoming denominational differences, these churches have played an essential role in the ecumenical movement by pushing the issue of church and mission and the need for a vision of unity as a core element of mission theology.[22]

In the 1990s, the term 'missional church' emerged in the North American discussion with the intention of joining ecclesiological and missiological perspectives within a *missio Dei* approach and discerning their impact on local churches' self-understanding and witness.[23] Soon this became a lively and creative international network of people concerned with witness of churches in post-modern contexts, with influence both on Evangelical and ecumenical thinking on church and mission within a *missio Dei* approach.[24]

Key to the debates on the relationship between church and mission is the connection between Faith and Order (F&O) and CWME. The relationship between these two WCC commissions, both indirect outcomes of Edinburgh, has not always been warm and respectful. However, when they were co-operating, this had a positive influence on the WCC's struggle for unity. Only more recent examples can be shared here.[25] In the mid-1980s, both commissions entered such a period of co-operation and dialogue following the publication of two major papers, *Baptism, Eucharist and Ministry* (BEM) and the *Ecumenical Affirmation on Mission and Evangelism* (*EA*). In the debates, CWME would emphasise diversity in

member-churches, earlier IMC member-councils, churches not related to WCC, and a large spectrum of mission and para-church structures. The progressive enlargement of membership possibilities in CWME's by-laws testifies to the increasing openness to quite diverse mission actors. In that sense, the criteria mentioned in §64 replace earlier moves towards full structural integration at national or regional levels.

[22] Thomas Best, 'United and Uniting Churches as Models of Mission and Unity', in Gibaut and Jörgensen, *Called to Unity*, 141-53. cf. *TTL*, §68.

[23] Darrell Guder (ed), *Missional Church: A Vision for the Sending of the Church in North America* (Grand Rapids, MI: Eerdmans, 1998).

[24] Reference is made to 'The Gospel and our Culture Network'. Martin Reppenhagen, 'The Missional Church and the "Homo areligiosus"', in Viggo Mortensen and Andreas Nielsen (eds), *Walk Humbly with the Lord: Church and Mission Engaging Plurality* (Grand Rapids, MI, and Cambridge, UK: Eerdmans, 2010), 167-83. In the same book, Darrell Guder also criticises the fact that 'missional' has become a buzzword and reformulates the original intention of the introduction of that terminology. Darrell Guder, 'Theological Formation for Missional Practice', in Mortensen and Nielsen, *Walk Humbly*, 307-08.

[25] On the recent convergence between F&O and CWME, cf. also John Gibaut, 'From Unity and Mission to Koinonia and Missio Dei: Convergences in WCC Ecclesiology and Missiology towards Edinburgh 2010', in Gibaut and Jörgensen, *Called to Unity*, 73-88.

unity and a contextualised approach to church and mission, rooted in a kenotic Christology, whereas F&O leant more weight on unity in diversity, the theological basis for ordained ministry, and the reference to the classical confessions of faith, traditions and ecclesiologies. Common convictions were also reached, as is best illustrated by the following quote: 'Mission belongs to the very nature of the church. Mission is also the response of a community of faith and love to the action of the Triune God, Creator of all, who calls the community members to be disciples and sends them forth into the world. All aspects of the church's life… Worship, witness, service… are shaped by the missionary nature and vocation of its very life.' This is taken from a group report submitted to the F&O Plenary Commission in Budapest 1989![26]

Following the Canberra Assembly, co-operation between both commissions became less intense until a fresh start was made in 2000, which introduced fifteen years of close dialogue and increasingly common understanding on some basics such as the reference to *missio Dei*, the specific role of the church in God's mission, the apostolic dynamics of church and Christian life, a holistic understanding of witness and its scope, increasingly including not only the whole of humanity, but also the whole of creation.[27] CWME gave more attention to ecclesiological issues than it had done in past, when it had a tendency to oppose a *missio Dei* theology to an approach emphasising the witness of the church.[28] F&O's study processes pointed much more often to mission than was the case in earlier papers. The specificities of each methodology did not disappear, F&O still giving more attention to the classical ecclesiological differences that had grown out of historical traditions, in particular the denominational ones, whereas CWME rooted its reflections more clearly in contextual or liberational theologies, and gave more attention to developments in the Evangelical and Pentecostal movements.[29] The result of such intense collaboration and dialogue is visible in the two reference documents adopted in 2012 by the WCC Central Committee and presented to the 2013

---

[26] Thomas Best (ed), *Faith and Order 1985-1989. The Commission Meeting at Budapest 1989* (WCC Faith and Order Paper No. 148 (1990)), 285.

[27] Cf. the concluding remarks on the common consultation in Höxter-Brenkhausen in 2000 by F&O and CWME which I wrote, as secretary of the CWME, together with Alan Falconer, director of F&O: 'Editorial', in *International Review of Mission,* 90.358 (July 2001), thematic issue on ecclesiology and mission, 227-31.

[28] Around the same period, the World Evangelical Fellowship's (now the World Evangelical Alliance) Missions Commission also gave more attention to ecclesiological considerations when reflecting on mission. See W.D. Taylor (ed), *Global Missiology for the 21st Century: The Iguassu Dialogue* (Grand Rapids, MI: Baker and WEF, 2000).

[29] The most recent developments within F&O, and in particular the nomination of a new director from the global South, could increase the similarities in theological approaches between the two commissions.

Busan Assembly: *The Church – Towards a Common Vision* and *Together towards Life – Mission and Evangelism in Changing Landscapes*.

## Mission and Unity

Already at Edinburgh 1910, some were convinced that unity was not only a condition for missions' success, but also an aim of mission: '... for the achievement of the ultimate and highest end of all missionary work – the establishment in these non-Christian lands of Christ's one Church – real unity must be attained.'[30]

Several contributions of mission work and theology to the search for the visible unity of the church have already appeared in the first parts of this chapter. Other specific mission approaches to unity also deserve attention. Major mission agencies were, at least within Protestantism, structurally interdenominational and overcame also national barriers up to a certain degree. As such, they embodied aspects of visible unity which were out of reach for many individual churches. In those cases where from the 1970s onwards such mission agencies could transform themselves into church communions in and for mission, the link between church and mission unity was even strengthened. Unfortunately, cultural and economic developments summarised under the term 'post-modernity' increasingly challenge the relevance of such church communities for mission. Charity regulations favour individualism and denominationalism also in mission.[31]

Cross-cultural missionaries or fraternal workers, in particular when they assume their ministry as servants, abandoning earlier dominating roles, are also visible signs of the catholicity of the church, of unity over cultural or national, more seldom of denominational, barriers. This sign-role gives them lasting value in terms of mission and unity in North and South, even when or where their technical competences might no longer be needed.

Evangelism is most closely related to unity. Indeed, evangelism can even be considered the test of true ecumenism.[32] This is particularly the case when evangelism is understood as calling to faith in Christ and to

---

[30] World Missionary Conference 1910, *Report of Commission VIII*, 5.

[31] In 2002, CWME and three historic mission bodies, Cevaa – Community of Churches in Mission, the Council for World Mission and the United Evangelical Mission together convened a major consultation that allowed for a reflection on the lasting value of, and new challenges to, their vision and practice of partnership in mission: *International Review of Mission,* 91.363 (October 2002), Toward the Fullness of Life: Intercontextual Relationships in Mission. That same consultation provided important thematic input for the planning of the 2005 World Mission Conference.

[32] An expression used several times by Philip Potter, late CWME director and WCC General Secretary. Cf. Jacques Matthey, 'Evangelism, still the Enduring Test of our Ecumenical – and Missionary Calling', in *International Review of Mission,* 96, Nos 382/383 (July/October 2007), 355 (see also references in footnote 1).

discipleship as a member of a church. Authentically ecumenical evangelism happens when such calling respects existing churches and leaves interested non-church-related persons free to choose the community they want to join, which may not necessarily be the church of the evangelist. Such evangelism truly contributes to unity, but requires at least some recognition of authentic Christian teaching and life in other churches. The related and much debated issue is the distinction between evangelism and proselytism, the latter being seen in mission matters as the major obstacle to unity. It is not the task of this chapter to go into details. Suffice to refer to the bilateral dialogues between the Roman Catholic Church and Pentecostals in the 1990s, where commonalities and differences appeared clearly. The Pentecostal team in the dialogues affirmed that 'proselytism is a disrespectful and uncharitable recruitment of committed members of Christian communities by persons from other Christian communities… All those who have not repented, believed and are not following Christ are to be evangelized'.[33] Most could agree with parts of the definition, but not with the understanding of who can be considered an authentic church member, due to differing ecclesiologies and soteriologies.

After the IMC Willingen Conference in 1952, missiological perspectives opened up to renewed consideration of God's own mission, encompassing a much larger horizon than just church co-operation or unity. Social, racial and economic issues entered the agenda of missiology with unprecedented weight, although in authentic heritage from earlier IMC debates. WCC priorities such as the Programme to Combat Racism, the struggle for human rights in opposition to dictatorial regimes, increasing attention to the plight and agency of the poor, both in and outside churches, development and gender issues, but also the new interreligious dialogue programme, led mission theologies to consider unity as a challenge not only for Christians, but for the whole of humanity.[34] Unity as a goal of God's own mission in the world brought Christians and churches to involve themselves in witness to and with the world on a large scale, encompassing all mentioned conflict areas.[35] The horizon for unity was nothing less than the Kingdom of God. These developments grew also in the Roman Catholic Church and among open Evangelicals, particularly in the global South. At times, concern for

---

[33] Veli-Matti Kärkkäinen, *Ad Ultimum Terrae: Evangelization, Proselytism and Common Witness in the Roman Catholic Pentecostal Dialogue (1990-1997)* (Frankfurt: Peter Lang, 1999), 204-05. This remains the key study on that most important dialogue and as such also on major issues related to evangelism and proselytism.

[34] The same is true for F&O. Following the Uppsala Assembly in 1968, F&O launched a major study process in 1971 on 'The Unity of the Church and the Unity of Mankind', revived in Lima in 1982 under a new heading. See *Church and World: The Unity of the Church and the Renewal of Human Community* (Geneva: WCC Faith and Order Paper No. 151 (1990)).

[35] *TTL,* §45.

the unity of churches lost visibility, at least in missiology linked with the WCC, in particular where the notion of ecumenism would be enlarged to mean dialogue and relationships with people of all religions.[36] In more recent years, the issue of inclusivity has increasingly shaped the debate on mission and unity.

Several very active networks related to CWME enriched the approach towards inclusivity and unity, both in church and society.[37] As one embodiment of the year-long study process on Gospel and Cultures, the multicultural ministry network helped to face challenges resulting from mission and migration for church communities in terms of the capacity of people from different cultural backgrounds to live and celebrate God together. Due to the ever-increasing number of migrants all over the world, this challenge to unity will become key in any future missiology.[38] In terms of social justice, the Urban and Rural Mission network (URM) never ceased to challenge missiologists and mission practitioners to consider justice as a pre-condition for genuine unity, both in church and society.[39] Most of these concerns are shared by the networks of Indigenous Peoples who in addition draw on age-old wisdoms also for the inclusion of nature, environment and creation in the understanding of mission and unity.

The contribution of the Ecumenical Disability Advocates Network (EDAN) to the issue of mission and unity deserves special mention. Together with F&O, EDAN undertook a serious study on challenges brought by people living with disability to church community life and service. Without due consideration of the physical, economic and spiritual needs of people living with disability, without thankful attention to and reception of their specific and unique gifts by the community, no authentic unity can be attained. '(The church) is an earthly reflection of a divine unity that is at the same time worshipped as Trinity. It is a community of people with different yet complementary gifts. It is a vision of wholeness as well as of healing, of caring and of sharing at once… Every child and every adult, those with disabilities and those without disabilities alike, will bring

---

[36] In my personal view, an unfortunate terminological development. 'Wider ecumenism' should be restricted to contacts and co-operation with all churches and Christian movements that are not participating in the classical ecumenical movement. For the other, essential, mission mandate, it is clearer to refer to 'Interreligious dialogue' or 'interreligious relations'.

[37] *TTL*, §14.

[38] See, among many other books, Jehu J. Hanciles, *Beyond Christendom. Globalization, African Migration, and the Transformation of the West* (Maryknoll, NY: Orbis Books, 2008); Sebastian C.H. Kim and Kirsteen Kim, *Christianity as a World Religion* (London and New York: Continuum, 2008), on this matter in particular the last chapter.

[39] D. Mukarjee and K. Labi, 'Urban Rural Mission' in N. Lossky, J.M. Bonino, J. Pobee, T.F. Stransky, G. Wainwright, P. Webb (eds), *Dictionary of the Ecumenical Movement,* 2nd edition (Geneva: WCC, 2002), 1182-1184. The URM network was related programmatically to CWME until 2009.

specific and special gifts and talents to the church… thus we can truly be 'A Church of All and for All' – a church which reflects God's intention for humankind.'[40]

The EDAN interim statement refers and contributes to late twentieth and early twenty-first century developments in the search for mission and unity. Since the early 1990s, the term *koinonia* has shaped ecclesiological reflections on unity.[41] Around the period of the 1991 Canberra Assembly, mission started to be understood in terms of healing and reconciliation, leading to this being a strong emphasis in the years 2000-2005. If God's mission aims at uniting all that exists, reconciling all in Christ through means that only God fully knows, then unity and reconciliation are the core of the gospel message.[42] Unity should not only be understood in terms of a means to give credibility to the gospel. It is the content of the mission of the church to point to Christ's offer of personal reconciliation with God, to discern where the Holy Spirit empowers people of all convictions to heal wounds of divisions, to strive for human and social community, and to overcome all barriers on the way to visible church unity. The reflection on political reconciliation processes highlighted the conditions that allow for reconciliation in justice, avoiding false peace and disillusionment. In turn, this also brought wisdom to the difficulties and conditions involved in the struggle for church unity – these are to be understood as processes of reconciliation. In such a perspective, it is part of the church's mission to struggle for visible unity, if the gospel is to have any meaning for a world in conflict.[43]

As *TTL* rightly hints, the various aspects of unity are interdependent. Neglecting one might jeopardise the other: 'Attempts to achieve unity must be in concert with the biblical call to seek justice. Our call to do justice may sometimes involve breaking false unities that silence and oppress. Genuine unity always entails inclusivity and respect for others.'[44]

The enlargement of the vision of God's mission that started in the 1950s reached a provisionally final stage in including the whole of creation in the understanding of the relation between mission and unity: 'There is a need to open up our reflections on church and unity to an even wider

---

[40] 'A church of All and for All. An Interim Statement', in A.S. Fritzson and S. Kabue, *Interpreting Disability: A Church of All and for All* (Geneva: WCC, 2004), §85 and 89. A more recent EDAN statement, taking into account the way in which churches responded to the challenges, is in process of revision.

[41] The term became prominent at the 1991 Canberra Assembly of the WCC. Cf. also Gibaut, 'From Unity and Mission to Koinonia'.

[42] See the CWME study document for Athens, 'Mission as Ministry of Reconciliation', in Matthey, *You are the Light of the World*, 90-126. Cf. also *TTL*, §19 and 20.

[43] Jacques Matthey, 'Some reflections on the significance of Athens', in Matthey, *Come Holy Spirit*, 327-41.

[44] *TTL*, §69.

understanding of unity: the unity of humanity and even the cosmic unity of the whole of God's creation.'[45] Both the common message issued by the 2010 Edinburgh Conference and the recent WCC mission document – as well as Evangelical, Orthodox and Catholic positions – now include creation as an integral part of God's and our mission. Unity then provides the horizon of our faith and hope in referring to the eschatological restoration of creation, the elimination of all suffering and evil, and the full communion of all that exists with God. 'The Triune God invites the whole creation to the Feast of Life, through Jesus Christ who came 'that they may have life, and may have it in all its fullness' (John 10:10, REB), through the Holy Spirit who affirms the vision of the reign of God, 'Behold, I create new heavens and a new earth!' (Isaiah 65:17, KJV).'[46]

---

[45] *TTL,* §61.
[46] *TTL,* §112.

# WORSHIP

Ruth A. Meyers

Over the course of the twentieth century, renewal of worship has gone hand-in-hand with the ecumenical movement. By the end of the century, the diversity of liturgical expression that emerged in western Christianity during the sixteenth-century Protestant Reformation had begun to coalesce in a common liturgical structure shared among a number of worshipping traditions.[1] Christians from many different traditions are more open than ever to borrowing texts, music and ritual practices from one another. Yet the rise of Pentecostalism has also meant a continuing breadth of Christian worship practices and patterns.

These liturgical developments proceeded in large measure apart from twentieth-century missiological scholarship and practice. Anglican scholar J.G. Davies began his 1966 book *Worship and Mission* with the lament that 'worship and mission are treated as two totally distinct objects of theological investigation; they are placed in isolated compartments without possibility of cross-fertilization and without the question of their unity being raised at all'.[2] By the end of the twentieth century, however, the situation had begun to change, as Lutheran liturgical scholar Thomas Schattauer noted: 'Much recent reflection about liturgy and mission has been motivated by questions about inculturation or contextualization in those parts of the world that have received patterns of worship from European and North American missionaries. The advent of a post-Christian era in the West has encouraged significant reflection about the forms of worship appropriate to this new missional situation.'[3]

## The Liturgical Movement

Beginning in the early twentieth century, a grassroots liturgical movement spread through Europe and North America, fostering renewal and revitalization of worship in Roman Catholic, Anglican and Lutheran

---

[1] Frank C. Senn, *Christian Liturgy: Catholic and Evangelical* (Minneapolis, MN: Fortress Press, 1997), 645-51; Clayton J. Schmit, *Sent and Gathered: A Worship Manual for the Missional Church* (Grand Rapids, MI: Baker Academic, 2009), 57-78.

[2] J.G. Davies, *Worship and Mission* (New York: Association Press, 1967 [1966]), 9.

[3] Thomas H. Schattauer, 'Liturgical Assembly as Locus of Mission', in T.H. Schattauer (ed), *Inside Out: Worship in an Age of Mission* (Minneapolis, MN: Fortress Press), 1.

churches, and to some extent in churches in the Reformed and Methodist traditions. Building upon a rediscovered biblical theology of the church as the mystical body of Christ, leaders of the liturgical movement sought to foster active participation of the entire assembly in worship and to deepen Christian commitment in the world as a visible outworking of the assembly's worship. Although a connection between worship and mission was implicit in the aims of the liturgical movement, leaders of the movement did not explain the evangelical and social implications of worship in terms of mission.[4]

The liturgical movement first flourished in Benedictine abbeys on the European continent: Solesmes in France, Beuron and Maria Laach in Germany, and Maredsous and Mount Cesár in Belgium. It quickly moved beyond the monastery walls. In an address given at the 1909 Malines Conference, Lambert Beauduin from Mount Cesár called for translation of the Latin missal so that the laity could understand and so participate and be formed by the liturgical texts. A Liturgical Week at Louvain, Belgium, followed in 1911, and during Holy Week 1914, the abbey of Maria Laach held a Liturgical Week for lay people. A decade later, the Roman Catholic liturgical movement was launched in the United States at the Benedictine Abbey of St John's in Collegeville, Minnesota.

Development of liturgical scholarship was a key element of the liturgical movement. Discoveries of ancient documents yielded new understandings of the early development of Christian liturgy. New journals and other publications explored the history and theology of liturgy. The classic text *Das christliche Kultmysterium* by Odo Casel, monk of Maria Laach, set forth a theology of the paschal mystery of Christ crucified and risen, a mystery made present in liturgical celebration.[5] *The Shape of the Liturgy* by Anglican Benedictine Gregory Dix identified a fourfold shape of the eucharist (take the bread and wine, bless them, break the bread, give the bread and wine) common to ancient Christian liturgies.[6] Both a theology of paschal mystery and Dix's emphasis on structure have had widespread ecumenical influence.

The liturgical movement went far beyond monasteries and the halls of academia. Lutheran scholar Frank Senn explains, 'The path-breaking work

---

[4] For example, in *Worship in Transition: The Liturgical Movement in the Twentieth Century* (New York: Continuum, 1995), John Fenwick and Bryan Spinks note the concurrence of the liturgical movement and the ecumenical movement (Introduction, 3-4), and the characteristics of the liturgical movement that they identify include 'an emphasis on proclamation and social involvement' (Chapter 1, 10-11), but Fenwick and Spinks never mention mission explicitly in their discussion of characteristics.

[5] Odo Casel, *Das christliche Kultmysterium* (Regensburg: F. Pustet, 1932); English trans. *The Mystery of Christian Worship and Other Writings* (Westminster Press, MD: Newman Press and London: Darton, Longman & Todd, 1962).

[6] Gregory Dix, *The Shape of the Liturgy* (London: Dacre Press, 1945).

of the monasteries was disseminated into the wider church through well-attended conferences, congresses, and institutes; and by the work of associations, clubs, centres, and societies that studied the liturgy, published tracts and monographs, conducted conferences and workshops, and modeled liturgical celebrations.'[7] In the Church of England, the Parish Communion movement emerged during the 1930s, as texts by Anglicans Henry de Candole and Gabriel Hebert encouraged a renewed understanding of the corporate nature of eucharistic celebration, drawing from the theology of the Roman Catholic liturgical movement.[8] A decade later, the Parish and People movement in England disseminated the ideas of the liturgical movement. In the Episcopal Church in the United States, Associated Parishes for Liturgy and Mission was founded in 1946 with similar aims. In the United States during the 1950s, Lutheran liturgical renewal flourished, its leaders borrowing styles of architecture, music, ceremony and vestments from Anglican tradition, and liturgical renewal movements also began in Reformed and Methodist churches.[9]

### *The Second Vatican Council*

In a watershed moment for twentieth-century liturgical renewal, on 4th December 1963, the Second Vatican Council of the Roman Catholic Church promulgated its first conciliar document, the 'Constitution on the Sacred Liturgy'.[10] The theological principles of the liturgical movement and their practical outworking are evident throughout. A theology of the church as the body of Christ undergirds the document: 'In the liturgy the whole public worship is performed by the mystical body of Jesus Christ, that is, by the head and his members.'[11] Liturgy is at the centre of the life of the church, 'the summit toward which the activity of the Church is directed' and 'the fount from which all her power flows'.[12] Hence liturgy requires 'full, conscious, and active participation' by all the faithful.[13]

---

[7] Senn, *Christian Liturgy*, 620.

[8] Henry de Candole, *The Church's Offering: A Brief Study of Eucharistic Worship* (1935); H. de Candole, *The Sacraments and the Church: A Study of the Corporate Nature of the Church* (1935); A. Gabriel Hebert, *Liturgy and Society: The Function of the Church in the Modern World* (London: Faber & Faber, 1935); A. G. Hebert (ed), *The Parish Communion: A Book of Essays* (London: SPCK, 1937).

[9] Senn, *Christian Liturgy*, 624-25.

[10] Constitution on the Sacred Liturgy, *Sacrosanctum Concilium*, Solemnly Promulgated by His Holiness Pope Paul VI, 4th December 1963: www.vatican.va/archive/hist_councils/ii_vatican_council/documents/vat-ii_const_19631204_sacrosanctum-concilium_en.html (accessed 28th July 2015; hereafter cited as *SC*).

[11] *SC* para 7.

[12] *SC* para 10.

[13] *SC* para 14.

The introductory paragraphs of the Constitution acknowledge the relationship of liturgy with evangelism ('Before men can come to the liturgy, they must be called to faith and to conversion') and to 'the works of charity, piety, and the apostolate'.[14] But neither evangelism nor Christian ministry in the world are acknowledged as aspects of mission, and most of the document focuses on reform of the liturgy. The council called for revision of liturgical books, including texts as well as rubrics guiding ceremonial action. While Latin would remain the foundational liturgical language for the Roman Church, translation into the vernacular would be permitted, and the liturgy could be adapted to different cultures.

Following the promulgation of the Constitution, revision of liturgical books began. A new missal was published in 1970, and regional conferences of bishops were directed to prepare editions in the vernacular.[15] The post-Vatican II reforms adopted many liturgical elements introduced in other churches during the sixteenth-century reformations, including use of the vernacular; a new emphasis on scripture, preaching and congregational song; and communion with both bread and wine. In the late twentieth century, many Protestant churches were influenced by the theology articulated in the Constitution on the Sacred Liturgy and subsequent reforms.[16]

A notable outcome of the post-Vatican II reforms is the emergence of an ecumenical lectionary. In its guidance for revision of the eucharistic liturgy, the Constitution directed, 'The treasures of the bible are to be opened up more lavishly, so that richer fare may be provided for the faithful at the table of God's word.'[17] Proposals for multi-year sequences of readings were advanced during the 1950s in European liturgical centres, owing to the rise of biblical scholarship as well as liturgical studies that show the significance of scripture in Sunday worship and the liturgical year in ancient churches. In 1969, the new three-year *Lectionary for Mass: Sundays and Feast Days* was approved and mandated for use beginning on the first Sunday of Advent 1971.[18]

Soon after the Roman Catholic Church introduced the *Lectionary for Mass*, several North American church bodies adapted it for their own use. Commentaries and homiletical resources soon followed, and pastors began to gather in ecumenical study groups. But each body that introduced the lectionary also revised it in some way. In 1978, the Consultation on Common Texts, an ecumenical body formed in North America in the mid-

---

14 *SC* para 9.

15 Fenwick and Spinks, *Worship in Transition*, 66-68.

16 James F. White, *A Brief History of Christian Worship* (Nashville, TN: Abingdon, 1993), 147.

17 *SC* para 51.

18 Fred Kimball Graham, 'Introduction', in Consultation on Common Texts, *The Revised Common Lectionary, Twentieth Anniversary Annotated Edition* (Minneapolis, MN: Fortress Press, 2012), xiii-xv.

1960s to develop agreed English-language versions of commonly used liturgical texts, turned its attention to lectionary issues. Their work led to the *Common Lectionary* in 1983, and a process of study and trial use resulted in the 1993 *Revised Common Lectionary*. This lectionary has been adopted in many churches throughout the world, extending far beyond English-speaking churches.[19] It has fostered ecumenical conversation as well as the development of worship resources, and it has encouraged Christians from different worshiping traditions to recognize a common biblical heritage, thus contributing to a renewal of mission thinking.

### Worship and Culture

From its origins in the first century, Christianity has taken root in different cultural contexts, and those diverse contexts have influenced Christian worship. In recent decades, scholars have increasingly recognized a complex relationship between worship and culture.

The Constitution on the Sacred Liturgy called for provision for 'legitimate variations and adaptations to different groups, regions, and peoples, especially in mission lands, provided that the substantial unity of the Roman rite is preserved'.[20] In its discussion of specific reforms, the document mentioned only the possibility of adapting elements of indigenous initiation rites in mission lands; the provision of a shorter baptismal rite, particularly for use by catechists in mission lands; and the incorporation of local music traditions.[21] Here, mission is understood as an expansion from the geographical centre of Rome to the global South and East.

While the Constitution called for adaptation of worship, theologians soon began using the neologism 'inculturation'. Roman Catholic theologian Anscar Chupungco defined liturgical inculturation as 'the process whereby the texts and rites used in worship by the local church are so inserted in the framework of culture, that they absorb its thought, language, and ritual patterns'. But, he continued, 'the cultural elements to be assimilated must undergo a critical evaluation.'[22] In contexts where the local culture differs significantly from that of the Roman rite, Chupungco called for liturgical creativity, that is, the composition of new liturgical texts and ritual elements.[23]

Recognition of the need for liturgical inculturation was not solely a concern of Roman Catholics. In the ecumenical openness of the late twentieth century, scholars and leaders in other churches also began to

---

[19] Graham, 'Introduction', xviii-xxv.
[20] *SC* para 38.
[21] *SC* paras 65, 68, 119.
[22] Anscar Chupungco, *Liturgies of the Future: The Process and Methods of Inculturation* (New York and Mahwah, NJ: Paulist, 1989), 29.
[23] Chupungco, *Liturgies of the Future*, 34-35.

explore the relationship between worship and culture.[24] In the mid-1990s, the Lutheran World Federation undertook a global study on worship and culture, bringing together an international and ecumenical group of scholars in a series of consultations. The second of these consultations resulted in the Nairobi Statement on Worship and Culture, which asserted:

> Christian worship relates dynamically to culture in at least four ways. First, it is transcultural: the same substance for everyone everywhere, beyond culture. Second, it is contextual: it varies according to the local situation (both nature and culture). Third, it is counter-cultural, challenging what is contrary to the gospel in a given culture. Fourth, it is cross-cultural: it makes possible sharing between different local cultures.[25]

By presenting a nuanced overview of the complex relationship between worship and culture, the Nairobi Statement makes a significant contribution to contemporary missiological imperatives to discern God's Spirit at work in local culture[26] and to challenge aspects of local culture that contradict the gospel.

Many of the efforts towards inculturation of worship in the late twentieth century focused on the need to inculturate worship in non-western contexts, not only in the global South and East but also in diaspora communities in the global North. Christians began to recognize that what had been considered universal forms of worship were actually reflections of the European cultures from which the missionaries came. Some Christians have made deliberate efforts to contextualize their worship so that it is a more authentic expression of the local context.[27]

As Christians in the global North have begun to recognize their post-Christendom context, some churches are exploring appropriate forms of worship in this emerging context. Acknowledging the need for local congregations to respond to their own contextual realities, *Together*

---

[24] See, for example, the findings and essays from a 1989 International Anglican Liturgical Consultation in David R. Holeton (ed), *Liturgical Inculturation in the Anglican Communion, including the York Statement 'Down to Earth Worship'* (Alcuin/GROW Liturgical Study 15; Nottingham, UK: Grove Books, 1990); Maren C. Tirabassi and Kathy Wonson Eddy, *Gifts of Many Cultures: Worship Resources for the Global Community* (Cleveland, OH: Pilgrim Press, 1995).

[25] Lutheran World Federation, 'The Nairobi Statement on Worship and Culture' (1996), in Gláucia Vasconcelos Wilkey (ed), *Worship and Culture: Foreign Country or Homeland?* (Grand Rapids, MI, and Cambridge, UK: Eerdmans, 2014), 138.

[26] *TTL*, §27.

[27] For example, in video recordings in *The Dancing Church around the World* (Mahwah, NJ: Paulist, 2004), Thomas Kane shows the use of indigenous music and dance in churches in Africa, Spain, the South Pacific and the United States. Charles Farhadian (ed), *Christian Worship Worldwide: Expanding Horizons, Deepening Practices* (Grand Rapids, MI, and Cambridge, UK: Eerdmans, 2007) includes several case studies of Roman Catholic, Protestant and Evangelical congregations in the non-Western world.

*towards Life* notes, 'in the secularizing global North, new forms of contextual mission such as "new monasticism", "emerging church", and "fresh expressions", have redefined and revitalized churches... Some churches in the global North now meet in pubs, coffee houses, or converted movie theatres.'[28]

## Contributions from Eastern Orthodoxy

In recent decades, Orthodox theologians have pointed out the integral relationship between the Divine Liturgy (the eucharist) and mission. Describing mission as 'the liturgy after the liturgy', Orthodox theologian Ion Bria explains, 'The eucharistic liturgy is not an escape into an inner realm of prayer, a pious turning away from social realities; rather, it calls and sends the faithful to celebrate 'the sacrament of the brother' outside the temple in the public market-place, where the cries of the poor and marginalized are heard'.[29] This impulse towards mission is grounded in the theological understanding of liturgy as an entrance into the presence of the Triune God and a celebration of the heavenly liturgy. Encountering the divine presence in worship, Christians are transformed and then sent forth to embody this presence in the world.[30]

While affirming the importance of Christian witness in the world, Bria also points out that 'under the burden of despotic and totalitarian regimes, the *Kyrie eleison* of the modest and sometimes hidden Sunday liturgy was the only collective cry for truth, love, and mercy'.[31] In such desperate circumstances, the celebration of the eucharist is itself an act of witness, a proclamation of God's eternal saving love and God's promise of a new heaven and a new earth. Such witness in the face of dire circumstances can remind Christians in every time and place that their gathering for worship is also a form of witness, a proclamation of the significance of God's reconciling love.

Bria is not uncritical of his Orthodox tradition. He notes a decreased involvement of people in liturgy and the communion, an ignorance of the Bible, and an attachment to ancient languages that are no longer spoken by the people. He also underscores the importance of challenging unjust structures of society, an imperative that Orthodox Christianity has sometimes ignored.[32] Bria calls for a renewed ecclesiology of communion,

---

[28] *TTL,* §72.

[29] Ion Bria, *The Liturgy after the Liturgy: Mission and Witness from an Orthodox Perspective* (Geneva: WCC, 1996), 20.

[30] Stephen B. Bevans and Roger P. Schroeder, *Constants in Context: A Theology of Mission for Today* (Maryknoll, NY: Orbis Books, 2009), 295.

[31] Bria, *The Liturgy after the Liturgy*, 22.

[32] Bria, *The Liturgy after the Liturgy*, 23-24.

connecting the proclamation of the reign of God and 'the building up of the body of Christ in history as sacrament of the kingdom'.[33]

In addition to a communion ecclesiology that shapes mission, Orthodox understandings and practices of liturgy have offered insights to western Christians. As the liturgical movement developed in the West, its leaders found in Eastern Orthodoxy reminders of ancient liturgical practices, including regular celebration of the eucharist by the community and the use of diverse languages. Western Christians have also borrowed more directly from Eastern practices. The Church of South India, an organic union of Anglicans, Methodists, Presbyterians and Congregationalists, introduced an epiclesis (invocation of the Spirit) and acclamations by the people as well as the passing of the Peace from the Syrian Orthodox liturgy of St James. Eucharistic Prayer 4 in the 1970 Roman missal is an adaptation of the anaphora of St Basil, and several churches in North America have included versions of this prayer in their contemporary worship books.[34]

## Pentecostal Worship

Alongside developments in Roman Catholic and Protestant churches rooted in the sixteenth-century reformations, by the middle of the twentieth century Pentecostalism had become a major worldwide influence. The Pentecostal tradition emerged in the first decade of the twentieth century, erupting in the Azusa Street revival led by William Seymour in Los Angeles, California. 'Hundreds received baptism of the Spirit as evidenced by speaking in tongues; hundreds were healed; and thousands came to observe the spectacle and remained to praise God for the work they saw before their eyes.'[35] Elements of the Pentecostal revival have roots in earlier Protestant traditions, particularly the nineteenth-century Methodist Holiness movement, and Pentecostal-type movements also appeared in Asia beginning in the mid-nineteenth century.[36] But Pentecostals understand their life and worship to be shaped primarily by the apostolic church, especially as depicted in the book of Acts.

Pentecostalism spread quickly throughout the world, becoming rooted in South America, Africa, Europe and Asia. In many places, Pentecostals have incorporated elements of indigenous religious traditions into their worship. A key characteristic is the gift of tongues, not only speaking in tongues but also interpretation and discernment of the Spirit in what is spoken. Healing, another gift of the Spirit, is often part of worship. Foot washing as well as water baptism and the Lord's Supper are usually understood as scriptural ordinances rather than as sacraments. Baptism of the Holy Spirit, evidenced

---

[33] Bria, *The Liturgy after the Liturgy*, 26.
[34] Fenwick and Spinks, *Worship in Transition*, 95-98.
[35] James F. White, *Protestant Worship: Traditions in Transition* (Louisville, KY: Westminster / John Knox, 1989), 195.
[36] Bevans and Schroeder, *Constants in Context*, 273.

by speaking in tongues, is considered a higher gift than baptism with water, and the gift may then be practised not only in the assembly for worship but also in personal prayer.

Pentecostals value spontaneity in worship, and although predictable patterns usually develop, outbursts of the Spirit may occur during preaching or prayer, or at any other moment. Prayer is rarely scripted. Any member of the assembly may voice prayer, whether in ordinary speech or in tongues. Sometimes many members of the assembly speak prayer simultaneously. Praying with one or both arms uplifted is common. Testimony to God's saving action, whether in one's own life or in that of another, may be voiced in the form of a prayer of thanksgiving.

Pentecostals believe that the various gifts of the Spirit are given to individuals for building up the body of Christ (1 Corinthians 12), and as a result worship is highly participatory. Moreover, the distribution of the gifts of the Spirit cuts across lines of race, class, gender and every other human division, including laity and clergy. For the first half of the twentieth century, 'Pentecostals were those who were on the lowest rung of the social and economic order; they were oppressed and impecunious'.[37] Many congregations have worshipped in storefront churches, a context that not only suits budgetary needs but also provides a familiarity and accessibility, hospitable especially to those who may be on the margins. The storefront context is also well-suited to the mission emphasis of Pentecostalism, taking its cue from the Spirit-driven mission in Acts.

In the 1960s, the Pentecostal movement burst into mainline American churches when an Episcopal priest, Dennis Bennett, announced that he had received the gift of tongues.[38] Within a few years, this charismatic renewal made its way to Lutheran, Methodist, Presbyterian and Roman Catholic churches. While initially many in those churches responded with hostility, gradually most accepted neo-Pentecostals. Elements of Pentecostal worship, such as speaking in tongues, spontaneous acclamations during preaching, spontaneous prayer, and prayer and song with uplifted arms, are now accepted in some mainline congregations.[39] Nevertheless, Mennonite scholars Eleanor Kreider and Alan Kreider have recently suggested that 'many Western Christians need to learn from the Pentecostals that the Spirit is at work during the services, as worship leaders allow for spontaneity as well as structure'.[40]

---

[37] White, *Protestant Worship*, 197.

[38] See Dennis Bennett, *Nine O'Clock in the Morning* (Plainfield, NJ: Logos International, 1970).

[39] Telford Work, 'Pentecostal and Charismatic Worship', in Geoffrey Wainwright and Karen B. Westerfield Tucker (eds), *The Oxford History of Christian Worship* (New York: Oxford University Press, 2006), 581.

[40] Alan Kreider and Eleanor Kreider, *Worship and Mission after Christendom* (Scottsdale, PA, and Waterloo, Ontario: Herald Press, 2011), 128.

## Ecumenical Convergence: *Baptism, Eucharist, and Ministry*

The 1927 Lausanne Conference on Faith and Order marked the beginning of multilateral ecumenical dialogue on questions of theology, sacraments and ministry that had been divisive for western Christianity since the sixteenth-century reformations. Over the next fifty years, a process of study involved local churches and members of what in 1948 became the Faith and Order Commission of the World Council of Churches. Decades of patient, careful dialogue culminated in Lima, Peru, at the 1982 meeting of the Faith and Order Commission, which adopted *Baptism, Eucharist and Ministry* (*BEM*) as a statement of doctrinal convergence. The *BEM* statement was widely distributed to churches around the world, and the Faith and Order Commission invited official responses from churches at the highest appropriate level of authority; six volumes of these responses were subsequently published.[41]

The Preface to *BEM* ties the study to mission in the twentieth century: 'As the churches grow into unity, they are asking how their understandings and practices of baptism, eucharist and ministry relate to their mission in and for the renewal of human community as they seek to promote justice, peace and reconciliation. Therefore our understanding of these cannot be divorced from the redemptive and liberating mission of Christ through the churches in the modern world.'[42] Here the document reflects theological understandings of mission as they emerged in the twentieth century. Mission is not the expansion of the church from a geographic centre, but rather is the redemptive and liberating work of Christ in which churches engage in their particular contexts.

In the section on the eucharist, *BEM* describes worship as an act of mission: 'The very celebration of the eucharist is an instance of the Church's participation in God's mission in the world.' That same mission takes place in the world through proclamation, service and 'faithful presence'. This mission is not limited to designated missionaries, but rather the entire eucharistic community 'is nourished and strengthened for confessing by word and action the Lord Jesus Christ who gave his life for the salvation of the world'. The imperative for mission challenges the separate communion tables of Christians: 'Insofar as Christians cannot unite in full fellowship around the same table to eat the same loaf and drink from the same cup, their missionary witness is weakened at both the individual and corporate levels.'[43]

---

[41] Max Thurian (ed), *Churches Respond to BEM,* 6 vols (WCC Faith and Order Paper Nos 129, 132, 135, 137, 143, 144 (1986)).

[42] Preface, *Baptism, Eucharist and Ministry* (WCC Faith and Order Paper No. 111 (1982)), vi; hereafter referred to as *BEM.*

[43] *BEM*, Eucharist paras 25, 26.

The Preface to *BEM* gives a nod to culture, claiming that the 'driving force [for the *BEM* text] is frequently contextual and contemporary'.[44] But the document says little about the intersection of worship and culture.[45] A decade later, the Ditchingham Report set forth principles and criteria for liturgical inculturation.[46] This report also links worship and mission, asserting that a recognition of their 'indissoluble relationship', along with theological convergence and liturgical renewal, were creating 'the momentum driving the churches towards koinonia in worship'.[47]

## 21st Century Challenges

Contemporary theologies of mission propose that mission is multi-dimensional, consisting of a number of elements. Some theologians include liturgy among the tasks of mission.[48] This perspective requires a dynamic model that understands worship as both an enactment of mission and an experience of empowerment for Christian mission in the world.[49] Led by the Spirit, Christians 'participate in the mission of love that is at the heart of the life of the Trinity'.[50]

As one dimension of mission, worship celebrates and enacts God's mission of reconciling love and justice. Christian assemblies who understand their worship as a form of mission practise radical hospitality, welcoming all and offering a foretaste of the reign of God. Their worship transforms them into being just communities practising radical hospitality in the world.[51] Worship is also prophetic, challenging unjust structures and proclaiming a vision of God's redemptive love. Christians who recognize that 'worship (*leitourgia*) is inextricably linked with witness (*martyria*), service (*diakonia*), and fellowship (*koinonia*)' engage actively in 'the

---

[44] *BEM*, Preface, vi.

[45] See *BEM*, Baptism, Commentary on para 21, regarding 'misunderstandings' of baptism in particular contexts; and *BEM*, Eucharist, Commentary on para 28, regarding the question of the use of local food and drink.

[46] Ditchingham Report (Ditchingham, UK, August 1994), paras 39-41; https://www.oikoumene.org/en/resources/documents/wcc-programmes/ecumenical-movement-in-the-21st-century/member-churches/special-commission-on-participation-of-orthodox-churches/sub-committee-ii-style-ethos-of-our-life-together/ditchingham-report-faith-and-order (accessed 31st July 15).

[47] Ditchingham Report, para 26.

[48] Bevans and Schroeder, *Constants in Context*, 350-51; Schattauer, 'Liturgical Assembly as Locus of Mission', 1-19.

[49] In a recent book, I propose two such models: a Möbius strip and a spinning top. See Ruth A. Meyers, *Missional Worship, Worshipful Mission: Gathering as God's People, Going Out in God's Name* (Grand Rapids, MI, and Cambridge, UK: Eerdmans, 2014), 34-36, 40-45, and passim.

[50] *TTL*, §18.

[51] *TTL*, §46-47.

liturgy after the liturgy', going forth from their assemblies to do God's work in the world.[52]

Mission is also multi-directional.[53] Christians in every part of the world are coming to understand that mission takes place in their neighbourhoods. Moreover, as mission increasingly takes place *from* the margins rather than *to* the margins,[54] Christians are experiencing the richness of a plurality of cultures that is a gift of the Spirit. Where diverse cultural communities worship together, 'culture can engage one another authentically and... culture can enrich the gospel'.[55] The complex relationship of worship and culture explicated in the Nairobi Statement suggests that worship is both particular and universal, uniting all in Christ while celebrating God's presence in diverse contexts.

Finally, a renewed appreciation of mission offers the possibility of deeper union among Christians and churches. 'Mission spirituality that flows from liturgy and worship reconnects us with one another and with the wider creation.'[56] In weekly public worship, Christian assemblies bring together people who have been engaging in mission in the world and now carry with them the needs and hopes of the world. Empowered by the Spirit and in communion with one another, worshippers offer praise, proclaim the good news of God's steadfast mercy and love revealed in Christ, and offer intercession for the needs of the world. Many assemblies also gather around the eucharistic table, where all are welcomed and fed. The assembly then goes forth, the Spirit leading them to continue to participate in God's mission in the world.[57] Christians may worship in different ways, with different cultural expressions, yet a common commitment to the mission of God unites them with one another and with all creation.

---

[52] *TTL,* §17, 74, 85. See Schmit, *Sent and Gathered,* 43-55.
[53] *TTL,* §106.
[54] *TTL,* §6.
[55] *TTL,* §100.
[56] *TTL,* §104.
[57] Meyers, *Missional Worship, Worshipful Mission*, 43.

# HEALING

## Manoj Kurian

In 1948, the Constitution of the World Heath Organisation defined health as 'a state of complete physical, mental and social well-being and not merely the absence of disease or infirmity'.[1] The definition continues to elaborate the phenomenon of health as a fundamental human right: 'The enjoyment of the highest attainable standard of health is one of the fundamental rights of every human being without distinction of race, religion, political belief, economic or social condition.' In 1989, the Christian Medical Commission of the World Council of Churches offered the following definition of health to the WCC's central committee: 'Health is a dynamic state of well-being of the individual and society, of physical, mental, spiritual, economic, political, and social well-being – of being in harmony with each other, with the material environment and with God.'[2]

The Christian understanding of health, healing and the healing ministry is related to the Christian understanding of salvation and the realization of the reign of God. This realization is the 'new creation' that the biblical prophets announced and anticipated as 'shalom'. Shalom can be described as an ultimate state of reconciled and healed relationships between creation and God, between humanity and God, humanity and creation, and between humans as individuals and as groups or societies. Each act of healing is a sign of the realization of shalom.

### Healing in the Ministry of Jesus

According to the Gospel of John, only some of the miracles and actions of Jesus Christ were recorded (John 21:25). Of the thirty-seven miracles performed by Jesus recorded in the Gospels, twenty-seven were related to healing – including four that involved raising from the dead, five that related to food and abundance, and five that illustrated his power over nature.

Apart from the fact that healing was a central feature of Jesus's ministry, he also wanted his followers to continue his work and endowed them with

---

[1] World Health Organisation, *Constitution of the World Health Organisation*, 1948: www.who.int/governance/eb/constitution/en/

[2] World Council of Churches, *Healing and Wholeness – The Churches' Role in Health*, Report of a study by the Christian Medical Commission (Geneva: WCC, 1990): http://difaem.de/fileadmin/Dokumente/Publikationen/Dokumente_AErztliche_Mission/healing_wholeness.pdf

the authority to do so. The missionary instruction in each of the first three (synoptic) gospels connects the proclamation of the word of God with deeds, and explicitly mentions the healing ministry:

> He (Jesus) called to him the twelve disciples and gave them authority over unclean spirits, to cast them out, and to heal every disease and every infirmity… These twelve Jesus sent out, charging them… 'Preach as you go, saying, 'The kingdom of God is at hand.' Heal the sick, raise the dead, cleanse the lepers, cast out demons.'[3]

His disciples followed suit.

> Are any among you sick? They should call for the elders of the church and have them pray over them, anointing them with oil in the name of the Lord. The prayer of faith will save the sick, and the Lord will raise them up; and anyone who has committed sins will be forgiven. Therefore confess your sins to one another, and pray for one another, so that you may be healed. The prayer of the righteous is powerful and effective.[4]

The early church took Jesus' healing ministry seriously, and Christianity affirms the centrality of the church as a healing community and proclaims Christ as the healer of the world.[5] The mentoring and training, grounded in love, which Jesus gave his disciples, ensured that the gospel reached across the continents. The mandate was given to his disciples and therefore to all of us, is to heal (Matthew 10:1) as part of the holistic mission of Christ. His teachings were so revolutionary that he said that his followers could achieve even greater things than him (John 14:11-13). The followers of Christ believed that they are not alone and work in the eternal and practical perspectives that the Lord Jesus provided.

The hallmarks of the healing nature of the Lord Jesus Christ include:

- His compassionate and approachable nature where he touched many people (Luke 18:15, 16)
- His sensitivity to the needs of people, especially the vulnerable, where he was 'touched' and responded by healing (Luke 8:42b-48)
- His willingness to listen and openness to change (Mark 7:24b-30)
- His unwillingness to accept delay in the alleviation of suffering (Luke 13:10-13)
- His authority over traditions and evil forces, and his willingness to empower others by sharing this authority (Mark 6:1-3, 7, 53, 56)
- His teaching that one needs to step outside one's comfort zone and empathize (the Beatitudes)
- Serving and loving others as oneself (John 13:34-35)

---

[3] Matthew 10:1, 5, 7.

[4] James 5:14-16.

[5] DIFAEM and WCC, 'Witnessing to Christ today: Promoting health and wholeness for all', German Medical Mission (DIFAEM) and WCC, 2010: www.difaem.de/fileadmin/dev-difaem/files/Publikationen/Grundsatzarbeit/Witnessing_to_Christ_today.pdf

- Seeing the divinity of the other and the sanctity of serving the marginalized (Matthew 25:31-40)
- Considering the whole community as part of the one body of Christ (1 Corinthians 12:12).

### Healing in the Ministry of the Church

The church, from its earliest days, defined its ministry and mission as one that offers wholesome life-giving healing in response to people's diverse needs. Indeed, a significant factor in the growth of the early church was the fact that it presented itself as a healing movement and agent in the societies within which it took root with the gospel. Its distinctive attitude to the sick, the weak and the vulnerable marked it out and found expression particularly through the monastic movement. Through wars, epidemics and all the vicissitudes of human life, Christianity across the centuries has been marked by its commitment to healing ministry, which has taken many different forms. The Athens conference of CWME, held in 2005, paid special attention to the church's call to be a healing community. As one of its preparatory papers affirmed:

> It belongs to the very essence of the church – understood as the body of Christ created by the Holy Spirit – to live as a healing community, to recognize and nurture healing charisms and to maintain ministries of healing as visible signs of the presence of the kingdom of God.[6]

A fundamental change occurred with the rise of modern science, technology and medicine in the western world during the eighteenth century and beyond. New discoveries and developments provided medicine with effective means to cure diseases and the church with new possibilities for rediscovering its healing ministry. At the same time, medicine came to be understood technically as the application of knowledge to cure malfunctioning of body or mind. This could lead to a less holistic understanding and to neglect of the spiritual dimension. Nonetheless, as knowledge of effective healing methods increased, Christians felt a moral duty to provide these opportunities to all people in need. During the nineteenth and twentieth centuries, many missionary societies believed that it was an essential part of their role to provide healing for the sick in the countries where they were operating.

Mission societies perceived that health care institutions could reach many people with the gospel. The effectiveness of the healing methods supported the credibility of the proclamation of the good news of Jesus

---

[6] Preparatory Paper No. 11 'The Healing Mission of the Church', in Jacques Matthey (ed), *Come Holy Spirit, Heal and Reconcile! Called in Christ to be Reconciling and Healing Communities – Report of the WCC Conference on World Mission and Evangelism, Athens, Greece, May 9-16, 2005* (Geneva: WCC, 2008), 91-112 at 103.

Christ. Through the missionary movement, Christian charity contributed to the construction of hospitals and clinics in many different countries of the global South. At the beginning of modern medical missions, an important motivation to create health care institutions was also the need to protect the health of the missionaries who suffered from many diseases unknown in their countries of origin.[7] By the middle of the twentieth century, the societies had founded hospitals, dispensaries and leprosariums all over the world. These establishments provided scientifically based medicine and contributed significantly to the health care systems of many countries.[8] Currently, faith-based organizations (FBOs) are among the major health providers in developing countries, providing, for example, an average of some 40% of health services in sub-Saharan Africa. FBOs' core values lead them to offer compassionate care to people with a long-term commitment to societies, closely aligning with community needs.[9]

At the same time, it has to be recognised that Christian mission was closely connected with the western colonial rule which prevailed in much of Africa and Asia during the nineteenth and twentieth centuries. In many instances, the colonised were dispossessed of their land, cultures, livelihoods and industry, and were reduced to fuelling the industrial revolution of the colonial powers. Conversion to the Christian faith in sub-Saharan Africa and Asia did not protect millions of local people from the brutal impact of colonisation that impoverished their societies. In the role of coloniser, western Christians saw it as their moral duty to civilise those they encountered. Part of their civilising programme was western education, which often resulted in the colonised adopting the coloniser's language, culture and worldview and losing their own.[10] In many colonised regions, local knowledge on healing was negatively impacted as missionaries worked against traditional healers, associating them with indigenous faiths and superstitions and as impediments to the missionary enterprise. These actions drove traditional medicine underground.[11]

---

7 See Christopher H. Grundmann, 'Gesandt zu heilen. Aufkommen und Entwicklung der Ärztlichen Mission im neunzehnten Jahrhundert', in *Missionswissenschaftliche Forschungen,* Bd. 12, Gütersloh, 1992.

8 Christoph Benn and Erlinda Senturias, 'Health, Healing and Wholeness in the Ecumenical Discussion', in *International Review of Mission,* 90.356/357 (2001), 7-25.

9 See Ted Karpf and Alex Ross (eds), *Building From Common Foundations, The World Health Organization and Faith-Based Organizations in Primary Healthcare*, World Health Organization, 2008.

10 Musa Dube, 'Consuming a Colonial Cultural Time Bomb: Translating Badimo into Demons in the Setswana Bible (Matthew 8.28-34, 15.22, 10.8)', in *Journal for the Study of the New Testament,* 73 (1999), 33-59, at 34.

11 Fhumulani M. Mulaudzi, 'Synergy between Indigenous Knowledge Systems, Modern Health Care System and Scientific Research – A Vision for the 21st Century', in *HEALTH SA GESONDHEID,* 6.4 (2001), 14-20.

However, the healing ministry of the mission organisations gave an alternative to the dominant narrative of colonisation. The selfless and sacrificial work of Christian missionary health personnel, establishing health care centres in remote and rural regions, which were neglected by colonial administrations, is a very inspiring testimony and a message of hope. The pioneering work continued to catalyse and mobilise care for whole communities, valuing individuals while seeing the person as part of the larger community. The mission churches provided the roots of vibrant volunteerism and a sense of calling and vocation to those involved in the church-related health services. In the field of health, church-related organisations have pioneered in successfully working against unjust pricing of medicine and campaigning for health for all, and in providing credible and affordable alternates to for-profit health care providers.

## Trends in Understanding the Healing Mission of the Church

By the mid-twentieth century, questions were being raised about expenditure on curative medicine and services that accounted for more than 90% of the resources of the healing ministry. The Tübingen I and II Consultations co-organized by the World Council of Churches (WCC), the Lutheran World Federation (LWF) and the German Institute for Medical Mission (DIFÄM), in 1964 and 1968 addressed many of these questions. These processes called for an integrated witness where medical work could be correlated with social work, nutrition, agriculture and community development, recognizing that that medical care was only a component of a diversity of disciplines, all of which were necessary to promote and maintain health. This led to the formation of the Christian Medical Commission (CMC) in 1968. The CMC assisted in the reorientation of the churches' health care – to be evolved into a more comprehensive and community oriented service.

With CMC's close working relationship with the World Health Organization (WHO) in Geneva, the experience of the grassroots in the issues of community health were channelled to the international, inter-governmental body. The churches were able to influence and give quality experiential and experimental input into a joint study process – by the WHO and UNICEF – called, 'Alternative approaches to meeting basic health needs of populations in developing countries'. Health care services were tailored to the needs of the communities with the local population being involved in the formulation of the policy and delivery of the system. This process led to the development of Primary Health Care. The Primary Health Care philosophy stressed an integrated approach to prevention and cure, and promoted health services both for the community and the individual. This was adopted by the WHO in 1977, and implied a radical shift in the priorities of the WHO, with global implications in decentralizing health care and granting greater rights and responsibilities to people in the management of their health. The contribution of the churches to the evolution of Primary Health Care thinking and practice is a lasting contribution to public health.[12]

In the 1970s, Christian communities began to train village health workers at the grassroots level. Equipped with essential drugs and simple methods, these workers were able to treat most common diseases and to promote the use of clean water and better hygienic conditions. They facilitated the introduction of small health centres that offered low-cost in-patient care, as well as pre-natal and early childhood health services. In these new decentralised health care systems, many mission hospitals began to play an essential role by acting as intermediaries between local village health services and the centralised state-supported hospitals.

Faith-based provision of health services has been a cornerstone of the global response to HIV from the earliest days of the HIV and AIDS epidemic. Africa, which has 10% of the world's population, but 25% of the global disease burden, is home to nearly a third of all people living with HIV and AIDS, with some countries in Southern Africa having HIV prevalence rates above 20%. In this context, faith-based health care providers deliver a large proportion of comprehensive HIV care to millions of people on a daily basis. With their holistic engagement and collaboration with communities, they can ensure effective biomedical responses to epidemics and health emergencies. But it has to be noted that many faith-based health services work under severe constraints, especially regarding their workforce.[13] This heroic role of health professionals on the frontlines of dealing with epidemics is further evident from the fact that a significant proportion of the more than 200 doctors, nurses and other health care workers who have died of Ebola since June 2014 worked in hospitals and health centres run by churches.

While specialized health services, and the professionals needed to run them, remain an integral part of Christian mission in many parts of the world, there has recently been a recovery of the place of the local congregation in the healing mission of the church. The Athens CWME conference in 2005 heard that 'the local congregation or Christian community is the primary agent for healing… The way a network of mutual support, of listening and of mutual care is maintained and nurtured in a local congregation expresses the healing power of the church as a whole. All basic functions of the local church have a healing dimension also for the wider community: the proclamation of the word of God as a message of hope and comfort, the celebration of the Eucharist as a sign of

---

[12] Socrates Litsios, 'The Christian Medical Commission and the Development of WHO's Primary Health Care Approach', in *American Journal of Public Health,* 94/11 (November 2004), 1884-93.

[13] See B. Schmid, E. Thomas, J. Olivier and J.R. Cochrane, 'The contribution of religious entities to health in sub-Saharan Africa', in African Religious Health Assets Programme (ARHAP), 2008.

reconciliation and restoration, the pastoral ministry of each believer, individual or community intercessory prayer for all members and the sick in particular'.[14]

The worship of the church is in itself a healing ministry: 'Joining the others as a community of believers, being liberated from guilt and the burdens of life, experiencing even unbelievable cures, being enflamed by the experience of singing and of praise, are a tremendously healing experience.'[15] In particular, the celebration of the Eucharist is a healing act at the heart of the life of the church: 'The Eucharistic liturgy provides… the setting and visible expression for God's healing presence in the midst of the church and through her in mission to this broken world.'[16] Spiritual gifts also have a part to play in the healing ministry of the church, and among them is the gift of healing. The report to the Athens CWME conference counselled: 'All gifts of healing within a given community need deliberate encouragement, spiritual nurture, education and enrichment – but also a proper ministry of pastoral accompaniment and ecclesial oversight. Charisms are not restricted to the so-called "supernatural" gifts which are beyond common understanding and/or personal worldview, but hold to a wider understanding in which both talents and approaches of modern medicine, alternative medical approaches as well as gifts of traditional healing and spiritual forms of healing have their own right.'[17]

Recent times have seen a growing recognition that modern western systems of health care represent no more than one strand in a healing mission that comprehensively engages the human situation. Ecumenical thinking has also been challenged by the rise of Pentecostal-Charismatic movements with their emphasis on the spiritual dimension of healing and awareness of the need to cast out evil spirits in certain situations – the ministry of deliverance. The fast growth of Neo-Pentecostalism, Charismatic and prosperity paradigm churches, especially in the global South, is in part due to the emphasis that they placed on what Hansjörg Dilger refers to as 'healing the wounds of modernity'.[18] The negative impact of economic globalisation on the vulnerable economies of the South has resulted in underdeveloped health care systems. The impact of HIV/AIDS especially in Africa and the slow response of government health care systems to address the socio-economic factors that perpetrate the

---

[14] Jacques Matthey (ed), *Come Holy Spirit, Heal and Reconcile! Called in Christ to be Reconciling and Healing Communities – Report of the WCC Conference on World Mission and Evangelism, Athens, Greece, May 9-16, 2005*. Geneva: WCC, 2008., 104.

[15] Matthey, *Come, Holy Spirit*, 106.

[16] Matthey, *Come, Holy Spirit*, 105.

[17] Matthey, *Come, Holy Spirit*, 105.

[18] Hansjörg Dilger, 'Healing the Wounds of Modernity: Salvation, Community and Care in a Neo-Pentecostal Church in Dar Es Salaam, Tanzania', in *Journal of Religion in Africa,* 37.1 (2007), 59-83.

disease enabled the response of Christian religious groups that claimed to offer healing to people without hope. Such groups offer the social, spiritual and economic support as forms of their networks of healing and support in urban contexts of suffering.

These pneumatological paradigm churches enter into the meaning systems of traditional culture and cosmologies of healing to declare that God can do the impossible and that faith heals, overcoming evil in all shapes and forms and meeting the needs of contemporary life. Ecumenical understanding has been enriched by learning from these churches.

Equally, ecumenical engagement with issues of justice has sharpened awareness of the reality that individuals are only likely to enjoy good health when they live in a healthy society and a healthy ecology. There is need today for a comprehensive and holistic understanding of health and healing. As stated in the new WCC mission affirmation *Together towards Life* (*TTL*): 'Health is more than physical and/or mental well-being, and healing is not primarily medical. This understanding of health coheres with the biblical-theological tradition of the church, which sees a human being as a multi-dimensional unity, and the body, soul, and mind as interrelated and interdependent. It thus affirms the social, political, and ecological dimensions of personhood and wholeness.'[19]

This creates a mandate for the churches to be engaged in healing mission in a wide range of ways which together meet the challenges of our times. As *TTL* observes: 'The Spirit empowers the church for a life-nurturing mission, which includes prayer, pastoral care, and professional health care on the one hand, and prophetic denunciation of the root causes of suffering, transformation of structures that dispense injustice, and pursuit of scientific research on the other.'[20] This opens up many practical ways in which churches can participate in healing mission, as suggested by *TTL*: 'There are many ways in which churches can be, and are, involved in health and healing in a comprehensive sense. They create or support clinics and mission hospitals; they offer counselling services, care groups, and health programmes; local churches can create groups to visit sick congregation members. Healing processes could include praying with and for the sick, confession and forgiveness, the laying on of hands, anointing with oil, and the use of charismatic spiritual gifts.'[21]

## Conclusion

The state of global health calls us to act as individuals and as communities to:

---

[19] *TTL*, §51.
[20] *TTL*, §50.
[21] *TTL*, §53.

- Challenge and work to overcome poverty, social inequity and injustice;
- Challenge patriarchy and work for the empowerment of women;
- Give greater priority to the welfare of children and mothers;
- Influence the promotion of a positive lifestyle and diet;
- Strive for greater engagement of health-related issues at the community level, and to promote their ownership in finding sustainable solutions;
- Build solidarity and empathy among and across communities;
- Work for greater investment in health and the welfare of communities;
- To see health and healing through the lens of our faith.

Faith communities carry the great legacy of human endeavour, ingenuity and achievement, diversity, culture and wisdom through millennia. With the grace of God, we can collectively mobilize this rich experience and legacy to bring about a positive transformation of society. Our faith and our foundational values dictate that everyone has a fundamental right to health and well-being!

# CULTURE

Daesung Lee and Stephen Bevans SVD

## Introduction

'Grace supposes culture, and God's gift becomes flesh in the culture of those who receive it.' These are the words of Pope Francis in his 2013 Apostolic Exhortation *Evangelii Gaudium*, and they are words that reveal the intimate and intricate connection between mission – God's mission, shared by the church – and the ways that human beings make sense of the world, or human culture.[1] If 'God's gift' of the gospel is truly to be received, the way it is witnessed to and proclaimed must take into account the way it is understood in contexts and cultures that may be very different from the contexts and cultures of those who witness and proclaim – missionaries. Indeed, 'culture' is one of the six 'constants' that are always part of the way the church engages in mission as it tries to participate in the work of the triune missionary God. Along with the centrality of Christ and the ecclesial and eschatological nature of mission, along with concerns with the nature of salvation and the nature of the human person, the church's missionary effort needs always to work within and continually grapple with the gift, the challenges, the grace, and the sinfulness of culture.[2]

'Culture', of course, is a notoriously difficult concept to define. Clifford Geertz has famously described culture as a 'system of inherited conceptions expressed in symbolic forms by means of which people communicate, perpetuate, and develop their knowledge about an attitude toward life.'[3] Thus a culture is like a web of interconnected values, customs, practices, kinship relationships and the like, creating the 'world' in which people live. Robert Schreiter speaks of this understanding as an 'integrated' approach to culture, and goes on to speak also of 'global' concepts of culture wherein a worldview or meaning structure is not so much inherited as constructed, often as a way of addressing a power imbalance.[4] Bernard Lonergan

---

[1] Pope Francis, Apostolic Exhortation *Evangelii Gaudium* (*EG*): http://w2.vatican.va/content/francesco/en/apost_exhortations/documents/papa-francesco_esortazione-ap_20131124_evangelii-gaudium.html, 115.

[2] See Stephen B. Bevans and Roger P. Schroeder, *Constants in Context: A Theology of Mission for Today* (Maryknoll, NY: Orbis Books, 2004), 32-72.

[3] Clifford Geertz, *The Interpretation of Cultures* (New York: Basic Books, 1973), 89, quoted in Gerald A. Arbuckle, *Earthing the Gospel: An Inculturation Handbook for the Pastoral Worker* (Maryknoll, NY: Orbis Books, 1990), 28.

[4] See Robert J. Schreiter, *The New Catholicity: Theology between the Global and Local* (Maryknoll, NY: Orbis Books, 1997), 46-61.

distinguishes between 'classicist' and 'empiricist' notions of culture. The former is normative, and would consider other cultures 'primitive' or 'undeveloped'. The latter is simply the way that peoples organize their worlds. In this view of culture, there are no 'high' or 'low' cultures. Cultures are neither normative nor universally valid. Culture is simply the way that peoples have sought and continue to seek to make sense out of their lives in particular situations. While they may be flawed, and in some cases seriously, cultures are basically healthy and good.[5]

What this chapter proposes to do is, in a first part, to survey the ways that culture has been understood in the ecumenical conversation that has been going on in the past one hundred years in the aftermath of the historic 1910 World Mission Conference in Edinburgh. Although it will mainly focus on that conversation within the World Council of Churches (WCC) and its Commission on World Mission and Evangelism (CWME) – and so include the Orthodox churches – it will also include conversations within Roman Catholicism and Evangelical churches. A second section will focus on an in-depth presentation of the role of culture in the WCC's latest document on mission, *Together towards Life: Mission in Changing Landscapes*. It will then conclude with a sketch of some of the challenges of the dynamic of mission and culture that mission might face in the future.

As the Second Vatican Council proclaimed in one of its most beautiful passages, one of the most important tasks of missionaries is to 'learn, by sincere and patient dialogue, what treasures a generous God has distributed among the nations of the earth', at the same time working 'to refurbish them, to set them free, and bring them under the dominion of God their savior'.[6] This is the dynamic that this chapter will explore, as churches from various traditions have discovered in the last century the importance and challenge of culture in their missionary work.

## Mission and Culture in the Ecumenical Movement

### *The World Missionary Conference, Edinburgh, 1910*

The Report of Commission VII of the 1910 Edinburgh Missionary Conference contained the statement that 'the reproach that missionaries desire to Europeanise the inhabitants of mission lands, if ever true, is now absurdly false'. Brian Stanley observes, however, that such a statement 'was not permitted to affect the fundamental categorization of cultures

[5] Bernard J.F. Lonergan, *Method in Theology* (London: Dartman, Longman & Todd, 1972), xi.

[6] Vatican Council II, Decree on the Mission Activity of the Church, *Ad Gentes*: www.vatican.va/archive/hist_councils/ii_vatican_council/documents/vat-ii_decree_19651207_ad-gentes_en.html, 11.

which provided the organizing framework for the report itself'.[7] That framework categorized civilizations in a way that ranked local cultures from 'low' to 'high',[8] very much under the influence of colonial and Enlightenment thinking, and reflecting the current state of the emerging discipline of anthropology. It was this thinking against which V.S. Azariah protested in his famous speech about racism and prejudice among missionaries in the Indian church, ending with his famous plea for personal relationships between British and Indian Christians: 'Give us FRIENDS!'[9] Nevertheless, as Stanley reports, one delegate from Scotland wrote that 'the spirit of nationalism, so deeply stirring in all lands, found utterance again and again at the Conference'. He went on to say that:

> It is not English speech and English thought on which the new churches in the Mission-field are to be formed: else they would be foreign churches. China, Japan, India must bring their own traditions and their own passion of patriotism into a Church of Christ, truly become also the Church of China, Japan, India. Missions exist to make missions unnecessary.[10]

These words are not exactly focused on culture, since the term and idea had not yet fully emerged at this time. But the emphasis is clear, and such emphasis of respect and autonomy of local traditions and customs would only grow in the years ahead.

### *1910 to 1961: The International Missionary Council*

One of the most significant moves of the 1910 Edinburgh Conference was the establishment of a Continuing Committee that became in 1921 the International Missionary Council (IMC). Its first conference was held in 1928 in Jerusalem, and although the issue of culture was not discussed head on, the conference was notable for the number of indigenous delegates present, and for its discussion of the relationship between the 'younger' and 'older' churches. Especially among the Chinese delegates, there was a call

---

[7] World Missionary Conference, 1910, *Report of Commission VII* (Edinburgh and London: Oliphant, Anderson & Ferrier; and New York, Chicago and Toronto: Fleming H. Revell Company, n.d. [1910]), 94; Brian Stanley, *The World Missionary Conference, Edinburgh 1910* (Grand Rapids, MI: Eerdmans, 2009), 258.

[8] See Stanley, *The World Missionary Conference*, 254-60.

[9] World Missionary Conference, 1910, *History and Records of the Conference Together with Addresses Delivered at the Evening Meetings* (Edinburgh and London: Oliphant, Anderson & Ferrier; and New York, Chicago and Toronto: Fleming H. Revell Company, n.d. [1910]), 315.

[10] *Life and Work: The Church of Scotland Magazine and Mission Record*, 32:8 (August 1910), 244, quoted in Stanley, *The World Missionary Conference*, 111.

for greater autonomy in church government, with a plea that local churches be recognized *as* churches in their own right.[11]

Culture was also not the immediate issue at the IMC's second conference in Tambaram, Madras, India, in 1938. The issue was the relation of Christianity to other faiths, sparked by W.E. Hocking's and others' more liberal *Rethinking Mission* on the one hand, and Hendrik Kraemer's more conservative *The Christian Message in a Non-Christian World* on the other, the book issued as a preparation for the conference.[12] The point of debate was whether God was in some way present within religions other than Christianity, an important question for the goodness and holiness of culture, given the close connection of some religions (e.g. Hinduism) with particular cultures (e.g. in India). What became increasingly clear nonetheless was that mission was being done more and more under the direction of local indigenous churches. Although Kraemer's work had strongly attacked the *Volkskirke* movement pioneered by Bruno Gutmann and Christian Keysser in the early years of the century, the contextual nature of that approach was vigorously defended at the conference, despite what some theologians were making of it in Nazi Germany.[13]

As Wesley Ariarajah observes, when the next congress of the IMC took place in Whitby, Canada, in 1947, the world had become a radically different place after six long years of World War. The colonial structure of the world, under the dominance of Europe and North America, was swiftly coming to and end, and with it the rise of nationalism and pride in local cultures. 'This new reality produced the next stage for the debate on gospel and culture.'[14]

Such discussion was rooted, as previously, in the identity of the local churches. But local identity was more than simply having indigenous leadership. It was about recognizing the importance and value of the local culture in which the churches lived and participated in the developments that the new nationalism was promoting. As Ariarajah writes: 'In no way could churches become partners in nation-building if they considered the religion and culture of the majority of the peoples with whom they lived to be in complete 'discontinuity' with their new life in Christ.'[15]

---

[11] See Timothy Yates, *Christian Mission in the Twentieth Century* (Cambridge: CUP, 1994), 66-67.

[12] See William Ernest Hocking (ed), *Rethinking Missions: A Laymen's Inquiry after One Hundred Years* (New York: Harper & Brothers, 1932); Hendrik Kraemer, *The Christian Message in a Non-Christian World* (London, 1938).

[13] On the *Volkskirke* movement, see Yates, *Christian Mission in the Twentieth Century*, 34-56. On the defence of the movement at Tambaram, see Yates, 102-21.

[14] S. Wesley Ariarajah, *Gospel and Culture: The Ongoing Discussion within the Ecumenical Movement* (Geneva: WCC, 1994), 10.

[15] Ariarajah, *Gospel and Culture*, 11.

Two ideas emerged in the late 1940s and 1950s (at Whitby in 1947, at Willingen, Germany, in 1952, and at Accra, Ghana, in 1957) that were to have impact on the understanding of the importance of culture in missionary work. The first was the idea of 'partnership', a notion that relativized the importance of the foreign mission sending agencies and once more emphasized the autonomy of the local church, local leadership and local culture. The second was the emergence of the importance of *missio Dei*, an understanding of mission that focused less on the church than on the world. God was working in the *world*, within history, within cultures. The church's task was to work with God in bringing that saving work to visibility.[16] Both concepts, so vital to contemporary missiology, would on the one hand challenge mission to its core in the coming years and, on the other, offer a basis for a continuing appreciation for the role of culture in missionary work.

### *Integration of the IMC with the World Council of Churches*

In 1961, at the third Assembly of the World Council of Churches, which had been inaugurated in 1948, the IMC was fully integrated into this larger body. By this time the call for the importance of cultures had become very clear in the light of growing independence of nations from colonial rule and the continued maturity of local churches. The final report of the Assembly states emphatically that western culture is not to be considered normative, and that such an insistence is actually 'a hindrance to the spread of the gospel and a stumbling block to those of other traditions'.[17] Strongly implied is the mandate to preach the gospel in ways that are relevant and challenging to the cultures that the gospel encounters.

With the integration of the IMC into the WCC, the Division of World Mission and Evangelism (DWME – now the Commission on World Mission and Evangelism or CWME) was created to attend particularly to matters of mission and evangelism. It held its first conference in 1963 in Mexico City on the theme of 'Mission in Six Continents' – again emphasizing the integrity of local, indigenous churches and their missionary identity. No longer was mission simply 'from the West to the rest,' with the western superiority that such an idea implied, but a mission marked by cultural identity and integrity.

---

[16] Ariarajah, *Gospel and Culture*, 18-19.

[17] *The New Delhi Report – The Third Assembly of the WCC* (London: SCM, 1962), 98, quoted in Ariarajah, *Gospel and Culture*, 25.

### *The Second Vatican Council and Roman Catholicism on Mission and Culture*

In this first half of the twentieth century, the relationship between mission and culture was growing and developing within Roman Catholicism as well. The year 1919 saw the first of five 'Mission Encyclicals' written by Popes Benedict XV, Pius XI, Pius XII and John XXIII, all of which emphasized the importance of the education of indigenous clergy, thus implying the importance of the local church and local culture. In 1925 a large-scale exhibit of 'Mission Art' at the Vatican Museum had a far-reaching effect on attitudes towards local cultures in 'mission countries'. In the third of the encyclicals, Pius XII's *Evangelii Praecones*, what missiologist James Kroeger calls its 'greatest novelty' was the Pope's commendation of local customs and 'time-honored observances of pagan peoples'. As the Pope writes: 'The Church does not wish to eradicate any good tradition, artistic production or custom of any people. Its mission is to preserve, elevate and sanctify these things in the spirit of the Gospel.'[18]

The full maturation of this development was reached at the Second Vatican Council (1962-1965), certainly the most important event in Roman Catholicism, and perhaps the most important religious event in the twentieth century.[19] Already in the first document approved by the Council, its document on liturgy, there was included a substantial section on the adaptation of liturgical practices to various local cultures. Pius XII's words in *Evangelii Praecones* find echo in the document's insistence that the church 'respects and fosters the spiritual adornments and gifts of the various races and peoples. Anything in their way of life that is not indissolubly bound up with superstition and error, it studies with sympathy and, if possible, preserves intact'.[20] The Council's Constitution on the Church in the Modern World lays special emphasis on the importance of culture in the church's engagement with the contemporary world. Alluding to the fact that culture has always been important in the church's life and mission, the Constitution insists that culturally sensitive preaching 'ought to remain the law of all evangelization. For thus the ability to express Christ's message in its own way is developed in each nation, and at the same time there is fostered a living exchange between the Church and the

---

[18] See James Kroeger, 'Papal Mission Wisdom: Five Mission Encyclicals 1919-1959', in Stephen Bevans (ed), *A Century of Catholic Mission* (Oxford: Regnum, 2013), 93-100. The quotation from Pius XII is found on 97.

[19] See Robert J. Schreiter, 'The Impact of Vatican II', in Gregory Baum (ed), *The Twentieth Century* (Maryknoll, NY: Orbis Books, 1999), 158; John W. O'Malley, *What Happened at Vatican II* (Cambridge, MA: The Belknap Press at Harvard University Press, 2008), 1.

[20] Vatican Council II, Constitution on the Divine Liturgy, *Sacrosanctum Concilium*: www.vatican.va/archive/hist_councils/ii_vatican_council/documents/vat-ii_const_19631204_sacrosanctum-concilium_en.html, 37.

diverse cultures of people'.[21] In the second chapter of the second part of the document there appears for the first time in an official Roman Catholic document an extended reflection on the nature and importance of culture.[22]

The document on the church's mission is also distinguished by a rich and generous understanding of the importance of culture in the church's missionary work. The term 'culture' appears in the document no less than ten times, and while there is always the call to purify and heal the culture of the peoples among whom missionaries work, there is always the encouragement to respect and immerse themselves within that culture as well. In paragraph 9 we hear an echo of Pius XII's words of wisdom in this regard: 'Whatever truth and grace are to be found among the nations, as a sort of secret presence of God, this [missionary] activity frees from all taint of evil and restores to Christ its maker...'[23] As quoted in the introduction to this chapter, paragraph 11 calls missionaries to a 'sincere and patient dialogue' with culture. Paragraph 22 calls for what eventually will be called the inculturation of theology.[24]

### *Uppsala 1968 and the Emergence of the Lausanne Movement*

The 1968 Assembly in Uppsala, Sweden, held in the midst of the great cultural shifts of the 1960s with its optimistic humanism, the sexual revolution, and the widespread student protests in the United States and Europe in the spring of that year, resulted in an atmosphere of radical thinking and rebellion. Led by Dutch theologian Johannes Hoekendijk, cries were raised against the church and its missionary task in favour of a radical understanding of God's mission that bypassed the church and was worked out immediately in the world. In such an understanding, the church needed to get out of the way, or at most point to the work that God was doing in the world. God needs no help in 'articulating himself'.[25]

The reaction to Uppsala by the more conservative Evangelical members of the Assembly was quite strongly negative – so much so that they formed a new body in contrast to the WCC that was eventually called the Lausanne Movement for World Evangelization. Paragraph 10 of the *Lausanne*

---

[21] Vatican Council II, Constitution on the Church in the Modern World, *Gaudium et Spes*: www.vatican.va/archive/hist_councils/ii_vatican_council/documents/vat-ii_const_19651207_gaudium-et-spes_en.html, 44.

[22] *Gaudium et Spes*, 53-62.

[23] *Ad Gentes*, §9.

[24] *Ad Gentes*, §11, 22.

[25] Roger Bassham, *Mission Theology: 1948-1975. Years of Worldwide Creative Tension. Ecumenical, Evangelical, and Roman Catholic* (Pasadena, CA: William Carey Library, 1979), 81. See also James A. Scherer, *Gospel, Church, and Kingdom: Comparative Studies in World Mission Theology* (Minneapolis, MN: Augsburg, 1987), 119-21. Here I am following quite closely Bevans and Schroeder, *Constants in Context*, 290-91.

*Covenant*, the brief document that was the result of the movement's landmark International Congress on World Evangelization in 1974, deals with 'Evangelism and Culture'. Here the document notes the intrinsic connection between 'churches deeply rooted in Christ and closely related to their culture'. Because God created the world, some part of each culture is 'rich in beauty and goodness', but because women and men are fallen, every culture is 'tainted with sin and some of it is demonic'. This short paragraph recognizes that missionary work in the past has often exported western culture rather the gospel, but it charges missionaries today to 'seek to transform and enrich culture, all for the glory of God'.[26] In a significant article about gospel and culture in the Lausanne Movement, Tite Tiénou observes that after the Lausanne Conference, and especially after a significant consultation at Willowbank, Bermuda, in 1978, Evangelicals began publishing widely in the area of contextual theology.[27] Interestingly, however, the second International Congress for World Evangelization in Manila, Philippines, in its *Manila Manifesto* gives scant, if any, attention to the question of culture.[28]

### *Bangkok and Evangelii Nuntiandi*

The Bangkok CWME conference of 1973 is remembered more perhaps by its call for a 'moratorium' on foreign missions, but there was also a clear call for a theology and ministry that was deeply culturally aware and sensitive. 'Proper theology includes reflection on the experience of the Christian community in a particular place, at a particular time.'[29] One can see the influence here of the establishment at the WCC of the Fund for Theological Education (FTE), headed by the Taiwanese theologian Shoki Coe, who was in many ways the one who coined the phrase 'contextual theology'.[30]

The same year as the Lausanne Conference, 1974, saw a Vatican Synod of Bishops that addressed the issue of evangelization. This was in the light

---

[26] Lausanne Committee for World Evangelization, *The Lausanne Covenant,* 10, in James A. Scherer and Stephen B. Bevans (ed), *New Directions in Mission and Evangelization 1, Basic Statements 1974-1991* (Maryknoll, NY: Orbis Books, 1992), 255.

[27] Tite Tiénou, 'Gospel and Cultures in the Lausanne Movement', in Margunn Serigstad Dalle, Lars Dalle and Knud Jørgensen (ed), *The Lausanne Movement: A Range of Perspectives* (Oxford: Regnum, 2014), 156-69.

[28] Lausanne Committee for World Evangelization, the *Manila Manifesto*, in Scherer and Bevans (ed), *New Directions 1*, 292-305.

[29] *Bangkok Assembly 1973* (Geneva: WCC, 1973), 74, quoted in Ariarajah, *Gospel and Culture*, 29.

[30] Shoki Coe, 'Contextualizing Theology', in Gerald H. Anderson and Thomas F. Stransky (eds), *Mission Trends No. 3: Third World Theologies* (Grand Rapids, MI: Eerdmans, 1976), 19-24.

of deep questioning of the very concept of mission that arose from some of the openness to other religions and the world's cultures that was expressed at Vatican II. The Synod itself was unable to produce a final document, and so asked Pope Paul VI if he would draw their contentious discussions together in a document of his own. The result was, in 1975, the Apostolic Exhortation *Evangelii Nuntiandi*, a landmark document on mission that continued Vatican II's openness to the world's religions and cultures, and expressed this openness in a particularly powerful way. 'The split between gospel and culture,' Paul VI wrote, is no doubt 'the drama of our time', and so the church must view culture as an ally rather than as an enemy or as something neutral. 'What matters is to evangelize man's culture and cultures (not in a purely decorative way, as it were, by applying a thin veneer, but in a vital way, in depth and right to their very roots) …'[31]

### *Nairobi 1975 and Mission and Evangelism*

Two years after Bangkok and a year after *Evangelii Nuntiandi,* the WCC's fifth Assembly in Nairobi spoke powerfully to the fact that 'commitment to Jesus Christ takes different cultural forms. This is an expression of the church's catholicity'. Christians are to relate to culture 'critically, creatively, redemptively'.[32] Ariarajah suggests that the perspective at the Nairobi Assembly 'marks the culmination of a particular entry point into the gospel and culture debate'. In fact, subsequent mission congresses of the CWME have not gone much further in the discussion. The 1980 mission conference in Melbourne, Australia, and the 1983 Vancouver WCC Assembly basically 'point in the same general direction'. Such a direction Ariarajah sums up in six points: the importance of striking roots in culture; the rejection of the normativity of western culture; the importance of a culturally sensitive missionary work; the insistence on the ambiguity of culture and its need for gospel purification; the acknowledgement of culture as a dynamic reality; and the need for mutual learning from various cultures.[33]

The WCC's 1982 document on mission, *Mission and Evangelism: An Ecumenical Affirmation* – up until 2012 its only comprehensive statement on mission since the IMC's integration into the WCC in 1961 – has a short but significant statement on the 'inculturation of the gospel'. The document connects such a process of inculturation with the Incarnation, and insists that it is more than an intellectual enterprise, but one of participation in the life of the poor. As the document expresses it, *'Solidarity is the best*

[31] Paul VI, Apostolic Exhortation *Evangelii Nuntiandi* (*EN*): http://w2.vatican.va/content/paul-vi/en/apost_exhortations/documents/hf_p-vi_exh_19751208_evangelii-nuntiandi.html, 20.
[32] David M. Paton (ed), *Breaking Barriers. Nairobi 1975* (Geneva: WCC, 1976), 79, quoted in Ariarajah, *Gospel and Culture*, 33.
[33] Ariarajah, *Gospel and Culture*, 33-34.

*teacher of common cultural values'*. It also calls for a recognition of the plurality of cultures and their validity, concluding that 'the visions of the nations coming from the East, the West, the North and the South to sit at the final banquet of the kingdom should always be before us in our missionary endeavour'.[34]

At the beginning of the San Antonio mission conference in 1989, then-director of the CWME, Christopher Duraisingh, also connected the question of mission and culture with issues of justice, particularly justice for women. This conference had no particular section on the question of mission and culture, but recognized the mission/culture dynamic as a kind of 'transversal' that ran through the entire conference. While at one level this can be seen as an advance in the discussion of the relationship between mission/gospel and culture, at another, as the report of the CWME at the 1991 Canberra Assembly admitted, there had been no substantial progress in understanding this dynamic.[35]

### *Salvador de Bahia*

The last conference on world mission and evangelism of the twentieth century was held at Salvador de Bahia, Brazil, in 1996, and it specifically focused on 'The Gospel in Diverse Cultures'. The conference 'insisted on the richness of cultural variety as God's gift, but also on the gospel imperative to link the affirmation of one's cultural identity with an openness to other identities'. While recognizing the equality and dignity of all cultures, it also emphasized their ambiguity. 'In its relation with cultures, the gospel may be illuminated, but also obscured', and so mission needs both to be open to culture and to challenge it as well.[36]

### *Edinburgh 2010,* the Cape Town Commitment, *and Evangelii Gaudium*

A search of the proceedings of the Edinburgh 2010 Centennial Celebration reveals that the word 'culture' appears 169 times in various contexts and meanings. It appears in discussions of mission among other faiths, of mission and contemporary secular culture, in the context of today's multicultural world in which the gospel in preached. The theme of culture, however, was not one of the nine 'official' themes of the conference. It was rather, like women's issues, a 'transversal' that ran throughout all the themes. In a real sense, it seems, the issue of mission and culture at Edinburgh 2010 had reached a certain maturity that it pervaded all the discussions there, and was rather taken for granted. It is somewhat

---

[34] *Mission and Evangelism: An Ecumenical Affirmation*, 16-17.

[35] See Ariarajah, *Gospel and Culture*, 43-45.

[36] Conference on World Mission and Evangelism, Salvador de Bahia: www.mission2005.org/index23fc.html?id=564&L=&type=98

unfortunate, however, that the theme of culture is not mentioned in the conference's nine-point *Common Call*.[37]

Tite Tiénou admits that little attention was paid to the gospel/culture dynamic in mission in the second Lausanne Congress in 1989 or at Cape Town in 2010 (the Evangelicals' own commemoration of the 1910 Edinburgh Conference). However, he insists, the Lausanne Movement has been 'a major contributor to global and Evangelical conversations on the issue of Gospel and culture'. Tiénou says that the *Cape Town Commitment's* view of the importance of culture in the missionary enterprise can be summed up in one sentence in the text: 'We long to see the Gospel embodied and embedded in all cultures, redeeming them from within so that they may display the glory of God and the radiance of Christ.'[38]

Three weeks after the Tenth General Assembly of the WCC in Busan, South Korea, and the publication of *Together towards Life* (which will be discussed in detail below), the newly-elected Pope Francis issued his extraordinary Apostolic Exhortation, *Evangelii Gaudium*. The main emphasis of the document was to call the Roman Catholic Church to be a thoroughly missionary church, to be a church of 'missionary disciples' 'for the evangelization of the world rather than for its self-preservation'.[39] Culture, however, plays a significant part in this lengthy document. 'Grace supposes culture,' writes Pope Francis. 'In the Christian customs of an evangelized people, the Holy Spirit adorns the Church, showing it new aspects of revelation and giving it a new face.' He insists that 'we would not do justice to the logic of the incarnation if we thought of Christianity as monocultural and monotonous'. He speaks powerfully of the 'evangelizing power of popular piety', suggesting that it is a *locus theologicus*, a genuine source for theological reflection and pastoral action.[40]

The second section of this chapter will focus exclusively on *Together towards Life*, the 2012 mission statement of the CWME and the latest WCC statement on the relation of mission and culture.

## Together towards Life

*Together towards Life* (*TTL*)[41] is a significant landmark in the history of ecumenical missiology. It addresses most of the issues that have arisen in regard to church and mission since 1910 in a compact statement of 12,500

---

[37] See 'Edinburgh 2010 Common Call', in Kirsteen Kim and Andrew Anderson (eds), *Edinburgh 2010: Mission Today and Tomorrow* (Oxford: Regnum, 2011), 1-2.

[38] Tiénou, 'Gospel and Cultures', 169, quoting *The Cape Town Commitment: A Confession of Faith and a Call to Action* Part I, paragraph 7.

[39] *EG* 24, 27.

[40] See *EG* 115-118; 122-26.

[41] *TTL*.

words. In regard to the issue of culture, *TTL* is an important milestone. When we focus on the explicit usage of the term 'culture', there are two sections where culture receives extensive attention: first, the section entitled 'Local Congregations: New Initiatives' (§72-79) where the role of local congregations in creating intercultural and multicultural ministry is emphasized; and secondly, the section entitled 'Evangelism and Cultures' (§97-100) where the plurality of cultures is considered as the gift of the Spirit that enriches gospel. However, even when *TTL* does not use the term 'culture' explicitly, by using expressions such as context, world, life-worlds, realities, society, social location, social systems, community of humanity, or *oikoumene,* the issue of culture is treated throughout the entire text of *TTL* as a cross-cutting, transversal theme. Overall, *TTL* offers a very significant paradigm shift in mission's relation with culture by emphasizing these features.

### *Fullness of Life as the Criterion of Mission and Cultures*

The most significant characteristic of *TTL* is that it is founded upon an unmistakably clear theological emphasis on fullness of life as the Triune God's ultimate concern for the world. Life in its fullness functions as the single overarching principle that binds diverse considerations into a coherent whole (§102). The first paragraph of *TTL* makes it clear that God the Creator constantly works in the world to affirm and safeguard life, that affirming life in all its fullness is the ultimate concern of Jesus Christ who is the Life of the world, and that the Holy Spirit is the Life-giver who sustains and empowers life. Accordingly, denial of Life is a rejection of God of Life, and mission is bearing common witness to the vision of abundant life in God (§1). This distinctive theological stance makes *TTL* appealing to diverse Christian traditions in today's world by showing faithful adherence to the Trinitarian Christian tradition and by emphasizing the urgent responsibilities of the church to spread the gospel of Life through mission and evangelism.

A radical shift in the view of culture is also closely related with this theme of life. According to *TTL*, where there is affirmation of life, there is the presence of God. By applying this criterion of the fullness of life, various complicated debates in the past can be aligned around an easily recognizable and agreeable guideline. Through this guideline, *TTL* helps us deal discerningly with diverse controversial issues such as the evaluation of human culture in general, the assessment of specific cultures, and the church's appropriate responses to important cultural changes arising from the introduction of the concepts such as plurality, margins, globalization, and the shift of Christianity's centre of gravity.

## *A Positive View of Culture*

*TTL* sees culture in very positive light. This is made very clear in the following paragraphs: 'We value each and every human culture…' (§110); 'Respect all people and human cultures…' (§90-c). 'God's Spirit can be found in all cultures that affirm life' (§93). Among the 59 occurrences of word 'culture' in *TTL*, 48 of the cases are used with a positive connotation. This affirmative view of culture is a logical consequence of the aforementioned overarching theological theme of the fullness of life.

However, it is important to note that the positive view of culture is not to be taken categorically. There is considerable subtlety and discernment in *TTL*'s treatment of culture. While it regards human beings' cultural achievements as basically good, contributing to the affirmation of life, it takes a critical stance towards any tendency to value only one's own culture or civilization, which is considered as superior to others. It clearly condemns any tendency to see other cultures as uncivilized or untamed. Enforcement of uniformity is seen as life-denying because it discredits the uniqueness, liveliness and diversity of life (§99).

The long history of the negative view of culture in the church, as exemplified in the debates on gospel versus culture, is related to the naïve conviction that the gospel can be separated from culture. Without any awareness of the pluralist concept of culture or the need to affirm subaltern or marginal cultures, for many Christians it was not easy to recognize the heavy cultural imprint on their own perception of the gospel. Many missionary endeavours operated on the basis of the wrong presupposition that 'Western forms of Christianity are the standards by which others' adherence to the gospel should be judged' (§98). The new cultural awareness informing *TTL* opens up the possibility of acknowledging that God is present in all life-affirming cultures (§22, 27). Mission, then, is 'not to bring God along, but to witness to the God who is already there' (§94), in unfamiliar cultural settings.

## *From Cultural Uniformity to Appreciation of Diversity and Marginality in Cultures*

One of the significant contributions of *TTL*'s view of culture is its appreciation of cultures from diverse contexts, and particularly from the margins. To understand its innovative nature, we need to look back on the history of Christian mission. For many centuries, Christian mission operated on the basis of the geographical expansion of Christian civilization from the centre to the ends of the earth (§5). For many Christians, there was only one standard culture and all other cultures were a hindrance to understanding the gospel (§98) – Lonergan's 'classical' notion of culture. *TTL*'s new view of culture is formulated against the background of the acknowledgement of the church's mistakes and sincere repentance (§33).

The second background for this view of culture has to do with today's changing landscapes. There are many reasons why the old concept of cultural uniformity cannot work any more. *TTL* recognizes the following as crucial changes: increased multicultural interactions as a result of the globalization and the advance of communication technology (§9), the secularization of the global North, the shifting of the centre of gravity of Christianity to the global South and East (§106), large-scale worldwide multi-directional migration (§70), the emergence of many intercultural communities of faith (§100), and the widespread influence of the post-modernism.

The third background for this new view of culture is found in the insights and findings of Cultural Studies, particularly their positive evaluation of subaltern cultures as self-regulating sub-cultures with the potential for resisting and reshaping the dominant culture – Schreiter's 'global' understanding of culture. Such insights have transformed the way culture is understood in related fields. Even though *TTL* does not use sources from Cultural Studies directly, its new view of culture can be understood against the background of changes brought about by advances in Cultural Studies.

*TTL*'s emphasis on the concepts of diversity and margins in cultures signals an important paradigm shift in the history of Christian mission. Diversity is listed as one of four key concepts of mission today (§11). *TTL*'s high regard for diversity is clearly expressed in these passages: 'a plurality of cultures is a gift of the Spirit' because it deepens the understanding of our own faith and our understanding of others (§100); unity in the Holy Spirit is unity in diversity (§66); in the plurality and complexity of today's world 'we acknowledge that there is inherent value and wisdom in diverse life-giving spiritualities' (§93).

The two concepts of margins and diversity stand on the debris of the concepts of centre and uniformity of culture. 'Margins', which is similar to 'the poor and the oppressed' in Liberation Theology, is a broad term. It includes the estranged, the outcast, the untouchable, the sick, the vulnerable, the minority and the underprivileged. Living on the margins means exclusion from justice and dignity (§38). The voices of the margins have been denied by those who are at the centre. The traditional concept of mission was the expansion of the gospel from the centre to the margins. People on the margins were considered merely as the recipients of mission. *TTL* states that these roles are now reversed in mission (§6). The people on the margins have a special gift to discern what is life-affirming and what is life-destroying through their experiences (§107). The cultures of the margins are reservoirs of hope, perseverance, solidarity and collective resistance against evil (§38). Marginalized people 'are agents of mission and exercise a prophetic role which emphasizes that fullness of life is for all' (§107). Through this paradigm shift we come closer to the image of authentic mission shown in Jesus who embraces and befriends those who are most marginalized in society (§37).

### *Mission as Counter-Cultural Resistance*

Even though *TTL* views cultures in a positive light, such a view is not unconditional. *TTL* is aware of the problems caused by life-denying cultures influenced by evil spirits, the forces of death (§102). Christian mission is called to discern and confront such cultures. In today's world, there are many forms of life-denying cultures: the idol worship in the global free-market economy which promises it will save the world through unlimited economic growth and the accumulation of undue wealth (§7, 108); all forms of discrimination through unjust social structures or stereotypes; any forces that promote falsehood, injustice, oppression (§91); excessive greed and unlimited consumption; and the worship of mammon. Often times, life-denying cultures deceive by presenting themselves as good news. So, Christian mission should develop keen discernment with the help of experts in diverse fields and through the wisdom and insights from the margins. The church needs to reaffirm that the gospel is liberative and transformative (§91).

Transformative mission should resist life-denying cultures which keep expanding their influence over the world. In this sense, mission is counter-cultural resistance against the dominant life-denying cultures (§108). In modern times, fighting against evil is similar to being engaged in a culture war. When evil possesses immense power like the Roman Empire, there will be persecutions and martyrdoms. In any situation, the church ought to remember that authentic mission is faithfully following the example of Christ by carrying the cross and emptying oneself (§92).

*TTL*'s view of culture, distilled in these four characteristics, addresses many difficult issues expressed in the discussions on culture by diverse mission organizations. *TTL*'s view of culture reflects up-to-date scholarship in related fields. *TTL*'s assessment of the changing landscapes of today's world is well substantiated. *TTL* will, surely, become a new ground upon which any further discussions on mission-culture relationships should rely.

*TTL* is a like a still photo-shot taken from a lengthy video which shows the history of ecumenical missiology. It is taken at a timely moment and aesthetically reflects the images of the important moments from the past to the present time. What are prominent in those images are: the goodness of culture, appreciation of the diversity and marginality of culture, and recognition of the power of evil in the world requiring mission to be counter-cultural resistance. All these are embraced by the principle of fullness of life. We live in a changing (not changed) world. We don't know what kind of unheardof challenges (something like extra-terrestrial intelligence?) awaits us in the future. In due time, we will again have to search for the opportune moment and for the best angle to record the scene.

In the meantime, *TTL* will serve as a hermeneutical horizon within which diverse meaningful vistas can be opened up under the overarching principle of the fullness of life.

## Conclusion: The Hopes and Challenges of the Future

In an oft-printed and oft-cited essay, Andrew Walls speaks about a double movement in terms of Christianity and culture, a movement that 'has its origin in the Gospel itself'. On the one hand, there is what Walls calls the 'indigenizing principle' that recognizes that God in Christ takes people where they are and who they are, 'with our group relations; with that social conditioning that makes us feel at home in one part of human society and less at home in another'. On the other hand, however, Walls speaks of 'the pilgrim principle'. Not only does God take people where they are; God takes them to transform them into the people God wants them to be.[42]

One can see this dynamic moving through the whole history of mission, from Paul's struggle and adaptation with Athenian culture in Acts 17, through Justin's discovery of 'seeds of the Word' in Hellenistic philosophy, through Celtic and Benedictine monasticism's preservation of cultural artefacts, to Cyril and Methodius, Matteo Ricci, Samuel Crowther and Henry Venn. This past century in particular has highlighted this dynamic, as is seen from this chapter's account of it in ecumenical conversation since 1910.

What might the future bring? One would hope for greater strides in local expressions of Christianity, from ways to celebrate liturgy to ways of training for ministry and organizing the structure of the church to articulations of theology.

One would hope, as *TTL* implicitly acknowledges, that a greater consciousness of the changing understanding of culture as being more connected with power dynamics in particular situations, especially in terms of marginalized peoples. In this regard, one challenge would be to think more in terms of 'context' – personal and social experiences, social locations, changing and impinging global realities – as well as in terms of culture as such.

One would hope also for a continued search for connecting dialogue with other religious ways, so often inextricably connected with culture, and local cultures themselves.

One would hope, too, for a greater dialogue *among* the Conciliar, Roman Catholic and Evangelical churches. The challenge here is to move away from our denominational silos and begin working together for greater partnership in imagining and bringing about a truly inculturated

---

[42] Andrew F. Walls, 'The Gospel as Prisoner and Liberator of Culture', in Walls, *The Missionary Movement in Christian History* (Maryknoll, NY: Orbis Books, 1996), 7-9.

Christianity. One small step in this regard has been taken in the final number of the *International Review of Mission* for 2015, which attempts to reflect on *Evangelii Gaudium* in dialogue with *TTL* and the *Cape Town Commitment*.[43]

In addition, one could hope that the church would rise to the challenge today of becoming truly *intercultural* in the way it lives its internal community life (*ad intra*) and the way it witnesses to and preaches the gospel (*ad extra*). Interculturality involves a mutually critical interaction between one culture and another, or among various cultures and contexts in a multicultural community or missionary situation.[44]

A final hope, and perhaps the greatest challenge, would be for the churches to engage together in a critical yet open dialogue with secular cultures, particularly those in the West and Australasia. If, to answer Lesslie Newbigin's haunting question positively, the West is to be converted, it will be done as a result of a critically appreciative dialogue with the genuine values and rightful critique of Christianity that secularism articulates.[45]

'Grace supposes culture.' Pope Francis gives us an important watchword for our missionary activity, one that is in itself a resounding and formidable challenge.

---

[43] *International Review of Mission*, 104.2 (2015).

[44] In this regard, see Roger Schroeder, 'Interculturality and Prophetic Dialogue', in *Verbum SVD,* 54, 1 (2013), 8-21; Lazar T. Stanislaus and Martin Üffing (ed), *Intercultural Living* (Vol. I) and *Intercultural Mission* (Vol. II) (Sankt Augustin, Germany: Steyler Missionswissenschaftliches Institut, 2015).

[45] Lesslie Newbigin, 'Can the West Be Converted?: www.newbigin.net/assets/pdf/85cwbc.pdf

# OTHER FAITHS

## Peniel Rajkumar

### Introduction

Since the onset of the modern ecumenical movement – now identified with the 1910 Edinburgh World Missionary Conference (WMC)[1] – very few questions have as critically captured the attention of mission studies as the question of 'other faiths'. Starting with John R. Mott's memorable watchword, which set the scene for Edinburgh 1910, 'the evangelization of the world in this generation', to the affirmation that 'dialogue and (interreligious) co-operation for life are integral to mission and evangelism' by the recent ecumenical affirmation on mission and evangelism produced by the World Council of Churches,[2] mission has often been conceived vis-à-vis other faiths, albeit in diverse ways.[3]

Despite its polyvalence, the narrative surrounding mission and the question of other faiths since Edinburgh 1910 has yielded lessons worth rehearsing and revisiting today. This chapter resorts to such rehearsing and revisiting as a way of providing a critical cartography (mapping) of the complex and polysemic (multi-layered) relationship between mission and other faiths which can foster and foreground future discourses on 'mission and other faiths' in a fruitful manner.

The mapping of 'mission and other faiths' in modern ecumenical history is one which can be charted in terms of quests and the questions they provoke(d). Multiple theological quests have sought to make sense of mission vis-à-vis other faiths and out of the interstitial spaces of this interface have emerged many questions which help us to better comprehend the complex intersection of mission and other faiths. A cartography of the relationship between mission and other faiths that focuses on these quests and questions has the potential to capture both the indicative (what mission vis-à-vis other faith is/has been) as well as the imperative (what mission vis-à-vis other faiths ought to be) dimensions of mission.

---

[1] Stephen Neill, *A History of Christian Missions* (Grand Rapids, MI: Eerdmans, 1964), 554.

[2] *TTL,* §110.

[3] Popular Christian perceptions of people of other faiths across mission history have included understanding the other as 'an enemy of God', 'as potential convert', 'as primitive superstition', 'an unfulfilled seeker', 'a storehouse of culture', 'companion in struggle' and 'as a partner in dialogue'. See M. Thomas Thangaraj, 'Religious Pluralism, Dialogue and Asian Christian Responses', in Sebastian C.H. Kim (ed), *Christian Theology in Asia* (Cambridge: CUP, 2008), 157-78, at 159-62.

## Mission and Other Faiths: A (hi)story of Quests and the Questions They Provoke(d)

Several important quests have been made in modern mission history to engage with the question of other faiths.

### *Mission* over *Dialogue (Edinburgh 1910)*

Though much has been mentioned about the Edinburgh 1910 WMC's preoccupation with the 'evangelisation of the world in this generation' and the emphasis on 'missionary expansionism', less attention has been given to the ground-breaking work of Commission IV of the conference which worked on the theme 'Missionary Message in Relation to Non-Christian Religions' employing a global questionnaire.[4] Its report, based on the 187 responses received to the questionnaire, was widely hailed at the 1910 conference as 'perhaps the greatest theological achievement of the conference'.[5] Thoroughly unanticipated and completely overwhelming, the responses received posed 'a fundamental challenge to some of the unexamined assumptions and presuppositions about other religious traditions which underpinned the Missionary Conference'.[6] The 'then dominant Anglo-American fulfilment theology of religions – that non-Christian religions were *praeparatio evangelica*' which formed the leitmotif of the Commission's questionnaire and report, was debunked as being neither 'monolithic nor unchallenged' across the world.[7]

---

[4] Assuming that the Commission's findings would benefit from experiential evidence from the mission fields, Commission IV embarked on a sound and novel methodology of soliciting responses to important questions concerning Christian relationships with other faiths from local missionaries across the world, employing a questionnaire which was specifically prepared for the purposes of the conference. For a detailed treatment of the work of Commission IV, see chapter 8 of Brian Stanley's *The World Missionary Conference, Edinburgh 1910* (Grand Rapids, MI: Eerdmans, 2009). Wesley Ariarajah says: "The questions requested information on number of points about Christian relationships with other religious traditions: What are the doctrines and observances in other faiths that seem to give genuine help and consolation to devotees in their religious life? What are the chief moral, intellectual and social hindrances to their responding to Christianity? What are the points at which people of other religious traditions are dissatisfied with their own religious communities and faith? What are possible points of contact between the Gospel message and religious life of others?" See S. Wesley Ariarajah, 'Interreligious Dialogue and Mission in Protestant Theology', in *Modern Believing,* 51.3 (2010), 38-47, at 39-42.

[5] Peter Phan, 'The World Missionary Conference, Edinburgh 1910: Challenges for Church and Theology in the 21st Century, in *International Bulletin of Missionary Research,* 34.2 (April 1910), 105-08, at 107.

[6] Ariarajah, 'Interreligious Dialogue and Mission', 40.

[7] Phan, 'The World Missionary Conference', 107.

Commission IV ushered in certain significant shifts in missiological thinking concerning other faiths. These included: a) taking other religious traditions 'with the theological seriousness they deserved' without treating them as 'primitive', 'preparatory', 'naturalistic', 'or 'devoid of revelation';[8] b) unanimously commending 'an attitude of openness and humility towards non-Christian religions'[9] and adopting an attitude of 'listening to and learning from the other faiths with a view of grasping their "meaning" for their believers';[10] and c) seeking to understand the doctrinal formulations of other religious traditions, and the spiritual search behind those formulations, instead of dismissing them on the grounds of their incompatibility and inconsistency with the gospel message.[11] Ironically, despite its theological value, the report of Commission IV had little impact on the overall report of the Edinburgh conference and was overridden by the explicit support for John Mott's vision of world evangelisation.[12] One cannot but wonder what the shape of mission would have been had Edinburgh 1910 embraced the voices and visions reflected in these responses to Commission IV's questionnaires.

### *Mission* or *Dialogue* *(Tambaram 1938, Nairobi 1975 and Chiang Mai 1977)*

The thinking about mission vis-à-vis other faiths provoked by Commission IV of the Edinburgh 1910 conference resurfaced in the second World Mission Conference in Jerusalem in 1928 which in its message 'articulated an appreciative apprehension' of the truth of other religions as not being discontinuous with the Truth in Christianity.[13] This was followed by the Hocking Commission's report on 'Rethinking Missions' which proposed that 'the relation between religions must take increasingly hereafter the form of a common search for truth'.[14] Alarmed by such liberalism, the

---

[8] Ariarajah, 'Interreligious Dialogue and Mission', 41.

[9] Phan, 'The World Missionary Conference', 107.

[10] Ariarajah, 'Interreligious Dialogue and Mission', 41

[11] The overall contributions of Commission IV of Edinburgh 1910 are of salutary value. According to Ariarajah: 'The Commission IV at the Missionary Conference of Edinburgh 1910 was bold enough to think in a radically different way about peoples of other religious traditions. This was made possible because they did their theology on the basis of the reflections of those who were in real dialogue with religions and cultures at the local level. A century later, we are yet to pick up their baton of courage or to harvest the full benefits of their radical re-thinking': Ariarajah, 'Interreligious Dialogue and Mission', 47.

[12] Unfortunately, the original idea of publishing the 187 responses in their entirety had to be reluctantly cancelled in 1911: Phan, 'The World Missionary Conference', 106. See also Ariarajah, 'Interreligious Dialogue and Mission', 42.

[13] Diana L. Eck, 'The Religions and Tambaram: 1938 and 1988', in *International Review of Mission,* 77.307 (July 1988), 375-89, at 379.

[14] W.E. Hocking, *Rethinking Missions* (New York: Harper & Brothers, 1932), 47.

debate on mission and other faiths was reborn in a remarkably exclusive manner in the third conference of the International Missionary Council held at Tambaram, India, in 1938.[15] Dutch missiologist Hendrik Kraemer's complex preparatory document *The Christian Message in a Non-Christian World,* while advocating a positive attitude towards other religions, emphasised the radical discontinuity of the gospel with all religions on grounds of 'biblical realism' – something which met with stiff opposition at the conference.[16]

Kraemer outlined the danger of compromising the Christian message in trying to relate to other religions.[17] Thereby, Tambaram brought to the surface a tension between mission and dialogue which has ever since remained a prominent and persistent topic in theological discourses. As Stanley Samartha, the first Director of the WCC's Sub-Unit on Dialogue puts it, 'Underlying the challenge of Tambaram is the difficult but important question of the relation between mission and dialogue in a religiously plural world.'[18] One only needs to read the chapter on 'Dialogue or Mission: Can the Tension be Solved?' in Ariarajah's book *Not Without My Neighbour* to realise that this tension between Mission and Dialogue has ever since been the stuff of 'ecu-lore'.

The tension that Tambaram evoked resurged dramatically in the 'dialogue controversy' at the Nairobi Assembly in 1975. When the WCC's Sub-Unit on Dialogue with People of Other Faiths and Ideologies presented the report of its working group on 'Seeking Community with People of Other Faiths and Ideologies', it met with accusations of betrayal of Christian mission founded on 'the three classical fears' of the missionary movement: 'syncretism', 'compromising the uniqueness of Christ' and 'loss of urgency of mission'.[19] Samartha says that an important issue Nairobi raised for 'careful theological reflection' was: 'Does dialogue blunt

---

[15] Gerald Anderson, 'The Theology of the Christian Mission at Edinburgh and Succeeding World Conferences', abstract of a PhD dissertation submitted to Boston University, 1960; Metropolitan Coorilos Geevarghese, 'Towards and Beyond Edinburgh 2010: A Historical Survey of Ecumenical Missiological Developments since 1910', in *International Review of Mission,* 99.390 (April 2010), 6-19, at 8.

[16] See Daryl Balia and Kirsteen Kim (eds), *Edinburgh 2010,Witnessing to Christ Today* (Vol. II), chapter on Theme Two: Christian Mission Among Other Faiths, 34-60, at 36.

[17] Mark Heim, 'Mission and Dialogue: 50 Years after Tambaram', in *The Christian Century,* 105.11 (6th April 1988), 340-43, at 340.

[18] Stanley J. Samartha, 'Mission in a Religiously Plural World: Looking Beyond Tambaram 1938', in *International Review of Mission*, 77.307 (July 1988), 311-24, at 311.

[19] Wesley Ariarajah, *Not Without My Neighbour: Issues in Interfaith Dialogue* (Geneva: WCC, 1999), 102.

the cutting edge of mission? Is it a substitute for proclamation? What is the relation between dialogue, witness and mission?'[20]

Of the various quests to overcome the difficulties caused by the 'mission or dialogue' debate, the theological consultation on 'Dialogue in Community' held in Chiang Mai in April 1977 remains a landmark – not least for 'the wide degree of agreement and mutual understanding' that the consultation statement achieved.[21] Its major points include the rejection of dialogue 'as a secret weapon in the armoury of an aggressive Christian militancy', but rather adopting it as 'a means of living out our faith in Christ in service of community with our neighbours'.[22] Significant is its recognition of the necessity of 'the spirit of dialogue' in giving witness which enabled the participants to 'not see dialogue and the giving of witness as standing in contradiction to one another'. [23] The statement further affirmed:

> Indeed, as we enter dialogue with our commitment to Jesus Christ, time and again the relationship of dialogue gives opportunity for authentic witness. Thus, to the member-churches of the WCC we feel able with integrity to commend the way of dialogue as one in which Jesus Christ can be confessed in the world today; at the same time we feel able with integrity to assure our partners in dialogue that we come not as manipulators but as genuine fellow-pilgrims, to speak with them of what we believe God to have done in Jesus Christ who has gone before us, but who now seek to meet anew in dialogue.[24]

This remarkably fresh theological approach to mission and dialogue was later adapted to form the theological basis of the *Guidelines on Dialogue with People of Living Faiths and Ideologies* which was adopted at the 1979 Kingston meeting of the Central Committee of the WCC. But to say that Chiang Mai completely resolved the tension between Mission and Dialogue would be far-fetched. The tension continued in remarkable ways![25]

---

[20] Stanley J. Samartha, 'Guidelines on Dialogue', in *The Ecumenical Review,* 31.2 (April 1979), 155-62, at 156.

[21] Minutes of the WCC Central Committee held in Geneva 1977, 26.

[22] *Dialogue in Community: Statement and Reports of a Theological Consultation, Chiang Mai, Thailand, 18-27 April 1977* (Geneva: WCC, 1977), 16.

[23] *Dialogue in Community,* 18.

[24] *Dialogue in Community*, 18.

[25] At the commemoration of the fifty years since the Tambaram conference, held in Tambaram in 1988, one of the participants, Mark Heim, said:

A look back at Tambaram 1938 cannot solve the tension between mission and dialogue any more than the meeting fifty years later could clearly point the way towards its future resolution. Yet the participants in Tambaram 1988 may have played some part in broadening the discussion of that tension, and in helping the church to understand that mission and dialogue are parts of one issue, not two isolated and alternate or opposing special interests': Heim, 'Mission and Dialogue', 343.

### *Mission* as *Dialogue:*[26] *Vatican II and Beyond*

A discussion on the relation of mission with other faiths would be incomplete without considering the Second Vatican Council's 'Declaration on the Relation of the Church to Non-Christians' – *Nostra Aetate* (*NA*) – proclaimed by his Holiness Pope Paul VI on 28th October 1965.[27]

In many ways, *NA* is an important signpost of the transition of Christian attitudes towards non-Christians in modern mission history. Recognised as a watershed document in inter-faith relations, *NA* has been considered to be 'a conversion to the "providential mystery of otherness" for the life of the church, and as a call to extend and deepen that conversion'.[28] Among the several commendable achievements of *NA* are its positive affirmation of other religions as providing 'answer to the unsolved riddles of human existence' and reflecting a 'ray of that Truth [*radius veritatis*] which enlightens all men (sic)'. [29] Frequently quoted among its affirmations is its declaration that 'the Catholic Church rejects nothing [*nihil reicit*] which is true and holy in these religions'.[30] It is important to note that the theological advancements of *NA* had to be taken into account in the shaping of *Ad Gentes,* the mission declaration that emerged out of Vatican II which clearly emphasised: 'Before the missionary begins his work by witness and preaching, the Holy Spirit, the giver of life, is already active.'[31]

This affirmation questioned the very rationale for missionary activity – 'why bring the good news to a place where it already exists?'[32] The fruit of

---

[26] The 1984 document on 'The Attitude of the Church Towards the Followers of Other Religions: Reflections and Orientations on Dialogue and Mission', produced by the Pontifical Council for Interreligious Dialogue, asserted that Mission includes 'the dialogue in which Christians meet the followers of other religious traditions in order to walk together toward truth and to work together in projects of common concern': paragraph 13. For a full text of the document, visit: www.shinmeizan.com/en/documents/72-2-pontifical-council-for-interreligious-dialogue. See the brief section on 'Mission as Dialogue' in 'Appendix 1 – Theme One: Foundations for Mission', in Emma Wildwood and Peniel Rajkumar (eds), *Foundations for Mission,* Regnum Edinburgh Centenary Series (Oxford: Regnum, 2013), 279.

[27] For a full text of this brief document see: www.vatican.va/archive/hist_councils/ii_vatican_council/documents/vat-ii_decl_19651028_nostra-aetate_en.html

[28] Mary C. Boys, SNJM, 'What *Nostra Aetate* Inaugurated: A Conversion To The 'Providential Mystery of Otherness', in *Theological Studies,* 74 (2013), 73-104, 73.

[29] *Nostra Aetate,* §2, in Austin Flannery (ed), *Vatican Council II: The Concilliar and Post Concilliar Documents* (revised edition) (Collegeville, MN: Liturgical, 1984).

[30] *Nostra Aetate*, §2.

[31] Cited in Kristin M. Colberg, 'The Omnipresence of Grace: Revisiting the Relationship between *Ad Gentes* and *Nostra Aetate* 50 Years Later', in *Missiology: An International Review,* 42.2 (2014), 181-94, at 187.

[32] Vatican II's reflections on other religions had radical implications for mission. As Kristin M. Colberg says: 'Vatican II's assertion that God's grace precedes the presence of missionaries and that it can have a salvific effect apart from any explicit

such an unsettling development however was the realisation of the need for a 'dynamic and renewed view of mission'.[33] It was agreed that 'the council's affirmation of the Christian experience of divine grace as abundant and dynamic does not exclude a strong account of missionary outreach, but demands it'.[34] Thus in many ways Vatican II challenged Christians to articulate mission by acknowledging the intrinsic value of other faiths and in creative fidelity to the gospel of Christ.

*Nostra Aetate,* which was, in the words of Cardinal Bea, 'an important and promising beginning',[35] triggered a renewed interest within the Roman Catholic Church in connecting Mission with Dialogue – especially among the Asian churches which affirmed dialogue as 'the way of being Church in Asia', 'the method for doing theology in Asia', and 'the mode of the Church's mission'.[36] The Federation of Asian Bishop's Conference

---

proclamation of God's word gave the impression that what had been perhaps the most forceful argument in favour of explicit missionary activity was no longer valid. If God's inexhaustible love cannot be frustrated, then why engage in the difficult and often misinterpreted task of travelling across the globe to bring the good news to a place where it already exists?' Colberg, 'The Omnipresence of Grace', 189-90.

[33] Colberg, 'The Omnipresence of Grace', 190.

[34] Colberg, 'The Omnipresence of Grace', 190.

[35] Cardinal Bea was the President of the then Secretariat (now Pontifical Council) for Promoting Christian Unity and was instrumental in the production of *Nostra Aetate*; J. Oesterreicher, 'The Declaration on Non-Christian Religions', in Vorgrimmler (ed), *Commentary on the Documents of Vatican II,* Vol. III (New York: Herder & Herder, 1968), 1-154, at 130, cited in Colberg, 'The Omnipresence of Grace', 185.

[36] Edmund Kee-Fook Chia, 'Mission as Dialogue: An Asian Roman Catholic Perspective', in Ogbu U. Kalu, Peter Vethanayagamony and Edmund Kee-Fook Chia (eds), Mission After Christendom: Emergent Themes in Contemporary Mission (Louisville, KY: Westminster John Knox Press, 2010), 144 -54, at 147. The Federation of Asian Bishops' Conference which emerged in 1972 following Vatican II identified four modes of interreligious dialogue, namely:

- The dialogue of life – which involves informal, ongoing sharing of life and friendship in day-to-day life;
- The dialogue of collaborative action – which fosters collaboration in the defence and promotion of justice, peace and ecological wholeness;
- The dialogue of theological reflection – which involves enrichment by and a deeper understanding of the beliefs and practices of other religions; and
- The dialogue of spiritual experience – which brings people together at a deeper level to both share their specific spiritual traditions and practices with each other and share in common spiritual experiences.

For more, see Peter C. Phan, 'Christian Social Spirituality: A Global Perspective', in Philomena Cullen, Bernhard Hoose and Gerard Mannion (eds), *Catholic Social Justice: Theological and Practical Explorations* (London: T. & T. Clark, 2007), 18-40, at 32; Michael Amalados, 'Dialogue', in R.S. Sugirtharajah and Virginia Fabella

(FABC) born post-Vatican II in 1972 understood dialogue as 'Triple Dialogue' – i.e. dialogue with Asian religions, Asian cultures and Asia's poor.[37] Triple dialogue, as an integral process involving inculturation, interreligious dialogue, and integral liberation, was seen as enabling the Asian church to address the issues of Asia's poverty and Asia's multi-religiosity under the evangelising mission of the church in Asia.[38]

Several critical questions have overflowed from the many quests to make sense of mission vis-à-vis other faiths. Since these questions continue to water the fertile ground of missional imagination and missiological thinking even today, it would be important to review them.

### Questions of Pneumatology and Christology

One of the popular ways in which Christian ecumenical discourses have affirmed the validity of the religious experience and traditions of other religions is by taking recourse to the language of the presence and activity of the Spirit in other religions.[39] The WCC's *Guidelines on Dialogue with People of Living Faiths and Ideologies* (1979) raises the question: 'Is it right and helpful to understand the work of God outside the Church in terms of the Holy Spirit?' The Baar statement on 'Theological Perspectives on Plurality' produced by the WCC's Programme on Interreligious Dialogue and Co-operation in January 1990 declared: 'We affirm unequivocally that God the Holy Spirit has been at work in the life and

---

(eds), *Dictionary of Third World Theologies* (Maryknoll, NY: Orbis Books, 2002), 111-14.

[37] Virginia Fabella, 'The Roman Catholic Church in the Asian Ecumenical Movement', in Ninan Koshy (ed), *A History of the Ecumenical Movement in Asia,* Vol. II (Hong Kong: World Student Christian Federation, Asia Pacific Alliance of YMCAs and Christian Conference of Asia), 116.

[38] Roman Catholic missiologist Edmund Chia explains 'triple dialogue' as follows: 'In the context of Asia, inculturation is brought about, first of all through the dialogue with Asia's poor, in view of facilitating their integral liberation. Second, because the other religions have their own views of what liberation and salvation mean and because the majority of Asia's poor owe their allegiance to these other religions, the process of inculturation, which entails the church's dialogue with the poor, must also include dialogue with the religions. In short, inculturation, interreligious dialogue, and the process of integral liberation are mutually involving ministries, all of which are integral to the evangelising mission of the church in Asia'; Edmund Chia, 'Wanted: Interreligious Dialogue', in *Studies in Interreligious Dialogue,* 12.1 (2002), 101-10, cited in Chia, 'Mission as Dialogue', 148.

[39] Of course, not always have Christians agreed upon the presence of divine activity in other faiths. One needs to remember the 1983 WCC Vancouver Assembly's rejection of the use of the phrase 'God's creative hand in the life of people of other faiths' in its report on 'Witness in a Divided World'.

traditions of peoples of living faiths.'[40] This contrasts with the tone of *Mission and Evangelism in Unity Today,* the preparatory paper for the 2005 CWME conference held in Athens, which seeks to clearly avoid the 'temptation to separate the presence of God or the Spirit, from the Son of God, Jesus Christ'.[41] *Together towards Life,* while acknowledging that God's Spirit... 'can be found in all cultures that affirm life', goes on to say that 'we do not fully understand the workings of the Spirit in other faith traditions'.[42]

There is an inherent dilemma in all these discourses on discerning the Spirit in other religions. This is brought out perceptively by the Pentecostal Asian American theologian Amos Yong as follows:

> If we discern the Spirit using Christian (e.g. biblical) criteria, we end up either 'christianizing' the other insofar as we find the Spirit to be present, or 'demonizing' the other insofar as we find the Spirit absent. In the former case, we appear to have allied ourselves with Rahner's idea of 'anonymous Christianity', and thus opened ourselves up to all the difficult counter-questions generated by such a position, not the least of which is that we have imposed our own categories on religious others who are distinct from ourselves and have their own self-understandings. In the latter case, not only have we arrived at theologically charged rhetoric liable to be abused socially and politically, but we have also done so by declaring religious others void of certain goods and values as determined by criteria external to them.[43]

---

[40] See Section IV: 'The Holy Spirit and Religious Plurality' of the Barr Statement: Theological Perspectives on Plurality (Statement of a theological consultation held in Barr, Zurich, Switzerland, in January 1990, organised by the WCC's Programme on Interreligious Dialogue and Co-operation as part of preparations for the Canberra Assembly. The Barr statement says:

Everything which belongs to 'love, joy, peace, patience, kindness, goodness, faithfulness, gentleness, self-control' is properly to be recognised and acknowledged as the fruit of the activity of the Holy Spirit. (Gal. 5.22-23, cf. Rom. 14.17).

We are clear, therefore, that a positive answer must be given to the question raised in the Guidelines on Dialogue (1979): 'Is it right and helpful to understand the work of God outside the Church in terms of the Holy Spirit?' (para 23).

[41] The WCC's Commission on World Mission and Evangelism's 2005 conference held in Athens offered four criteria as a way of discerning the signs of the Spirit. They are ecclesial (that which confesses Jesus as Lord), personal and life-changing (that in which there is evidence of the fruit of the Spirit), charismatic (that which empowers the practising of the gifts of the Spirit with love), and ethical (that which identifies with the poor). See Kirsteen Kim, 'Come, Holy Spirit: Who? Why? How? So What?' in Jacques Matthey (ed), *Come Holy Spirit, Heal and Reconcile!* Report of the WCC Conference on World Mission and Evangelism, Athens, Greece, May 2005 (Geneva: WCC, 2008), 155ff.

[42] *TTL,* §93.

[43] Amos Yong, 'The Holy Spirit and the World Religions: On the Christian Discernment of Spirit(s) 'after' Buddhism', in *Buddhist-Christian Studies,* 24.1 (2004), 191-207, at 192.

Yong poses a stiff challenge to all those who attempt to accord validity to other religious traditions employing a Christian pneumatological framework. The validity and integrity of our theological claims to respect other religions stands or falls vis-à-vis our position in relation to the dilemma Yong raises.

The salvific significance of Christ in our relationships with other faiths has also been a persistent and perennial question.[44] As the San Antonio mission conference of 1989 aptly captured it: 'We cannot point to any other way of salvation than Jesus Christ; at the same time we cannot set limits to the saving power of God. There is a tension between these affirmations which we acknowledge and cannot resolve.'[45]

The attempts of John Hick[46] and Stanley J. Samartha to resolve this tension through a theocentric shift need attention. In his *The Rainbow of Faiths,* Hick argued:

> ... in order to make sense of the idea that 'the great world religions are all inspired and made salvific by the same transcendent influence, we have to go beyond the historical figure of Jesus to a universal source of all salvific transformation. Christians may call it the cosmic Christ or the eternal Logos; Hindus and Buddhists may call it the Dharma; Muslims may call it Allah; Taoists may call it the Tao; and so on. But what we then have is no longer (to put it paradoxically) an exclusively Christian inclusivism, but a plurality of mutually inclusive inclusivisms...[47]

[44] Two important meetings which dealt with this issue are:

a) The Zurich Consultation of the WCC held in May 1970 to evaluate an earlier interreligious meeting held in Ajaltoun, Lebanon, in March 1970 to consider the theme 'Dialogue between Men (sic) of Other Faiths – Present Discussions and Future Possibilities'. The consultation was of the view that mission is concerned 'with discovering Christ where he already is holding all things together, with making Christ known so that men (sic) may consciously receive and share in his work of moving all things to their fulfilment in his kingdom, the Kingdom of love, and with receiving Christ as he makes himself known to us through his activity in, and through followers of, other faiths and commitments': 'Christians in Dialogue with Men of Other Faiths', in *International Review of Mission,* 59.236 (October 1970), 382-91, at 385.

b) A Mission/Dialogue Consultation of the WCC held 26th-29th January 1988 in Mahabalipuram, India, on the theme 'Christian Witness in a Pluralistic World', which dealt at considerable length with the theme of 'Christology and Salvation in the Mission of God'. For a report on this consultation, see Jean Stromberg, 'Christian Witness in a Pluralistic World: Report on a Mission/Dialogue Consultation', in *International Review of Mission,* 77.307 (July 1988), 412-36.

[45] San Antonio, Section 1 report, paras 26 and 29.

[46] John Hick's Copernican Revolution in Christian theology of religions ushered in through his 1973 book *God and the Universe of Faiths* (Macmillan) argued that the recognition of the religious values of other religions required a theocentric shift.

[47] Hick argued for leaving aside the historical figure of Jesus of Nazareth in favour of 'a non-historical, or supra-historical, Christ figure or Logos'... effectively 'a name for the worldwide and history-long presence and impact upon human life of

Similarly, embracing the Hindu idea of Mystery – as an 'ontological basis for tolerance' – Samartha too argued for a theocentric Christology to emphasise both the distinctiveness of Christian mission as well to foster interreligious relationships:

> No one could have anticipated in advance the presence of God in the life and death of Jesus of Nazareth. There is an incomprehensible dimension to it. That Jesus is the Christ of God is a confession of faith by the Christian community. It is indeed normative to Christians everywhere, but to make it 'absolutely singular' and to maintain that the meaning of the mystery is disclosed only in one particular person at one particular point, and nowhere else, is to ignore one's neighbours of other faiths, who have other points of reference. To make exclusive claims for our particular tradition is not the best way to love our neighbours as ourselves.[48]

Samartha revises his Christology as a means through which 'the particularity and distinctiveness of Christian mission' can be restated in a way 'that co-operation with neighbours of other faiths for common purposes in society is not seen as a betrayal of mission but as the context in which the Christian witness to God's saving work in Jesus Christ becomes transparently clear'.[49]

Other notable attempts to reconcile the issue of 'salvation only through Christ' with 'respecting the integrity of other faiths' are Mark Heim's idea of many salvations, in which he argues that that one cannot talk of salvation in the singular but 'salvations' in the plural, given the intrinsic difference in religious understandings of salvation,[50] and Ariarajah's proposal for a 'composite Christology' for a 'holistic vision of salvation'.[51] The recent

---

the Divine, the Transcendent, the Ultimate, the Real': John Hick, *The Rainbow of Faiths* (London: SCM, 1995), 22-23.

[48] Stanley Samartha, 'The Cross and the Rainbow', in John Hick and Paul F. Knitter (eds), *The Myth of Christian Uniqueness* (London: SCM, 1987), 75-76.

[49] Stanley Samartha, *One Christ Many Religions: Towards a Revised Christology*, 3rd Indian edition, 171.

[50] Mark Heim, *Salvations: Truth and Difference in Religion* (Maryknoll, NY: Orbis Books, 1995).

[51] Wesley Ariarajah, *Your God, My God, Our God: Rethinking Christian Theology for Religious Plurality* (Geneva: WCC, 2012), 144. Arguing how 'we cannot arrive at a theology of religions that takes the experience of the peoples of other religious traditions seriously without radically reinterpreting the traditional Christian notions of salvation and the role of the cross in it', Ariarajah says: "My own sense is that we need a new 'composite Christology' that envisions a 'holistic salvation' understood at the personal, social and all other dimensions of human life. In doing so, it should hold together Jesus the teacher, healer, life-giver, the one who initiated the reign of God, and the one who mediates our life in God. This Christology could include some of the new dynamic understandings of what the death of Jesus on the cross and faith in resurrection can mean in our day. We also need to place this Christology-soteriology in the context of all other witnesses to God's saving work in the world, and God's overall mission of healing God's creation. We can, as

document on Christian Self-Understanding produced by the WCC's programme on Interreligious Dialogue and Co-operation responds to the Christological question in a persuasive way: 'We see Christ as a specific saving gift to all creation, not a replacement for or denial of God's presence and power through many other means.'[52] Pneumatology and Christology will be two issues that will push mission theology to widen the horizons of its imaginations critically and creatively so that our witness to the hope that is within us in a pluralistic world is both compassionately Christian and passionately interreligious. This demands theological integrity and interreligious sensitivity.

### Mission and the Question of Culture

In contexts where religions and culture are intimately intertwined, mission has to contend with the issue of the clash of cultures where mission is accused of cultural erosion through the superimposition of a set of cultural values foreign to local cultures. Triumphalism has doubtlessly caused great cultural damage – especially where colonialism employed Christianity to aid its economic and political agendas through the myth of Christian superiority and moral co-option. However, an indiscriminate and wholesale affirmation or romanticising of local/native culture can be morally dubious because of the ambiguity of culture itself. The historical connections between mission, colonialism and culture are complex.[53]

Perhaps one of the points in the ecumenical movement when this conflict between Christianity and culture surfaced as a missiological issue was in the WCC's CWME conference held in Salvador de Bahia, Brazil, in 1996. The conference recognised that there are 'life-denying and oppressive elements in cultures which reject fundamental values of human relationships' (I.3). Therefore the conference was critical and cautious about concepts such as inculturation which were thus far seen as bringing mission into closer contact with religions and cultures. Dr Musimbi R.A. Kanyaro from Kenya called upon the churches to 'move beyond a theology of inculturation and to put culture itself under scrutiny, in order to determine whether it promotes justice, life, peace and liberation, or whether it diminishes and dehumanizes people'.[54]

---

Christians, affirm without any hesitation that we have such a large vision and hope for the world because of our belief that 'God was in Christ' reconciling the world unto Godself and has called us to become Christ's disciples to participate in this work": Ariarajah, *Your God, My God, Our God*, 145.

[52] 'Who Do We Say That We Are? Christian Identity in a Multi-Religious World', in *The Ecumenical Review,* 66.4 (December 2014), 458-501, at 475.

[53] See Philip Jenkins, 'Imperial Missionaries?' in *Christian Century,* 26th November 2014, 45.

[54] Cited in Jacques Matthey, 'Salvador Among the World Mission Conferences of this Century', in *International Review of Mission,* 86.340/341, 19-26, at 20-21.

Revisiting the question of mission and local cultures today would entail being perceptive about how power is embedded between and within cultures, and evaluating culture from the perspectives of the margins – i.e. the ones oppressed by culture.[55] We need to be critical about politically expedient worldviews, which in the name of not offending the religio-cultural sensibilities of some religious and cultural elite, offer tacit complicity to internal injustices inherent in cultures. Mission and dialogue discourses should feel free to denounce religiously validated cultural practices like for example casteism and Zionism without the guilt of religious supremacy, and make the perspectives of the marginalised and oppressed the touchstone for evaluating culture.[56] Probably the biggest

---

[55] The complex intersection of mission, colonialism and culture is brought out in a study entitled 'Mission At and From the Margins: Patterns, Protagonists and Perspectives', undertaken under the auspices of the Centenary Celebrations of the Edinburgh 1910 conference. The study points out how mission provided the space for the Dalit (formerly 'untouchable') communities to resist the 'internal colonialism' of the caste system which is an integral part of the Hindu religion. The study says: "… Dalit entanglements with missionaries are much more complex than patron-client or colonizer-colonized relationships. The conditions created by mission were seen as a liberative-transformative space by Dalit communities for self-assertion and reclamation of their place in society rather than as components of the colonizing process. Dalit communities, which had no stake in local power, viewed those in their own country who had power as 'colonizers'. For them, the conversion experience of which they were the primary agents helped in their quest for freedom from oppression. In this, the conditions of mission played and continue to play the role of midwife": Joseph Prabhakar Dayam and Peniel Jesudason Rufus Rajkumar, 'Mission At and From the Margins: Patterns, Protagonists and Perspectives – A Critical and Constructive Contribution to the Edinburgh 2010 Conference', in Peniel Jesudason Rufus Rajkumar, Joseph Prabhakar Dayam and I.P. Asheervadham (eds), *Mission At and From the Margins: Patterns, Protagonists and Perspectives* (Oxford: Regnum, 2014), 3-9, at 8.
Despite all the problems associated with colonialism and the ideals of the enlightenment, the discourses of the anti-caste social reformers Jyothiba Phule and B.R. Ambedkar (who were in many ways very critical of colonialism) help us to understand how, in the context of caste-based Brahmanical colonialism, 'British colonialism inadvertently made available certain normative and cognitive tools with which to fight Brahmanical colonialism', and, using the enlightenment-based ideal of civil society, 'aimed to reconstitute intra-human and human-divine relationships on a higher level of egalitarianism'. See Mahesh Gavaskar, 'Colonialism within Colonialism: Phule's Critique of Brahmin Power', in S.M. Michael (ed), *Dalits in Modern India: Vision and Values*, 2nd edition (New Delhi: Sage Publications), 91-107, at 92.

[56] Dialogue which indiscriminately embraces the religion and culture of the other faces the danger of being counter-intuitive to the purposes of the marginalized. Ariarajah recounts his encounter with an Indian bishop who denounced the credibility of the dialogue programme of the WCC on the grounds that WCC's partners in Hindu-Christian dialogue were oppressors of the Dalits (who were previously known as 'untouchables'). For the bishop being in dialogue with

question for both mission and dialogue in today's context where religions and cultures are being exposed for their oppression and marginalization is whether they can be counter-culturally reshaped as solidarity with the margins in contexts where cultures can be dominant and oppressive.[57]

## Mission and the Question of Conversions

One of the crucial questions in the debates relating to mission and dialogue has been the questions of religious conversions. An indication of its importance was the publication of 'Christian Witness in a Multi-Religious World: Recommendations for Conduct', jointly produced by the Pontifical Council for Christian Unity (PCID), WCC's Programme on Interreligious Dialogue and Co-operation (WCC-IRDC) and the World Evangelical Alliance (WEA) which sought to engage the issue. There are two issues which merit attention:

First, there is need for a more robust political understanding of conversions, especially in contexts of majoritarian religious assertion like India where the rhetoric of conversion is often employed to intimidate minorities and curtail the religious freedom of the marginalised to validate the opinion that the 'most pervasive legal threat faced by Indian Christians today' is 'the aspersion that they are either victims or perpetrators of forced or fraudulent religious conversions'.[58]

---

dominant-caste Hindus 'would be to compromise; it would amount to a tacit approval of the caste system by the Christian partners'. More importantly, it would amount to 'a lack of concern for and solidarity with the oppressed community'. S. Wesley Ariarajah, *Not Without My Neighbour* (Geneva: WCC, 1991), 80.

[57] Shanta Premawardhana, former Director of the Interreligious Dialogue and Co-operation programme of the WCC, suggests that, in a context where there is a growing recognition of the nexus between dominance, power and religion, 'our partners in dialogue are not necessarily those religious leaders who are a part of the exploitative structures, but those who suffer from exploitation': Shantha Premawardhana, 'The Strange Exorcist', in *Masihi Sevak: Journal of Christian Ministry,* 34.2 (August 2009), 61-70, at 63.

[58] Nandini Chatterjee, *The Making of Indian Secularism: Empire, Law and Christianity, 1830-1960* (New York: Palgrave Macmillan, 2011), 242. The Global Anglicanism Project Report (Episcopal Church Foundation, 2005) gives us a comprehensive picture of how the language of conversion can be used against Christianity:

The North Indian states of Gujarat (2003) and, more recently, Rajasthan (2005) have passed anti-conversion laws prohibiting conversion through force, fraud or allurement. While most people, including Christians, readily condemn such methods, application of the law by conservative 'Hindutva groups' can be broad. In one case, non-Christian students who failed an examination in a Christian school alleged they were failed because they refused to become Christian. Even basic expressions of Christian faith can be defined as coercive, regardless of how they were uttered: *The Vitality and Promise of Being Anglican, The Global Anglicanism Project* (Episcopal Church Foundation, 2005), 23.

Second is the issue of the agency and autonomy of those who choose to convert (especially those concerning historically marginalised communities). More often than not, implicit in the mission and dialogue discourses on conversion is a tacit tendency to be dismissive about the capacity of marginalised people to make religious choices. Marginalised people are rendered as 'objects' of mission – as those who are susceptible to monetary and materialistic inducements. A good indication of this pejorative attitude in mission discourses is the colonial epithet 'rice-Christians' used for Dalit converts in India.[59] These discourses insinuate an elitist view of freewill and autonomy through their essentialising of the marginalised as 'incapable of distinguishing motives and inexperienced in the exercise of their own judgement'.[60] Such views constitute social Darwinism as they solely target the marginalised. Today there is a need to move away from such understandings of conversion which blur the lines between consent, co-option and coercion, and between freedom, force and fraud.

The challenge for proponents of mission and dialogue is to carry out their respective agendas – of affirming proclamation and avoiding proselytism – employing an epistemology which does not denigrate the marginalised as merely 'objects' of their agenda and understands conversion within a wider intersection of religious freedom, human dignity, economic and political interests, and social privilege and power. Both *Christian Witness in a Multi-Religious World* and *Together towards Life* make reference to religious freedom and human dignity when discussing the issue of conversions.

## Mission and Multiple-Religious Affiliations

One important question that the present context of religious plurality poses for mission concerns the shape of mission in a context where people claim multiple religious affiliations. Multiple religious belonging or multiple religious participation is now explicitly being acknowledged as a valid religious identity and a viable mode of being religious today. Two recent conferences on the theme 'Exploring Hybridity, Embracing Hospitality' organised by the WCC's Programme on Interreligious Dialogue and Co-operation in Chennai (October 2014) and Cleveland (April 2015) served to highlight the point that Multiple Religious Belonging as a phenomenon and practice is not a concern of academic theology alone or the by-product of post-modern supermarket spiritualities but a real phenomenon in mainline

---

[59] Missionaries in colonial South India cast aspersions on the conversion motives of Dalits who were considered 'out-castes' (and were previously known as 'untouchables') and denied them baptism on the grounds that their conversions were motivated by reasons of food and livelihood.

[60] Gauri Viswanathan, 'Literacy and Conversion in the Discourse of Hindu Nationalism', in *Race and Class,* 42.1 (2000), 4.

churches which prevails in plural forms. In the Cleveland meeting, clergy in mainline Christian denominations who simultaneously embraced practices of another faith, faith practitioners who were always nurtured in two faiths as a result of being born from interreligious marriages, and ordinary people for whom living between and within two religious /spiritual traditions was just the norm, all testified to the ability of a person to participate in more than one religious tradition.

Multiple religious belonging poses unprecedented challenges for traditional understandings of mission because the boundary between the Christian self and the non-Christian 'other' no longer exists. There is need for a paradigmatic shift in conceiving of mission. What this phenomenon of multiple religious belonging enables mission to see is the relative redundancy of earlier models of 'doing' mission as now the context and conditions of doing mission are radically altered. The agent of mission is no longer 'purely' Christian. Therefore does it still make sense to talk of Christian foundations for mission?

One question ahead of us is whether this is a 'crisis' or *krisis* (opportunity) of new foundations for mission. Multiple religious belonging forces a revisiting of traditional understandings of Christian commitment, salvation, in a changed context. In a context where there are possibilities for 'inclusi-vising' mission – by not pitting 'me' against the 'other' – one of the ways mission can be conceived is probably as a response to the pastoral challenges that multiple-belongers face within structures which refuse to acknowledge the possibility that faith and believing can be hybridised and hyphenated.

## (In) Conclusion

According to the noted missiologist Lamin Sanneh, 'For all of us pluralism can be a rock of stumbling but for God it is the cornerstone of universal design.'[61] This chapter sought to portray how the (hi)story of Christian mission vis-à-vis other faiths within the modern ecumenical movement has involved, on the one hand, ensuring that mission does not stumble in the face of religious plurality, and on the other hand, seriously taking up the challenge of building a world of justice, peace, healing and reconciliation on this cornerstone of God. There are several other issues that could have been discussed on the theme 'mission and other faiths'. This chapter, though furnishing only the most representative issues that have defined the debate between mission and dialogue in (in)decisive ways, has nevertheless sought to view the debate in an intersectional manner, bringing in the matrices of culture, politics and colonialism (to name a few) – all of which impinge upon missiological thinking today. It is with the hope that this

---

[61] Lamin Sanneh, *Translating the Message: The Missionary Impact on Culture* (Maryknoll, NY: Orbis Books, 1989), 29.

intersectional analysis will open up concomitant issues for discernment, debate and dissent in changing mission contexts that the incompleteness of this chapter is embraced. In its incompleteness it testifies that the (hi)story of missions may not be just about the unresolved questions of the past, or the changing contexts of the present but also the unknown opportunities of the future. The challenge is to traverse this unknown future as pilgrims – steadfast in our faith, sustained by a common hope and serving each other selflessly through love.

# FORMATION

## Martin W.H. Robra

### Formation for Life-Affirming Mission and Transformative Action

Formation for life-affirming mission and transformative action is the task that follows from the statement of the Commission on World Mission and Evangelism (CWME): *Together towards Life: Mission and Evangelism in Changing Landscapes* (*TTL*).[1] Theological education, ministerial and lay formation, continuing ecumenical formation, theological education by extension (TEE) and various other terms – they all point to particular dimensions and methods of the broader process of equipping people for their life and witness as Christians. Going beyond a more narrow understanding of training or education, the term 'formation' refers here 'to the whole process of equipping, enabling, raising awareness, shaping or transforming attitudes and values'.[2] It corresponds to education as lifelong learning 'enabling people to lead a responsible and mature life in which conflicting experiences can be integrated and relationships with those who are different can be established' rather than 'education as the process through which people are introduced in the traditions and norms of a given community'.[3] The *Joint Working Group between the Roman Catholic Church and the World Council of Churches* underlined in 1993: 'Ecumenical Formation is an essential part of the process of building community in the one household of God.'[4]

The *TTL* document does not explicitly refer to theological education and formation itself, but it provides theological foundations for reflections on formation for life-affirming mission. Some vital impulses for this essential dimension of the life of the churches are being presented in the *Practical*

---

[1] Jooseop Keum (ed), *Together towards Life: Mission and Evangelism in Changing Landscapes – with a Practical Guide* (Geneva: WCC, 2013).

[2] Konrad Raiser, 'Fifty Years of Ecumenical Formation: Where Are We? Where Are We Going?' in *The Ecumenical Review,* 48.4 (1996), 440-56, at 440 – the term *formation* is used in this sense ecumenically since the 1965 Gazzada statement on laity formation.

[3] Raiser, 'Fifty Years', 445.

[4] Joint Working Group between the Roman Catholic Church and the WCC, *Ecumenical Formation: Ecumenical Reflections and Suggestions,* in Joint Working Group between the Roman Catholic Church and the WCC, *Seventh Report* (Geneva/Rome: WCC/PCPCU, 1998), 53-59; also *The Ecumenical Review,* 45.4 (1993), 490-94, para 16.

*Guide* that accompanies the statement, focusing on four of its central themes:

1. Spirit of Mission: Breath of Life, which involves the 'formation of leaders gifted with discernment' (*TTL* §35) and ready to 'empty themselves of their privileges for the sake of the disempowered (*TTL* §33). Through the gift of the Holy Spirit they embrace *metanoia* (repentance) as a process of transformation'.[5]
2. Spirit of Liberation: Mission from the Margins, which requires 'genuine liberation' (*TTL* §100) as 'an indispensable gift of the Spirit that must embrace all creation'; 'good missional leadership creates, space, invites and empowers others to come in and express their gifts' (*TTL* §47).[6]
3. Spirit of Community: Church on the Move, which calls in response to the impact of globalization and migration 'for intercultural missional formation of leaders' (*TTL* §§75-76), and requires 'new guidelines to facilitate authentic engagement in evangelism' (*TTL* §90);[7]
4. Spirit of Pentecost: Good News for All, which inspires 'transformative missional formation' recognizing 'that the *missio Dei,* being in mission, is greater than loyalty to denominational and local identities' – 'identity is a gift from God, which needs to be celebrated and explored, resulting in what is life-giving to all'; leadership formation needs 'to ensure that outreach and proclamation are evangelism and not proselytism.'[8]

The emphasis on the Holy Spirit opens the horizon beyond humanity towards God's creation and the life-giving power of God's redemptive and transformative love, realizing already in the here and now signs of God's reign to come. Mission as participation in *missio Dei* begins at the margins among marginalized and subaltern communities and opens the space for mutual empowerment, life-affirming action and the sharing of the Good News of God's gift of life in Christ. The value of diverse contexts is affirmed, together with the need for inter-contextual and inter-cultural dialogue and co-operation also with people of other faiths in the transformative dynamic towards the promise of life in its fullness.

## The Changing Context of World Christianity and the Journey from Edinburgh 1910 Onwards

The *Practical Guide* points to a number of major challenges to theological education and formation in view of the changing global and ecclesial

---

[5] *TTL*, 51.
[6] *TTL*, 51
[7] *TTL*, 64
[8] *TTL*, 71-72.

landscapes and the existing power asymmetries and inequalities that still reflect to a large extent the colonial and neo-colonial past. Formation is thus described as process of transformation of loyalties and identities towards a new community of life in the Holy Spirit.

The *TTL* statement and the practical guide build on:

- the account of the history of ecumenical education and formation,
- analysis of contemporary challenges in the different regions and globally,
- contextual reflections on the role of education and formation in Christian mission, and
- some very concrete proposals for action that are the results of the preparatory study process to the Edinburgh 2010 Centenary of the 1910 World Missionary Conference, the event itself and the follow-up in research and publications.[9]

The document is informed by the changing context of world Christianity:

- from the colonial period, the time of the two world wars, processes of de-colonisation, nation-building and continuing neo-colonial oppression to post-colonial realities marked by the impact of the globalization of markets and media, and the migration of millions of people leading to growing diversity,
- the shift of the centre of gravity of world Christianity towards the South and the East, together with the growth of Pentecostal, Neo-Pentecostal, Charismatic and African Independent Churches,

---

[9] See especially the Regnum Edinburgh Centenary Series volume on theological education and formation; Stephen Bevans, Teresa Chai, Nelson Jennings, Knud Joergensen and Dietrich Werner (eds), *Reflecting on and Equipping for Christian Mission* (Oxford: Regnum, 2015). The *Report of Study Group VI on Theological Education and Formation* was published in Daryl M. Balia and Kirsteen Kim (eds), *Witnessing to Christ Today,* Edinburgh 2010, Volume II (Oxford: Regnum, 2010), 148-74. The WCC Ecumenical Theological Education (ETE) programme published a series of handbooks on theological education in world Christianity with Regnum and a global study report: Dietrich Werner, David Esterline, Namsoon Kang, Joshva Raja (eds), *Handbook of Theological Education in World Christianity: Theological Perspectives, Ecumenical Trends, Regional Surveys* (Oxford: Regnum, 2010); see also the series of handbooks on Africa (with Isabel Phiri), Asia (with Hope Antone, Hyjun Bae, Wati Longchar and Huang Po Ho), Orthodox Theological Education and Ecumenism (with Pantelis Kalaitzidis, Cyril Hovorun, Aikaterina Pekrido and Tom Fitzgerald), and Dietrich Werner and Namsoon Kang, 'Global Study Report of the WCC on the Future of Theological Education in World Christianity', in Melisande Lorke and Dietrich Werner (eds), *Ecumenical Visions for the 21st Century: A Reader for Theological Education, Supplemental Readings* (Geneva: WCC, 2013), 115-76. Some of these and many other important resources of the process can be accessed at: https://www.oikoumene.org/en/resources/documents/wcc-programmes/education-and-ecumenical-formation/ete/edinburgh-2010-study-group (accessed 1st August 2015).

- the rise of new voices from post-colonial, gender, ecological, ecumenical, interreligious, and other perspectives, and
- a new geo-political landscape with competing poles of economic, political and military power, new alliances (such as BRICS – Brazil, Russia, India, China, South Africa), and new forms of violence and war involving new actors.[10]

This body of work presents a striking continuity of power imbalances with the tendency to impose generalized frameworks that are reflecting the situation in Europe and North America. This refers for instance to the concept of secularization, the dominance of the economy over all other dimensions of life, and heavily institutionalized forms of education that require important financial resources, etc. In contrast, motivating stories of contextualized vital and inspiring forms of education were shared that are deeply rooted in the lives and spirituality of all God's people and sensitive to the voices and contributions of the poor and marginalized.[11] This refers for instance to the emergence of TEE – 'Theological Education by Extension',[12] now often read as 'Transformative Equipping and Education' or 'Tools to Equip and Empower'.[13] The Edinburgh 2010 process helped to bridge the gap between educators, scholars and leaders with Evangelical, Pentecostal and Charismatic self-understanding and identity, and those from Orthodox, Roman Catholic, Anglican and diverse Protestant traditions.

Kenneth R. Ross demonstrates in his analysis of the texts of the two commissions of the 1910 Edinburgh Missionary World Conference concerned with education and formation (Commissions III and V)[14] that, in certain contrast to the prevailing vision of a Christianized planet, some perspectives anticipating future developments surfaced:

> From the distance of 100 years the flaws of Edinburgh 1910 are all too apparent. Yet its prescience and prophetic qualities also come into view. Its passion for forms of education which would serve the emergence of truly indigenous forms of Christianity proved to have great resonance through the 20th century. Theologically, the Conference anticipated the concentration on such themes as inculturation and contextualization that would be key to maturity for the 'younger churches'. Its insistence that such a process of

---

[10] Cf. Martin Robra, 'The Ecumenical Movement in the Context of World Christianity in the 21st Century', in Lorke and Werner, *Ecumenical Visions*, 7-15.

[11] Cf. for instance, Ross Kinsler (ed), *Diversified Theological Education: Equipping All God's People* (Pasadena, CA: WCIU Press, 2008).

[12] See Ross Kinsler (ed), *Ministry by the People: Theological Education by Extension* (Geneva: WCC / Maryknoll, NY: Orbis Books, 1983.

[13] Graham Aylett and Tim Green, 'Theological Education as a Tool for Twenty-First Century Mission', in Chai et al, *Reflecting on and Equipping for Christian Mission,* 56-71.

[14] Kenneth R. Ross, 'Perspectives on Education and Formation from the World Missionary Conference, Edinburgh 1910', in Bevans et al, *Reflecting on and Equipping for Christian Mission,* 21-33.

indigenization would necessarily be led by indigenous leaders and its consequent prioritization of the formation of such leaders proved to be of far-reaching significance.[15]

## The Theological Education Fund

The implementation of ideas and recommendations of Edinburgh 1910 was blocked by World War I. Little changed in regard to theological education organized in the framework of the four classical disciplines of biblical, historical, systematic and practical theology, with ethics subsumed in systematic theology and the education of missionaries referred to special seminaries or just left to itself. Against this background, participants in the 1938 World Missionary Conference in Tambaram, India, stated: 'The worst element in all initiatives in Christian mission is theological education.'[16] It was at Tambaram that representatives of the so-called 'Younger Churches' became for the first time the majority at a World Missionary Conference. The participants called for a listening and dialogical approach to mission with an emphasis on the local church and the theological education required for it. They re-stated Edinburgh 1910 recommendations, for instance the use of vernacular languages rather than the colonial languages in theological education.[17]

But again, the next World War interrupted the follow-up to the conference. It took another twenty years until the Theological Education Fund of the International Missionary Council (IMC) was established at the IMC Assembly in 1958 in Accra, Ghana. After the integration of the IMC into the WCC in 1961, the fund continued to operate from London where it was based.[18]

The three decisive marks of TEF's work were:

- quality, combining intellectual rigour, spiritual maturity and commitment,

---

[15] Ross, 'Perspectives on Education and Formation, 35.

[16] Cf. Ofelia Ortega, 'Contextuality and Community', in *International Review of Mission*, 98.388 (2009), 25-36, at 25, quoting Petros Vassiliadis, 'The Need for Change in Theological Education: Presidential Address. The IV Congress of the World Conference of Associations of Theological Institutions (WOCATI), 31st May-7th June 2008', Thessaloniki, 1.

[17] Mark Laing, 'Recovering Missiological Ecclesiology in Theological Education', in Ebenezer D. Dazan and Frampton F. Fox (eds), *Missiological Education: Theological Integration and Contextual Implications* (New Delhi: Centre for Mission Studies, 2009), 41-72, at 52-53.

[18] For this and the following see John S. Pobee, 'Education', in Nicholas Lossky et al (eds), *Dictionary of the Ecumenical Movement*, 2nd edition (Geneva: WCC, 2002), 384-89. A key educational initiative of the WCC is the Ecumenical Institute, Château de Bossey, that was already established in 1946. Bossey has been a laboratory of ecumenical learning and contributed significantly to reflections on ecumenical learning and education in the WCC – see Raiser, 'Fifty Years',

- authenticity, involving critical encounter with each cultural context in the design, purpose and shape of theological education, and
- creativity, understood as promoting new approaches of the churches obedience in mission.

The fund chose the following points of emphasis for different periods:

1958-1965: support for indigenous and interdenominational places and institutions for theological education in the global South;

1965-1970: development of new curricula for churches of the global South and new teaching materials written by theologians from the South;

1970-1977: critique of western concepts of theological education and the call for contextualization of both forms of ministry and forms of theological education in the South.

Desmond Tutu served TEF in the early seventies as Africa director at the time when Shoki Coe introduced the concept of contextualization to the broader discussion. TEF co-operated within the WCC with the Office of Education which was set up in 1969 following a call of the Uppsala Assembly.[19] The office included sub-sections on adult education, theological education and church education, and a fund for education among children and adults. The office worked with the understanding of education as lifelong learning and teaching as a two-way process. Paulo Freire, author of the *Pedagogy of the Oppressed,* worked with the office on the adult education desk. He strengthened the influence of Liberation Theology in the WCC: the poor are to be subjects of their own history and literacy/education is a process of liberation in action and reflection.

With a new mandate, in 1977 the TEF became the Programme on Theological Education (PTE). The PTE was to give attention to:

- the influence of context and culture in theology and ministerial formation,
- the need to liberate theological education and ministerial formation and practices from bondages which hamper faithfulness in their life and witness,
- cross-cultural discussion of key aspects of theological education, and
- the integration of gender concerns.

The 1983 Vancouver Assembly underlined that education is constitutive of the church and that Christian education as a whole

- transcends barriers
- is action-oriented
- is done in community

---

[19] In 1971 the World Council on Christian Education also joined the WCC; and in 1972 the World Collaboration Committee for Christian Lay Centres, Academies and Movements for Social Concern was established (known since 1997 as *oikosnet*).

- means learning together (detecting the local in the global and the unfamiliar)
- is inter-cultural
- is a total process – social and religious learning are not separated from each other but constitute a unity.[20]

PTE translated this vision into action as a global network, with funding available for capacity-building and in close co-operation with the WCC scholarship programme. PTE developed with contributions of gifted leaders such as Samuel Amirtham, John Pobee and Ofelia Ortega. The continuity of the emphasis on learning in community, contextualized education and processes of intercontextual exchange, and the need for intercultural and interreligious co-operation, is obvious. PTE continued to operate within the CWME with its commitment to mission. PTE's points of emphasis reflected the understanding of mission promoted by the 1973 Bangkok World Mission Conference.

In parallel, the process of regional and global networking among Evangelical educators and institutions of education for mission and evangelism intensified. Important regional associations developed from the 1960s onwards. The Theological Assistance Program (TAP) of the World Evangelical Alliance (WEA) was formed in 1968 and became the WEA Theological Commission.[21] Like PTE, TAP promoted Theological Education by Extension (TEE) and assisted in faculty development and the publication of teaching material. Supported by the Theological Commission, the International Council of Accrediting Associations, now the International Council for Evangelical Theological Education, was created in 1980, fostering dialogue and co-operation at the international level.

The foundation of the Society for Pentecostal Studies in 1970 as an academic network which is also involved in bilateral theological dialogues was a first step at the international level in the world of Pentecostal and Charismatic churches.[22] Representatives of regional associations that were formed in the meantime took the initiative for a World Alliance for Pentecostal Theological Education (WAPTE) in 2008 in Singapore. WAPTE was endorsed by the Pentecostal World Fellowship in 2009.[23]

---

[20] Ulrich Becker, 'Ecumenical Learning', in Nicholas Lossky et al (eds), *Dictionary of the Ecumenical Movement*, 379-80.

[21] www.worldevangelicals.org/tc/about.htm (accessed 1st August 2015).

[22] http://storage.cloversites.com/societyforpentecostalstudies/documents/history.pdf (accessed 1st August 2015).

[23] http://wapte.org/about/history (accessed 1st August 2015).

## New Horizons for Theological Education and Formation – from the 1990s to 2013

The changing ecclesial landscape and the shift of the centre of gravity of world Christianity, together with the challenges of inter-faith dialogue and co-operation, began to impose themselves increasingly on the ecumenical agenda during the 1990s. Both the Ecumenical Institute at Bossey and the Programme on Ecumenical Theological Education (ETE), as it was now called, began to address these challenges systematically. To overcome separations and competitive relationships of the past, pro-active steps were taken by both sides to forge new links between ecumenical and Evangelical and Pentecostal scholars, theological networks and communities. Among those engaged in bridge-building was the Oxford Centre for Mission Studies which was founded in 1983. Fruitful exchange intensified and participation broadened after the 1998 WCC Assembly in Harare. The emerging Global Christian Forum started to function as a platform for the building of trust, exchange and shared reflections for all Christian traditions, churches and communities.[24]

The preparatory process for the Edinburgh Centennial contributed significantly to intensive research and discussion on ecumenical formation and theological education in world Christianity with the involvement of all relevant actors concerned.[25] The 'Report of parallel session on theological education – Edinburgh 2010' summarized the results of the discussion during the conference.[26] The report lists the following as 'most important challenges for reshaping and strengthening theological and missionary training':

a. Disparity in the availability of resources for theological education between the North and the South and within several regions;
b. The tremendous rise in the number of higher education students in the South in General, and the rise in applications for theological study programmes in particular;
c. The growing interest of Pentecostal churches in theological education programmes;
d. The urgent needs prevailing in many contexts to create more space for women in
e. theological education, theological leadership and in the ministries of the church;

[24] Huibert van Beek (ed), *Revisioning Christian Unity. The Global Christian Forum* (Oxford: Regnum, 2009).
[25] See footnote 9 above.
[26] https://www.oikoumene.org/en/resources/documents/wcc-programmes/education-and-ecumenical-formation/ete/edinburgh-2010-study-group/report-on-edinburgh-2010-session-on-the-future-of-theological-edcuation-in-the-21st-century (accessed 1st August 2015).

f. The lack of common quality standards and mutual recognition between theological schools of different contexts, denominational background and theological orientation;
g. Denominational fragmentation of the international landscape of theological education institutions;
h. The grave lack of scholarships and grants available for higher studies in theological education and the increasing difficulties of churches in funding their institutions of theological education;
i. Changing structural conditions of theological education (the move in some contexts away from church-related seminaries towards state-funded departments of religious studies);
j. The fundamental implications of global migration movements, and changing and increasingly diverse constituencies for programmes of theological education.

The report underlined concern for the education of children who represent 30% of world Christianity (para 8). It called for interdisciplinary and holistic methodologies overcoming compartmentalization, integrating academic learning, spirituality and education for ministerial service, contextualizing teaching materials, and strengthening gender-sensitivity and the inclusion of marginalized and subaltern communities (para 9). Affirming the value and 'strategic role of non-formal and non-residential forms of theological training', the report advocated a better 'balance between formal and non-formal, residential and non-residential forms of theological education' (para 10).

Common concerns included:

- the central role of the Bible as the Word of God in theological education, and the need for a 'new hermeneutic of the work of the Holy Spirit' (para 11),
- the role of the ecumenical and global dimensions and the task of reclaiming 'the public space for theology and for Christian witness by facing the burning issues of today's society' (para 12),
- the necessity of 'bridging the gap between theory and practice' inspired also by different 'models of theological learning and teaching' with some of them having an even longer history (para 13),
- the creative tension between the common basis of theological education in the Scriptures and Christian traditions, and the need for contextualization (para 14),
- creation of new spaces for inter-contextual exchange of resources, teaching staff, students, teaching materials, etc. – for instance, through a 'worldwide Online Network among theological educators of diverse theological traditions' (para 15),
- integration of the concerns and perspectives of marginalized groups and subaltern communities in the curricula for theological

education: 'Theological education in the presence of the other' (para 16),

- 'development of general Christian education both in universities and in private or public schools' (para 17), and
- Opening spaces for interdenominational education by including students of other traditions and support for interdenominational education by giving up past privileges and the sharing of resources and decision-making (para 18).

## An Unfinished Agenda

The Edinburgh 2010 process and the work on the CWME mission statement (*TTL*) have raised research, reflection and debate on mission and missional formation to a new level. This is true for the inclusiveness of the processes in terms of different Christian traditions and communities, and to a large extent also regarding the inclusion of perspectives of marginalized and subaltern communities. It is also true in terms of the new theological insights regarding the role of the Holy Spirit presented by *TTL*.

The present generation is privileged to build common reflection and practice on these achievements. The emphasis on the Holy Spirit has still far more to offer concerning the care for creation and people, a vital basis for theological reflection, the understanding of relationships among Christians and with people of different faith communities, and – in the more narrow interest of missional formation – regarding curricula, methodologies and co-operation for life-affirming mission and transformative action.

It would be unacceptable if the level of dialogue and co-operation among representatives of different Christian traditions that was reached so far would weaken again and give way to different 'camps' of world Christianity. Simplifying, but probably not oversimplifying, important features of the present situation, they can be described as three overlapping circles of a) those emphasizing the unity of the church expressed and realized by the role of (male) bishops, b) those focusing on 'truth' regarding moral values (especially concerning issues of body and sexuality), and c) those who see the urgent need for dialogue and co-operation of all Christians and all people of goodwill in response to contemporary threats to life. These trends cut across different traditions and contexts.

In this situation, it is worthwhile to listen again to the wisdom of Willem Visser 't Hooft, who was to become the first General Secretary of the World Council of Churches (WCC) in 1948. He underlined at the inauguration of the Ecumenical Institute Château de Bossey in 1946:

> ... the centre – i.e. the Institute – must have a truly ecumenical character. It should be the place where men and women of all the member-churches of the ecumenical movement learn together, receiving and giving, learn to struggle

> one for the other, and where they thus accept the tension between truth and unity which is at the basis of any true ecumenical community.[27]

After many years of reflection on hermeneutics and the diversity of cultures and religions, we would perhaps prefer a different language. But still today we understand that the tension between 'truth and unity' to which Visser 't Hooft refers is a consequence and vital expression of the existing diversity of traditions, cultures and values in truly ecumenical communities that cut across boundaries of ethnic or national identities and loyalties and are committed to overcome existing power dynamics and inequalities. Not allowing the different circles to fall apart is a shared task of all who are faithful to participation in *missio Dei* – being together in mission and trying together to be authentic witnesses to Christ and the Good News of the Gospel in the world of today.

---

[27] Quoted in Raiser, 'Fifty Years', 442.

# DISCIPLESHIP

Benjamin Conner

'There is no participation in Christ without participation in his mission in the world.'[1]

Lesslie Newbigin

## Introduction

Christian discipleship, at an analytic minimum, can be described as responding to and following Jesus Christ with the goal of union with God through Christ and in the power of the Holy Spirit.[2] One notable feature about the ecumenical movement's contribution to contemporary understandings of discipleship, according to Lesslie Newbigin, is that the ecumenical movement has connected discipleship with mission and evangelism because it participates with Christ in God's ongoing redemptive mission in the world. Within the ecumenical movement, there are numerous expressions of what following entails and requires, and these differences relate to fundamental and often unreconciled understandings of the relationship between church, mission, society and gospel as well as perceptions of what God is doing in history.

---

[1] Norman Goodall (ed), *Missions under the Cross: Addresses delivered at the enlarged meeting of the Committee of the International Missionary Council at Willingen, Germany, 1952, with statements issued by the meeting* (London: Edinburgh House Press, 1953), 190.

[2] Different definitions of Christian discipleship and what a disciple is (*discipulus*, *mathetes*, learner) will emphasize one aspect over another, but one core or unifying affirmation is that Christian discipleship involves *following* Jesus. The call to discipleship, according to Dietrich Bonhoeffer, is: 'Follow me, run along behind me'… It gives us no intelligible programme for a way of life, no goal or ideal to strive after. It is not a cause which human calculation might deem worthy of our devotion, even the devotion of ourselves' (Dietrich Bonhoeffer, *The Cost of Discipleship* (New York: Collier Books Macmillan Publishing, 1963), 62). According to Karl Barth, discipleship is related to *akolouthein*, the verb 'to follow', which reminds us that the event of following Jesus cannot be enclosed in a general concept – it is a response to a specific calling. In his words, 'the call to discipleship is the particular form of the summons by which Jesus discloses and reveals himself to individuals in order to claim and sanctify them as his own, and as his witnesses in the world' (Karl Barth, *The Call to Discipleship* (Minneapolis, MN: Fortress Press, 2003), 7).

However discipleship has been conceived in the ecumenical movement, it has always indicated the importance of shaping and forming *people* to be and do certain things in response to the missionary calling of a missionary God. Therefore, in order to distinguish and benefit from the different conceptions of discipleship in the ecumenical movement, it is essential to examine ecumenical visions of who the people of God are, the laity, and what they are called to do and be, their vocation, because ecumenical understandings of Christian discipleship are often framed in terms of the people of God who are being discipled towards some end.

It is interesting to note that the *Dictionary of the Ecumenical Movement* does not include an entry on 'discipleship'.[3] Perhaps this is because discipleship is simply implicit in every aspect of the ecumenical movement as the entire movement could be interpreted in relation to responding to the call of Christian discipleship. Given the overwhelmingly broad scope of discipleship in the ecumenical movement, this chapter, for the sake of focus and clarity, will engage only one facet of the larger conversation – the ecumenical understanding of discipleship as articulated in relationship to the laity. If, as I have suggested, the key question for understanding discipleship is correlated to the issue of supporting Christians in following Christ and preparing them to participate in God's ongoing redemptive work in the world, then ecumenical perceptions of the role and calling of the laity should provide fertile ground for apprehending how many in the ecumenical movement have understood Christian discipleship.

## Christian Discipleship: Presumptions and Challenges

Expressions of Christian discipleship in the ecumenical movement have been articulated in response to challenges: challenges to the faith, challenges to the church, and challenges to the missionary enterprise. At that first great ecumenical missionary conference, Edinburgh 1910, it could be argued that the legitimacy of the missionary enterprise or whether or not such a conference was a faithful way of responding to the gospel was not questioned. The faithful response of discipleship was for the so-called Christian nations to organize for mission, to evaluate and marshall their resources, and to participate in advancing 'the evangelization of the world in this generation' (the SVM [Student Volunteer Movement] watchword, the spirit of which impacted the tenor of the conference).[4] The outbreak of

---

[3] Nicholas Lossky et al (ed), *Dictionary of the Ecumenical Movement*, 2nd edition (Geneva: WCC Publications, 2002).

[4] As Denton Lotz reminds us, 'The leaders of the Edinburgh Conference, its chairman [John Mott] and secretary [J.H. Oldham], were all men from the student movement, influenced by the urgency of the watchword's appeal' (Denton Lotz, 'The Evangelization of the World in this Generation: The Resurgence of a Missionary Idea among the Conservative Evangelicals' (Dissertation, University of Hamburg, 1970), in Thomas Shivute, *The Theology of Mission and Evangelism in*

World War I in 1914 not only compromised the missionary effort but also called into question the entire modern missionary enterprise. The issue that challenged the authenticity of Christian discipleship was that the message of the gospel was clothed in western cultural baggage which was not congruent with the relationships between the messengers or the contexts in the global South that was their focus. The ecumenical historian W.R. Hogg comments, 'The war inflicted no greater disaster upon the Christian missionary enterprise than its rupture of the bonds of Christian love.'[5] Indeed, the war called into question the authenticity and depth of the discipleship of western Christianity.[6]

In this global context of conflict, the call of discipleship required, on the one hand, that Christians 'establish a counter-good' by harnessing every resource and power that was available to them to advance the missionary mandate.[7] On the other hand, the increasing influence of the phenomenon of secularization in the West was also calling into question the validity and relevance of Christian mission that was indirectly linked with the rise of military conflicts. The challenge for the so-called western 'sending' countries, restoring their missionary and evangelization advance in the global South, involved more than mere reorganization; it called for theological engagement and contextual analysis of their own culture.

In 1928, Rufus Jones noted that the 'greatest rival of Christianity in the world to-day is not Islam, or Buddhism, or Hinduism, or Confucianism, but a worldwide secular way of life and interpretation of the nature of things'.[8]

---

*the International Missionary Council from Edinburgh to New Delhi*, 32, note 30). For a brief yet substantial history of the watchword, see Dana L. Robert, 'The Origin of the Student Volunteer Watchword: "The Evangelization of World in This Generation"', in *International Bulletin of Missionary Research* 10.4 (October 1986).

[5] W.R. Hogg, *Ecumenical Foundations: A History of the International Missionary Council and its Nineteenth-Century Background* (Eugene, OR: Wipf & Stock, 2002).

[6] As John Flett has argued, 'The West had considered itself a Christian civilization, yet the war revealed the impotence of Christianity, even among its greatest supporters' (J.G. Flett, 'From Jerusalem to Oxford: Mission as the Foundation and Goal of Ecumenical Social Thought', *International Bulletin of Missionary Research* 27.1 (January 2003), 17-22, 17).

[7] As one author suggested, 'The war itself comes as a challenge to the disciples of the Kingdom to call into being by the mercy of God a work which might never have been but for this tragedy' (E. Shillito, 'The Sweep of War', in *International Review of Mission*, 8 (1919), 443).

[8] R.M. Jones, 'Secular Civilization and the Christian Faith', in *The Jerusalem Meeting of the International Missionary Council, March 24-April 8, 1928* (New York: International Missionary Council, 1928), 230. The forces that were secularizing, in the sense that Jones was employing the term, were mechanistic science (a scientific interpretation of the universe and its concomitants 'rationalism' and 'naturalism', the emergence of 'new historical methods'), the industrial

The impact of secularization, according to Jones, was the withdrawal of western society from the church, and 'absorbing' interest in purely secular (as opposed to 'spiritual') interests, the disintegration of life into disparate fields and spheres, and the marginalization of the 'prestige and sacred character of the Church'.[9]

Emil Brunner argued that only 'true theology' can free Christianity from secularism by struggling with the powers of the *Zeitgeist*.[10] However, 'true theology' cannot be limited to merely doctrinal or ideological formulations. Rather, within the context of Christian discipleship, it calls for radical engagement with the secularism that involves appropriate training of the laity to positively impact the world through their different professions to challenge the maxims of the secular worldview.[11]

### Discipleship and the Emergence of the Laity

The laity became, in the theology of the ecumenical movement, both a concrete strategy of ecclesial influence in a rapidly changing world and a conceptual place to consider the changing landscape for Christian discipleship. The Life and Work Movement that initially engaged the concept of lay discipleship in ecumenical circles and their role in evangelization, played a pioneering role in this regard.[12]

In the preparatory documents associated with the Life and Work's Oxford Conference on Church, Community and State (1937), J.H. Oldham considered the predicament of the church and determined that religion had come to be considered 'one department among others, instead of something that is concerned with the whole of life'.[13] Oldham's call was for the church to restore its influence by becoming laicized. The laity must be prepared as part of an ecclesial strategy of influence, he argued, suggesting, 'The church as an organized society stands outside the activities of the social and political life. The Christian laity participates in these activities. Transformation from within is immeasurably more effective than any influence that can be brought to bear from without.'[14] The witness and action of the laity is the way that the church will transform society but, Oldham recognized, to this point the church's discipleship had not been

---

revolution and urbanization, 'widespread loss of faith in immortality' and the failure of the Church.

[9] Jones, 'Secular Civilization', 239.

[10] Emil Brunner, 'Secularism as a Problem for the Church', in *International Review of Mission,* 19 (1930).

[11] Emil Brunner, 'Secularism as a Problem for the Church', in *International Review of Mission,* 19 (1930).

[12] W.A. Visser 't Hooft and J.H. Oldham, *The Church and Its Function in Society* (Chicago, IL and New York: Willett, Clark & Company, 1937), 106.

[13] Visser 't Hooft, *The* Church, 176.

[14] Visser 't Hooft, *The* Church, 176.

adequate for supporting them in this task. 'Many lay men and women who are conscious of religious need long in their secret hearts for the help they feel the church might give them,' he argues, 'but they do not find that the church satisfies that need.'[15]

According to Visser 't Hooft, the following issues must be addressed to support the action of the laity in living out the 'obligations of the Christian life'.[16] First, the church must be connected more deeply with the exigencies of lay life in the world, for example, by providing clarity for the laity who are dealing with issues related to life in the workforce. Second, the church needs to offer ethical guidance to the laity for concrete situations that might arise in the public sphere. Finally, the larger congregations must offer smaller groups of Christians more intimate settings 'for the purpose of mutual help in Christian witness and action'.[17] These groups could be described as discipleship groups that have the aim of attending to the fitness of lay witness and they –

> … may be local, having as their primary concern the social evils of a particular town or rural area. Their objects may be primarily spiritual, i.e. to sustain and fortify through prayer and fellowship those who seek to advance the cause of righteousness, to relieve distress and to serve the common good in various forms of public activity.[18]

The *telos* of this notion of discipleship arcs towards the Kingdom of God, advocates a deeper and more faithful participation in the ongoing mission of God in the world and, therefore, towards social justice, the relief of distress, responsibility to one's neighbourhood, and prophetic conflict.

The role of church leaders is, then, to clarify for the laity the consequences of Christian responsibility and offer guidance as to what kind of behaviour the gospel calls forth in particular circumstances.

The concern that impactful social engagement and mission require preparing the laity for life and witness in a complex world was also recognized at the inaugural meeting of the World Council of Churches in 1948[19] and also at the WCC gatherings at Amsterdam and Evanston.[20] The

---

[15] Visser 't Hooft, *The Church*, 178.

[16] Visser 't Hooft, *The Church*, 180.

[17] Visser 't Hooft, *The Church*, 181.

[18] Visser 't Hooft, *The Church*, 181-82.

[19] W.A. Visser 't Hooft (ed), *The Official Report Man's Disorder and God's Design,* Volume V, The First Assembly of the World Council of Churches (New York: Harper & Brothers, 1949), 154. According to the inaugural WCC meeting, 'The laity requires strengthening through biblical and theological study and discussion with special reference to the bearing of Christian faith upon daily life'. The report stated further: 'For it is through the laity that the Church has the greatest and most natural opportunity to show in and to the world that the message of the Bible, and all that the Church is committed to by obedience to its Lord, are relevant to the real problems and needs of man in every age, and not least our own. Only by the witness of a spiritually intelligent and active laity can the Church meet the

issues were given sustained attention through the Ecumenical Institute at Bossey and through ecumenical publications like *Laymen's Work* and *Laity*.

## Discipleship and a Laity that is Coming of Age

A pertinent question for the ecumenical movement is: Who or what sets the agenda for Christian discipleship? Prior to the 1950s, discipleship was focused on the preparing laity to bear the church into the world – into the university, the academy, the factory, the family and the political realm – and be responsible Christians in their everyday lives as community members, employees and family members. The church supported the discipleship of the Christian in the following way: 'The real task is for the church to become genuinely and active present, there where she already is' present in the lives of believers and as they navigate political and vocational issues. Strategically, it is through preparing the laity to live rightly in the world, and through the power of the Spirit and in the name of the church, that the world might 'be restored to health and life'.[21] Responsibility was one of the key words to describe discipleship at this time.

Responsible Christians asked such questions as, 'What do we mean by "Christian Witness" in the case of a social worker serving in a secular organization?' Discipleship requires that the church prepare Christians to be responsible and ethical in their various callings and thereby to be faithful witnesses. Christians must be trained so they can 'see the meaning of faith for social problems'.[22] The Ecumenical Institute took up the questions that were raised by the ecumenical movement and by other lay movements, and imagined the discipleship of the laity in the following way: 'Programmes must take up the questions and needs of human society so that Christians may be helped to respond to them through prophetic witness and healing service.'[23]

---

modern world in its actual perplexities and life situations.' The proposal to create an Ecumenical Institute was offered in response to such concerns.

[20] 'It is the laity who draw together work and worship; it is they who bridge the gulf between the Church and the world, and it is they who manifest in word and action the Lordship of Christ over that world which claims so much of their time and energy and labour' (W.A. Visser 't Hooft (ed), *The Evanston Report: The Second Assembly of the World Council of Churches* (New York: Harper Books, 1955), 161). It is in faithfully executing their vocation in the midst of a 'secular' job, called to obedience and service wherever they are. What are Christian vocation and witness in the context of this particular occupation or profession? Discipleship is the response of faith that answers such questions.

[21] *Laymen's Work* 1 (May 1951), 9.

[22] *Laymen's Work* 1, 12.

[23] Hans-Reudi Weber, *A Laboratory for Ecumenical Life: The Story of Bossey 1946-1996* (Geneva: WCC, 1996), 7.

Certainly one of the most significant contributions of the Ecumenical Institute for the developing understanding of Christian discipleship in the ecumenical movement was the affirmation, through publications and programmes, of the notion of professional life as vocation. Specialized meetings enabled teachers to think through how the Christian faith might impact teaching from the basics of humanist assumptions to the specifics of complex subjects. Medical doctors, people involved in industry and other professionals gathered together to look at 'human relationships within a production-oriented society'.[24] Additional conferences related to living as disciples in the world were held for artists, politicians, lawyers, journalists and social workers. Along with conferences that supported particular vocational groups, there were conferences that addressed specific issues in the modern world like social welfare, family and the meaning of work. In terms of Christian discipleship, *the point in all of this was to equip the laity for their witness in the world* – which, of course, begs the question, What is the world? Consequently, the Institute offered consultations on the meaning of the secular, the meaning of history, and the significance of sociology for understanding and navigating social structures, institutions and relationships. The Institute was supported in its efforts by the ecumenical publication, *Laity*.

While no single prevailing understanding of discipleship dominated the pages of *Laity*, one can discern important affirmations of past conceptions and anticipations of future trajectories. Discipleship may still be summarized, from the standpoint of the church's responsibility to the laity, as 'the training of the laity for their ministry in the world'[25] because their ministry is one of being in the world faithfully. In this perspective on discipleship, to disciple the laity is to help them to become 'adult' and to give them a proper 'biblical orientation'. Consider the impact of Hans-Ruedi Weber's and Suzanne de Dietrich's Bible studies for orienting the discipleship of Christians who are to be in, yet not of, the world. In this vision, every baptized Christian must be supported by a church that understands the world and that offers disciplines that are portable enough to be 'translated into very concrete ways and lines of conduct',[26] right down to addressing issues related to the 'right use of time and money'.[27]

While the world is in view in this vision, discipleship, following Christ, is still grounded in the Biblical text and in the rhythm of being gathered into the church and being sent from the church. According to Frère Francois (Taizé community): 'Spiritual retreats should be understood as a means of training laity, with a view of their witness in the world, their apostolate and their obedience.' The disciplines are an essential aspect of a

[24] Weber, *A Laboratory*, 40.

[25] *Laity: reprints from Laity 2-6* (Geneva: Department on the Laity, WCC, May 1962), *Laity* 2, 3.

[26] *Laity*, 25.

[27] *Laity*, 26.

kind of evangelical discipleship that always has the calling of the disciple as a messenger in view.

The view of discipleship as gathering into and sending by the church is balanced by another view that emerged around the same time, an almost competing view that has a dissimilar assessment of the church and a different understanding of where the presence of God and strength for faithful witness can be found. In an effort to combat 'church narcissism',[28] this competing approach to discipleship aims at preparing Christians for dialogue with the world in the effort of jointly imagining a more humanized world. This line of thinking is adequately captured and summarized by theologian Hans Hoekendijk:

> Wherever in our apostolate we *see a convincing demonstration of Christ's solidarity with the world, we* will clearly have to be present *in* this world with solidarity, not just now and then in a sortie from the ecclesiastical enclave, only to return thereafter with great speed, but *permanently*, because we know that as Christians we have our *Sitz im Leben* (life situation) in the world, not in the church. In the world one must live as a 'child of the kingdom, that has been planted on the acreage of the world'.[29]

What then, does it mean to disciple the laity if living comfortably and authentically as humans in the world is their calling? Put baldly:

> This training does not aim at extending a knowledge of dogma, improving evangelism, nor raising the level of professional ethics. Nor is this training concerned with the growth of the Church as an organization or the increase of its influence as an institution in the world. On the contrary, the object of this training is to improve the functioning of society and the creation among members of an insight into the connection between the daily order of things and the hidden kingdom of God.[30]

By 1958 the conversation about Christian discipleship pivoted on an interpretation of Dietrich Bonhoeffer's so-called 'worldly Christianity', a Christianity that has come of age, and called the church to 'no longer lament over the process of secularization, but rejoice in it'.[31] The challenge of Christian discipleship was to move 'out of our pious isolation to a deep commitment to the affairs of this world'.[32] As I will explain below, discipleship was moving out of religion and into history. Newbigin's phrase from the Introduction ('There is no participation in Christ without participation in his mission in the world') was being applied in ways that he had neither imagined nor intended.[33]

---

[28] *Laity*, 29.

[29] Johannes Christiaan Hoekendijk, 'Apostolate: The Communicating with Fellow Travelers', in *The Church Inside Out* (UTS, NY: 1966), 54.

[30] *Laity*, 31.

[31] *Laity*, 105.

[32] *Laity*, 100.

[33] In speaking about the integration of the IMC and the WCC in 1961, Newbigin laments that mission, the church and discipleship were not oriented as he had

In the 1960s, secularization changed, in the estimation of many in the ecumenical movement, from being a problem that stood in the way of evangelization to being the animating theological doctrine for faithful evangelism. This mindset prepared the way for new conceptions of discipleship that were imagined in response to the question of what Christians were being formed to do and be in the world.

## Out of Religion and Into History

By appealing to Bonhoeffer's notion of Jesus as the 'Man for others', the Missionary Structure of the Congregation project of the Department on Studies in Evangelism promoted an understanding of true transcendence (or union with Christ, which was noted earlier as the goal of Christian discipleship) as living a life for others. The cultural marginalization of the church, which had been relegated to the sphere of the private and the sacred, was now inconsequential and even providential as faithful discipleship had its power and purpose in the secular world. Discipleship, under such conditions, involves recasting secular work as a 'work of holiness', following Charles West's directive to 'strengthen the true secularity' of the secular person.[34]

Discipleship is still, in agreement with the Oxford Conference, about preparing Christians to be responsible, but history (the now, the *saeculum*, this age), and not the church, must be the place where God's action and presence are sought. Christians who become present in the world will be able to discern *Christus extra muros ecclesiae*.[35] Since God is present in the 'actual life situation of every [person]', then discipleship must involve 'entering into partnership with God in history'.[36] Whereas secularization

imagined: 'There were important areas, however, where I have to confess that *I failed to achieve what I had hoped for as the result of integration*. I hoped that we would be able to use the resources of a world organization to identify and direct resources to places where there were great opportunities for evangelism... but it had to be admitted that there was much less enthusiasm for the direct preaching of the Gospel and the building up of the Church than for technical assistance and political action': Lesslie Newbigin, *Unfinished Agenda: An Autobiography* (Grand Rapids, MI: Eerdmans, 1985), 205-06.

[34] C.A. Coulson, 'A Secular World? – God and Things', in *Laity* 16 (November 1963), 36. See also Charles C. West, '*Consultation on 'the Meaning of the Secular'* (Bossey, Switzerland: Ecumenical Institute, 1959).

[35] 'Christ outside the walls of the Church.' This argument is advanced in ecumenical circles by Walter Hollenweger in 'Christus Extra et Intra Muros Ecclesiae', in WCC Department on Studies in Evangelism and Thomas Wieser (ed), *Planning for Mission: Working Papers on the New Quest for Missionary Communities* (New York: U.S. Conference for the WCC, 1966).

[36] WCC Department on Studies in Evangelism Western European Working Group and WCC Department on Studies in Evangelism North American Working Group, *The Church for Others, and the Church for the World: A Quest for Structures for*

might *de-churchify* discipleship, it was argued, it cannot *de-Christianize* it. Transcendence is achieved by immersion into the present – by moving out of religion (which focuses on transcendence and the metaphysical) and into history (the present, this age, this world, the secular). The disciple must join God who is already at work in the world that has 'come of age'. Christian discipleship is itself portrayed as a secular, worldly movement so that *kenosis*, presence and participation in the world become essential themes of discipleship.[37]

## Discipleship in the Ecumenical Movement Today: Back to the Church

There is no way to offer a comprehensive picture of discipleship in the ecumenical movement. In promoting the narrative that in the ecumenical movement discipleship moved out of religion and into history, I recognize that I am giving scant attention to the important contributions of the Orthodox theologians and the concept of missionary discipleship as participation in 'the liturgy after the liturgy' (Ion Bria). And I am overlooking the many contributions of the Faith and Order Movement, including the conferences and papers that culminated in the ecumenical best-seller, *Baptism, Eucharist, and Ministry* (The Lima Document or BEM), a document that grounds discipleship in a baptismal ecclesiology and offers a contrasting story-line to mine.

And, although non-Europeans certainly contributed to the documents and discussions I have engaged above, I have not adequately attended to

---

*Missionary Congregations. Final Report of the Western European Working Group and North American Working Group of the Department on Studies in Evangelism* (Geneva: WCC, 1967), 14.

[37] What does discipleship look like when it is moving out of religion and into history? Christian discipleship involves testing the spirits that are at work around us, discerning God's action and considering how God might be drawing us into the action, whether it be reforming and supporting public education, engaging civil rights movements, participating in urban service training, supporting voluntary services in the cities, engaging issues of housing, employment, poverty, social welfare, discrimination, participating in city renewal movements, or challenging unjust social institutions. Theological reflection must be guided by sociological analysis. Discipleship in this era had shifted from the 'gathering and sending' model of earlier days to a diffused model where the is little talk of how God forms Christians in the church and much more about how God is at work in grassroots community organizations like the Los Angeles Goals Project initiated by the Department of City Planning and Public Policies (WCC, *The Church for Others*, 120-24). Christian discipleship was not churchly, but was instead a participation in what Hans Hoekendijk termed 'shalomization' or humanization.

discipleship in the context of the 'great new fact of our era'[38] or accounted for the challenges and insights that other faith traditions might have for Christian discipleship – a particularly important contribution of the ecumenical movement. According to Weber, 'The Bible had to be read also with the eyes of Asians, Africans, Latin Americans and Pacific Islanders, from the perspective of the oppressed and the poor, enriched by the experience and insights of women.'[39] Ministry from the margins is one of the central affirmations in the new affirmation on Mission and Evangelism (*Together towards Life: Mission and Evangelism in Changing Landscapes*) – insights from discipleship in the ecumenical church will continue to inform the shape and spirit of Christian mission in the future.

My omissions are partly for the sake of expediency, but also because the shift of discipleship moving out of religion and into history is, to my mind, the seismic shift that continues to impact the ecumenical movement in the most significant ways. There has, however, recently been a trend back towards the church, and this comes in part due to the initiative of Faith and Order and partly due to developing understandings of evangelism in the context of a continually changing world.

According to Konrad Raiser, former General Secretary of the WCC (1993-2003), the southern shift in the centre of Christianity and the increasing secularization of the West, combined with the reality of globalization, has created the need for a new understanding of the laity. In earlier ecumenical discussions of the laity, the laity were understood to be representatives of the church in the secular world. Their witness corresponded with their faithfulness as responsible Christians in various roles in society and was enlivened by the rhythmic spiritual breathing of gathering and sending. Today, Christian discipleship is often understood as participating in wide-ranging movements and initiatives related to justice, the environment, and confronting 'anonymous centres of power'.[40] Globalization and its concomitants require a new profile and programme of discipleship for the laity in order to help them face 'global threats to survival'.[41]

The vision for Christian discipleship (still related to participation in the ongoing redemptive mission of God) is 'the rebuilding of viable, non-exclusive social forms that will produce a community with a human face in which human dignity is recognized, basic human needs are satisfied, and

---

[38] From the sermon William Temple preached at his enthronement as Archbishop of Canterbury. William Temple, *The Church Looks Forward* (London: Macmillan, 1944), 2.

[39] Weber, *A Laboratory*, 8.

[40] Konrad Raiser, 'Profile of the Laity in the Ecumenical Movement: Towards a New Definition', in Nicholas Apostola (ed), *A Letter from Christ to the World: An Exploration of the Role of the Laity in the Church Today* (Geneva: WCC, 1998), 12-22, at 17.

[41] Raiser, 'Profile of the Laity', 19.

the diversity of cultural identities and human talents is duly recognized'.[42] Under such conditions, discipleship is preparing Christians to join in movements of justice, peace and 'the integrity of creation'.[43] In many ways, the ecumenical movement is still considering what it means for Christian discipleship to move out of religion and into history. Recently, however, the ecumenical movement is recovering the importance of connecting discipleship and evangelism with the life and spiritual resources of the church.

Three very important documents from the joint study programme on Ecclesiology and Ethics conducted by Faith and Order and the WCC's Justice, Peace and Creation team (*Costly Unity, Costly Commitment* and *Costly Obedience*), and a report from the ecumenical conversation on evangelism (*Evangelism Today: New Ways for Authentic Discipleship*) are representative of this shift. While not official statements, they represent the cross-current of conversation surrounding discipleship, evangelism and mission in the ecumenical movement today and offer a middle position between church-centred discipleship prior to the 1950s and Christian discipleship that has moved out of religion and into history.

The documents recognize the formative value of ecclesial practices for shaping the laity, and for forming congregations and individuals for faithful and concrete witness/actions in the world. In terms of discipleship, 'The heart of Christian moral formation lies in worship, through which the story of salvation is re-enacted in the modes of prayer, proclamation, and sacrament.'[44] What the documents represent is the fact that congregations practise witness together,[45] and preparing congregations to embody witness should orient the goals and disciplines of Christian discipleship. *Evangelism Today* acknowledges that the 'mere humanization of Christian mission' is not an adequate vision for discipleship and evangelism.[46] What is proposed instead is a vision of liturgical formation that shapes and nurtures internal habits, establishes patterns of life, and provides new lenses for viewing the world along with 'new energy to bear witness in it'.[47]

The ecumenical concept of discipleship that had moved out of religion and into history is now returning to the church, not to escape from the influence of the world, not with a naïve understanding of the relationship

---

[42] Raiser, 'Profile of the Laity', 18.

[43] Raiser, 'Profile of the Laity', 19.

[44] Thomas F. Best and Martin Robra (eds), *Ecclesiology and Ethics: Ecumenical Ethical Engagement, Moral Formation and the Nature of the Church* (Geneva: WCC, 1997), 66-67.

[45] For a deeper discussion of practising witness, see Benjamin T. Conner, *Practicing Witness: A Missional Vision of Christian Practices* (Grand Rapids, MI: Eerdmans, 2011).

[46] WCC, 'Evangelism Today: New Ways for Authentic Discipleship', in *International Review of Mission,* 103.1 (April 2014), 131.

[47] Best and Robra. *Ecclesiology and Ethics*, 67.

between church and culture, nor imagining that the church is a total culture that is somehow apart from the world. The turn back to the church is for the sake of strengthening disciples through faithful Christian practices, and the turn represents the recognition that immersion in the world without the guidance of the church has often led to 'malformation'. As *Costly Obedience* suggests, 'Discipleship finds resources in many complexly interacting elements of churchly life: the education of lay persons, the preparation of pastors, moral discourse in family and congregation, the experience of seeking to serve the wider community. Liturgical formation, in the Lord's supper and in our common baptism, is fundamental to all other kinds of formation.'[48]

The concept of discipleship in the Ecumenical Movement has always been set within larger conversations related to mission and evangelism. And while ecumenical understandings of the demands of Christian discipleship have changed as discipleship has moved out of religion into history and back to the church again, the affirmation has remained the same: 'There is no participation in Christ without participation in [God's] mission in the world.'

[48] Best and Robra, *Ecclesiology and Ethics*, 56.

# PARTNERSHIP AND RESOURCE-SHARING

Dongsung Kim

## Introduction

Christians are called to share the good news of God's kingdom in every place and at all times. The Christian churches have carried out this vocation through their ministries of mission and evangelism, service and proclamation. In so doing, they have developed strategies and methods that have sought to enable each church, as equal members of the one Body of Christ, to benefit from as well as to contribute to this common endeavour. This chapter will explore how the ideals and practice of ecumenical sharing has developed within the ecumenical movement, focusing specifically on the developments within the activities of the World Council of Churches, wherein the so-called four streams of the modern ecumenical movement – Faith and Order, Life and Work, Christian Education, and Mission and Evangelism – have historically been located. I will seek to examine how ecumenical sharing evolved over the years by focusing on the discourse as it developed in relation to the work of the International Missionary Council (IMC), later to become the Department and then the Commission on World Mission and Evangelism of the WCC. This is because sharing ecumenically has been a concern and interest of the modern Protestant missionary movement from its very early period, and also, in my view, because of the systematic engagement with the issue which has occurred within the structures of the IMC over the years. As such, this chapter will engage with the various reports and documents relating to particular meetings and conferences of the IMC as well as other departments of the WCC which were influenced by the turn of events and direction in which the discussions evolved over the years.

Sharing of resources within and beyond the life of the Christian church has been part of its identity and mission from the very earliest periods of its history. According to the Pauline Epistle to the Romans (15:26), we find reference to the monetary gifts that the churches in Macedonia and Achaia had collected for 'God's people' in need (Romans. 15:26). The interesting point of this sharing was that the Gentile church provided the financial resources for the church in Jerusalem. In other words, the church on the margins was providing for the church in the centre, and this sharing was an expression of solidarity and not mere charity. In this sense, the first expression of inter-church aid in the first century was instrumental in building up the universal church and establishing the bonds of fellowship as the one body of Christ. Also noteworthy is the purpose for this inter-church aid or ecumenical sharing of resources. It was not only to secure the survival of the church in Jerusalem, but also to ensure that its missionary vocation could be sustained and strengthened. The ecumenical sharing of resources possessed a missionary nature with the resources shared serving as an investment of sorts in ensuring the continuation of the witness and service of the local Christian church.

Within the modern ecumenical movement since the beginning of the twentieth century, the development of inter-church aid and ecumenical sharing of resources was instrumental in fostering reconciliation in war-torn Europe as the ravaged communities struggled to overcome the brutal years of violence and hatred. With the changing socio-political landscape which followed the tumultuous years of warfare, the scope of inter-church aid also experienced a shift. Its focus and scope expanded beyond Europe to other parts of the world. The decolonization process in Asia and Africa, as well as other parts of the world that followed World War II, reached its heights of impact after the 1950s, and this led to the establishment of many independent states. In a similar manner, the churches within these new states also sought to establish themselves as independent entities distinct from the Eurocentric mission bodies that led to their establishment. With the rise of self-awareness and a growing desire for self-reliance, the western mission-founded churches of the global South began to challenge the established ecclesial principles and underpinning political ideology, processes and theological foundations for sharing between churches. One of the issues that emerged for debate was the nature of their future ecclesial relationship. Concerns and even objections were raised to the nature of inter-church aid being a one-directional flow from the rich to the poor, the churches of the North to the churches of the South, and from the powerful to the powerless.

It is within this evolving ecumenical landscape that the practice and concept of ecumenical resource-sharing emerged as:

> … a framework for new relationships that would free the churches from traditional roles of being either a sending (giving) or a receiving body, and enable them to overcome structures of inequality and dependency between rich and poor.[1]

The genesis of the concept 'Ecumenical Sharing of Resource' (ESR) originated as a study process after the Nairobi Assembly of the WCC in 1976.[2] The Central Committee of the WCC called for:

> … a study on the ecumenical sharing of resources, to study all existing methods of sharing resources, both human and financial, to seek new and

[1] Huibert van Beek, 'Ecumenical Sharing of Resources', in Nicholas Lossky, José Míguez Bonino, John Pobee, Tom F. Stransky, Geoffrey Wainwright and Pauline Webb (eds), *Dictionary of the Ecumenical Movement* (Geneva: WCC, 2002), 382.
[2] van Beek, 'Ecumenical Sharing of Resources', 382.

> more ecumenical methods, and to relate the whole issue to the World Council's search for the unity of the Church.[3]

Ecumenical resource-sharing was therefore motivated by a missio-economic paradigm for just relationships to become normative within the economic sphere of missional relationship between the churches of the global North and South. The relationship between the churches, irrespective of one's material wealth or otherwise, should be based on 'spiritual sharing and solidarity'.[4] This meant that the emphasis of sharing resources was to facilitate 'Fullness of life for all' and meant mutual challenge and equipping of each other based upon principles of mutuality and reciprocity.

According to the WCC document on the ecumenical sharing of resources, the followers of Jesus are 'all receivers in the first instance, and that Christ is the one who gives everything to all'.[5] Acknowledging this indicates that 'sharing is not a matter of one giving to another, but of all receiving together', while noting that 'no one can receive anything except what is given from heaven' (John 3:29).[6] This affirmation repudiates an economic model of ownership that is privatized, belittles the sovereignty of God and denies life in community that benefits the common good. Everything, including ourselves, is created by God, 'the father of every good and perfect thing' (James 1:7).[7] Seen in this light, 'sharing' is not simply about giving or receiving but 'is rather the way in which we seek to be what we are within an interrelated human community'.[8] In this sense, sharing, as a 'responsive relation to others, is indeed the costly discipleship to which God calls us and for which Jesus has set the pattern before us'.[9] This means that sharing is a confessional act of faith in which the church proclaims her message through her acts of sharing because 'all the resources held by the churches are given to them in trust by God'.[10] Through its sharing, the church expresses its conviction that 'the almighty God has given us an opportunity to use his resource in order to show

---

[3] WCC, *Empty Hands – An Agenda for the Churches: A Study Guide on the Ecumenical Sharing of Resources for use by Churches, Local Congregations and Other Groups* (Geneva: WCC, 1980), 4.

[4] Unit IV – Sharing and Service, *New Approaches to Development – Ecumenical Formation Seminar Report* (Geneva: WCC, 1996), 6.

[5] Tracy Early, *Simply Sharing – A Personal Survey of How Well the Ecumenical Movement Shares its Resources* (Geneva: WCC, 1980), 20.

[6] Early, *Simply Sharing*, 21.

[7] Francis Stephanos, 'An African Perspective: Challenging the Power Structure', in Knut Edvard Larsen and Knud Jørgensen (eds), *Power and Partnership* (Oxford: Regnum, 2014), 62.

[8] Ghana Robinson (ed), *Sharing and Living – A Study on the Ecumenical Sharing of Resources in India* (Madurai, India: Nepolean Press, 1983), 2.

[9] Ghana Robinson (ed), *Sharing and Living*, 2.

[10] David Gill (ed), *Gathered for Life: Official Report, Sixth Assembly of the World Council of Churches* (Geneva: WCC, 1983), 63.

compassion, love, respect and care for our fellow human beings and nature'.[11] As such, the ecumenical sharing of resources is one of the ways in which the church fulfils its ministry of witness, service and mission in the world. The sixth Assembly of the WCC that was held in Vancouver acknowledged this when it declared that:

> The ministry of sharing is a challenge to the churches to practise what they are called to be: sharing communities which seek to do justice, taking the side of all those who are denied their share in the fullness of life that God has promised.[12]

In a later document recommending ESR as a process for study and action for the churches, the WCC Central Committee further elaborated on the understanding and practice of the concept with the statement that 'our participation in sharing has its origin in our ministry as a Church and our relations with one another as members of the same body'.[13]

The Vancouver Assembly further noted that 'sharing is rooted in the very nature of the Triune God as a "community of sharing" characterised by dynamic and creative mutuality', and that 'the Church's sharing and healing ministry originates from the very life and mission of Christ himself'.[14] It is therefore important for the church to regard the responsibility of sharing resources as being part of its vocation and stewardship. This is why 'sharing and healing begin at a personal level, but they become societal both on local and ecumenical levels'.[15] However, sharing of the Christian church goes beyond its borders and embraces 'the whole inhabited earth' (*oikoumene*) while also characterizing the relationship that we have with our neighbours.[16]

A significant achievement of the Vancouver Assembly was the recognition that the churches needed a new model of sharing and that 'the donor-receiver type of relationship must give way to relationships which facilitate the sharing of decision-making and power'.[17] This 'donor-receiver type of relationship' had passed its sell-by date because the political era of colonial rule had given way to the rise of independent nation-states that demanded a different model of political relationship. This also had major impact on the relationship that evolved between mission agencies and the local churches that they founded. The ecumenical movement under the umbrella of the WCC also recognised that the politico-ecclesial environment in which the sharing of resources took place had radically

---

[11] Stephanos, 'An African Perspective: Challenging the Power Structure', 62.
[12] Gill, *Gathered for Life,* 63.
[13] WCC, *Empty Hands*, 10.
[14] 'Report of the Issue Group on Healing and Sharing Life in Community' in Gill, *Gathered for Life.* 62.
[15] 'Report of the Issue Group on 'Healing and Sharing Life in Community', 62.
[16] WCC, *Empty Hands*, 10.
[17] 'Report of the Issue Group on Healing and Sharing Life in Community', 62.

changed and that a more just and life-affirming model was needed. It also announced that 'bilateral or confessional patterns of sharing should be challenged so that the churches may grow towards greater ecumenical sharing on local, regional and international levels'.[18]

As the debate on the practice, processes and theological foundations for sharing developed throughout the years, there was also a shift in the understanding of resources within the ecumenical movement. At the outset much of the inter-church aid was financial in that it involved the transferring of money from the giver to the receiver. However, in subsequent decades the churches came to recognize that the church had much more to share than simply money. The manifold gifts that the church has received from Christ included 'insights into the gospel arising from cultural heritage, commitment to liberation and involvement in the struggle, and sharing in the suffering and pain of other members of the body of Christ'.[19] No church, regardless of where it is situated geographically, socially or economically, is without something that can be shared with others. Each person, as a child of God, is uniquely endowed with 'some understanding of life and its value, some strength of purpose, some sense of direction, some unique, individual expression of humanity'.[20]

The ecumenical vision which is present in the spirit and principles of the ecumenical sharing of resources is a broad understanding of resources which include 'spirituality, culture and human resources as well as finance and material goods'.[21] As the Central Committee of the WCC affirmed during their 1980 meeting in Geneva, 'every church, rich or poor, needs to recognize the greatness of its wealth in being the people of God'.[22] This wealth of the church takes many forms, as already described above, and it is in sharing these very gifts that the Christians 'mutually enrich one another and build up one another in the fullness of Christ'.[23] The recognition that all Christian churches, regardless of where they are situated within the socio-economic order, have resources gifted to them by God is important as it strengthens the integrity and worth of one's self-identity as a member of the body of Christ. The acknowledgement of gifts held by all as God's people is also important in shaping the perspectives and framework for sharing as it provides the possibility for humility, respect and a strong sense of mutuality to inform them. Knowing that our wealth in Christ as the body of Christ is not determined by material or financial terms is what enables us as Christians to hold out our hands to one another in hope and expectation that God will fill us, together.

---

[18] 'Report of the Issue Group on Healing and Sharing Life in Community', 62.

[19] Unit IV – Sharing and Service, *New Approaches to Development*, 6.

[20] Early, *Simply Sharing*, 71.

[21] van Beek, 'Ecumenical Sharing of Resources', 382.

[22] WCC, *Empty Hands*, 7.

[23] WCC, *Empty Hands*, 7.

During the 1970s two specific examples of institutions intentionally searching for methods, processes and structures that could give expression to the ideals of resource sharing between churches took shape. The first example is the Evangelical Community for Apostolic Action (CEVAA) which was established in 1971 by 'different churches in Europe... Africa and the Pacific, linked with missionary societies' as they transformed 'their relationships in order to establish a community of partners in mission'.[24] The transformed relationship reflected a desire to enter together into a covenant as churches which are 'working together in the mission of evangelisation' and reflected:

> The search by the churches of the south for their own autonomy in relation to the missionary societies and the churches of the north, their concern to take up their different responsibilities and their desire to reflect upon their resources and their identity.[25]

However, the creation of CEVAA was not a simple process nor could it be likened to 'a victory parade' and 'came at the cost of many difficulties'. This was because those who were responsible for the transformation 'were not content with a few cosmetic retouches to what was there. They aimed at a thorough-going reform to correspond to the missionary demands of the church today'.[26] These efforts for transformation began as early as 1954 when the Paris Evangelical Missionary Society (PEMS) began exploring how to reorganise its structure. Through a prolonged process of consultation and joint action, the Paris Evangelical Missionary Society finally adopted the proposal for a new organic structure and 'the Paris Evangelical Missionary Society dissolved itself, 30th October 1971. On this same date, the Evangelical Community for Apostolic Action was created'.[27]

A distinctive characteristic of CEVAA is that this community of churches –

> is not a 'single centre' unifying the churches. It functions as a 'multi-centre'; that is, it is the place where many relations uniting the churches come together. It thereby gives rise to a community life made up of relations and collaborations that favour the discovery and realisation of a worldwide

---

[24] Samuel K. Ada, 'CEVAA: From a Missionary Society to a Community of Churches in Mission', in *International Review of Mission*, 76.304 (October 1987), 505.

[25] Ada, 'CEVAA: From a Missionary Society to a Community of Churches in Mission', 505.

[26] Ada, 'CEVAA: From a Missionary Society to a Community of Churches in Mission', 514.

[27] Ada, 'CEVAA: From a Missionary Society to a Community of Churches in Mission', 515.

> mission in the service of a world of solidarity. This goes beyond mere inter-church aid to an organism made for service, communion and dialogue.[28]

Not only does CEVAA provide a different level of engagement and mutuality in action; it also provides a different process or mechanism for sharing power in decision-making as 'decisions are taken jointly on the international level' where a representative of each member-church is present. This enables a structure and decision-making process whereby, 'in principle, no church imposes its decision on others'.[29] The actions necessary for carrying out these decisions are then 'entrusted to member-churches and organisms who share responsibility for them',[30] with each member contributing 'the spiritual, human and financial resources at its disposal, according to what each has received from the Lord'.[31]

The other example is the Council for World Mission (CWM) with its historic roots in the London Missionary Society (LMS). The Congregational Council for World Mission, formed in 1966 by the Congregational Church in England and Wales, was renamed as the Council for World Mission in 1973. However, it was only in 1977 that the Council for World Mission came to embody 'a radically different conception of mission' which in turn 'influenced the creation of a new strategy for engagement in world mission'.[32] It is important to recognise that CWM 'emerged not as a traditional missionary society' but rather 'understands itself as a fellowship of churches, which are themselves involved in mission, acting locally and seeking partners globally'.[33] It was, and continues to be, 'a community of churches, from the north and the south, that have covenanted together to challenge and to enable each other for mission and, as equal partners, to share their gifts and needs for mission'.[34] Much like the structure of CEVAA, the Council for World Mission, by constituting itself as a council in which 'a place is allocated to each participating church' seeks to provide 'opportunity for effective

---

[28] Ada, 'CEVAA: From a Missionary Society to a Community of Churches in Mission', 516.
[29] Ada, 'CEVAA: From a Missionary Society to a Community of Churches in Mission', 517.
[30] Ada, 'CEVAA: From a Missionary Society to a Community of Churches in Mission', 516.
[31] Ada, 'CEVAA: From a Missionary Society to a Community of Churches in Mission', 518.
[32] Maitland Evans, 'The Council for World Mission's Partnership in Mission Model', in *International Review of Mission*, 76.304 (October 1987), 458. See also, Barrie Scopes, 'The Shaping of the Council for World Mission', in *International Review of Mission*, 76.304 (October 1987), 452-53.
[33] Christopher Duraisingh, 'CWM's First Decade and Beyond', in *International Review of Mission*, 76.304 (October 1987), 474.
[34] Duraisingh, 'CWM's First Decade and Beyond', 474.

participation by member-churches at the strategic levels of decision-making'.[35]

Along with the two historical models described above, a recent organic transformation took place in the Association of Churches and Missions in South West Germany (EMS), founded in 1972. As the Association grew in partnership with churches in Asia, Africa and the Middle East, it evolved as an international mission organisation with a first international consultation organised in 1983 under the title 'Sharing in Obedience' which was attended by two delegates from each member- and partner-organization. The final message from this consultation states:

> All Christians share in obedience, in order to live and proclaim the Gospel of Jesus Christ and to spread the Kingdom of God on earth. The members of the body of Christ acknowledge that all of them depend on each other, help each other and complement each other. All have received gifts and all can pass on gifts.[36]

In 2012 EMS celebrated its 40th anniversary and adopted a new constitution as well as a new name where the abbreviation 'EMS' is no longer derived from a mission 'in South-west Germany', but signifies rather an 'Evangelical Mission in Solidarity'. With this new constitution and self-understanding, the Evangelical Mission in Solidarity presents itself:

> As a fellowship of churches and missions in Europe, Africa, Asia and the Middle East with equal rights in our 'Common Witness', we learn from each other and support each other. We stand on the foundation of the Gospel of Jesus Christ. In word and deed, we participate in God's mission in our world. In solidarity we stand up for one another, and for justice, peace, the integrity of creation and the dignity of all mankind.[37]

The example of EMS shows that the ecumenical movement continues to seek opportunities for discerning together structures, processes and methods that can build humility, respect and mutuality in the relationship between churches.

More recently, during a consultation in Malawi organised by the World Council of Churches and ACT Alliance (Action by Churches Together for Development) on the relationship between churches and specialised ministries in September 2014, a different term, 'assets', was presented as a potential alternative reference that could enable the churches to move beyond the historical baggage held by the term 'resources' as this has primarily been identified as money. The term 'assets' provides more space and opportunity to refer to gifts already existing within a church and allows

---

[35] Evans, 'The Council for World Mission's Partnership in Mission Model', 459.

[36] https://ems-online.org/en/about-us/who-we-are/the-history (accessed 14th October 2015).

[37] https://ems-online.org/en/about-us/who-we-are/the-history (accessed 14th October 2015).

the church to explore more broadly what is available without being limited to finances as it is used in other contexts beyond economics. Exploring assets allows the church to assess the social, cultural as well as religious experiences and gifts at its disposal.

In his recent article, 'Mapping Out and Mobilising Diaconal Assets', Kjell Nordstokke identifies two categories of assets that can be found in Christian churches – tangible and intangible assets – which can contribute to strengthening the sharing of resources between churches.[38] The tangible assets he refers to are practice, institutions and structures, human resources, economic resources and communication resources. On the other hand, intangible assets are identified as the collective memory of the past, rites and rituals, ethos and relations, along with trust and moral authority.[39]

The practice of the ecumenical sharing of resources is more than simply the exchange of money or other materials. It is, foremost, about establishing right relationships. In this vein it is interesting to note that one of the intangible assets that the church possesses is its network of global relationships. The church, wherever it is situated and regardless of size or perceived strength, is a member of the one body of Christ. All Christian churches around the world confess that they believe one holy catholic and apostolic church as a fundamental foundation of their faith. The shared confession implies that the Christian church is equal in stature and heritage. This has significant implications for how the churches relate to one another, particularly in terms of sharing ecumenically.

Given that the discussion of sharing resources ecumenically originated from the Christian church's deliberations on mission, it is not surprising to see that the earliest discussions on the significance of partnership was also raised in the missionary context. From as early as the third World Mission Conference which was held in Tambaram, India, in 1938 the issues of co-operation and unity were explored which affirmed the importance of right relationships between churches of the global North and the global South. The report of the Tambaram conference states:

> We believe that cooperation is in line with the will and purpose of God, and that it is thus essentially Christian. We would urge that not only between churches in each field but also in the relations between the older and the younger churches, cooperation should be regarded as the governing principle.[40]

---

[38] Kjell Nordstokke, 'Mapping Out and Mobilising Diaconal Assets', in Stephanie Dietrich, Knud Jørgensen, Kari Karsrud Korslien and Kjell Nordstokke (eds), *Diakonia as Christian Social Practice: An Introduction* (Oxford: Regnum, 2014).

[39] Stephanie Dietrich, Knud Jørgensen, Kari Karsrud Korslien and Kjell Nordstokke (eds), *Diakonia as Christian Social Practice: An Introduction* (Oxford: Regnum, 2014), 217-9.

[40] International Missionary Council (ed), *The World Mission of the Church – Findings and Recommendations of the Meeting of the International Missionary*

During the subsequent meetings of the IMC, such as those in Whitby, Ontario, Canada, in 1950 and the meeting in Willingen, Germany, in 1952, the theological foundations and practice of sharing resources ecumenically were further probed and discussed. Throughout the development of the discourse on partnership, the focus was on mutuality and respect, and the recognition that each partner had the capacity to be responsible. In addition, the most important basis for fostering a relationship of mutuality and interdependence as an expression of true partnership was the conviction that, as members of the one body of Christ, all were equal.

At no point in the history of the discussions on the ecumenical sharing of resources was the notion of independence offered as a viable alternative to partnership. Rather, the proper sharing of resources ecumenically was regarded as promoting the unity of the church. In this sense, the discussions and deliberations on the ecumenical sharing of resources can be understood as confirming the ideal that 'the corrective for paternalism is not independence, but interdependence, and interdependence comes with a deeper understanding of the nature of unity in Christ and of the situation in which other members of the body of Christ live'.[41]

An important element in partnership is the recognition by the churches that they are one, sharing in the common baptism of faith in Christ Jesus. This aspect of our commonality as a faith community has been emphasized again and again over the years. As René Padilla remarked, 'Giving and receiving cannot be maintained unless there is between the churches a mature relationship based on the Gospel. If the Church ceases to be a community in which people share a common meaning derived from the Gospel, sooner or later there is a return to the old ways of paternalism and dependence'.[42] A similar observation was made by Francis Stephanos who argued that, 'if Christians are to take interdependence seriously, they need to realize that they share a common life – the resurrection life'.[43]

As the one body of Christ, the churches around the world are compelled, in their sharing of ecumenical resources, to ensure that the method of sharing is reflective of the values of the relationship that they have in Christ. The churches must therefore constantly remind themselves that:

> True partnership implies mutual support for the identity and all aspects of the work and the well-being of each of the partners. It is comprehensive, with no

---

*Council, Tambaram, Madras, India, December 12-29, 1938* (London, New York: International Missionary Council, 1939), 153.

[41] C. René Padilla, 'Partnership' in Unit IV – Sharing and Service', in *New Approaches to Development*, 45.

[42] Padilla, 'Partnership' in Unit IV', 45.

[43] Padilla, 'Partnership' in Unit IV', 45.

> limits as to what the relationship should embrace. It is built on respect, trust, accountability and genuine two-way communication.[44]

It could be argued that if Christ must be truly present in ministries of service and sharing of the church, then it is important to build the relationship and establishes the processes of mutuality based on the life and ministry of Christ himself, therefore: 'The model of partnership that Jesus gives us is that of servanthood – partnership which is expressed in compassion, humility, obedience and in a genuine spirit of service to the point of sacrificing oneself'.[45] The church must maintain the attitude and conviction that, as equal members in the body of Christ, we have the responsibility as a new creation of reflecting Christ in our acts of sharing. According to Francis Stephanos, 'Partners who dispense resources are stewards of the resources of God and let others be equal players to share the resources in the manner that will benefit all members and maintain dignity'.[46]

Therefore when one delves into the plethora of documents, statements, expressions of intent and goodwill that can be found throughout the history of the modern ecumenical movement on the ideals of ecumenical sharing of resources and partnership, it could be assumed that the process of sharing had reached the pinnacle of an effective, meaningful and constructive relationship of mutuality, respect and trust. Yet, the reality of the relationship between churches is one where the commitment and interest of partnership is still in jeopardy, and the ecumenical sharing of resources as reflecting the right relationships of a community of sharing are limited. The obstacles to realizing these ideals are present in churches of the global North as well as the South.

Does this mean, then, that and the process of ecumenical sharing of resources can never reach the ideal to which the ecumenical movement has been aspiring? According to Konrad Raiser, former General Secretary of the WCC:

> The vision of ecumenical sharing offers a real opportunity for a new beginning and the theology of sharing itself is not an abstract idea, but rather an important aid to interpreting our own experiences and a pointer towards the sources which can constantly renew the strength for sharing.[47]

---

[44] Knut Edvard Larsen and Knud Jørgensen, 'Editorial Introduction – Exploring Models for Power and Partnership' in Knut Edvard Larsen and Knud Jørgensen (eds), *Power and Partnership* (Oxford: Regnum, 2014), 2.

[45] Stephanos, 'An African Perspective: Challenging the Power Structure', 74.

[46] Stephanos, 'An African Perspective: Challenging the Power Structure', 74.

[47] Konrad Raiser, 'Towards a Sharing Community' in Huibert van Beek (ed), in *Sharing Life – Official Report of the WCC World Consultation on Koinonia: Sharing Life in a World Community, El Escorial, Spain, October 1987* (Geneva: WCC), 18.

More concretely, the source and strength which enables one to persevere in hope is that a true and faithful commitment to the sharing relationship necessitates the church recognising that mutuality is only possible in 'the freedom granted by the Spirit of God'.[48]

Raiser reiterated that the ecumenical movement has not been without success in sharing its resources ecumenically, promoting changes in attitudes and perspectives, and fostering and promoting the sharing of non-material resources.[49] Raiser also noted that the churches in the North and the South have been mutually enriched through the sharing of 'spiritual perceptions and ideas, music and songs, prayers and living testimonies'.[50]

Throughout the history of the modern ecumenical movement the desire to see the churches sharing their resources ecumenically, with the whole of the *oikoumene*, has been a prominent and lasting topic. That the churches continue to discuss and debate the issue, as well as deliberate on how best to practise it, signifies that it continues to be a theme of interest. Even more, it implies that sharing ecumenically is, as was noted previously, an integral part of how the church can and should exist in this world, as a community of sharing and fostering just relationships.

---

48 Raiser, 'Towards a Sharing Community', 19.
49 Raiser, 'Towards a Sharing Community', 19.
50 Raiser, 'Towards a Sharing Community', 21.

# CONTEXTUALISATION

Katalina Tahaafe-Williams

If the twentieth century could be classified as mission's ecumenical century, then it could also be described as the century that gave us a world Christianity that no longer appeared predominantly white and western. African scholar Akintunde Akinade defines world Christianity as the 'new global configuration of the Christian faith in all its hues and colours', including the varieties of local expressions and the ways they interact with one another.[1] The Scottish theologian Andrew Walls stated that the 'most remarkable century in the history of the expansion of Christianity has been the twentieth'.[2] While it can be argued that at the time Christian decline in the West was already apparent, this was not the case in other parts of the world, especially in the global South.[3] According to American historian Dana Robert, more than seventy per cent of the world's Christian population in the early twentieth century were Europeans.[4] However, by the end of the century, African and Latin American Christians alone made up almost fifty per cent of the world Christian populations, not counting the Christian populations of Asia and Oceania.

Clearly, a demographic transformation in world Christianity took place which saw a shift in Christian identity from the western to the southern hemisphere. This was a massive shift not just in population and geography,

---

[1] Akintunde E. Akinade, 'Hans Küng', in Miguel A. de la Torre and Stacey M. Floyd-Thomas (eds), *Beyond the Pale: Reading Theology from the Margins* (Louisville, KY: Westminster John Knox Press, 2011), 232.

[2] Andrew F. Walls, *The Cross-cultural Process in Christian History* (Maryknoll, NY: Orbis Books, 2002), 64.

[3] The language used to name the parts of the globe that are not 'western' or part of what is known as 'the West' continues to be problematic. Without exception, all such terms (e.g. non-western, non-European, Third World, Developing World, non-white) implicitly convey the notion that the West is superior and all the rest are inferior. I have resorted to using the term 'global South' simply because it is the term I found most used in the contemporary literature I have researched. Further, the idea of the East was also absorbed into the Eurocentric ideological discourse of 'the West and the Rest' which promoted the 'ineradicable distinction between Western superiority and Oriental inferiority'. See Edward W. Said, *Orientalism: Western Concepts of the Orient* (Harmondsworth, UK: Penguin, 1985).

[4] Dana L. Robert, 'Shifting Southward: Global Christianity since 1945', in Paul W. Chilcote and Laceye C. Warner (eds), *The Study of Evangelism: Exploring a Missional Practice of the Church* (Grand Rapids, MI, and Cambridge, UK: Eerdmans, 2008), 118.

but also in cultural and world outlook. Robert Schreiter quotes the German theologian Karl Rahner who described this situation as:

> the church moving from a predominantly Hellenistic worldview into the era of a world church, characterised by a pluralism in worldview and multiplicity of new pastoral and theological problems unprecedented in Christian history.[5]

Combined with a socio-political environment that saw the processes of decolonisation to independence empowering former colonised nations with the confidence to shake off European domination, we witness the emerging demand for and debate over what has become widely known in the world church, especially within missiological and theological circles, as *contextualisation.*

My intention in this chapter is to highlight some significant developments in contextualisation in the twentieth century, and to discuss key challenges that may pick up some of the themes in the new WCC Mission Affirmation: *Together towards Life* (*TTL*)[6] which students of *TTL* may find useful as they seek to apply it in their communities and churches, mission activities, ministries and lives.

As a child born in Tonga and brought up in the Methodist Church, I thought Christianity was a western religion. In my childish imagination, when I thought of what God might look like, I pictured an image of a white man with long white hair and beard. This is not surprising, given that western Christian missions in the colonised territories had been in existence for at least four centuries. Add to that the rather ambiguous relationship between western missions and European imperialism and you have an environment where non-western minds and imaginations were conditioned to think that the Christian faith originated in the West when in fact it was born in the East.

Western cultural and religious dominance were so pervasive that even in a small island kingdom in the South Pacific, western Eurocentric representations of what it meant to be Christian were uncritically accepted as normative. The pictures of Jesus that hung on our church walls and family homes portraying him at any stage in his life on earth from infancy to adulthood were consistently of a very white European male. The picture books in my Sunday School class that I loved to look at with such fascination had the whole holy family radiant with peaches-and-cream complexions. The films of Christ's crucifixion that were viewed at Easter and cried over with such anguish, had characters, including that of Jesus, with distinctly white European features.

In the hot tropical climate of the South Pacific, proper attire for Sunday worship worn by Tongan women were British Victorian-style clothes that covered the body from neck to toe, while men had to wear jackets and ties.

---

[5] Robert J. Schreiter, *Constructing Local Theologies* (Maryknoll, NY: Orbis Books, 2001), xi.
[6] *TTL*.

In the Eucharist the congregants received the body and blood of Christ in bread and wine (grape juice for us good Methodists, of course!) which were not easily acquired in a Tongan village. However, if anyone dared to suggest an alternative use of the flesh and the juice of the indigenous coconut as sacramental elements, the uproar would be deafening! So it was acceptable to use the British religio-cultural Methodist-contextualised bread and grape juice for the body and blood of Christ *(which I contend are not necessarily the Biblical/traditional bread and wine used by Jesus in Palestine)*, but it was inconceivable that local church leaders and members would consider the use of the flesh and juice of the beloved coconut! Hymns were sung with gusto that told of the need to be washed by the blood of Jesus in order to be 'white as snow' and thereby to be pure and worthy. Liberationist ethicist Miguel de la Torre and womanist ethicist Stacey Floyd-Thomas concur that many in marginalised situations are 'conditioned from childhood to see and interpret reality through the eyes of the dominant culture'.[7] One could say that in this situation western Christian conditioning was quite thorough so that anything white western was superior and therefore to be internalised, imitated and/or adopted.

Clearly, western Christianity had intentionally brought the gospel to the non-western world in deeply enculturated western forms. Inevitably and increasingly, Christian populations in Asia, Africa and Latin America began to question what was perceived as imposed alien cultural categories and forms. As Asian theologian Hwa Yung explained, there was an 'increasing dissatisfaction with a Western Christianity as against an indigenous variety', and a growing desire for a confident self-identity.[8]

In significant ways, the Protestant ecumenical movement was instrumental in bringing the visible presence and voices of Christians from the global South to the forums of world mission thinking and theological discourse. Beginning at the Edinburgh 1910 World Missionary Conference and continuing through to the 1938 International Missionary Conference in Tambaram, India, the presence of representatives from new churches in the global South was more visible than at any mission conferences held earlier.[9] After World War II, however, it was clear that reactions against European colonialism in the global South included rejecting western Christian missionaries with accusations of 'paternalism, racism and cultural imperialism'.[10] Ironically, Christianity in the global South continued to grow rapidly, even as the demand for a moratorium on western missionaries became more intense. A significant part of that growth came

---

[7] Miguel A. de la Torre and Stacey M. Floyd-Thomas, *Beyond the Pale: Reading Theology from the Margins* (Louisville, KY: Westminster John Knox Press, 2011), xxiii.

[8] Hwa Yung, *Mangoes or Bananas? The Quest for an Authentic Asian Christian Theology* (Oxford: Regnum, 1997), 1.

[9] Walls, *The Cross-Cultural Process*, 64.

[10] Robert, 'Shifting Southward', 122.

in the form of indigenous independent Pentecostal churches, for example, within the African context, the African Initiated Churches (AICs).[11]

Robert credits contextualisation with the explosion of Christian growth in the global South, stating that, while the scholars were busy debating theological concepts, the people at the grassroots who received the gospel message went about 'retranslating it into cultural modes that fitted their worldviews and met their needs'.[12] The implication is that, without the mission professionals and elites noticing, indigenous Christians demonstrated their effectiveness as interpreters of Christianity to their own people so that, even before the missionaries and colonisers had left, the gospel was already being contextualised. In short, this was a remarkable example of the marginalised being the agents of mission and evangelism.

Within Roman Catholic circles there was also a growing mood for renewal in the church.[13] The idea of interpreting the gospel in terms of local contexts and circumstances began to gain strong support, as was the case at the Second Vatican Council in the early 1960s. This gave the impetus for Latin American bishops who gathered at Medellin in Colombia in 1968 to articulate their profound concerns over the alarming level of poverty in Latin America, and to officially endorse this idea of contextualisation in the form of what was becoming widely known as the *theology of liberation.*[14] By the early 1970s both Catholics and Protestants were engaging with this radical understanding of mission and theology using terms like *contextualisation, localisation, indigenisation, inculturation,* and *adaptation.*[15] In the last quarter of the twentieth century a growing awareness and wider acceptance of human experience as integral to mission and to the classical sources of theology, namely, scripture and tradition, were quite evident.

The renowned South African missiologist David Bosch credited the nineteenth century German scholar Friedrich Schleiermacher with pioneering the contextual approach to theology, as Schleiermacher was the first to assert that all theologies are shaped by the context in which they emerge.[16] Though Schleiermacher did not go far enough with his contextual approach, he opened the door to challenge the very notion of a 'pure' message.[17] In his terms, all texts including the biblical text were influenced by the contexts and circumstances in which they were written. As Bosch

---

[11] Robert, 'Shifting Southward', 133.
[12] Robert, 'Shifting Southward', 125.
[13] Robert J. Schreiter, *Constructing Local Theologies* (Maryknoll, NY: Orbis Books, 2001), 2.
[14] Gustavo Gutierrez, *A Theology of Liberation: History, Politics, and Salvation* (London: SCM, 1974), 5.
[15] Schreiter, *Constructing Local Theologies,* 2.
[16] David J. Bosch, *Transforming Mission: Paradigm Shifts in Theology of Mission* (Maryknoll, NY: Orbis Books, 1991), 422.
[17] Bosch, *Transforming Mission,* 422.

framed it, 'It was impossible to penetrate to a residue of Christian faith that was not already, in a sense, interpretation.'[18] Bosch therefore maintained that 'from the beginning the missionary message of the Christian church incarnated itself in the life and world of those who had embraced it'.[19] Likewise, contextual theologians Stephen Bevans and Roger Schroeder made very clear that 'mission has always engaged in what is today called the process of inculturation or contextualisation', and listed key figures in the history of the church who have practised contextualisation in how they witnessed to and proclaimed the gospel, from the apostles of Jesus, to the Patristic Fathers, through the Reformation and right up to the present day.[20] So while it was from the Christians of the global South that the contextual approach to mission and theology was brought to the fore in the twentieth century, contextual mission and theology are not novel to the Christian faith nor indeed to European contextual theology!

In this vein, one could further name *European* theology, *Euro-American* theology, and *Western* theology as contextual theologies because, according to Bevans:

> There is no such thing as 'theology'; there is only *contextual* theology: *feminist* theology, *black* theology, *liberation* theology, *Filipino* theology, *Asian-American* theology, *African* theology, and so forth. Doing theology contextually is not an option, nor is it something that should only interest people from the Third World, missionaries who work there, or ethnic communities within dominant cultures. The contextualisation of theology – the attempt to understand Christian faith in terms of a particular context – is really a theological imperative.[21]

Of course, Christianity in both western and non-western contexts had not yet become fully conscientised to that phenomenon and it is arguable that many western missionaries at the time were shocked and took offence at the changing missiological and theological landscape! But once indigenous Christians were awakened to their own discomfort in struggling to relate to the gospel message in foreign terms, they demanded not only that they be free to contextualise it for their own realities, but that the world church should recognise and accept that contextual theology is *the* way to do theology. They began to set the agenda for mission and there would be no turning back. Bevans and Schroeder agree that Christians in both the global South and in the West came to the realisation that 'what had pretended to be a *universal* theology was in fact one that *universalised* theological

---

[18] Bosch, *Transforming Mission,* 422.
[19] Bosch, *Transforming Mission*, 421.
[20] Stephen B. Bevans and Roger P. Schroeder, *Constants in Context: A Theology of Mission for Today* (Maryknoll, NY: Orbis Books, 2004), 385.
[21] Stephen B. Bevans, *Models of Contextual Theology* (Maryknoll, NY: Orbis Books, 2001), 3.

expression according to what amounted to a local theology developed in Europe'.[22]

Even with that realisation, perhaps the most serious challenge to contextualisation is western Christianity's resistance, continuing lack of recognition, and failure to take seriously the contextual nature of theology in how it does theology in the West. There continues to be a certain air of arrogance among the ranks of western theologians, in the academy and seminaries, where the prevailing attitude is that 'they know what theology is and that everyone else has to submit to their judgment when theologising'.[23] Missiologist Stan Nussbaum suggests that this might be because –

> Western theologians generally think and write as if knowing, understanding, and explaining are the only valid aims of theology. They rarely get their hands dirty in history, taking the side of the poor and experiencing life from their perspective.[24]

Perhaps it is simply an oblivion to just how culturally conditioned western mission and theological thinking and presuppositions are. Perhaps it is more about a reluctance to let go of privileged positions in the centre of power and make room for the *other*, for the *marginalised*. De la Torre and Floyd-Thomas promote the view that doing theology from the centre of power and privilege not only assists in normalising and legitimising the social location and theological status of the dominant culture, but also enables a process of self-justification and legitimising of the socio-political status quo.[25] Bevans and Schroeder suggest that western theology's reluctance to take contextualisation seriously may have something to do with the risk and pain involved in confronting the fact that western Christianity has been marred by colonial expansionism, racism and assumptions of cultural superiority.[26]

It would seem that the Hellenistic mindset Rahner thought had been left behind with the advent of world Christianity still dominates western theology. So much so that the classical binaries of principle versus application, objective versus subjective, continue to shape western theological approaches. The implication of course is that western theology falls under the superior principle-objective mode, while contextual theologies such as Liberation Theology fall under the inferior application-subjective mode. Unfortunately, this stigma of inferiority continues to

---

[22] Bevans and Schroeder, *Constants in Context*, 386.

[23] John Fuellenbach, 'The Theology of Liberation', in William Jenkinson and Helene O'Sullivan (eds), *Trends in Mission: Toward the 3rd Millennium* (Maryknoll, NY: Orbis Books, 1991), 75.

[24] Stan Nussbaum, *A Reader's Guide to Transforming Mission: A Concise, Accessible Companion to David Bosch's Classic Book* (Maryknoll, NY: Orbis Books, 2005), 108.

[25] Torre and Floyd-Thomas, *Beyond the Pale,* xxiii.

[26] Bevans and Schroeder, *Constants in Context*, 388.

hinder active self-conscious contextual theologising and mission in western Christian contexts.

De la Torre and Floyd-Thomas describe the uphill battle that contextual theologians from the global South and from migrant diasporic communities in the West often face when they question or challenge Eurocentric theological perspectives –

> Those relegated to the margins of theological discourse are always welcomed to 'colour' the conversation, as long as the supremacy of Eurocentric theological thought is not radically challenged. Scholars from marginalised communities who engage in questioning or debunking Eurocentric theological perspectives are usually ignored, their scholarship dismissed as lacking 'academic rigor'.[27]

This assessment resonates with my own experiences in western church circles and theological forums. Often the views and challenges I offer are dismissed as coming from an apparently aggressive minority ethnic woman, or alternatively I get patronised as just another person with a *chip on her shoulder*. What irks even more is the very surreal experience of having a white male or female in the same forum make a point you made first, and seeing their input being treated as insightful and valuable while yours is totally ignored and you wonder whether you have said anything at all or you just imagined having said it! It is irksome and surreal because in such moments there is a sense of utter invisibility. Over the years I have tried different postures and projections of my voice and body language when I speak in such forums to see if I am better received and heard. Then I realised I could not possibly carry that problem too! There are no medals for the never-ending effort dedicated to honing one's skills at getting under the skin of an alien dominant culture and mastering an alien dominant tongue in order to articulate, to communicate, to be heard. There is no acknowledgment of the years spent in building strength and resilience to survive that dominant racist culture. There certainly is no respect for refusing to be co-opted and be fitted in a box *they* have constructed. In that kind of climate, to be a contextual theologian one must develop a thick skin. Darrell Whiteman contends that 'good contextualisation offends people for the right reasons',[28] and Walls concurs when he intimates that to be faithful to Christ will often put one at odds with one's society.[29]

Liberation Theology and its methodological use of inculturation are two of the most prominent and well-known forms of contextualisation. They also appear to be the best matched with marginalised and indigenous Christian populations and communities, and this is not surprising for they emerged out of precisely those contexts. It was Latin American scholar

---

[27] Torre and Floyd-Thomas, *Beyond the Pale,* xxiv.

[28] Darrell L. Whiteman, 'Contextualisation: The Theory, the Gap, the Challenge', in *International Bulletin of Missionary Research,* 21.1 (January 1997), 2.

[29] Andrew Walls, 'The Gospel as the Prisoner and Liberator of Culture', in *Missionalia,* 10.3 (November 1982), 98-99.

Gustavo Gutierrez who brought the theology of liberation to world attention when his book of the same name was published in the early 1970s.[30] Emerging out of a situation in Latin America of abject poverty and oppression for millions of its peoples, Liberation Theology seeks to engage with socio-political reality in ways that could overcome such human desperation and hopelessness.

Roman Catholic theologian John Fuellenbach explains that it is a theology that demands 'a radical commitment to the plight of the poor in order to help them to change the situation through an active engagement for social justice and human rights'.[31] It asks questions of the gospel and what it has to say to such situations or risk being totally irrelevant. A significant feature of Liberation Theology is its insistence that taking a preferential option for the poor does not mean doing things for the poor. Rather, it is about ensuring that the poor are free to exercise their human agency in ways they choose. It is ensuring that, as marginalised Christians, the poor are full partners in God's mission and hence are agents and bearers of mission.

In *TTL*, the church affirms that marginalised people are agents of mission exercising a prophetic role that emphasises fullness of life for all, and commits to acting in justice, solidarity and inclusivity as the marks of mission from the margins.[32] Gutierrez's expressed vision made clear that in his view there will be –

> an authentic theology of liberation only when the oppressed themselves can freely raise their voice and express themselves directly and creatively in society and in the heart of the People of God, when they themselves account for the hope, which they bear, when they are the protagonists of their own liberation.[33]

Whereas the process of contextualisation involves a particular theology engaging with the reality of its local context, in the case of inculturation the theological concern is to do with cultural empowerment and freedom. Oppression is seen in terms of cultural imperialism across cultural lines, so the key theological task according to Nussbaum is to free each culture from alien cultural domination.[34] In his recent encyclical *Evangelii Gaudium,* Pope Francis details the request by the Bishops of Oceania that the church develop an 'understanding of the truth of Christ' that integrates the traditions and cultures of the region, and to require missionaries to use it in co-operation with indigenous Christians to ensure that the faith and life of the church is expressed in legitimate forms appropriate to each culture.[35]

---

[30] Gustavo Gutierrez, *A Theology of Liberation: History, Politics, and Salvation* (London: SCM, 1974).
[31] Fuellenbach, 'The Theology of Liberation', 74.
[32] *TTL,* §39.
[33] Gutierrez, *The Theology of Liberation*, 268.
[34] Nussbaum, *A Reader's Guide*, 112.
[35] Pope Francis, *Evangelii Gaudium* (Strathfield, NSW: St Pauls, 2013), 93.

This is inculturation. Bosch views inculturation as far more radical than some of the liberation theologies and certainly more so than some of its former manifestations, i.e. *adaptation*, *accommodation*, and *indigenisation*, because it is about making the gospel at home in a particular culture.[36] However, he warns against making the gospel so at home in that particular culture that it becomes co-opted and thereby loses its ability to illumine, inform, enlighten and challenge that culture.[37] Bevans listed six models of inculturation including translation, anthropological, praxis, synthetic, transcendental and counter-cultural, and explains that, while each may have an affinity with a particular context (e.g. counter-cultural is the most appropriate in securalised post-modern European or North American context), no one model is absolute.[38]

Vietnamese-American theologian Peter Phan sees the significance of contextualisation for the growth and health of Christianity when he states that 'on the success of inculturation will hang the future of the church'.[39]

We have seen the impact of indigenous contextual mission during the colonial era and at the exodus of colonisers and western missionaries from the global South. The profound and inspiring point of that moment in history was that world Christianity saw grassroots indigenous and marginalised Christians in action! In other words, the church and the mission of God are flourishing and growing through the agency of the marginalised!

It is estimated that by 2025 there will be 2.6 billion Christians in the world with 633 million living in Africa, 640 million in Latin America, 460 million in Asia, and 555 million in Europe.[40] Whilst not surprising, this continuing reality of the radical shift in the demographics of world Christianity should surely compel us to rethink our mission and theological formulations and strategies. This is exactly the vision and hope of *TTL*.[41] It affirms that mission movements are emerging from the global South and East and that rethinking our mission and theological formulations involves rooting our mission practice in these contexts and cultures as well as acting to confront structures that oppress and dehumanise contrary to the values of God's reign.[42]

Given the unprecedented level of global migration with its very public and visible implications for the world church, western Christianity is certainly seeing growth and vitality in the diasporic and multicultural churches and communities, in stark contrast to the decline that is now so common in the western church. There is a sort of reverse contextualisation

---

36 Nussbaum, *A Reader's Guide*, 112.
37 Bosch, *Transforming Mission*, 455.
38 Bevans, *Models of Contextual Theology*, 37.
39 Bevans and Schroeder, *Constants in Context,* 388.
40 Akinade, 'Hans Küng', 232.
41 *TTL,* §39.
42 *TTL,* §39.

going on here. Christian migrants arriving in the West bring with them their understandings and practices of Christianity (which might have been taught to them by western missionaries in the first place but now it is 'tradition'). They set up communities and plant diasporic churches where they live and witness in ways that mirror what happened back home. As a matter of fact, what these migrants are doing is taking the gospel and making it feel at home within their own minority ethnic diasporic communities. So it is a bit like contextualising in a bubble. They are surrounded by western society and culture, and they have created a diasporic bubble where they contextualise the gospel message they receive from the wider church in the shape of the 'tradition' they brought with them. The pros and cons of such a monoculturally entrenched approach to being church in diaspora are open for debate. But the point for now is that these are marginal Christian communities actively living out their faith in a kind of ironically contextual way – and they are strong, vibrant, thriving and growing, on the margins! For they are certainly not at the centre!

Yet it could be argued that the western churches are not paying serious attention. Contextualising patterns of mission practice initiated by migrant churches are emerging within western contexts that could have a truly profound impact in the whole life and vitality of western Christianity as has happened in the global South. By not paying serious attention, the older western churches are missing golden opportunities for really innovative and creative mission practices that could contribute to their missional renewal. For what could be more innovative and creative than contextualisation? The strength of contextualisation is that it helps us bridge the gap between our talking and our walking, between our theorising and our action, between our theologising and our authentic praxis. The experiences of migrant/multicultural churches in the West and of indigenous independent churches in the global South demonstrate that contextualisation helps build strong churches! Non-contextualised Christianity tends to engage people only at very superficial levels, so that at best what you get is a kind of 'split-level Christianity'.[43] This is what Yung calls 'nominal Christianity' where the gospel has not penetrated deep into individual and communal consciousness so as to engage meaningfully with human needs and aspirations.[44] Yung believes that nominal Christianity is prevalent in world Christianity, and I would add that it is western Christianity that is most susceptible and vulnerable to it.

This is why mission from the margins is so vital for the renewal of the life of the world church, especially in the West. Marginal peoples are experts in contextualisation. With very few material resources and often under extremely dire circumstances, they are innovatively and creatively going about doing the mission of God. De la Torre and Floyd-Thomas

---

[43] Whiteman, 'Contextualisation: The Theory, the Gap, the Challenge', 3.
[44] Hwa Yung, *Mangoes or Bananas?* 4.

make the point that the margins provide a 'double-consciousness' that helps illuminate and expose realities that the centre is bound to miss.[45] *TTL* is fully in sync when it states that 'People on the margins have agency, and can often see what, from the centre, is out of view'.[46] Doing mission from the margins allows for contextualisation to unmask the centre's taken-for-granted mission and theological presuppositions. It allows for Bevans' and Schroeder's notion of 'prophetic dialogue' as the new paradigm of mission for the 21st century.[47] But ultimately our contextual imperative takes its cue from our Lord's incarnation itself. There is nothing abstract about God incarnate. Henri Nouwen would insist: 'It has everything to do with the tangible, audible, and visible experience of God, an experience so real that it becomes the foundation of life.'[48] Knowing that, how can we not go and do likewise?

---

45 De la Torre and Floyd-Thomas, *Beyond the Pale,* xxv.
46 *TTL,* §15.
47 Bevans and Schroeder, *Constants in Context*, 387. The notion of 'prophetic dialogue' prioritises dialogue between gospel and context and, combined with good listening and discerning skills, you have a formula for effective contextual mission.
48 Gustavo Gutiérrez, *We Drink from Our Own Wells: The Spiritual Journey of a People* (Maryknoll, NY: Orbis Books, and Melbourne, Vic: Dove Communications, 1984), viii.

# TRANSFORMATION

Nico A. Botha

### Introduction: A Characterisation of Transformation

The difficulty in designating and describing the concept 'transformation' could be likened to the complexities around recounting a term like 'globalisation'. It has not been easy either to define Christian mission and its concomitant discipline of missiology. The South African missiologist David Bosch spoke of mission as being 'indefinable'.[1] There is a downside and an upside which the trickiness of characterizing transformation throws up. On the one hand, the lack of a clear-cut characterisation renders the task of tracing transformation in mission over a century virtually impossible. On the other hand, it opens up the prospect of looking at transformation from diverse angles and perspectives.

The introductory paragraph should not necessarily detract from attempts at describing transformation, albeit not in clinical terms. A few examples must suffice. First, in order to develop some understanding of transformation, a striking example in the ecumenical world comes from the Lutheran World Federation document[2] that describes transformation as 'an ongoing process of total reorientation of life with all its aspirations, ideologies, structures, and values'. It is a continuous process of rejection of that which dehumanizes and desecrates life, and adherence to that which affirms the sanctity of life and gifts in everyone, and promotes peace and justice in society. Transformation engages and changes all who are a part of it. In that manner, transformational *diakonia* helps to overcome so-called *helpers' syndromes*, practices and relationships that separate 'we' from 'they'. In the end, no-one escapes vulnerability. We all need to be transformed, reconciled and empowered. For that reason, we are all in need of *diakonia* – first of all God's *diakonia* as revealed in Jesus Christ, and then as mutual care and accompaniment of one another. Transformation is clearly a process, but at the same time, transformation envisions the achievement of certain goals, arriving at a new situation where human dignity is more respected with peace and justice for more people. Thus, transformation is closely related to what also may be defined as social

[1] David J. Bosch, *Transforming Mission: Paradigm Shifts in Theology of Mission* (Maryknoll, NY: Orbis Books, 2003), 9.

[2] Kjell Nordstokke (ed), Diakonia in Context: Transformation, Reconciliation, Empowerment – An LWF Contribution to the Understanding and Practice of Diakonia (Geneva: Lutheran World Federation, 2009), 43-44.

change, progress or development. From a theological point of view, transformation is a reminder of God's constant renewal of creation (Latin: *creatio continua*), as every morning we experience the darkness of night being transformed into the light of a new day breaking forth. As people of God, we see transformation as God's gracious gift for which we owe praise and service. It links diaconal work with the admonition of St Paul who told the believers not to 'be conformed to this world but be transformed by the renewal of your mind, that you may prove what is the will of God, what is good and acceptable and perfect' (Romans 12:2). Therefore, transformation rejects conformism. It expresses an alternative way of experiencing God's will in relationship to all God's creation.

As the Mission in Context document reads:

> … transformation, perceived in the light of Christ's resurrection, is the unfolding of the potential life-giving nature of all creation and an expression of the working of God's grace in nature. It is the ongoing work of the Holy Spirit to effect transformation in and through the Church to the whole world.[3]

Perhaps the German missiologists Faix and Weissenborn are unintentionally assisting in breaking down the very rich definition offered by the Lutheran World Federation by drawing attention to seven elements of transformation in their chapter on *Transformation als Aspekt der Soteriologie*[4] (Transformation as an Aspect of Soteriology). They interpret transformation as the all-encompassing challenge of God's reign. Space does not allow for any manner of elaboration on the seven elements, so they will merely be enumerated: it is present as well as something for the future; it includes soul and body; it is personal or individualistic and communal; it is momentary as well as a process; it is worked by the Spirit as well as being embodied by Christians; it is word, deed and being; and finally, it comes from God into the world.[5] The ensuing discussion therefore shows diverse elements of what is contained in the above-mentioned characterisation, as well as in the breakdown offered by Faix and Weissenborn.

In this chapter, liberty is taken to introduce different perspectives of transformation, relating to Christian mission from 1910 to 2010. First, transformation is looked at from a philosophical perspective with specific reference to the changes in thought-patterns and epistemologies brought about by shifts from the Enlightenment paradigm to a more post-modern mode of thinking. Secondly, the question is posed as to why, for example, Bosch uses the term 'transforming' in the title of his life work,

---

[3] Nordstokke, 'Diakonia', 44.

[4] Tobias Faix and Thomas Weissenborn, 'Transformation als Aspekt der Soteriology', in Rainer Ebeling and Afred Meier (eds), in *Missionale Theologie* (Marburg an der Lahn: Verlag der Francke-Buchhandlung, 2009), 113-20.

[5] Faix and Weissenborn, 'Transformation', 116-20.

*Transforming Mission,*[6] but does not even begin to offer some specific characterisation of transformation. Thirdly, a strong focus is on transformation in social, political, cultural and economic modes in relation to Christian mission. For this purpose, the thinking on transformation is traced in terms of the world mission conferences of the International Missionary Council (IMC), and after the fusion between the IMC and the World Council of Churches (WCC) in New Delhi, India, in 1961, the conferences under the auspices of the Commission on World Mission and Evangelism (CWME), Lausanne, as well as some individual scholars.

## Philosophical Transformation

The term 'philosophical' is used in very a broad sense to include shifts and transformation in missionary thinking since Edinburgh 1910, as well as hard-core philosophical transformation – for example, post-modernism – in its implications for mission.

What passes the review first is a brief investigation into how the missionary message was transformed over the twentieth century. Perhaps it is important to say from the outset that these shifts were profoundly informed by different cultural trends. A further issue is to reveal the underlying assumption that in the Bible, the book of Christians, and the church, there is no obvious concept of mission found, meaning that mission is a Christian construction which has undergone many changes, at least more than ten times during the past century.

Before and after Edinburgh 1910, mission was understood in terms of 'expansionism'. More concretely, western churches were required to expand into countries that had not yet been fully 'missionised'. The emphasis was on individual conversions, or in the Von Zinzendorf jargon, 'winning souls for the Lamb'. Disastrously, this has led to mission and colonialism becoming fellow travellers. In a country like Germany, the very specific protuberance or prominence of such an understanding of mission has been the notion of the *volkskirche,* or the establishment of 'national ethnic churches'. The effect of such a kind of missionary understanding on a country like South Africa is well recorded and not up for any further discussion in this chapter.

The Jerusalem 1928 mission conference saw a deconstruction of mission concepts in following a binary approach to the secularism-mission dialectic.[7] Doing mission in a divided world meant for this conference that the only possible relationship was dualistic or binary in terms of a Christian 'mission versus secularism' construct.

---

[6] Bosch, *Transforming Mission.*
[7] *Christian Century*, 10th May 1928, 1.

Amazingly, but true as early as the 1930s, what is today a common understanding of mission as holistic – 'meeting the whole of human need'[8] – emerged. Still, in the 1930s another important trend which saw the light was an understanding of mission in relation to, or meeting, other faiths;[9] and indeed, still in the 1930s a compelling notion of mission as partnership in evangelism[10] came to the fore with the inclusion of what was then still known as the 'younger churches'.

Turning quickly from the IMC mission conferences to the coming into being of the WCC in 1948, the fusion of the 'Faith and Order' and the 'Life and Work' Commissions gave rise to an understanding of mission as 'ecumenical witness'.[11] Up till then, mission had been understood very much in ecclesiological terms as an activity or enterprise of the *church*.

The Willingen 1952 conference of the IMC brought about a fundamental transformation from a church-centric mission to an understanding of mission as God's mission, with its deep and profound theological thinking of mission as emanating from the heart of God, and based on earlier reflections of Barth, Hartenstein and Kähler, the conference gave rise to the artefact *missio Dei.*[12] This has indeed been quite a radical transformation, espoused particularly by the Dutch missiologist, Hoekendijk, in his understanding of mission based on the God-world-church scheme. For Hoekendijk, the church was nothing but an instrument of mission, with mission as the only reason for its existence and, consequently, completely relativised. Mission was now interpreted as participating in God's mission.

To conclude the fifty years since Edinburgh 1910 of what is indeed a cursory perspective on what is loosely understood as philosophical and studious transformation, the attention turns to the 1958 mission conference at Achimota in Ghana. The Achimota conference was made famous by the resolution of the IMC to merge with the WCC. Clearly, the foundation for

---

[8] Daniel J. Adams (ed), *From East to West: Essays in Honour of Donald Bloesch* (Lanham, MD: University Press of America, 1997), 99.

[9] Stanley H. Skreslet, *Comprehending Mission: The Questions, Methods, Themes, and Prospects of Missiology* (Maryknoll, NY: Orbis Books, 2012), 117; Daryl Balia and Kirsteen Kim, *Witnessing to Christ Today,* Edinburgh 2010 Vol. II (Oxford: Regnum, 2010), 36.

[10] Wolfgang Gunther and Guillermo Cook, 'World Missionary Conferences', in Karl Muller, Theo Sundermeier, Stephen B. Bevans, Richard H. Bliese (eds), *Dictionary of Mission: Theology, History, Perspectives* (Maryknoll, NY: Orbis Books, 2006), 504.

[11] Mark Beach (ed), *Introducing the World Council of Churches. A Common Journey of Faith* (Geneva: WCC, 2013), 5; Balia and Kim, *Witnessing to Christ Today*, 201.

[12] Stephen B. Bevans and Roger P. Schroeder, *Constants in Conflict: A Theology of Mission for Today* (Maryknoll, NY: Orbis Books, 2004), 290; John G. Flett, *The Witness of God: The Trinity, Missio Dei, Karl Barth, and the Nature of Christian Community* (Grand Rapids, MI: Eerdmans, 2010), 152.

understanding mission as 'mission in unity' was laid here, though the main emphases were on presence and dialogue.

Perhaps, and arguably so, one of the most radical transformations in mission occurred at the Mexico City conference in 1963. A complete overhaul of mission understanding, albeit to a large extent only theoretical, took place. Mission was transformed as a departure from the slogan 'from the West to the rest since the best is in the West', to mission in six continents. If this is not creating too much of a caricature, the understanding was that the entire world is a mission field, not just particular geographical areas of it. A further issue at Mexico City was an epistemological break with the Jerusalem binary of Christian mission versus secularism to a more creative interpretation of the relationship between the two. Consequently, Mexico City opted for the more dynamic term 'secularisation' rather than 'secularism', which creates the impression of a closed system to be resisted rather than to be engaged creatively with the gospel.

Furthermore, the 1960s began to witness a greater participation of Africans, Asians and Latin Americans, taking mission by storm with their stories of oppression and exploitation, struggle and hope. This resulted in mission being viewed more and more as liberation (Bosch).[13] Key terms from the gospel – for example, salvation – found a more comprehensive and contextual interpretation, culminating in another major transformation at the Melbourne 1980 conference where very profound missiological thinking took place about the plight of the poor of the world. From the perspective of God's kingdom missions were to exercise a preferential option for the poor, following God in his choice for the poor. There were other interpretations of mission, still in the period between 1970 and 1990 – for example, mission was seen as inter-church aid, proclamation, dialogue and church growth.

## Transforming Mission: David J Bosch

One of the intriguing speculations about Bosch's world-renowned book is why the term used in the title of the book does not find any further reflection in it.

In a personal discussion, Prof. Piet Meiring from Pretoria and Prof. Kritizinger from Unisa, Pretoria, who both knew David Bosch well, concurred that he did not find it necessary to work out his understanding of 'transforming' in any pertinent fashion, since this is profoundly constituted by the thirteen elements of his Emerging Ecumenical Paradigm. What is of course very transformative is Bosch's metaphorical understanding of mission. His consistent description and analysis of 'mission as', rather than

---

[13] Bosch, *Transforming Mission*, 432-46.

'mission is', is in itself a major transformation from clinical, watertight definitions to a more open-ended understanding of mission.

Hans Küng had numerous discussions with David Bosch in South Africa in 1986. During public meetings Küng often referred to the six epochs in the history of Christianity, the six major paradigms operative in the church through the centuries. Building upon the theory of paradigm shifts proposed by the natural scientist Thomas Kuhn, Küng explained the way transformation took place in the church over twenty centuries, from early Christianity till the contemporary era. Küng and Bosch agreed to a remarkable degree on interpreting mission according to paradigm shifts, and it came as no surprise that David Bosch, when he conceived his magnum opus on Transforming Mission, used Küng's – as well as Kuhn's – arguments as a springboard for his study.[14]

Christian mission, Bosch wrote, helped in its own way to transform the world. In the same process, the church's mission was profoundly influenced and transformed by *the world*, to which it was sent. The many facets of transformation, aptly described in Part 3 of his book, reiterate the truth time and again. That Bosch had it right becomes clear when one studies the discussions at the great ecumenical gatherings since Edinburgh 1910, and by reading the statements and decisions made by these gatherings.[15] Mission at its core has been a process of transformation, *in both directions*.

In Tina Ahonen's study on Bosch,[16] she refers to Bosch's unwavering belief that 'Christians make a difference to this world'. In a footnote she factors in a lengthy citation from Bosch to illustrate the point about his clear understanding of the involvement of the Christian community in God's mission of transforming the world:

> 'We know,' Bosch asserts, 'that evil, injustice, hatred, estrangement, prejudice and fear will never entirely disappear from the face of the earth before the kingdoms of this world are finally consummated in the Kingdom of God. But the moment we allow this harsh reality to paralyse and sabotage our efforts, we can no longer pray the Lord's Prayer – "thy kingdom come, thy will be done, on earth as in heaven". To offer that prayer implies believing that Christians make a difference to this world… the community of those who are enjoying the foretaste of perfection – should get involved in God's mission of transforming the world.'[17]

---

[14] Bosch, *Transforming Mission*, 181-89.

[15] Bosch, *Transforming Mission,* 301-03, 338-39, 369-74, 376-78.

[16] Tina Ahonen, *Transformation through Compassionate Mission: David J Bosch's Theology of Contextualization* (Helsinki: Luther-Agricola-Society, 2003), 114-15.

[17] David J. Bosch, 'The Kingdom of God and the Kingdoms of This World', in *Journal of Theology for Southern Africa,* 29 (December 1979), 3-13.

## Reflections on Transformation in Diverse Modes

This rather broad and generalising heading is aimed at creating space for reflections on transformation in its interconnectedness to theology or missiology, and special reference to the world mission conferences. Perhaps an important disclaimer is necessary. On the issue of transformation in its linkages to theology and missiology, a random selection of individual authors has been made and, with reference to the world mission conferences, it is necessary to point out that an exhaustive discussion on all of them is impossible in a chapter as limited as this.

The most that is achievable is to let examples, or perhaps more aptly illustrations, illuminate the message of transformation. The random and slightly arbitrary selection of authors is meant to substantiate thinking on transformation at the world mission conferences.

## Whitby 1947: Stephen Neill on Revolution

The brief discussion on Whitby 1947, the fourth mission conference, under the auspices of the International Missionary Council, focuses on Part 1 of the conference report under the heading *World in Ferment.*[18] The particular reference is to the thinking of one of the foremost mission stalwarts, Stephen Neill.[19] The underlying assumption here is that his input at Whitby speaks to the question of transformation. In fact, in Neill's perspective, his ecclesiological construct is that of a church at the forefront of radical transformation. Indeed, 'From the beginning, and in its essential nature, the Church has been revolutionary. Christ sent it out as an explosive, corrosive, destructive force'.[20]

An intriguing part of his exposition is locating the revolutionary church in the context of the Roman Empire. In a reflection on transformation, this is paramount in the following sense: *there is no depoliticized, individualized understanding of the church.* As then, so now, the matrix in which the church exists is empire. In identifying the church as 'the tiny charge of dynamite', [21] Neill suggests that, when placed under the Roman Empire, it blew 'the whole thing sky high'. In his understanding, such reality is also reflected in the overthrow of the temple of the great Diana in Ephesus. Conversely, for Neill the truth of God as embodied by the church, is not one-sidedly a destructive and a corrosive force, but equally a force for the reshaping of the world: 'The Church is also the mother and nurse of the nations.' A rather intriguing but controversial aspect of the reflection on

---

[18] C.W. Ranson, *Renewal and Advance: Christian Witness in a Revolutionary World* (London: Edinburgh House Press, 1948), 206-22.

[19] Stephen Neill, 'A Revolutionary Church', in Ranson, *Renewal and Advance*, 62-84.

[20] Neill, 'A Revolutionary Church', 64.

[21] Neill, 'A Revolutionary Church', 65.

the church as revolutionary is Neill's take on Marx and Engels.[22] Based on a sense of symbolism, he draws attention to the centenary of the Communist Manifesto in 1948, a year after Whitby. Without being able to trace this and in full awareness of the fact that Marx has broken radically with all forms of religion, particularly Christianity, he still poses the question whether ultimately there was not 'something inchoately Christian' in their option for the underdog.

Based on this very cursory look at the views advanced by Neill at Whitby all those years ago, we can see that ideas on transformation in Christian mission should be kept in creative tension with secular ideas on transformation. Put slightly differently, Christian mission and the concomitant discipline of missiology will contribute immensely to the transformation of the world if a critical discourse between the two is kept alive. This is the DNA, the determinant of mission in post-modern fashion.

## Bangkok 1973: Salvation to the World Today

Highly relevant to any discussion on transformation is Section II report of the Bangkok 1973 mission conference on salvation and social justice.[23] In accepting the reality that in a book on Ecumenical Missiology which introduces a diversity of topics, some measure of overlapping between chapters is unavoidable, the simple argument will be that the Section II report speaks eloquently to the issue of transformation. It contains an important disclaimer to the effect that the focus on the social, economic and political aspects of the gospel in no way denies the personal and eschatological dimensions of salvation. The implications of the work of this Section for any reflection on mission as transformation are quite challenging.

First, there has been an understanding that the transformation of social, economic and political structures is an instruction from God. Based on Luke 4:18-19, the mission of Christ by the Father in the power of the Holy Spirit was to declare God's love to the poor, to nurse the wounds of the broken-hearted, to liberate captives, to restore sight to the blind, and to free the oppressed. All of this was to be wrought through the death, cross and resurrection of Jesus Christ. Salvation was understood as something where human beings were called to participate and where they were offered life in its fullness in a divided world. Secondly, salvation or transformation in these terms was first and foremost aimed at the liberation of the church and of Christians. Thirdly, such salvation reflects four dimensions, namely: the struggle for economic justice and against the exploitation of human beings by human beings, the struggle for human dignity in the face of political

---

[22] Ranson, *Renewal and Advance,* 72-73, 189.

[23] Pauline Webb, *Salvation Today* (London: SCM, 1974), 40-51; Bosch, *Transforming Mission,* 384, 393, 396-99.

oppression, the struggle for solidarity in the face of the alienation of human beings, and the struggle for hope against the hopelessness in individual lives.

The only serious criticism of Bangkok 1973 pertaining to the Section II report is the omission of any reflection on the devastation caused by the prevailing geo-economic system to the earth. In his world-renowned and acclaimed book, *Earth Community, Earth Ethic*, Rasmussen traces the havoc created to mother earth by the successive agricultural, industrial and information and resources revolutions.[24] In a fascinating and mind-blowing fashion, he pleads for a 'homecoming', as a return to the *oikos,* a reconciliation of sorts with mother earth.

## Lausanne 1974 to Wheaton 1983. Tizon: Radical Evangelicals and Transformation

Any reflection on transformation will be incomplete without the profound thinking on the issue in Evangelical mission circles, with particular reference to Lausanne. Space is lacking to engage the documents emanating from the Lausanne Movement in any serious manner. Instead, what is reflected upon here is the excellent study by Tizon,[25] in which he deals with missionary thinking on transformation in a profound way. The focus in his study is on how in radical Evangelical circles the complex term 'transformation' is used and developed. A striking feature of Tizon's[26] treatment of the term is his notion, and one supposes in following Bosch, 'Mission as Transformation'. *Is this a correction of Bosch's omission of transformation from his elements which make up the Emerging Ecumenical Paradigm?*

One issue that is overlooked quite often and to which Tizon[27] draws attention is that, though Bosch does not offer any substantial definition of transformation in *Transforming Mission*, he does, however, show two meanings of the term. As an adjective, the term 'transforming' describes mission as a society, culture and reality changing movement and as a movement being transformed itself. The avoidance of the subject-object terminology (the subject is mission, and the object is society, culture and reality), used by Tizon, is deliberate. Though the point he makes, on how Bosch understands transformation without working it out in his mammoth book, is important, the subject-object scheme of things which, on a different level, Bosch deconstructs in his critique of the Enlightenment paradigm, remains problematic. To identify mission as the subject, and

---

[24] Larry L. Rasmussen, *Earth Community, Earth Ethics* (Maryknoll, NY: Orbis Books, 1997) 53-74.

[25] Al Tizon, *Transformation after Lausanne: Radical Evangelical Mission in Global-Local Perspective* (Oxford:: Regnum, 2008).

[26] Tizon, *Transformation,* 4.

[27] Tizon, *Transformation*, 6-7.

society and culture as object, is to reinvent the binary, creating dualism between the two. More often than not there are very helpful elements in society and culture which contribute to change rather than serving as hindrances. Conversely, there are sometimes elements in mission which are detrimental to transformation.

Be that as it may, a hugely creative moment with Tizon[28] is the description of transformation based on the global-local construction. Borrowing from Schreiter[29] in his global-local perspective on the history, theology and practice of mission, Tizon identifies four reasons why such a construction is 'timely and necessary'. First, it 'has done much to elevate social concern in evangelical mission thought'. Secondly, if this is interpreted correctly, context is taken seriously as a source of mission theology. Thirdly, Tizon calls into service the 'bridges' to show how the global-local construct can bring evangelical, ecumenical and Catholic mission traditions together 'for issues of social justice'. He goes on to assert that 'by laying out a socially informed, holistic, integrative – in a word, Transformational – missiology, we encourage genuine Christian ecumenism'. Fourthly, Tizon believes that the global-local lens as a rendering of *Mission as Transformation* may add to 'ongoing creative thinking among theologians, missiologists, and social scientists concerning the tension between the global/universal and the local/particular'.[30]

Then again, what is the theological or biblical grounding of *Mission as Transformation* in the understanding of evangelical mission? The answer to this question has been given in the Wheaton 1983 statement on Transformation in which, the goal of transformation is captured in the biblical vision of the Kingdom of God.[31] Some feminists and womanist theologians may suggest that the metaphor of Kingdom should be avoided in favour of the reign of God. Nevertheless, the statement's interpretation of transformation as a new way of being human in submission to the Lord is incisive – once again feminists and womanists may object to the title 'Lord'. In simple terms, the statement then spells out the social, political and economic consequences of such a new life: bringing peace, overcoming prejudices, sharing basic resources, working for greater participation of people in the decisions which affect their lives, and an equal receiving from others and giving of themselves. The Christological grounding of this being is 'growing up in Christ', and the pneumatological grounding is 'dependent on the work of the Holy Spirit'.[32]

---

[28] Tizon, *Transformation*, 11-13.
[29] Robert J. Schreiter, *The New Catholicity: Theology between the Global and Local* (Maryknoll, NY: Orbis Books, 1997), 3-4.
[30] Tizon, *Transformation,* 12-13.
[31] Tizon, *Transformation*, 247.
[32] Stephen Neill, 'A Revolutionary Church', 62-84.

## Salvador 1996: Kanyoro's Cultural Hermeneutics

In my 1996 interview with Mercy Oduyoye on the moratorium call, she thought that if there was still any relevance at all to this type of call, it could only be a call for a moratorium on patriarchy in the African Church.[33] The ideas expounded by Kanyoro at the mission conference in Salvador de Bahia, Brazil, in 1996 tie in with what Oduyoye said the same year.[34] In coining her 'cultural hermeneutics', she reflects on what she understands as her accumulated experiences and expresses wariness of glibly accepting culture and, by so doing, tolerating unjust behaviour. Looking at the evolution of her ideas on cultural hermeneutics it would be safe to predicate this on transformation. She writes:

> For generations, African women have unquestioningly obeyed all that society prescribes for them in the name of culture. Child marriages, female circumcision and the rites of passage from birth to death, whether useful or harmful, are imposed on African women simply because it is 'our culture'. This might be taken to mean that what is culture is natural, good and unavoidable. Culture has silenced many women in Africa. It has hindered them from experiencing Jesus' liberating promise of abundant life for all (John 10:10).[35]

In essence, her cultural hermeneutics is aimed at the scrutiny of cultures themselves. In her understanding there are a number of basic underlying assumptions on cultural hermeneutics in its African garb. First, it is an analysis and interpretation of culture to discern liberative as well as oppressive elements. Secondly, it creates space for the telling of stories of their own experiences, and the reading and understanding of the Bible in context. Thirdly, cultural hermeneutics is geared towards renewal or, in the context of this chapter, transformation in that harmful elements in culture are unmasked and holistic ones are affirmed. This is setting, the context for confession and forgiveness in the power of the Holy Spirit.

## Edinburgh 2010: Children as Agents of Transformation

At the centenary celebrations of Edinburgh in 2010, refreshing ideas on children in mission emerged. These are not simply reflections on how adults should respond more aptly in theology and the church to the situation of children, but thoughtful suggestions on acknowledging children as agents of mission. One such creative suggestion is to identify children as agents of transformation. In rather simple terms it is stated that '...

---

[33] Interview by Nico A. Botha with Mercy A. Oduyoye in Nairobi, August 1996.

[34] Musimbi R.A. Kanyoro, 'Called to One Hope: The Gospel in Diverse Cultures', in Christopher Duraisingh, *Called to One Hope: The Gospel in Diverse Cultures* (Geneva: WCC, 1998), 96-110.

[35] Kanyoro, 'Called to One Hope', 104.

throughout history God has used children as his willing instruments'.[36] In narrative mode, Edinburgh 2010 has taken note of the diverse ways in which God calls children into service as instruments of change. The stories of Patricia of Santa Mesa, Moko and Selfin of Poso and Pronchai, the Hmong are lined up to illustrate the point. Patricia's story is about working for transformation through disciple-making in an area in the Philippines which is described as '… a breeding ground for thieves, criminals, and sex workers'.[37] Moko's and Selfo's story is on transformation or reconciliation in a context of grave violence in Indonesia, and in Prochai's story he emerges as an 'environmental ambassador' in Thailand in a situation where deforestation is rife.[38] If this will not be construed as mere sloganeering, one could say in acknowledging children as serious agents of transformation: *If the adults mess up, let the children clean up.*

### Transformation as a Response to Post-modernity

The final and concluding section of this chapter is triggered by discussions between the author and Dr Rudolph Meyer, a close friend of the late Beyers Naudé in the Christian Institute (CI), and erstwhile anti-apartheid activist and editor of the CI journal, *Pro Veritate.*[39] As a knowledgeable scholar on post-modernism, he raised convincing arguments on why any discussion on transformation would be incomplete without some engagement with post-modernity.

From approximately the 1950s to the 1970s far-reaching changes occurred in many areas of life. Kirk states that:

> In contradistinction to comprehensive and globalising theories of science, economics, technology, law and not least in Christianity and mission, post-modernity proposes a reading of history always bound by limited, context-specific, fallible, and therefore constantly revisable perspectives.[40]

Post-modernity, says Tizon,[41]

> … refers to a different way to understand the world. The most fundamental claim of post-modernity it seems, is that the Enlightenment has failed. A breakdown of such a claim boils down to the following: … that human rationality, ingenuity, industrialization and determination have led not to a

---

[36] Balia and Kim, *Witnessing to Christ Today*, 126.
[37] Balia and Kim, *Witnessing to Christ Today*, 126.
[38] Balia and Kim, *Witnessing to Christ Today*, 126.
[39] A Christian monthly journal of the Christian Institute, called *Pro Veritate* (For the Truth), was published from the 1950s to 1976 when it was banned by the apartheid government. The journal testified in the name of Christ against injustice in society, politics, economics and labour. Rudolph Meyer was its final editor from 1970 to 1976.
[40] J. Andrew Kirk, 'Post-modernity', in John Corrie (ed), *Dictionary of Mission Theology: Evangelical Foundations* (Nottingham, UK: IVP, 2007), 299.
[41] Tizon, *Transformation*, 85.

better world, but to an unjust world, in which elitist, hegemonic, and dehumanizing forces have created new kinds of cultural, economic, and socio-political inequities.

The question arises: why is post-modernism and its core dimension of deconstruction so vitally important for mission, and particularly mission as transformation? In proceeding with a discussion on deconstruction in its relevance for mission as transformation, it is to be conceded up front that it can quite easily be construed as a negative description. It is, however, a rather positive objective indication maintaining that knowledge of the real, as the presence of an object, its in-depth meaning, and knowledge extending itself all the way to the object as a thing-in-itself, is *invalid.* The real object always 'slips' away and always eludes the signifier. The thing in itself always escapes.

In mission and its accompanying discipline of Missiology, and indeed in theology in general, the point made about deconstruction is perhaps best illustrated by the metaphorical narrative of the paradise which human beings cannot reach or enter – we are permanently 'outside': we live out of reach of the ultimate, away from the final – incomplete and limited. Here, we cannot reach the ultimate meaning of our lives – we cannot contact God directly, as there is no 'straight', objective connection, *except through faith.*

Deconstruction is to be as positive and assisting as to 'hope and pray' continuously and to try and reach the 'real', whatever it may be. It is also expressed in Hebrews 11:29 as: 'These were all commended for their faith, yet none of them received what had been promised.' One of the main aims of deconstruction is dismantling invalid efforts and claims to reach the ultimate real, especially God; it shuns pretences, shams, fabrications, façades and deceit. It always hopes and longs… 'We see through a faint copper plate (a mirror), into a puzzle'. The hope is always there to experience someday 'face to face'… (1 Corinthians13).

The implications of this for mission as transformation could be put in simple terms. Even when we think that we have a firm grip on issues of liberation and transformation in personal, communal, social, cultural, political and economic terms, the danger of disarray is constantly looming large. In addition, that is why we can only proceed as understood by Tizon 'with more cultural sensitivity, humility, and an emphasis on relationships over impersonal programs'.[42] Furthermore, Tizon is clear that post-modernity in itself has not yet provided humanity with a viable alternative to modernity. [43] Or perhaps it would be closer to the truth to suggest that the gains of post-modernism have not yet permeated the way we go about life in general and mission in particular.

---

[42] Tizon, *Transformation*, 86.
[43] Tizon, *Transformation*, 86.

## Conclusion

This chapter regards transformation as one of the most striking developments in mission, especially from 1910 to 2010. Transformation challenges missionaries, missiologists and the churches worldwide comprehensively. This is visible in the mission conferences and modifications in mission understanding which are delineated, as well as the major metamorphosis from modernism to post-modernism in contemporary society, science, biblical interpretation, and also mission. It is a new way of life, of thinking, of caring, of loving, of responsibility, and of joy. Above all, this ubiquitous missional transformation makes room for the Holy Spirit to crown Christ as Saviour of the whole world towards renewal, and the glorification of almighty God.

# JUSTICE

Chammah J. Kaunda and Roderick R. Hewitt

## Introduction

The modern ecumenical movement's journey with issues of justice over the last century mirrors the global crises since World War I that exposed the human struggle for justice and peace amidst conflictive forces of violence and death that have since continued to mutate and spread like wildfire throughout the world. The essence of this struggle is to be found in the inhumane and anti-creation dispensing of power by imperial forces that unleash death upon God's creation. The mechanistic coming together of political, economic and military power (empire), seeks control over the life forms and resources of the earth to use for its own selfish and unjust global agenda.

The key objective of this chapter is to present some highlights of key programmatic expressions of the modern ecumenical movement since 1910 that have promoted and demonstrated how the church's missional commitment to justice has resisted forces of empire that deny people fullness of life. The church's missional identity and vocation demands that it serves as vanguard of God's justice and peace in the world. In order to appreciate the context of the modern era, a brief overview is required to identify the legacy of justice that was bequeathed to the modern church.

The locus of ecumenical discourse on justice began with a missiological reading of the biblical narrative. The stories of God's relationship with humanity and creation are clothed in language that speaks of peace (*shalom*), righteousness (right living) and the well-being of all within God's household (*oikos*). How power is dispensed within any relationship will ultimately shape whether justice (that is, ethically and morally right action) has been carried out. God's justice (*shaphat* and *mishpat)* becomes most active in contexts where life-denying and unjust exercise of power prompts those who are oppressed to seek God's intervention (Exodus 3:15). Those who are recipients of God's justice enter into a covenantal relationship with God to practise his standard of justice in their relationship with others. Not only should justice shape the lifestyle of individuals with God and with one another but also justice should shape the political and economic ethics of a nation.

## The Kingdom of God and God's Justice in Relation to the Modern Era

In approaching the theme of justice in the twentieth century, this chapter highlights some of the development of the concept of justice within the ecumenical movement of the World Council of Churches since its inception in 1948. In order to set the stage, it is imperative to revisit the 1910 Edinburgh World Missionary Conference because it sets the stage for what Mark MacDonald refers to as the 'institutional church's captivity to the mindset of Western culture'.[1] This description by MacDonald aptly described the dilemma faced by the church of 1910 with its Christianisation model of the world that was made synonymous with the political goals of western civilization steeped in the world order of colonialists' power and policies.

Therefore, the Stockholm 1925 Life and Work conference had a minimalist perspective on the urgency of justice as a missiological imperative and its focus reflected the agenda of the political status quo. The Jerusalem World Mission Conference of 1928 did address the social relevance of the Kingdom of God by calling for a rejection of the worship of money as 'the religion of a capitalist society'. We begin to detect some tentative signs of the ecumenical movement identifying consensus around how biblical perspectives on the Kingdom of God oppose modern secularism and the global structures of exploitation in the economic system of colonialism.[2] The 1937 Oxford Conference on 'Church, Community and State' marked a shift when the church sought to re-enter into strategic partnership with the state and later found out the hard way how easily the church's mission to justice can be compromised – with the rise of the fascist totalitarian state. The global economic crisis of the 1930s ushered in fascism as a political order in parts of Europe that wreaked havoc on millions of lives through World War II. The Oxford Conference on 'Church, Community and State' argued for the church to become a servant of justice rather than the lord thereof.[3]

The church's identity is not under any obligation to uncritically support any political or economic ideology but should be critical of every economic exploitation and marginalization. This means that the churches should work towards a preferential option for workers who are treated unjustly.[4] The

---

[1] Mark MacDonald, 'Our agenda, as we wake up': www.anglicanjournal.com/articles/our-agenda-as-we-wake-up#sthash.UYvYSSvo.dpuf (accessed 11th November 2015).

[2] Nicholas Lossky et al (eds), *Dictionary of the Ecumenical Movement,* 2nd edition (Geneva: WCC, 2002).

[3] Joseph H. Oldham, *The Churches Survey Their Task: The Report of the Conference at Oxford, July 1937, on Church, Community and State* (London: Allen & Unwin, 1937).

[4] Michael Kinnamon and Brian E. Cope (eds), *The Ecumenical Movement: An Anthology of Key Texts and Voices* (Geneva: WCC, 1997).

church is therefore expected to demonstrate its solidarity with people and contexts where justice is denied.

### A New Ecumenical Era for Justice?

The founding of the World Council of Churches in 1948 brought with it a restoration of the church's missional responsibility to 'balance freedom, justice and the control of power'[5] that involves working for the emergence of a just and responsible society. The 1948 Assembly focused on what the mission of God means for human society and emphasized the gospel's realistic impact on the lives of people in concrete contexts of injustice. Reinhold Niebuhr, with his Christian Realism approach, was highly influential in the development of the WCC's social thought.[6] The religio-political fallout from the two world wars had exposed deficiencies in the two forms of political 'religions' that dominated the minds of the people at that time. One model focused on a kind of morally cynical worship of force, and the other on morally sentimental and utopian ideals that used revolutionary force to build a purely classless society. The Christian faith as practised by the church within the context of western colonialism was inconsistent at times in its attitude to structural injustices like slavery that oppressed vulnerable people. What they experienced was a Christian faith that was celebrated by western nations and a church that claimed to be morally and ethically superior to other civilizations and cultures, but which also embraced a political and economic system that was built on oppressing the labourers. Niebuhr argues that 'the first task of the Christian Church was to interpret the sorrows and distresses, agonies and pains, through which the world was passing, and recognize the hand of God in them, and to see beyond the crises because there was a divine judgment upon the sins that are travails of the nations'.[7]

The emerging WCC programme on justice therefore called for a return to Christianity that reflected the justice, peace and love of God in society instead of relying on secular idealism and its false promises.[8] Reliance on secular idealism, secular law and uncritical Christian legalism would not promote social justice; therefore, the missional church ought to work for the peace of nations by translating the revolutionary gospel of Jesus to speak to the diverse expressions of oppression.

---

[5] Lossky et al, *Dictionary,* 556.
[6] Kinnamon and Cope, *The Ecumenical Movement,* 281.
[7] Kinnamon and Cope, *The Ecumenical Movement,* 280.
[8] Kinnamon and Cope, *The Ecumenical Movement,* 282.

## The Responsible Society in a World Perspective

The WCC Amsterdam Assembly of 1948 had proposed 'Responsible Society' as a frame of action for the church's missional engagement in the world. The concept was regarded as 'a criterion by which [to] judge all existing social orders and at the same time a standard to guide [human beings] in the specific choices [they] have to make'.[9] By 'responsible society', it meant a society 'where freedom was the freedom of men [and women] who acknowledge responsibility for justice and public order and where those who hold political authority and economic power are responsible for its exercise, and the people whose welfare is affected by it'.[10]

'Responsible society' was postulated, not as an alternative social or political system, but as a criterion by which all existing social orders would be judged, and to influence the specific choices that are employed to make such judgments. However, the notion of 'Responsible society' was found to be ideologically biased to a western worldview of the world's economic (dis)order and justice which proved irrelevant to the situation in these newly independent countries in the global South, especially in Africa.[11] Yet the concept had some value as justice cannot exist where a few people abuse social and political power by denying the majority their socio-economic and political freedom. This report encouraged the exercise of justice at all levels of society: families, work places, young peoples' teams, tribal groups and associations, and Christian congregations.[12]

## Christian Social Responsibility and the Programme to Combat Racism

The Second Assembly of the WCC, at Evanston in 1954, affirmed that Christian social responsibility was centred on the mighty acts of God, revealed in Jesus Christ as Lord, and that God created the world, and all time was embraced within his eternal purpose centred on justice and peace.[13] Everything about social justice ought to revolve around the lived experience of Jesus and his interaction with the human family and the rest of creation. His experiences have set an example that invites women and

---

[9] Edward Duff, *The Social Thought of the World Council of Churches* (New York: Associate Press, 1956), 117.

[10] Kinnamon and Cope, *The Ecumenical Movement,* 283.

[11] Peter Lodberg, 'Justice and Peace in a World of Chaos', in John Briggs et al (eds), *A History of the Ecumenical Movement: Volume 3, 1968-2000* (Geneva: WCC, 2004), 323-43; Paul Abrecht, 'From Oxford to Vancouver: Lessons from Fifty Years of Ecumenical Work for Economic and Social Justice', in *The Ecumenical Review,* 40.2 (1988), 147-68.

[12] Kinnamon and Cope, *The Ecumenical Movement,* 284.

[13] Kinnamon and Cope, *The Ecumenical Movement*, 282.

men to live in life-giving and just relationships of promise and obedience to God's purpose in the world.

Racism has remained one of the most unjust humanly created instruments of oppression that has been used by imperial powers. The colonial governments had legitimized the enslavement of people where legalized racism provided cheap labour to strengthen their economy. Even after slavery was abolished in the British colonies in 1834, other forms of racism continued in other societies during the twentieth century. The WCC Evanston Assembly stated that 'any form of segregation based on race, color or ethnic origin is contrary to the gospel and is incompatible with the Christian doctrine of man [woman] and with the nature of the church of Christ' (WCC Evanston Assembly, 1954).[14]

Therefore, racism was identified as a grave issue of injustice. The move to create a Programme on Racism gained momentum from churches from the global South that pressured the 1968 Uppsala WCC Assembly to give programmatic priority to the elimination of institutional racism. The apartheid ideology of the minority white South African government made racism its official policy from 1948. Racial segregation and other issues of social injustice had also flourished in the countries of South America and the southern states of the United States of America that culminated in the assassination of Martin Luther King in 1968. The Programme to Combat Racism (PCR) was therefore established in 1969 at the WCC Central Committee meeting at Canterbury, UK. In the 1970s and 1980s, the PCR played a highly visible and controversial role in mobilizing international debate and action against the white minority government of South Africa. Churches were called to support churches and groups in South Africa that worked towards overcoming apartheid to promote justice and peace.

## A Post-Colonial Discourse on Justice

This chapter argues that it was the global decolonisation process that followed World War II, and the rise of different contextual theologies of liberation in Africa, Asia and Latin America and the Caribbean, that restored the centrality of justice to the missional mandate of the modern church and the ecumenical movement. The justice paradigm of Liberation Theology exposed the alliance of Euro-American imperial forces with western theological, ecclesial and missionary agenda that created military-backed regimes that unleashed suffering and death upon oppressed peoples. The different theologies of liberation achieved some success in contributing to the disempowering political systems of oppression. However, the much more entrenched control of the economy by unjust financial capitalistic

---

[14] Baldwin Sjollema, 'The Archives of the World Council of Churches' Programme to Combat Racism': www.brill.com/sites/default/files/ftp/downloads/31985_Brochure.pdf (accessed 13th November 2015).

power systems remains an unfinished agenda in the cause of achieving global justice.

The contemporary ecumenical discourse on justice is constructed on the perspective that it is indivisible, not only as a matter of ethical and theological conviction, but in praxis that affirms 'the conviction that justice, peace and creation are bound together'.[15] The different programmatic expressions of the WCC such as *Just, Participatory and Sustainable Society* (JPSS), the conciliar process for *Justice, Peace and the Integrity of Creation* (JPIC), the *Theology of Life* (TOL) and, most recently, *Pilgrimage of Justice and Peace* (PJP) have built on the insights of previous ecumenical discussions that challenge the churches to make sacrificial commitments to justice, peace and creation within their unique and changing social contextual landscapes.

## Just, Participatory and Sustainable Society (JPSS)

The WCC's quest in the 1970s for a 'just, participatory and sustainable society' was a response to growing recognition of the persistence of poverty and misery and of ecological degradation threats. To a great extent, these issues were legacies from the underdevelopment policies of the colonial era that shaped many nations of the global South. Therefore, the WCC Nairobi Assembly in 1975 gave new emphases to justice issues linked with science and technology, militarism and disarmament, ecology and human survival, and the role of women in the church and society which were all part of the growing liberation theological paradigm. Philip Potter, the former WCC General Secretary, emerged as a key voice in the transition from the older colonial paradigm to a post-colonial ecumenical social thought paradigm.[16] The focus on justice issues mandated by the Nairobi Assembly was followed up by the Assemblies held in Vancouver in Canada in 1983 and Canberra in Australia in 1991. These Assemblies offered continuous advocacy for churches to define what it meant to be a missional church in the world by taking concrete action on the threats to life in the areas of justice, peace and the integrity of creation.

Other justice-focused programmes emerged, such as *Towards a Church of the Poor* and *Faith, Science and the Future.*[17] *Towards a Church of the Poor* was undertaken to produce documents to explore the relationships between the poor and the organized church in the medieval periods. The idea behind *Towards the Church of the Poor* was for the church to identify with the poor, to encourage preferential options for the poor, and to further

---

[15] WCC, 'Justice, Peace and Creation': www.wcc-coe.org/wcc/what/jpc/hist-e.html (accessed 13th November 2015).

[16] Lewis Mudge, 'Ecumenical Social Thought', in John Briggs, Mercy Amba Oduyoye and Georges Tsetsis (eds), *A History of the Ecumenical Movement, Volume 3, 1968-2000* (Geneva: WCC, 2004), 279-321, at 290.

[17] Mudge, 'Ecumenical Social Thought', 290.

identification and solidarity with the poor as means of promoting justice in the oppressive world.

## Justice, Peace and the Integrity of Creation (JPIC)

The ecumenical focus on justice expanded to include other emphases such as the promotion of human rights that included socio-economic and political rights. The 1983 Vancouver Assembly, for example, called for an interrelated study of justice, peace and the integrity of creation. This emphasis on the integrity of creation marked the beginning of an intentional focus within the ecumenical movement to address issues concerning environmental degradation and climate change caused by rogue human behaviour. In contexts of systemic injustice, the church's mission should resist and reject all socio-economic systems that contribute to the disintegration of life.

JPIC was therefore developed to engage WCC member-churches in a conciliar process of mutual commitment to justice, peace and the integrity of creation as a priority. JPIC was originally intended only for advocacy within the WCC member-churches but the Vancouver Assembly in 1983 extended the call to all non-member-churches because 'humanity is now living in the dark shadows of an arms race more intense and of systems of injustice more widespread than the world has ever known'.[18] The programme emphasized the need for churches to confess anew the Christian faith and repent of past silence in contexts of systemic oppression where the powers of death in racism, sexism, caste oppression, economic exploitation, militarism, violation of human rights, and the misuse of science and technology reign.

The WCC Seoul Convocation (1990) on JPIC focused on urgent questions of human survival and called for stronger conciliar fellowship in the ecumenical movement around shared moral principles. The convocation argued that, in the exercise of power, all human actions are ultimately accountable to God. However, the ecclesial diversity that exists in the ecumenical movement meant that the level of commitment to the 'conciliar process' varied, and some churches opted out of ecclesiological commitment which they were unprepared to make in the quest for justice and peace.

## Militarism, Disarmament and Peace

Another important threat to life that robbed people of justice and human dignity throughout the twentieth century was the growing militarism

---

[18] Preman Niles, 'Ecumenical Dictionary: Justice, Peace and the Integrity of Creation': www.wcc-coe.org/wcc/who/dictionary-article11.html (accessed 13th November 2015).

promoted by the global arms industry and the stark consequences of nuclear proliferation. Since the Amsterdam Assembly in 1948, the WCC has consistently stated that 'the part which war plays in our present international life is a sin against God and a degradation of man, while the discovery of atomic and other new weapons renders widespread and indiscriminate destruction inherent in the whole conduct of modern war'.[19]

This ecumenical focus on the threats posed by global militarism was raised again at the Second Assembly in Evanston in 1954 where the delegates stressed that 'the development of nuclear weapons makes this an age of fear. True peace cannot rest on fear'.[20] It could be argued that the voice of the ecumenical movement has served to drive the global movement for the development of the Nuclear Non-Proliferation Treaty (NPT).[21] At the fourth WCC Assembly in Uppsala, Sweden in 1968, a report entitled 'Towards Justice and Peace in International Affairs' was adopted by the Assembly. It also adopted a statement on 'further steps' to avoid nuclear conflict. The sixth Assembly in Vancouver in 1983 condemned the production, deployment and use of nuclear weapons as 'a crime against humanity... The nuclear weapons issue is, in its import and threat to humanity, a question of Christian discipline and faithfulness to the Gospel'.[22] All the WCC Assemblies recognized the threat of militarism in destroying global peace and in spreading economic injustice and underdevelopment among the world's poor. Therefore the production, development and use of nuclear weapons were classified as a crime against humanity and must be condemned on ethical and theological grounds. At the WCC Harare Assembly in 1998 it was emphasized that the communities of faith must become 'agents of reconciliation and peace with justice in homes, churches and societies as well as in political, social and economic structures at the global level'.[23]

The International Peace Convocation held in Kingston, Jamaica, in 2011 called for the protection of the innocent in the face of injustice, war and violence, and advocated total nuclear disarmament and control of the proliferation of small arms around the world.[24] This message was reiterated

---

[19] Peter Weiderud, 'The WCC concern for nuclear disarmament and non-proliferation' (12th March 2005): https://www.oikoumene.org/en/resources/documents/commissions/international-affairs/peace-and-disarmament/nuclear-weapons/the-wcc-concern-for-nuclear-disarmament-and-non-proliferation (accessed 13th November 2015).

[20] Weiderud, 'The WCC concern for nuclear disarmament and non-proliferation'.

[21] For more information, see US Department of the State – Office of the Historian, 'Milestones: 1961-1968': https://history.state.gov/milestones/1961-1968/npt (accessed 11th November 2015).

[22] WCC, 'Statement on the Way of Just Peace' (8th November 2013): https://www.oikoumene.org/en/resources/documents/assembly/2013-busan/adopted-documents-statements/the-way-of-just-peace (accessed 11th November 2015).

[23] WCC, 'Statement on the Way of Just Peace'.

[24] Mathews G. Chunakara, *Building Peace on Earth* (Geneva: WCC, 2013).

at the WCC Busan Assembly in 2013, set in the context of the ongoing Korean conflict and threat of nuclear war, and the gathering again called for nuclear weapons to be made illegal.

## The Ecumenical Decade of Churches in Solidarity with Women

Gender issues have been a challenge for the ecumenical movement because of the difference in the ecclesiological thinking of the member-churches of WCC. In spite of these challenges, the ecumenical movement has embraced the need to promote women's rights as a justice issue mandated by the gospel of Christ. Through collaboration with religious and civil societies partners around the world, a department on the co-operation between men and women in the Church and Society programme was established in 1954 and developed to become a programme desk of the WCC in 1974. Feminist theologians critiqued patriarchy and expressed anger at gender injustice against women, even within the ecumenical movement. In response, the WCC launched an ecumenical Decade of Solidarity with Women in 1988 which was concluded with a presentation at the eighth Assembly in Harare in 1998.[25] The programme was built on the United Nations Decade for Women from 1976 to 1975.

At the end of the Decade at the Harare Assembly in 1998, the delegates suggested four major themes as a means of promoting justice that would impact on women's lives in the world: a) Economic; b) Social Justice; c) Women's Participation in the Church; and d) Racism and Violence against Women. The Decade brought together various groups to reflect on the concerns of gender, justice and violence. These concerns were to: a) empower women to challenge oppressive structures; b) affirm the contribution of women in their churches and society; c) give visibility of their engagement in the struggle for peace, justice and integrity of creation; d) enable churches to free themselves from racism, sexism, classism and discrimination; and e) encourage church action in solidarity with women.[26] The Decade declared gender-based violence and sexism in the church as a sin and called for steps to be taken to achieve justice for women.

## Decade to Overcome Violence (DOV): Church Seeking Reconciliation

The WCC Decade to Overcome Violence was launched in 2001 in Berlin, Germany, in response to the global context of pervasive violence that threatened all forms of life. The DOV called on churches to become 'aware

[25] WCC, 'Together on the Way – *8.2. Response to the plenary on the Ecumenical Decade – Churches in Solidarity with Women*' (1999): www.wcc-coe.org/wcc/assembly/fprc2e-e.html (accessed 10th November 2015).
[26] WCC, 'Together on the Way'.

of the urgent need to overcome violence that has pervaded [human lives], the world, and the whole created order'. The programme was launched in response to peoples' 'deep yearning for the restoration of justice and building lasting peace grounded in justice'.[27]

Through these objectives, the WCC envisaged challenging churches and civil societies to work together in promoting justice and peace-building in the world. DOV, which ran from 2001 to 2010, focused on Peace in the Community, Peace with the Earth, Peace in the Market, and Peace among Peoples. The International Ecumenical Peace Convocation that was held in Kingston, Jamaica, in 2011 brought to an end the DOV with the recognition that peace could not be achieved in the world if there was no justice. Therefore a new methodological approach to justice and peace was launched that was synthesized as 'just peace'.

### An Ecumenical Call to Just Peace

Since 2011, the WCC took a radical shift in the discussion on justice and peace to postulate for 'just peace' as a framework of analysis and criteria for ethical action. The call to just peace was received by the Central Committee meeting in Geneva in February 2011 to commence studying, reflection, collaboration and common action. This was a direct response to the recommendations of the WCC Assembly in Porto Alegre, Brazil, in 2006, and further developed the insights gleaned from the 'Decade to Overcome Violence, 2001-2010'. The call for just peace was therefore launched at the International Ecumenical Peace Convocation (IEPC) held in Kingston, Jamaica, in 2011. The focus on the work of just peace embraced four key areas of recognized threats to life on a global scale: in *the community* – so that all may live free from fear; with *the earth* – so that life is sustained; in *the market-place* – so that all may live with dignity; and among *the nations* – so that human lives are protected. Central to this call was the affirmation that there can be no peace anyway without justice; while the opposite is also true.[28]

The theme of the tenth assembly in Busan, South Korea, in 2013 also embraced the focus on justice and peace – 'God of life, lead us to justice and peace' – that gave birth to the current programmatic emphasis on *The Pilgrimage of Justice and Peace* as an ecumenical praxis. The message of the tenth Assembly affirmed the churches' desire to move together. The WCC perceives the *Pilgrimage of Justice and Peace* as neither a journey towards a concrete geographical place nor merely an activist action, but a transformative journey in which God is the one who invites believers to begin anticipating the world that the Triune God unfolds by describing and

---

[27] Simon Oxley, *Telling the Truth About ourselves and our World* (Geneva: WCC, 2009), 8.
[28] WCC, *Companion to Just Peace* (Geneva: WCC, 2011), 2.

re-describing the world in the context of ecology, economy, peace or human dignity.[29]

### Ecumenical Chronicle Life, Justice, and Peace for All: A Call to Action

This programme was mainly based on issues that relate to economic justice. It is a call to action necessitated by people and the earth being in peril due to over-consumption of some growing inequalities as shown in the persistent poverty of many in contrast to the extravagant wealth of a few.[30] The WCC makes a case that the life of the global community would end if the sins of egotism, callous disregard and greed, which lie at the root of these crises, are not addressed. With a sense of urgency, this dialogue is brought to the churches as a call for action, born of a profound hope and belief that 'an economy of life is not only possible, it is in the making, and God's justice lies at its very foundation'.[31] This dialogue addresses the destructive economic variance between the global North and the global South because it fosters economic injustice. The focus on economic issues as an area for faith confession emerged during the 2004 ecumenical gathering at Accra, Ghana, that culminated in the adoption of the *Covenanting for Justice in the Economy and the Earth* process that outlined theological convictions that addressed the threats to life in the economic and environmental injustices of the contemporary global economy. Issues surrounding poverty, wealth and ecology, and the impact of economic globalization, became urgent agenda items for ecumenical reflection.

In the 2013 ecumenical focus on *Economy of Life for All Now: An Ecumenical Action Plan for a New International Financial and Economic Architecture,* the ecumenical community outlined action areas for churches in tackling public finance and debt, regulation of the financial sector, and global economic governance with the aim of realizing ethical, democratic, just and sustainable financial and economic systems.[32]

---

[29] WCC, 'An Invitation to the Pilgrimage of Justice and Peace' (2014): www.oikoumene.org/en/resources/documents/central-committee/geneva-2014/an-invitation-to-the-pilgrimage-of-justice-and-peace (accessed 13th November 2015).

[30] WCC, 'Economy of Life, Justice, and Peace for All: A Call to Action' (2012): https://www.oikoumene.org/en/resources/documents/wcc-programmes/public-witness-addressing-power-affirming-peace/poverty-wealth-and-ecology/neoliberal-paradigm/agape-call-for-action (accessed 13th November 2015).

[31] WCC, 'Economy of Life'.

[32] WCC, 'Economy of Life for All Now: An Ecumenical Action Plan for a New International Financial and Economic Architecture' (2014): www.oikoumene.org/en/resources/documents/wcc-programmes/public-witness-addressing-power-affirming-peace/poverty-wealth-and-ecology/economy-of-life-for-all-now-an-ecumenical-action-plan-for-a-new-international-financial-and-economic-architecture (accessed 11th November 2015).

## Pilgrimage of Justice and Peace: An African Case Study of Ancestral Land Justice

This chapter concludes by using the important issue of land justice within the African context to highlight the urgency of addressing issues of injustice in the world. Displacement from ancestral lands continues to be a source of bitterness among many African ethnic groups. In the name of progress, many ethnic groups have been internally displaced from their ancestral land because of unjust political and economic motives. Places that most ethnic groups considered as sacred and sources of their well-being have been desacralized and destroyed. Many African people believe that the Supreme Being as the creator of the whole universe is intertwined with their ancestral land with fauna and flora and entrenched with the social, political and spiritual dimensions of their lives.[33] This brings a direct link with African spirituality since, like many indigenous peoples, African communities have set great importance on their relationship to their ancestral land. In this perspective, the land did not belong to any human being but people belong to the land, which is given by God.

Many conflicts during the period of colonialism, and even since the independence of African nations, are related to the theft of ancestral land. Land has therefore become a justice issue that has influenced the United Nations Declaration on the Rights of Indigenous Peoples. However, political leaders tend to pay very little attention to implementing these rights in most African nations. For example, a clear case of land injustice is present among the Himba people of Kaokoland in Namibia who have been struggling since European colonialism. This struggle continues with the Namibian government trying to erect a large dam for hydro-electric power at Epupa Falls which would mean displacing hundreds of Himba people, disrupting their traditional way of life, and infringing their traditional land rights.[34] The Himba people are a small ethnic group with a population of about 20,000. They argued that their rights have been downtrodden and that decisions about their future imposed on them by the Namibian government are unjust. There has been a clash between economic development of the 350 square kilometres of ancestral lands, that the government argues is in the national interest, and the just rights of the Himba people to their sacred grave sites and grazing lands, and to protect the land against massive ecological damage on water systems.[35] As Craig Matthew puts it in his documentary film *Ochre and Water*: 'For the Himba and in the words of the chief headman, Kapika, "The land is an absolute. If you take away this

---

[33] Robert Hitchcock and Diana Vinding (eds), *Indigenous Peoples' Rights in Southern Africa* (Copenhagen: IWGIA, 2004).

[34] Hitchcock and Vinding, *Indigenous Peoples' Rights.*

[35] Terese Sveijer, 'Himba people's fight against Planned Construction of the Dam', in *Indigenous Affairs*, 3/4 (July-December 1997), 12-17.

land, then there is no longer a Himba.'"[36] The Himba people's just struggle for land rights represents an important part of the wider global struggle where land once owned by the local people has been corruptly transferred and expropriated by an unjust legal system and given to a wealthy minority elite, many of whom had no desire to develop the land.

The ecumenical programmes on *Together towards Life* and the *Pilgrimage of Justice and Peace* must therefore include the global struggle for land justice, especially in contexts such as the occupied land of Palestine and Irian Jaya (West Papua) where continuous land theft is denying people justice with fullness of life. The WCC support of indigenous people in ancestral land-related claims must therefore be treated as a spiritual and human rights issue because without it a dignified life is not possible. The call to the *Pilgrimage of Justice and Peace*, with its missional affirmation through *Together towards Life* (*TTL*), is very relevant to indigenous peoples in their struggles to defend ancestral land rights. Accompanying them in their struggles will prove significant in journeying 'together towards life'.

## Conclusion

Justice and peace have occupied pride of place within the ministry of the WCC since its inception in 1948. Issues of justice have centred on economic, political, gender and environmental justice. The road of justice is not an easy one as there are too many roadblocks and unspeakable dangers. The WCC has achieved some success in its global justice advocacy in spite of the many threats to life that are denying people and the wider creation fullness of life. The search to promote values and practices of justice and peace, and to work towards an inclusive community in which women and children, indigenous peoples, minorities, refugees and migrants, racially and ethnically oppressed peoples, can find unconditional love, security, respectability, equal opportunity and rights must never be surrendered to the unjust imperial systems of this world.

---

[36] National GeoGraphic Traveller South Africa, 'Travel tactics for a changing world: smart traveller': www.fotolambro.com/HimbaTravels.pdf (accessed 13th November 2015).

# MARGINS

## Deenabandhu Manchala

> Jesus said to them, 'Have you never read in the Scriptures: "The stone the builders rejected has become the cornerstone; the Lord has done this, and it is marvellous in our eyes"?' (Matthew 21:42 NIV).

'Mission from the Margins' is an approach that affirms exactly this vision of mission as one done, not from positions of power and privilege, but with empty hands, in resistance to powers, and in struggle for life with dignity and justice.

'Mission from the Margins' is the contribution of those who represented the experiences of the marginalized communities – anti-racism and Dalit movements, indigenous peoples, people with disabilities, and migrant workers, in the work of the WCC's Just and Inclusive Communities during 2006-2013. Presenting margins as the signpost for mission today, this chapter asserts the agency of the marginalized and their experience as authentic bases for mission, and then goes on to define mission as: i) struggle and resistance, ii) seeking justice and inclusivity, and iii) healing and wholeness. To put it differently, it focuses not on those on the margins but on those at the centre as the ones in need of healing and restoration.

This emphasis on the 'margins' marks a significant milestone in the ecumenical movement's consistent engagement with issues of life and people as the core of its vocation of fostering unity and mission. The enormous human suffering and divisions caused by two world wars, interspersed with genocides, famines, and the proliferation of various instruments and institutions of injustice that drew strength from certain cultures of domination and discrimination, dispossessing large sections of people around the world, inspired and influenced the ecumenical movement in the twentieth century.[1] Through the World Council of Churches, churches have participated in struggles against racism, apartheid and military dictatorships, and of the Australian Aborigines, the indigenous peoples of South and Central America, the Palestinians against occupation, people with disabilities, and similar issues. This has helped the churches to

---

[1] In the WCC-led ecumenical initiatives, the concerns and issues of people from the global South, and of social justice, began to be more pronounced all the way from the WCC's Assembly in New Delhi in 1961. The 'Church and Society' conference in Geneva in 1966, the 'Towards the Church of the Poor' conference in Cyprus in 1978, the convocation on 'Justice, Peace and Integrity of Creation' in Seoul in 1989, and the 'Ecclesiology and Ethics' study during the 1990s, were some of the major milestones along the way.

converge their visions and actions more intentionally towards an inclusive society.[2]

However, 'God's option for the poor', a theme that arose from the churches' engagement in contexts of intense poverty in Latin America, broke new ground.[3] By ascribing epistemological privilege to the poor and other subjugated voices, it inspired the creative surge of Liberation Theology. Simultaneously, similar theological formulations, such as Black Theology, African theologies, Feminist and womanist theologies, the Dalit and Minjung theologies and many others, arising out of people's struggles for life, began to challenge the dominant discourse, demanding change in the churches' self-understanding and their vocation.

Within the distinct missiological stream of the Commission for World Mission and Evangelism too, *Mission and Evangelism: An Ecumenical Affirmation* (1982) singled out the poor as the crucial criterion for testing the effectiveness of mission. It affirmed that the 'church's relation to the poor was not simply a question of social ethics; it was a matter of faithfulness to the gospel itself… Christ demonstrated that centrality by moving towards those who are on the margins – to the point of dying "outside the gate" (Heb. 13:12)… Such concern (for the poor) is not only a matter of speaking to the poor or for them, but of listening to their distinctive voices and standing with them against political and economic systems of oppressive inequity'.[4] Even as it held the poor as recipients of the gospel, it nevertheless affirmed their agency: 'Who but the church of the poor can preach with integrity to the poor of the world? In these ways we see the poor churches of the world as the bearers of mission.'[5] The preparations for the centenary celebrations of the 1910 World Missionary Conference in Edinburgh in 2010 inspired fresh reflections on mission in a world that was radically different. It was recognized that the church was now a global reality, highly diverse and located predominantly in the global South. Engaging with hard questions and existential challenges brought by people from many parts of the world, it was able to affirm the collective experience of the marginalized as a foundation for mission.[6]

---

[2] See Lukas Vischer, 'Major Trends in the Life of the Churches', in John Briggs, Mercy Amba Oduyoye and Georges Tsetsis (eds), *A History of the Ecumenical Movement, Volume 3, 1968-2000* (Geneva: WCC, 2004).

[3] The two Latin American bishops' meetings in Medellin (1968) and Puebla (1979) are considered to be watershed events. Gustavo Gutierrez and Cardinal Gerhard Ludwig Muller, *On the Side of the Poor: the Theology of Liberation* (Maryknoll, NY: Orbis Books, 2015), 39.

[4] Birgitta Larson and Emilio Castro, 'From Missions to Mission', in Briggs, Oduyoye and Tsetsis (eds), *A History of the Ecumenical Movement,* 128.

[5] Section 4 of the Statement. Quoted in Briggs, Oduyoye and Tsetsis (eds), *A History of the Ecumenical Movement, Volume 3,* 128.

[6] It must said that some were suspicious as to whether the idea of mission from the margins was in response to the reality of the former recipients – the people and

While all along these different streams, the concerns of those treated unjustly remained on the agenda, and were referred to as 'the poor', what makes 'Mission from the Margins' distinctive is its emphasis on the agency of the marginalized and their visions as crucial for authentic mission in the world today. It underlines a new consciousness of Christian faith and vocation in an increasingly marginalized and marginalizing world.

The purpose of this chapter, therefore, is not to insist further on the agency of the margins but to point out what such a mission might mean for the churches as they affirm their participation in God's mission.

## The Risk of Semantics

The statement uses the term 'margins' to suggest all those who are yearning for justice and for life with dignity. At the outset, it is necessary to recognize that the term 'margins' is prone to both misrepresentation and misinterpretation. First, 'margins' belongs to the language of the centre. It seems to hold people as objects or a category. By avoiding naming them as *people*, it takes the focus off the reasons why they are marginalized.[7] Further, it seems to suggest that in an essentially centripetal social dynamic, it is inevitable that some are on the margins for a variety of reasons. The privileges of being at the centre and the misfortunes of being on the margins thus become normative and inevitable, and so are the consequent responses. Secondly, it is an unfair categorization of all who are pushed to the sides for a variety of reasons. Those on the margins are not a homogeneous group, and there are many forces and factors that marginalize people. Most often, marginalized people are referred to, in the language of economics, as 'the poor'. Their condition of being poor is the result of many other marginalizing forces at work, and these manage to hide themselves under the cover of this broad categorization. Thirdly, 'margins' is a fluid concept. Not all those who experience marginalization follow the same trajectory as those who experience multiple or intense forms of marginalization. But the powerful few may claim marginal status whenever their power and prominence are in danger. Ironically, the powerless may be the majority but they remain on the margins. And lastly, there are 'margins' within 'margins', and so are the value orientations that sustain and legitimize marginalization among the marginalized. Each of these deserves

---

churches in the South now as active agents of mission and evangelization in many parts of the world.

[7] 'These generalizations are produced by positions of control – (and) are indeed not just after-effects but direct manifestations of the power structures that repress these groups – and thus miss the reality of the people, hinder real options for the margins, and repress people even further': Joerg Rieger, 'Liberating God-Talk: Postcolonialism and the Challenge of the Margins', in Catherine Keller, Michael Nausner and Mayra Rivera (eds), *Postcolonial Theologies: Divinity and Empire* (St Louis, MO: Chalice Press, 2004), 211.

recognition and response, but for them the category of 'margins' does not help.

Therefore, 'margins' is relative to perception and interpretation, and by provoking semantics one can hide the causes and dynamics of marginalization, the faces of the forces as well as of the victims.[8] The continued reference to 'Mission from the Margins' without this consciousness may valourize the marginalized, promote patronization, and in turn veil the causes of marginalization – the core of what this concept aims to address.

## Unveiling the Veiled

Incidentally, those at the centre are constantly at work circulating certain myths to insist that marginalization is self-imposed, and that some are poor because they are lazy, not smart enough, or ontologically inferior, basically to deflect scrutiny of their own privileged positions. Unfortunately, traditional mission expressions are influenced by this perception of marginalized people as those to be pitied and helped rather than those who are sinned against.

A necessary first step, therefore, is to come to an awareness of the faces and names of those whom we refer to as inhabiting the margins. A cursory look at some of these would reveal the truth about the reasons for their marginalization. The hundreds and thousands of refugees of war from Africa, the Middle East, and many parts of the world, the Palestinians who are punished for their resistance to occupation, the African Americans who are pushed further to make space for white privilege, the aboriginal Australians and the First Nation people in the Americas whose faces are veiled to hide historical crimes, the children who are trafficked and are fleeing in order to escape the wars of the drug lords in Central America, women who are deprived of education and employment, and even the right to life, in many parts of the world, the Pacific Islanders who live on the brink of being submerged, the nearly 90,000 war widows in Sri Lanka, millions of rural and urban poor, forced migrant workers, child labourers, climate refugees, physically disabled people and people maimed in wars and land mines, and the nearly 250 million discriminated Dalits in South Asia. Indeed, the list is awfully endless. Besides these, there are hundreds and thousands of people in every society who are deliberately excluded from opportunities and participation so that those at the centre feel special and privileged in the face of mass deprivation.

---

[8] This was exactly the risk that the draft of the new WCC mission statement *Together towards Life* ran into when it was first introduced at the Pre-Assembly gathering in Manila in 2012. The section on 'Mission from the Margins' provoked a lengthy, rather tiresome, debate on the meaning and location of the margins and the centre, suggesting that it is often unsettling to step outside the box, particularly when that step is towards the 'not-so-mainstream', and the 'not-so-glorious'.

## Unmasking the Powers

Who then are these that push millions to the margins? Once again, these too are many: individuals and collectives, and institutions and structures that sustain themselves by making and ensuring that certain values and cultures are normative and acceptable. Foremost among these is the insatiable greed for power and wealth, which makes millions poor, hungry, homeless, dispossessed and dehumanized. What more can we say about this when it is acknowledged widely that a mere 2% own 90% of the world's wealth? People, communities, nations, and political and economic structures are in the grip of this collective egotistic disorder that seeks self-elevation by causing mass deprivation in order to feel powerful and invulnerable. Second is the role of certain cultures, anthropological theories and the concomitant values that ascribe status and privilege to a few by holding others to be inferior and expendable. Patriarchy, racism, casteism, ageism, ableism, and excessive and irresponsible assertion of identity are some of these, perpetuating the disenfranchisement and dehumanization of those who do not fit into the normative scheme of dominant powers. Third come some dominant religious traditions and institutions that lend support and legitimacy to the marginalizing forces. By constantly nurturing and accentuating the notion of 'the other', and 'the other' as hostile or inferior, these justify sometimes even ruthless expressions of discrimination and exclusion.[9] By legitimizing marginalization of others as a part of the divine scheme, these religious belief systems diminish whatever consciousness their adherents may have, and by holding that this world is an illusion and the best is yet to come, they anaesthetize their victims from revolting and asserting their rights.[10]

In sum, the forces that sanctify greed for wealth and power, the cultures and traditions that nurture domination and discrimination, and the religious and cultural resources that encourage the rejection and exploitation of 'the other' are those that cause and sustain marginalization. As such, 'Mission

---

[9] 'Most world religions, including Christianity, while furthering their self-perpetuating missions, have played a major role in this process of 'othering'. Operating alongside nationalism, ethnicity, racism, patriarchy, and in my context casteism, religions have always encouraged people to nurture inflated self-understandings and detrimental understandings of those who do not belong to their fold. In fact, this common but often ignored trait of "othering" has been the source of most evils': Deenabandhu Manchala, 'Migration: An Opportunity for Broader and Deeper Ecumenism', in Elaine Padilla and Peter C. Phan (eds), *Theology of Migration in the Abrahamic Religions* (New York: Palgrave Macmillan, 2014), 159.

[10] C.S. Song puts this succinctly: 'Faith and theology… have reduced believers to inactivity not only in matters of faith but also in relation to their social and political responsibilities. How easy it is, then, for them to become, on the one hand, objects of exploitation and, on the other, unconscious or unwilling collaborators of evil social and political forces!': C.S. Song, *Jesus, The Crucified People* (New York: Crossroad, 1990), 209.

from the Margins' involves confronting cultures and systems, and transforming them through just and life-affirming alternatives. Unfortunately, these forces and cultures are also present and even rampant in many churches. An option such as this calls for introspection and transformation from within.

## God's Mission with the Marginalized

It is in the light of this agenda of mission that we need to understand afresh the oft-repeated affirmation: 'God opts for the poor.' We may perhaps replace the term 'the poor' with 'marginalized people' and thus keep the focus on different forces and experiences of marginalization. First of all, God loves marginalized people not because they are innocent and pitiable but primarily because they are victims of the unbridled and insatiable greed of some for power and wealth. As Daniel Groody says, 'Christ came to live as a poor person not because poverty itself has any intrinsic value but to criticize and challenge those people and systems that oppress the poor and compromise their God-given dignity.'[11] In fact, the whole Biblical tradition itself is an account of God's continuous intrusion whenever life is abused, denied and destroyed to satiate this greed.

Secondly, Jesus embraces liberation of the oppressed as the core of his ministry and dares the powers by taking sides with the despised and discriminated people of his time, thus challenging religious and cultural traditions that deny rights and dignity to some – women, Gentiles, widows, lepers, people with disabilities and tax collectors. In other words, God's justice in Jesus Christ is a biased justice, neither neutral and universalistic, nor forensic, but biased towards the victims of cultures and traditions that keep people in bondage, both the victim and the aggressor alike. Therefore, he preaches repentance to the powerful and the privileged which, when they change, becomes good news to the poor.

Thirdly, in defiance of the norms and values that create and sustain hatred, fear and rejection of 'the other', Jesus chooses a counter-strategy of opting for the 'othered' people of his time. So much so that, against popular images of the Divine, we find, in Jesus, a victim God – betrayed, forsaken, tortured, killed, maimed, mocked and ridiculed – all experiences that those who have been pushed to and beyond the margins go through. 'From this social location he undermines all the world's categories, which deprecate and dehumanize, rejecting the idols which classify and segregate human beings based on social labels such as superior or inferior, rich or poor, worthy or unworthy. Instead, Jesus reveals the truth that all human beings have an essential, inalienable dignity given by God.'[12] The promise of

---

[11] Daniel G. Groody, *Globalization, Spirituality and Justice* (Maryknoll, NY: Orbis Books, 2007), 195.
[12] Groody, *Globalization, Spirituality and Justice,* 49.

fullness of life for all can be a reality only when some stop behaving as if their lives were more important and valuable than others.[13]

## The Mission of the Marginalized

'Through their struggles in and for life, marginalized people are reservoirs of the active hope, collective resistance and perseverance that are needed to remain faithful to the promised reign of God,' says *TTL*.[14] The many movements and initiatives of marginalized people around the world today testify to their determination to resist and expose the forces that deprive them of their rights and dignity. Their struggles for economic justice, rights and self-determination, and against displacement and discrimination, present themselves as signs of a new social order. Further, they are not only exploding the myth of the manipulative centre but also articulating alternative visions arising from their resistance to injustice. They are also rejecting ideologies and identities imposed on them.[15] These movements may be fluid and vulnerable to various forces and dynamics; but through their struggles, they offer hope and alternative visions that reflect the goals of God's mission. Therefore, their resources of experience and perspective,[16] and strategies and struggles, are not merely subject-matter for theological reflection 'but are places where theories and ideas are produced'.[17] Traces of such counter-culture are present in the gospel

---

[13] As Orlando Costas says that the 'call to conversion is not an invitation to soothe guilty consciences, to reinforce one's privileged status, and to give one strength to continue to be part of an oppressive social system. It is, rather, to turn from personal sins and from alliances with the oppressive structures of this world, to join the struggle of God's kingdom against the forces of evil, of injustice, exploitation and repression': Orlando E. Costas, *Christ Outside the Gate: Mission Beyond Christendom* (Maryknoll, NY: Orbis Books, 1984), 14.

[14] *TTL*, §39.

[15] For example, the worst victims of India's heinous caste system were called by many names over the centuries – untouchables, outcastes, fifth castes, depressed castes, low castes, Harijans, etc. But today they call themselves 'Dalits', meaning crushed, torn, crumpled and oppressed. With each assertion of their Dalit identity, they indict the dominant society for its cruelty and hold it responsible for their 'dalitness'. Such trends are seen among many subaltern and hitherto subjugated communities. Their new names and ideological movements also reject patronizing attitudes but solicit solidarity and participation.

[16] As *TTL*, §38 says: 'People on the margins have agency, and can often see what, from the centre, is out of view.'

[17] Rieger, 'Liberating God-Talk, 204. Rieger also shares another useful insight: 'Truth is that which has been pushed below the surface in specific situations... This sort of truth cannot be determined once and for all... but must be discovered time and again along the way... Truth thus conceived can only be perceived from the margins. It has to do with the underside of things... Truth needs to be sought – and can be found – in the tensions and conflicts of life... It might be said that truth – created in repression and thus full of pressure – harbours its own energy sources

tradition too, especially in the choices that Jesus and the first community made.[18]

## Church in God's Mission with the Marginalized

'Mission from the margins', therefore, is guided by the vision of a world based on mutuality and interdependence. It hopes for a polity of justice and freedom which allows the space and possibility for all to celebrate God's gift of life. As such, it is neither about marginalizing those who have been at the centre nor about reducing the margins through superficial expressions of inclusion. However, calling churches to join this mission of God from the margins may imply that churches are at the centre. This is not true in most cases, even in the predominantly Christian West. In an increasingly diverse and secularized world, churches are increasingly finding themselves on the margins. How then do churches participate in God's mission in ways that are more in response to theological convictions rather than existential compulsions, and to the gospel call rather than to survival needs? The following possibilities may be considered as part of a reflection on the way forward.

First, when marginalization is the result of the irresponsible exercise of power, the churches' neutrality and subtle forms of glorification of power do not make them credible to be a part of this movement of God with marginalized people. Instead, churches need to follow Jesus who rejected all forms of hegemonic and dominating power but opted for models of power that nurture and affirm life and healing. 'Both injustice and violence have to do with assertions of power – power to dominate, intimidate, control, and exploit. The traces and glorification of such concepts of power are rampant in our social and ecclesial structures, ideologies, theologies, liturgies, and even in interpersonal and institutional dynamics.'[19] The option for 'Mission from the Margins', then, is an option to give up

---

that reshape desire and instigate transformation.' Rieger, 'Liberating God-Talk, 217.

[18] Warren Carter in his *Matthew and the Margins: A Sociopolitical and Religious Reading* (Maryknoll, NY: Orbis Books, 2005) makes interesting comparisons to prove margins as God's preferred site. He lists: instead of law, the synagogue tradition and imperial ideology, the community looks to Jesus and the prophets; instead of commitment to the emperor, commitment to the one crucified by the emperor; instead of *pax romana*, they opt for the hope of the Kingdom of God; no embracing but critiquing powers; no sustaining the order, but shaking up the order; power not to lord over but to serve; instead of hierarchical and patriarchal structures, they opt for an egalitarian and communitarian life; no violence but active resistance; and instead of wealth, sharing as a source of prosperity and life-giving.

[19] Deenabandhu Manchala, 'Theological Reflections on Pilgrimage', in *Ecumenical Review,* 66.2 (July 2014), 140.

privileges of power and to subject oneself to be scorned, scrutinized and trivialized like the marginalized.

Secondly, churches need to evolve themselves from being mere religious communities to being moral communities, upholding the values that sustain and celebrate life through their own being and actions. This implies overcoming the life-denying practices of sexism, racism, casteism, and different forms and expressions of discrimination and phobias both within and around, as part of their witness to being the signs of God's reign to come. In response to the reality of increasing plurality, the discourse on Christian unity is now annotated with the language of hospitality and inclusion. As those denied identity and taken advantage of by many devious expressions of unity and community, the marginalized are suspicious of such attempts. Therefore, there is need to deconstruct the terms 'hospitality' and 'inclusion' because the notions of power are implied in them. 'Hospitality involves guest and host… In this experience, the host has the power and prerogative to offer hospitality… the manner and extent of it are often based on the social identity and location of the guest…'[20] Likewise, inclusion too implies 'the notion of "*normative/norm*" and the binary notion of "insider/outsider" with the "insider inviting the outsider" into the normative space. Someone is choosing to include someone else! The fundamental question then is, who includes whom?'[21] Therefore, 'hospitality without justice is oppressive and dehumanizing. Similarly, inclusion without hospitality is nothing more than charity'.[22]

Thirdly, a just, open and inclusive world does not flow forth because of the church's preaching or missiological reflections. Those who enjoy power do not give it up and those who gain through injustice do not stop being unjust. Instead, this transformation begins with those who are marginalized and with those who are indignant about injustice. Churches need to be a part of this stream and, wherever possible, facilitate dialogue and partnership – among faith communities, and with movements and initiatives committed to this vision of the world. The report of a study on 'mission in the experience of the Dalits', holds that 'understanding mission as having a midwifery role has significant implications because primarily mission does not become the monopoly of ecclesiastical Christianity… Rather, understanding mission as creating the conditions for liberation

---

[20] 'Hospitality, Inclusion and Justice: A theological reflection in response to old and new forms of discrimination and exclusion – a continuing conversation among the members of the Core Group of, and others related to, the WCC programme on Just and Inclusive Communities': WCC Consultation, Nagpur, India, December 10-14, 2009: www.oikoumene.org/en/resources/documents/wcc-programmes/unity-mission-evangelism-and-spirituality/just-and-inclusive-communities/theological-reflection-in-response-to-old-and-new-forms-of-discrimination (accessed 6th July 2015).

[21] 'Hospitality, Inclusion and Justice'.

[22] 'Hospitality, Inclusion and Justice'.

helps us to understand mission as a process which opens itself to further the liberative agendas of other organizations, groups and bodies which may have their base outside the church but yet are involved in the issues of justice'.[23] Therefore, the unity that the church seeks is for the mission of bringing all things and people together, irrespective of the conditions and restrictions that society imposes.[24]

Fourthly, it calls for an engagement with theologies of life, theologies emerging out of struggles against injustice, discrimination and oppression. These theologies alone can liberate the churches to break free of the tendency to maintain neutral positions and refuse to legitimize the perpetuation of unjust and oppressive structures and forces. Joerg Rieger advocates: 'Theology that develops resistance to the powers of exclusion may help to develop new models that prove useful in restructuring not only the process of theological reflection but also the church and, ultimately, even society at large.'[25] The credibility of the churches' witness today, therefore, depends on their ability to re-anchor themselves in the theologies and system of knowledge arising out of multi-religious contexts and in contexts of people's struggles for life, justice and dignity. On the other hand, affirmation of faith in the God of life cannot remain mere verbal activity confined to liturgy and theological articulations in the context of concrete historic struggles of people for life. When poverty and injustice are a creation of irresponsible assertion by oppressive powers, leading to the denial of life for many, then exposing, resisting and transforming all forces that create such conditions is an essential form of Christian obedience. Whether churches with all their institutional interests and power structures have the courage and inclination to join this pilgrimage of life of the poor, is a moot question. The challenge here is the reluctance to let go of burdensome structures, archaic systems of knowledge, and often

---

[23] Deenabandhu Manchala, Joseph Prabhakar Dayam and Peniel Rajkumar, 'When Margins Inform and Reform Mission: Dalit Experiences as Foundations for Mission Theology', in Emma Wildwood and Peniel Rajkumar (eds), *Foundation for Mission,* Regnum Edinburgh Centenary Series, Vol. XIII (Oxford, Regnum: 2013), 41.

[24] Further, the 'Global Platform for Theological Reflection 2010 Unity and Mission Today: Voices and Visions from the Margins', a conference held at Bucharest, Romania, from 4 to 10 October 2010, found that 'Mission is an activity in the struggle for life, and to that extent, mission could also be re-conceived as enabling everybody to participate in the discovery of one's own and our collective humanity. The marginalized people become the agents of mission and unity': www.oikoumene.org/en/resources/documents/wcc-programmes/unity-mission-evangelism-and-spirituality/just-and-inclusive-communities/global-platform-for-theological-reflection-2010 (accessed 6th July 2015).

[25] Joerg Rieger, *God and the Excluded* (Minneapolis, MN: Fortress Press, 2001), 3.

redundant theological formulations, and to open oneself to the margins in order to listen to what God is saying and asking the churches to do.[26]

In conclusion, the mission of God with the marginalized today implies setting aside seemingly endless prescriptions on mission and getting engaged in the life-world of marginalized people, among whom God is present in their sighs and clamour for life and justice. 'After all, the church belongs to a faith tradition that is built around the memory of the one who defied the power and glory of the contemporary political and religious establishments, and proposed life-affirming alternatives by commending the act of a widow who gave only two small copper coins as greater than those who gave huge sums; applauding the prayer of the scorned tax collector as more acceptable than that of the glorified Pharisee; valuing the faith of the despised gentile more than that of his own centuries-old religious tradition; defying the protocols and traditions of rituals and propriety for the sake of the healing the sick; and teaching his disciples that to have and wield power is to be a servant, and even goes to extent of being one by washing their feet on the night before he was killed. In fact, much of the biblical tradition is driven by this counter-culture, unveiling to us the locale of God's presence and power among the Last, the Lost and the Least. These for Jesus are God's VIPs and his partners, and so should they be for the church too!' [27]

---

[26] Jürgen Moltmann challenges: 'Every theology which claims to be Christian must come to terms with Jesus' cry on the cross… In the face of Jesus' death-cry to God, theology becomes impossible or becomes possible only as specifically Christian theology. Christian theology… must come to terms with the cry of the wretched for God and for freedom out of the depths of the sufferings of this age. Sharing in the sufferings of this time, Christian theology is truly contemporary theology': *The Crucified God: The Cross of Christ as the Foundation and Criticism of Christian Theology* (New York, Evanston, San Francisco and London: Harper & Row, 1973), 153.

[27] See Deenabandhu Manchala, 'Relocating Theological Education in a Marginalized Context', Bangalore: Board of Theological Education of the Senate of Serampore College, 2015.

# ENVIRONMENT

Ernst M. Conradie

## Introduction

The relatedness of the three terms included in the title of this contribution is nowadays widely accepted in missiological circles. Since Edinburgh (1910) Christian mission can only be undertaken ecumenically, although this does not necessarily reflect missionary praxis. At least since Vancouver (1983) and Seoul (1990), it is widely acknowledged in ecumenical circles that mission includes an environmental dimension. Likewise, ecumenical fellowship is situated in a particular social and environmental context – given the etymological connections between the 'whole inhabited world' (*oikoumene*), ecology (the underlying logic of the household) and economy (the rules for housekeeping) on the basis of the Greek root *oikos* (household).

However, the relationships between these terms remain contested since each may be used as an umbrella concept that includes the others. Is mission not one dimension of the ecumenical movement, alongside the quest for unity, faith and order, social responsibility, education and worship?[1] Or does the ecumenical movement itself form part of God's mission? Or is Christianity one religious tradition alongside others so that the whole Christian tradition forms part of the emergence of symbolic consciousness (alongside culture, music and science) within the human species, which forms part of the evolution of life within the environment of the earth as a planet in a vast universe? Or does the creation and evolutionary history of the universe form part of the mission of the Triune God? In each case, these questions reveal theological differences and power relations.

In this contribution I will address such questions through a brief survey of crucial insights that emerged within the history of the modern ecumenical movement in general, and in Christian eco-theology in particular. I need to admit that this survey is tendentious and offers only one version of a story (situated mainly in reformed literature emerging from within the South African context) that can only be properly reconstructed through ecumenical participation, and therefore has to be corrected by other contributions within this volume.

---

[1] For a recent discussion of 23 notions of ecumenicity, see Ernst M. Conradie (ed), *Notions and Forms of Ecumenicity: South African Perspectives* (Stellenbosch, RSA: Sun Press, 2013).

The structure of this essay was conceived while sitting at Cape Maclear, Lake Malawi, with an injured leg, not able to go for a swim. This is a place of incredible beauty and tranquillity, where the tension between affluent tourists and poor villagers, a stone's throw away, is all too obvious. While the legacy of (foreign) mission is equally obvious, the natural beauty is deeply contaminated by deforestation, over-fishing and localised over-population, not to mention political conflict over scarce resources.

## The Agents of Mission Revisited

In classic rhetoric, four core questions have to be addressed: Who says what to whom with what intended effect? In missiological terms these questions become: Who sends whom to whom with what agenda?[2] In the modern ecumenical movement these questions have been answered in diverging ways with many twists and turns, given diverging soteriological, cultural (and economic), ecclesiastical and developmental notions of mission. I suggest that this may help us to understand how environmental concerns have come to be included in missionary agendas, or inversely, how 'mission' became a dimension of environmental concerns.

In classic (Nicene) ecumenical theology, it was assumed that it is God the Father who sends the Holy Spirit to do God's work of creation, salvation and consummation on the basis of what Jesus Christ has done 'for us and our salvation'. The Spirit is commissioned by the Father and thus 'proceeds' from the Father. Note that the work of the Creator Spirit, the 'Giver of Life', includes participation in the Triune God's work of creation (*creatio*) so that it would be incorrect to say that the Spirit is sent to creation (*creatura*), 'the world', the earth or the land. Mission is situated within the whole work of God (*oikounomia tou Theou*), which is an even broader category than God's mission.[3] The work of salvation takes place 'through the prophets' by providing the means of salvation (including the inspiration of the Scriptures) and by using the church as an instrument so that the formation, edification (through word and sacrament), fellowship, ministries and missions of the church forms part of the mission of the Spirit. In Nicene missiology, the movement of the Spirit is towards the consummation of all things through the resurrection of the dead and the 'life of the world to come'.

In ecumenical missiology, this pneumatological understanding of mission is captured in *Together towards Life* (2013), alongside the Christological focus of *Mission and Evangelism: An Ecumenical*

---

[2] See also Ernst M. Conradie, 'Creation at the Heart of Mission', in *Missionalia,* 38:3 (2010), 380-96.

[3] See Steve de Gruchy, 'Agency, Sin and Grace: Protestant Reflections on Mission and Creation', in Lukas Vischer (ed), *Witnessing in the Midst of a Suffering Creation: A Challenge for the Mission of the Church* (Geneva: WCC, 2007), 97-114 (111).

*Affirmation* (1982). However, it took more than a century of controversy to arrive at such ecumenical consensus. In what follows I will reconstruct a brief narrative of this process.[4]

In the nineteenth century, mission was understood primarily as the activities of various para-church agencies operating in a cross-cultural context to proclaim the gospel, to convert the heathen (and to save their souls from damnation), to plant churches and to establish Christianity in non-western contexts. Given denominational equivalents to the colonial 'scramble for Africa' (and colonial resources elsewhere), mission gradually morphed to become the activities of various denominations (no longer of para-church organisations) operating in cross-cultural contexts to proclaim the gospel, to win converts (or proselytes) and to establish new congregations that would strengthen a particular confessional tradition. It was soon realised that this required the self-governance, the still elusive self-sustenance, and self-extension of so-called daughter churches. On this basis, the insight gradually dawned that mission was primarily the mission of the church, that mission was ecclesial, church-centred. Conversely, the sending church itself came to be understood in missionary (or better, missional) terms, prompting a missionary ecclesiology (Karl Barth). The conclusion was that the church was missionary by its very nature, that it was inappropriate to speak about church *and* mission, that the church was the one that is sent, not the one that is sending. This insight could not hide abiding tensions between so-called mother and daughter churches, but by the Whitby conference of 1947 a new formula was endorsed that mission described a partnership or churches to proclaim the gospel together in six continents. In *Together towards Life* (Busan 2013), this insight was radicalised to speak of mission *from* the margins, not only *to* the margins. Nevertheless, in some Evangelical and Pentecostal circles (e.g. by Donald McGavran), church growth was still being regarded, well beyond the 1980s, as the very goal of mission.

This ecclesiocentric understanding of mission was radicalised and subsequently undermined by the retrieval of a more classic understanding of mission as being God's mission (*missio Dei*). The focus shifted from a mission-centred church to the belief that the church and its missions (plural) form part of *missio Dei.* There is a church because there is mission. Mission is thus understood in the context of the doctrine of the Trinity and not soteriology or ecclesiology. The emphasis on God's mission should be understood within the context of a Barthian critique of religion and of Christianity in particular. This was the lasting response of dialectic theology to the legitimacy crisis experienced in western Christianity following the two world wars. The criterion against which the moral

[4] I am drawing here especially from the magisterial overview offered by David J. Bosch in *Transforming Mission: Paradigm Shifts in Theology of Mission* (Maryknoll, NY: Orbis Books, 1991), 368-93.

bankruptcy of western culture and Christianity alike is measured is God's mission, not ours.

Such insights led to two important shifts that each decentralised the role of the church in God's mission:

First, God's mission is not primarily to the church but to the world in order to establish God's reign. The church cannot be equated with God's reign. The church is therefore nothing but an instrument used by the Spirit in the coming of God's reign. Given the waning influence of the church in so-called secular societies, some concluded that the church is only one such instrument and perhaps not even the most important one used by God. If King Cyrus could be hailed as the servant of Yahweh, the Spirit may also use other instruments, including progressive organisations, development agencies, technological innovations and so forth. This suggests the radical *in*significance of the church. In the Dutch theology of the apostolate (Arnold van Ruler and J.C. Hoekendijk), a dynamic notion of the church as participating in the movement of the Spirit was proposed. The church was even described as a 'sociological impossibility' since any institutionalisation would tend to hamper this movement. It would be to fossilise the movement of a bird in flight. In the ecumenical climate of the 1960s and 1970s, with a widespread loss of confidence in the institutional church, it seemed that inside the church there was no salvation! It was still possible to describe mission as God's work but this was then understood as a rich, metaphorical re-description of the human quest for well-being or of progressive notions of social responsibility.

Secondly, the locus where the Spirit is believed to be at work shifted with this 'turn to the world', the orientation of the church towards the world, that coincided with the turning of the world away from the church.[5] For some, the Spirit works primarily in the institutional church and its governance structures in order to establish a visible sign of God's reign in the world. Others place the emphasis on the church as an organism, and thus on the vocations of the laity in the world, but then outside the church as an institution. For yet others, the world becomes the primary locus of the Spirit's mission. The church is perhaps the only organisation that does not exist for its own sake, but for the sake of its non-members. The church need not gather the whole world into itself as a haven of salvation but exists through its mission for the sake of the world. One is not human in order to become a Christian; one becomes a Christian in order to become human (again). The goal of mission is understood as humanisation, not as Christianisation. Culture is not subservient to the gospel; the gospel is necessary so that human cultures can flourish. Moreover, the world provides the agenda in this regard. The church only exists as a church *for* others (Dietrich Bonhoeffer), it is best understood as a servant church

---

[5] See Karl Barth, *Church Dogmatics, Volume IV.3.1: The Doctrine of Reconciliation* (Edinburgh: T. & T. Clark, 1961), 18-38 (37).

(Avery Dulles), and since the church cannot claim that it knows what is best for others, perhaps as a church *with* others (Theo Sundermeier). The gospel is not an aim in itself but is there for the sake of the well-being of the world (Arnold van Ruler).

Willie Jonker, an eminent twentieth-century South African reformed theologian, puts it aptly: 'At the very moment when the world turned away from the Church and the illusion of the so-called corpus Christianum fell away, the Church became free for a new awareness of its mission and its calling to be a witness in the world.'[6] This suggests a tendency to relativise the church: 'The Spirit is not restricted to the church but is operative in the whole world to accomplish the salvation that is intended for the world, and in some sense is already present in the world.'[7] The church is therefore not absolutely necessary for the salvation of the world, but the world is absolutely necessary for the existence of the church. Accordingly, mission is best associated with the social agenda of churches situated in civil society in various local contexts, for example in terms of proclaiming the 'social gospel', caring for the needy, engaging in 'charity', 'development', social and economic justice, peace-making and perhaps earthkeeping.

This turn to the world prompted a further pendulum shift in which it is nowadays widely recognised that the church is not merely an instrument of the Holy Spirit but also a sign, symbol and sacrament of God's coming reign (Melbourne 1980). It may be a fragile and not a triumphalist sign, a sign of the cross, but it is not as insignificant as secularised interpretations of God's mission seem to suggest. The conversion of the church is needed but the gospel provides the agenda for such transformation. There is a distinction between the community we are and the one we long for. The blurring of the boundaries between church and world is neither in the interest of the church nor of the world. The church's mode of being in the world is being different from the rest of the world. The world needs to be challenged by the radical demands of the gospel. The church, and Christian theology, can only be relevant only within the wider world as long as it sticks to its own cause. The mode of belonging to the world is through antithesis. The church is always provisional, the firstfruits of the coming harvest, an experimental garden, an alternative community (David Bosch), an eschatological community (Jürgen Moltmann). It has sociological but also theological qualities so that the church cannot be equated with any other organisation or voluntary association.[8] There needs to be a creative tension between the realisation of God's reign on earth and the role of the

[6] See W.D. Jonker, 'Turning to the World: On Karl Barth's Interpretation of the Modern Era', in Johan Mouton and Bernard C. Lategan (eds), *The Relevance of Theology in the 1990s* (Pretoria, RSA: HSRC, 1994), 535-48 (539).

[7] Jonker, 'Turning to the World', 543.

[8] See John W. de Gruchy, 'Christian community', in John W. de Gruchy and Charles Villa-Vicencio (eds), *Doing Theology in Context: South African Perspectives* (Cape Town, RSA: David Philip, 1994), 125-38.

church as a pointer to that.[9] These insights prompt ongoing reflections on the place of the church in the whole household of God[10] – which is widely acknowledged to extend far beyond the institutional church and, indeed, has cosmic dimensions.

## Views on the World

The turn to the world that was evident in ecumenical theology in the 1960s pre-empted and acted as a bridge between traditional church-centred theologies and twentieth-century contextual theologies. One may suggest that the term 'world' was still open to interpretation, so that some theologies focused on the human psyche (habits of the heart), family life and sexuality, while others focused on cultural issues such as indigenisation, civil religion, consumerism or the impact of technology. Yet others became concerned with the relationship between theology and the arts, literature, philosophy or with dialogue with other religious traditions. Some became immersed in the political economy, while yet others focused on the bio-physical environment. One also needs to recognise the burgeoning interest in the entire cosmos that is evident in current discourse on science and theology. In each case, this 'turn to the world' is evident.

There is no need to play off a theological interest in the personal, the social, the cultural, the religious, the biophysical and the scientific against each other. All the better contributions recognise the need for a multi-dimensional approach even though the relationships between these spheres are construed in diverging ways. It is also not surprising that this 'turn to the world' was eventually captured under umbrella terms such as contextual theology or public theology. What these approaches have in common is a resistance to ecclesiocentric theologies, a sense of ecumenicity that is wider than a concern over church unity and a multi-dimensional notion of mission that encompasses but also extends well beyond ecclesial missions.

My sense is that this 'turn to the world' set the parameters for subsequent debates on the relationship between mission, ecumenical fellowship and the environment. Diverging interpretations of the turn to the world remain possible, if only because of different cosmological views of the world or socially constructed worldviews. Nevertheless, this 'turn to the

[9] See Bosch, *Transforming Mission*, 381.

[10] See Ernst M. Conradie, 'The whole household of God (*oikos*): Some ecclesiological perspectives: Part 1 & 2', in *Scriptura,* 94 (2007), 1-28. See also the forthcoming volume edited by Clive W. Ayre and Ernst M. Conradie, *The Church in God's Household: Protestant Perspectives on Ecclesiology and Ecology* (submitted to Cluster Publications, 2015). This volume places the church within a missiological framework and explores the ecological significance of various dimensions of mission in chapters on *leitourgia*, *kerygma*, *diakonia*, *koinonia*, *martyria* and *ecclesia*.

world' influenced all subsequent debates on God's mission, ranging from self-secularising theologies to a Barthian universalism, from understanding the world as a process (following Whitehead, Cobb and others) to the panentheistic views that are now common in indigenous theologies, eco-theologies and in discourse on science and theology alike.

### Shifts in Environmental Concerns

The emergence of Christian eco-theology followed in the wake of this turn to the world. Although environmental concerns may be traced back to the early history of Christianity and is inspired, for example, by the medieval examples of Hildegard of Bingen and Francis of Assisi, self-conscious and overt forms of eco-theology emerged only in the 1960s with early exponents such as Hendrikus Berkhof, Thomas Berry, John Cobb, Paul Santmire and Joseph Sittler, most of whom were also deeply involved in the ecumenical movement. It is not possible to offer a brief history of subsequent developments in eco-theology here. Instead, one may point to shifts in the way in which environmental challenges have been understood in secular discourse since the first global environmental conference that was held in Stockholm in 1972. I suggest that the following twists and turns, each symbolised by a particular landmark conference or report, may be identified.

Before the 1970s, environmental discourse had focused mainly on issues around nature conservation and preservation, i.e. the protection of pristine areas from commercial agriculture, mining, industry and urban development. The famous *Limits to Growth* report to the Club of Rome (1972) signalled an emerging concern over population growth (when there were less than 4 billion humans on earth, compared with the current 7.3 billion). Besides issues around food production, the concern was over non-renewable resources, including fossil fuels and minerals. This concern gradually shifted to debates on the sustainable use of renewable resources, signalled by the Brundtland report on *Our Common Future* (1987). The focus on the carrying capacity of the land was prompted by concerns over fresh water, deforestation, the erosion of topsoil, plummeting fish stocks and a rapid loss of biodiversity. While early debates had centred on the sustainability of economic growth, efficiency and the need for sustainable development, later debates had shifted to the very notion of sustainability. The question was not only how long the use of non-renewable resources could be sustained or how it could be sustained (technologically), but what it was that had to be sustained, i.e. what such scarce resources were to be used for. While some focused on the need for sustainable livelihoods, others critiqued the perceived need to sustain expanding consumerist lifestyles, industrialised capitalism or even western forms of civilisation.

The Earth Summit held in Rio de Janeiro in 1992 signalled a shifting emphasis towards the victims of environmental destruction, including the human victims. This had been prompted by the loss of species but also by the social ecology movement, the animal welfare, animal rights and animal liberation movements, and by a wide range of indigenous, eco-feminist and social justice movements that were concerned over the plight of refugees, the victims of climate change, exposure to toxic waste (associated with environmental racism), the plight of farm workers, factory workers and mine workers, and by the adverse environmental conditions to which the poor and marginalised, especially women and children, were exposed. The argument was that the daily problems experienced by the poor were of an environmental and not merely an economic nature. The focus therefore shifted to the interplay between economic inequalities, violent forms of conflict and environmental destruction (also captured in the ecumenical call for 'Justice, Peace and the Integrity of Creation') and the role of ideological distortions around gender, race and class associated with environmental injustices.

The further shifts in environmental discourse are best understood in terms of climate change and therefore with understanding the environment as being indeed a truly global concern. The focus was no longer on nature conservation, limited resources or on carrying capacity but on the absorption capacity of the biosphere – to absorb the waste products of industrialised societies, especially carbon dioxide but also municipal, toxic and nuclear waste. The UN protocol adopted at Kyoto in 1997 signalled a recognition of the need for a political solution to a problem on which there was already sufficient scientific consensus at that time, a consensus that obtained higher levels of probability with each subsequent report released by the Inter-Governmental Panel on Climate Change (IPCC). Although mustering sufficient political will remain elusive, it seems that the technological means are already available to address climate change, while the economic costs have been calculated to be quite feasible as, for example, the *Stern Review on the Economics of Climate Change* (2006) suggests. Although the task is gigantic, it can be captured in one sentence, namely, to transform the energy basis of the entire global economy from an over-reliance on fossil fuels to sustainable alternatives within the period between 1990 and 2050, of which the first two decades were the most important.

Two further shifts were signalled by the Conference of the Parties held at Copenhagen (COP 15, 2009) and COP 21 held in Paris (2015). The inability at Copenhagen to reach an agreement that would limit an increase in average global surface temperature to below 2 degrees Celsius above pre-industrial levels suggested that the problem was not merely political, economic or technological but that it be understood in terms of limits to the kind of rapid social change on a voluntary basis that was required.[11]

[11] The different forms of limits involved (limited resources, limited absorption capacity and limits to social change) were analysed by Larry Rasmussen in a

Societies can and do change, but the scale of the required change and the relatively long time frame seemed to pose intractable problems. This prompted an interest in theories of, and mechanisms for, social change. What if trusted strategies such as education, marketing, punishment (through self-imposed taxes), policy-making, social engineering, management, calls for responsibility and prophetic warnings all fail to deliver the required change promptly enough?[12] Clearly, such social change is necessary in order to muster political will and for change to be effective.

It is too early to comment on the significance of the Conference of the Parties held in Paris in November 2015, but it was remarkable to observe the apocalyptic language used in preparatory documents and statements released prior to the conference. As many suggest, this might have been our 'last chance' to prevent catastrophic climate change by the end of the 21st century through international policy. There is much debate on irreversible environmental thresholds that will have apocalyptic consequences if and when they are transgressed. Ironically, such apocalyptic language is pre-empted in millennial expectations and in post-apocalyptic literature and films alike. Indeed, what if it is already too late? How would that shape our understanding of God's mission and God's loving care for creation?

## Anticipated Further Shifts in Thinking about Mission, Environment and Ecumenism

It is fair to say that Christian discourse on the environment largely mirrors the shifts in secular environmental discourse as sketched above. This is true even though in some Christian circles the focus remains on issues around nature conservation and the environmental stewardship of land, while others are concerned over environmental justice or climate justice.[13] Even if there is an emerging consensus that earthkeeping forms a dimension of mission, there are diverging views on what such mission entails, given shifting views on 'the environment' – views that are influenced more by secular than by theological considerations.

This correlation between secular and Christian discourse on the environment may be partly due to the quite significant ecumenical participation in environmental movements. This would be entirely

---

brilliant early article entitled, 'The future isn't what it used to be: 'Limits to growth' and Christian ethics', in *Lutheran Quarterly,* 27 (1975), 101-11.

[12] See Ernst M. Conradie, 'Contemporary Challenges to Christian Ecotheology: Some Reflections on the State of the Debate after Five Decades', in *Journal of Theology for Southern Africa,* 147 (2013), 106-123.

[13] There is a huge corpus of Christian literature on the highly contested notion of environmental stewardship. For a critique of this notion and a survey of different rationales for Christian earthkeeping, see Ernst M. Conradie, *Christianity and Earthkeeping: In Search of an Inspiring Vision* (Stellenbosch, RSA: Sun Press, 2011).

appropriate, given the need for collaboration between governments, business, industry and civil society alike. Within civil society (which is a highly contested terrain) there is an obvious need for co-operation between the full array of social movements and organisations, especially amongst religious traditions, to protect our common home. There is a welcome, quite widespread, recognition that climate change, for example, is not merely a technological, political or economic problem. It is a moral issue since those who contribute very little to the problem will suffer the consequences disproportionally. This is reiterated in concerns over climate justice and in calls for differentiated responsibilities, adaptation and technological transfer. Moreover, there is an emerging recognition that climate change is also a spiritual problem. If one knows what to do and how to do it, and has the means, but still finds oneself unable to muster the necessary moral energy, will, leadership and imagination to do so, all this points towards a spiritual and not merely a moral problem. This is recognised in many statements by religious leaders, most recently in Pope Francis's encyclical *Laudato Si* (June 2015).[14]

However, there is another side to this spirit of collaboration. This is prompted by debates on the *Christian* roots of environmental degradation. This is supported by: a) the correlation between historic carbon emissions and those countries where Christianity was influential by the advent of the industrial revolution, b) the tacit ideological legitimation of neo-liberal capitalism and consumerist aspirations in many Christian contexts, and c) the popularity of preaching the prosperity gospel in so-called developing economies. If industrial capitalism did not simply result from the spirit of Protestantism (Max Weber), one may argue that Christians were not quick enough to warn about its side-effects (including the plight of impoverished workers), or to resist the ideological tendencies (e.g. consumerism) that legitimised and incentivised economic activities causing environmental destruction.

If that is taken into account, it seems that Christians and therefore also the ecumenical movement could contribute something quite particular to global efforts to address environmental challenges that no other organisation or movement can. To fail do so in the name of a spirit of collaboration would be irresponsible. What is that particular contribution that only Christians can make? My impression is that this question is seldom addressed and often underplayed. Where it is addressed, this is typically done in the form of retrieving ecological wisdom from the symbols embedded within particular confessional traditions, liturgies and spiritualities. Given Christian complicity in the root causes of environmental destruction, one would wonder whether a confession of guilt

---

[14] See also the document produced by the Climate Change Committee of the South African Council of Churches, entitled *Climate Change – A challenge to the churches in South Africa* (Marshalltown, RSA: SACC, 2009).

and not only a confession of faith may not be more appropriate.[15] This may well revolutionise dialogue with other religious traditions – for example, if the Muslim victims of rising sea levels in Bangladesh were taken as the cue for such a confession.

There is more at stake though and this comes more closely to the heart of the ecumenical movement itself, given the deep denominational and theological divisions within the larger Christian tradition. While Christians in some contexts contribute disproportionately to carbon emissions, Christians in other contexts are or will increasingly become the victims of climate change. Given the way in which political power blocks tend to protect their own interests in negotiations on climate change, it is sad to note that ecumenical fellowship between churches and Christians living in such countries are unable to bridge such divides through common witness, a quest for justice and peace-making. One may imagine what a difference common public witness across such political divides could make to the legitimacy of protecting national interests at any Conference of the Parties. Clearly, the quality of fellowship between churches provides a test case for the credibility of their witness to the mission of the Triune God in the world. This is the inexorable crux where the interplay between God's mission, ecumenical fellowship and environmental challenges will be at stake in the next few decades.

[15] See Ernst M. Conradie, 'Confessing Guilt in the Context of Climate Change: Some South African Perspectives', in *Scriptura,* 103 (2010), 134-52.

# GENDER

Lilian C. Siwila

## Introduction

This chapter examines the contours of women's experiences and contributions to mission work by tracing how they negotiated the gender challenges that they faced throughout their work. According to Predelli and Muller, much of the literature on women and their work in mission organisations suggest that women were talked about as the 'other or totally neglected'.[1] This is despite their immense contribution to Christian mission. In the general global discourse on the value of women's involvement in Christian mission, many have been classified as assistants or helpers who worked alongside men to support the men, but never as the leaders of the community because of socialised gender-perception and ecclesial endorsement of men being the preferred leaders.[2] The work done by the men set the standard for what was classified as missionary work. Within an ecclesial environment where women were deemed not to be qualified to enter the ordained ministry because it was reserved for the males, the classification of work done by the women was seen as social work and was not regarded as mission but service to the community.[3] In response to these perceptions concerning women's involvement in mission work, this chapter uses ecumenical perspectives of partnership in mission as demonstrated in the London Missionary Society (LMS) work in Zambia to interrogate ways in which men and women understood gender dimensions in mission work. The chapter also challenges some of the ambivalences in the understanding of gender in relation to mission that have been reflected during this period. It concludes by postulating a gendered approach to mission calling and service that affirms the contributions of men and women.

## Gender Division of Labour in Mission Stations

Ideas about gender dynamics among western missionaries played a critical role in organising work and giving meaning to their mission projects in the

---

[1] Line Nyhagen Predelli and Jon Muller, 'Piety and Patriarchy: Contested Gender Regimes in Nineteenth-Century Evangelical Mission', in M.T. Huber and Nancy C. Lutkehaus (eds), *Gendered Mission: Women and Men in Missionary Discourses and Practice* (Ann Arbor, MI: University of Michigan Press, 1999), 67-112.
[2] Predelli and Muller, 'Piety and Patriarchy'.
[3] Predelli and Muller, 'Piety and Patriarchy'.

global South. Mission organisations like the LMS within Zambia held a conservative view on women's involvement in mission activities. Due to the patriarchal nature and construct of most of the Protestant mission organisations, mission work took on ambiguous and ambivalent gender perspectives that allowed male missionaries to emphasise their supremacy over women missionaries. Predelli and Muller state that Protestant missions have not been simply patriarchal but male-dominant in the form of organisational control.[4] Despite these challenges, male missionaries also realised that they needed to rely on the service of women in some of the mission activities.[5] This resulted in a gendered division of labour in the administration of mission work. Services such as teaching, nursing, and training women in housewifery and domestic work were regarded as women's work and consequently classified as a lower priority and lower paid mission work.[6] Within the division of labour practised in the mission stations of western missionaries, evangelism and preaching were accorded a high priority and were viewed as men's mission work.[7] Despite this perception, Hill and Hunter argue that mission has been historically viewed as a women's cause because women missionaries were seen to be suitable to work with native women since they had more freedom and opportunities for contact with native women than male missionaries.[8] In Escobar's memory of women in mission, he presents a detailed account of scholars who have expressed the value and contribution of women to mission work and their contribution to missionary literature.[9] It could be argued that in most cases this literature was used to confine women to specific roles such as literacy, hygiene, homecraft and other types of domestic work.

Another factor that affected gender division of labour in mission stations was the idea of hiring and evaluating personnel according to an objective standard. Rita Smith Kipp argues that women who made themselves available for mission work were sometimes hired to 'act as men' when it came to professional matters. However, their lack of access to theological education or the privilege of ordination meant that many women were classified as lay missionaries and therefore came to their professions without formal theological training. They relied on experiences which did

---

[4] Predelli and Muller, 'Piety and Patriarchy', 68.
[5] Predelli and Muller, 'Piety and Patriarchy', 68.
[6] Predelli and Muller, 'Piety and Patriarchy', 68.
[7] Predelli and Muller, 'Piety and Patriarchy', 68.
[8] See also Jane Hunter, *Gospel of Gentility: American Women Missionaries in Turn of the Century in China* (New Haven, CT: Yale University Press, 1984). Also Patricia Hill, *The World their Household: The American Women's Foreign Mission Movement and Cultural Transformation 1870-1920* (Ann Arbor, MI: University of Michigan Press, 1995).
[9] Samuel J. Escobar, 'Mission Studies – Past, Present and Future', in Robert L. Gallagher and Paul Hertig (eds.), *Landmark Essays in Mission and World Christianity* (Maryknoll, NY: Orbis Books, 2009), 244-63.

not fully prepare them for the work ahead.[10] Commenting further on this bureaucratic mode of hiring, Kipp identified this kind of approach as a contributing factor to the way in which male missionaries from the West underestimated the competence of their female colleagues in the mission field. The persistence of gender stereotypes which was driven by these factors was also motivated by missions' bureaucratic structures.[11]

Hierarchical bureaucracy, associated with patriarchy and gendered as male, was embraced by churches that engaged in mission in the global South. In order to address this setback, there was need for gender mainstreaming of these bureaucratic organisations that controlled mission work. The gendered nature of bureaucracy meant that men controlled the decision-making of the organisations on behalf of women. This caused resistance among some women missionaries who had an alternative vision of gender justice in mission understanding and practice. This was evident in the work of Mabel Shaw whose work at the Girls' Boarding School in Mbereshi, Zambia, encountered a number of bureaucratic challenges from the LMS.[12] Although her work ethic was ridiculed as arrogant and feminine, Shaw's reaction was in response to the bureaucratic male leadership within the LMS that seemed to downgrade the concept of mutuality and partnership in mission.

In order for questions about gender relationships in mission within the African context to be effectively interrogated, it is important to also examine the relationship that emerged between missionaries and the different groups of people with whom they interacted at their mission stations and the wider society in which they were located, such as the native people, owners of capital, and their workers, politicians and the judiciary. This kind of gender perception was consistent with the dominant cultural worldviews of the western political landscape that informed and shaped the governance model of their mission stations within the global South. Colonial policies within Zambia focused on setting control between the colonizer and the colonised which were embedded in gender constructs. This is because gender inequalities were also reflected in colonial discourses.[13] Therefore, the presence of western-founded mission stations within Zambia as exhibited in the work of the LMS was coloured by

---

[10] Rita Smith Kipp, 'Why Can't a Woman be More like a Man? Bureaucratic Contractions in the Dutch Missionary Society', in Huber and Lutkehaus, *Gendered Mission*, 145-77, at 146.

[11] Kipp, 'Why Can't a Woman be More like a Man?', 146.

[12] Sean Morrow. '"No Girl Leaves School Unmarried": Mabel Shaw and the Education of Girls at Mbereshi, Northern Rhodesia, 1915-1940', in *The International Journal of African Historical Studies*, 19.4 (1986), 601-35.

[13] The work of Huber and Lutkehaus (eds), *Gendered Mission*, provides a detailed account of this debate. Most of the authors in this volume have demonstrated in detail a gendered analysis on the relationship between the mission field and the missionaries who worked in these mission fields.

cultural, race and class prejudices that informed the embedded patriarchy within the system of governance. It could be argued that western missionaries within Zambian society embodied patriarchal ideologies that kept women in positions of servitude. Therefore, as missionaries engaged in working particularly with African women, an embedded patriarchal construct shaped the agenda of the mission station and grossly restricted efforts for mutual partnership between men and women and a need for a holistic, gendered approach to mission. Despite all these gender ambivalences within the London Mission Society's missional understanding and practice, especially within the African context of Zambia, they emerged as a pro-active western Protestant mission organisation that promoted the autonomy of women in developing mission projects that served the needs and interests of native women.

One transformational example is expressed through the work of the female missionaries at the Mabel Shaw Girls' Mission School which was expressly dedicated to the care of women missionaries.[14] Shaw, who was the founder of the school, proposed that the school be administered by single women missionaries whom she thought did not have the same opportunities as their male counterparts did to work in the mission field abroad. The call for an all-inclusive mission was also the emphasis of the LMS during the period of sending its missionaries to the mission field in Africa. Although many missionaries were condemned for not being all-inclusive in their mission work, to some extent they still maintained the call for all humanity to go into the world and preach the gospel. Phiri argues that the concept of mutual sharing should reject the imperialistic tendency to expect the sharing to be one-sided. This is based on the assumption that only certain people in the partnership have something to share.[15] The theology of partnership in the mission project should be seen beyond gender. Mission work done in the sharing of the common project would go beyond gender, race and culture boundaries in an effort to serve life.

## Decade of the Churches on Women and Mission

Having presented an overview of the gender dynamics that shaped western missional attitudes and practice towards women who served within the context of the global South, attention will be given next to examining the phenomenon as expressed within one mission station within Zambia. The next area of interrogation between mission and gender gives attention to the period of the 'Churches in Solidarity with Women' which was born out of a need to focus on women's issues within the ecumenical agenda of the

---

[14] Morrow, 'No Girl Leaves School Unmarried'.

[15] Isabel Apawo, 'Partnership in Mission: A Critical Appraisal of the Partnership of Women and Men', in Desmond van der Water (ed), *Postcolonial Mission: Power and Partnership in World Christianity* (Upland, CA: Sopher Press, 2010), 61-77.

church and wider society. This chapter argues that a gendered perspective on the *Ecumenical Decade on Churches in Solidarity with Women* challenged the ecumenical movement to find non-patriarchal ways of reading women's missional contribution into the history of the church. Despite the invaluable contribution of women's involvement in mission work, it has not been adequately recognised and recorded in the history of world mission.[16] According to Heider-Rottwilm:

> The decision by WCC central committee in 1987 to declare the Decade was based on the recognition that the much-vaunted community between men and women would remain an illusion so long as we failed to identify and combat factors disrupting and dividing the community… By deciding on the Ecumenical Decade, the churches co-operating in the WCC committed leadership, which is largely male-dominated, to work towards eliminating such relationships of violence.[17]

This focus by the WCC signalled that systemic imbalance in recognition of women's missional contribution in the church could only be addressed, not by mere exhortation but through intentional corrective efforts. Throughout the Decade, a number of suggestions on how the churches through their predominantly male leadership could address issues that negatively affect women's missional contribution were made. A major concern raised in the WCC project was the need for the full participation of women in the decision-making of the church at all levels. Progress on the work towards solidarity with women was discussed in most of the WCC Assemblies during this period. Llewellyn, reflecting on the WCC's emphasis on the *Ecumenical Decade on Churches in Solidarity with Women*, argued that the core issue faced by the churches was that of revisiting their unenlightened position on the role of women within the church.[18] The author warned that if, at the end of the Decade, there was no real life-giving difference experienced by women, then the church's very being would have been seriously ruptured.[19] Using a gendered framework on mission and the church, it becomes imperative to continuously challenge the church to revisit its contribution to the call for churches to be in solidarity with women.

The Ecumenical Decade should be seen as one way in which the ecumenical body has attempted to encourage gender advocacy in mission. As an initiative that aimed at bringing the concerns of women onto the ecumenical agenda, the Decade also became a period in which the church

---

[16] See Escobar, 'Mission Studies – Past, Present and Future'.

[17] Antje Heider-Rottwilm, 'Violence Against Women: A Challenge to the Churches' Solidarity', in *The Ecumenical Review, Churches in Solidarity with Women: A Mid-Decade Assessment*, 46.2 (April 1994), 172-77, at 173.

[18] Hallett Llewellyn, 'The Ecumenical Decade: A Gift to the Churches?', in *The Ecumenical Review, Churches in Solidarity with Women: A Mid-Decade Assessment,* 46.2 (April 1994), 186-90.

[19] Llewellyn, 'The Ecumenical Decade: A Gift to the Churches?', 186-90.

had to reflect on the ways in which it had progressed in its response to issues affecting women. Llewellyn calls it a period of 'a new walking with women where repeated acts of forgiveness and creative repentance would flow'[20] from the patriarchal structures of the church that have hindered women's full participation in the mission of the church. The *Ecumenical Decade on Churches in Solidarity with Women* agenda called for a gendered missional journey that turned 'pyramids to circles'[21] where all God's people gathered round the table as partners of equals in the ministry of the gospel. This meant placing much more emphasis on shared leadership, decision-making and the training of women to take up leadership roles, and for men to intentionally let go and make space for women to equally share their gifts in leading the church and her mission. In this way, women would then be capable of participating in the leadership roles of the church. Heider-Rottwilm cautions that the ecumenical decade was not a decade for women but a decade for the churches to be in solidarity with women.[22] The statement must be understood in line with accountability on the side of the church. The Decade was supposed to be a time for the church to rediscover and use its prophetic voice to advocate the full participation of women in the work of the church and find other gender-affirming ways of being church that is all-inclusive. It was also a period to remind the church of the need to repent and to be reconciled with women for the sin of negligence in upholding women's roles in the ministry and mission of the church.

One of the main hindrances to gendered mission that keeps women from being adequately recognised for missional contributions within the church and wider society is the issue of sexism that has been used as a phenomenon to exclude women from full participation. Philip Potter, a former WCC general secretary, argued that:

> Neither men nor women will become truly human unless this disease of sexism is diagnosed and cured. It will be one world of women and men together or no world at all. And we are still a world in state of becoming. Sexism, like racism, is sin. Only in Christ can we become renewed to be authentic human beings as men and women.[23]

---

[20] Llewellyn, 'The Ecumenical Decade: A Gift to the Churches?'

[21] In most of her writing, Letty Russell placed much emphasis on the round-table theory when addressing issues of gender. As a feminist, she believed that, unless both men and women are brought to the round table, issues of hierarchy will always hinder the call for a partnership of equals between men and women. In her work on women in mission, Russell used the framework of 'African Women Theologians – The Circle' to emphasise the need for mutual partnership in mission. See also Letty M. Russell, 'God, Gold, Glory and Gender: A Postcolonial View of Mission', in *International Review of Mission*, 93.368 (January 2004), 39-49.

[22] Heider-Rottwilm, 'Violence Against Women', 117.

[23] Philip Potter, *Sexism in the 1970s: Discrimination Against Women: A Report of the WCC Consultation* (Geneva: WCC, 1975), 33.

Sexism has therefore been a longstanding enemy to mainstreaming gender in church and society through the use of sexist language, symbols and approaches in presenting the mission of the church. Sexism has also portrayed women as the weaker sex, with the intention of reflecting the 'who' they are as women and not 'what' they are as human beings created in the image of God. One of the aims of this *Ecumenical Decade on Churches in Solidarity with Women* was to call for shared partnership in mission. Therefore the challenge posed by sexism should be central to the gender discourse of the mission agenda. This would entail focusing on different forms of gender-based violence that manifested themselves through sexism. Within church circles, violence against women has in many cases worked as a hindrance to a gendered missional approach. The mere fact that women are sometimes excluded from full participation, even in the ministry of the Eucharist due to their gender, is a form of violence which challenges gender equality. Policies that sometimes govern the mission of the church also incorporate strong sexist language that excludes women from leadership positions in the church. Instead of bringing together men and women in partnership in mission, sexism has in many ways become a reaction to the effective and life-giving mission work of the church.

## Together towards Life: A Theology of Partnership of Men and Women in Mission

This chapter adopts the concept of *Together towards Life* by focusing on one of the themes which is 'Mission from the Margins'. The contemporary involvement of women in mission demonstrates pro-active methods in neutralising the negative legacy of the past. Women are responding with life-affirming alternative strategies to challenges that threaten their participation in the church's ministry and mission. They pose new questions that relate to the post-modern context that bear witness to the enslaving and prostituting relationship that has evolved between the global socio-economic system and the dominant religious context that shapes the church's missional identity and witness. Keum states that the changing landscape of church and mission provides an opportunity for fresh thinking and new forms of action that involves a change of emphasis from partnership towards mission to 'Together towards Life'.[24] This new and changing landscape must also factor into its changing dynamics, the role that gender must play if the missional objective of seeking for fullness of life is to be realised. According to *Together towards Life*:

> Mission has been understood as a movement taking place from the centre to the periphery, and from the privileged to the marginalised of society. Now people at the margins are claiming their key role as agents of mission and

[24] *TTL*, 43.

> affirming mission as transformation. This reversal of roles in the envisioning of mission has strong biblical foundations because God chose poor, the foolish and the powerless (1 Cor. 1:18-31) to further God's mission of justice and peace so that life may flourish.[25]

The document confirmed that it is the poor that lived on the margins of their society and women are the majority of those that are deemed poor. There is a correlation with this socio-economic phenomenon and the reality that it has always been women and the poor who did not have an opportunity for full participation in the mission of the church because they became the object rather than the subject of mission. According to Russell, in the development of the modern missionary movement, the gospel message was combined with the patriarchal, imperialist and social legacy of the Greco-Roman empire that gave the church of the global North unchecked powers to introduce mission that had imperialistic ideology in the nineteenth century.[26] This however should no longer be the case because of the socio-political and economic trends that are changing the landscape of global Christianity. Christianity is no longer thought of as a product from the North to the South and 'crossing oceans to heathen lands'. Rather, the contemporary era has embraced 'mission from everywhere to everywhere' and involves home-based commitment to all humanity, including women. The current approach to mission begins with the heart of God and love for all humanity and creation. This means building communities of men and women working together towards serving life which includes all God's creation. *TTL* is therefore about the church becoming the communion of Christ's disciples and an inclusive community that exists to bring healing and reconciliation to the world.[27] This communion is commissioned to invite those on the margins to come into the centre so that the church becomes a communion of believers working towards a common project.[28]

Lastly, reflecting on the concept of gender and mission during this period, I can also conclude that gender issues need to be understood within the framework of power relations. Mission during the twentieth-century era was carried along by power relations more than a relationship between men and women. This was seen in power dynamics between and among mission projects, power between the North and the South, and power between the elite and those in the lower class within the mission field. Therefore a call for a theology of partnership of equals today will require an investigation on how the church has in the 21st century defined power dynamics between men and women. To what extent has the call for 'Together towards Life' been viewed through gender lens?

---

[25] *TTL,* §6.
[26] Russell, 'God, Gold, Glory and Gender'.
[27] *TTL,* §7
[28] Phiri, 'Partnership in Mission', 61-77.

## Conclusion

This chapter has sought to analyse the concept of gender and its relationship with how the church expressed its ministry and mission. It examined the way in which gender discourses played themselves out at different times and in different contexts during the twentieth century. The chapter has found that issues of gender took on ambivalent stances. The ambivalences in gender discourses also affected the way in which mission work progressed. In conclusion, if the mission work of the churches is to be effective in the contemporary era then there is need to address gender issues that disadvantage the participation of women. The 21st-century concept of mission is about a call for partnership that goes beyond gender, class, race and other social constructs that affect the dialogue on gender equality. Partnership in mission in a post-colonial period entails the understanding that all humans are called to be missionaries in their context. Finally, gender and mission should challenge the church to create a new awareness of the increasing diversities in discussions of gender, and learn to celebrate difference with an emphasis on unity in diversity.

# MIGRATION

## Gemma Tulud Cruz

### The Migration Landscape

Mobility is as old as the human species. In fact, it is regarded as an engine of human history. Borders have been re-drawn, people's stories have been rewritten, and identities and subjectivities have been transformed, because individuals, groups or masses of people took the risk to cross borders by land, sea or air.

The twentieth century saw large movements of people across borders for various reasons. European colonial expansion which extended into the first half of the twentieth century involved the movement of peoples from three continents – from the more or less sixty-one million Europeans, including missionaries, who moved to the settlement colonies, to the thousands of people from the colonies who moved or were forced to move e.g. as slaves. The social upheavals brought by the two world wars, meanwhile, led to a considerable movement of refugees and asylum seekers.

The second half of the twentieth century saw the rise of particular types and waves of migration. There was the guest worker who came under a temporary permit system aimed at the importation of temporary contract labourers. France and Germany ran such programmes in the 1960s and 1970s, importing labourers largely from Algeria and Turkey respectively. About the same time a parallel pattern was seen in the oil-rich Middle Eastern countries which imported cheap unskilled labour from south and south-east Asian. This movement of workers intensified globally in the 1980s when the world economy rapidly evolved new forms of integration. Women also became more visible as independent migrants at this time. Last but not least, the end of the twentieth century saw the increase of clandestine or unauthorised movements of people, particularly unskilled workers, refugees and asylum seekers, a phenomenon which took on unprecedented proportions in the 21st century, not only in volume but also in the often tragic nature of these movements, as destination countries instituted more stringent and more restrictive immigration policies.[1]

---

[1] For a more substantive historical discussion of the migration of groups mentioned in this section, see Gemma Tulud Cruz, *Toward a Theology of Migration: Social Justice and Religious Experience* (New York: Palgrave Macmillan, 2014).

Nevertheless, the 21st century has been called 'the age of migration'[2] mainly because there are more people on the move in the world today than ever before. A July 2014 UN report notes that, globally, there were 232 million international migrants.[3] More disturbingly, a June 2014 UN refugee agency reports that there were now 51.2 million refugees, asylum seekers, and internally displaced people worldwide, the highest since World War II.[4] Today, about 3% of the world's population are migrants. While the percentage may seem minuscule, it actually represents a lot of people. In fact, if all migrants in the world were to come together to constitute a country, theirs would be the world's fifth most populous.

## Shifts in Missiological Approaches

Christian mission's close link with migration is not a new phenomenon. The most extensive missionary movement in Christianity's history, for example, corresponded with one of the great migrations in human history, namely, European expansion, especially between 1800 and 1925. Theological reflection on the close relationship between migration and mission, however, were not common until fairly recently.[5] This is due in part to the fact that it is also only fairly recently that migration has started to be considered as *locus theologicus*.[6] One of the earlier notable documents that address Christian mission in the context of migration is

---

[2] See Stephen Castles and Mark Miller, *The Age of Migration: International Population Movements in the Modern World,* 4th edition (Basingstoke, UK: Palgrave Macmillan, 2009).

[3] See 'International Migration and Development Report', Report of the Secretary General at the 69th Session of the United Nations General Assembly, 20th July 2014: www.un.org/en/ga/search/view_doc.asp?symbol=A/69/207 (accessed 10th June 2015).

[4] UNCHR, 'World Refugee Day: Global forced displacement tops 50 million for first time since post-World War II era': www.unhcr.org/53a155bc6.html (accessed 15th June 2015).

[5] See Gioacchino Campese CS, 'Mission and Migration', in Stephen Bevans (ed), *A Century of Catholic Mission* (Oxford: Regnum, 2013), 247-60, for an example. Note also recent journals entirely devoted to mission and migration. E.g. *Exchange: Journal of Missiological and Ecumenical Research,* 43.1 (2014) which focused on the topic 'Christian Communities Facing Migration'; and *Mission Studies,* 32.2 (2015) where five out of six articles come from the 'Migration, Religion, and Identity' study group conducted at the International Association for Mission Studies (IAMS) conference, Toronto, 2012.

[6] One of the earliest explicit theological treatments may be found in Carmen Lussi, 'Human Mobility as a Theological Consideration', in Solange Lefebvre and Luis Carlos Susin (eds), *Migration in a Global World*, Concilium 2008/5 (London: SCM, 2008), 50. For an instructive survey on the emergence of migration as *locus theologicus,* see Gioacchino Campese CS, 'The Irruption of Migrants: Theology of Migration in the 21st Century', in *Theological Studies,* 73 (2012), 3-32.

*Exsul Familia* (1952), which is considered as the Catholic Church's *Magna Carta* on migration. The World Council of Churches document that came out of the 1995 global ecumenical consultation in Ethiopia on the churches' response to the forced displacement of peoples is particularly noteworthy as it covers a wide range of missiological issues and responses in relation to people on the move.[7]

As in the past century, the challenges and gifts associated with the plight of people on the move in contemporary times, almost half of whom are Christians,[8] constitute an important context for Christian mission. Within the churches' missiological responses to uprooted people one can discern some shifts to which this essay now turns.[9]

## From Religious to Pastoral

From time immemorial, Christian churches understood and practised mission in the context of people on the move primarily in terms of tending to migrants' religious needs. In colonial times many missionaries came, or were sent, to take care of the religious needs of compatriots on the move such as soldiers, merchants and their families. While mission among migrants continues to be animated by this vision and approach, other more personal, psycho-social and ethnic needs of migrants slowly took on equal (sometimes greater) importance as more people moved in groups and in greater numbers, and settled in ethnic enclaves. Since the 1920s, every Ukrainian community in Saskatchewan, Canada, has had the so-called Ukrainian National House which is actually a church and a hall where people can get together. Today, these churches, whether Orthodox or Catholic, remain a source of well-being, security and meaning. They also serve as a conduit into Ukrainian heritage and a bridge across generations.[10]

For many migrants, however, the church is not just the principal site of celebration for ethnic identity and community. It is also their refuge in times of crisis and their home when they want to shout for joy. Not surprisingly, and more especially so in the 21st century when there is greater recognition and more opportunity for the exercise of cultural rights, roles for the clergy would tend to be more service-oriented, or strongly informed and guided by practical needs. In traditional societies, where most migrants originate, the clergy are usually experts in religious rituals and scriptures. In the context of contemporary migration, however, members of

---

[7] See Sara Stephens, *The Prophetic Mission of Churches in Response to Forced Displacement of People: A Global Ecumenical Consultation* (Geneva: WCC, 1996).

[8] Todd Johnson and Gina Bellofatto, 'Migration, Religious Diasporas and Religious Diversity', in *Mission Studies,* 29 (2012), 8-9.

[9] 'Shift' is used here not in terms of 'either-or' but 'both-and'; in other words, in terms of a fluid continuum.

[10] Janet Mancini Billson, *Keepers of the Culture: The Power of Tradition in Women's Lives* (New York: Lexington Books, 1995), 345, 368.

the clergy are sought for various kinds of help, particularly those that are normally defined as pastoral work. Witness, therefore, has now become strongly associated with '*with*ness', while mission as 'accompaniment' is more strongly practised.

Jacqueline Maria Hagan, for example, notes the increasing practice of migration counselling among ministries in the western highlands of Guatemala for prospective migrants. Services sought by migrants from their priests or pastors range from group prayer (with the migrants and their families and, sometimes, with church members) before setting off by foot towards the Mexican border, or asking their priest or pastor to meet with their *coyote*[11] to determine whether the guide is honest or a scoundrel.[12] Many Christian groups themselves become a direct part of the migrants' actual journey.[13] In the context of the Americas, these include the Scalabrinians, a Catholic religious congregation, who operate a network of migrant shelters along the US-Mexico and Mexico-Guatemala borders that provides spiritual, religious and practical support for unauthorized migrants in transit. There is also the group called Samaritan Patrol, a coalition of Quakers, Jews, Methodists, Catholics and Presbyterians, which has volunteers that roam the desert in jeeps and vans, from daybreak to nightfall, to offer water to migrants in distress.[14]

## From Charity to Justice

The churches have undoubtedly long been involved in missionary work among people on the move. The biblical command to the Israelites to love the stranger, as they were also strangers in Egypt (Deuteronomy 10:19) enshrines the missionary task of every Christian to care for migrants. Up until the last quarter of the twentieth century, the missionary work that the churches have done among migrants was arguably largely confined to charity or charitable services. In the US, for example, national ecclesiastical structures in the Catholic Church ministering to new immigrants or refugees began only in 1920 when the National Catholic Welfare Conference established a Department of Immigration after the World War

---

[11] A *coyote* is a guide who takes migrants across international borders in exchange for money.

[12] Jacqueline Maria Hagan, *Migration Miracle: Faith, Hope and Meaning on the Undocumented Journey* (Cambridge, MA: Harvard University Press, 2008), 2.

[13] See Jacqueline Maria Hagan, 'The Church vs the State: Borders, Migrants, and Human Rights', 96-101 and Cecilia Menjivar, 'Serving Christ in the Borderlands: Faith Workers Respond to Border Violence', in Pierrette Hondagneu-Sotelo (ed), *Religion and Social Justice for Immigrants* (New Brunswick, NJ: Rutgers University Press, 2007), 110-15.

[14] Pierette Hondagneu-Sotelo, *God's Heart Has No Borders: How Religious Activists Are Working for Immigrant Rights* (Berkeley, CA: University of California Press, 2008), 141-43.

I. The US Bishops' Migration and Refugee Services itself was established only in 1965.[15]

Around the last quarter of the twentieth century, when assimilationist discourses gave way to the idea of integration and destination, countries increasingly became more restrictive in their immigration policies resulting in dangerous clandestine journeys by migrants, while pastoral work for migrants also started to evolve more strongly from largely addressing the effects by providing economic, physical and psychological assistance, to targeting the causes, including those of a more political nature.[16] As Elizabeth Ferris noted on the heels of post-Cold War conflicts that led to the widespread forced displacement of people, 'Increasingly the Churches are called to become more active in addressing the causes of uprooting of people'.[17] Thus, in addition to ecclesiastical structures and organizations serving migrants and refugees, what are known today as FBOs (faith-based organizations) increasingly took on important missionary roles in the context of migration. Anglican priest and theologian Susanna Snyder, for example, looks at the FBOs that deal with asylum seekers in the UK and proposes three strengths that these religious bodies have to offer – namely, transcendent motivation, organisational nature and strategies, and resource mobilisation.[18]

This evolution of the understanding of the churches' mission to people on the move also had implications for the idea of hospitality as a critical biblical missionary call and challenge in the context of migration. More specifically, the understanding and practice of hospitality shifted towards what Christine Pohl regards as subversive hospitality[19] or what Evangelical

---

[15] Angelyn Dries, OSF, 'Catholic Mission in North America 1910-2010', in Bevans, *A Century of Catholic Mission*, 59.

[16] This could be seen in the presentations in the above-mentioned global ecumenical consultation in Ethiopia in 1995. Two years earlier, a similar event sponsored by the WCC was held by the churches in Asia. See conference proceedings in Christian Conference of Asia, *Uprooted People in Asia: Conference on Migrant Workers, Refugees and Internally-Displaced Communities in Asia. Hong Kong, 22-26 November 1993* (Hong Kong: Christian Conference of Asia, 1995).

[17] Elizabeth Ferris, 'Crisis Situations, Humanitarian Assistance, Preventive Measures and Churches' Response', in Matthews George Chunakara (ed), *Rights of Internally Displaced People: Asian Churches' Response* (Hong Kong: Christian Conference of Asia, 2000), 37.

[18] See Susanna Snyder, *Asylum-Seeking, Migration and Church* (Farnham, UK: Ashgate, 2012). See also Alexia Salvatierra and Peter Heltzel, *Faith-Rooted Organizing: Mobilizing the Church in Service to the World* (Downers Grove, IL: IVP, 2013); and Erin Wilson, 'Much to be Proud of, Much to be Done: Faith-Based Organizations and the Politics of Asylum in Australia', in *Journal of Refugee Studies,* 24.3 (2011), 548-64.

[19] See Christine D. Pohl, 'Responding to Strangers: Insights from the Christian Tradition', in *Studies in Christian Ethics,* 19.1 (2006), 82. A more substantive

Lutheran church pastor the Rev. Alexia Salvatierra calls 'prophetic hospitality'.[20] To be sure, the massive, global, and sometimes tragic,[21] nature of human mobility towards the end of the twentieth century – and, even more, in the current century – has compelled the churches to move beyond charity to justice.

For Mary Jo Leddy, a Canadian who is widely recognized for her work with refugees in Toronto, Christian missionary work from the perspective of justice in the context of migration requires and begins with conversion – the change of mind and heart and moral imagination – through an encounter and personal relationship with a refugee. Leddy posits that this ethical moment – that is, the encounter with a migrant or refugee – is the moment when we are 'summoned, addressed, and commanded… the time of annunciation and visitation… For many, the encounter with a real person called "refugee" evokes feelings of profound compassion that lead to practical forms of kindness. It is within this reach of mercy that the necessity (and near impossibility) of justice begins to emerge'.[22] Making justice possible means that 'arguments about the economic, political and social implications of migration must first find a reference in the human face of the migrant or else the core issues at stake become lost and easily distorted. If we do not get the human face of the migrant right, a just society is not possible'.[23] This idea of focusing on the human person and their dignity is reiterated by Thomas Albinson, World Evangelical Alliance Ambassador for Refugees, Displaced and Stateless People, by pointing out the need for putting a face on the numbers and valuing human life above other agendas.[24]

---

treatment may be found in Pohl's earlier work, *Making Room: Recovering Hospitality as a Christian Tradition* (Cambridge, MA: Eerdmans, 1999).

[20] See Alexia Salvatierra, '"Do Not Neglect to Show Hospitality": Sanctuary and Immigrant Justice', in L. Dykstra and C. Myers (eds), *Liberating Biblical Study: Scholarship, Art and Action in Honor of the Center and Library for the Bible and Social Justice* (Eugene, OR: Wipf & Stock, 2011), 213-20. See also Ched Myers, 'Our God is Undocumented: Sanctuary and Prophetic Hospitality', in Ched Myers and Matthew Colwell (eds), *Our God is Undocumented: Biblical Faith and Immigrant Justice* (Maryknoll, NY: Orbis Books, 2012), 53-72.

[21] See, for example, Nick Squires, 'Italy mourns 300 dead in Lampedusa migrant boat tragedy': www.telegraph.co.uk/news/worldnews/europe/italy/10355661/Italy-mourns-300-dead-in-Lampedusa-migrant-boat-tragedy.html (accessed 20th June 2015).

[22] Mary Jo Leddy, 'When the Stranger Summons: Spiritual and Theological Considerations for Ministry', in *New Theology Review*, 20.3 (August 2007), 6-7.

[23] Daniel Groody, 'The Church on the Move: Mission in an Age of Migration', in *Mission Studies*, 30 (2013), 36.

[24] See Thomas Albinson, 'A Christian Response to the Humanitarian Crisis in the Mediterranean': www.worldea.org/news/4555/a-christian-response-to-the-humanitarian-crisis-in-the-mediterranean (accessed 25th July 2015).

Pierette Hondagneu-Sotelo, for example, points to Christian groups and activists who played a role in the struggle for immigrant rights in post-1965 and post-9/11 America, particularly those who responded to the death and violence at the US-Mexico border, and Christian clergy defending the labour rights of Latino immigrants. *Borderlinks*, an ecumenical organization founded by Presbyterian minister Rick Ufford-Chase, even offers experiential education and border tours for US citizens as it seeks to provide a theological understanding of conflicts and inequalities at the US-Mexico border. These and other groups arose in the 1990s and combine advocacy, service and civil disobedience. Hondagneu-Sotelo reckons that they constitute a new civil society of biblically-inspired social action groups and are, in a sense, direct heirs to a well-known pro-migrant movement in the US in the 1980s known as The Sanctuary Movement. This movement, led by a lay Quaker named Jim Corbett, aided and advocated just treatment for Central American refugees, particularly Guatemalans and Salvadorans who had been detained and denied legal status as officially sanctioned refugees. The movement's actions on behalf of migrants took a radical turn when Presbyterian minister John Fife, followed by five San Francisco Bay churches, publicly declared his church as a sanctuary church. The letter sent by Fife to the US attorney general goes straight to the point:

> We are writing to inform you that Southside United Presbyterian Church will publicly violate the Immigration and Nationality Act, Section 274 (A). We have declared our church as a 'sanctuary' for undocumented refugees from Central America… We believe that justice and mercy require that people of conscience actively assert our God-given right to aid anyone fleeing from persecution and murder. The current administration of US law prohibits us from sheltering these refugees from Central America. Therefore we believe the administration of the law to be immoral, as well as illegal… Obedience to God requires this of all of us.[25]

It is common knowledge that the migration of peoples, particularly those who are forced to move, is embedded in local and global inequalities. Thus the churches understand, especially in view of horrific deaths of large numbers of migrants in the Mediterranean witnessed in 2014 and 2015, that in the context of human dislocation, there can be no meaningful mission without costly incarnation since 'this may entail advocating justice in regard to migration policies and resistance to xenophobia and racism' (*TTL* §70). As Jonathan Bonk contends:

> To be a Christian entails recognizing and resisting the terrible reductionisms of all self-serving nationalisms, tribalisms, and racisms – and their ever-attendant legalisms – that undervalue or even dismiss the stranger, the refugee, or the immigrant, or the enemy. When we co-operate in such

[25] Renny Golden and Michael McConnell, *Sanctuary: The New Underground Railroad* (Maryknoll, NY: Orbis Books, 1986), 46, as quoted in Hondagneu-Sotelo, *God's Heart Has No Borders*, 145.

> systemic reductionism we subvert our own identities as men and women created in the image of God, since we yield to Caesar something to which Caesar has no ultimate claim – human beings, including ourselves. *Legality*, for Christians, can never be an acceptable substitute for *justice*.[26]

## From Mission *to* Migrants to Mission *of* Migrants

The title of this section is perhaps ironic as missionaries are, in most cases, migrants themselves. Many of the great Christian missionaries such as William Carey and Matteo Ricci crossed borders. But while missionary work used to be largely centred in the less developed countries and was mainly done by westerners, the whole world is now a mission field because of the 'death of distance'[27] and because of the shift in Christian demographics. As *TTL* §5 points out: 'Today we are facing a radically changing ecclesial landscape described as 'world Christianity' where the majority of Christians either are living or have their origins in the global South and East', and that 'migration has become a worldwide, multi-directional phenomenon which is reshaping the Christian landscape.' In other words, mission is now everywhere, including the West, not just because of the structures and processes associated with globalization but also because of changes within the churches themselves.

Indeed, mission in the context of migration arising from globalization has changed or expanded not just the mission field. It also brought other forms of spreading the gospel, e.g. travelling evangelists and short-term missions.[28] Other creative ways differing from the traditional 'soil-based' church planting, which are facilitated by the disappearance of geographic barriers, include 'bus churches' for the diaspora in limited access contexts and churches on the high seas, aboard ships, including cruise ships and ocean liners.[29] In addition, mission in the context of migration arising from globalization expanded the objects of missionary activity as migrants and

---

[26] Jonathan Bonk, 'Whose head is this and whose title?' Presidential address delivered at the International Association for Mission Studies 13th Quadrennial Conference, Toronto, 15th August 2012: https://sites.google.com/a/iams2012.org/toronto-2012 (accessed 5th July 2015).

[27] Albino Barrera, OP, 'Mission in a Globalized Economy', in James Kroeger (ed), *The Gift of Mission: Yesterday, Today and Tomorrow* (Maryknoll, NY: Orbis Books, 2013), 161.

[28] See Mäite Maskens, 'Mobility among Pentecostal Pastors and Migratory Miracles', in *Canadian Journal of African Studies,* 46.3 (2012), 397-409. A broader survey of missionaries on the move in contemporary times may be seen in Claire Brickell, 'Geographies of Contemporary Christian Mission(aries)', in *Geography Compass,* 6/12 (2012), 725-39.

[29] Enoch Wan, *Diaspora Missiology: Theory, Methodology and Practice* (Portland, OR: Institute for Diaspora Studies, 2011), 132.

refugees become targets of missionary activity.[30] As Steven Ybarrola argues, using studies he has conducted in the evangelical churches in the Basque country of Spain, liminality can make people more receptive to the gospel.[31] In the context of the diaspora, Enoch Wan attributes the receptivity to the gospel to the experience of being in transition.[32] Some Christian groups even aggressively target migrants, whether they have moved to a country for good or are there only short-term, e.g. contract workers or seafarers.[33] One such group is *MoveIn*, a Christian group in Toronto, who took up residence in neighbourhoods where many new immigrants live. With a cup of cold water in one hand and the good news in the other, they pray that the migrants will discover Christ's love.[34] What is interesting is that most of these missionaries are immigrants or former migrants themselves. Thus, mission in the context of migration arising from globalization has also changed the face of the missionary from white, western or European to a Christian person of colour from the global South.

The missionary potential of (im)migrants, particularly from the global South, is immense as they reach out not only to their kin or compatriots in their adopted country, country of origin or other countries.[35] In the case especially of diaspora Christian individuals and congregations[36] they, in many cases, expand their missionary efforts to other members of the host society[37] and, in some cases, to other countries. Evidence for the former is the increasing role of migrants in what they perceive as the (re)-evangelization of Europe, giving rise to terms such as reverse-mission.[38] It

---

[30] See P. Nyiri, 'Moving Targets: Chinese Christian Proselytizing among Transnational Migrants from the People's Republic of China', in *European Journal of East Asian Studies,* 2.2 (2003), 263-301.

[31] Steven Ybarrola, 'Anthropology, Diaspora and Mission', in *Mission Studies* 29 (2012), 85.

[32] Wan, *Diaspora Missiology,* 132.

[33] In some cases, these temporary migrant workers become missionaries themselves. See, for example, Sadiri Emmanuel Santiago B. Tira, *Filipino Kingdom Workers: An Ethnographic Study in Diaspora Missiology* (Pasadena, CA: William Carey International University Press, 2012).

[34] Wan, *Diaspora Missiology,* 132.

[35] The Vietnamese diaspora in North America, for instance, conducts evangelistic work among Vietnamese, not just in their adopted country but also in Vietnam, Cambodia, Cameroon, Mali and Taiwan: Wan, *Diaspora Missiology,* 238-46.

[36] A more comprehensive and recent distillation of mission in/among the diaspora could be found in Chandler Im and Amos Yong (eds), *Global Diasporas and Mission* (Portland, OR: Wipf & Stock, 2014).

[37] Enoch Wan and Anthony Casey, *Church Planting Among Immigrants in US Urban Centers: The 'Where', 'Why' and 'How' of Diaspora Missiology in Action* (Portland, OR: IDS, 2014).

[38] This is particularly true among African migrants. Afe Adogame has a substantive body of work on this topic. See, for example, Afe Adogame, *The African Christian Diaspora: New Currents and Emerging Trends in World Christianity* (London: Continuum, 2013); 'Transnational Migration and Pentecostalism in Europe', in

must be noted, of course, that the missionary work of migrants is not confined to evangelism.[39]

What is clear is that mission in the context of migration is not only about mission *to* migrants but also mission *of* migrants. In fact, the mission for the local church, according to Stephen Bevans, is 'not only to respond to migrants' needs and to accompany them on their journey but also to call and equip them for ministry, both within the church and within the world'.[40] Jehu Hanciles echoes this perspective in the case of immigrant churches. Hanciles argues that immigrant churches potentially have a missionary function, not only because they represent the most effective instruments through which immigrants can impact wider society, but also because they model religious commitment, apply the message of the gospel directly to daily exigencies, and comprise communities that interact on a daily basis with other marginalized segments of society.[41] Immigrant churches in many developed countries, for example, play a strategic role, whether they like it or not, since they are predominantly located in urban neighbourhoods and are often forced to occupy the most unlikely places – cramped living rooms, hotel ballrooms, thousands of shop fronts, rented halls or office buildings, even ornate churches whose membership has declined – they serve constituencies (both immigrant and native) long abandoned by more established and affluent congregations.[42] Churches

---

*PentecoStudies: An Interdisciplinary Journal for Research on the Pentecostal and Charismatic Movements,* 9.1 (2010), 56-73; and 'African Christians in a Secularizing Europe', in *Religion Compass,* 3.4 (2009), 488-501. See also Jehu Hanciles, 'Migrants as Missionaries, Missionaries as Outsiders: Reflections on African Christian Presence in Western Societies', in *Mission Studies,* 30 (2013), 64-85; Richard Burgess, 'Bringing Back the Gospel: Reverse Mission Among Nigerian Pentecostals in Britain', in *Journal of Religion in Europe,* 4 (2011), 429-49; Danielle Koning, 'Place, Space, and Authority: The Mission and Reversed Mission of the Ghanaian Seventh-day Adventist Church in Amsterdam', in *African Diaspora,* 2.2 (2009), 203-26; and Gerrie ter Haar, *Halfway to Paradise: African Christians in Europe* (Cardiff, UK: Cardiff Academic Press, 1998).

[39] See Matthew Colwell, 'From Immigrant to Immigrant Justice Organizer: Moises Escalante', and 'Proclaiming Liberty to the Captives', in *Our God is Undocumented,* 73-90 and 107-22 respectively. See also Vedaste Nyazabino, 'The Role of Refugee-Established Churches in Integrating Forced Migrants: A Case Study of Word of Life Assembly in Yeoville, Johannesburg', in *HTS Theological Studies,* 66.1 (2010), 1-9.

[40] Stephen Bevans, 'Mission *among* Migrants, Mission *of* Migrants', in Daniel Groody and Gioacchino Campese (eds), *A Promised Land, A Perilous Journey: Theological Perspectives on Migration* (Notre Dame, IN: University of Notre Dame Press, 2008), 101.

[41] Jehu Hanciles, *Beyond Christendom: Globalization, African Migration and the Transformation of the West* (Maryknoll, NY: Orbis Books, 2008), 277-78.

[42] See the story of two large African-led Christian groups in Europe, the Church of the Embassy of the Blessed Kingdom of God for all Nations (Kiev, Ukraine), and Kingsway International Christian Centre or KICC (London) as described in J.

built or established by (im)migrants themselves often become veritable centres of social and religious life.[43] As *TTL* §71 reminds us: 'God's hospitality calls us to move beyond binary notions of culturally dominant groups as hosts, and migrant and minority peoples as guests.' Hospitality in the context of migration, in other words, ought to be understood not so much as hospitality *to* strangers but hospitality *of* strangers and, consequently, mission as a discipleship of equals.

## The Challenges Ahead

Mission in the context of migration drives home the point that mission is a shared calling and vocation of all Christians, no matter who they are and wherever they may be. However, at no time is the idea of mission as shared and borderless stronger than ever before than in this age of migration, when globalization-induced human mobility has reached unprecedented proportions, and Christian migrants, who are predominantly from the global South, bring with them not only different ways of practising Christianity but also a relatively strong faith commitment that includes evangelism.

The previous section has attempted to describe some of the shifts in the missionary orientation and practice of the churches as a result of the intensification of migration as well as changes in the factors, faces and conditions associated with contemporary human mobility, particularly among Christians. These shifts are, of course, just the tip of the iceberg. The immense geographic boundaries that globalization has shrunk, and the plural societies that contemporary migration created or intensified, means that there are other existing, as well as emerging, missionary challenges that remain largely unaddressed. There is, for example, the transnational challenge.[44] There is much missionary promise in using and engaging not only migrants' transnational networks but also the churches' very own transnational networks. Related to this is the digital challenge. While most churches have a digital presence, there is also much potential that could be tapped in using digital technology for doing mission in the context of migration. The overwhelming majority of migrants are 'digital natives' so the possibilities are endless. Then there is also the interreligious challenge. How do we respectfully observe the limits and possibilities of evangelism

---

Kwabena Asamoah-Gyadu, '"To The Ends of the Earth": Mission, Migration and Impact of African-led Pentecostal Churches in the European Diaspora', in *Mission Studies,* 29 (2012), 23-44.

[43] See, for example, Fenggang Yang, 'Chinese Gospel Church: The Sinization of Christianity', in Helen Rose Ebaugh and Janet Chafetz (eds), in *Religion and the New Immigrants: Continuities and Adaptations in Immigrant Congregations* (Walnut Creek, CA: Altamira Press, 2000), 89, 97-98, 101-02.

[44] See, for example, Kirsteen Kim, 'Editorial', in *Mission Studies,* 32. 2 (2015), 175-76.

among migrants who are not Christians? Moreover, how do we practise mission as interreligious hospitality in a way that is praxological and doxological?[45] Last but not least, and perhaps the most critical of the challenges, is the intercultural challenge. How do we realize the church of the Pentecost in faith communities, especially in multicultural societies? While it is true and good that immigrants can use most local churches for their own services, Martin Luther King's statement that the most segregated hour of the week is 11:00 a.m. on Sunday morning still rings true in places of worship worldwide as power differentials and various forms of differences inhibit the formation of inclusive churches.

Miriam Adeney gives voice to the heart of the challenge with the following questions:

> Should multi-ethnic churches – and therefore merged mission – be the goal? Do separate ethnic churches perpetuate divisions? Or is cultural identity so foundational that ethnic churches are a blessing? Should [US] ministry of the future expect to be multilingual, or is that a passing phase?
>
> How can majority-culture churches partner in mission with ethnic churches? In our hegemonic context, is it realistic to believe that churches of the less powerful can exert significant influence?[46]

It does not help, argue Martha Fredericks and Dorottya Nagy, in their guest editorial for the most recent issue of the journal *Mission Studies,* that the key missiological concepts of 'inculturation' and 'contextualization' tend to presume a single definable culture or context with respect to which the gospel is inculturated/contextualized, which may not be the case with migrants. Moreover, both processes, Fredericks and Nagy point out, favour a form of assimilation, whereas the challenge for migrant communities fleeing oppression is to maintain their threatened tradition.[47] *TTL* §75 eloquently gives voice to the challenge:

More than ever before, local congregations today can play a key role in emphasizing the crossing of cultural and racial boundaries and affirming cultural difference as a gift of the Spirit. Rather than being perceived as a problem, migration can be seen as offering new possibilities for churches to rediscover themselves afresh. It inspires opportunities for the creation of intercultural and multi-cultural churches at local level. All churches can create space for different cultural communities to come together and embrace exciting opportunities for contextual expressions of intercultural mission in our time.

---

45 M. Thomas Thangaraj, 'Embracing God's Hospitality in a Multi-Religious World', in *CTC Bulletin,* XXVIII.1 (December 2012), 22-24.

46 Miriam Adeney, 'Colorful Initiatives: North American Diasporas in Mission', in *Missiology: An International Review,* XXXIX.1 (January 2011), 7-8.

47 Martha Fredericks and Dorottya Nagy, guest editorial in *Mission Studies,* 32.2 (2015), 177-79.

What is clear is that unity is a powerful theme in Scripture (Gal. 3:28). Equally central, however, is the emphasis on vibrant creativity that gives birth to diversity.

# SECTION THREE

# TOGETHER TOWARDS LIFE

## Introduction

This section is focused on the 2012 World Council of Churches Mission Affirmation *Together Towards Life*. It offers first the entire text of the document, followed by an essay that outlines its genesis and development. Further essays analyse the text from a variety of confessional and contextual perspectives. The section concludes with an essay that considers the challenge of missional formation in light of *Together Towards Life*.

# TOGETHER TOWARDS LIFE

## New WCC Affirmation on Mission and Evangelism

The Commission on World Mission and Evangelism (CWME) has, since the WCC Porto Alegre Assembly in 2006, been working towards and contributing to the construction of a new ecumenical mission affirmation. The new statement will be presented to the WCC 10th Assembly at Busan, Republic of Korea, in 2013. Since the integration of the International Missionary Council (IMC) and the World Council of Churches (WCC) in New Delhi in 1961, there has been only one official WCC position statement on mission and evangelism which was approved by the central committee in 1982, *Mission and Evangelism: An Ecumenical Affirmation.* This new mission affirmation was unanimously approved by the WCC central committee on 5th September 2012 at its meeting on the island of Crete, Greece. It is the aim of this new ecumenical discernment to seek vision, concepts and directions for a renewed understanding and practice of mission and evangelism in changing landscapes. It seeks a broad appeal, even wider than WCC member churches and affiliated mission bodies, so that we can commit ourselves together to fullness of life for all, led by the God of Life!

## Together towards Life: Introducing the Theme

1. We believe in the Triune God who is the creator, redeemer, and sustainer of all life. God created the whole *oikoumene* in God's image and constantly works in the world to affirm and safeguard life. We believe in Jesus Christ, the Life of the world, the incarnation of God's love for the world (John 3:16).[1] Affirming life in all its fullness is Jesus Christ's ultimate concern and mission (John 10:10). We believe in God, the Holy Spirit, the Life-giver, who sustains and empowers life and renews the whole creation (Gen. 2:7; John 3:8). A denial of life is a rejection of the God of life. God invites us into the life-giving mission of the Triune God and empowers us to bear witness to the vision of abundant life for all in the new heaven and earth. How and where do we discern God's life-giving work that enables us to participate in God's mission today?

---

[1] Unless otherwise indicated, Bible quotations are from the New Revised Standard Version (NRSV). Abbreviations used for other translations include KJV (Authorized/King James Version), NIV (New International Version), and REB (Revised English Bible).

2. Mission begins in the heart of the Triune God and the love which binds together the Holy Trinity overflows to all humanity and creation. The missionary God who sent the Son to the world calls all God's people (John 20:21), and empowers them to be a community of hope. The church is commissioned to celebrate life, and to resist and transform all life-destroying forces, in the power of the Holy Spirit. How important it is to 'receive the Holy Spirit' (John 20:22) to become living witnesses to the coming reign of God! From a renewed appreciation of the mission of the Spirit, how do we re-envision God's mission in a changing and diverse world today?

3. Life in the Holy Spirit is the essence of mission, the core of why we do what we do and how we live our lives. Spirituality gives the deepest meaning to our lives and motivates our actions. It is a sacred gift from the Creator, the energy for affirming and caring for life. This mission spirituality has a dynamic of transformation which, through the spiritual commitment of people, is capable of transforming the world in God's grace. How can we reclaim mission as a transformative spirituality which is life-affirming?

4. God did not send the Son for the salvation of humanity alone or give us a partial salvation. Rather, the gospel is the good news for every part of creation and every aspect of our life and society. It is therefore vital to recognize God's mission in a cosmic sense and to affirm all life, the whole *oikoumene*, as being interconnected in God's web of life. As threats to the future of our planet are evident, what are their implications for our participation in God's mission?

5. The history of Christian mission has been characterized by conceptions of geographical expansion from a Christian centre to the 'unreached territories,' to the ends of the earth. But today we are facing a radically changing ecclesial landscape described as 'world Christianity' where the majority of Christians either are living or have their origins in the global South and East.[2] Migration has become a worldwide, multi-directional phenomenon which is reshaping the Christian landscape. The emergence of strong Pentecostal and charismatic movements from different localities is one of the most noteworthy characteristics of world Christianity today. What are the insights for mission and evangelism – theologies, agendas and practices – of this 'shift of the centre of gravity of Christianity'?

6. Mission has been understood as a movement taking place from the centre to the periphery, and from the privileged to the marginalized of society. Now people at the margins are claiming their key role as agents of mission and affirming mission as transformation. This reversal of roles in the envisioning of mission has strong biblical foundations because God chose

---

[2] See Todd M. Johnson and Kenneth R. Ross (eds), *Atlas of Global Christianity, 1910-2010* (Edinburgh: Edinburgh University Press, 2009).

the poor, the foolish, and the powerless (1 Cor. 1:18-31) to further God's mission of justice and peace so that life may flourish. If there is a shift of the mission concept from 'mission *to* the margins' to 'mission *from* the margins,' what then is the distinctive contribution of the people from the margins? And why are their experiences and visions crucial for re-imagining mission and evangelism today?

7. We are living in a world in which faith in mammon threatens the credibility of the gospel. Market ideology is spreading the propaganda that the global market will save the world through unlimited growth. This myth is a threat not only to economic life but also to the spiritual life of people, and not only to humanity but also to the whole creation. How can we proclaim the good news and values of God's kingdom in the global market or win over the spirit of the market? What kind of missional action can the church take in the midst of economic and ecological injustice and crisis on a global scale?

8. All Christians, churches, and congregations are called to be vibrant messengers of the gospel of Jesus Christ, which is the good news of salvation. Evangelism is a confident but humble sharing of our faith and conviction with other people. Such sharing is a gift to others which announces the love, grace, and mercy of God in Christ. It is the inevitable fruit of genuine faith. Therefore, in each generation, the church must renew its commitment to evangelism as an essential part of the way we convey God's love to the world. How can we proclaim God's love and justice to a generation living in an individualized, secularized, and materialized world?

9. The church lives in multi-religious and multi-cultural contexts and new communication technology is also bringing the people of the world into a greater awareness of one another's identities and pursuits. Locally and globally, Christians are engaged with people of other religions and cultures in building societies of love, peace, and justice. Plurality is a challenge to the churches and serious commitment to inter-faith dialogue and cross-cultural communication is therefore indispensable. What are the ecumenical convictions regarding common witnessing and practicing life-giving mission in a world of many religions and cultures?

10. The church is a gift of God to the world for its transformation towards the kingdom of God. Its mission is to bring new life and announce the loving presence of God in our world. We must participate in God's mission in unity, overcoming the divisions and tensions that exist among us, so that the world may believe and all may be one (John 17:21). The church, as the communion of Christ's disciples, must become an inclusive community and exists to bring healing and reconciliation to the world. How can the church renew herself to be missional and move forward together towards life in its fullness?

11. This statement highlights some key developments in understanding the mission of the Holy Spirit within the mission of the Triune God (*missio Dei*)

which have emerged through the work of CWME. It does so under four main headings:

Spirit of Mission: Breath of Life
Spirit of Liberation: Mission from the Margins
Spirit of Community: Church on the Move
Spirit of Pentecost: Good News for All

Reflection on such perspectives enables us to embrace dynamism, justice, diversity, and transformation as key concepts of mission in changing landscapes today. In response to the questions posed above, we conclude with ten affirmations for mission and evangelism today.

## Spirit of Mission: Breath of Life
## The Mission of the Spirit

12. God's Spirit – *ru'ach* – moved over the waters at the beginning (Gen. 1:2), being the source of life and the breath of humankind (Gen. 2:7). In the Hebrew Bible, the Spirit led the people of God – inspiring wisdom (Prov. 8), empowering prophecy (Isa. 61:1), stirring life from dry bones (Ezek. 37), prompting dreams (Joel 2), and bringing renewal as the glory of the Lord in the temple (2 Chron. 7:1).

13. The same Spirit of God, which 'swept over the face of the waters' in creation, descended on Mary (Luke 1:35) and brought forth Jesus. It was the Holy Spirit who empowered Jesus at his baptism (Mark 1:10) and commissioned him for his mission (Luke 4:14, 18). Jesus Christ, full of the Spirit of God, died on the cross. He gave up the spirit (John 19:30). In death, in the coldness of the tomb, by the power of the Holy Spirit he was raised to life, the firstborn from the dead (Rom. 8:11).

14. After his resurrection, Jesus Christ appeared to his community and sent his disciples in mission: 'As the Father has sent me, so I send you' (John 20:21-22). By the gift of the Holy Spirit, 'the power from on high,' they were formed into a new community of witness to hope in Christ (Luke 24:49; Acts 1:8). In the Spirit of unity, the early church lived together and shared her goods among her members (Acts 2:44-45).

15. The universality of the Spirit's economy in creation and the particularity of the Spirit's work in redemption have to be understood together as the mission of the Spirit for the new heaven and earth, when God finally will be 'all in all' (1 Cor. 15:24-28). The Holy Spirit works in the world often in mysterious and unknown ways beyond our imagination (Luke 1:34-35; John 3:8; Acts 2:16-21).

16. Biblical witness attests to a variety of understandings of the role of the Holy Spirit in mission. One perspective on the role of the Holy Spirit in mission emphasizes the Holy Spirit as fully dependent on Christ, as the Paraclete and the one who will come as Counsellor and Advocate only after Christ has gone to the Father. The Holy Spirit is seen as the continuing presence of Christ, his agent to fulfill the task of mission. This understanding

leads to a missiology focusing on sending out and going forth. Therefore, a pneumatological focus on Christian mission recognizes that mission is essentially christologically based and relates the work of the Holy Spirit to the salvation through Jesus Christ.

17. Another perspective emphasizes that the Holy Spirit is the 'Spirit of Truth' that leads us to the 'whole truth' (John 16:13) and blows wherever he/she wills (John 3:8), thus embracing the whole of the cosmos; it proclaims the Holy Spirit as the source of Christ and the church as the eschatological coming together (*synaxis*) of the people of God in God's kingdom. This second perspective posits that the faithful go forth in peace (in mission) after they have experienced in their eucharistic gathering the eschatological kingdom of God as a glimpse and foretaste of it. Mission as going forth is thus the outcome, rather than the origin, of the church, and is called 'liturgy after the Liturgy.'[3]

18. What is clear is that by the Spirit we participate in the mission of love that is at the heart of the life of the Trinity. This results in Christian witness which unceasingly proclaims the salvific power of God through Jesus Christ and constantly affirms God's dynamic involvement, through the Holy Spirit, in the whole created world. All who respond to the outpouring of the love of God are invited to join in with the Spirit in the mission of God.

## Mission and the Flourishing of Creation

19. Mission is the overflow of the infinite love of the Triune God. God's mission begins with the act of creation. Creation's life and God's life are entwined. The mission of God's Spirit encompasses us all in an ever-giving act of grace. We are therefore called to move beyond a narrowly human-centred approach and to embrace forms of mission which express our reconciled relationship with all created life. We hear the cry of the earth as we listen to the cries of the poor and we know that from its beginning the earth has cried out to God over humanity's injustice (Gen. 4:10).

20. Mission with creation at its heart is already a positive movement in our churches through campaigns for eco-justice and more sustainable lifestyles and the development of spiritualities that are respectful of the earth. However, we have sometimes forgotten that the whole of creation is included in the reconciled unity towards which we are all called (2 Cor. 5:18-19). We do not believe that the earth is to be discarded and only souls saved; both the earth and our bodies have to be transformed through the Spirit's grace. As the vision of Isaiah and John's revelation testify, heaven and earth will be made new (Isa. 11:1-9; 25:6-10; 66:22; Rev. 21:1-4).

---

[3] See Ion Bria, *The Liturgy after the Liturgy: Mission and Witness from an Orthodox Perspective* (Geneva: WCC, 1996). The term was originally coined by Archbishop Anastasios Yannoulatos and widely publicized by Ion Bria.

21. Our participation in mission, our being in creation, and our practice of the life of the Spirit need to be woven together, for they are mutually transformative. We ought not to seek the one without the others. If we do, we will lapse into an individualistic spirituality that leads us to believe falsely that we can belong to God without belonging to our neighbour, and we will fall into a spirituality that simply makes us feel good while other parts of creation hurt and yearn.

22. We need a new conversion (*metanoia*) in our mission which invites a new humility in regard to the mission of God's Spirit. We tend to understand and practice mission as something done by humanity *to* others. Instead, humans can participate in communion *with* all of creation in celebrating the work of the Creator. In many ways creation is in mission to humanity; for instance, the natural world has a power that can heal the human heart and body. The wisdom literature in the Bible affirms creation's praise of its Creator (Ps. 9:1-4; 66:1; 96:11-13; 98:4; 100:1; 150:6). The Creator's joy and wonder in creation is one of the sources of our spirituality (Job 38–39).

23. We want to affirm our spiritual connection with creation, yet the reality is that the earth is being polluted and exploited. Consumerism triggers not limitless growth but rather endless exploitation of the earth's resources. Human greed is contributing to global warming and other forms of climate change. If this trend continues and earth is fatally damaged, what can we imagine salvation to be? Humanity cannot be saved alone while the rest of the created world perishes. Eco-justice cannot be separated from salvation, and salvation cannot come without a new humility that respects the needs of all life on earth.

## Spiritual Gifts and Discernment

24. The Holy Spirit gives gifts freely and impartially (1 Cor. 12:8-10; Rom. 12:6-8; Eph. 4:11) which are to be shared for the building up of others (1 Cor. 12:7; 14:26) and the reconciliation of the whole creation (Rom. 8:19-23). One of the gifts of the Spirit is discernment of spirits (1 Cor. 12:10). We discern the Spirit of God wherever life in its fullness is affirmed and in all its dimensions, including liberation of the oppressed, healing and reconciliation of broken communities, and the restoration of creation. We also discern evil spirits wherever forces of death and destruction of life prevail.

25. The early Christians, like many today, experienced a world of many spirits. The New Testament witnesses to diverse spirits, including evil spirits, 'ministering spirits' (i.e. angels, Heb. 1:14), 'principalities' and 'powers' (Eph. 6:12), the beast (Rev. 13:1-7), and other powers – both good and evil. The apostle Paul also testifies to some spiritual struggle (Eph. 6:10-18; 2 Cor. 10:4-6) and other apostolic writings contain injunctions to resist the devil (James 4:7; 1 Pet. 5:8). The churches are called to discern the work of the life-giving Spirit sent into the world and to join with the Holy Spirit in bringing about God's reign of justice (Acts 1:6-8). When we have discerned the Holy Spirit's

presence, we are called to respond, recognizing that God's Spirit is often subversive, leading us beyond boundaries and surprising us.

26. Our encounter with the Triune God is inward, personal, and communal but also directs us outward in missionary endeavour. The traditional symbols and titles for the Spirit (such as fire, light, dew, fountain, anointing, healing, melting, warming, solace, comfort, strength, rest, washing, shining) show that the Spirit is familiar with our lives and connected with all the aspects of relationship, life, and creation with which mission is concerned. We are led by the Spirit into various situations and moments, into meeting points with others, into spaces of encounter, and into critical locations of human struggle.

27. The Holy Spirit is the Spirit of wisdom (Isa. 11:3; Eph. 1:17) and guides us into all truth (John 16:13). The Spirit inspires human cultures and creativity, so it is part of our mission to acknowledge, respect, and co-operate with life-giving wisdoms in every culture and context. We regret that mission activity linked with colonization has often denigrated cultures and failed to recognize the wisdom of local people. Local wisdom and culture which are life-affirming are gifts from God's Spirit. We lift up testimonies of peoples whose traditions have been scorned and mocked by theologians and scientists, yet whose wisdom offers us the vital and sometimes new orientation that can connect us again with the life of the Spirit in creation, which helps us to consider the ways in which God is revealed in creation.

28. The claim that the Spirit is with us is not for us to make, but for others to recognize in the life that we lead. The apostle Paul expresses this by encouraging the church to bear the fruits of the Spirit which entail love, joy, peace, patience, kindness, generosity, faithfulness, and self-control (Gal. 5:23). As we bear these fruits, we hope others will discern the love and power of the Spirit at work.

## Transformative Spirituality

29. Authentic Christian witness is not only in *what* we do in mission but *how* we live out our mission. The church in mission can only be sustained by spiritualities deeply rooted in the Trinity's communion of love. Spirituality gives our lives their deepest meaning. It stimulates, motivates and gives dynamism to life's journey. It is energy for life in its fullness and calls for a commitment to resist all forces, powers, and systems which deny, destroy, and reduce life.

30. Mission spirituality is always transformative. Mission spirituality resists and seeks to transform all life-destroying values and systems wherever these are at work in our economies, our politics, and even our churches. 'Our faithfulness to God and God's free gift of life compels us to confront idolatrous assumptions, unjust systems, politics of domination and exploitation in our current world economic order. Economics and economic justice are

always matters of faith as they touch the very core of God's will for creation.'[4] Mission spirituality motivates us to serve God's economy of life, not mammon, to share life at God's table rather than satisfy individual greed, to pursue change towards a better world while challenging the self-interest of the powerful who desire to maintain the status quo.

31. Jesus has told us, 'You cannot serve God and mammon' (Matt. 6:24, KJV). The policy of unlimited growth through the domination of the global free market is an ideology that claims to be without alternative, demanding an endless flow of sacrifices from the poor and from nature. 'It makes the false promise that it can save the world through creation of wealth and prosperity, claiming sovereignty over life and demanding total allegiance, which amounts to idolatry.'[5] This is a global system of mammon that protects the unlimited growth of wealth of only the rich and powerful through endless exploitation. This tower of greed is threatening the whole household of God. The reign of God is in direct opposition to the empire of mammon.

32. Transformation can be understood in the light of the Paschal mystery: 'If we have died with Christ, we will also live with him; if we endure, we will also reign with him' (2 Tim. 2:11-12). In situations of oppression, discrimination, and hurt, the cross of Christ is the power of God for salvation (1 Cor. 1:18). Even in our time, some have paid with their lives for their Christian witness, reminding us all of the cost of discipleship. The Spirit gives Christians courage to live out their convictions, even in the face of persecution and martyrdom.

33. The cross calls for repentance in light of misuse of power and use of the wrong kind of power in mission and in the church. 'Disturbed by the asymmetries and imbalances of power that divide and trouble us in church and world, we are called to repentance, to critical reflection on systems of power, and to accountable use of power structures.'[6] The Spirit empowers the powerless and challenges the powerful to empty themselves of their privileges for the sake of the disempowered.

34. To experience life in the Spirit is to taste life in its fullness. We are called to witness to a movement towards life, celebrating all that the Spirit continues to call into being, walking in solidarity in order to cross the rivers of despair and anxiety (Ps. 23, Isa. 43:1-5). Mission provokes in us a renewed awareness that the Holy Spirit meets us and challenges us at all levels of life, and brings newness and change to the places and times of our personal and collective journeys.

35. The Holy Spirit is present with us as companion, yet is never domesticated or 'tame.' Among the surprises of the Spirit are the ways in

---

[4] *Alternative Globalization Addressing Peoples and Earth (AGAPE): A Background Document* (Geneva: WCC, 2005), 13.

[5] World Alliance of Reformed Churches, *The Accra Confession: Covenanting for Justice: in the Economy and the Earth* (2004), §10.

[6] Edinburgh 2010, *Common Call* (2010), §4.

which God works from locations which appear to be on the margins and through people who appear to be excluded.

### Spirit of Liberation: Mission from the Margins

36. God's purpose for the world is not to create another world, but to re-create what God has already created in love and wisdom. Jesus began his ministry by claiming that to be filled by the Spirit is to liberate the oppressed, to open eyes that are blind, and to announce the coming of God's reign (Luke 4:16-18). He went about fulfilling this mission by opting to be with the marginalized people of his time, not out of paternalistic charity but because their situations testified to the sinfulness of the world, and their yearnings for life pointed to God's purposes.

37. Jesus Christ relates to and embraces those who are most marginalized in society, in order to confront and transform all that denies life. This includes cultures and systems which generate and sustain massive poverty, discrimination, and dehumanization, and which exploit or destroy people and the earth. Mission from the margins calls for an understanding of the complexities of power dynamics, global systems and structures, and local contextual realities. Christian mission has at times been understood and practiced in ways which failed to recognize God's alignment with those consistently pushed to the margins. Therefore, mission from the margins invites the church to re-imagine mission as a vocation from God's Spirit who works for a world where the fullness of life is available for all.

### Why Margins and Marginalization?

38. Mission from the margins seeks to counteract injustices in life, church, and mission. It seeks to be an alternative missional movement against the perception that mission can only be done by the powerful to the powerless, by the rich to the poor, or by the privileged to the marginalized. Such approaches can contribute to oppression and marginalization. Mission from the margins recognizes that being in the centre means having access to systems that lead to one's rights, freedom, and individuality being affirmed and respected; living in the margins means exclusion from justice and dignity. Living on the margins, however, can provide its own lessons. People on the margins have agency, and can often see what, from the centre, is out of view. People on the margins, living in vulnerable positions, often know what exclusionary forces are threatening their survival and can best discern the urgency of their struggles; people in positions of privilege have much to learn from the daily struggles of people living in marginal conditions.

39. Marginalized people have God-given gifts that are under-utilized because of disempowerment and denial of access to opportunities and/or justice. Through struggles in and for life, marginalized people are reservoirs of

the active hope, collective resistance, and perseverance that are needed to remain faithful to the promised reign of God.

40. Because the context of missional activity influences its scope and character, the social location of all engaged in mission work must be taken into account. Missiological reflections need to recognize the different value orientations that shape missional perspectives. The aim of mission is not simply to move people from the margins to centres of power but to confront those who remain the centre by keeping people on the margins. Instead, churches are called to *transform* power structures.

41. The dominant expressions of mission, in the past and today, have often been directed *at* people on the margins of societies. These have generally viewed those on the margins as recipients and not as active agents of missionary activity. Mission expressed in this way has too often been complicit with oppressive and life-denying systems. It has generally aligned with the privileges of the centre and largely failed to challenge economic, social, cultural, and political systems which have marginalized some peoples. Mission from the centre is motivated by an attitude of paternalism and a superiority complex. Historically, this stance has equated Christianity with Western culture and resulted in adverse consequences, including the denial of the full personhood of the victims of such marginalization.

42. A major common concern of people from the margins is the failure of societies, cultures, civilizations, nations, and even churches to honour the dignity and worth of *all* persons. Injustice is at the roots of the inequalities that give rise to marginalization and oppression. God's desire for justice is inextricably linked with God's nature and sovereignty: 'For the Lord your God is God of gods and Lord of lords… who executes justice for the orphan and the widow, and who also loves the strangers, providing them food and clothing' (Deut. 10:17-18). All missional activity must, therefore, safeguard the sacred worth of every human being and of the earth (see Isa. 58).

## Mission as Struggle and Resistance

43. The affirmation of God's mission (*missio Dei*) points to the belief in God as One who acts in history and in creation, in concrete realities of time and contexts, who seeks the fullness of life for the whole earth through justice, peace, and reconciliation. Participation in God's ongoing work of liberation and reconciliation by the Holy Spirit, therefore, includes discerning and unmasking the demons that exploit and enslave. For example, this involves deconstructing patriarchal ideologies, upholding the right to self-determination for Indigenous peoples, and challenging the social embeddedness of racism and casteism.

44. The church's hope is rooted in the promised fulfillment of the reign of God. It entails the restoration of right relationships between God and humanity and all of creation. Even though this vision speaks to an

eschatological reality, it deeply energizes and informs our current participation in God's salvific work in this penultimate period.

45. Participation in God's mission follows the way of Jesus, who came to serve, not to be served (Mark 10:45); who tears down the mighty and powerful and exalts the lowly (Luke 1:46-55); and whose love is characterized by mutuality, reciprocity, and interdependence. It therefore requires a commitment to struggle against and resist the powers that obstruct the fullness of life that God wills for all, and a willingness to work with all people involved in movements and initiatives committed to the causes of justice, dignity, and life.

## Mission Seeking Justice and Inclusivity

46. The good news of God's reign is about the promise of the actualization of a just and inclusive world. Inclusivity fosters just relationships in the community of humanity and creation, with mutual acknowledgement of persons and creation, and mutual respect and sustenance of each one's sacred worth. It also facilitates each one's full participation in the life of the community. Baptism in Christ implies a lifelong commitment to give an account of this hope by overcoming the barriers in order to find a common identity under the sovereignty of God (Gal. 3:27-28). Therefore, discrimination of all types against any human beings is unacceptable in the sight of God.

47. Jesus promises that the last shall be first (Matt. 20:16). To the extent that the church practices radical hospitality to the estranged in society, it demonstrates commitment to embodying the values of the reign of God (Isa. 58:6). To the extent that it denounces self-centredness as a way of life, it makes space for the reign of God to permeate human existence. To the extent that it renounces violence in its physical, psychological, and spiritual manifestations both in personal interactions and in economic, political, and social systems, it testifies to the reign of God at work in the world.

48. In reality, however, mission, money, and political power are strategic partners. Although our theological and missiological language talks a lot about the mission of the church being in solidarity with the poor, sometimes in practice it is much more concerned with being in the centres of power, eating with the rich, and lobbying for money to maintain ecclesial bureaucracy. This poses particular challenges to reflect on what is the good news for people who are privileged and powerful.

49. The church is called to make present God's holy and life-affirming plan for the world revealed in Jesus Christ. This means rejecting values and practices which lead to the destruction of community. Christians are called to acknowledge the sinful nature of all forms of discrimination and to transform unjust structures. This call places certain expectations on the church. The church must refuse to harbour oppressive forces within its ranks, acting instead as a counter-cultural community. The biblical mandate

to the covenant community in both testaments is characterized by the dictum: 'It shall not be so among you' (Matt. 20:26, KJV).

## Mission as Healing and Wholeness

50. Actions towards healing and wholeness of life of persons and communities are an important expression of mission. Healing was not only a central feature of Jesus' ministry but also a feature of his call to his followers to continue his work (Matt. 10:1). Healing is also one of the gifts of the Holy Spirit (1 Cor. 12:9; Acts 3). The Spirit empowers the church for a life-nurturing mission, which includes prayer, pastoral care, and professional health care, on the one hand, and prophetic denunciation of the root causes of suffering, transformation of structures that dispense injustice, and pursuit of scientific research, on the other.

51. Health is more than physical and/or mental well-being, and healing is not primarily medical. This understanding of health coheres with the biblical-theological tradition of the church, which sees a human being as a multi-dimensional unity and the body, soul, and mind as interrelated and interdependent. It thus affirms the social, political, and ecological dimensions of personhood and wholeness. Health, in the sense of wholeness, is a condition related to God's promise for the end of time as well as a real possibility in the present.[7] Wholeness is not a static balance of harmony but rather involves living-in-community with God, people, and creation. Individualism and injustice are barriers to community building and therefore to wholeness. Discrimination on grounds of medical conditions or disability – including HIV and AIDS – is contrary to the teaching of Jesus Christ. When all the parts of our individual and corporate lives that have been left out are included, and wherever the neglected or marginalized are brought together in love such that wholeness is experienced, we may discern signs of God's reign on earth.

52. Societies have tended to see disability or illness as a manifestation of sin or a medical problem to be solved. The medical model has emphasized the correction or cure of what is assumed to be the 'deficiency' in the individual. Many who are marginalized, however, do not see themselves as 'deficient' or 'sick.' The Bible recounts many instances where Jesus healed people with various infirmities but, equally importantly, he restored people to their rightful places within the fabric of the community. Healing is more about the restoration of wholeness than about correcting something perceived as defective. To become whole, the parts that have become estranged need to be reclaimed. The fixation on cure is thus a perspective that must be overcome in order to promote the biblical focus. Mission should foster the full participation of people with disabilities and illness in the life of the church and society.

---

[7] *Healing and Wholeness: The Churches' Role in Health* (Geneva: WCC, 1990), 6.

53. Christian medical mission aims at achieving health for all in the sense that all people around the globe will have access to quality health care. There are many ways in which churches can be, and are, involved in health and healing in a comprehensive sense. They create or support clinics and mission hospitals; they offer counselling services, care groups, and health programmes; local churches can create groups to visit sick congregation members. Healing processes could include praying with and for the sick, confession and forgiveness, the laying on of hands, anointing with oil, and the use of charismatic spiritual gifts (1 Cor. 12). But it must also be noted that inappropriate forms of Christian worship, including triumphalistic healing services in which the healer is glorified at the expense of God and false expectations are raised, can deeply harm people. This is not to deny God's miraculous intervention of healing in some cases.

54. As a community of imperfect people, and as part of a creation groaning in pain and longing for its liberation, the Christian community can be a sign of hope and an expression of the kingdom of God here on earth (Rom. 8:22-24). The Holy Spirit works for justice and healing in many ways and is pleased to indwell the particular community which is called to embody Christ's mission.

## Spirit of Community: Church on the Move
## God's Mission and the Life of the Church

55. The life of the church arises from the love of the Triune God. 'God is love' (1 Jn. 4:8). Mission is a response to God's urging love shown in creation and redemption. 'God's love invites us' (*Caritas Christi urget nos*). This communion (*koinonia*) opens our hearts and lives to our brothers and sisters in the same movement of sharing God's love (2 Cor. 5:18-21). Living in that love of God, the church is called to become good news for all. The Triune God's overflowing sharing of love is the source of all mission and evangelism.

56. God's love, manifest in the Holy Spirit, is an inspirational gift to all humanity 'in all times and places',[8] and for all cultures and situations. The powerful presence of the Holy Spirit, revealed in Jesus Christ, the crucified and risen Lord, initiates us into the fullness of life that is God's gift to each one of us. Through Christ in the Holy Spirit, God indwells the church, revealing God's purposes for the world, and empowering and enabling its members to participate in the realization of those purposes.

57. The church in history has not always existed but, both theologically and empirically, came into being for the sake of mission. It is not possible to separate church and mission in terms of their origin or purpose. To fulfill God's missionary purpose is the church's aim. The relationship between church and mission is very intimate because the same Spirit of Christ who

---

[8] WCC Commission on Faith and Order, *Baptism, Eucharist and Ministry* (WCC Faith and Order Paper No. 111 (1982)), §19.

empowers the church in mission is also the life of the church. At the same time as he sent the church into the world, Jesus Christ breathed the Holy Spirit into the church (John 20:19-23). Therefore, the church exists by mission, just as fire exists by burning. If it does not engage in mission, it ceases to be church.

58. Starting with God's mission leads to an ecclesiological approach 'from below.' In this perspective it is not the church that has a mission but rather the mission that has a church. Mission is not a project of expanding churches but of the church embodying God's salvation in this world. Out of this follows a dynamic understanding of the apostolicity of the church: apostolicity is not only safeguarding the faith of the church through the ages but also participating in the apostolate. Thus the churches mainly and foremost need to be missionary churches.

## God's Mission and the Church's Unity

59. Living out our faith in community is an important way of participating in mission. Through baptism, we become sisters and brothers belonging together in Christ (Heb. 10:25). The church is called to be an inclusive community that welcomes all. Through word and deed and in its very being, the church foretastes and witnesses to the vision of the coming reign of God. The church is the *coming together* of the faithful and their *going forth* in peace.

60. Practically as well as theologically, mission and unity belong together. In this regard, the integration in 1961 of the International Missionary Council (IMC) and the World Council of Churches (WCC) was a significant step. This historical experience encourages us to believe that mission and church can come together. This aim, however, is not yet fully accomplished. We have to continue this journey in our century with fresh attempts so that the church becomes truly missionary.

61. The churches realize today that in many respects they are still not adequate embodiments of God's mission. Sometimes a sense of separation between mission and church still prevails. The lack of full and real unity in mission still harms the authenticity and credibility of the fulfillment of God's mission in this world. Our Lord prayed 'that they may all be one… so that the world may believe' (John 17:21). Thus mission and unity are intertwined. Consequently there is a need to open up our reflections on church and unity to an even wider understanding of unity: the unity of humanity and even the cosmic unity of the whole of God's creation.

62. The highly competitive environment of the free market economy has unfortunately influenced some churches and para-church movements to seek to be 'winners' over others. This can even lead to the adoption of aggressive tactics to persuade Christians who already belong to a church to change their denominational allegiance. Seeking numerical growth at all costs is incompatible with the respect for others required of Christian disciples. Jesus became our Christ not through power or money but through his self-emptying (*kenosis*)

and death on the cross. This humble understanding of mission does not merely shape our methods but is the very nature and essence of our faith in Christ. The church is a servant in God's mission and not the master. The missionary church glorifies God in self-emptying love.

63. The Christian communities in their diversity are called to identify and practice ways of common witness in a spirit of partnership and co-operation, including through mutually respectful and responsible forms of evangelism. Common witness is what the 'churches, even while separated, bear together, especially through joint efforts, by manifesting whatever divine gifts of truth and life they already share and experience in common.'[9]

64. The missionary nature of the church also means that there must be a way that churches and para-church structures can be more closely related. The integration of the IMC and the WCC brought about a new framework for consideration of church unity and mission. While discussions of unity have been very concerned with structural questions, mission agencies can represent flexibility and subsidiarity in mission. While para-church movements can find accountability and direction through ecclesial mooring, para-church structures can help churches not to forget their dynamic apostolic character.

65. The Commission on World Mission and Evangelism (CWME), the direct heir of Edinburgh 1910's initiatives on co-operation and unity, provides a structure for churches and mission agencies to seek ways of expressing and strengthening unity in mission. Being an integral part of the WCC, the CWME has been able to encounter new understandings of mission and unity from Catholic, Orthodox, Anglican, Protestant, Evangelical, Pentecostal, and Indigenous churches from all over the globe. In particular, the context of the WCC has facilitated close working relationships with the Roman Catholic Church. A growing intensity of collaboration with Evangelicals, especially with the Lausanne Movement for World Evangelization and the World Evangelical Alliance, has also abundantly contributed to the enrichment of ecumenical theological reflection on mission in unity. Together we share a common concern that the whole church should witness to the whole gospel in the whole world.[10]

66. The Holy Spirit, the Spirit of unity, unites people and churches too, to celebrate unity in diversity both pro-actively and constructively. The Spirit provides both the dynamic context and the resources needed for people to explore differences in a safe, positive and nurturing environment in order to grow into an inclusive and mutually responsible community.

---

[9] Thomas F. Best and Günther Gassmann (eds), *On the Way to Fuller Koinonia: Official Report of the Fifth World Conference on Faith and Order, Santiago de Compostela 1993* (WCC Faith and Order Paper No. 166 (1994)), 254.

[10] See 'The Whole Church Taking the Whole Gospel to the Whole World: Reflections of the Lausanne Theology Working Group' (2010).

## God Empowers the Church in Mission

67. Through Christ in the Holy Spirit, God indwells the church, empowering and energizing its members. Thus mission becomes for Christians an urgent inner compulsion (1 Cor. 9:16) and even a test and criterion for authentic life in Christ, rooted in the profound demands of Christ's love, to invite others to share in the fullness of life Jesus came to bring. Participating in God's mission, therefore, should be natural for all Christians and all churches, not only for particular individuals or specialized groups.[11]

68. What makes the Christian message of God's abundant love for humanity and all creation credible is our ability to speak with one voice, where possible, and to give common witness and an account of the hope that is in us (1 Pet. 3:15). The churches have therefore produced a rich array of common declarations, some of them resulting in uniting or united churches, and of dialogues, seeking to restore the unity of all Christians in one living organism of healing and reconciliation. A rediscovery of the work of the Holy Spirit in healing and reconciliation, which is at the heart of today's mission theology, has significant ecumenical implications.[12]

69. While acknowledging the great importance of 'visible' unity among churches, nonetheless unity need not be sought only at the level of organizational structures. From a mission perspective, it is important to discern what helps the cause of God's mission. In other words, unity in mission is the basis for the visible unity of the churches; this also has implications for the order of the church. Attempts to achieve unity must be in concert with the biblical call to seek justice. Our call to do justice may sometimes involve breaking false unities that silence and oppress. Genuine unity always entails inclusivity and respect for others.

70. Today's context of large-scale worldwide migration challenges the churches' commitment to unity in very practical ways. We are told: 'Do not forget to entertain strangers, for by so doing some people have entertained angels without knowing it.' (Heb. 13:2, NIV). Churches can be a place of refuge for migrant communities; they can also be intentional focal points for intercultural engagement.[13] The churches are called to be one to serve God's mission beyond ethnic and cultural boundaries and ought to create multicultural ministry and mission as a concrete expression of common witness in diversity. This may entail advocating justice in regard to migration policies and resistance to xenophobia and racism. Women, children, and undocumented workers are often the most vulnerable among migrants in all

---

[11] 'Mission and Evangelism in Unity', CWME Study Document (2000), §13.

[12] See 'Mission as Ministry of Reconciliation', in *You Are the Light of the World: Statements on Mission by the World Council of Churches 1980-2005*, Jacques Matthey (ed) (Geneva: WCC, 2005), 90-162.

[13] 'Report of WCC Consultation on Mission and Ecclesiology of the Migrant Churches, Utrecht, Netherlands, 16th-21st November 2010', in *International Review of Mission*, 100.1, 392 (April 2011): 104-07.

contexts. But women are also often at the cutting edge of new migrant ministries.

71. God's hospitality calls us to move beyond binary notions of culturally dominant groups as hosts, and migrant and minority peoples as guests. Instead, in God's hospitality, God is host and we are all invited by the Spirit to participate with humility and mutuality in God's mission.

## Local Congregations: New Initiatives

72. While cherishing the unity of the Spirit in the one Church, it is also important to honour the ways in which each local congregation is led by the Spirit to respond to its own contextual realities. Today's changed world calls for local congregations to take new initiatives. For example, in the secularizing global North, new forms of contextual mission such as "new monasticism,", "emerging church," and "fresh expressions," have redefined and revitalized churches. Exploring contextual ways of being church can be particularly relevant to young people. Some churches in the global North now meet in pubs, coffee houses, or converted movie theatres. Engaging with church life online is an attractive option for young people thinking in a non-linear, visual, and experiential way.

73. Like the early church in the Book of Acts, local congregations have the privilege of forming a community marked by the presence of the risen Christ. For many people, acceptance or refusal to become members of the church is linked with their positive or negative experience with a local congregation, which can be either a stumbling block or an agent of transformation.[14] Therefore it is vital that local congregations are constantly renewed and inspired by the Spirit of mission. Local congregations are frontiers and primary agents of mission.

74. Worship and the sacraments play a crucial role in the formation of transformative spirituality and mission. Reading the Bible contextually is also a primary resource in enabling local congregations to be messengers and witnesses to God's justice and love. Liturgy in the sanctuary only has full integrity when we live out God's mission in our communities in our daily life. Local congregations are therefore impelled to step out of their comfort zones and cross boundaries for the sake of the mission of God.

75. More than ever before, local congregations today can play a key role in emphasizing the crossing of cultural and racial boundaries and affirming cultural difference as a gift of the Spirit. Rather than being perceived as a problem, migration can be seen as offering new possibilities for churches to re-discover themselves afresh. It inspires opportunities for the creation of intercultural and multi-cultural churches at local level All churches can create space for different cultural communities to come together and

---

[14] Christopher Duraisingh (ed), *Called to One Hope: The Gospel in Diverse Cultures* (Geneva: WCC, 1998), 54.

embrace exciting opportunities for contextual expressions of intercultural mission in our time.

76. Local congregations can also, as never before, develop global connections. Many inspirational and transformative linkages are being formed between churches that are geographically far apart and located in very different contexts. These offer innovative possibilities but are not without pitfalls. The increasingly popular short-term 'mission trips' can help to build partnerships between churches in different parts of the world but in some cases place an intolerable burden on poor local churches or disregard the existing churches altogether. While there is some danger and caution around such trips, these exposure opportunities in diverse cultural and socio-economic contexts can also lead to long-term change when the travellers return to their home community. The challenge is to find ways of exercising spiritual gifts which build up the whole church in every part (1 Cor. 12-14).

77. Advocacy for justice is no longer the sole prerogative of national assemblies and central offices but a form of witness which calls for the engagement of local churches. For example, the WCC Decade to Overcome Violence (2001-2011) concluded with a plea in the International Ecumenical Peace Convocation that 'churches must help in identifying the everyday choices that can abuse and promote human rights, gender justice, climate justice, unity and peace.'[15] Local churches' grounding in everyday life gives them both legitimacy and motivation in the struggle for justice and peace.

78. The church in every geo-political and socio-economic context is called to service (*diakonia*) – to live out the faith and hope of the community of God's people, witnessing to what God has done in Jesus Christ. Through service the church participates in God's mission, following the way of its Servant Lord. The church is called to be a diaconal community manifesting the power of service over the power of domination, enabling and nurturing possibilities for life, and witnessing to God's transforming grace through acts of service that hold forth the promise of God's reign.[16]

79. As the church discovers more deeply its identity as a missionary community, its outward-looking character finds expression in evangelism.

## Spirit of Pentecost: Good News for All
## The Call to Evangelize

80. Witness (*martyria*) takes concrete form in evangelism – the communication of the whole gospel to the whole of humanity in the whole

---

[15] 'Glory to God and Peace on Earth: The Message of the International Ecumenical Peace Convocation', WCC, Kingston, Jamaica, 17th-25th May 2011, 2.

[16] '*Diakonia* in the Twenty First Century: Theological Perspectives', WCC Conference on Theology of *Diakonia* in the 21st Century, Colombo, Sri Lanka, 2nd-6th June 2012, 2.

world.[17] Its goal is the salvation of the world and the glory of the Triune God. Evangelism is mission activity which makes explicit and unambiguous the centrality of the incarnation, suffering, and resurrection of Jesus Christ without setting limits to the saving grace of God. It seeks to share this good news with all who have not yet heard it and invites them to an experience of life in Christ.

81. 'Evangelism is the outflow of hearts that are filled with the love of God for those who do not yet know him.'[18] At Pentecost, the disciples could not but declare the mighty works of God (Acts 2:4; 4:20). Evangelism, while not excluding the different dimensions of mission, focuses on explicit and intentional articulation of the gospel, including 'the invitation to personal conversion to a new life in Christ and to discipleship.'[19] While the Holy Spirit calls some to be evangelists (Eph. 4:11), we all are called to give an account of the hope that is in us (1 Pet. 3:15). Not only individuals but also the whole church together is called to evangelize (Mark 16:15; 1 Pet. 2:9).

82. Today's world is marked by excessive assertion of religious identities and persuasions that seem to break and brutalize in the name of God rather than heal and nurture communities. In such a context, it is important to recognize that proselytism is not a legitimate way of practicing evangelism.[20] The Holy Spirit chooses to work in partnership with people's preaching and demonstration of the good news (see Rom. 10:14-15; 2 Cor. 4:2-6), but it is only God's Spirit who creates new life and brings about rebirth (John 3:5-8; 1 Thess. 1:4-6). We acknowledge that evangelism at times has been distorted and lost its credibility because some Christians have forced 'conversions' by violent means or the abuse of power. In some contexts, however, accusations of forced conversions are motivated by the desire of dominant groups to keep the marginalized living with oppressed identities and in dehumanizing conditions.

83. Evangelism is sharing one's faith and conviction with other people and inviting them to discipleship, whether or not they adhere to other religious traditions. Such sharing is to take place with both confidence and humility and as an expression of our professed love for our world. If we claim to love God and to love our fellow human beings but fail to share the good news with them urgently and consistently, we deceive ourselves as to the integrity of our love for either God or people. There is no greater gift we can offer to our fellow human beings than to share and or introduce them to the love, grace, and mercy of God in Christ.

---

[17] *Minutes and Reports of the Fourth Meeting of the Central Committee*, WCC, Rolle, Switzerland, 1951, 66.

[18] The Lausanne Movement, the *Cape Town Commitment*, 2010, Part I, 7(b).

[19] See Congregation for the Doctrine of the Faith, *Doctrinal Note on Some Aspects of Evangelization*, No. 12, 2007, 489-504.

[20] WCC Central Committee, *Towards Common Witness: A Call to Adopt Responsible Relationships in Mission and to Renounce Proselytism* (1997).

84. Evangelism leads to repentance, faith, and baptism. Hearing the truth in the face of sin and evil demands a response – positive or negative (John 4:28-29; cf. Mark 10:22). It provokes conversion, involving a change of attitudes, priorities, and goals. It results in salvation of the lost, healing of the sick, and the liberation of the oppressed and the whole creation.

85. 'Evangelism,', while not excluding the different dimensions of mission, focuses on explicit and intentional articulation of the gospel, including 'the invitation to personal conversion to a new life in Christ and to discipleship.'[21] In different churches, there are differing understandings of how the Spirit calls us to evangelize in our contexts. For some, evangelism is primarily about leading people to personal conversion through Jesus Christ; for others, evangelism is about being in solidarity and offering Christian witness through presence with oppressed peoples; others again look on evangelism as one component of God's mission. Different Christian traditions denote aspects of mission and evangelism in different ways; however, we can still affirm that the Spirit calls us all towards an understanding of evangelism which is grounded in the life of the local church where worship (*leiturgia*) is inextricably linked with witness (*martyria*), service (*diakonia*), and fellowship (*koinonia*).

## Evangelism in Christ's Way

86. Evangelism is sharing the good news both in word and action. Evangelizing through verbal proclamation or preaching of the gospel (*kerygma*) is profoundly biblical. However, if our words are not consistent with our actions, our evangelism is inauthentic. The combination of verbal declaration and visible action bears witness to God's revelation in Jesus Christ and of his purposes. Evangelism is closely related to unity: the love for one another is a demonstration of the gospel we proclaim (John 13:34-35) while disunity is an embarrassment to the gospel (1 Cor. 1).

87. There are historical and contemporary examples of faithful, humble service by Christians, working in their own local contexts, with whom the Spirit has partnered to bring about fullness of life. Also, many Christians who lived and worked as missionaries far away from their own cultural contexts did so with humility, mutuality, and respect; God's Spirit also stirred in those communities to bring about transformation.

88. Regrettably, sometimes evangelism has been practiced in ways which betray rather than incarnate the gospel. Whenever this occurs, repentance

---

[21] It is important to note that not all churches understand evangelism as expressed in the above. The Roman Catholic Church refers to 'evangelization' as the *missio ad gentes* [mission to the peoples] directed to those who do not know Christ. In a wider sense, it is used to describe ordinary pastoral work, while the phrase 'new evangelization' designates pastoral outreach to those who no longer practise the Christian faith. See 'Congregation for the Doctrine of the Faith, Doctrinal Note on Some Aspects of Evangelization'.

is in order. Mission in Christ's way involves affirming the dignity and rights of others. We are called to serve others as Christ did (cf. Mark 10:45; Matt. 25:45), without exploitation or any form of allurement.[22] In such individualized contexts, it may be possible to confuse evangelism with buying and selling a 'product', where *we* decide what aspects Christian life we want to take on. Instead, the Spirit rejects the idea that Jesus' good news for all can be consumed under capitalist terms, and the Spirit calls us to conversion and transformation at a personal level, which leads us to the proclamation of the fullness of life for all.

89. Authentic evangelism is grounded in humility and respect for all and flourishes in the context of dialogue. It promotes the message of the gospel, of healing and reconciliation, in word and deed. 'There is no evangelism without solidarity; there is no Christian solidarity that does not involve sharing the message of God's coming reign.'[23] Evangelism, therefore, inspires the building of inter-personal and community relationships. Such authentic relationships are often best nourished in local faith communities and based in local cultural contexts. Christian witness is as much by our presence as by our words. In situations where the public testimony to one's faith is not possible without risking one's life, simply living the gospel may be a powerful alternative.

90. Aware of tensions between people and communities of different religious convictions and varied interpretations of Christian witness, authentic evangelism must always be guided by life-affirming values, as stated in the joint statement on 'Christian Witness in a Multi-Religious World: Recommendations for Conduct':

a. Rejection of all forms of violence, discrimination and repression by religious and secular authority, including the abuse of power – psychological or social.

b. Affirming the freedom of religion to practice and profess faith without any fear of reprisal and or intimidation. Mutual respect and solidarity which promote justice, peace and the common good of all.

c. Respect for all people and human cultures, while also discerning the elements in our own cultures, such as patriarchy, racism, casteism, etc. that need to be challenged by the gospel.

d. Renunciation of false witness and listening in order to understand in mutual respect.

e. Ensuring freedom for ongoing discernment by persons and communities as part of decision-making.

---

[22] World Council of Churches, Pontifical Council for Interreligious Dialogue, and World Evangelical Alliance, *Christian Witness in a Multi-Religious World: Recommendations for Conduct* (2011).

[23] The San Antonio Report, 26; CWME, *Mission and Evangelism: An Ecumenical Affirmation* (1982), §34; Duraisingh, *Called to One Hope*, 38.

f. Building relationships with believers of other faiths or no faith to facilitate deeper mutual understanding, reconciliation and co-operation for the common good.[24]

91. We live in a world strongly influenced by individualism, secularism, and materialism and by other ideologies that challenge the values of the kingdom of God. Although the gospel is ultimately good news for all, it is bad news for the forces which promote falsehood, injustice, and oppression. To that extent, evangelism is also a prophetic vocation which involves speaking truth to power in hope and in love (Acts 26:25; Col. 1:5; Eph. 4:15). The gospel is liberative and transformative. Its proclamation must involve transformation of societies with a view to creating just and inclusive communities.

92. Standing against evil or injustice and being prophetic can sometimes be met with suppression and violence, and thus consequently lead to suffering, persecution, and even death. Authentic evangelism involves being vulnerable, following the example of Christ by carrying the cross and emptying oneself (Phil. 2:5-11). Just as the blood of the martyrs was the seed of the church under Roman persecution, today the pursuit of justice and righteousness makes a powerful witness to Christ. Jesus linked such self-denial with the call to follow him and with eternal salvation (Mark 8:34-38).

### Evangelism, Inter-faith Dialogue and Christian Presence

93. In the plurality and complexity of today's world, we encounter people of many different faiths, ideologies, and convictions. We believe that the Spirit of Life brings joy and fullness of life. God's Spirit, therefore, can be found in all cultures that affirm life. The Holy Spirit works in mysterious ways and we do not fully understand the workings of the Spirit in other faith traditions. We acknowledge that there is inherent value and wisdom in diverse life-giving spiritualities. Therefore, authentic mission makes the 'other' a partner in, not an 'object' of mission.

94. Dialogue is a way of affirming our common life and goals in terms of the affirmation of life and the integrity of creation. Dialogue at the religious level is possible only if we begin with the expectation of meeting God who has preceded us and has been present with people within their own contexts.[25] God is there before we come (Acts 17) and our task is not to bring God along, but to witness to the God who is already there. Dialogue provides for an honest encounter where each party brings to the table all that they are in an open, patient and respectful manner.

95. Evangelism and dialogue are distinct but interrelated. Although Christians hope and pray that all people may come to living knowledge of the Triune God, evangelism is not the purpose of dialogue. However, since

---

[24] See *Christian Witness in a Multi-Religious World.*

[25] See WCC, *Baar Statement: Theological Perspectives on Plurality* (1990).

dialogue is also 'a mutual encounter of commitments,' sharing the good news of Jesus Christ has a legitimate place in it. Furthermore, authentic evangelism takes place in the context of the dialogue of life and action and in 'the spirit of dialogue' – 'an attitude of respect and friendship.'[26] Evangelism entails not only proclamation of our deepest convictions, but also listening to others and being challenged and enriched by others (Acts 10).

96. Particularly important is dialogue between people of different faiths, not only in multi-religious contexts but equally where there is a large majority of a particular faith. It is necessary to protect rights of minority groups and religious freedom, and to enable all to contribute to the common good. Religious freedom should be upheld because it flows from the dignity of the human person, grounded in the creation of all human beings in the image and likeness of God (Gen. 1:26). Followers of all religions and beliefs have equal rights and responsibilities.[27]

### Evangelism and Cultures

97. The gospel takes root in different contexts through engagement with specific cultural, political, and religious realities. Respect for people and their cultural and symbolic life-worlds are necessary if the gospel is to take root in those different realities. In this way it must begin with engagement and dialogue with the wider context in order to discern how Christ is already present and where God's Spirit is already at work.

98. The connection of evangelism with colonial powers in the history of mission has led to the presupposition that Western forms of Christianity are the standards by which others' adherence to the gospel should be judged. Evangelism by those who enjoy economic power or cultural hegemony risks distorting the gospel. Therefore, they must seek the partnership of the poor, the dispossessed, and minorities, and be shaped by their theological resources and visions.

99. The enforcement of uniformity discredits the uniqueness of each individual created in the image and likeness of God. Whereas Babel attempted to enforce uniformity, the preaching of the disciples on the day of Pentecost resulted in a unity in which personal particularities and community identities were not lost but respected – they heard the good news in their own languages.

100. Jesus calls us out of the narrow concerns of *our* own kingdom, *our* own liberation, and *our* own independence (Acts 1:6) by unveiling to us a larger vision, and empowering us by the Holy Spirit to go 'to the ends of the earth' as witnesses in each context of time and space to God's justice,

---

[26] Pontifical Council for Inter-Religious Dialogue, *Dialogue and Proclamation: Reflection and Orientations on Interreligious Dialogue and the Proclamation of The Gospel of Jesus Christ* (1991), §9.

[27] See *Christian Witness in a Multi-Religious World.*

freedom, and peace. Our calling is to point all to Jesus, rather than to ourselves or our institutions, looking out for the interests of others rather than our own (see Phil. 2:3-4). We cannot capture the complexities of the scriptures through one dominant cultural perspective. A plurality of cultures is a gift of the Spirit to deepen our understanding of our faith and one another. As such, intercultural communities of faith, where diverse cultural communities worship together, is one way in which cultures can engage one another authentically and where culture can enrich gospel. At the same time, the gospel critiques notions of cultural superiority. Therefore, 'the gospel, to be fruitful, needs to be both true to itself and incarnated or rooted in the culture of a people … We need constantly to seek the insight of the Holy Spirit in helping us to better discern where the gospel challenges, endorses or transforms a particular culture'[28] for the sake of life.

## Feast of Life: Concluding Affirmations

101. We are the servants of the Triune God, who has given us the mission of proclaiming the good news to all humanity and creation, especially the oppressed and the suffering people who are longing for fullness of life. Mission – as a common witness to Christ – is an invitation to the 'feast in the kingdom of God' (Luke 14:15). The mission of the church is to prepare the banquet and to invite all people to the feast of life. The feast is a celebration of creation and fruitfulness overflowing from the love of God, the source of life in abundance. It is a sign of the liberation and reconciliation of the whole creation which is the goal of mission. With a renewed appreciation of the mission of God's Spirit, we offer the following affirmations in response to the question posed at the beginning of this document.

102. *We affirm that the purpose of God's mission is fullness of life (John 10:10) and that this is the criterion for discernment in mission.* Therefore, we are called to discern the Spirit of God wherever there is life in its fullness, particularly in terms of the liberation of the oppressed peoples, the healing and reconciliation of broken communities, and the restoration of the whole creation. We are challenged to appreciate the life-affirming spirits present in different cultures and to be in solidarity with all those who are involved in the mission of affirming and preserving life. We also discern and confront evil spirits wherever forces of death and negation of life are experienced.

103. *We affirm that mission begins with God's act of creation and continues in re-creation, by the enlivening power of the Holy Spirit.* The Holy Spirit, poured out in tongues of fire at Pentecost, fills our hearts and makes us into Christ's church. The Spirit which was in Christ Jesus inspires us to a self-emptying and cross-bearing life-style and accompanies God's people as we seek to bear witness to the love of God in word and deed. The Spirit of truth

---

[28] *Called to One Hope*, 21-22; 24.

leads into all truth and empowers us to defy the demonic powers and speak the truth in love. As a redeemed community we share with others the waters of life and look for the Spirit of unity to heal, reconcile, and renew the whole creation.

104. *We affirm that spirituality is the source of energy for mission and that mission in the Spirit is transformative.* Thus we seek a re-orienting of our perspective between mission, spirituality, and creation. Mission spirituality that flows from liturgy and worship reconnects us with one another and with the wider creation. We understand that our participation in mission, our existence in creation, and our practice of the life of the Spirit, are woven together, for they are mutually transformative. Mission that begins with creation invites us to celebrate life in all its dimensions as God's gift.

105. *We affirm that the mission of God's Spirit is to renew the whole creation.* 'The earth is the Lord's and everything in it' (Ps. 24:1, NIV). The God of life protects, loves, and cares for nature. Humanity is not the master of the earth but is responsible to care for the integrity of creation. Excessive greed and unlimited consumption which lead to continuous destruction of nature must end. God's love does not proclaim a human salvation separate from the renewal of the whole creation. We are called to participate in God's mission beyond our human-centred goals. God's mission is to all life and we have to both acknowledge it and serve it in new ways of mission. We pray for repentance and forgiveness, but we also call for action now. Mission has creation at its heart.

106. *We affirm that today mission movements are emerging from the global South and East which are multi-directional and many-faceted.* The shifting centre of gravity of Christianity to the global South and East challenges us to explore missiological expressions that are rooted in these contexts, culture, and spiritualities. We need to develop further mutuality and partnership, and affirm interdependence within mission and the ecumenical movement. Our mission practice should show solidarity with suffering peoples and harmony with nature. Evangelism is done in self-emptying humility, with respect towards others and in dialogue with people of different cultures and faiths. It should, in this landscape, also involve confronting structures and cultures of oppression and dehumanization that are in contradiction to the values of God's reign.

107. *We affirm that marginalized people are agents of mission and exercise a prophetic role which emphasizes that fullness of life is for all.* The marginalized in society are the main partners in God's mission. Marginalized, oppressed, and suffering people have a special gift to distinguish what news is good for them and what news is bad for their endangered life. In order to commit ourselves to God's life-giving mission, we have to listen to the voices from the margins to hear what is life-affirming and what is life-destroying. We must turn our direction of mission to the actions that the marginalized are taking. Justice, solidarity, and inclusivity are key expressions of mission from the margins.

108. *We affirm that the economy of God is based on values of love and justice for all and that transformative mission resists idolatry in the free-market economy.* Economic globalization has effectively supplanted the God of Life with mammon, the god of free-market capitalism that claims the power to save the world through the accumulation of undue wealth and prosperity. Mission in this context needs to be counter-cultural, offering alternatives to such idolatrous visions because mission belongs to the God of Life, justice, and peace, and not to this false god who brings misery and suffering to people and nature. Mission, then, is to denounce the economy of greed and to participate in and practice the divine economy of love, sharing, and justice.

109. *We affirm that the gospel of Jesus Christ is good news in all ages and places and should be proclaimed in the Spirit of love and humility.* We affirm the centrality of the incarnation, the cross, and the resurrection in our message and also in the way we do evangelism. Therefore, evangelism always points to Jesus and the kingdom of God rather than to institutions, and it belongs to the very being of the church. The prophetic voice of the church should not be silent in times that demand this voice be heard. The church is called to renew its methods of evangelism to communicate the good news with persuasion, inspiration, and conviction.

110. *We affirm that dialogue and co-operation for life are integral to mission and evangelism.* Authentic evangelism is done with respect for freedom of religion and belief, for all human beings as images of God. Proselytism by violent means, economic incentive, or abuse of power is contrary to the message of the gospel. In doing evangelism it is important to build relations of respect and trust between people of different faiths. We value each and every human culture, and recognize that the gospel is not possessed by any group but is for every people. We understand that our task is not to bring God along but to witness to the God who is already there (Acts 17:23-28). Joining in with the Spirit, we are enabled to cross cultural and religious barriers to work together towards life.

111. *We affirm that God moves and empowers the church in mission.* The church as the people of God, the body of Christ, and the temple of the Holy Spirit, is dynamic and changing as it continues the mission of God. This leads to a variety of forms of common witness, reflecting the diversity of world Christianity. Thus the churches need to be on the move, journeying together in mission, continuing in the mission of the apostles. Practically, this means that church and mission should be united and that different ecclesial and missional bodies need to work together for the sake of life.

112. The Triune God invites the whole creation to the Feast of Life, through Jesus Christ who came 'that they may have life, and may have it in all its fullness' (John 10:10, REB), through the Holy Spirit who affirms the vision of the reign of God, 'Behold, I create new heavens and a new earth!' (Isa. 65:17, KJV). We commit ourselves together in humility and hope to the mission of God, who recreates all and reconciles all. And we pray, 'God of Life, lead us into justice and peace!'

# RESPONDING TO THE CHANGED LANDSCAPE OF THE 21ST CENTURY: THE PROCESS AND CONTENT OF *TOGETHER TOWARDS LIFE*

Kirsteen Kim

*Together towards Life: Mission and Evangelism in Changing Landscapes* (*TTL*) is only the second World Council of Churches (WCC) policy statement on mission and evangelism. The first, *Mission and Evangelism: An Ecumenical Affirmation* (*EA*) was ratified by the WCC Central Committee in 1982 after several attempts to produce an acceptable text.[1] *EA* was the WCC response to two important documents of the previous decade: the *Lausanne Covenant* (*LC*) produced at the International Congress on World Evangelization in 1974 and the apostolic exhortation of Pope Paul VI, *Evangelii Nuntiandi,* in 1975. Within the WCC, it interpreted the lively debate on mission and evangelism at the General Assembly in Nairobi in 1975, and it was very much influenced by the World Mission Conference organised by CWME in Melbourne, Australia, in 1980.[2] The influence of Latin American Liberation Theology, which was at its height at the time, is evident in the text, which was commended for its 'holistic, encompassing approach to mission, highlighting both the call to a clear witness to Jesus Christ and the promised Kingdom of God, as well as the mandate to live in solidarity with those exploited and rejected by social and economic systems'.[3]

By the beginning of the 21st century, the need for a new WCC policy statement on mission and evangelism was urgent because of the 'changing landscapes'[4] in which mission was happening. The Commission on World

---

[1] WCC, *Mission and Evangelism: An Ecumenical Affirmation*, in Jacques Matthey (ed), *'You are the Light of the World': Statements on Mission by the World Council of Churches 1980-2005* (Geneva: WCC, 2005), 4-38.

[2] Jacques Matthey, 'Mission and Evangelism: An Ecumenical Affirmation: Presentation', in Matthey, *'You are the Light of the World'*, 1-3; Lausanne Committee for World Evangelization, *The Lausanne Covenant* (1974), available at: www.lausanne.org; Paul VI, *Evangelii Nuntiandi*: Apostolic exhortation on Evangelism Today, available at: www.vatican.va; David M. Paton (ed), *Breaking Barriers*. The Official Report of the Fifth Assembly of the World Council of Churches, Nairobi, 1975 (Geneva: WCC, 1976); WCC, *Your Kingdom Come: Mission Perspectives*. Report on the World Conference on Mission and Evangelism, Melbourne, Australia, 12th to 25th May 1980 (Geneva: WCC, 1980).

[3] Matthey, 'Mission and Evangelism', 3.

[4] *TTL* subtitle.

Mission and Evangelism (CWME), reconstituted after the Assembly in Porto Alegre, Brazil, in 2006, began work on a new statement by identifying four contemporary challenges for mission: pneumatology and spirituality, the market economy and marginalisation, church and mission, and evangelism. Working groups formed in 2008 for each of these produced the four main parts of the new statement: Spirit of mission, Spirit of liberation, Spirit of community, and Spirit of Pentecost. In this chapter, following this outline, I shall consider how, in the process of writing *TTL*, CWME embraced changes in the theological landscape and applied these new insights to the interrelated socio-economic, ecclesial and religious contexts in which mission and evangelism are carried out. I shall conclude with a brief consideration of the significance of *TTL*.

## Theological Landscape: Breath of Life

Comparing *TTL* with the earlier mission statement, *EA*, the most obvious shifts are in the theological themes which run through the documents: from reference to Christology and the Kingdom (or reign) of God to attention to the Holy Spirit and life. *EA* highlighted 'mission in Christ's way' (§§28-30), following the 'servant king' (§§6-8). It saw the church primarily as the body of Christ, which continues Christ's sacrificial ministry of mediating between God and his creation through its proclamation and witness (§§6, 8, 20, 47). By framing the second WCC statement on mission and evangelism pneumatologically, CWME signalled that *TTL* was intended to complement *EA* rather than replace it. At the same time, the pneumatological approach is a sign of continuity since it is construed in *TTL* as within the *missio Dei* theology (*TTL* §§1-2), which had shaped ecumenical mission theology in a Trinitarian way since the meeting of the International Missionary Council in Willingen, Germany, in 1952.[5] The understanding of mission as participating in the sending of the Triune God was strengthened during the 1970s by Orthodox theologians, especially through their spokesperson Ion Bria,[6] and used in the 1982 statement to emphasise particularly the link between mission and unity (see especially *EA* §§1, 3, 5, 20-21). Bria drew particular attention to the role of the Holy Spirit as the foundation of mission: 'The "sending" of mission is essentially the sending of the Spirit (John 14.26), who manifests precisely the life of God as communion' (1 Cor. 13.13).[7] *TTL* continues this focus in its first main section and in its framing.

---

[5] IMC, 'The Missionary Calling of the Church', in 'Quarterly Notes, No. 16, October 1952', in *International Review of Mission,* 41.4 (Oct 1952), i-xii, at ii-iii.

[6] See, for example, Ion Bria, 'Confessing Christ Today', in *International Review of Mission,* 64.253 (Jan 1975), 67-74; 'The Liturgy After the Liturgy', in *International Review of Mission,* 67.265 (Jan 1978), 86-90; 'On Orthodox Witness', in *International Review of Mission,* 69.276-77 (Oct 1979-Jan 1980), 527-28.

[7] Bria, *Go Forth in Peace*, 3.

In its interpretation of 'mission in Christ's way, *EA* focused on the Synoptic Jesus who preached the Kingdom of God (Preface, 5, 6, 14, 20). In the post-colonial context in which *EA* was produced, 'kingdom' was reinterpreted as 'reign' rather than expanding territory[8] and, moving beyond the duality of 'evangelism' and 'social action' (*LC* §4 and §5), *EA* emphasised that God's reign encompassed both personal conversion (*EA* §§10-13) and social justice (§§31-36). In Matthew and Mark, Jesus repeatedly speaks of 'the kingdom', while 'Spirit' as a reference to God is rare, but Luke's gospel has a more developed pneumatology and in Luke's sequel to his gospel, the book of Acts, the Spirit takes centre stage as 'the guiding and driving force of mission'.[9] In John's gospel, 'kingdom' occurs in only three verses, whereas 'Spirit' or 'Paraclete' are frequently used. Furthermore, in the Pauline corpus the word 'Spirit' occurs over ten times more often than 'kingdom'.[10] The terms 'kingdom' and 'Spirit' occur in parallel in several New Testament verses (Matt. 12.28; John 3.5; Luke 4.18-19); these represent a general pattern in which both 'Spirit' and 'kingdom' function to describe God's work in history.[11] For example, the restoration of the kingdom for which the disciples were looking (Acts 1.6) is answered by the promise of the Holy Spirit, 'power from on high' (1.8; Luke 24.49). The two terms hang together in a Trinitarian doctrine of the kingdom: 'The Spirit is the one who makes the kingdom of God, the kingdom of love and justice, real in Jesus' life, and in the life of his followers. The Spirit is the Spirit of this kingdom (John 3:3-5).'[12] Since 'kingdom' and 'Spirit' are in many respects parallel terms in Scripture, the choice of one over the other is a contextual one.[13] In CWME, the shift from an almost exclusively Christocentric view of mission to embrace a more pneumatological one was already apparent in a text from 2000: 'Mission and Evangelism in Unity Today' (MEUT).[14]

---

[8] Following the post-World War II New Testament scholarship of Ernst Käsemann, who spoke at the Melbourne conference in 1980, Krister Stendahl, who led the Bible studies at Melbourne, Oscar Cullmann, who was the doctoral supervisor of David Bosch, and others.

[9] David J. Bosch, *Transforming Mission: Paradigm Shifts in Theology of Mission* (Maryknoll, NY: Orbis Books, 1991), 113.

[10] Timothy Gorringe, *Redeeming Time: Atonement through Education* (London: Darton, Longman & Todd, 1986), 89.

[11] Gorringe, *Redeeming Time*, 71.

[12] Mike Higton, *Christian Doctrine* (London: SCM, 2008), 80, commenting on Jürgen Moltmann, *The Trinity and the Kingdom of God: The Doctrine of God* (London: SCM, 1981).

[13] See also Kirsteen Kim, 'Edinburgh 1910 to 2010: From Kingdom to Spirit', in *Journal of the European Pentecostal Theological Association,* 30.2 (2010), 3-20.

[14] CWME, 'Mission and Evangelism in Unity Today', in Matthey, *'You are the Light of the World'*, 62-89. See also Jacques Matthey, 'Mission and Evangelism in Unity Today: Presentation', in Matthey, *'You are the Light of the World'*, 59-61.

The sending of the Spirit in mission to which Orthodox theologians drew attention was not first at Pentecost but in the very act of creation. The creative work of God led to the conception of Jesus Christ and the gathering of the church as eschatological gathering (*synaxis*). Continued Orthodox insistence on the need for proper attention to pneumatology in ecumenical theology led the first WCC General Assembly to have a pneumatological theme: the seventh Assembly held at Canberra, Australia, in 1991, which discussed, 'Come, Holy Spirit, renew the whole creation'.[15] The papers in preparation for the Assembly, other presentations there and the responses afterwards, revealed the potential of pneumatology for a holistic, environmentally concerned and inclusive theology of mission.[16] However, in the event, the approach was divisive because the treatment of the Holy Spirit in relation to creation and to other spirits and powers was insufficiently rigorous, and this led to accusations of syncretism from both Orthodox and Evangelical participants.[17] Fourteen years after the Canberra Assembly, the conference on mission and evangelism organised by CWME in Athens in 2005 at the invitation of the Greek Orthodox Church dared to revive the topic of pneumatology in the WCC. This time it was approached with caution and under the irenic theme, 'Come, Holy Spirit, heal and

---

[15] Michael Kinnamon (ed), *Signs of the Spirit*: Official Report of the Seventh Assembly of the World Council of Churches, Canberra, 1991 (Geneva: WCC, 1991). A pneumatological approach to mission is found in previous WCC general assemblies. At the New Delhi Assembly in 1961, the power of the Holy Spirit to bring about God's purposes in the whole creation was frequently mentioned, although the theology of the 'cosmic Christ' prevailed. See, John Nagpur, 'New Delhi 1961: The Third Assembly of the World Council of Churches', in *International Review of Mission,* 51/202 (Apr 1962), 137-52. At the Uppsala Assembly of 1968, there was an emphasis on the freedom of the Spirit, while the Spirit's life-giving work made possible theologically the Assembly's affirmation of humanisation and development as a legitimate part of the church's task: WCC, *The Uppsala Report 1968: Official Report of the Fourth Assembly of the World Council of Churches* (Geneva: WCC, 1968). The pneumatological reasoning for a broad understanding of Christian mission was very clearly expressed at Uppsala by John V. Taylor, a prominent theologian, in his subsequent book about the Holy Spirit and mission, *The Go-between God* (London: SCM, 1972).

[16] A good selection of these can be found in *Ecumenical Review,* 41.3 (1989) and in *International Review of Mission,* 80.319-20 (1991). The Assembly provided rich resources of creation pneumatology for the development of theologies of eco-justice through the JPIC (Justice, Peace and the Integrity of Creation) programme: see David G. Hallman (ed), *Ecotheology: Voices from South and North* (Geneva: WCC, 1994).

[17] For analysis of the pneumatological issues raised at Canberra, see Kirsteen Kim, *The Holy Spirit in the World: A Global Conversation* (Maryknoll, NY: Orbis Books, 2007); Kirsteen Kim, 'Spirit and "Spirits" at the Canberra Assembly of the World Council of Churches, 1991', in *Missiology: An International Review,* 32.3 (2004), 349-65.

reconcile'.[18] One of the documents prepared by CWME for Athens, 'Mission as Ministry of Reconciliation', drew attention to the Holy Spirit as the agent of reconciliation,[19] a theme which runs throughout the new statement. In *TTL* the Spirit's ministry of reconciliation is most often connected with creation. *TTL* calls for 'mission with creation at its heart' (§20), which moves 'beyond a narrowly human-centred approach and to embrace forms of mission which express our reconciled relationship with all created life' (§19).

In *TTL*, there is an integral relationship between personal encounter with Jesus Christ in the Spirit and participation in the church's mission. In the 1980s, Latin American liberation theologians, belatedly, connected the declaration of Jesus that 'the Spirit of the Lord is upon me' with the liberation he proclaimed (Luke 4.18) and developed a spirituality of liberation.[20] *TTL* takes this mission spirituality further and connects it with the liberation and reconciliation of the whole creation (§21). 'Spirituality' is often used for a kind of religion that is not expressed in worldly activity, but in worship, meditation and often introspection. 'Mission', on the other hand, is associated with activism, with goals and strategy, so 'mission spirituality' sounds like a contradiction in terms[21] and mission studies does not often overlap with spiritual theology.[22] However, the potential of the *missio Dei* paradigm understood pneumatologically for the development of mission spirituality had been revealed at the Canberra Assembly through the dialogue with spiritualities of indigenous peoples, reflection on women's spirituality, and the ecological agenda. In its development of 'transformative spirituality' (§3, 29-35), *TTL* shows that mission is a spiritual endeavour and spiritual life is missional since both are human

---

[18] For documentation of the Athens conference, see Jacques Matthey (ed), *Come, Holy Spirit, Heal and Reconcile. Report of the World Council of Churches Conference on Mission and Evangelism, Athens, May 2005* (Geneva: WCC, 2008). For background, see Kim, *The Holy Spirit in the World.*

[19] CWME, 'Mission as Ministry of Reconciliation', in Matthey, *Come, Holy Spirit, Heal and Reconcile*, 92-126.

[20] Gustavo Gutiérrez, *We Drink from Our Own Wells: The Spiritual Journey of a People* (Maryknoll, NY: Orbis Books, and Melbourne, Vic: Dove Communications, 1984), 138, n.1; Gustavo Gutiérrez, 'Theology as Wisdom', in T.K. John (ed), *Bread and Breath: Essays in Honour of Samuel Rayan SJ* (Anand, Gujarat: Gujarat Sahitya Prakash, 1990), 3-5, at 4.

[21] Robert Schreiter, 'The Theology of Reconciliation and Peacemaking for Mission', in Howard Mellor and Timothy Yates (eds), *Mission, Violence and Reconciliation* (Sheffield, UK: Cliff College Publishing, 2004), 11-28.

[22] A point addressed by Robert Davies Hughes, III, *Beloved Dust: Tides of the Spirit in the Christian Life* (New York: Continuum, 2008).

responses to impulses produced by the mission of the Spirit in the whole creation. Mission spirituality is mission 'in the Spirit'.[23]

As well as reflecting Protestant-Orthodox dialogue within the WCC, the Athens conference also reached out to Pentecostal churches and charismatic movements. Their growth, and the emergence in the intervening period of Pentecostal and charismatic theology,[24] meant that pneumatology, spirituality, and even discussion of spirits, had become more common across traditions and around the world – and this helped the discussion at Athens to avoid accusations of syncretism. Another preparatory document by CWME, 'The Healing Mission of the Church', related healing to the work of the Spirit, concepts of spiritual powers and gifts of healing.[25] This is reflected in the section in *TTL* on mission as healing and wholeness (§50-54). Furthermore, the Commission's committed involvement in the Edinburgh 2010 (centenary) project confirmed that a pneumatological approach would have an appeal beyond WCC member-churches to reach all strands of Christianity.[26] In many ways, the climate was right to approach time-worn topics from a fresh, pneumatological perspective, which seemed to capture the moment and reached across the churches from Orthodox to Pentecostal, from Catholic to Quaker. *TTL* incorporates references to spiritual gifts and discernment of spirits encouraged by spiritual renewal movements (§24-25). In fact, it revisions Christian mission as beginning with the spiritual activity of discerning the spirits in order to discover the movement of the Spirit of God in the world and join with it (§18, 25, 110).

If mission is 'finding out where the Holy Spirit is at work and joining in',[27] then learning to recognise the presence and work of the Spirit is crucially important. The Holy Spirit's life-giving nature is the most prominent feature of *TTL*, which takes its cue from John 10.10b: 'I came that they may have life, and have it abundantly' (§1, 102, 112). Although there was a strategic aim in choosing 'life' as the theme of the new mission

---

[23] Jürgen Moltmann, *The Church in the Power of the Spirit* (London: SCM, 1977); Kirsteen Kim, *Mission in the Spirit: The Holy Spirit in Indian Christian Theologies* (Delhi: ISPCK, 2003).

[24] For example, Pentecostal theology of mission was brought together in Harold D. Hunter and Peter D. Hocken (eds), *All Together in One Place: Theological Papers from the Brighton Conference on World Evangelization* (Sheffield, UK: Sheffield Academic Press, 1993).

[25] CWME, 'The Healing Mission of the Church', in Matthey, *Come, Holy Spirit, Heal and Reconcile*, 129-62.

[26] See the 'Common Call' of Edinburgh 2010 which can be downloaded from the project website: www.edinburgh2010.org. Catholic, Orthodox, Protestant (ecumenical and evangelical), Pentecostal and indigenous churches were full members of this project. See also the Regnum Edinburgh Centenary Series published by Regnum Books, Oxford: www.ocms.ac.uk/regnum/edinburgh.

[27] Kirsteen Kim, *Joining in with the Spirit: Connecting World Church and Local Mission* (London: SCM, 2012).

statement because it would allow for a direct contribution to the theme of the WCC's thirteenth assembly, which was decided in 2011 to be 'God of life, lead us to justice and peace', the decision was entirely consistent with the established approach of CWME, as shown in the earlier document, MEUT. The great ecumenical creed of Nicaea-Constantinople defines the Holy Spirit as 'the Giver of Life' (*TTL* §1). The structure of the Nicene Creed makes it clear that we cannot reduce the life of the Spirit to some kind of 'purely spiritual' or church life that is separated from biological and natural life. The Spirit is the life-giver because the Spirit is co-creator with the Father and the Son. In *TTL*, the life of the church is set within the Triune God's creative activity to bring life to the world. In the preparation of the text, and at the pre-Assembly conference in Manila in 2012, at which delegates helped to hone the text, CWME spent some time reflecting on how the Spirit is related scripturally to each of the elements of creation: wind, water, fire and earth itself.

Because it takes life as the key marker of the Christian spirit, *TTL* expresses openness to engagement with all agencies that are life-affirming, such as liberation and development initiatives of various sorts, whether they are faith-based or not, while resisting the forces of death (§1, 3-4, 27, 49, 90, 93-4, 102, 106-7). This gives grounds for co-operation and alliances in mission with communities of other faiths and with secular bodies. Because Christians are committed to Jesus Christ, the life of the world, they have a particular understanding of what constitutes abundant life to share with the rest of humanity (*TTL* §1).

Having embraced a mission pneumatology, CWME working groups applied this to the most significant aspects of the changed landscape since 1982.

## Socio-economic Landscape: Mission from the Margins

Changes in the theological landscape were not isolated from the significant socio-economic changes that took place in the thirty years between 1982 when *EA* was published and 2012 when *TTL* was finalised. The ending of the Cold War after the collapse of the USSR and the Eastern Bloc in the late 1980s ushered in a new world order. Many of the changes brought socio-economic and political benefits as the dictatorships of the right as well as the left from which *EA* called for liberation collapsed, and new democracies emerged in Latin America, Europe, Asia and Africa. However, struggles for identity and self-determination led to new outbreaks of conflict often within nations. It was in large part as a response to this global context, and in the middle of the WCC Decade to Overcome Violence,[28] that the Athens conference expressed a new understanding of mission as reconciliation. The conference showed that 'mission does not belong to us,

[28] Details available at: www.overcomingviolence.org.

but is the mission of God, who is present and active as Holy Spirit in church and world… to heal, reconcile and empower us so that, as individuals and communities, we may become and share signs of peace, forgiveness, justice and unity, and renounce hatred, violence, injustice and divisions'.[29] *TTL* builds on this theology of reconciliation and takes a step beyond *EA*'s call for liberation when it repeatedly links the two themes together (*TTL* §§24, 43, 101). Recognising the danger that action for liberation could degenerate into activism or even violence,[30] *TTL* insists that Christian efforts at social liberation must also look beyond the achievement of justice towards a reconciled society. Having a vision for future reconciliation with our enemies, the struggle must be waged in a way that does not breed future resentment but bears witness to the rightness of our cause through extending Christian love (Matt. 5.43-48).[31]

The post-Cold War era is often characterised as the era of globalisation. Globalisation may be thought of benignly as 'a process… which embodies a transformation in the spatial configurations of social relations and transactions… generating transcontinental or inter-regional flows'.[32] In this sense, it has been going on for many centuries, and Christian mission may be regarded as a globalising movement.[33] The changes brought about are varied, not uniform, and some are excluded, or exclude themselves, from aspects of globalisation, but no-one on the planet is unaffected by it.[34] Although they do not necessarily originate with the most powerful, in the era since 1945, global developments have tended to be driven by the USA. Whereas the globalisation brought about by the British Empire was expressed mainly in terms of territorial expansion, the USA holds power through non-governmental organisations, international corporations and local elites which carry its cultural influence around the globe. In both

---

[29] Conference website: www.mission2005.org.

[30] Jacques Matthey, 'Reconciliation, *Missio Dei* and the Church's Mission', in Mellor and Yates, *Mission, Violence and Reconciliation*, 113-37.

[31] Donal Dorr, *Mission in Today's World* (Blackrock, Dublin: Columba Press, 2000), 128; cf. Miroslav Volf, *Exclusion and Embrace: A Theological Exploration of Identity, Otherness and Reconciliation* (Nashville, TN: Abingdon Press, 1996), 105.

[32] David Held, Anthony McGrew, David Goldblatt and Jonathan Perraton, *Global Transformations: Politics, Economics and Culture* (Stanford, CA: Stanford University Press, 1999), 16.

[33] See, for example, Dana L. Robert, *Christian Mission: How Christianity Became a World Religion* (Oxford: Wiley-Blackwell, 2009); Sebastian C.H. Kim and Kirsteen Kim, *Christianity as a World Religion* (London: Bloomsbury, 2013).

[34] Anthony Giddens, *Runaway World: How Globalization is Reshaping Our Lives,* 2nd edition (London: Profile Books, 2002), 6-19.

cases, military might and control of the global economy undergird global power but today's imperialism is disguised as 'soft power'.[35]

If the global context for mission is thought of as 'empire', then raising the profile of the alternative kingdom of Christ, king of kings, was perhaps the most intelligible way of conveying the power of the gospel, as indeed was done at the World Missionary Conference in Edinburgh in 1910.[36] But in many respects, pneumatology – the language of Spirit, spirit(s) and spirituality – resonates with a form of globalisation that relies less on territorial expansion and more on hegemony by means of global flows, communications and cultural influences. The organic metaphors are also in keeping with the theology of the Spirit who moves in and over the creation. Furthermore, given that the movement of the Spirit is unpredictable (John 3.8), pneumatology allows for multi-directional movements in a way that the top-down analogy of kingship does not. As with the use of the 'kingdom' analogy, use of 'Spirit' may support as well as subvert the world order.[37] Nevertheless, in *TTL*, the Spirit is aligned with life-affirming forces (§2) as the Spirit of liberation and empowerment who overcomes the powers of evil and brings fullness of life for all (§36-37). The theology of the Holy Spirit that informs *TTL* is one that is subversive of human power structures, mindful that the Spirit speaks from the margins and empowers the prophets.

The issue of mission and power was a lively topic in the Edinburgh 2010 project[38] and CWME continued this interest in *TTL*. It did so, both in view of the abuse of power in Christian mission in the colonial period (§27, 98) and today, for example in some forms of prosperity theology, the lack of accountability of some 'para-church' agencies (§64), and also due to the unequal power relations of globalisation. Since globalisation affects people differently depending on their situation, it was a deliberate decision on the part of CWME not to try and describe the contemporary landscape in detail.[39] However, in solidarity with Christian sisters and brothers who are less able to articulate their views internationally, and in the tradition of the prophets, *TTL* draws particular attention to devastating socio-economic and ecological effects produced by the triumph of the 'market ideology' (§7, 31). Some enthusiasts for contemporary globalisation argued that a self-

---

35 Joseph S. Nye Jr, *The Paradox of American Power: Why the World's Only Superpower Can't Go it Alone* (Oxford: OUP, 2002); Niall Ferguson, *Colossus: The Rise and Fall of the American Empire* (London: Penguin, 2004), 1-29.

36 Brian Stanley, *The World Missionary Conference, Edinburgh 1910* (Grand Rapids, MI: Eerdmans, 2009), title of chapter 1.

37 Kim, 'Edinburgh 1910 to 2010'.

38 'Theme Four: Mission and Power', in Daryl Balia and Kirsteen Kim (eds), *Edinburgh 2010: Witnessing to Christ Today* (Oxford: Regnum, 2010), 86-115; Atola Longkumer, Jorgen Skov Sorenson and Michael Biehl, *Mission and Power* (Oxford: Regnum, 2016).

39 A more detailed analysis of the effects of globalisation is found in MEUT, 18-30.

regulating and universal economic system would facilitate liberal democratic political systems and therefore more just societies.[40] However, through the AGAPE process, the WCC heard otherwise and sought an alternative globalisation which would eradicate poverty, challenge wealth accumulation and safeguard ecological integrity.[41]

The response of *TTL* to the socio-economic landscape was expressed especially in the second theme of 'mission from the margins'. It drew on the understanding that poverty, wealth and ecology are integrally related and was informed by several initiatives: *Oikotree*, which submitted a paper to CWME in 2011 entitled 'Mission in the Context of Empire: Putting Justice at the Heart of Faith';[42] the work of the WCC's 'Just and Inclusive Communities' programme;[43] and Dalit experience in India, which stressed the agency of the marginalised.[44] 'Mission from the margins' was a development of the concern for the poor expressed in *EA* to include all categories of marginalisation. Whereas *EA* advocated mission *to* the poor and *with* the poor (§§32-36), *TTL* challenges 'the perception that mission can only be done by the powerful to the powerless' and, asserting that 'People on the margins have agency, and can often see what, from the centre, is out of view' (§38), recognises mission *from* the margins that 'works for a world where the fullness of life is available for all' (§37).

### Ecclesial Landscape: Church on the Move

Especially in its treatment of the option for the poor, *EA* continued the model of mission as done by 'the West to the rest', whereas *TTL* responds to the 'shift of the centre of gravity' of Christianity from the North and West to the global South and East, to which Andrew Walls first drew attention from the 1970s.[45] For demographic reasons alone, developments

---

[40] E.g. Francis Fukuyama, *The End of History and the Last Man* (New York: Free Press, 1992).

[41] WCC, 'Economy of Life, Justice, and Peace for All: A Call to Action' (19th July 2012): www.oikoumene.org (accessed 10th July 2015).

[42] *Oikotree* is an ecumenical space open to people of all faiths who share a concern for justice and the healing of the nations, and is sponsored by the Council for World Mission (CWM), the World Communion of Reformed Churches (WCRC) and the WCC: *Oikotree* 'About Us': www.oikotree.org (accessed 10th July 2015).

[43] Just and Inclusive Communities brings together WCC work on racism, migration, indigenous peoples, Dalits and people with disabilities: www.oikoumene.org/en/what-we-do/just-and-inclusive-communities (accessed 16th July 2015).

[44] See Peniel Rajkumar, Joseph Dayam and I.P. Asheervadham (eds), *Mission at and from the Margins: Patterns, Protagonists and Perspectives*, Regnum Edinburgh Centenary Series (Oxford: Regnum, 2014).

[45] Andrew F. Walls, *The Missionary Movement in Christian History: Studies in the Transmission of Faith* (Maryknoll, NY: Orbis Books, 1996); Andrew F. Walls, *The Cross-cultural Process in Christian History: Studies in the Transmission and Appropriation of Faith* (Maryknoll, NY: Orbis Books, 2002).

outside the West will increasingly define the future of Christianity and of mission.[46] Walls' work has also given rise to the paradigm of world Christianity, which has many facets in addition to the statistical. For example, it treats Christianity as a world religion; it draws attention to new movements arising outside the West; and it is a way of de-centring Europe, which has been overly dominant in the study of theology and church history.[47] The Edinburgh project was organised to highlight world Christianity, and *TTL* uses it as one of its main frameworks for analysis (§5).

Awareness of world Christianity transformed the view of the ecclesial landscape. A diversity of new and independent Christian movements has become apparent in the last few decades. The growth of new movements means that increasing numbers of Christians belong to churches which are local or independent and do not relate to any of the global confessional families with their origins in Europe. 'Independency' is the predominant form of Christianity in Africa and Asia.[48] Even where a church belongs in name to a particular global denomination, its practice and identity in a new context may diverge so significantly from others of the same denomination that the family resemblance breaks down.[49]

One of the main stimuli for new movements has been the growth, especially since the liberalisation of many economies worldwide, of Pentecostal or Spirit-type churches, which are in keeping with post- or late-modern capitalist societies in that they tend to preach a form of prosperity gospel and see themselves as transnational.[50] However, serious study of, and engagement with, Pentecostalism, New Religious Movements and indigenous spiritualities has given legitimacy to many of these as expressions of faith parallel in many ways with New Testament churches.[51]

---

[46] Philip Jenkins, *The Next Christendom: The Coming of Global Christianity* (Oxford: OUP, 2002).

[47] William B. Burrows, Mark R. Gornik and Janice A. McLean (eds), *Understanding World Christianity: The Vision and Work of Andrew F. Walls* (Maryknoll, NY: Orbis Books, 2011).

[48] Todd M. Johnson and Kenneth R. Ross (eds), *Atlas of Global Christianity, 1910-2010* (Edinburgh: Edinburgh University Press, 2009), 70-71.

[49] There is likely to be further weakening in the confessional families related to churches of European origin because many nations with large Protestant populations, such as South Korea, Brazil, Nigeria and China, are rising on the global economic and political stage and developing their own mission movements, while the European churches decline relatively in wealth, and the ties provided by development activities grow less significant. Kim and Kim, *Christianity as a World Religion*, 227-28.

[50] Harvey Cox, *Fire from Heaven: The Rise of Pentecostal Spirituality and the Reshaping of Religion in the Twenty-first Century* (New York: Cassell, 1996); David Martin, *Pentecostalism: The World Their Parish* (Oxford: Blackwell, 2002).

[51] Among the pioneers of this scholarship were Walter Hollenweger, *The Pentecostals* (London: SCM, 1969; ET 1972) and Andrew F. Walls (see above).

The WCC was slow to adjust to this new landscape of Christianity. New movements, particularly those initiated in Africa, were initially dismissed by western churches as hopelessly syncretistic because of their affinity with indigenous religions which were regarded as superstitions.[52] Pentecostal and other new movements were experienced by older churches as a threat rather than as examples of the boundary-breaking nature of the Spirit's work. Such churches were not mentioned in *EA*. *TTL*, however, continuing CWME's inclusive work, recognises Evangelical, Pentecostal, and indigenous churches (§65). In a world of many churches, *TTL* condemns inter-church competition (§62) and calls for the unity in the midst of diversity. However, this unity is not western-led uniformity but inclusivity and mutuality (§59, §66), common witness (§63) and collaboration in mission (§60-61, 64).

*TTL* urges this togetherness on the theological basis of the 'rediscovery of the work of the Holy Spirit in healing and reconciliation' (§68). It also points out that true unity and peace are never at the expense of justice and therefore 'unity in mission is the basis for the visible unity of the churches' (§69). From the outset of its third main section, *TTL* sets the church and its unity in the context of the mission of the Triune God both in its origin and in its destiny (§§55-58). During collaboration with CWME between the ninth (Porto Alegre) and tenth (Busan) Assemblies, the WCC Commission on Faith and Order came to a similar conclusion and produced a significantly reshaped ecclesiological statement.[53] Within this *missio Dei* paradigm, the church is missionary by its very nature and local congregations are centres of mission (§§72-79).

Contemporary global flows also include the movement of people. Migration is a key issue within the debate about poverty, wealth and ecology but it is also an ecclesiological issue as Christians and churches are 'on the move'.[54] So-called 'migrant churches' are a feature of many cities where they challenge received paradigms of church life.[55] The

---

[52] John S. Pobee and Gabriel Ositelu II, *African Initiatives in Christianity: The Growth, Gifts and Diversities of Indigenous African Churches* (Geneva: WCC, 1998), 27.

[53] Compare Commission on Faith and Order, The Nature and Mission of the Church (WCC Faith and Order Paper No. 198 (2005)) with Commission on Faith and Order, *The Church: Toward a Common Vision* (WCC Faith and Order Paper No. 214 (2013)): www.oikoumene.org (accessed 16th July 2015). See also articles in *International Review of Mission,* 99.1 (2010), which records the joint consultation of CWME and the Commission in Faith and Order in Hungary in 2009.

[54] Subtitle of ecclesiology section of *TTL*.

[55] For recent studies of migrant churches, see these examples relating to African churches in Europe: Afe Adogame, *The African Christian Diaspora: New Currents and Emerging Trends in World Christianity* (London: Bloomsbury Academic, 2013); Gerri ter Haar, *Halfway to Paradise: African Christians in Europe* (Cardiff, UK: Cardiff Academic Press, 1998); Claudia Währisch-Oblau, *The Missionary Self-*

commissioners received a paper on the implications of migration from ENFORMM, the Ecumenical Network for Multicultural Ministry.[56] It reflected on how the worldwide spread of Christianity as recorded in the New Testament was due not only to the deliberate sending activity of the church, but also due to migration movements. The Roman Empire, like most empires, dispossessed and displaced individuals and whole communities. Persecutions, like those recorded in Acts 8, 11 and 18, caused Christians to scatter or relocate. As well as such involuntary movement, the Empire also facilitated mobility for some, like Paul himself, his fellow tentmakers Priscilla and Aquila and Lydia, the business woman from Asia Minor (Acts 16). This was facilitated by the already existing Jewish diaspora, which extended from Pontus in the north of Asia Minor south to Egypt, from Rome in the west to Elam, east of Arabia (Acts 2.9-11), as shown in the missionary journeys of the apostle Paul, who in most cities found a Jewish community.[57]

Although missionaries move from one place to another, much mission theology has assumed that churches are geographically static in keeping with the European pattern of settled church life in parishes and national churches. Missionaries 'planted' churches and rarely encouraged them to think of themselves as missionary beyond their own context. Moreover, the *missio Dei* paradigm, in stressing the missionary nature of the local church, has downplayed movement between churches or of churches. Despite this, many of the growing churches in Africa, Asia and Latin America see themselves as sending and mobile. To the discomfort of many western Christians, they refuse to stay where they were planted. *TTL* responds to these challenges by calling for mutual hospitality at the invitation of the Spirit (§70). It also advocates multicultural ministry and globally connected churches (§75, §76). The statement characterises the church as a movement of the Spirit and, thus animated by the Spirit, it is naturally a missionary movement (§57). Because the Spirit is dynamic and powerful, the church lives and acts in the power of the Spirit, and the church moves and changes; it does not, it cannot, stay still.

At the heart of the shift to world Christianity in *TTL* lies a rediscovery of the nature of the church's catholicity, not primarily in terms of differences

---

*perception of Pentecostal/charismatic Church Leaders from the Global South in Europe: Bringing Back the Gospel* (Leiden: Brill, 2009).

[56] ENFORMM, 'Churches in Ecumenical Transition: Towards Multicultural Ministry and Mission' (2011).

[57] For insight into the colonial and diaspora context of early Christian mission, see, *inter alia,* Udo Schnelle, *Apostle Paul: His Life and His Theology*, trans. M.E. Boring (Grand Rapids, MI: Baker Academic, 2005); Alexander J.M. Wedderburn, *A History of the First Christians* (London: T. &T. Clark, 2004); Dale T. Irvin and Scott W. Sunquist, *History of the World Christian Movement*, Vol. I (Maryknoll, NY: Orbis Books, 2001); R. Geoffrey Harris, *Mission in the Gospels* (Peterborough, UK: Epworth, 2004).

in doctrine and polity but as spatial or geographical diversity, which was the primary sense in which the first councils of the church understood it. No longer is the unity envisaged chiefly a denominational one; it is also a cultural and regional one. The ecumenism of the colonial period that gave birth to the WCC tended to assume that overcoming differences between the historic churches of Europe would unite Christians globally. Today, this is no longer the case and new expressions of catholicity are being sought from different regions of the world – for example, through the Global Christian Forum. The new catholicity must also recognise that many of the newer churches are organised differently from the traditional churches of Europe. Many of the newer churches of our age – especially neo-Pentecostal ones – do not understand themselves as national but as international, and they may exist primarily as local congregations. For various reasons, migrant churches may not settle or integrate into the local religious landscape.[58] These are Christians without borders and churches on the move – arguably much like the churches of the book of Acts. In view of the historical diversity of world Christianity and the different contexts in which faith is practised, *TTL* keeps an open mind about models of church polity and affirms Christian diversity, while encouraging a truly global conversation to discern the Holy Spirit (§69, §§72-75).

## Religious Landscape: Good News for All

The final major change in the landscape for mission and evangelism since 1982 to which *TTL* responded was the growth in complexity of societies due to globalisation, particularly in the sense of religious plurality. Especially since 9/11, there has been heightened tension between people of different faiths, and further 'excessive assertion of religious identities and persuasions that seem to break and brutalize in the name of God rather than heal and nurture communities' (§82). In this climate, the word 'witness' – *martyria* in Greek – was taking on the meaning of the English 'martyr' due to the persecution of Christians (§32). Despite this, *TTL* nevertheless follows *EA* in promoting dialogue as the basis for relationships with people of other faiths (§§93-96; *EA* §§43-45). That is 'an honest encounter' in an 'open, patient and respectful manner' (§94). Dialogue in the WCC was grounded theologically in the belief that 'the Spirit of God is constantly at work in ways that pass human understanding and in places that to us are least expected' (§43). It was another way in which pneumatology was being developed in ecumenical discourse in the 1970s and 1980s.[59] *TTL*

[58] For the circumstances of Korean diaspora churches, see Sebastian C.H. Kim and Kirsteen Kim, *A History of Korean Christianity* (Cambridge: CUP, 2014).

[59] See WCC, *Guidelines on Dialogue with People of Living Faiths and Ideologies* (Geneva: WCC, 1979); Stanley Samartha, 'The Holy Spirit and People of Other Faiths', in Emilio Castro (ed.), *To the Wind of God's Spirit: Reflections on the Canberra Theme* (Geneva: WCC, 1990), 50-63.

affirms the presence and working of the Holy Spirit in all faith traditions and spiritualities that bring 'joy and fullness of life' (§93). Reflecting the work of CWME in the 1990s, following the frictions of the Canberra Assembly, *TTL* affirms that the gospel takes root in different cultures (§97) and the result is diverse communities (§§98-100).[60]

Nevertheless, *TTL* is mindful that the most immediate result of the outpouring of the Spirit at Pentecost was the preaching of the gospel and the appeal to repent and believe. As well as dialogue, *EA* also insisted that witness to the message of salvation 'should be rendered to all' (§42), and recognised the tension, later famously articulated at the WCC conference on mission and evangelism at San Antonio, Texas, in 1989: 'We cannot point to any other way of salvation than Jesus Christ; at the same time we cannot set limits to the saving power of God.'[61] *TTL* explains and resolves that tension by focusing on the role of the Holy Spirit in interreligious relations. The Spirit both creates the medium in which the dialogue takes place and is also the power for salvation. At one and the same time, the Spirit emboldens the witness and is the source of the love between neighbours of different faiths. Moreover, 'the Holy Spirit chooses to work in partnership with people's preaching and demonstration of the good news... but it is only God's Spirit who creates new life and brings about rebirth' (§82).

The final main section of *TTL* is the first WCC statement on evangelism. In *EA*, the emphasis in dialogue was on hearing and receiving from others. Although witness was described as 'evangelistic' and *EA* insisted that 'There is no evangelism without solidarity' (§34; cf. *TTL* §89), it contained no sustained treatment of the second part of CWME's brief. *TTL* defines evangelism as a particular form of mission: 'Mission activity which makes explicit and unambiguous the centrality of the incarnation, suffering, and resurrection of Jesus Christ' (§80).[62] It is a particular expression of mission or witness which includes an 'invitation to personal conversion to a new life in Christ' (§85). In addition to drawing attention to the Holy Spirit as the agent of evangelism and conversion (§82), another major contribution of *TTL* is to establish the link of evangelism with prophecy (§§91-92). The Spirit gives the prophetic boldness to speak truth to power. *TTL* combines the prophetic and more religious dimensions of Christian witness in several ways: first, it focuses on the way of Jesus in the gospels rather than on the missionary methods of Paul (§§86-92); second, by advocating a dialogical approach to evangelism that affirms diversity (§§93-100); and third, by returning to a definition of the WCC from 1951, which was later adapted

---

[60] Christopher Duraisingh (ed), *Called to One Hope: The Gospel in Diverse Cultures*, Report of the Conference of the Commission on World Mission and Evangelism, Salvador, Brazil, 1996 (Geneva: WCC, 1998).

[61] WCC, *The San Antonio Report*, F.R. Wilson (ed) (Geneva: WCC, 1990), 32 (Section I 26).

[62] This terminology was set out in MEUT, 7.

by evangelicals: evangelism is 'the communication of the whole gospel to the whole of humanity in the whole world' (§80; cf. *LC* §6).

Whereas in *EA* the main issue pertaining to evangelism was its perceived opposition to social action, *TTL* approaches evangelism within the context of fraught interreligious relations and controversy about conversion from one religion to another (§82). In reflecting on the topic, CWME was greatly helped by the involvement of some commissioners in the production in 2011 of the document *Christian Witness in a Multi-Religious World: Recommendations for Conduct* jointly by the WCC, the Catholic Church and the World Evangelical Alliance.[63] *TTL* likewise calls for 'authentic evangelism' which rejects violence, affirms freedom of religion, respects peoples and cultures, practises mutual respect and facilitates reconciliation (§90). The statement thus, on the one hand, affirms proclamation while, on the other hand, reigning in proselytisers (§82, §110) and salesmen (§88) whose activities are not only contrary to the Spirit of Christ but also threaten community cohesion in various parts of the world.

All too often, evangelism has been a strategy for church growth, an unfinished task for the church, or an urgent call for the missionary, forgetting that it is only the Holy Spirit who brings about conversion (§82). Rather, in pneumatological perspective, evangelism is a spirituality, 'the outflow of hearts that are filled with the love of God for those who do not yet know him' (§81). It involves not only announcing good news in Christ but also affirming and discerning the wider presence and activity of the Holy Spirit 'wherever life in its fullness is affirmed' (§24). The Edinburgh 2010 project linked mission spirituality with authentic discipleship.[64] *TTL* continues this model of witness and evangelism in the spirit and the way of Christ (§§86-92). In authentic or Christ-like evangelism, words are consistent with actions and 'love for one another is a demonstration of the gospel we proclaim' (§86). There is an emphasis throughout *TTL* on following Christ by self-emptying or kenotic mission and on vulnerability and humility in evangelising (e.g. §§8, 23, 33, 62, 71, 87, 89, 92, 106). Evangelism 'is grounded in humility and respect for all and flourishes in the context of dialogue' (§89) 'with the expectation of meeting God who has preceded us and has been present with people within their own contexts' (§94).

Good news must be shared, and so the statement declares: 'There is no greater gift we can offer to our fellow human beings than to share and introduce them to the love, grace and mercy of God in Christ' (§83). Evangelism, in this sense, is at the heart of mission. It leads to repentance, faith and baptism (§84). It is the sharing of ourselves and our life in Christ

---

[63] Available from the websites of each of the respective bodies.

[64] Cf. Theme 9 of the study process of the Edinburgh 2010 centenary project, which was entitled: 'Mission spirituality and authentic discipleship'. See Balia and Kim, *Edinburgh 2010*, 222-44.

while 'also listening to others and being challenged and enriched by others' (§95).

## Together towards Life

In preparing *TTL*, CWME defined ecumenical mission in the 21st century by responding to changed landscapes: theological, socio-economic, ecclesial and religious. As a result of a seven-year process, *TTL* emerged as a consensus document from the commission and its wider network that includes not only WCC member-churches and mission bodies – Protestant and Orthodox – but also Catholic, Evangelical and Pentecostal representatives. As it turns out, *TTL* was produced at a fruitful moment when other major global Christian bodies were reflecting on mission and evangelism. *TTL* can fruitfully be compared with the *Cape Town Commitment* of the Lausanne Movement, published in 2011[65] and Pope Francis's apostolic exhortation *Evangelii Gaudium* (*The Joy of the Gospel*) of late 2013, which draws on the proceedings of 2012 synod of bishops as well as other sources.[66] All three documents share the concerns of *TTL* for a Trinitarian theology of mission, integral or holistic mission, missionary congregations and transmission of the gospel message. However, in any comparison, certain characteristics of *TTL* will stand out. The most distinctive feature of *TTL* is its consistent pneumatological approach of 'mission in the Spirit', which facilitates other insights such as mission as discerning and affirming life, transformative spirituality, a dynamic understanding of the church and prophetic evangelism.[67] In each of its other main themes, *TTL* makes distinctive contributions which are not features of either the *Lausanne Covenant* or *Evangelii Gaudium*. In its treatment of the socio-economic landscape, *TTL* draws attention to mission *from* the margins. In dealing with the ecclesial landscape, *TTL* gives particular attention to the mobility of churches. With regard to the religious landscape, *TTL* stresses the complementarity of evangelism and dialogue.

The confluence of these documents gives great hope for mission that is even more ecumenical and reflects the church's catholicity. I look forward to seeing the response to changed landscapes, as expressed in *TTL*, being

---

[65] Lausanne Movement, *The Cape Town Commitment: A Confession of Faith and a Call to Action* (Peabody, MA: Hendrickson, 2011). See also: www.lausanne.org and the chapter by Allen Yeh in this book.

[66] Francis I, *Evangelii Gaudium: The Joy of the Gospel*, Apostolic Exhortation on the Proclamation of the Gospel in Today's World (London: Catholic Truth Society, 2013): www.vatican va. For the historical, ecclesial and theological background to *Evangelii Gaudium*, see Paul Grogan and Kirsteen Kim (eds), *The New Evangelization: Faith, People, Context and Practice* (London: Bloomsbury, 2015). See also the chapter by Stephen Bevans in this book.

[67] Evangelii Gaudium also pays particular attention to the work of the Holy Spirit, although pneumatology does not provide the whole framework as it does in *TTL*.

implemented in the WCC and member-churches. I believe it will make a rich and distinctive contribution to the churches' participation in the mission of God through the Spirit in the name of Jesus Christ to create a new heaven and a new earth.

# *Together towards Life*: A Catholic Assessment

Madge Karecki, SSJ-TOSF

## Introduction

As I read an account[1] of the development of the World Council of Churches' (WCC) document *Together towards Life: Mission and Evangelism in Changing Landscapes* (*TTL*), I became interested both in its theological foundation and the landscapes that were included. The description written by Kirsteen Kim rang true with me and I found it to be very engaging. When I was asked to write a Catholic response to *TTL* for publication in the *International Bulletin of Missionary Research*,[2] I went back to it and found much food for thought. My task in this essay is not to report, but to assess the document using a Catholic lens. My lens has been calibrated and focused on post-Vatican II Catholic mission documents. I have chosen certain elements that I will use for my assessment: *Ad Gentes* (*AG*), *Evangelii Nuntiandi* (*EN*), *Redemptoris Missio* (*RM*), *Doctrinal Note* (*DN*), *Evangelii Gaudium* (*EG*), and *Laudato Si'* (*LS*). They have much in common, and hopefully this will be revealed as we move along through the assessment.

## The Theological Foundation – Trinitarian Mission

The Second Vatican Council, particularly in *Ad Gentes*, stressed the 'missionary nature of the church', basing it on the very nature of the Trinity as a sending community. It was this document that provided the Catholic Church with a theology of mission that was not based on missionary work,

---

[1] An account by Kirsteen Kim, Professor of Theology and World Christianity at Leeds University. She served as vice-moderator of the WCC's Commission on World Mission and Evangelism and chair of the drafting group for *Together towards Life.* Her presentation at the intercontinental conference of MISAL (Missionary Societies of Apostolic Life) in London in May 2014 bears the same title as the WCC document. A link to her presentation can be found on the Missionaries of Africa website: www.africamission-mafr.org/misal_london_2014.htm

[2] Madge Karecki, 'A Missiological Reflection on 'Together towards Life: Mission and Evangelism in Changing Landscapes', in *International Bulletin of Missionary Research,* 38:4 (2014), 191-92. Sections of this essay have been developed from this article.

but rather on the mission identity of the whole church. The origin of mission is the very life of the Father, Son and Holy Spirit. The sending action of the Father, through which he sends the Son, whose mission is a gradual revelation of the Father's will and plan for all humanity, is the foundation of the Catholic Church's teaching on mission. The Father, then, through the mediation of the Son, sends the Holy Spirit, and the Holy Spirit continues to send the ecclesial assembly. This is a key area of agreement of Catholic mission theology with *TTL* (§11, §43). It also reflects the intention of the drafting committee: 'The new statement aims to promote renewed appreciation of the mission of the Spirit… as the Life-giver as stated in the creeds of Nicaea and Constantinople.'[3] Within this renewed appreciation for the Holy Spirit, *TTL* nevertheless asserts that 'a pneumatological focus on Christian mission recognizes that mission is essentially christologically based and relates the work of the Holy Spirit to the salvation through Jesus Christ'. The Holy Spirit is seen 'as the continuing presence of Christ, his agent to fulfil the task of mission' (§16).

Attention is placed firmly on 'the Triune God who is the creator, redeemer and sustainer of all life' (§1). This is accompanied by a forthright conviction that 'mission begins in the heart of the Triune God and the love which binds together the Holy Trinity overflows to all humanity and creation' (§2). It is the Gospel of John that demonstrates this most clearly in chapters 14–16. Here the focus is on how the Spirit will act in the community of believers. Jesus assured the apostles that the 'Holy Spirit whom the Father will send will teach you all things and will remind you of everything I have said to you' (John 14:26). Senior and Stuhlmueller point out that the presence of the Holy Spirit is to enrich the post-resurrection community and strengthen its faith so that they can bear witness to Jesus as the true Son of God.[4] In its Spirit-prompted mission to the world, the church discovers the true meaning of the Word made flesh. *TTL* §3 echoes this same idea: 'Life in the Holy Spirit is the essence of mission, the core of why we do what we do, and how we live our lives. Spirituality gives deepest meaning to our lives and motivates our actions.' This emphasis on the inner dynamics of the Trinity does not in any way diminish the mission of Jesus; instead it is an enrichment of our understanding of the *missio Dei* as revealed in Jesus in the Gospels.

Biblical and historical sources testify that both the celebration of the liturgy and mission were the most striking hallmarks of the early Christian community. It was in the context of worship that the community of believers experienced the presence of Christ through the action of the Holy Spirit. This was the birth of mission spirituality. *TTL* makes this point when it affirms that the Holy Spirit is the source of energy for mission (§104). In

---

[3] Kim, 'Together towards Life', 1.

[4] Donald Senior and Carroll Stuhlmueller, *The Biblical Foundations for Mission* (Maryknoll, NY: Orbis Books, 1983), 287-88.

the end, *TTL* calls all of us to transformation, a deep conversion that hopefully leads us to shape the choices we make in a way that gives witness to our commitment to participation in God's mission in the world.

Cardinal Walter Kasper, writing about Pope Francis, observed that the Pope's thought develops between two poles of 'encounter and praxis',[5] meaning that Pope Francis works in reality. He analyzes a situation, talks with others, prays, then sets in motion a plan of action based on discernment. He is praxis-oriented and the action is for the common good. It is a method that can be used in mission in the context of any of the landscapes described in *TTL* – in fact, in any landscape.

## The Landscape of Creation

'Creation's life and God's life are entwined' (*TTL* §19). This document and the recently published encyclical by Pope Francis, *Laudato Si': On Care for Our Common Home*[6] both give a clear expression to creation as a gift of God's love.

> Nature is usually seen as a system which can be studied, understood and controlled, whereas creation can only be understood as a gift from the outstretched hand of the Father of all, and as a reality illuminated by the love which calls us together into universal communion (*LS* §76).

This is a key convergence from a Catholic point of view. *TTL* invites humanity to a 'new conversion' and a 'new humility' (§22) in relationship to creation. Pope Francis incorporated not only his own thoughts, but also those of his predecessors Pope Saint John XXIII, Blessed Pope Paul VI, Pope Saint John Paul II, and Pope Emeritus Benedict XVI who urged human beings to take cognizance of the devastation of the planet through excessive damage from pollution and the exploitation of the earth's natural resources.

The core concern of *TTL* and *LS* is what is happening to God's gift to all humanity, especially to poor people who are deprived of the earth's goods because of the rapacious appetites that cry out for immediate gratification. *TTL* §21 stresses that 'our participation in mission, our being in creation, and our practice of the life of the Spirit, need to be woven together, for they are mutually transformative'. The 'new conversion' called for in the document invites humans to 'participate in communion *with* all creation in celebrating the work of the Creator' (*TTL* §22). In that communion we come together in a common dance learning to step lightly upon the earth and celebrating God's gift to us. It is well known that the Greek word *oikos*

---

[5] See Walter Kasper, *Pope Francis' Revolution of Tenderness and Love: Theological and Pastoral Perspectives*, trans. William Madges (New York: Paulist, 2014), 19.

[6] Pope Francis, *Laudato Si': On Care for our Common Home* (Washington, DC: United States Conference of Catholic Bishops' Conference, 2015).

meaning 'house' is the root of 'eco' which forms the words 'ecology', 'economy', and 'ecumenical'.

Pope Francis has added to this trio of words by bringing to the attention of the human community the need for consideration of human ecology, a phrase first used by Pope Saint John Paul II in his encyclical letter, *Centesimus Annus* (*CA*). Referencing this letter, Pope Francis writes that:

> The destruction of the human environment is extremely serious, not only because God has entrusted the world to us men and women, but because human life is itself a gift which must be defended from various forms of debasement. Every effort to protect and improve our world entails profound changes in lifestyles, models of production and consumption, and the established structures of power which today govern societies (*LS* §5).

*TTL* §23 echoes these observations and clearly states that the greed of humanity is contributing to the global warming and climate change that leads to the disfigurement and damage of the earth, and adds more burdens to the lives of poor people. As Christians, we have a responsibility to care for our common home. If we allow our societies to continue to be obsessed with power and profit, we will continue to not only destroy the earth, but also deprive our sisters and brothers of their share of the earth's resources.[7]

This is a challenge that calls for a profound commitment to the common good, something that many people in the western world do not find easy because of individualism and materialism. Anthropologist and missiologist Paul Hiebert has pointed out that people from the western world tend to judge people by what they own, and judge success by the material goods they have accumulated.[8] This is an assault on human dignity. 'Authentic human development has a moral character. It presumes full respect for the human person, but it must also be concerned for the world around us and take into account the nature of each being and of its mutual connection in an ordered system' (*LS* §5).

## The Landscapes of Mission on the Margins

The widening gap between rich and poor is a reality for countries throughout the world. 'In many ways, inequality is not just a financial issue,' notes Richard Wike.[9] He cites the UN Secretary-General's Special

---

[7] See Ilia Delio, Keith Douglass Warner and Pamela Wood, *Care for Creation: A Franciscan Spirituality of the Earth* (Cincinnati, OH: St Anthony Messenger Press, 2007), 25.

[8] Paul G. Hiebert, *Anthropological Insights for Missionaries* (Grand Rapids, MI: Baker Academic, 2008), 115.

[9] Richard Wike, 'With 41% of global wealth in the hands of less than 1%, elites and citizens agree inequality is a top priority', in *FactTank* (8th November 2014), Pew Research Center website: www.pewresearch.org/fact-tank/2014/11/08/with-41-of-global-wealth-in-the-hands-of-less-than-1-elites-and-citizens-agree-inequality-is-a-top-priority

Adviser on Post-2015 Development Planning, Amina Mohammed, who has skilfully pointed out that 'inequality is a major problem, in part, because it is linked with so many other challenges, such as "poverty, environmental degradation, persistent unemployment, political instability, violence and conflict"'.[10]

Mission history is filled with expressions of missionary activity that viewed people on the margins of their societies as passive recipients. The drafters of *TTL* drew attention to the fact that such an approach 'is too often complicit with oppressive and life-denying systems' (§41). Further, they judge that this approach was 'generally aligned with the privileges of the centre and largely failed to challenge economic, social, cultural and political systems which have marginalized some peoples' (§41). Pope Francis, commenting on just such an approach to mission, says: 'We have to state, without mincing words, that there is an inseparable bond between our faith and the poor' (*EG* §48). Faith and life cannot be separated. This is why a praxis-oriented and communal method of mission is essential. From a Catholic perspective, the task of evangelization, to use the words of the Pope, 'demands the integral promotion of each human being' (*EG* §182).

*TTL* reminds us that 'people on the margins, living in vulnerable positions, often know what exclusionary forces are threatening their survival and can best discern the urgency of their struggles; people in positions of privilege have much to learn from the daily struggles of people living in marginal conditions' (§38). In the light of this important observation about the perspective of people on the margins of society, in *TTL* there is an even stronger call made to the member-churches of the WCC to not just move people from the margins to the centres of power, but to learn to confront those who sit at these centres – to '*transform* power structures in society' (§40). 'Participation in the *missio Dei* requires a willingness to be of service to all others in all the realities of life. Whatever form of service is rendered needs to be characterized by mutuality, reciprocity and interdependence' (*TTL* §45). In this, words and deeds find concrete expression of our commitment to those on the margins, and in the process, we gain the ability to see more clearly the human dignity inherent in all people as our sisters and brothers in Christ Jesus.

In a world where inequality is considered one of the most important challenges facing every country, and where in 'developed and developing countries alike, the poorest half of the population often controls less than 10% of its wealth',[11] churches cannot ignore the forces that result in the disempowerment of people on the margins because others want to maintain the status quo and keep their profits high. This is what Pope Francis has named 'an economy of exclusion' (*EG* §53). Though the Catholic Church

---

[10] Wike, 'With 41%', citing Amina Mohammed, *Deepening Income Inequality*, World Economic Forum website: http://reports.weforum.org/outlook-global-agenda-2015/top-10-trends-of-2015/1-deepening-income-inequality

[11] Amina Mohammed, *Deepening Income Inequality*, 1.

has a long record of social teaching, the Pope places great importance on working for the common good. It is no longer possible to claim that religion should be restricted to the private sphere and that it exists only to prepare souls for heaven. We know that God wants his children to be happy in this world too, even though they are called to fulfilment in eternity, for he has created all things 'for our enjoyment' (1 Tim. 6:17), the enjoyment of everyone. It follows that Christian conversion demands reviewing especially those areas and aspects of life 'related to the social order and the pursuit of the common good' (*EG* §182).

Clearly, there is a high level of agreement between the vision presented in *TTL* and the Catholic position on mission to people on the margins or peripheries of societies developed in Pope Francis's apostolic exhortation, *EG*. The situation of people on the margins often becomes complicated because of immigration issues. Church communities can be places of refuge for people who are struggling with issues surrounding their legal status. Churches are called to move beyond ethnic and cultural boundaries to come to the aid of all people in need and work to create multicultural communities. *TTL* §70 recommends advocacy work to promote justice in regard to legislation for people who want to settle in countries legally. Welcoming immigrants from various countries can enrich the life of nations if support is given to their integration into the larger society. This belongs to what Pope Francis calls a 'culture of encounter':

> People in every nation enhance the social dimension of their lives by acting as committed and responsible citizens, not as a mob swayed by the powers-that-be. Let us not forget that 'responsible citizenship is a virtue, and participation in political life is a moral obligation'.[12] Yet becoming a people demands something more. It is an ongoing process in which every new generation must take part: a slow and arduous effort calling for a desire for integration and a willingness to achieve this through the growth of a peaceful and multi-faceted culture of encounter (*EG* §220).

The word 'encounter' is used in *TTL* in relation to God, people of other faiths, different spiritualities and with people who are different from us. This is most especially true when it comes to immigrants. We can add to their insecurities in being in a new land, or we can help them to feel at home in their new environment. Articles in *TTL* are especially cogent on this point. 'We are led by the Spirit into various situations and moments, into meeting points with others, into spaces of encounter, and into critical locations of human struggle' (§26). In meeting and working with immigrants and poor people, we can find ourselves faced with questions that challenge our commitment to Christ. In *TTL* §45 we meet another challenge to our thinking about immigrants in the context of God's hospitality. Usually sociologists and anthropologists use the binary notions

---

[12] United States Conference of Catholic Bishops, Pastoral Letter: *Forming Conscience for Faithful Citizenship* (November 2007), 13.

of dominant groups as hosts, and minority groups as guests, in issues of cultural adjustment. *TTL* §71, deepening the discussion on immigration issues, puts the issues in the context of Christian life: 'In God's hospitality, God is host and we are all invited by the Spirit to participate with humility and mutuality in God's mission.'

## The Landscapes of Solidarity

There is a thread that runs consistently throughout the text, that poor people must be the concern of the Christian community. It should give witness to the world of our commitment to a Gospel way of life that can truly be called 'evangelical'. In *TTL* we find this same idea put more profoundly:

> To experience life in the Spirit is to taste life in its fullness. We are '… called to witness to a movement toward life, celebrating all that the Spirit continues to call into being, walking in solidarity in order to cross the rivers of despair and anxiety (Ps. 23, Isa. 43:1-5). Mission provokes in us a renewed awareness that the Holy Spirit meets us and challenges us at all levels of life and brings newness and change to the places and times of our personal and collective journeys (*TTL* §34).

Solidarity with poor people is meant to spur us on to take transformative action for ourselves and for the poor. We ourselves are called to conversion and to give preference to the needs of poor people. It is what Henri Nouwen called 'downward mobility'. Nouwen meant that one would need to choose voluntarily to scale down one's way of living for the sake of the common good. Nouwen learned many lessons from letting go of possessions, but also egotistical self-concerns. Indeed, downward mobility is what is needed to be able to meet everyone's legitimate needs for quality of life. Pope Francis wrote strongly and forthrightly about the need for basic human rights to be available to all people for the common good.

> In the present condition of global society, where injustices abound and growing numbers of people are deprived of basic human rights and considered expendable, the principle of the common good immediately becomes, logically and inevitably, a summons to solidarity and a preferential option for the poorest of our brothers and sisters (*LS* §158).

To learn to think about the unity of the human family, people have to be exposed to others and to various ways of living. *TTL* §72 urges a local congregation to respond 'to its own contextual realities'. Mission trips and short-term mission service opportunities often help to stimulate members of local congregations to consider making a longer-term commitment to a specific mission location (*TTL* §76). Such experiences expose people to other cultures as well as to the possibility of developing relationships that are based on common concerns, solidarity and mutuality, equally enriching the local congregation and the global partners. Real solidarity with people creates an atmosphere of trust and mutual support, and we learn to work together with others for something bigger than ourselves. Both *TTL* and

Catholic teaching support such efforts because they help people to see their mission experience in the light of faith. Although Christian churches often work in a spirit of unity in meeting the needs of people who are oppressed or suffering, a deeper unity that is rooted in our common faith is still not a reality. Efforts have been made on many fronts, but there are still stumbling blocks on the path to unity.

## The Landscapes of Unity

The unity that was brought through the joining together of the International Missionary Conference (IMC) and the evangelism desk of the WCC in 1961, to become the Commission on World Mission and Evangelism, was indeed a cause for rejoicing. The efforts at collaboration among the Orthodox, Anglican, Protestant, Pentecostal and indigenous churches has resulted in closer relationships and greater consensus on issues concerning worldwide mission. Catholics are now playing a role in the WCC, as evidenced by their participation in the General Council charged with organizing the Edinburgh Conference.

John Paul II linked ecumenism and mission in his encyclical letter *Redemptoris Missio* (*RM*) where he wrote that 'the missionary thrust belongs to the very nature of the Christian life, and is also the inspiration behind ecumenism' (*RM* §1). The structure of *TTL* reflects its foundation in a Trinitarian theology of mission in a way that gives special attention to the work of the Holy Spirit. This resonates with the theology of a Trinitarian mission presented in the *Decree on the Church's Missionary Activity* (*AG* §2). *TTL* reflects these same elements of a theology of mission rooted in the life of the Trinity.

*TTL* §10 links the creative and abiding presence of the Trinity with working for unity in mission. 'The church is a gift of God to the world for its transformation towards the Kingdom of God. Its mission is to bring new life and announce the loving presence of God in our world. We must participate in God's mission in unity, overcoming the divisions and tensions that exist among us, so that the world may believe and all may be one' (John 17:21). As *TTL* §60 rightly stated: 'Mission and unity belong together', and unity is a reality rooted in baptism. Through baptism, the Trinity indwells all Christians and the Trinity continues to send us out to proclaim the Kingdom of God. Nevertheless, 'the lack of full and real unity in mission still harms the authenticity and credibility of the fulfilment of God's mission in the world… mission and unity are intertwined' (*TTL* §61). If we, as Christians, can work together on other issues that affect humanity and the whole of creation, then we need to open up ways to widen a process of discussion among all the churches that leads to concrete steps of working for unity.

For Catholics, the Second Vatican Council was a turning point in terms of ecumenism. This resulted in a very robust effort to engage in dialogue with various Orthodox traditions, the Anglican Communion, Lutheran World Federation, World Methodist Conference, World Alliance of Reformed Churches, Baptist World Alliance, Disciples of Christ, Pentecostals, Evangelicals and the Mennonites. All these dialogues continue because they are born out of the desire for unity instead of the 'scandal of disunity', and out of the need for common witness. There is now in the Catholic Church a sincere openness to ecumenism.

*TTL* §69 is indeed crucial: 'From a mission perspective, it is important to discern what helps the cause of God's mission.' The answer, no doubt, is that the steadfast concern for unity must be evident at every level of church life; otherwise we compromise our commitment to *missio Dei.* Paul VI expressed it well:

> It is the test of the credibility of Christians and of Christ Himself. As evangelizers, we must offer Christ's faithful not the image of people divided and separated by unedifying quarrels, but the image of people who are mature in faith and capable of finding a meeting-point beyond the real tensions, thanks to a shared, sincere and disinterested search for truth. Yes, the destiny of evangelization is certainly bound up with the witness of unity given by the Church (*EN* §77).

The early Christian community was of 'one heart and one mind' (Acts 4:32), and the witness of their lives was an attractive sign to others of the difference Christ makes in the lives of believers. The care shown to people in need (Acts 6:1-7; Matthew 25:31-40; James 2:5-8) was a striking image of God's own love for them. Christians have always engaged in mission through care for people in need, and this opened the way for them to accept the Gospel.

## The Landscapes of Mission and Evangelism

Within the Catholic Church, Paul VI's summation of the ideas raised at The Synod on Evangelization (1974) inspired the use of the word 'evangelization' in missiological literature. His use of the term 'evangelization' instead of 'mission' helped to clarify the role of evangelization within the missionary enterprise, but also caused confusion. Instead of shedding light on the relationship of evangelization to mission, evangelization is treated as something completely unrelated to mission; or, as one colleague explained, mission is something that is done in other countries, evangelization is something which is done in one's home country! This is certainly not the Catholic position. Nevertheless, some Catholic dioceses have created separate offices for evangelization and for mission. This only compounds the confusion because the erroneous distinction between mission and evangelization is cemented into the institutional structure of a diocese.

Evangelization and witness are primary elements of Catholic teaching on mission. They are intimately related aspects of mission, but mission is the wider category that includes other expressions which have long been part of mission as well as those which have arisen in contemporary contexts for mission. There is a footnote in *TTL* §85 which, though true, is not complete. Two articles in the *Doctrinal Note* deserve attention:

> The term *evangelization* has a very rich meaning. In the broad sense, it sums up the Church's entire mission: her whole life consists in *accomplishing* the *traditio Evangelii,* the proclamation and handing-on of the Gospel, which is 'the power of God for the salvation of everyone who believes' (Rom. 1:16) and which, in the final essence, is identified with Jesus Christ himself (1 Cor. 1:24). Understood in this way, evangelization is aimed at all humanity. In any case, *to evangelize* does not mean simply to teach a doctrine, but to proclaim Jesus Christ by one's words and actions, that is, to make oneself an instrument of his presence and action in the world (*DN* §2).

Furthermore, the *DN* acknowledges the fact of contextualization as a factor in the work of evangelization, and the necessary sensitivity that should characterize what I prefer to call missionary evangelization:

> Evangelization also involves a sincere dialogue that seeks to understand the reasons and feelings of others. Indeed, the heart of another person can only be approached in freedom, in love and in dialogue, in such a manner that the word which is spoken is not simply offered, but also truly witnessed in the hearts of those to whom it is addressed. This requires taking into account the hopes, sufferings and concrete situations of those with whom one is in dialogue. Precisely in this way, people of good will open their hearts more freely and share their spiritual and religious experiences in all sincerity. This experience of sharing, a characteristic of true friendship, is a valuable occasion for witnessing and for Christian proclamation (*DN* §8).

*TTL* reflects on mission in articles 67-79 and on evangelism in 80-100. Though various elements of mission are considered, such as witness, unity, immigration, liturgy, twinning, advocacy and service, a connection is made in the last sentence that makes up §79. This sentence makes the connection between mission and evangelism: 'As the church discovers more deeply its identity as a missionary community, its outward-looking character finds expression in evangelism.' Despite the conviction one can sense in these words, a question remains: What are all the other dimensions mission if not outward-looking?

The longer section on evangelism – surprisingly, at least to this author – includes sections that as a missiologist, I would consider in conjunction with mission: individualism, secularism and materialism (§91), interreligious dialogue (§93), and cultural issues (§97-100). Now, it is true that there are no hard-and-fast distinctions, but long before proclamation goes on, in the preparation for mission these issues need to be clearly dealt with so that, as the community of faith engages in mission, they have been made aware of the importance of these aspects of mission praxis under the guidance of the Holy Spirit, informed by sound missiological principles.

## Conclusion

In the light of the challenges of changing landscapes, the way forward might benefit from the development of some serious discourse around changing how thinking about mission is presented. We need to look at mission as a way of life, not as only a work. This would then be a more inclusive way of looking at missionary identity rooted in baptism. *TTL* uses the word 'humility' nine times §23, 71, 83, 87, 89, 106, 109 and 112. In each instance, humility is linked with some of the central aspects of missionary life. The first time it is used in the text is in connection with conversion: 'We need a new conversion (*metanoia*) in our mission which invites a new humility in regard to the mission of God's Spirit.' This is another aspect of preparation for missionary encounters that needs to be revisited because it is the very foundation of how the Holy Spirit works to prepare people not only for mission, but for the whole of Christian life. It prepares us for a life of gradual and systemic attitudes that mark *kenosis*, and manifests itself in choices that lead to self-emptying so that mission in Christ's way shapes mission praxis.

From a Catholic perspective, *TTL* serves to remind the entire Christian community that we must, through common witness and solidarity with those most in need, reveal God's desire and invitation that all humanity and all creation share in the 'Feast of Life through Jesus Christ' (§112). *TTL* rightly affirms the church's missionary identity and reasserts the need for us as Christians to commit ourselves anew to live in ways that give witness to God's revelation in Jesus, that all 'may have life, and have it abundantly' (John 10:10). Though there are differences in ecclesiology, sacramental practice and institutional structures that shape mission thinking, there are many more areas of commonality that can benefit the Catholic Church. This is a document that needs to be studied, reflected upon and implemented in ways that actually bring about justice, peace and unity for the sake of humanity and all creation. In this way, the reign of God can become not merely a promise but a foretaste of God's mission to the world in its ultimate fullness.

Scripture texts taken from the *Holy Bible, NRSV Catholic Version, Anglicized Text* (London: Darton, Longman & Todd, 2005).

# *TOGETHER TOWARDS LIFE*: AN ORTHODOX ASSESSMENT

Petros Vassiliadis

The year 2012, the year of the official adoption of the New Mission Statement, entitled *Together towards Life: Mission and Evangelism in Changing Landscapes,* by the Central Committee of WCC, meeting in Crete, Greece, marked the end of a long period of Christian mission in modern times. The same year another document, also important from a missiological point of view, was released: the AGAPE Call for Action, entitled *Economy of Life, Justice, and Peace for All: A Call for Action*, finalized at the Global Forum and AGAPE Celebration in Bogor, Indonesia, in June 2012. This latter document, repeating many ideas of the former WCC document, was not only addressed to the member-churches of WCC, to all Christians worldwide and to people of faith in general, but also to all partners from the secular establishment (political, social, etc.), who shared common ethical values. Both documents were the main focal points of reflection in the tenth General Assembly of WCC, which met in Busan, South Korea, on the theme: *God of life, lead us to justice and peace* (30th October-8th November 2013). The Busan General Assembly was the second in Asia in the history of this privileged ecumenical organization in the 65 years of its life, after the historic meeting in New Delhi in 1961, which was significant for two reasons: the full integration of the Orthodox Christian family into the ecumenical movement, and the importance it laid on inter-faith encounter and dialogue. The year 2013 also marked the release of another mission document of great magnitude: the personal encyclical of Pope Francis *Evangelii Gaudium.*[1]

The interdependence, therefore, of Orthodox Christianity with the new paradigm in Christian mission, underlined in all these mission documents that changed in a positive manner the route of our Christian witness to the world, is what initially the Orthodox expected to be the first step the ecumenical movement should take, even before the 1910 Edinburgh mission conference, which is considered in the West as the beginning of the ecumenical era.[2] The famous Circular Letters of the Orthodox Ecumenical

---

[1] See chapters by Madge Karecki and Stephen Bevans in this book.

[2] According to Thomas E. FitzGerald, 'even before the Edinburgh Conference, the Orthodox Church of Constantinople, known as the Ecumenical Patriarchate, began a new series of discussions on issues related to church divisions as early as the year 1902. On 12th June of that year, Patriarch Joachim III addressed an encyclical…':

Patriarchate in 1902, 1904, and later in 1920, addressing all Christian churches, insisted that social and other practical activities of the churches should not be postponed until complete doctrinal agreement was achieved. Only through co-operation on social issues and joint commitment in the name of Christ for the sake of humanity, the circular went on, can a visible unity of the church be accomplished.[3] Of course, for unspecified reasons, the Orthodox interest in the course of time shifted to an exclusive quest for church unity, depriving the urgent quest for the unity of humankind of Orthodox energy and theological reflection.[4]

This is what all Orthodox committed to ecumenism expected from global Christian mission, and particularly its ecumenical branch, namely, the Commission on World Mission and Evangelism (CWME) of WCC. In one of the last Messages of the Primates of the Orthodox Churches, it was clearly stated that:

> Orthodox Christians share responsibility for the contemporary crisis of this planet with other people, whether they are people of faith or not, because they have tolerated and indiscriminately compromised on extreme human choices, without credibly challenging these choices with the word of faith. Therefore, they also have a major obligation to contribute to overcoming the divisions of the world. [5]

These divisions, to a certain extent due to the failure or shortcomings of modernity on issues of justice, peace, the integrity of creation and the world economy, are among the consequences of individualism. The latter being one of the pillars of modernity, and the ensuing absolute, unconditional,

---

*The Ecumenical Movement: An Introductory History* (Westport, CT: Praeger Publishers, 2004), 82.

[3] Cf. Encyclical of the Ecumenical Patriarchate, 1920: 'Unto the Churches of Christ Everywhere', in Gennadios Limouris (ed), *Orthodox Visions of Ecumenism: Statements, Messages and Reports on the Ecumenical Movement 1902-1992* (Geneva: WCC, 1994), 9-11. As interpreted by the first General Secretary of the WCC and historian Visser 't Hooft, this important principle was one of the key requirements of the ecumenical movement (cf. *Minutes and Reports of the Twelfth Meeting of the Central Committee, Rhodes, Greece, August 19-27* (Geneva: WCC, 1959), 95-97. See also §12 *Unitatis redintegratio*, of the Vatican II Decree on Ecumenism.

[4] More on this in Stylianos Tsompanidis, 'The Ecumenical Process of *AGAPE* (Alterative Globalization Addressing People and Earth): An Orthodox Perspective', in *A Testimony to the Nations: A Vigintennial Volume Offered to the Ecumenical Patriarch Bartholomew* (Thessaloniki 2011), 905-23 (in Greek). Also his *Orthodoxie und Ökumene. Gemeinsam auf dem Weg zu Gerechtigkeit, Frieden und Bewahrung der Schöpfung* (Münster, Hamburg and London, 1990), especially chs. I, 1.3, II, 2 and II, 1.

[5] §6 of the *Message of the Primates of the Orthodox Churches,* disseminated *urbi et orbe* by the ultimate authority of the Orthodox Church, namely the Synod of the Primates of the independent (Autocephalous) Orthodox Churches, issued on 12th December 2008.

uncontrolled freedom of the individual in all aspects of life (sexual freedom, legally protected freedom in accumulating wealth, etc.), has been heralded as the new faith after the Enlightenment. Looking at the ambivalence of modernity, many Christian theologians and activists (and many more faithful from other religions, I suppose) insist that there must be a criterion to judge what should be saved from the values and achievements of modernity and what should be discarded. The latest neo-liberal form of the free-market economy, has changed power balances, shifting modernity from being the 'midwife' of human rights to their murderer. On the basis of the old principles of modernity, the present world economic system is increasingly falling back into totalitarian trends. Only if the world listens again carefully and gleans from the shared wisdom of religions and other age-old ethical traditions, can the positive values of the modern paradigm be renewed and revitalized. It is for this reason that from all religious quarters we speak of *liberation of modernity*.[6]

The most tangible aspect of this liberation has to do with the revered *Universal Declaration of Human Rights.* In view of the breakdown of the International Convention on Climate Change in Copenhagen a few years ago, just to mention one example, it became clear – at least in religious circles – that human rights are largely ineffective if they are not accompanied by human responsibilities. People of faith nowadays believe that the values and principles that form part of a common world ethic need not only public declaration but also a call for international legal endorsement.

The struggle, however, of Christians and faithful of other religions to promote a Universal Declaration of Human Responsibilities is not just a diplomatic initiative aiming at introducing moral values to the global agenda at the expense of the values of modernity and the democratic achievements of the Enlightenment. It resulted from the pressure of prophetic and charismatic figures and theological movements for social and ecological justice from a faith perspective. Economic justice is a concept developed by the churches and the ecumenical movement with a view to achieving the equitable sharing of resources and power as essential prerequisites for human development and ecological sustainability. Long before a universal concern (political, scientific, etc.) and advocacy concerning the dangerous effects of climate change were developed, theologians from all religious quarters put a critical question to their own religious institutions: 'Will the churches have the courage to engage with the 'values' of a profit-oriented way of life as a matter of faith, or will they withdraw into the 'private' sphere? This is the question our churches must

---

[6] This is the general message of an international, interdisciplinary, inter-faith project, in which Orthodox institutions participated, analyzed in the recently published book by Ulrich Duchrow and F.J. Hinkelammert, *Transcending Greedy Money: Interreligious Solidarity for Just Relations* (New York: Palgrave Macmillan, 2012).

answer or lose their very soul,'[7] declared a WCC consultation of Eastern and Central European Churches on the problem of economic globalization at the dawn of the third millennium. This paved the way for *TTL* together with the *Call for Action,* which appeals for 'building a common voice, fostering ecumenical co-operation, and ensuring greater coherence for the realization of an Economy of Life for all'.[8]

Furthermore, the Orthodox Primates clearly affirmed that:

> The gap between rich and poor is growing dramatically due to the financial crisis, usually the result of manic profiteering by economic factors and corrupt financial activity, which, by lacking an anthropological dimension and sensitivity, does not ultimately serve the real needs of mankind. A viable economy is that which combines efficacy with justice and social solidarity.[9]

Therefore, Christian churches slowly, but steadily, started being concerned about two interrelated aspects of globalization: ecology and economy, both stemming from the Greek word *oikos* (household), and both carrying inherently the notion of communion *(koinonia),* so dear and revered in all Christian denominations, but definitely rooted deeper in the Orthodox tradition. The timely response of His All Holiness Ecumenical Patriarch Bartholomew on environmental issues, inasmuch as he expressed concern on the preservation of God's creation, as articulated through universally acknowledged endeavours (projects, conferences, etc.), have gained him the nickname 'The Green Patriarch'.

On a theoretical level, however, the most significant and crucial decision, shared now by most religions, is the conviction that, from a faith perspective, economy and ecology cannot be dealt with separately. This interrelatedness is in line with a similar conviction in the ecumenical movement, which for almost half a century had being examining justice and peace as inseparable entities, even at a time when the superpowers during the Cold War insisted on prioritizing them in differing and opposite ways.

In the wider ecumenical movement, Christians, in co-operation with their partners in inter-faith dialogue, came to the conclusion that 'various aspects of climate, ecological, financial, and debt crises are mutually dependent and reinforce each other. They cannot be treated separately any more'.[10] People of faith –

> discern the fatal intertwining of the global financial, socio-economic, climate, and ecological crises accompanied in many places of the world by the suffering of people and their struggle for life. Far-reaching market liberalization, deregulation, and unrestrained privatisation of goods and

---

[7] Rogate Mshane, *Globalization: WCC-JPC,* presented at the Harare WCC Assembly: *The Responsibility of World Religions for Ecology, the World Economic System, and the International Law.*

[8] *Economy of Life, Justice, and Peace for All: A Call for Action,* §23.

[9] Message of the Primates, §8.

[10] Economy of Life, §10.

> services are exploiting the whole Creation and dismantling social programs and services and opening up economies across borders to seemingly limitless growth of production.[11]

Needless to say, faithful from all religions must join forces to this end, and not fight one another. Hostility between them is a betrayal of religion. And the battle for achieving a legally established Universal Declaration of Human Responsibilities cannot be won unless it is fought by a united front of people of faith. If all religious leaders and religious communities take action similar to the ecological initiatives of Patriarch Bartholomew, a new and better world will undoubtedly rise. And this is certainly the will of God!

With regard to *TTL* itself,[12] we should remind ourselves that Orthodoxy and Mission are two terms that at a first glance seem quite incompatible; at least, to western historians of mission.[13] When in 1910 the historic gathering of missionaries across denominational boundaries took place in Edinburgh, in order to launch interdenominational missionary co-operation, Orthodoxy was completely marginal. In their deliberations, there were only references to the Oriental (sic) or Greek churches, always within the framework of western (mainly Protestant) missions. Even in the following generation, no article on the importance of mission was written by Orthodox theologians.[14] The initiatives of the Ecumenical Patriarchate at the dawn of the twentieth century, inviting all Christians to address together the great challenges of the new century, were brought later to the attention of the wider Christian world.

The encounter of Orthodoxy itself with world Christian mission has not always been a happy one. The missional dimension of the Orthodox Church was rediscovered just over a generation ago, thanks to the efforts and theological arguments of the former moderator of CWME, His Beatitude Anastasios (Yannoulatos), Archbishop of Tirana, Durrës and All Albania.[15] The theological discussion about mission, originally with Protestantism

---

[11] Economy of Life, §10. This is something that was painfully felt in Greece by the majority of its citizens during the recent economic crisis.

[12] Most of what follows is based on an earlier article of mine under the title, 'An Orthodox Assessment of the New Mission Statement', in *International Review of Mission,* 102 (2013), 174-78.

[13] More in the collective Volume I edited under the title *Orthodox Perspectives on Mission*, Regnum Edinburgh Centenary Series 17 (Oxford: Regnum, 2013), which was actually prepared as an Orthodox input to the WCC General Assembly held in Busan, South Korea, in 2013.

[14] More in Athanasios Papathanasiou, 'Tradition as Impulse for Renewal and Witness: Introducing Orthodox Missiology', in *International Review of Mission,* 100:2 (2011), 203-15.

[15] Archbishop Anastasios Yannoulatos, 'Discovering the Orthodox Missionary Ethos', in Ion Bria (ed), *Martyria-Mission: The Witness of the Orthodox Churches* (Geneva: WCC, 1980), 20-29; also Anastasios Yannoulatos, *Mission in Christ's Way* (Geneva: WCC and Brookline: HC Orthodox Press, 2010), 117-34.

within the framework of the activities of WCC, and after Vatican II also with Catholicism, has awakened the importance of mission for the Orthodox Church.

However, a significant contribution to the overall deliberations for an ecumenical mission theology in the form of a mission statement had to wait till a missionary awareness of the various *autocephali* Orthodox Churches was accomplished. Gradually, in addition to Archbishop Anastasios, other Orthodox theologians, who were actively involved one way or another with the ecumenical movement, and particularly with the CWME of WCC, most notably the late Prof. Ion Bria, made significant contributions to the development of contemporary mission theology. Themes emphasised by the Orthodox include: the dimension of *martyria* in mission over against an offensive and sometimes arrogant mission, the Trinitarian importance of the *missio Dei* theology, and the liturgical aspect of Christian witness in the form of 'the liturgy after the liturgy'. These emphases have been gleaned from the richness of the Christian tradition of the undivided church, as well as from the wealth of the Orthodox missionary heritage, especially St Cyril and Methodius' evangelization of the Slavs, and of Europe in general. Though at first the Orthodox approach to mission could be difficult for western missiologists and missionaries to understand, Orthodox mission theologians have nonetheless become invaluable players in the field of contemporary Christian missiology.

During the last fifty years, i.e. from the time of the admission of Orthodox Churches into membership of the WCC in 1961, there have been two official statements and one study document on mission and evangelism. The 1982 document *Mission and Evangelism: An Ecumenical Affirmation,* was officially approved by the Central Committee of WCC. The 2000 document *Mission and Evangelism in Unity Today,* was adopted by CWME as a Study Document. The new mission statement, *Together towards Life: Mission and Evangelism in Changing Landscapes*, was unanimously approved by the WCC Central Committee held in Crete, Greece, on 5th September 2012.

The 1982 mission statement is traditional, reflecting a mainly Protestant understanding of mission. Though it was translated into languages such as Greek,[16] it was never embraced or wholeheartedly followed by Orthodox missionaries and missiologists. The Orthodox did not feel at home with its theological arguments or its overall aura. By contrast, the 2000 *Mission and Evangelism in Unity Today* document was shaped, to a significant extent, by a substantial Orthodox contribution. This, however, exposed it to criticism from Protestant, particularly Evangelical, missiologists, and this may have been the reason why it never acquired universal acceptance or

[16] Cf. Ion Bria and Petros Vassiliadis, *Orthodox Christian Witness,* EKO 1 (Katerini, Greece: Tertios Press, 1989), 177-200 (in Greek).

official approval by the entire WCC in the form of a decision by its Central Committee.

Both the 1982 statement and the 2000 mission study paper attempted to bring into actuality the traditional (western and eastern respectively) understanding of mission. However, they both fell short with regard to adaptation to the rapidly changing landscapes. The third millennium required concrete affirmations in the context of emerging new challenges, especially with regard to the growing pluralistic situation and the world economic system, and a renewed philosophy and language. In addition, the widening of the spectrum of Christian missionaries, ranging from the historically traditional churches (Orthodox and Catholic) and the traditional mainstream Protestant ecclesial communities, to the new vibrant and charismatic ones (Evangelical and Pentecostal), required the statement to have a broader appeal. Indeed, it was required to look even wider than WCC member-churches and affiliated mission agencies, so that all Christians could commit themselves together to fullness of life for all, led by the God of Life! It was into this situation that *TTL* came into being.

Of course, any new statement concerning the Christian imperative of mission would be wholeheartedly welcome from an Orthodox perspective. This one, however, seems in addition to fulfil some of the expectations of the Orthodox, especially in areas of crucial theological importance. First of all, its Trinitarian, as well as pneumatological, basis (§1) is of great importance. The Orthodox always insist that all fundamental aspects of Christian theology – creation of the entire cosmos by God, redemption in Christ and salvation through the church, but beyond its historic boundaries in the power of the Holy Spirit, etc. – are all conceived as the natural consequence of the inner dynamics of the Triune God, i.e. of the communion and love that exists within the Holy Trinity. Applied to mission, this Trinitarian basis can have tremendous effect in helping Christian missionaries to avoid imperialistic or confessionalistic attitudes. 'Trinitarian theology points to the fact that God's involvement in history aims at drawing humanity and creation in general into this communion with God's very life. The implications of this assertion for understanding mission are very important: mission does not aim primarily at the propagation or transmission of intellectual convictions, doctrines, moral commands, etc., but at the transmission of the life of communion that exists in God.'[17]

One could also add some further points: the ecclesial dimension of mission, the implicit liturgical aspect (although not fully articulated in the direction of the Eucharistic approach to mission, especially in view of the affirmation in §17), the explicit environmental and inter-faith consequences of an authentic Christian witness, and the clear connection between mission

[17] Ion Bria (ed), *Go Forth in Peace: Orthodox Perspectives on Mission* (Geneva: WCC, 1985), 3.

and unity,[18] are all profound theological aspects, very familiar to the Orthodox tradition. The importance of inter-faith dialogue (instead of an aggressive and triumphalistic mission), on the basis of the economy of the Spirit (side by side, of course, with the economy of the Word/Christ),[19] and the integrity of creation with the ensuing environmental missional ethos,[20] must certainly please not only Orthodox missiologists, but also theologians engaged in the quest for the visible unity of the Church of Christ. To my knowledge, it is the first time that a mission statement has made such a strong and direct appeal: 'We are called to participate in God's mission beyond our human-centred goals. God's mission is to all life and we have to both acknowledge it and serve it in new ways of mission. We pray for repentance and forgiveness, but we also call for action now. Mission has creation at its heart' (§105).

The strong spiritual dimension that permeates the whole document is yet another positive point the Orthodox can immediately endorse. 'Authentic Christian witness is not only in *what* we do in mission but *how* we live out our mission. The church in mission can only be sustained by spiritualities deeply rooted in the Trinity's communion of love' (§29). Closely connected also are the spirit of humility and the imperative of repentance in mission. The cross, states the document, 'calls for repentance in the light of misuse of power and use of the wrong kind of power in mission and in the church' (§33). For generations, even centuries, the triumphalistic character in doing mission overwhelmed the humble quintessence of the Christian message and attitude, the Pauline affirmation that 'God was pleased through the foolishness of what was preached to save those who believe' (1 Corinthians 1:21).

This brings us to the heart of the new mission statement, namely, that in the third millennium Christian mission, in addition to the proclamation of the Good News, should address structural sin, expressed in the intertwined contemporary crises, the economic and environmental, from the perspective of the marginalized (§36): '[Christians] are called to acknowledge the sinful nature of all forms of discrimination and transform unjust structures' (§49), and that 'all missional activity must... safeguard the sacred worth of every human being and of the earth' (§42).

The third millennium, in which all Christians are called to witness to the gospel, is characterized by a deep and prolonged crisis, caused by the world economic system; and their mission cannot be authentically pursued

---

18 'Practically, as well as theologically, mission and unity belong together' (§60).

19 (Metropolitan of Mount Lebanon) Georges Khodr, 'Christianity in a Pluralistic World: The Economy of the Holy Spirit', in *The Ecumenical Review* 23 (1971), 118-28.

20 (Ecumenical Patriarch) Bartholomew Archontonis, *Encountering the Mystery: Understanding Orthodox Christianity Today* (New York, London, Toronto, Sydney and Auckland: Doubleday, 2008).

without addressing this structural evil. In this respect, the 2012 AGAPE 'Call for Action' is clearly echoed in one of the final affirmations of *TTL*:

> Economic globalization has effectively supplanted the God of life with mammon, the god of free-market capitalism that claims the power to save the world through the accumulation of undue wealth and prosperity. Mission in this context needs to be counter-cultural, offering alternatives to such idolatrous visions because mission belongs to the God of life, justice and peace, and not to this false god who brings misery and suffering to people and nature (§108).

Such a strongly socially-oriented missionary appeal, of course, is not something new in the recent history of the missionary branch of the WCC. Some forty years ago, and only in the second decade after the integration of the IMC and the WCC, it was one of the reasons that caused a dramatic split in the world missionary movement with the creation of the Evangelical Lausanne movement. This time, however, the profound biblical, theological and spiritual argumentation can hardly provide any reasonable excuse for theological disagreement on the part of the Evangelicals or the Pentecostals. It surely is hopeful and timely to witness in recent times encouraging initiatives for encounter, reflection and discussion among Evangelical/Pentecostal and Orthodox representatives. It may not be accidental that, with both Evangelicals and Pentecostals, the Orthodox are engaged in a very constructive theological dialogue. It is also notable that since the time of the 2005 Athens World Mission Conference, and particularly in the 2010 Edinburgh centenary celebrations, they have been central players shaping the development of ecumenical missiology.

# *TOGETHER TOWARDS LIFE*: AN ECUMENICAL PROTESTANT ASSESSMENT

Thomas Kemper

Let me say at the outset that my interest in and excitement about *Together towards Life: Mission and Evangelism in Changing Landscapes* (*TTL*) are based on its potential value as a teaching document on Christian mission in a world where that mission is truly global and moves with ease across national, cultural, economic, social and denominational boundaries. I find it an excellent resource for introducing an exploration of mission history, contemporary mission theology and future mission praxis.

### What does 'Protestant Ecumenical' mean?

But to write about it under the rubric 'An Ecumenical Protestant Assessment' raises challenges for me. One dramatic example of the changing mission landscape addressed in *TTL* is the difficulty today of delineating an 'ecumenical Protestant' community with a distinctive Protestant missiological perspective. Such once existed, and much of the content of the document, as well as the process out of which it comes, is rooted in a predominantly Protestant ecumenical tradition, a tradition now significantly enlarged, as *TTL* itself bears witness, by interaction with evangelical Protestant, Roman Catholic, Eastern Orthodox, and Pentecostal perspectives. This history merits brief introductory notice here.

It was impossible to miss an ecumenical Protestant perspective on mission and evangelism at the 1910 World Missionary Conference in Edinburgh. Indeed, the event was predominantly Protestant and the mostly European and American participants shared an optimistic expectation that by working together they could bring the world to Christ in one generation. Such was **the** ecumenical Protestant perspective.

Although tempered by the tragedy of two world wars, Edinburgh's spirit of Protestant co-operation infused the International Missionary Council and the other mostly Protestant organizational streams that produced the World Council of Churches after World War II. This would remain the epitome of ecumenical thought and action for much of the twentieth century. The churches of this movement were primarily the historical Protestant communions of Europe, both established and dissenting, and their North American implants, which today form the Protestant 'mainline': Anglican, some Baptist, Congregationalist, Lutheran, Methodist, Moravian and Presbyterian/Reformed. These churches also constitute what is often called 'conciliar Protestantism', comprised of those denominations participating in local, regional and national ecumenical agencies, whether in the US, Europe or the global South. They are commonly seen as advancing social as well as spiritual agendas.

But the ecumenical impulse would outdistance its Protestant origins. By the 1980s, when I was doing my studies in missiology and later as a missionary in Brazil, 'ecumenical' incorporated more than Protestants in the fields of mission and evangelism. The Second Vatican Council had taken place. Protestants were being influenced by Roman Catholic Liberation Theology. In Brazil some of my most effective mission partners in street ministry were Roman Catholic nuns. Other partners were evangelical Protestants and a few Pentecostals.

'Ecumenical' is often used in contrast to 'Evangelical', but that is an increasingly dubious missional distinction. The success and maturing of the Lausanne Movement from its formation in 1974 to the *Cape Town Commitment* of 2010 showed that 'Evangelicals', too, are collaborative, also embrace social action, while the work of the World Council's Commission on World Mission and Evangelism indicates that 'ecumenicals', too, are evangelical, and also engage in evangelization.

I find no distinctively 21st-century 'Protestant ecumenical' mission platform or perspective, such as that represented by the International Missionary Council and then, to a large degree, the World Council of Churches, in the twentieth century. It seems to me that the historical Protestant ecumenical perspective on mission has been replaced by a larger awareness, and for that I thank God. Moreover, the mission-founded churches of Africa, Asia and Latin America are sources of new mission enthusiasm that stretches the contours of historical Protestant ecumenical thinking.

My own perspective is that of a Methodist, a theological Wesleyan, influenced by the Protestant ecumenical past, very sympathetic to the Lausanne Movement, instructed by my interaction with Catholic colleagues, especially in the Divine Word Order, and attentive to sundry Orthodox theologians. I am Protestant from a minority background, moved by circumstance into a large global context, the CEO of a large mission agency in daily contact with mission worldwide. In that process I have learned an important ecumenical lesson; namely, that one's context within the community of churches affects how one sees the church as a whole and understands the scriptural mission mandates in ecumenical perspective.

I grew up in the United Methodist Church in Germany, a small community to which ecumenical participation was enormously important. We gained recognition and status from ecumenical collaboration. We also learned a great deal about evangelism and mission from the larger Lutheran and Catholic churches. I was surprised to discover that the sizeable American embodiment of United Methodism, related to a truly global constituency, did not value ecumenical involvement as much as that I had experienced in Germany, or even while serving as a missionary in Brazil. Bigness seems to breed ecumenical isolation. The chief executive of a US ecumenical relief organization begged me to attend meetings of the heads of its member-churches. 'The United Methodists haven't seen it as important to meet with the leaders of mostly small denominations,' he said. I have been attending the meetings, sometimes with impatience, I will admit, as I am becoming increasingly aware that mission perspectives are significantly moulded by context and expectation.

## Mission in the Future

What will Christian mission be like in the future? We know already that mission tomorrow will not be the exclusive domain of European and North American institutions or energy. The pendulum of Christian growth has already swung to the global South, where religious faith is expanding even as it contracts in the old missionary-sending lands. Mission zeal for conversions to Jesus Christ is pulsating in the global South. Many expressions of Christianity are growing, for example, in Africa and Asia, and reaching into the global North and West; Pentecostalism is gaining traction everywhere. Will *TTL* speak to this situation? Can it enrich mission in the global South? Could it contribute to the renewal of church life in the older mission-sending lands? Possibly. I hope so.

*TTL* is an excellent manual with the potential for strengthening Christian mission in general and for drawing the churches closer together in the practice of mission. I say this from experience, having used it with multicultural groups of young persons and adults, laity and clergy, and ethnically mixed audiences. I have found that young mission professionals on the staff of my agency draw upon *TTL* in their work with new church starts, congregational revitalization, and social and health ministries in the US and on the international level. I have rarely encountered an ecumenical mission statement that in my context has generated as much attention and proved to be as useful as *TTL*.

## Teaching Themes and Hopes

I find four *TTL* themes particularly useful in mission education, and I have elsewhere cited these four as components for evaluating and shaping mission going forward.[1] The four are the concept of *missio Dei*, reliance on the Holy Spirit, 'mission from the margins', and health and wholeness as components of mission. Here, I want to briefly treat each of these expressed as hopes.

---

[1] Thomas Kemper, 'The Missio Dei in Contemporary Context'. in *International Bulletin of Missionary Research,* 38 (October, 2014), 188-90.

- I hope that the study of *TTL* will help the whole church to understand the enormity of what it means to say that mission is God's mission.
- I hope that the study of *TTL* will lead us to real and renewed reliance on the Holy Spirit.
- I hope that the study of *TTL* will better equip us to take seriously the fact that mission is coming from the margins, and allow God to reform our inherited mission theology and activities in ways that welcome and respect this reality.
- I hope that the study of *TTL* will lead to a lasting embrace of health and healing as expressions of mission without letting the humanitarian overcome the spiritual dimension of wholeness.

## *Missio Dei*

*TTL* is neither an historical nor a theological explication of *missio Dei* but it is a good place to begin a study of the implications of a term used across the broad spectrum of Christianity today. Virtually all theological perspectives affirm mission as 'God's mission', but understandings are not the same among all users. The Latin term clearly means that mission belongs to God, but what does this mean operationally for the church and for Christian discipleship? The meaning is not self-evident. Is the church the channel of God's mission, or is it the church's duty to look for and join God in mission staked out by the divine in social, political and economic spheres? Is it a matter of participating in a course God sets, or allowing God to guide the existing ships of faith? These two perspectives have competed and sometimes coalesced since the term began to gain currency in the 1950s, entering the ecumenical mission vocabulary at a 1952 International Missionary Council conference in Willingen, Germany.[2] The most informative theological and historical investigation of *missio Dei* is David Bosch's *Transforming Mission: Paradigm Shifts in Theology of Mission.*[3]

*TTL* offers this definition:

> The affirmation of God's mission (*missio Dei*) points to the belief in God as One who acts in history and in creation, in concrete realities of time and contexts, who seeks the fullness of life for the whole earth through justice,

---

[2] For a discussion of the use of the term in missiology, see Tormod Engelsviken, '*Missio Dei:* The Understanding and Misunderstanding of a Theological Concept in European Churches and Missiology', in *International Review of Mission*, Vol. XCII, No. 367 (2003), 481-97, and Jacques Matthey, 'Missiology in the World Council of Churches: Update: Presentation, History, Theological Background and Emphases of the Most Recent Mission Statement of the World Council of Churches', in *International Review of Mission*, 90, No. 359 (2001), 429-30.

[3] David J. Bosch, *Transforming Mission: Paradigm Shifts in Theology of Mission* (Maryknoll, NY: Orbis Books, 1991).

> peace and reconciliation. Participation in God's ongoing work of liberation and reconciliation by the Holy Spirit, therefore, includes discerning and unmasking the demons that exploit and enslave. For example, this involves deconstructing patriarchal ideologies, upholding the right to self-determination for indigenous peoples, and challenging the social embeddedness of racism and casteism.[4]

This sounds like agreement with the participatory option. Yet, at another place, the community of faith as bearer of mission is invoked:

> Mission begins in the heart of the Triune God and the love which binds together the Holy Trinity overflows to all humanity and creation. The missionary God who sent the Son to the world calls all God's people (John 20:21), and empowers them to be a community of hope. The church is commissioned to celebrate life, and to resist and transform all life-destroying forces, in the power of the Holy Spirit.[5]

Another strong affirmation of the role of the church in God's mission comes in §10:

> The church is a gift of God to the world for its transformation towards the kingdom of God. Its mission is to bring new life and announce the loving presence of God in our world. We must participate in God's mission in unity, overcoming the divisions and tensions that exist among us, so that the world may believe and all may be one (John 17:21). The church, as the communion of Christ's disciples, must become an inclusive community and exists to bring healing and reconciliation to the world. How can the church renew herself to be missional and move forward together towards life in its fullness?[6]

Section 8 further asserts: 'All Christians, churches and congregations are called to be vibrant messengers of the gospel of Jesus Christ, which is the good news of salvation. Evangelism is a confident but humble sharing of our faith and conviction with other people.'[7]

I find it invigorating that non-exclusive interpretations of the operation of *missio Dei* are found in *TTL*. This inclusiveness offers the opportunity to investigate common or differing perspectives of mission according to theological stream or denominational doctrines and confessions. All of us need to comb through our particular tradition to gain theological clarity on mission historically, and to learn how choices are currently made about mission functionality. There are many, many styles and options for mission and evangelism. How do we determine which embody or represent *missio Dei*? This is an essential question for mission in the future and is one closely related to the issue of reliance on the Holy Spirit.

---

[4] *TTL,* §43.
[5] *TTL,* §2.
[6] *TTL,* §10.
[7] *TTL,* §8.

## The Holy Spirit

Some power besides human effort must sustain mission commitment, especially when mission is seen as belonging to God. Historically and psychologically, that power is the Holy Spirit, the progenitor and prime actor in *missio Dei. TTL* is seriously Trinitarian with regard to the nature of God. The Spirit is active in creation. The Spirit empowers Jesus at baptism and in ministry, sustains him in crucifixion, and acts in resurrection. The Spirit is universally present and provides the incentive for mission: 'By the Spirit we participate in the mission of love that is at the heart of the life of the Trinity… All who respond to the outpouring of the love of God are invited to join in with the Spirit in the mission of God.'[8]

The Trinitarian framework no doubt reflects Orthodox influence, and the strong Spirit emphasis, Pentecostal contributions. Perhaps *TTL* has such strong appeal to me because my first reading of it came in the wake of months of work on a mission theology statement for the United Methodist General Board of Global Ministries, part of that time as a director before I was staff of the agency. We struggled to write a relatively short statement that took account of scripture, history, experience and reason – matters important to Methodists. Methodism was born as a mission movement and never moved away from it, yet seeks to restate its basic nature in successive generations. The last such United Methodist statement, 'Grace Upon Grace: God's Mission and Ours' in 1988 has continuing value, but we needed a succinct affirmation in a social media era. Our goal was 850 words, and we accomplished it with a great deal of prayer. I was not surprised by the instructive insight into the nature of God's mission that came from local pastors and laity.

The Holy Spirit became our guide and also the organizing theological concept via the Trinity in our statement, which begins with confession of our mission as *missio Dei*. It moves from creation, to the incarnation of undying love in Jesus Christ, to the community of faith animated and sustained by the Spirit in pursuit of God's purposes in the world.

We found hope and determination by keeping the focus on *ru'ach*:

> God's Holy Spirit calls the church into being for mission. The Church is one sign of God's presence in the world and of God's intention in creation. In response to God's call and the leading of the Holy Spirit, women and men, young and old, of all nations, stations and races, and in all times and places, unite as the living body of Christ to join God's mission of redemption, bearing witness to God's presence in the world.[9]
>
> Transforming witness, sustained by the Spirit, is the substance of mission.

---

[8] *TTL,* §18.

[9] General Board of Global Ministries, The United Methodist Church, 'Theology of Mission Statement': www.umcmission.org/Learn-About-Us/About-Global-Ministries/Theology-of-Mission

> The Church in Mission lifts up the name of Jesus in thought, word and deed, proclaiming Jesus Christ as 'the Word become flesh' through its own incarnate living; deeds of love; and service, healing and renewal.[10]

An affirmation of the universal presence of God follows, with the statement concluding with an opening to God's new challenges in the future:

> The Spirit is always moving to sweep the church into a new mission age. With openness and gratitude we await the leading of the Spirit in ways not yet seen as God continues to work God's purposes out in our own day in a new way.[11]

I go into the details of my own organization's understanding of the role of the Holy Spirit in mission to underscore the value of *TTL*'s Spirit-based theology to a real community of mission practitioners in the 21st century.

### 'Mission from the Margins'

The phrase 'Mission from the Margins' is one of the most valuable teaching tools in *TTL* because it is so dramatic and fresh. It testifies to the global nature of the church, to the inclusion of the poor in the community of faith, and to the demand for greater equality in awareness and respect for Christian witness and service.

This awareness that an old mission paradigm is no longer sound or possible is well stated in *TTL*:

> Mission has been understood as a movement taking place from the centre to the periphery, and from the privileged to the marginalized of society. Now people from the margins are claiming their key role as agents of mission and affirming mission as transformation. This reversal of roles in the envisioning of mission has strong biblical foundations because God chose the poor, the foolish and the powerless (1 Corinthians 1:18-31) to further God's mission of justice and peace so that life may flourish.[12]

The concept and reality of mission from the margins has developed in concert with the shift of Christianity's centre of gravity from the West to the global South and East. In that respect, it is not as prophetic as it is simply descriptive, but it requires a significant shift in the direction of mission perception. The inherited presumption was that mission comes from well-established, well-funded, institutional-centred churches and is directed towards the poor, marginalized parts of the world, notably in Africa, Asia and Latin America. This has long been under challenge by the mission-founded and indigenous churches of the global South, at least since the IMC conference held in Whitby, Canada, in 1947. At Whitby, the younger churches made it clear that they intended to assume a greater role

---

[10] GBGM, 'Theology of Mission Statement'.
[11] GBGM, 'Theology of Mission Statement'.
[12] *TTL*, §6.

in selecting the missionaries they would receive, and intended, as they were able, to become part of the church's evangelization and service.

The presentations given and papers written at Whitby speak of 'partnership in obedience to God' in identifying with God's mission.[13] Churches in some former mission-receiving countries – I think of such diverse places as South Korea, Brazil and Nigeria – have become primary players in the practice and support of world mission; movement has been slower in most areas, though not in intention and zeal. While still financially dependent upon American and European support, our United Methodist missionaries are today at least 50% from the global South.

I have experienced a sense of partnership in obedience to God with Christian refugees from Africa coming to Europe, where they infuse struggling traditional congregations with new vigour and mission vision.

*TTL* states the case in moving away from the perception that 'mission can only be done by the powerful to the powerless… People on the margins have agency, and can often see what, from the centre, is out of view'.[14]

'Agency' is an essential quality of mission, and faith, hope and love are agencies even more than dollars, organization and educational resources. Those on the margins are often gifted with great agency: faith, hope and love and, as *TTL* states, 'people in positions of privilege have much to learn from the daily struggles of people living in marginal conditions'.[15]

Let us, however, not polarize here. At the margins and at the centre we find gifted people engaged in God's mission. However, at the margins and at the centre we also find a lack of human and civil liberty, and there can be places with no organizational stability or transparent financial systems. Partnership then also requires action to ensure human rights, access to educational opportunities and, most of all, respect for those who bring the gospel of Jesus Christ from the margins. And partnership in obedience to God means that those with material abundance have the responsibility of facilitating mission from the margins.

## Health and Healing

Health and healing have long been parts of practical Christian service, but seldom recognized in theological statements on mission and evangelism. That these themes are prominent in *TTL* is in no small part the outcome of decades of reflection and advocacy by the WCC's Christian Medical Commission, and work within the WCC Commission on World Mission and Evangelism. The 2005 World Missionary Conference explored the topic 'Come, Holy Spirit, Heal and Reconcile', with the subtitle, 'Called in

---

13 Charles W. Ranson (ed), *Renewal and Advance: Christian Witness in a Revolutionary World* (London: Edinburgh House, 1948).
14 *TTL,* §38.
15 *TTL,* §38.

Christ to be Reconciling and Healing Communities'. A great strength of *TTL*'s affirmation is its holistic approach, and this gives me hope that missiologists, missionaries and church members in the future will understand, in the words of the statement, that 'Health is more than physical and/or mental well-being, and healing is not primarily medical'.[16] *TTL* offers a biblical view of health that embraces spiritual, emotional and physical aspects of life. This view sees 'a human being as a multi-dimensional unity, and the body, soul, and mind as interrelated and interdependent. It thus affirms the social, political and ecological dimensions of personhood and wholeness'.[17]

Health, in *TTL*, is a 'sense of wholeness', and God's mission of wholeness incorporates not only persons but families, communities and the fullness of creation. As I have written, 'This emphasis on community as an ingredient of health and wholeness: 1) recognizes that congregations today are becoming involved in local and global health mission and ministry, and 2) promotes the expansion of this form of the *missio Dei.*'[18]

An understanding of health, healing and wholeness as expressions of God's grace – as mission, not human charity – is gaining acceptance, even enthusiasm, in my United Methodist Church. Real grassroots interest undergirds our new unit on Global Health at the General Board of Global Ministries. This responds in part to expansion of community-based primary health care by missionaries and volunteers, and partnership with non-profit and governmental organizations. It found broad acceptance through an anti-malaria campaign in Africa that depended upon community-based training and volunteers. 'What else can we do together and with partners?' church members asked. Energy has been generated for a new wholeness campaign, based on Jesus' assurance in John 10 of 'abundant life'. Tentatively called: 'Abundant Life – Our Promise to Children', the campaign, likely to be launched in 2016 at the United Methodist General Conference, pledges the church to reach one million children with life-saving interventions by 2020, as part of a broad-based collaborative effort to significantly improve global health for all by 2035.

There is a danger to be avoided in expanding attention to health ministries, and the same applies to church-based response to natural and human-caused disasters – the danger of letting the humanistic and altruistic motives overshadow the theological and spiritual aspects of mission. It is often easier to advertise response to hunger, suffering, homelessness and disease than it is demonstrate that Christian service is a response to divine grace, not an end in itself. Of course, Christian disaster relief and follow-up community development, health ministries and the promotion of human rights make no distinction as to religious affiliation, nationality, ethnicity,

---

[16] *TTL,* §51.
[17] *TTL,* §51.
[18] Kemper, 'The Missio Dei in Contemporary Context', 189.

gender or sexual orientation. The objectives are to give evidence to God's love for all, to indicate that the church as the instrument of divine grace cares about the entire human family. Recipients may not be aware of the spiritual and missional motivation, but the providers certainly must be.

In using *TTL* in mission education with regard to health and wholeness, this paragraph is essential:

> Actions towards healing and wholeness of life of persons and communities are an important expression of mission. Healing was not only a central feature of Jesus' ministry but also a feature of his call to his followers to continue his work (Matt. 10:1). Healing is also one of the gifts of the Holy Spirit (1 Cor. 12:9; Acts 3). The Spirit empowers the church for a life-nurturing mission, which includes prayer, pastoral care and professional health care on the one hand, and prophetic denunciation of the root causes of suffering, transformation of structures that dispense injustice, and pursuit of scientific research on the other.[19]

It really is about God.

## Conclusion

*Together Toward Life: Mission and Evangelism in Changing Landscapes* has become a valuable resource in the library of mission resources of the United Methodist Church. It was at the centre of the March/April, 2015 issue of *New World Outlook*, our bi-monthly mission magazine. The overall theme was 'Reflections on Mission and Evangelism', and featured perspectives on *TTL* from various cultures and theological points of view. We use it in missionary training. We feature responses to it by staff members on our website. The overall tone and content of the statement track well with our experience of mission in a time when we believe that the Holy Spirit is truly at work in changing mission landscapes.

---

[19] *TTL*, §50.

# *TOGETHER TOWARDS LIFE*: AN EVANGELICAL ASSESSMENT

Samuel Escobar

For this Evangelical commentary on *Together towards Life* (*TTL*) to make sense to the reader, this writer has to describe the perspective from which he is writing.[1] During a recent trip from Spain to Brazil over the Atlantic Ocean, I had time to read *TTL* and reflect about Christian mission in relation to it. I was attending a theological consultation in São Paulo, at which the Latin American Theological Fraternity (LATF) celebrated its 45th anniversary. With my colleagues René Padilla and Pedro Arana, we had been among the signers of the *Declaración de Cochabamba*, the founding document with which we launched the LATF in 1970. One of the joys of this celebrative occasion in São Paulo was to meet a new generation of theologians which were pursuing the vision of the LATF. We were guests of the Baptist Church of Agua Branca, one of the liveliest Evangelical churches I have visited recently. Among the people I met was Alzira Nascimento, the director of the mission department of the church.

Alzira was a missionary in Angola for seventeen years, during the civil war, and is now a professor and promoter of mission work. She is also a missiologist who reflects systematically about her practice in the light of God's word. I was struck by sections of her recent book *Evangelização ou Colonização?*[2] which are very similar in content and style to the text of the *TTL*. Her experiences in the context of post-colonial Angola made her question the primary missionary approach that she had been practising until then. She had to learn to overcome the tendency to treat people in her mission service as *objects* instead of *subjects*. She had to learn the difference between evangelization and colonization. It was not easy. She came to realize that the colonialist paradigm was deeply entrenched in the missionary practice of her church, both at home and abroad. Her book reflects missiology at its best, particularly in relation to the practice of mission. In my view, Evangelical missiologists like Alzira will be the ones primarily working with the agenda set by *TTL*.

---

[1] This chapter is an expanded version of Samuel Escobar, 'Together towards Life: Mission and Evangelism in Changing Landscapes', in *International Bulletin of Missionary Research*, 38/4 (October 2014), 193-95.

[2] Alzira Nascimento, *Evangelização ou Colonização?* (Viçosa, Brazil: Ultimato, 2015).

## A Brief Historical Approach

When my generation founded the Latin American Theological Fraternity (LATF) back in 1970, we were part of a growing number of Evangelical pastors, missionaries and theological educators searching for answers to questions that came from our evangelistic and missionary commitment and activity.[3] It was a vocation to serve the theology emerging from churches that were relatively new at the time, committed to evangelization and fast-growing within the overall framework of a Christendom in decline. As Evangelical theologians, we found ourselves on the margins of the dominant cultural establishments of our countries but at the centre of the missionary action of our churches. We were part of communities that saw the world as a territory to be 'conquered for Christ', and the gospel as a transforming message that was going to bring forth a new spiritual, social and political creation, even though there was no clear 'project' to visualize the outcome of that process.[4]

For our generation it was obvious that liberation theologies born in Roman Catholic soil could offer no adequate answers for urgent questions about the meaning of the gospel and the evangelistic mission of the church. We acknowledged, however, promising signs in the post-Vatican II self-criticism, in the return to biblical sources and in the emphasis on relating theology and praxis.[5] On the other hand, we perceived much of the theology developed in the 1960s and 1970s within the ecumenical foci related to the World Council of Churches as a theology that, in spite of its impressive academic dress, was shaped by a disposition and stance that reflected the uncertainties and the fatigue of a declining Protestantism in Europe.[6] Catholic liberation theologies were heavily dependent on the assumption that Latin America was a 'Christian continent', and their ecumenical Protestant counterparts would not question that assumption. In

---

[3] For a history and evaluation of the LATF, see Sharon E. Heaney, *Contextual Theology for Latin America: Liberation Themes in Evangelical Perspective* (Carlisle, UK: Paternoster, 2008); Daniel Salinas, *Latin American Evangelical Theology in the 1970s* (Leiden: Brill, 2009).

[4] I use the word 'project' in the sense described by Paul Freston in 'In Search of an Evangelical Political Project for Brazil: A Pentecostal 'Showvention', in *Transformation,* 9/3 (July-Sept 1992); especially 31.

[5] For a later elaboration of these points, see C. René Padilla, 'Liberation Theology: an Appraisal', in Daniel S. Schipani (ed), *Freedom and Discipleship* (Maryknoll, NY: Orbis Books, 1989); Emilio A. Núñez, *Liberation Theology* (Chicago, IL: Moody Press, 1985); and Samuel Escobar, *Liberation Themes in Reformational Perspective* (Sioux Center, IA: Dordt College Press, 1989).

[6] See the foundational documents of the Latin American Theological Fraternity in Pedro Savage (ed), *El debate contemporáneo sobre la Biblia* (Barcelona, Spain: Ediciones Evangélicas Europeas, 1972); see Samuel Escobar, 'Identity, Future and Mission of Latin American Protestantism', in *Theological Fraternity Bulletin* 1/2 (1978).

such theologies, there was no room for the fundamental evangelistic stance of our churches.

It became clear for us as Evangelical theologians that we had to engage in the development of a contextual theology that would aim to be 'forged in the heat of Evangelical reality in Latin America, in faithfulness to the Word of God'.[7] We perceived that such theology could not limit itself to be 'an adaptation of an existing theology of universal validity to a particular situation… aided by benevolent missionary paternalism'.[8] Rather, its aim would be to offer 'a new open-ended reading of Scripture with a hermeneutic in which the biblical text and the historical situation become mutually engaged in a dialogue whose purpose is to place the Church under the Lordship of Jesus Christ in its particular context'.[9]

This agenda was followed in the 1970s, 1980s and 1990s up to the present, and the participation of Latin American Evangelicals in the consultations and debates of these decades contributed to an ongoing dialogue in the Evangelical world and beyond. After all those years, the tone and the content of *TTL*, echoing also the voice of many churches, came as a surprise as much as a challenge! To read an official statement on mission and evangelism from the World Council of Churches that reflects so many of the concerns expressed by Evangelicals through the years is exciting indeed.

In 2010 we celebrated the centennial of Edinburgh 1910, and then in 2014 we were celebrating forty years of the *Lausanne Covenant* and the movement that followed it. In fact, the *TTL* affirmation has reminded me of what I consider providential convergences for Christian mission in the mid-1970s. First, in 1974 Evangelicals gathered in Lausanne and issued the *Lausanne Covenant*, which reaffirmed commitment to mission and evangelism. But the Covenant also contained a critical reflection about the way in which evangelism and mission were carried out up to that moment, with a call to repentance and a commitment to explore realistically a more Christ-like way of going about it.

That same year the Synod of Bishops of the Roman Catholic Church asked Pope Paul VI to issue a renewed call to evangelism, and in 1975 he promulgated the Apostolic Exhortation *Evangelii Nuntiandi* about evangelization in the modern world. The same year the WCC had its fifth Assembly in Nairobi with renewed attention to the themes of mission and evangelism. Missiologist James A. Scherer says that, in Nairobi, 'Assembly statements about "confessing Christ" had a strongly Christocentric, Trinitarian and churchly ring, echoing Eastern Orthodox and Roman

---

[7] Samuel Escobar, 'Biblical Content and Anglo-Saxon Trappings in Latin American Theology', in *Occasional Bulletin,* Latin American Theological Fraternity, 3 (October 1972); 2.

[8] René Padilla, 'Biblical Foundations: a Latin American Study', in *Evangelical Review of Theology,* 7/1 (1983), 86.

[9] René Padilla, 'Biblical Foundations: a Latin American Study'.

Catholic influence but also responding to evangelical criticisms'.[10] Soon after, in 1982, the first WCC mission and evangelism affirmation was published.

The chronicle, by Jooseop Keum, published in the *International Bulletin of Missionary Research* in April 2014, provides a fascinating description of the setting from which *TTL* came into being.[11] Though its structure and the style are different from the *Cape Town Commitment* that came out of the Lausanne III gathering in South Africa in 2010, I find that there are also important theological convergences between the two.

## Trinitarian Conviction and Pneumatological Emphasis

At several key points *TTL* affirms a Trinitarian position. The first and second paragraphs are clear theological statements in this regard and the missiological unfolding of the faith which is affirmed comes in §3:

> Life in the Holy Spirit is the essence of mission, the core of why we do what we do, and how we live our lives. Spirituality gives deepest meaning to our lives and motivates our actions. It is a sacred gift from the Creator, the energy for affirming and caring for life. This mission spirituality has a dynamic of transformation which, through spiritual commitment of people, is capable of transforming the world in God's grace. How can we reclaim mission as transformative spirituality which is life-affirming?

Though Trinitarian in its foundation, the document has what I would call a pneumatological structure. However, my own missiological emphasis on Christology resonates with the statement in §16: 'Therefore, a pneumatological focus on Christian mission recognises that mission is essentially christologically based and relates the work of the Holy Spirit to the salvation through Jesus Christ.' The four main sections of *TTL* are built upon statements about the nature of the Holy Spirit: the Spirit of mission, the Spirit of liberation, the Spirit of community and the Spirit of Pentecost. I find it significant that the section about liberation is connected with the affirmation of 'mission from the margins'.

Probably many Evangelical pastors, teachers and even theologians would not relate the work of the Holy Spirit to liberation the way *TTL* does. But in the last three decades I have followed the search for a renewed understanding of the role of the Holy Spirit and the way he works. Let me mention a couple of milestones which address key theological themes from a liberationist perspective. In 1992 Eldin Villafañe, a Pentecostal theological educator published his book *The Liberating Spirit: Toward an*

---

[10] James A. Scherer, *Gospel, Church and Kingdom: Comparative Studies in World Mission Theology* (Eugene, OR: Wipf & Stock, 2004), 40.

[11] Jooseop Keum, 'Shift in the Center of Gravity for the Ecumenical Movement? WCC Busan Assembly and the Korean Churches', in *International Bulletin of Missionary Research,* 38/2 (April 2014), 64-67.

*Hispanic American Pentecostal Social Ethic.*[12] Villafañe was the founder and director of the Center for Urban Ministerial Education (CUME) in Boston. In 1986 Joseph Comblin, a respected Belgian Catholic missionary and liberation theologian published (originally in Portuguese) his book *The Holy Spirit and Liberation.*[13] Both these works anticipated in important ways the relationship between pneumatology and liberation which we find in *TTL*.

These days in Spain, mission is taking place in new and creative forms. I know of several Latin American evangelical women migrants who earn their living caring daily for old people in Madrid or Valencia, and share with them spontaneously the good news of God's love in Christ. They would never describe this as actual 'mission' work. I can also think of a young Argentinian missionary in North Africa who is a soccer coach and thus can reach dozens of teenagers with whom at some points he can talk about Jesus Christ in a spontaneous and natural manner.

In a way, we have witnessed the end of the imperial age of mission in which the gospel was presented 'from above' by Spanish conquistadores, British merchants and American enthusiasts who sometimes followed too closely the colonial or neo-colonial patterns of their nations. Now the younger churches are carrying on mission 'from below', not only through missionaries but also through Filipino maids in Muslim countries, illegal immigrants in the United States and African university students in Europe. As *TTL* states in §15: 'The Holy Spirit works in the world often in mysterious and unknown ways beyond our imagination' (Luke 1:34-35; John 3:8; Acts 2:16-21). We missionaries and missiologists must be ready for surprises as the Spirit keeps mission going, in his own way. The agenda for the future is very well stated in §106: 'We affirm that today mission movements are emerging from the global South and East which are multi-directional and many-faceted. The shifting centre of gravity of Christianity to the global South and East challenges us to explore missiological expressions that are rooted in these contexts, culture, and spiritualities.'

I find it necessary to state a point of clarification: §38 of *TTL* about margins and marginalization describes the emergence of a new missionary movement: 'Mission from the margins seeks to counteract injustices in life, church and mission. It seeks to be an alternative missional movement against the perception that mission can only be done by the powerful to the powerless, by the rich to the poor, or by the privileged to the marginalized.' This paragraph seems to attribute to the new missionary movement a kind of fighting attitude with what one could interpret as a vindictive intention and tone. In the attitude of Latin American or Korean missionaries that I have observed through the years, the joy of obedience and a sense of

---

[12] Eldin Villafañe, *The Liberating Spirit: Toward an Hispanic American Pentecostal Social Ethic* (Lanham, MD: University Press of America, 1992).

[13] Joseph Comblin, *The Holy Spirit and Liberation* (London: Burns & Oates, 1989).

privilege seem to be the predominant mood and attitude, in spite of their limited resources and the lowliness of their social status.

## Widening the Meaning of Spirituality

The above-quoted paragraph also has a reference to spirituality which is then developed in §29-35, in the section on 'Transformative spirituality'. In the Evangelical tradition, missionaries have been known as spiritual giants. Their exercise of the spiritual disciplines has been an inspiration and example. I trace it back to the strong influence of Pietism in the development of the Protestant missionary movement. *TTL* has kept several of the key elements of this tradition but it also calls us to a *transformative spirituality*: 'Mission spirituality resists and seeks to transform all life-destroying values and systems wherever these are at work in our economies, our politics, and even our churches' (§30).

Later on, in §48, *TTL* invites us to a painful self-examination: 'In reality, however, mission, money and political power are strategic partners. Although our theological and missiological talk says a lot about the mission of the church being in solidarity with the poor, sometimes in practice it is much more concerned with being in the centres of power, eating with the rich and lobbying for money to maintain ecclesial bureaucracy. This poses particular challenges to reflect on what is the good news for people who are privileged and powerful.'

A moving case of missionary self-examination is described by Gerald M. Costello in his book *Mission to Latin America: The Successes and Failures of a Twentieth Century Crusade*.[14] This book gives an account of the crisis of conscience that was experienced by many American Catholic missionaries in the 1950s and 1960s when they realized that their church was part of the political machinery that in certain cases exploited the poor in Latin America. The new awareness made many of them practise 'a preferential option for the poor' long before the Bishops adopted it in the now famous Conference of Medellín (1968). Some of them paid with their lives or were ostracized by the national hierarchies, and their self-examination preceded the coming of liberation theologies.

In spite of the 'preferential option for the poor' that the Roman Catholic Church started to practise in the late 1960s, popular forms of Protestantism continued to grow. One could say that in Latin America the poor seemed to take a preferential option for Protestantism, a situation that made some theologians in Latin America feel perplexed and full of questions. They call to mind John the Baptist who, when he was imprisoned and the situation developed differently from his expectations, sent his disciples to ask Jesus 'Are you the one who was to come or should we expect someone else?'

---

[14] Gerald M. Costello, *Mission to Latin America: The Successes and Failures of a Twentieth Century Crusade* (Maryknoll, NY: Orbis Books, 1979).

(Matthew 11:3). Jesus' answer was a simple call to consider the facts: 'Go back and report to John what you hear and see: the blind receive sight, the lame walk, those who have leprosy are cured, the deaf hear, the dead are raised, and the good news is preached to the poor. Blessed is the man who does not fall away on account of me' (Matthew 11:4-6). Today, perplexed theologians are also invited to look at the facts of an emerging 'Third Church'.[15] It is the emerging church of the poor, of oral theology, narrative preaching, dreams and visions, signs and wonders, and the transformative spiritual power which at given points does far more for the poor than the elaborate social agendas of traditional denominations. Maybe in North and South the time has come for theologians to do on a global scale what Richard Mouw calls 'consulting the faithful', i.e. intellectuals learning from popular religion.[16]

## Mission and Freedom of Religion

I find relevant and necessary the statements in the final paragraphs of *TTL* about the nature of mission and evangelism (§109), and dialogue and co-operation in mission (§110), particularly after having participated in the origins of the Lausanne movement since 1966, when in the Berlin Congress of Evangelism John Stott invited us to reconsider the Great Commission in the Gospel of John. Working together with René Padilla on the development of a concept of mission that would have Christological structure, we found Stott's emphasis in Berlin refreshing and seminal. By the time of the Lausanne Congress in 1974, the follow-up to the Berlin process with regional congresses in Europe, Asia, the USA, Canada and Latin America had confirmed the validity and relevance of what we had been trying to do in Latin America under René Padilla's leadership.[17]

What I find missing in *TTL* is a more specific and detailed reference to mission in the context of post-Christendom situations, like the one in which I now live in Spain. §10 states: 'Authentic evangelism is done with respect to freedom of religion and belief, for all human beings, as images of God. Proselytism by violent means, economic incentive or abuse of power is contrary to the message of the gospel. In doing evangelism, it is important to build relations of respect and trust between people of different faiths.'

---

[15] The expression was coined by missiologist Walbert Bühlman to describe the new global church, contrasting it with the dominant Eastern Church of the first thousand years of our era, and the dominant Western Church of the second millennium.

[16] Richard Mouw, *Consulting the Faithful* (Grand Rapids: Eerdmans, 1994).

[17] I have described this process in Chapter 1 of my book *The New Global Mission* (Leicester, UK: IVP, 2003), and in the Chapter I contributed to Jeffrey P. Greenman and Gene L. Greene (eds), *Global Theology in Evangelical Perspective* (Leicester, UK: IVP, 2012). René Padilla's theological contribution to the Lausanne movement is gathered in his book *Mission Between the Times: Essays on the Kingdom,* revised and updated (London: Langham Monographs, 2010).

Evangelical missionaries in Spain find themselves doing mission in one of the most traditional contexts of Christendom. The Roman Catholic Church has lost much of the power of social coercion that it had until the 1970s, the point at which Spain had to adopt religious freedom if it wanted to become part of the European Union. Nevertheless, the church still has money, power, properties and an array of educational institutions, many of which are partially supported by the state. It is indeed sad to realise that in most cases when bishops raise their voice it is in order to defend old privileges. In the past, the church attempted to create a negative image of Protestants, while Spanish bishops bitterly opposed the concept of religious freedom during Vatican II. Thus, the evangelistic activity of Evangelical churches, instead of being occasionally perceived as proselytistic, can be seen as the manifestation of the existence of other ways to live out Christianity.

With few exceptions, there is no co-operation in mission between Catholics and Protestants in Spain. Among the exceptions one could mention the co-operation between Catholics and Protestants in the Bible Society. Since 2008 they have been working together on an inter-confessional translation of the Bible, an attempt that finds growing acceptance in Spain and Latin America. Moreover, some Protestants are part of the Juan XXIII Theological Association that has an annual theological congress attended by as many as 1,500 theologians. The Association, however, does not enjoy the blessing of the Bishops. A book published in 2010 compiled the final declarations or messages of the first thirty congresses that met since 1981. On certain points the concept of mission that these declarations present comes very close in language and style to sections of *TTL*.[18]

For many Catholics the Protestant presence is a non-issue. I was very happy when I received my copy of the *Atlas of Global Christianity* edited by Todd M. Johnson and Kenneth R. Ross, published for the centennial of Edinburgh 1910.[19] Rosemary Dowsett and I had contributed a chapter about Evangelicals, and I was fascinated and thankful for the final product. However, I felt disappointed and saddened when I read the chapter about Southern Europe: Spain, Portugal and France, among other countries. Not once in the whole chapter are Protestants mentioned. It appeared as if they simply did not exist.

In spite of the above-mentioned facts, there is a Protestant missionary presence at work in Spain, and missionaries are trying to learn how to co-operate with the small existing Protestant churches, and at the same time how to shape mission in response to the present historical and cultural situation. In 2013 I spoke at a gathering of Latin American missionaries in

---

[18] Asociación de teólogos/as Juan XXIII, *Congresos de Teología.* (Madrid: *Mensajes*, 2010).

[19] Todd M. Johnson and Kenneth R. Ross (eds), *Atlas of Global Christianity, 1910-2010* (Edinburgh: Edinburgh University Press, 2009).

Europe. Over a hundred of them met at Torrox, near Málaga, representing fifteen countries. After that I crossed the peninsula to Seville in order to teach an intensive course about Christian mission organized by Irismenio Ribeiro, a Brazilian missionary who leads an extension theological centre for the region. It was hosted by the Baptist church of Montequinto, where the pastor is Stella Maris Merlo, an Argentinian who has been serving as a missionary in Spain for 33 years. During the course we prayed for a team of Spanish missionaries that serve in Equatorial Guinea in West Africa under the European Baptist Mission. At meals we were hosted by Gladys, a lady from El Salvador, a hardworking immigrant, and one of the hundreds of Latin American volunteers that are active in Spanish churches these days. This is the reality of the global church in the 21st century, and as I experience it in Spain, I cannot but praise the Lord as I trace back this reality to the two centuries of missionary work that have preceded us.

On the other hand, it is rather puzzling, how the Roman Catholic Church in Spain, despite its ageing clergy and the continuous loss of popularity among the population, sends abroad a strong missionary force of 14,000 men and women. There are, for instance, 969 Spanish missionaries in Perú, 968 in Venezuela, 666 in Argentina, 26 in China, 17 in Indonesia, and 116 in India.[20] The presence of these missionaries in Latin America is focused among the poorest segments of society and in remote areas. Some of them, such as Pedro Casaldaliga in Brazil or the six Jesuits who were killed in El Salvador, have been very vocal in their defence of the poor and in their opposition to structures of injustice and exploitation.

Through instruments such as the above-mentioned Atlas we have at our disposal an incredible amount of data about peoples, nations, sociological trends and cultural patterns. Some of us are also familiar with a formidable set of missionary institutions, denominational and interdenominational, each one with their agendas that reflect their theological convictions as well as an accumulated wisdom that cannot be despised. There is data that cannot be changed but institutions and patterns need to be open to change. *TTL* provides inspiration, theological foundations and challenging questions. As we practise our mission, we must be attentive to the Holy Spirit. We also have to be attentive to new and spontaneous missionary developments in unexpected places which may contain suggestions as to the way in which the existing missionary enterprise may be reformed. This should not be difficult for people who believe in an *ecclesia reformata semper reformanda*. And we can add that the renewal of spiritual vitality has had an impact on mission when it has been matched with creativity in regard to structures and methods.

---

[20] 'Más de 14,000 misioneros españoles dan su vida en el mundo para dar a conocer el Evangelio': www.religionenlibertad.com/artículo=25466 (accessed 28th June 2013).

# *TOGETHER TOWARDS LIFE*: A PENTECOSTAL ASSESSMENT

Timothy T. N. Lim

This chapter appraises *Together towards Life* (*TTL*) after a concise account of global Pentecostalism, its ecumenical dialogues, and missional expressions.[1] The appraisal examines aspects of *TTL* that Pentecostals would affirm, are likely to affirm, and not amenable to agree, with reasons and sources for further investigation.

### Global Pentecostalism

Contemporary global Pentecostalism traces its origins to William Seymour and an outpouring of the Holy Spirit at Azusa Street in 1901.[2] Reports uncover other indigenous Pentecostal outpourings before, during and after 1901, both at Azusa Street and elsewhere (e.g. Pyongyang).[3] In our milieu, global Pentecostalism contributes to societal transformation and the renewal of Christianity.[4] Pentecostalism transmutes into various streams (classical, neo-Pentecostal, charismatic, neo-charismatic and 'third wave'). Occasionally, some streams maintain exclusivity from other streams. Nearly all share similar phenomenological experiences of the Spirit – Spirit baptism, *glossolalia*, manifold operations of charismata, power encounters,

---

[1] Readers may also be interested in my review essay, 'Comparative Pneumatology in Together towards Life, Evangelii Gaudium, and the Cape Town Commitment', in *International Review of Mission* 104.2 (2015) 203-16.

[2] Mel Cecil Robeck Jr,, *Azusa Street Revival* (Nashville, TN: Thomas Nelson, 2006).

[3] A.H. Anderson, 'Pentecostalism in East Asia: Indigenous Oriental Christianity?', in *Pneuma,* 22:1 (Spring 2000), 115-32; Young-Hoon Lee, 'Korean Pentecost: The Great Revival of 1907', in *Asian Journal of Pentecostal Studies,* 4:1 (2001), 73-83; Hwa Yung, 'Endued with Power: The Pentecostal-Charismatic Renewal and the Asian Church in the Twenty-First Century', in *Asian Journal of Pentecostal Studies* 6:1 (2003), 63-82, esp. 68-69; Sung Won Yang, *The Influence of the Revival Movement of 1901-1910 on the Development of Korean Christianity* (Southern Baptist Theological Seminary, 2002).

[4] Allan Heaton Anderson, *To the Ends of the Earth* (Oxford: OUP, 2013); Allan Heaton Anderson, 'To All Points of the Compass', *Enrichment Journal* (Springfield, MO: The General Council of the Assemblies of God, Spring 2006); Donald E. Miller, Kimon H. Sargeant and Richard Flory (eds), *Spirit and Power* (Oxford: OUP, 2013).

healing, exorcism and deliverance ministries.[5] Phenomenological explanations do not fully account for the multi-complex religious, socio-economic-political, divine-temporal engagements or the religious community despite the similar, confluential and convergent narratives about the experiences of the Holy Spirit.[6] The movement's diversity is shaped by global, cultural, theological-ecumenical, linguistic and indigenous expressions in various social locations.[7] And because of the plurality of localized expression, it is almost impossible to gather a team to speak representatively for the varieties within this movement.[8] Statistics report nearly 18,810 independent, indigenous, post-denominational groups of global neo-charismatics, 1,500 intra-denominations in North America, and another fifteen hundred Pentecostal denominations in Chile.[9] The challenges for this global movement abound, as does its potential.[10]

## Pentecostals in Ecumenical Dialogue

Ecumenical dialogues have been continuing across various communions.[11] Pentecostals have moved from being a marginalized community to becoming an invited dialogue partner at world, national and regional levels. Pentecostal dialogue with other churches is no longer a novelty.[12] The Joint Consultative Group between the World Council of Churches and Pentecostals formed in 2000 has paved the way for Pentecostal participation in bilateral and multilateral meetings.[13] The *Focolare*

---

[5] W. Paul Williamson and Ralph W. Hood, 'Spirit Baptism: A Phenomenological Experience', in *Mental Health, Religion and Culture,* 14:6 (2011), 543-59; Peter D. Neumann, *Pentecostal Experience.* Princeton Theological Monograph 187 (Eugene, OR: Wipf & Stock, 2012).

[6] Stephen C. Torr, *A Dramatic Pentecostal/Charismatic Anti-Theodicy* (Eugene, OR: Pickwick, 2013), 107. See also Vinson Synan and Amos Yong (eds), *Global Renewal Christianity* (Lake Mary, FL: Charisma House, 2015), 4 vols.

[7] Wonsuk Ma, Veli-Matti Kärkkäinen and J. Kwabena Asamoah-Gyadu, *Pentecostal Mission and Global Christianity* (Eugene, OR: Wipf & Stock and Oxford: Regnum, 2014), 'Introduction', 3.

[8] Wolfgang Vondey, *Pentecostalism and Christian Unity*, Vol. II (Eugene, OR: Cascade, 2012), 4, 9, 10, cf. 1-31.

[9] Ed van der Maas and Stanley M. Burgess (eds), *The New International Dictionary of Pentecostal and Charismatic Movements* (Grand Rapids, MI: Zondervan, 2002), xx.

[10] Nigel Paul Willis, *The Pentecostal Movement, Its Challenges and Potential* (Frankfurt: Peter Lang, 2013).

[11] Example of reports: https://ecumenism.net/docu/dialogue.htm (2015) (accessed 25th April 2015).

[12] Wolfgang Vondey, 'Presuppositions for Pentecostal Engagement in Ecumenical Dialogue', in *Exchange,* 30:1 (Brill, 2001), 344-58.

[13] Pentecostals participate in the WCC's Commissions on Faith and Order, World Mission and Evangelism, and in more than forty national councils of churches and

movement's course on ecumenism at Castelgandolfo, Italy, in April 2014, emphasized Pentecostal and Charismatic expressions in Protestant and Catholic Christianity.[14] The Vatican claims 120 million Charismatic-renewed faithful worldwide, and with the blessing of various Popes, though not without resistance from some Catholic bishops.[15]

The longest-standing dialogue with Pentecostals, the International Catholic-Pentecostal Dialogue, has continued since 1972 and recently entered its sixth phase. Though Pentecostals showed distrust for theology at the first Quinquennium of the dialogue, Pentecostals engaged in topics of vital importance for Pentecostal-Catholic relations in subsequent phases of dialogue.[16] Hollenweger's lament of the difficulties (in 1999) has since been replaced with Cecil Robeck's appraisal of being warmly welcomed by Catholics although, internally, many Pentecostals are still suspicious about ecumenism.[17]

Reformed-Pentecostal dialogue has entered the third cycle. The first two official dialogues occurred in 1996-2000 and 2002-2011, between the World Alliance of Reformed Churches and the Pentecostal World Conference.[18] In November 2014, the World Communion of Reformed

---

other ecumenical agencies. Pentecostals have ongoing dialogues with Roman Catholics (since 1972), World Communion of Reformed Churches, formerly World Alliance of Reformed Churches (since 1996), Lutheran World Federation (since 2005), and World Alliance (since 2011), and have entered informal conversations as steps towards dialogue with the Anglican Communion, Mennonite World Conference, and the Synodal Committee for Inter-Orthodox and Inter-Christian Affairs of the Ecumenical Patriarchate of Constantinople.

[14] www.focolare.org/en/news/2014/04/29/dialogo-con-i-pentecostali (29th April 2014) (accessed 5th February 2015).

[15] Kilian McDonnell (ed), *Open the Windows* (South Bend, IN: Greenlawn Press, 1989), cited from Cecil M. Robeck Jr,, 'Creative Imagination and Ecumenism in Light of Global Demographic Changes': lecture delivered 4th February 2013 at Catholic University of America for Washington Theological Consortium, 19, 18-19, n. 23.

[16] Juan Usma Gomez, 'Dialogue with Pentecostals', Eternal World Television Network (2001): https://www.ewtn.com/library/curia/pccupent.htm (accessed 9th June 2015).

[17] Walter J. Hollenweger, 'Roman Catholics and Pentecostals in Dialogue', in *The Ecumenical Review,* 51:2 (April 1999), 147-59; Cecil M. Robeck Jr, 'Cooperation and the Promotion of Unity: A Pentecostal Perspective', David A. Kerr and Kenneth R. Ross (ed), *Edinburgh 2010: Mission Then and Now* (Oxford: Regnum, 2009), 290-303; I analyzed the suspicion, not just of Pentecostals, but also of Anabaptists, Baptists, Evangelicals and Presbyterians, towards ecumenism in 'Recognition and Reception: Towards a Joint Commemoration of the Reformation in 2017', in *Ecclesiology*, Part III.

[18] Cecil M. Robeck, 'First International Reformed-Pentecostal Dialogue', in *Journal of Ecumenical Studies,* 33:3 (June 1996), 442; 'Word and Spirit, Church and World', Pentecostal-Reformed Dialogue 1996-2000: https://ecumenism.net/archive/docu/2000_pent_warc_word_spirit_church_world.pdf (2000) and http://pctii.org/

Churches, the Reformed Church of Hungary and the classical Hungarian Pentecostals held an international dialogue focusing on 'mission' in Berkfürdö, Hungary. Both communions appreciate the principles of mission theologically, and recognize differences in the way mission is practically expressed.[19]

Lutherans, under the umbrella of the Lutheran World Federation, have been dialoguing with other church families since the 1960s. International conversation with Trinitarian Pentecostals, which formally began in 2004, continued for another six years in Strasbourg, Pasadena, Zurich and Tampere. The exchange focuses on how each tradition encounters Christ in their various charismas, sacraments and rites, and on each communion's mutual response to the other historically.[20]

Baptists and Pentecostals have agreed to seek common ground, a significant step because of their history of mutual repudiations.[21] Historically, Baptists and Pentecostals disagree about the implications of receiving the Scriptures as the final authoritative revelation for churches of all ages, the continuing work of the Holy Spirit in the life of believers and the church after the apostolic age (known as cessationism and non-cessationism respectively), and the understanding of sanctification and perfectionism (depending on their roots in Calvinistic theology or Arminian theology respectively). While Baptists increasingly adopt Pentecostal modes of worship, Duke University's Baptist theologian Curtis Freeman insists that Baptists are not 'Bapticostals'.[22] Or is a shift to accept Pentecostals possible after the International Missions Board of the Southern Baptist Convention revision of its policy to admit missionary candidates

---

cyberj/cyberj8/WARC.html (20th December 2001); Cecil M. Robeck, 'The Challenge of the Pentecostal Movement and the First Dialogue Results on the World Level': Strasbourg Institute Lecture 2011: http://strasbourginstitute.org/wp-content/uploads/2012/10/Seminar2011-Strasbourg-LWF-Dialogue-Cecil-ROBECK.pdf (2012); and http://reformatus.hu/mutat/10397/ (7th January 2015) (accessed 5th February and 25th April 2015).

[19] http://wcrc.ch/news/wcrc-opens-new-round-of-dialogue-with-pentecostals/ (5th December 2014) (accessed 25th April 2015).

[20] www.strasbourginstitute.org/dialog/lutherisch-pfingstlerischer-dialog (Institut für Ökumenische Forschung, 2015) (accessed 5th February 2015); Lutherans and Pentecostals in Dialogue (Institut für Ökumenische Forschung in Strasbourg, and David du Plessis Center for Christian Spirituality, in Pasadena, and the European Pentecostal Charismatic Research Association in Zurich, 2015).

[21] http://baptistnews.com/archives/item/7022-baptists-pentecostals-seek-common-ground (20th December 2011), and http://ecclesialtheology.blogspot.com/2012/08/update-on-baptist-pentecostal-dialogue.html (9th Aug 2012) (accessed 5th February 2015).

[22] Curtis Freeman, 'Pentecostal Power', in *Baptist News Global* (25th May 2012): https://baptistnews.com/opinion/commentaries/item/7452-pentecostal-power (assessed 10th June 2015).

who speak in tongues, a Pentecostal/Charismatic phenomena of the Spirit?[23] Still, the prospects for better relations are hopeful.

Pentecostals have historically adopted a pacifist position as far back as 1917 until the Assemblies of God embraced nationalism and militarism.[24] The historic, mutual contempt between Pentecostals and Mennonites[25] has been ameliorated with dialogues between the Mennonite Church USA and the Church of God Cleveland taking place in 2005 and 2006.[26]

Despite some internal puristic tendencies, the movement has maintained its harbinger role for plurality. Though it may be too early to claim that Pentecostalism is making waves in ecumenism, the hopeful developments in these dialogues show that it has reversed an older negative assessment regarding its potential for participation in collaborative, ecumenical mission.[27]

## Pentecostal Missional Expressions

Pentecostal mission expressions are as diverse as the movement's plurality.[28] Several biblical promises provide the foundational premise and approach for Pentecostals' obedience to the Great Commission mandate (Matthew 28): 'You shall receive power when the Holy Spirit comes upon you' (Acts 1:8), the continuing fulfilment of Joel's prophecy on dreams, visions and manifestations of the Spirit (Acts 2:17; Joel 2:28), with healing and restoration as a regular manifestation that continues in Peter's reply: 'Silver and gold I have none' (Acts 3:6-16). Nimi Wariboko claims that the Pentecostal Spirit, who gives the many tongues of the Spirit in the church, is the Pentecostal principle that allowed these many missional manifestations.[29] Among some Charismatics, the gospel mission emphasises the message of prosperity, health and wealth, which proponents

---

[23] www.religionnews.com/2015/05/14/southern-baptists-open-ranks-missionaries-speak-tongues/ (14th May 2015) and Southern Baptist Convention's perspectives: www.sbc.net/faqs.asp (both accessed 9th June 2015).

[24] Paul Alexander, *Peace to War* (Telford, PA: Cascadia, 2009); Paul Alexander, *Pentecostals and Nonviolence: Reclaiming a Heritage* (Eugene, OR: Wipf & Stock, 2012), 350.

[25] Alan Kreider, *Social Holiness; A Way for Living for God's Nation* (Eugene, OR: Wipf & Stock, 2008; previously published as *Journey Toward Holiness* (Scottdale, PA: Herald Press, 1987), 15-16.

[26] Cheryl Bridges Johns, 'Overcoming the Holy Spirit Shyness in the Life of the Church', in *Vision,* 13:1 (Spring 2012), 6-15.

[27] www.pctii.org/cyberj/cyberj5/bundy.html (accessed 9th June 2015); cf. the dated article by David Bundy, 'The Ecumenical Quest for Pentecostalism', in *Cyberjournal for Pentecostal-Charismatic Research*, n.d.

[28] Ma, Kärkkäinen and Asamoah-Gyadu, *Pentecostal Mission and Global Christianity*.

[29] Nimi Wariboko, *The Pentecostal Principle: Ethical Methodology in New Spirit* (Grand Rapids, MI: Eerdmans, 2011).

read to be implicit in Paul's wishes for the soul's prosperity (3 John 1:2).[30] Global Pentecostalism and Charismaticism have become agents and witnesses of the Spirit's renewal despite the historic churches' contestation of the movement's claims.[31]

Not all missional expressions are affiliated with historic classical Pentecostals. Newer indigenous movements, such as African Initiated Churches, and the Pentecostal-like China house church movements, have been observed.[32] The social and political expressions of Pentecostal mission and witness in North America, Latin America, Africa and Asia, continue to expand, and these theologians, social and political scientists have analyzed these movements.[33] Recent trajectories include a systematic Pentecostal missiology.[34] Do these ecumenical, missional developments within renewal movements (Pentecostals and Charismatic Christianity) signal a positive reception of *TTL*?

### Renewed Mission and Evangelism Affirmation

CWME's desire to include older, historic, and newer Christian churches is evident when *TTL* begins with Nicea's Trinitarian position. Though Pentecostals were not major conversational partners in the World Council of Churches' dialogue towards convergence on *Confessing One Faith* in the 1990s, Pentecostals have gradually participated in discussions on *The Nature and Mission of the Church,* and *The Nature and Purpose of the Church*, both of which eventually became foregrounds to the convergence

---

[30] This Charismatic prosperity teaching has received several criticisms. For instance, Timothy Lim, 'Blessings in the Prophets and the Wisdom: A Response to Charismatic Christian Hermeneutics and a General Application for Christian Living', in *Evangelical Review of Society and Politics Special Edition on Money, Prosperity and Economics,* 6:1/2 (2012/2013), 77-103.

[31] Ma, Kärkkäinen and Asamoah-Gyadu, *Pentecostal Mission and Global Christianity*, 1.

[32] Here I register that most Chinese house church movements would not affiliate themselves with historic Pentecostals or Charismatics, despite sharing similar spiritual passion and Pentecostal-like phenomena.

[33] E.g. Timothy J. Steigenga, *The Politics of the Spirit: The Political Implications of Costa Rica and Guatemala* (Lanham, MD: Lexington Books, 2002); Donald E. Miller and Tetsunao Yamamori, *Global Pentecostalism: The New Face of Social Engagement* (Berkeley, CA: University of California Press, 2007); Ruth Marshall, *Political Spiritualities: the Pentecostal Revolution in Nigeria* (Chicago, IL: University of Chicago Press, 2009); Michael Wilkinson and Steven M. Studebaker (eds), *A Liberating Spirit: Pentecostals and Social Action in North America* (Eugene, OR: Wipf & Stock, 2010); Miller, Sargeant, Flory (eds), *Spirit and Power.*

[34] Amos Yong, *The Missiological Spirit: Christian Mission Theology in the Third Millennium Global Context* (Eugene, OR: Cascade, 2014).

text, *The Church: Towards a Common Vision*.[35] With the exception of Oneness Pentecostals,[36] Pentecostals and Charismatics would strongly welcome *TTL*'s Trinitarian basis of Christian mission as rooted in God who creates, redeems and sustains life with his incarnational love for the world, and his empowerment of the church for renewing the whole creation.

Pentecostalism has always emphasized the ministry of the Holy Spirit in empowering believers for sanctification and in the work of the gospel, although perspectives vary on whether the 'finished work of Christ' on the cross translates into Christians attaining sinless perfection instantly or gradually in this temporal life; the variations depend on whether they are Wesleyan, Keswick or Classical Holiness in conceiving the triumphant Christian life.[37] Still, as Jesus has instructed, the disciples of Christ are to wait for the Spirit to anoint them for ministry. Despite the empowerment on the Day of Pentecost (Acts 1–2), churches disagree as to whether Christ's disciples in each subsequent era have to receive the Spirit's manifold charismas for manifold service.[38]

The Introduction to *TTL* provides the strongest rationales for multi-faceted missional expression.[39] As Pentecostal-Evangelical systematician and missional theologian Amos Yong argues, 'The plurality of tongues of the Spirit' will give witness to the manifold works of the Spirit of the one God so that the church may fulfil her missionary thrust![40] Hence, Christian mission is rightly understood 'in a cosmic sense, and to affirm all life, the whole *oikoumene*, as being interconnected in God's web of life'.[41] 'Life in the Holy Spirit' is conceived as 'the essence of mission', identity, being and doing of Christians.[42] At least two Pentecostal theologians have recently affirmed life in the Spirit as missional, albeit without documenting

---

[35] See Wolfgang Vondey, 'Pentecostal Perspectives on The Nature and Mission of the Church: Challenges and Opportunities for Ecumenical Transformation', in Paul M. Collins and Michael A. Fahey (eds), *Receiving 'The Nature and Mission of the Church'* (New York: T. & T. Clark, 2008), 55-68.

[36] Gregory A. Boyd, *Oneness Pentecostals and the Trinity* (Grand Rapids, MI: Baker, 1992); Bruce Tucker, *Oneness Pentecostal Churches* (New York: Xlibis, 2011); Matthew J. Cawthorn, *American Oneness Pentecostalism* (CreateSpace, 2012).

[37] Charles W. Burtner, and Robert E. Chiles (eds), *John Wesley's Theology* (Nashville, TN: Abingdon, 1982), 141.

[38] Some argue that Pentecost is a once-and-for-all event and not repeatable. Others suggest that believers in each era need their initial and continual filling with the Spirit.

[39] *TTL,* §1-11, especially §1-4, 8, 10.

[40] E.g. Amos Yong, *The Spirit Poured Out on All Flesh* (Grand Rapids, MI: Baker Academic, 2005), 26, 124, 173.

[41] *TTL,* §4.

[42] *TTL,* §3.

any awareness of *TTL*.[43] Thus, all Christians and churches are God's messengers and gifts to, and for loving and transforming, the world.[44] *TTL* underscores the need for healing and reconciliation among the churches towards communal inclusivity and unity for her mission.[45]

*TTL* would appeal to many Pentecostals and Charismatics for various reasons. *TTL*'s explicit recognition of the Trinity in Christian mission – when CWME significantly adumbrates the Spirit of Christian mission and the Spirit's operation in Christian mission – is a favourable change from the Spirit's less prominent role in WCC's earlier mission text, *Mission and Evangelism: An Ecumenical Affirmation* (1982)! *TTL*'s recognition of the renewal movements' global expansion and expressions could correct the historic and mainline churches' negative reception of these global renewal movements in the middle of the twentieth century.[46] While it may be a far cry to say that Pentecostals are now accepted in all churches and traditions, communions outside the Pentecostal movement are more willing to befriend believers outside their fold, even if these communions are still not in theological agreement with Pentecostals, as evidenced in the many dialogue reports. Still, many non-Pentecostal and non-Charismatic churches have renewed their worship services to become more contemporary, or at least participatory, thanks to the 'Spirit-led' worship renewal movements within this diverse tradition that have unfortunately also created 'music wars' when they deviated from the liturgies and practices of classical Christian worship.[47] *TTL*'s multi-faceted recognition of the local praxes to faith, and acknowledgement of the plurality of Pentecostal self-

---

[43] Andrea D. Snavel and Joel P. Okamoto, *Life in the Spirit* (Eugene, OR: Pickwick, 2015).

[44] *TTL*, §8, 10.

[45] *TTL*, §8, 10. Unlike *TTL*'s introduction, *EA* begins with the scandal of the churches' divisions before explicating the biblical, theological and ecumenical grounds and convictions for mission and witnessing. Thus, *TTL* would be ecumenically more inviting for churches.

[46] *TTL*, §5. *TTL* is right in how Christians identify who, where and what the 'centre' of Christianity is, while the outreach missions have been changing as a result of a) the global expansion of Christianity, which is by no means only a consequence of the successes of Pentecostalism (which §5 seems to imply), b) the phenomenon of migration, and c) the increasing trajectory of the margins recognizing themselves as agents of mission (rather than as the targets or recipients of mission). After the introduction, *TTL* did admit to the churches' historic faults in mission when churches denigrated local wisdom and local cultures in their missional history to indigenous peoples (cf. *TTL*, §27).

[47] For a global Pentecostal expression of worship, see Monique M. Ingalls and Amos Yong (eds), *The Spirit of Praise* (Penn State University Press, 2015). For a different perspective, see Ruth C. Duck, *Worship for the Whole People of God* (Louisville, KY: Westminster John Knox, 2013). For a historic perspective, see James F. White, *Introduction to Christian Worship*, 3rd edition (Nashville, TN: Abingdon, 2001).

understandings, are important because Pentecostals are experiential in their faith and thus do not receive well a singular, universal concept and practice of the church.[48]

Pentecostals in the Majority World are likely to welcome *TTL*'s dual-direction of pursuing mission. To the older paradigm of 'mission to the margins', *TTL* now adds 'mission from the margins' of the 'powerless', 'the poor', and 'marginalized'. *TTL* affirms that missions could move in both directions simultaneously. *TTL* recognizes that the margins possess God-given gifts for serving both in their own contexts and in transnational contexts. They could use their gifts 'to counteract injustices in life, church, and mission' because they experienced the 'misuse of power and use of the wrong kind of power in mission and in the church' from the rich, the powerful, and western centres of power. According to *TTL*, because the western missionary enterprise had unfortunately perpetuated injustices rather than furthering 'the causes of justice, dignity and life',[49] the shift in missional paradigm towards 'mission from the margins' is now desirable. The change will find favour with Pentecostals, not merely because *TTL* is now embracing a liberation ethos, articulated decades ago.[50] Rather, *TTL*'s explicit encouragement of 'mission from the margins' affirms that those at the margins have something to teach the rest of the mainstream churches that have marginalized them.[51] Churches at the margins are also God's missional instruments not just to their own local contexts but also to the dominant and powerful in western Christianity. As Kenneth Ross' interpretation of *TTL* in the context of 'liquid modernity' has suggested (and with insights from Lamin Sanneh), re-evangelization of the western world may occur from the Spirit who actually brings about the transmigration of people in a global world![52]

However, certain formulations in *TTL* may or may not excite some Pentecostals and Charismatics. The reception on these formulations may range from ambivalence to rejection. The first ambivalence concerns *TTL*'s framing of mission inclusively.[53] The current approach towards inclusivity may inhibit a positive reception, especially by churches that see Christian

---

[48] Simon Chan, 'Mother Church: Toward a Pentecostal Ecclesiology', in *PNEUMA,* 22:2 (Fall 2000), 177-208.

[49] *TTL,* §33, 38, 39-42, 45, 46-49.

[50] Liberation theology is much older, although the ethos entered Pentecostal expression only in recent decades, as seen in R. Andrew Chesnut, *Born Again in Brazil* (New York: Rutgers University Press, 1997); Samuel Solivan, *Spirit, Pathos, and Liberation*, *Journal of Pentecostal Theology,* Supplement 14 (New York: Bloomsbury T. & T. Clark, 1998).

[51] E.g. Chad M. Bauman, *Pentecostals, Proselytization, and Anti-Christian Violence in Contemporary India* (Oxford: OUP, 2015), ch. 3, 70-93.

[52] Kenneth R. Ross, 'Together towards Life in the Context of Liquid Modernity', in *International Review of Mission,* 103.2 (November 2014), 249-50; cf. 240-55; Lamin Sanneh, *Summoned from the Margin* (Grand Rapids, MI: Eerdmans, 2012).

[53] *TTL,* §8-10.

mission either as a counter-cultural force or as focusing primarily on eternal salvation. Though *TTL* has duly acknowledged these perspectives, the inclusive framing will be difficult for some in the Renewal tradition to embrace, for the following reasons.

*TTL* suggests that evangelism could be understood, not just as the proclamation of the gospel leading the unbeliever to conversion, but also as the witnessing of Christian mission in social justice and solidarity with the poor, oppressed and marginalized.[54] The crux for a proper reception on *TTL*'s views on evangelism boils down to: what constitutes evangelism and gospel proclamation? To be sure, *TTL* affirms that the fundamental basis of their faith and the thrust of the gospel rest on the eternal salvific revelation of Jesus Christ: this explicit affirmation of Christ as the thrust of the gospel might help Evangelicals and Pentecostals overcome their prior assessment of WCC's Justice, Peace and Integrity of Creation projects (JPIC) as liberal deviations from the gospel.[55] As we now know, some Pentecostals in the Majority World have expressed their faith counter-culturally when they explicitly seek to be conduits of societal transformation through concrete projects in social justice advocacy, but even these social witnesses are conducted without relegating the direct proclamation of the salvific message of Jesus Christ.[56] *TTL*'s inclusivity and reframing of what counts as evangelism would remain a challenge: Pentecostals and Charismatics, together with Evangelicals, would be likely to disagree with *TTL*'s acceptance of solidarity as a form of evangelism, and *TTL*'s relegation of the direct proclamation of Jesus Christ's salvation message as only 'an essential part of the way we convey God's love to the world'. In Renewal and Evangelical understanding, evangelism is not merely an aspect of

---

[54] *TTL*, §85.

[55] *TTL*, §9; Jonas Jonson and Norman A. Hjelm, *Wounded Visions* (Grand Rapids, MI: Eerdmans, 2013). That said, apart from a few dissenting voices, Pentecostals would readily affirm the need to co-operate with 'other religions and cultures in building societies of love, peace and justice' in our 'multi-religious and multi-cultural' world. Daniel Castello, *Revisioning Pentecostal Ethics* (Cleveland, TN: CPT Press, 2012) proposes an eschatological reframing of Pentecostal moral theology to allow the possibility of Pentecostal mission in the world. Though Castello did not directly address issues of social advocacy, justice, and ecological care, the appropriation is well within an application of Castello's work (cf. Castello, *Revisioning Pentecostal Ethics*, 51). Monte Lee Rice, 'Renewing the Pentecostal Vision and Witness of the Justified People of God', in *Asian Journal of Pentecostal Studies*, 16:2 (August 2013), 85-98, offers an example of a Pentecostal social witness.

[56] David H. Lumsdaine (ed), *Evangelical Christianity and Democracy in Asia* (Oxford: OUP, 2009); Allan Anderson and Edmond Tang (eds), *Asian and Pentecostal* (Oxford: Regnum, 2nd edition, 2011).

Christian proclamation; evangelism is primarily about the saving of souls eternally: salvation is the gospel itself![57]

Nonetheless, *TTL* and Renewal churches can affirm that social witnessing does not exclude evangelism. As *TTL* states, because 'the mission of God's Spirit encompasses us all in an ever-giving act of grace … we are therefore called to move beyond a narrowly human-centered approach and to embrace forms of mission which express our reconciled relationship with all created life'.[58] *TTL* rightly points out that to presume that believers can seek eternal salvation without caring for JPIC is 'to falsely believe [that] we can belong to God without belonging to our neighbour', and in so doing, 'fall into a spirituality that simply makes us feel good while other parts of creation hurt and yearn'.[59] Also, *TTL* explains that Christian proclamation and witness as 'good news for all' should not succumb to forces of individualism, secularism and materialism 'that end up 'promoting falsehood, injustice and oppression': the caveat would be a lesson for Pentecostal mission, given Pentecostals' varying approaches to secularity and materiality, as we shall shortly examine.[60]

On another aspect of *TTL*'s inclusive missional framing, the inter-faith position articulated in *TTL* may also find an ambivalent reception. *TTL*'s inter-faith position is also rather mild in its presentation. One could easily read *TTL*'s position as arguing for an open, inclusive and collaborative listening and dialogue with other religions towards their shared responsibilities as part of humanity in the protection of religious liberty and solidarity.[61] Here, Pentecostals are unlikely to fully stand with *TTL*, though promoting religious liberty and solidarity are certainly part of Christian witness![62] On the whole, since Pentecostal reflection on its mission is still

---

[57] *TTL,* §8. Here, *TTL*'s use of direct proclamation as 'an essential' in the larger backdrop of the churches' wider witness implies, albeit unintentionally, that direct witness is one among other messages of the gospel witness; the relegation of evangelism as only an essential remains a problem for renewal readers. Nonetheless, the clarification of a more moderate perspective in *TTL,* §19-23 that Christian mission would seek the flourishing of creation eco-justice, and respect of the earth and advocacy for the oppressed and marginalized, against the backdrop of §83 that conceives evangelism as the sharing of faith and conviction with other people as the ultimate gift to another fellow human being, would be more acceptable to renewal readers.

[58] *TTL,* §19.

[59] *TTL,* §21.

[60] *TTL,* §91.

[61] *TTL,* §93-96.

[62] Tony Richie, *Speaking by the Spirit* (Lexington, KY: Emeth Press, 2011); Tony Ritchie, *Towards a Pentecostal Theology of Religions* (Cleveland, TN: CPT Press, 2013); for a more inclusive and pluralistic voice, see Steven M. Studebaker, 'Christian Mission and the Religions as Participation in the Spirit of Pentecost', in Amos Yong and Clifton Clarke (eds), *Global Renewal, Religious Pluralism, and the Great Commission* (Lexington, KY: Emeth Press, 2011), 71-95.

emerging, one could speculate that Pentecostals are likely to concur with aspects in *TTL* that conceive salvation through evangelism and witnessing through advocacy as necessary to the gospel and the mission of the church, although they would not affirm *TTL*'s relegation of direct proclamation or a subdued role in interreligious engagement.[63]

It would also be interesting to see how Pentecostals and especially Charismatics would respond to both *TTL*'s rejection of the saving power of the market economy and mammon, and *TTL*'s acknowledgement of communicating the gospel in the global market economy.[64] On the one hand, Pentecostals and Charismatics, including factions that embrace a prosperity gospel, seem to use this-worldly materiality as a means or a platform for proclaiming the gospel.[65] Thus, *TTL*'s introduction in §7 and commentary in §31 may offer a pushback for Pentecostals. *TTL*'s point would definitely not affect groups that see 'the creation of wealth and prosperity' as an end in itself.[66] On the other hand, Pentecostal and Charismatic spirituality would agree with *TTL* that transformational mission would 'confront idolatrous assumptions, unjust systems, politics of domination and exploitation in our current world economic order' so that the church would be motivated 'to serve God's economy of life, not mammon, to share life at God's table rather than satisfy individual greed, to pursue change for a better world'.[67] On either spectrum, there will be respondents who will embrace or critique *TTL*'s rejection of the market economy and mammon: the litmus test will be whether economy and mammon are regarded as a means and instruments of the gospel or ends in themselves. Amid the political economy of exchange, Amos Yong argues that an informal economy is at work when believers share and exchange goods and services in the spirit of Christian love, and hence one cannot totally reject the capabilities of economy and mammon, despite the real dangers of misusing or abusing them.[68]

Ecclesiology underlies the missional expression of the church, and thus one would expect *TTL* to give substantial treatment to the church. *TTL* speaks accurately about the gift of the church to the world: the church

---

[63] Ma, Kärkkäinen and Asamoah-Gyadu, *Pentecostal Mission and Global Christianity*. Norbert Hintersteiner, 'From Cultural Translation to Interfaith Witness: The Intercultural Transformation of Missiology', in Linda Hogan, Solange Lefebvre, Norbert Hintersteiner and Felix Wilfred (eds), *From World Mission to Inter-religious Witness*. Concilium 2011/1 (London: SCM, 2011), 85-94.

[64] *TTL*, §7.

[65] Amos Yong and Katherine Attanasi (eds), *Pentecostalism and Prosperity* (New York: Palgrave Macmillan, 2012); Calvin L. Smith, 'The Politics and Economics of Pentecostalism: A Global Survey', in *The Cambridge Companion to Pentecostalism* (Cambridge: CUP, 2014), 175-94.

[66] *TTL*, §31.

[67] *TTL*, §30.

[68] Amos Yong, *In the Days of Caesar* (Grand Rapids, MI: Eerdmans, 2010), 304-10.

transforms society by bringing new life and announcing God's love and presence. *TTL* also affirms the fundamental ecclesiological unity of the church on the basis of the Trinitarian vision, and hopes to facilitate the churches' unitive witness as disciples of Christ and as agents of healing and reconciliation to the world.[69] Pentecostals would concur here. As Peter Althouse suggests, Pentecostal ecclesiology is anchored in the missional life of the Triune God: the church becomes the sent and sending community to live out its mission.[70] Nonetheless, *TTL* frames its ecclesiology to inclusivity without offering substantial qualifiers: the lack of nuance about what sort of inclusivity would characterize the gospel-centric community of disciples is unlikely to find acceptance with puristic churches in Evangelical and Pentecostal communities, although to a certain extent, the gospel would prize inclusivity. Pentecostal churches, as with Evangelical communities, would wish to remind the drafters of *TTL* that the gospel is also exclusivist – whoever believes in Jesus Christ as Lord and Saviour shall be saved and those who deny Christ will be denied by the Father (Matthew 10:33; 1 John 2:22-23)![71]

*TTL* drafters may have wanted a wide reception of the text, and hence *TTL* is not formulated only with exclusivist churches, like Pentecostals and Evangelicals, in mind. Still, I wish that *TTL* had presented their alternative model without needing readers to choose between their preferred inclusivity or the implicit contrasting exclusivist approach to gospel mission. *TTL* remains attractive because it clarifies that Christian mission, as a step towards welcoming others, entails not just the practice of hospitality to aid inclusivity, but also implies the crossing of boundaries. The notions of hospitality and crossing boundaries are certainly not foreign to Pentecostal spiritual ethos; from the beginnings of Pentecostalism, it was called a harbinger for plurality. Nonetheless, the movement still has much to do to expand its inclusivity.[72] Thus, *TTL* has unwittingly offered some correctives for Pentecostals and Evangelicals.

> §25: The churches are called to discern the work of the life-giving Spirit sent into the world and to join with the Holy Spirit in bringing about God's reign of justice (Acts 1:6-8). When we have discerned the Holy Spirit's presence,

---

[69] *TTL,* §10.

[70] Peter Althouse, 'Towards a Pentecostal Ecclesiology: Participation in the Missional Life of the Triune God', in *Journal of Pentecostal Theology,* 18:2 (2009), 230-45. For a wider study of Pentecostal ecclesiology, both theological and empirical, see Mark Cartledge, 'Renewal Ecclesiology in Empirical Perspectives', *PNUEMA* 36 (2014), 5-24.

[71] Clifton Shane, 'Pentecostal Ecclesiology: A Methodological Proposal for a Diverse Movement', in *Journal of Pentecostal Theology,* 15:2 (2007), 213-32.

[72] Amos Yong, *Hospitality and the Other* (Maryknoll, NY: Orbis Books, 2008) engages hospitality in the interreligious arena. Still, the principle of hospitality and its applied implication towards crossing boundaries would not be inconceivable for ecclesiology or ecclesiological mission.

> we are called to respond, recognizing that God's Spirit is often subversive, leading us beyond boundaries and surprising us.[73]
>
> §26: We are led by the Spirit into various situations and moments, into meeting points with others, into spaces of encounter and into critical locations of human struggle.[74]
>
> §33: Mission provokes in us a renewed awareness that the Holy Spirit meets us and challenges us at all levels of life, and brings newness and change to the places and times of our personal and collective journeys.[75]
>
> §44: The church's hope is rooted in the promised fulfilment of the reign of God. It entails the restoration of right relationships between God and humanity and all of creation. Even though this vision speaks to the eschatological reality, it deeply energizes and informs our current participation in God's salvific work in this penultimate period.[76]

Whether Pentecostals will receive the Spirit's invitation and *TTL*'s pneumatological mission proposal remains to be seen. Many of *TTL*'s encouragements, which could offer correctives for renewal churches, have been raised in one way or another by the late Baptist-Evangelical Renewal theologian Clark Pinnock's programmatic essay, 'Church in the Power of the Holy Spirit'.[77] The question then becomes: Will renewal churches advance the themes in their respective contexts in global, collaborative missions, outside their own communions in the coming era?

---

[73] *TTL*, §25.
[74] *TTL*, §26.
[75] *TTL*, §34.
[76] *TTL*, §44.
[77] Clark H. Pinnock, 'Church in the Power of the Holy Spirit: The Promise of Pentecostal Ecclesiology', in *Journal of Pentecostal Theology*, 14:2 (2006), 147-65.

# *TOGETHER TOWARDS LIFE* AND THE CAPE TOWN COMMITMENT

Allen Yeh

The words 'evangelical' and 'ecumenical' have unfortunately been used in opposition to each other from the mid-twentieth century onwards. The reason this is unfortunate is that their respective meanings are 'about the good news' and 'about unity'. The *euaggelion* and the *oikoumene* are two things that Jesus calls all Christians to, and their interplay is at the heart of mission. It has been said that 'mission is the mother of ecumenism' because mission is so large that it requires an integrated co-operation inter-denominationally to achieve its goals. Para-church organizations are a case in point. They usually have missional functions but consist of Christians from a wide variety of denominations. The mission trumps parochial identity. But if one were to read Jesus' high priestly prayer in John 17, especially vv. 20-23, he prays, 'that they may be brought to complete unity. Then the world will know that you sent me and have loved them even as you have loved me'. If the unity of the church is a missiological sign to the world, then perhaps the inverse is also true: 'Ecumenism is the mother of mission'.

However, despite the fact that the Edinburgh 1910 World Missionary Conference is considered by many to be the birthplace of the modern ecumenical movement, it produced two 'children' that have often been seen as the opposite of each other: the World Council of Churches (WCC) and the Lausanne Committee for World Evangelization (LCWE). However, Andrew Walls says that this is not as it should be: 'Both "ecumenical" and "evangelical" today have their roots in Edinburgh 1910. If each will go back to the pit whence both were dug, each may understand both themselves and the other better.'[1]

It is perhaps not the fault of the missiologists or the missionaries that this unnecessary rivalry has occurred; rather, it can be traced to a development which had its origins prior to Edinburgh 1910, namely, the Fundamentalist-Modernist Controversy which took place largely in the United States and set the tone of western Christianity for about a century. The two most representative men of this era were a Presbyterian named J. Gresham Machen who wrote a book called *Christianity and Liberalism* (1923),

---

[1] Andrew F. Walls, cit. Kenneth R. Ross, 'The Centenary of Edinburgh 1910: Its Possibilities', in *International Bulletin of Missionary Research,* 30/4 (October 2006), 177-79, at 178.

representing the Fundamentalist side, and a Baptist named Harry Emerson Fosdick who preached a sermon called 'Shall the Fundamentalists Win?' (1922) representing the Modernist side. The Fundamentalists stood for 'truth' often at the expense of 'unity', and the Modernists stood for 'unity' often at the expense of 'truth'. This false dichotomy of 'conservative' versus 'liberal' perpetuated for decades and has often coloured people's perceptions of what Lausanne and the WCC are about. Both organizations have produced significant documents on evangelism and ecumenism, and this chapter aims to explore their two most recent articulations of mission: *Together towards Life* (2012) and the *Cape Town Commitment* (2010), showing that there is far more in common between the two than is obvious on the surface.

## The *Cape Town Commitment*

The *Cape Town Commitment* (*CTC*) will be addressed first because it was earlier in chronology. This was the third such major document produced by Lausanne, one coming out of each of their major Congresses: the *Lausanne Covenant* which came out of Lausanne, Switzerland, in 1974 (when the movement was named); the *Manila Manifesto* which was birthed out of Manila, Philippines, in 1989; and *CTC* itself from Cape Town, South Africa, in 2010. Lausanne III was called the 'most diverse gathering ever' of Christian leaders in history by *Christianity Today*[2] and *CTC* was a much-needed addition (as opposed to revision) to the two previous documents. In the Preamble to *CTC*, it states its reaffirmation to the other two:

> *First*, we remain committed to the task of bearing worldwide witness to Jesus Christ and all his teaching. The first Lausanne Congress (1974) was convened for the task of world evangelization. Among its major gifts to the world church were: (i) The *Lausanne Covenant*; (ii) a new awareness of the number of unreached people groups; and (iii) a fresh discovery of the holistic nature of the biblical gospel and of Christian mission. The Second Lausanne Congress, in Manila (1989), gave birth to more than 300 strategic partnerships in world evangelization, including many that involved co-operation between nations in all parts of the globe.
>
> And *second*, we remain committed to the primary documents of the Movement – the *Lausanne Covenant* (1974), and the *Manila Manifesto* (1989). These documents clearly express core truths of the biblical gospel and apply them to our practical mission in ways that are still relevant and challenging. We confess that we have not been faithful to commitments made in those documents. But we commend them and stand by them, as we seek to discern how we must express and apply the eternal truth of the gospel in the ever-changing world of our own generation.

---

[2] John W. Kennedy, 'The Most Diverse Gathering Ever', in *Christianity Today*, 54/9 (29th September 2010), 66.

The references to (ii) unreached people groups and (iii) holistic mission heavily influenced much of the language in the *Lausanne Covenant* and were a result of plenary addresses by Ralph Winter and C. René Padilla, respectively, during the Lausanne I Congress which was convened by Billy Graham.[3] These were probably the most memorable and seminal parts of that Congress other than the production of (i), the *Lausanne Covenant* itself, of which the chief architect was John Stott.

The *Lausanne Covenant*'s Evangelical pedigree is clear because it coheres with David Bebbington's Quadrilateral, the classic definition of what an Evangelical is. The Bebbington Quadrilateral consists of biblicism, crucicentrism, conversionism and activism.[4] The *Lausanne Covenant* was written in fifteen paragraphs, of which only ten actually deal with missional issues such as conversionism and activism.[5] The other five are actually systematic treatments of theological commitments that all Evangelicals share, including biblicism and crucicentrism.[6]

The *Manila Manifesto* has not had the same lasting influence that the *Lausanne Covenant* had,[7] nor did the Lausanne II Congress have the same memorable historical impact. Still, it is worth mentioning because *CTC* stands on the shoulders of both documents and both Congresses, and the *Manila Manifesto* was important for what it contributed at the time. It consisted of 21 theological and missiological affirmations which solidify Evangelical identity, followed by twelve points which fall into three main categories: The Whole Gospel;[8] The Whole Church;[9] and The Whole World.[10] Much of the purpose of this document had to do with addressing interdenominational and inter-agency partnerships, especially with the AD

---

[3] Ralph D. Winter, 'The Highest Priority: Cross-Cultural Evangelism', and René Padilla, 'Evangelism and the World', in J.D. Douglas (ed), *Let the Earth Hear His Voice* (Minneapolis, MN: World Wide Publications, 1975), 213-41 and 116-46.

[4] David Bebbington, *Evangelicalism in Modern Britain* (London: Unwin Hyman, 1989), 2-3.

[5] 4. The Nature of Evangelism; 5. Christian Social Responsibility; 6. The Church and Evangelism; 7. Co-operation in Evangelism; 8. Churches in Evangelistic Partnership; 9. The Urgency of the Evangelistic Task; 10. Evangelism and Culture; 11. Education and Leadership; 12. Spiritual Conflict; 13. Freedom and Persecution.

[6] 1. The Purpose of God; 2. The Authority and Power of the Bible; 3. The Uniqueness and Universality of Christ; 14. The Power of the Holy Spirit; 15. The Return of Christ.

[7] One potential explanation could simply be that the first often has more impact and influence than subsequent editions; another is that *The Lausanne Covenant* has a conciseness that its sequels do not have.

[8] 1. Our Human Predicament; 2. Good News for Today; 3. The Uniqueness of Jesus Christ; 4. The Gospel and Social Responsibility; 5. God the Evangelist.

[9] 6. The Human Witness; 7. The Integrity of the Witnesses; 8. The Local Church; 9. Co-operating in Evangelism.

[10] 10. The Modern World; 11. The Challenge of AD 2000 and Beyond; 12. Difficult Situations.

2000 and Beyond movement.[11] But theologically, it was a further updating, incorporating concepts like *missio Dei*, mission in the context of world Christianity ('from everyone to everywhere'), ecumenical openness to non-Evangelicals, and challenges like modernity, communism, pluralism and persecution.

The *Cape Town Commitment* (2010) came much longer after the *Manila Manifesto* (1989) than *Manila* came after the *Lausanne Covenant* (1974). Part of the reason is that the Lausanne movement became somewhat dormant in the 1990s to be revitalized under the leadership of Doug Birdsall from 2004. But as a result, the world had changed massively in the intervening period. Between 1989 and 2010, the world had witnessed 9/11, the advent of the Internet and a shift to popular post-modernism, as three examples of massively consequential changes to the world's political, technological and philosophical landscapes. Clearly, Lausanne had some catching up to do.

*CTC* was different from its predecessors in that it was written both before *and* after the Congress. Part I, 'For the Lord we love' (the confession of faith), had started five years prior to the Lausanne III Congress in Cape Town, South Africa, and was presented in its final version there. Part II, 'For the world we serve' (the call to action), was the result of a listening process begun three years before Lausanne III, continued throughout the Congress, and finished a year later. 'Love' was the framing word for Part I, as it was developed in ten sub-points.[12] Part II consisted of six key issues which became the structure of the Congress.[13] The link between Parts I and II can be seen as either: belief and praxis; or, primary truths and secondary issues. The World Evangelical Alliance assisted in the production of this document, showing a further co-operative spirit.

Some of the new or missing issues that *CTC* addressed that were not in the previous iterations included: oral cultures, seminaries, cities, children, prayer, HIV/AIDS, homosexuality, creation care and egalitarianism.

---

[11] After the movement ended in 2001, it was continued in another form as the Joshua Project. The AD 2000 and Beyond movement was originally a breakaway from the Lausanne movement.

[12] 1. We love because God first loved us; 2. We love the living God; 3. We love God the Father; 4. We love God the Son; 5. We love God the Holy Spirit; 6. We love God's Word; 7. We love God's world; 8. We love the gospel of God; 9. We love the people of God; 10. We love the mission of God.

[13] A. Bearing witness to the truth of Christ in a pluralistic, globalized world; B. Building the peace of Christ in our divided and broken world; C. Living the love of Christ among people of other faiths; D. Discerning the will of Christ for world evangelization; E. Calling the Church of Christ back to humility, integrity and simplicity; F. Partnering in the body of Christ for unity in mission.

## Together towards Life: Mission and Evangelism in Changing Landscapes

Similar to the *Cape Town Commitment* being the third in a series, *Together towards Life* (*TTL*) was not the first of its kind. This document was preceded by the 1982 text, *Mission and Evangelism – an Ecumenical Affirmation* (*EA*) which was prepared by the WCC's Commission on World Mission and Evangelism.[14] Similar to *CTC* and the earlier documents in its series, *TTL* differed from its predecessor in length (40 pages instead of 15) and in topics. *EA*'s seven points[15] are similar to the *Lausanne Covenant* in that they cover evangelism, social justice, holistic mission, etc. The main difference between them is not related to their content but to their 'colour'. *EA* is more corporate in its call than the *Lausanne Covenant*: e.g. conversion is not just of people but of nations and families; the gospel is meant to transform structures, not just individuals; it emphasizes the physical public presence of the church, not just its spiritual presence; mission is not just verbal and physical, but it's about the totality of the Lordship of Christ; and the agency of the powerless and solidarity with the poor are affirmed.

*EA* actually has more resonance with the *Manila Manifesto*, e.g. in its call to grapple with issues of modern technology, ecumenism and world Christianity. Perhaps these similarities are not surprising, considering that *EA* is closer chronologically to Lausanne II than Lausanne I. But it not only anticipates *Manila* but *CTC* as well, in its emphasis on love: 'Conversion happens in the midst of our historical reality and incorporates the totality of our life, because God's love is concerned with that totality',[16] and 'In all communications of the Gospel, power must be subordinate to love'.[17] Perhaps one of the reasons the Evangelical community has been late to 'catch up' is because of the lingering effects of the Fundamentalist-Modernist Controversy, where the former camp majored on truth/theology and the latter camp emphasized unity/love. It seems, however, there is now a coalescing of the Evangelical and ecumenical communities in comparing *CTC* with *TTL*.

This evokes earlier attempts to achieve convergence. One of the points of contention in the *Manila Manifesto* is under Section 9, Co-operating in Evangelism: 'Some of us are members of churches which belong to the World Council of Churches and believe that a positive yet critical participation in its work is our Christian duty. Others among us have no link with the World Council. All of us urge the World Council of Churches

---

[14] *International Review of Mission,* 61.284 (1982), 432-37.

[15] 1. Conversion; 2. The Gospel to all Realms of Life; 3. The Church and its Unity in God's Mission; 4. Mission in Christ's Way; 5. Good News to the Poor; 6. Mission in and to Six Continents; 7. Witness among People of Living Faiths.

[16] *Mission and Evangelism: An Ecumenical Affirmation,* §11.

[17] *Mission and Evangelism: An Ecumenical Affirmation,* §28.

to adopt a consistent biblical understanding of evangelism.' In addition to this, Evangelicals drafted a letter at the WCC's sixth Assembly in Vancouver, Canada, in 1983, stating:

1. Although the WCC Central Committee had approved (1982) an illuminating and thoroughly evangelical study: Mission and Evangelism – an Ecumenical Affirmation, we were disappointed that it was not referred to in any plenary address. We were gratified that the Affirmation received strong support in the Programme Guidelines Committee Report, in other reports and in the Assembly's Message to the Churches. No ecumenical document has been so welcomed by evangelicals. Actually, evangelical counsel was widely sought in its preparation. Furthermore, the Assembly did not give central place to the shameful fact that at this late hour in the history of the church, more than three billion have yet to hear the Gospel of Christ – despite Christ's mandate that it be proclaimed to all peoples. We did not feel that the Assembly adequately treated either Gospel proclamation or the invitational dimensions of evangelism.
2. On occasion, terminology became fuzzy and theology worse. For example, while the Assembly frequently heard that sin brings social alienation, little was said about spiritual alienation – from God himself. As a result, the redemptive dimension of Christ's sufferings on the Cross was not particularly stressed. Moreover, while larger issues of social ethics were frequently treated, more personal ethical concerns rarely surfaced. In sum, there were times when we wished that evangelical voices in the churches were given the prominence accorded some theological mavericks. Fortunately, in the issue and discussion groups, we heard evangelical men and women participate whose evident concern was to remind fellow delegates of the biblical authority and witness to the issues under review. Evangelicals are convinced that if Jesus Christ is the life of the world, his claim that his words are spirit and life (John 6:63) should not be downplayed.[18]

Other points which may have caused Evangelicals consternation are the use of the word 'moratorium' on mission (to be fair, 'Moratorium does not mean the end of the missionary vocation nor of the duty to provide resources for missionary work, but it does mean freedom to reconsider present engagements and to see whether a continuation of what we have been doing for so long is the right style of mission in our day… There can never be a moratorium of mission, but it will always be possible, and sometimes necessary, to have a moratorium for the sake of better

[18] 'An Open Letter: Evangelicals at the Sixth Assembly of the WCC', in *Mid-Stream,* 23.1 (1984), 130.

mission'[19]), and Christians needing to receive 'witness' from those of other faiths (the clarification of this being: 'Life with people of other faiths and ideologies is an encounter of commitments. Witness cannot be a one-way process, but of necessity is two-way: in it, Christians become aware of some of the deepest convictions of their neighbours. It is also the time in which, within a spirit of openness and trust, Christians are able to bear authentic witness, giving an account of their commitment to the Christ, who calls all persons to himself'[20]). One of the reasons that *TTL* came into being was to address such concerns. But it was also a necessary update, as the time between *EA* and *TTL* (thirty years) was much longer than between the *Manila Manifesto* and the *Cape Town Commitment* (21 years).

*TTL* is structured with 112 paragraphs listed under four main sections, each of which has four sub-sections, all centred on the Spirit. It updates *Mission and Evangelism – an Ecumenical Affirmation* for our times, not only highlighting contemporary issues but creating a robust theological framework which was missing from *EA*.

## The *Cape Town Commitment* and *Together towards Life*

There is much to be affirmed about the similarities between these two documents. Both begin with the Triune God and the importance of *missio Dei*. They both grapple with massive social changes in this world. Creation care is featured prominently in each document. There is a mutual awareness of world Christianity as the backdrop of all mission work that we do today, that mission is polycentric and multi-dimensional, and that migration is a global reality for many people today. Both documents have a call to repentance and humility, for ourselves to be renewed and freed from sins such as materialism and paternalism. At the same time, both contain cautions about the abuse of spiritual gifts such as false prophets and a prosperity gospel. Ecumenical unity is a shared goal. Respectful evangelism is affirmed while proselytism is decried. Religious freedom and ethnic diversity are values to be cherished, as they symbolize dignity for all peoples. Instead of the false dichotomy of Evangelicals caring only about theology/truth and ecumenicists being concerned only with unity/love, *CTC* emphasizes love as its main controlling paradigm, while *TTL* is much more heavily theological than its predecessor *EA*.

However, the differences are also stark: *CTC* tends to lean in a more Christocentric direction,[21] whereas *TTL*'s accent is more pneumato-centric. This is obvious in noting that *CTC* mentions only the Second Person of the

[19] Point 6.
[20] Point 7.
[21] This is especially seen in Part I, Sec. 1, which describes the God we love, and Sec. 8, which articulates what the Gospel is; and in all of Part II.

Trinity in the titles of all six sections of Part II,[22] while *TTL* mentions only the Third Person of the Trinity in the titles of all four sections of the entire document.[23] Another major difference is their approach to theology. *CTC* devotes fully half of its document to theology and the other half to praxis. *TTL* is more integrative, weaving theology and praxis throughout each of its 112 paragraphs. *CTC* asserts many core beliefs in its Part I, while *TTL* asks many questions, following each of its first ten theological statements, wondering aloud how convictions will impact eventual action. The implications are: *CTC* sees theology as the foundation upon which to do mission, without which we would not be properly rooted. *TTL*, on the other hand, uses theology as a launching point for praxis, basically not seeing propositional truths as ends in and of themselves but rather for how they can aid the cause of mission.

For all the agreements on the definition of 'mission' in the two documents, perhaps the sections in *TTL* that Evangelicals would understand most differently would be the following:

> §22: 'We tend to understand and practice mission as something done by humanity to others. Instead, humans can participate in communion with all of creation in celebrating the work of the Creator. In many ways creation is in mission to humanity; for instance, the natural world has a power that can heal the human heart and body.'

§32 delineates the cross as a panacea for earthly rather than spiritual ailments:

> 'In situations of oppression, discrimination and hurt, the cross of Christ is the power of God for salvation (1 Cor. 1:18). Even in our time, some have paid with their lives for their Christian witness, reminding us all of the cost of discipleship. The Spirit gives Christians courage to live out their convictions, even in the face of persecution and martyrdom.'

§46 talks about the purpose of baptism initiating people into the act of inclusivity:

> 'The good news of God's reign is about the promise of the actualization of a just and inclusive world. Inclusivity fosters just relationships in the community of humanity and creation, with mutual acknowledgement of persons and creation, and mutual respect and sustenance of each one's sacred worth. It also facilitates each one's full participation in the life of the community. Baptism in Christ implies a lifelong commitment to give an account of this hope by overcoming the barriers in order to find a common identity under the sovereignty of God (Gal. 3:27-28).'

---

[22] It is worth clarifying that in Part I, Sec 5, it says: 'Our engagement in mission, then, is pointless and fruitless without the presence, guidance and power of the Holy Spirit… All we do in the name of Christ must be led and empowered by the Holy Spirit.'

[23] Still, in §16, it says: 'A pneumatological focus on Christian mission recognizes that mission is essentially christologically based and relates the work of the Holy Spirit to the salvation through Jesus Christ.'

Many of these come from the section on marginalization (Sec. 2, 'Spirit of Liberation: Mission from the Margins'), whereas just about everything under the section on evangelism (Sec. 4, 'Spirit of Pentecost: Good News for All') would be language quite familiar to Evangelicals.

*CTC*, in contrast, has a heavy emphasis on Truth, but not understood as simply propositional statements. As Part II, Sec. A ('Bearing witness to the truth of Christ in a pluralistic, globalized world') says:

> 'Jesus Christ is the truth of the universe. Because Jesus *is* truth, truth in Christ is (i) personal as well as propositional; (ii) universal as well as contextual; (iii) ultimate as well as present.

Part II, Sec. B ('Building the peace of Christ in our divided and broken world') articulates the role of the cross as restoring relationships and pathways:

> 'Reconciliation to God is inseparable from reconciliation to one another. Christ, who *is* our peace, *made* peace through the cross, and *preached* peace to the divided world of Jew and Gentile. The unity of the people of God is both a fact ("he made the two one"), and a mandate ("make every effort to preserve the unity of the Spirit in the bond of peace"). God's plan for the integration of the whole creation in Christ is modelled in the ethnic reconciliation of God's new humanity.'

And Part II, Sec. F ('Partnering in the body of Christ for unity in mission') describes baptism as the consummation of evangelism:

> Both tasks [evangelism and church planting] are integrated in the Great Commission, where Jesus describes disciple-making in terms of evangelism (before 'baptizing them') and 'teaching them to obey all that I have commanded you'.

These are nuanced approaches. *CTC* would see diversity as more ethnic and cultural, *TTL* as more a matter of giving the marginalized an equal voice. *TTL* would affirm life as more justice-oriented, while *CTC* sees it as more spiritual. *CTC* would view unity as more inter-agency co-operation rather than denominational as *TTL* would. The old Evangelical and ecumenical camps still hold some sway.

Yet, *CTC* and *TTL* are not mutually exclusive. The 'L' in *TTL* stands for *Life* and that is something all Christians can affirm. Perhaps by forging new Evangelical ('about the Gospel') and ecumenical ('about unity) alliances, both groups can allow one another to address areas which need bolstering. §65 of *TTL* holds out the greatest hope of this becoming a reality:

> 'A growing intensity of collaboration with Evangelicals, especially with the Lausanne Movement for World Evangelization and the World Evangelical Alliance, has also abundantly contributed to the enrichment of ecumenical theological reflection on mission in unity. Together we share a common concern that the whole church should witness to the whole gospel in the whole world.'

# *TOGETHER TOWARDS LIFE* AND THE *EVANGELII GAUDIUM*: LIFE AND JOY IN DIALOGUE

Stephen Bevans, SVD

## Introduction: Two Major Documents on Mission

The year 2013 was an extraordinary one for both missiologists and ecumenists. In early November that year, the World Council of Churches' Commission on World Mission and Evangelism (CWME) presented its new document on mission *Together towards Life* (*TTL*) to the delegates of its tenth Assembly in Busan, South Korea. Later that month, Pope Francis published his first Apostolic Exhortation, entitled *Evangelii Gaudium* (*EG*) or, in English, *The Joy of the Gospel.*

Pope Francis's Apostolic Exhortation had its origins in the Vatican's 2012 Synod of Bishops on the theme of the 'New Evangelization'.[1] Since 1975, with the publication of Paul VI's *Evangelii Nuntiandi (EN)*,[2] it has been the custom of the Pope to issue a document (technically called an Apostolic Exhortation) to reflect on the discussions of the Synods of Bishops that are held at various intervals in Rome. Pope Francis's document is his reflection on the 2012 Synod, although in the document he widens his understanding of evangelization and mission and uses the term 'New Evangelization' only twelve times. It seems that neither *TTL* nor *EG*

---

[1] The term 'New Evangelization' had its origin in several talks by Pope John Paul II throughout his pontificate. He spoke of the need for an evangelization that was new 'in its ardour, methods and expression' (see John Paul II, Discourse to the XIX Assembly of CELAM (9th March 1983), 3: *L'Osservatore Romano*: Weekly Edition in English, 18th April 1983, 9: AAS 75 (1983), 778. Although the focus was wider, John Paul emphasized the need for such an evangelization within the more secularized countries of Europe, North America, Australia and New Zealand. Subsequently, Pope Benedict XVI established the Pontifical Council for the New Evangelization and announced that the 'New Evangelization' would be the topic for the 2012 Synod of Bishops (See Benedict XVI, Apostolic Letter *Ubique et Semper*: www.vatican.va/holy_father/benedict_xvi/apost_letters/documents/hf_ben-xvi_apl_20100921_ubicumque-et-semper_en.html). See also Stephen Bevans, 'Beyond the New Evangelization: A Missionary Church for the Twenty-First Century', in Richard R. Gaillardetz and Edward P. Hahnenberg (eds), *A Church with Open Doors: Catholic Ecclesiology for the Third Millennium* (Collegeville, MN: The Liturgical Press, 2015), 3-22.

[2] Paul VI, Apostolic Exhortation *Evangelii Nuntiandi* (*EN*): http://w2.vatican.va/content/paul-vi/en/apost_exhortations/documents/hf_p-vi_exh_19751208_evangelii-nuntiandi.html

had influenced writing of the other, although, as we will see, several of the themes and issues treated in the documents are similar.

Both documents' main focus is on mission – God's mission, *missio Dei* – in which the church subsequently shares as a graced privilege and task. The goal of that mission, for *TTL*, is the abundant *life* that the gospel brings (John 10:10), and the commitment to oppose all that opposes life; *EN* emphasizes the *joy* that is the result of accepting that gospel, and the joy with which the gospel is witnessed to and preached. But each document includes a substantial ecumenical sensitivity as well. This is naturally so in regards to *TTL*, since it is the product of a body dedicated to ecumenical practice and witness. As that document insists, 'practically as well as theologically, mission and unity belong together', even though it admits that 'we have to continue this journey in our century with fresh attempts so that the church becomes truly missionary' (§60). *EG*'s recognition of the ecumenical dimensions of mission is less pronounced since it is a document addressed primarily to members of the Roman Catholic Church, but towards the end of the document, in a special section on ecumenical dialogue, Francis writes that 'the credibility of the Christian message would be much greater if Christians could overcome their divisions', and that 'we must never forget that we are pilgrims journeying alongside one another' (*EG* §244). Although, as I've pointed out, neither document is influenced by the other, the reference to the word 'journey' in both passages is quite felicitous, especially since this dovetails quite nicely with the WCC's emphasis in the next several years on an ecumenical 'pilgrimage of justice and peace'.[3]

What this chapter intends to accomplish is to put *TTL* and *EG* in dialogue with each other so that the ecumenical journey or pilgrimage undertaken by both the WCC and the Roman Catholic Church can be more clearly delineated. We might say that we are putting Life and Joy in dialogue. Since Kirsteen Kim's essay summarizes the contents of *TTL*, this essay will offer only a brief summary of *EG*, and then certain commonalities will be highlighted, followed by a reflection on some of the differences of emphasis in each document. A final section will suggest several areas in which each document, as the result of the pilgrimage so far, has learned and can learn from the other.

## *EG*: Summary

*EG* is a much larger document than *TTL*, over twice its size. It consists of eighteen introductory paragraphs and five subsequent chapters, and has

[3] See Dagmar Heller, 'Reflections on the Pilgrimage of Justice and Peace', in *The Ecumenical Review,* 66/2 (July 2014), 135-38: http://onlinelibrary.wiley.com/doi/10.1111/erev.12090/abstract. WCC: www.oikoumene.org/en/what-we-do/ pilgrimage-of-justice-and-peace

been described by Pope Francis himself as the 'plan of my Pontificate'.[4] Because of its length, it is very rich and impossible to summarize briefly, but we can offer some of its main points, taking up more details later. Chapter One is entitled 'The Church's Missionary Transformation' (*EG* §§19-49), and calls for a church that 'goes forth' as 'a community of missionary disciples' (*EG* §24). The Pope explains this as taking a 'missionary option... capable of transforming everything' (*EG* §27), as putting 'all things in a missionary key' (§34), as being 'A Mother with an Open Heart' (see the title of I.V). Chapter Two is named 'Amid the Crisis of Communal Commitment' (*EG* §§50-109) and is a lengthy reflection on 'the context in which we all have to live and work' (*EG* §50). The Pope speaks against an 'Economy of Exclusion' and the 'Idolatry of Money', challenges that come from Culture and Urbanization, the temptations of 'spiritual workers', and the challenge of laity, women's participation, and laity in the church. Chapter Three takes up a reflection on 'The Proclamation of the Gospel' (*EG* §§110-175), insisting that this is the task of the entire People of God as it engages in inculturation, personal witness, and uncovering the resources of the piety of ordinary Christians. Included in this section is an extended treatment of the homily given especially at the Sunday celebration of the Eucharist. Chapter Four deals with 'The Social Dimension of Evangelization' (*EG* §§176-258), and focuses on what has already become a hallmark of Francis's papacy: the commitment to and inclusion of the poor in the work of evangelization. Francis also includes in this chapter reflections on the common good, the dialogue of peace, and ecumenical and interreligious dialogue. Chapter Five outlines a mission spirituality under the title 'Spirit-Filled Evangelizers' (*EG* §§258-88) and ends with a thoughtful and powerful reflection on Mary, the Mother of Evangelization.

## *TTL* and *EG*: Commonalities

### *A Missionary Church*

The very first line of *TTL* is very much in line with the now traditional WCC and CWME perspective of *missio Dei*: 'We believe in the Triune God who is the creator, redeemer and sustainer of all life. God created the whole *oikoumene* in God's image and constantly works in the world to affirm and safeguard life.' God's mission calls for a missionary church: 'God invites us into the life-giving mission of the Triune God and empowers us to bear witness to the vision of abundant life for all in the new

---

[4] This is on the word of the Prefect of the Congregation of the Evangelization of Peoples, Cardinal Fernando Filone, in a talk he gave (attended by the author), entitled 'Mission in *Evangelii Gaudium*' at a conference at the Pontifical Urbaniana University in Rome in April 2015.

heaven and new earth' (§1). Later on in the document, in the chapter that specifically focuses on the church, we read that 'the life of the church arises from the love of the Triune God' (§55), and that the church, 'both theologically and empirically, came into being for the sake of mission' (§57). Even though there is no note on the allusion, the reference to Faith and Order's 2013 document *The Church: Toward a Common Vision* (also presented at the 2013 Busan Assembly) is clear: 'It is not possible to separate church and mission in terms of their origin or purpose. To fulfil God's missionary purpose is the church's aim' (§57).[5]

Although Francis alludes to the passage in Vatican II's decree on mission activity that adopts the *missio Dei* perspective for the Roman Catholic Church (*EG* §179), he rather surprisingly does not cite it in a footnote.[6] There is, nevertheless, no doubt that, for Francis, 'by her very nature the Church is missionary' (*EG* §179). Indeed, realizing the centrality of missionary activity in the church would lead to the deeper realization that 'missionary outreach is *paradigmatic for all the Church's activity*' (*EG* §15). Francis writes that the church is a church that 'goes forth as a community of missionary disciples' (*EG* §24), a description of the church from the Latin American Bishops' conference at Aparecida, Brazil, that he has taken as his own.[7] He calls for pastoral ministry to be done in a 'missionary style' (*EG* §35), and to 'put all things in a missionary key' (*EG* §34). Again, with the Latin American Bishops, he urges the church to be 'permanently in a state of mission' (*EG* §25).[8] Perhaps most extraordinarily, however, he writes that he dreams 'of a 'missionary option', that is, a missionary impulse capable of transforming everything, so that the Church's customs, ways of doing things, times and schedules,

---

[5] See Commission on Faith and Order, *The Church: Towards a Common Vision* (TCTCV): www.oikoumene.org/en/resources/documents/commissions/faith-and-order/i-unity-the-church-and-its-mission/the-church-towards-a-common-vision. In the 'Historical Note' of this document (TCTCV 46), it is acknowledged that the CWME document had a strong influence on the final version. This is true especially of the first chapter. See Stephen Bevans, 'Ecclesiology and Missiology: Reflections on Two Recent Documents from the World Council of Churches', in *Dialog: A Journal of Theology*, 54/2 (Summer 2015), 126-34.

[6] The reference is Vatican Council II, Decree on the Mission Activity of the Church, *Ad Gentes (AG)*: www.vatican.va/archive/hist_councils/ii_vatican_council/documents/vat-ii_decree_19651207_ad-gentes_en.html, 2. As we will see in the following section, the lack of the *Missio Dei* perspective is one of the key points of difference between *EG* and *TTL*. Rather remarkably, the Vatican II document on mission is never cited in the Apostolic Exhortation.

[7] Conference of Latin American Bishops, Fifth General Conference at Aparecida, Brazil, 2007: www.aecrc.org/documents/Aparecida-Concluding%20Document.pdf. It should be mentioned that, as Archbishop of Buenos Aires, Argentina, the then Cardinal Jorge Mario Bergoglio was the chair of the writing group of this document.

[8] Aparecida Document, 551.

language and structures can be suitably channelled for the evangelization of today's world rather than for her self-preservation' (*EG* §27).

## *Care of Creation*

A second commonality that *TTL* and *EG* share is a concern for the care of creation as something integral to the mission and life of the church. This concern is a major one in *TTL*, and one of its major contributions to missionary thinking and practice today. *TTL* speaks of mission as the 'overflow of the infinite love of the Triune God', and so creation is understood as God's first act of mission (§19). Right from the beginning, therefore, mission is a call to move from an anthropocentric understanding to one that has the entire creation at its heart. Because of this, 'our participation in mission, our being in creation, and our practice of the life of the Spirit, need to be woven together, for they are mutually transformative' (§21). Salvation is not a merely spiritual reality, but one that involves cosmic wholeness and healing (§29). Consequently, rather than thinking about a mission *to* creation (or, as will be repeated later in the document, *to* other humans), Christians are in mission *with* creation. Indeed, 'in many ways creation is in mission to humanity; for instance, the natural world has a power that can heal the human heart and body' (§22). Nevertheless, mission with creation calls for its protection and care by human beings, especially in the light of the exploitation and pollution that humanity has caused (§29).

The care and protection of creation is not a major theme in *EG*, although it has been a prominent feature of Pope Francis's pontificate, included in the homily as his installation as Pope in March 2013, and reiterated many times since. In June 2015, he issued a lengthy encyclical, *Laudato Si'*, 'On the Care of our Common Home'.[9] Because the Pope addresses the encyclical to all women and men in the world, he does not connect ecological concern with the mission of the church directly, but he does do so in *EG*, towards the end of the document. Here Francis speaks of creation as one of the poor 'who are frequently at the mercy of economic interests or indiscriminate exploitation'. As the Pope says quite eloquently, 'Thanks to our bodies, God has joined us so closely to the world around us that we can feel the desertification of the soil almost as a physical ailment, and the extinction of a species as a painful disfigurement. Let us not leave in our wake a swath of destruction and death which will affect our own lives and those of future generations' (*EG* §215). All Christians, the Pope concludes, 'are called to watch over and protect the fragile world in which we live, and all its peoples' (*EG* §216).

---

[9] Pope Francis, Encyclical Letter *Laudato Si'*: http://w2.vatican.va/content/francesco/en/encyclicals/documents/papa-francesco_20150524_enciclica-laudato-si.html

### *Mission from the Margins*

The other major feature of *TTL* – in fact, its 'defining perspective' according to one of the document's principal authors[10] – is the idea of 'Mission from the Margins'. *TTL* insists on a reversal of thinking about mission. Classically, mission was conceived as a rich, powerful centre going to poor, powerless people on the world's margins. However, such a perspective only contributes to the continuation of oppression and marginalization. People on the margins, however, can offer important lessons to those at the centre. 'People on the margins have agency, and can often see what, from the centre, is out of view. People on the margins, living in vulnerable positions, often know what exclusionary forces are threatening their survival and can best discern the urgency of their struggles' (§38), and marginalized people have gifts that only they can bring to the missionary effort (§39). As such, people on the margins are 'reservoirs of the active hope, collective resistance and perseverance' that the entire church needs to witness to and proclaim the reign of God (§39). Mission should no longer be directed *at* people, but *with* people, acknowledging the agency that people on the margins have. 'The marginalized in society are the main partners in God's mission' (§107). Such a commitment to the dignity and power of people on the margins gives new emphasis and energy to working for justice and inclusivity for the poor, since it calls for the poor themselves to claim the agency that is truly theirs.

*EG* does not use the phrase 'Mission from the Margins', but it has the same understanding of the importance of the poor as the church's primary evangelizers. This is particularly true in a sub-section of Chapter Four, 'The Inclusion of the Poor in Society' (*EG* §§187-216). On the one hand, the Pope is clear that 'each individual Christian and every community is called to be an instrument of God for the liberation and promotion of the poor, and for enabling them to be fully a part of society' (*EG* §187). This involves, in the first place, real solidarity with all peoples, and a recognition of their right to equal dignity and participation in society's processes (*EG* §§188-90). But, in a way that echoes *TTL*, the Pope speaks of the need to learn from the poor, for 'they have much to teach us'. 'The new evangelization is an invitation to acknowledge the saving power at work in their lives and to put them at the center of the Church's pilgrim way.' Christians are called to find Christ in the poor, to lend their voice to their causes, but – more importantly in the light of *TTL*'s insights – to listen to them and 'to embrace the mysterious wisdom which God wishes to share with us through them' (*EG* §198).

---

[10] Metropolitan Geevarghese Coorilos, 'God of Life, Lead Us to Justice and Peace: Some Missiological Perspectives', in *International Review of Mission,* 102/1 (396) (April, 2013), 9.

### *Critique of the Global Economy*

Particularly in the introductory statements at the beginning and the summary affirmations at the end, *TTL* is extremely critical of today's global economy. 'We are living in a world in which faith in mammon threatens the credibility of the gospel' and critiques a 'market economy' that promises to save the world through 'unlimited growth' (§7). Today's globalized economy, *TTL* claims, 'has effectively supplanted the God of Life with mammon', and so mission has to be counter-cultural, prophetic action, 'offering alternatives to such idolatrous visions' (§108). Such strong language is repeated in the body of the document. Unlimited growth promoted by the free market 'is an ideology that claims to be without alternative' (§31), amounting to idolatry. Jesus Christ, the document says, confronts and transforms all that denies life, including 'cultures and systems which generate and sustain massive poverty, discrimination and dehumanization, and which exploit or destroy people and the earth' (§37).

Although Francis puts in a good word for business as a 'noble vocation' (*EG* §203), he is equally critical of any kind of business that does not work ultimately for the common good and for the equal distribution of goods to all (*EG* §§202-08). Perhaps his most devastating critique comes in the second chapter of the Apostolic Exhortation. Citing the fifth Commandment, 'Thou shalt not kill', Francis writes that 'today we also have to say 'Thou shalt not' to an economy of exclusion and inequality' because 'such an economy kills' (§53). Referring to today's consumer culture in which people buy things, use them for a while, and then throw them away, Francis compares this to a 'disposable' or throwaway culture that is spreading. In this new development of the free market economy (*EG* §54), 'those excluded are no longer society's underside or its fringes or its disenfranchised – they are no longer even a part of it. The excluded are not the "exploited" but the outcast, the "leftovers"' (*EG* §53). Again, Francis writes, 'The culture of prosperity deadens us; we are thrilled if the market offers us something new to purchase; and in the meantime all those lives stunted for lack of opportunity seem a mere spectacle; they fail to move us' (§54). The answer to all of this, then, is a resounding 'No to the New Idolatry of Money' (*EG* §§55-56), 'No to a Financial System which Rules Rather Than Serves' (*EG* §§57-58), and 'No to the Inequality which Spawns Violence' (*EG* §§59-60). Anticipating the subtitle of his encyclical on protecting creation, *Laudato Si'*, Francis writes: 'Economy, as the very word indicates, should be the art of achieving a fitting management of our common home, which is the world as a whole' (*EG* §206). Those involved in the pursuit of economic growth need to be keenly aware, in today's global economy, of the global repercussions of every economic or financial decision.

### *Evangelism, Culture, Inter-faith Dialogue, and Spirituality*

*TTL* includes a chapter on Evangelism, which it describes as seeking to share the good news of the gospel 'with all who have not yet heard it', and so inviting 'them to an experience of life in Christ' (§80). *EG* begins with a long, enthusiastic section to encourage Christians to share the 'joy of the Gospel', by which 'those who accept [Jesus'] offer are set free from sin, sorrow, inner emptiness and loneliness' (*EG* §1).

For *TTL*, Evangelism includes both sensitivity to culture and commitment to interreligious dialogue. 'Respect for people and their cultural and symbolic life-worlds are necessary if the gospel is to take root in those different realities' (§97), the document insists. It also insists on understanding that 'God is there before we come (Acts 17) and our task is not to bring God along, but to witness to the God who is already there' (§94). Dialogue, therefore, is an essential part of mission. Pope Francis places great emphasis on culture in the process of evangelization, observing astutely that 'we would not do justice to the logic of the incarnation if we thought of Christianity as monocultural and monotonous' (*EG* §117). His treatment of interreligious dialogue is not as extensive as his treatment of culture, but he clearly is in continuity with the church's teaching that it is an essential part of the church's missionary activity (*EG* §§250-54).[11] He insists, however, that true openness to 'the other' does not compromise the convictions of either side and avoids a 'facile syncretism' (*EG* §251).

Both documents call for a deep spirituality to accompany the church's missionary work. *TTL* develops this briefly, speaking of a 'transformative spirituality' that works for justice and 'provokes in us a renewed awareness that the Holy Spirit meets us and challenges us at all levels of life, and brings newness and change to the places and times of our personal and collective journeys' (§34, see §§29-35). *EG* devotes an entire chapter to the cultivation of 'Spirit-filled evangelizers', who are rooted in contemplation of God's Word (*EG* §264), moving beyond self-regard (*EG* §272), and dedicated to prayer (*EG* §§281-83).

## *TTL* and *EG*: Differences

The commonalities in *TTL* and *EG* greatly outweigh their differences, but there are several significant differences that need to be mentioned as the two documents are put in dialogue with one another.

---

[11] This essential connection is implied rather than expressly stated. For such a statement, see John Paul II, Encyclical Letter, *Redemptoris Missio* (*RM*): http://w2.vatican.va/content/john-paul-ii/en/encyclicals/documents/hf_jp-ii_enc_07121990_redemptoris-missio.html, 55.

### *Missio Dei*

The missionary nature of the church in *TTL* is rooted firmly, as we have said already, in a Trinitarian perspective of *missio Dei*. 'Mission begins in the heart of the Triune God', and 'the missionary God who sent the Son to the world calls all God's people (John 20:21), and empowers them to be a community of hope' (§2). In contrast, as mentioned above, the church's missionary nature in *EG* is spoken of without any reference to the Trinity or God's mission (see *EG* §179). There is, nevertheless, a subtle understanding that the church's mission is indeed Christians' participation in the prior mission of God. The church is a 'mystery rooted in the Trinity', 'whose ultimate foundation is found in the free and gracious initiative of God' (*EG* §111). The church is a 'community of missionary disciples', that 'knows that the Lord has taken the initiative, he has loved us first (1 John 4:19), and therefore we can move forward, boldly take the initiative, going out to others, seek those who have fallen away, stand at the crossroads and welcome the outcast' (*EG* §24). God sends the Spirit into Christians' hearts, Francis writes at the beginning of the chapter about the proclamation of the gospel, to transform Christians and help them to respond to God's love by the way they live. Christ sends the church on mission to be a sacrament of God's love. In the act of evangelization, the church 'co-operates as an instrument of that divine grace which works unceasingly and inscrutably' (*EG* §112). The Trinitarian formula is not expressed as clearly in *EG* as in *TTL*, but it is there.

### *The Holy Spirit*

One of the most important features of *TTL* is its emphasis on 'the mission of the Holy Spirit within the mission of the Triune God' (§11). From the beginning, the Spirit 'moved over the waters' (Gen. 1:2), bringing life to humankind and wisdom and prophecy to Israel. This same Spirit, *TTL* notes, came upon Mary 'and brought forth Jesus', and commissioned Jesus for mission at his baptism, raised him to life after his resurrection, and through the risen Christ was poured on the Jesus community at Pentecost, anointing them for mission (§12-15). Christians 'by the Spirit... participate in the mission of love that is at the heart of the life of the Trinity' (*EG* §18). Today, the Spirit 'works in the world often in mysterious and unknown ways beyond our imagination' (§15). Because of this, 'the claim that the Spirit is with us is not for us to make, but for others to recognize in the life we lead' (§28). References to the Holy Spirit abound in the document (e.g. §§56, 66-67, 85, 87, 93, 101-12), so much so that some critics have claimed that the document lacks a true Christological focus.[12]

[12] I refer especially to a discussion I had with several Finnish theologians in August 2013.

Such Christological focus is not lacking, however, in *EG*, and there is certainly not as strong an emphasis on the Spirit. *EG*'s first line is 'The joy of the Gospel fills the hearts and lives of all who encounter Jesus… With Christ, joy is constantly born anew' (*EG* §1). For Francis, life 'in the Spirit' 'has its source in the heart of the risen Christ' (*EG* §2). Francis therefore begins his Apostolic Exhortation with a strong evangelistic appeal: 'I invite all Christians, everywhere, at this very moment, to a renewed personal encounter with Jesus Christ, or at least an openness to letting him encounter them; I ask all of you to do this unfailingly each day' (*EG* §3). A bit further on in the document, Francis writes: 'Jesus can also break through the dull categories with which we would enclose him, and he constantly amazes us by his divine creativity. Whenever we make the effort to return to the source and to recover the original freshness of the gospel, new avenues arise, new paths of creativity open up, with different forms of expression, more eloquent signs, and words with new meaning for today's world' (*EG* §11). Like Trinitarian language, language referring to the Spirit is present, and rather abundantly, but used rather incidentally. While the word 'Spirit' appears less than a hundred times, the words 'Jesus' and 'Christ' appear over three hundred times. The emphasis is clearly Christological.

### *Internal Church Issues*

Not surprisingly, *TTL*'s focus on concrete issues internal to the church is much more general than that of Pope Francis. As a WCC document, *TTL* can only offer general guidelines for action, whereas Francis can speak very specifically. Accordingly, he speaks intriguingly of his own role as Pope and of the need to de-centralize power in the church to make room for the role of local bishops and conferences of bishops in particular areas (*EG* §§16, 31-32). He reminds priests that the confessional – in which is celebrated the sacrament of reconciliation – 'must not be a torture chamber' (*EG* §44), and emphasizes that 'the Eucharist, although it is the fullness of sacramental life, is not a prize for the perfect but a powerful medicine and mercy for the weak'. In the same paragraph he warns that Baptism should not be withheld from parents who seek it for their children (*EG* §47). His message of a church with open doors (*EG* §§46-49) has been greeted by Catholics as a fresh approach in pastoral practice that focuses on making the church a community that attracts rather than challenges or even repels (see *EG* §14).

## ***TTL* and *EG*: Learning from One Another**

It is remarkable, in reading both documents, how much the churches and ecclesial communities of the WCC and the church of Roman Catholicism have already learned from one another in this last century in which ecumenical dialogue and co-operation has been a prominent feature in the church's life. From the mutual suspicion that marked the Protestant, Catholic and Orthodox churches at the 1910 World Mission Conference at Edinburgh, to the mutual trust as pilgrims that Pope Francis calls for in *EG* §244, is a transformation that can only be the result of God's grace. That pilgrim journey (*TTL* §60) is not complete, but there is no question that the quest for unity is one to which both the WCC and the Roman Catholic Church are committed.

On the side of the *TTL*, there is evidence of learning from Catholicism in its rather new emphasis on 'transformative spirituality' (§29-30) in which 'worship and sacraments play a crucial role' (§74). A Catholic reading *TTL* would feel very much at home. But it is also clear that Catholic thinking about mission has learned a great deal over the years from their Orthodox and Protestant sisters and brothers on the journey. The foremost of these learnings is the radical missionary nature of the church which, although it appears within the Catholic tradition as well, was most clearly articulated in the twentieth century at the 1954 conference of the International Missionary Council (predecessor of CWME) in Willingen, Germany.[13] While, as we have noted, the conviction is not expressed strongly in *EG* in terms of the Trinitarian *missio Dei*, it is expressed forcefully in terms of Pope Francis's 'missionary option' (*EG* §27) and the call to be a church of 'missionary disciples' (*EG* §24).

Could more be learned by engaging *TTL* and *EG* in dialogue? Certainly. Catholic mission thinking embodied in *EG* could learn much from a stronger, more intentional development of the Holy Spirit and the Spirit's role in salvation history and the church's missionary life. *TTL* in turn could profit by a more explicit Christological reading of the text. The Christology is there, of course, but in the light of *EG* it could be made more explicit and pervasive.

There is a need for both documents to reflect more deeply and consistently on *TTL*'s pioneering reflections on 'Mission from the Margins'. Both documents offer much wisdom on this fresh and ground-breaking perspective, but WCC members and Roman Catholics have just begun to think about mission from this angle. As Christendom continues to unravel, and as the churches of the global South become more and more prominent in the church's missionary activity, this new missiological perspective will need to be reflected upon more carefully.

Finally, *TTL*'s rather earnest tone could learn from Pope Francis's breezy, quotable, and sometimes even humorous, style, one that embodies the title of his document: *The Joy of the Gospel*. The Pope has been quoted extensively about his remark that Christians should not seem like women and men who live as though there were only Lent without Easter, that they

[13] The great Roman Catholic ecclesiologist Yves Congar acknowledged this influence on Vatican II's *Ad Gentes*. See Yves Congar, 'Principes Doctrineaux', in Johannes Schütte (ed), Vatican II: *Activité Missionaire d'lÉglise*, Unam Sanctam 67 (Paris: Éditions du Cerf, 1967), 186.

should not live life as though they had just come back from a funeral, that they should not live like 'sourpusses' (*EG* §85). On the other hand, the perspective of *TTL* that mission is about the promotion of Life in all its forms, and the opposition to any persons or forces that oppose or oppress it, is one that Roman Catholics need to ponder and develop more fully as well. That the gospel is about life is something that women and men need to hear today – indeed, many think that the church and the gospel stand for just the opposite![14] Life and Joy, therefore, need to be in a mutually fruitful dialogue. Reading these powerful documents together can do just that. It is this kind of mutually appreciative and mutually critical dialogue from which the ecumenical movement can profit today.

[14] See Peter Cruchley Jones, ''You Have Not Sought the Lost: A Reflection from Europe on the WCC Theme', in *International Review of Mission,* 102/1 (396) (April 2013), 69-81.

# *TOGETHER TOWARDS LIFE* AND THE CONTEXT OF THE GLOBAL SOUTH

Roderick Hewitt

## Introduction

The topic calls for a critical engagement with the contextual realities of the Global South in conversation with the changing landscape of Christianity as articulated in the World Council of Churches document, *Together towards Life: The Changing Landscape of Christianity in the 21st Century* (hereafter *TTL*). The issues that will emerge in this exploration are construed from key terms of Global South, Changing Landscape, and Christianity. Each concept will require clarification in what is meant because they are shaped by unique contextual nuances in meaning.

This chapter begins by identifying what is meant by the term 'Global South' and then proceeds to describe and critique the characteristics of that phenomenon. It will then proceed to postulate the different ways in which the landscape of Christianity has and is changing in response to the contextual challenges of the Global South. The subject under discussion will be deeply influenced by the author's identity and vocation that has been shaped primarily by missional formation within the Global South. The first point of reference is the context of the Caribbean region – a melting pot of cultures from Europe, Africa, Asia and the Americas. In this region, it may be best to speak about 'seascape' rather than 'landscape'. The diverse small islands, in which a Euro-American brand of Christianity dominates the religio-cultural setting with an overlay of other religious expressions from Africa and Asia, have given birth to a pulsating syncretistic mixing of different cultures that has made the people open to external influences.[1] The second hermeneutical lens has been shaped by missional experiences through service with the Council for World Mission.[2] Thirdly, ecumenical and missiological learning through decades of involvement in the WCC Commission for World Mission and Evangelism

---

[1] Roderick R. Hewitt, 'Sun, Sand, Sea, Reggae! The Challenge of Tourism for Church and Society in the Caribbean', in Caesar D'Mello, Wati Longchar and Philip Mathew (eds), *Deconstructing Tourism: Who Benefits? A Theological Reading from the Global South* (Kolkata, India: SCEPTRE, 2013).

[2] CWM was created in 1977 and incorporates the London Missionary Society (1795), the Commonwealth Missionary Society (1836), and the (English) Presbyterian Board of Missions (1847): www.cwmission.org/index.php/about-us (accessed 3rd July 2015).

(CWME); and, finally, theological and ministerial formation perspectives through ongoing academic research work. These resources will be used to interrogate the key question of this chapter: 'What are the ways in which the urgent issues that give shape to the realities of life in the Global South converse with the missiological affirmations of the *TTL* document?'

## What is the Global South?

The term Global South is used in this paper to describe the concept 'Third World' which was popularly used during the East-West tensions and Cold War era between the USA and the former USSR that emerged after World War II.[3] Those developing countries that existed primarily in Latin America and the Caribbean, Africa, most of Asia and the Pacific Islands, were prejudicially classified by the more wealthy northern countries as 'Third World'. Although there are different understandings of what constitutes the Global South, the phenomenon is characterised by contexts that Volker Boege, Anne Brown, Kevin Clements and Anna Nolan describe as the hybrid political order of emerging states.[4] In a comparative analysis of the Global North and Global South economies in 2010, E.L. Odeh states:

> While Global North countries are wealthy, technologically advanced, politically stable and ageing as their societies tend towards zero population growth, the opposite is the case with Global South countries. While Global South countries are agrarian-based, dependent economically and politically on the Global North, the Global North has continued to dominate and direct the Global South in international trade and politics.[5]

Among these states are emerging expressions of different brands of democracies in which many citizens do not have equal entitlement or access to the scarce benefits of state services. Countries such as China, India, Brazil and South Africa had more advanced and developed economies than the typical Third World country and therefore did not readily embrace the concept to describe their identity, but political and economic changes driven by globalisation and greater investment in technology since the 1990s have led them to embrace the concept of Global South to describe their status in political solidarity with those countries that were previously classified as Third World. The term 'Global South' has therefore emerged as a contemporary expression to describe how

---

[3] The term was popularized by the Brandt Commission reports published in 1980 and 1983.

[4] Volker Boege, Anne Brown, Kevin Clements and Anna Nolan, *On Hybrid Political Orders and Emerging States: State Formation in the Context of 'Fragility'*: http://edoc.vifapol.de/opus/volltexte/2011/2595/pdf/boege_etal_handbook.pdf (accessed 2nd July 2015).

[5] L.E. Odeh, 'A Comparative Analysis of Global North and Global South Economies', in *Journal of Sustainable Development in Africa,* 12/3 (2010) 1.

developing economies, most of which are in the Southern hemisphere,[6] are coping with the onslaught of the socio-economic impact of globalisation on their different societies. It is worth noting however that the concept of 'Global South' cannot strictly be linked with socio-economic problems affecting only those countries that exist to the south of the Equator.

## The Context of the Global South

The contemporary era has seen increasing state fragility, failure and even collapse in parts of the Global South that has engendered violent conflict and the disintegration of societies.[7] According to Krasner and Pascual, state fragility constitutes 'one of the most important foreign policy challenges of the contemporary era'.[8] Increasing state fragility constitutes a receptive environment for extremist political and religious groups to engage in transnational terrorism, providing safe havens for human trafficking, and trading in illegal weapons, drugs and commodities.[9] Developmental issues of poverty and inequality cannot be adequately addressed with the full national focus that is required because of overriding security threats. Therefore, within many political contexts of the Global South:

> One cannot be sure about what it means to live in a nation-state or in communities. Social change has resulted in pluralities and diversities that sometimes breed conflict, and many persons are no longer willing to give their allegiance to any centre. Democracy in the contemporary neo-liberal model functions like a bubble in a very delicate state of existence that can easily burst and have its life-sustaining contents spilt.[10]

State formation with 'Western-style' democratic models of governance has failed in many contexts to meet the basic needs of people in the Global South. Poor quality of governance therefore constitutes a burning issue in many countries of the Global South. Political parties that evolved from popular liberation movements that successfully fought colonialism have proved to be also weak in fostering good government. The paradox is that these political movements of liberation have won electoral victory of the political left, but the economic power has remained with the political right

---

[6] With the two exceptions of the economies of Australia and New Zealand.

[7] Examples of South Sudan, Somalia, Syria and Iraq.

[8] S.D. Krasner and C. Pascual, 'Addressing State Failure', in *Foreign Affairs,* 84/4 (2005), 153-63.

[9] The rise of groups such as Boko Haram in Northern Nigeria, El Shabbah in Somalia, Islamic State (ISIS) in Iraq and Syria, the Lord's Resistance Army in Uganda, the FRAC Group in Colombia, and many other such groups in Asia, have all emerged in contexts of fragile states.

[10] Roderick R Hewitt, 'Spirituality for Democracy: Spiritual resources for democratic participation in the 21st century', in *Verbum et Ecclesia* (2014), 35(3), Art. #1345, 7 pages: http://dx.doi. org/10.4102/ve.v35i3.1345

that produced a 'democracy' that produces progressive poverty, high inequalities and exclusion for the common people.

The forces of neo-liberal globalization seek global domination and this has resulted in the creation of the liberalization and deregulation of markets. Instead of globalisation serving primarily as an opportunity for building more just global relations between nations, this global system promotes the insatiable consumption of human and natural resources to serve contexts of expanding economic, social and ecological imbalances. This deceptive and enslaving instrument of development masks itself as working in the best interests of all. It uses the language of 'Free Trade' that in practice is experienced as an unfair system designed to ensure that wealthy northern economies continue to access and exploit the commodities of underdeveloped and developing nations of the Global South. The market has therefore become a system organised for cheating the poorer nations whose economies cannot be distributed according to market logic alone. Daley and Cobbs Jr. refer to this as a 'misplaced concreteness of the market because of its false claim that:

> Its strengths are to be found in its capacity to use independent, decentralised decisions to give rise not to chaos… Individual consumers know their preferences better that anyone else and act directly to satisfy them in the market-place. Individual producers know their own capacities and options better than anyone else and they too act on this information in the market.[11]

The rosy picture of national well-being painted by this perspective belies the awesome forces of violence and injustice that are unleashed by this dehumanizing force that is designed to enrich the few at the expense of denying fullness of life, especially to those who live on the margins of society. The toxic combination of the forces of a dysfunctional state and economy have produced an intractable problem of refugees and migrants moving away from war, ethnic and religious conflicts, and economic instability to any place and by whatever means, to seek peace and a better future. In such situations, women and children are the most vulnerable. The political and economic realities that characterised the context of the Global South have to a great extent been heightened by influences caused by the dominating world power relationships that embody the controversial concept of 'Empire'. The nuanced understanding of the concept was popularised in the ecumenical debates and became embedded in the Accra Declaration (2004) of the World Alliance of Reformed Churches (WARC):

> The convergence of economic, political, cultural, geographic and military imperial interests, systems and networks for the purpose of amassing political power and economic wealth. Empire typically forces and facilitates the flow

[11] H.E. Daley and J.B. Cobbs Jr, *For The Common Good: Redirecting the Economy Towards Community, the Environment, and a Sustainable Future* (Boston, MS: Beacon Press, 1898), 44-45.

> of wealth and power from vulnerable persons, communities and countries to the more powerful.[12]

The Global South is still 'work in progress'. There are immeasurable positive assets of human development that have been accomplished but there are also intractable challenges. The rich and pulsating kaleidoscope of cultures, the potentially wealthy but underdeveloped resources, young and growing populations – all represent positive potential to be harnessed for development of the people. The different systems of government that have evolved since independence are still expiring pains because they have been in existence for a relatively short time period of time. Their experience of independence did not necessarily produce the formation of a strong and mature state that was politically and economically equipped to offer effective management of their developmental challenges. The threats to life in many states that are weak, fragile, failing, failed and collapsed have accentuated to precipitous proportions in the core areas of politics and good governance, economy and ecology, religion and culture. It is these areas that the changing landscape of Christianity and the mission of the church advocated in *TTL* must address.

## Church Presence and Christian Witness in the Global South

Whereas in the global North, most Christians live in countries where Christianity is the majority religion, this is the opposite in the Global South where in many contexts millions of Christians live as minorities in plural communities. The key terms of Christians, Christianity and Church are used for their sociological significance rather than their specific theological meanings to describe religious followers, their ideology and institutions that impact on the cultures in which they live. This broad scope of understanding of the key terms is necessary for engaging with the issues raised in *TTL* and exploring ways in which they affect fullness of life in the pluralistic and changing landscapes of the Global South. According to the Global Christianity report of the Pew Forum:

> In 1910, about two-thirds of the world's Christians lived in Europe, where the bulk of Christians had been for a millennium, according to historical estimates by the Center for the Study of Global Christianity. Today, only about a quarter of all Christians live in Europe (26%). A plurality – more than a third –are now in the Americas (37%). About one in every four Christians

---

[12] *The ACCRA Confession*, developed and published by the North American Covenanting for Justice Working Group (RCA Communication and Production Services, 2007), 6.

> lives in sub-Saharan Africa (24%), and about one in eight is found in Asia and the Pacific (13%).[13]

Christianity and the church's mission has been a force for good in many parts of the Global South in improving the lives of people. However, it must also be recognised that some expressions of the faith have contributed to instability in societies that deny people fullness of life. In some areas, fundamentalist religious fervour has gained momentum, reshaping the identities and actions of people in ways that have resulted in clashes and violent conflicts.

The central theme of *TTL* is the affirmation of fullness of life, constructed in a triune framework in which God the Creator is affirmed as the giver of life, Jesus as the Saviour for the whole universe and the Holy Spirit as the sustainer that empowers life and renews the whole creation (Genesis 2:7; John 3:8). This missional document has received a warm reception from churches in the Global South for being Biblically centred and contextually relevant to the issues that impact on the changing landscape of Christianity. In the geographical expansion of Christianity since 1910, the ecclesial landscape of the global South has become the locus where the majority of the world's Christian population resides or have their origins. If at the beginning of the twentieth century only Europe could claim to be the centre for global Christianity, then the contemporary landscape does not give that status to any single continent or region. The changing landscape of Christianity has resulted in the Global North no longer being able to dominate global Christianity in the same way that it did one hundred years ago.[14] It no longer has veto powers or monopoly to determine the identity, vocation and witness of global Christianity.

*TTL* identified the following shifts in global Christianity since 1980:

- Majority of Christians either are living or have their origins in the Global South and East.
- Migration has become a worldwide, multi-directional phenomenon which is reshaping the Christian landscape.
- The emergence of strong Pentecostal and charismatic movements from different localities is one of the most noteworthy characteristics of world Christianity today.
- People at the margins are claiming their key role as agents of mission and affirming mission as transformation.

---

[13] Pew Forum from the Center for the Study of Global Christianity at Gordon-Conwell Theological Seminary in South Hamilton, MS. Pew Research Center's Forum on Religion and Public Life, *Global Christianity* (December 2011), 9.

[14] According to the Pew Report, 'the fastest growth in the number of Christians over the past century has been in sub-Saharan Africa (a roughly sixtyfold increase, from fewer than nine million in 1910 to more than 516 million in 2010) and in the Asia-Pacific region (a roughly tenfold increase, from about 28 million in 1910 to more than 285 million in 2010)': Pew Research Center's Forum on Religion and Public Life, *Global Christianity*, 10.

- The church lives in multi-religious and multicultural contexts and new communication technology is also bringing the people of the world into a greater awareness of one another's identities and pursuits.[15]

The values that undergird *TTL*'s focus on the life-giving, life-saving and life-sustaining character and mission of the Triune God are pertinent to the contextual realities of the Global South. As Christianity, through the mission of different churches, makes increasing inroads into different contexts, this has led to fresh questions being raised about the understanding and praxis of God's mission. The societal challenges of wealth, poverty, ecology, political violence, corruption, migration, and law and order instability can no longer be neglected by churches that seek to be missional because these threats impact upon the fundamental well-being of all people.[16]

The spread of Christianity in the Global South is communicated less by what is read and more by what is seen, heard and recited.[17] Therefore, this methodology of transmission and reception of the gospel will more likely result in followers who express greater passion towards what they embrace and what motivates them to engage in action. A radical shift has therefore taken place over the last century in the quantity and quality of missional agents. The decline of long-term, full-time professional missionaries from the Global North to the South has been replaced by short-term, part-time and lay missional agents. Also, a significant rise in local indigenous mission agents is facilitating the growth of Christianity in the Global South.

The continuing changing landscape of Christianity has seen the advancement of Pentecostal and Charismatic types of churches as the dominant shapers of how Christianity engages with the social, cultural, economic and political culture. This brand of Christianity is significantly influenced by what can be classified a strategic alliance with the powerful influence of the USA's brand of evangelical Christianity that journeys in partnership with the global political, cultural and economic agenda of their imperial foreign policy that promotes the continuing educational, economic, cultural and political power of the West.[18] The continuing

---

[15] *TTL,* §5, 9.

[16] Church and Society Commission, Consejo Latinoamericano de Iglesias and Conference of European Churches, CEC-CLAI Globalization Final Report: *Threats and challenges of globalization: Churches in Europe and Latin America in dialogue* (September 2010).

[17] J. Philip and J.J. Myers, 'The New Faces of Christianity: Believing the Bible in the Global South': https://www.carnegiecouncil.org/studio/multimedia/20061011/5399.html/_res/id=sa_File1/The_New_Faces_of_Christianity.pdf (accessed 3rd July 2015).

[18] M.F. Shaw, 'Robert Wuthnow and World Christianity: A Response to Boundless Faith', 179: www.internationalbulletin.org/issues/2012-04/2012-04-179-shaw.pdf (accessed 2nd July 2015).

growth of Christianity seems to suggest multi-faceted reasons. Significant is the fact that population growth is being experienced at a phenomenally faster rate than in most countries in the Global North which are experiencing increasing gentrification in their population and an overall low birth rate that varies from -0.2 to a high +0.2%.[19]

The fast growth rate of Christianity must therefore be linked with the growth in population within many countries of the Global South. It could therefore be argued that the significant growth of Christianity in many parts of the global South (primarily Africa, Latin America and Asia) may be directly linked with rapid population growth. The religious movements of Pentecostalism and Charismatics, with their attractively packaged products that appeals to the world of youth culture, would be the beneficiaries of that growth in membership.[20] Significantly, it is in these geographical areas where the USA's spheres of political, economic and cultural influences are present that its brand of evangelical, Pentecostal and Charismatic Christianity is making impact.[21] According to Shaw, the American churches are (*fast*) becoming airports of a new globalization.[22] The third major factor that facilitates the growth of Christianity is the effectiveness of indigenous independent missional groups that evangelise without any reference to external partnerships of support by missionary networks from the West such as the evangelising work of the Karen people of Burma (Myanmar).[23]

*TTL* envisages the missional reformation of church that will give leadership to the issues that pose the most severe threats to life. It offers a broader understanding of the missional challenge facing the Church in the contemporary era that removes the understanding of salvation from its classical anthropocentric bias to a broader 'all creation' perspective. For example, in the context of the global, this church's mission must include advocacy for climate justice that involves working assiduously for climate protection, advocacy of international policies in favour of ecological debt to those vulnerable countries in the South, cancellation of illegitimate debts that enslave developing nations, advocating national food sovereignty, available and affordable quality health care and access to clean water as a

---

[19] World Population Data Sheet is an annual report: http://data.worldbank.org/indicator/SP.POP.GROW (accessed 4th July 2015).

[20] For a fresh paradigm perspective to understand the current role of Western mission in world Christianity, see D. Miller and T. Yamamori, *Global Pentecostalism: The New Face of Christian Social Engagement* (California: University of California Press, 2007).

[21] According to Shaw, 'Robert Wuthnow and World Christianity', 180. North American Christianity of American churches spent over $4 billion on overseas ministries.

[22] Shaw defines globalization as an embodiment of paradoxes in which a mixture of 'economic, political and cultural forces that produces the paradox of sameness and diversification': Shaw, 'Robert Wuthnow and World Christianity', 180.

[23] J.C. Riley, *An Unpredictable Gospel: American Evangelicals and World Christianity, 1812-1920* (New York: Oxford University Press, 2012), xi, 311.

human right.[24] This missional understanding of fullness of life is also referred to as 'The Economy of Life' because it places the whole *oikoumene* – the household of God – at the centre of the Church's mission:

> The Economy of Life cares for land and sea, the whole inhabited Earth, which has its own God-given integrity. It is against the commoditization of all aspects of nature, including water, air, forests and other commons. The bounty of creation is not a commodity to be plundered; rather, it is a divine gift to celebrate life through mutual sharing. The Economy of Life is where all creation glorifies God, the Creator, Redeemer and Sustainer, so that all may reach fullness of life (John 10:10).[25]

The ecumenical focus on addressing the global issues of the interconnectivity between poverty, wealth and ecology are central to the threats to life in the Global South. The WCC's Alternative Globalization Addressing People and Earth (AGAPE) global conference of 2012 offers an apt analysis of the challenges facing the churches:

> Theologies of human arrogance and domination… have failed to question and even legitimated systems and ideologies founded on unlimited growth, accumulation and exploitation of 'natural resources' … we have turned a blind eye to ecological destruction and the plight of victims of globalisation… we neglected to examine and change our own production, consumption and investment behaviour… we confess our complicity in systems of oppression.[26]

*TTL*'s vision of life envisions intentional interdependence between politics, economics and civil society where financial markets are guided by human and environmental concerns. The global financial and economic regime must no longer be based on neo-liberal principles such as unlimited profit maximisation and growth but, on the contrary, must be founded on the goal of provisioning for life. The mission of the church must also regard itself as an economic agent that advocates and embodies the core values of: economy from an ethical standpoint, embedding the market economy in a social and cultural context, ensuring the ecological and social sustainability of competition, and strengthening the primacy of politics in a global context.[27]

*TTL* calls for a re-evaluation of the way in which evangelism is understood and practised in the multi-religious and multicultural contexts

---

[24] *Threats and challenges of globalization*: Churches in Europe and Latin America in dialogue, Church and Society, Commission Consejo Latinoamericano de Iglesias and Conference of European Churches, 23-38.

[25] WCC, *The Economy of Life: An Invitation to Theological Reflection and Action: Theological Consultation on Economy of Life* (27th-30th October 2014), Chennai, India.

[26] J.C. Riley, *An Unpredictable Gospel*, xi, 311.

[27] Evangelical Church of Westphalia, 'Re-modelling the Social Market', Altstädter Kirchplatz 5 / D-33602 Bielefeld, Germany: www.evangelisch-in-westfalen.de, quicklink 257-58.

in which many Christians live. In addition, the new communication technology that has entered many unprepared communities and transformed traditional methods of networking into global networking, calls for attention in terms of how it affects identity. The movement of migrants into many cities has resulted in the presence of many different global religions. This changing environment of religious plurality constitutes a serious challenge to the churches, and new ways must be found to engage inter-faith dialogue that is characterized by reciprocity, shunning proselytization and instead embracing respectful cross-cultural communication.

Finally, *TTL* has introduced 'mission from the margins' as a fresh understanding of the contemporary mission of the church. Within the global context, people who live on the margins usually live in a permanent state of vulnerability, being excluded from active participation in the political and economic decisions that shape their lives. Although they make up a large number of the people that attend church, they are often objects rather than subjects of the church's mission. In some cases, those that live on the margins are deceived by corrupt 'prosperity preachers' with promises of healing and financial well-being, but often they are then fleeced through religious systems of greed that benefit the few powerful elites within the group. The churches in the South will need to experience a cathartic repentance because their hands are not clean in their mission with people that live on the margins. The transformation needed does not call simply,

> To move people from the margins to centres of power but to confront those who remain the centre by keeping people on the margins. Instead, churches are called to *transform* power structures.[28]

## Conclusion

One must be very careful not to exaggerate the claims of Christianity in the Global South as though the phenomenon has led to the emergence of independent, self-propagating, self-financing and self-governing churches and Christian movements. As mentioned earlier in this chapter, the changing landscape of global Christianity has to a great extent been shaped by forces linked with the phenomenon of globalisation. In this driving force, religious movements are not immune from this infectious force. In the same way that western missionary Christianity became an accompaniment of colonialism, the contemporary growth of Christianity in the global South is accompanied by the phenomenon of globalisation. Therefore, this chapter argues that the umbilical cord of the Global North that influences and controls global Christianity still continues today through the contemporary era through the phenomenon of globalisation.

---

[28] *TTL*, §6.

American Christianity continues to influence the growth of Christianity in the Global South because of the USA's continued role as a superpower that promotes its trade, finance, travel, culture and mass media, especially through its foreign aid programme. Therefore, as Wuthnow has argued, despite the demographic shift to the Global South, 'the notion of a shift of influence… cannot be inferred from such evidence.'[29] He therefore dismisses the claim of a global shift in Christianity from North to South as a 'hyperbole', and argues that it is still the impact of western missionary Christianity that is shaping the growth of Christianity in the Global South and that a key component of the growth is a higher birth rate.[30]

The threats to life in the Global South are not reducing, and this makes the missional challenge of the church even more urgent. However, in the midst of the threats people still celebrate. They never surrender to any of the life-denying forces that are at work but demonstrate 'a never giving up' resilience. Darkness will never overcome light and death will never overcome life. It is these people that set the agenda for the church's mission.

[29] Shaw, 'Robert Wuthnow and World Christianity', 181.
[30] Shaw, 'Robert Wuthnow and World Christianity', 181.

# *TOGETHER TOWARDS LIFE* AND THE CONTEXT OF THE GLOBAL NORTH

Kenneth R. Ross

### A New Frontier

Evidence abounds of a recession of Christian faith in the global North.[1] With minor local variations, there is an unmistakable trend: church attendance is in decline, numbers of baptisms are reducing, numbers of church weddings are reducing, numbers of church funerals are reducing. It has become perfectly possible to live one's life in many parts of the global North without participation in, or even much awareness of, the Christian faith. The sharp decline in religious identity and participation is evidenced by innumerable surveys. The results of the 2011 Scottish Census, for example, show that those identifying themselves as 'Church of Scotland' fell from 42% in 2001 to 32% in 2011. Meanwhile, those identifying themselves as 'no religion' rose from 28% in 2001 to 37% in 2011.[2] While religious affiliation and practice is higher in the USA than in Europe, a similar trend is evident there. The Pew Research Center reported in 2015 that its 'major new survey of more than 35,000 Americans finds that the percentage of adults who describe themselves as Christians has dropped by nearly eight percentage points in just seven years, and from 78.4% in an equally massive Pew Research survey in 2007 to 70.6% in 2014. Over the same period, the percentage of Americans who are religiously unaffiliated – describing themselves as atheist, agnostic or 'nothing in particular' – has jumped more than six points, from 16.1% to 22.8%.[3] How can we account for such changes?

Charles Taylor suggests that we have moved '… from a condition in 1500 in which it was hard not to believe in God, to our present situation just after 2000, where this has become quite easy for many. A way of

---

[1] A more extended version of this chapter can be found in Kenneth R. Ross, '*Together towards Life* in the Context of Liquid Modernity: Mission and Evangelism in the Age of Secularization', in *International Review of Mission,* 103.2, 399 (2014), 240-55.

[2] Scotland's Census 2011: Shaping our Future – Detailed Characteristics on Ethnicity, Identity, Language and Religion in Scotland: www.scotlandscensus.gov.uk/news/census-2011-detailed-characteristics-ethnicity-identity-language-and-religion-scotland (accessed 20th March 2014).

[3] Pew Research Center, 'Religious Landscape Study', www.pewforum.org/religious-landscape-study/ (accessed 2nd May 2015).

putting our present condition is to say that many people are happy living for goals which are purely immanent; they live in a way that takes no account of the transcendent.'[4] Despite centuries of Christian influence on their culture, language, literature, architecture, politics and values, many in the global North are opting to live with a frame of reference in which Christian faith has practically no place. As Reinhard Hempelmann observes: 'We talk about "inculturation" when the gospel finds a place in a certain cultural context. In our society today, Christian faith is in a stage of "exculturation".'[5] This presents a new, hitherto unexplored, frontier for Christian mission.

Lesslie Newbigin, a generation ago, was a pioneer in urgently drawing the attention of the churches to this new frontier which they now have to face. At a time when it was still widely assumed that the global North was the 'home base' of Christianity and that mission was something to be done elsewhere in the world, Newbigin demonstrated how far the tables had turned. For him, as a missionary returning from India to the UK in the 1970s, this was a profoundly personal experience. He described his experience of ministry on return to England as '… much harder than anything I met in India. There is a cold contempt for the gospel which is harder to face than any opposition… England is a pagan society and the development of a truly missionary encounter with this very tough form of paganism is the greatest intellectual and practical task facing the Church'.[6] This led him to pose what has proved to be the great unanswered mission question of our time: 'What would be involved in a missionary encounter between the gospel and this whole way of perceiving, thinking and living that we call "modern Western culture"?'[7]

Thirty years later, there can be little doubt that there was accuracy and acuity to Newbigin's analysis. While there is a resurgence of religion worldwide, there is also an advance of secularism, particularly in the global North but also making its mark wherever western culture exercises influence. How far does *Together towards Life* address this reality?

## The New Frontier: Wider and Stronger

In assessing the context of the global North, while acknowledging the prophetic quality of Newbigin's analysis, it is also necessary to recognize significant developments which have occurred since his time. The

---

[4] Charles Taylor, *A Secular Age* (Cambridge, MA, and London: The Belknap Press of Harvard University Press, 2007), 143.

[5] Reinhard Hempelmann, 'The Context of Christian Witness in the 21st Century', in *International Review of Mission,* 92.364 (2003), 45-55, at 47.

[6] Lesslie Newbigin, *Unfinished Agenda: An Autobiography* (Grand Rapids: Eerdmans, 1985), 249.

[7] Lesslie Newbigin, *Foolishness to the Greeks: The Gospel and Western Culture* (Geneva, World Council of Churches, 1986), 1.

secularizing trends identified by Newbigin in the 1980s have intensified during the subsequent decades. The strident voices of the 'New Atheists' have enjoyed a high profile in the global North. Scholars like Richard Dawkins and Christopher Hitchens have not only made the case for atheism but have powerfully argued that religion is a divisive, violent and destructive force in human life.[8] Though their rhetoric, ironically, in some respects mirrors the religious fundamentalism to which they are opposed, they have succeeded in creating an environment where it is no longer taken for granted that religion is on the side of virtue. It is not difficult to puncture their complacent assurance that, while religion fosters ignorance, fanaticism and violence, atheism is enlightened, tolerant and progressive.[9] Nonetheless, they have had some considerable success in giving religion a bad name. This is evident, for example, in the work of groups which campaign to end religious observance in the public education system.

The context for Christian mission in much of the global North is one of repudiated Christianity. Conscious rejection of Christianity presents a challenging context for the church's witness today. A yet greater difficulty, however, for Christian mission is the direction which has been taken by late modernity during recent decades. Its celebrated 'incredulity towards metanarratives'[10] has continued to deconstruct and demolish any attempt to establish a stable way of understanding reality. This has been described as 'liquid modernity'. What makes modernity liquid, according to Zygmunt Bauman, is 'its self-propelling, self-intensifying, compulsive and obsessive "modernization" as a result of which, like liquid, none of the consecutive forms of social life is able to maintain its shape for long'.[11] Whereas an evangelistic strategy in earlier times could identify the 'plausibility structure' of any given context and establish points of contact for the gospel, this has become much more difficult and improbable in the fluid context prevailing today. A continuously changing and ever more fragmented and atomized society presents a challenge yet more severe than that discerned by Newbigin a generation ago.

What does *TTL* have to offer to those at work on this new frontier? In its introduction it acknowledges the question: 'How can we proclaim God's love and justice to a generation living in an individualized, secularized, and materialized world?'[12] When it considers local congregations, it recognizes

---

[8] See Richard Dawkins, *The God Delusion* (London: Bantam, 2006); Christopher Hitchens, *God Is Not Great: How Religion Poisons Everything* (London: Atlantic Books, 2007).

[9] See e.g. Terry Eagleton, *Reason, Faith, and Revolution: Reflections on the God Debate* (New Haven and London: Yale University Press, 2009).

[10] Jean-Francois Lyotard, *The Postmodern Condition: A Report on Knowledge* (Manchester: Manchester University Press, 1984), xxiv-xxv.

[11] Zygmunt Bauman, *Culture in a Liquid Modern World* (London: Polity Press, 2011), 11.

[12] *TTL,* §8.

both a new context and new initiatives: '… in the secularizing global North, new forms of contextual mission such as "new monasticism", "emerging church" and "fresh expressions" have redefined and revitalized churches.'[13]

Nonetheless, at first reading, *TTL* might seem to be little engaged with the liquid modern culture of the secularized western world. It might be argued that a mission affirmation at the beginning of the 21st century ought to have been more explicit in acknowledging this particular and unprecedented context. Its methodology, however, is to start from the content of the faith – 'We believe in the Triune God…'[14] – and to unfold its meaning in ways that address the contemporary situation. This chapter argues that this methodological approach succeeds in offering critically important suggestions as to the shape and direction of Christian mission in the context of the liquid modernity of the global North, though there are points where it might have been helpful to make these more explicit.

## Mission in Pneumatological Mode

A distinctive feature of *TTL* is that it speaks of mission in terms of the Holy Spirit. While the spirituality of those engaged in mission has always been vital, this is now foregrounded in a new way: 'Life in the Holy Spirit is the essence of mission, the core of why we do what we do and how we live our lives. Spirituality gives the deepest meaning to our lives and motivates our actions.'[15] This talks the language of people immersed in the culture of 'liquid modernity' who struggle to connect with heavily institutional religion but yearn for a viable spirituality.

For the understanding and experience of Christian faith, *TTL* marks a departure from the privileging of the rational and cerebral which was adopted in an attempt to come to terms with the European Enlightenment. This was always a reductionist approach and its shortcomings have been laid bare, particularly by the worldwide revolution known as Pentecostalism which has recovered the spiritual core of New Testament Christianity.[16] Besides Pentecostalism, many other branches of the church, in their own way, are rediscovering the spiritual dimension – as demonstrated by the positive reception accorded to *TTL* by so many different church constituencies.

Given the discrediting of religion and widespread aversion to heavily institutional forms of organization, there is an urgent need for the spiritual

---

[13] *TTL,* §72; see further, Jonathan R. Wilson, *Living Faithfully in a Fragmented World: From* After Virtue *to a New Monasticism* (Cambridge: Lutterworth, 2010); David Goodhew, Andrew Roberts and Michael Volland, *Fresh! An Introduction to Fresh Expressions of Church and Pioneer Ministry* (London: SCM, 2012).

[14] *TTL,* §1.

[15] *TTL,* §3.

[16] See further, Wonsuk Ma and Kenneth R. Ross (eds), *Mission Spirituality and Authentic Discipleship* (Oxford: Regnum, 2013).

quality of Christianity to be demonstrated. Unfolding the meaning of Christian mission in terms of the Holy Spirit is a timely initiative. It is intriguing and inviting language. It challenges everyone to look beyond their dogmatic defences to discover the authenticity of life in the Spirit. Such is the mystery of the Spirit that all are reminded of their finitude and vulnerability, while all may be inspired by possibilities of growth and transformation.

Admittedly, there is an element of risk in taking a pneumatological approach in a liquid modern culture. Will distinctive points of Christian faith also end up being dissolved? Though *TTL* itself could hardly be more firmly anchored in Trinitarian and Christological belief, questions might be raised about the direction of travel. Such questions are acknowledged in *TTL* by the emphasis it places on 'discernment of spirits'.[17] Still, when 'affirmation of life' is given as the key criterion for such discernment, does it win in terms of communication and solidarity at the cost of losing clarity and definition? Gerrit Noort, on the basis of Dutch responses to *TTL*, has suggested that 'a critical step has been taken without sufficient theological debate about the implications for mission'.[18]

This is a healthy area of debate since the journey of inculturation invariably raises the question as to whether faithfulness to the gospel has been sustained in the necessary quest for relevance. Mission has to walk that fine line. Meeting a liquid modern culture with an open, pneumatological understanding of mission may entail an element of risk, but is this not the kind of risk that every true missionary would recognize? The recent work of Ben Quash helpfully opens up what is involved in the dialectic between what is 'given' in Christ and what is 'found' as the gift of the Spirit: 'The givens come alive only in this indefinitely extended series of encounters with new circumstances, and the Christian assumption ought to be that no new-found thing need be construed as a threat to what has been given, for we have to do with the same God both in the given and in the found. The God who has "stocked our backpack for the journey", so to speak, also "places things in our path", up ahead of us.'[19] Such a perspective gives the courage needed to meet a new context with the confidence evoked in *TTL*, that 'God is there before we come…'[20]

## Mission and Social Transformation

Lest anyone imagine that the pneumatological turn in the understanding of mission would lead in an entirely other-worldly direction, *TTL* does not

---

[17] *TTL*, §24.
[18] Gerrit Noort, '"So What?" – Dutch Responses to the New Mission Statement', in *International Review of Mission*, 102.2 (397), November 2013, 191-98, at 195.
[19] Ben Quash, *Found Theology: History, Imagination and the Holy Spirit* (London: Bloomsbury, 2013), xiv.
[20] *TTL*, §30.

lose time before turning to questions of economics and economic justice. Given the growing inequality and injustice of today's world, it might be expected that there would be a great political movement aiming to put things right. However, as Pope Francis has observed: 'Something has happened to our politics… It is out of ideas…'[21] Faced with gross injustice on a global scale, it seems that politics has been eviscerated and rendered impotent. As Collier and Esteban have argued: '… the culture of economism leads ultimately to a form of totalitarianism, where the only thing demanded from all political institutions is not to interfere with the "free working of the market" – a euphemism for the freewheeling and dealing of the money oligarchy that dominates the world economy and makes a charade of democratic institutions.'[22]

*TTL* is perhaps at its most trenchant when confronting the domination of the global free market: 'This is a global system of mammon that protects the unlimited growth of wealth of only the rich and powerful through endless exploitation. This tower of greed is threatening the whole household of God. The reign of God is in direct opposition to the empire of mammon.'[23] If the note of spirituality in some respects says 'yes' to our liquid culture, the affirmation that it is a *transformative* spirituality provides a thundering, prophetic 'no' to a central tenet of late modernity – its claim of supremacy for the global free market. For those who are troubled by the acute inequality and injustice found in today's context, for those who want to believe that 'another world is possible', *TTL* uncompromisingly meets their concerns.

It will also strike a chord with the many who are concerned by trends towards ecological devastation. Again, *TTL* has strong words: 'Consumerism triggers not limitless growth but rather endless exploitation of the earth's resources… Eco-justice cannot be separated from salvation, and salvation cannot come without a new humility that respects the needs of all life on earth.'[24] It is apparent that the culture of economism and consumerism is coming unstuck against the magnitude of the ecological crisis now unfolding. The scale of the crisis is such that it is clearly not resolvable within the limitations of the normal political cycle. It may be that only a vision inspired by faith will suffice to create the resources needed to resolve it. By integrating mission more closely than ever before with a theology of creation, and by nurturing a transformative spirituality which embraces all life on earth, *TTL* addresses crucial points of concern on which late modern culture appears to lack answers. Prophetic critique is offered along with a call to a form of spirituality which can effect transformation.

---

[21] Paul Vallely, *Pope Francis: Untying the Knots* (London: Bloomsbury, 2013), 29.
[22] Jane Collier and Rafael Esteban, *From Complicity to Encounter: The Church and the Culture of Economism* (Harrisburg, PA: Trinity Press, 1998), 39.
[23] *TTL*, §31.
[24] *TTL*, §23.

## Mission from the Margins

The currently prevailing social and economic system leaves many people marginalized. *TTL* not only recognizes this but takes a radical and surprising direction when it suggests that it is the marginalized who are the agents of the mission of God, the vanguard of transformation. Here it is necessary to acknowledge that Christianity has been used ideologically to support a global economic system governed from the centre. Much missionary engagement operated on the presuppositions of this view of the world and became, whether intentionally or not, complicit in the system. It is in this context that *TTL* calls for a fundamental repositioning of Christian mission so that it operates not from the centre but from the margins: 'People on the margins have agency, and can often see what, from the centre, is out of view.'[25]

It is from the margins that Lamin Sanneh discerns possibilities for a re-evangelization of the secularized world: '... the evangelization ferment of the frontier contains forces of renewal that can banish the growing shadows of materialism spreading over Europe, and thus open the way for the return of theistic faith there. Instead of bemoaning the slide into neo-paganism and rehashing old theological assurances in response, the West can recapture the initiative it unwittingly surrendered in its costly pact with secularism.'[26] A key feature of the 'changing landscapes' is the large-scale migration which is bringing the peoples of the world together as never before. This creates new possibilities for missional engagement. TTL holds open the possibility that effective mission to late modern culture might come from unexpected quarters, from those regarded as marginalized who now '... re-imagine mission as a vocation from God's Spirit who works for a world where the fullness of life is available for all.'[27]

## Mission and the Life of the Church

One quarter of the *TTL* text is devoted to the life of the church. In today's context, it may be already a counter-cultural move to speak of 'living out our faith in community'.[28] In the context of liquid modernity, as Zygmunt Bauman explains '... networks replace structures, and an uninterrupted game of connecting to and disconnecting from those networks, and the never-ending sequence of connections and disconnections, replace determination, allegiance and belonging'.[29] By insisting that mission finds

[25] *TTL,* §38.
[26] Lamin Sanneh, *Summoned from the Margin: Homecoming of an African* (Grand Rapids, MI: Eerdmans, 2012), 232.
[27] *TTL,* §37.
[28] *TTL,* §59.
[29] Bauman, *Culture in a Liquid Modern World*, 14.

expression in the communal life of the church, *TTL* challenges current trends and offers an alternative view of the purpose of life.

*TTL*'s insistence on mission and church being inextricably intertwined may touch a raw nerve in the context of late modernity. As Alasdair Macintyre concluded his devastating account of the loss of moral bearings in the western world: 'We are waiting not for a Godot, but for another – doubtless very different – St Benedict.'[30] This was a note which resonated with Lesslie Newbigin and informed his conviction that '... the only possible hermeneutic of the gospel is a congregation which believes it'.[31] If anything, today the process of disintegration has gone much further and the need for a convincing and viable form of church life is yet more urgent. This is not to take a conservative option. Rather, it is to look for that renewed form of church life which will be accessible to people formed by the culture of liquid modernity.

## Mission Embracing Plurality

An irreducible feature of late modernity is the fact that we live in close proximity to 'others', including those who profess a different religion and/or understand ultimate reality in a different way. Wolfgang Welsch has suggested that plurality is *the* key issue in post-modernity.[32] In that case, *TTL*'s approach to plurality has a great bearing on the question of its applicability and usefulness in the liquid modern context.

TTL's contribution, working out of its pneumatological understanding of mission, is to encourage an open and adventurous approach: 'We believe that the Spirit of Life brings joy and fullness of life. God's Spirit can be found in all cultures that affirm life.'[33] It fosters an engaging approach, making the radical and thought-provoking suggestion that 'authentic mission makes the "other" a partner in, not an "object" of, mission.'[34] This points the way towards a public witness to the gospel which engages a context of plurality.

*TTL* emphasizes the importance of dialogue. Rather than regarding dialogue and evangelism as separate, or even opposed, approaches, *TTL* proposes that they are interrelated: 'Although Christians hope and pray that all people may come to a living knowledge of the Triune God, evangelism is not the purpose of dialogue. However, since dialogue is also "a mutual

---

30 Alasdair MacIntyre, *After Virtue: A Study in Moral Theory*, 3rd edition (London: Duckworth, 2007), 263.

31 Lesslie Newbigin, *The Gospel in a Pluralist Society* (London: SPCK, 1989), 232.

32 Wolfgang Welsch, *Unsere Postmoderne Moderne* (Darmstadt, Germany. 1991); cf. Jan-Olav Hendriksen, 'Multifaceted Christianity and the Postmodern Condition: Reflections on its Challenges to Churches in the Northern Hemisphere', in Rolv Olsen (ed), *Mission and Postmodernities* (Regnum: Oxford, 2011), 3-21, at 6.

33 *TTL*, §93.

34 *TTL*, §93.

encounter of commitments", sharing the good news of Jesus Christ has a legitimate place in it.'[35] Might the plurality of liquid modernity function for Christian mission as, in the words of Tomás Halik, 'a summons to a new Areopagus'?[36] *TTL* seems to point in this direction with its proposal that 'Evangelism entails not only proclamation of our deepest convictions, but also listening to others and being challenged and enriched by others'.[37] By recovering the spiritual roots of the faith and fostering an open, dialogical approach to a context of plurality, *TTL* offers an understanding of mission which has traction in the liquid modernity of the global North.

## Mission and Proclamation

The note of confidence is clearly evident in *TTL*'s call to evangelize: 'Evangelism is mission activity which makes explicit and unambiguous the centrality of the incarnation, suffering and resurrection of Jesus Christ without setting limits to the saving grace of God. It seeks to share this good news with all who have not yet heard it and invites them to an experience of life in Christ.'[38] This includes 'the invitation to personal conversion to new life in Christ and to discipleship'.[39] It is important that *TTL* in this way opens up the personal dimension of faith and discipleship. It will be for those who consider it in the context of liquid modernity to further explore what this will mean in terms of meeting the personal existential crisis that is a common feature of the late modern world. Charles Taylor detects much evidence of '… a profound dissatisfaction with a life encased entirely in the immanent order. The sense is that this life is empty, flat, devoid of higher purpose'.[40] The discontents of late modernity can act as an invitation for Christian witness.

Perhaps it is the question of what it means to be human which offers the most promising ground on which Christian evangelists might meet with contemporaries whose outlook is shaped by liquid modernity. Charles Taylor suggests that '… for any liveable understanding of human life, there must be some way in which this life looks good, whole, proper, really being lived as it should'. He suggests that 'the swirling debate between belief and unbelief, as well as between different versions of each, can… be seen as a debate about what real fullness consists in'.[41] The question of what it means to be truly human is an urgent one in today's liquid modernity and offers

[35] *TTL,* §95.
[36] Tomás Halik, 'The Soul of Europe: An Altar to the Unknown God', *International Review of Mission,* 95.378/379, 265-70, at 269.
[37] *TTL,* §95.
[38] *TTL,* §80.
[39] *TTL,* §85.
[40] Taylor, *A Secular Age*, 506.
[41] Taylor, *A Secular Age*, 600.

perhaps the most promising point of engagement for the Christian proclamation.

Pope Francis, in *Evangelii Gaudium*, seeks to engage the emotional level, observing, for example, that 'our technological society has succeeded in multiplying occasions of pleasure, yet has found it very difficult to engender joy'.[42] Perhaps it is the joy of the gospel that holds the key to touching the heart of a post-modern generation? Neither institutional authority nor rhetorical brilliance makes much impression in the context of liquid modernity. This is a disillusioned, distrustful and suspicious age. Hence the value of expressing the faith in an emotional key.

The ministry of proclamation in our contemporary situation is not unconnected with the witness for social justice and transformation outlined above. It is worth recalling the words of David Bosch: 'As we call people (back) to faith in God through Jesus Christ, we must help them to articulate an answer to the question: "What do we have to become Christians *for*?" At least part of the answer to this question will have to be: 'In order to be enlisted into God's ministry of reconciliation, peace and justice on earth.'[43] With this in view, *TTL* makes the point that 'the gospel is liberative and transformative. Its proclamation must involve transformation of societies with a view to creating just and inclusive communities'.[44] To have integrity in the context of liquid modernity, evangelism must be a matter of encounter that is transformative for all involved, as together we discover new ways in which the gospel meets the crisis of our time

## Conclusion: Challenging Relevance

Lesslie Newbigin liked to recall a phrase coined by A.G. Hogg to describe what it takes to communicate the good news of Jesus Christ: 'Challenging relevance'. As Newbigin explained: 'The Gospel must be heard as relevant. It must speak of things which are real things in the life of the hearer. It must therefore begin by accepting his issues, using his models and speaking his language. But relevance alone is not enough. The Gospel must at the same time challenge the whole worldview of the hearer.'[45] This chapter has attempted to show how *Together towards Life* strikes notes which resonate in the context of liquid modernity while also making a call to conversion and transformation. It offers, in short, 'challenging relevance'.

The importance of this is underlined by the realization that secularization is no temporary blip. It represents a permanent reshaping of human consciousness from which ever fewer of the human community remain

[42] *Evangelii Gaudium,* §7.

[43] David J. Bosch, *Believing in the Future: Toward a Missiology of Western Culture* (Valley Forge, PA: Trinity Press, 1995), 34.

[44] *TTL,* §91.

[45] See Geoffrey Wainwright, *Lesslie Newbigin: A Theological Life* (Oxford: OUP, 2000), 196.

immune. Pervasive liquid modernity defines the context for mission and evangelism in the world of the 21st century. Bert Hoedemaker stated the scale of the challenge: 'The problem of secularization... requires a reformulation of the goals, means, and motives of mission. Beyond that, it requires a rethinking of the position of Christianity in a religiously and culturally plural world, even a reconstruction of its tradition in that perspective.'[46] In many respects, *TTL* has stepped up to this challenge, even if its response is often implicit and inviting further development.

With its orientation to the spiritual dimension of life, its robust challenge to the culture of economism, its solidarity with those on the margins, its insistence that faith must be expressed in community, its unhesitating embrace of plurality, and its confidence in the power of the gospel to address the human crisis, TTL suggests a series of points of engagement with the culture of liquid modernity. The task ahead is to critique, deepen, exemplify and expand its suggestions. TTL may then come to be regarded as a ground-breaking resource for mission and evangelism in the context of the global North.

---

[46] Bert Hoedemaker, *Secularization and Mission: A Theological Essay* (Harrisburg, PA: Trinity Press, 1998), 40.

# *Together towards Life* and Contemporary Asian Theology

Atola Longkumer

'The past should not be resurrected in order to justify oppression in the present, but rather it should be retold to enable the liberation of all' – Kwok Pui Lan.[1]

'... Christianity is also slowly coming of age in this vast continent, reaching a critical mass both demographically and intellectually, so much so that important breakthroughs are likely to emerge in the next couple of decades' – Felix Wilfred.[2]

## Introduction

A paradoxical condition prevails in contemporary Asian society. On the one hand, there is much freedom for many people and from many aspects of societal circumstances and cultural expectations. Yet, on the other hand, restraint and suppression for many from different dimensions of society are existential realities. Today's Asia presents a multiplicity of possibilities as well as difficulties, conditioned by the socio-economic locations of communities. An undeniable phenomenon of modern Asia is the explosion of economic growth and the inevitable changes this has ushered into Asian communities. WCC/CWME's mission document *Together towards Life* (hereafter *TTL*), provides a critical resource for Christian mission at an opportune time, particularly with its emphasis on the Spirit as the source and foundation of mission.

*Spiritus* as breathing and life-giving, enabling and transforming humanity towards the Kingdom of God, presents a liberating encounter marked by freedom from all forms of oppression and suppression – the human condition of sinfulness, selfishness, greed and a structured hierarchy of domination.[3] In the context of contemporary Asia, a spirit of freedom, as derived and sustained by the good news as taught and lived out by Jesus of Nazareth, needs continued, critical and constructive articulation. *TTL* celebrates life and calls on communities of faith to enable life to flourish as

---

[1] Kwok Pui Lan, *Introducing Asian Feminist Theology* (Cleveland, OH: Pilgrim Press, 2000), 18.

[2] Felix Wilfred, 'General Introduction', in Felix Wilfred (ed), *The Oxford Handbook of Christianity in Asia* (New York: Oxford University Press, 2014), 2.

[3] *TTL*, §10.

God intends for his creation. This chapter will argue that contemporary Asian theology needs to articulate a spirit of freedom. There is need for a theology informed by *TTL*'s vision of Christian mission as proclaiming the good news to all humanity and creation,[4] bringing forth new life and announcing the loving presence of God in our world,[5] and a theology informed by the challenges and opportunities of contemporary Asia. In having this conversation, contemporary Asian theology advocates a spirit of freedom from suppression and the negation of embedded power structures such as religious fundamentalism, ecclesiastical rigidity, parochial socio-cultural practices, and divisive political and economic forces.

## *Together towards Life* and the Context of Contemporary Asia

*TTL* was prepared by a global community of theologians and mission scholars, relatively representative in denominational, gender and regional perspectives. The participation of Evangelicals, Orthodox, Protestants and Roman Catholics is reflected in the document. The leadership of Asian theologians – Jooseop Keum, the Secretary of the CWME, and Geevarghese Mor Coorilos, the Moderator of the CWME – in the production of the document itself lends significance for Asian Christians. Since the 1982 document *Mission and Evangelism: An Ecumenical Affirmation, TTL* in 2012 is the most significant document that redefines, redirects and renews the understanding and practice of mission for the church.[6] It has received critical acclaim and reviews from scholars of missions and from a variety of church traditions. Among these, the review by missiologist Stephen B. Bevans demonstrates the value and relevance of *TTL* for Christian missions.[7]

Some of the distinctive features of *TTL* are: the emphasis on the role of the Holy Spirit for mission as the initiator and enabler of the transformation of people and cultures towards the loving God (*TTL* §34); the recognition

---

[4] *TTL,* §101.

[5] *TTL,* §10.

[6] Other church and mission documents have followed, sharing common vision of a healed, restored humanity by the Good News of the Gospel: see *Evangelii Gaudium* (The Joy of the Gospel), 2013, Apostolic Exhortation by Pope Francis: www.vatican.va/evangelii-gaudium/en; the *Cape Town Commitment* by the Lausanne Movement: www.lausanne.org/content/ctc/ctcommitment (accessed 27th July 2015).

[7] See Stephen Bevans, 'Together towards Life: Reflections on the Proposed WCC Mission Statement', in www.cmsm.org/forum/forum_fall13_WCC_Statement.html June 2015 (accessed 20th June 2015). See also Byung Joon Chung, 'An Assessment of Together towards Life: Korean Responses', in *International Review of Mission,* 102.2 (November 2013), 199-204; Petros Vassiliadis, 'An Orthodox Assessment of the New Mission Statement', in *International Review of Mission,* 102.2 (November 2013), 174-78.

of the structural sins of socio-economic discrimination and exploitation of the creation (*TTL* §§30, 49); Christian mission as characterised by striving towards a life that is nourishing for all, as encapsulated in the following passage: 'Jesus Christ relates to and embraces those who are most marginalized in society, in order to confront and transform all that denies life. This includes cultures and systems which generate and sustain massive poverty, discrimination and dehumanization, and which exploit and destroy people and the earth' (*TTL* §37).

The theme of evangelism in relation to Christian mission is addressed comprehensively, clarifying the myopic limitations that have often centred on human efforts and church traditions. The proclamation of the good news has also too often been undertaken in a way which leads to cultural exclusivism. In contrast to these limitations, *TTL* states emphatically that 'evangelism is sharing one's faith and conviction with other people and inviting them to discipleship, whether or not they adhere to other religious traditions… it leads to repentance, faith and baptism… It provokes conversion, involving a change of attitudes, priorities and goals. It results in salvation of the lost, healing of the sick, and the liberation of the oppressed and the whole creation' (*TTL* §§83, 84). Taking cognizance of the criticism of Christian mission for its often parochial tendencies and good intentions gone awry in actual expression, *TTL* underlines the core of Christian mission as God's unlimited grace revealed in the life and work of Jesus. Therefore it is crucial to understand that in mission, 'Jesus calls us out of our narrow concerns of our own kingdom, our own liberation, and our own independence' (Acts 1:6) by unveiling to us a larger vision, and empowering us by the Holy Spirit to go 'to the ends of the earth' as witnesses, in each context of time and space, to God's justice, freedom and peace. Our calling is to point all to Jesus, rather than to ourselves or our institutions, looking out for the interests of others rather than our own' (*TTL* §100).

The clarity and commitment for a renewed and relevant Christian mission expressed in *TTL* adds impetus to contemporary theology as it offers both affirmation and a critique of Asian multiple contexts. Today's Asia presents both 'promises and crises'[8] with unprecedented developments taking place in the continent. Contemporary Asia is experiencing unprecedented economic growth, while simultaneously the misery of the poor and the powerless is most vividly reflected in the migration of labourers from and within Asia.[9] Contemporary Asia is also marked by

---

[8] Pui Lan, *Introducing Asian Feminist Theology*, 12.

[9] For an excellent theological analysis of the phenomenon of migration, wherein the magnitude and the experience of migrants make it imperative to make migration a locus of theology, see Gemma Cruz, *An Intercultural Theology of Migration: Pilgrims in the Wilderness* (Leiden: Brill, 2010). In 2012, CCA-CATS VII, Seoul, Asian theologians deliberated on the theme of hospitality within the migration

frequent environmental tragedy amidst rapid construction of modern infrastructure. After the Fukushima nuclear disaster, the collapse of unsafe factory buildings in Bangladesh, the creation of the Asian Infrastructure Investment Bank (AIIB), the discovery of the mass graves of suspected migrants in Malaysia, the growing assertion of a Hindutva ideology in India, endemic gender violence (most vividly illustrated in the rape of a medical student in Delhi, 2012), tension surrounding the South China Sea – amongst many other events – contemporary Asian theology cannot ignore the shift of the geopolitics of the region, and the cost in human lives and the environment by a profit-making economic force. Additionally, the growing response to Christianity and the significance of Christianity in many Asian nations needs to be considered in articulating a contemporary Asian theology.[10] Anri Morimoto states, 'From inception throughout its history of two millennia, Christian theology has always been contextualised.'[11] Hence, contemporary Asian theology arises from the contexts of 'promises and crises' of a rapidly changing Asia. A contemporary Asian theological articulation incorporates the lament of the marginalised on one hand while, on the other, it enunciates the empowerment delivered in the incarnation event that radically inaugurated a spirit of freedom from all forms of domination. Prior to elaborating more on the theme of freedom in contemporary Asian theology, a brief discussion of the term 'Asia' is necessary.

---

phenomenon as a resource for Asian theology: www.cca.org.hk/clusters/fmu/programs/cats7/cats7-call.htm (accessed 23rd July 2015).

[10] Christianity as integral to many communities in Asia is a consensus among historians, theologians and sociologists: see *The Oxford Handbook of Asian Christianity*; Peter C. Phan (ed), *Christianities in Asia* (Oxford: Wiley-Blackwell, 2010); Georg Evers, *The Churches in Asia* (New Delhi: ISPCK, 2005); Sebastian C.H. Kim and Kirsteen Kim, *Christianity as a World Religion* (London: Continuum, 2008). Each Asian country has many historical texts on Christianity from micro-contexts. For instance, for some recent publications, see Leonard Fernando and George Gispert-Sauch, *Christianity in India: Two Thousand Years of Faith* (New Delhi: Oxford University Press, 2004); Robert Eric Frykenberg, *Christianity in India: From Beginnings to the Present* (New York: Oxford University Press, 2008); Sebastian C.H. Kim and Kirsteen Kim, *A History of Korean Christianity* (Cambridge: CUP, 2014), Daniel H. Bays (ed), *Christianity in China: From the Eighteenth Century to the Present* (Stanford: Stanford University Press, 1999); Mark R. Mullins (ed), *Handbook of Christianity in Japan* (Leiden: Brill, 2003). A helpful list of Asian Christians and Christianity is Scott W. Sunquist (ed), *A Dictionary of Asian Christianity* (Grand Rapids, MI: Eerdmans, 2001).

[11] Anri Morimoto, 'Asian Theology in the Ablative Case', in *Studies in World Christianity,* 17.3 (2011), 201-15.

## 'Asia is Many': A Myriad Asian Theologies

Douglas J. Elwood, in the volume he edited on Asian theology in the last quarter of the twentieth century, stated emphatically, 'Asia is not one but many.'[12] A single, or even a few, representative contexts or articulations, cannot comprehensively portray Asia in its entirety. It is known that the idea of the continent of Asia is more a convenient term tracing back to the antiquity period and solidified during medieval times as the planet was divided into three parts: the continents of Asia, Europe and Africa.[13] However, to understand Asia today, it is essential to take account of its complex diversities and multi-layered socio-cultural and economic contexts. In fact, keen awareness of the differences and plurality of circumstances in Asia serves as a *raison d'être* for a theology that exposes the victims produced by the differences and a theology that explicates a reality of freedom from the entanglement of the oppressive and contesting differences. In other words, taking cognizance of the plurality of contexts in Asia is vital to any articulation of theology in contemporary Asia.[14] A contemporary theology of Asia, therefore, includes not only the geographical nation-states of the continent of Asia, but is aware of the many Asias demarcated by socio-economic locations.

It is therefore aware that Asia is a growing economic region, Asia is a source of cheap labour (both skilled and unskilled) for the global economy,

---

[12] Douglas J. Elwood, 'Asian Christian Theology in the Making: An Introduction', in Douglas J. Elwood (ed), *Asian Christian Theology: Emerging Themes,* revised version (Philadelphia, PA: Westminster Press, 1980), 23-39.

[13] Folker Reichert, *Das Bild der Welt im Mittelalter* (Darmstadt, Germany: Wissenschaftliche Buchgesellschaft, 2013), 9-42.

[14] Among the many resources that define, describe and delineate Asia in its diverse regions, see Todd M. Johnson and Kenneth R. Ross (eds), *Atlas of Global Christianity, 1910-2010* (Edinburgh: Edinburgh University Press, 2009), 134-53; Samuel Hugh Moffett, *A History of Christianity in Asia,* 2 vols (Maryknoll, NY: Orbis Books, 1998); Namsoon Kang, 'Re-constructing Asian feminist theology: toward a glocal feminist theology in an era of neo-Empire(s)', in Sebastian C.H. Kim (ed), *Christian Theology in Asia* (Cambridge: CUP, 2008), 205-26; Nami Kim, 'Cutting Edges: "my/our" comfort not at the expense of somebody else: Toward a Critical Global Feminist Theology', in *Journal of Feminist Studies in Religion*, 21.2 (Fall 2000), 75-94. Among the many Asian scholars and theologians who have provided critical commentary on the term 'Asian' and cautioned against homogeneity is Nami Kim, 'The "Indigestible" Asian: The Unifying Term "Asian" in Theological Discourse', in Rita Nakashima Brock, Jung Ha Kim, Kwok Pui Lan and Seung Ai Yang (eds), *Off the Menu: Asian and Asian North American Women's Religions and Theology* (Louisville, KY: Westminster John Knox Press, 2007), 23-43; Nami Kim, 'Which Postcolonialism? The Relevance of Resistance Postcolonialism to Postcolonial Asia', in *Asian Christian Review,* 6.1 (2012), 23-35; Peter C. Phan (ed), *Christianities in Asia* (Oxford: Blackwell, 2011), 2-8; Wong Wai Ching, 'Negotiating for a Postcolonial Identity of "the Poor Women" in Asia', in *Journal of Feminist Studies of Religion*, 16.2 (Fall, 2000), 5-23.

Asia is the cradle of ancient civilizations, and Asia is the home of mushrooming religious communities. Asia has produced critical contextual theologies and continues to pose critical interrogation to a Eurocentric theology that has for long held sway in Christianity.[15] Assessing theology from a global perspective, Stephen B. Bevans affirms this fact, stating, 'Asian Christians are engaged in some of the most exciting and creative theologizing in the world today.'[16] A contemporary Asian theology also acknowledges the historical fact of Asia as the cradle of Christianity, which ironically has encountered the most vehement resistance from other ancient civilizations.[17] Contemporary Asian theology includes critical awareness of the tremendous impact of Christianity in Asian cultures and societies. As Felix Wilfred writes, 'The impact of Christianity in Asia cannot be overestimated; it led to intellectual revolutions, religio-cultural confrontations and social conflicts, but also to fundamental transformation of Asian societies.'[18] By the same token, the encounter of Christianity with Asian cultures also occasioned critical theological questions often seen in theological controversies as well as the expansion of theological perspectives, in the process transforming Christianity.[19]

Given Asia's multiple contexts and plurality of cultures and a history spanning millennia, the articulation of theology must entail not just one theology but rather a myriad theologies. Any theology is rooted in lived contexts of faith communities and expressed within socio-cultural locations. Contemporary Asian theology therefore is markedly plural in content and aspiration, and consciously avoids the perils of expressing a homogeneous theological discourse. With these points in mind, we proceed to present a theology of contemporary Asia arising from diverse contexts, calling for radical commitment to a spirit of freedom as a mark of the mission of the Triune God expressed in the work of the Holy Spirit.

---

[15] To name a few, Aloysius Peiris, R.S. Sugirtharaj, Kwok Pui Lan, Sebastian C.H. Kim, Mary John Mananzan, Chung Hyun Kyun, K.C. Abraham, Felix Wilfred, Amos Yong, Gemma Cruz, Wati Longchar, Peter C. Phan, Anri Morimoto, among others. Apart from these, there is an earlier generation of Asian theologians, for which see Douglas J. Elwood (ed), *Asian Christian Theology: Emerging Themes;* and for a helpful bibliography of Asian Christian Theologies in three volumes, see John C. England et al, *Asian Christian Theologies: A Research Guide to Authors, Movements, Sources* (Maryknoll, NY: Orbis Books, 2002).

[16] Stephen B. Bevans, *An Introduction to Theology in Global Perspective* (Maryknoll, NY: Orbis Books, 2009), 311.

[17] Felix Wilfred, *The Oxford Handbook of Asian Christianity*, 2. For a Catholic Church perspective, see Georg Evers, *The Churches in Asia*, xx-xxi.

[18] Wilfred, *The Oxford Handbook of Asian Christianity*, 2.

[19] Wilfred, *The Oxford Handbook of Asian Christianity*, 2.

## The Spirit of Freedom: A Mark of Contemporary Asian Theology

*TTL* emphasises a pneumatological focus on Christian mission, making it clear that mission is directed by the work of the Holy Spirit to proclaim salvation through Jesus Christ (*TTL* §16). Mission is to witness to the flourishing of life that Jesus Christ announced through his life and work, wherein the Holy Spirit empowers and enables the transformation and affirmation of life. This understanding of mission as an act of the Triune God expressed by the Holy Spirit is described under four main headings in *TTL*: Spirit of Mission: Breath of Life, Spirit of Liberation: Mission from the Margins, Spirit of Community: Church on the Move, Spirit of Pentecost: Good News for All (*TTL* §11). A close reading of these four dimensions of the mission of the Holy Spirit within the mission of the Triune God reveals a spirit of freedom that runs through the four sections in the document (*TTL* §§30, 33, 43, 44, 54, 66, 70, 94). A commitment to freedom from different aspects of subjugation and restraint is a pronounced distinction of *TTL* in its articulations of mission. The mission of the Triune God is an invitation to 'the Feast of Life, through Jesus Christ who came "that they may have life, and may have it in all its fullness" through the Holy Spirit who affirms that vision of the reign of God' (*TTL* §112). A spirit of freedom as a mark of contemporary Asian theology is discussed under three major categories: the proclamation of freedom in the good news, the cultures of Asia, and ecclesial unity.

## The Proclamation of Freedom in the Good News

Asia is home to a number of indigenous peoples who were, historically, among the most responsive groups of people to the work of Christian mission. For instance, from the remote highlands sandwiched between India and Myanmar, are the Chins, Mizos and Nagas. Likewise the Torajas in Indonesia are people who are identified by their oral cultures and affinity to the natural world around them. Such peoples comprise a sizeable Christian population in the continent. Not only is Christianity a meaningful presence but these communities are becoming an important source of South-to-South evangelism, as Philip Jenkins defines the efforts of taking Christianity beyond one's community in the phenomenon of Christianity's shift to the global South.[20] To be sure, response to Christianity in the continent is not isolated to these indigenous communities. The statistics of growth of Christian presence in Asia is significant, although Christianity is still a minority religion in most nation-states of Asia.[21]

---

[20] Philip Jenkins, *The Next Christendom: The Coming of Global Christianity* (New York: Oxford University Press, 2002).

[21] David Barrett and Todd M. Johnson, *World Christian Trends, AD 20-AD 2200: Interpreting the Annual Christian Megacensus* (Pasadena, CA: William Carey Library, 2001); Johnson and Ross, *Atlas of Global Christianity, 1910-2010.*

There is a plethora of keen analyses on the response and embrace of Christianity, and a fundamental consensus is the freedom experienced by communities in the transition to the new religion, notwithstanding the acute critique in terms of imposition and often supposed cultural destruction. While not trivialising the critique of aspects of mission that were influenced by imperial power and cultural superiority, it is also fair to recognise that transmission of Christian values were transformational for many communities. Christian mission was indeed Good News for many of the marginalised, politically suppressed, culturally ridiculed and economically deprived – measured from the unstoppable modern *geist* that was set apace by globalisation and imperialism.[22] Despite the resistance from external forces and the limitation inherent in the church, Christianity continues to attract people, as illustrated by the growing number of adherents to Christianity in the region.[23] The mega-churches in the Republic of Korea, the Philippines and India, the personal stories of converts themselves, and the existence of indigenous mission activities, all attest to the fact that Christianity provides meaning to millions in Asia.[24]

---

[22] An excellent analysis for illustrating the social-political empowerment afforded by marginalized peoples, such as indigenous peoples, is the example of the tribals or *adivasis* of India, as rightly stated by Frykenberg: 'Moreover, modern education and literacy in Roman script has not only given them easy access to all of India but to the entire Anglophone world'; see Frykenberg, *Christianity in India,* 422; Wong Wai Ching Angela, although critical of 'the hegemony and homogeneity of Western modernity' invariably linked with Christianity, she acknowledges the enormous impacts and development it initiated in Asia: see her, 'Modernity and Change of Values: Asian Christian Negotiations and Resistance', in Wilfred, *The Oxford Handbook of Asian Christianity*, 200-214; Christine Lienemann-Perrin, Atola Longkumer and Afrie Songco Joye (eds), *Putting Names with Faces: Women's Impact in Mission History* (Nashville, TN: Abingdon Press, 2012); Kwok Pui Lan, *Chinese Women and Christianity, 1860-1927* (Atlanta, GA: Scholars Press, 1992); Naw Eh Tar Gay, 'Tribal Women in Asian Churches', in Hope Antone, Wati Longchar, Hyungju Bae, Huang Po Ho and Dietrich Werner (eds), *Asian Handbook for Theological Education and Ecumenism* (Taiwan: PTCA, 2013), 368-76.

[23] For instance, despite the complex relationship between the state and Christianity, by all measures, Christianity persists to exist and attract adherents in China: see Fenggang Yang, *Religion in China: Survival and Revival Under Communist Rule* (New York: Oxford University Press, 2012).

[24] David Martin, *Pentecostalism: The World Their Parish* (Oxford: Wiley-Blackwell, 2002); Allan Anderson, *An Introduction to Pentecostalism: Global Charismatic Christianity* (New York: Cambridge University Press, 2004); Julie Ma and Wonsuk Ma present a missiology of Pentecostal/Charismatic churches with case studies of growing Pentecostal/Charismatic churches in Asia:, see Julie C. Ma and Wonsuk Ma, *Mission in the Spirit: Towards a Pentecostal/Charismatic Missiology* (Oxford: Regnum, 2010); David Martin, 'Issues Affecting The Study of Pentecostalism in Asia', in Allan Anderson and Edmond Tang (eds), *Asian and Pentecostal: The Charismatic Face of Christianity in Asia* (Oxford: Regnum, 2005), 27-36.

This aspect of freedom and meaning-making experienced in Christianity cannot be ignored in contemporary Asian theology. In this, it is critically important to note that *TTL* clarifies the practice of evangelism as an embodiment of Christ-like values, balancing verbal proclamation and authentic action (*TTL* §86). Hence, it is both a sharing of one's faith in the Triune God, leading to an invitation to a transformed life in Jesus Christ, and deeds of compassion springing from the commitment to the vision of inclusive justice inherent in God's revelation in Jesus Christ. Informed by a renewed clarification of the church activities of evangelism as proclamation of life abundant in Jesus Christ, and that 'mission is not a project of expanding churches but of the church embodying God's salvation in the world' (*TTL* §58), contemporary Asian theology seeks to include proclamation of the good news as seen in the incarnation event. Christianity is potentially about good news of freedom from oppressive systems and their inherent web of domination. This also forms a part of the reason for the resurgence of Christianity in the South. Wilfred affirms that Christianity brought 'a message that came to us through Jesus Christ, which is credible not because of its presumed metaphysical basis, but through its radical appeal to our deeper humanity and the contingencies of our lives (individual and collective), and indeed through Jesus' unconditional love and grace, and through his becoming one in solidarity with the poor'.[25]

In the light of *TTL* and its vision of the flourishing of life for all, an explicit and persuasive articulation of the freedom inherent in the Gospel as seen in the life and work of Jesus of Nazareth is made imperative in any discourse on contemporary Asian theology.

### Cultural Constrains and the Freedom of the Gospel

The concept and practice of culture remains a perennial and provocative topic in formulating theological discourse and in the practice of mission. The gamut of contextual theologies is a product of the challenges posed to theology and mission by the diversity of human cultures encountered by the gospel. Stephen B. Bevans' *Models of Contextual Theology* remains a resourceful text for a comprehensive theological appreciation of cultures.[26] A discussion on the etymology and taxonomy of the term 'culture' is not the intent here; however, 'a thick description' can be reduced to emphasize

---

[25] Felix Wilfred, *Asian Public Theology: Critical Concerns in Challenging Times* (New Delhi: ISPCK, 2010), 186.

[26] Stephen B. Bevans, *Models of Contextual Theology* (Maryknoll, NY: Orbis Books, 2002). See also Volker Kuster, *Einfuhrung in die Interkulturelle Theologie* (Gottingen: Vandenhoeck & Ruprecht, 2011), where Kuster argues that diverse cultures and their cognates inform and are imperative in doing an intercultural theology. Christianity challenges and is indigenized by the cultures of the place – see further Andrew F. Walls, *The Missionary Movement in Christian History: Studies in the Transmission of Faith* (Maryknoll, NY: Orbis Books, 1996), 26-36.

that culture is understood as the defining and distinctive practices, beliefs and behaviours of human societies that also serve as identifiers of communities.[27] In the Asian context, the use of culture is accentuated by the invariable plurality of cultures. If culture is broadly understood as a signifier of communities, it then includes the variety of cognates of human society: gender roles, caste, class, rituals, myths, stories, economic production modes, religiosity, habits of consumption, authority, ownership and social kinship among others. Each of these cognates of society presents a complex concept, rationale and expression, often intertwined with another aspect of the society in question. Put in a simplified way, the adherence of these dimensions of society in turn contributes to the demarcation of cultural boundaries.

From the perspective of Christian mission and theology, the cultural signifiers have often been criticised, obliterated by coercion, ridiculed, reformulated and re-adapted into the new religion: Christianity. However, there has been a paradigm shift in appropriating cultures of communities which have been Christianised. For instance, in the context of indigenous cultures and Christianity, the Federation of Asian Bishops' Conference (FABC) declared the resourcefulness of the cultures: 'Much of the indigenous peoples' worldview and ethos is compatible with the Christian faith, [hence] the traditional beliefs, rites, myths and symbols of indigenous peoples provide material for developing indigenous theologies and liturgical ceremonies.'[28] Appreciation of diverse cultures and the encounter of the Good News are also affirmed by *TTL*, which states: 'The gospel takes root in different contexts through engagement with specific cultural, political, and religious realities. Respect for people and their cultural and symbolic life-worlds are necessary if the gospel is to take root in those different realities' (*TTL* §96). The firm conviction that the Triune God is the source and goal of life enlightens the faithful to appreciate diverse human cultures as inspired by the Spirit, and this conviction also enables mission 'to acknowledge, respect, and cooperate with life-giving wisdoms in every culture and context'(*TTL* §27).

While respect for diverse cultures enables the encounter between many different categories of others and enhances dialogue, it is important to note that culture also presents a complicated dilemma in terms of the intricate web of power upholding the status quo. Human cultures also present constraints and oppressive structures. There are human cultural practices that discriminate, exclude, negate and dehumanise – for instance, the Brahmanical religio-social hierarchy that produced and perpetuates caste

---

[27] Clifford Geertz, *Interpretation of Cultures* (New York: Basic Books, 1973); Kathryn Tanner, *Theories of Cultures: A New Agenda for Theology* (Minneapolis, MN: Augsburg Fortress Press, 1997).

[28] Federation of Asian Bishops' Conference (FABC), *The Spirit at Work in Asia Today* (Hong Kong, 1998).

hierarchy, victimising Dalits and tribals in India.[29] Patriarchy, tribalism, land rights, gender roles and economic production rights are often tied to cultures which are parochial, alienating and exclusive. In such cultural contexts, the Spirit enables radical, courageous witness to Christ, the liberator of all oppressive structures, and the Spirit empowers a mission of integrity towards inclusive justice and freedom. The insights of Walter Brueggemann motivate a contemporary Asian theology that is prophetic in advocating freedom, as 'the task of prophetic ministry is to nurture, nourish and evoke a consciousness and perception alternative to the consciousness and perception of the dominant culture around us'.[30] The mission of the Triune God expressed in the work of the Holy Spirit emphatically presented in *TTL*, offers an alternative perception of socio-cultural realities wherein 'people see their own history in the light of God's freedom and his will for justice'.[31]

## Ecclesial Unity and a Spirit of Freedom

Mission and Unity was Theme Eight of Edinburgh 2010. The study group included Evangelical, Orthodox, Pentecostal and Ecumenical participants. A significant document reviewed was prepared by the Roman Catholic *Institut Africain des Sciences et la Mission* in Kinshasa. The study group reiterated the theological and biblical foundations for Christians to exist as the Body of Christ united as a community by the confession of Christ as the Lord who proclaims the Kingdom of God, in whom there is reconciliation and fellowship.[32] The issue of mission and unity has been the source of a deep wound in the history of Christian mission: 'Parallelisms, competitions, conflicts and divisions on what was then called "the mission fields" gravely undermined the credibility of the witness of the love of Christ', causing a scandal to the good news of freedom in Christ.[33] Unfortunately, these divisions from the heyday of mission are a sad legacy in many Christian contexts in Asia, wherein competitions, conflicts, bias and the isolation of fellow Christians exist. A contemporary Asian theology is required to participate in a reconciled Christian fellowship for common witness to Christ and his good news of freedom.

---

[29] One of the earliest and most brilliant critiques of caste practice as a distinct mark of Hinduism came from Bhimrao Ambedkar, a Mahar (an 'untouchable' as defined by Brahmanical cultural criteria): see B.R. Ambedkar, *Annihilation of Caste: Annotated Critical Edition,* with an Introduction by Arundhati Roy (New Delhi: Navayana Publishing, 2014 [1936]).

[30] Walter Brueggemann, *The Prophetic Imagination,* 2nd edition (Minneapolis, MN: Fortress Press, 2001), 3.

[31] Brueggemann, *The Prophetic Imagination*, 116.

[32] Daryl Balia and Kirsteen Kim (eds), *Edinburgh 2010: Witnessing to Christ Today* (Oxford: Regnum, 2010), 209.

[33] Balia and Kim, *Edinburgh 2010*, 200.

With keen awareness of the historical divisions, *TTL* has continued the drive to work towards unity among different church traditions, affirming: 'Together we share a common concern that the whole church should witness to the whole gospel in the whole world' (*TTL* §65). Further, *TTL* calls on the different Christian traditions to come together for partnership in common witness to Christ: 'The Christian communities in their diversity are called to identify and practise ways of common witness in a spirit of partnership and co-operation, including through mutually respectful and responsible forms of evangelism' (*TTL* §63). In sharing a common call to witness to Christ, partnership in evangelism has significant potential to pave the way for greater unity and inclusive fellowship (*TTL* §§85, 86). A contemporary Asian theology needs to articulate and participate in forging ecclesial unity, as enabled by the Holy Spirit to overcome historically constructed divisions: 'The Holy Spirit, the Spirit of unity, unites people and churches too, to celebrate unity in diversity both pro-actively and constructively' (*TTL* §66).

## Conclusion

A contemporary Asian theology in the light of *TTL* will be forged in the crucible of critical and candid conversation with the many Asian cultures and contexts. The conversation is undergirded by a fundamental faith in the good news that Jesus of Nazareth proclaimed. Further, Asian contemporary theological articulations espouse a radical reality of freedom as enabled by the Holy Spirit. A life of flourishing and freedom for every citizen of every community is the objective and mark of contemporary Asian theological discourse in all its diversity. Written a decade after the devastation of Hiroshima and Nagasaki by the atomic bomb, the words of the hymn, *Here, O Lord, Your Servants Gather*[34] by Tokuo Yamaguchi, written during the 14th World Council of Christian Education Convention, Tokyo, 1958, continue to inspire Asian theological articulation marked by freedom in Jesus Christ for the many cultures and peoples of Asia:

> Many are the tongues we speak, scattered are the lands
> Yet our hearts are one in God, One in love's demands
> E'en in darkness hope appears, calling age and young;
> Jesus teacher, dwell with us, For you are the truth.
> Grant, O God, an age renewed, filled with deathless love;
> Help us as we work and pray, send us from above
> Truth and courage, faith and power, needed in our strife;
> Jesus Master, be our Way, be our Truth, our Life.

[34] www.umcdiscipleship.org/resources/history-of-hymns-here-o-lord-your-servants-gather (accessed 28th July 2015).

# *TOGETHER TOWARDS LIFE* AND CONTEMPORARY PACIFIC THEOLOGY

Cliff Bird

## Introduction: Two Statements

> We believe that the mission of the churches is the mission of our Lord Jesus Christ. At the beginning of his ministry, he proclaimed that he was sent to preach the good news to the poor, to set the prisoners free, feed the hungry, cloth the naked and to proclaim the time of salvation (Luke 4:18-19). In essence, this is the central message of our Lord's image of the "Kingdom of God". In this respect, we hold that the mission of the church is God's mission and we are God's instruments... We hold that the characteristics of God's mission are that it is life-giving, life-saving, justice-seeking, healing and reconciling. These become the tasks of the church in the current context of a globalised world.[1]

> Mission begins in the heart of the Triune God and the love which binds together the Holy Trinity overflows to all humanity and creation. The missionary God who sent the Son to the world calls all God's people (John 20:21), and empowers them to be a community of hope. The church is commissioned to celebrate life, and to resist and transform all life-destroying forces, in the power of the Holy Spirit.[2]

The above two quotations are significant in various ways, two of which are that the statements are quite recent and were produced within two years of each other; their gist resonates in various ways with a very strong and clear focus on the primacy of life. In the light of this, the current chapter is an interactive and reflective engagement of *Together towards Life* (*TTL*) and contemporary theology in the Pacific Island Countries (PICs). This approach seeks to establish the relevance and resonance of key affirmations of *TTL* with the PICs' contemporary theology. In this way, too, the chapter is quite focused and does not delve into the history of missions in general in the PICs.[3] However, elements of shifts in mission theology and theological

---

[1] 'The Mission Call from Viwa to the Pacific Churches', Viwa Island, Fiji, 17th April 2010, 1. This 'mission call' was the outcome of the third missionary conference which was organised by the Pacific Conference of Churches (PCC), Pacific Theological College (PTC) and the South Pacific Association of Theological Schools (SPATS). The conference was attended by all the member-churches of the PCC. The first mission conference was in 1961 and the second one in 1985.

[2] *TTL*, §2.

[3] For an informative and engaging overview of the history of missions to the PICs, see the trilogy by John Garrett: *To Live Among the Stars: Christian Origins in*

perspectives over time will be highlighted as indications of developments in theological thinking regionally, and of the influence of global theological emphases and flows. Admittedly, it is impossible within the prescribed length of this chapter to cover the entire range of theological thinking in the region. What is presented here is a representative selection of contemporary Pacific theology.

## Salvation of Souls Then and Now

In order to appreciate the shifts in theological perspectives since the intrusion by western missionaries into the Pacific at the close of the eighteenth century and throughout the nineteenth century, it is necessary to state at the outset that the primary goal of missionary activities was for the salvation of the heathens through the gospel of Jesus Christ. This followed from the great spiritual awakening in the eighteenth century as noted by Garrett: 'Missionary activity was a product of great religious changes in Europe and America.'[4] The LMS Fundamental Principle, which was formulated in May 1796, expressed the evangelical zeal to '… send… the glorious Gospel of the Blessed God to the heathen'.[5] Other mission agencies also had very similar conversion-oriented theologies. *From Darkness to Light in Polynesia*, for instance, was not simply the title of the book by W.W. Gill but was the great theme of the missionary project throughout the Pacific. What David Hilliard said about missionaries in Melanesia resonated with other parts of the Pacific, namely, that they [missionaries] tended to regard traditional religion 'as a collection of absurd superstitions – "filthy", "degrading", "horrible" and "cruel".'[6] The call by missionaries to abandon traditional religions and cultures and to convert to and embrace Christianity echoed throughout the islands. The Christian God was presented in terms of power encounters and complete distinction from the gods of traditional religions. This is typified in how one missionary for instance described the Christian God as 'the Great Outsider'.[7] Bernard Thorogood laments that 'by such a contrast the pre-Christian life of the islands was condemned as darkness and the mode established by the missions was affirmed as light. The sharpness of the

---

*Oceania* (Geneva: WCC, 1982); *Footsteps in The Sea: Christianity in Oceania to World War II* (Geneva: WCC, 1992); *Where Nets Were Cast: Christianity in Oceania Since World War II* (Geneva: WCC, 1997).

[4] Garrett, *To Live Among the Stars*, 8.

[5] The LMS missionaries arrived on Tahiti on 5th March 1797. See Marama Gaston Tauira, 'The Phase of "Translation": The LMS Missionaries' Labour in Tahiti 1797-1860', in *The Pacific Journal of Theology*, II.14 (1995), 17-19.

[6] David Hilliard, 'Protestant Mission in Solomon Islands: 1849 – 1942', (PhD thesis, Australian National University, 1966), 497. (see KR-TG email of 23 Feb).

[7] See Alan R. Tippett, *Solomon Islands Christianity: A Study in Growth and Obstruction* (New York: Friendship Press, 1967).

conversion experience was emphasised: from the Bible such a dramatic contrast is justified'.[8] Given the historical context out of which such a theology of mission developed, caution must be exercised to not over-criticise missionaries to the Pacific. It is indeed noteworthy and heartening that the mission theology of *TTL* highlights the importance and necessity of people's cultures and symbolic worlds for the meaningful transmission of the good news of God.

While there have been significant shifts and transformations in theological thinking and perspectives (which will be discussed shortly), this rather narrow and limited theology of mission, which stresses the salvation of souls, persists still. In a major research that was conducted in most of the churches in the Pacific, one of the main findings is that an individualistic and futuristic understanding of salvation is a characteristic feature of new religious groups as well as some historic mainline churches.[9] Two examples could be taken as representing this finding: the New Methodist Christian Fellowship in Fiji, for instance, has the words 'Souls to Jesus' inscribed on many public places, including all vehicles owned by the church. The church's slogan is 'Souls to Jesus at Any Cost'; the Methodist Church in Fiji, which is by far the largest historic mainline church in the country, through its Connexional Plan 2015-2019, has as its 'Pillar One – Salvation of People' and its 'Key Strategic Area 1 – Salvation of Souls'.[10] One major difference between these two is that, whereas the New Methodist Christian Fellowship emphasis on salvation is so other-worldly-focused and detached from the realities of earthly life, the Methodist Church in Fiji situates and connects its emphasis with current and emerging contexts and the lived experiences of the people. This divergence connects directly with a more fundamental theological issue, which is Christological in nature and substance: the theology of salvation and the role of Jesus Christ and faith in Jesus Christ.

## *Together towards Life* and Contemporary Pacific Theology

There is no consensus amongst theologians in the Pacific on the question of what description or label should be given for 'Pacific-specific theology'. It would seem that theologians are content with the variety in theological perspectives and articulations. Nevertheless, I would argue that the various theological perspectives could be viewed in what I would like to describe as 'themes of contemporary Pacific theology'. I say 'themes' because in one way or other all the theological articulations in the Pacific have one

---

[8] Bernard Thorogood, 'After 200 Years – The LMS Legacy', in *The Pacific Journal of Theology*, 2.14 (1995), 5-15.

[9] Manfred Ernst (ed). *Globalisation and the Re-Shaping of Christianity in the Pacific Islands* (Suva: Pacific Theological College, 2006).

[10] 'Methodist Church in Fiji: Pillars and Key Strategic Areas': Connexional Plan 2015-2019, unpublished document.

thing in common, namely, all are contextual and are outgrowths of the contextual dynamics and particularities of the people. These theological themes are not independent of each other, but are interconnected, and are not exhaustive.

## Cultures, Cultural Identity and the Gospel

The biggest breakthrough for theology in the Pacific as well as for the developing world in general was in terms of the broadening of sources for theology to recognise 'context' in addition to the Bible and Christian traditions.[11] Bevans points out further that cultures were a necessary and crucial part of context.[12] The use and acceptance of the 'contextualisation' of theology was official by the early 1970s,[13] and contextual theology, with the primary use of and reliance on cultures and symbolic systems, took off in the PICs. *TTL* states categorically that 'the gospel takes root in different contexts through engagement with specific cultural, political and religious realities. Respect for people and their cultural and symbolic life-worlds are necessary if the gospel is to take root in those different realities'.[14] There are two interrelated developments to this realisation for theology in the Pacific. The first development resonated strongly with the *TTL* statement: the gospel needs cultures in order to enter into the meaning-making systems and processes of the people. The realisation, especially on the part of later missionaries, was/is that meaningful communication of the gospel cannot, and indeed must not, be done outside the cultures of a people. What Paulo Koria said is quite representative of this Pacific perspective:

> Linguistic idioms, proverbial sayings, imagery, symbolism, metaphors and the like, are all viable means for communicating the substance of the Gospel message… there are local stories, parables, island folk tales, legends, myths, narratives both oral and literary, which our Pacific people have accumulated and treasured as a communal source of knowledge. All these, together with customs, social etiquette, traditions, philosophies, religious beliefs, concepts, etc. have provided Pacific people with the means of understanding the world and reality. Taken together, they form a system of meaning by which life in the Pacific is lived. Because theology has to do with the totality of human life, all these resources are important for the expression and articulation of the Christian faith.[15]

---

[11] See Stephen Bevans, *Models of Contextual Theology* (Maryknoll, NY: Orbis Books, 2002), 9-15.

[12] Bevans, *Models of Contextual Theology*, 9-15.

[13] Todd M. Johnson, 'Contextualization: A New-Old Idea', in *The International Journal for Frontier Missions* 4 (1987), 1-4. Johnson points out that it was Shoki Coe who first coined the term 'contextualization'.

[14] *TTL*, §97.

[15] Paulo Koria, 'Moving Toward a Pacific Theology: Theologising with Concepts', in *The Pacific Journal of Theology* 2:22 (1999), 3-14.

The second development builds on the first and is implied in what Koria says above. Not only were cultures a necessary medium for communicating the gospel – cultures were also an important source or starting point for theology. Theological articulations in the region from the 1960s drew heavily on cultures, particularly cultural worldviews, values, symbols, concepts, rituals, proverbs and processes. The seminal 'coconut theology' of Havea in the 1960s,[16] the 'grassroots theology' of Boseto in the 1980s and 1990s,[17] the '*vanua* (land) theology' of Tuwere in the 1990s and early 2000s,[18] the 'eco-theology' of Tofaeono[19] at the turn of the millennium, and the '*moana* (sea/ocean) theology' of Halapua[20] in the late 2000s, to name a few, were all rooted in and derived from elements of cultures in the Pacific. Meo describes the cultural-traditional values of 'inclusiveness, reconciliation, unity, participation, dialogue, partnership, fellowship, sharing and service' as hallmarks and gems of Pacific communities.[21] In a declaration, the contemporary significance of cultures for Pacific people and theology was affirmed and endorsed by all the heads and leaders of churches in the Pacific at a landmark conference in 2000: '... the traditional values of the Pacific Island societies are similar to Kingdom values... We

---

[16] Sione, 'Amanaki Havea, 'Christianity in the Pacific Context', in *South Pacific Theology: Papers from Consultation on Pacific Theology, Papua New Guinea, January 1986* (Parramatta: Regnum Books and World Vision International South Pacific, 1986). Although Havea's theological thinking was published only later, he began to articulate such thinking in the 1960s and 1970s.

[17] Leslie Boseto has published a number of his writings. See his *I Have a Strong Belief* (Goroka, Papua New Guinea: Unichurch Books and The Melanesian Institute, 1983); 'God as Community – God in Melanesian Theology', in *The Pacific Journal of Theology,* 2.10 (1993), 41-48; 'Toward a Pacific Theology of Reality', in *The Pacific Journal of Theology* 2.12 (1994), 53-61; *Lauru Land Conference of Tribal Community: Philosophy, Theology and Guiding Principles* (Suva: Pacific Conference of Churches, 1995.)

[18] See the following works by Ilaitia Sevati Tuwere; 'Making Sense of the Vanua (Land) in the Fijian Context: A Theological Exploration' (PhD thesis, Melbourne College of Divinity, 1992); 'Indigenous People's Struggle for Land and Identity: An Account from Fiji. Indigenous People's Struggle for Land Identity in the Pacific: A Joint Seminar of the World Council of Churches Indigenous People's Programme, the Pacific Desk of the World Council of Churches, and the Pacific Conference of Churches', Fiji, September 2000, unpublished paper; *Vanua: Towards a Fijian Theology of Place* (Suva: Institute of Pacific Studies/University of the South Pacific, 2002).

[19] Ama'amalele Tofaeono, *Eco-Theology: AIGA – The Household of Life, A Perspective from Living Myths and Traditions of Samoa* (Erlangen, Germany: Erlangen Verl. Für Mission und Okumene, 2000).

[20] Winston Halapua, *Waves of God's Embrace: Sacred Perspectives from the Ocean* (Norwich, UK: Canterbury Press, 2008), and '*Theomoana.* Toward an Oceanic Theology', in *Concilium*, 5 (2010), 23-33.

[21] Jovili Iliesa Meo, 'Gems of the Pacific: Sharing and Service', in *The Pacific Journal of Theology,* 2.16 (1996), 84-101.

are not saying that traditional values… are identical with the Kingdom of God preached by Jesus… if lived traditions are put together, they offer viable alternatives to the destructive ways associated with globalisation.'[22] The reversal of early missionary demonisation and relegation of cultures to lower-level spirituality, coupled with the reaffirmation of various positive and life-affirming elements of cultures, were progressive movements in theology in the Pacific.

## The Primacy and Fullness of Life

The title *Together towards Life* holds two key themes: life – life in all its fullness – and the journey towards life as a corporate and communal commitment and undertaking, not a solo venture. This life is rooted in and emanates from the very life of the Triune God: God the Creator who willed and continues to will creation ever anew; the Spirit, the life-giver who sustains and empowers all life – human and non-human – and renews the whole creation; Jesus, the Christ whose vision and passion it is for all God's people to enjoy abundant life. At the very heart of God's mission in and for and with the world is life: 'God's mission is nothing less than the sending of the Holy Spirit from the Father through the Son into the world, so that this world should not perish but live. The Gospel of John tells us quite simply what it is that is brought into the world from God through Christ: *life*.'[23]

The centrality and significance of life is a key theme in Pacific theology. This theme has been expressed in various and related ways over time: '… most fundamental value… continuation, protection, maintenance and celebration of Life',[24] a common ground of 'Pacificness' and Christianness' in any Pacific theology is their 'life-centredness',[25] 'ancestral theo-cosmic convictions… conserving the ecology of life'[26] and 'primacy of life'[27] as characteristic of a unique Pacific contribution to global theological reflection in an age of climate change. The life of which Pacific theologians speak is not compartmentalised but is one complete whole, and includes and at the same time transcends biological life. This is obvious from the

---

[22] *Island of Hope: A Pacific Alternative to Economic Globalisation* (Geneva: WCC, 2002), 91.

[23] Jürgen Moltmann, *The Source of Life: The Holy Spirit and the Theology of Life* (London: SCM, 1997), 19.

[24] Darrell Whiteman, 'Melanesian Religions: An Overview', in Ennio Mantovani (ed), *An Introduction to Melanesian Religions* (Goroka, Papua New Guinea: The Melanesian Institute, 1984), 91.

[25] John Havea, 'A Reconsideration of *Pacificness* in a Search for a South Pacific Theology', in *The Pacific Journal of Theology,* 2.10 (1993), 5-16.

[26] Tofaeono, *Eco-Theology: AIGA*, 186.

[27] Philip Gibbs, 'Emerging Indigenous Theologies in Oceania', in *Concilium,* 5 (2010), 34-44.

languages of the Pacific where life is immediately and directly connected with breath and spirit. It is also life in relationships and interrelationships with and between people, between people and their immediate environments, and between people and the divine. Along the kataphatic (or cataphatic) tradition, primacy and fullness of life in Pacific cultures could be stated as the human desire for well-being and fulfilment in every aspect of life, be it health, success, fecundity, respect, honour and egalitarianism. Along the apophatic tradition, it could be stated as the absence of forces that stand in destruction tension with life, such as sickness, conflicts, in-fecundity, poverty, dishonour and death. This view and understanding of the primacy and fullness of life resonates well with the affirmation in *TTL*. In Pacific contemporary theology, life is experienced as one whole and at the same time is interconnected.

## Interconnectedness of Life

*TTL* is clear that God's mission is primarily for the fullness of life in all its dimensions. 'Theology of interconnectedness' is how theologians of the Pacific describe this miracle and mystery of life. The land, sea and atmosphere and all lives therein are interconnected. This land-sea-atmosphere web of life has readability characteristics that enable people to live in a meaningful relationship with their environments.[28] Whiteman speaks of life as one integrated whole where the physical, spiritual, sacred and secular dovetail.[29] Tuwere[30] and Bird[31] speak of the interconnectedness of the rhythms and processes of the land with those of the ocean and the moon in the sky, and of how human life is intricately interwoven with these rhythms and processes;[32] Tofaeono speaks of the interconnectedness of human life with the divine and other existents; Halapua,[33] concurring with Hau'ofa,[34] speaks of how the oceans and seas connect the islands of the Pacific rather than separating them. Underlying all of this is the assurance that fullness of life is only possible within the interconnectedness of all life. Boseto says, 'Our existence and our survival can never be separated from our land and sea. Our life in God is in creation. God is our bread of life and our water of life in our land and sea… Our tropical forest is the home and

[28] Cliff Bird, 'Hermeneutics of Ecology and its Relationship to the Identity of the Oikos in Oceania', in *The Pacific Journal of Theology* 2.46 (2011), 19-33.
[29] Whiteman, *Melanesian Religions*, 88.
[30] Tuwere, *Vanua* (2002).
[31] Cliff Bird, '*Pepesa* – The Household of Life: A Theological Exploration of Land in the Context of Change in Solomon Islands' (PhD thesis, Charles Sturt University, Australia, 2008).
[32] Tofaeono, *Eco-Theology – AIGA*.
[33] Halapua, *Waves of God's Embrace*.
[34] Epeli Hau'ofa, *A New Oceania: Rediscovering our Sea of Islands* (Suva: University of the South Pacific in association with Beake House, 1993.)

garden of many species as well as our human communities… Our land and sea are us and we are them. Do not separate us. If you do so, you are murdering us.'[35]

Implicit in the above statement by Boseto is that, in the Pacific theo-cosmological interpretation, salvation is inseparable from the interconnectedness of all life. The earlier missionary tendency to both spiritualise and abstract salvation to some purely futuristic existence in heaven has come under criticism from academic theologians. Amongst others, Tuwere contends that we cannot speak of salvation without also speaking of the *vanua* (land-sea),[36] a position which Bird also articulates.[37] Within the worldviews and experiences of Pacific peoples, the following could be argued:[38] salvation was temporal and pragmatic in the sense that it was time-related and earth-oriented; salvation was experienced in connection with the immediate environment in which people live, thus highlighting the saving and healing qualities of the flora, fauna and maritime life; and salvation was seen and experienced in terms of the basic human welfare of the communities which was lived out within the context of their environments. *TTL* makes a similar affirmation: 'In many ways creation is in mission to humanity; for instance, the natural world has a power that can heal the human heart and body.'[39] The salvation Pacific theologians speak of is not some low 'mundane matters' in contrast to the Christian 'great spiritual salvation of man' [*sic*] as earlier alleged by Tippett;[40] it is God's salvific, healing, gracious and interactive presence within the 'very [exceedingly] good'[41] creation that God has joyfully willed into being. The life-nurturing and life-affirming qualities of the land-sea-atmosphere are an inherent and integral part of God's work of creating, after which God 'was refreshed'.[42] The mission of God through the permeating and renewing presence of the Spirit and through the enfleshed Word neither nullified nor replaced the interconnectedness of life which was part and parcel of God's original creation and vision. For Pacific theology, God's mission reaffirms this primacy of interconnected life, and

---

[35] Leslie Boseto, 'Do Not Separate Us from Our Land', in *The Pacific Journal of Theology,* 2.13 (1995), 69-72.

[36] Tuwere, *Vanua.*

[37] Cliff Bird, 'Re-conceptualising Salvation: Some Insights from a Solomon Islands Culture toward a Relevant Theology of Salvation for Today', in *The Pacific Journal of Theology,* 2.42 (2009), 23-39.

[38] Bird, 'Re-conceptualising Salvation' (2009).

[39] *TTL,* §22.

[40] Alan Tippet, *Verdict Theology in Missionary Theory: a collection of addresses and discussions that were prepared for a special week of missionary presentations at Lincoln Christian College and Seminary* (Pasadena, CA: William Carey Library, 1973), 21. See also his *Aspects of Pacific Ethnohistory* (Pasadena, CA: William Carey Library, 1973.)

[41] Genesis 1:31, Expanded Bible.

[42] Exodus 31:17, New Revised Standard Version.

through both the *paraclete* and the life, ministry, death and resurrection of Jesus Christ, God walks and lives with humanity, not only to say. 'Walk ye this way'[43] so as not to miss the mark of God's vision for creation again, but also to keep reminding humanity that the life-denying, life-negating and life-destroying forces have been overcome. Peoples of the Pacific are called to celebrate life, life in all its fullness, life in all its interconnectedness.[44]

## Eco-Theology: Oikos of God and Oikos of Life

Home and household are important themes in Pacific theology. Pacific peoples have a deep sense of attachment to place, to home;[45] even now with migration, Pacific people continue to have a strong sense of belonging to their motherland, and to their particular 'place' in it. The land and sea comprise the immediate and tangible *oikos* or home for the people of the Pacific. In fact, the everyday life of the majority of people in PICs is grounded primarily in an interrelatedness of land and sea and atmosphere.[46] At the same time, the land and sea is home to many other existents[47] – flora and fauna and others. All these do not live outside the economy (Greek *oikos-nomos*) of God. As *TTL* affirms, 'Creation's life and God's life are entwined'.[48]

With the growing threats and worsening impacts of anthropogenic climate change for the PICs, especially the low-lying atoll island countries,[49] the focus on *home* as a theological issue is a pertinent one. Tuwere,[50] Tofaeono,[51] and Bird[52] deal centrally with the theological construct of *oikos*. Theology of home is founded on the interconnectedness of life between human beings and their environments. Home or *oikos* is

---

[43] See Isaiah 30:21; Jeremiah 7:23.

[44] See Bird, 'Re-conceptualising Salvation'.

[45] See Tuwere, *Vanua*.

[46] Edvard Hviding, *Guardians of Marovo Lagoon: Practice, Place and Politics in Maritime Melanesia* (Honolulu, HI: University of Hawaii Press, 1996). See also Te'o I. J. Fairbairn and DeLisle Worrell, *South Pacific and Caribbean Islands: A Comparative Study* (Brisbane, Australia: The Foundation for Development Co-operation, 1996).

[47] Tofaeono, *Eco-Theology: AIGA*.

[48] *TTL*, §19.

[49] Patrick Nunn, 'Bridging the Gulf Between Science and Society Imperatives for Minimizing Societal Disruption from Climate Change in the Pacific', in A. Sumi et al (eds), *Adaptation and Mitigation Strategies for Climate Change* (New York: Springer, 2010). Nunn summarizes the threat in the Pacific area to be: a) temperature rise, at least 2.5°C higher in 2100 than in 1990, but perhaps even more; b) sea level rise, projected by the IPCC to be a maximum of 58cm; and c) more storms (235).

[50] Tuwere, *Vanua* (2002).

[51] Tofaeono, *Eco-Theology: AIGA – The Household of God*.

[52] Bird, '*Pepesa* – The Household of Life'.

about our 'sea of islands'[53] and the Earth, and is intricately connected with both economics (Greek *oikos-nomos*) and ecology (Greek *oikos-logos*). *Oikos-nomos* means rules of the home or rules of the household. *Oikos-logos* means the study of the home or household; it is the study of the way things relate to make the home or household work. These two belong together, as de Gruchy points out: 'At heart, economy and ecology should cohere; after all, they are both about the earth, our *oikos*, or home. Ecology, as *oikos-logos*, concerns the wisdom of how our home functions; and economy, as *oikos-nomos*, is about the rules that should govern the way we run our home.'[54] Mindless and rampant capitalism, with its doctrine of more economic growth, is being pushed at the expense of ecological integrity and justice.

'For Pacific people, anthropogenic climate change is an issue of justice – those who contribute least to global warming and the climate change-induced sea level rise are the ones who are affected most. The Pacific Conference of Churches (PCC) is leading the way for churches to speak out for justice and seek alternatives. In their *Island of Hope* declaration, the heads and leaders of all churches in the Pacific identified family life, communal relationships, environment, spirituality and traditional economy as Pacific alternatives to the destructive impacts of economic globalisation.[55] In a declaration in Kiribati in 2004, the WCC and WCC member-churches in the Pacific stated as follows: 'Here on the small atoll islands of Kiribati, the impacts of human-induced climate change are already visible. The sea level is rising. People's homes are vulnerable to the increasingly high tides and storm surges. Shores are eroding and the coral reefs are becoming bleached. The water supplies and soil fertility are being threatened by the intrusion of salt water. Weather patterns are less predictable, posing risks to fisher-folk and farmers.'[56] Climate change is perhaps the biggest threat to the *oikos* of many Pacific people today. The PCC has taken this further in an attempt to rethink the household of God in Oceania concept with the addition of sufficiency, solidarity, inclusiveness and participation as hallmarks of the *oikos* of God in the Pacific.[57] The *TTL*

---

[53] Hau'ofa, *A New Oceania*.

[54] Steve de Gruchy, 'An Olive Agenda: First Thoughts on a Metaphorical Theology of Development', unpublished paper.

[55] *Island of Hope,* 192-94.

[56] 'The Otin Taai Declaration: A Statement and Recommendations from the World Council of Churches and WCC member-churches in the Pacific' (6th-11th March 2004, Tarawa, Kiribati).

[57] 'Rethinking the Household of God in the Pacific: Towards Sufficiency and Solidarity, Inclusiveness and Participation. Concept Paper to Oceania Island Leaders' (Pacific Conference of Churches, 2010), unpublished paper. See also 'Rethinking the Household of God in the Pacific – Literature Review' (Pacific Conference of Churches, 2013), unpublished paper.

affirms that creation will not be destroyed but will be renewed and redeemed. This affirmation is at the heart of the Pacific theology of home.

## Being Church in Mission in the Pacific Today

What does being church in the Pacific mean? How do the churches engage in mission in the context of rapid change? If the mission of God is centrally about abundant life as affirmed in *TTL*, how might the churches ensure that God's people do actually enjoy such abundant life? In the light of all these pertinent questions, the 'Mission Call from Viwa' acknowledged and affirmed 'the call of God for the churches to again engage in new and innovative ways in mission activity', and that the 'present context in the Pacific requires much solidarity, unity and witness by the churches as our issues are converging in many ways'.[58] The 'Mission Call' identifies and affirms 'today's [six] mission fields': theology and the meaning of mission in the Pacific context; politics, justice and governance; development and social challenges; multicultural societies – race relations and nation-building; political and gender violence; poverty, wealth and ecology.[59] What stands out is that almost all the 'mission fields' affirmed transcend the earlier missionary understanding and practice of mission. What is called for is the life-giving and life-nurturing presence of God's Spirit through the churches in spheres beyond their walls. What is implicit in the mission affirmation is the challenge to shift from one way of *being* church to another (or others) that frees and enables it to engage in innovative and fresh mission activities. This is also an affirmation of *TTL*.

However, to be able to engage in innovative mission activities, a church needs to be more self-aware, self-reflective and self-analytical because the church's self-understanding determines to a large degree its responses to challenges that are external to its inner life. For Pacific churches, this involves several aspects, including the following:[60] the institution of the church and its capacity and adaptability to respond to problems and challenges faced by its members and others; the capability of the church in engaging in appropriate hermeneutics, its willingness to let go of interpretations that deny and negate life, and its openness to accept hermeneutical alternatives and interpretations that affirm and protect life; the willingness of the church to burst its theological boundaries and abandon theologies, doctrines and policies that dehumanise and deny fullness of life; the realisation by churches that worship does not happen only, and end, within the walls of its church buildings, but continues in the

---

[58] 'The Mission Call from Viwa', 2.

[59] 'The Mission Call from Viwa', 2-4.

[60] Bird, Cliff, 'Deep Sea Thinking: A Call to 21st Century Oceania Churches for (Self)-Critical Awareness and Prophetic Presence in the Context of "Seas of Change"'. Paper presented at the Third Consultation of Bread for the World Partners in Oceania, Sonaisali, Fiji, October 2013.

events and situations of daily life; that the Body and Blood of Christ and the word of God must be afforded their healing, life-affirming and transforming presence in the world outside the church walls, where the battered, bruised, beggars, homeless, sex workers, ordinary folk and perceived sinners have their being. It is also where the powers-that-be have their being and shape the being of others. As Tissa Balasuriya points out, 'The Eucharist has an *extraordinary potential* for being an agent of *personal and global transformation*'[61], and as Izunna Okonkwo says, 'By extending the liturgical celebration of Christ's memorial sacrifice into real life, one can talk of the link the Eucharist has with social transformation.'[62] All of this means bringing the church into the lived experiences of people rather than expecting them to turn up in church. This is one way of *being* church that takes seriously God's mission to bring fullness of life to all people.

## Conclusion

*TTL* as an affirmation of God's mission has much in common with contemporary Pacific theology, as this brief sketch has demonstrated. There is much more in contemporary Pacific theology that could be written but space does not allow. One of the biggest challenges for contemporary Pacific theology is to move beyond the zones of comfort and familiarity, and to begin to really and truly engage in mission activities affirmed in 'The Mission Call from Viwa' and in *TTL*. This is a challenge that must be addressed because it is a challenge that opens and widens doors, brightens horizons, and enlivens hope for God's fullness of life to be enfleshed in humanity and in all creation.

---

[61] Tissa Balasuriya, *Eucharist and Human Liberation*, in Quest Series 50 (Colombo, Sri Lanka: Centre for Society and Religion, 1977), 82.

[62] Izunna Okonkwo, 'The Eucharist as Community Builder: Eucharistic Communion and Social Transformation' (Glasgow, UK: n.d.).

# *TOGETHER TOWARDS LIFE* AND CONTEMPORARY LATIN AMERICAN THEOLOGY

Néstor Míguez

> Now people at the margins are claiming their key role as agents of mission and affirming mission as transformation. This reversal of roles in the envisioning of mission has strong biblical foundations because God chose the poor, the foolish and the powerless (1 Cor. 1:18-31) to further God's mission of justice and peace so that life may flourish (TTL §6).

The history of Christian missions in Latin America is mostly a history of conquest, impositions, cultural alienation and humiliation, amidst a dreadful genocide and the devastation of natural resources. In the first half century (1500-1550) of the conquest by European powers (Iberian Christianity), the native population was cut to a half.[1] Far from good news, evangelization resulted in the oppression of the native people, exploitation and even massacres and the degradation of creation.[2] It is true that some voices were lifted in defence of the indigenous peoples and their rights,[3] but an overview shows that the forces that came into the continent from the so-called Christian world mixed their beliefs with a thirst for gold, riches and prestige, with very little consideration of the content of the Gospel they claimed to present or represent.[4] Though it was justified as a civilizing enterprise, 'evangelization' resulted in compulsory conversions, forced labour and the dreadful experience of oppression.

Despite that false start, the power of the Gospel found its way in, and the Spirit created a renewed faith among many of the local people. Not only recently, but even in the struggles for their rights and dignity (in 17th and 18th centuries), many aboriginal leaders appealed to the Scriptures and the

---

[1] There are different interpretations of the causes of this demographic catastrophe. The numbers are also subject to discussion. The invasion, the conquest wars, ecological changes, diseases unknown to the local population, forced labour and the cultural and social destruction, all contributed to the decimation of the original native population. But overall, most studies agree that the population suffered extreme reduction, both in numbers and dignity.

[2] See Eduardo Galeano, *Open Veins of Latin America* (New York: Monthly Review Press, 1973).

[3] The Dominican Friar Bartolomé de las Casas was the most outspoken defender of the indigenous population. See Gustavo Gutiérrez, *Las Casas: In Search of the Poor of Jesus Christ*, trans. Robert R. Barr (Maryknoll, NY: Orbis Books, 1993).

[4] See Gustavo Gutiérrez, *Dios o el oro de las Indias* (Lima: CEP, 1989).

sufferings of the Christ to defend their cause.[5] Also, during the days of the Independence wars (19th century), we can find people and movements that took inspiration from the Christian message and affirmed their right to freedom from an understanding of the Gospel which made them confront, on many occasions, their church institutions.

The evangelical missionaries who came to the continent in the 19th and 20th centuries also understood that their missions had a beneficial and educational purpose, though many despised native beliefs and promoted cultural alienation, contributing to the dominion of the new neo-colonial powers.[6] Protestantism grew little during the first years of those missions. It experienced a larger growth under the impact of the Pentecostal churches, but their theology was almost totally imported. Yet, in many cases, a certain syncretism between Pentecostal experience and local popular culture gave these churches a vernacular flavour.

However, especially in the second half of the 20th century, there grew a new awareness of the liberating power of the Christian message, with an impact that ran through the different Christian churches and confessions. This mobilized millions of Christians into a new reading (*relectura*) of the Bible, and a life-giving engagement in the struggles for social justice and the integrity of creation. This gave birth to a new ecumenical theological stream, Latin American Liberation Theology.

This movement spread into all Latin American countries, notwithstanding strong repression from dictatorships and foreign intervention.[7] It took different forms and shades according to local situations, and also to the different subjects that expressed their particular claims and concerns: native people, women, Afro-descendants, urban workers and peasants, ecological militants, migrants and exiles. At the same time, we must acknowledge the growth of a certain Pentecostal fundamentalism and so-called 'Prosperity theology'. (Not all Pentecostals are fundamentalist; in Latin America there are also very progressive and

---

[5] See the defence of Tupac Amaru in his trial in front of the Spanish Court, in Daniel Bruno and Néstor Míguez, 'History of the Bible in Latin America', in John Riches (ed), *The New Cambridge History of the Bible* (Cambridge: CUP, 2015), 427-60; and the writings and drawings of Guamán Poma de Ayala, in Néstor Míguez, 'Sociopolitical Context of Postcolonial Studies in Latin America', in Joseph Duggan (ed), *Pressing On: Next Generation of Indecent Theologians*, Borderless Press.

[6] See Jean-Pierre Bastian, *Historia del protestantismo en América Latina* (México, Ediciones CUPSA, 1990).

[7] In 1969, Nelson Rockefeller made a trip to various countries in Latin America and issued a document known as 'The Rockefeller Report on Latin America'. In it he explicitly mentions the 'danger' of the new theological trends in Latin American churches and theology. In similar fashion, the so-called 'Santa Fé Document', prepared in 1980 for President Reagan, established the political lines for the relationship of North and South America, including the need to control the Latin American churches and their theology.

ecumenical Pentecostal churches and theologians). That provides us with a very complex panorama when trying to consider the contemporary situation of Latin American theologies and church mission. Yet, since fundamentalism and prosperity theology is not a Latin American product, even if in many cases adapted to local conditions, I will concentrate on those theological trends that we can envision as 'together towards life'. In doing this, we try to show the contribution Latin American churches can offer to the witness of the Reign of God in our world today.

## Suma Qamaña, 'the Good Living'[8]

> We affirm that the purpose of God's mission is fullness of life (John 10:10) and that this is the criterion for discernment in mission. Therefore, we are called to discern the Spirit of God wherever there is life in its fullness, particularly in terms of the liberation of the oppressed peoples, the healing and reconciliation of broken communities, and the restoration of the whole creation. We are challenged to appreciate the life-affirming spirits present in different cultures and to be in solidarity with all those who are involved in the mission of affirming and preserving life. We also discern and confront evil spirits wherever forces of death and negation of life are experienced (TTL §102).

This expression, in the Aymara language, has become a useful slogan for the new theological trends in Latin America. It is the gift of the Spirit through the ancestral cultures of the original peoples of this land. *Suma Qamaña* (the good life; or *Ñande reko* – our harmony, in the Guarani language) involves not only human relationships, but also, in its traditional and ancestral use, the way that humans relate to the *Pachamama* (Mother Earth), *Inti* (the Sun and skies God), the *Achachilas* (the mountains/the ancestors). It rests on community mutual support. In the Guarani tradition, it relates to the *ivi maraei*, the 'land without hardships' (or worries; it can also be translated as 'the land without evil'), presided over by the Moon deity. The Bolivian government has established that *Suma Qamaña* (or *sumac kawsay* in Quechuan) should be the goal of every law and governmental action, and so it is mentioned in the Preamble of the new Constitution of the Multinational State of Bolivia. Similar concerns have been expressed by the Ecuadorian authorities and other Latin American political leaders.

*Suma Qamaña* is not 'living better', as a western understanding might propose, in the sense of having more goods or comfort, 'The best things in life are not things.'[9] Obviously, it is about housing and education, health

---

[8] For an introduction to the origin and meaning of this term, see Javier Albó, 'Suma Qamaña = El buen convivir' available at: https://sumakkawsay.files.wordpress.com/2009/06/albo_sumaqamana.pdf (accessed June 2015).

[9] The sentence was 'tweeted' by one of the people who recovered their identity after being kidnapped in childhood by the military dictatorship in Argentina. The

and work – that is, the totality of living conditions. But it is also about freedom and collective dignity, about family life and spiritual welfare, about equality and integrity. But most of all, and as a summary of all these, it is about the way to 'get along well' among people, and between people and the whole of creation. It presupposes the possibility of a certain harmony. Yet that harmony cannot be a static equilibrium, a motionless ideal, where everything reaches its perfection as in ancient Greek philosophy, and the homeostatic tendencies of today. Life is motion, change, unexpected events and situations, and harmony is to learn how to deal with these happenings in peace and justice. In the Guaraní understanding, it is a constant pilgrimage in search of the land without worries, the Moon Valley. But that *ivi maraei* is neither a spiritual post-mortem ideal nor an unreachable worldly utopia, but a way of life, an understanding of life based on hope.

That is to say, it includes most of the assertions of the Latin American Liberation Theology of the 1970s, the struggle for Human Rights under the repressive dictatorships of the late 1970s and 1980s, and adds the contribution of the new theological trends that are concerned with gender, ethnic and class identity and ecology. It provides a way of understanding all these different approaches as part of an all-embracing concept of life. Yet, we must not be idealistic: *Suma Qamaña* is a concept that flourishes in the indigenous agricultural environment. It now has to be rethought in new situations, where people live in crowded cities, where the economy is related to different industries, where the simple life of the self-supporting village (if it was ever simple) has turned into the complex life and economy of a globalized world described in the WCC Document *TTL* (especially §7, 9 and 31). If by this motto we propose a way back into an idealized primeval life, we will do little favour to the real needs and living conditions of people today. 'Good living' is to be related to the problems and challenges that modernity has brought, to which we must respond in a creative and responsible way, and not by shying away into a utopian and irretrievable past.

## The Earth and the Poor

> We are therefore called to move beyond a narrowly human-centred approach and to embrace forms of mission which express our reconciled relationship with all created life. We hear the cry of the earth as we listen to the cries of the poor and we know that from its beginning the earth has cried out to God over humanity's injustice (Gen. 4:10) (TTL §19).

---

'Abuelas de Plaza de Mayo' were able to identify more than 115 of those kidnapped as babies by the military when their parents were assassinated or disappeared, and restore them to their true identity and to their remaining families.

Sometimes we find a kind of implicit 'either/or' in the debate about poverty and ecology. On the one hand, some ecological trends tend to emphasize the preservation of nature as a goal in itself, without any deep concern for the social implications of ecology. On the other hand, some political leaders who promote inclusion and development, well intended in the sense of raising up those impoverished in society, are relatively careless about the environmental damage done to the places where those same people have lived and will live through generations.

The common problem in both approaches is the 'top-down' direction in which many proposals are made or decisions taken. Often those in power pretend to know what is best and what should be done, but they do it from an idealistic stand or a disengaged position, when not in the egotistic drive of self-interest. No matter how well intentioned they might be, they declare their message before hearing the real concerns and wisdom of the people. This error has been the unhappy way of Christian mission through centuries, and can now be repeated even by those who consider themselves engaged and progressive. Without a pondered dialogue on the part of all concerned, and an ear attentive to the whispers of creation, guided by the Spirit that empowered creation, nothing good or sustainable will emerge.

No real concern for the environment can be conceived without a concern for the people, especially for those more vulnerable, poor and oppressed.[10] No real ecological wisdom will come without hearing the claims of those who toil every day in the hardships of daily living, who have to struggle with unproductive land, with floods and drought, or work in poisonous factories. At the same time, no real social progress can be made or justice be found if we consider nature just as a resource and not as a gift to be cared for. Some development programmes that today may offer alleviation of poverty might tomorrow result in the destruction of the living conditions for those same people or their descendants. But the preservation of a depopulated land does not solve the problem either.

Sustainability must consider the needs of the people as part of the health of creation. Social and economic justice cannot be separated from the care of other living creatures or the environment. That is what we read in *Suma Qamaña.* This is also why we have to overcome a static concept of nature. The current concept of nature that emerged from modernity is that of a self-perpetuating entity, a universe with its laws and regularities, with its own equilibrium. Some naturalists think that human activity should not interfere and that, when it does, it creates chaos. In many ways, that understanding is related to deism, in the sense of a God that launched the universe and left it on its own. If God does not interfere, why should humans? It is interesting to note, as we shall see later, that defenders of the neo-liberal imperial

---

[10] A similar concern has been expressed at great length and with careful study in the 2015 Encyclical by Pope Francis: *Laudato Si'*.

economy use this same kind of argument in order to avoid any regulation of the total free market.

A theological understanding of creation should be able to overcome this idea of nature (that is not valid even for the most advanced scientific vision of today) in order to see the dynamic interaction of many factors, including human culture, social justice and economic developments. One of the conflicts that we find today in political and social discourse is the problem of exclusion, of the marginalization of the people from access to the basic needs of life (*TTL* §§36-42); therefore, there is a need to include the excluded. But a question remains: to include where? If inclusion, as understood by some social development ideology, is to make the excluded part of the same system that excluded them, to include people in a mode of production that is polluting land, air and water, the remedy is worse than the malady. The question is not inclusion in this way, but rather: 'Inclusivity fosters just relationships in the community of humanity and creation, with mutual acknowledgement of persons and creation and mutual respect and sustenance of each one's sacred worth' (*TTL* §46). It is not only inclusion as a social goal, but transformation.

> Transformation can be understood in the light of the Paschal mystery: 'If we have died with Christ, we will also live with him; if we endure, we will also reign with him' (2 Timothy 2:11-12). In situations of oppression, discrimination and hurt, the cross of Christ is the power of God for salvation (2 Corinthians 1:18). Even in our time, some have paid with their lives for their Christian witness, reminding us all of the cost of discipleship. The Spirit gives Christians courage to live out their convictions, even in the face of persecution and martyrdom (TTL §32).

## The People and the Empire

> Jesus has told us, 'You cannot serve God and mammon' (Matt. 6:24, KJV). The policy of unlimited growth through the domination of the global free market is an ideology that claims to be without alternative, demanding an endless flow of sacrifices from the poor and from nature. 'It makes the false promise that it can save the world through creation of wealth and prosperity, claiming sovereignty over life and demanding total allegiance, which amounts to idolatry.'* This is a global system of mammon that protects the unlimited growth of wealth of only the rich and powerful through endless exploitation. This tower of greed is threatening the whole household of God. The reign of God is in direct opposition to the empire of mammon (TTL §31).
>
> *World Alliance of Reformed Churches, *The Accra Confession: Covenanting for Justice in the Economy and the Earth* (2004), §10.

In the biblical narrative, we find time and again this opposition between the people and the empire. It is not only the presence of empires with their military and political violence (which unfortunately we still see), but what we may call the 'Spirit of Empire'.[11] It is the attempt of the powerful to accumulate power and wealth without limit, subjugating all people. But it is also the temptation of some elites of subalternized nations who seek the protection of empires and negotiate their own petty power over against the common people of their own societies. And this can happen also with those who invoke God, as the prophets of old declare many times (Amos 5, Hosea 12, Isaiah 1, Jeremiah 7, to mention only a few examples). In the biblical narrative, we can clearly see the case of Ezra and Nehemiah who, in order to build the Second Temple, reject the *'am ha'aretz,* the people of the land. Nehemiah, with the use of torture (Nehemiah 13:25), forces Jews married to non-Jewish women to oust their wives and children for the sake of purity,[12] that same purity and the same Temple that Jesus condemns (Matthew 21:12-14; Luke 21:1-6). Even if Nehemiah pleads for God's blessing at the end of the book, we can see in him imperial power and local elite prejudice working together against life. It is that kind of sectarian Judaism that Jesus wants to transform and that Paul rejects.

So it is also with the new post-modern Empire, as described in *TTL*. The name of the globalized post-modern Empire is 'free market'. It is ironic enough that this so-called *free* market is imposed with the help of the armed forces and institutional violence. In the name of freedom, innocent people are bombed from unmanned planes, suspects are tortured and kept captive without trial, and cutbacks in social welfare are imposed while banks are baled out. And even worse, these are defended as something 'natural'. The rules of economy are presented as if they were part of human evolution, a kind of God-given equilibrium (the invisible hand) that prevents chaos.[13] Humans are expected to blindly follow market laws, and not interfere out of moral apprehension or well-intended but useless intentions. Yet the outcome is evident: the market satisfies the desires of the rich and neglects the needs of the poor. Less than 15% of the world's population enjoys more than 80% of the world's resources, while the overwhelming majority is left with what remains, and the poorest 20% have less than 1.3%.[14]

---

[11] See Néstor Míguez, Joerg Rieger and Jung Mo Sung, *Beyond the Spirit of the Empire: New Perspectives on Theology and Politics* (London: SCM, 2009).

[12] In those times, to expel a woman or a child from a community was almost equal to a death sentence, or at least suffering the perils of poverty, hunger and defencelessness. According to Nehemiah, even Moses would have had to banish his wife and children! (Exodus 2:21-22; Numbers 12:1).

[13] So it was defended by Friedrich von Hayek, one of the ideologists of the free market, in his Nobel Price speech: 'The Pretence of Knowledge': www.nobelprize.org/nobel_prizes/economic-sciences/laureates/1974/hayek-lecture.html

[14] United Nations Report on World Population: *El estado de la población mundial 2001*: *www.unfpa.org/swp/2001/espanol/ch01.html.* See also: www.worldhunger.org/articles/Learn/world%20hunger%20facts%202002.html.

From a theological point of view, we should apply to market laws the same critique that Paul makes against the Law as a device: it is the law of greed and covetousness; it is the law that ends in sin and death (Romans 7:7-11). Against that injustice of the law of the market, in which everything has a price (there is nothing free in the free market), there is the justice of grace, the priceless victory of life over death, of the salvation of human life against the condemnation of the law (Romans 5).[15]

Imperial practices, ideology and spirit, destroy the people, create prejudice and disunity, and expel and oppress. Through the whole Old Testament and in the history of the Christian church, we can see how the imperial spirit brings about division, injustice and death. While the God-given mandate is to create a people, empires destroy them. Abraham is called to form a people that would be a blessing for all peoples (Genesis 12:3), and Moses is elected to free that people from the slavery of the Egyptian Empire. Yet, when Israel, against Samuel's warning (1 Samuel 8), chooses to have a king 'as other nations', that kingship becomes oppressive, and ends up dividing the people and pitting one side of Israel against the other. We are to condemn imperial practices and ideology, not only because of economic and social harm, but also because of their cultural and spiritual consequences. We need to grow in our awareness of how that ideology, that economic practice, and the idolatrous and sacrificial character of the Empire, affects our subjectivity, how it influences our culture, our way of seeing things and even our faith.

But it is not simply that we are called to adopt an anti-imperialist stand. Rather, the issue is what we are *for*, the positive action of love. In Latin American theology and politics, the concept of 'people' (in the sense of the Greek *laos,* or the Latin *populus*) becomes central. In the rebirth of democratic rule, after the criminal dictatorships of the past century, the real meaning of the rule of the people has to be rethought. Is democracy only a way to elect authorities, a system of government, a way to manage state affairs? Or is it something more profound, a construction of dignity that arises from the deep roots of being human in the image of God, of considering the integrity of all humans in their mutual relationships and amidst creation? Is it not the mandate to meet the needs of the needy, to respond to the claims of the *populus*? Some recently elected governments in Latin America arose from the social struggles of the workers. Both President Lula in Brazil and President Morales in Bolivia were the heads of workers' unions before being elected to office. They have aimed to take care of social inequalities, to make a better distribution of the goods necessary for living, to overcome poverty. Curiously enough, they are contemptuously called 'populist', as if responding to the real demands of the *populus* was a sin against democracy instead of its fulfilment.

---

[15] See Néstor Míguez: 'Grace in Pauline Theology: Political and Economic Projections', in *Neotestamentica,* 46.2 (2012), 287-98.

What we aspire to, in the political arena, working *together towards life*, is to go beyond the formalities of democracy (after all, the Empire uses formal democratic methods in its dominant countries) and respond to the people, to construct a people, what we have called a *laocracy*.[16] That is, to be able to hear the cry of the oppressed, as Jesus did, always surrounded by the *laos*, in order to heal, bless, feed, educate, and give sense and meaning to the life of the despised by the elites and the powerful. That is, to live up to the hope of freedom in the Messianic promise (Rom. 8:18-27).

It is true, the rule of the people is not always the rule of nature nor the rule of God, and even these popular governments have serious ecological and political demands to face. Similarly, the preservation and growth of the church in its institutional dimension is not our goal, but to build church unity in the wider concept of the people of God (*laos tou Theou*) (*TTL* §§67-71). It is the dynamics of the interaction between social justice, the wisdom of ancient inhabitants and care for creation, together with the witness of our faith, that can guide us in a way of life that can become *Suma Qamaña*.

## The Art of Dialogue

> Dialogue is a way of affirming our common life and goals in terms of the affirmation of life and the integrity of creation. Dialogue at the religious level is possible only if we begin with the expectation of meeting God who has preceded us and has been present with people within their own contexts. God is there before we come (Acts 17) and our task is not to bring God along, but to witness to the God who is already there. Dialogue provides for an honest encounter where each party brings to the table all that they are in an open, patient and respectful manner (TTL §94).

Paul, in Romans 7, recognizes the ambiguity of our human condition. Far from being a defect, we recognize that ambiguity is necessary for open dialogue. When we become aware of our own flaws and failures, we will be more inclined to hear the other and learn from others instead of judging them. In Latin America, inter-faith dialogue cannot be limited to the great world religions, but has to take into account the many different native visions of the cosmos, the ancient cults of the original peoples and the diversity of spiritual learning brought by the different migrations, forced or voluntary.

There is little place for formal dialogue and doctrinal discussion. Meeting the other is a live experience that traverses peoples and cultures in the quest for good living. This is certainly a decisive matter in our continent, where more than five centuries of western domination has influenced every field of human life. So-called syncretism is the rule, not the exception. It cannot be considered as a defect in the missionary

---

[16] For the concept of laocracy, see Míguez, Rieger and Jung, *Beyond the Spirit*, chapter 6.

enterprise, but as the outcome of the way in which local people can really take hold of the Gospel message, out of their own categories and understanding, from their own way of feeling, reasoning and worshipping.

In Latin America, notwithstanding our different ethnic precedence, cultural background or religious stance, we are all transcultural (forgive the neologism) in our being. We are, more than in an intercultural dialogue, in a transcultural setting, where even language can give testimony to how the words and modes of expression have mixed in such a way that we use them without really knowing from which cultural trend they might have originated. The same thing happens with the arts, whether sculpture, pictorial or musical, in literature and artisan's craftsmanship.[17] Dialogue occurs within one's own community and even within one's own self. Our ambiguity is the uncertainty of all human beings, but also the product of our history and our hopes. Only fear born out of prejudice and haughtiness takes steps to deny our pluralistic heritage, and generates a shameful negation of what we really are. The true dialogue of faith is the assertion of our own diversity, and should be considered a unique opportunity to enjoy the plurality of which we are part.

The 'feast of life' in Latin America has many different musical sounds and dances. We will hear some dominant languages in many versions and, at the same time, the many languages of native peoples and migrant groups. We will appreciate the different skin shades of the original people, the Latin conquerors, of the blond north and East European migrants, together with people of African descent whose ancestors were brought in by slavery, or the many *mestizo* whose origins lie in the extensive interweaving that occurred. But it would be congregated around the *Suma Qamaña*, the search for good living.

## Working towards Life in Mission

How does this affect our theological understanding and education? How does this affect Christian mission? Traditional missions, whether the Catholic conquest or the evangelical mission wave, despised and condemned as superstition and demonic the local religions and visions of the cosmos. Yet, these prove today to have a better perception of the complex relationships of the universe than the rationalist and logocentric understanding brought about by the conceptual theology and dogmatism, or the exalted spiritualism imported from the North Atlantic missionary centres. The mission of the Christian faith today in Latin America is the fourfold task of caring for and enjoying the richness of creation, of building a people with its agreements and also its conflicts, of searching for social justice in the continent with the most uneven distribution of wealth, and thus proclaiming, in open dialogue and witness, hope in the life that, by

[17] See Míguez, 'Sociopolitical context'.

grace, we receive from the Creator God, in Jesus, the Messiah and the life-giving breath of the Spirit, the community of Godself that inspires human community.

# *TOGETHER TOWARDS LIFE* AND CONTEMPORARY AFRICAN THEOLOGY

Kenneth R. Ross

It is well known that Africa has been the scene of dramatic growth of Christianity, with the number of professing Christians increasing from an estimated 11,663,000 to 494,668,000 between 1910 and 2010.[1] As a result, the continent has become an important theatre for the exploration of the meaning of Christian faith. This exploration has been undertaken principally at a local level and in African languages. In recent decades, the results of this engagement with the faith have found expression also in more formal theological work. Three main trends can be discerned in contemporary African theology: inculturation, liberation and reconstruction.[2] This essay will consider the new World Council of Churches mission affirmation *Together towards Life* (*TTL*) using the lens provided by these three leading trends. First, however, there is a more fundamental matter to consider.

## The World of Spirit

Of great importance to communities right across the African continent is the world of spirit. Besides the physical world that is perceptible to our senses, Africans have been alert to the unseen world of the spirit as an equally valid sphere in shaping human life and destiny. In fact, the spirit world is considered the ultimate source of power. It has therefore been a source of perplexity to many that the new faith of Christianity, as introduced by western missionaries, seemed to have little connection with the spiritual dimension of life. They have found it compelling and convincing in many ways, but there has been a mismatch at the spiritual level, explained by Andrew Walls in these terms: 'Western theology is in general too small for Africa; it has been cut down to fit the small-scale

---

[1] Todd M. Johnson and Kenneth R. Ross (eds), *Atlas of Global Christianity, 1910-2010* (Edinburgh: Edinburgh University Press, 2009), 112.

[2] See further, Francis Anekwe Oborji, 'Theology', in Kenneth R. Ross, J. Kwabena Asamoah-Gyadu and Todd M. Johnson (eds), *Christianity in Sub-Saharan Africa: Edinburgh Companions to Global Christianity, Vol. 1* (Edinburgh: Edinburgh University Press, forthcoming 2017); see further, Francis Anekwe Oborji, *Trends in African Theology since Vatican II: A Missiological Orientation,* 2nd edition (Rome: Leberit Press, 2005).

universe demanded by the Enlightenment, which set and jealously guarded a frontier between the empirical world and the world of spirit. Much of humanity lives in a larger, more populated universe, in which the frontier is continually being crossed. It is a universe that comprehends what Paul calls the principalities and powers. Such is the background of the majority of the world's Christians, and it requires a theology that brings Christ to bear on every part of that universe.'[3] In pursuit of such a theology, Africans have created their own spiritual movements – whether by forming African Independent ('spirit') churches, joining the Pentecostal movement that is a dynamic force in today's Africa, or renewing the life and worship of their mission-founded churches so as to give them a more spiritual quality.

It is therefore music to the ears of African Christians to find *TTL* acknowledging the world of spirit that has always been of great importance to them: 'The early Christians, like many today, experienced a world of many spirits. The New Testament witnesses to diverse spirits, including evil spirits, 'ministering spirits' (i.e. angels, Heb. 1:14), 'principalities' and 'powers' (Eph. 6:12), the beast (Rev. 13:1-7), and other powers – both good and evil. The apostle Paul also testifies to some spiritual struggle (Eph. 6:10-18; 2 Cor. 10:4-6) and other apostolic writings contain injunctions to resist the devil (James 4:7; 1 Pet. 5:8)'.[4] More than in any previous ecumenical statement of the meaning of mission, *TTL* is a Holy Spirit document. Its confidence in the Holy Spirit leads it to engage spiritual reality with confidence: 'One of the gifts of the Spirit is the discernment of spirits (1 Cor. 12:10). We discern the Spirit of God wherever life in its fullness is affirmed and in all its dimensions, including liberation of the oppressed, healing and reconciliation of broken communities, and the restoration of creation. We also discern evil spirits wherever forces of death and destruction of life prevail.'[5] Thinking of Christian mission in these terms puts it on a wavelength that will have a wide reach in Africa.

The call to engage the spiritual level is foundational to *TTL*. Its introduction includes the following statement that will strike a chord in Africa: 'Life in the Holy Spirit is the essence of mission, the core of why we do what we do and how we live our lives. Spirituality gives the deepest meaning to our lives and motivates our actions. It is a sacred gift from the Creator, the energy for affirming and caring for life. This mission spirituality has a dynamic of transformation which, through the spiritual commitment of people, is capable of transforming the world in God's grace.'[6] Such an orientation goes a long way towards answering the African cry for a more spiritual expression of the faith. We turn our attention now

---

[3] Andrew F. Walls, 'Commission One: "Carrying the Gospel to all the Non-Christian World"', in David A. Kerr and Kenneth R. Ross (eds), *Edinburgh 2010: Mission Then and Now* (Oxford: Regnum, 2009), 27-40 at 38.

[4] *TTL*, §25.

[5] *TTL*, §24.

[6] *TTL*, §3.

to another major concern of African theology – to ascertain whether or not it is met by the affirmations of *TTL*.

## Inculturation of the Gospel

The first generation of African theologians, whose work was being published from the 1970s, were greatly preoccupied with countering the widely-held view that Christianity was a western religion imposed upon Africa. As Desmond Tutu wrote: '[The missionaries] have consciously or unconsciously sought to Europeanise us before they could Christianize us. They have consequently jeopardised the entire Christian enterprise since Christianity has failed to be rooted sufficiently deeply in the African soil, since they have tended to make us feel somewhat uneasy about what we could not alter even if we had tried until doomsday – our Africanness.'[7] *TTL* strikes a chord with African sensibilities when it admits: 'The connection of evangelism with colonial powers in the history of mission has led to the presupposition that Western forms of Christianity are the standards by which others' adherence to the gospel should be judged.'[8] It issues a ringing call to the churches to take an entirely different direction:

> The Spirit inspires human cultures and creativity, so it is part of our mission to acknowledge, respect and co-operate with life-giving wisdoms in every culture and context. We regret that mission activity linked with colonization has often denigrated cultures and failed to recognize the wisdom of local people. Local wisdom and culture which are life-affirming are gifts from God's Spirit. We lift up testimonies of peoples whose traditions have been scorned and mocked by theologians and scientists, yet whose wisdom offers us the vital and sometimes new orientation that can connect us again with the life of the Spirit in creation, which helps us to consider the ways in which God is revealed in creation.[9]

African theologians who have struggled long and hard to express Christian faith in terms of African culture will surely feel vindicated by this Spirit-centred affirmation of indigenous wisdom and culture offered by *TTL*.

In fact, they have already advanced a long way down the path proposed by *TTL*. As Kwame Bediako has observed: 'The main thrust of African Christian scholarship has been the argument that "conversion" to Christianity must be coupled with cultural continuity. In its specific application to Africa, the argument has meant that, against all the odds, space had to be made for a positive pre-Christian religious heritage in the African Christian consciousness on the grounds that "religion informs the

---

[7] Desmond M.B. Tutu, 'Some African Insights and the Old Testament', in Hans-Jürgen Becken (ed), *Relevant Theology for Africa* (Durban, RSA: Lutheran Publishing House, 1973), 40-46 at 41.

[8] *TTL*, §98.

[9] *TTL*, §27.

African's life in its totality".'[10] In order to open up such space, African theologians set out to express Christian faith in terms of African culture. This led them into a sustained dialogue with African Traditional Religion. This was something that had been implicit in the engagement of African communities with the Christian message but was now articulated through the work of scholars like John Mbiti and Bolaji Idowu.[11] Mbiti called on African Christians to express in theological terms the leading role they now occupied in world Christianity, the goal being to bring to expression an African Christianity that is both fully African and fully Christian.

The central question in this enterprise was expressed by Congolese theologian Bénézet Bujo in these terms: 'In which way can Jesus Christ be an African among the Africans according to their own religious experience?'[12] The attempt to answer this question has involved understanding Christ in terms of categories familiar within African culture such as liberator, ancestor, firstborn son, master of initiation, healer, king, chief, mediator, saviour, and redeemer with power. Particularly potent has been the idea of Christ as ancestor which seems to have suggested itself independently to numerous African theologians in different parts of the continent. It has been expounded in great depth by Bujo himself, by John Pobee of Ghana[13] and by Charles Nyamiti of Tanzania in his seminal work, *Christ as Our Ancestor: Christology from an African Perspective.*[14] These theologians found it meaningful to speak of Jesus as Ancestor par excellence, for in him are fulfilled all the qualities and virtues that Africans ascribe to their ancestors. In other words, the historical Jesus fulfils the highest ideals ascribed to the ancestors in African thought – he heals, he cures, he raises the dead, and so on. In short, he imparts life force in all its fullness. This love and power he bequeaths, after death, to his disciples. It is precisely in his death and resurrection, with its soteriological meaning, that Jesus transcends the ancestors. Considering the meaning of faith in Christ in terms of the cherishing of ancestors found throughout Africa is one way in which theologians such as Bujo, Pobee and Nyamiti have sought to root Christian faith in African reality.

---

[10] Kwame Bediako, *Christianity in Africa: The Renewal of a Non-Western Religion* (Maryknoll, New York: Orbis Books, and Edinburgh: Edinburgh University Press, 1995), 77.

[11] See E. Bolaji Idowu, *Olodumare: God in Yoruba Belief* (London: Longmans, 1962); E. Bolaji Idowu, *African Traditional Religion: A Definition* (Maryknoll, New York, Orbis Books: 1974); John S. Mbiti, *African Religions and Philosophy* (London: Heinemann, 1969); John S. Mbiti, *Introduction to African Religion* (London: Heinemann, 1975).

[12] Bénézet Bujo, *African Theology in its Social Context* (Maryknoll, New York: Orbis Books, 1992), 75.

[13] John S. Pobee, *Towards an African Theology* (Nashville, TN: Abingdon Press, 1979).

[14] Charles Nyamiti, *Christ as Our Ancestor: Christology from an African Perspective* (Eldoret, Kenya; Gaba Publications, 1984).

In its section on 'Evangelism and Cultures', *TTL* calls for an approach that is deeply rooted in the kind of inculturation that has been championed by African theologians: 'The gospel takes root in different contexts through engagement with specific cultural, political and religious realities. Respect for people and their cultural and symbolic life-worlds are necessary if the gospel is to take root in those different realities. In this way it must begin with engagement and dialogue with the wider context in order to discern how Christ is already present and where God's Spirit is already at work.'[15] This is a mandate which has already been taken up and fulfilled with remarkable results, though the enterprise is still in its first generation and ripe for further development. African theologians are already actively mining their cultural heritage so as to be able to contribute fully to the expression of Christian faith envisaged by *TTL*: 'We cannot capture the complexities of the scriptures through one dominant cultural perspective. A plurality of cultures is a gift of the Spirit to deepen our understanding of our faith and one another.'[16]

African theologians, in turn, may bring to the wider *oecumene* the kind of challenge expressed in the words of John Mbiti: 'There cannot be theological conversation or dialogue between North and South, East and West, until we can embrace each other's concerns and stretch to each other's horizons. Theologians from the southern continents believe that they know about most of the constantly changing concerns of older Christendom. They would also like their counterparts from the older Christendom to come to know about their concerns of human survival.'[17] The time is ripe for a pilgrimage of true theological reciprocity and mutuality. The steps in this direction taken by *TTL* will be welcomed within African Christianity as something long overdue.

## The Cry for Liberation

Deep in the soul of African Christians lies the yearning for their faith to be rooted in their culture. The quest for inculturation remains fundamental. Yet there is another cry to which African theologians have felt obliged to respond. There are urgent social, political and economic questions to be addressed. A theology of inculturation, on its own, may not be enough. As Desmond Tutu has written: 'I fear that African theology has failed to produce a sufficiently sharp cutting edge. It has indeed performed a good job by addressing the split in the African soul, and yet it has by and large failed to speak meaningfully in the face of a plethora of contemporary

---

[15] *TTL,* §97.

[16] *TTL,* §100.

[17] John S. Mbiti, 'Theological Impotence and Universality of the Church', in Gerald H. Anderson and Thomas F. Stransky (eds), *Mission Trends No. 3: Third World Theologies* (New York: Paulist, and Grand Rapids, MI: Eerdmans, 1976), 6-18 at 17.

problems which assail the modern African. It has seemed to advocate disengagement from the hectic business of life, because very little has been offered that is pertinent, say, about the theology of power in the face of the epidemic of coups and military rule, about development, about poverty and disease and other equally urgent present-day issues.'[18] The need to address the multi-faceted crisis in which Africa has been embroiled in its recent history has concentrated the mind of many African theologians.

Perhaps the most representative is Jean-Marc Éla who has sought to articulate theology out of his pastoral experience with the Kirdi people of Tokombèrè village in northern Cameroon and turn it into a theological paradigm. For Éla, the shock which the local church might have experienced through its pastoral experience was the realization that even though a greater part of Africa is a deeply and massively Christian region, 'it tends to remain a veritable empire of hunger'.[19] He asks the question: how could the local church co-exist with such a situation without 'shocking' it with the gospel? In his writings, Éla captures various angles of this 'shock' as he describes the frustration, the apparently meaningless existence, the extreme and paralyzing poverty, the violation of basic human rights, the colonial and neo-colonial violence, and the multinational exploitation, as well as hunger experienced by the people. It is this 'rough ground' that, according to Éla, provides the unique context and challenge for Christianity and theology in Africa today: 'Our practice of Christian faith faces a major challenge from African men and women who agonize over where their next meal is coming from.'[20]

Éla has no hesitation in facing up to these harsh realities now presenting themselves in post-colonial Africa: 'The battles for independence gave birth in the hearts of so many Africans to hope for a new world. But after more than twenty years of experience with democracy African-style, independence has turned out to be a sham and a decoy. For many, the situation is worse than it was before. Black persecutes, tortures, murders black…'[21] While he is by no means unsympathetic to inculturation theology, Éla's analysis leads him to be critical of an African theology that seems to assume that African society and churches 'can achieve their identity by considering only anthropological and cultural problems'.[22] In his view, such preoccupation with cultural identity could be a dangerous alibi, employed so as to ignore the more burning issues in contemporary

[18] Desmond Tutu, 'Black Theology/African Theology: Soul Mates or Antagonists?', in James S. Cone and Gayraud S. Wilmore, *Black Theology: A Documentary History, Vol. I 1966-79, 2nd edition* (Maryknoll, New York: Orbis Books, 1993), 385-92 at 386.

[19] Jean-Marc Éla, *My Faith as an African* (Maryknoll, New York: Orbis Books, 1988), 87.

[20] Éla, *My Faith as an African*, 87.

[21] Jean-Marc Éla, *African Cry* (Maryknoll, New York: Orbis Books, 1986), 46.

[22] Éla, *My Faith as an African,* 118.

Africa. What is needed instead, according to Éla, is an inculturation which is relevant to the culture that is being born out of daily struggles of Africans for survival.

The daily social and political realities which shape African life form the context in which theology requires to be done. 'In our environment,' Éla contends, 'our faith does not ask questions about the sex of angels or the infallibility of the Pope; instead we question the lack of any genuine application of the critical function inherent in Christian faith. How can we show that the African church is blocked by an ecclesiastical praxis that is, in fact, a kind of museum of narrow moralism, a ritualistic sacramentalism, a disembodied spirituality and a withering dogmatics?'[23] Éla himself attempts to give a lead in awakening the critical function inherent in Christian faith: 'We have been permanently reduced, it seems, to a situation where poverty and oppression surround a few islands of affluence. A multitude of the oppressed are up against an elite that always tends to reinforce its position of power by setting up a system whose results are clear.'[24] Éla is not afraid to identify the forces which operate to create such a situation: 'Almost everywhere throughout the black continent, the various forms of coercive apparatus of the multinationals guarantee optimal conditions for the over-exploitation of human labour and natural resources.'[25]

The 'cry' articulated by Éla and others finds an emphatic answer in *TTL*. While it grounds Christian mission, more fundamentally than ever before, in spirituality, it is clear that what it seeks to promote is a *transformative* spirituality[26] – one which is fully engaged with the kind of realities with which Éla is concerned. 'Mission spirituality,' argues *TTL*, 'motivates us to serve God's economy of life, not mammon, to share life at God's table rather than satisfy individual greed, to pursue change toward a better world while challenging the self-interest of the powerful who desire to maintain the status quo.'[27] It quotes from an earlier WCC document to ground its commitment to transformation and justice: 'Our faithfulness to God and God's free gift of life compels us to confront idolatrous assumptions, unjust systems, and the politics of domination and exploitation in our current world economic order. Economics and economic justice are always matters of faith as they touch the very core of God's will for creation.'[28]

*TTL* is perhaps at its most trenchant when addressing the injustice inherent in the prevailing economic system of globalization: 'The policy of unlimited growth through the domination of the global free market is an

---

[23] Éla, *My Faith as an African*, 153.
[24] Éla, *My Faith as an African*, 89-90.
[25] Éla, *My Faith as an African*, 89.
[26] *TTL*, §29.
[27] *TTL*, §30.
[28] *Alternative Globalization Addressing Peoples and Earth (AGAPE): A Background Document* (Geneva: WCC, 2005), 13; cf. *TTL*, §30.

ideology that claims to be without alternative, demanding an endless flow of sacrifices from the poor and from nature.'[29] In offering a prophetic critique of the currently prevailing system of economic globalization, *TTL* quotes from the 2004 'Accra Confession' of the World Alliance of Reformed Churches: 'It makes the false promise that it can save the world through creation of wealth and prosperity, claiming sovereignty over life and demanding total allegiance, which amounts to idolatry.'[30] An answer to Jean-Marc Éla's 'African cry' can be found when *TTL* strikes a confrontational note: 'This is a global system of mammon that protects the unlimited growth of wealth of only the rich and powerful through endless exploitation. This tower of greed is threatening the whole household of God. The reign of God is in direct opposition to the empire of mammon.'[31]

The need to counter systems of injustice and bring liberation to the oppressed has perhaps had no clearer articulation on the African continent than it has in the Black Theology of South Africa.[32] In a highly polarised situation where power, wealth and privilege were concentrated on one side, and poverty, oppression and suffering on the other, proponents of Black Theology like Mokgethi Motlhabi, Allan Boesak and Manas Buthelezi took up the biblical theme that God takes sides with the oppressed, just as God did when the people of Israel were being oppressed in Egypt. In the perspective of Black Theology, the social location of the theologian is critical to the formation of a proper understanding of God. When the church has moved to the centre of society and is identified with the rich, the powerful and the dominant, then it becomes so much bound up with their interests that it finds it impossible to come to terms with the God of the Bible. It is only those who look from the margins, from the vantage point of poverty and suffering, who are in a position to understand the God who revealed himself to the poor and suffering, as indicated in the biblical record. For its own integrity, theology must move out to the margins of society and see things with the eyes of the poor.

Advocates of Black Theology will surely feel that their point has been taken when they find that 'mission from the margins' is one of the most distinctive and provocative emphases of *TTL*: 'Mission from the margins recognizes that being in the centre means having access to systems that lead to one's rights, freedom and individuality being affirmed and

---

[29] *TTL*, §31.

[30] World Alliance of Reformed Churches, *The Accra Confession: Covenanting for Justice: in the Economy and the Earth* (2004), §10; cf. *TTL*, §31.

[31] *TTL*, §31.

[32] See Mokgethi Motlhabi, 'Black Theology: A Personal View', in Basil Moore (ed), *Black Theology: the South African Voice* (London: C. Hurst & Co.,1973); Allan A. Boesak, *Black Theology Black Power* (London: Mowbray, 1978); Allan A. Boesak, *Black and Reformed* (Maryknoll, New York: Orbis Books, 1984); Manas Buthelezi, 'African Theology and Black Theology', in Becken, *Relevant Theology for Africa*, 18-24.

respected; living on the margins means exclusion from justice and dignity. Living on the margins, however, can provide its own lessons. People on the margins have agency, and can often see what, from the centre, is out of view.'[33] One of the core convictions of *TTL* is that it is precisely from the margins that authentic Christian mission can be undertaken. It works from the basis that 'Jesus Christ relates to and embraces those who are most marginalized in society, in order to confront and transform all that denies life. This includes cultures and systems which generate and sustain massive poverty, discrimination and dehumanization, and which exploit or destroy people and the earth. Mission from the margins calls for an understanding of the complexities of power dynamics, global systems and structures and local contextual realities'.[34] The understanding that mission needs to be undertaken from the margins is one that connects with both African Theology and Black Theology.

## Time for Reconstruction

Just as African theology of inculturation was criticised for its lack of attention to the social, political and economic dimensions of life, so the corrective efforts of theologians like Jean-Marc Éla have been subject to criticism for offering a Liberation Theology that begins and ends only in lamentations without showing a way of 'getting out of the jungle'. It is perhaps significant that Allan Boesak entitled the final chapter of his book on Black Theology, 'Beyond the Sorrow Songs'.[35] A sense that there was need for a more constructive theology was the inspiration for a conference called by the All Africa Conference of Churches in Mombasa in 1991. The Cold War had ended, the apartheid system in South Africa was finally crumbling, and soon there would be talk of an African Renaissance. There was a need for a theology which would engage these new realities. The response to this challenge generated by the Mombasa conference was styled a theology of reconstruction, with Kenyan theologian Jesse Mugambi as its chief architect.[36] This new theological direction was not an abrupt departure since it continued to emphasise the themes of inculturation and liberation, but it did bring a new awareness of the responsibility of theologians to contribute, in a positive way, to the transformation of society.

This was a call to which theologians in different parts of the continent were ready to respond. Notable work was done, for example, by Charles

---

[33] *TTL,* §38.
[34] *TTL,* §37.
[35] Boesak, *Black Theology*, 123-52.
[36] See Jesse N.K. Mugambi, *From Liberation to Reconstruction: African Christian Theology after the Cold War* (Nairobi: East African Educational Publishers, 1995); Jesse N.K. Mugambi, *Christian Theology and Social Reconstruction* (Nairobi: Acton, 2003).

Villa-Vicencio in South Africa, Kä Mana of the DRC, and Valentin Dedji of Cameroon.[37] In the view of these theologians of reconstruction, both inculturation and liberation responded to a situation of ecclesiastical and colonial bondage which no longer obtains. In place of the inculturation-liberation paradigm, which they saw as 'reactive', they sought to install a 'pro-active' theology of reconstruction. Instead of being preoccupied with the ascendancy of liberation over inculturation or vice versa – a matter which is still of great debate – advocates of a theology of reconstruction call for an innovative transcendence of both. It is theology addressed to the public domain, seeking to bring a vision of Christ crucified and risen to bear on the challenges of creating new social, political and economic structures in Africa.

The African theology of reconstruction will find its concerns are voiced also in *TTL*. The new WCC mission statement is inspired by a lofty theological vision, but is equally aware that this vision needs to be brought to expression in concrete terms in our contemporary societies:

> The affirmation of God's mission (*missio Dei*) points to the belief in God as One who acts in history and in creation, in concrete realities of time and contexts, who seeks the fullness of life for the whole earth through justice, peace and reconciliation. Participation in God's ongoing work of liberation and reconciliation by the Holy Spirit, therefore, includes discerning and unmasking the demons that exploit and enslave. For example, this involves deconstructing patriarchal ideologies, upholding the right to self-determination for indigenous peoples, and challenging the social embeddedness of racism and casteism.[38]

A significant contribution to the theology of reconstruction has been made by African women theologians, such as Mercy Oduyoye, Musimbi Kanyoro and Isabel Phiri, who have sharply questioned the hierarchical and discriminatory patterns which have prevailed both in church and society.[39] Their critique finds an echo in *TTL* with its insistence that, 'Participation in God's mission follows the way of Jesus, who came to serve, not to be served (Mark 10:45); who tears down the mighty and powerful and exalts the lowly (Luke 1:46-55); and whose love is characterized by mutuality, reciprocity and interdependence. It therefore requires a commitment to

---

[37] Charles Villa-Vicencio, *A Theology of Reconstruction: Nation-Building and Human Rights* (Cambridge: CUP, 1992); Kä Mana, *L'Afrique va-t-elle Mourir: Bousculer L'imaginaire Africain. Essai D'éthique Politique* (Paris: Éditions du Cerf, 1991), Valentin Dedji, *Reconstruction and Renewal in African Theology* (Nairobi: Acton, 2003).

[38] *TTL*, §43.

[39] See Mercy Amba Oduyoye and Musimbi R.A. Kanyoro (eds), *The Will to Arise: Women, Tradition, and the Church in Africa* (Maryknoll: New York, 1992); Mercy Amba Oduyoye, *Daughters of Anowa: African Women and Patriarchy* (Maryknoll, New York: Orbis Books, 1995); Isabel Apawo Phiri, *Women, Presbyterianism and Patriarchy: Religious Experience of Chewa Women in Central Malawi* (Blantyre: CLAIM, 1997).

struggle against and resist the powers that obstruct the fullness of life that God wills for all, and a willingness to work with all people involved in movements and initiatives committed to the causes of justice, dignity and life.'[40]

Another contribution of African women theologians has been to promote a collaborative, collective, rather than individualist, approach to the task of theology. This concern is also evident in the theology of reconstruction, with reference being made to the conversational and communicative styles in African cultures, which are captured in the writings of some African scholars with the word *palaver*. Drawing on strong African traditions of resolving issues through community discussion, theologians like Agbonkhianmeghe Orobator have advocated a more conversational and communicative mode of doing theology.[41] This sense of interrelation and reciprocity, which draws on currents that run deep in African life, chimes in well with the *TTL* affirmation: 'The good news of God's reign is about the promise of the actualization of a just and inclusive world. Inclusivity fosters just relationships in the community of humanity and creation, with mutual acknowledgement of persons and creation, and mutual respect and sustenance of each one's sacred worth.'[42] It is also notable that one quarter of *TTL* is devoted to 'Spirit of Community: Church on the Move' – the communal expression of Christian faith.[43]

## Conclusion

Space does not allow for the exploration of other features of *TTL* that resonate with contemporary African theology, such as the need to relate mission to the flourishing of creation,[44] the call to confident but sensitive evangelism,[45] or the importance of dialogue with people of other faiths as a 'mutual encounter of commitments'.[46] However, by noting the spiritual key in which *TTL* is set and tracing its relevance to the leading concerns of African theologians – inculturation, liberation, and reconstruction – it is already apparent that this is a mission affirmation which has embraced major issues facing Christianity in Africa today. There is good reason to believe that it will prove to be a highly relevant text for the consideration of

---

[40] *TTL,* §45.

[41] See Agbonkhianmeghe E. Orobator (ed), *Reconciliation, Justice and Peace: The Second African Synod* (Maryknoll, New York: Orbis Books, 2011); Agbonkhianmeghe E. Orobator (ed), *Theological Re-imagination: Conversations on Church, Religion, and Society in Africa* (Nairobi: Paulines, 2014).

[42] *TTL,* §46.

[43] *TTL,* §55-79.

[44] *TTL,* §19-23.

[45] *TTL,* §80-88.

[46] *TTL,* §89-96.

mission questions in Africa, and to be confident that its emphases will be broadened and deepened as they are explored in the African context.

# *TOGETHER TOWARDS LIFE* AND CONTEMPORARY WESTERN THEOLOGY

Beate Fagerli

## Introduction

This chapter will attempt to give some perspectives on the document *Together towards Life (TTL)* based on input from some western churches. To give a fuller account of western theology in dialogue with *TTL* would not be possible in this format. While preparing this article, information and material was collected from churches in Europe and North America, by contacting colleagues in church and mission, asking for official responses or personal reflections on *TTL*. Some of these will be presented at the beginning of this chapter. In order to single out certain themes for further discussion, parts of the contemporary missiological discussion in Norway will be presented. Based on this, this chapter will suggest some main challenges for western churches as well as challenges for continued missiological discussion in the World Council of Churches (WCC) and the Commission on World Mission and Evangelism (CWME). The theological perspectives presented here will therefore basically be the perspectives coming from certain historic churches in Northern Europe, predominantly from Protestant traditions and from the evangelical movement.

## Background

After the WCC Central Committee's approval of *TTL* in 2012, the document was widely distributed to churches and organisations. Since responses to my request for information on the reception of *TTL* in the churches are limited, this article cannot do justice to all contemporary western theology. It is therefore based on feedback largely received from Northern Europe.[1] However, these responses indicate that the content and style of *TTL* has made it well suited for further study. It seems *TTL* has been widely distributed within churches and mission organisations. Many

[1] In preparing this article, an informal request was sent to colleagues in a number of churches. Information on reception processes have come from the Evangelical Lutheran Church of Finland, the Finnish Missionary Council, Church of Sweden, the Evangelical Lutheran Church in Denmark, the Danish Mission Council, the Scottish Episcopal Church, the Church of Scotland, the Church of England, as well as the Christian Council of Norway, the Church of Norway and the Norwegian Mission Council.

churches, organisations, mission boards or Christian councils have translated the document, initiated studies locally, and made it the topic of thematic consultations and ecumenical dialogues. The document is also being studied in missiological departments of educational institutions.

The informal responses received have overall been positive to, and even enthusiastic about, *TTL*. The feedback suggests that the angle chosen in the document, by anchoring the concept of God's mission (*missio Dei*) in the Trinitarian God, and developing a pneumatological perspective rooted in Trinitarian theology throughout the document, provide renewed and refreshing missiological insight. Furthermore, although the definition of mission is very broad, many churches seem to agree with *TTL*'s overall definition of mission given in the first part of the document (*TTL* §§1-11). A holistic scope of mission which includes not only all people, but the whole of creation, is also much appreciated (e.g. *TTL* §20). The importance of the shift of the centre of gravity for world Christianity from the West to the South and East is recognized by western churches. Also, the responses seem to agree that the concluding affirmations of the document (*TTL* §§101 and 112) provide an updated view on mission.

On a more critical note, the feedback received from different churches raises questions on some of the topics in the document. One important question concerns the use of the term 'marginalized' and the concept of 'mission from the margins'. It is not felt that Jesus is making a case for the poor that seems to be critically questioned. Rather, it is the definition of 'margins', and who makes that definition, which raises a question. Has the document been written *by* the marginalised, or for the marginalised, or is the use of 'marginalisd' a way of idealising 'the other'?[2]

Another main point of criticism seems to be linked with the understanding of evangelism and what it entails. Although the pneumatological reading of God's mission rooted in a Trinitarian understanding is much appreciated, several churches and mission bodies seem to be expressing the fact that they miss a deeper Christological understanding of mission.[3] Some questions are raised regarding the use of scriptural passages, which in places seem to be somewhat arbitrary or slightly superficial. The most significant questions are raised in connection with Jesus' teaching on the coming of the Reign of God and the understanding of what salvation means in regard to this.[4]

---

[2] Email from the Revd Dr Tomi Karttunen of the Evangelical Lutheran Church of Finland, 11th June 2015, summarising analyses of *TTL* offered in the (Finnish language) *Journal of Mission Theology*, Vol. 16 (2013).

[3] Email from Tomi Karttunen, 11th June 2015.

[4] Rolf Kjøde, 'Spirit of Pentecost: Good news for all! An approach to evangelization and dialogue'. Paper presented at the Missiological Forum, Oslo, 22nd November 2012: http://norme.no/aktuelt/detaljer/journey-together-again

In order to try to understand the content of these questions, we will look more closely at contemporary missiological discussion in Norway in the wake of *TTL*.

## Mission from the Margins

Following the Central Committee's approval of *TTL* in 2012, the Norwegian Council for Mission and Evangelism (NORME) invited Dr Jooseop Keum, the director of CWME, to introduce the document at a Missiological Forum day in Oslo, Norway, on 22nd November 2012. His introduction was on 'Dynamism and Diversity',[5] and was followed by a number of responses to different parts of *TTL* given by Norwegian church leaders, ecumenists and missiologists. The responses were largely very positive. The Revd Knut Refsdal, the General Secretary of the Christian Council of Norway, put it as follows:

> It is my hope that this document can contribute to the building of bridges between different directions within the churches and guide us all towards a deeper understanding of what it means to be church in our time.[6]

The document also inspired thoughts on mission at the heart of the very being of the church, as well as on the link between mission and ecumenism. The Rt Revd Helga Haugland Byfuglien, the presiding bishop of the Church of Norway, picked up from *TTL* the need for the church to be on the move, because God is on the move. This movement is created by God's love, which always reaches beyond itself. *TTL*'s potential as an ecumenical study project for church unity and mission as the essence of being church was thereby highlighted. From there she goes on to describe how mission and ecumenical theology are intertwined, linking it with the geographical shift in mission:

> … if mission is the essence of the **entire** Church… if mission belongs to the **whole** church, not only to churches of western societies, mission is ecumenical and something that we need to do together. Churches in the West must be influenced by the mission activity of churches from the South. The reason for this is that context always influences missional activity. The social location of all engaged in mission must therefore be taken into account.[7]

It seems Bishop Helga Byfuglien grasps a key point in *TTL*: that the shift of the centre of world Christianity must influence the way we do mission, and that 'mission from the margins' may provide a necessary change of perspective. She does not understand this change of perspective to be

---

[5] Jooseop Keum, 'Dynamism and Diversity: An Ecumenical perspective on Mission in Changing Landscapes', Missiological Forum, 22nd November 2012.

[6] Knut Refsdal, 'Together towards Life'. Presentation given at the Missiological Forum, Oslo, 22nd November 2012.

[7] Helga Haugland Byfuglien, 'Spirit of community: Church on the move'. Presentation given at the Missiological Forum, Oslo, 22nd November 2012.

exclusive, however, but as inclusive: '... so is the gospel of Christ a gospel that does not belong only to one part of the world, but to the entire world, crossing all cultures and nations.' However, since Refsdal was giving a response to the *TTL* chapter 'Spirit of Liberation: Mission from the Margins', he raised a question regarding this perspective:

> One last comment and question regarding the terms 'margins' and 'centre': I understand the rationale behind this terminology. Nevertheless, as I read the Bible, and especially the teachings of Jesus, who again and again turned things upside down, the only people that are located on the margins are those that believe that they are in the centre. Are we among them? If so, we have to rethink this terminology.[8]

As I understand Refsdal, he is not against a change of perspective, but questions whether the terms 'margins' and 'centre' are useful when describing a change of perspective based on the teaching of Jesus, who turns perspectives upside down. The use of this terminology was discussed further, raising questions about who the marginalised are, and in which context. What is a majority and a minority when defining who the marginalised are? Is a polarised division between people living on the margins and people at the centre an accurate description in any context? This question is particularly relevant with regard to the aim of mission as described in *TTL*:

> The aim of mission is not simply to move people from the margins to the centres of power but to confront those who remain the centre by keeping people on the margins. Instead, churches are called to *transform* power structures (*TTL* §40).

From Finland, another question is raised regarding the concept 'mission from the margins', and whether it tends to idealise the notion of 'the other'.[9] The Theological Commission of the Council on Ecumenical and International relations in the Church of Norway has noted that the term 'marginalised' has become a central term in several ecumenical documents. But since the meaning of 'marginalised' is dependent on which context it is being used, a clearer definition and further analysis of the understanding of the terms 'power' and the 'centres of power' would be useful.[10]

All these questions may seem to rise from the perspective of a western context, historically understood to be at the 'centres of power'. In that case, churches and mission in the western world should be directly challenged by the change of perspective *TTL* brings. This, however, may be to oversimplify the question of context.

---

[8] Knut Refsdal, 'Together towards Life'.

[9] Email from Tomi Karttunen, 11th June 2015.

[10] From the Theological Commission's discussion on the WCC document *Diakonia in the Twenty First Century: Theological Perspectives*, minutes of the Theological Commission meeting, 4th-5th October 2012.

In Denmark, Dr Anna Marie Aagaard, a well-known missiologist, gave a keynote address on 'Spirit and Mission' to the Danish Mission Council in 2014.[11] She gives a positive account of the renewal of the pneumatological understanding of mission in *TTL*. However, towards the end of her address, she looks at the phrase in the title of *TTL* '… in changing landscapes', and asks for a more in-depth analysis of why the landscapes (in which mission takes place) are changing. In a time of globalisation and climate change, it is easy to get the feeling that things are out of hand, she says: the world is out of control. In such a context, fear has become a worldview. This must be part of the background for understanding mission in changing landscapes. Mission must challenge fear as a worldview.

## The Reign of God

Another central theme running through *TTL* is the understanding of Jesus′ teaching on the coming of the Reign of God as a world where fullness of life is available for all.[12] There seems to be no contradiction to this understanding from the material we have collected from the churches. But several questions related to the understanding of Christ′s role in the coming of the reign of God have been raised. Although supportive of the Trinitarian basis of *TTL*, feedback from Finland indicates that a weakness of the document is that the pneumatological approach rules out Christology. As a consequence, it becomes unclear why reconciliation is needed.[13] Although the incarnation, death and resurrection of Christ are mentioned (§56, 80), *TTL* does not develop the theme as central to the reconciliation between God and Creation.[14]

At the Missiological Forum in November 2012, I was asked to give a short response to *TTL* with a special consideration of the future.[15] In this presentation I referred back to the WCC Conference on World Mission and Evangelism in Athens in 2005, and the two main themes of that conference: healing and reconciliation. *TTL* has taken up and developed the

---

[11] Dr Anna Marie Aagaard: 'Ånd og Mission', keynote address given at the Danish Mission Council in 2013: https://soundcloud.com/dansk-missionsrad/anna-marie-aagaard-nd-og (accessed 17th June 2015).

[12] *TTL,* §37, 44, 46, 56, 67, 88, 91, 102.

[13] Email from Tomi Karttunen, 11th June 2015

[14] This view does not take into account the work of CWME on 'Reconciliation as a new paradigm for Mission', following the Conference on World Mission and Evangelism in 2005. See J. Matthey (ed), *Come Holy Spirit, Heal and Reconcile! Called to be Reconciling and Healing Communities – Report of the WCC Conference on World Mission and Evangelism, Athens, Greece* (Geneva: WCC, 2008), and *International Review of Mission*, 103.2 (399) (November, 2014): 'Evangelism as Discipleship' (entire volume).

[15] Beate Fagerli, 'Mission and Evangelism today and for the future – Mission in Dialogue, Dialogue in Mission', Missiological Forum, Oslo, 22nd November 2012.

pneumatological focus from the Athens conference, and a holistic view on healing in mission is set out. But the theme of reconciliation has not received the same kind of attention in *TTL*, at least not from a Christological point of view. In classical western theology, the concept of reconciliation is closely connected with the death and resurrection of Christ, which is God's ultimate act in reconciling the sinful world with the Creator. The point of my input was the need for dialogue between a classical western understanding of salvation and *TTL*'s notion of the Reign of God.

The question of *TTL*'s view of salvation became a major issue at the Missiological Forum. First, the Revd Dr Tormod Engelsviken gave a historical account of the dialogue between CWME and the World Evangelical Alliance,[16] where he outlined the main reasons and the main obstacles for co-operation between CWME and the evangelical movement. Traditionally, evangelical mission has given priority to the proclamation of salvation through faith in Jesus Christ. Jesus' teaching on the coming of the Reign of God has thus been related to faith in Christ defeating death, where salvation is understood strictly as eternal life for the faithful. For the evangelical movement, one of the main obstacles to co-operation with the WCC has been that the WCC has not given enough priority to proclamation of the Gospel understood as the only way to salvation.

This understanding of salvation was reiterated by the input of the Revd Rolf Kjøde, the then General Secretary of Normisjon, a major mission organisation in Norway. In his input he makes a comparison between *TTL* and the *Cape Town Commitment* (*CTC*):[17]

> I struggle to find clear expression in *TTL* about the ultimate goal of the gospel and consequently of God's mission through his church: eternal salvation. In its preamble, *CTC* is very clear on what it calls 'unchanged realities': the lostness of human beings in sin and rebellion under the judgement of God. This is the background for the Gospel, which saves us through faith in Jesus Christ alone, a salvation which stretches far beyond death and resurrection in the coming Kingdom of God.[18]

Kjøde's input must be seen in the light of the invitation to join the CWME given by Dr Jooseop Keum to NORME, where Kjøde's organisation Normisjon is a member. The invitation is historic, as the Norwegian Mission Council (NORME's predecessor) left the International Missionary Council (IMC) in 1961, when IMC joined the WCC. NMC left on the grounds of disagreement over the question of a leading norm for

---

[16] Tormod Engelsviken, 'Some perspectives on Mission and Evangelisation the last thirty years'. Paper given at the Missiological Forum, Oslo, 22nd November 2012.

[17] The *Cape Town Commitment*, © The Lausanne Movement, 2011. The document can be downloaded at: www.lausanne.org/content/ctc/ctcommitment

[18] Rolf Kjøde, 'Spirit of Pentecost: Good news for all! An approach to evangelization and dialogue'.

theology and mission.[19] Through his response, Kjøde turned the invitation down:

> Although I am in favour of good relations and forums for conversation, we must admit that the gap between the evangelical and the ecumenical movement is still so significant on decisive questions that we should still journey separately.[20]

The missiological discussion in Norway continued between representatives of the ecumenical and evangelical movements through meetings and in journals. Evangelical representatives clearly expressed the conviction that the positive change in church ecumenism regarding views on evangelism was a signal that the churches of the South and East were being strengthened at the expense of more liberal ones in the North and West.[21] This not only expresses what, from an evangelical point of view, is seen as a positive development in documents like *TTL*. It also presupposes that churches in the East and South now have greater influence on what is said in ecumenical documents, and assumes that these churches are less liberal than those in the North and West. This point is reiterated in the desire that the evangelical voice of the Church of Norway can help voices from the South and East to be further strengthened against the liberal understanding with which westerners have too long dominated church ecumenics.[22]

This point of departure is based on a certain traditional Lutheran theology, where 'faith alone' has priority for salvation. Salvation is understood as eternal salvation for the faithful, located in an after-life. God has a linear plan for salvation, which takes place in a particular salvation history, which differs from human history. When the coming of the Kingdom of God is understood in this way, it rules out the possibility of the church being actively instrumental in the coming of the Kingdom within human history. The urgent missionary task of the church is therefore conversion of all people to faith in Christ, with a particular priority for the unreached. Whether a dualistic and linear understanding of salvation history makes any sense everywhere in the world, or in most churches, is doubtful. Whether churches in the South and East in general are less liberal must therefore be questioned. Nevertheless, a continued dialogue on salvation is called for.

---

[19] An account of the discussion has been given in Beate Fagerli and Knud Jørgensen, 'Together towards Life: Norwegian reflections', in *International Review of Mission*, 103.1 (398) (April, 2014).

[20] Rolf Kjøde, 'Spirit of Pentecost: Good news for all! An approach to evangelization and dialogue'.

[21] Øyvind Åsland and Rolf Kjøde in *Dagen*, a Christian daily newspaper, January 2013. See also: http://norme.no/aktuelt/detaljer/journey-together-again

[22] Øyvind Åsland and Rolf Kjøde in *Dagen,* January 2013.

## Concluding Remarks

Although based on limited material, we can draw some conclusions on certain issues that have come up for discussion based on *TTL*, at least in Northern Europe.

### *Mission in a World on the Margins*

Feedback from some churches in Northern Europe indicates that the concept of 'mission from the margins' is difficult to grasp if it is not further defined. Looking more closely into the current state of missiological discussion in Norway, we see that there seem to be several reasons for this reaction. It is often assumed that western churches in general are not living on the margins. In that sense, Bishop Byfuglien´s response at the Missiological Forum could be understood positively: that to be true to God´s mission, western churches need to welcome the perspective of the marginalised. Refsdal´s reading of the Bible, however, suggests that Jesus turns all perspectives upside down. Therefore, the categorisation of people into 'powerful' or 'marginalised' may be challenged by Scriptures itself.

Feedback from churches and missiological discussions implies that churches in the West don´t necessarily see themselves as the centre of power any longer, or as opposed to the marginalised. This is partly as the picture is changing because of the secularisation of society. The centre of Christianity is moving to the South and East, and western churches are losing ground. Many traditional western churches are losing their privileges and influence, and struggling to survive. Partly also, the picture is changing because of migration. Although growing in numbers, many western migrant churches find themselves living on the margins when it comes to establishing themselves and gaining access to rights and resources. Thus, changes in church demography complicates the picture and makes it difficult, even meaningless, to understand 'mission from the margins' based on a traditional understanding of the North/South divide. Also, 'mission from the margins' may be understood philosophically. This has led some churches to question whether this is a way of looking at the marginalised as 'the other', thereby risking cementing the old divide between 'us' and 'them'.

Finally, western churches have welcomed *TTL*'s inclusion of the whole of creation into the understanding of salvation. Increased awareness of climate change has led many churches to actively engage in climate justice, locally and globally. In many western societies, this means opposing political authorities, challenging economic priorities, and encouraging a 'green shift' by upholding the hope of re-creation as an alternative to a dying creation. The earth itself is living on the margins, increasing risk for all aspects of life. It is in this context that Professor Aaagard talks about mission being a calling to encourage hope in the midst of a worldview of fear. This is an important insight when reflecting further on the definition of 'mission from the margins'.

### *Reconciliation and the Reign of God*

*TTL* explores a pneumatological approach of mission. Based on the answers presented at the beginning of this article, it seems that many western churches welcome this. However, some miss a more Christological approach. From the limited material we have looked at, it has not been possible to discern whether this means that some churches lack a traditional understanding of the starting point for mission in *TTL*, based in Jesus′ calling and sending of his disciples (Matthew 28:18-20), or whether they lack a Christological reasoning for mission based on Jesus′ act of reconciliation through his death and resurrection. *TTL* does not explicitly incorporate Christological reflection on reconciliation as it has been developed in CWME during and after Athens 2005. We may therefore assume that further reflections on a Christological view on reconciliation linked with *TTL*′s pneumatolocigal insights on mission would be welcomed. The reflection process around reconciliation as a new paradigm for mission may be of use in this regard.[23]

On one hand, the missiological discussion in Norway reflects a development similar to that between WCC and the evangelical movement. The churches and the evangelical movement do come together to discuss God′s mission, and have come closer on a number of areas. In this regard, *TTL* has been well received. However, the discussion shows quite clearly that parts of the evangelical movement do not find the soteriological reasoning they are looking for in *TTL*, which is their very starting point for, and essence of, mission. A major challenge for a continued common journey will therefore be to further explore mission and the Reign of God from a soteriological perspective.

Not being able to present a full view on *TTL* and western theology, I nevertheless hope some important matters arising from current discussion on *TTL* have been presented. These are as much challenges to western churches and the evangelical movement as to the global ecumenical movement.

---

[23] See, for instance, Robert Schreiter, 'Mission as a Ministry of reconciliation – Norwegian Contributions'. Keynote address at the 2013 O.G. Myklebust Memorial Lecture at the Norwegian School of Theology, Oslo, 29th January 2013.

# *TOGETHER TOWARDS LIFE* AND THE CHALLENGE OF MISSIONAL FORMATION

Bård Mæland

## Introduction

What does it mean to 'walk by the Spirit' (Galatians 5:16)? And what does it mean that we, every human being, and even the creation at large, shall receive 'fullness of life' (John 10:10) by the coming of Jesus Christ? Reading such New Testament passages *after* having studied *Together towards Life* (*TTL*) certainly adds some perspectives to these biblical texts. This is so because of the prominence of pneumatology and the focus on 'life' in *TTL*, but also because these notions capture so well the core of the Gospel and the Reign of God.

Yet, what impact should such passages and the whole approach of *missio Spiritus* for the sake of life have for our lives and service as Christians? This is the question I want to pursue in this chapter. For these texts are not merely informative excerpts from the Bible; they are *formative* texts, meant to be embodied in a missional life of individual Christians, but also of congregations and the entire church of Jesus Christ.

The methodology I employ is to search for perspectives and concepts in *TTL* to explore, that together may throw some important light on the challenge of missional formation.

Before I move on, let me propose a very simple working definition of 'formation', which is 'the development of something into a particular thing or shape'.[1] Employing such a definition of *TTL* could help us rephrase missional formation below. I also want to make clear from the beginning that this chapter is not about theological education as such, nor about training missionary professionals more specifically, even though our analysis of missional formation based on *TTL* may have many implications for such training and formation. I have therefore included a separate section on this. All in all, this chapter is therefore about how a missional life shaped by the challenges brought forward by *TTL* may inspire, form and develop Christians in their thoughts and actions as participants in God's ongoing mission in the world.

---

[1] See http://dictionary.cambridge.org/dictionary/british/formation (accessed 7th August 2015).

## The Pragmatics of Mission as a Foundation for any Missional Formation

Having said all this, I have already stated a fundamental point about *TTL* from the perspective of missional formation: the understanding of mission and evangelism in *TTL* is not primarily concerned with missional *understanding* and the *idea* of God's mission, but with understanding *and* commitment, practice and action.

A 'proof' of this is the practical guide that was added to *TTL* after the January 2013 meeting of the working group of the Commission for World Mission and Evangelism in Kochi, India. The concern was to bring *TTL* into 'missional action'. Hence, simply reading the *TTL* with its added practical guide one realizes that *TTL* is a markedly pragmatic (Greek *pragma,* a thing done, a fact) document. It aims at commitment, and it should have an impact far beyond becoming an interesting ecumenical document on mission and evangelism adding to the stockpile of ecumenical readings. Based on this observation, it is no surprise when the editor of *TTL*, CWME Secretary Dr Jooseop Keum, in his foreword states that:

> The CWME is thankful to God that the world church and mission bodies of the WCC have been able to reach a common *understanding of and commitment to* God's mission today. The commission is also grateful that the affirmation is provoking fresh interest in the new vision of ecumenical mission *thinking and action* (vii; my emphases).

Hence, if anything, at least 'commitment', 'action' and 'practice' are part of what missional formation aims at, according to *TTL*, and this makes *TTL* challenging. Put differently, one cannot be missional, nor participate in the mission of God and the Spirit merely in theory. Rather, on the contrary, *TTL* aims at a journey and a process 'towards' life (viii). Consequently, *TTL* reveals a missional 'intention'.[2]

Of course, this pragmatic aim of *TTL* has vast implications for how mission is thought of, discussed and done in all kinds of learning environments, from the academic classroom to the communal life of a congregation. Put simply, as soon mission is made a theme in such learning sites, one should expect to be challenged to act and commit oneself. But how should it be done? This brings me to a second observation with relevance to my reading of *TTL*.

## Formation through Discernment – Seeing with the Spirit

The notion of discernment is important in *TTL*, and for several reasons. The document itself begins with a quite programmatic statement: 'It is the aim

[2] J.J. (Dons) Kritzinger, 'Training for Mission: Some Thoughts on Theological and Missionary Training in South Africa', in *Missionalia,* 30.1 (2002), 122-31; cited in Xolile Simon, 'Mission and Frontier-crossing and Identity Formation: An Integrating Contextual Missiology', in *Scriptura* 100 (2009), 89-103, at 92.

of this new ecumenical discernment to seek vision, concepts and directions for a renewed understanding and practice of mission and evangelism in changing landscapes.'[3] Again, we see how understanding and practice are kept intimately together. However, what interests us here is how 'discernment' seemingly does an integrative job in gathering together such notions as 'vision', 'concepts' and 'directions'. I will make an effort below to demonstrate how discernment is pivotal for integrating the theoretical and practical ideas of what it means to be missional.

Still, missional discernment does not work in a vacuum, but depends on the concept of God's mission in the world, and ultimately God's own mission in the world, for liberation, justice, peace – or, to use the L-word of *TTL*, Life! Hence, discernment is a theological discernment about God's own actions in the world in order to prepare for our own participation in God's mission.[4] So, what are the ways discernment is used in *TTL*?

The section on 'Spiritual Gifts and Discernment' (§24-28) makes spiritual discernment a theme, or better, discernment of the Spirit's work. This relates first to discerning 'the work of the life-giving Spirit sent into the world', which calls for response and action: 'When we have discerned the Holy Spirit's presence, we are called to respond.'[5] Again, we see how *missio Spiritus* and life are made central themes in this document.

It is very interesting to see how the churches are made the subjects of such discernment: 'The churches are called to discern the work of the life-giving Spirit sent into the world and to join with the Holy Spirit in bringing about God's reign of justice (Acts 1:6-8).'[6] This may be understood as an institutional discernment (e.g. churches making strategic decisions about where the Spirit is at work, and where the church as an organization should prioritize their commitments), but such an understanding would appear awkward in the light of the document at large. There is reason to argue that, in this, we see rather a democratization of discernment, namely, to the whole church and all its members. Participation in God's mission is not an elitist endeavour for just a few, but for everyone. This conclusion is backed by an empirical argument, namely, that it is those who experience affirmations of life, or threats to life, who are best placed to discern God's life-giving mission in the world.

The strongest proof of this can be found in the section on 'Why Margins and Marginalization?' (§38ff), where another key issue of *TTL* comes to the fore, namely, mission from the margins:

> People on the margins have agency, and can often see what, from the centre, is out of view. People on the margins, living in vulnerable positions, often know what exclusionary forces are threatening their survival, and can best discern the urgency of their struggles; people in positions of privilege have

---

[3] *TTL*, §3.
[4] *TTL*, §4.
[5] *TTL*, §25.
[6] *TTL*, §25.

> much to learn from the daily struggles of people living in marginal conditions.[7]

The logic seems to be: those who experience the lack of fullness of life most should be the prime interpreters of what 'fullness of life' is, and is not. Hence, *TTL* put it bluntly: 'The marginalized in society are the main partners in God's mission,' and it is their 'special gift to distinguish what news is good for them and what news is bad for their endangered life'.

Yet, this is not their responsibility exclusively, because to discern what the life-giving Gospel is all about belongs also to those of the 'centre', whatever 'centre' should imply: 'Wherever the neglected or marginalized are brought together in love such that wholeness is experienced, we may discern signs of God's reign on earth.'[8] One may perhaps say that wherever the responsibility for discernment is shared, the primary capacity to discern rightly belongs to those who are closest to whatever may threaten life.

From this it follows that, as soon as one distinguishes the absence of life-sustenance, one also knows what life-giving mission must look like. In such situations, discernment is not enough, but needs to be followed by a 'confrontation of evil spirits wherever forces of death and negation of life are experienced'. When the *TTL* describes the 'view from the margins', its language is thus sharpened considerably:

> Participation in God's ongoing work of liberation and reconciliation by the Holy Spirit, therefore, includes discerning and unmasking the demons that exploit and enslave. For example, this involves deconstructing patriarchal ideologies, upholding the right to self-determination for indigenous peoples, and challenging the social embeddedness of racism and casteism.[9]

Apart from this strong language, to which I will return, we also see here how the whole notion of God's work, the mission of God, etc. is the point around which everything else revolves in *TTL*. Therefore also, any discernment must centre round this, as a mode of participating in God's mission (cf. the quotation above). To do this successfully, one needs the guidance of the Holy Spirit: 'We need constantly to seek the insight of the Holy Spirit in helping us to better discern where the gospel challenges, endorses or transforms a particular culture for the sake of life.'[10]

Consequently, so far, missional formation along the 'discernment route' seems to consist of the following components: a) It is all about deciphering how God is at work to secure life and to counter life-threatening forces, b) such discernment is best done by people most affected by whatever diminishes life, c) yet all others also share the same responsibility to discern and act, and lastly, d) we need the insightful guidance of the Spirit

---

[7] *TTL*, §38.
[8] *TTL*, §51, in the section on 'Mission and Healing and Wholeness'.
[9] *TTL*, §43, in the section on 'Mission and Struggle and Resistance'.
[10] *TTL*, §100.

– the Life-Giver – to discern how God is active for the sake of abundant life.

There is, however, no doubt in *TTL* as to how the criterion for discernment is to be formulated:

> We affirm that the purpose of God's mission is fullness of life (John 10:10) and that this is the criterion for discernment in mission. Therefore, we are called to discern the Spirit of God wherever there is life in its fullness, particularly in terms of the liberation of the oppressed peoples, the healing and reconciliation of broken communities, and the restoration of the whole creation.[11]

It seems that the role of right discernment is so much emphasized in *TTL* that it has as one of its implications that no unity among the churches can be found without a common discernment of such issues as justice, inclusion and respect: 'Attempts to achieve unity must be in concert with the biblical call to seek justice. Our call to do justice may sometimes involve breaking false unities that silence and oppress. Genuine unity always entails inclusivity and respect for others.'[12] Hence, true ecumenism depends on a true participation in God's life-affirming and death-defying activity in the world.

*TTL* sees this struggle as one which requires good co-operation with people of other cultures and religious traditions. In non-conventional language, *TTL* here speaks of 'life-affirming spirits present in different cultures'.[13] To work in such co-operation is not to enter into foreign territory outside the domain of the church. As has been rather conventional ecumenical thinking for a long time, God's work is not limited to the church, and hence not limited by cultural, religious or other borders. The theological corollary for this is basically that 'Christ is already present' and 'God's Spirit is already at work'.[14]

## Formation by Hope – a Force for Today's Struggles

As we know from stories of trial and struggle, hope can play an immense role in fighting forces which threaten to destroy and ruin persons and organisations. With the emphasis on marginalization in *TTL*, it is no wonder that the resources of hope are mobilized for the sake of affirming life. I will now look into how hope may have formative challenges for mission.

The first time hope is mentioned in *TTL*, mission, power and community are kept together: 'The missionary God who sent the Son to the world calls all God's people (John 20:21), and empowers them to be a community of

---

[11] *TTL*, §102, in the section on 'Feast of Life: Concluding Affirmations'.
[12] *TTL*, §69.
[13] *TTL*, §102.
[14] *TTL*, §97, in the section on 'Evangelism and Culture'.

hope.'[15] This seems to be clearly in parallel with the disciples of Christ, following his resurrection: 'by the gift of the Holy Spirit, "the power from on high", they were formed into a new community of witness to hope in Christ (Luke 24:49; Acts 1:8).'[16] It belongs to the nature of hope that, despite its future orientation, it works in the present. Hence, eschatology is experienced as an actual reality through hope. That this eschatological-actual reality is regarded as powerful in *TTL* can be seen from various passages. A very obvious example is this one:

> The church's hope is rooted in the promised fulfilment of the reign of God. It entails the restoration of right relationships between God and humanity and all creation. Even though this vision speaks to an eschatological reality, it deeply energizes and informs our current participation in God's salvific work in this penultimate period.[17]

In *TTL,* such participation is related to suffering and the 'groaning' of Romans 8: 'As a community of imperfect people, and as part of a creation groaning in pain and longing for its liberation, the Christian community can be a sign of hope and an expression of the Kingdom of God here on earth (Rom. 8:22-24).'[18] Moreover, such participation in God's mission to provide life here and now certainly looks different from the viewpoint of marginalized people who lack basic resources and conditions for a 'life in its fullness'. For them, the hope may be comparably stronger and more important:

> Marginalized people have God-given gifts that are under-utilized because of disempowerment and denial of access to opportunities and/or justice. Through struggles in and for life, marginalized people are reservoirs of the active hope, collective resistance and perseverance that are needed to remain faithful to the promised reign of God (§39).

Thus, through hope an otherwise disempowered situation receives resources for perseverance and action. Similarly, the promise is also stronger for the ones who in this life did not enjoy the same gifts:

> Jesus promises that the last shall be first (Matthew 20:16). To the extent that the church practises radical hospitality to the estranged in society, it demonstrates commitment to embodying the values of the reign of God (Isaiah 58:6).[19]

In some passages this is fleshed out in a warlike manner, using words like 'confrontation' of evil spirits and cultures of oppression and dehumanization, and that 'demonic forces' should be defied. Hence the Gospel is not only good news to everyone:

---

[15] *TTL,* §2.
[16] *TTL,* §14.
[17] *TTL,* §44.
[18] *TTL,* §54.
[19] *TTL,* §47.

> Although the gospel is ultimately good news for all, it is bad news for the forces which promote falsehood, injustice and oppression. To that extent, evangelism is also a prophetic vocation which involves speaking truth to power in hope and in love (Acts 26:25; Col. 1:5; Eph. 4:15).[20]

Hence, Gospel, Spirit, hope, life and love seems to go well together with struggle, confrontation and war against evil spirits. In this, our hope comes from the divine intervention through the sending of his Son: 'The church in every geo-political and socio-economic context is called to service (*diakonia*) – to live out the faith and hope of the community of God's people, witnessing to what God has done in Jesus Christ.'[21]

What we see here is certainly a formative challenge of hope, for hospitality and resistance alike, deeply based in what I described as the eschatological-actual reality of the community that God shaped after the resurrection of Christ. A Christian hope in Christ and the coming of the Kingdom of God challenges the church to be inclusive and confrontational at the same time.

## Missional Formation and Leadership in TTL – Diagnosis and Remedies

How can missional action, discernment and hope be trained in a formative environment? In this part of the chapter, I will first explore how *TTL* itself makes formation an issue, and then move to voices from both the global South and North, and how they view the formative challenges of making God's mission central to their theologies and ecclesiologies.

*Together towards Life* does not say very much directly about formation and education. What it does say, however, is important, and may work as a point of departure for pursuing the issue through other voices.

First, *TTL* emphasises how the congregation and congregational life is a primary place of formation:

> Worship and the sacraments play a crucial role in the formation of transformative spirituality and mission.[22]

Also, reading the Bible contextually is important as this '[enables] local congregations to be messengers and witnesses to God's justice and love' (§74). The missional aspects of worship, sacraments and contextual Bible studies, however, can only be assessed against what we could call the 'pragmatic criterion' of '[living] out God's mission in our communities in our daily life'. Hence, 'local congregations are… impelled to step out of their comfort zones and cross boundaries for the sake of the mission of God' (§74).

---

[20] *TTL,* §106.
[21] *TTL,* §78.
[22] *TTL,* §74.

Secondly, with this as a backdrop, the Practical Guide of *TTL* sees a challenge for churches, in particular pertaining to a crisis in leadership:

> The new mission affirmation also has significant implications for education and formation. Many church communities look in vain for leaders who enable them to move forward in the power of the Spirit, offering fullness of life for all. *Together towards Life* provides resources to meet this crisis of leadership.[23]

The resources are found in the Practical Guide, and of course prepared well in *TTL* itself, as my analysis has shown. The approach to resolving the leadership crisis is to '[involve] all members of the faith community, employing their unique spiritual gifts to discern and address the critical missionary challenges facing us today'.[24] Again, we see how a 'decentred' approach is employed in *TTL*, as well as how discernment is central for the issue of formation.

We shall now move on to see how a similar diagnosis of the lack of adequate missional formation and leadership, and how relevant remedies are prescribed by missiologists from different parts of the global church, as well as from different kinds of missiological conversations.

## The Need for an Overhaul of Theological Education for the Sake of Missional Formation? Voices from the Global South

In his article, 'Evangelism as Discipleship: Implications for Theological Education and Leadership Formation',[25] South Africa-based Jamaican missiologist Roderick R. Hewitt calls for 'an overhaul of seminary- and university-based theological education careerism, because they serve as an encumbrance to nurturing effective contextual witness of churches'.[26] His concern is primarily directed to what he sees as a lack of 'dialogue, respect and relationship built on reciprocity'.[27] Writing from an Anglo-Caribbean context, with particular reference to Jamaica, he writes about colonial and neo-colonial evangelization strategies, where people were left without practically any viable option for rejecting 'the message of Jesus'.

Hewitt is critical towards both seminaries and university-based theological education. Whereas the former has become too concerned with numerical growth and the financial stability of the churches, the latter with its 'bias to Eurocentric orthodoxy and hermeneutics' has often produced ministers without the ability 'to inspire and connect because it lacks authenticity and spirituality', are 'unable to pray, preach and witness with

---

[23] *TTL,* Practical Guide, 44-45.
[24] *TTL,* Practical Guide, 44-45.
[25] Roderick Hewitt, 'Missional Leadership Formation: Embodiment of Together towards Life', in *International Review of Mission*, 103.1 (2014), 144-47.
[26] Hewitt, 'Missional Leadership Formation', 200.
[27] Hewitt, 'Missional Leadership Formation', 202.

authenticity and confidence', ignore the felt needs of people, and are clergy-centred, overlooking the strategic importance of the laity.[28] Hewitt asserts for both kinds of formation that they have become 'disconnected and disorientated leaders from the church's missional task'.[29]

Hewitt has been central in the WCC Commission for World Mission and Evangelism and the *TTL* process.[30] In his article, he relates his diagnosis of theological formation to the *TTL*. What he finds in *TTL* makes him do at least two important things: a) The church must widen its horizon from a focus on individual converts to the wider impact of salvation for humanity and the entire creation in the name of the 'God of life'.[31] It is this God, best expressed in the life of Jesus, that people look to in order to receive 'greater personal experiences of the Spirit', b) Future pastoring must concern itself with what takes place at the margins, which Hewitt especially interprets as the displacement of the church from the centre of culture to the contested environment of religiously pluralistic societies.[32] The way to meet these challenges is to recruit, train and form persons who are willing to operate without the 'comfort zone' of majority churches, and to earn respect through sacrificial service. The kind of missional leadership that Hewitt deduces from this is a 'transformational spirituality' that will 'empower leaders to respond effectively to the diverse spiritual needs of people for wholesome living'.[33]

The best thing about university-based formation (what he describes as 'evangelism through education'!) is that it provides an informed faith and quality teachers of theology, and has often also an open ecumenical approach to theology and church.[34] But more is needed! Highlighting the Daniel figure of the Hebrew Bible as an example, candidates should also be 'equipped in intercultural learning and be ready to witness, full of God's Spirit, and must dare to speak truth to power and not be afraid to serve God on the margins of a pluralistic society'.[35] If such an amalgam of the best from seminaries and universities can be achieved, then, according to Hewitt, 'it may be possible to facilitate the emergence of new or fresh ways or expressions of being church'.[36]

Another missiologist with a strong foothold in the global South is Wonsuk Ma, a long-term director of the Oxford Centre for Mission Studies,

---

[28] Hewitt, 'Missional Leadership Formation', 205, 206, 208 and 212.
[29] Hewitt, 'Missional Leadership Formation', 214.
[30] Kenneth R. Ross, Eva Christina Nilsson, and Roderick Hewitt, 'Implementation of the New Mission Affirmation: Together towards Life', in *International Review of Mission,* 103.1 (2014), 71-76.
[31] Hewitt, 'Missional Leadership Formation', 209-10.
[32] Hewitt, 'Missional Leadership Formation', 210-12.
[33] Hewitt, 'Missional Leadership Formation', 210.
[34] Hewitt, 'Missional Leadership Formation', 204.
[35] Hewitt, 'Missional Leadership Formation', 212.
[36] Hewitt, 'Missional Leadership Formation', 212.

who in a recent article has made 'theological and missional formation' a theme within the context of what he understands as the 'New Christianity'.[37] In this article, he places a strong emphasis on the role of lay people and the local congregation. He does so by talking about 'bottom up-theologies' and that local congregations will gain increased importance for theological education. What we saw in Hewitt above as a rather sharp distinction between theological education (seminaries/universities), on the one hand, and people's needs and lives, on the other, has been moved even further in Ma. Whereas Hewitt describes how academic theology has ignored spirituality and congregational life, Ma puts the local congregation and its leadership in command of theological education. The leader of a congregation, often a part-time minister, will lead the theological process. Thus, the connection between theology and mission will be much closer than in the past, and only this way can lived theology get its right place with due attention to context and how the Gospel is relevant to every aspect of human life. According to Ma, there is no such thing as pure (academic) theology and, admittedly, what he maintains comes close to a revolution in the order of church practice and academic theology, of which he is well aware ('This is a very tall order'!).[38] Most interestingly, Ma sees this re-ordering as a result of the failure of western theology, and of global South taking over as a church power – from the margins, and against all odds of resource estimates:

> The new mission players from mission fields, struggling with resources, and culturally and politically 'weak' places, have the potential not only to revitalize Christian mission but also to restore the right 'rules of missionary engagement' as informed by the New Testament.[39]

So, independent of the state of power and resources, what Wonsuk Ma predicts is a reformation of theological formation by the global South in order to strengthen the relationship between theologizing and everyday life of ordinary people who very often will also be marginalized one way or another. In this, we hear a voice and a tone rather similar to that of Roderick R. Hewitt. These voices are the more important as there are trends that clearly show a weakening of formation – as seen, for example, in the shrinking number of denominational seminaries in parts of the world, especially in the global North.[40]

---

[37] Wonsuk Ma, 'Theological and Missional Formation in the Context of "New Christianity"', in *The Ecumenical Review*, 66.1 (2014), 53-64.
[38] Ma, 'Theological and Missional Formation', 54.
[39] Ma, 'Theological and Missional Formation', 64.
[40] Dietrich Werner, 'Theological Education in the Changing Context of World Christianity – An Unfinished Agenda: Global and Ecumenical Perspectives from the Edinburgh 2010 Process and Beyond'. Lecture at the convocation of Philadelphia Lutheran Theological Seminary, 5th October 2010 and the meeting of the Board of the Foundation for Theological Education for South East Asia (FTESEA): www.ftesea.org/WernerLecture.pdf

## Voices from the West/North – a Return to 'Missional' Theology and the Primacy of Apostolicity

It is easy to find fertile ground for such proposals for missional engagement and priorities, even though contexts may differ.

One such example is Darrell Guder, long-term professor of 'missional and ecumenical theology' at Princeton Theological Seminary. In his presidential address, when elected president of the American Society of Missiology some years ago, he made 'Missio Dei: Integrating Theological Formation for Apostolic Vocation' a theme.[41]

Guder is well-known from the 'missional church conversation' in the United States, where it has been a core issue to move away from ecclesio-centrism 'toward understanding the identity and purpose of the church within God's mission, subordinate to and focused upon God's purposes'.[42] The adjective 'missional' has been coined within this 'conversation'. Guder is well aware of the situation within western academic theology, where mission has simply been omitted from the mainstream theological imagination, and instead has had to be worked up as a permanent scaffolding, supporting other theological disciplines.[43] Against such a view, Guder maintains that 'we would not need that scaffolding if our theological work were shaped by the *missio Dei*, if the entire doctrinal enterprise were, in diverse ways, truly focused upon the formation and equipping of the church for its apostolate'.[44] He therefore raises suggestive questions such as:

> What does a thoroughly trinitarian definition and explication of the *missio Dei* mean for the task of theological formation of missional servant leaders of the church? How do our theological disciplines, as they have evolved over the centuries of Christendom, come together around the central task of missional equipping? How does apostolic vocation define and integrate theological formation?[45]

On the one hand, such questions reflect an approach to theology, mission and formation as found in *TTL*, as well as in Hewitt and Ma, with its emphasis on *missio Dei*, sent-ness and formation, even though the immediate context of Guder is 'Christendom' as found in western cultures, with a Christian majority culture and often strong state-church relationships. As the state-church relationship and the public role of the church has rapidly been weakening in most western countries during recent decades, the time is ripe for the church to reconsider what it means to be the (apostolic) church and to take part in *missio Dei*. With such a focus,

---

[41] Darrell Guder, 'Missio Dei: Integrating Theological Formation for Apostolic Vocation', in *Missiology: An International Review*, 38.1 (2009), 63-74.

[42] Guder, 'Missio Dei: Integrating', 65.

[43] Guder, 'Missio Dei: Integrating', 65 and 67.

[44] Guder, 'Missio Dei: Integrating', 66.

[45] Guder, 'Missio Dei: Integrating', 64.

members and funding are not the main issues. Rather the contrary, to be a truly apostolic church, being 'witnesses for God's mission through everything that we are, that we say, and that we do',[46] what is needed is 'conversion':

> Congregations in our culture struggle with their missional vocation when the demands of institutional maintenance and the desire for organizational success assert themselves. I find more and more reasons to insist that the challenge before us is not one merely of renewal, or re-tooling, but of conversion – the conversion of the church to its radically simple missional vocation. Since conversion is a work of God's Spirit and is not under our control, our theological formation for apostolic vocation must be done in a posture of patient and confident prayer.[47]

There may be many ways to form a missional vocation. But, citing David Bosch, with immediate relevance for this chapter and in line with the spirit (!) of *TTL*, I think Darrell Guder resonates with *TTL*, Hewitt and Ma, when he hits the nail on the head in his address: 'It is not simply to receive that people are called to become Christians, but rather to give life.'[48] That is a broad perspective on mission, and a strong incentive to missional formation. I think this is the direction towards which missional formation is challenged to navigate.

## Conclusion

*TTL* not only raises the challenge of missional formation; it also provides perspectives and concepts that can revitalize a discussion of this issue as well as formational processes and 'journeys'.

First, one may argue that the very pragmatic aim of mission, traditionally and as expressed in *TTL*, provides a foundation for working with the issue of missional formation. Secondly, we have seen how selected foci, such as discernment and hope, may throw light on how *TTL* challenges us with respect to this issue. Lastly, based on what *TTL* itself has to say about missional formation, and how missional formation is perceived as a major challenge for both churches and institutions of theological education, there is reason to suggest that working on missional formation is not only a good approach to conversing with *TTL*, but is also an issue that makes clear what is at stake for the churches and God's mission in today's world of very different life-affirming and life-threatening forces, mechanisms and contexts. In this, there is no room for working on spirituality, liturgy and mission as separated entities.[49] One must take an integrative approach to both what it means to be a church

[46] Guder, 'Missio Dei: Integrating', 70.
[47] Guder, 'Missio Dei: Integrating', 73.
[48] Guder, 'Missio Dei: Integrating', 70.
[49] See Kenneth Berding, 'At the Intersection of Mission and Spiritual Formation in the Letters of Paul', in *Journal of Spiritual Formation and Soul Care* 6:1 (2013).

(identity) and how best to participate in God's mission at a particular place at a given time (context).[50]

[50] See Simon, 'Mission and Frontier-crossing'.

# Conclusion
# Together in God's Mission: The Prospects for Ecumenical Missiology

Jooseop Keum

Why should we be ashamed of the gospel, if our mission is life-affirming, not life-denying?

Why should we be ashamed of the gospel, if our mission is witnessing to the Kingdom of God, not our own kingdom?

Why should we be ashamed of the gospel, if our news is good to the suffering people in Galilee, not to the powers in Jerusalem?

Gospel, discipleship, courage, dynamism, passion, joy and hope… These were the words in my mind after the approval of the new mission statement at the tenth WCC Assembly, held in Busan, South Korea, in November 2013. The history of mission during the last century has been marked by many divisions and tensions, sometimes even misrepresentation of God's mission. Accusations and negative images of the missionary movement too much characterized our missiological debates during the past century. This is not to say that there were not mistakes to be corrected or wrongs to be put right. The development of authentic missiology depends on constructive criticism.

In my daily prayers during the drafting process of *Together towards Life*, I prayed, 'O God, may this new mission statement provoke a fresh interest in and commitment to world mission, that this new mission statement may create a positive image of mission so that the ecumenical missionary movement can be rejuvenated, re-energized in the power of the Holy Spirit!'

Peter Cruchley-Jones, a Welsh missiologist, evaluated: '*TTL* offers many horizons for those who would look out from the church doors at the changed landscapes of the world. The horizons and hermeneutics of justice, evangelism, dialogue, healing and unity are all gathered up under the overarching rainbow presence of the Holy Spirit in mission. *TTL* is full of hope and passion, as befits a mission affirmation, and offers itself as a fresh impetus for the Church to cross her own threshold and borders and locate herself in the joys and struggles of the world God loves. The title alone invites and charms us out of ourselves, queries our choice of direction and companion, and challenges all our aims and desires to be life-giving and life-affirming.'[1] Given that, it seems no small leap of faith to imagine that the church, with all its bureaucracies, anxieties and vanities, can be trusted to be a true partner of the Holy Spirit in this mission and vision of life which moves far beyond the aims of the institutional church. Yet the statement strongly affirms that the Holy Spirit calls us to be a church on the move together towards life.

The question is: how can we live it out? How can we make an elephant dance in cold weather? The cold weather of cynicism against religions, the cold weather of a maintenance and reductionist approach in an age of church decline. It is becoming extremely difficult to share the story of Jesus Christ in secularized societies. People look at Christians as aliens who still believe that the way of Jesus is the true way to live our lives. It may be that we, the people of mission, have still survived. But survival mode is not what the Risen Christ wants us to live out and to carry forth.

## Mission Spirituality

The conclusion of *TTL*'s practical guide reminds us that, following the crucifixion of Jesus, 'the doors of the house where the disciples had met were locked for fear of the Jews' (John 20:19).[2] In today's world, disciples of Jesus can find many reasons to be afraid. We could easily be tempted to lock the doors and concern ourselves with self-preservation. The gospel, however, points in a different direction. Jesus came and stood among them saying: 'Peace be with you. As the Father has sent me, so I send you' (20:21). Hiding behind locked doors was not their calling. Instead they were sent on a mission modelled after the mission of Jesus. Finally, he breathed on them and said, 'Receive the Holy Spirit' (20:22).

Pope Francis summons us: 'Let us recover and deepen our enthusiasm, the delightful and comforting joy of evangelizing, even when it is in tears that we must sow.'[3] Retreat is not part of our missionary gene. Our Lord called us, 'Don't be afraid' and 'Go in peace' to the world. Indeed, mission begins when the church meets the world, when Christians join in the mission of the Spirit which is already present and at work in the world. The pneumatological focus on mission in *TTL* is not merely theological jargon. Nor is it a copyright of the Pentecostal movement. *TTL* affirms, 'Mission spirituality has a dynamic of transformation which, through spiritual commitment of people, is capable of transforming the world in God's grace.'[4] In order to live out 'Together towards Life', the ecumenical

---

[1] Peter Cruchley-Jones, 'Together towards Life & Missional Congregation', CWME Consultation on Missional Formation, 19th-24th October 2014, Pietermaritzburg, RSA, 1.

[2] *TTL*, §72.

[3] *Evangelii Gaudium*, 10.

[4] *TTL*, §3.

missionary movement has to be empowered by the Holy Spirit which is transformative and life-giving.

Therefore, I would like to suggest that a pneumatological paradigm for Christian mission in the pluralist context has to be continuously the focus for ecumenical missiology today.[5] If the previous studies of mission have mainly focused on the theological dimension of Christian mission with emphasis on rigorous rationale, systematic justification and methodological development, the distinctive contribution of *TTL* can be to shift missiological discussions so that they are conducted not only from a theological angle but also from the spiritual perspective. In this way, *TTL* points the direction for missiology in the Post-Enlightenment, post-western, and post-Christendom contexts of world Christianity.

## Quality of Discipleship

The disciples dared to open the locked doors of their gated community. They went to people and encountered their daily challenges and hardships. Although they were small in number, poor in material terms, powerless in politics, marginalised in their religious tradition, they took courage to meet the people who were still hungry and sick, hopeless about their future. How then were the disciples able to create a new community of faith and hope after the experience of Pentecost?

In chapter 13 of the book of Acts, there was a shift of the centre of gravity in mission from Jerusalem to Antioch. The Christians in Antioch elected five leaders for their mission and ministry. One of them, together with Paul and Barnabas, was Simeon from Niger. A new-born religious community in Antioch, now taking the name 'Christian', elected a black African slave as their leader. Under the Roman Empire, the prevailing power of that time, slaves were treated no better than livestock. The election of a slave as leader of the community was such a shock that it stirred up the whole society, ultimately the entire Greco-Roman world! There was neither discrimination nor exclusion from the good news of salvation. In this way, powerful witness to the values of the gospel of the Kingdom of God was offered by the disciples. Indeed, it was a sign of hope and transformation for those people who were living in a hopeless situation.

We believe that the gospel has a power to transform the world – personality, value, class, system and society. The gospel of the Kingdom of God challenges the world that keeps the *status quo* of the hopeless situation. The world was not able to silence the small group of disciples. We, as the servants of God, have a mission to share the Good News to all humanity and creation which is longing for hope in their life. There is God's preferential love for the receivers of the good news in this process.

---

[5] See further, Amos Yong, *The Missiological Spirit: Christian Mission Theology in the Third Millennium Global Context* (Eugene, OR: Cascade, 2014).

The receivers are the ones to judge whether the news delivered to them is good or bad. The news which Jesus spread across Galilee was news of salvation – but it was utterly bad news for the people in Jerusalem because they understood the good news as a serious threat to their political, economic and religious powers and privileges. They had a strong faith, not in Jesus but in their money, power and religious hierarchy. Therefore, they crucified Jesus in order to silence this news so that they could continue enjoying their perpetual privileges.

What news are we sharing with the world today? Are we not talking only to ourselves? Are we not talking only in familiar and comfortable settings? Jesus did not start his movement of the Kingdom of God in the temple; rather, he began his ministry 'outside the gate' among the vulnerable people. If our eyes are turned towards the peoples at the margins, we will not need to be ashamed of the proclamation of the Good News. If we are bringing something really good to them, we have to take the courage to share the story of Jesus Christ.

People will know by the instinct of their hearts who we are. People know by the instinct of their hearts whether we do really believe in the vision of the new heavens and earth. *TTL* has beautifully expressed the reality that 'mission is the overflow of the infinite love of the Triune God'.[6] There are so many ways to share the love of God in this troubled world! Even in public spaces, the Holy Spirit is present and active. Therefore, we should pray for a fresh outpouring of the Spirit to empower our engagement with people and society. It is time to question ourselves as ecumenical mission leaders and workers: 'Are we true disciples of the gospel?' In my view, this question is more important than any other academic missiological discourse in today's context. It is not a matter of numbers or resources. It is the quality of discipleship that will prove decisive. It is time for the issues of authentic discipleship to be given priority attention in ecumenical missiology, given today's context where faith in mammon is threatening the credibility of the gospel.

## Religion, Violence and Peace

The increasing levels of conflict that give rise to massive numbers of deaths, ethnic cleansing, the increase of displaced people on a large scale, and other acts of violence particularly committed against women and children, are a matter of profound concern for our mission. Particularly disturbing aspects of the violence we witness today are the inhuman conditions in which uprooted people are forced to live. Even basic human rights are ignored and war crimes perpetrated against women and children are so terrible that it is difficult to believe they are happening in the 21st century.

---

[6] *TTL*, §19.

In many cases, religion has fuelled the escalation of conflicts. Even within the same religion, different sects and factions justify the conflicts in the name of their particular doctrinal convictions. Some argue that it is politicians who actually cause the conflicts and justify them in the name of religion. Even so, there remains the question, 'Can we refuse together to serve as the emperor's clothes?' The core of the teachings of the major world religions is wisdom of life. If we are preaching on the nature and salvation of life, we should be able to work together to safeguard life. Religion is a powerful source of peace and reconciliation in conflict situations, if we are able to work together. This is why the WCC is strongly committed to inter-faith dialogue and co-operation for life.

Individual churches often feel helpless in the face of such developments as war and violence. Therefore, it is necessary to expand our understanding of mission as common inter-faith witness in our community as well as in the public square. Public witness takes 'the world's' agenda as a missional agenda. We need to seek together to offer distinctive and constructive insights from our treasury of faith to help in the building of healing and reconciling communities. The ecumenical history of public witness testifies that unity in mission or common witness is a powerful source and symbol of solidarity and support and encouragement to overcome conflicts and violence. The WCC launched the 'Pilgrimage of Justice and Peace' at its tenth Assembly in Busan, South Korea, in 2013 as an overarching programmatic strategy to affirm life in the context of increasing conflict and violence on a global scale. Therefore, it is an imperative for ecumenical missiology today to actively contribute to the pilgrimage of justice and peace through developing a missional pilgrimage.

## A Theology of Hospitality

Today, about 250 million people are on the move, carrying with them their cultural and religious backgrounds. At least 75 million have permanently settled in new lands and around half of them are Christians. Migration has become a worldwide and multi-directional phenomenon which is radically reshaping the Christian landscape. Today's context of large-scale worldwide migration challenges the churches' commitment to mission and unity in very practical ways because of the fact that many migrant churches are existing separately from the churches in the lands where they have settled. Churches can be a place of refuge for migrant communities; they can also be intentional focal points for inter-cultural engagement. The churches are called to be one to serve God's mission beyond ethnic and cultural boundaries, and so ought to create multicultural ministry and mission as a concrete expression of common witness in diversity. This may entail advocating justice in regard to migration policies and resistance to xenophobia and racism.

One of the reasons for the success of the missionary movement was its practice of hospitality. One of the key themes of the pneumatological approach in mission is the Spirit's mission of hospitality together with charisma, dynamism, healing, diversity and transformation. A fruit of mission spirituality is *shalom*: 'Go in peace'. God's *shalom* provokes a radical hospitality overcoming hostility. Martin Luther King Jr said: 'I have decided to stick with love; hate is too great a burden to bear.' God's *shalom* introduces the mission of a transforming hospitality of justice. Justice is not only a standard that rejects the evil of hostility and hatred towards refugees and migrants, but is also the power to transform hatred and hostility into hospitality. God's hospitality is unconditional and eschatological. It is not God's mission merely to extend an invitation to the guests and treat them nicely. Rather, this is a matter of ontological mission, of being together as one family in God's *shalom* – a missional vision of unity.

Pentecostal missiologist Amos Yong introduces three elements that constitute a pneumatological theology of hospitality:

1. Christian hospitality is grounded upon the hospitable God who through the incarnation has received creation to himself and through Pentecost has given himself to creation. God gives of himself by the Holy Spirit at Pentecost to all flesh, and by doing so welcomes and embraces all humanity; at another level, human beings receive the gift of God, effectively hosting the Spirit of God in their bodies.
2. Christian hospitality is enacted by the charismatic practice of the church as its members are empowered by the Holy Spirit. The hospitality of God is thus embodied in a hospitable church whose members are empowered by the Holy Spirit to stand in solidarity and serve with the sick, the poor and the oppressed (Luke 4:18-19).
3. Christian hospitality is realizable in a world of many faiths only when it is reciprocated by those in other faiths, and such reciprocity is made possible by the Spirit who is poured out on all flesh.[7]

In God's hospitality, there is no discrimination between the poor and the rich, between the Jew and the Gentile, between male and female, between centrality and marginality. God calls us to a new relationship of mutual hospitality, not only at the margins but also at the centre, not only within Christianity but also with other faiths, and not only the receivers of the news but also those who bring it need to be ready to be transformed through the encounter of marginality. A pneumatological theology of hospitality is an important missiological theme in the context of religious plurality and migration. Therefore the development of an ecumenical missiology of hospitality is urgently needed today.

It is the God of *missio Dei* who will continue to knock the gates of the church in the face of refugees and migrants. The term 'refugees and migrants' is not only a sociological term. In this 21st century of

[7] Yong, *The Missiological Spirit*, 88-92.

globalisation, it represents a reality that calls for constant attention from every Christian who follows in the footsteps of Jesus Christ. Migration is a mission issue and the theology of hospitality is the theological agenda today!

## The Younger Generation

Globally, young people are turbulent. They are yearning to work, and yet finding themselves on the fringes of society, marginalized and excluded politically and economically. The competition and stress to fight for their future is at a level that is unprecedented in human history. Many of them have not been able to get even their first proper jobs. In some situations, this dismal reality has become fertile ground for religious extremism.

How are we addressing this issue through our missional work? Can the current structures and ways of working in the church and the ecumenical movement attract many young people? Agnes Abuom, moderator of the WCC central committee, stressed, in an address to the committee: 'If there is a growing sense that the global ecumenical movement is losing its prophetic cutting edge and instead becoming more and more institutionalized and bureaucratic, it is also because it has slowly but steadily been losing its youthfulness… Therefore, to bring back prophetic dynamism and movement emphasis into the ecumenical movement, we need to let the young generation own and define the ecumenical movement.'[8]

We need deliberately to invite and encourage young people if we want to revitalize the ecumenical missionary movement, if we want to have fresh visions in mission (Joel 2:28). It is time to take radical measures. It is important that we change ourselves to fit into the new generation, rather than asking them to fit into ours.

## Equipping Congregations and Future Leaders

Will *TTL* help in enabling local congregations to be missional? Chammah Kaunda and Roderick Hewitt claim that the missional formation process of *TTL* should be intentionally interdisciplinary and ecumenical, taking seriously the theological education that shapes its development and examining whether the local congregation remains the primary agent of God's mission in the world. The pedagogical task needs to be reframed within the contextual model of missiological education for the formation of

[8] Agnes Abuom, 'Moving Together Towards Communities of Justice and Peace', Moderator's Address, WCC Central Committee, 2nd-8th July 2014, Geneva, 5.

missional leaders. New forms of pedagogical transformation have to emerge that may facilitate fullness of life.[9]

Undoubtedly, *TTL* has significant implications for education and formation. It has already been widely taught in theological schools. It also suggests a new approach to missional leadership formation that involves all members of faith communities, employing their unique spiritual gifts to discern and address the critical missionary challenges facing us today and encouraging them to join in the mission of the Holy Spirit. Therefore, it is vital that ecumenical missiology should generate the resources and materials for missional formation based on *TTL* at the various levels of churches and mission bodies. The present volume is a fine example of what needs to be done. As CWME looks forward to its next world mission conference in 2018, it will engage in further work towards a process of missional formation, a pedagogical and contextualizing process of *TTL*. Work is underway to develop a missiological curriculum for the training of future mission leaders in theological schools, modules for equipping local congregations, and continuing education courses for missionaries and mission workers.

## Convergence between Ecumenical and Evangelical Understandings of Mission

In the changing landscape of mission today, it is questionable whether the dichotomy of ecumenical and evangelical perspectives is still relevant to envisioning the future of world Christianity. One could also ask the question whether it is rather a hindrance to 'reformulating' the future of mission. In fact, it is imperative to articulate a new approach to revitalize mission through convergence and co-operation between the ecumenical and evangelical understandings of mission. It is vital to seek a way of overcoming the missiological confrontations of the last century and to attempt to develop a new synergy between the two approaches.

One of the most significant missiological developments in the early years of the 21st century has been an increasing exchange and mutual respect between the ecumenical and evangelical movements of mission. Edinburgh 2010 has enlarged the fellowship and led to reconciliation among different mission streams. It has increased confidence among the partners involved, allowed for the sharing of power and provided space to each. Its final aim was relational, reaching in the long-term a form of *koinonia* in mission. CWME intentionally remained in a more supporting role for Edinburgh 2010 to nurture the fellowship. CWME was open in

---

[9] Chammah J. Kaunda and Roderick R. Hewitt, '"Together towards Life": Reconceptualising Missio-Formation in the Changing Landscape of World Christianity'. CWME Consultation on Missional Formation, 19th-24th October 2014, Pietermaritzburg, RSA, 20.

Edinburgh for constant updates, modifications and reformulations of its own positions on mission and evangelism, in the search for a new consensus on the matter.

An analysis of the *Common Call* produced at the Edinburgh conference shows that positions defended for decades by CWME have now become somewhat common ground: *missio Dei*, empowerment and humility, creation as scope of mission, the holistic content of the gospel, mission from everywhere to everywhere, unity and mission. There has also been a particular emphasis on pneumatology, where one can discern the influence of Pentecostal traditions. Indeed, Edinburgh 2010 was a moment of celebration, healing and convergence of the missionary movement.

*TTL* also affirms that evangelism is at the centre of Christian mission. The new mission statement has four main chapters – on spirituality, margins, church and evangelism. It is important to note that the entire section on evangelism was drafted jointly by the World Evangelical Alliance Theological Commission and the CWME evangelism desk. The co-operation between WCC and WEA in the work of the 'Recommendations for Conduct'[10] and the new mission statement is a remarkable achievement – something that we could not have dreamt of during the last century, and a sign of overcoming the dichotomy and bringing synergy to our approach in mission.

Healing the wounds of division in world mission, nurturing the current co-operative relationship, and leading to a new opportunity of common witness to the good news of Jesus Christ in a world where the credibility of the Christian faith has been seriously challenged, is a significant task of ecumenical missiology.

## Mission and Ecumenism

What can be the role of mission at this current juncture in the history of the ecumenical movement? During the last century, the missionary movement has both inspired and given shape to the modern ecumenical movement as the churches have sought to respond to the challenges of history and to be witnesses to the good news of Jesus Christ for the world through visible unity. However, we are facing a sharp challenge to define the vision and relevance of the ecumenical movement within the changing ecclesial and global landscape of today.

There are three vantage points with regard to the distinctive role of mission within the wider ecumenical movement. First, mission can play a prophetic role in bringing together unity and justice discourses in the ecumenical movement. Mission provides a holistic approach that helps to affirm the integrity of the ecumenical movement because of the way in which it connects people and contexts. Mission can play a unique role in

[10] *TTL*, §90.

connecting the scattered streams of the ecumenical movement today and strengthening the synergy between them, a point emphasized in *TTL*. This does not mean that mission is claiming a self-centred approach where we see our tradition as more important than others. Rather, it is placing mission in a position of serving the whole ecumenical movement.

Secondly, mission can play a creative role in the midst of dilemmas between movement and institution by bringing new vision to the ecumenical movement. It is inevitable that we develop institutions as a means of trying to secure the integrity of the movement. However, over time, the institution can lose the vision for the movement and fall into the temptation to only serve its self-interest. In such a situation, mission can provide the bridge between movements and institutions, through missiological imagination and action. As witnessed in the history of CWME, traced in Section 1 of this book, mission has constantly pioneered a new paradigm for the ecumenical movement.

Thirdly, mission has a distinctive role between the church and development agencies within the WCC. Vladimir Fedorov reminds us that, 'In 1961, the World Council of Churches entered into mission, not the opposite.'[11] Our forebears had an ambitious plan to challenge and transform churches to become missionary congregations, recognizing the role of the church as the primary agent of mission. In spite of this ambitious project, we must ask, 'Where is the location of mission in the WCC today?' What place can it find between the hierarchy of the church and the power of the resources of the development agencies?

Mission is all about the face-to-face encounter of people. It is about the stories of God's people responding to the calling to be common witnesses to the hope in Jesus Christ. Mission has an important role in reclaiming the human face, the powerful stories and testimonies of God's people, an experience that we have all enjoyed throughout our time together towards life. The human stories of all God's people contributing to God's mission in the power of God's Spirit can serve as a continuous and much-needed challenge to the church and the ecumenical movement. If mission fails in this role, it is doubtful whether the ecumenical movement can remain relevant among the generation who are living in the secularised context. Therefore, it is highly important to put the mission agenda at the heart of the church and the ecumenical movement today and tomorrow.

> The Triune God invites the whole creation to the Feast of Life, through Jesus Christ who came 'that they may have life, and may have it in all its fullness' (John 10:10), through the Holy Spirit who affirms the vision of the reign of God, 'Behold, I create new heavens and a new earth!' (Isaiah 65:17). We commit ourselves together in humility and hope to the mission of God, who

---

[11] Archpriest Vladimir Fedorov, 'The Wind of Change: An Orthodox Point of View', in *International Review of Mission,* 101.2 (2012), 405.

recreates all and reconciles all. And we pray, 'God of life, lead us to justice and peace'[12]

[12] *TTL*, §112.

# Bibliography

## Primary Sources


Aagaard, Anna Marie, 'Ånd og Mission'. Keynote address given at the Danish Mission Council, 2013.

Abuom, Agnes, 'Moving Together Towards Communities of Justice and Peace'. Moderator's Address, WCC Central Committee, 2nd-8th July 2014, Geneva.

*Alternative Globalization Addressing Peoples and Earth (AGAPE): A Background Document.* Geneva: WCC, 2005.

Anderson, Gerald, 'The Theology of the Christian Mission at Edinburgh and Succeeding World Conferences'. Abstract of PhD dissertation submitted to Boston University, 1960.

*Bangkok Assembly 1973: Minutes and Report of the Assembly of the Commission on World Mission and Evangelism.* Geneva: WCC, 1973.

*Baptism, Eucharist, and Ministry.* Geneva: WCC, 1982.

*Barr Statement: Theological Perspectives on Plurality.* Statement of a Theological Consultation held in Barr, Zurich, Switzerland, in January 1990 organised by the WCC's Programme on Interreligious Dialogue and Co-operation as part of preparations for the Canberra Assembly.

Benedict XVI, Pope, *Ubique et Semper*, 2010.

Best, Thomas (ed), *Faith and Order 1985-1989: The Commission Meeting at Budapest 1989.* WCC Faith and Order Paper No. 148. Geneva: WCC: 1990.

Bird, Cliff, 'Deep Sea Thinking: A Call to 21st Century Oceania Churches for (Self)-Critical Awareness and Prophetic Presence in the Context of "Seas of Change"'. Paper presented at the Third Consultation of Bread for the World Partners in Oceania, Sonaisali, Fiji, October 2013.

Bonk, Jonathan, 'Whose Head is This and Whose Title?' Presidential address delivered at the International Association for Mission Studies 13th Quadrennial Conference, Toronto, 15th August 2012.

Byfuglien, Helga Haugland, 'Spirit of Community: Church on the move'. Paper presented at the Missiological Forum, Oslo, 22nd November 2012.

Christian Conference of Asia, *Uprooted People in Asia: Conference on Migrant Workers, Refugees and Internally-Displaced Communities in Asia: Hong Kong, 22-26 November 1993.* Hong Kong: Christian Conference of Asia, 1995.

*Christian Witness in a Multi-Religious World: Recommendations for Conduct* (2011): https://www.oikoumene.org/en/resources/documents/wcc-programmes/interreligious-dialogue-and-cooperation/christian-identity-in-pluralistic-societies/christian-witness-in-a-multi-religious-world

Church and Society Commission Consejo Latinoamericano de Iglesias & Conference of European Churches, 2010. CEC-CLAI Globalization Final Report: *Threats and Challenges of Globalization: Churches in Europe and Latin America in Dialogue.*

Commission on Faith and Order, *The Church: Toward a Common Vision.* WCC Faith and Order Paper No. 214. Geneva: WCC, 2013.

Commission on Faith and Order, *The Nature and Mission of the Church.* WCC Faith and Order Paper No. 198. Geneva: WCC, 2005.

Conference of Latin American Bishops, Fifth General Conference at Aparecida, Brazil, 2007: www.aecrc.org/documents/Aparecida-Concluding%20Document.pdf
Congregation for the Doctrine of the Faith, *Doctrinal Note on Some Aspects of Evangelization*. 3rd December 2007: www.vatican.va/roman_curia/congregations/cfaith/documents/rc_con_cfaith_doc_20071203_nota-evangelizzazione_en.html
Constitution on the Sacred Liturgy, *Sacrosanctum Concilium*. Solemnly Promulgated by His Holiness Pope Paul VI, 4th December 1963.
Cruchley-Jones, Peter, '*Together Towards Life* & Missional Congregation'. CWME Consultation on Missional Formation, 19th-24th October 2014, Pietermaritzburg, RSA.
CWME, 'Mission and Evangelism in Unity Today', in Jacques Matthey (ed), *'You are the Light of the World': Statements on Mission by the World Council of Churches 1980-2005*. Geneva: WCC, 2005, 62-89.
CWME, 'Mission as Ministry of Reconciliation', in Jacques Matthey (ed), *'You are the Light of the World': Statements on Mission by the World Council of Churches 1980-2005*. Geneva: WCC, 2005, 92-126.
CWME, 'The Healing Mission of the Church', in Jacques Matthey (ed), *'You are the Light of the World': Statements on Mission by the World Council of Churches 1980-2005*. Geneva: WCC, 2005, 129-62.
De Gruchy, Steve, 'An Olive Agenda: First Thoughts on a Metaphorical Theology'. Unpublished paper.
*Dialogue in Community: Statement and Reports of a Theological Consultation, Chiang Mai, Thailand, 18-27 April 1977*. Geneva: WCC, 1977.
Duraisingh, Christopher (ed), *Called to One Hope: The Gospel in Diverse Cultures*. Report of the Conference of the Commission on World Mission and Evangelism, Salvador, Brazil, 1996. Geneva: WCC, 1998.
Edinburgh 2010, 'Common Call', in Kirsteen Kim and Andrew Anderson (eds), *Edinburgh 2010: Mission Today and Tomorrow*. Oxford: Regnum, 2011, 1-2.
Engelsviken, Tormod, 'Some Perspectives on Mission and Evangelisation the last thirty years'. Paper presented at the Missiological Forum, Oslo, 22nd November 2012.
*Evangelii Nuntiandi,* Apostolic Exhortation of Pope Paul VI, promulgated on 8th December 1975.
Fagerli, Beate, 'Mission and Evangelism Today and for the Future – Mission in Dialogue, Dialogue in Mission'. Missiological Forum, Oslo, 22nd November 2012.
Faith and Order Commission of the World Council of Churches, *Ditchingham Report*. Ditchingham, UK, August 1994.
Federation of Asian Bishops' Conference (FABC), *The Spirit at Work in Asia Today*. Hong Kong, 1998.
Flannery, Austin (ed), *Vatican Council II: The Conciliar and Post Conciliar Documents.* Wilmington, DE: Scholarly Resources, 1975.
Francis I, *Evangelii Gaudium.* Strathfield, NSW: St Paul Publishers, 2013.
Francis I, Encyclical Letter '*Laudato Si', On Care for our Common Home.* 24th May 2015: http://w2.vatican.va/content/francesco/en/encyclicals/documents/papa-francesco_20150524_enciclica-laudato-si.html

Francis I, *Evangelii Gaudium: The Joy of the Gospel*. Apostolic Exhortation on the Proclamation of the Gospel in Today's World. London: Catholic Truth Society, 2013.

Gairdner, W.H. Temple, *'Edinburgh 1910': An Account and Interpretation of the World Missionary Conference*. Edinburgh and London: Oliphant, Anderson & Ferrier and New York, Chicago and Toronto: Fleming H. Revell, 1910.

Gairdner, W.H. Temple and John Raleigh Mott, *Echoes from Edinburgh, 1910: an Account and Interpretation of the World Missionary Conference*. New York, Chicago and Toronto: Fleming H. Revell, 1910.

General Board of Global Ministries, The United Methodist Church. 'Theology of Mission Statement': www.umcmission.org/Learn-About-Us/About-Global-Ministries/Theology-of-Mission

Gill, David (ed), *Gathered for Life – Official Report, 6th Assembly of the World Council of Churches*. Geneva: WCC, 1983.

Gomez, Juan Usma, 'Dialogue with Pentecostals'. Eternal World Television Network, 2001.

Goodall, Norman (ed), *Missions Under the Cross: Addresses delivered at the Enlarged Meeting of the Committee of the International Missionary Council at Willingen, Germany, 1952; with Statements issued by the Meeting*. London: Edinburgh House Press, 1953.

Goodall, Norman (ed), *Uppsala Speaks: Section Reports of the Fourth Assembly of the World Council of Churches Uppsala 1968*. Geneva: WCC, 1968.

Hollenweger, Walter J, 'Christus Extra Et Intra Muros Ecclesiae', in WCC Department on Studies in Evangelism (ed), *Planning for Mission: Working Papers on the New Quest for Missionary Communities*. New York: Conference for the WCC, 1966

International Missionary Council (ed), *The World Mission of the Church – Findings and Recommendations of the Meeting of the International Missionary Council, Tambaram, Madras, India, December 12-29, 1938*. London, New York: International Missionary Council, 1939.

John Paul II, Encyclical Letter *Centesimus Annus*, 1st May 1991: http://w2.vatican.va/content/john-paul-ii/en/encyclicals/documents/hf_jp-ii_enc_01051991_centesimus-annus.html

John Paul II, Encyclical Letter *Redemptoris Missio: On the Permanent Validity of the Church's Missionary Mandate*. 7th December 1990. Washington, DC: Office of Publishing and Promotions Services, United States Catholic Conference.

John Paul II, Discourse to the XIX Assembly of CELAM (9th March 1983), 3: *L'Osservatore Romano*. Weekly edition in English, 18th April, 9: AAS 75 (1983), 778.

Joint Working Group between the WCC and the Roman Catholic Church. 'The Challenge of Proselytism and the Calling to Common Witness', 25th September 1995, in J. Gros, H. Meyer and W.G. Rush (eds), *Growth in Agreement II, Reports and Agreed Statements of Ecumenical Conversations on a World Level, 1982-1998*. Grand Rapids, MI: Eerdmans and Geneva: WCC, 2000, 891-99.

Joint Working Group between the Roman Catholic Church and the WCC, *Ecumenical Formation: Ecumenical Reflections and Suggestions. Seventh Report*. Geneva and Rome: WCC-PCPCU, 1998, 53-59.

Jones, Rufus M., 'Secular Civilization and the Christian Faith', *The Jerusalem Meeting of the International Missionary Council, March 24-April 8, 1928*. New York: International Missionary Council, 1928.

Kaunda, Chammah J. and Roderick R. Hewitt, '*Together Towards Life*: Reconceptualising Missio-Formation in Changing Landscape of World Christianity'. CWME Consultation on Missional Formation, 19th-24th October 2014, Pietermaritzburg, RSA.

Keum, Jooseop, 'Dynamism and Diversity: An Ecumenical Perspective on Mission in Changing Landscapes'. Paper presented at the Missiological Forum, Oslo, 22nd November 2012.

Keum, Jooseop (ed), *Together towards Life: Mission and Evangelism in Changing Landscapes.* Geneva: WCC, 2013.

Kim, Kirsteen, 'Come, Holy Spirit: Who? Why? How? So What?', in Jacques Matthey (ed), *Come Holy Spirit, Heal and Reconcile!* Report of the WCC Conference on World Mission and Evangelism, Athens, May 2005. Geneva: WCC, 2008.

Kim, Kirsteen, 'Together Towards Life: Mission and Evangelism in Changing Landscapes'. Paper presented at the MISAL (Missionary Societies of Apostolic Life) conference, London, May 2014: www.africamission-mafr.org/misal_london_2014.htm

Kinnamon, Michael (ed), *Signs of the Spirit.* Official Report of the Seventh Assembly of the World Council of Churches, Canberra, 1991. Geneva: WCC, 1991.

Kjøde, Rolf, 'Spirit of Pentecost: Good news for all! An Approach to Evangelization and Dialogue'. Paper presented at the Missiological Forum, Oslo, 22nd November 2012.

*Laity: reprints from Laity 2-6.* Geneva: Department on the Laity, WCC, May 1962.

Latourette, Kenneth Scott and William Richey Hogg, *Tomorrow is Here: A Survey of the World-wide Mission and Work of the Christian Church.* London: Edinburgh House Press, 1948.

Lausanne Committee for World Evangelization, *The Manila Manifesto*, in James A. Scherer and Stephen B. Bevans (eds), *New Directions in Mission and Evangelization I.* Maryknoll, NY: Orbis Books, 1992, 292-305.

Lausanne Movement, *The Cape Town Commitment: A Confession of Faith and a Call to Action.* Peabody, MA: Hendrickson, 2011.

*Laymen's Work* No.1. Geneva: WCC, May 1951.

Matthey, Jacques (ed), *Come Holy Spirit, Heal and Reconcile! Called in Christ to be Reconciling and Healing Communities – Report of the WCC Conference on World Mission and Evangelism, Athens, Greece, May 9-16, 2005*. Geneva: WCC, 2008.

Matthey, Jacques, 'Mission and Evangelism: An Ecumenical Affirmation: Presentation', in Jacques Matthey (ed), *'You are the Light of the World': Statements on Mission by the World Council of Churches 1980-2005.* Geneva: WCC, 2005, 1-3.

'Melbourne Conference Section Reports – Good News for the Poor', in *International Review of Mission,* 69, 276-77 (October 1980-June 1981), 388-96.

Methodist Church in Fiji, 'Pillars and Key Strategic Areas'. Connexional Plan 2015-2019.

Minutes of the WCC Central Committee held in Geneva 1977, 26.

*Mission and Evangelism: An Ecumenical Affirmation.* Geneva: WCC, 1983.

Newbigin, Lesslie, 'The Missionary Dimension of the Ecumenical Movement', in *The Ecumenical Review,* 14:2 (1962), 207-15.

Oldham, Joseph H., *The Churches Survey Their Task: The Report of the Conference at Oxford, July 1937, on Church, Community and State*. London: Allen & Unwin, 1937.

Orchard, Ronald K. (ed), *The Ghana Assembly of the International Missionary Council 28th December to 8th January, 1958.* London: Edinburgh House Press, 1958.

Orchard, Ronald K. (ed), *Witness in Six Continents: Records of the Meeting of the Commission on World Mission and Evangelism of the World Council of Churches held in Mexico City, December 8th to 19th, 1963.* London: Edinburgh House Press, 1964.

Paton, David M. (ed), *Breaking Barriers*. The Official Report of the Fifth Assembly of the World Council of Churches, Nairobi 1975. Geneva: WCC, 1976.

Refsdal, Knut, 'Together Towards Life'. Paper presented at the Missiological Forum, Oslo, 22nd November 2012.

*Report of Study Group VI on Theological Education and Formation*, in Daryl M. Balia and Kirsteen Kim (eds), *Witnessing to Christ Today*. Regnum Edinburgh 2010 Series, Vol. II. Oxford: Regnum, 2010, 148-74.

'Rethinking the Household of God in the Pacific – Literature Review'. Suva, Pacific Conference of Churches, 2013.

'Rethinking the Household of God in the Pacific: Towards Sufficiency and Solidarity, Inclusiveness and Participation'. Suva, Pacific Conference of Churches, 2010.

Robeck Jr., Cecil M., 'Creative Imagination and Ecumenism in Light of Global Demographic Changes'. Lecture delivered at Catholic University of America for Washington Theological Consortium, 4th February 2013.

'Salvation and Social Justice, Report of Section II, CWME Assembly, Bangkok, 1973', in Michael Kinnamon and Brian E. Cope (eds), *The Ecumenical Movement: An Anthology of Key Texts and Voices.* Geneva: WCC and Grand Rapids, MI: Eerdmans, 1997.

Schreiter, Robert, 'Mission as a Ministry of Reconciliation – Norwegian Contributions'. Lecture given at the 2013 O.G. Myklebust Memorial Lecture, MF – Norwegian School of Theology, Oslo, 29th January 2013.

Sjollema, Baldwin, 'The Archives of the World Council of Churches' Programme to Combat Racism' www.brill.com/sites/default/files/ftp/downloads/31985_Brochure.pdf

Tambaram Madras Series, Vol. I, *The Authority of the Faith.* London: Oxford University Press, 1939.

Tambaram Madras Series, Vol. II, *The Growing Church.* London: Oxford University Press, 1939.

Tambaram Madras Series, Vol. IV, *The Life of the Church.* London: Oxford University Press, 1939.

'The Christian Life and Message in Relation to Non-Christian Systems'. *Report of the Jerusalem Meeting of the International Missionary Council, March 24th-April 8th, 1928, Vol. I.* London: Oxford University Press, 1928.

*The Lausanne Covenant*, 1974, in J.D. Douglas (ed), *Let The Earth Hear His Voice: Official Reference Volume, Papers and Responses*, Minneapolis, MN: World Wide Publications, 1975, 2-9.

'The Mission Call from Viwa to the Pacific Churches'. Mission document produced by the Pacific Conference of Churches, Pacific Theological College, and South Pacific Association of Theological School, Viwa, Fiji, 2010.

*The New Delhi Report: The Third Assembly of the World Council of Churches, 1961*. London: SCM, 1962.

*The Vitality and Promise of Being Anglican, The Global Anglicanism Project*. Episcopal Church Foundation, 2005.

*The World Mission of the Church: Findings and Recommendations of the Meeting of the International Missionary Council, Tambaram, Madras, India, December 12-29, 1938*. London: International Missionary Council, 1939.

*Together Towards Life: Mission and Evangelism in Changing Landscapes*. Geneva: WCC, 2012.

'Towards Common Witness: A Call to Adopt Responsible Relationships in Mission and to Renounce Proselytism', in *'You are the Light of the World': Statements on Mission by the World Council of Churches 1980-2005*. Geneva: WCC, 2005, 39-58.

Tuwere, Ilaitia Sevati, 'Indigenous People's Struggle for Land and Identity: An Account from Fiji. Indigenous People's Struggle for Land Identity in the Pacific: A Joint Seminar of the World Council of Churches Indigenous People's Programme, Pacific Desk of the World Council of Churches, and the Pacific Conference of Churches'. Suva, 2000.

Unit IV – Sharing and Service, *New Approaches to Development – Ecumenical Formation Seminar Report*. Geneva: WCC, 1996.

United States Conference of Catholic Bishops Pastoral Letter. *Forming Conscience for Faithful Citizenship*. November 2007.

van Beek, Huibert (ed), *Sharing Life – Official Report of the WCC World Consultation on Koinonia: Sharing Life in Community*. Geneva: WCC, 1989.

Vatican Council II, *Ad Gentes*. Decree on the Missionary Activity of the Church. 7th December 1965.

Vatican Council II, Constitution on the Divine Liturgy. *Sacrosanctum Concilium*. 4th December 1963.

Vatican Council II, Constitution on the Church in the Modern World. *Gaudium et Spes*. 7th December 1965.

Visser 't Hooft, W.A. (ed), *The Official Report Man's Disorder and God's Design Volume V, The First Assembly of the World Council of Churches*. New York: Harper & Brothers, 1949.

Visser 't Hooft, W.A. (ed), *The Evanston Report: The Second Assembly of the World Council of Churches*. New York: Harper Books, 1955.

Weiderud, Peter, 'The WCC concern for Nuclear Disarmament and Non-proliferation'. 2005: www.oikoumene.org

Werner, Dietrich, 'Theological Education in the Changing Context of World Christianity – An Unfinished Agenda: Global and Ecumenical Perspectives from the Edinburgh 2010 Process and Beyond'. Lecture at the convocation of Philadelphia Lutheran Theological Seminary, 5th October 2010 and the meeting of the Board of the Foundation for Theological Education for South East Asia (FTESEA).

Wilson, Frederick R. (ed), 'Section Reports: Melbourne Conference', in *International Review of Mission,* 69, 276-77 (1980), 388-436.

Wilson, Frederick R. (ed), *The San Antonio Report: Your Will be Done: Mission in Christ's Way*. Geneva: WCC, 1990.

World Alliance of Reformed Churches, *The Accra Confession: Covenanting for Justice in the Economy and the Earth*. Geneva: WARC, 2004.

World Council of Churches, 2013: www.oikoumene.org/en/what-we-do/pilgrimage-of-justice-and-peace

World Council of Churches, 'An Invitation to the Pilgrimage of Justice and Peace' (2014): www.oikoumene.org

World Council of Churches, *Church and World: The Unity of the Church and the Renewal of Human Community*. WCC Faith and Order Paper No. 151. Geneva: WCC, 1990.

World Council of Churches, 'Economy of Life for All Now: An Ecumenical Action Plan for a New International Financial and Economic Architecture' (2014): www.oikoumene.org

World Council of Churches, 'Economy of Life, Justice, and Peace for All: A Call to Action'. (19th July 2012): www.oikoumene.org

World Council of Churches, *Guidelines on Dialogue with People of Living Faiths and Ideologies*. Geneva: WCC, 1979.

World Council of Churches, *Healing and Wholeness – The Churches' Role in Health*. Report of a Study by the Christian Medical Commission. Geneva: WCC, 1990.

World Council of Churches, Justice, Peace and Creation': www.wcc-coe.org/wcc/what/jpc/hist-e.html

World Council of Churches, *Minutes and Reports of the Fourth Meeting of the Central Committee, Rolle (Switzerland), August 4-11, 1951*. Geneva: WCC, 1951.

World Council of Churches, 'Mission and Evangelism: An Ecumenical Affirmation' (1982), in Jacques Matthey (ed), *'You are the Light of the World': Statements on Mission by the World Council of Churches 1980-2005*. Geneva: WCC, 2005, 4-38.

World Council of Churches, Roman Catholic Church and World Evangelical Alliance, *Christian Witness in a Multi-Religious World: Recommendations for Conduct*. Geneva: WCC, 2011.

World Council of Churches, 'Statement on the Way of Just Peace' (8th November 2013): www.oikoumene.org

World Council of Churches, 'Together on the Way – Response to the plenary on the Ecumenical Decade – Churches in Solidarity with Women': www.wcc-coe.org/wcc/assembly/fprc2e-e.html

World Council of Churches, *The Church for Others, and the Church for the World: A Quest for Structures for Missionary Congregations: Final Report of the Western European Working Group and North American Working Group of the Department on Studies in Evangelism*. Geneva: WCC, 1967.

World Council of Churches, *The San Antonio Report*. F.R. Wilson (ed). Geneva: WCC, 1990.

World Council of Churches, *The Uppsala Report 1968: Official Report of the Fourth Assembly of the World Council of Churches*. Geneva: WCC, 1968.

World Council of Churches, 'Towards Common Witness: A Call to Adopt Responsible Relationships in Mission and to Renounce Proselytism'. Document commended by the 1997 WCC Central Committee to all member-churches, in Jacques Matthey (ed), *You are the Light of the World: Statements on Mission by the World Council of Churches 1980-2005*. Geneva: WCC, 2005, 39-58.

World Council of Churches, *Your Kingdom Come: Mission Perspectives*. Report on the World Conference on Mission and Evangelism, Melbourne, Australia, 12th-25th May, 1980. Geneva: WCC, 1980.

World Health Organisation, *Constitution of the World Health Organisation,* 1948: www.who.int/governance/eb/constitution/en
*World Mission and Evangelism: Salvation Today: Bangkok, 29th December-8th January 1973*. Vol. IX. Geneva: WCC and Commission on Mission and World Evangelism, 1972.
World Missionary Conference, 1910, *Carrying the Gospel into all the Non-Christian World.* Report of Commission I. Edinburgh and London: Oliphant, Anderson & Ferrier and New York, Chicago and Toronto: Fleming H. Revell, 1910.
World Missionary Conference, 1910, *The Church in the Mission Field.* Report of Commission II. Edinburgh and London: Oliphant, Anderson & Ferrier and New York, Chicago and Toronto: Fleming H. Revell, 1910.
World Missionary Conference, 1910, *Education in Relation to the Christianisation of National Life*. Report of Commission III. Edinburgh and London: Oliphant, Anderson & Ferrier and New York, Chicago and Toronto: Fleming H. Revell, 1910.
World Missionary Conference, 1910, *The Missionary Message in Relation to Non-Christian Religions.* Report of Commission IV. Edinburgh and London: Oliphant, Anderson & Ferrier and New York, Chicago and Toronto: Fleming H. Revell, 1910.
World Missionary Conference, 1910, *The Training of Teachers: with Supplement.* Report of Commission V. Edinburgh and London: Oliphant, Anderson & Ferrier and New York, Chicago and Toronto: Fleming H. Revell, 1910.
World Missionary Conference, 1910, *The Home Base of Missions.* Report of Commission VI. Edinburgh and London: Oliphant, Anderson & Ferrier and New York, Chicago and Toronto: Fleming H. Revell, 1910.
World Missionary Conference, 1910, *Missions and Governments*. Report of Commission VII. Edinburgh and London: Oliphant, Anderson & Ferrier and New York, Chicago and Toronto: Fleming H. Revell, 1910.
World Missionary Conference, 1910, *Co-operation and the Promotion of Unity.* Report of Commission VIII. Edinburgh and London: Oliphant, Anderson & Ferrier and New York, Chicago and Toronto: Fleming H. Revell, 1910.
World Missionary Conference, 1910, *The History and Records of the Conference.* Edinburgh and London: Oliphant, Anderson & Ferrier and New York, Chicago and Toronto: Fleming H. Revell, 1910.
World Missionary Conference, 1910, *Statistical Atlas of Christian Missions: Containing a Directory of Missionary Societies, a Classified Summary of Statistics, an Index of Mission Stations, and a Series of Specially Prepared Maps of Mission Fields.* Edinburgh: World Missionary Conference, 1910.
*'You are the Light of the World': Statements on Mission by the World Council of Churches 1980-2005.* Geneva: WCC, 2005.
*Your Kingdom Come: Mission Perspectives – Report on the World Conference on Mission and Evangelism, Melbourne, Australia, 12-25 May 1980.* Geneva: WCC, 1980.

## Secondary Sources

'A Century of Ecumenical Missiology', in *International Review of Mission,* 100.393 (November 2011).

Abrecht, Paul, 'From Oxford to Vancouver Lessons from Fifty Years of Ecumenical Work for Economic and Social Justice', in *The Ecumenical Review,* 40:2 (1988), 147-68.

Adeney, Miriam, 'Colorful Initiatives: North American Diasporas in Mission', in *Missiology: An International Review,* 39:1 (January 2011), 5-23.

Adogame, Afe, 'African Christians in a Secularizing Europe', in *Religion Compass,* 3:4 (2009), 488-501.

Adogame, Afe, *The African Christian Diaspora: New Currents and Emerging Trends in World Christianity.* London: Bloomsbury, 2013.

Adogame, Afe, 'Transnational Migration and Pentecostalism in Europe', in *PentecoStudies: An Interdisciplinary Journal for Research on the Pentecostal and Charismatic Movements,* 9:1 (2010), 56-73.

Ahonen, T., *Transformation through Compassionate Mission: David J. Bosch's Theology of Contextualization.* Helsinki: Luther-Agricola-Society, 2003.

Albinson, Thomas, 'A Christian Response to the Humanitarian Crisis in the Mediterranean': www.worldea.org/news/4555/a-christian-response-to-the-humanitarian-crisis-in-the-mediterranean

Alexander, Paul, *Peace to War.* Telford, PA: Cascadia, 2009.

Alexander, Paul, *Pentecostals and Nonviolence: Reclaiming a Heritage.* Eugene, OR: Wipf & Stock, 2012.

Althouse, Peter, 'Towards a Pentecostal Ecclesiology: Participation in the Missional Life of the Triune God', in *Journal of Pentecostal Theology,* 18:2 (2009), 230-45.

Amalados, Michael, 'Dialogue', in R.S. Sugirtharajah and Virginia Fabella (eds), *Dictionary of Third World Theologies.* Maryknoll, NY: Orbis Books, 2002.

Ambedkar, B.R., *Annihilation of Caste: Annotated Critical Edition.* Introduction by Arundhati Roy. New Delhi: Navayana Publishing, 2014 [1936].

Amirtham, Sam and John S. Pobee (eds), *Theology by the People.* Geneva: WCC, 1986.

Anderson, A.H., 'Pentecostalism in East Asia: Indigenous Oriental Christianity?', in *Pneuma,* 22:1 (Spring 2000), 115-32.

Anderson, A.H., 'To All Points of the Compass', in *Enrichment Journal.* Springfield, MO: General Council of the Assemblies of God, Spring 2006.

Anderson, Allan, *An Introduction to Pentecostalism: Global Charismatic Christianity.* Cambridge: CUP, 2004.

Anderson, Allan, *Spreading Fires: The Missionary Nature of Early Pentecostalism.* London: SCM, 2007.

Anderson, Allan, *To the Ends of the Earth Pentecostalism and the Transformation of World Christianity.* Oxford: OUP, 2013.

Anderson, Allan and Edmond Tang (eds), *Asian and Pentecostal.* 2nd edition. Oxford: Regnum, 2011

Antone, Hope, Wati Longchar, Hyungju Bae, Huang Po Ho and Dietrich Werner (eds), *Asian Handbook for Theological Education and Ecumenism.* Taiwan: PTCA, 2013.

Arbuckle, Gerald A., *Earthing the Gospel: An Inculturation Handbook for the Pastoral Worker.* Maryknoll, NY: Orbis Books, 1990.

Archontonis, Bartholomew, *Encountering the Mystery: Understanding Orthodox Christianity Today*. New York, London, Toronto, Sydney and Auckland: Doubleday, 2008.

Ariarajah, S. Wesley, *Gospel and Culture: The Ongoing Discussion within the Ecumenical Movement.* Geneva: WCC, 1994.

Ariarajah, S. Wesley, 'Interreligious Dialogue and Mission in Protestant Theology', in *Modern Believing,* 51.3 (2010).

Ariarajah, Wesley, *Not Without My Neighbour: Issues in Interfaith Dialogue.* Geneva: WCC, 1999.

Ariarajah, Wesley, *Your God, My God, Our God: Rethinking Christian Theology for Religious Plurality.* Geneva: WCC, 2012.

Asamoah-Gyadu, J. Kwabena, 'Pulling Down Strongholds: Evangelism, Principalities and Powers and the African Pentecostal Imagination', in *International Review of Mission,* 96.382-83 (2007), 306-21.

Asamoah-Gyadu, J. Kwabena, '"To the Ends of the Earth": Mission, Migration and the Impact of African-led Pentecostal Churches in the European Diaspora', in *Mission Studies,* 29 (2012), 23-44.

Attanasi, Katherine and Amos Young, *Pentecostalism and Prosperity: The Socio-Economics of the Global Charismatic Movement.* New York: Palgrave Mcmillan, 2012.

Aylett, Graham and Tim Green, 'Theological Education as a Tool for Twenty-first Century Mission', in Teresa Chai, Stephen B. Bevans, Dietrich Werner, J. Nelson Jennings and Knud Jøergensen (eds), *Reflecting on and Equipping for Christian Mission.* Oxford: Regnum, 2015, 56-71.

Ayre, Clive W. and Ernst M. Conradie (eds), *The Church in God's Household: Protestant Perspectives on Ecclesiology and Ecology.* Pietermaritzburg, RSA: Cluster Publications, forthcoming.

Bailyes, Alan J., 'Evangelical and Ecumenical Understandings of Mission', in *International Review of Mission,* 85.339 (1996), 485-503.

Balasuriya, Tissa, *Eucharist and Human Liberation.* Quest Series 50. Colombo: Centre for Society and Religion, 1977.

Balia, Daryl and Kirsteen Kim (eds), *Edinburgh 2010: Witnessing to Christ Today.* Oxford: Regnum, 2010.

Barker, Chris, *The SAGE Dictionary of Cultural Studies*. London: Sage Publications, 2004.

Barrera, Albino O.P., 'Mission in a Globalized Economy', in James Kroeger (ed), *The Gift of Mission: Yesterday, Today and Tomorrow*. Maryknoll, NY: Orbis Books, 2013, 157-63.

Barrett, David and Todd M. Johnson, *World Christian Trends, AD 20-AD 2200: Interpreting the Annual Christian Megacensus.* Pasadena, CA: William Carey Library, 2001.

Barth, Karl, *Church Dogmatics, Volume IV.3.1: The Doctrine of Reconciliation.* Edinburgh: T. & T. Clark, 1961.

Bassham, Roger, *Mission Theology: 1948-1975. Years of Worldwide Creative Tension, Ecumenical, Evangelical, and Roman Catholic.* Pasadena, CA: William Carey Library, 1979.

Bastian, Jean-Pierre, *Historia del protestantismo en América Latina.* México: Ediciones CUPSA, 1990.

Bauman, Chad M., *Pentecostals, Proselytization, and Anti-Christian Violence in Contemporary India*. Oxford: OUP, 2015.

Bauman, Zygmunt, *Culture in a Liquid Modern World.* London: Polity Press, 2011.
Bays, Daniel H. (ed), *Christianity in China: From the Eighteenth Century to the Present.* Stanford, CA: Stanford University Press, 1999.
Bebbington, David, *Evangelicalism in Modern Britain.* London: Unwin Hyman, 1989.
Becker, Ulrich, 'Ecumenical Formation', in John Briggs, Mercy Amba Oduyoye and Georges Tsetsis (eds), *A History of the Ecumenical Movement Volume 3, 1968-2000.* Geneva: WCC, 2004, 175-93.
Becker, Ulrich, 'Ecumenical Learning', in Nicholas Lossky et al (ed), *Dictionary of the Ecumenical Movement.* 2nd edition. Geneva: WCC, 2002, 379-80.
Bediako, Kwame, *Christianity in Africa: The Renewal of a Non-Western Religion.* Maryknoll, NY: Orbis Books and Edinburgh: Edinburgh University Press, 1995.
Benn, Christoph and Erlinda Senturias, 'Health, Healing and Wholeness in the Ecumenical Discussion', in *International Review of Mission,* 90 356-357 (2001), 7-25.
Berding, Kenneth, 'At the Intersection of Mission and Spiritual Formation in the Letters of Paul', in *Journal of Spiritual Formation & Soul Care,* 6:1 (2013).
Berger, Iris, 'Women in East and Southern Africa', in I. Berger & F. White (eds), *Women in Sub-Saharan Africa: Restoring Women to History.* Bloomington, IN: Indiana University Press, 1999, 5-60.
Berneburg, Erhard, *Das Verhältnis von Verkündigung und sozialer Aktion in der evangelikalen Missionstheorie.* Wuppertal, Germany: Brockhaus, 1997.
Best, Thomas, 'United and Uniting Churches as Models of Mission and Unity', in John Gibaut and Knud Jørgensen (eds), *Called to Unity For the Sake of Mission.* Oxford: Regnum, 2014, 141-53.
Best, Thomas F. and M. Robra (eds), *Ecclesiology and Ethics: Ecumenical Ethical Engagement, Moral Formation and the Nature of the Church.* Geneva: WCC, 1997.
Bevans, Stephen B., *An Introduction to Theology in Global Perspective.* Maryknoll, NY: Orbis Books, 2009.
Bevans, Stephen B., 'Beyond the New Evangelization: A Missionary Church for the Twenty-First Century', in Richard R. Gaillardetz and Edward P. Hahnenberg (eds), *A Church with Open Doors: Ecclesiology for the Twenty-first Century.* Collegeville, MN: The Liturgical Press, 2015, 3-22.
Bevans, Stephen B., 'Ecclesiology and Missiology: Reflections on Two Recent Documents from the World Council of Churches', in *Dialogue: A Journal of Theology,* 54:2 (Summer 2015), 126-34.
Bevans, Stephen B., 'Mission *among* Migrants, Mission *of* Migrants', in Daniel Groody and Gioacchino Campese (eds), *A Promised Land, A Perilous Journey: Theological Perspectives on Migration.* Notre Dame, IN: University of Notre Dame Press, 2008, 89-106.
Bevans, Stephen B., 'Mission at the Second Vatican Council: 1962-1965', in Stephen B. Bevans (ed), *A Century of Catholic Mission: Roman Catholic Missiology 1910 to the Present.* Oxford: Regnum, 2013, 101-11.
Bevans, Stephen B., *Models of Contextual Theology.* Maryknoll, NY: Orbis Books, 2002.
Bevans, Stephen B. and Katalina Tahaafe-Williams (eds), *Contextual Theology for the Twenty-first Century.* Cambridge: James Clarke, 2012.
Bevans, Stephen B. and Roger P. Schroeder, *Constants in Context: A Theology of Mission for Today.* Maryknoll, NY: Orbis Books, 2008.

Beyerhaus, Peter, *Bangkok 73: The Beginning or End of World Mission?* Grand Rapids, MI: Zondervan, 1974.

Billson, Janet Mancini, *Keepers of the Culture: The Power of Tradition in Women's Lives.* New York: Lexington Books, 1995.

Bird, Cliff, 'Hermeneutics of Ecology and its Relationship to the Identity of the Oikos in Oceania', in *The Pacific Journal of Theology* 2:46 (2011), 19-33.

Bird, Cliff, '*Pepesa* – The Household of Life: A Theological Exploration of Land in the Context of Change in Solomon Islands'. PhD thesis. Charles Sturt University, Australia, 2008.

Bird, Cliff, 'Re-conceptualising Salvation: Some Insights from a Solomon Islands Culture toward a Relevant Theology of Salvation for Today', in *The Pacific Journal of Theology,* 2:42 (2009), 23-39.

Bittlinger, A. (ed), *The Church is Charismatic: The World Council of Churches and the Charismatic Renewal.* Geneva: WCC, Renewal and Congregational Life, 1981.

Boege, Volker, Anne Brown, Kevin Clements and Anna Nolan, *On Hybrid Political Orders and Emerging States: State Formation in the Context of 'Fragility'*: http://edoc.vifapol.de/opus/volltexte/2011/2595/pdf/boege_etal_handbook.pdf

Boesak, Allan A., *Black and Reformed.* Maryknoll, NY: Orbis Books, 1984.

Boesak, Allan A., *Black Theology Black Power.* London: Mowbray, 1978.

Bosch, David J., *Believing in the Future: Toward a Missiology of Western Culture.* Valley Forge, PA: Trinity Press, 1995.

Bosch, David J., 'Church Growth Missiology', in *Missionalia,* 16.1 (1988), 13-24.

Bosch, David J., 'The Melbourne Conference: Between Guilt and Hope', in *International Review of Mission,* 69.276-77 (1980), 512-18.

Bosch, David J., *Transforming Mission: Paradigm Shifts in Theology of Mission.* Maryknoll, NY: Orbis Books, 1991.

Boseto, Leslie, 'Do Not Separate Us from Our Land', in *The Pacific Journal of Theology,* 2:13 (1995), 69-72.

Boseto, Leslie, 'God as Community-God in Melanesian Theology', in *The Pacific Journal of Theology,* 2:10 (1993), 41-48.

Boseto, Leslie, *I Have a Strong Belief.* Goroka, Papua New Guinea: Unichurch Books and The Melanesian Institute, 1983.

Boseto, Leslie, *Lauru Land Conference of Tribal Community: Philosophy, Theology and Guiding Principles.* Suva: Pacific Conference of Churches, 1995.

Boseto, Leslie, 'Toward a Pacific Theology of Reality', in *The Pacific Journal of Theology,* 2:12 (1994), 53-61.

Boyd, Gregory A., *Oneness Pentecostals and the Trinity.* Grand Rapids, MI: Baker, 1992.

Boys, Mary C., SNJM, 'What *Nostra Aetate* Inaugurated: A Conversion To The "Providential Mystery of Otherness"', in *Theological Studies,* 74 (2013).

Bria, Ion, 'Confessing Christ Today', in *International Review of Mission,* 64.253 (Jan 1975), 67-74.

Bria, Ion (ed), *Go Forth in Peace: Orthodox Perspectives on Mission.* Geneva: WCC, 1985.

Bria, Ion, 'On Orthodox Witness', in *International Review of Mission,* 69.276-77 (Oct 1979-Jan 1980), 527-28.

Bria, Ion, 'The Liturgy after the Liturgy', in *International Review of Mission,* 67.265 (Jan 1978), 86-90.

Bria, Ion, *The Liturgy after the Liturgy: Mission and Witness from an Orthodox Perspective*. Geneva: WCC, 1996.
Bria, Ion and Petros Vassiliadis, *Orthodox Christian Witness*. Katerini, Greece: Tertios Press, 1989.
Brickell, Claire, 'Geographies of Contemporary Christian Mission(aries)', in *Geography Compass,* 6:12 (2012), 725-39.
Briggs, John, Mercy Amba Oduyoye and Georges Tsetsis, *A History of the Ecumenical Movement, Vol.III, 1968-2000*. Geneva: WCC, 2004.
Bright, Bill, *The Four Spiritual Laws*: http://crustore.org/four-laws-english
Brinkman, Martien E., *Progress in Unity? Fifty Years of Theology in the World Council of Churches: 1945-1995: A Study Guide*. Louvain: Peeters Press and Grand Rapids, MI: Eerdmans, 1995.
Brueggemann, Walter. *The Prophetic Imagination*. 2nd edition. Minneapolis, MN: Fortress Press, 2001.
Brunner, Emil, 'Secularism as a Problem for the Church', in *International Review of Mission,* 19.76 (October 1930), 495-511.
Bujo, Bénézet, *African Theology in its Social Context*. Maryknoll, NY: Orbis Books, 1992.
Bundy, David, 'The Ecumenical Quest for Pentecostalism', in *Cyberjournal for Pentecostal-Charismatic Research* 5 (February 1999).
Burgess, Richard, 'Bringing Back the Gospel: Reverse Mission Among Nigerian Pentecostals in Britain', in *Journal of Religion in Europe,* 4 (2011), 429-49.
Burrows, William B., Mark R. Gornik and Janice A. McLean (eds), *Understanding World Christianity: The Vision and Work of Andrew F. Walls*. Maryknoll, NY: Orbis Books, 2011.
Burtner, Charles W. and Robert E. Chiles (eds), *John Wesley's Theology*. Nashville, TN: Abingdon Press, 1982.
Buthelezi, Manas, 'African Theology and Black Theology', in Hans-Jürgen Becken (ed), *Relevant Theology for Africa*. Durban, RSA: Lutheran Publishing House, 1973, 18-24.
Campese, Gioacchino C.S., 'Mission and Migration', in Stephen B. Bevans (ed), *A Century of Catholic Mission*. Oxford: Regnum, 2013, 247-60.
Campese, Gioacchino C.S., 'The Irruption of Migrants: Theology of Migration in the 21st Century', in *Theological Studies,* 73 (2012), 3-32.
Carter, Warren, *Matthew and the Margins: A Sociopolitical and Religious Reading*. Maryknoll, NY: Orbis Books, 2005.
Cartledge, Mark, 'Renewal Ecclesiology in Empirical Perspectives', in *PNUEMA,* 36 (2014), 5-24.
Castello, Daniel, *Revisioning Pentecostal Ethics*. Cleveland, TN: CPT Press, 2012.
Castles, Stephen and Mark Miller, *The Age of Migration: International Population Movements in the Modern World*. 4th edition. Basingstoke, UK: Palgrave MacMillan, 2009.
Castro, Emilio, *Freedom in Mission: The Perspective of the Kingdom of God*. Geneva: WCC, 1985.
Cawthorn, Matthew J., *American Oneness Pentecostalism*. CreateSpace, 2012.
Chai, Teresa, Stephen B. Bevans, Dietrich Werner, J. Nelson Jennings and Knud Jørgensen (eds), *Reflecting on and Equipping for Christian Mission*. Oxford: Regnum, 2015.
Chan, Simon, 'Mother Church: Toward a Pentecostal Ecclesiology', in *PNEUMA,* 22:2 (Fall 2000), 177-208.

Chatterjee, Nandini, *The Making of Indian Secularism: Empire, Law and Christianity, 1830-1960*. New York: Palgrave Macmillan, 2011.

Chesnut, R. Andrew, *Born Again in Brazil*. New York: Rutgers University Press, 1997.

Chia, Edmund Kee-Fook, 'Mission as Dialogue: An Asian Roman Catholic Perspective', in Ogbu U. Kalu, Peter Vethanayagamony and Edmund Kee-Fook Chia (eds), *Mission After Christendom: Emergent Themes in Contemporary Mission*. Louisville, KY: Westminster John Knox Press, 2010.

Chia, Edmund, 'Wanted: Interreligious Dialogue', in *Studies in Interreligious Dialogue,* 12.1 (2002).

Chilcote, Paul W. and Laceye C. Warner (eds), *The Study of Evangelism: Exploring a Missional Practice of the Church*. Grand Rapids, MI: Eerdmans, 2008.

'Christians in Dialogue with Men of Other Faiths', in *International Review of Mission,* 59.236 (October 1970), 382-39.

Chunakara, Mathews G., *Building Peace on Earth*. Geneva: WCC, 2013.

Chung, Byung Joon, 'An Assessment of Together Towards Life: Korean Responses', in *International Review of Mission,* 102.397 (November 2013), 199-204.

Chupungco, Anscar, *Liturgies of the Future: The Process and Methods of Inculturation*. New York and Mahwah, NJ: Paulist, 1989.

Clements, Keith, *Faith on the Frontier: A Life of J.H. Oldham*. Edinburgh: T. & T. Clark and Geneva: WCC, 1999.

Clifton, Shane, 'Pentecostal Ecclesiology: A Methodological Proposal for a Diverse Movement', in *Journal of Pentecostal Theology* 15:2 (2007), 213-32.

Cobb, Kelton, *The Blackwell Guide to Theology and Popular Culture*. Malden, MA: Blackwell, 2005.

Coe, Shoki, 'Contextualizing Theology', in Gerald H. Anderson and Thomas F. Stransky (eds), *Mission Trends No. 3: Third World Theologies*. Grand Rapids, MI: Eerdmans, 1976, 19-24.

Colberg, Kristin M., 'The Omnipresence of Grace: Revisiting the Relationship between *Ad Gentes* and *Nostra Aetate* 50 Years Later', in *Missiology: An International Review,* 42.2 (2014).

Coleman, Robert, *The Master Plan of Evangelism*. Grand Rapids, MI: Revell Publishing, 1963.

Collier, Jane and Rafael Esteban, *From Complicity to Encounter: The Church and the Culture of Economism*. Harrisburg, PA: Trinity Press, 1998.

Colwell, Matthew, 'From Immigrant to Immigrant Justice Organizer: Moises Escalante', in Ched Myers and Matthew Colwell (eds), *Our God is Undocumented: Biblical Faith and Immigrant Justice*. Maryknoll, NY: Orbis Books, 2012, 73-90.

Colwell, Matthew, 'Proclaiming Liberty to the Captives', in Ched Myers and Matthew Colwell (eds), *Our God is Undocumented: Biblical Faith and Immigrant Justice*. Maryknoll, NY: Orbis Books, 2012, 107-22.

Comblin, Joseph, *The Holy Spirit and Liberation*. London: Burns & Oates, 1989.

Congar, Yves, 'Principes Doctrineaux', in Johannes Schütte (ed), Vatican II: *Activité Missionaire de l'Église*. Unam Sanctam 67. Paris: Éditions du Cerf, 1967.

Conner, Benjamin T., *Practicing Witness: A Missional Vision of Christian Practices*. Grand Rapids, MI: Eerdmans, 2011.

Conradie, Ernst M., *Christianity and Earthkeeping: In Search of an Inspiring Vision.* Stellenbosch, RSA: SUN Press, 2011.

Conradie, Ernst M., 'Confessing Guilt in the Context of Climate Change: Some South African Perspectives', in *Scriptura,* 103 (2010), 134-52.

Conradie, Ernst M., 'Contemporary Challenges to Christian Ecotheology: Some Reflections on the State of the Debate after Five Decades', in *Journal of Theology for Southern Africa,* 147 (2013), 106-23.

Conradie, Ernst M., 'Creation at the Heart of Mission', in *Missionalia,* 38:3 (2010), 380-96.

Conradie, Ernst M., 'The Whole Household of God (oikos): Some Ecclesiological Perspectives: Parts 1 & 2', in *Scriptura* 94 (2007), 1-28.

Conradie, Ernst M. (ed), *Notions and Forms of Ecumenicity: South African Perspectives.* Stellenbosch, RSA: Sun Press, 2013.

Coorilos, Geevarghese, 'God of Life, Lead Us to Justice and Peace: Some Missiological Perspectives', in *International Review of Mission,* 102.396 (April 2013), 5-16.

Costas, Orlando E., *Christ outside the Gate: Mission Beyond Christendom.* Maryknoll, NY: Orbis Books, 1984.

Costello, Gerald M., *Mission to Latin America: The Successes and Failures of a Twentieth Century Crusade.* Maryknoll, NY: Orbis Books, 1979.

Coulson, C.A., 'A Secular World? – God and Things', in *Laity,* 16 (November 1963).

Cox, Harvey, *Fire from Heaven: The Rise of Pentecostal Spirituality and the Reshaping of Religion in the Twenty-first Century.* New York: Cassell, 1996.

Cox, James L., 'Jerusalem 1928: Its Message for Today', in *Missiology: An International Review* 9:2 (April 1981), 139-53.

Cracknell, Kenneth, *Justice, Courtesy and Love: Theologians and Missionaries Encountering World Religions 1846-1914.* London: Epworth Press, 1995.

Crane, William H., 'Dropping the S', in *International Review of Mission,* 58.230 (1969), 141-44.

Cruchley Jones, Peter, 'You Have Not Sought the Lost: A Reflection from Europe on the WCC Theme', in *International Review of Mission,* 102.396 (April 2013), 69-81.

Cruz, Gemma, *An Intercultural Theology of Migration: Pilgrims in the Wilderness.* Leiden: Brill, 2010.

Cruz, Gemma Tulud, *Toward a Theology of Migration: Social Justice and Religious Experience.* New York: Palgrave Macmillan, 2014.

Daley, H.E. and Cobbs J.B. Jr, *For The Common Good.* Boston, PA: Beacon Press, 1989.

Davies, J.G., *Worship and Mission.* London: SCM, 1966 and New York: Association Press, 1967.

Davis, O., *Theology of transformation: Faith, Freedom, and the Christian Act.* Oxford: OUP, 2013.

Dawkins, Richard, *The God Delusion.* London: Bantam, 2006.

Dawson, David G., 'The Church and the Edinburgh Missionary Conference', in *Missiology: An International Review,* 39:2 (April 2011), 157-73.

De Gruchy, John W., 'Christian Community', in John W. de Gruchy & Charles Villa-Vicencio (eds). *Doing Theology in Context: South African Perspectives.* Cape Town, RSA: David Philip, 1994, 125-38.

De Gruchy, Steve, 'Agency, Sin and Grace: Protestant Reflections on Mission and Creation', in Lukas Vischer (ed), *Witnessing in the Midst of a Suffering Creation: A Challenge for the Mission of the Church*. Geneva: WCC, 2007, 97-114.

De Haan, M.J., *Mission on the Margin*. Pietermaritzburg, RSA: Cluster Publications, 2010.

De La Torre, Miguel A. and Stacey M. Floyd-Thomas (eds), *Beyond the Pale: Reading Theology from the Margins*. Louisville, KY: Westminster John Knox Press, 2011.

De Masa, Jose M., 'Mission and Inculturation', in Stephen B. Bevans (ed), *A Century of Catholic Mission: Roman Catholic Missiology 1910 to the Present*. Regnum Edinburgh 2010 Series, Vol. XV. Oxford: Regnum, 2013.

Dedji, Valentin, *Reconstruction and Renewal in African Theology*. Nairobi: Acton, 2003.

Delio, Ilia, Keith Douglass Warner and Pamela Wood. *Care for Creation: A Franciscan Spirituality of the Earth*. Cincinnati, OH: St Anthony Messenger Press, 2007.

Deng Zhaoming, 'Indigenous Chinese Pentecostal Denominations', in Allan Anderson and Edmond Tang (eds), *Asian and Pentecostal: The Charismatic Face of Asian Christianity*. Oxford: Regnum and Baguio City: APTS Press, 2005.

Dietrich, Stephanie, Knud Jørgensen, Kari Karsrud Korslien and Kjell Nordstokke (eds), *Diakonia as Christian Social Practice – An Introduction*. Oxford: Regnum, 2014.

Dilger, Hansjörg, 'Healing the Wounds of Modernity: Salvation, Community and Care in a Neo-Pentecostal Church in Dar Es Salaam, Tanzania', in *Journal of Religion in Africa,* 37.1 (2007), 59-83.

Dorr, Donal, *Mission in Today's World*. Blackrock, Dublin: Columba Press, 2000.

Dries, Angelyn, OSF, 'Catholic Mission in North America 1910-2010', in Stephen B. Bevans (ed), *A Century of Catholic Mission*. Oxford: Regnum, 2013, 58-66.

Dube, Musa, 'Consuming a Colonial Cultural Time Bomb: Translating Badimo into Demons in the Setswana Bible (Matt. 8.28-34; 15.22; 10.8)', in *Journal for the Study of the New Testament,* 73 (1999), 33-59.

Duchrow, Ulrich and F.J. Hinkelammert. *Transcending Greedy Money: Interreligious Solidarity for Just Relations*. New York: Palgrave Macmillan, 2012.

Duck, Ruth C., *Worship for the Whole People of God*. Louisville, KY: Westminster John Knox, 2013.

Duff, Edward, *The Social Thought of the World Council of Churches*. New York: Associate Press, 1956.

Duraisingh, Christopher, 'Editorial', in *International Review of Mission,* 79.313 (1990), 1-5.

Eagleton, Terry, *Reason, Faith, and Revolution: Reflections on the God Debate*. New Haven and London: Yale University Press, 2009.

Early, Tracy, *Simply Sharing – A Personal Survey of How Well the Ecumenical Movement Shares its Resources*. Geneva: WCC, 1980.

Ebeling, R. & A. Meier, (Hrsg) *Missionale Theologie*. Marburg an der Lahn, Germany: Verlag der Francke-Buchhandlung, 2009.

Eck, Diana L., 'The Religions and Tambaram: 1938 and 1988', in *International Review of Mission,* 77.307 (July 1988).

Éla, Jean-Marc, *African Cry*. Maryknoll, NY: Orbis Books, 1986.
Éla, Jean-Marc, *My Faith as an African*. Maryknoll, NY: Orbis Books, 1988.
Elwood, Douglas J., 'Asian Christian Theology in the Making: An Introduction', in Douglas J. Elwood (ed), *Asian Christian Theology: Emerging Themes*. Philadelphia, PA: Westminster Press, revised edition, 1980, 23-39.
ENFORMM, 'Churches in Ecumenical Transition: Towards Multicultural Ministry and Mission', in *International Review of Mission*, 101.394 (2012).
Engelsviken, Tormod, '*Missio Dei:* The Understanding and Misunderstanding of a Theological Concept in European Churches and Missiology', in *International Review of Mission*, 92.367 (2003), 481-97.
England, John C. et al, *Asian Christian Theologies: A Research Guide to Authors, Movements, Sources*. Maryknoll, NY: Orbis Books, 2002.
Ernst, Manfred (ed), *Globalisation and the Re-Shaping of Christianity in the Pacific Islands*. Suva: Pacific Theological College, 2006.
Escobar, Samuel, 'Biblical Content and Anglo-Saxon Trappings in Latin American Theology', in *Occasional Bulletin*, Latin American Theological Fraternity 3 (October 1972).
Escobar, Samuel, 'Identity, Future and Mission of Latin American Protestantism', in *Theological Fraternity Bulletin*, 1:2 (1978).
Escobar, Samuel, *Liberation Themes in Reformational Perspective*. Sioux Center, IA: Dordt College Press, 1989.
Escobar, J. Samuel, 'The Missiological Significance of Latin American Protestantism', in *International Review of Mission*, 100.393 (November 2011), 232-43.
Escobar, Samuel, *The New Global Mission*. Leicester, UK: IVP, 2003.
Escobar, Samuel, 'Together Towards Life: Mission and Evangelism in Changing Landscapes', in *International Bulletin of Missionary Research*, 38:4 (October 2014), 193-95.
Evers, Georg, *The Churches in Asia*. New Delhi: ISPCK, 2005.
Fabella, Virginia, 'The Roman Catholic Church in the Asian Ecumenical Movement', in Ninan Koshy (ed), *A History of the Ecumenical Movement in Asia, Vol. II*. Hong Kong: World Student Christian Federation, Asia Pacific Alliance of YMCAs and Christian Conference of Asia, 116.
Fagerli, B. and K. Jørgensen, 'Together Towards Life: Norwegian reflections', in *International Review of Mission*, 103.398 (April 2014), 135-43.
Faggioli, Massimo, *Vatican II: The Battle for Meaning*. New York: Paulist, 2012.
Fairbairn, Te'o I.J. and DeLisle Worrell, *South Pacific and Caribbean Islands: A Comparative Study*. Brisbane, Australia: The Foundation for Development Co-operation, 1996.
Farhadian, Charles E. (ed), *Christian Worship Worldwide: Expanding Horizons, Deepening Practices*. Grand Rapids, MI and Cambridge, UK: Eerdmans, 2007.
Farquhar, J.N., *The Crown of Hinduism*. London: Oxford University Press, 1913.
Federov, Vladimir, 'The Wind of Change: An Orthodox Point of View', in *International Review of Mission*, 101.395 (November 2012), 404-06.
Fenwick, John and B. Spinks, *Worship in Transition: The Liturgical Movement in the Twentieth Century*. New York: Continuum, 1995.
Ferguson, Niall, *Civilization: The West and the Rest*. New York: Penguin, 2011.
Ferguson, Niall, *Colossus: The Rise and Fall of the American Empire*. London: Penguin, 2004.

Fernando, Leonard and George Gispert-Sauch, *Christianity in India: Two Thousand Years of Faith.* New Delhi: Oxford University Press, 2004.

Ferris, Elizabeth, 'Crisis Situations, Humanitarian Assistance, Preventive Measures and Churches' Response', in Matthews George Chunakara (ed), *Rights of Internally Displaced People: Asian Churches' Response*. Hong Kong: Christian Conference of Asia, 2000, 31-42.

FitzGerald, Thomas E., *The Ecumenical Movement: An Introductory History.* Westport, CT: Praeger Publishers, 2004.

Flannery, Austin (ed), *Vatican Council II: The Concilliar and Post Concilliar Documents,* revised edition. Collegeville, MN: Liturgical, 1984.

Flett, John G., 'From Jerusalem to Oxford: Mission as the Foundation and Goal of Ecumenical Social Thought', in *International Bulletin of Missionary Research,* 27.1 (January 2003).

Flett, John G., *The Witness of God: The Trinity, Missio Dei, Karl Barth and the Nature of Christian Community.* Grand Rapids MI: Eerdmans, 2010.

Fredericks, Martha and Dorottya Nagy, 'Guest Editorial', in *Mission Studies,* 32:2 (2015), 177-79.

Freeman, Curtis, 'Pentecostal Power', in *Baptist News Global* (25th May 2012).

Freston, Paul, 'In Search of an Evangelical Political Project for Brazil: A Pentecostal "Showvention"', in *Transformation,* 9:3 (July-Sept 1992).

Friesen, J. Stanley, *Missionary Responses to Tribal Religions at Edinburgh 1910.* New York: Peter Lang, 1996.

Fritzson, A.S. and S. Kabue, *Interpreting Disability: A Church of All and for All.* Geneva: WCC, 2004.

Frykenberg, Robert Eric, *Christianity in India: From Beginnings to the Present.* New York: Oxford University Press, 2008.

Fukuyama, Francis, *The End of History and the Last Man.* New York: Free Press, 1992.

Galeano, Eduardo, *Open Veins of Latin America.* New York: Monthly Review Press, 1973.

Garrett, John, *Footsteps in the Sea: Christianity in Oceania to World War II.* Geneva: WCC, 1992.

Garrett, John, *To Live Among the Stars: Christian Origins in Oceania.* Geneva: WCC, 1982.

Garrett, John, *Where Nets Were Cast: Christianity in Oceania Since World War II.* Geneva: WCC, 1997.

Gavaskar, Mahesh, 'Colonialism within Colonialism: Phule's Critique of Brahmin Power', in S.M. Michael (ed), *Dalits in Modern India: Vision and Values.* 2nd edition. New Delhi: Sage Publications, 2007.

Gay, Naw Eh Tar, 'Tribal Women in Asian Churches', in Hope Antone, Wati Longchar, Hyungju Bae, Huang Po Ho and Dietrich Werner (eds), *Asian Handbook for Theological Education and Ecumenism.* Taiwan: PTCA, 2013, 368-76.

Geertz, Clifford, *The Interpretation of Cultures.* New York: Basic Books, 1973.

Geevarghese, Metropolitan Coorilos, 'Towards and Beyond Edinburgh 2010: A Historical Survey of Ecumenical Missiological Developments since 1910', in *International Review of Mission,* 99.390 (April 2010).

Gibaut, John, 'From Unity and Mission to Koinonia and Missio Dei. Convergences in WCC Ecclesiology and Missiology towards Edinburgh 2010', in John Gibaut and Knud Jørgensen (eds), *Called to Unity For the Sake of Mission*. Oxford: Regnum, 2014, 73-88.

Gibaut, John and Knud Jørgensen (eds), *Called to Unity For the Sake of Mission*. Oxford: Regnum, 2014.

Gibbs, Philip, 'Emerging Indigenous Theologies in Oceania', in *Concilium,* 5 (2010), 34-44.

Giddens, Anthony, *Runaway World: How Globalization is Reshaping Our Lives.* 2nd edition. London: Profile Books, 2002.

Goodhew, David, Andrew Roberts & Michael Volland, *Fresh! An Introduction to Fresh Expressions of Church and Pioneer Ministry.* London: SCM, 2012.

Gorringe, Timothy, *Redeeming Time: Atonement through Education.* London: Darton, Longman & Todd, 1986.

Greenman, Jeffrey P. and Gene L. Greene (eds), *Global Theology in Evangelical Perspective.* Leicester, UK: IVP, 2012.

Grogan, Paul and Kirsteen Kim (eds), *The New Evangelization: Faith, People, Context and Practice.* London: Bloomsbury, 2015.

Groody, Daniel G., *Globalization, Spirituality and Justice.* Maryknoll, NY: Orbis Books, 2007.

Groody, Daniel, 'The Church on the Move: Mission in an Age of Migration', in *Mission Studies,* 30 (2013), 27-42.

Grundmann, Christopher H., 'Gesandt zu heilen. Aufkommen und Entwicklung der Ärztlichen Mission im neunzehnten Jahrhundert', in *Missionswissenschaftliche Forschungen,* Bd. 12, Gütersloh, Germany: 1992.

Guder, Darrell L., 'Evangelism and the Debate Over Church Growth', in *Interpretation,* 48:2 (April 1994), 145-55.

Guder, Darrell, 'Missio Dei: Integrating Theological Formation for Apostolic Vocation' (Presidential address), in *Missiology: An International Review,* 38:1 (2009).

Guder, Darrell (ed), *Missional Church: A Vision for the Sending of the Church in North America.* Grand Rapids, MI: Eerdmans, 1998.

Gutiérrez, Gustavo, *A Theology of Liberation*. London: SCM, 1988.

Gutiérrez, Gustavo, *Dios o el oro de las Indias*. Lima: CEP, 1989.

Gutiérrez, Gustavo, *Las Casas: In Search of the Poor of Jesus Christ.* Trans. Robert R. Barr. Maryknoll, NY: Orbis Books, 1993.

Gutiérrez, Gustavo, 'Theology as Wisdom', in T.K. John (ed), *Bread and Breath: Essays in Honour of Samuel Rayan SJ.* Anand, Gujarat: Gujarat Sahitya Prakash, 1990, 3-5.

Gutiérrez, Gustavo, *We Drink from Our Own Wells: The Spiritual Journey of a People.* Maryknoll, NY: Orbis Books and Melbourne: Dove Communications, 1984 and Maryknoll, NY: Orbis Books, 2003.

Günther, Wolfgang, 'The History and Significance of World Mission Conferences in the 20th Century', in *International Review of Mission,* 92.367 (2003), 521-37.

Hagan, Jacqueline Maria, *Migration Miracle: Faith, Hope and Meaning on the Undocumented Journey.* Cambridge, MA: Harvard University Press, 2008.

Hagan, Jacqueline Maria, 'The Church vs. the State: Borders, Migrants, and Human Rights', in Pierrette Hondagneu-Sotelo (ed), *Religion and Social Justice for Immigrants*. New Brunswick, NJ: Rutgers University Press, 2007, 96-101.

Halapua, Winston, '*Theomoana*: Toward an Oceanic Theology', *Concilium,* 5 (2010).

Halapua, Winston, *Waves of God's Embrace: Sacred Perspectives from the Ocean.* Norwich, UK: Canterbury Press, 2008.
Halik, Tomás, 'The Soul of Europe: An Altar to the Unknown God', in *International Review of Mission,* 95.378-79 (2006), 265-70.
Hallencreutz, Carl F., *Kraemer Towards Tambaram: A Study in Hendrik Kraemer's Missionary Approach.* Uppsala, Sweden: Gleerup, 1966.
Hallman, David G. (ed), *Ecotheology: Voices from South and North.* Geneva: WCC, 1994.
Hanciles, Jehu J., *Beyond Christendom: Globalization, African Migration, and the Transformation of the West.* Maryknoll, NY: Orbis Books, 2008.
Hanciles, Jehu, 'Migrants as Missionaries, Missionaries as Outsiders: Reflections on African Christian Presence in Western Societies', in *Mission Studies,* 30 (2013), 64-85.
Harris, R. Geoffrey, *Mission in the Gospels.* Peterborough, UK: Epworth, 2004.
Hau'ofa, Epeli, *A New Oceania: Rediscovering Our Sea of Islands.* Suva: University of the South Pacific, 1993.
Havea, John, 'A Reconsideration of *Pacificness* in a Search for a South Pacific Theology', in *The Pacific Journal of Theology,* 2:10 (1993), 5-16.
Havea, Sione 'Amanaki, 'Christianity in the Pacific Context', in *South Pacific Papers from Consultation on Pacific Theology.* Parramatta, Australia: Regnum and World Vision International South Pacific, 1986.
Hawn, C. Michael, *One Bread, One Body: Exploring Cultural Diversity in Worship.* Bethesda, MD: Alban Institute, 2003.
Heaney, Sharon E., *Contextual Theology for Latin America: Liberation Themes in Evangelical Perspective.* Carlisle, UK: Paternoster, 2008.
Heim, Mark, 'Mission and Dialogue: 50 Years After Tambaram', in *The Christian Century,* 105.11 (6th April 1988).
Heim, Mark, *Salvations: Truth and Difference in Religion*, Maryknoll, NY: Orbis Books, 1995.
Held, David, Anthony McGrew, David Goldblatt and Jonathan Perraton, *Global Transformations: Politics, Economics and Culture.* Stanford, CA: Stanford University Press, 1999.
Heller, Dagmar, 'Reflections on the Pilgrimage of Justice and Peace', in *The Ecumenical Review,* 66:2 (July 2014), 135-38.
Hempelmann, Reinhard, 'The Context of Christian Witness in the 21st Century', in *International Review of Mission,* 92.364 (2003), 45-55.
Hendriksen, Jan-Olav, 'Multifaceted Christianity and the Postmodern Condition: Reflections on its Challenges to Churches in the Northern Hemisphere', in Rolv Olsen (ed), *Mission and Postmodernities.* Regnum: Oxford, 2011.
Hewitt, R.R., 'Evangelism as Discipleship', in *International Review of Mission,* 103.399 (November 2014), 200-14.
Hewitt, R.R., 'Spirituality for Democracy: Spiritual Resources for Democratic Participation in the 21st Century'. *Verbum et Ecclesia* 35:3 (2014).
Hewitt, R.R., 'Sun, Sand, Sea, Reggae! The Challenge of Tourism for Church and Society in the Caribbean', in Caesar D'Mello, Wati Longchar and Philip Mathew (eds), *Deconstructing Tourism: Who Benefits? A Theological Reading from the Global South.* Kolkata, India: SCEPTRE, 2013.
Hewitt, Roderick, 'Missional Leadership Formation: Embodiment of Together towards Life', in *International Review of Mission,* 103.398 (2014), 144-47.
Hick, John, *The Rainbow of Faiths.* London: SCM, 1995.

Hiebert, Paul G., *Anthropological Insights for Missionaries.* Grand Rapids, MI: Baker Academic, 2008.
Higton, Mike, *Christian Doctrine.* London: SCM, 2008.
Hill, Patricia, *The World their Household: The American Women's Foreign Mission Movement and Cultural Transformation 1870-1920.* Ann Arbor, MI: University of Michigan, 1985.
Hilliard, David Lockhart, 'Protestant Mission in Solomon Islands 1849-1942'. PhD thesis. Australian National University, 1966.
Hintersteiner, Norbert, 'From Cultural Translation to Interfaith Witness: The Intercultural Transformation of Missiology', in Linda Hogan, Solange Lefebvre, Norbert Hintersteiner and Felix Wilfred (eds), *From World Mission to Inter-religious Witness.* Concilium 2011:1. London: SCM, 2011, 85-94.
Hitchcock, Robert and Diana Vinding (eds), *Indigenous Peoples' Rights in Southern Africa.* Copenhagen: IWGIA, 2004.
Hitchens, Christopher, *God Is Not Great: How Religion Poisons Everything.* London: Atlantic Books, 2007.
Hocking, W.E. (ed), *Rethinking Missions: a Laymen's Inquiry after One Hundred Years.* New York and London: Harper & Brothers, 1932.
Hoedemaker, Bert, *Secularization and Mission: A Theological Essay.* Harrisburg, PA: Trinity Press, 1998.
Hoekendijk, Johannes C., *The Church Inside Out.* Philadelphia, PA: Westminster Press, 1966.
Hogg, William Richey, *Ecumenical Foundations: A History of the International Missionary Council and its Nineteenth Century Background.* New York: Harper & Brothers, 1952 and Eugene, OR: Wipf & Stock, 2002.
Hollenweger, Walter J., *Pentecostalism: Origins and Developments Worldwide.* Peabody, MA: Hendrickson, 1997.
Hollenweger, Walter J., 'Roman Catholics and Pentecostals in Dialogue', in *The Ecumenical Review,* 51:2 (April 1999), 147-59.
Hollenweger, Walter J., *The Pentecostals.* London: SCM, 1969 and ET 1972.
Hondagneu-Sotelo, Pierette, *God's Heart Has No Borders: How Religious Activists are Working for Immigrant Rights.* Berkeley, CA: University of California Press, 2008.
Hopkins, C. Howard, *John R. Mott 1865-1955: A Biography.* Geneva: WCC and Grand Rapids, MI: Eerdmans, 1979.
Hughes, Rebecca, 'The Legacy of Mabel Shaw', in *International Bulletin of Missionary Research,* 37:2 (April 2013), 105-08.
Hughes, III, Robert Davies, *Beloved Dust: Tides of the Spirit in the Christian Life.* New York: Continuum, 2008.
Hunter, Harold D. and Peter D. Hocken (eds), *All Together in One Place: Theological Papers from the Brighton Conference on World Evangelization.* Sheffield, UK: Sheffield Academic Press, 1993.
Hunter, Jane, *Gospel of Gentility: American Women Missionaries in Turn of the Century China.* New Haven, CT: Yale University Press, 1984.
Hviding, Edvard, *Guardians of Marovo Lagoon: Practice, Place and Politics in Maritime Melanesia.* Honolulu, HI: University of Hawaii Press, 1996.
Idowu, E. Bolaji, *African Traditional Religion: A Definition.* Maryknoll, NY: Orbis Books, 1974.
Idowu, E. Bolaji, *Olodumare: God in Yoruba Belief.* London: Longmans, 1962.

Im, Chandler and Amos Yong (eds), *Global Diasporas and Mission.* Portland, OR: Wipf & Stock, 2014.
IMC, 'The Missionary Calling of the Church' in 'Quarterly Notes', No. 16, October 1952: *International Review of Mission,* 41.64 (October 1952), i-xii.
Ingalls, Monique M. and Amos Yong (eds), *The Spirit of Praise.* Penn State University Press, 2015.
'International Migration and Development Report'. Report of the Secretary General at the 69th Session of the United Nations General Assembly, 20th July 2014: www.un.org/en/ga/search/view_doc.asp?symbol=A/69/207
Irvin, Dale T. and Scott W. Sunquist, *History of the World Christian Movement, Vol. I.* Maryknoll, NY: Orbis Books, 2001.
*Island of Hope: A Pacific Alternative to Economic Globalisation.* Geneva: WCC, 2002.
Jenkins, Philip, 'Imperial Missionaries?', in *Christian Century,* 26th November 2014.
Jenkins, Philip, *The New Faces of Christianity: Believing the Bible in the Global South.* Oxford: OUP, 2008.
Jenkins, Philip, *The Next Christendom: The Coming of Global Christianity.* Oxford: OUP, 2002.
Jenkins, William and Helene O'Sullivan (eds), *Trends in Mission: Toward the 3rd Millennium.* Maryknoll, NY: Orbis Books, 1991.
Johns, Cheryl Bridges, 'Overcoming the Holy Spirit Shyness in the Life of the Church', in *Vision,* 13:1 (Spring 2012), 6-15.
Johnson, Todd M., 'Contextualisation: A New-Old Idea', in *The International Journal for Frontier Mission,* 4 (1987), 1-4.
Johnson, Todd and Gina Bellofatto, 'Migration, Religious Diasporas and Religious Diversity', in *Mission Studies* 29 (2012), 3-22.
Johnson, Todd M. and Kenneth R. Ross (eds), *Atlas of Global Christianity, 1910–2010.* Edinburgh: Edinburgh University Press, 2009.
Jonker, W. D. (Willie), 'Turning to the World: On Karl Barth's Interpretation of the Modern Era', in Johan Mouton & Bernard C. Lategan (eds), *The Relevance of Theology in the 1990s.* Pretoria, RSA: HSRC, 1994, 535-48.
Jonson, Jonas and Norman A. Hjelm, *Wounded Visions.* Grand Rapids, MI: Eerdmans, 2013.
Kang, Namsoon, 'Re-constructing Asian Feminist Theology: Toward a Glocal Feminist Theology in an Era of Neo-Empire(s)', in Sebastian C.H. Kim (ed), *Christian Theology in Asia.* Cambridge: CUP, 2008, 205-26.
Karecki, Madge, 'A Missiological Reflection on "Together towards Life: Mission and Evangelism in Changing Landscapes"', in *International Bulletin of Missionary Research,* 38:4 (2014).
Kärkkäinen, Velli-Matti, *Ad ultimum terrae: Evangelization, Proselytism and Common Witness in the Roman Catholic Pentecostal Dialogue 1990-1997.* Frankfurt: Peter Lang, 1999.
Karotemprel, S. (ed), *Following Christ in Mission: A foundational course in mission.* Nairobi: Pauline Publications, 1995.
Karpf, Ted and Alex Ross (eds), *Building From Common Foundations, The World Health Organization and Faith-Based Organizations in Primary Healthcare.* World Health Organization, 2008.
Kasper, Walter, *Pope Francis' Revolution of Tenderness and Love: Theological and Pastoral Perspectives.* Trans. William Madges. New York: Paulist, 2014.

Keller, Timothy, *Preaching: Communicating Faith in an Age of Skepticism.* New York: Viking, 2015.

Kemper, Thomas, 'The Missio Dei in Contemporary Context', in *International Bulletin of Missionary Research,* 38 (October 2014), 188-90.

Kerr, David A. & Kenneth R. Ross (ed), *Edinburgh 2010: Mission Then and Now.* Oxford: Regnum, 2009.

Keshkegian, F.A., *Redeeming Memories: A Theology of Healing and Transformation.* Nashville, TN: Abingdon Press, 2000.

Keum, Jooseop, 'Beyond Dichotomy: Towards a Convergence Between the Ecumenical and Evangelical Understanding of Mission in Changing Landscapes', in Margunn Serigstad Dahle, Lars Dahle and Knud Jørgensen (eds), *The Lausanne Movement: A Range of Perspectives.* Oxford: Regnum, 2014, 383-98.

Keum, Jooseop, 'Shift in the Center of Gravity for the Ecumenical Movement? WCC Busan Assembly and the Korean Churches', in *International Bulletin of Missionary Research,* 38:2 (April 2014), 64-67.

Khodr, George, 'Christianity in a Pluralistic World: The Economy of the Holy Spirit', in *The Ecumenical Review* 23 (1971), 118-28.

Kim, Kirsteen, 'Edinburgh 1910 to 2010: From Kingdom to Spirit', in *Journal of the European Pentecostal Theological Association,* 30.2 (2010), 3-20.

Kim, Kirsteen, 'Editorial', in *Mission Studies,* 32:2 (2015), 175-76.

Kim, Kirsteen, *Joining in with the Spirit: Connecting World Church and Local Mission.* London: SCM, 2012.

Kim, Kirsteen, *Mission in the Spirit: The Holy Spirit in Indian Christian Theologies.* Delhi: ISPCK, 2003.

Kim, Kirsteen, '"Spirit and Spirits" at the Canberra Assembly of the World Council of Churches, 1991', in *Missiology: An International Review* 32.3 (2004), 349-65.

Kim, Kirsteen, *The Holy Spirit in the World: A Global Conversation.* Maryknoll, NY: Orbis Books, 2007.

Kim, Kirsteen and Andrew Anderson (eds), *Edinburgh 2010: Mission Today and Tomorrow.* Oxford: Regnum, 2011.

Kim, Nami, 'Cutting Edges: "My/our" comfort not at the Expense of Somebody Else: Toward a Critical Global Feminist Theology', in *Journal of Feminist Studies in Religion*, 21:2 (Fall 2000), 75-94.

Kim, Nami, 'The "Indigestible" Asian: The Unifying Term "Asian" in Theological Discourse', in Rita Nakashima Brock, Jung Ha Kim, Kwok Pui Lan, Seung Ai Yang (eds), *Off the Menu: Asian and Asian North American Women's Religions and Theology.* Louisville, KY: Westminster John Knox Press, 2007, 23-43.

Kim, Nami, 'Which Postcolonialism? The Relevance of Resistance Postcolonialism to Postcolonial Asia', in *Asian Christian Review* 6:1 (2012) 23-35.

Kim, Sebastian C.H. and Kirsteen Kim, *A History of Korean Christianity.* Cambridge: CUP, 2014.

Kim, Sebastian C.H. and Kirsteen Kim, *Christianity as a World Religion.* London and New York: Continuum, 2008 and London: Bloomsbury, 2013.

Kinnamon, Michael (ed), *Signs of the Spirit.* Official Report of the Seventh Assembly of the World Council of Churches, Canberra, 1991. Geneva: WCC, 1991.

Kinnamon, Michael and Brian Cope (eds), *The Ecumenical Movement: An Anthology of Key Texts and Voices.* Geneva: WCC, 1997.

Kinsler Ross (ed), *Diversified Theological Education: Equipping All God's People.* Pasadena, CA: WCIU Press, 2008.
Kinsler, Ross (ed), *Ministry by the People: Theological Education by Extension.* Geneva: WCC and Maryknoll, NY: Orbis Books, 1983.
Kipp, Rita Smith, 'Why Can't a Woman be more like a Man? Bureaucratic Contractions in the Dutch Missionary Society', in M.T. Huber and N.C. Lutkehaus (eds), *Gendered Mission: Women and Men in Missionary Discourses and Practice.* Michigan: University of Michigan 1999, 145-77.
Kirk, J.A., 'Postmodernity', in J. Corrie (ed), *Dictionary of Mission Theology: Evangelical Foundations.* Nottingham, UK: IVP, 2007.
Kobia, Samuel, 'Cooperation and the Promotion of Unity. A World Council of Churches Perspective', in David A. Kerr and Kenneth R. Ross (eds), *Edinburgh 2010: Mission Then and Now.* Oxford: Regnum, 2009.
Koning, Danielle, 'Place, Space, and Authority: The Mission and Reversed Mission of the Ghanaian Seventh-day Adventist Church in Amsterdam', in *African Diaspora* 2:2 (2009), 203-26.
Koria, Paulo, 'Moving Toward a Pacific Theology: Theologising with Concepts', in *The Pacific Journal of Theology* 2:22 (1999), 3-14.
Kraemer, Hendrik, *The Christian Message in a Non-Christian World.* London: Edinburgh House Press and New York: Harper, 1938.
Krasner, S.D. and C. Pascual, 'Addressing State Failure', in *Foreign Affairs* 84:4 (2005), 153-63.
Kreider, Alan, *Social Holiness: A Way for Living for God's Nation.* Eugene, OR: Wipf & Stock, 2008; previously published as *Journey Toward Holiness.* Scottdale, PA: Herald Press, 1987.
Kreider, Alan and E. Kreider, *Worship and Mission after Christendom.* Scottdale, PA and Waterloo, Ontario: Herald Press, 2011.
Kritzinger, J.J. (Dons), 'Training for Mission: Some Thoughts on Theological and Missionary Training in South Africa', in *Missionalia,* 30:1 (2002).
Kroeber, Alfred Louis and Clyde Kluckhohn, *Culture: A Critical Review of Concepts and Definitions.* New York: Vintage Books, 1952.
Kroeger, James, 'Papal Mission Wisdom: Five Mission Encyclicals 1919-1959', in Stephen B. Bevans (ed), *A Century of Catholic Mission.* Oxford: Regnum, 2013, 93-100.
Kupchan, C.A., *No One's World: The West, the Rising Rest, and the Coming Global Turn.* Oxford: OUP, 2012.
Kuster, Volker, *Einfuhrung in die Interkulturelle Theologie.* Gottingen: Vandenhoeck & Ruprecht, 2011.
Laing, Mark T.B., *From Crisis to Creation: Lesslie Newbigin and the Reinvention of Christian Mission.* Eugene OR: Pickwick, 2012.
Laing, Mark, 'Recovering Missiological Ecclesiology in Theological Education', in Dazan, Ebenezer D. and Frampton F. Fox (eds), *Missiological Education: Theological Integration and Contextual Implications.* New Delhi: Centre for Mission Studies, 2009, 41-72.
Laing, Mark, 'The Church is the Mission: Integrating the IMC with the WCC', in *International Review of Mission,* 100.393 (November 2011), 216-31.
Lang, Gottfried O. and Grattan T. Brown, 'Culture', in Robert L. Fastiggi (ed), *New Catholic Encyclopedia Supplement 2012-2013: Ethics and Philosophy.* Detroit, MI: Gale, 2013.

Larsen, Edvard and Knud Jørgensen (eds), *Power and Partnership*. Oxford: Regnum, 2014.

Larsson, Birgitta and Emilio Castro, 'From Missions to Mission', in John Briggs, Mercy Amba Oduyoye and George Tsetsis (eds), *A History of the Ecumenical Movement, Vol. III, 1968-2000*. Geneva: WCC, 2004, 125-48.

Latourette, Kenneth Scott, 'Ecumenical Bearings of the Missionary Movement and the International Missionary Council', in Ruth Rouse and Stephen Charles Neill (eds), *A History of the Ecumenical Movement 1517-1948*. 4th edition. Geneva: WCC, 1994, 351-402.

*Laymen's Foreign Mission Enquiry, Supplementary Series*. 7 vols. New York: Harper & Brothers, 1933.

Leddy, Mary Jo, 'When the Stranger Summons: Spiritual and Theological Considerations for Ministry', in *New Theology Review*, 20:3 (August 2007), 5-14.

Lee, Jung Young, *Marginality: The Key to Multicultural Theology*. Minneapolis, MN: Fortress Press, 1995.

Lee, Young-Hoon, 'Korean Pentecost: The Great Revival of 1907', in *Asian Journal of Pentecostal Studies* 4:1 (2001), 73-83.

Lienemann-Perrin, Christine, Atola Longkumer and Afrie Songco Joye (eds), *Putting Names with Faces: Women's Impact in Mission History*. Nashville, TN: Abingdon Press, 2012.

Lim, Timothy T.N., 'Blessings in the Prophets and the Wisdom: A Response to Charismatic Christian Hermeneutics and a General Application for Christian Living', in *Evangelical Review of Society and Politics Special Edition on Money, Prosperity and Economics*, 6:1-2 (2012-13), 77-103.

Lim, Timothy T.N., 'Comparative Pneumatology in Together Towards Life, Evangelii Gaudium, and the Cape Town Commitment', in *International Review of Mission* 104.2 (2015).

Lim, Timothy T.N., 'Recognition and Reception: Towards a Joint Commemoration of the Reformation in 2017', in *Ecclesiology* (forthcoming).

Limouris, Gennadios (ed), *Orthodox Visions of Ecumenism: Statements, Messages and Reports on the Ecumenical Movement 1902-1992*. Geneva: WCC, 1994.

Litsios, Socrates, 'The Christian Medical Commission and the Development of WHO's Primary Health Care Approach', in *American Journal of Public Health*, 94/11 (November 2004), 1884-93.

Lodberg, Peter, 'Justice and Peace in a World of Chaos', in John Briggs et al (eds), *A History of the Ecumenical Movement: Volume III, 1968-2000*. Geneva: WCC, 2004, 323-43.

Lonergan, Bernard J.F., *Method in Theology*. London: Dartman, Longman & Todd, 1972.

Longkumer, Atola, Jorgen Skov Sorenson and Michael Biehl, *Mission and Power*. Oxford: Regnum, forthcoming.

Lorke, Melisande and Dietrich Werner (eds), *Ecumenical Visions for the 21st Century: A Reader for Theological Education*. Geneva: WCC, 2013.

Lossky, Nicholas et al (ed), *Dictionary of the Ecumenical Movement*. Geneva: WCC and Grand Rapids, MI: Eerdmans, 1991.

Lucy, Niall, *Beyond Semiotics: Text, Culture and Technology*. A. & C. Black, 2001.

Lumsdaine, David H. (ed), *Evangelical Christianity and Democracy in Asia*. Oxford: OUP, 2009.

Lussi, Carmen, 'Human Mobility as a Theological Consideration', in Solange Lefebvre and Luis Carlos Susin (eds), *Migration in a Global World.* Concilium 2008/5. London: SCM, 2008, 49-60.
Lyotard, Jean-Francois, *The Postmodern Condition: A Report on Knowledge.* Manchester, UK: Manchester University Press, 1984.
Ma, Julie C. and Wonsuk Ma, *Mission in the Spirit: Towards a Pentecostal/Charismatic Missiology.* Oxford: Regnum, 2010.
Ma, Wonsuk, 'Theological and Missional Formation in the Context of "New Christianity"', in *The Ecumenical Review,* 66:1 (2014).
Ma, Wonsuk and Kenneth R. Ross (eds), *Mission Spirituality and Authentic Discipleship.* Oxford: Regnum, 2013.
Ma, Wonsuk, Veli-Matti Kärkkäinen and J. Kwabena Asamoah-Gyadu (eds), *Pentecostal Mission and Global Christianity.* Eugene, OR: Wipf & Stock and Regnum, 2014.
MacDonald, Mark, 'Our agenda, as we wake up'. 6th November 2015: www.anglicanjournal.com/articles/our-agenda-as-we-wake-up
MacIntyre, Alasdair, *After Virtue: A Study in Moral Theory.* 3rd edition. London: Duckworth, 2007.
Mana, Kä, *L'Afrique va-t-elle Mourir: Bousculer L'imaginaire Africain: Essai d'Éthique Politique.* Paris: Éditions du Cerf, 1991.
Manchala, Deenabandhu, 'Mission as struggle for justice: From the perspective of those who are denied Justice', in George Mathew Nalunnakkal and A.P. Athyal (eds), *Quest for Justice: Perspectives on Mission and Unity.* ISPCK, NCCI and Gurukul, India, 2000.
Manchala, Deenabandhu, *Relocating Theological Education in a Marginalized Context.* Bangalore, India: Board of Theological Education of the Senate of Serampore College, 2015.
Manchala, Deenabandhu, 'Theological Reflections on Pilgrimage', in *Ecumenical Review,* 66.2. Geneva: WCC (July 2014), 140.
Manchala, Deenabandhu, Joseph Prabhakar Dayam and Peniel Rajkumar, 'When Margins Inform and Reform Mission: Dalit experiences as Foundations for Mission Theology', in Emma Wildwood and Peniel Rajkumar (eds), *Foundation for Mission.* Oxford: Regnum, 2013.
Marshall, Ruth, *Political Spiritualities: the Pentecostal Revolution in Nigeria.* Chicago, IL: University of Chicago Press, 2009.
Martin, David, 'Issues Affecting the Study of Pentecostalism in Asia', in Allan Anderson and Edmond Tang (eds), *Asian and Pentecostal: The Charismatic Face of Christianity in Asia.* Oxford: Regnum, 2005, 27-36.
Martin, David, *Pentecostalism: The World Their Parish.* Oxford: Blackwell, 2002.
Martin, Hugh, *Beginning at Edinburgh: A Jubilee Assessment of the World Missionary Conference 1910.* London: Edinburgh House Press, 1960.
Maskens, Mäite, 'Mobility among Pentecostal Pastors and Migratory Miracles', in *Canadian Journal of African Studies,* 46:3 (2012), 397-409.
Matthey, Jacques, 'Continuités et ruptures entre les deux conférences d'Edimbourg 1910 et 2010', in *Perspectives Missionnaires* 60:2 (2010), 21-37.
Matthey, Jacques, 'Evangelism, still the Enduring Test of our Ecumenical and Missionary Calling', in *International Review of Mission,* 96.382-83 (July-October 2007).
Matthey, Jacques, 'Integration of Church and Mission: the Challenge of Melbourne', in *International Review of Mission,* 70.280 (October 1981), 259-66.

Matthey, Jacques, 'Milestones in Ecumenical Missionary Thinking from the 1970s to the 1990s', in *International Review of Mission,* 88.350 (1999), 291-303.
Matthey, Jacques, 'Missiology in the World Council of Churches: Update: Presentation, History, Theological Background and Emphases of the Most Recent Mission Statement of the World Council of Churches', in *International Review of Mission,* 90.359 (2001), 427-43.
Matthey, Jacques, 'Mission et évangélisation dans l'optique de Lausanne, Rome et Genève', in *Perspectives Missionnaires,* 10 (1985), 36-50.
Matthey, Jacques, 'Reconciliation, Missio Dei and the Church's Mission', in Howard Mellor and Timothy Yates (eds), *Mission, Violence and Reconciliation.* Sheffield, UK: Cliff College Publishing, 2004, 113-37.
Matthey, Jacques, 'Salvador among the World Mission Conferences of this Century', in *International Review of Mission* 86.340-41 (1997), 19-26.
Maxey, James A., *From Orality to Orality: A New Paradigm for Contextual Translation of the Bible.* Eugene OR: Cascade Books, 2009.
Mbiti, John S., *African Religions and Philosophy.* London: Heinemann, 1969.
Mbiti, John S., *Introduction to African Religion.* London: Heinemann, 1975.
Mbiti, John S., 'Theological Impotence and Universality of the Church', in Gerald H. Anderson and Thomas F. Stransky (eds), *Mission Trends No. 3: Third World Theologies.* New York: Paulist and Grand Rapids, MI: Eerdmans, 1976, 6-18.
McClung Jr., L. Grant. 'Evangelism', in Stanley M. Burgess (ed), *International Dictionary of Pentecostal and Charismatic Movements.* Revised and expanded edition. Grand Rapids MI: Zondervan, 2002.
McDonnell, Kilian (ed), *Open the Windows.* South Bend, IN: Greenlawn Press, 1989.
McGavran, Donald A., *Bridges of God: A Study in the Strategy of Mission.* Eugene OR: Wipf & Stock 2005 [1955].
McGavran, Donald A. 'Salvation Today', in Ralph Winter (ed), *The Evangelical Response to Bangkok.* Pasadena, CA: William Carey Library, 1973, 27-32.
McGavran, Donald A., *Understanding Church Growth.* Third edition. Revised and edited by C. Peter Wagner. Grand Rapids MI: Eerdmans, 1990.
McGavran Donald A. and Win Arn, *Ten Steps for Church Growth.* New York: Harper & Row, 1977.
McIntosh, Gary (ed), *Evaluating the Church Growth Movement.* Grand Rapids MI: Zondervan, 2004.
Mendonca, Clemens, 'Mission According to the Catholic Church in Asia: A New Way of Being Church', in Wonsuk Ma and Kenneth R. Ross (eds), *Mission Spirituality and Authentic Discipleship.* Regnum Edinburgh 2010 Series, Vol. XV. Oxford: Regnum, 2013.
Menjivar, Cecilia, 'Serving Christ in the Borderlands: Faith Workers Respond to Border Violence', in Pierrette Hondagneu-Sotelo (ed), *Religion and Social Justice for Immigrants.* New Brunswick, NJ: Rutgers University Press, 2007, 110-15.
Meo, Jovili Iliesa, 'Gems of the Pacific: Sharing and Service', in *The Pacific Journal of Theology,* 2:16 (1996), 84-101.
Meyers, Ruth A., *Missional Worship, Worshipful Mission: Gathering as God's People, Going Out in God's Name.* Grand Rapids, MI and Cambridge, UK: Eerdmans, 2014.
Míguez, Néstor, 'Grace in Pauline Theology: Political and Economic Projections', in *Neotestamentica,* 46:2 (2012), 287-98.

Míguez, Néstor, 'Sociopolitical Context of Postcolonial Studies in Latin America', in Joseph F. Duggan (ed), *Pressing On: Next Generation of Indecent Theologians*. Northampton, UK: Borderline Press, forthcoming.

Míguez, Néstor and Daniel Bruno, 'History of the Bible in Latin America', in John Riches (ed), *The New Cambridge History of the Bible*. Cambridge: CUP, 2015, 427-60.

Míguez, Néstor, Joerg Rieger and Jung Mo Sung, *Beyond the Spirit of the Empire: New Perspectives on Theology and Politics*. London: SCM, 2009.

Miller, Donald E., Kimon H. Sargeant and Richard Flory (eds), *Spirit and Power*. Oxford: OUP, 2013.

Miller, Donald E. and Tetsunao Yamamori, *Global Pentecostalism: The New Face of Social Engagement*. Berkeley, CA: University of California Press, 2007.

Moffett, Samuel Hugh, *A History of Christianity in Asia:* Vols I and II. Maryknoll NY: Orbis Books, 1998.

Mohammed, Amina, *Deepening Income Inequality*. World Economic Forum: http://reports.weforum.org/outlook-global-agenda-2015/top-10-trends-of-2015/1-deepening-income-inequality

Moltmann, Jürgen, *The Church in the Power of the Spirit*. London: SCM, 1977.

Moltmann, Jürgen, *The Crucified God: The Cross of Christ as the Foundation and Criticism of Christian Theology*. New York, Evanston, San Francisco and London: Harper & Row, 1973.

Moltmann, Jürgen, *The Source of Life: The Holy Spirit and the Theology of Life*. London: SCM, 1997.

Moltmann, Jürgen, *The Trinity and the Kingdom of God: The Doctrine of God*. London: SCM, 1981.

Morimoto, Anri, 'Asian Theology in the Ablative Case', in *Studies in World Christianity*, 17:3 (2011), 201-15.

Morrow, Sean, '"No Girl Leaves School Unmarried": Mabel Shaw and the Education of Girls at Mbereshi Northern Rhodesia 1915-1940', in *The International Journal of African Historical Studies*, 19:4, Boston University African Studies Centre (1986), 601-35.

Morrow, Sean, 'The Missionary in Bernard Shaw's *Black Girl*', in Stanley Weintraub (ed), *Shaw: The Annual of Bernard Shaw Studies, Vol. VI*. Pennsylvania State University Press, 1986, 5-12.

Motlhabi, Mokgethi, 'Black Theology: a Personal View', in Basil Moore (ed), *Black Theology: the South African Voice*. London: C. Hurst & Co., 1973.

Mott, John R., *The Decisive Hour of Christian Missions*. New York: Student Volunteer Movement for Foreign Missions, 1912.

Mott, John R., *The Evangelization of the World in This Generation*. London: Student Volunteer Missionary Union, 1900.

Mouw, Richard, *Consulting the Faithful*. Grand Rapids, MI: Eerdmans, 1994.

Mudge, Lewis, 'Ecumenical Social Thought', in John Briggs, Mercy A. Oduyoye and Georges Tsetsis (eds), *A History of the Ecumenical Movement, Volume III, 1968-2000*. Geneva: WCC, 2004, 279-321.

Mugambi, Jesse N.K., *Christian Theology and Social Reconstruction*. Nairobi: Acton, 2003.

Mugambi, Jesse N.K., *From Liberation to Reconstruction: African Christian Theology after the Cold War*. Nairobi: East African Educational Publishers, 1995.

Mukarjee, D. and K. Labi. 'Urban Rural Mission', in N. Lossky, J.M. Bonino, J. Pobee, T.F. Stransky, G. Wainwright, P. Webb (eds), *Dictionary of the Ecumenical Movement.* Second edition. Geneva: WCC, 2002, 1182-84.

Mulaudzi, Fhumulani M., 'Synergy between Indigenous Knowledge Systems, Modern Health Care System and Scientific Research – A Vision for the 21st Century', in *Health SA Gesondheid,* 6.4 (2001), 14-20.

Mullins, Mark R. (ed), *Handbook of Christianity in Japan.* Leiden: Brill, 2003.

Myers, Ched, 'Our God is Undocumented: Sanctuary and Prophetic Hospitality', in Ched Myers and Matthew Colwell (eds), *Our God is Undocumented: Biblical Faith and Immigrant Justice.* Maryknoll, NY: Orbis Books, 2012, 53-72.

Nagpur, John, 'New Delhi 1961: The Third Assembly of the World Council of Churches', in *International Review of Mission,* 51.202 (April 1962), 137-52.

Nascimento, Alzira, *Evangelização ou Colonização?* Viçosa, Brazil: Ultimato, 2015.

Neill, Stephen, 'A Revolutionary Church', in C.W. Ranson (ed), *Renewal and Advance: Christian Witness in a Revolutionary World.* London: Edinburgh House Press, 1948

Neill, Stephen, *A History of Christian Missions.* Grand Rapids, MI: Eerdmans, 1964.

Neill, Stephen, *The Church and Christian Union.* London: OUP, 1968.

Netland, Harold, *Encountering Religious Pluralism: The Challenge to Christian Faith & Mission.* Downers Grove, IL: IVP, 2001.

Neumann, Peter D., *Pentecostal Experience.* Princeton Theological Monograph 187. Eugene, OR: Wipf & Stock, 2012.

Newbigin, Lesslie, *Foolishness to the Greeks: The Gospel and Western Culture.* Geneva: WCC, 1986.

Newbigin, Lesslie, 'Mission to Six Continents', in Harold E. Fey (ed), *The Ecumenical Advance: A History of the Ecumenical Movement Vol. II, 1948-1968.* 3rd edition. Geneva: WCC, 1970, 171-97.

Newbigin, Lesslie, *The Gospel in a Pluralist Society.* London: SPCK, 1989.

Newbigin, Lesslie, *Unfinished Agenda: An Autobiography.* Grand Rapids, MI: Eerdmans, 1985.

Newbigin, Lesslie, *Unfinished Agenda: An Updated Autobiography.* Geneva: WCC, 1993.

Niebuhr, H. Richard, *Christ and Culture.* San Francisco, CA: HarperSanFrancisco, 2001.

Niles, Preman D., 'Ecumenical Dictionary: Justice, Peace and the Integrity of Creation'. November 2003: www.wcc-coe.org/wcc/who/dictionary-article11.html

Noort, Gerrit, '"So What?" – Dutch Responses to the New Mission Statement', in *International Review of Mission,* 102.397 (November 2013), 191-98.

Nordstokke, K. (ed), *Diakonia In Context: Transformation, Reconciliation, Empowerment: An LWF Contribution to the Understanding and Practice of Diakonia.* Geneva: LWF, 2009.

Norheim, Bård-Eirik Hallesby, 'The Global Youth Culture: Targeting and Involving Youth in Global Mission', in T. Engelsviken, E. Lundeby, and D. Solheim (eds), *The Church Going Glocal: Mission and Globalisation.* Regnum Edinburgh 2010 Series, Vol. VI. Oxford: Regnum, 2011.

Nouwen, Henri, *The Selfless Way of Christ: Downward Mobility and the Spiritual Life.* Maryknoll, NY: Orbis Books, 2007.

Núñez, Emilio A., *Liberation Theology.* Chicago: Moody Press, 1985.

Nunn, Patrick, 'Bridging the Gulf Between Science and Society: Imperatives for Minimizing Societal Disruption from Climate Change in the Pacific', in A Sumi et al. (eds), *Adaptation and Mitigation Strategies for Climate Change.* New York: Springer, 2010.

Nussbaum, Stan, *A Reader's Guide to Transforming Mission.* Maryknoll, NY: Orbis Books, 2005.

Nyamiti, Charles, *Christ as Our Ancestor: Christology from an African Perspective.* Eldoret, Kenya: Gaba Publications, 1984.

Nyazabino, Vedaste, 'The Role of Refugee-Established Churches in Integrating Forced Migrants: A Case Study of Word of Life Assembly in Yeoville, Johannesburg', in *HTS Theological Studies,* 66:1 (2010), 1-9.

Nye Jr., Joseph S., *The Paradox of American Power: Why the World's Only Superpower Can't Go It Alone.* Oxford: OUP, 2002.

Nyiri P., 'Moving Targets: Chinese Christian Proselytizing among Transnational Migrants from the People's Republic of China', in *European Journal of East Asian Studies,* 2:2 (2003), 263-301.

Oborji, F.A., *Concepts of Mission: The Evolution of Contemporary Missiology.* Maryknoll, NY: Orbis Books, 2006.

Oborji, Francis Anekwe, 'Theology', in Kenneth R. Ross, J. Kwabena Asamoah-Gyadu and Todd M. Johnson (eds), *Christianity in Sub-Saharan Africa: Edinburgh Companions to Global Christianity, Vol. I.* Edinburgh: Edinburgh University Press, forthcoming 2017.

Oborji, Francis Anekwe, *Trends in African Theology since Vatican II: A Missiological Orientation.* 2nd edition. Rome: Leberit Press, 2005.

Odeh, L.E., 'A Comparative Analysis of Global North and Global South Economies', in *Journal of Sustainable Development in Africa,* 12:3 (2010), 338-48.

Oduyoye, Mercy, *Daughters of Anowa: African Women and Patriarchy.* Maryknoll, NY: Orbis Books, 1995.

Oduyoye, Mercy Amba and Musimbi R.A. Kanyoro (eds), *The Will to Arise: Women, Tradition, and the Church in Africa.* Maryknoll, NY: Orbis Books, 1992.

Oesterreicher, J., 'The Declaration on Non-Christian Religions', in Herbert Vorgrimmler (ed), *Commentary on the Documents of Vatican II, Vol. III.* New York: Herder & Herder, 1968.

Okonkwo, Izunna, 'The Eucharist as Community Builder: Eucharistic Communion and Social Transformation'. Glasgow, UK, n.d.

Olsen, Rolv (ed), *Mission and Postmodernities*. Regnum Edinburgh 2010 Series, Vol. 10. Oxford: Regnum, 2011.

O'Malley, John W., *What Happened at Vatican II?* Cambridge, MA: The Belknap Press at Harvard University Press, 2008.

Orobator, Agbonkhianmeghe E. (ed), *Reconciliation, Justice and Peace: The Second African Synod.* Maryknoll, NY: Orbis Books, 2011.

Orobator, Agbonkhianmeghe E. (ed), *Theological Re-imagination: Conversations on Church, Religion, and Society in Africa.* Nairobi: Paulines, 2014.

Ortega, Ofelia, 'Contextuality and Community', in *International Review of Mission,* 98.388 (2009), 25-36.

Oxley, Simon, *Telling the Truth About Ourselves and our World* (17th-25th May 2011, Kingston, Jamaica). Geneva: WCC, 2009.

Oyaliwola, David, 'Joseph Ayodele Babalola', in *Dictionary of African Christian Biography*: www.dacb.org/stories/nigeria/babalola2_joseph.html

Pachuau, Lalsangkima, 'Ecumenical Missiology: Three Decades of Historical and Theological Development (1951-1982)', in Lalsangkima Pachuau (ed), *Ecumenical Missiology: Contemporary Trends, Issues and Themes*. Bangalore, India: United Theological College, 2002, 29-50.

Padilla, René, 'Biblical Foundations: A Latin American Study', in *Evangelical Review of Theology*, 7:1 (1983).

Padilla, René, 'Evangelism and the World', in J.D. Douglas (ed), *Let the Earth Hear His Voice*. Minneapolis, MN: World Wide Publications, 1975, 116-46.

Padilla, C. René, 'Liberation Theology: an Appraisal', in Daniel S. Schipani (ed), *Freedom and Discipleship*. Maryknoll, NY: Orbis Books, 1989.

Padilla, C. René, *Mission Between the Times: Essays on the Kingdom*. Revised and updated edition. London: Langham Monographs, 2010.

Padilla, René, 'The Unity of the Church and the Homogeneous Unit Principle', in Wilbert Shenk (ed), *Exploring Church Growth*. Eugene, OR: Wipf & Stock, 2010.

Panourgiá, Neni, 'Culture', in *International Encyclopedia of the Social Sciences*. William A. Darity Jr. (ed), 2nd edition. Vol. II. Detroit: Macmillan Reference USA, 2008.

Papathanasiou, Athanasios, 'Tradition as Impulse for Renewal and Witness: Introducing Orthodox Missiology', in *International Review of Mission*, 100.393 (2011), 203-15.

Paton, David M. (ed), *Breaking Barriers: Nairobi 1975*. Geneva: WCC, 1976.

Phan, Peter C., 'Christian Social Spirituality: A Global Perspective', in Philomena Cullen, Bernhard Hoose and Gerard Mannion (eds), *Catholic Social Justice: Theological and Practical Explorations*. London: T. & T. Clark, 2007.

Phan, Peter C. (ed), *Christianities in Asia*. Oxford: Wiley-Blackwell, 2010.

Phan, Peter, 'The World Missionary Conference, Edinburgh 1910: Challenges for Church and Theology in the 21st Century', in *International Bulletin of Missionary Research*, 34.2 (April 1910).

Philip, T.V., *Edinburgh to Salvador: Twentieth Century Ecumenical Missiology – A Historical Study of the Ecumenical Discussions on Mission*. Delhi: SPCK and Tiruvalla, India: CSS, 1999.

Phiri, Isabel Apawo, 'Partnership in Mission: A Critical Appraisal of the Partnership of Women and Men', in Desmond van der Water (ed), *Postcolonial Mission: Power and Partnership in World Christianity*. Sopher Press, 2010, 61-77.

Phiri, Isabel Apawo, *Women, Presbyterianism and Patriarchy: Religious Experience of Chewa Women in Central Malawi*. Blantyre: CLAIM, 1997.

Pinnock, Clark H., 'Church in the Power of the Holy Spirit: The Promise of Pentecostal Ecclesiology', in *Journal of Pentecostal Theology*, 14:2 (2006), 147-65.

Plantinga, Richard J., 'Missionary Thinking about Religious Plurality at Tambaram 1938: Hendrik Kraemer and His Critics', in Lamin Sanneh and Joel Carpenter (eds), *The Changing Face of Christianity: Africa, the West and the World*. New York: Oxford University Press, 2005.

Pobee, John S., 'Education', in Nicholas Lossky et al (eds), *Dictionary of the Ecumenical Movement*. 2nd edition. Geneva: WCC, 2002, 384-89.

Pobee, John S., *Towards an African Theology.* Nashville, TN: Abingdon Press, 1979.

Pobee, John S. and Gabriel Ositelu II, *African Initiatives in Christianity: The Growth, Gifts and Diversities of Indigenous African Churches.* Geneva: WCC, 1998.

Pohl, Christine D., *Making Room: Recovering Hospitality as a Christian Tradition.* Cambridge: Eerdmans, 1999.

Pohl, Christine D., 'Responding to Strangers: Insights from the Christian Tradition', in *Studies in Christian Ethics,* 19:1 (2006), 81-101.

Pope-Levison, Priscilla, 'Evangelism in the WCC. From New Delhi to Canberra', in James A. Scherer and Steven B. Bevans (eds), *New Directions in Mission and Evangelization 2: Theological Foundations.* Maryknoll, NY: Orbis Books, 1994.

Predelli, Line Nyhagen and Muller, Jon, 'Piety and Patriarchy: Contested Gender Regimes in Nineteenth-Century Evangelical Mission', in M. T. Huber and N. C. Lutkehaus (eds), *Gendered Mission: Women and Men in Missionary Discourses and Practice.* Michigan: University of Michigan, 1999, 67-112.

Premawardhana, Shantha, 'The Strange Exorcist', in *Masihi Sevak: Journal of Christian Ministry* 34.2 (August 2009).

Pui Lan, Kwok, *Chinese Women and Christianity, 1860-1927.* Atlanta, GA: Scholars Press, 1992.

Pui Lan, Kwok, *Introducing Asian Feminist Theology.* Cleveland, OH: The Pilgrim Press, 2000.

Quash, Ben, *Found Theology: History, Imagination and the Holy Spirit.* London: Bloomsbury, 2013.

Raiser, Konrad, 'Fifty Years of Ecumenical Formation: Where Are We? Where Are We Going?', in *The Ecumenical Review,* 48.4, 440-56.

Raiser, Konrad, 'Profile of the Laity in the Ecumenical Movement: Towards a New Definition', in Nicholas Apostola (ed), *A Letter from Christ to the World: An Exploration of the Role of the Laity in the Church Today.* Geneva: WCC, 1998.

Rajkumar, Peniel, Joseph Dayam, I.P. Asheervadham (eds), *Mission at and from the Margins: Patterns, Protagonists and Perspectives.* Regnum Edinburgh Centenary Series, Oxford: Regnum, 2014.

Ranson, Charles W. (ed), *Renewal and Advance: Christian Witness in a Revolutionary World.* London: Edinburgh House, 1948.

Rasmussen, L.L., *Earth Community, Earth Ethics.* Maryknoll, NY: Orbis Books, 1998.

Rasmussen, Larry, 'The Future Isn't What It Used To Be: "Limits to growth" and Christian Ethics', in *Lutheran Quarterly,* 27 (1975), 101-11.

Reichert, Folker, *Das Bild der Welt im Mittelalter.* Darmstadt, Germany: Wissenschaftliche Buchgesellschaft, 2013.

Reppenhagen, Martin, 'The Missional Church and the "Homo Areligiosus"', in Viggo Mortensen and Andreas Osterlund Nielsen (eds), *Walk Humbly with the Lord: Church and Mission Engaging Plurality.* Grand Rapids, MI and Cambridge, UK: Eerdmans, 2010, 167-83.

Rice, Monte Lee, 'Renewing the Pentecostal Vision and Witness of the Justified People of God', in *Asian Journal of Pentecostal Studies,* 16:2 (August 2013), 85-98.

Richie, Tony, *Speaking by the Spirit.* Lexington, KY: Emeth Press, 2011.

Richie, Tony, *Towards a Pentecostal Theology of Religions.* Cleveland, TN: CPT Press, 2013.

Rieger, Joerg, *God and the Excluded*. Minneapolis, MN: Fortress Press, 2001.
Rieger, Joerg, 'Liberating God-Talk: Postcolonialism and the Challenge of the Margins', in Catherine Keller, Micheal Nausner and Mayra Rivera (eds), *Postcolonial Theologies: Divinity and Empire*. St Louis, MO: Chalice Press, 2004, 204-20.
Riley, J.C., *An Unpredictable Gospel: American Evangelicals and World Christianity, 1812-1920*. New York: Oxford University Press, 2012.
Robeck Jr., Cecil M., 'Cooperation and the Promotion of Unity: A Pentecostal Perspective', in David A. Kerr and Kenneth R. Ross (eds), *Edinburgh 2010: Mission Then and Now*. Oxford: Regnum, 2009, 290-303.
Robeck Jr., Cecil M., 'First International Reformed-Pentecostal Dialogue', in *Journal of Ecumenical Studies,* 33:3 (June 1996).
Robeck Jr., Cecil M., *The Azusa Street Mission and Revival: The Birth of the Global Pentecostal Movement*. Nashville, TN: Thomas Nelson, 2006.
Robeck Jr., Cecil M., 'The Challenge of the Pentecostal Movement and the First Dialogue Results on the World Level'. Strasbourg Institute Lecture 2011.
Robeck Jr., Cecil M., 'Word and Spirit, Church and World'. Pentecostal-Reformed Dialogue 1996-2000.
Robert, Dana L., *American Women in Mission: A Social History of Their Thought and Practice*. Macon, GA: Mercer University Press, 1996.
Robert, Dana L., *Christian Mission: How Christianity Became a World Religion*. Oxford: Wiley-Blackwell, 2009.
Robertson, R., *Globalization: Social Theory and Global Culture*. London: Sage Publications, 1992.
Robinson, Ghana (ed), *Sharing and Living – A Study on the Ecumenical Sharing of Resources in India*. Madurai, India: Nepolean Press, 1983.
Robra, Martin, 'The Ecumenical Movement in the Context of World Christianity in the 21st Century', in Melisande Lorke, and Dietrich Werner (eds), *Ecumenical Visions for the 21st Century: A Reader for Theological Education*. Geneva: WCC, 2013, 7-15.
Ross, Kenneth R., *Edinburgh 2010: Springboard for Mission*. Pasadena, CA: William Carey International University Press, 2009.
Ross, Kenneth R., 'Edinburgh 2010: The Common Call', in *Forum Mission*, Band 7 (2011), 192-202.
Ross, Kenneth R., 'Perspectives on Education and Formation from the World Missionary Conference, Edinburgh 1910', in Teresa Chai, Stephen B. Bevans, Dietrich Werner, J. Nelson Jennings and Knud Jørgensen (eds), *Reflecting on and Equipping for Christian Mission*. Oxford: Regnum, 2015, 26-35.
Ross, Kenneth R., 'The Centenary of Edinburgh 1910: Its Possibilities', in *International Bulletin of Missionary Research,* 30:4 (October 2006), 177-79.
Ross, Kenneth R., '*Together Towards Life* in the Context of Liquid Modernity: Mission and Evangelism in the Age of Secularization', in *International Review of Mission,* 103.399 (2014), 240-55.
Ross, Kenneth R., Eva Christina Nilsson, and Roderick Hewitt, 'Implementation of the New Mission Affirmation: Together Towards Life', in *International Review of Mission,* 103.398 (2014), 71-76.
Salinas, Daniel, *Latin American Evangelical Theology in the 1970s*. Leiden: Brill, 2009.
Salvatierra, Alexia, '"Do Not Neglect to Show Hospitality": Sanctuary and Immigrant Justice', in L. Dykstra and C. Myers (eds), *Liberating Biblical Study:*

*Scholarship, Art and Action in Honor of the Center and Library for the Bible and Social Justice.* Eugene, OR: Wipf & Stock, 2011, 213-20.
Salvatierra, Alexia and Peter Heltzel, *Faith-Rooted Organizing: Mobilizing the Church in Service to the World.* Downers Grove, IL: IVP, 2013.
Samartha, Stanley J., 'Guidelines on Dialogue', in *The Ecumenical Review,* 31.2 (April 1979).
Samartha, Stanley J., 'Mission in a Religiously Plural World: Looking Beyond Tambaram 1938', in *International Review of Mission,* 77.307 (July 1988).
Samartha, Stanley, *One Christ Many Religions: Towards a Revised Christology.* Maryknoll, NY: Orbis Books, 1991.
Samartha, Stanley, 'The Cross and the Rainbow', in John Hick and Paul F. Knitter (eds), *The Myth of Christian Uniqueness.* London: SCM, 1987.
Samartha, Stanley, 'The Holy Spirit and People of Other Faiths', in Emilio Castro (comp.), *To the Wind of God's Spirit: Reflections on the Canberra Theme.* Geneva: WCC, 1990, 50-63.
Sanneh, Lamin, *Summoned from the Margin: Homecoming of an African.* Grand Rapids, MI: Eerdmans, 2012.
Sanneh, Lamin, *Translating the Message: The Missionary Impact on Culture.* Maryknoll, NY: Orbis Books, 1989.
Santiago-Vendrell, Angel D., *Contextual Theology and Revolutionary Transformation in Latin America: The Missiology of M.R. Shaull.* Eugene, OR: Pickwick Publications, 2010.
Savage, Pedro (ed), *El debate contemporáneo sobre la Biblia.* Barcelona, Spain: Ediciones Evangélicas Europeas, 1972.
Schattauer, Thomas H. (ed), *Inside Out: Worship in an Age of Mission.* Minneapolis, MN: Fortress Press, 1999.
Scherer, James A., 'Church, Kingdom and *Missio Dei*: Lutheran and Orthodox Correctives to Recent Ecumenical Mission Theology', in Charles van Engen et al (eds), *The Good News of the Kingdom: Mission Theology for the Third Millennium.* Eugene OR: Wipf & Stock, 1993.
Scherer, James A., *Gospel, Church and Kingdom: Comparative Studies in World Mission Theology.* Minneapolis, MN: Augsburg, 1987 and Eugene, OR: Wipf & Stock, 2004.
Scherer, James A. and Stephen B. Bevans (eds), *New Directions in Mission & Evangelization 1: Basic Statements.* Maryknoll, NY: Orbis Books, 1992.
Schmemann, Alexander, *For the Life of the World: Sacraments and Orthodoxy.* Second, revised and expanded edition. Crestwood, NY: St Vladimir's Seminary Press, 1973.
Schmid, B., E. Thomas, J. Olivier and J.R. Cochrane, 'The Contribution of Religious Entities to Health in Sub-Saharan Africa', in *African Religious Health Assets Programme* (ARHAP), 2008.
Schmit, Clayton J., *Sent and Gathered: A Worship Manual for the Missional Church.* Grand Rapids, MI: Baker Academic, 2009.
Schnelle, Udo, *Apostle Paul: His Life and His Theology.* Trans. M.E. Boring. Grand Rapids, MI: Baker Academic, 2005.
Schreiter, Robert J., *Constructing Local Theologies.* Maryknoll, NY: Orbis Books, 2001.
Schreiter, Robert J., 'The Impact of Vatican II', in Gregory Baum (ed), *The Twentieth Century.* Maryknoll, NY: Orbis Books, 1999.

Schreiter, Robert J., *The New Catholicity: Theology between the Global and Local.* Maryknoll, NY: Orbis Books, 1997.
Schreiter, Robert J., 'The Theology of Reconciliation and Peacemaking for Mission', in Howard Mellor and Timothy Yates (eds), *Mission, Violence and Reconciliation.* Sheffield, UK: Cliff College Publishing, 2004, 11-28.
Schroeder, Roger, 'Interculturality and Prophetic Dialogue', in *Verbum SVD,* 54.1 (2013), 8-21.
Segovia, F.F. (ed), *Towards a New Heaven and a New Earth: Essays in honor of Elizabeth Schussler Fiorenza.* Maryknoll, NY: Orbis Books, 2003.
Senior, Donald and Carroll Stuhlmueller, *The Biblical Foundations for Mission.* Maryknoll, NY: Orbis Books, 1983.
Shaull, Richard and Waldo Cesar, *Pentecostalism and the Future of the Christian Churches: Promises. Limitations. Challenges.* Grand Rapids, MI: Eerdmans, 2000.
Shaw, M.F., 'Robert Wuthnow and World Christianity: A Response to Boundless Faith': www.internationalbulletin.org/issues/2012-04/2012-04-179-shaw.pdf
Shillito, Edward, 'The Sweep of War', in 'A Survey of the Effect of War upon Missions', in *International Review of Mission,* 8.32 (October 1919), 433-43.
Simon, Xolile, 'Mission and Frontier-crossing and Identity Formation: An Integrating Contextual Missiology', in *Scriptura* 100 (2009).
Siwila, Lilian, 'Problematizing a "Norm": A Religio-cultural Gender Analysis of Child Marriage in the Context of HIV and AIDS', in *Journal of Gender and Religion in Africa,* 17:1 (July 2011).
Smith, Calvin L., 'The Politics and Economics of Pentecostalism: A Global Survey', in *The Cambridge Companion to Pentecostalism.* Cambridge: CUP, 2014, 175-94.
Smith, James K.A., *Desiring the Kingdom: Worship, Worldview and Cultural Formation.* Grand Rapids, MI: Baker Academic, 2009.
Snyder, Susanna, *Asylum-Seeking, Migration and Church.* Farnham, UK: Ashgate, 2012.
Solivan, Samuel, *Spirit, Pathos, and Liberation*, in Journal of Pentecostal Theology Supplement 14. New York: Bloomsbury T. & T. Clark, 1998.
Song, C.S., *Jesus, The Crucified People,* New York: Crossroad, 1990.
South African Council of Churches. *Climate Change – A challenge to the churches in South Africa.* Marshalltown, RSA: SACC, 2009.
Stanislaus, Lazar T. and Martin Üffing (eds), *Intercultural Living* (Vol. I) and *Intercultural Mission* (Vol. II). Sankt Augustin, Germany: Steyler Missionswissenschaftliches Institut, 2015.
Stanley, Brian, 'Edinburgh 1910 and the Genesis of the *IRM*', in *International Review of Mission,* 100.393 (November 2011), 149-59.
Stanley, Brian, *The World Missionary Conference, Edinburgh 1910.* Grand Rapids, MI and Cambridge, UK: Eerdmans, 2009.
Steigenga, Timothy J., *The Politics of the Spirit: The Political Implications of Costa Rica and Guatemala.* Lanham, MD: Lexington Books, 2002.
Stephens, Sara, *The Prophetic Mission of Churches in Response to Forced Displacement of People: A Global Ecumenical Consultation.* Geneva: WCC, 1996.
Steuernagel, Valdir, *The Theology of Mission in its Relation to Social Responsibility Within the Lausanne Movement.* Chicago, IL: Lutheran School of Theology, 1988.

Stott, John, 'The Significance of Lausanne', in *International Review of Mission,* 64.255 (1975), 288-94.
Stromberg, Jean S., 'Christian Witness in a Pluralistic World: Report on a Mission/Dialogue Consultation', in *International Review of Mission,* 77.307 (July 1988), 412-36.
Stromberg, Jean S., 'Ecumenical Affirmation on Mission and Evangelism – a Review', in *International Review of Mission*, 90.358 (2001), 243-52.
Studebaker, Steven M., 'Christian Mission and the Religions as Participation in the Spirit of Pentecost', in Amos Yong and Clifton Clarke (eds), *Global Renewal, Religious Pluralism, and the Great Commission*. Lexington, KY: Emeth Press, 2011, 71-95.
Sugden, Chris, *Gospel, Culture and Transformation.* Oxford: Regnum, 2000.
Sugden, Chris and Vinay Samuel, *Mission as Transformation.* Eugene, OR: Wipf & Stock, 2009.
Sunquist, Scott W. (ed), *A Dictionary of Asian Christianity.* Grand Rapids, MI: Eerdmans, 2001.
Sveijer, Terese, 'Himba People's fight against Planned Construction of the Dam', in *Indigenous Affairs,* 3/4 (July-December 1997), 12-17.
Swamiraju, T., 'Subaltern Movements: Insights from Interfaith Dialogue', in Marina Ngursangzeli Behera (ed), *Interfaith Relations after One Hundred Years: Christian Mission among Other Faiths.* Regnum Edinburgh 2010 Series, Vol. VIII. Oxford: Regnum, 2011.
Synan, Vinson and Amos Yong (eds), *Global Renewal Christianity,* Vol. I. Lake Mary, FL: Charisma House, 2015.
Tan, Jonathan Y., 'Mission as Witness and Proclamation', in Stephen B. Bevans (ed), *A Century of Catholic Mission: Roman Catholic Missiology 1910 to the Present*. Regnum Edinburgh 2010 Series, Vol. XV. Oxford: Regnum, 2013.
Tanner, Kathryn, *Theories of Cultures: A New Agenda for Theology*. Minneapolis, MN: Augsburg Fortress Press, 1997.
Tauira, Gaston Marama, 'The Phase of Translation: The LMS Missionaries Labour in Tahiti, 1797-1860', in *The Pacific Journal of Theology,* 2:14 (1995), 17-19.
Taylor, Charles, *A Secular Age.* Cambridge, MA & London: The Belknap Press of Harvard University Press, 2007.
Taylor, John V., *The Go-between God.* London: SCM, 1972.
Taylor, W.D. (ed), *Global Missiology for the 21st Century: The Iguassu Dialogue.* Grand Rapids, MI: Baker and WEF, 2000.
Temple, William, *The Church Looks Forward.* London: Macmillan, 1944.
Ter Haar, Gerrie, *Halfway to Paradise: African Christians in Europe.* Cardiff, UK: Cardiff Academic Press, 1998.
Thangaraj, M. Thomas, 'Embracing God's Hospitality in a Multi-Religious World', in *CTC Bulletin,* 28:1 (December 2012), 22-24.
Thangaraj, M. Thomas, 'Religious Pluralism, Dialogue and Asian Christian Responses', in Sebastian C.H. Kim (ed), *Christian Theology in Asia.* Cambridge: CUP, 2008.
Thorogood, Bernard, 'After 200 Years – The LMS Legacy', in *The Pacific Journal of Theology,* 2:14 (1995), 5-15.
Tiénou, Tite, 'Gospel and Cultures in the Lausanne Movement', in Lars Dahle, Margunn Serigstad Dahle and Knud Jørgensen (eds), *The Lausanne Movement – A Range of Perspectives.* Regnum Edinburgh 2010 Series, Vol. XXII. Oxford: Regnum, 2014, 156-69.

Tippett, Alan, *Solomon Islands Christianity: A Study in Growth and Obstruction.* New York: Friendship Press, 1967.

Tippett, Alan, *Verdict Theology in Missionary Theory: a collection of addresses and discussions that were prepared for a special week of missionary presentations at Lincoln Christian College and Seminary.* South Pasadena, CA: William Carey Library, 1973.

Tira, Sadiri Emmanuel Santiago B., *Filipino Kingdom Workers: An Ethnographic Study in Diaspora Missiology.* William Carey International University Press, 2012.

Tizon, Al, 'Evangelism and Social Responsibility: The Making of a Transformational Vision', in Margunn Serigstad Dahle, Lars Dahle and Knud Jørgensen (eds), *The Lausanne Movement: A Range of Perspectives*. Oxford: Regnum, 2014.

Tizon, A., *Transformation after Lausanne: Radical Evangelical Mission in Global-Local Perspective.* Waynesboro, GA: Regnum Books, 2008.

Tofaeono, Ama'amalele, *Eco-Theology: AIGA – The Household of Life, A perspective from Living Myths and Traditions of Samoa.* Erlangen, Germany: Erlangen Verl. Fur Mission und Okumene, 2000.

Torr, Stephen C., *A Dramatic Pentecostal/Charismatic Anti-Theodicy.* Eugene, OR: Pickwick, 2013.

Tsompanidis, Stylianos, 'The Ecumenical Process of *AGAPE* (Alterative Globalization Addressing People and Earth): An Orthodox Perspective', in *A Testimony to the Nations: A Vigintennial Volume Offered to the Ecumenical Patriarch Bartholomew.* Thessaloniki, 2011, 905-23 (in Greek).

Tsompanidis, Stylianos, *Orthodoxie und Ökumene: Gemeinsam auf dem Weg zu Gerechtigkeit, Frieden und Bewahrung der Schöpfung.* Münster, Hamburg and London, 1990.

Tucker, Bruce, *Oneness Pentecostal Churches*. New York: Xlibis, 2011.

Tutu, Desmond, 'Black Theology/African Theology: Soul Mates or Antagonists?' in James S. Cone and Gayraud S. Wilmore, *Black Theology: A Documentary History, Vol. I, 1966-79,* 2nd edition. Maryknoll, NY: Orbis Books, 1993, 385-92.

Tutu, Desmond M.B , 'Some African Insights and the Old Testament', in Hans-Jürgen Becken (ed), *Relevant Theology for Africa.* Durban, RSA: Lutheran Publishing House, 1973, 40-46.

Tuwere, Ilaitia Sevati, 'Making Sense of the Vanua (Land) in the Fijian Context: A Theological Exploration'. PhD thesis. Melbourne College of Divinity, 1992.

Tuwere, Ilaitia Sevati, *Vanua: Toward a Fijian Theology of Place.* Suva: Institute of Pacific Studies/University of the South Pacific, 2002.

UNCHR, 'World Refugee Day: Global forced displacement tops 50 million for first time since post-World War II era': www.unhcr.org/53a155bc6.html

Vallely, Paul, *Pope Francis: Untying the Knots.* London: Bloomsbury, 2013.

Van Beek, Huibert, 'Ecumenical Sharing of Resources', in Nicholas Lossky, José Míguez Bonino, John Pobee, Tom F. Stransky, Geoffrey Wainwright and Pauline Webb (eds), *Dictionary of the Ecumenical Movement.* Geneva: WCC, 2002, 382-83.

Van Beek, Huibert (ed), *Revisioning Christian Unity: The Global Christian Forum.* Oxford: Regnum, 2009.

Van der Maas, Eduard and Stanley M. Burgess (eds), *The New International Dictionary of Pentecostal and Charismatic Movements*. Grand Rapids, MI: Zondervan, 2002.
Van Lin, Jan, *Shaking the Fundamentals: Religious Plurality and Ecumenical Movement*. Amsterdam and New York: Editions Rodopi, 2002.
Van Rheenen, Gailyn (ed), *Contextualization and Syncretism: Navigating Cultural Currents*. Pasadena, CA: William Carey Library, 1996.
Vasconcelos Wilkey, Gláucia (ed), *Worship and Culture: Foreign Country or Homeland?* Grand Rapids, MI and Cambridge, UK: Eerdmans, 2014.
Vassiliadis, Petros, 'An Orthodox Assessment of the New Mission Statement', in *International Review of Mission,* 102.397 (November 2013), 174-78.
Vassiliadis, Petros, *Orthodox Perspectives on Mission*. Regnum Edinburgh Centenary Series 17, Oxford: Regnum, 2013.
Vicedom, Georg F., *The Mission of God: An Introduction to a Theology of Mission*. Trans. Gilbert A. Thiele and Dennis Hilgendorf. St Louis, MO: Concordia Press, 1965.
Villa-Vicencio, Charles, *A Theology of Reconstruction: Nation-Building and Human Rights*. Cambridge: CUP, 1992.
Villafañe, Eldin, *The Liberating Spirit: Toward an Hispanic American Pentecostal Social Ethic*. Lanham, MD: University Press of America, 1992.
Visser 't Hooft, W.A. and J.H. Oldham. *The Church and Its Function in Society*. Chicago, IL: Willett, Clark & Company, 1937.
Viswanathan, Gauri, 'Literacy and Conversion in the Discourse of Hindu Nationalism', *Race and Class,* 42.1 (2000).
Volf, Miroslav, *Exclusion and Embrace: A Theological Exploration of Identity, Otherness and Reconciliation*. Nashville, TN: Abingdon Press, 1996.
Volf, Miroslav, 'Materiality of Salvation: An Investigation in the Soteriologies of Liberation and Pentecostal Theologies', in *Journal of Ecumenical Studies,* 26:3 (1989), 447-67.
Vondey, Wolfgang, *Pentecostalism and Christian Unity, Vol. II*. Eugene, OR: Cascade, 2012.
Vondey, Wolfgang, 'Pentecostal Perspectives on the Nature and Mission of the Church: Challenges and Opportunities for Ecumenical Transformation', in Paul M. Collins and Michael A. Fahey (eds), *Receiving 'The Nature and Mission of the Church'*. New York: T. & T. Clarke, 2008, 55-68.
Vondey, Wolfgang, 'Presuppositions for Pentecostal Engagement in Ecumenical Dialogue', in *Exchange,* 30:1 Brill (2001), 344-58.
Wagner, C. Peter, *Strategies for Church Growth*. Eugene OR: Wipf & Stock, 1989.
Währisch-Oblau, Claudia, *The Missionary Self-Conception of Pentecostal/Charismatic Church Leaders from the Global South in Europe: Bringing Back the Gospel*. Leiden: Brill, 2009.
Wainwright, Geoffrey, *Lesslie Newbigin: A Theological Life*. Oxford: OUP, 2000.
Walls, Andrew F., 'Farquhar, John Nicol', in Nigel M. de S. Cameron (ed), *Dictionary of Scottish Church History and Theology*. Edinburgh: T. & T. Clark, 1993, 315.
Walls, Andrew F., 'Commission One: "Carrying the Gospel to all the Non-Christian World"', in David A. Kerr and Kenneth R. Ross (eds), *Edinburgh 2010: Mission Then and Now*. Oxford: Regnum, 2009.

Walls, Andrew F., *The Cross-Cultural Process in Christian History: Studies in the Transmission and Appropriation of Faith*. Maryknoll, NY: Orbis Books and Edinburgh: T. & T. Clark, 2002.
Walls, Andrew F., 'The Gospel as the Prisoner and Liberator of Culture', in *Missionalia,* 10:3, 1982.
Walls, Andrew F., *The Missionary Movement in Christian History: Studies in the Transmission of Faith*. Maryknoll, NY: Orbis Books, 1996.
Wan, Enoch, *Diaspora Missiology: Theory, Methodology and Practice*. Portland, OR: Institute for Diaspora Studies, 2011.
Wan, Enoch and Anthony Casey, *Church Planting Among Immigrants in US Urban Centers: The 'Where', 'Why' and 'How' of Diaspora Missiology in Action.* Portland, OR: IDS, 2014.
Wariboko, Nimi, *The Pentecostal Principle: Ethical Methodology in New Spirit*. Grand Rapids, MI: Eerdmans, 2011.
Watkins, Ralph, 'The Underground: The Living Mural of a Hip-Hop Church', in Ryan Bolger (ed), *The Gospel after Christendom: New Voices, New Cultures, New Expressions*. Grand Rapids, MI: Baker Academic, 2012.
Weber, Hans-Ruedi, *A Laboratory for Ecumenical Life: The Story of Bossey 1946-1996*. Geneva: WCC, 1996.
Wedderburn, Alexander J.M., *A History of the First Christians.* London: T. & T. Clark, 2004.
Werner, Dietrich, 'Evangelism from a WCC Perspective: A Recollection of an Important Ecumenical Memory, and the Unfolding of a Holistic Vision', in *International Review of Mission,* 96.382-83 (2007), 183-203.
Werner, Dietrich, 'Missionary Structure of the Congregation', in Nicholas Lossky et al (ed), *Dictionary of the Ecumenical Movement.* Geneva: WCC and Grand Rapids, MI: Eerdmans, 1991, 699-701.
Werner, Dietrich, David Esterline, Namsoon Kang, Joshva Raja (eds), *Handbook of Theological Education in World Christianity: Theological Perspectives, Ecumenical Trends, Regional Surveys.* Oxford: Regnum, 2010.
Werner, Dietrich and Namsoon Kang, 'Global Study Report of the WCC on the Future of Theological Education in World Christianity', in Melisande Lorke and Dietrich Werner (eds), *Ecumenical Visions for the 21st Century: A Reader for Theological Education.* Geneva: WCC, 2013, 115-76.
West, Charles C., *Consultation on 'The Meaning of the Secular'.* Bossey, Switzerland: Ecumenical Institute, 1959.
White, James F., *Introduction to Christian Worship*. 3rd edition. Nashville, TN: Abingdon Press, 2001.
Whiteman, Darrell L., 'Contextualisation: The Theory, The Gap, The Challenge', in *International Bulletin of Missionary Research,* 21:1 (1997).
Whiteman, Darrell, 'Melanesian Religions: An Overview', in Ennio Mantovani (ed), *An Introduction to Melanesian Religions.* Goroka, Papua New Guinea: The Melanesian Institute, 1984.
'Who Do We Say That We Are? Christian Identity in a Multi-Religious World', in *The Ecumenical Review,* 66. 4 (December 2014), 458-501.
Wike, Richard, 'With 41% of global wealth in the hands of less than 1%, elites and citizens agree inequality is a top priority', in *FactTank,* Pew Research Center: www.pewresearch.org/fact-tank/2014/11/08/with-41-of-global-wealth-in-the-hands-of-less-than-1-elites-and-citizens-agree-inequality-is-a-top-priority

Wild-Wood, Emma and Peniel Rajkumar (eds), *Foundations for Mission.* Regnum Edinburgh Centenary Series, Oxford: Regnum, 2013.

Wilfred, Felix, *Asian Public Theology: Critical Concerns in Challenging Times.* New Delhi: ISPCK, 2010.

Wilfred, Felix (ed), *The Oxford Handbook of Christianity in Asia.* New York: Oxford University Press, 2014.

Wilkinson, Michael and Steven M. Studebaker (eds), *A Liberating Spirit: Pentecostals and Social Action in North America.* Eugene, OR: Wipf & Stock, 2010.

Williams, Raymond, 'Culture and Civilization', in Paul Edwards (ed), *Encyclopedia of Philosophy.* New York: Macmillan, 1967.

Williamson, W. Paul and Ralph W. Hood. 'Spirit Baptism: A Phenomenological Experience', in *Mental Health, Religion & Culture,* 14:6 (2011), 543-59.

Willis, Nigel Paul, *The Pentecostal Movement, Its Challenges and Potential.* Frankfurt: Peter Lang, 2013.

Wilson, Erin, 'Much to be Proud of, Much to be Done: Faith-Based Organizations and the Politics of Asylum in Australia', in *Journal of Refugee Studies,* 24:3 (2011), 548-64.

Wilson, Jonathan R., *Living Faithfully in a Fragmented World: From* After Virtue *to a New Monasticism.* Cambridge: Lutterworth, 2010.

Wimber, John and Kevin Springer, *Power Evangelism.* San Francisco, CA: Harper & Row, 1986.

Winter, Ralph D. (ed), *The Evangelical Response to Bangkok.* South Pasadena, CA: William Carey Library, 1973.

Winter, Ralph D., 'The Highest Priority: Cross-Cultural Evangelism', in J.D. Douglas (ed), *Let the Earth Hear His Voice.* Minneapolis, MN: World Wide Publications, 1975, 213-41.

Wong Wai Ching, Angela, 'Modernity and Change of Values: Asian Christian Negotiations and Resistance', in Felix Wilfred (ed), *The Oxford Handbook of Asian Christianity.* New York: Oxford University Press, 200-14.

Wong Wai Ching, Angela, 'Negotiating for a Postcolonial Identity of "the Poor Women" in Asia', in *Journal of Feminist Studies of Religion,* 16:2 (Fall 2000), 5-23.

World Council of Churches, *Empty Hands – An Agenda for the Churches: A Study Guide on Ecumenical Sharing of Resources for Use by Churches, Local Congregations and Other Groups*. Geneva: WCC, 1980.

World Council of Churches, 'Evangelism Today: New Ways for Authentic Discipleship', in *International Review of Mission,* 103.398 (April 2014).

Wrogemann, Henning and Claudia Währisch-Oblau (eds), *Witchcraft, Demons and Deliverance – A Global Conversation on an Intercultural Challenge*. Münster, Germany: LIT-Verlag, 2015.

Yang, Fenggang, 'Chinese Gospel Church: The Sinization of Christianity', in Helen Rose Ebaugh and Janet Chafetz (eds), *Religion and the New Immigrants: Continuities and Adaptations in Immigrant Congregations*. Walnut Creek, CA: Altamira Press, 2000, 89-107.

Yang, Fenggang, *Religion in China: Survival and Revival Under Communist Rule.* New York: Oxford University Press, 2012.

Yang, Sung Won, *The Influence of the Revival Movement of 1901-1910 on the Development of Korean Christianity.* Louisville, KY: Southern Baptist Theological Seminary, 2002.

Yannoulatos, Anastasios, 'Discovering the Orthodox Missionary Ethos', in Ion Bria (ed), *Martyria-Mission: The Witness of the Orthodox Churches*. Geneva: WCC, 1980, 20-29.

Yannoulatos, Anastasios, 'The Purpose and Motive of Mission', in *International Review of Mission*, 54.215 (1965), 281-97.

Yannoulatos, Anastasios, *Mission in Christ's Way*. Geneva: WCC and Brookline, MA: Holy Cross Orthodox Press, 2010.

Yates, Timothy, *Christian Mission in the Twentieth Century*. Cambridge: CUP, 1994.

Ybarrola, Steven, 'Anthropology, Diaspora and Mission', in *Mission Studies*, 29 (2012), 79-94.

Yong, Amos, *Hospitality and the Other*. Maryknoll, NY: Orbis Books, 2008.

Yong, Amos, *In the Days of Caesar*. Grand Rapids, MI: Eerdmans, 2010.

Yong, Amos, 'The Holy Spirit and the World Religions: On the Christian Discernment of Spirit(s) "after" Buddhism', in *Buddhist-Christian Studies*, 24:1 (2004).

Yong, Amos, *The Missiological Spirit: Christian Mission Theology in the Third Millennium Global Context*. Eugene, OR: Cascade, 2014.

Yong, Amos, *The Spirit Poured Out on All Flesh*. Grand Rapids, MI: Baker Academic, 2005.

Yong, Amos and Katherine Attanasi (eds), *Pentecostalism and Prosperity*. New York: Palgrave Macmillan, 2012.

Yung, Hwa, 'Endued with Power: The Pentecostal-Charismatic Renewal and the Asian Church in the Twenty-First Century', in *Asian Journal of Pentecostal Studies* 6:1 (2003), 63-82.

Yung, Hwa, *Mangoes or Bananas? The Quest for an Authentic Asian Christian Theology*. Oxford: Regnum, 1997.

# List of Contributors

**Stephen Bevans** is a priest in the Roman Catholic missionary congregation of the Society of the Divine Word (SVD) and Louis J. Luzbetak, SVD Professor of Mission and Culture (Emeritus) at Catholic Theological Union, Chicago, USA. His many books include *Models of Contextual* Theology (1992, 2002), *Constants in Context: A Theology of Mission for Today* (with Roger P. Schroeder), and *A Century of Catholic Mission* (edited, 2013, in the Regnum Edinburgh 2010 Series) Past president of the American Society of Missiology (2006) and a member of WCC Commission on World Mission and Evangelism.

**Nico Botha** is Professor in Missiology at the University of South Africa; tentmaking minister in the Uniting Reformed Church in Southern Africa; General Secretary of the Southern African Missiological Society, and Executive member of the International Association for Mission Studies. Author of many articles and book chapters on missiology, Reformed theology and contextual theology.

**Cliff Bird** is an ordained minister of the United Church in the Solomon Islands. Currently employed by the Methodist Church in Fiji, and is Regional Co-ordinator for UnitingWorld (Uniting Church in Australia) in the Pacific region. Earlier, was senior lecturer and head of the Theology and Ethics department of the Pacific Theological College in Suva, Fiji. Areas of interest include gospel-cultures dynamics, ecology and economics, theology and human rights and responsibilities, gender theology, being church today.

**Benjamin T. Conner** is Associate Professor of Christian Discipleship at Western Theological Seminary in Holland, Michigan, USA. Academic interests lie at the intersection of missiology, disability studies and practical theology. Publications include *Practicing Witness: A Missional Vision of Christian Practices* (Eerdmans) and *Enabling Witness: Perspectives on Mission and Disability* (IVP Academic).

**Ernst M. Conradie** is Senior Professor in the Department of Religion and Theology at the University of the Western Cape, South Africa, where he teaches Systematic Theology and Ethics. Specializes in eco-theology and is author of two recent monographs: *Saving the Earth? The Legacy of Reformed Views on 'Re-creation'* (LIT Verlag, 2013), and *The Earth in God's Economy: Creation, Salvation and Consummation in Eco-logical Perspective* (LIT Verlag, 2015).

**Gemma Tulud Cruz** is Senior Lecturer in Theology at the Australian Catholic University in Melbourne. Author of *An Intercultural Theology of Migration: Pilgrims in the Wilderness* (Brill, 2010), and *Toward a Theology of Migration: Social Justice and Religious Experience* (Palgrave Macmillan, 2014).

**Samuel Escobar** is from Peru and worked with his wife Lilly as a missionary to universities with the International Fellowship of Evangelical Students in several Latin American countries and Canada. From 1985 to 2005 was Professor of Missiology at Eastern Baptist Theological Seminary (now Palmer Theological Seminary) in Pennsylvania. Currently teaches at the Baptist Theological Seminary in Madrid.

**Beate Fagerli,** Cand. Teol., is a lay theologian, working as senior adviser in ecumenical theology in the Church of Norway's Council on Ecumenical and International Relations. Previously worked with Conference of European Churches, WWC (CWME), and World Student Christian Federation.

**Roderick Hewitt,** PhD, is Associate Professor in Systematic Theology and Academic Leader, Research and Higher Degrees, at the School of Religion, Philosophy and Classics, University of KwaZulu-Natal, South Africa. Has held various leadership positions in ecumenical organisations: Executive Secretary for Education in Mission and, later, Moderator of the Council for World Mission; also Moderator of the Synod of the United Church in Jamaica and the Cayman Islands for two terms. Author of *Church and Culture: An Anglo-Caribbean Experience in Hybridity and Contradiction* (Cluster, 2012).

**Madge Karecki,** SSJ-TOSF, DTh, is the Assistant National Director of the Pontifical Mission Societies in the USA. Serves as a consultant to the United States Conference of Catholic Bishops' Committee on Evangelization and Catechesis. Spent 22 years in South Africa, and returned to the USA after serving as the President of St Augustine College in Johannesburg.

**Chammah J. Kaunda,** PhD, is a post-doctoral research fellow in *Christelike Spiritualiteit*/Christian Spirituality at the University of South Africa (*Universiteit van Suid-Afrika*), Pretoria. He is particularly interested in how African religio-cultural heritage can inform African theology, Christianity and politics, theological education, African Pentecostal theology, missiology and ecumenical theology.

**Thomas Kemper** is the General Secretary of the General Board of Global Ministries of the United Methodist Church, responsible for personnel, projects and mission partnerships in more than 130 countries. A native of Germany, Kemper was the first person from outside the USA elected to lead a United Methodist agency. A missionary in Brazil 1986-1994, and served as mission leader for the German Central Conference of the United Methodist Church, and as Director of Ecumenical Learning at the Lippische Landeskirche, a regional church of the Association of Protestant churches in Germany.

**Jooseop Keum** is Director of the Commission on World Mission and Evangelism of the WCC. Also editor of the *International Review of Mission*, the missiological journal that owes its inception to the Edinburgh World Missionary Conference in 1910. Teaches ecumenical missiology at the Presbyterian University and Theological Seminary in Seoul, South Korea, and at Stellenbosch University in South Africa. An ordained minister of the Presbyterian Church of Korea, earlier served the Council for World Mission as Executive Secretary of its Mission Programme.

**Dongsung Kim** is Programme Executive, Diakonia and Capacity Building, WCC. Also Book Review Editor of the *International Review of Mission*. Also an ordained minister of the Presbyterian Church of Korea.

**Kirsteen Kim,** PhD, is Professor of Theology and World Christianity at Leeds Trinity University, UK, editor of *Mission Studies*, journal of the International Association for Mission Studies, and an editor of the Regnum Edinburgh Centenary Series. Her most recent monograph (with Sebastian C.H. Kim) is *A History of Korean Christianity* (Cambridge University Press, 2014).

**Dr Manoj Kurian** is a Malaysian doctor with 22 years' experience working with churches in policy, advocacy and programme management. Currently Co-ordinator of the WCC-Ecumenical Advocacy Alliance. Also an adjunct faculty at the College of Public Health, Kent State University, USA.

**Dae Sung Lee** is Professor of Systematic Theology at United Graduate School of Theology of Yonsei University, Seoul, South Korea. Serves also as a university chaplain and as a Senior Pastor of a university church.

**Timothy T.N. Lim** tutors at King's Evangelical Divinity School, London, and adjunct teaches at Regent University School of Divinity, Virginia Beach, USA. Also a candidate as a teaching elder of the Presbyterian Church (USA), and holds dual church membership with Bethesda Chapel in Singapore. Has published extensively on theology, missions and ecumenism, and is the author of *Ecclesial Recognition,* forthcoming from Brill.

**Dr Atola Longkumer,** a Baptist from Nagaland, North-East India, currently teaches Religions and Missions at the South Asia Institute of Advanced Christian Studies, Bengaluru, South India. Her recent writings include *Putting Names with Faces: Women's Impact in Mission History*, co-edited with Christine Lienemann-Perrin and Afrie Songco Joye (Abingdon Press, 2012).

**Dr Bård Mæland** is a professor of Systematic Theology at the School of Mission and Theology, Stavanger, Norway, where he has served as President since 2010. Is also a member of the WCC Commission for World Mission and Evangelism.

**The Rev. Dr Deenabandhu Manchala**, a theologian from India and a former co-ordinator of the Just and Inclusive Communities Programme of the WCC, is Area Executive for Southern Asia in the Global Ministries of the United Church of Christ and Disciples of Christ, Cleveland, Ohio.

**Jacques Matthey,** from Switzerland, is a retired Protestant pastor and missiologist. Served earlier as General Secretary of the Mission Department of the French-speaking Protestant Churches of Switzerland between two spells of service with the WCC, first as organiser of the CWME Melbourne conference in 1980, and later as programme executive for mission study, secretary of the Commission on World Mission and Evangelism, and editor of the *International Review of Mission*.

**Ruth A. Meyers** is Dean of Academic Affairs and Hodges-Haynes Professor of Liturgics at Church Divinity School of the Pacific, Berkeley, California. From 2009 to 2015, she chaired the Episcopal Church's Standing Commission on Liturgy and Music.

**Néstor O. Míguez** was born in Rosario, Argentina, in 1948. A minister of the Evangelical Methodist Church in Argentina, is also President of the Argentinean Federation of Evangelical Churches. He also serves as Professor Emeritus in I.U. ISEDET (Instituto Superior Evangélico de Estudios Teológicos), Buenos Aires, in the areas of New Testament and Systematic Theology.

**Peniel Jesudason Rufus Rajkumar**, an ordained minister of the Church of South India, is Programme Executive for Interreligious Dialogue and Co-operation with the WCC. Publications include *Dalit Theology and Dalit Liberation: Problems, Paradigms and Possibilities* (Ashgate, 2010), *Asian Theology on the Way: Christianity, Culture and Context* (edited, London: SPCK and Minneapolis: Fortress Press), *Foundations for Mission* (co-edited with Emma Wildwood, Regnum, 2012), and *Mission At and From* *the Margins: Patterns, Protagonists and Perspectives* (co-edited, Regnum, 2014).

**Martin Robra** is a pastor of the Evangelical Church in Germany and a long-serving staff member of the WCC. Moved from the field of social and environmental ethics to ecumenical relations and currently works with the team on ecumenical education and formation, focusing on continuing ecumenical formation.

**Kenneth R. Ross,** from Scotland, is parish minister at Netherlorn, Argyll, and an Honorary Fellow of Edinburgh University School of Divinity. Also a former General Secretary of the Church of Scotland Board of World Mission. Having served earlier as Professor of Theology at the University of Malawi, retains close links with Malawi where he was given the clan name 'Ngozo' by Chief Champwiti in 2011. Recent publications include the *Atlas of Global Christianity* (Edinburgh University Press, 2009) and *Roots and Fruits: Retrieving Scotland's Missionary Story* (Regnum, 2014).

**Dr Lilian Cheelo Siwila** is a lecturer in the School of Religion, Philosophy and Classics under the discipline of Systematic Theology and Gender. Has worked with a number of ecumenical bodies, and is a member of the Circle of Concerned African Women Theologians.

**Katalina Tahaafe-Williams** is a Tongan-born Australian currently serving as Programme Executive in Mission and Evangelism with the WCC. Has worked with the United Reformed Church, UK, and with the Uniting Church in Australia, and has a PhD in Multicultural Ecclesiology and Mission from the University of Birmingham, UK.

**Petros Vassiliadis,** emeritus professor of the Aristotle University of Thessaloniki, Greece, is the President of the Center for Ecumenical, Missiological and Environmental Studies 'Metropolitan Panteleimon Papageorgiou', a former Orthodox commissioner of WCC's Commission on World Mission and Evangelism (1998-2006), and President of the World Conference of Associations of Theological Institutions/Educators.

**Claudia Währisch-Oblau** heads the Evangelism Department of the United Evangelical Mission, a communion of 35 churches on three continents. Holds a PhD in Religious Studies/Intercultural Theology from Heidelberg University and is the co-editor of *Mission Continues: Global Impulses for the 21st Century* (Regnum 2010).

**Dr Allen Yeh** is Associate Professor of Intercultural Studies and Missiology at Biola University near Los Angeles, California. Co-editor (with Chris Chun) of *Expect Great Things, Attempt Great Things: William Carey and Adoniram Judson, Missionary Pioneers* (Wipf & Stock, 2013).

# INDEX

Arnon (



# Goede mannen

Nijgh & Van Ditmar
Amsterdam

FSC
www.fsc.org
RECYCLED
Papier gemaakt van gerecycled materiaal
FSC® C004472

Eerste druk 2018
Tweede druk (e-book) 2018
Derde druk 2018

www.arnongrunberg.com
www.nijghenvanditmar.nl


Omslag Studio Ron van Roon
Foto auteur Ringel Goslinga
Typografie Zeno Carpentier Alting
NUR 301 / ISBN 978 90 388 0535 1

# GOEDE MANNEN

Ander werk van Arnon Grunberg:

*Blauwe maandagen*
Roman 1994
*Figuranten*
Roman 1997
*De troost van de slapstick*
Essays 1998
*De heilige Antonio*
Novelle 1998
*Het veertiende kippetje*
Scenario 1998
*Liefde is business*
Gedichten 1999
*Fantoompijn*
Roman 2000
*De geschiedenis van mijn kaalheid*
(oorspr. verschenen onder de
naam Marek van der Jagt)
Roman 2000
*De Mensheid zij geprezen*
Lof der Zotheid 2001
*Amuse-gueule*
Vroege verhalen 2001
*Monogaam*
(Marek van der Jagt)
Boekenweekessay 2002
*Gstaad*
(Marek van der Jagt)
Roman 2002
*De asielzoeker*
Roman 2003
*Grunberg rond de wereld*
Verhalen 2004
*Het aapje dat geluk pakt*
Novelle 2004
*De joodse messias*
Roman 2004
*De techniek van het lijden*
Essays 2005
*Grunbergbijbel*
Het beste uit de Bijbel 2005
*Tirza*
Roman 2006
*Omdat ik u begeer*
Brieven 2007
*Ik ging van hand tot hand*
(Marek van der Jagt)
Verzameld werk 2008
*Onze oom*
Roman 2008
*Kamermeisjes en soldaten*
Journalistieke reportages 2009
*Het verraad van de tekst*
Albert Verwey-lezing 2009
*Huid en Haar*
Roman 2010
*Brieven aan Esther*
Brieven 2011
*De Mensendokter*
Raadgevingen 2011
*Voetnoot*
Columns 2012
*De man zonder ziekte*
Roman 2012
*De receptioniste*
Verhaal 2012
*Buster Keaton lacht nooit*
Filmessays 2013
*De christelijke nacht en de*
*mechanische rede*
Frederik Muller-lezing 2013
*Apocalyps*
Verhalen 2013
*Voetnoot 2*
Columns 2014
*Het bestand*
Roman 2015
*Moedervlekken*
Roman 2016
*Aan nederlagen geen gebrek*
Brieven 2016
*Het tweede bestand*
Verhaal 2017
*Thuis ben je*
Columns 2017
*De dagen van Leopold Mangelmann*
Keuze uit de archieven 2017
*De eerste boze burger*
Essay 2017
*Alle Voetnoten*
Columns 2018

# Inhoud

# I

# *De C-ploeg*

# 1

De Pool deed wat hij zijn hele leven al wilde doen, hij was brandweerman. Eigenlijk heette hij Geniek Janowski, maar iedereen noemde hem de Pool en op een gegeven moment had hij die bijnaam geaccepteerd zoals je borstelige wenkbrauwen accepteert. Hij begon zijn oorspronkelijke naam te vergeten. Die naam speelde ook geen grote rol meer in zijn leven, alleen voor gemeentelijke instanties, banken, verzekeringen en zijn vader was hij nog Geniek Janowski. Het was een moeilijke naam, voor niet-Polen althans, en het grootste gedeelte van de wereld bestond uit niet-Polen. Als hij nou gewoon in Polen had gewoond was er geen probleem geweest maar nu moest hij iedereen steeds weer uitleggen dat het 'Gen' was en dat de 'g' werd uitgesproken als in het Duitse 'gut' en dan 'jek', Genjek. Zijn collega's waren hem als eerste de Pool gaan noemen toen hij ruim zestien jaar geleden begon in de C-ploeg. Daar was hij opgeleid tot brandwacht en later tot brandwacht eerste klas. Ze hadden hem getest op hoogte- en dieptevrees en op claustrofobie, ze hadden onderzocht of hij een teamspeler was. Hij had hoogte- noch dieptevrees en aan claustrofobie leed hij ook niet. Daar kwam nog eens bij dat hij een aardige teamspeler was, maar Geniek vonden ze te ingewikkeld, de mannen van de C-ploeg, en Beckers had gezegd: 'Die naam past ook niet bij jou.' Alleen al daarom was Geniek 'de Pool' als een geuzennaam gaan beschouwen, de mannen vonden dat die naam namelijk wel bij hem paste. En na een jaar of twee in de C-ploeg was hij van top tot teen de Pool, alsof hij eindelijk was geworden wie hij altijd al was geweest.

Nu, op deze mistige novemberochtend zat hij tussen zijn collega's in de kamer van de ploegchef te wachten tot

Beckers zijn mond open zou doen. De Pool hield van de mist, hij vond alle weertypes prima maar voor nevel had hij een zwak. Het landschap mocht er zijn en de mist maakte het nog mooier. De bomen, de heuvels, de velden, de Pool wandelde graag door de mist. Hoe sneller hij de stad uit was hoe beter.

De ploegchef had zijn mannen bij elkaar geroepen omdat Beckers iets wilde vertellen en al wist de C-ploeg ongeveer wat – de ploegchef had hen ingelicht, details had hij achterwege gelaten, twee zinnen, meer had hij niet nodig gehad – toch zaten ze gespannen rond de tafel. Alsof ze examen moesten doen, alleen waarvoor wisten ze niet. Alle mannen keken naar de Pool. Verwachtten ze dat niet Beckers maar hij iets ging vertellen?

Neel van de administratie liep langs en zwaaide vrolijk. Een paar jaar geleden was er voor het eerst een vrouw in de C-ploeg gekomen, die het niet lang had uitgehouden. Niet omdat ze een vrouw was maar omdat ze niet bij de groep paste, omdat ze moeilijk deed, kritiek had op het eten dat de brandweermannen met zoveel toewijding kookten. Toen hadden ze een grap met haar uitgehaald. Ze hadden de kamer waar ze sliep volgestopt met oude meubels en matrassen zodat ze niet meer naar binnen kon. Brandweerhumor. Beckers had het initiatief genomen. Practical jokes, daarin was Beckers goed. Zoals ze ooit naar de vrouw hadden gekeken zo keken ze nu naar de Pool.

Hij had het gevoel dat hij precies wist welke woorden Beckers zou gebruiken, ze waren ongeveer op hetzelfde moment in de C-ploeg begonnen. Als hij zich met iemand hier verwant voelde was het Beckers, ondanks alle verschillen. Beckers was bijvoorbeeld een echte carnivoor. Een goede kerel. Ze hoorden bij elkaar, ze werkten al zo lang samen.

Deze ochtend zaten ze anders bij elkaar dan op andere ochtenden, als ze om een uur of zeven in de Wacht samenkwamen. En ook anders dan 's avonds als ze in diezelfde Wacht hun avondeten naar binnen werkten, haastig omdat je nooit wist wanneer ze je nodig hadden. En als ze je nodig hadden kwam het geregeld voor dat je pas uren later terugkwam en je je amper kon herinneren dat in de Wacht een bord ijskoud eten op je stond te wachten. Soms was het vlees al aardig aan het verkleuren want de kwaliteit ervan liet te wensen over, wat geen wonder was met hun budget.

Er waren er altijd een paar bij die weinig zeiden, het liefst helemaal niets. Ze zaten te puzzelen of ze keken een filmpje op hun telefoon. Meestal dezelfden, de zwijgers, maar zo stil als nu was het nooit. Alsof ze in de kerk zaten, terwijl ze daar toch niet heen gingen, hun ouders gingen daar al amper meer heen, behalve de vader van de Pool, die was met geen stok uit de kerk te slaan. Die kwam liever in de kerk dan in het café. Zijn God was nog niet dood, zijn God was nog springlevend.

De Pool voelde aan een korstje op zijn neus. Hij wist niet hoe dat daar was gekomen. Van de kat misschien, die hij drie dagen daarvoor uit een boom had moeten plukken. Het dier bleek niet gered te willen worden, althans niet door de Pool.

Aan het eind van de tafel zat Beckers, die al een tijdje met zorgverlof was en die nu het woord zou gaan nemen, want daarvoor was hij verschenen, maar hij bleef zwijgen. Hij had een plastic bekertje met cappuccino uit de automaat in zijn hand en hij staarde naar het bekertje, terwijl hij toch een verhaal te vertellen had. De mannen vonden het ongepast hem aan te moedigen en ze vonden het nog ongepaster om zelf verhalen te gaan vertellen, terwijl ze dat goed konden – ook de zwijgers hadden iets te vertellen, zelfs de jonge Nelemans, hoewel ze het erover eens waren dat Nelemans, die in zijn vrije tijd liederen zong die hij zelf had geschreven, weinig te zeggen had en ze snoerden hem geregeld de mond maar dat deden ze plagerig, nooit gemeen. Ze waren niet gemeen, de mannen van de C-ploeg, als ze iets waren dan was het goed, ze zouden zichzelf goeie kerels noemen. De C-ploeg was de beste ploeg en hoewel iedere ploeg dat ongetwijfeld van zichzelf vond meenden zij dat zij meer redenen hadden dat te geloven, omdat ze stuk voor stuk fatsoenlijke mannen waren die niets anders wilden dan fatsoenlijk zijn, met het hart op de juiste plaats. Al had Nelemans nog meer ambities, hij probeerde door te breken als zanger met zijn liederen die hij zelf had geschreven en die vrolijk waren, om te lachen, want er waren al genoeg treurige liederen, er was al genoeg begrafenismuziek. Hij had gezworen dat hij ook na zijn doorbraak in de muziek de C-ploeg trouw zou blijven. Hij kende niet zoveel zingende brandweermannen en hij was van plan de eerste te worden. Ja, Nelemans wilde een zingende brandweerman worden.

De Pool keek naar Nelemans, de jongste van de groep. De zingende brandweerman hoefde zich amper te scheren, misschien zou hij zich nooit echt hoeven te scheren, en hij keek bedrukt alsof hij een reprimande verwachtte, alsof hem weer eens de mond zou worden gesnoerd. De Pool wilde dat Beckers eindelijk ging vertellen wat ze al wisten, dan waren ze ervan af, dan konden ze aan het werk. Hoewel hun werk natuurlijk voor een groot gedeelte bestond uit wachten was er een verschil of je wachtte op een brand of een ongeluk of dat je aan het wachten was op het verhaal van Beckers. De Pool dacht aan zijn zoon Jurek, die over tien dagen twaalf zou worden. Ze hadden hem Jurek genoemd omdat Wen vond dat Geniek en Jurek zo goed klonk, Geniek en Jurek, Jurek en Geniek, maar niemand noemde hem nog Geniek. Zelfs zijn eigen zoon had het tegenwoordig over de Pool. Als hij van school kwam vroeg Jurek aan zijn moeder: ‘Is de Pool thuis?’ Terwijl de jongen kon weten dat zijn vader thuis was, de Pool had 24 uur dienst en was dan twee dagen thuis om vervolgens weer 24 uur dienst te hebben, een ritme dat hem beviel, een ritme waarmee niet alleen hij maar het hele gezin was gaan samenvallen. De vader had het gevoel dat de zoon het alleen vroeg opdat de vader het kon horen, opdat de vader wist hoe hij genoemd werd, ook in zijn eigen huis: de Pool.

Hij vatte het liefkozend op, het was de puberteit of de prepuberteit. Als de zoon tegen zijn moeder zei: 'Heeft de Pool weer wat aan te merken?' of 'Gaat het weer eens niet zoals de Pool het wil?' liet de vader het van zich af glijden. Zo waren pubers, zo waren jongens van die leeftijd. Meisjes schenen heel anders te zijn, daar had hij geen ervaring mee.

'Je mag ook papa zeggen,' had de Pool een keer gezegd. 'Gewoon papa, zoals je me vroeger altijd noemde.' Maar de prepuberteit was hard en volgens sommige deskundigen niet te onderscheiden van de puberteit. De Pool zelf kon zich niet herinneren ooit zo'n tiener te zijn geweest. Vanaf zijn achtste was hij alleen met zijn vader geweest, een goede en rechtschapen man die brutaliteit noch tegenspraak duldde.

Hoe hij als puber was geweest deed er niet toe, je moest jezelf niet als maatstaf nemen had hij gelezen in een boek over het opvoeden van pubers en dat deed hij daarom ook niet, hij nam zichzelf niet als maatstaf. Ook zonder dat boek zou het niet in hem zijn opgekomen.

Ooit waren de Pool en zijn zoon onafscheidelijk geweest, hij was als een god voor Jurek geweest. Jurek wilde ook brandweerman zijn. Alles moest geblust worden. De Pool had zich als kind vooral aangetrokken gevoeld tot de zwaailichten, de glimmende wagens en de stoere mannen in hun pakken, die mens en dier kwamen redden. Stoer wilde de Pool zijn en dat was hij op zijn eigen manier ook, onverschrokken, hij wilde redden wat er te redden viel. De helpende hand wilde hij bieden, als niemand meer naar binnen durfde wilde hij naar binnen gaan.

Jurek had willen worden zoals zijn vader, hij klom in zijn vader zoals andere kinderen in bomen klimmen, maar zoals het weer kon omslaan zo was Jurek omgeslagen. De prepuberteit was gekomen, noodweer in de zomer.

Geniek Janowski had zich er volledig bij neergelegd dat zijn zoon hem tegenwoordig 'de Pool' noemde, alsof hij ook in zijn eigen woonkamer de vreemdeling moest blijven die hij alleen al was door zijn naam. Het belangrijkste was dat hij van Jurek hield, zijn eigen vlees, zijn eigen zoon, en dat Jurek van hem hield. Hij begreep dat het liefde was, de plagerijtjes, de pesterijtjes, de norsheid – de liefde van een kind, van een prepuber, die niet meer wist hoe je dat moest doen, liefde uiten, liefde laten blijken. Het was ook moeilijk, liefde.

Geniek was niet in Polen geboren en hoewel hij Pools kon verstaan en ook redelijk sprak was het niet zijn eerste taal. Hoe dan ook sprak hij weinig, net als zijn vader. Zijn vader was naar Limburg gekomen als aspergesteker en hij was blijven hangen aan een Duits meisje dat daar in een pannenkoekenboerderij werkte, in de keuken, Genieks moeder, die op 33-jarige leeftijd na een ziekbed was overleden. Op de rouwkaart had gestaan: 'Na veel strijd en lijden is in Gods ontferming opgenomen onze dierbare vrouw en moeder Ulrike Janowski-Zimmermann.'

En dat stond er ook in het Duits en Pools. Als achtjarige zei die ontferming de Pool niets, pas later begon hij te begrijpen wat er met ontferming werd bedoeld. Al had de vader het na het sterven van zijn vrouw regelmatig over de hemel gehad.

Genieks vader, die van aspergesteker was opgeklommen tot IT-specialist, woonde tegenwoordig in Haarlem met een nieuwe vrouw en twee nieuwe kinderen en zijn springlevende God. Geniek had een halfbroer en een halfzus, nog niet eens tieners, zo oud als zijn eigen zoon. Hij zag zijn halfbroer en halfzus hooguit een keer per jaar. De vader van de Pool had zijn zoon te kennen gegeven dat hij hem niet meer zo vaak hoefde te zien. 'Je herinnert me aan de dood, aan het verleden dat dood is,' had de vader gezegd toen Geniek achttien was en op het punt stond om uit huis te gaan. 'We moeten allebei een nieuw leven beginnen. Beter voor ons beiden.'

De man had de rouw te boven willen komen, de pijn om het verlies van zijn jonge Duitse vrouw, die te vroeg was gestorven, zo jong horen mensen niet te sterven en daarom had hij zijn zoon ook maar halfdood verklaard. Om de pijn te verzachten, om er niet voortdurend aan te hoeven denken. Zo was Geniek een soort wees geworden. Hij nam het zijn vader niet kwalijk, hij begreep het. Die man was een nieuw leven begonnen, een nieuw gezin, een nieuw huis in een nieuwe stad, hij wilde niet achtervolgd worden door het oude leven dat naar de dood rook. De Pool sloot ook niet uit dat hijzelf naar de dood rook, alleen al vanwege zijn beroep. Als brandweerman kwam je geregeld met de dood in aanraking, als iemand voor de trein sprong mocht de brandweer het lichaam van de rails en de locomotief krabben, want daar voelden de broeders van de ambulance zich te goed voor, die waren er voor de levenden, en de politie had er ook geen trek in, die hielden niet van schoonmaken, en als politie en ambulance het lieten afweten dan mocht de brandweer het opknappen. Zo was het, zo zat de wereld nu eenmaal in elkaar. Protesteren had geen zin. Je mond houden en doen wat er van je verwacht werd, dát had zin. Zo had de Pool Jurek ook opgevoed.

De Pool hield van zijn vader, een echte Pool die correct Nederlands sprak met een zwaar accent. Omdat hij van hem hield accepteerde hij het zwijgen en de afwezigheid van de man, al vond hij het voor Jurek weleens moeilijk als die vroeg: 'Waarom wil opa niets met ons te maken hebben? Waarom is opa zo boos op ons?'

Dat ging hem door merg en been, de vragen van het

kind. Dan legde de Pool uit dat opa niet boos was en dat hij onder andere omstandigheden ook een goede en misschien wel uitstekende opa zou zijn geweest, maar dat oma jong was gestorven en dat opa daarom voor het verleden was weggerend, een beetje zoals mensen uit een brandend huis rennen.

Andere mensen noemden het gemankeerd, zijn vrouw bijvoorbeeld. 'Je vader is een gemankeerd man,' zei ze weleens maar dat soort woorden gebruikte de Pool niet. Wat had je aan dat soort woorden? En daarom legde hij het op zijn eigen manier uit aan zijn zoon, tot Jurek er niet meer naar vroeg en op een gegeven moment ook niet meer mee naar Haarlem wilde op die ene dag per jaar, eerste kerstdag, dat opa bereid was zijn verleden toe te laten in zijn woonkamer. Een paar uur mocht het verleden dan op opa's banken en aan opa's eettafel zitten, al snel kreeg opa het toch benauwd en moest het verleden weer terug naar waar het vandaan kwam, waar het thuishoorde, waar het allemaal begonnen was, Zuid-Limburg. Het werd opa te veel, je kon het aan zijn gezicht zien, hij liep blauw aan, begon te zuchten en te steunen alsof hij geen lucht kreeg. Zijn nieuwe vrouw en zijn nieuwe kinderen bemoeiden zich er niet mee. Ja, ze vroegen wel: 'Gaat het? Wil je een glaasje water?' Meer als een formaliteit. Ze lieten hem begaan, ze leken een beetje bang voor hem, voor de grote oude Pool die blauw aanliep in Haarlem.

Tegen zichzelf zei de jonge Pool dat vroeg of laat alle mensen wees werden, dat ze daartoe voorbestemd waren en dat het uiteindelijk niet veel uitmaakte wanneer het gebeurde. Wees was wees. Misschien was het goed dat het vroeg gebeurde, dan was je ervan af.

Uiteindelijk was hij bij de brandweer gegaan omdat hij ervan overtuigd was dat brand geblust moest worden, dat je het redden van mensen niet aan God of aan andere mensen moest overlaten, dat je het zelf moest doen. Als kind had hij altijd al 'brandweerman' gezegd wanneer mensen hem vroegen wat hij later wilde worden. Zonder dat hij zich kon voorstellen dat dit ooit zou gebeuren. Hij had nooit bovenmatig veel vertrouwen gehad dat zijn verlangens vervuld zouden worden. Maar dit verlangen was vervuld en andere verlangens waren ook vervuld, een vrouw, een kind, een huis. Wat wil een mens nog meer?

Beckers zei nog steeds niets, maar er liepen tranen over zijn wangen, de man huilde waar iedereen bij was. Hij wendde zich discreet af, ging een beetje verzitten, staarde nog indringender naar de cappuccino dan daarvoor, er was alleen het gesnik te horen. De Pool kon een gevoel van schaamte niet onderdrukken en tegelijkertijd voelde hij ook medelijden. Was dit wat er over was van Beckers? Dit snikkende lichaam dat ooit de meest competitieve volleybalspeler van de C-ploeg was geweest?

Als ze niet hoefden uit te rukken speelden ze een paar keer per week volleybal om de conditie op peil te houden, Beckers had altijd gespeeld alsof er geen alternatief was voor winnen en nu zat hij daar te snikken. Er was weinig over van zijn bravoure, van de man die volleybal speelde om de tegenstander te verpletteren.

De Pool had met Beckers onder de douche gestaan, daar spraken ze over hun kinderen, over het gezin, daar werden grappen gemaakt over vrouwen, daar werden zorgen gedeeld. De namen van zijn dochters stonden op Beckers' linkerbovenarm. Ja, hij had veel met Beckers gedeeld maar nog nooit had hij hem zien huilen. Hij vond huilen privé, hij wilde Beckers niet zien huilen en daarom bekeek hij de mok waarin zijn lauwe koffie zat, een mosgroene mok, en hij vroeg zich af wat hij Jurek voor zijn verjaardag moest geven. De jongen wilde een iPhone maar dat vond de Pool overdreven, nee niet overdreven, hij was er gewoon tegen omdat hij wist wat er met die iPhone ging gebeuren, daarmee werd niet gebeld, mensen belden allang niet meer met telefoons, alleen als het echt niet anders ging werd de telefoon nog weleens gebruikt waarvoor de telefoon was uitgevonden. Pubers keken porno op hun telefoon, jongens, de Pool had gehoord over meisjes die het ook deden. Zijn vrouw zei wel dat ze het ding zo konden afstellen dat porno kijken onmogelijk was en dat de meeste jongens in de klas van Jurek een smartphone hadden maar de Pool vertrouwde het niet, hij zei: 'Onze Jurek is slim, slimmer dan de techniek.' Hij begreep wel dat het gevecht dat hij tegen porno voerde gedoemd was te mislukken maar hij vond twaalf te jong. Als je twaalf was hoorde je niet als je thuiskwam van school onder de dekens te kruipen om naar neukende mannen en vrouwen te kijken en God mocht weten wat er nog meer te zien was op die pornofilms van tegenwoordig. De Pool wist natuurlijk wel ongeveer wat er te zien was en juist daarom voerde hij zijn oorlog, want hij ambieerde naast een goede brandweerman ook een goede vader te zijn.

Beckers haalde zijn neus op en de mannen luisterden hoe Beckers zijn neus ophaalde en ze keken hem niet aan. Ze dachten ongetwijfeld allemaal wat de Pool dacht, dat je niet naar andermans tranen moest kijken en dat je die ook niet aan andere mensen moest laten zien en eigenlijk hoopte de Pool dat het alarm zou gaan, dat ze nu moesten uitrukken, naar een grote, uitslaande brand, daarop hoopte hij, hoewel het natuurlijk beter was als dat soort branden niet plaatsvonden. De Pool moest niks hebben van dit soort medelijden. En uiteindelijk, toen ze het met z'n allen niet meer uithielden, zei Beckers: 'Jullie weten allemaal dat mijn vrouw al een tijdje ziek is. Het zag ernaar uit dat het goed ging, dat ze schoon was...'

De man haalde opnieuw zijn neus op, de collega die al een tijdje met verlof was om voor vrouw en kinderen te zorgen. Toen hij zijn emoties onder controle leek te hebben zei hij: 'Het is teruggekomen, twee weken geleden bleek bij onderzoek dat het is teruggekomen, en de artsen zeggen dat ze nu niets meer kunnen doen, dat ze er alleen slechter van kan worden, dat het nu gewoon morfine is en...'

Beckers keek niet meer opzij, hij keek naar beneden, naar zijn cappuccino en toen naar zijn schoot en de ploegchef zei: 'Jezus, Beckers, jezus.' En de andere mannen zeiden niets, ze staarden voor zich uit of ze tuurden naar hun koffie. De Pool had wel iets willen zeggen maar hij begreep dat als er één moment geschikt was om te zwijgen het nu was. Beckers wreef over zijn gezicht en zijn ogen, hij zette het bekertje op tafel en hij zei: 'Van het weekend had ik in het ziekenhuis al het gevoel dat het niet goed was, ze wilde niet meer eten, al zeiden de verplegers: "Laten we het even aankijken." Er waren ook niet zoveel artsen vanwege het weekend. Mijn vrouw wil niet naar huis, ze voelt zich veiliger in het ziekenhuis.'

De ploegchef knikte. Hij zei: 'Dat begrijp ik, dat ze zich daar veiliger voelt. Ze weet zelf het beste wat ze nodig heeft.'

Beckers slikte en hij sprak bijna zakelijk: 'Het is een kwestie van dagen hebben ze gezegd. Het gaat nu heel snel. Ik merk het ook aan haar. Ze vecht niet meer. Ze heeft het opgegeven. De kinderen merken het natuurlijk ook maar we hebben nog niets verteld. Dat moet ik nu wel snel doen. Ik wilde met mijn vrouw overleggen hoe we het precies gingen aanpakken. We dachten ook aan school... School gaat gewoon door.'

Beckers haalde zijn neus weer op en de Pool herinnerde zich dat zijn moeder aan het begin van de zomer was gestorven. De juf had gezegd: 'Ga maar naar het ziekenhuis, Geniek. Je kunt nu beter daar zijn dan hier.' Hij had zijn spullen gepakt en had de bus naar het ziekenhuis genomen en daar lag ze te sterven. Kort daarop begon de grote vakantie.

Misschien was het beter voor kinderen als hun ouders stierven in de schoolvakantie en toen dacht hij dat dit juist niet beter was want dan was de hele vakantie verpest. En even meende hij dat hij zijn zoon die binnenkort jarig was toch een smartphone moest geven.

'Klote,' zei de ploegchef. 'Dat is heel erg klote, Beckers.'

En de mannen knikten want dat was het, klote, veel meer viel er niet over te zeggen. Ze lieten het spreken aan Beckers over en aan de ploegchef, die namens hen sprak en die na een korte pauze zei: 'Als we iets voor je kunnen doen, laat het ons weten.'

En weer viel er een stilte. Beckers wist niet wat hij moest zeggen, zoveel was duidelijk, hij wilde ook niet gaan, niet naar het ziekenhuis en niet naar zijn kinderen, hij wilde hier blijven, bij zijn collega's, en de mannen staarden voor zich uit, een enkeling mompelde iets, woorden van instemming, woorden van troost. Klote, kut, we denken aan je. Dat soort woorden. De Pool probeerde zich het gezicht van de vrouw van Beckers voor de geest te halen en toen dat van zijn eigen vrouw en van zijn moeder. De herinneringen aan zijn moeder waren verbleekt, wat hij zich vooral herinnerde waren de bezoeken aan het ziekenhuis, een onbestemd verdriet. Het vermoeden van gevaar. Angst. Dat laatste vooral. Angst dat hij alleen zou blijven met zijn vader. Nou ja, hij was alleen gebleven met zijn vader en het was meegevallen, de angst was groter geweest dan noodzakelijk.

Even later stond de ploegchef op, om aan te geven dat het gesprek was afgelopen, dat ze verder moesten, hoe klote het ook allemaal was.

Beckers nam afscheid van de mannen. Sommigen gaven hem een hand, anderen drukten hem tegen zich aan en eigenlijk wist de Pool niet zo goed wat hij moest doen, toen besloot hij Beckers ook maar tegen zich aan te drukken en even voelde hij de natte wangen van de man. Hij rook het zweet, aftershave en vaag de geur van ziekenhuis. Hij drukte zijn vriend tegen zich aan omdat hem als troost even niet veel anders te binnen schoot.

De ploegchef zei: 'Je hebt onze nummers, aarzel niet te bellen als we iets voor je kunnen doen. Of kom langs.'

Beckers knikte, eerst langzaam en toen steeds sneller alsof de woorden van de ploegchef ook pas langzaam tot hem doordrongen. Aan de manier waarop hij knikte begreep de Pool dat hij niet zou bellen en dat het ook wel even kon duren voor hij weer langskwam.

Toen Beckers weg was zei de ploegchef: 'Ik weet dat je het niet mag zeggen, toch ben ik ontzettend blij dat het mij niet overkomt. Je zult kinderen hebben en dan dit...'

De mannen knikten. Ook zij waren blij dat het hun niet overkwam, allemaal, ze wisten dat je dat niet mocht zeggen en ze waren ook blij dat de ploegchef het wel had gezegd.

De Pool, die vanavond zou koken, ging met Nelemans en de autospuit naar de supermarkt om boodschappen te doen. Vroeger was dat niet nodig geweest, dan kon er op de fiets naar de supermarkt worden gegaan, maar met de bezuinigingen moesten ook degenen die boodschappen deden paraat staan als er iets misging en daarom ging hij met de autospuit.

'Klote voor Beckers,' zei Nelemans. 'Het leek wel alsof hij weken niet gegeten had. Zag je hoe mager hij was? En die gelige huid.'

De Pool knikte. 'Als je verdriet hebt smaakt het eten je niet,' zei hij, 'en als je bang bent vergeet je te eten.'

Daarna startte hij de auto. Ze gingen shoarmavlees kopen, patat lag nog in de diepvries.

## 2

De vrouw van de Pool stond met een glas water in haar hand voor de spiegel. Ze nam een slok, zette het glas neer en ging verder met het epileren van haar wenkbrauwen. Ze had die avond een feest en voor bijzondere gelegenheden epileerde ze haar wenkbrauwen. Aan haar man had ze een keer gevraagd: 'Is het nodig?' En hij had geantwoord: 'Nee van mij hoeft het niet, ik vind je wenkbrauwen goed zo.'

Voor feesten werkte ze haar wenkbrauwen nog wel bij, voor de feestganger die wellicht anders over haar wenkbrauwen dacht dan haar eigen man.

Met een stylingtang had ze al wat nonchalante krullen in haar donkerblonde haren gedraaid.

'Je bent vroeg,' zei ze.

Hij kuste haar, eerst op de wang, toen op de mond, hij nam haar in zijn armen, hij gaf haar een tongzoen. Het was belangrijk om je vrouw een tongzoen te geven als je 24 uur in de kazerne was geweest, als je kinderen en bejaarden uit over de kop geslagen auto's had moeten bevrijden, junks van een verstikkingsdood had moeten redden omdat ze niet meer roken dat alles aanbrandde, dan moest je je vrouw zoenen wanneer je thuiskwam. Soms vergat hij het, vandaag niet. Voor je het wist verdween de tongzoen uit je leven, was het iets wat je alleen nog in een film of een televisieserie zag.

Zijn vrouw beantwoordde de zoen, maar na een paar seconden maakte ze zich los uit zijn omhelzing. 'Lieverd,' zei ze, 'lieverd,' ze streek hem over de wang en daarop ging ze verder met het epileren. Eén wenkbrauw was al gedaan. Haastig deed ze het en toch nauwkeurig. Al die jaren dat hij haar kende was ze nauwelijks aangekomen. Ze had een meisjesachtig lichaam behouden, zelf zei ze vaak lachend: 'Ik verbrand mijn eten snel, daar kan ik ook niets aan doen.'

Hij duwde haar teder opzij en waste zijn gezicht, zonder zeep, met lauw water. De badkamer was goed opgeruimd, ze waren allebei ordentelijke mensen, ze hielden niet van chaos om zich heen.

De Pool had zijn vaste rituelen bij thuiskomst. Na een dienst ging hij eerst naar de badkamer, waste zijn handen, zijn gezicht en dronk daarna in de keuken een kop groene thee. Als vrouw en kind het huis uit waren kroop hij nog een uur, maximaal anderhalf uur, afhankelijk van hoe de nacht was verlopen, onder de dekens. Dat was luxe, dat uur alleen in bed, in een stil huis, al was het natuurlijk niet altijd stil geweest, er waren ooit babygeluiden te horen geweest in het huis van de Pool, gebrabbel, gejengel, gehuil. Een peuter die op het bed sprong als de Pool net was gaan liggen, het vreugdevolle weerzien met papa.

'Ik kom altijd om deze tijd,' zei hij, met zijn hand op de schouder van de vrouw die hij vaak 'mijn lieve vrouw' noemde.

'Halfacht,' zei ze, 'het is nu twintig over zeven.'

Wendela heette ze, al werd ze zo nooit genoemd. Wen was het, heel soms Wentje – een half dozijn koosnaampjes was de revue gepasseerd inclusief 'speertje van me', omdat ze altijd al spichtig was geweest. In haar jeugd werd ze op school 'de speer' genoemd. Dat 'speertje van me' kon ze niet waarderen, en de koosnaampjes waren geleidelijk uit hun leven verdwenen, tot zij 'lieverd' was geworden en 'mijn lieve vrouw' en hij 'schat' en soms ook 'mijn man', tegenover derden. 'Dat moet u met mijn man bespreken.'

Jurek noemde zijn moeder ook geen mama, het mocht niet, hij noemde haar Wen, dat vond ze prettiger. Lang geleden had ze tegen haar zoon gezegd: 'Ik ben bang dat je vader mij straks ook "mama" gaat noemen. Dat vind ik vreselijk, van die mannen die hun vrouw "mama" of "moeder" noemen. Mijn vader deed dat. Het sluipt erin. Dus zeg maar gewoon Wen.' Ze wilde voor de Pool een vrouw blijven en wat hem betreft was ze dat ook gebleven, ze was niet veranderd in een moeder. Ooit had hij gezegd: 'Ik zal je echt niet zomaar "mama" gaan noemen, laat die jongen gewoon "mama" zeggen.' Het had niet geholpen, ze wilde dat haar zoon Wen zei.

Ze was nu klaar met epileren en wreef over haar slapen.

'Heb je hoofdpijn?' vroeg hij.

'Een beetje,' zei ze. 'Zal zo over zijn. Ik heb twee paracetamolletjes genomen.' Ze trok een groen jurkje aan dat mooi bij haar ogen paste en dat ze speciaal voor dit feest had laten stomen.

'Dit staat je sexy,' zei de Pool.

Ze gingen naar beneden. In de keuken zat Jurek achter een boterham met vlokken, hij keek een film op het mobieltje van zijn moeder. 'Zet dat uit,' zei de Pool, maar er gebeurde niets.

De Pool deed de waterkoker aan, hij wreef over het korstje op zijn neus.

'Zet dat uit,' zei hij nog een keer. Hij probeerde het mobieltje af te pakken, er ontstond een kleine worsteling, het lukte de Pool het ding uit de handen van zijn zoon te trekken. Hij legde het op het aanrecht terwijl zijn vrouw bezig was yoghurt in een bakje te doen. Ze schilde een peer, sneed die in kleine stukken en mengde het fruit door de yoghurt. De Pool volgde de geroutineerde bewegingen van zijn vrouw. Mooie bewegingen, juist omdat ze zo geroutineerd waren. Zo vanzelfsprekend. Als iemand iets goed kon, dan was het ook mooi om ernaar te kijken.

'Kun je niet ontbijten zonder een scherm?' vroeg hij aan zijn zoon toen de peer helemaal door de yoghurt was gemengd. 'Verteert het eten slechter als je niet naar een scherm staart? Denk je dat je ziek wordt zonder?'

‘Waar moet ik dan naar staren?’ vroeg de jongen. ‘Naar jou? Denk je dat het zo leuk is om jou te zien?’

Het water begon te koken. De Pool pakte de thee, deed het zakje in een mok, wachtte nog een paar seconden tot de waterkoker afsloeg en tegen zijn vrouw zei hij: ‘Het is jouw telefoon, hij hoeft niet aan je telefoon te zitten. Er bestaat zoiets als privacy. Ook in een gezin.’

Ze was juf, kleuterjuf. De kleuters schenen met haar weg te lopen, terwijl ze in haar eigen huis de opvoeding grotendeels aan haar man overliet, althans dat vond de Pool. Ze had altijd een excuus voor de jongen, hij mocht zelfs met haar mobieltje naar de wc en daar bleef hij dan een uur lang tot de Pool het niet meer uithield, op de deur klopte en vroeg: ‘Wat ben je daar aan het doen Jurek, wat gebeurt er? Heb je hulp nodig?’

‘Ik ben aan het poepen,’ luidde het antwoord meestal. Waarop de Pool terugriep: ‘Onzin, zo lang zit geen mens te poepen. Niemand poept een uur lang, zelfs demente bejaarden niet. Kom eruit met die telefoon.’

Het was een gevecht, de opvoeding, vooral als het kind zich opsloot op de wc. Moest je de deur intrappen? En wie zette die deur er dan weer in? Moest opvoeding zo kostbaar zijn? Als het moest, als het voor de bestwil van de jongen was dan moest de wc-deur worden ingetrapt. Een brandweerman trapte soms deuren in en een vader ook.

Hij nam een slok van zijn thee, nog te heet, de Pool was een man die chronisch zijn tong verbrandde. Ongeduldig was hij. Dat moest hij afleren, het ongeduld. Terwijl hij van zijn thee nipte gaf Wen haar telefoon aan de jongen terug die weer naar het scherm begon te staren. Het geluid stond zacht, toch kon je goed horen dat het een gewelddadige film was.

‘Ik heb dat ding net afgepakt,’ siste de Pool. ‘Waar ben je mee bezig? Bij het ontbijt moord en doodslag? Is dat echt nodig?’

'Ze kijken allemaal,' zei zijn vrouw. 'Ze leren er ook van, denk je dat kinderen er beter van worden als je de wereld voor ze verstopt?' Ze omhelsde haar man, ze kwam tot zijn kin. Zachtjes kneep ze in zijn flanken alsof zijn lichaam deeg was dat gekneed moest worden. 'Niet zo ouderwets,' zei ze. 'Niet zo ouderwets. We leven in het nu.'

Toen de mok thee voor de helft leeg was gedronken ging hij naar zijn zoon toe, hij bracht zijn mond bij het oor van de jongen. 'Doe je best op school,' zei de Pool. 'Je toekomst hangt ervan af, je leven hangt ervan af, nu niet je best doen is later armoe lijden.'

Soms, ondanks al het sarcasme, ondanks alle pogingen afstand te bewaren omhelsde de jongen zijn vader, alsof hij weer klein was, alsof alles vergeven en vergeten was, deze ochtend knikte hij alleen, zonder het scherm uit het oog te verliezen. De Pool legde een hand op het hoofd van de jongen, twijfelde even of hij nog iets anders moest doen, affectie moest tonen, iets moest zeggen, hij wist zelf niet wat en uiteindelijk ging hij naar boven, poetste zijn tanden, waste zijn gezicht voor de tweede keer, wat hij anders nooit deed, kleedde zich uit en ging in bed liggen, terwijl zijn zoon zich beneden klaarmaakte om naar school te gaan. Het was een kwartier fietsen en in het begin van zijn middelbareschoolcarrière had hij weleens geklaagd over regen en kou, of hij niet met de bus mocht, of ze hem wilden halen met de auto. Tegenwoordig ging hij zonder tegensputteren op de fiets, door regen en sneeuw, door hagel en onweer. Dat gevecht was gewonnen.

De Pool lag in bed maar hij sliep niet, hij staarde naar de muur en het plafond en luisterde naar de geluiden in en om het huis die zo vertrouwd waren, Jurek die de deur dichtsloeg, Jurek die zijn fiets pakte. Dat laatste kon hij niet echt horen, toch zag hij het voor zich.

Zijn vrouw kwam binnen, ging op bed zitten, ze had haar schoenen nog niet aan, verder was ze klaar voor de dag, voor het feest. Een collega werkte twintig jaar op de school, het zou groot gevierd worden, met een buffet. Twintig jaar was een mensenleven. Dan was de investering in een buffet goed te verdedigen.

'Hoe is het met Jurek?' vroeg hij. 'Zijn er nieuwe cijfers binnen?'

Het eerste jaar op de middelbare school. Wiskunde ging niet goed, er gebeurden merkwaardige dingen tijdens proefwerken wiskunde, alsof hij tijdens de toets de meest elementaire kennis van getallen was vergeten. 'Slordig, hij is slordig,' had de wiskundejuf gezegd op een ouderavond, de Pool vreesde dat het meer was dan slordigheid. De Pool was bang dat de jongen niet wilde, dat wiskunde hem niets kon schelen, dat de proefwerken hem niets konden schelen, dat hij misschien wel wiskunde haatte en de Pool vroeg zich af wat de jongen dan wel kon schelen behalve de filmpjes die hij op de smartphone van zijn moeder keek.

Wen schudde haar hoofd. 'Hij doet zijn best,' zei ze. 'Hij doet wat hij kan. Geef hem wat ruimte.'

De Pool wreef over zijn arm. Hij vroeg: 'Wordt hij niet te oud voor vlokken? Altijd vlokken. Waarom eet hij niet eens kaas op zijn brood?'

Er kwam geen antwoord. Ze keek naar haar nagels en hij keek mee, ze zou die nagels vast nog lakken, ergens aan het eind van de middag – als de wenkbrauwen werden gepileerd, dan werden de nagels ook gelakt.

Toen zei de Pool: 'De vrouw van Beckers gaat dood.'

Wen keek hem even aan, hij wendde zijn blik af, krabde aan de stoppels op zijn kin. Ze ging op bed liggen en ze keek naar het plafond en hij keek naar zijn vrouw, hoe ze daar lag. Ze zag er goed uit, blakend eigenlijk, een mooie vrouw. Hij was ooit verliefd op haar geworden, hij wist niet meer waarom, omdat zij het was, daarom vermoedelijk. De Pool geloofde de mensen niet die precies wisten waarom ze verliefd waren geworden, de humor, de lach, de ogen.

Leugentjes omdat je iets moest zeggen als mensen je dat soort vragen stelden. Wat mensen steeds vaker deden trouwens, ze wilden alles van je weten, ze konden de stilte niet verdragen. Zijn vrouw kon de stilte niet verdragen. 'Zeg iets, man,' had ze geroepen toen ze een paar weken geleden zonder kind uit eten waren vanwege hun huwelijksdag. 'Zeg iets. Ik hou het niet uit.'

Toen had hij wel iets gezegd. Als dat erbij hoorde, bij de liefde, dat gepraat, dan was hij best bereid iets te zeggen. 'Ik ben aan het nadenken,' had hij gezegd.

En zij had haar stoel naar achteren geschoven en was naar buiten gerend, hij ging achter haar aan, er brandde een kaars op hun tafel, er zaten oude mensen in ongetwijfeld dure pakken in het restaurant, ze keken hem na, dat kon hem niets schelen; als zijn vrouw het restaurant uit rende dan liet hij haar niet alleen. En toen stonden ze buiten, het sneeuwde, natte sneeuw maar toch. Ze trilde en ze zei: 'Je zegt altijd: wat kan ik voor je doen? Wat heb je nodig? Hoe kan ik het je naar de zin maken? Maar wat wil jij, Geniek? Wat wil jij in godsnaam?'

Hij voelde de natte sneeuw. Ze stonden op de parkeerplaats van het restaurant. Veel te duur voor wat het was. Wat wilde hij? Het zijn vrouw naar de zin maken. 'Ik moet erover nadenken,' zei hij en hij proefde het vocht op zijn lippen. Terwijl hij met zijn tong over zijn lippen ging keek hij naar de dure auto's die voor het te dure restaurant geparkeerd stonden en hij besefte dat hij het verkeerde antwoord had gegeven. Ik wil jou, had hij moeten zeggen en dat zei hij toen ook: 'Ik wil jou.' En hij had haar in zijn armen genomen en ze hadden gehuild, gezoend en gehuild, anders dan Beckers had gehuild, heel anders. Beckers had om de dood gehuild en zij huilden om het leven en hij was weer naar binnen gegaan en had de rekening betaald, ze hadden alleen het voorgerecht op, maar hij had alles betaald. 'Het staat vast al op het vuur, het hoofdgerecht, ik betaal er wel voor,' had hij gezegd, en ze waren naar huis gereden, met een noodvaart, alsof ze dood wilden, en thuis hadden ze gevreeën, in de vestibule, ze hadden geen tijd gehad ergens anders heen te gaan. En toen ze klaar waren bleven ze daar liggen, op de deurmat, als honden. Tot hij was opgestaan en had gezegd: 'Ik ga een tosti maken, want we hebben honger.' Het kind logeerde bij een vriendje en de Pool maakte vier tosti's die ze opaten in de woonkamer, in hun blootje; normaal pakte ze altijd een ochtendjas, of ze sloeg een handdoek om, ze was op een rare manier preuts, zijn vrouw, maar die dag niet. Ze zat poedelnaakt op de bank met twee tosti's. Ze leek helemaal tevreden en toen de tosti's op waren had ze geconstateerd: 'Nu zeg je weer niets.' Zo hadden ze hun huwelijksdag gevierd, een week of drie geleden, en het was een mooie viering geweest, een heel mooie viering, al had Wen dan misschien gevonden dat hij te weinig sprak, maar dat maakte hij op andere manieren wel weer goed. Op andere momenten.

'Wat rot,' zei ze nadat ze een tijd stil naast hem had gelegen met haar armen onder haar hoofd. 'Zo oud is ze niet.' Ze haalde diep adem, alsof ze geen haast had om naar haar werk te gaan, zo haalde ze adem voor ze in slaap viel als ze 's avonds in bed nog een serie aan het kijken waren en de slaap haar overmande, ook al was het spannend, ook al wilde ze graag weten wie het gedaan had, de slaap overmande haar, dan zuchtte ze diep. 'Rot ook voor de kinderen,' zei ze. 'Die zijn nog best jong, toch?'

'Pubers geloof ik. Niet zo heel jong meer.'

De Pool was normaal niet echt moe na een dienst, hij sliep ook op de kazerne goed. Eigenlijk ging hij vooral uit plichtsbesef thuis nog een uurtje slapen. Vanochtend voelde hij zich echt moe, uitgeput, alsof hij de hele nacht op de been was geweest, terwijl hij juist had kunnen doorslapen.

'Nou,' zei Wen na een tijd, 'dan zal Beckers een nieuwe moeder voor zijn kinderen moeten zoeken.' Ze kwam overeind, trok haar schoenen aan, ze zat met de rug naar haar man toe en hij kriebelde met een hand over haar schouder, gedachteloos en toch bezorgd. Hij besefte dat hij niet zoveel kon zeggen als ze hem zouden vragen: 'Wat is je vrouw voor iemand?' Ja, 'kleuterjuf,' zou hij zeggen, 'ze is kleuterjuf. En moeder. Ze houdt ervan als de boel een beetje opgeruimd is.' En daarna zou het stil worden. Misschien zou hij nog zeggen: 'Ze is mijn vrouw,' al was dat feitelijk overbodige informatie.

'Ik weet niet precies hoe laat ik terug ben,' zei ze, nog steeds met haar rug naar hem toe. 'Ik heb beloofd Magda na het feest thuis te brengen. Het eten voor Jurek en jou staat in de koelkast. Je hoeft het alleen op te warmen.'

'Ik had zelf kunnen koken,' zei de Pool.

'Ik dacht, ik doe het wel. Het is je vrije dag.'

Ze ging naar beneden en kwam toen toch weer naar boven met haar jas. De Pool opende en sloot zijn ogen, hij opende en sloot ze. 'Ik ga er vanmiddag even heen,' zei hij zacht. Er zat iets in zijn keel. Hij werd verkouden, het heerste. Of misschien was hij gewoon schor.

'Waarheen?'

'Naar de vrouw van Beckers. Dat lijkt me wel zo netjes.'

Wen stond klaar om naar de kleuterschool te gaan, ze had haar jas aan, de autosleutels in de hand, haar tas over de linkerschouder, zoals altijd, zoals vijf ochtenden per week. 'Nee,' zei ze, 'daar ga jij niet heen.'

De Pool bleef zijn ogen openen en sluiten en hij kon zich herinneren dat hij dat als kind een keer had gedaan toen hij vroeg wakker was geworden op zijn verjaardag, om te kijken wat er met het licht gebeurde, om te kijken hoe je het licht kon laten verdwijnen. Het verdween nooit helemaal. Hij was hartje zomer jarig en als iets hem nerveus maakte als kind was het wel zijn eigen verjaardag. Hij kon er niet van slapen.

'Ze is bijna dood,' zei hij. 'Wat maakt het uit?'

Het was een grauwe dag, er was weinig licht, je kon het laten verdwijnen.

'We hebben een afspraak, we hebben iets afgesproken, Geniek, lang geleden, ik heb me aan de afspraak gehouden, het enige wat jij hoeft te doen is je er ook aan houden. Meer niet. Meer hoef je niet te doen.'

'Nou ja, een afspraak. Je hebt me iets verboden en ik hou me eraan. Ik heb me er al die tijd aan gehouden.'

'Niet als je er nu heen gaat. Dan hou je je er niet aan. Dus dat moet je niet doen. Dat moet je gewoon niet doen.'

De Pool richtte zich op. 'Ze is vrijwel dood,' zei hij. 'Wat kan het jou schelen? Het is een kwestie van fatsoen. Even gedag zeggen. Meer niet.'

Ze knoopte haar jas dicht. 'Geniek,' zei ze, 'als jij vandaag naar de vrouw van Beckers gaat dan wil ik jouw vrouw niet meer zijn.'

Ze ging naar beneden, en de Pool trok een ochtendjas uit de kast en hij ging achter haar aan. Hij liep achter zijn vrouw de trap af, zij liep door. In de vestibule haalde hij haar in, hij versperde haar de weg. Dit was anders dan die keer in het restaurant.

'Wat is er?' vroeg ze. 'Ik moet gaan.'

Hij haalde een hand over zijn hoofd, alsof er nog haar zat, hij bestudeerde haar gezicht, hij meende iets in haar gezicht te zien, iets van herkenning, iets van bevestiging dat ze niet meende wat ze zei, dat ze gewoon geschrokken was van de dood, de naderende dood. Hij probeerde haar te zoenen, zoals die avond op de parkeerplaats van het restaurant toen ze hun huwelijksdag vierden. De natte sneeuw, veel te vroeg voor de tijd van het jaar. De dure auto's. De tosti's. De toenadering. Nu trok ze haar hoofd weg.

'Ik moet erheen,' zei hij. 'Het is een kwestie van fatsoen, gewoon even gedag zeggen. Beterschap wensen, omdat er toch altijd een wonder kan gebeuren. Meer niet. Omdat het straks waarschijnlijk niet meer kan. Ik zou niet meer in de spiegel kunnen kijken als ik wegbleef. Dat moet jij begrijpen.'

'Nee,' zei ze, heel rustig en heel kalm, ze keek hem aan en in haar blik zag hij dat ze eigenlijk al vertrokken was, ze keek hem aan alsof hij een vreemde was, een klusjesman die zijn werk niet goed had gedaan en die daarom streng moest worden toegesproken, 'dat begrijp ik niet. Je gaat er niet heen. Je hebt daar niets te zoeken. Ze zitten niet op je te wachten. Het is de vrouw van Beckers, het is niet jouw vrouw. Ik ben jouw vrouw. Laat die mensen met rust.'

Ze probeerde zich langs hem te wringen, hij versperde haar de weg zoals hij mensen de weg versperde die een brandend huis probeerden binnen te dringen, voor hun eigen bestwil, ze wilden er nog iets uit halen, een konijn of een muntenverzameling. Moesten ze niet doen, hun leven was belangrijker dan dat konijn of die muntenverzameling. En hij dacht aan zijn vader die het verleden had afgezworen als een slechte gewoonte en uiteindelijk zei hij: 'Ik heb nooit iets uitgelegd, ik heb altijd gedacht: het komt nog wel een keer, dan verklaar ik het allemaal, maar nu weet ik dat die keer er niet komt als ik er niet naartoe ga vandaag,' en hij streelde zijn vrouw met de rug van zijn hand over haar wang. 'Wen,' zei hij, 'begrijp me toch.'

Ze schudde haar hoofd. 'Voor jou gaat ze niet dood,' zei ze, 'voor jou zal ze altijd blijven leven en alleen al daarom wil ik niet dat jij erheen gaat.'

Ze glipte langs hem heen en hij liet haar begaan, hij liep wel achter haar aan, in zijn ochtendjas, op blote voeten, door de plassen, tot hij bij haar auto was, ze zat al achter het stuur, ze deed het raampje naar beneden. 'Je vat kou,' zei ze. 'En de buren zien je.'

'Is er iemand anders?' vroeg hij. 'Is dat het?'

Ze zuchtte zoals ze zuchtte voor ze in slaap viel. Toen reed ze weg en de Pool wachtte nog even want hij had het idee dat ze aan het eind van de straat zou keren en terugrijden, maar ze kwam niet terug en uiteindelijk liep hij naar binnen. In de keuken stonden de vlokken nog op tafel. Hij pakte het pak, bestudeerde het, zette het toen in de kast en legde en passant nog een vergeten vork in de afwasmachine.

Het was niet genoeg. Dit hier, het was allemaal niet genoeg, daarom zat zijn zoon elke ochtend, nee elk moment van de dag op de smartphone van zijn moeder, omdat het niet genoeg was.

In de badkamer veegde hij zijn voeten schoon. Hoe kon Wen nu nog zo moeilijk doen over de vrouw van Beckers? Veel tijd om erover na te denken had hij niet, hij wilde nog wat slapen en 's middags naar het ziekenhuis. Uiteindelijk zou ze het begrijpen, Wen, hij zou het zo uitleggen dat ze mild werd. Hij zou zo spreken dat er geen misverstand mogelijk was.

# 3

De Pool was lang. Behalve dat hij Pool was of als zodanig werd beschouwd werd hij ook bepaald door zijn lengte. Hij was bijna 1 meter 90. En tanig. Hij was iets aangekomen, in de loop der jaren, maar zijn lichaam was goed onderhouden. Hoe kon je de ander redden als je lichaam je in de steek liet omdat je het niet goed had onderhouden? In kledingwinkels hadden ze het vaak over een moeilijke maat, terwijl er toch meer mensen in Nederland moesten rondlopen zoals hij. En de langste was hij zeker niet, zo uitzonderlijk was 1 meter 90 ook weer niet. Hij kende een paar mannen die nog langer waren en al stak hij boven een hoop mensen uit, niet boven zijn vorige ploegchef. Ze zagen hem van verre aankomen, dat wel, dat gevoel had hij vanaf zijn vijftiende; waar hij ook heen ging, ze zagen hem van verre aankomen.

Voor de kast aarzelde hij, zoals Wen soms ook een halfuur voor de kast kon staan voor ze uitging. Een trainingspak vond hij merkaardig als je iemand voor het laatst ging bezoeken, een echt pak was ook weer zo formeel, alsof diegene al begraven was terwijl hij nog in het ziekenhuis lag. Halfdood weliswaar, maar ademend, nog niet helemaal dood. Zoveel pakken had hij ook niet, alleen zijn trouwpak. Uiteindelijk koos hij voor een donkere trui en een spijkerbroek.

Hij schoor zich zorgvuldig, voorzichtig, hij wilde zich niet snijden. Vandaag niet.

Hoewel hij wist dat hij waarschijnlijk Beckers zou tegenkomen en vermoedelijk ook de kinderen van Beckers, had hij het zo uitgekiend dat hij een minuut of tien voor het begin van het bezoekuur arriveerde, misschien waren ze er dan nog niet. En anders begrepen ze vast wel dat hij even langskwam. Een collega, een goede collega, hij was een paar keer bij hen thuis geweest in een niet eens zo ver verleden, hij had met de kinderen gespeeld, hij had hen hoog de lucht in getild, niet alle drie, maar wel een of twee, althans zo herinnerde hij het zich. De kinderen van Beckers zouden wel weten wie de Pool was en wat hij daar kwam doen.

Onderweg kocht hij een boeketje bloemen. 'Vrolijke kleuren,' zei hij tegen de verkoopster. De dood mocht op de stoep staan, hij wilde niet met lege handen komen en ook niet met een rouwboeket.

Bij de informatiebalie van het ziekenhuis zei hij: 'Ik kom voor Beckers, mevrouw Beckers.'

De dame van de informatiebalie keek in haar computer: 'We hebben drie mevrouwen Beckers, bij welke moet u zijn?' vroeg ze. 'Op welke afdeling ligt ze?'

Hij had geen idee op welke afdeling ze lag. Oncologie, heette het zo? Of interne geneeskunde? Waar had zijn moeder eigenlijk gelegen? 'Je moeder is nu op een plek waar ze het vast beter heeft dan bij ons en ooit zul je haar weer zien,' had zijn vader gezegd. De Pool had zich schuldig gevoeld dat hij zijn moeder miste, omdat ze ergens was waar ze het beter had dan bij de levenden. Daarom was hij op een gegeven moment gestopt met dat missen.

'Deze mevrouw Beckers gaat binnenkort dood,' zei hij en hij bracht het boeket van zijn linker- naar zijn rechterhand.

'Daar heb ik niet zoveel aan,' antwoordde de dame. 'Er gaan hier heel veel mensen binnenkort dood. Hebt u misschien een voornaam?'

'Frieda,' antwoordde hij, 'Frieda Beckers.'

Toen vond ze de informatie die hij nodig had, de dame. Ze gaf hem de verdieping en het kamernummer en ze legde uit hoe hij moest lopen, hij bedankte vriendelijk en vervolgens wandelde hij naar de kamer van mevrouw Beckers, langzaam, steeds langzamer eigenlijk. Had Wen niet gelijk gehad? Zat ze op hem te wachten? Voor wie ging hij daar heen? Wat viel er nog uit te leggen?

In dit ziekenhuis had zijn moeder gelegen, hier had hij als achtjarige gelopen. In zijn herinnering had het er anders uitgezien, hadden de gangen eindeloos geleken, uren had hij door die gangen gedwaald. Met sommige patiënten was hij bevriend geraakt, hij had aan hun bed gestaan alsof hij familie van hen was en van zijn vader had hij elke dag geld gekregen voor een ijsje. Dan ging hij naar beneden om een ijsje te halen, omdat de oude Pool, de echte Pool, niet had gewild dat het kind getuige was van het sterven. Nee, zijn vader wilde het kind niet met de dood confronteren. Het was een mooie zomer geweest. Een verpleegster had hem nog een cadeautje gegeven, een modelvliegtuig dat hij zelf in elkaar moest zetten, daarvoor was lijm nodig, die zat er alleen niet bij en uiteindelijk was het vliegtuig nooit in elkaar gezet. Eerst belandde het op zolder, daarna in de vuilnisbak.

De vrouw van Beckers lag op een kamer met twee bedden, één bed was vrij. Het ziekenhuis had doorzichtig plastic over het lege bed gedrapeerd. Vanuit het raam zag je wat groen. Ooit had de vrouw van Beckers tegen hem gezegd dat Heerlen de lelijkste stad van Nederland was, maar de Pool had ermee leren leven, zoals je leert leven met een wrat op je wang.

Man en kinderen stonden in stilte om het bed toen de Pool binnenkwam. Ze keken om, ze leken niet eens verbaasd. Hij groette met een handgebaar, er kwam geen reactie.

Even bleef hij bij de ingang staan, niet ver van de wastafel, toen deed hij een paar stappen naar voren. Het rook niet naar ziekenhuis in de kamer, meer naar mens, naar ziek en zweterig mensenvlees. De Pool kon de vrouw van

Beckers niet goed zien en hij wilde zich niet naar voren dringen. De logeplaatsen waren niet voor hem bestemd.

'Weten jullie nog wie ik ben?' vroeg hij aan de kinderen, drie meisjes. Ze waren groot geworden, de oudste was al bijna een vrouw. Ze leek niet op haar moeder. Hij probeerde zich te herinneren hoe de dochters heetten, er schoot hem niets te binnen. Hij wist alleen nog dat Beckers vreesde dat zijn dochters er op een dag met een Arabier of Afrikaan vandoor zouden gaan. Omdat de meisjes niet antwoordden, omdat ze hem alleen aankeken zei hij uiteindelijk zelf: 'Ik ben de Pool.' Ze bleven hem aankijken maar hun gezichtsuitdrukking verried niets. Hij kon er niet uit opmaken of ze nog wisten wie de Pool was of dat ze gewoon niet begrepen waarover hij het had.

Tegen Beckers zei hij: 'Ik dacht, ik kom even langs.'

Beckers draaide zich om, knikte en toen richtte hij zijn blik weer op zijn vrouw, die in het ziekenhuisbed lag te sterven. De Pool vroeg zich af waarom ze niet gingen zitten, Beckers en zijn drie dochters. Je kon toch ook zitten naast een stervende.

Hij wist niet waar hij de bloemen moest laten want het nachtkastje stond vol met bekers en medicijnen en kaarten, dus bleef hij staan met het boeket in zijn handen, op gepaste afstand van het gezin. Na een paar minuten legde hij het toch maar op het bed dat leeg was.

'Ze slaapt,' zei Beckers.

De kinderen staarden naar hun moeder. En ook Beckers staarde naar zijn slapende vrouw.

Hij zag dat alle drie de meisjes een hand op de arm van hun moeder hadden gelegd, alsof ze wilden voorkomen dat ze weg zou gaan, alsof ze het sterven konden tegenhouden door aan de arm van hun moeder te gaan hangen. Beckers zelf had zijn handen op de dekens gelegd.

Op dat moment kwam een mevrouw van het ziekenhuis langs met drinken. Een opluchting, vond de Pool. Afleiding. De dood was inderdaad niets voor kinderen.

'Wil mevrouw wat drinken?' werd er gevraagd. 'Ik heb ook een tomatensoepje.'

'Doe maar appelsap,' zei Beckers en de Pool zag dat er nog twee volle bekers appelsap op het nachtkastje stonden.

Hij bleef staan, op de tweede rang, achter de gezinsleden, je kwam niet om meteen weer weg te gaan. Op het lege bed lag zijn boeket, de bloemen leken nu al niet meer vers. Hij keek om zich heen maar zag niets dat als vaas dienst kon doen. Een verpleegkundige zou zich wel over de bloemen ontfermen, het ging om het gebaar. Vrolijke kleuren. Ze had altijd van vrolijke kleuren gehouden.

De dame met het drinken ging weer weg, er stonden nu drie bekers appelsap op het nachtkastje, en vervolgens gebeurde er niets, iedereen bleef staan, iedereen wachtte. Tot Beckers zich omdraaide en in de wc verdween.

Eindelijk kon de Pool haar goed zien. Hij wist wat hij had kunnen verwachten, hij had zich op het ergste voorbereid en toch schrok hij. De dood begon zoveel eerder dan de dood. Er was al zoveel uit haar gezicht weggevreten, hij herkende haar amper, haar lichaam lag onder de dekens en daar leek eveneens weinig van over, terwijl ze altijd iets molligs had gehad. De oudste dochter had al borstjes, dat zag hij wel, ze keken hem weer aan, alle drie, hij zou ze op straat niet herkend hebben. Het was uiteindelijk de jongste die zei: 'Jij bent toch die collega van mijn vader?'

De oudste zei: 'Ssst.'

En de Pool zei: 'Klopt, dat ben ik, vroeger kwam ik weleens bij jullie thuis.'

Meer werd er niet gezegd. De Pool lustte wel wat appelsap, zijn mond was kurkdroog, maar hij kon moeilijk het appelsap van de vrouw van Beckers pakken, ook al stonden er drie bekers die ze vermoedelijk zelf niet meer zou drinken. En de meisjes bleven hem aanstaren, niet vijandig, evenmin vriendelijk, alsof de Pool bij de naderende dood van hun moeder hoorde, alsof hij een van de verschijningsvormen van die dood was.

'Het is warm hier,' zei hij.

Beckers kwam terug. De Pool had van alles voorbereid om te zeggen als hij even alleen zou zijn met de vrouw van Beckers. Nu de dood zo dichtbij was moest de stilte worden verbroken. Hij had willen uitleggen waarom hij indertijd niets meer had laten horen, waarom hij haar berichten genegeerd had, waarom hij haar had geblokkeerd. Hij had moeten kiezen en hij had gekozen, de enige keuze die een man die een goede man wil zijn had kunnen maken. Daarom had hij gezwegen.

'Waar ben je?' had ze gevraagd, 'waarom hoor ik niets?' Hij was hard geweest zoals mannen hard kunnen zijn, hij had gedaan alsof ze dood was, zoals het hem was opgedragen. Op den duur was hij het zelf gaan geloven, de vrouw van Beckers was voor hem dood geweest tot haar man erover begon dat ze doodziek was. Zij moest twee keer sterven.

Het is een kleine stad, Heerlen, maar de enkele keer dat hij haar was tegengekomen had hij zich verstopt, met een behendigheid die hem zelf verraste, alsof verstoppen een talent van hem was. Om te voorkomen dat het weer begon, daarom maakte hij zich af en toe onzichtbaar.

Uiteindelijk waren de Beckers naar een dorp in de buurt verhuisd en had hij zich niet meer hoeven verstoppen, want ze kwam nooit meer in de stad.

Ik heb gekozen voor mijn jongen, had hij willen zeggen als Beckers en zijn kinderen er niet waren geweest en de vrouw van Beckers niet had liggen slapen. Dan had hij gezegd dat dit de enige keuze was die hij had kunnen maken en dat hij daarom was gevlucht, niet voor het verleden zoals zijn vader maar voor de hartstocht, en hij zou het weer doen. De hartstocht was niet goed voor een mens. Zo kon een mens niet leven, met hartstocht, er kwam niets meer uit zijn handen.

De Pool wist nu vrijwel zeker dat ze haar ogen niet meer zou opendoen, niet waar hij bij was, niet dit bezoekuur en vermoedelijk ook niet de bezoekuren erna en toen hij dat eenmaal besefte besloot hij weg te gaan. Hij had geen spijt dat hij was gekomen maar langer wachten was zinloos.

'Ik ga ervandoor,' zei de Pool.

'Ik zie je wel weer,' zei Beckers.

En toen deed de Pool het toch, hij wrong zich tussen de meisjes naar voren, bracht zijn mond naar het gelige oor en fluisterde: 'Jij hebt me getroost.' Meteen daarna stapte hij weer naar achteren.

Bij de deur bleef hij staan en zei: 'Er komt iets in plaats van het verdriet. Ik weet het uit ervaring. Er komt iets erna.'

Hij wist niet of ze hem hadden gehoord, toch was het goed dat hij dat had gezegd. Je moest iets meer zeggen dan 'klote', hoewel dat het allemaal samenvatte.

Nog even wachtte hij, toen liep hij naar beneden en in het cafetaria waar hij als kind altijd een ijsje had gekocht bestelde hij een Fanta. Aan een tafeltje keek hij op zijn telefoon en zag dat zijn jongen hem een sms had gestuurd, zijn jongen die zo graag een smartphone wilde. 'Mag ik bij Daan blijven? We gaan ook huiswerk maken,' stond er. De Pool keek naar zijn telefoon, hij schudde zijn hoofd, er waren toch afspraken gemaakt, door de week werd er niet bij vriendjes gespeeld, niet zolang de cijfers niet omhooggingen. Toen belde hij zijn jongen op en eigenlijk had hij precies dat willen zeggen, je kent de afspraken, kom onmiddellijk naar huis, er wordt niet gespeeld bij Daan. Waar Daan was zou vast geen huiswerk worden gemaakt, hij had die Daan twee of drie keer gezien, het leek hem een jongen die principieel geen huiswerk maakte, zo'n figuur die nog liever doodging dan aan zijn huiswerk te beginnen, maar omdat hij bij de vrouw van Beckers was geweest, omdat hem dat week had gemaakt, de vrouw die eruitzag alsof ze gelyncht was, het dode verleden dat nu zo levend en zo vers aanvoelde, omdat je ook coulant moest zijn als opvoeder zei hij tegen zijn jongen dat het goed was, zolang er maar echt huiswerk werd gemaakt, dat hij om zeven uur thuis moest zijn en dat ze dan samen gingen eten. Samen zouden ze het eten opwarmen dat Wen in de koelkast had gezet, samen zouden ze de tafel dekken en terwijl ze aten zouden ze samen een gesprek voeren. Hij benadrukte wat ze allemaal samen zouden doen maar de jongen ging er niet op in. Daarop dronk de Pool het blikje Fanta bijna in één keer leeg. Vervolgens liet hij een boer, het ontglipte hem, waarvoor hij zich schaamde, want er zaten mensen naast hem.

De dame van de kiosk kwam de tafel schoonmaken. 'Jij bent toch brandweerman?' zei ze. 'Mijn zoon wil bij de brandweer.'

'Een mooi beroep,' antwoordde de Pool. 'Het mooiste beroep dat er bestaat.' Hij stond op. Hij meende het. Anders dan vroeger, als kind had hij het geïdealiseerd, nu wist hij wat het werkelijk inhield. Minder spannend dan gedacht, wel prachtig.

Hij reed naar het dorp waar de Beckers woonden, vandaar kon je goed wandelen. Beckers had de stad te druk gevonden, te gevaarlijk voor zijn kinderen. De Pool had het adres opgezocht op Google Street View en reed langs het huis van de Beckers. Hij bekeek het huis grondig. Het zag er goed onderhouden uit. Er stond een grote boom voor die veel licht wegnam. Verder was het een dorp zoals veel dorpen, met een kerk, een café, een hoofdstraatje, tevens doorgangsstraat, en daaromheen de heuvels waar hij graag fietste en wandelde.

Aan de rand van het dorp parkeerde hij zijn auto, hij keek op zijn telefoon. Geen nieuwe berichten van zijn jongen en ook niet van Wen. Het was namiddag, in de late herfst, geen al te beste tijd voor een wandeling door de heuvels. Het begon te hagelen, toch had de Pool behoefte om te gaan lopen, om de bomen te zien, om een stam aan te raken, geen mensen tegen te komen. Niet dat hij iets tegen mensen had, hij wilde ze immers redden, maar soms wilde hij ook vergeten dat ze er waren.

Vandaag lukte het vergeten niet, deze middag was hij ingehaald door het verleden. Hij zou een flinke wandeling maken tot vlak bij de Belgische grens om zijn voorsprong op het verleden weer te vergroten, om de herinneringen van zich af te schudden. Borys en Jurek. Er waren twee jongens geweest.

# II

## *Hij weigerde het beest Manja te noemen*

# 1

Er was een oudste geweest, een eerstgeborene die ze Borys hadden genoemd. Een stille jongen, lang en dun, een bonenstaak. Hij zou waarschijnlijk net zo groot worden als zijn vader, misschien wel groter, maar hij was vooral stil. Doodstil. De juf van groep acht had gezegd: 'Soms vergeet je dat Borys er is, hoewel hij boven iedereen uitsteekt, alleen niet met zijn cijfers.'

Borys was twaalf en hij zat altijd achterin, het liefst onderuitgezakt. Zo was hij nu eenmaal. Van reizen hield hij niet, op vakantie vroeg hij: 'Wanneer gaan we weer naar huis?' en ook niet van vriendjes, als er eens een jongetje uit de buurt aanbelde of Borys buiten wilde komen spelen zei hij: 'Zeg maar dat ik er niet ben.' Het liefst was hij thuis in z'n eentje of met zijn jongere broer, die hij zijn babybroertje noemde. Omdat Wen vond dat een leven zonder vrienden niet goed was drong ze aan dat hij iets deed om vrienden te maken. Lief zijn voor je babybroertje was prima, beter dan je broertje mee willen geven aan de vuilnisman, een verlangen dat zij goed kende uit haar eigen jeugd. Maar er was meer op deze wereld, vooral als je een kind was. Hij moest het huis uit, want zo maakte je vrienden, door naar buiten te gaan, de wereld in te trekken.

Soms vreesde de Pool dat zijn oudste jongen dat niet wilde, nu niet en nooit niet, maar die vrees sprak hij niet uit, hij was bang dat het zijn vrouw zou ontrieven. Al waren haar opvattingen over opvoeding ruimhartig – 'kinderen weten zelf heel goed wat rechtvaardigheid is,' zei ze, 'zelfs peuters weten dat' – toch hield ze niet van tegenspraak. Zij wist hoe hun jongens in elkaar zaten.

Op basketbal wilde Borys niet, hoewel dat gezien zijn

lengte voor de hand lag. Ze hadden het hem een paar keer voorgesteld maar hij zag er niets in. 'Andere jongens smeken hun ouders of ze op basketbal mogen,' zei de Pool. 'Laat ze lekker smeken,' antwoordde Borys. Hij wilde op geen enkele sport en dat terwijl hij atletische talenten had. Hij was een paar maanden lid geweest van een atletiekclub waar hij zich verdienstelijk had gemaakt in polsstokhoogspringen en hordelopen, de trainer had beweerd dat hij het ver had kunnen schoppen, maar uiteindelijk wees Borys het polsstokhoogspringen en het hordelopen ook af. Hij wilde er niet meer heen. 'Ik ben echt het liefste thuis,' had hij tegen zijn ouders gezegd. 'Ik ga al naar school, waarom moet ik nog ergens anders naartoe?'

Wen zei: 'Dat is niet normaal en niet gezond.' Zij kon het weten, ze was kleuterjuf, ze had een half dozijn abnormale en ongezonde kinderen voorbij zien komen. De Pool hechtte aan gezondheid en normaliteit. Hij vroeg zich af hoe zijn oudste jongen zonder die twee zaken iets kon bereiken op deze wereld.

Er kleefde nog een ander ongemak aan de stille jongen. Ongemak, het was een woord dat bij zijn jongen paste en ook bij de Pool. Soms was Borys niet op tijd voor de wc, alsof hij een oude man was of een tweejarig kind dat nog niet helemaal zindelijk is. Het was begonnen zonder dat ze er erg in hadden. En dat terwijl hij vroeg zindelijk was geworden. Hij was een snelle prater geweest, snel met lopen, snel op het potje, met alles was hij snel. Een intelligent kind, hadden de mensen altijd gezegd, al had zijn oma, Wens moeder, een paar keer gezegd dat Borys 'een oude ziel' had. Wens moeder nam reïncarnatie serieus. Later zei de vrouw van het consultatiebureau: 'Hij is wel vroegwijs.' Dat was waar, de jongen zei op zesjarige leeftijd dingen waarvan de Pool niet begreep waar hij het vandaan haalde. Wen zei: 'Dat pikt hij ergens op en dat herhaalt hij, dat doen slimme kinderen. Leren is imiteren. Hij weet zelf niet wat het betekent.'

Na de paasvakantie had Borys een terugval gekregen. Toen was het begonnen. Hij kwam thuis met poep in zijn broek. Hij had niets gezegd, Wen ontdekte het toen ze zijn vieze broek in een hoek van de badkamer vond. Eerst dachten ze: een ongelukje, kan iedereen gebeuren. Borys schaamde zich, daarom zei hij niets, daarom had hij de vieze broek weggemoffeld. Het was ook gênant.

Maar toen gebeurde het weer en nog een keer. Het gebeurde regelmatig, poep in de broek was geen uitzondering meer. Zoveel ongelukjes kon een mens niet hebben, ook geen twaalfjarige.

Er waren dagen, soms zelfs anderhalve week, dat het niet gebeurde, dat Wen 's ochtends als de Pool terugkwam van de kazerne zachtjes zei: 'Volgens mij hebben we het lek gedicht.'

En twee dagen later was er dan toch weer poep in de broek. Vaak meerdere keren op een dag. Eerst meende Wen dat het alleen op school gebeurde, maar ze kwamen er al snel achter dat Borys er overal last van had, bijvoorbeeld in de supermarkt en tijdens een gezinsuitje. Alleen niet thuis, daar gebeurde het nooit. Wen werd moe van het wassen. Ze moest nieuwe broeken voor de jongen kopen omdat alle broeken in de was zaten.

Ze praatten met hun jongen. 'Als je aandrang voelt moet je meteen naar de wc,' zei Wen. En de Pool zei: 'Je moet niet wachten, ook al is de juf aan het woord, je steekt gewoon je vinger op en je gaat naar de wc.'

'Maar ik voel het niet,' antwoordde de jongen, 'ik voel niets en als ik het wel voel is het te laat.'

Wen ging met Borys naar de huisarts. De ouders vonden dat hij het probleem zelf aan de dokter moest uitleggen, hij poepte weliswaar nog in zijn broek maar hij was geen klein kind meer.

's Avonds vertelde Wen aan haar man hoe het was gegaan, dat hun jongen had gezegd: 'Als ik op de wc ga zitten gebeurt er niets en als ik niet op de wc zit komt het er plotseling uit. Ik kan er niets aan doen.' Ze voegde eraan toe: 'Hij kon het uitstekend uitleggen, hij was niet verlegen.'

De huisarts, een man met een baard en een bril die ze al jaren hadden maar die ze nauwelijks zagen, ze waren zelden ziek – de Janowski's waren kerngezond – had hem diarreeremmers voorgeschreven. Even leek dat te helpen, toen kwam de jongen toch weer thuis met een poepbroek. 'Ik kan er niet meer tegen,' zei Wen, 'ik word er gek van. Moeten we Borys net als zijn broertje weer luiers omdoen?' Ze had tranen in haar ogen gehad en het waren de tranen geweest die de Pool de ernst van de situatie hadden doen inzien.

De juf wilde met de ouders spreken. Ook dat nog. Ze zei dat de andere kinderen niet meer naast Borys wilden zitten, omdat hij stonk. Ze zei dat dit echt een probleem was, het was haar ook opgevallen dat hij regelmatig stonk. Ze had met hem gesproken, hij had ontwijkende antwoorden gegeven op haar vragen, daarom had ze de ouders bij zich geroepen, vanwege de overlast die de stank bezorgde. 'Het gaat soms meer over de geur in de klas dan over spellen,' zei de juf, 'dat is voor niemand goed, ook voor Borys niet. Hij ligt de laatste tijd niet meer lekker in de groep.'

De ouders zaten er verslagen bij, vooral de Pool. Zijn jongen zorgde voor overlast. De brandweer moest een einde maken aan overlast, in zijn eigen gezin kon hij de overlast niet de baas. Dat zijn jongen voor stankoverlast zorgde vatte de Pool persoonlijk op. Alsof hij het zelf was die stonk, alsof zijn jongen alleen de stank van de vader verspreidde.

'Kunt u voortaan niet een raam openzetten als u het ruikt?' had hij gevraagd.

'Dat is geen oplossing,' had de juf geantwoord, 'en hoeveel ramen moeten we openzetten? Moeten we soms met z'n allen buiten gaan zitten omdat Borys niet op tijd naar de wc kan gaan?'

'Het is niet dat hij niet wil,' had Wen gezegd. 'Hij wil het best, het lukt hem alleen niet. We zijn bij de dokter geweest en die zegt dat het een darmprobleem is.'

'Darmprobleem of geen darmprobleem, hoe gaan we dit oplossen?' had de juf gezegd. 'Misschien moeten jullie eens naar een psycholoog. Die poep zit tussen de oren, ik ken niemand op die leeftijd die structureel te laat is voor het toilet.'

Ze sprak het woord 'structureel' langzaam en nadrukkelijk uit.

De juf moest de ontreddering op het gezicht van de Pool hebben gezien, want meteen daarna zei ze: 'Verder is hij de vriendelijke, stille jongen die hij altijd is geweest. Hij haalt voldoendes, al kan hij beter. Laat Borys eens met iemand praten. Misschien zit hij ergens over in?'

Met die woorden werden de ouders naar huis gestuurd.

Ze spraken weer met hun zoon. Ze vroegen wat er was, of hij hun iets moest vertellen. Was er iets wat hem verdrietig maakte? 'Zit je ergens over in?'

Maar hij had zoals gewoonlijk niets te vertellen, hij zat nergens over in en niets maakte hem verdrietig, helemaal niets. Zelfs het poepen in de broek niet, zei hij. En hij voegde eraan toe dat hij alles best vond.

Hij had zich in zijn hoek genesteld met zijn broertje, een nakomertje, eigenlijk een ongelukje, en hij zweeg. Wen vertelde hem dat ze bij de juf waren geweest, om te praten – het woord 'stank' vermeed Wen – en dat de juf had geadviseerd naar een psycholoog te gaan.

De jongen haalde zijn schouders op. 'Een psycholoog is voor gekken,' zei hij. 'Waarom doet iedereen zo moeilijk? Het zit toch in mijn broek?'

'Ze ruiken het,' zei de Pool, die zich niet meer kon inhouden en hij schudde zijn jongen door elkaar, 'ze ruiken het, begrijp je dat niet? Je bent niet gek, maar ze ruiken heel goed wat er in je broek zit want de mensen zijn ook niet gek. Je doet het om ons te pesten. Je doet het omdat je een hekel aan ons hebt.' Steeds wilder rammelde hij de jongen door elkaar, tot Wen de Pool wegtrok, die anders altijd de rust zelve was, en de jongen begon te huilen, want hij werd nooit door elkaar gerammeld. In de keuken zei Wen: 'Het heeft geen zin zo tegen hem tekeer te gaan, dat maakt het alleen erger.'

'Jij kan er toch ook niet meer tegen?' antwoordde de Pool. Hij ademde zwaar, meer van de emotie dan van de inspanning. Hij was niet alleen lang maar ook in goede conditie. Zijn lichaam was een instrument dat hij met zorg onderhield.

'We doen wel wat de juf zegt,' antwoordde ze. 'We nemen hem mee naar een psycholoog. Het is geen darmprobleem, anders zou het ook in het weekend gebeuren.'

Daarna gingen ze weer de woonkamer in. De jongen zat tegen de verwarming met zijn babybroertje naast zich en Wen vertelde hem dat hij zich geen zorgen hoefde te maken, dat ze met iemand gingen praten en dat dan alles in orde kwam.

De jongen knikte, Wen verdween naar de keuken en de Pool vroeg of de jongen een spelletje met hem wilde spelen. De jongen zei: 'Laat me maar even. Het is goed zo.' De Pool wist dat het niet goed was en hij pakte zijn jongen weer beet, zijn grote jongen, die even terugdeinsde, hij ging snel door zijn knieën en hij tilde de grote jongen als een veertje op, alsof er een brand woedde en hij de brandweergreep moest toepassen om Borys het huis uit te slepen en hij zei: 'Het maakt me niet uit dat je stinkt, andere mensen ruiken je stank, maar ik vind dat je lekker ruikt. Geloof me, je papa vindt dat je heerlijk ruikt.'

De Pool wilde niet mee naar de psycholoog, het leek hem meer iets voor moeder en zoon dan voor het hele gezin. De grote vakantie kwam eraan, daarna ging de jongen naar de brugklas en dan werd misschien alles anders, op de nieuwe school zou het beter gaan.

Een paar weken later vertelde Wen tijdens het avondeten hoe de afspraak met de psycholoog was verlopen. Het broertje zat te brabbelen in zijn stoel, af en toe kwam er iets verstaanbaars uit (auto, hap, poesje, aai), echt praten kon je het nog niet noemen. De rest van het gezin kauwde onverstoorbaar op het eten – de stilte bracht het gezin nader tot elkaar, had de vader van de Pool beweerd en de Pool zelf vond dat hij daar gelijk in had. Borys ontfermde zich gretig over het laatste stukje van de worst die Wen bij de biologische slager had gekocht, want ze was tegen plofkippen en varkensstallen waar de varkens amper konden ademen en het daglicht nooit zagen. Ook varkens hadden recht op daglicht voor ze werden verwerkt tot worst. Zo was Wen, een goede vrouw, goed voor iedereen, voor kleuters en varkens.

'Vertel,' zei de Pool toen zijn mond leeg was.

Ze zei dat de psycholoog best aardig was geweest en aan hun jongen had gevraagd of hij veel stress had. En hoe het op school ging en thuis, hoe het daar ging, of hij vriendjes had en hobby's.

'En wat heb je geantwoord?' vroeg de Pool. Hij voegde er zachtjes aan toe: 'Mogen de mensen geen geheimen meer hebben? Moeten ze alles van ons weten?'

De jongen spoelde zijn mond met een slok water en daarna zei hij: 'Dat ik niet goed wist waar hij het over had.'

'Heb je stress?' vroeg de Pool. De jongen schudde zijn hoofd. 'Ik heb geen stress,' zei hij en Wen vertelde dat de psycholoog had gezegd dat het misschien verstandig was als de jongen op vaste tijden op de wc ging zitten, bijvoorbeeld na het avondeten of 's ochtends voor hij naar school ging, ook als er geen aandrang was. En of de jongen aan yoga wilde doen. Maar de jongen had resoluut gezegd dat hij niet aan yoga wilde doen, nu niet en later ook niet.

'Hebben jullie stress?' vroeg de jongen. Zijn bord was nu leeg. 'Krijgen jullie stress van mij?'

'Wij hebben geen stress,' zei de Pool. 'Wij zijn een normaal gezin. Stress heb ik weleens als ik een brandend huis in moet, maar daar denk je niet over na, je bent getraind om alles te doen zonder erover na te denken, daarom heb je eigenlijk geen stress. Daar is geen tijd voor. Want we komen met z'n zessen aan en we willen met z'n zessen ook weer terug naar de kazerne. Eigen veiligheid eerst.'

Niemand reageerde op wat de Pool zei. Misschien was zijn gezin van mening dat hij zijn brandweerverhalen op de kazerne moest laten.

Wen nam een slok water, ook zij spoelde haar mond om de etensresten uit alle hoeken en gaten te verwijderen. De hulpverlener had het consult beëindigd met de vraag of het hele gezin niet eens langs moest komen.

Wen had geantwoord dat ze dat met haar man moest bespreken. Ze nam de jongste op haar schoot, ze veegde met zijn slabbetje zijn gezicht schoon. De Pool zei: 'Misschien kun je beloven het gewoon niet meer in je broek te doen? En weet je wat, als je het twee weken hebt volgehouden, dan krijg je een cadeau van ons. Wat zou je willen hebben? Wat wil je van ons hebben als je twee weken niet in je broek hebt gepoept?'

Andere jongens speelden nog met Lego Technic, ze voetbalden of ze speelden spelletjes op de computer, hun jongen deed dat allemaal niet, heel af en toe gamede hij, maar zelfs dat leek eerder een verplicht nummer. Er zat weinig passie in hun jongen, hij bekeek de wereld met een licht verveelde blik alsof hij alles al had gezien en niets hem echt beviel en dat verontrustte de ouders. Hoe kon je zo jong al zo verveeld zijn?

'Geef maar geld,' zei de jongen. 'Als ik het twee weken volhoud moet je me maar wat geld geven.'

De Pool dacht even na en antwoordde toen: 'Als je het twee weken volhoudt dan krijg je tien euro van me. Vind je dat redelijk?'

'Maak er twintig van,' zei de jongen en in de keuken vertelde Wen zachtjes dat dit waanzin was. Wat moest de jongen denken? Dat hij geld kon verdienen door niet in zijn broek te poepen?

Een paar dagen ging het goed en de Pool zei trots tegen zijn vrouw: 'Zie je wel?' Op de kazerne had hij er nog steeds niet over gesproken, hij sprak sowieso weinig over thuis, alleen onder de douche tegenover Beckers had hij het zich veroorloofd tijdens het inzepen een opmerking te maken dat zijn oudste jongen darmproblemen had. Beckers zei dat kinderen altijd wat hadden, darmproblemen, verkoudheden, pukkels, ingegroeide teennagels. Zijn middelste dochter was een tijd doodsbang geweest voor vreemde wc's. 'En voor mannen met een baard,' voegde hij eraan toe. Het was vanzelf overgegaan.

Borys hoefde niet te worden uitbetaald want voordat er twee weken waren verstreken zat er toch weer wat in de broek en toen concludeerde Wen dat het geen stress was, maar gewoon gebrek aan vrienden. Borys zei wel dat hij geen vrienden nodig had en dat hij het liefst met zijn broertje speelde, maar misschien was dat stoerdoenerij en poepte hij in zijn broek omdat hij het niet meer uithield. Omdat hij vrienden miste, omdat hij contact miste. De poep was een noodkreet.

'Nee,' zei de Pool, 'dat denk ik niet. Poep is geen noodkreet.'

## 2

Het naar school gaan werd een drama, die laatste weken voor de vakantie. Borys verstopte zich, weigerde te fietsen, zei dat hij wel ging lopen en deed dit dan niet. Dan moest de Pool achter hem aan, terwijl de jongen zich aan lantaarnpalen vastklemde omdat hij niet naar school wilde. Ook aan bomen klemde hij zich vast. De Pool rukte hem los, want niet naar school gaan kon natuurlijk niet, dan kreeg je de kinderbescherming of de leerplichtambtenaar achter je aan. En de vader van de Pool had altijd gezegd: 'Gedraag je keurig en onopvallend, zodat de mensen hier niet slecht over de Polen zullen denken.' En als de Pool Borys dan had losgerukt dreef hij hem voort, zoals de herdershond een onwillig schaap voortdrijft. Voor de bestwil van de jongen. Ja, zo was het, Borys was het schaap en de vader de herdershond.

Er moest iets gebeuren, dus drongen ze nog meer aan. Was er misschien toch iets wat Borys wilde? Iets wat hij wel leuk vond? Behalve thuis met zijn broertje spelen? Ze noemden van alles op, van goochelen tot de padvinderij, van een cursus programmeren tot de muziekschool. 'Ieder mens heeft een hobby,' zei de Pool. 'Neem jij er nou alsjeblieft ook een.'

'Wat is jouw hobby dan?' vroeg de jongen.

Feitelijk was de Pool een man zonder hobby's, al kon je natuurlijk zeggen dat hij van zijn hobby zijn werk had gemaakt. De brandweerkazerne was zijn hobby.

Na een korte stilte antwoordde de Pool dan toch: 'De tuin, tuinieren is mijn hobby.'

Er ging een week voorbij en toen zei Borys op een ochtend: 'Geef me een pony. Ik wil wel een pony.'

Wen en de Pool waren verrast. Niet eerder had hun oudste jongen belangstelling laten blijken voor dieren in het algemeen of voor pony's in het bijzonder. Voor honden was hij zelfs een beetje bang en dat terwijl hij verder niet angstig was aangelegd. Hij was zo stil, je wist niet wat er in hem omging, misschien was hij al jaren aan het broeden op een pony zonder dat hij iemand daarover iets had verteld.

De ouders begrepen niet zo goed wat hun boomlange jongen met een pony moest. Ondanks zijn lengte paste hij nog prima op een pony, ook die dieren kwamen tenslotte in verschillende formaten voor, maar toch, een pony, waar kwam dat vandaan? Het stemde Wen argwanend. 'Zijn er andere jongens in jouw klas die een pony hebben?' vroeg ze. 'Alleen meisjes,' antwoordde Borys. En daar liet hij het bij en Wen vroeg niet verder.

Eerst sputterde Wen tegen, ze vond een pony overdreven. 'Voor hetzelfde geld is hij er na één week op uitgekeken,' zei ze, 'gewoon eerst eentje huren,' maar uiteindelijk was ze toch gevoelig gebleken voor de argumenten van haar man. 'Als het beest echt van hem is,' zei de Pool, 'dan ontwikkelt hij na verloop van tijd misschien ook een andere relatie tot mensen, echte relaties.' En daar voegde hij licht wanhopig aan toe: 'Als onze jongen een pony wil, dan kopen we die voor hem. Verder wil hij namelijk niets. Helemaal niets.'

Zo was de Pool. Als dat de oplossing was, dan moest er gehandeld worden. Hij was zo blij dat Borys eindelijk iets wilde dat hij fanatiek naar een pony begon te zoeken. En hij vond een pony op een boerderij bij hen in de buurt, op het internet vond je alles.

'Ik heb een geschikt dier voor je gevonden,' zei de Pool en hij stompte zijn zoon vaderlijk tegen de schouder. 'Mooi,' zei Borys.

De Pool wilde van de koop een uitje maken. Het was

iets wat hen zou binden, zo stelde hij zich dat voor, dat als Borys oud was hij zich nog ontroerd zou herinneren hoe hij op een dag samen met zijn vader een pony had aangeschaft. Misschien zou hij zijn kinderen later vertellen over de dag dat hij met opa een pony had gekocht.

Op een zaterdagmiddag reden ze erheen. Een oude man zat voor het raam, verder was er niemand te bekennen, alleen een kat liep over het erf. De boerderij maakte een vervallen en wat naargeestige indruk maar vermoedelijk maakten alle boerderijen die indruk. De Pool wilde in elk geval de moed erin houden, het was een belangrijke dag, al hingen de wolken laag en had het de hele ochtend geregend. Hij zei tegen zijn oudste jongen: 'Ergens moet hier jouw pony zijn.' En hij streelde de jongen over zijn hoofd, sloeg hem zachtjes op zijn rug, zoals vaders dat met hun jongens doen. Op dat moment klopte de boer tegen het raam en hij wenkte dat ze binnen moesten komen. Een kromme vinger wenkte, een hand zwaaide.

Er hing een geblokt gordijn voor het deurraam van de boerderij. Via een keuken waar afwas van een paar dagen stond kwamen ze in een woonkamer. De boer zat in een rolstoel voor het raam. De woonkamer stond vol met meubels die van voor de Tweede Wereldoorlog leken te komen. Het hout van een ladekast zag er half vermolmd uit. Op tafel stonden borden met etensresten. Een suikerpot. Brood op een servet. Het rook er naar een mengeling van open haard, mest en oud eten.

De hand van de boer waarmee hij had gewenkt rustte nu in zijn schoot. Een hand die vaak in de grond had gezeten, of in dieren. Wellicht had de boer geholpen met bevallingen.

Borys moet hebben gevoeld dat hij een andere wereld binnenstapte, een andere wereld in een andere tijd, want hij pakte zijn vader bij de hand, wat hij anders zelden deed. De vader zelf wilde het ontspannen houden, opdat zijn jongen nog jaren later met plezier aan deze zaterdagmiddag zou denken. Het was vooral dat, vreesde de Pool, wat ontbrak in het leven van zijn jongen, plezier. Toen hij dat eens tegen Wen had gezegd antwoordde ze: 'En jij dan, geef jij het goede voorbeeld? Straal jij plezier uit?'

Juist vandaag wilde de Pool plezier uitstralen, het moest een fijne namiddag worden, vooral voor zijn oudste jongen, die eindelijk iets wilde. De Pool zei: 'We komen voor de pony, ik heb gebeld, dit is mijn jongen, Borys. Het is voor hem.'

Hij had de gewoonte ontwikkeld te benadrukken dat de jongen en hij bij elkaar hoorden, omdat de jongen soms kon doen alsof zijn vader een volstrekte vreemde was, zelfs op zijn eigen verjaardagfeestje. Eerst weigerde de jongen vriendjes uit te nodigen, hij wilde zijn verjaardag niet vieren. Hij zag ertegen op als tegen een executie en als er dan met moeite een lijst van tien klasgenootjes was opgesteld die uiteindelijk door de jongen werd teruggebracht tot vijf of zes kinderen, zat hij erbij alsof hij er niet bij hoorde, alsof zijn ouders niet zijn ouders waren, zijn klasgenoten niet zijn klasgenoten en zijn verjaardag niet zijn verjaardag was. En een keer toen ze op vakantie waren in Zeeland, ze zaten in een restaurant en ze hadden ruzie gehad, zei de jongen verbeten tegen de ober: 'Ik ken deze mensen niet.'

Daarop had de Pool hem een draai om zijn oren gegeven, waar de ober bij stond en de Pool had gezegd, luid en duidelijk: 'Wij zijn je ouders, Borys.' De ober had onthutst gekeken, maar hij liet het erbij, bracht de bestelling en hield zich de rest van de avond op de vlakte.

Het was om die reden dat de Pool nadrukkelijk over 'mijn jongen' of 'onze jongen' sprak, dat de mensen wisten hoe de vork in de steel zat als ze eraan twijfelden. Maar nu hield de jongen de hand van zijn vader vast en was er voor de Pool geen reden te onderstrepen dat deze jongen bij hem hoorde en hij bij de jongen. Het was duidelijk dat zij onlosmakelijk met elkaar waren verbonden. Toch deed hij het gewoontegetrouw. Onze jongen. Mijn jongen.

De boer in de rolstoel had een stoppelbaard, op zijn handen zaten bulten, hij zei: 'Duw me even naar de stal, de knecht is bezig.'

De Pool pakte de rolstoel vast en duwde hem door de woonkamer, langs het eten, hij kon niet goed zien wat het was, pap leek het wel, misschien was het soep, langs de keuken en vervolgens over een drassig pad. De boer liet met zijn hand zien hoe ze moesten lopen, hij zei niets, hij gebaarde alleen. Af en toe tilde hij zijn rechterhand met de bulten op en wees in de richting van de stal. Er waren meerdere stallen.

Achter hen sjokte de jongen in het trainingspak dat hij bij voorkeur droeg, met de capuchon, hij hield van capuchons. Wen zei: 'Hij verstopt zich in zijn capuchon.' De Pool zei: 'Zijn capuchon is zijn schild.'

Telkens bleef de rolstoel in de modder steken. Dit was geen pad voor invaliden. Het liefst had de Pool de boer uit zijn rolstoel getild en over zijn schouder naar de stal gedragen, maar dat was onbeleefd. Hij was hier niet als brandweerman gekomen, hij was hier om een pony te kopen en dan tilde je de verkoper niet zomaar uit zijn rolstoel, al was dat vermoedelijk het beste geweest. Af en toe draaide de Pool zich om en dan zag hij Borys stappen over het natte pad. Het leek alsof de jongen niet goed wist waar hij heen ging, alsof hij zich niet meer kon herinneren dat hij niets wilde behalve een pony.

Eindelijk waren ze in de stal. Er was plaats voor zeker twaalf paarden of andere dieren, misschien wel meer, maar er stond nog maar één pony. 'Ik heb ze allemaal weggedaan,' zei de boer, 'in een rolstoel kun je niet voor de beesten zorgen. Ik heb alleen nog wat schapen en koeien, daar zorgt de knecht voor. De kinderen willen het niet overnemen. Boer zijn is niets voor de kinderen. Ze vinden het vies.'

De boer pakte de hand van de Pool zoals de jongen dat eerder had gedaan, hij kneep erin alsof hij zich wilde optrekken en hij zei: 'Niemand heeft meer respect voor de boeren. En jij ook niet. Dat zie ik aan je.'

Zoveel bitterheid zat er in de oude man, zoveel woede op de wereld, die met alles wat er misging toch eigenlijk een prima wereld was, en zoveel kracht zat er nog in de hand waarmee hij de Pool had vastgegrepen. De Pool wilde niet over boeren praten en ook niet over respect, hij wilde een pony kopen en hij zei tegen zijn jongen: 'Daar is je pony.'

De pony was wit of grijs, dat was in dit licht niet goed te zien, er zaten vlekken op het dier en hij wist ook niet of die vlekken van de modder kwamen of dat die bij het dier hoorden, dat deed er ook niet toe. Hij zou het dier voor zijn jongen kopen, daarna gingen ze naar huis. Misschien samen nog ergens iets drinken en proberen tegen beter weten in een gesprek te voeren.

'Iedereen eet vlees, maar de boeren die voor dat vlees hebben gezorgd, die het met moeite vet hebben gemest, die zijn vies, dat zijn schoften,' zei de boer en de Pool was bang dat de stille jongen in de war zou raken van de woorden van de oude boer. De Pool gaf de jongen een zetje en toen liep Borys naar de pony.

De boer zei: 'Ze heet Manja. Ze kan behoorlijk gemeen zijn. Een vals kreng is het. Ze heeft al haar broers en zussen overleefd. Zo zijn de valse krengen, die worden het oudst.'

'Nou, dat zal toch wel meevallen,' zei de Pool hard, zodat zijn jongen het zou horen, 'pony's zijn lieve beesten.'

'Jullie weten niets van dieren,' zei de boer en hij hees zich op aan de hand van de Pool om beter te gaan zitten. Daarna liet hij die hand eindelijk los. 'Jullie uit de stad weten er niets van. Alles is zielig tegenwoordig, behalve de boer zelf.'

'We wonen hier vlakbij,' zei de Pool.

Hij zag hoe zijn jongen zijn hand door de tralies van het hek stak.

'Vlakbij begint de stad,' zei de boer. 'Jij praat niet alsof je hiervandaan komt.'

'Mijn vader is een Pool,' zei de Pool, 'en mijn moeder kwam uit Duitsland. Ik ben opgegroeid in Heerlen, heb een tijd in de Peel gewoond, daarna in de Randstad tot ik weer in Heerlen belandde.'

'O, je bent dus een buitenlander,' zei de boer.

Het leek alsof de pony zijn jongen negeerde. De Pool wist niets van dieren, hij kon zich niet voorstellen dat dit een gemene pony was, dat er echt gemene pony's op de wereld te vinden waren, anders stonden de kinderboerderijen toch niet vol met pony's?

'Hoeveel wilt u ervoor hebben?' vroeg de Pool zachtjes.

'Achthonderd,' zei de boer. 'Ze gaat nog jaren mee. Kerngezond en ijzersterk. Vals, maar daar wen je wel aan.'

Dat vond de Pool wat veel. 'Vierhonderd,' zei hij.

'Zevenhonderd,' zei de boer.

'Vijfhonderd,' zei de Pool. 'Ik ben brandweerman,' voegde hij eraan toe, 'ik ben niet rijk.'

'Rijker dan ik,' zei de boer. 'Ik wed dat elke brandweerman rijker is dan ik. Zeshonderdvijftig omdat het voor die jongen is. Aan jou heeft hij niets. Dat zie je zo.'

Misschien was de boer zélf een gemenerik, maar gemeen of niet, de Pool wilde geen ruzie, hij wilde uitsluitend de pony.

'Ik bied zeshonderd,' fluisterde de Pool. Hij liet de belediging passeren. Doen alsof je niets gehoord hebt. Je kon je werk als brandweerman, misschien wel elk werk het beste doen als je regelmatig deed alsof je niets gehoord had. En de boer zei dat zeshonderd goed was mits er meteen en contant werd afgerekend. Hij moest het paspoort van de pony even zoeken, de knecht had het ergens neergelegd, ze zouden het wel vinden, er moest alleen contant worden afgerekend. Dat was belangrijk.

De pony had de jongen eindelijk gezien, ze leken contact te maken, mens en dier, pony en jongen. Uit zijn portemonnee haalde de Pool vier briefjes van honderd en twee van vijftig en vijf van twintig. Hij telde het geld twee keer na, het was een smak geld, maar dat beest zou Borys helpen en hij gaf het geld aan de boer. Het was meer dan waarop hij had gerekend, een collega had hem verteld dat drie- of vierhonderd al veel was voor een pony op leeftijd, maar als ze zonder pony naar huis gingen zou Borys teleurgesteld zijn.

'Manja was van mijn kleindochter, die heeft er geen interesse meer in. Geen interesse en geen tijd. Rij me terug. Dan zoek ik het paspoort.'

De Pool greep de rolstoel vast en ze reden terug over het modderige pad, door de keuken met de stapels afwas en de woonkamer waar de etensresten nog op tafel stonden.

'Zet me maar hier,' zei de boer. Hij nam meteen een hap van de pap die misschien geen pap was. Toen reed hij zelf, voortvarender dan de Pool had gedacht, naar een bureautje vol met rotzooi dat ook al aardig vermolmd was en na een paar minuten had de boer het paspoort van de pony in handen. Hij legde het met een klap op tafel.

'Zo,' zei hij, 'nu is het dier van jou. Neem je haar vandaag nog mee?'

De jongen stond in de deuropening tussen woonkamer en keuken. Verlegener dan hij normaal was.

De Pool opende het paspoort. Ze heette inderdaad Manja.

'Ik vroeg me eigenlijk af of ze hier kon blijven. Tot ik iets gevonden heb.' Hij stak het paspoort in zijn zak.

De boer keek hem aan, peinzend en op een eigenaardige manier ook sluw, alsof hij hier allang op had gerekend.

Stedelingen die een pony kochten zonder te weten wat ze daarmee moesten, de boer leek het soort te kennen.

'Honderd voor de stal, honderdvijftig voor het voer. Per maand. Ze vreet je arm, dat valse kreng. Het is een koopje.'

'Die stal staat leeg,' zei de Pool na een lange stilte. Hij voelde dat hij op de proef werd gesteld, niet alleen door de boer, ook door zijn jongen. Het kon nog steeds misgaan en hij vreesde dat de jongen zich zonder pony meer en meer zou terugtrekken, nog stiller zou worden, tot er alleen stilte van hem overbleef. 'Het is een beetje vreemd dat ik huur moet betalen voor iets wat toch leeg staat. Ik betaal graag voor het eten van het dier, maar ik ben... Het is niet dat ik...'

De boer zat weer aan tafel. Hij had zich daar behendig heen gemanoeuvreerd en hij nam een paar happen. Toen zei hij: 'Als jullie een dier nodig hebben weten jullie ons te vinden. Maar het moet wel allemaal gratis, niet? Wij en onze beesten mogen niets kosten. Vijfenzeventig voor de huur, honderdvijfentwintig voor het vreten van dat kreng. Als dat je niet bevalt kun je haar nu meteen meenemen.'

De boer sprak over de pony alsof ze een ex van hem was die hij niet kon uitstaan. Zou de boer überhaupt nog een vrouw hebben?

'Je kunt nu betalen voor de rest van de maand,' zei de boer, 'dan hebben we dat gehad. En dan altijd op de eerste. Komt de jongen af en toe naar het dier kijken, of zien we hem verder nooit meer, net als mijn kleindochter?'

'De jongen zal hier een keer per week naartoe gaan, toch, Borys? Misschien vaker.'

Borys knikte.

'Hij kan vanaf ons huis hierheen fietsen.' De Pool keek naar zijn jongen, die weer knikte.

'Wat gaat hij eigenlijk met de pony doen?' vroeg de boer. 'Erop rijden?'

Er viel een stilte.

'Wat ga je ermee doen?' vroeg de Pool voor de zekerheid.

'Ik ga haar verzorgen,' zei Borys.

De boer haalde zijn schouders op. 'Hij doet maar,' zei hij. 'Je begint als serieuze boer en je eindigt als kinderboerderij.'

Een man met een zwart petje kwam binnen. Hij was nog langer dan de Pool, lang en mager was hij en zijn mond stond een beetje scheef.

'Dat is de knecht,' zei de boer.

De knecht knikte. Hij wilde de borden pakken maar de boer zei: 'Laat staan. Ik ben aan het eten.'

Daarop verdween de knecht weer, de Pool hoorde hem in de keuken scharrelen en van boven klonk het geluid van krakende planken. Misschien zat er toch een vrouw aan de boer vast. Iemand die de trap niet meer af kon. De Pool kende dat soort gevallen. Als het ernstig werd moest de brandweer eraan te pas komen.

'Morgen of overmorgen komt de jongen terug, dan heeft hij het geld bij zich,' zei de Pool.

'Goed,' zei de boer. 'Laat hem tegen het raam tikken.' Hij nam nog een paar happen en de Pool zag nu dat het champignonsoep was wat de boer zat te eten, koude champignonsoep. Hij kon de champignons nu zelfs een beetje ruiken.

Ze gaven de boer een hand. Eerst de Pool en toen zijn jongen, hij had de jongen naar voren moeten duwen.

In de auto zweeg de jongen zoals altijd, maar toen de Pool vroeg: 'Ben je blij met de pony?' zei de jongen: 'Ja, heel blij.'

Ze stopten bij een McDonald's waar ze frietjes en cola bestelden. De Pool vroeg of de jongen nog iets anders wilde, maar hij zei: 'Nee, mama wacht op ons met het eten.' Hij was ondanks zijn zwijgzaamheid een lieve en behulpzame jongen.

Ze dronken hun cola en ze aten hun frietjes en terwijl de Pool pogingen deed het gesprek gaande te houden, gingen zijn gedachten steeds weer naar de boer in zijn rolstoel.

'Het is niet te ver fietsen, toch?' vroeg de Pool.

'Nee,' zei zijn jongen.

'Waarom wilde je eigenlijk een pony?'

'Gewoon. Leek me leuk.'

De Pool stopte een laatste frietje in zijn mond. 'Wil je net als ik later bij de brandweer?' vroeg hij, want hij voelde dat dit een bijzonder moment was, dichter bij zijn jongen was hij lange tijd niet geweest.

'Nee,' zei Borys.

'Weet je wat je dan wilt?'

'Nee,' zei Borys. 'Nog niet.'

'Maar je gaat wel af en toe naar die pony hè?' vroeg de Pool. 'Laat dat dier daar niet alleen staan.'

'Nee,' zei Borys, 'dat doe ik niet.'

Ze stapten in de auto en in de auto overhandigde de Pool het paspoort van de pony aan zijn oudste zoon. 'Dit is voor jou,' zei hij, 'het is jouw beest, jij moet het paspoort bewaren.' Daarop reden ze naar huis en pas toen ze hadden geparkeerd zei de jongen: 'Dank je, papa, dank je dat je die pony voor me hebt gekocht.' Hij keek zijn vader niet aan toen hij dat zei, hij keek recht voor zich uit, alsof de Pool niet in de auto zat maar ervoor stond.

# 3

Zo kreeg Borys een pony die Manja heette en zoals de jongen had beloofd ging hij er eerst twee keer per week heen en later zelfs vier tot vijf keer per week. Op een gegeven moment zat hij er elke dag. Wen was opgelucht, ze zei tegen haar man dat het een uitstekend idee was dat ze de pony voor hun jongen hadden aangeschaft, veel beter dan eerst een pony huren of lenen. Dat het feit dat het dier van Borys was en van niemand anders hem had geholpen naar buiten te gaan. Ze zei dat hij zich echt kon hechten aan die pony. Manja was feitelijk mens en sport ineen. 'Goed dat je dit hebt doorgezet,' zei ze tegen haar man. 'Hij lijkt er met plezier heen te gaan. Ik hoef hem niet aan te moedigen. Hij gaat helemaal uit zichzelf naar de boer. Hij houdt blijkbaar van pony's.'

Dat was waar, aanmoediging was overbodig en het had er ook alle schijn van dat het beter ging met poepen in de broek. Wen hield het bij in haar telefoon. Van gemiddeld zes keer per week kwam het nu nog maar een keer per week voor. En de Pool hoefde hem ook nog nauwelijks van lantaarnpalen los te rukken. De jongen ging de laatste weken zonder al te veel tegenzin naar school.

De ouders werden niet meer door de juf op het matje geroepen en de Pool zei: 'We hebben het lek gedicht.'

'Laten we afwachten,' antwoordde Wen. 'Niet te vroeg juichen.' Altijd de angst om te vroeg te juichen. Als je veel van kinderen wist dan wist je dat je nooit te vroeg moest juichen.

'Die juffrouw van hem heeft meer over de stank van Borys gepraat dan over Borys zelf,' zei de Pool.

Wen haalde haar schouders op. Als kleuterjuffrouw was

ze solidair met de juf. 'Ze heeft zoveel kinderen in de klas,' zei ze, 'ze kan niet van elk kind wakker liggen. Borys moet leren voor zichzelf op te komen. En dat lukt hem ook wel. Hij heeft jouw karakter, hij zegt niet veel, hij kan een beetje nors zijn, maar hij zet wel door.'

De basisschool werd afgesloten met een musical over een bootreis. Borys was een van de zeven matrozen. Na afloop zei Wen dat ze trots op hem was en de Pool zei dat hij een goede matroos was geweest en dat die matrozenpet hem prachtig stond. Borys glunderde. De Pool had zich die avond ongemakkelijk gevoeld, tussen de andere ouders in het publiek, alsof hij daar niet hoorde. Hij vreesde dat ze zagen dat hij niet echt een vader was, dat ze zagen dat hij een bedrieger was. Iemand die voor vader speelde zonder dat te zijn, iemand die alles speelde zonder iets echt te zijn, behalve brandweerman misschien, dat was hij van top tot teen.

De zomervakantie brak aan. Op tien dagen Kreta na zat Borys vrijwel de hele zomer bij de pony. Ook toen de brugklas begon bleef Manja zijn dierbaarste kameraad. Zijn cijfers waren behoorlijk, voor biologie zelfs uitstekend. Op vragen van zijn ouders hoe het op school ging antwoordde hij dat er veel werd gerookt en dat sommige meisjes zich al opmaakten. Over een meisje werd gezegd, zei hij, dat ze in de poederdoos was geboren. Meer liet hij niet los.

Soms doorbrak de Pool de stiltes tijdens het avondeten door te vragen hoe het met de pony ging, want hij weigerde het beest Manja te noemen. Hij zou allang vergeten zijn hoe ze heette als zijn jongen niet af en toe aan het dier refereerde als Manja. 'En hoe is het met de boer?' vroeg de Pool. Want dat wilde hij ook weten. Als hij eerlijk was interesseerde die boer hem meer dan de pony.

'Die zie ik nooit,' zei Borys.

'Nooit? Die zie je nooit?'

'Nee,' zei de jongen, 'alleen als ik hem geld moet geven. De knecht zie ik weleens.'

De Pool luisterde naar het getik van hun bestek, Wen voerde het jochie een prakje, het zei: 'Ape, ape, ape.' Zijn lievelingsknuffel was een aap en de naam van die knuffel werd telkens herhaald, vooral tijdens het eten, als een gebed, tot de Pool er gek van werd. Borys had nooit zoveel gesproken, hij had ook nooit echt een lievelingsknuffel gehad.

Een dag later, toen het goot van de regen en hun oudste jongen om zes uur nog niet thuis was van de boerderij, besloot de Pool Borys op te halen. In zulk weer kon je de jongen niet laten fietsen, bovendien wilde de Pool weleens met eigen ogen zien hoe het met het beest ging waarvoor hij volgens sommige van zijn collega's te veel had betaald. Onderhandelen lag hem niet. De boer was zijn meerdere geweest. Iets in de blik van de man had de Pool een onbehaaglijk gevoel gegeven, hij had zich ontmaskerd gevoeld. Ook daar werd hij ontmaskerd. Of was het de rolstoel geweest? Hij had van alles verwacht bij een boer maar geen rolstoel.

Onder de douche op de kazerne had hij het een keer over de pony gehad. Er werden grapjes over gemaakt, er werd gelachen. De mannen wisten elkaars kwetsbaarheden feilloos te vinden. Zo waren ze. De C-ploeg vergat veel, maar nooit de zwakke plekken van de ander, dat noemden ze plagen. Een geintje.

Tijdens het douchen maakten ze niet alleen geintjes. Ze spraken ook over dingen die ze tijdens de dienst hadden meegemaakt, een kind met zoveel brandwonden dat het twijfelachtig was of het het zou halen. Ze zeiden tegen elkaar dat ze eigenlijk wilden weten hoe het verderging met het kind. Ze trokken mensen uit brandende huizen, hoe het afliep met die mensen hoorden ze niet. Meestal was dat goed, soms waren ze nieuwsgierig. Dat vertelden ze elkaar als ze samen douchten na het sporten. Je moest wel in conditie blijven als je mensen uit brandende huizen wilde sleuren. Je kon dit werk ook niet tot je vijf- of zevenenzestigste doen en het was vermoedelijk daarom dat veel brandweermannen er nog een beroep bij hadden, omdat ze wisten dat het brandweerleven snel voorbij kon zijn. Een collega van de Pool importeerde bijvoorbeeld wijn, veel brandweermannen waren ernaast klusser. Alleen de Pool had geen ander baantje. Hij was uitsluitend brandweerman, niets anders dan dat. In het verleden had hij zich voor loodgieter of schilder uitgegeven maar het was hem niet bevallen en zijn opdrachtgevers waren ook niet onder de indruk geweest van zijn capaciteiten om wc's te ontstoppen.

Er gingen weleens weken voorbij zonder brandwonden van kinderen waarover ze konden spreken. Eigenlijk was er betrekkelijk weinig brand in het leven van de brandweerman. Waar de burger zijn ellende niet meer aankon daar kwam de brandweerman tevoorschijn en dat had dikwijls niets met brand te maken, van een kat in een boom tot een overstroming, alleen ellende van de ziel, daar had de brandweerman niets mee te schaften.

En er waren dagen dat ze zwijgend het zweet en de viezigheid van hun lichamen wasten en in het schuim van elkaars zeep gingen staan en keken naar elkaars behaarde ruggen, elkaars beginnende kaalheid, elkaars billen, elkaars vetkwabben. Soms knepen ze lachend in elkaars vetkwabben, omdat ze elkaar al zo lang kenden.

De regen was overgegaan in motregen, de Pool zette zijn ruitenwissers op de laagste stand en hij dacht aan die zaterdag dat hij met zijn jongen naar de boer was gereden. Dat was een mooie dag geweest, hij had niet voor vader gespeeld, die dag wás hij vader.

De Pool parkeerde zijn auto op precies dezelfde plek als toen ze de pony gingen kopen. Hij liep rechtstreeks naar de stal, ook al tikte de boer weer tegen het raam.

Het pad was bezaaid met plassen. Onder een zeil lag een dode koe, de poten staken eronderuit. De Pool bleef staan, haalde zijn neus op. Wat zag zijn jongen in deze plek? Wat zocht hij hier?

Voor de stal zag hij de fiets van zijn jongen. Een dure fiets, zo op de grond gesmeten. Zo waren jongens. Goed dat hij hem was komen halen. Borys zou blij zijn dat hij niet op zijn fiets door de regen naar huis hoefde.

De Pool, die hoe ouder hij werd steeds meer zijn best deed om een andere vader te zijn dan die van hem was geweest, ging de stal in. Het viel hem op hoe donker het hier was, hoe onherbergzaam, zelfs voor een dier leek het hem geen pretje op deze plek te wonen, maar vermoedelijk hadden dieren andere opvattingen over onherbergzaamheid dan mensen.

Hij zag zijn jongen nergens. Een hok stond open, daar kon Borys zijn. Langzaam liep hij ernaartoe. Hij voelde een druppel aan zijn neus hangen. Was dit een plek voor een twaalfjarige jongen? Had hij niet beter bij zijn babybroertje kunnen zitten? Wat was daar eigenlijk zo erg aan? Misschien zonder vrienden, maar in elk geval veilig. En een broertje kon ook een vriend zijn.

Toen zag hij zijn jongen. In het donkerste gedeelte van het hok stond hij naast de pony. Het kind was aan het prevelen. Ja, het was nog echt een kind, ondanks zijn lengte. De pony maakte geen geluid. De Pool bleef staan, de jongen had hem niet gezien, niet gehoord, de vader stond bij de ingang van het hok alsof hij niet zeker wist of hij naar binnen of naar buiten moest, hij wist alleen dat hij zijn jongen niet wilde storen.

Hij kon niets verstaan van wat zijn jongen zei, dat deed er ook niet toe. Zijn jongen praatte niet met mensen, zijn jongen praatte met dieren. Met een oude pony waarvoor de Pool te veel geld had betaald, maar als het zijn jongen gelukkig maakte dan was het een goede investering. Alleen nu bekroop de twijfel hem. Ze hadden gewild dat hun jongen vriendjes maakte, maar ze hadden toch echt aan mensen gedacht, niet aan een bejaarde pony.

Hij hoorde iemand de stal binnenkomen, draaide zich

om en zag de knecht. 'De boer wil je spreken,' zei de knecht met zijn uitdrukkingsloze blik, hij hield afstand alsof hij bang was. Hij keek de Pool ook niet aan, hij keek de stal in, langs de Pool.

Nu had ook de jongen zijn vader gezien, hij rukte zich los uit zijn eigen geprevel, liep naar zijn vader en vroeg toen: 'Wat doe je hier?' Hij leek niet blij, eerder boos, onaangenaam verrast.

'Ik kom je halen,' zei de Pool. 'Het giet. Gooi je fiets maar in de achterbak, dan gaan we naar huis.' En toen bedacht hij dat hij als vader, als goede vader, interesse moest tonen in het dier van zijn zoon. Hij vroeg: 'Hoe is het met haar?'

'Ze hinkt,' zei de jongen. 'Ze is gevallen.'

'De boer wil je spreken,' zei de knecht, harder nu, dwingender. 'Kom mee.' De knecht was een man die bevolen werd en bevelen uitdeelde.

'Blijf hier op me wachten,' zei de Pool tegen Borys. 'Of wil je mee? Het is zo vochtig hier. Hoe hou je het uit?'

'Ik blijf hier,' zei de jongen en hij keek naar zijn vader, niet onvriendelijk, eerder onderzoekend.

Achter de knecht liep de Pool over het modderige pad. Langs de dode koe onder het zeil, langs een nog levende kat. 'Moet je het allemaal alleen doen op deze boerderij?' vroeg de Pool onder het lopen. Mannen onder elkaar, dan maakte je een praatje.

De knecht haalde zijn schouders op. 'Altijd gedaan,' mompelde hij en hij hield de keukendeur open. Net als die zaterdag ging de Pool door een vervuilde keuken naar de woonkamer waar de boer in zijn rolstoel bij het raam zat, naar buiten staarde alsof hij televisie aan het kijken was. De knecht was niet mee naar binnen gegaan. Door het raam zag de Pool hoe de knecht over het erf liep. Ook een beetje mank leek het wel.

'U wilde me spreken,' zei de Pool.

De boer draaide zich langzaam om met zijn rolstoel, het manoeuvreren leek hem nu meer moeite te kosten dan de laatste keer. Hij kuchte, er kwam gepiep uit zijn neus. Met zichtbare moeite reed hij naar de tafel, de Pool hielp niet, hij had geleerd dat ongevraagde hulp mensen ook boos kon maken. Met een hand onder zijn kin ondersteunde de boer zijn hoofd, een kop vol groeven had de man, zijn huid leek van klei, en hij monsterde de Pool, zonder gêne, zonder haast. Er bleef maar gepiep uit de neus van de man komen.

Wist de boer nog waarom hij hem had laten komen? Hij keek alsof hij amper meer wist wie de Pool was.

'Jouw kind,' zei hij uiteindelijk, 'heeft het hok open laten staan. Toen is ze naar buiten gegaan en in de beek terechtgekomen. De knecht heeft haar met moeite uit de beek gehaald. Sindsdien is ze kreupel, stokkreupel. Het is jouw beest, het is jouw beslissing maar jij bent geen boer, jij weet niets van dieren. Ik zou haar laten afmaken, zo snel mogelijk. Ik ken een paardenslager hier in de buurt, misschien brengt ze nog iets op. Veel zal het niet zijn. Ik weet wat je zeggen wil, dat is zielig. Maar dat is niet zielig, laten leven is zielig. Voor zo'n beest is leven zielig.'

Eerst had de Pool met de boer over de prijs van de pony moeten onderhandelen, toen over de prijs van haar voedsel, nu moest hij over haar bestaansrecht onderhandelen.

'Ik heb haar net gekocht,' zei de Pool, 'nu moet ik zeker een nieuwe pony kopen? Daar heb ik geen geld voor. Mijn jongen is blij met het beest. Hij is hier elke dag. Hij leeft hier zowat. We zien hem amper. Hij houdt van dat beest.'

Zonder het te willen verhief hij zijn stem. De bekentenis dat hij geen geld had maakte hem emotioneel. Niet het weinige geld zelf maar de bekentenis dat er niet genoeg was. En de jongen die ze amper nog zagen, ook dat was een onaangename bekentenis. Eigenlijk moest je zeggen dat hun jongen in de stal leefde. Het ging beter met hem, dat wel. In de stal, daar was hij opgeknapt.

De boer had zijn ogen gesloten. 'Ik heb geen pony's meer.' Hij opende zijn ogen, knipperde een paar keer, plukte met zijn vrije hand aan zijn wenkbrauwen alsof hij wilde voelen of ze er nog zaten. 'Dit was de laatste. Over een of twee jaar gaat het hier dicht, als ik het zo lang uithoud. Je kind heeft de staldeur open laten staan. Had hij niet moeten doen. Hij is geen kleuter meer. Hij heeft verantwoordelijkheid te nemen.'

De Pool zette zijn handen op tafel. Het kleed dat erop lag deed hem denken aan een vloerkleed. 'Ik laat haar niet afmaken,' zei de Pool. 'Voor mijn jongen is die pony alles. Of ze hinkt of mank loopt doet er niet toe. Dat beest wil leven, zoals wij allemaal willen leven.'

'Jij weet niets van dieren,' zei de boer met hardere stem, zijn kin nog altijd ondersteunend met zijn rechterhand. 'Jij weet niet wat de dieren willen. Jij weet amper wat je zelf wil.'

De Pool haalde zijn neus op. 'Deze pony is van mijn jongen, hij heeft ook nog wat te zeggen.'

'Laat hem iets zeggen,' zei de boer rustig. 'Tegen mij heeft hij tot nu toe niets gezegd. Ik kan je tot niets dwingen. Ik geef je alleen advies.'

Hij manoeuvreerde zich naar het raam en keek weer naar buiten. De knecht liep met een kruiwagen langs. Wilde de boer aangeven dat het gesprek was afgelopen?

'Ik heb liever kou dan warmte,' zei de boer na een tijd op een andere toon. 'De zomers bevallen me niet meer. Droog. Heet. Dan weer drijfnat. Extreme zomers, daar moet ik niets van hebben.' Misschien sprak hij tegen zichzelf.

De Pool bleef staan omdat hij het gevoel had dat hij nog iets moest zeggen. Hij staarde naar de rug van de boer, naar de schouders, en hij kon zich niet losmaken van die aanblik, kon zich er niet toe zetten om naar buiten te gaan, zijn jongen te halen.

‘Mijn vrouw ligt boven,’ zei de boer op dezelfde toon. ‘Ze komt haar bed niet meer uit. Maar ze wil nergens heen. Ze wil hier sterven, in haar eigen bed. Geef haar eens ongelijk. Niemand mag haar helpen. Dat gaat tegen haar geloof in. De dood moet vanzelf komen. De knecht voert haar alsof ze een zuiglam is, mijn vrouw. Ik kan het niet. Ik kom amper meer boven. Heb er de kracht niet voor. Wat valt er ook te zien? Ik zie haar nog een keer per maand. Omdat de kinderen dat willen. Die tillen me dan naar boven en dan laten ze me aan mijn vrouw zien en dan zeggen ze tegen haar: “Daar is je man.” En dan kijkt mijn vrouw, dan kijkt ze. Maar ze heeft niets te zeggen. Ze is niet dement, ze heeft gewoon niets meer tegen me te zeggen. Goed, zo willen de kinderen het, dat we elkaar nog een keer per maand zien. Er komt wel weer een nieuwe pony. Wat is een paar honderd euro voor een brandweerman? Vroeger kregen wij boeren subsidie. Nu niet meer. Ons soort boeren niet. Als ik zoveel geld had gehad als de grote boeren had ik je het geld teruggegeven van je pony, maar ik heb het niet. Ik kan het me niet permitteren. Ook een dier verdient het niet met pijn rond te lopen. Dat zou een brandweerman moeten weten.’

‘Het dier wil leven,’ zei de Pool, ‘pijn of geen pijn. Kan er geen veearts naar haar komen kijken?’

Hij zag niet meer dan een stuk van de rug van de boer, de schouders, het achterhoofd. Er groeide nog veel haar op het hoofd van de boer, grijs en vettig, maar het groeide wel.

De boer schudde zijn hoofd. ‘Zo’n veearts kost meer dan twee nieuwe pony’s bij elkaar. En wat denk je wat die gaat zeggen? Laten inslapen. Ik zeg: afmaken. Hij zegt: laten inslapen. Daar betaal je je dan blauw voor.’

Nog even bleef de Pool staan, hij wilde het gesprek wel voortzetten maar hij wist niet hoe. Uiteindelijk ging hij terug naar de stal.

De jongen praatte nu niet meer met het beest, hij stond er gewoon naast en de Pool zei: 'Kom, we gaan.' Zonder op antwoord te wachten liep hij naar buiten, pakte de fiets van de jongen, sleurde de fiets als een onwillig dier mee naar de auto. Pas halverwege draaide hij zich om en zag dat de jongen hem niet achterna was gekomen. Toen riep hij zijn naam, hij bleef nog even wachten en riep nog een keer, 'Borys.' Eindelijk kwam het kind tevoorschijn, ondanks de regen treuzelde hij.

In de auto zei de Pool tegen zijn jongen: 'De boer zegt dat de pony moet worden afgemaakt. Dat het beter voor haar is. Stokkreupel zou het beest zijn.' De jongen zweeg. Hij staarde voor zich uit, hij deed alsof hij niets had gehoord, hij deed alsof de Pool niet bestond. Even wachtte de vader, je moet een kind de tijd geven, maar toen ze bijna thuis waren en er nog altijd geen reactie was gekomen, zei hij: 'Ik praat tegen je, kun je me antwoord geven? Kun je ophouden te doen alsof ik niet besta? Moet dat beest worden afgemaakt of niet? Kun je ophouden te doen alsof ik een spook ben? Ik besta. Ik ben je vader.'

'Niet doodmaken, alsjeblieft,' zei de jongen.

# 4

Thuis herhaalde de Pool wat de boer had gezegd en Wen reageerde anders dan hij had verwacht. Ze was praktisch, op het zakelijke af. Als iets kapot was moest het worden vervangen. De Pool daarentegen bewaarde graag dingen omdat je nooit kon weten wat je er nog aan had en misschien ook stiekem omdat hij eraan gehecht was, omdat een ding weggooien toch voelde alsof je een levend wezen in de vuilnisbak deponeerde. Overbezorgd was Wen ook nooit geweest. Niet dat hij dat wel was, maar als brandweerman wist hij dat het om de eerste minuten ging. Als je levens wilde redden moest je dat snel doen. Toen Borys nog klein was en weleens eten en andere dingen van de grond raapte en in zijn mond stopte zei Wen meestal alleen: 'Daar wordt hij sterker van.' De Pool haalde het allemaal uit de mond van zijn jongen, soms met moeite, dan weigerde de jongen zijn mond te openen en moest de Pool er twee vingers in wurmen.

Deze levensinstelling van Wen – haar moeder noemde het levenskunst – was vast niet alleen van toepassing op kapotte huishoudartikelen, ook op pony's. Nuchter, onsentimenteel, wat natuurlijk niet hetzelfde was als liefdeloos. Daarom had hij verwacht dat ze zou zeggen: 'Wegdoen. Doen wat de boer zegt. We kopen wel een nieuwe.'

Wegdoen was in het geval van de pony een ander woord voor afmaken, al moest de Pool toegeven dat wegdoen beter klonk. Het deed ertoe hoe je de dingen noemde. Je kon dingen zo omschrijven dat mensen er vrede mee hadden. Een kleuterjuffrouw moest daar alleen al vanwege haar beroep bedreven in zijn en Wen was er ook thuis bedreven in.

Maar deze avond had Wen haar doelgerichtheid laten

varen. Toen ze eindelijk haar mond opendeed om te reageren op het vonnis van de boer zei ze: ‘Dat lijkt me helemaal niets. Borys is aan dat dier gehecht, toch, Borys?’

De jongen keek strak voor zich uit en hij zei: ‘Manja is bang.’ De Pool had gezien hoe de jongen in de stal had gestaan, hij was getuige geweest van een teder moment tussen zijn jongen en het beest. Nu hij dat had gezien kon hij het niet vergeten. Hij had gehoord hoe zijn jongen met het beest had gesproken, niet even, nee, minutenlang en vermoedelijk deed hij dat elke dag, was dat het belangrijkste wat hij met dat beest deed. Niet erop rijden, niet borstelen zoals meisjes doen, maar ertegen praten. Omdat hun jongen niet of nauwelijks met mensen wilde spreken praatte hij met dat dier en omdat de Pool getuige was van dat praten zei hij: ‘Ja, dat beest betekent veel voor hem. Maar ze is niet bang, Borys. Ze is mank. Ze is stokkreupel, zei de boer.’ En hij begon Borys te strelen. Als er niet gepraat kon worden moest er worden gestreeld.

De ouders waren het erover eens, het beest moest gered worden, het beest redden was Borys redden. Zo simpel was het. Redden was de typische taak van een brandweerman en alleen al daarom had de Pool spijt dat hij in de auto bijna zijn geduld was verloren. Zo iemand wilde hij niet zijn, een schreeuwende, vloekende vader. ‘We laten dat beest niet afmaken,’ zei hij met een kordaatheid die hem verraste want hij was er zelf nog niet helemaal van overtuigd dat het echt het beste was voor de pony, zo’n boer wist waarover hij sprak. Maar hij had geen keus, pony en zoon waren aan elkaar verbonden, ze mochten niet gescheiden worden. Nu niet in elk geval. Later, als hun jongen sterker was, misschien dan.

‘Kun je aan de boer vragen of er een veearts naar haar kan komen kijken?’ vroeg hij daarom aan Borys. ‘Zeg maar dat je vader het betaalt. Dat hij zich daar geen zorgen over hoeft te maken. De Pool betaalt de veearts.’

De jongen knikte. Veel emotie was er van zijn gezicht niet af te lezen, maar de vader wist zeker dat Borys blij was.

Het zou een hoop geld kosten, zo'n veearts, aan verzekeren had hij niet gedacht, als dat überhaupt mogelijk was geweest. Bestond er eigenlijk een ziektekostenverzekering voor pony's? Hij had geen idee, het maakte niet uit. Voor verzekeringen was het hoe dan ook te laat. Desnoods gingen ze volgende zomer niet naar Kreta. Een huisje in Duitsland was goedkoper en daar kon het ook mooi weer zijn.

Aangezien het poepen in de broek nu geheel tot stilstand was gekomen – Borys deponeerde zijn vuiligheid weer zoals alle gezonde mensen deden gewoon in het toilet – en zowel de Pool als zijn vrouw ervan overtuigd was dat dit was te danken aan de pony, zette de Pool vaart achter de redding van het beest.

Elke avond vroeg hij of er al nieuws was over de komst van de veearts en elke avond kwam er een vaag antwoord van hun jongen. Over een paar dagen, de boer wist het niet, de boer sliep en de jongen durfde hem niet wakker te maken, de knecht was ermee bezig, tot het uiteindelijk tot de Pool begon door te dringen: hun jongen durfde niet met de boer te praten. De jongen was bang voor de boer, zelfs al ging het om de redding van zijn pony. Zo'n zoon hadden ze, een tikkeltje bangig, maar hij zou veranderen. Later zou hij met de mensen gaan spreken. De angst zou verdwijnen zoals pukkels verdwijnen.

Twee weken na zijn laatste bezoek aan de boer vroeg de Pool voor de zekerheid nog eens naar de gezondheidstoestand van de pony. Je wist het niet, voor hetzelfde geld lag het beest onder een stuk zeil omdat de boer nog geen tijd had gehad het te laten weghalen en durfde de jongen zijn ouders niet te vertellen dat de pony uit haar lijden was verlost. Borys belastte zijn omgeving niet graag met slecht nieuws.

'Ze hinkt,' zei de jongen. Tot verbazing van zijn ouders stond de stille jongen op en hij deed voor hoe het kreupele beest zich door het leven sloeg. Het was een merkwaardig tafereel. Hun oudste zoon die zijn kreupele pony imiteerde. Hij hinkte door de woonkamer, Borys. Vader en moeder keken toe en daarna keken ze elkaar aan.

'Voor pony's bestaan er helaas geen rolstoelen,' merkte de Pool op, want ook deze avond wilde hij het luchtig houden. 'Maar we gaan er iets aan doen. We gaan dat dier helpen. We laten haar niet aan haar lot over.'

De eerstvolgende vrije dag reed hij aan het eind van de middag naar de boerderij. Hij zou met de boer praten, eerst zou hij om een veearts vragen, daarna zou hij er een eisen, hij zou met zijn vuist op tafel slaan als gewoon eisen niet tot de gewenste resultaten leidde en mocht de boer hem dan nog niet willen helpen zou hij er zelf achteraan gaan. Er was vast iemand in de C-ploeg die een betrouwbare veearts kende.

Zoals de vorige keren zat de boer voor het raam, dit keer werd er niet gewenkt. De Pool moest bekennen dat hij zelf ook een beetje bang was voor deze boer, dat hij zich onbehaaglijk voelde door de man, zijn monologen, zijn waarheden, zijn levenshouding. Zijn onverzorgde haar. De Pool was bij de brandweer gegaan om de mensen te helpen. Natuurlijk waren er ook andere redenen geweest, het avontuur, de droom van het kind dat hij geweest was, de werktijden, maar iets in hem wilde de burger helpen. Deze man in zijn rolstoel geloofde niet in hulp, wilde er niets van weten. Dat ongeloof stond de Pool tegen, het maakte hem onzeker. Op een bepaalde manier zelfs woedend.

Met minder aarzeling dan de twee voorgaande keren liep hij naar de stal. De koe was weggehaald. Het zeil lag er nog maar er lag niets meer onder. De Pool staarde even naar het zeil terwijl hij zijn broek ophees en zich afvroeg hoeveel dode beesten daar al hadden gelegen.

Hij liep de stal in en riep: 'Borys.' Er kwam geen reactie maar dat verbaasde hem niet want de jongen reageerde zelden als ze hem riepen. Hij kwam wel naar beneden en ging aan tafel zitten maar nooit riep hij: 'Ik kom al.' Of: 'Hier ben ik.' Hij werd geroepen en hij verscheen. En dan deed hij wat hij doen moest, hij at zijn bord leeg.

Het hok stond open en eerst zag de Pool alleen het dier. Niemand stak deze namiddag een monoloog af. Het dier had nog nooit een kik gegeven en zou daar vandaag ook niet mee beginnen. De pony keek hem aan en toen zag hij in een hoek helemaal achter in de stal de jongen op zijn hurken zitten. Zijn broek op de knieën. En hij keek, de jongen keek terug, geen woord kwam over zijn lippen, hij keek zijn vader alleen maar strak aan.

Het plan om zijn jongen te omhelzen, hem tegen zich aan te drukken, hem de warmte te geven waarnaar zijn jongen verlangde, waarnaar elke jongen verlangde, daar kon de Pool zich nu niet toe zetten. Hij kwam dichterbij, de pony verroerde zich niet. Zoals de boer in zijn rolstoel bleef zitten, zo bleef de pony staan. Te oud en te stijf en waarschijnlijk ook te mank om nog veel te bewegen. Daar zat zijn jongen, zijn lange, stille, magere jongen, geen Pool, een echte Nederlander. Hij wilde zo graag trots zijn op zijn jongen, de vader, maar wat hij daar zag gaf hem weinig reden tot trots.

'Wat doe je daar?' vroeg de Pool.

'Ik ben aan het poepen,' zei de jongen en hij staarde nu voor zich uit. Niet alsof hij in trance was, eerder alsof hij zich concentreerde, alsof hij zich jaartallen probeerde te herinneren van een geschiedenisles.

'Toch niet in de stal?' zei de Pool en hij kwam iets dichter bij zijn jongen staan en hij legde zijn hand op het hoofd van de jongen. Dat kon wel. Omhelzen ging moeilijk in deze situatie, maar een hand kon op het hoofd van de jongen worden gelegd, een zorgzame, beschermende hand. 'Jij bent toch geen beest?' zei hij. 'Er zijn hier vast wc's waarvan je gebruik kunt maken. En hier in de stal is geen wc-papier, waar veeg je je in godsnaam mee af?'

Hij keek om zich heen alsof hij de jongen ervan verdacht allemaal rollen wc-papier achter in de stal te hebben verstopt.

'Hiermee,' zei de jongen en hij pakte stro en liet het aan zijn vader zien. Hij keek meewarig, alsof hij medelijden had met de man die niet begreep dat je je met stro kon afvegen.

'Hier gaan wij naar de wc,' zei de jongen en hij bleef op zijn hurken zitten want hij was aan het poepen en in zijn rechterhand hield hij het stro, vermoedelijk stro waar de pony al vaak op had gestaan, want de boer was gierig met stro. Het leek alsof de jongen zijn vader ervan wilde overtuigen dat hij een keurig opgevoede jongen was, dat hij zich goed afveegde, ook onder barre omstandigheden, ook in deze stal.

Wij. De Pool keek van het dier naar zijn jongen en weer terug naar het kreupele beest. 'Wat zegt de knecht ervan?' vroeg de Pool. 'Dit is toch geen mensen-wc? Moet de knecht jouw poep opruimen? Niet alleen die van het dier maar ook de uitwerpselen van een mens?'

Zijn jongen haalde de schouders op en het beest stond daar maar, onbeweeglijk. Of het pijn had of niet kon de Pool niet vertellen maar de onbeweeglijkheid baarde hem zorgen. 'Ik ga naar de boer,' zei hij. 'Blijf zitten. Ik kom zo terug.'

Hij zou dit later wel met zijn vrouw bespreken, eerst moest de veearts worden geregeld. Dat had prioriteit.

De Pool liep naar de boerderij, haastig, driftig bijna, opende de keukendeur zonder te kloppen en liep naar de woonkamer. De boer zat bij het raam in zijn rolstoel te slapen. De Pool bleef aan de andere kant van de tafel staan en hij rook weer die merkwaardige lucht, dit keer nog vermengd met zweet.

Van boven hoorde hij aanhoudend geklop komen. Het klonk steeds harder. Daarboven was iemand in nood. Het was alsof een kracht buiten de Pool om aan hem trok, iets of iemand herinnerde hem aan zijn ware missie: daarboven moest een levend wezen gered worden, de vrouw van de boer waarschijnlijk.

Voorzichtig opende hij de deur waarachter hij de trap vermoedde en vervolgens liep hij naar boven. De treden kraakten maar hij voelde zich geen inbreker, hij was het gewend huizen binnen te dringen. Zijn zelfverzekerdheid was terug. Het was het verantwoordelijkheidsgevoel van de brandweerman dat hem deze trap op leidde.

Een jongen die het over 'wij' had en daarmee zichzelf en een pony bedoelde. Een jongen die poepte naast zijn pony, in een koude, onverwarmde stal. Daar moest een vader zich zorgen om maken. Maar eerst moest hier iemand worden gered.

Zelfverzekerd was hij en toch gespannen. Ook al was er geen brand, hij was voorbereid op alles, hij was getraind om op alles voorbereid te zijn.

Het rook in het trappenhuis naar riool. Boven was een halletje met drie deuren. Hij opende de eerste deur, de geur van het riool werd sterker. Een kinderkamer, althans iets wat ooit een kinderkamer was geweest, er stond nog een ledikant. Hij opende een kast. Geen kleren, wat houten speelgoed. Blokken, niet meer van deze tijd. Lege lades. Een wastafel.

Hij opende de tweede deur. Daar lag ze, klaarwakker, ogen open, haar gezicht deed hem aan dat van een oude koningin denken, maar dan een onverzorgde versie.

Ze had hem gezien, geen woord kwam echter over haar lippen. Geen schreeuw, geen hulpgeroep, ze keek alsof ze hem had verwacht.

Hij kwam een paar passen dichterbij. Op een nachtkastje stond een bord met ontbijtkoek of iets wat daarop leek.

De koek was met boter of margarine besmeerd, het mes lag er nog naast. De Pool moest de neiging om te kokhalzen onderdrukken en dat terwijl hij niets tegen ontbijtkoek had, maar hoe het daar lag, zo armoedig, zo oud, zo onaangeroerd, daarvan werd hij misselijk. Het bord was gebroken geweest, iemand had de moeite genomen de twee helften weer aan elkaar te lijmen.

Ze zag er beter uit dan haar man, haar ogen waren helderder. Haar huid had minder te lijden gehad onder kou, zon en wind.

'Goeienavond.' Hij wilde zich voorstellen en even overwoog hij wat hij zou doen als de knecht nu binnenkwam. Hij zou zich betrapt voelen, ondanks het feit dat dit eigenlijk niet nodig was. Wat kon hij tegen de vrouw zeggen? Hebt u hulp nodig? Hebt u geklopt?

'Wie bent u?' vroeg ze. Haar stem klonk zwak en aarzelend maar ze sprak tenminste.

'Ik ben brandweerman,' zei de Pool. Hij deed zijn armen over elkaar.

Ze bekeek hem en schudde vervolgens haar hoofd. 'Dat bent u niet,' zei ze. Ze klonk overtuigd en misschien zelfs een tikkeltje teleurgesteld alsof ze liever had gehad dat hij dat wel was geweest.

'Ik ben in burger,' zei de Pool, 'ik heb een pony van uw man gekocht. Nu is ze kreupel.'

Ze knikte. Zachtjes zei ze: 'Aha.' Haar concentratie leek weg te ebben, ze keek naar de gele deken waaronder ze lag. Een oude, verwassen deken. Er zaten vlekken op die er in de wasmachine nooit uit waren gegaan. Tomatensoep of bloed. Of aardbeienjam. Ze richtte haar blik weer op hem. 'U bent lang,' zei ze.

Nog een paar passen deed de Pool en nu stond hij naast haar. Hij had haar kunnen strelen alsof ze zijn eigen moeder was. Het was vermoedelijk ongepast dat hij hier stond. Hij zocht een veearts, maar een brandweerman is gevoelig voor noodkreten. Brandweerman was je altijd, 24 uur per dag, ook op je vrije dagen, al zeiden sommige van zijn collega's dat het vroeger anders was. Vroeger zat je bij de brandweer, nu werkte je er.

De Pool zag dat de vrouw met riemen was vastgebonden, ouderwetse leren riemen die zoals alles in dit huis uit een andere eeuw leken te komen. Andere eeuw of geen andere eeuw, oude, verwarde mensen moesten niet worden vastgebonden aan hun bed en deze vrouw was niet eens verward. Hij legde zijn linkerhand op de gele deken maar zo dat hij het lichaam van de boerin niet raakte.

'Ze hebben u vastgebonden,' zei hij omdat hij niet zeker wist of ze zich daar zelf wel bewust van was en hij merkte dat hij nu toch weer aarzelde in welke hoedanigheid hij hier stond. Was hij de vader van zijn jongen, de vader die een veearts nodig had, of toch de man die burgers in nood wenste te helpen? Van nood leek hem hier wel degelijk sprake. Hoe kwam ze hier weg als er brand uitbrak? Alleen al vanwege de maatregelen die burgers konden en moesten nemen om zich te beschermen tegen brandgevaar, en dan met name tegen mogelijke rookontwikkeling, vond hij het onwenselijk dat de boer zijn vrouw op haar bed had vastgebonden.

'Bent u misschien vastgebonden, mevrouw?' vroeg hij voor de zekerheid. De eerste keer had hij het vastgesteld en toen was er geen reactie gekomen, vermoedelijk moest hij het gewoon vragen. Hij had het geleerd op de opleiding. Niet als een gek een brandend gebouw binnenstormen. Even denken voor je iets doet. Is er tijd te praten met de burger die het alarmnummer heeft gebeld, praat met hem. Hij kan informatie hebben die van levensbelang is.

'Ach.' Ze keek hem aan op zo'n manier dat hem het gevoel bekroop dat ze aan deze kwestie geen woorden wenste vuil te maken. Ze was vastgebonden, het hoorde er nu eenmaal bij, ze was eraan gewend geraakt.

Hij wilde naar beneden gaan, hier had hij verder niets te zoeken. Je moest je grenzen kennen, de burger in nood helpen was één ding, maar als een burger niet geholpen wenste te worden dan moest je, zeker als je geen dienst had, je uit de voeten maken.

Ze monsterde hem, met meer helderheid dan daarnet en het was deze blik die ervoor zorgde dat hij bleef staan.

'Ik heb al zo lang gewacht op de brandweer, ik heb al zo vaak gebeld,' zei ze. 'Vroeger. Maar jullie kwamen nooit. En op een gegeven moment ben ik ermee opgehouden.'

'Het alarmnummer?' vroeg de Pool.

Moest hij aanbieden haar iets rechterop te zetten? Ze lag daar zo ongelukkig. Hij deed het gewoon. Met een hand onder iedere oksel legde hij haar hoger op het kussen. Ze woog niets. Ondanks de riemen lukte het prima. Als ze zou willen kon ze ontsnappen, met een beetje moeite, maar kennelijk wilde ze dat niet.

'Ik kan allerlei nare dingen over mijn man vertellen,' sprak ze helder. 'Maar een vrouw staat achter haar man. Wat hij ook doet. Ze staat achter hem.'

'Zo is dat,' zei de Pool, 'en ik wil me ook niet met uw zaken bemoeien. Als uw man u wenst vast te binden aan het bed en u hebt daar verder geen bezwaar tegen, dan is dat iets tussen u en uw man. Maar als brandweerman moet ik u waarschuwen. Als brandweerman vind ik dat onverantwoord.' Hij keek om zich heen. 'U kunt zich misschien wel met enige moeite loswringen uit die riemen maar bij brand gaat er kostbare tijd verloren. Het is hier behoorlijk brandgevaarlijk. Dit is een oud huis, dat fikt zo weg.'

Zat Borys nog op zijn hurken in de stal? Hij moest met de boer praten. 'Mijn man wil niet dat ik naar beneden kom,' zei ze, 'dat werkt hem op de zenuwen, misschien omdat hij zelf niet meer boven kan komen. Het is nooit leuk als iemand anders wel kan wat jij niet meer kunt. En de knecht brengt me het eten. Hij aait me ook. Ik heb niets te klagen. Ik lig hier goed. Soms ga ik verliggen. In de ochtend word ik gewassen, dan loop ik wat door de kamer. Voor zover dat nog lukt. De knecht helpt me. Als het moet kan ik met mijn rechterhand op de muur kloppen, dan horen ze me beneden. De wereld buiten deze kamer is me veel te groot, te eng, ik zal het maar eerlijk zeggen, meneer de brandweerman, te groot en te eng.'

De Pool knikte bedachtzaam en begon in de richting van de deur te lopen.

'U bent lang,' zei ze weer.

Bij de deur zei hij: 'Ik zal met uw man over brandpreventie spreken. Nu ik hier toch ben.'

Ze zwaaide met haar hand. Of ze naar hem zwaaide of hem wenkte was onduidelijk. 'Dit is mijn nest,' zei ze. 'Ik lig hier goed. Soms hoor ik de radio van beneden. Of de tv. Het journaal. Mijn man zet de tv beneden altijd hard aan, zodat ik er ook nog wat aan heb. Muziek vind ik prima, maar als het journaal voorbijkomt kruip ik diep onder de dekens. Zelfs als je de beelden niet ziet... Ik wacht tot ik het weerbericht hoor. En dan heb ik vaak een uur nodig om bij te komen. Ik wil niet dat de wereld deze kamer binnendringt. Begrijpt u dat, meneer de brandweerman? Ik wil niet uit mijn nest worden gejaagd. Daarom moet u het maar niet met mijn man over brandpreventie hebben. Dat schopt alles in de war.'

Hij aarzelde weer. Moest hij haar nu beloven tegenover haar man te doen alsof hij hier nooit was geweest? Alsof hij haar nooit had gezien? Wilde ze het risico nemen te verbranden, in ruil voor rust?

'Ik moet gaan,' zei hij. 'Ik ben hier voor een veearts. Ik heb voor mijn jongen een pony gekocht van uw man en nu is ze ziek geworden. Kreupel.'

'Hebben we nog pony's? Ik dacht dat we helemaal geen beesten meer hadden.' Ze strekte haar hand naar hem uit, niet om hem vast te pakken, het was alsof ze wees, naar de stallen, naar waar de beesten waren geweest, waar zij zelf had gelopen toen de wereld nog niet te eng was.

Hij kwam weer dichterbij, hij moest fatsoenlijk afscheid van haar nemen, misschien de deken nog eens goed leggen. Hij wilde haar hand pakken maar hij greep verkeerd, hij pakte alleen haar wijzende vinger en daarom schudde hij die. Voorzichtig, want ze was broos. Helder maar broos.

Daarna liep hij snel weg. Hij sloot de deur, ze had hem nog nageroepen: 'Stoot uw hoofd niet.'

Hij ging rechtstreeks naar de boer, die nog altijd in zijn rolstoel zat te slapen. Hij legde een hand op de schouder van de man. 'O, jij bent het,' zei de boer. Zijn stem klonk weer hijgerig, het ademhalen kostte hem moeite.

'Ik ben hier voor de pony,' zei de Pool. 'Ik wil dat een veearts naar haar komt kijken. Mijn jongen is gehecht aan dat dier. Hij kan niet zonder haar.'

'Dat beest moet dood,' zei de boer. 'Die jongen van jou vindt wel weer een nieuw dier, pony's in overvloed. Veel te veel zelfs.'

'Ik heb het beest gekocht.' De Pool wilde zijn stem niet verheffen, maar hij wilde wel laten zien dat hij het meende en daarom sprak hij elk woord nadrukkelijk uit. 'Ik wil dat er een veearts naar haar komt kijken. Ook al staat het in uw stal, ik betaal voor dat dier.'

'Als jij betaalt voor de veearts zal ik hem bellen. Jullie weten alles beter. Jullie denken dat de dood een drama is.' Toen begon de boer te fluiten, althans hij deed pogingen om te fluiten, af en toe leek het echt ergens op en de Pool begreep dat de boer vroeger veel gefloten moest hebben en dat het gesprek nu was afgelopen. Hij floot om de bezoeker te verjagen en de bezoeker liet zich verjagen. Een andere keer zou hij over de brandpreventie beginnen en die merkwaardige gewoonte om oude mensen aan hun bed vast te binden.

In de stal zat de jongen nog altijd op zijn hurken en de

Pool, die eigenlijk had verwacht dat de jongen inmiddels wel klaar was, liep rechtstreeks op hem af, hij hurkte naast hem neer. De pony bleef stil staan, ze draaide alleen even haar hoofd om en bekeek vader en zoon met ogen waar de Pool niet goed tegen kon, omdat hij er een weemoed in zag, een stil verdriet. Verbeelding vermoedelijk, maar toch. Beesten wisten wat weemoed was.

'Waarom zit je hier nog steeds?' vroeg de Pool. 'Het is toch veel te koud hier. Waarom blijf je hier zitten?'

'Er komt nog niets uit,' zei de jongen, 'het duurt altijd even. En hier zit ik goed.'

De jongen ging met zijn hand door het stro naast hem en de vader steunde met zijn linkerhand op het vieze stro. Hij nam zich voor de knecht eens te vragen hoe vaak de stal eigenlijk werd uitgemest, de stal waarvoor hij betaalde.

'We gaan naar huis,' zei hij tegen zijn jongen. 'Er komt een veearts naar haar kijken.'

De jongen knikte. Hij stond op, pakte wat stro en streek daarmee tussen zijn billen. 'Ik veeg me altijd voor de zekerheid af,' zei hij. 'Ook als er niets uit is gekomen.'

De jongen deed zijn onderbroek omhoog en zijn broek, die zijn moeder in drie kleuren had gekocht.

De Pool pakte de fiets van Borys en dit keer liep hij niet vooruit, hij bleef naast zijn jongen lopen met de fiets aan de hand en de jongen zei: 'Manja is dol op winterpeen. Ze eet er op een middag wel vier of vijf op.'

# 5

'Ik ben ook jager,' zei de veearts.

Zijn naam had de Pool niet goed kunnen verstaan. Klep. Of Klemp. Het deed er ook niet toe. Ze stonden op het erf van de boer, die zich voor de verandering dit keer niet liet zien, en de veearts zelf leek inderdaad meer op een jager dan op een arts, meer iemand die van afschieten hield dan van genezen. Hij was een stuk ouder dan de Pool en hij stond erbij als een man die al dagelijks aan zijn pensioen dacht, alsof hij nog maar half veearts was, zijn ziel vooruit was gereisd naar de zuidkust van Spanje, maar desondanks had hij iets vitaals. Hij droeg een hoedje en daaronder vandaan kwamen enkele glimmende grijze haren.

Naast de Pool stond zijn jongen, het was een belangrijke dag voor hem. De Pool was nerveus, nu werd beslist over het leven van het dier en daarmee indirect over dat van zijn jongen. Hij trok de rits van zijn blauwe jack omhoog. Het jack was een overblijfsel van een wintersportvakantie. Ze waren erheen gegaan om het carnaval te ontlopen, maar wintersport was niets voor hem geweest, dat was iets voor andere mensen, een ander soort mensen. Wen had genoten, de Pool had zich niet thuis gevoeld in het wintersportdorp, het skiën was hem niet goed afgegaan, hij was bang om te vallen, te trots om dit toe te geven. 's Nachts hield de disco hem uit zijn slaap en toen ze na een week weer thuis waren en de Pool het speciaal voor deze reis aangeschafte jack ophing in de kast zei hij: 'Dat doen we nooit meer. Als onze jongens later zo nodig nog eens op een snowboard willen staan gaan ze maar naar SnowWorld hier om de hoek.' Zo'n jack weggooien was zonde, bovendien was het best warm. Vanochtend had hij het uit de kast gehaald, omdat hij de veearts zou ontmoeten. Hij wilde er fatsoenlijk uitzien voor de veearts.

'Jagen en genezen zijn niet met elkaar in tegenspraak,' zei Klep. 'De jager geneest door te jagen. Ik beleef er natuurlijk ook plezier aan, maar ik doe het uiteindelijk voor de dieren. Ik draag bij aan de instandhouding van het evenwicht in de natuur. De jager en de veearts leven in volstrekte harmonie met elkaar. Ik ben veearts geworden omdat ik van jagen hield en ik ben gaan jagen omdat ik van kinds af dierenarts wilde worden. Dat begrijpt niet iedereen, alleen de goede verstaander begrijpt het.'

De Pool wilde bij de goede verstaanders horen. In het bijzijn van de jager die ook veearts was besefte hij hoe graag hij dat wilde, alleen al daarom besloot hij de man te begrijpen. Niet dat hij veel met jagen had, hij had er ook niets tegen, hij vond het een onbegrijpelijke hobby. Dan had hij nog eerder begrip voor mensen die weekenden lang aan het vissen waren.

Klep had verder gesproken maar de Pool was afgeleid en daarom knikte hij wat tot hij merkte dat de veearts hem zwijgend aankeek, ongetwijfeld wachtend op een blijk van instemming, op iets meer dan alleen geknik. In verlegenheid gebracht mompelde de Pool: 'Zo is dat.'

'Wat is zo?' vroeg de veearts.

De Pool legde zijn linkerhand op het hoofd van Borys. 'Het gaat om zijn pony,' zei hij vervolgens zacht en toch indringend. 'Ze is in een beek gelopen en sindsdien is ze kreupel. We willen dat er iets aan gedaan wordt. We willen geen afscheid van haar nemen.'

'Ja, ja,' zei Klep ongeduldig. Irriteerde de pony hem? De Pool merkte nu voor het eerst op dat de arts met een licht accent sprak. 'We willen geen afscheid nemen,' vervolgde Klep. 'Dat wil niemand en als het dan toch moet kijken ze boos naar de arts. Dan doen ze alsof het aan hem ligt dat er afscheid moet worden genomen. De boeren zijn anders.

Die weten hoe het gaat in de natuur. Die zijn nog niet verpest met de gedachte dat alles zielig is. Goed, we gaan eens kijken.'

De veearts snelde vooruit, liet de Pool en zijn jongen achter zich, hij leek nog maar één doel te hebben: de stal. In zijn kaplaarzen rende hij over het modderige pad, het leek alsof hij expres de plassen uitzocht en daarin trapte als een ondeugend kind dat ontsnapt is aan de aandacht van zijn ouders. Hij keek niet op of om, snelde de stal binnen. De Pool en zijn jongen liepen achter hem aan. Een vaal zonnetje scheen. Borys ontweek de plassen zorgvuldig. Hij liep op gympen. De Pool had geprobeerd de hand van zijn jongen vast te pakken maar de jongen had zijn hand meteen weer losgetrokken. Hij leek zich te schamen voor de man in het wintersportjack, de man die zijn vader was.

In de stal liep Klep om de pony heen, betastte haar, klopte op haar rug, friemelde aan haar manen. 'Ah,' zei hij, 'mijn meisje. De laatste. Ze hadden hier wel twintig pony's en paarden en toen werd de boer ziek. Altijd kinderen over de vloer, twintig pony's en paarden. Hij wilde ze niet wegdoen. Ze begrijpen de natuur maar ze zijn eigenwijs, de boeren. In het begin heeft de knecht hem nog naar de stal gedragen, snel zagen ze in dat het gekkenwerk was en de meeste knechten hebben ook geen zin om met de boer te zeulen. Langzaam zijn de pony's en de paarden hier uitgestorven, de rest is met de meeste koeien verkocht. Niemand wilde dit meisje hebben.'

Klep sprak het woord 'uitgestorven' uit met een merkwaardig genoegen alsof dat de verdiende straf was voor de eigenwijsheid van de boer die zich niet had neergelegd bij zijn ziekte.

'Het zijn haar achterpoten,' zei de Pool.

De veearts schudde zijn wijsvinger. 'Bij paarden spreken we van benen, niet van poten. Het zijn edele dieren.'

De veearts benaderde het dier, bekeek de poten, kneep

wat in het vlees, liet het dier een poot optillen – de Pool weigerde over benen te beginnen, alleen mensen hadden benen – en toen hij een tijdje een soort van strekoefeningen met het beest had gedaan kwam hij terug naar de Pool en zijn jongen. De veearts veegde zijn hand af aan een zakdoek die hij vervolgens netjes opvouwde en weer in zijn broekzak stak. 'Het is een oud meisje,' zei hij en nam zijn hoed af. Nu werd zijn goedverzorgde grijze haar werkelijk zichtbaar, het glom van de gel. 'Een oud meisje,' herhaalde de arts en er klonk iets door in zijn stem wat een snik had kunnen zijn, alsof hij het over zijn eigen vrouw had, nog steeds een meisje, wel oud geworden. 'Ik kan haar medicijnen toedienen, dan kan ze een tijd voort. Maar weet je wat dat kost?'

'Wat is het alternatief?' vroeg de Pool. Hij wilde nog niet weten wat het kostte, niet waar de jongen bij was.

'De paardenslager,' zei de veearts en hij trok er een gezicht bij alsof hij goed kon begrijpen dat dit voor niemand een aantrekkelijk vooruitzicht was. 'We leven niet eeuwig,' zei Klep, nadat hij met zijn tong over zijn lippen was gegaan, 'de natuur moet zijn werk doen, maar niets vergaat werkelijk. De kleinste deeltjes zijn onvernietigbaar. Daaraan hou ik me vast. Voor mij is de dood niet meer dan een overgang van de ene toestand naar de volgende en welke toestand het aantrekkelijkst is moet nog blijken. Ik zie niet op tegen de dood, helemaal niet.'

De onverwoestbaarheid van de kleinste deeltjes leek de Pool een schrale troost voor zijn jongen. En dat gepraat over de overgang van de ene naar de andere toestand werkte hem ook op de zenuwen. Was hij daarom brandweerman geworden? Als leven en dood een kwestie was van een overgang van de ene naar de volgende toestand kon de brandweer net zo goed thuisblijven.

'Hoeveel kost dat?' fluisterde hij.

'Ik doe ook acupunctuur,' zei de veearts op een toon

alsof hij dit geheim nog niet eerder aan een wildvreemde had geopenbaard. 'Eigenlijk alleen voor renpaarden, in uitzonderlijke gevallen ook voor bejaarde paarden, als de eigenaar aan het dier hangt, het niet kan loslaten, zich een leven zonder niet kan voorstellen. Ik heb eens een man gehad...' De veearts begon steeds zachter en dieper te spreken, 'Die zei tegen mij: "Ik wil niet op een paard zitten, ik wil op míjn paard zitten. Het gaat me niet om paarden in het algemeen." Die kon geen afscheid nemen van zijn dier. Wel van zijn echtgenote, niet van zijn dier. Ja, dan kom je al snel bij mij terecht.'

De Pool greep de hand van zijn jongen en dit keer trok Borys zich niet los. 'Is er uitzicht op genezing?' De Pool voelde hoe hij zweette, alsof hij examen deed.

'Verlichting,' zei de veearts. 'Er is uitzicht op verlichting. Kijk, de eigenaren van renpaarden, en dan heb ik het over de crème de la crème, vragen niet voor niets aan mij of ik langs kan komen voor acupunctuur. Ik ben geen tovenaar maar er zijn eigenaren van renpaarden die tegen me zeggen: "Klep, jij hebt wonderen verricht." Medicijnen bieden verlichting, acupunctuur kan het meisje genezen.'

Nadat hij dat had gezegd wreef de veearts, hoewel dat volstrekt overbodig was, zijn haren glad en hij zette zijn hoedje weer op.

Met zijn vrije hand betastte de Pool zijn rechterwang, hij voelde aan zijn stoppels en zo terloops mogelijk vroeg hij: 'Wat kost dat, acupunctuur voor een pony?'

De veearts, die geen tovenaar was, alleen zo nu en dan wonderen verrichtte, bracht zijn mond naar het oor van de brandweerman en even dacht de Pool dat de man hem wilde kussen, maar hij wilde alleen een bedrag in het oor van de brandweerman fluisteren, een bedrag waarvan de Pool behoorlijk schrok. Eerlijk is eerlijk, hij schrok geweldig, hij werd misselijk van dat bedrag, hij merkte dat hij moest kokhalzen. Zijn jongen moet dat hebben gevoeld, want die rukte zich los en daarop zei de Pool meteen: 'Wat moet dat moet.'

'Akkoord,' zei de arts met een gematigd enthousiasme. Had hij de Pool ingeschat als iemand die zou zeggen: Dat is me te duur? Had hij hem ingeschat als iemand die te weinig geld had om de dieren om hem heen te redden van de ondergang? 'Ik kan er nu niet mee beginnen, want ik heb de spullen niet bij me, morgenmiddag heb ik een gaatje, dan zal ik doen wat ik kan voor dat arme, oude meisje.' En hij klopte de pony op haar rug, het beest zelf gaf geen kik.

'Naar welk adres moet de factuur?' vroeg de veearts terwijl hij zijn tas van het stro pakte.

Hij noteerde het adres van de Pool in een agenda, hij keek om zich heen naar de grote stal waar ruim twintig paarden in pasten, maar nu nog maar één zieke pony verbleef en liep toen samen met de Pool en de jongen naar buiten.

De arts praatte en praatte, hij was nu overduidelijk goedgehumeurd, hij zei dat de goede jager de beste dierenvriend was die hij zich kon voorstellen, hij vertelde wat hij allemaal geschoten had en hij voegde eraan toe dat hij op elk continent had gejaagd behalve Noord- en Zuid-Amerika en Australië. 'Verder overal,' zei hij, 'het is de enige luxe die ik me gun. En ik jaag met plezier in Nederland, maar het echte werk vindt natuurlijk in Afrika plaats. Daar beleef je de jacht anders, daar voel je nog iets van het oude jagen, het werkelijke jagen, daar schiet je ook eens op een ander dier dan een fazant of een hert, dat spreekt vanzelf. Lekker hoor, fazant. Een goede jager, en ik reken mijzelf tot de beste jagers die dit land rijk is, schiet zijn beesten niet dood, hij kietelt ze dood, hij kust ze dood.'

En toen waren ze weer bij de boerderij.

'Hoe weet ik of de behandeling aanslaat?' vroeg de Pool en de veearts die dieren dood kuste zei dat hij over een tijdje moest bellen. 'Je hebt mijn nummer toch? Hier is mijn kaartje.'

'Klepp', stond erop. 'Veearts'. Verder een adres en een telefoonnummer.

De Pool stak het in zijn zak en daarop stapte de dierenarts in zijn auto. Langzaam reed hij weg.

De Pool legde een hand op de schouder van zijn magere jongen en hij zei: 'We moeten natuurlijk nog even afwachten maar jouw pony hoeft niet naar de paardenslager. Daarvan kun je op aan. Geen paardenslager voor dat beest.'

De jongen knikte.

'Ben je blij?' vroeg de Pool.

'Hmm,' zei de jongen.

'Ben je echt blij?'

'Jaha,' zei de jongen. 'Zie je dat niet? Maar pap, geloof jij in acupunctuur? Wat is dat eigenlijk?'

'Naalden,' zei de Pool. 'Naalden die ze in je stoppen. Ik denk dat acupunctuur zal helpen, maar we moeten realistisch zijn. Jouw pony is niet de jongste meer. We gaan allemaal een keer dood. Het belangrijkste is dat we blij zijn dat het beter met je gaat. Je verstoorde stoelgang maakte ons zo wanhopig. Daar werden we zo verdrietig van.'

'Ik kon de stoelgang niet stoppen, het ging vanzelf.'

'Ja,' zei de Pool, 'het ging vanzelf. Jouw moeder en ik zijn toch blij dat het nu niet meer vanzelf gaat. Ook al poep je nu in de stal, naast dat beest, later moet je toch proberen niet meer in de stal naar de wc te gaan, maar gewoon naar de mensen-wc, dat doe ik ook. Ik ga ook niet in een stal op mijn hurken zitten. Ik moet er niet aan denken.'

'Nee,' zei de jongen. 'Dat is niets voor jou.'

'En je praat ook met dat beest?'

'Ja,' zei de jongen.

'Wat vertel je dat beest?'

De jongen haalde zijn schouders op. 'Van alles. Verhalen.'

‘Wat voor verhalen?’ wilde de Pool weten. ‘Wil je die niet aan mij vertellen, of aan je moeder? We weten zo weinig over je. Het is de puberteit. Die begint vroeg. Zegt je moeder. Maar je kunt toch een keer iets aan ons vertellen?’

‘Ik heb niet zoveel te vertellen. Het komt wel een keer, als ik tijd heb.’

En de Pool drukte zijn hand harder en liefdevoller op de schouder van zijn jongen en hij vroeg: ‘Zal ik je fiets in de auto gooien?’

De jongen antwoordde: ‘Nee, ik denk dat ik hier nog even blijf. Ik kom zo thuis.’

Borys liep weg, na een paar passen draaide hij zich om, kwam terug. ‘Dank je papa,’ zei de jongen. ‘Dank je voor die acupunctuur.’ En hij omhelsde zijn vader, kuste hem. De Pool schrok daarvan want dat gebeurde bijna nooit. Hij drukte zijn jongen tegen zich aan, heel stevig, en hij zei: ‘Dat spreekt toch vanzelf. Dat spreekt toch vanzelf, lieve jongen. Ik weet hoe belangrijk dat oude beest voor je is.’

Daarop rukte de jongen zich los. ‘Het is geen beest. Ze heet Manja.’

‘Nee, nee, geen beest,’ zei de Pool. Hij stapte in de auto en reed naar huis, terwijl hij besefte: die jongen heeft liefde nodig, meer liefde. Maar hoe geef je die? Meer strelen, vermoedde de Pool, meer knuffelen, meer aandacht. Er moest meer geknuffeld worden. Hij nam zich voor er meteen morgen mee te beginnen.

Thuis zei hij eerst niets, zijn vrouw was bezig in de keuken en hij hielp haar. Koken vond hij aangenaam, hij kookte graag voor de mannen op de kazerne. Ook al waren daar de middelen beperkt, hij probeerde er altijd iets feestelijks van te maken.

Wen was Thaise curry aan het maken en de Pool concentreerde zich op de sla die bij de curry werd geserveerd. Pas toen zijn vrouw eindelijk vroeg hoe het was gegaan met de veearts zei hij dat er waarschijnlijk wel een oplossing was gevonden. En daarna zei hij weer een tijdje niets en toen de sla zo ongeveer klaar was vertelde hij dat het beest acupunctuur zou krijgen. Wen begon te lachen. 'Serieus?' Ze lachte hard. Op de grond in de keuken speelde de jongste met een zeef, een pollepel en wat blokjes. Hij zei weer 'ape, ape, ape,' tot zijn moeder hem zijn aapje gaf.

'Serieus,' zei de Pool en vertelde dat de veearts renpaarden behandelde en daarmee resultaten boekte die sommige mensen 'wonderen' noemde en toen wilde Wen weten wat dat kostte, zo'n wonder, ja ze ging vlak voor haar man staan alsof ze hem wilde zoenen, alsof ze verliefd waren en elkaar nog maar een paar weken kenden, alsof hun verlangen nog niet was aangevreten door gewenning en tijd. 'Wat kost zo'n wonder?' vroeg ze. 'Wat moeten ze tegenwoordig hebben voor zo'n wonder?' De Pool keek naar de rijst in de pan, hij deed een pas opzij, roerde wat door de curry terwijl hij het bedrag noemde dat het wonder kostte. Per behandeling. Het was niet één keer een wonder en dan nooit meer, het moest herhaald worden. Wekelijks een wonder. Zoveel had hij begrepen. Zijn vrouw werd stil. Hij keek op. Ze was wit weggetrokken. Dat gebeurde anders nooit, niet als het om geld ging, niet als het om andere zaken ging. 'Jezus,' zei ze, 'dat beest wordt onze ondergang, Geniek.'

Geniek, dat zei ze zelden. Wen liep naar het andere eind van de keuken. Ze had bloemen gekocht, ze vond het fijn als er bloemen in huis waren. De bloemen stonden nog in het papier in een emmertje. Ze haalde het papier van de bos en begon de bloemen te snijden en te schikken. Ze was er lang mee bezig, ze deed het zorgvuldig en terwijl ze met het schikken bezig was zei ze nog een keer: 'Dat beest wordt onze ondergang.' Ze keek haar man niet aan, ze keek naar de bloemen en hij antwoordde: 'Doe niet zo dramatisch, dat is niets voor jou.'

De curry was klaar, hoefde alleen nog te worden opgediend. Wen bracht de vaas naar de woonkamer en toen ze terug was vroeg ze: 'Hoe gaan we dat betalen?'

'Dan gaan we niet naar Griekenland,' zei de Pool lichtelijk geïrriteerd. 'Dan gaan we naar de Eifel. Daar kun je huisjes huren voor bijna niets. Mijn moeder is er geboren.'

'Wat moet ik in de Eifel?' vroeg Wen. 'Wat moet ik daar? Dan kan ik net zo goed thuisblijven. Het regent in de Eifel. Ook al is je moeder er geboren. Ik wil er niet heen.'

'Het regent daar niet altijd,' zei de Pool, 'ook in de Eifel schijnt weleens de zon,' en hij tilde Wen op en hij zette haar op het aanrecht naast de snijplank waar hij net nog tomaten had gesneden voor de salade, alsof zijn verlangens nog niet waren aangevreten door sleur en tijdgebrek, die nu eenmaal bij de mensen horen. Een volwassene zonder tijdgebrek is een overbodig mens. 'Het is voor onze jongen. Ik had geen keus. Ik heb je toch verteld wat hij daar in de stal doet, hij praat met het beest, hij vertelt haar van alles en nog wat en hij gaat daar naar de wc in de stal. Hij poept niet meer in zijn broek omdat hij daar in de stal poept, naast dat beest zit hij daar op zijn hurken. Hij gebruikt stro als wc-papier, maar jij en ik, wij weten dat hij daar gelukkig is, dus wat maakt zo'n bedrag dan uit, desnoods haal ik het van mijn doorlopend krediet.'

Dat had hij niet moeten zeggen. Zijn vrouw, die al die tijd begripvol had geluisterd, liet zich van het aanrecht glijden. Ze zei: 'Ik heb een hekel aan schulden, dat weet je. Geen schulden. Ik kan niet tegen schulden. Ik kan er niet van slapen. Ik kan dan aan niets meer denken, alleen nog aan die schulden. Ook als we seks hebben, dan kan ik alleen nog aan onze schulden denken.' De Pool zei: 'Dan ga ik wel bijklussen op mijn vrije dagen. Ik zal eens aan de jongens op de kazerne vragen of ze iets weten.' Hij zei ook nog: 'Hij heeft meer liefde nodig. We moeten hem meer strelen.'

Toen kwam Borys thuis. Ze hoorden hem thuiskomen, ze hoorden hoe de voordeur werd geopend en gesloten, de jongen zei niets. Ze hoorden hoe hij de woonkamer in liep en toen ze gingen kijken zat hij in de woonkamer aan de eettafel want het was etenstijd.

'Heb je honger?' vroeg Wen.

'Niet echt,' zei de jongen.

'Je bent zo bezweet.'

'Ik heb hard gefietst.'

'Help je even met tafel dekken?'

'Ja,' zei hij en de lange jongen dekte de tafel in stilte. Hij deed het traag, eindelijk konden ze gaan zitten. Wen schepte de curry op en de Pool zei dat het lekker was. Jurek werd in zijn stoel gezet en kreeg een prakje, de Pool kauwde op de salade die hij zelf had gemaakt, tot hij zei: 'Dat dier krijgt acupunctuur. Ik heb het je moeder verteld en ze is blij.'

Wen knikte. 'Ja,' zei ze. 'Ik ben blij dat het dier nog even bij je kan blijven, dat het hopelijk heel lang bij je kan blijven. We zijn blij. Voor jou, Borys.'

Er verscheen een klein lachje op het gezicht van de jongen. En toen vroeg hij: 'Mag ik naar boven?'

'Er is nog mango,' zei Wen.

De jongen at zijn mango haastig, eigenlijk ongeïnteresseerd, het leek de Pool uitgesloten dat zijn jongen ervan genoot terwijl mango iets speciaals was, dat aten ze toch niet elke dag, en toen de jongen zijn portie naar binnen had gewerkt vroeg hij weer of hij naar boven mocht. Wen knikte. 'Ik hou van je,' riep de Pool zijn jongen na en toen zaten ze daar alleen met hun jongste zoon aan tafel, ze luisterden naar het gebrabbel van Jurek ('mango, mmm'), tot Wen hem uit zijn stoeltje tilde om hem naar bed te brengen. 'Hoe zouden ze dat doen?' vroeg ze, 'acupunctuur bij zo'n pony. Breinaalden?'

'Geen idee,' zei de Pool.

De Pool begon de tafel af te ruimen en daarna zei hij: 'Ik heb morgen dienst. Ik ga alvast in bed liggen.'

Hij kroop in bed en later, toen de beide jongens sliepen, kroop Wen bij hem en zijn verlangen was niet helemaal dood maar hij deed er niets mee, want morgen had hij dienst. Het verlangen bewaarde hij voor erna.

De volgende ochtend begroette hij op de kazerne zijn collega's, die eigenlijk zijn tweede familie waren. Hij bladerde wat door de krant, en de dag ging voorbij zoals veel dagen voorbijgingen, met sporten en wachten, de auto's controleren, een oefening. Twee keer rukten ze uit, twee keer was het loos alarm en aan het eind van de middag kregen ze bericht dat ze buiten hun inzetgebied naar een springer moesten. De andere kazerne had zijn handen vol aan een brand in de keuken van een bejaardentehuis.

Ze reden naar de springer. Politie was er al. Er stonden een hoop mensen op het perron. De intercity naar Amsterdam stond stil op het kleine station waar hij normaal gesproken langsraasde. Beckers zei: 'Ik heb altijd zo te doen met die machinisten.'

De Pool keek naar de mensen op het perron en naar de trein. Veel kinderen, jonge kinderen ook. Ze stonden verderop, ze wilden niet naar huis, ze kenden de springer vermoedelijk. De Pool was al in de buurt van de locomotief, waar het was afgezet, waar nieuwsgierige passanten niet meer mochten komen, alleen de hulpdiensten.

In de verte zag hij de ploegchef met de politie praten en met de kinderen die rugzakken om hadden, tassen en frisdrank in hun hand, koptelefoons op hun hoofd. Beckers stond naast de Pool te wachten, zijn handen in de zij. Beckers hield niet van dit soort klusjes, niemand hield ervan. 'Alleen al daarom zou ik nooit machinist willen worden,' zei Beckers.

De Pool wilde eindelijk de rails op gaan om het werk te doen dat eigenlijk geen werk was voor de brandweer, maar de ploegchef kwam naar hem toe en hij zei: 'Jij blijft hier.'

'Waarom?' vroeg de Pool.

'Jij blijft hier,' herhaalde de ploegchef.

'Waarom?' vroeg de Pool nog een keer.

De ploegchef haalde zijn hand over zijn mond en zei: 'Het is jouw jongen. Het is Borys.'

De Pool duwde de ploegchef opzij, hij duwde Beckers opzij, iedereen duwde hij opzij en hij ging als eerste het spoor op. Hij zou zijn jongen van de rails krabben.

Collega's kwamen achter hem aan en wilden hem tegenhouden maar hij sloeg hen van zich af.

Hij wilde helemaal alleen zijn jongen van de rails en van de locomotief krabben.

# III

## *Een wonder*

## 1

'We slepen je erdoorheen,' had de ploegchef gezegd. 'We laten jullie niet in de steek.'

De Pool had uiteraard verlof gekregen en zijn vrouw ook. Nu zaten ze thuis en ze liepen van de ene naar de andere kamer, van beneden naar boven en weer terug. Ze hielden hun jongste zoontje in hun armen, om de beurt, soms legden ze hem in zijn bedje, want hij moest slapen, hun armen werden moe, ze waren bang hem te laten vallen. Ze keken naar hem en ze wisten zonder dat ze dat hoefden uit te spreken dat ze allebei hetzelfde vreesden.

En de Pool vroeg aan zijn vrouw of hun jongste zoontje zijn broer miste, of hij merkte dat hij niet thuis was, of dat het voor hem meer leek alsof Borys op een schoolreisje was. Of ze het hem moesten vertellen, wilde de Pool weten, en wat ze dan zouden moeten vertellen? Wat drong er nu al tot hem door en wat niet? Moesten ze wachten tot later? De Pool vond wachten tot later beter, er kwam wel een moment om het te zeggen, als hij ouder was, als ze hem een foto konden laten zien, maar wanneer dan precies? En Wen zei: 'We kijken wel.' Ze tilde haar jongste zoontje op en bracht hem naar boven, naar de commode om zijn luier te verschonen. Wat zag zij als zij naar de jongen keek, die nu de enige jongen was, de jongen die ze misschien hadden verwaarloosd omdat alle aandacht was uitgegaan naar de poepbroeken en de pony en de stilte van zijn oudere broer, zijn zwijgzaamheid die soms op nukkigheid leek, zijn behoefte om alleen te worden gelaten, om niet te worden lastiggevallen, maar Wen had altijd gezegd: 'Zo zijn jongens. Meisjes zijn heel anders.'

Ze gingen de trap op en af en hij keek naar hun jongste

kind dat door het huis werd gedragen, maar de Pool zag alleen de rails. Hij had het gevoel dat hij vanaf nu ook Jurek op de rails zou zien, losse onderdelen, nooit meer een geheel. Hij was er niet bang voor, hij zou ook zo van deze jongen houden, gefragmenteerd en wel. De Pool zou van de linkervoet van Jurek houden, van de rechterarm en van een oor, een oog. Van elk lichaamsdeel afzonderlijk. God of wat voor God doorging moest er maar weer een geheel van maken.

De mannen van de C-ploeg kwamen langs, ze gingen op de bank in de woonkamer zitten en op extra stoelen die de Pool uit andere kamers had gehaald, er moesten nog wat tuinstoelen aan te pas komen, en de ploegchef zei: 'Als we te veel zijn moeten jullie het zeggen.'

'Jullie zijn niet te veel,' antwoordde de Pool.

De ouders van Wen kwamen, ze bleven niet lang want ze waren oud en het was zwaar voor hen. Ze somden alle familieleden op die er zelf voor hadden gekozen en dat waren er nog best wat. Een oudoom, een tante, een overgrootvader, een achternichtje, een neef. Toen ze niemand meer wisten op te sommen gingen ze de mensen in het dorp na die er zelf voor hadden gekozen en daarbij gingen ze ver terug, ongeveer tot 1950. Daarna refereerde de moeder van Wen nog aan mannen die zich hadden doodgedronken, want dat waren eigenlijk ook mannen die er zelf voor hadden gekozen. Ten slotte gingen ze naar huis, want ze wisten niet waar ze heen moesten met hun verdriet, ze wilden hun dochter er niet mee lastigvallen.

Er kwamen collega's van Wen op bezoek, zij kwamen met ernstige gezichten en sommigen van hen hadden betraande ogen. Die tranen stonden de Pool tegen, hij hield er niet van, het leek of de collega's van Wen zich verdriet toe-eigenden dat niet van hen was. De C-ploeg kwam opnieuw langs. Door hun harde stemmen waren de collega's van Wen niet meer hoorbaar. Het bezoek van Wen vertrok op een gegeven moment, de mannen van de C-ploeg bleven. Er was koffie en iemand had vlaai meegenomen. En de ploegchef zei nog een keer: 'We slepen je erdoorheen.' Hij was kort van stof, hij zei het hoognodige, maar wat hij zei was zinvol. Juist daarom respecteerde de Pool hem en hij had ook humor, al liet hij dat niet vaak blijken. Stille humor, verborgen humor.

Zo zat de Pool stil maar toch ook trots naast zijn mannen. Trots dat hij zulke collega's had, trots dat hij een vrouw en een zoon en een huis en een baan had, hij vertelde niet dat hij alleen nog losse onderdelen van zijn zonen zag, een linkervoet, een oor, een neus. De mannen wisselden anekdotes uit, ze haalden herinneringen op aan collega's die met pensioen waren gegaan en die van grappen en kattenkwaad hielden, het soort kattenkwaad dat tegenwoordig niet meer werd uitgehaald, niet meer werd getolereerd. Sommige mannen gingen weg en kwamen terug met bier maar over de reden dat ze hier zaten spraken ze niet, over de jongen die was verdwenen, die was gestruikeld, zo zei de Pool het als ernaar gevraagd werd. 'Hij is gestruikeld,' zei de Pool als het moest. De ene dood is een schande, de andere minder en de Pool was niet van plan te leven met meer schande dan strikt noodzakelijk.

Beckers ging naar de wc, hij kwam terug en hij zei: 'Jullie gang kan wel een likje verf gebruiken. Laat ons dat doen.' En Beckers en de andere mannen gingen verf halen om de gang te verven, terwijl de Pool en Wen in de woonkamer zaten met hun jongste zoontje op schoot. De Pool had willen meehelpen, maar Beckers zei: 'Blijf zitten. Wij doen dit wel.'

En Wen zei: 'Misschien moeten we op reis.'

De Pool antwoordde: 'Ik moet daar niet aan denken.'

Iemand van slachtofferhulp belde, of ze geheel vrijblijvend behoefte hadden aan een gesprek. 'Iemand van slachtofferhulp is aan de lijn,' zei de Pool tegen zijn vrouw.

'Of we geheel vrijblijvend behoefte hebben aan een gesprek.'

'Wij zijn geen slachtoffers,' zei Wen. 'En we hebben geen behoefte aan een gesprek.'

Dat herhaalde de Pool door de telefoon, de dame zei dat als ze er later misschien anders over zouden denken ze altijd konden bellen. Toen zei Wen: 'Laat maar komen, dan zijn we ervan af.' Ze huilde als niemand haar zag en niemand haar hoorde. Dan nam de Pool haar in zijn armen en hij zei: 'We hadden pech, we hebben ook lang geluk gehad.'

'Ja,' zei ze, 'lang hebben we geluk gehad. Hier moeten we alleen doorheen, hier moeten we ieder op onze eigen manier doorheen.'

Er kwam een mevrouw van slachtofferhulp en die praatte en stelde vragen en toen zei Wen: 'We gaan hier op onze eigen manier mee om, we hebben eigenlijk niemand nodig. Zeker geen professionals.'

'We zijn geen slachtoffers,' legde de Pool uit. 'We zijn de ouders van een jongen die pech had. We hebben nog een jongen en we gaan ervan uit dat die jongen geen pech zal hebben.'

Ze zaten stokstijf op de bank en toen de vrouw van slachtofferhulp opstond zei de Pool: 'Het verdriet is een uitslaande brand maar die brand gaan we met z'n tweeën blussen. Toch fijn dat u bent gekomen.'

Een paar dagen later kwam de C-ploeg om de gang af te maken en toen zei Beckers: 'Jullie slaapkamer kan vast ook een likje verf gebruiken. Vind je het goed als wij dat doen? Dat slaapt stukken beter, in een vers geverfde slaapkamer.'

Dat vonden de Pool en Wen prima, als ze dat bedoelden met 'we slepen jullie erdoorheen', dan moesten ze de slaapkamer een likje verf geven. Terwijl ze beneden zaten met hun jongste zoontje werd boven met meubels gesleept en daarna werd er geverfd.

Daarvoor was de ploegchef brandweerman geworden,

daarvoor waren de mannen van de C-ploeg brandweerman geworden, om mensen ergens doorheen te slepen. Al was het vroeger beter, toen er meer saamhorigheid was, de C-ploeg leefde nog in een verleden dat beter was geweest, de C-ploeg was niet modern, deze ploeg was anders. En de vrouwen van de mannen van de C-ploeg kwamen langs met eten. Ze zeiden: 'Jullie hebben vast geen zin om te koken.' De vrouw van Beckers kwam bij de mannen staan. Ze pakte de hand van de Pool en zei: 'Ik heb drie kinderen, ik zou willen dat ik er een aan jullie kon geven.'

'Dat is heel aardig,' zei de Pool. 'Maar dat hoeft niet.'

En ze aten, Wen en hij, ze aten met tegenzin maar ze aten. De vrouwen van de C-ploeg brachten nog meer eten en Wen en de Pool zeiden tegen elkaar dat het best lekker was, al proefden ze niet veel en al had de Pool nauwelijks honger en Wen zei: 'Ik heb al zoveel zoetigheid naar binnen gewerkt. Ik zit vol.' Maar ze had nauwelijks zoetigheid naar binnen gewerkt. Ze zaten gewoon vol. Propvol.

De mannen wilden verdergaan met verven, er waren nog kamers die ze niet hadden geverfd en ook die konden wel een fris kleurtje gebruiken, een was er zelfs over begonnen dat ze de riolering konden ontstoppen maar dat was nergens voor nodig. De riolering hoefde niet te worden ontstopt. De mannen wilden iets te doen hebben. Het stilzitten maakte hen gek. Dat begreep de Pool maar hij zei: 'Zo is het genoeg.' Want dat gesleep met meubels en dat geverf begon Wen op de zenuwen te werken.

In de pas geverfde gang stonden ze met z'n allen bij elkaar, de mannen van de C-ploeg, ze pasten er nauwelijks in, half op elkaar stonden ze, de een hing op de ander. De ploegchef maakte een foto en hij zei tegen de Pool: 'Kom erbij. Jij hoort erbij.' En toen werd er nog een foto gemaakt. Met z'n allen keken ze naar het schermpje, tevreden, verenigd, solidair, dit was wat kameraden waren, dit was erdoorheen slepen. Ze hadden er weer iemand doorheen gesleept.

Daarna ging al het bezoek weg en eindelijk waren ze alleen thuis, Wen en de Pool. Ze stonden voor hun bed als kinderen voor de kooi van de leeuw in de dierentuin en ze roken de verf in de slaapkamer. De mannen hadden het snel en goed gedaan. Ze gingen op hun bed liggen met hun jongste zoontje tussen hen in.

De Pool vroeg: 'Is die verflucht wel goed voor hem?' Maar Wen zei: 'Als wij ertegen kunnen, kan hij er ook tegen.'

De crematie was aan de Pool voorbijgegaan. Hij wist dat hij erbij was geweest, al voelde het niet zo. Hij had niets kunnen en niets willen zeggen, hij was naar voren gegaan op aandringen van Wen en daar had hij toch wat uit zijn mond gekregen: 'Ik kan niets zeggen.' Dat had hij gezegd. Op aanraden van Wen was hij zo blijven staan. 'Zo ben je toch normaal ook,' had Wen gezegd. 'Je staat daar en je zegt niet zoveel.' Daarom was hij daar blijven staan, zoals hij normaal was.

Wen had wel iets gezegd, heel mooi, heel ontroerend, wat ze precies had gezegd was hij vergeten, hij had er ook niet goed naar kunnen luisteren, en de juffrouw van de basisschool had gesproken en de mentor van de middelbare school, meer een kind dan een man, met een hoop jeugdpuistjes, en twee jongens uit de klas van Borys hadden een gedicht voorgedragen dat niet rijmde maar dat toch iedereen ontroerde en uit Haarlem was de vader van de Pool gekomen die niets met het verleden van doen wilde hebben maar voor deze gelegenheid maakte hij een uitzondering. Hij zat daar met zijn nieuwe gezinnetje en hij keek zoals hij altijd keek, dreigend en afwezig tegelijkertijd. Hij keek als iemand die besefte dat het leven niet om te lachen was maar zo keek hij niet alleen op crematies, zo keek hij ook op bruiloften en als hij vroeger naar de kermis ging keek hij net zo. Hij had de Pool omhelsd en de Pool had het laten gebeuren, de omhelzing door de vader die het verleden had afgezworen om het lijden te ontvluchten, en daarna had de Pool het gevoel dat zijn kaak van ijzer was. De Pool dacht dat zijn mond niet meer goed dichtging, alsof die klemde en altijd op een kier zou blijven staan. Gelukkig was de vader van de Pool niet begonnen over genade en de hemel, want hij was een man van de oude stempel en zulke mannen meenden dat er geen genade was voor hen die moedwillig waren gestruikeld. En de mannen van de C-ploeg zaten er, met hun vrouwen, sommigen hadden hun kinderen meegenomen. De oudere kinderen, die het wel konden verdragen, die je dit niet wilde besparen omdat het bij het leven hoorde. Voor wie het misschien wel goed was om het een keer mee te maken.

En toen was het voorbij. Ze gingen naar huis.

De ploegchef had gezegd: 'Laat weten als je weer bij ons terug wilt komen. Geen haast. De dingen hebben tijd nodig.'

De Pool nam zijn tijd, want de honger was niet teruggekomen, hij at met lange tanden, met meer dan normale tegenzin, soms had hij het gevoel dat hij moest kotsen als hij een hap naar binnen werkte. Om de drie dagen belde hij de ploegchef en hij zei: 'De dingen hebben nog iets meer tijd nodig.'

'Begrijp ik,' antwoordde de ploegchef.

Maar tegenover Wen wilde de Pool er niet over beginnen, hij wilde niet laten blijken dat hij op het punt stond over te geven als hij moest eten.

De dame van slachtofferhulp kwam nog een keer langs. 'We kunnen het echt alleen af,' antwoordde Wen. De dame liet haar visitekaartje achter en Wen zei tegen haar man: 'Ik hoef niet uit te huilen bij een onbekende.' De Pool knikte. 'Die lui van slachtofferhulp zijn hardnekkig.'

En na een week of drie was Wen het die zei: 'Ik ga aan het werk. Ik heb gebeld dat ik er morgen weer ben.'

‘Dat is goed,’ zei de Pool. ‘Ik denk dat ik ook weer eens ga beginnen. We moeten verder.’

‘We moeten verder,’ antwoordde Wen, ‘we hebben nog een kind.’

En die avond lagen ze in bed, Wen tikte op haar horloge en ze zei: ‘Het wordt wel weer eens tijd.’

‘Wat?’ vroeg de Pool.

Ze bleef maar op haar horloge tikken. ‘Wat wordt weer eens tijd?’ vroeg de Pool. ‘Waar heb je het over?’

Toen deed ze haar horloge af en legde het op het nachtkastje. ‘We hebben elkaar zo lang niet meer aangeraakt,’ zei ze. ‘Dat onze jongen er niet meer is betekent toch niet dat we elkaar niet meer hoeven aan te raken?’

Hij wilde het ook wel, haar aanraken, graag zelfs, en even deed hij het ook, met zijn grote handen, maar daarna zei hij: ‘Laten we in zijn kamer gaan kijken.’

Hij stond als eerste op en zij volgde hem naar de deur die ze al die dagen niet hadden geopend. Ze hadden er niet over gesproken, het was hun allebei duidelijk dat ze die kamer niet moesten betreden. Alleen toen Wen had gezegd dat het wel weer tijd werd om elkaar aan te raken had de Pool aan de kamer gedacht en hij was nieuwsgierig geworden. Hij wilde die kamer toch zien. In zijn onderbroek liep hij erheen en Wen volgde hem in haar nachthemd dat feitelijk niet meer was dan een te lang T-shirt. Hij opende de deur, deed het licht aan, hij snoof de geur op. Hier rook het nog naar de jongen, of verbeeldde hij zich dat?

Ze liepen op hun blote voeten door zijn kamer. Het bed was onopgemaakt, blauwe lakens, er zat een rode streep van een stift op de hoes die er in de was nooit uit was gegaan. Op de grond lag een onderbroek, de Pool raapte hem op, rook eraan. Het was alsof de jongen elk moment thuis kon komen. Computerspelletjes op de grond, wat kleren, niet eens heel veel, *Donald Ducks*, andere strips, voetbalplaatjes, een paar oude munten in een kast die hij ooit van een buurman had gekregen, waarna hij had verklaard: 'Ik denk dat ik oude munten ga verzamelen. Weten jullie hoe dat moet?' Vervolgens hadden ze hem nooit meer over oude munten gehoord.

Ze gingen naar zijn bureau: pennen, potloden, een dode mug, het paardenpaspoort, een oude skibril, een paar schriften. De Pool opende een schrift. Taaloefeningen. Een tweede schrift, meer taaloefeningen. Een derde schrift. Een bladzijde was uit het schrift gescheurd en er vervolgens weer in gestopt. Op die bladzijde stond: 'Ik heb geen vrienden. Ik zal nooit vrienden hebben. Ik heb nooit vrienden gehad.' Wen las over zijn schouder mee. De Pool sloot het schrift, legde het terug op precies de plek waar hij het had gevonden alsof niemand mocht weten dat hij in deze kamer was geweest. Toen gingen ze op het bed van hun jongen zitten.

Onder het hoofdkussen vonden ze een gymbroek en een reep chocolade die voor de helft was opgegeten, wit uitgeslagen. 'Ik heb zo vaak tegen hem gezegd,' zei Wen, 'eet geen chocola in bed. Daar krijg je vieze vlekken van.'

Haar stem klonk hees, alsof ze avondenlang in de kroeg had gezeten met sterkedrank en veel sigaretten.

'Ja,' zei de Pool. 'Dat heb je vaak gezegd.'

Hij stond op van het bed en Wen kwam achter hem aan, de chocolade nam ze mee. Ze sloten de deur van de kamer van hun jongen en allebei wisten ze zeker – ja, dat ze het allebei wisten daaraan twijfelde de Pool niet – dat ze die deur voorlopig niet meer zouden openen.

In hun kamer rook het niet naar de jongen maar nog altijd naar verf. Dit keer tikte Wen niet op haar horloge, het lag daar stil op haar nachtkastje. De Pool keek ernaar en hij besefte dat het leven verderging en dus ook het seksleven, dat ging net zo goed verder. Steeds verder en verder tot het stopte. Ze legde haar hoofd op zijn arm en ze zei: 'Hij had geen vrienden.'

'Kennelijk,' zei de Pool. Hij keek naar zijn vrouw en hij twijfelde er niet aan dat Wen zijn vrouw was maar hij wist even niet meer hoe het moest, intimiteit. Man zijn. Verlangen. Net als het verlangen naar eten, was ook dit verlangen gedoofd. Er was alleen nog een herinnering aan het verlangen. Vaag kon hij zich voor de geest halen hoe het was als je dat voelde.

Wen was bezig het alarm op haar telefoon in te stellen want morgen ging ze weer aan het werk. De kleuters hadden haar nodig.

'Ze stonden weleens voor de deur,' zei Wen, 'vriendjes. Vroeger. Dan zei hij altijd: zeg maar dat ik er niet ben. Hij wilde graag alleen zijn.'

'Zo is dat,' zei de Pool. 'Hij wilde graag alleen zijn.' En hij probeerde zijn Wen over haar hoofd te strelen, maar het ging niet goed. Hij kon de tederheid niet opbrengen. Zijn hand leek schuurpapier.

'Misschien hadden we verder door moeten vragen,' zei Wen, 'al heb ik dat zo vaak gedaan. Zo vaak.'

'Hij was een stille jongen,' zei de Pool. 'Onze Borys.' Moeheid overviel hem, toch wist hij dat hij niet zou kunnen slapen.

'Hadden we aan de juf moeten vragen of hij misschien gepest werd?' vroeg Wen. 'Of aan zijn mentor?'

'Waarom?' antwoordde de Pool. 'Was er aanleiding toe?'

'We kunnen het nog vragen.'

'Nu is het te laat,' zei de Pool.

'We hebben Jurek nog,' zei Wen terwijl ze met haar telefoon prutste, 'als Jurek ook zo stil is moeten we doorvragen. We zullen niet meer denken: zo is hij nu eenmaal.'

'Nee,' zei de Pool. 'Dat zullen we nooit meer denken.'

Hij deed het licht uit en terwijl hij wakker lag merkte hij dat ook Wen slapeloos naast hem lag maar allebei zeiden ze niets.

De volgende dag toen Wen naar haar werk was, de dingen hadden immers genoeg tijd gekregen, en de Pool alleen thuis was met zijn overgebleven jongen, hij had nog geen dienst, die begon pas de dag erna, werd hij in de middag gebeld. Het nummer stond niet in zijn telefoon.

'Ze is beter,' hoorde hij een mannenstem zeggen.

'Wie is beter?' vroeg de Pool.

Aan de andere kant van de lijn werd gelachen. 'Wie denk je zelf?' vroeg de stem.

'Ik weet het echt niet,' zei de Pool, met zijn overgebleven jongetje op zijn arm.

'Hier spreekt Klepp,' zei de stem nu plotseling scherp en met dat onmiskenbare lichte accent. 'Klepp heeft weer een wonder verricht. Klepp kan het niet laten, hij verricht om de haverklap wonderen. Het oude kreupele meisje is niet meer kreupel. Ze is nog wel oud, daar kan ik niets aan doen.'

'O jezus,' zei de Pool, 'de pony.'

'Ja de pony, over wie dacht je dan dat ik het had? Ben je het beest helemaal vergeten? Het ene moment is het leven een tranendal zonder het oude meisje, het andere moment weten ze niet meer wie het oude meisje is. Altijd hetzelfde met de mensen. De rekeningen zijn ook niet betaald.'

'De rekeningen,' zei de Pool en hij liep naar de keuken waar wat ongeopende post lag.

'Ja, de rekeningen,' herhaalde Klepp. 'Niet dat ik uitsluitend voor het geld werk, maar als ik van tevoren zeg wat een wonder kost dan wil ik toch ook graag voor dat wonder worden betaald als het eenmaal verricht is. Ik doe het niet voor het geld, maar ik moet ook leven. Ook de veearts staat niet boven het geld, al zou hij dat soms wel willen.'

Tussen de ongeopende post vond de Pool de rekeningen. Er waren drie brieven van Klepp, twee rekeningen en een herinnering.

'Weet u niet wat er gebeurd is?' vroeg de Pool. 'Hebt

u er niet over gelezen? Het heeft in de krant gestaan, de rouwadvertentie.'

'Wat had ik moeten lezen?' vroeg Klepp en hij klonk geergerd alsof het hem tegenstond dat er dingen in de krant stonden die niet over hem en zijn wonderen gingen.

'Onze jongen is er niet meer.'

Even was Klepp stil. Toen zei hij: 'Dat spijt me. Gecondoleerd. Dat spijt me enorm.' En daaraan voegde hij toe: 'Ik volg het regionale nieuws ook niet zo, ik lees eigenlijk alleen buitenlandse kranten.'

De Pool scheurde de enveloppen open en hoewel de bedragen hem bekend waren schrok hij er toch weer van, misschien nu nog meer omdat de jongen er niet meer was.

'Wil je het wonder nog zien?' vroeg Klepp. 'Zal ik toelichten wat ik heb gedaan? Misschien brengt het verlichting als je het wonder hebt gezien.' En voor het eerst klonk Klepp aarzelend alsof hij zelf ook besefte dat zijn wonderen het soort wonderen waren dat uiteindelijk niemand verlichting bracht.

'Ik wil het wel zien,' zei de Pool. 'Wanneer kunnen we afspreken?'

'Ik kan vanmiddag langskomen,' zei Klepp. 'Ik moet toch in de buurt van de boerderij zijn.'

De Pool zei dat hij er over een uurtje kon zijn. Hij propte de rekeningen in zijn achterzak en hees Jurek in een jasje, deed hem wanten aan, zette hem een muts op, gebreid door de moeder van Wen.

'We gaan de pony van je broer bekijken,' zei hij tegen zijn overgebleven jongen. 'We gaan een wonder bekijken.'

# 2

Voor zijn auto liep de jager met zijn hoedje op en zijn tas in zijn hand parmantig heen en weer alsof hij de wacht hield. De grond was kennelijk nog altijd te modderig voor de tas, ook al was het een oude tas die vast al met veel viezigheid in aanraking was gekomen.

Nadat de Pool zijn auto had geparkeerd en zijn overgebleven jongen uit het autostoeltje had getild hield de jager op met heen en weer lopen en werd hij weer veearts. Hij stond stil en keek met de strenge maar toch begrijpende blik van de autoriteit hoe de Pool met het kind op zijn arm naar hem toe kwam gelopen. Genezen was zijn vak, jagen slechts zijn hobby.

De boer zat weer voor het raam, zijn kin rustte op een hand. De Pool kon niet zien of de boer sliep of de boel in de gaten hield, hij had ook niet de moeite genomen goed te kijken. Het deed er niet meer toe wat de boer deed nu zijn jongen hier niet meer kwam. Zijn aandacht werd in beslag genomen door de veearts, op wie hij zijn hoop had gevestigd toen zijn jongen nog leefde, de veearts die rekeningen stuurde alsof de pony een renpaard was waarvoor kosten noch moeite gespaard dienden te worden. Nu hoefde er geen hoop meer op de veearts te worden gevestigd, de zaak hoefde alleen te worden afgehandeld. En was zijn jongen geen renpaard geweest voor wie alleen het beste goed genoeg was? Nee, een renpaard was de jongen niet geweest, eerder een knol die iets voorttrok wat hem te zwaar was.

'Nogmaals gecondoleerd,' zei Klepp. Hij sprak zacht alsof het een geheim was dat de peuter niet mocht horen. Het geheim van de dood, het geheim van het spreken over de dood. Daarna keek hij naar de jongen en hij vroeg: 'Is dat zijn broertje?'

'Dat is Jurek,' zei de Pool. 'Dat is onze andere jongen.'

De veearts kietelde de andere jongen onder zijn kin en over zijn wang en zijn neus en hij vroeg, opnieuw op die plechtige toon: 'Hoe is het eigenlijk gebeurd? Was hij ziek?'

'Hij is gestruikeld,' zei de Pool. 'Op het station. Toen de intercity naar Amsterdam voorbijkwam. Hij had die dag niet veel gegeten. Hij was duizelig.'

'Wat vreselijk,' zei de veearts. 'Had hij epilepsie? Komt ook bij dieren voor, maar anders.'

Zonder verder nog iets te zeggen liep hij naar de stal en de Pool kwam met de andere jongen op zijn arm achter hem aan. Nu hij hier over dit pad liep, waar hij alleen voor zijn jongen had gelopen, werd het verleden levendig, levendiger dan al die dagen dat hij met zijn vrouw rusteloos door het eigen huis had gedwaald. Toen was het verleden langzaam verbleekt, het was schimmig geworden, onwerkelijk, iets wat losstond van het nu en de toekomst. Het verleden leek alleen te hebben bestaan opdat je het kon vergeten, opdat je de deur naar dat verleden kon dichtdoen en je vervolgens kon zeggen: Dat was het dan. Die deur gaat nooit meer open. Hier op het erf van de boer voelde het anders en even had de Pool de sensatie dat hij voor de stal de fiets van zijn jongen zag liggen en dat hij in de stal de jongen naast het beest op zijn hurken zou zien zitten met stro in zijn hand, zijn vader verbaasd en verwijtend aankijkend, niet begrijpend waarom hij nu weer werd gestoord.

De veearts opende het hok. Het dier stond erbij zoals altijd, verstild, onaangedaan. Zoals de boer in zijn rolstoel voor het raam zat zo stond de pony in haar hok.

'Ja,' zei Klepp, 'het oude meisje heeft natuurlijk weinig aanspraak meer.' En hij kietelde het oude meisje op allerlei plekken met de vertrouwdheid van iemand die zijn leven lang jonge en oude meisjes heeft gekieteld.

Met Jurek op zijn arm deed de Pool een paar stappen dichterbij. Hoe zag het wonder eruit, dat wilde hij nu wel zien. Daarvoor was hij gekomen.

'We gaan even stappen,' zei Klepp. 'Buiten kun je het goed zien.'

Daarop leidde de veearts met gemak maar ook met een zekere ruwheid, ongeduldig eigenlijk, het oude meisje naar buiten, het modderige pad op dat naar het weiland voerde, want daar, zo had hij gezegd, zou hij het wonder demonstreren.

Het oude meisje liep naast de veearts, maar aangezien de Pool haar nog nooit eerder had zien lopen kon hij het verschil tussen het wonder en het gebrek aan wonder niet herkennen. Hij vroeg zich alleen af of dit het was, of hij hiervoor was gekomen.

'Niet meer kreupel,' zei de veearts, 'wel oud en eenzaam. Ze zal wel naar de paardenslager gaan.' En hij liet het beest nog een paar keer langs de Pool paraderen. Kennelijk wilde hij bewijzen dat zijn hoge rekeningen terecht waren, geen kwestie van hebzucht, een betrekkelijk bescheiden beloning voor een miraculeuze redding. Daarna leidde hij het dier weer haar hok in, waar de eenzaamheid en de ouderdom door het hooi en het dak draaglijk werden gemaakt. Er was genoeg gedemonstreerd, lang had het niet geduurd. Hier moest de Pool genoegen mee nemen.

Hij begreep er eigenlijk niets van. Niet waarom hij was gekomen en niet waarom de veearts hem had laten komen. Wilde de man er zeker van zijn dat de rekeningen ook onder deze omstandigheden werden betaald? Hij liep achter dier en man aan, verwonderd en nu ook tamelijk uitgeput. Deze plek viel hem zwaar, misschien nog zwaarder dan de kamer van zijn jongen, die voorlopig niet geopend zou worden. Alles hier deed hem aan zijn jongen en de afzonderlijke delen van die jongen denken. Met terugwerkende kracht leek het alsof de intercity naar Amsterdam dwars door deze stal raasde, dwars door de boerderij, dwars door het weiland. Het was de Pool gewoon niet eerder opgevallen. Hij dacht nu na over de paardenslager over wie de veearts net zo achteloos had gesproken als over het jagen, maar dan met minder enthousiasme. Het jagen was subliem, de paardenslager was hooguit noodzakelijk.

En toch weigerde de Pool te geloven dat de veearts uitsluitend voor de paardenslager wonderen verrichtte. Hij had hem daarop willen aanspreken. Dit is zonde, had hij willen zeggen, slachten is niet nodig. Ze is genezen. Maar nog voor hij dat kon doen zei de veearts: 'Voor menselijke consumptie zal ze niet meer geschikt zijn, in de dierentuin kunnen ze zo'n oud meisje altijd nog wel gebruiken.'

'Moet ze naar de dierentuin?' vroeg de Pool en hij sprak over het oude meisje alsof hij er al niets meer mee te maken had. Het woord 'dierentuin' had hem van zijn à propos gebracht. Het beest was van zijn jongen geweest en nu de jongen er niet meer was had hij zich over het dier moeten ontfermen. Hij verried Borys door dat niet te doen. Het was de autoritaire uitstraling van Klepp die hem in de verdediging drukte, die hem onderdanig maakte. De onderdanigheid had hij van zijn vader en in zijn vader had hij die onderdanigheid altijd veracht. De vader van de Pool was een bange man die zijn hoofd boog voor alles wat autoriteit en rijkdom uitstraalde.

'De dieren in de dierentuin moeten ook eten,' zei de veearts, 'maar zij stellen minder hoge kwaliteitseisen aan het voedsel dan wij mensen. Ik heb een wonder verricht dat de leeuw en de tijger straks zullen verorberen. Nou ja, zo gaat het.' En daarop tikte de arts de Pool gretig op zijn schouder. Hij deed het een beetje op dezelfde manier als waarop hij het oude meisje had gekieteld. 'Denk er rustig over na,' zei hij, 'geen haast. Het is jammer dat het voor niets was maar niets is echt voor niets. Overal is betekenis, alles betekent iets en de meeste dingen betekenen veel te veel, dat moet de arts elke dag opnieuw vaststellen en de jager ook. Ik ga alvast terug, dan zeg ik de boer nog even gedag. Die is ook oud en eenzaam.'

Daarna verliet de veearts het hok en de Pool bleef alleen met het oude meisje en zijn andere jongen op zijn arm die wat brabbelde. ('Ape, auto. Auto, ape.' Tot de Pool zei: 'Dat is geen ape, dat is een pony.') Hij liep door de stal, nog altijd onwennig zonder Borys, zonder zijn aanwezigheid, hij bekeek de hoek waar hij zijn jongen op de hurken had zien zitten maar er lag niets meer. 'Ja, hier,' zei hij tegen het kind op zijn arm, 'hier heeft jouw broer geleefd. Hier ging hij heen als hij uit school kwam.' Zo voelde het. Zijn jongen had in de stal geleefd, elders had hij geëxisteerd.

Het kind op zijn arm leek te kijken, het leek te luisteren, het overgebleven kind, verder reageerde het niet. Toen de Pool alle hoeken van de stal had bekeken, alsof hij toch nog verwachtte dat er sporen van zijn jongen te vinden waren, ging hij voor de pony staan, het oude meisje op wie wonderen waren verricht, wonderen die tevergeefs waren gebleken, daar kon de veearts noch het oude meisje zelf iets aan doen.

Hij keek het dier in de ogen en in die ogen zag hij niets en alles tegelijkertijd, alles wat je erin wilde kon je erin zien, maar niets was ook prima. 'Wat heeft hij jou allemaal verteld?' vroeg hij zacht. 'Wat heeft mijn jongen allemaal tegen jou gezegd?'

Een stekende jaloezie kwam in hem op. Rouw was een woord dat hij al die dagen had vermeden, rouw was iets voor anderen, mensen die niet sterk waren. Hij was verdrietig maar staand voor de pony besefte hij dat rouw niets was in vergelijking met de jaloezie die hij nu voelde. Zijn laatste weken had zijn jongen de voorkeur gegeven aan een oud en kreupel dier boven zijn eigen ouders. Zijn geheimen had hij met dat dier gedeeld. Goed, zijn ouders hadden hem gestimuleerd het huis uit te gaan, vrienden te maken, minder eenkennig te zijn maar moesten ze daarom worden ingeruild voor een pony? Hadden ze die straf verdiend? Had hij hen willen straffen, hun jongen, was zijn dood niets anders geweest dan een straf en waren zij te stom geweest om de reden voor de straf te begrijpen?

Het dier bleef maar kijken en even had de Pool de krankzinnige gedachte dat het oude meisje zou antwoorden, dat het hem alles zou vertellen wat hij wilde weten als hij het maar vroeg.

'Wat heeft hij jou allemaal verteld?' vroeg hij nog een keer, maar er kwam geen antwoord. Het dier reageerde niet op zijn stem, het stond stokstijf voor hem. Zou het net zo stokstijf voor de paardenslager staan? Zou het dan eindelijk spreken? Trok het dan eindelijk zijn bek open? Durfde het oog in oog met de dood eindelijk de waarheid te zeggen?

Zijn overgebleven jongen begon te jammeren. Had hij honger? Zat de muts te diep over zijn ogen? 'Rustig,' zei hij. 'We gaan zo naar huis.'

Even wilde de Pool het dier knuffelen zoals hij zijn jongen weleens had geknuffeld. Te weinig, maar toch. De Pool wilde het dier tegen zich aan drukken, het oude, eenzame dier dat volgens deskundigen naar de paardenslager moest worden gebracht, maar in plaats van te strelen sloeg hij. Hij sloeg met zijn vuist op de neus van de pony. Wie niet vrijwillig sprak moest leren onvrijwillig te spreken. Het dier begon te trillen, bleef hem aankijken. Het accepteerde de slag zoals het dit hok en het wonder had geaccepteerd. 'Neem me niet kwalijk,' zei de Pool en voorzichtig ging hij met zijn hand over het hoofd van het dier. 'Neem me niet kwalijk,' herhaalde hij. 'Oud meisje.'

Daarop verliet hij vlug het hok. Hier mocht niemand achter komen. Wat was er in hem gevaren? Hij had het dier van zijn jongen geslagen omdat het niet wilde spreken. Gelukkig had de overgebleven jongen geen idee wat er was gebeurd. Hij had gekeken maar hij had niets gezien. De Pool sloot het hek met de haast van een indringer. Zijn overgebleven jongen huilde nu en uit zijn jaszak haalde de Pool een koekje waarop de jongen begon te knabbelen.

Voor zijn auto wachtte Klepp. 'De boer wil je spreken,' verklaarde hij, zakelijker dan hij al die tijd daarvoor had gesproken. De lust om wonderen te verrichten en erover te vertellen leek te zijn verdwenen. 'Het spijt me dat het allemaal voor niets was,' zei Klepp. 'Ik heb mijn best gedaan, ik kwam te laat. Als ik eerder was gekomen, wie weet...'

'Eerder?' vroeg de Pool.

De veearts schudde zijn hoofd alsof de vraag onbetamelijk was. 'Ik weet voor wie je dit allemaal hebt willen doen. Haal maar tien procent van het totaalbedrag af. Dat is het minste.'

De zakelijkheid was mededogen. Tien procent was in elk geval iets.

'Dank u,' zei de Pool. Als zijn vrouw er was geweest had ze er twintig procent van gemaakt, maar zo was hij niet. Hij vond dit al lastig.

Jurek huilde nu niet meer en Klepp stapte in zijn auto. Zijn tas had hij op de achterbank gezet met een tederheid die de Pool verraste. Het leek alsof Klepp de chauffeur was van zijn tas, de tas waarmee hij wonderen verrichtte. Toen reed hij weg.

Daar zat de boer, die hem wilde spreken. Eerst dat afhandelen, daarna kon de Pool naar huis.

Dit keer hoorde de boer het bezoek binnenkomen, want hij wendde zijn rolstoel meteen na binnenkomst in de richting van de Pool en hij nam de bezoeker op. Van top tot teen. De konen van de boer waren rood en zijn huid was geliger dan de vorige keer. Hij opende zijn mond, om iets te zeggen meende de Pool, maar hij hoestte. Een rochel met slijm die hij niet uitspoog maar weer inslikte. Tussen zijn voortanden, ongetwijfeld een kunstgebit, kleefde iets groens, spinazie of een stukje sla, de Pool zei er niets van. Wat tussen de tanden van de mensen zat was hun eigen verantwoordelijkheid.

'U wilde me spreken,' zei de Pool.

De boer hoestte nog een paar keer, nu zonder dat er slijm loskwam. Toen zei hij: 'Ik neem aan dat je ervan af wilt.' Het spreken viel hem niet makkelijk, desondanks sprak hij met vuur, het vuur van de bitterheid waarop de Pool hem al eerder had betrapt.

'Ik heb nog geen beslissing genomen,' zei de Pool en hij verplaatste zijn jongste van zijn ene naar zijn andere arm.

'Het heeft niet geholpen,' ging de boer verder alsof de Pool niets had gezegd. 'Had ik je van tevoren kunnen vertellen. Mensen blijven niet leven voor een oud paard. Ze blijven niet leven voor een oud mens, laat staan voor een paard.'

'Waar hebt u het over?' vroeg de Pool en zijn gedachten dwaalden naar de boerin die boven vastgebonden op haar bed lag.

'Die jongen,' zei de boer en hij veegde met de rug van zijn linkerhand over zijn rode konen en de gelige, ongeschoren huid rondom de konen. 'Ik had het je kunnen vertellen toen je hier de eerste keer kwam. Ik heb hier veel kinderen gehad. Veel pony's, veel kinderen. Ooit was deze boerderij een kinderboerderij. En ik heb zelf kinderen opgevoed. Dat vergeten de mensen, dat de boer ook een vader is. En dan leer je de kinderen kennen zoals je de beesten kent. Je wilde het niet horen en ik praat niet tegen mensen die niet willen luisteren. Maar er was iets mis met de jongen. Ik heb hem een paar keer voor me gehad. De knecht bracht hem bij me. Hij was niet goed.'

'Niet goed?' De Pool schudde zijn hoofd. 'Er was niets mis met mijn jongen. Misschien was hij anders dan andere jongens. Stiller, liever. Hij deed geen vlieg kwaad, hij praatte met de dieren omdat hij de mensen niet vertrouwde, dat betekent niet dat er iets mis met hem was. Hij is gestruikeld, hij was duizelig, had die dag weinig gegeten, te weinig.'

Op tafel, onder en naast een bord lagen regionale kranten. De ogen van de Pool gleden over de kranten, zijn jongen was nieuws geweest. Geen groot nieuws, wel nieuws, ernstige ontregeling van het treinverkeer.

'Gestruikeld,' zei de boer en hij begon weer te hoesten.

'Het doet er ook niet toe. Ik ben u geen verantwoording verschuldigd. U wilde me spreken. Daarom sta ik hier. Over mijn jongen hoeven we het niet te hebben, die is er niet meer.'

'Wat ga je met die pony doen?' vroeg de boer, snakkend naar adem. 'Ik wil haar niet meer hebben. Dat beest moet weg. Ik ben de boel hier aan het afbouwen.'

'Niemand haalt haar weg zolang ik het niet wil.' De Pool draaide zich om, hij verliet de kamer. Hij groette de oude man niet hoewel hij nog even met het idee had gespeeld de vastgebonden boerin ter sprake te brengen. Vanuit het oogpunt van de brandpreventie. Als mensen hun partner wilden vastbinden op bed en die partner vond dat prima dan was dat verder geen zaak voor de brandweer en ook niet voor de politie. De mensen waren bevrijd van het juk van de kerk en de hoge heren. Er waren nog wel wat hoge heren over die de mensen wilden vertellen wat goed en wat slecht was maar ook van hen zouden ze weldra worden bevrijd. Alleen de regels van de brandpreventie golden nog, daarbuiten begon de vrijheid.

Op het erf gaf de Pool zijn overgebleven jongen nog een koekje. De knecht liep met een kruiwagen vol mest voorbij. De Pool riep hem na: 'Hé, wacht eens even.' Aangezien dat geen effect had ging hij naar de knecht toe. Pas toen zette de knecht de kruiwagen neer.

'De boer houdt ermee op?'

De knecht knikte. Een bonenstaak met zijn eeuwige, wat vuile zwarte petje op. Hij leek arrogant. Dat kon ook verlegenheid zijn, had de Pool op de kazerne geleerd.

'En wat ga jij doen?' vroeg hij aan de bonenstaak, omdat hij niet kon geloven dat de boerderij echt ophield te bestaan, dat hij hier niet meer naartoe zou kunnen.

'Andere boer,' zei de knecht. 'Net over de grens. Duitse boer. Ik werk hard. Doe alles. Vraag weinig.'

De knecht wilde doorlopen maar de Pool had toch nog een vraag. 'Heeft hij weleens met jou gepraat? Mijn jongen? Heeft hij iets tegen jou gezegd?'

'Jouw jongen.' De knecht schudde zijn hoofd. 'Hij zat altijd in de stal bij dat beest. Ze waren onafscheidelijk, die twee. Niet dat hij erop reed. Misschien beter ook. Ze was vast in elkaar gezakt als hij dat had gedaan.'

Daarop pakte de knecht zijn kruiwagen en de Pool ging naar zijn auto. Hij zette de jongen in het stoeltje op de achterbank. 'Beestje,' zei Jurek enthousiast. 'Beestje. Beestje.'

Terwijl de Pool naar huis reed stelde hij zich voor hoe hij het lot van het dier met Wen zou bespreken, of hij het in bed ter sprake zou brengen of tijdens het avondeten: 'Wat zullen we met de pony doen?' In bed was het beste, vlak voor ze seks hadden zou hij zeggen: 'Lieverd, we moeten het over de pony hebben.'

# 3

Er stond een vrouw voor zijn deur toen hij thuiskwam. Ze droeg een bontgekleurde regenjas en ze had een boodschappentas bij zich. Eerst herkende hij haar niet, maar toen hij dichterbij kwam zag hij dat het de vrouw van Beckers was. 'Ik moet aldoor aan jullie denken,' zei ze zonder hem verder te begroeten.

De Pool zocht naar zijn sleutels. Ze moest aldoor aan hem en zijn vrouw denken, daarom stond ze daar. Helemaal begrijpen deed hij het niet, maar er waren veel dingen die hij niet helemaal begreep. Daar moest je niet te lang bij stilstaan, dan ging je malen.

'Zal ik het kind even vasthouden?' vroeg ze.

'Nee hoor,' antwoordde de Pool. 'Gaat prima zo.' Even wierp hij een blik op zijn overgebleven jongen die daar stil en tevreden op zijn arm zat. Hij wilde zijn jongen een gevoel van veiligheid geven, van geborgenheid. Misschien had hij behoeftes van Borys over het hoofd gezien, misschien had hij gefaald als vader al zou hij zo gauw niet weten wat hij anders had moeten doen. Was het gebrek aan liefde geweest? Hij had altijd in de overtuiging geleefd dat hij van zijn oudste jongen hield zoals je van een mens kon houden, zoals de jongen zelf van dat beest had gehouden.

'Kom binnen,' antwoordde de Pool toen de deur eindelijk was geopend. Hij zette Jurek naast zijn houten trein op de grond, hij rook een poepluier, dat kon straks verholpen worden, lang zou het bezoek niet blijven. Daarna hing hij zijn jas op in de vestibule, waar de vrouw van Beckers nog altijd stond met de boodschappentas in haar hand. Aarzelend stond ze daar, verlegen. Ze leek te denken dat binnenkomen betekende dat ze in de vestibule moest blijven staan. 'Ik moet aldoor aan jullie denken,' zei ze weer, 'en toen dacht ik, ik haal wat lekkere dingen voor ze.' Uit haar tas pakte ze iets om aan de Pool te laten zien. 'Tiramisu, vinden jullie dat lekker?' De tiramisu gleed weer terug in de tas, alsof ze zelf begreep dat een bakje tiramisu niet kon troosten, dat ze er vanmiddag anders over had gedacht, dat ze in de supermarkt de hoop had gehad dat er zoiets bestond als eetbare troost.

Hij vroeg: 'Wil je je jas niet even uitdoen?' Ze zei dat dit niet nodig was, dat ze alleen was gekomen om iets af te geven en daarop zei de Pool: 'Wat aardig.' Aardig, dat was het. Attent.

In de woonkamer ging ze met haar jas aan op de bank zitten. Hij begon het te begrijpen, je krabde je jongen van de rails en dan kwamen de mensen met tiramisu langs. Vroeger waren er de hemel en wolkjes waarop engelen zaten, hij kon zich herinneren hoe ze tegen hem hadden gezegd dat zijn moeder nu met engelen op een wolkje zat. Een buurvrouw had dat gezegd, als hij zich niet vergiste. Maar de tijden waren veranderd, er waren geen wolken meer, althans niet met engelen, er waren alleen nog regenwolken. En tiramisu, die was er ook. De mensen waren bevrijd van de engelen en hun wolkjes en dat was beter zo.

De vrouw van Beckers stalde de etenswaren uit op de koffietafel. 'Zeg maar als jullie iets niet lekker vinden, dan neem ik het weer mee.' Ze had een grote boezem die op en neer ging, ze leek buiten adem te zijn. Hij moest denken aan de boer die ook zwaar had geademd. 'Wil je wat drinken?' vroeg hij, terwijl de vrouw van Beckers doorging met spullen uitstallen alsof ze van plan was winkeltje met de Pool te spelen.

'Ik moet er zo vandoor,' zei ze, 'ik heb drie kinderen thuis. Juist daarom moest ik aan jullie denken. En ik bleef maar aan jullie denken. Aan jou, hoe je daar zwijgend had gestaan bij de crematie. Zonder iets te zeggen. En toen had ik een ingeving, ik ging naar de supermarkt en kocht wat lekkers voor jullie.'

'Mijn vrouw heeft mooi gesproken,' zei de Pool.

Ze keek nu alsof ze bij nader inzien de ingeving zelf ook een beetje raar vond, maar ze kon niet meer terug. Ze zat hier met haar tiramisu en de andere lekkernijen.

'Wil je echt niets drinken?' vroeg de Pool. 'Thee? Koffie? Iets sterkers misschien?'

'Een kopje thee,' zei ze. 'Maar ik moet zo weer weg.' Ze frunnikte aan haar lange, donkerbruine haar.

In de keuken deed hij water in de waterkoker en in de kast keek hij welke soorten thee ze hadden. Hij legde wat theezakjes op een bordje zodat het bezoek zelf kon kiezen. Even vroeg hij zich af of hij van tiramisu hield. Hij wist het niet meer zeker. De eetlust was nog niet teruggekomen. Hij at vooral uit plichtsbesef.

Zwijgend dronk hij zijn thee tegenover de vrouw van Beckers, earl grey, zij had voor iets gekozen dat goed was voor de nachtrust hoewel het nog lang geen bedtijd was en zo zaten ze tegenover elkaar en hij keek naar de boodschappen die zij op tafel had uitgestald. Er zat van alles bij, zure haring en sardientjes in blik, wat camembert, oude kaas, en als in trance staarde hij beurtelings naar de boodschappen en dan weer naar de vrouw van Beckers. De vader van de Pool had indertijd troost gevonden bij engelen en de ondoorgrondelijke Eeuwige, tegenwoordig kwamen ze langs met camembert. Op een gegeven moment begreep de Pool dat hij iets moest zeggen. Ze konden hier niet blijven zitten. Als hij niets zou zeggen zat ze hier over een uur nog en Jurek had een poepluier.

'Het is aardig,' zei hij en hij tilde het blik sardientjes op, zette het vervolgens weer neer, 'het is lief, maar we hebben alles in huis.' Hij keek peinzend naar de sardientjes. Hij moest kokhalzen, hoewel hij vroeger graag sardientjes had gegeten. 'Mijn vrouw komt zo thuis,' zei hij, 'wil je op haar wachten?'

De vrouw van Beckers schudde haar hoofd. 'Ik moet gaan, de kinderen zitten alleen. De jongste is net geen vier. Een nakomertje. Net als bij jullie. De oudste past op. Mijn man is met een klus bezig.' Ze nam een slok thee en toen trok ze haar jas toch uit. 'Het is hier zo warm. Wanneer ben je eigenlijk jarig?'

Het duurde even voor de Pool antwoordde: 'Het weer slaat om. Ik ben in de zomer jarig.' Daarop ging de Pool naar boven om billendoekjes, crème en een nieuwe luier te pakken en hij legde zijn overgebleven jongen op de eettafel, zodat hij de luier kon verschonen en toch met de vrouw van Beckers kon blijven praten, die geen aanstalten maakte om de spullen die ze had uitgepakt weer in haar boodschappentas te stoppen.

Hij verschoonde Jurek wel vaker op de eettafel, hoewel Wen dat onprettig vond.

'Niet tegenstribbelen, Jurek,' zei hij, 'werk eens mee, lieverd.' En hij veegde de billen van de jongen met vijf vochtige doekjes schoon, iets waar zijn vrouw niet tegen kon, die zei altijd: 'Het kan met drie, vijf is overbodig.' Hij gebruikte er altijd minstens vijf om er zeker van te zijn dat de billen van de jongen goed schoon waren, hij hield van schone billen, en de vrouw van Beckers was opgestaan, ze kwam langzaam dichterbij, zag hij toen hij even had omgekeken.

'Gaat het?' vroeg ze belangstellend.

'Het zit vastgekleefd.'

De Pool had van alles tegen de overgebleven jongen willen zeggen, maar dat deed hij niet want de vrouw van Beckers was erbij en Jurek zelf zei alleen: 'Beestje, beestje, beestje.'

'Hoe doen jullie het?' vroeg de vrouw van Beckers. 'Hoe leven jullie verder? Ik denk niet dat ik het zou kunnen.'

Hij smeerde de billen in met crème, luieruitslag was

geen pretje. Hij smeerde de crème dik met lange halen over de billen en anus van de jongen, ook wat over de ballen om het zekere voor het onzekere te nemen en hij genoot van de geur van de crème, dat waren kleine dingen waarvan hij genoot. 'Het gaat verder,' zei hij zacht. 'Het leven. Hij is er, mijn vrouw is er, ik ben er. Ik ben niet gemaakt om op te geven.'

De Pool was klaar met verschonen en zette Jurek in de box. De jongen begon te huilen, hij liet hem jengelen.

De vrouw van Beckers stond er wat verloren bij met haar kopje thee in de hand. Hij zag dat ze ook huilde, net als zijn overgebleven jongen. Eerlijk gezegd stoorde het hem, niemand hoefde zich om hun verdriet te bekommeren. Slachtofferhulp niet, de vrouw van Beckers evenmin. Hij vroeg zich af wanneer zijn vrouw thuiskwam, die was een hele roedel huilende kleuters gewend. Die kon vast ook een huilende volwassene aan.

Toch had hij met de vrouw van Beckers te doen, met haar drie kinderen, hoe ze daar in zijn woonkamer tegen haar tranen vocht. Ze droeg een jurk met grote bloemen erop en een rits van voren. Dergelijke jurken droeg Wen nooit. Met een rits van voren.

Hij pakte de vrouw van Beckers zachtjes bij haar bovenarm, niet om haar het huis uit te zetten, maar om haar te troosten en hij zei: 'Je zet een knop om. Dat heb je geleerd als brandweerman, je zet gewoon een knop om.' En na een korte stilte: 'Het zal jou niet overkomen, het overkomt bijna niemand. Hij had pech.'

Ze knikte een paar keer. Ze leek niet geheel overtuigd, alsof ze nog altijd dacht dat het ook haar kon overkomen, dat pech besmettelijk was.

Hij zei: 'Ik wil je niet beledigen, maar neem de spullen weer mee. We hebben echt alles in huis.'

Gelaten begon ze haar etenswaren weer in te pakken, de zure haring en de sardientjes, de oude kaas en het stuk camembert, alles verdween in haar boodschappentas. Het was een nederlaag, zo zag het eruit, maar hij kon er niets aan doen, hij wilde die spullen niet. Ze was erbij gaan zitten. Tot ze bij de tiramisu kwam en toen zei ze met overslaande stem: 'Die hou je toch wel? Die is zo lekker.' Ze vocht tegen het snikken, ze vocht tegen zichzelf en het lukte haar niet, het vocht kwam uit haar ogen, ze trilde een beetje. Hij kon die tiramisu niet afwijzen en daarom zei hij dat ze die nog vanavond zouden eten en hij pakte de tiramisu aan alsof het een hostie was en met de tiramisu in zijn hand hurkte hij naast de vrouw van Beckers die op haar stoel zat. Hij keek recht in haar gezicht, hij zag de uitgelopen mascara en hij zei: 'Hij had een pony, die was alles voor hem. Die moet nu naar de paardenslager. Maar dat laat ik niet gebeuren. Daar steek ik een stokje voor.'

Hij bleef in de ogen van de vrouw van Beckers kijken. Hij had haar nooit echt aangekeken, je hoefde niet iedereen in de ogen te kijken, maar wat hij daar nu zag joeg hem meer schrik aan dan de dood en alleen al daarom zei hij: 'Nu moet je gaan.'

Hij kwam overeind, trok haar mee naar de vestibule, zij met de zware boodschappentas in haar hand en net voor hij de voordeur wilde openen zei ze: 'Mijn jas.' Ze ging terug naar de woonkamer en verscheen vervolgens met de regenjas over haar arm en ze fluisterde: 'Ik had al twee meisjes en toen kwam het nakomertje, nog een meisje, ik had ook best een jongen gewild. Ik wist niet dat hij een pony had, zielig voor dat dier.' Het vechten tegen het snikken had haar hees gemaakt. Daarop omhelsde de Pool haar om haar te bedanken voor de spulletjes die ze nu weer meenam en hij drukte haar tegen zich aan, met de tiramisu in zijn hand, alsof zij de pony van zijn jongen was in mensengedaante, zo drukte hij haar tegen zich aan, alsof ook de vrouw van Beckers gered moest worden van de paardenslager.

‘Leek Borys eigenlijk op jou?’ vroeg de vrouw van Beckers.

‘Niet echt,’ zei de Pool en toen opende hij de deur. Hij riep haar nog na: ‘Dank je voor alles.’

Ze bleef staan voor het huis, met de boodschappentas in haar hand, over haar arm de regenjas. Ze zwaaide en riep: ‘Bel me als je me nodig hebt. Laat me weten als ik iets voor je kan doen.’

Hij sloot de deur, ging naar de woonkamer, tilde de huilende jongen uit zijn box en liep door het huis, het kind op zijn rug kloppend en in zijn oor zingend, maar het huilen stopte niet. ‘Heb je pijn?’ vroeg de Pool. ‘Heb je honger?’

Eindelijk kwam Wen thuis, die de jongen van hem overnam en toen de jongen was getroost werd er pasta met paddenstoelen gemaakt. De Pool zei: ‘Er is tiramisu.’

Wen vroeg niet: ‘Waar komt die vandaan?’ Ze zei: ‘Dan eten we die na.’

Toen de tiramisu op tafel stond – ze probeerden ervan te genieten, met het grootmoedige acteertalent waarmee geliefden elkaars pijn proberen te verzachten – vond de Pool dat het tijd werd zijn vrouw aan het bestaan van de pony te herinneren. Niet in bed, nu al. Verliefdheid verdween, er kwam iets voor in de plaats en soms vreesde de Pool dat wat ervoor in de plaats kwam ook zou verdwijnen, maar nu hij zag hoe gewetensvol zij allebei hun toneelstukje opvoerden besefte hij dat het substituut van verliefdheid hen samenhield en daarom durfde hij het wonder te berde te brengen. ‘Zullen we het over de pony hebben?’ vroeg hij.

Ze keek hem aan met een gezicht alsof ze zelf niet kon begrijpen hoe ze dat was vergeten. Ze hadden zo aan hun jongen gedacht, om de een of andere reden was de pony aan hun aandacht ontsnapt.

‘Ja, de pony,’ ze keek naar het bakje tiramisu. ‘Goed dat je erover begint. Wat doen we ermee? Verkopen denk ik, niet?’

'Ik ben er vandaag geweest. Met de veearts. Hij heeft een wonder verricht.' De Pool kuchte. Het wonder zat hem dwars, maar hij moest erover praten.

Weer had hij het gevoel te moeten kokhalzen. De tiramisu was hem te zoet, hij dwong zichzelf om verder te eten, omdat je een knop moest kunnen omzetten maar ook om de vrouw van Beckers te eren, die in haar rare jurk etenswaren voor de Pool en Wen had gekocht, omdat ze hen had willen helpen met verder leven. Omdat ze dacht dat het haar ook kon overkomen.

Wen begon te lachen. 'Welk wonder? Die rekeningen die hij beloofd had te sturen? Bedoel je dat, met het wonder? Die afzetter.'

'Hij heeft de rekeningen gestuurd,' zei de Pool, 'en hij is geen afzetter.' Hij keek strak voor zich uit. Op zijn kinderstoeltje zat de overgebleven jongen. Wen voerde hem wat tiramisu. Ze veegde zijn mond af. Hij zat onder de cacao. 'Niet blazen,' zei ze. 'Gekkie. Niet blazen.'

'Het beest loopt niet meer mank,' verklaarde de Pool. 'Ik kan dat natuurlijk niet goed zien, ze lopen toch anders dan mensen, maar op mij maakte ze een gezonde indruk.' Hij tilde zijn lepel op, liet de lepel weer zakken, nam een hap en hij vroeg zich af wanneer het slikken geen gevecht meer zou zijn.

'We moeten er zo snel mogelijk van af,' zei Wen terwijl ze een bromvlieg volgde met haar ogen. 'Niemand bekommert zich nu om haar. Dat is zielig. Dat heeft die pony niet verdiend.'

Wat had ze dan wel verdiend, die pony? Moest ze worden gestraft omdat zij hun jongen niet had gered? Konden ze dat van een pony verwachten? Kon die iets wat de mensen niet hadden gekund? Had hun jongen gered kunnen worden? Allemaal vragen waarover de Pool niet wilde nadenken omdat dit niets opleverde. 'Ze begonnen over de paardenslager,' zei hij zacht, 'de veearts en de boer. Dat had Borys nooit gewild.'

'Maar Borys is er niet meer,' verklaarde Wen. Ze klonk boos. Alsof hij verzaakt had op school, spijbelde, alsof de dood een kwaadaardige vorm van spijbelen was en de doden zelf niets dan spijbelaars waren die er flink van langs moesten krijgen om ze dat spijbelen voor eens en voor altijd af te leren. 'Het doet er niet toe wat hij wilde. We moeten ervan af. Ga morgen naar de boer en zeg hem dat hij moet doen wat het beste voor de pony is.' Ze sloeg naar de bromvlieg.

'Ik wil niet dat de boer dat beslist,' zei de Pool nadrukkelijk. 'Jij hebt hem nooit gezien. Die man is oud en afgetakeld. Niet meer helemaal bij zinnen. En ja, ik vind dat we onze jongen iets verschuldigd zijn.'

Wen sloeg op tafel. Dat deed ze anders nooit. 'Hij is er niet meer,' riep ze, 'we zijn hem niets verschuldigd want hij is er niet meer. Deze jongen zijn we iets verschuldigd.' En ze stopte nog een lepel tiramisu in Jureks mond alsof ze hem nu vooral tiramisu verschuldigd was.

De jongen keek de Pool met grote ogen aan. Hij leek te begrijpen dat het over hem ging, hij begreep veel, in elk geval dat dacht de Pool, dat zijn beide jongens altijd veel hadden begrepen.

'Ik ben hem iets verschuldigd,' zei hij, nog zachter dan anders. Als zijn vrouw haar stem verhief ging hij zacht praten, want hij hield niet van ruzie. 'Ook al is hij er niet meer.'

Wen haalde de jongen uit zijn stoel, zette hem op haar schoot, veegde met het slabbetje over zijn mond, zijn lippen waren bruin van de cacao, ze kriebelde over zijn lichtblonde haar en uiteindelijk vroeg ze zonder haar stem te verheffen: 'Wat wil je in godsnaam met die pony gaan doen? Wil je erop gaan rijden?' Ze lachte, niet honend, eerder een beetje wanhopig. 'Je hebt nooit iets met dieren gehad. Zelfs niet met honden.'

'Ik heb niets met dieren,' zei de Pool. 'Ik red ze hooguit, als dat nodig is.'

'Ga me geen heldenverhalen vertellen over poesjes die je uit bomen hebt gered, alsjeblieft bespaar me dat, alleen omdat je geen afscheid kunt nemen van een doodzieke pony. Omdat je je hebt laten bedriegen door een veearts, omdat je niet weet wat een wonder is, omdat je goedgelovig bent. Had je je maar net zoveel zorgen gemaakt om Borys.'

Hij stond op, begon af te ruimen. 'We gaan die rekeningen niet betalen,' riep Wen. 'Ik wil gewoon met jou en Jurek naar Griekenland. Je zei toch dat als die pony te duur werd we wel naar de Eifel konden? Ik wil niet naar een somber huisje waar we twee weken lang doodvriezen alleen omdat jij je schuldig voelt. Ik wil naar Griekenland.'

'Ik voel me niet schuldig, maar ik ben verantwoordelijk voor dat beest,' zei de Pool, met de vieze borden in zijn hand.

'Voel je je dan niet verantwoordelijk voor ons?' vroeg Wen. 'Hebben alleen de doden recht op je aandacht?'

De Pool wilde toegeven dat de doden hem riepen, dat hun stemmen liefelijk klonken en soms ook dreigend, dat hun stemmen vaak levendiger waren dan die van de levenden, maar dat zei hij niet. Hij bracht de borden naar de keuken en daar likte hij met zijn vinger het bakje tiramisu leeg. Om te bewijzen dat hij boven zijn gekokhals stond, dat hij zijn aanhoudende misselijkheid kon overwinnen. De Pool wilde geen speelbal zijn van de omstandigheden. Hij stond boven de omstandigheden en toch vroeg hij zich even af of zijn vrouw gelijk had, dat hij goedgelovig was.

# 4

Dagenlang wist hij niet met wie hij kon praten over zijn voornemen een oude pony te redden en uiteindelijk wist hij niet meer zeker of hij dat dier wel moest redden, zoals mensen twijfelen aan hun relatie of hun roeping. Jarenlang hebben ze gedacht dat ze met bloemen en planten moesten werken en opeens denken ze, nee, misschien ben ik eerder een kapper.

Het einde van de maand naderde en de boer had gezegd dat als er dan geen beslissing was genomen hij de pony naar de paardenslager zou laten brengen.

Er waren momenten, bijvoorbeeld nadat ze waren uitgerukt en weer terug op de kazerne waren, dat de Pool met een helderheid die hem zelf verraste inzag dat het dwaasheid was zich om de pony te bekommeren, dat hij het dier niet moest proberen te scheiden van zijn noodlot. Tussendoor zag hij zijn jongen weer voor zich, in de stal, hij hoorde hem fluisteren zonder te verstaan wat hij zei en hij had het gevoel dat hij tot het eind van zijn leven dat gefluister zou horen zonder er ooit ook maar een woord van te verstaan. Maar hij zou zich blijven inspannen om er iets van op te vangen, al was het maar een voegwoord of een lidwoord. Als Wen hun jongen zo zou hebben gezien dan had ze anders gepraat, dan had ze anders gehandeld, maar ze had hem niet zo gezien en daarom was de paardenslager voor haar gewoon een slager zoals elke andere slager. Daarom was die pony voor haar niets dan een nog net levende biefstuk. En vond ze het prima dat leeuwen en tijgers in de dierentuin zich straks tegoed deden aan haar vlees. Ja, er waren momenten dat hij dacht dat hij gek werd van dat gefluister van hun jongen en dat hij wilde roepen:

Hou op met fluisteren, spreek verstaanbaar of hou je kop dicht.

Op een middag, toen hij eindelijk had besloten naar de boer te gaan en het beest terug te geven, terug aan de boer, terug aan zijn schepper, kreeg hij een ingeving. Hij pakte de auto maar hij reed niet naar de boer. Hij reed naar Beckers. Hij was er een keer eerder geweest, lang geleden, voor een feestje. Hij belde aan.

De vrouw van Beckers deed open.

'Is Beckers thuis?' vroeg hij.

Ze schudde haar hoofd.

'Wil je binnenkomen?' Ze droeg weer een vreemde jurk, dit keer met flamingo's erop, zonder rits van voren. Hij wist niet dat de vrouw van Beckers zo extravagant was. Beckers zelf was gewoontjes, zoals alle mannen van de C-ploeg eigenlijk gewoon waren, al waren ze op hun eigen manier ook bijzonder.

'Ik heb een vraag,' zei hij, 'dat kan misschien ook hier.'

'Kom verder, de kinderen zijn boven.' Ze pakte hem bij zijn mouw en trok hem zachtjes een paar centimeter verder naar binnen.

De keer dat hij hier was geweest op een feest kon hij zich alleen maar één kind herinneren, één kind dat dartel door de woonkamer had gedanst voordat het naar boven was gegaan, of misschien vergiste hij zich, misschien waren er toen al meer kinderen geweest. Van dat hele feest kon hij zich niet veel herinneren. Ook hij en Wen hadden gedanst. Ze hadden gedronken, te veel gedronken om naar huis te rijden. Ze hadden een taxi willen nemen en toen ze die niet konden krijgen omdat om de een of andere reden iedereen die avond een taxi wilde nemen waren ze naar huis gelopen. Dat kon hij zich herinneren, hoe ze naar huis waren gelopen en hoe hij geheel tegen zijn natuur in niet had kunnen ophouden met praten. Honderduit had hij verteld, maar halverwege de wandeling was hij stilgevallen en toen waren ze zonder te praten verder gelopen. Eerst hadden ze elkaars hand vastgehouden tot de Pool het warm had gekregen, hij had zijn hand losgetrokken en zo waren ze verdergegaan door de lege straten, langs de donkere huizen. Thuis lag hun jongen te slapen en de babysitter sliep ook op de bank. Hij had haar moeten wekken en toen hem dat was gelukt had hij haar betaald. Daarna waren Wen en hij in bed gaan liggen, ze waren te dronken en te moe om te vrijen, al was de lust er, de lust kon hij zich nog goed herinneren en Wen had gezegd: 'Ik ruik de alcohol. Je bent dronken.' Beckers had het feest gegeven omdat hij jarig was, een rond getal, en het een keer groot wilde vieren.

De Pool hing zijn jas niet op. De vrouw van Beckers had klaargestaan met een kleerhanger maar hij had zijn hoofd geschud. Hij volgde haar gedwee naar de keuken. Een keer had Wen tegen hem gezegd: 'Je bent zo lang en toch lijk je soms net een kleine jongen.' Zo voelde hij zich nu, een kleine jongen, maar hij wist waarom hij hier was. Hij had een missie.

'Jij hebt drie kinderen,' zei hij, staand naast het fornuis. Hij keek rond in de keuken die niet de zijne was en hij besefte dat dit een beetje een vreemde manier was om een gesprek te beginnen. Ze wist zelf hoeveel kinderen ze had. Toch knikte ze alsof het heel gewoon was voor een collega van haar man om aan te bellen en te zeggen: 'Je hebt drie kinderen.' Maar ja, zij had voor zijn deur gestaan met tiramisu, camembert en sardientjes.

Ze informeerde beleefd, bijna te beleefd, of hij iets wilde drinken en ze voegde er nog aan toe dat er appeltaart over was van gisteren. Waarom er gisteren appeltaart in huis was gehaald vertelde ze niet en de Pool vroeg er ook niet naar. Zin in appeltaart had hij niet, toch zou hij ook dat stuk appeltaart naar binnen werken zoals hij alles tegenwoordig naar binnen werkte en hij keek toe hoe ze een flink stuk afsneed. Het was zelfgebakken appeltaart zo te zien, ze deed er een klodder slagroom bij, dus die slagroom moest hij ook naar binnen werken, en daarna vroeg ze of hij naar de woonkamer wilde gaan of dat hij het hier staand wilde opeten. 'Hier,' zei hij. En zij merkte op: 'De oudste eet altijd staand in de keuken.' Mannen en hun eetgewoontes, kinderen en hun eetgewoontes, je hoefde haar niets te vertellen. Ze had alles gezien, alles meegemaakt. Ze keek toe hoe hij at en hij probeerde te verbergen dat hij het bijna niet binnen kon houden, hij hoopte dat het lukte, dat ze niets zou zien. En terwijl ze hem observeerde zei ze zacht dat ze nog altijd aan hem en zijn vrouw dacht, dat ze niet uit haar gedachten waren verdwenen. 'Mijn gedachten,' zei ze en ze schudde haar hoofd zoals je je hoofd schudt over een stout kind. Haar gedachten waren misschien net stoute kinderen. En ook hij schudde zijn hoofd, waarmee hij wilde zeggen dat ze niet aan Wen en hem hoefde te denken, dat iedereen aan zichzelf moest denken. Hij nam een grote hap, kauwde, hij vermaalde haar zelfgebakken appeltaart in zijn mond en terwijl hij dat deed zag hij voor zich hoe ze het deeg had gekneed, in deze keuken, met haar excentrieke kleren aan.

'Ik had je verteld over die pony,' zei hij toen zijn mond leeg was, 'de pony van Borys die genezen is door een wonder, en als je genezen bent door een wonder dan is de paardenslager zonde. Dat wonder heeft me ook heel wat gekost en nu dacht ik dat ze misschien iets voor een van jouw kinderen was. Ik hoef er verder niets voor te hebben, ik vind het zo zonde haar naar de paardenslager te brengen.'

'Zonde,' zei de vrouw van Beckers nadenkend, 'heel zonde. Maar mijn kinderen hebben het al zo druk. Met hun hobby's en hun vriendinnetjes, ze hebben amper tijd voor school. En de jongste is veel te jong voor zo'n dier.'

Hij voelde hoe zijn hand trilde waarmee hij het bordje vasthield waarop nog een half stuk appeltaart lag en wat al te vloeibare slagroom.

‘Ik wou dat ik je kon helpen,’ zei ze zacht en ze leek het bordje van hem te willen aannemen, ze leek te zien hoe hij trilde maar op het laatste moment trok ze haar hand terug.

Van boven klonk geschreeuw. ‘Ze hebben klasgenootjes te spelen,’ legde ze uit.

De Pool nam nog een hap en zette het bordje toen neer op het aanrecht. Hij had zijn best gedaan, er viel hem niets te verwijten. ‘Oké,’ zei hij. ‘Nou ja, je kunt het altijd proberen.’

‘Je kunt het altijd proberen,’ zei ze.

Hij liep de keuken uit en zij kwam achter hem aan. ‘Niet meteen weggaan, er zijn vast andere kinderen die je blij kunt maken met de pony. Alleen mijn kinderen... Nee.’

In de gang bij de voordeur trok ze hem weer aan zijn mouw. ‘Ik wil jullie zo graag troosten,’ zei ze, ‘zo graag. Weet je dat?’

Even keek hij haar aan, hij proefde haar appeltaart nog, hij wreef over zijn stekelharen, hij knipte het graag kort, zijn haar, als het aan hem had gelegen had hij alles weggeschoren, Wen vond een beetje haar fijn.

‘Jij bent de vrouw van Beckers,’ zei hij, ‘jij moet je man troosten.’

‘Ja, ik ben de vrouw van Beckers en dat zal ik ook altijd blijven. Mijn man hoeft niet te worden getroost. En ik kan me jullie nog herinneren toen jullie hier waren op dat feest en toen zag ik jullie weer na dat ongeluk. Zo anders. Begrijpelijk, daar niet van. Maar ik dacht, ik moet iets voor die mensen doen... Ik kan ze niet alleen laten.’

Ze sloeg haar armen om hem heen alsof ze wilde zeggen hoe letterlijk, hoe lichamelijk dat niet alleen willen laten was en eigenlijk viel hem nu pas op hoe klein ze was. Hij liet zich omhelzen, hij liet het toe en terwijl van boven de stemmen van spelende kinderen kwamen drukte hij haar tegen zich aan en ze had gelijk, tegen alle verwachting in had ze gelijk, er zat iets troostends in deze aanraking, iets wat naar de toekomst verwees en niet uitsluitend naar het verleden, iets wat bevrijdde, iets wat niet gevangenhield.

Het was onduidelijk wie wie omhelsde, maar hij liet haar niet los, zoveel was zeker, terwijl hij bleef luisteren naar de schreeuwende kinderen op de eerste verdieping en ontroering zich van hem meester maakte. Ontroering dat een vreemde had gezien dat zij getroost moesten worden, Wen en hij. Natuurlijk, zijn collega's hadden het ook gezien, voor hen bestond troost uit het afkrabben van oud behang, uit verven en renoveren en dat was toch iets anders dan troosten. En de dame van slachtofferhulp, die kwam echter alleen langs omdat niet getrooste mensen een gevaar voor zichzelf of voor de samenleving konden worden.

Al deze dingen schoten door zijn hoofd terwijl hij zijn mond naar de wang van de vrouw van Beckers bracht en hij haar rook, haar parfum, anders dan dat van Wen, hij kon het parfum van Wen niet uitstaan maar hij durfde er niets van te zeggen, het maakte hem misselijk. Dat kon je niet tegen je vrouw zeggen, dat haar parfum je misselijk maakte, vooral niet als ze dat parfum al jaren gebruikte. En zijn lippen gleden zacht over de wang van de vrouw die hem wilde troosten, ze gleden van haar oor naar haar mond, vlak voor zijn lippen die van haar konden raken gleed zijn mond terug in de richting van haar oor, ongeveer zoals een stofzuiger over het tapijt gleed, en toen zijn mond bij haar oor was aangekomen zei hij: 'Mijn vrouw heeft ook troost nodig.'

'Dat weet ik,' zei de vrouw van Beckers, 'dat besef ik maar al te goed. Maar zij is er nu niet. Eerst jij, dan je vrouw.'

Daarop rukte de Pool zich los uit haar armen. 'Wat zijn ze daarboven aan het doen?' vroeg hij. 'Breken je kinderen soms de boel af?'

'Ze spelen,' zei de vrouw van Beckers. 'Ze spelen, je moet ze een beetje ruimte gunnen.'

De Pool zei verder niets meer, hij draaide zich om en liep naar zijn auto. In zijn dashboardkastje vond hij een oud pepermuntje dat hij gedachteloos in zijn mond stak. Uiteindelijk startte hij de auto en reed naar huis. Als de kinderen en de vrouw van Beckers de pony niet wilden dan zou hij zelf voor dat beest gaan zorgen. Hij zou de dagen dat hij geen dienst had naar de boer gaan en zich over het dier ontfermen. De boer had wel gezegd dat alles dichtging, dat de beesten weggingen, maar de boer bleef daar vast wonen, samen met zijn vastgebonden vrouw. Hij vond hem geen type voor het verpleegtehuis. Dan kon zo'n eenzame pony daar ook blijven staan. En als het nodig was zou hij de stal zelf uitmesten.

Thuis hoorde hij zijn vrouw rommelen in de badkamer. Ze riep hem. Hij ging naar boven. Ze was bezig Jurek in bad te doen. Ze stond gebogen over de rand van de badkuip en ze zei: 'Je was er niet, dus ik heb hem zelf in bad gedaan.'

De Pool was vrolijk, zo vrolijk was hij lang niet geweest. Zelfs toen hun jongen er nog was en hij zwijgend aan tafel zat was de Pool niet zo vrolijk geweest. Dat was ook iets wat hij zichzelf verweet, zij het in stilte, dat hij niet genoeg genoten had van hun oudste jongen. Wen moest iets hebben gezien of geroken, want ze keek op van het bad, ze keek naar haar man, hij zag afkeuring in haar ogen – of was het wantrouwen? – en ze vroeg: 'Wat is er?'

'Niets,' zei hij.

Ze waste de overgebleven jongen. De jongen lachte, hij lachte meer dan zijn broer, dat was een goed teken, de Pool moest zelf ook lachen. Toen zei hij: 'Ik ga me om de pony bekommeren.'

Wen had rug en buik van de jongen ingezeept, ze wilde de zeep net gaan afspoelen en ze verstijfde. 'Wat?' vroeg ze, terwijl ze haar hand stil op de rug van de jongen hield, 'wat ga je doen?'

'Ik ga de pony redden. Ik ga haar verzorgen.'

'Verzorg hém,' zei Wen en ze begon driftig de zeep van de jongen af te spoelen. 'Red hém.' Dat wilde de Pool ook, Jurek verzorgen, hem voor zover nodig redden, maar hij vond dat er genoeg tijd over was om ook een pony te redden.

'Over een paar jaar heeft Jurek een dier waarmee hij kan spelen,' zei de Pool.

'Dan is dat beest allang dood en misschien wil hij liever voetballen. Of op straat hangen. Kun jij je voorstellen dat Jurek helemaal niet op een pony zit te wachten?' Ze spoelde het kind af.

'Misschien,' zei de Pool. Hij wilde niets doen wat Wen verdrietig of boos zou maken maar hij had een beslissing genomen.

Wen tilde de jongen uit het water en begon hem grondig af te drogen. 'Nee,' zei ze. 'Dat dier heeft ons alleen ongeluk gebracht. Laten we er afscheid van nemen. Wat wil je nog van die pony?'

De jongen was afgedroogd. Ze nam hem naar zijn kamertje en daar deed ze hem een luier om. De Pool volgde haar. 'Je krijgt hem niet terug,' zei ze, 'al koop je twintig pony's. Borys is weg. Leg je erbij neer. Hij is weg. Andere mensen krijgen een kindje met een spierziekte. Wij hebben dit gekregen. Nu zijn we met z'n drieën. Dat is ook goed.'

'Dat is ook goed,' zei hij zacht. 'Dat we met z'n drieën zijn is prima. Maar zij heeft dat niet verdiend. Wat kan zij eraan doen? Waarom moet zij ook dood?'

Wen kleedde de jongen verder aan. Het kind was stil, het leek te luisteren. 'Wij hebben dit ook niet verdiend,' zei ze, 'het gaat er niet om wat mensen en dieren verdienen. Wie krijgt wat hij verdient? Heb ik jou verdiend? Heb ik echt niets beters verdiend?'

De Pool liep de kamer uit en bleef voor de gesloten deur staan, de deur die naar de kamer van hun jongen leidde, de deur die ze niet meer zouden openen, niet dit jaar, misschien volgend jaar, ook dat was onzeker, waarschijnlijk zelfs niet volgend jaar, er was geen haast bij. Misschien zouden ze de deur van die kamer pas weer opendoen als ze oud waren en hun overgebleven jongen het huis uit was. Of ze gingen dood zonder dat ze die deur ooit nog hadden geopend. Dat was waarschijnlijk beter, nooit meer opendoen.

Tijdens het eten zei Wen dat het haar speet en ze legde haar hand op de arm van de Pool. Ze zei dat ze zich geen betere man kon voorstellen en dat het niet aardig was geweest om te zeggen dat ze iets beters had verdiend. Niet alleen onaardig, ook onwaar.

'Ach,' de Pool had zijn handen in elkaar gevouwen en hij bekeek zijn knokkels, 'ach, de dood bezorgt ons stress en dan zeg je dingen die je niet meent. Maar nu is de dood achter de rug, nu kunnen we de stress afbouwen.'

Ze kuste hem, eerst op zijn wang, zijn ongeschoren wang, en daarna pakte ze hem met beide handen vast, ze drukte haar mond op de zijne, ze duwde haar tong naar binnen en het kon haar kennelijk niets schelen dat hun overgebleven jongen aan tafel zat. Ze dacht vast en zeker dat hij te jong was om dit te onthouden of dat het wel goed voor hem was om dit te zien en de Pool moest kokhalzen. Hij vroeg zich af of zij niet moest kokhalzen, of zij niet misselijk was, hij had het haar willen vragen: Komt het eten bij jou niet omhoog? Maar hij zoende terug. Hij zoende zoals hij at, met een verantwoordelijkheidsgevoel dat niet van fanatisme te onderscheiden was. En in zijn stoeltje zat hun overgebleven jongen met zijn slab om en hij zei weer 'ape, beestje' en zo verder. Vanuit zijn ooghoeken zag de Pool hem zitten, tevreden eigenlijk, en hij zei: 'Laten we naar boven gaan.'

Hij was misselijk maar hij stond boven de misselijkheid. 'Het is lang geleden,' fluisterde ze in zijn oor. En ze zoende hem alsof ze elkaar net hadden ontmoet en verschrikkelijk verliefd waren, verliefder dan goed voor hen was, maar ze waren niet verschrikkelijk verliefd, ze hadden hun jongen verloren en hij had willen zeggen: De vrouw van Beckers wil ons troosten. Jou en mij.

Hij zoende Wen, aan wie hij niet twijfelde. Zijn misselijkheid was geen twijfel, zijn misselijkheid was een streek van het noodlot, zoals de intercity naar Amsterdam een smerige streek van het noodlot was geweest en ze zei: 'Ja, laten we naar boven gaan.'

Ze stond op, ze trok hem omhoog uit zijn stoel en hij liet zich omhoogtrekken, hij volgde haar als een puber en nog even keek hij om naar hun jongen die daar zo vredig in zijn stoeltje zat.

'Ik wil je,' zei ze op de trap en ze keek om naar haar Pool, die vocht met de maaltijd die hij net naar binnen had gewerkt. Het zuur kwam naar boven, hij slikte het weg. 'Wil je mij?' vroeg ze. 'Eindelijk wil ik je weer zoals ik je toen wilde. Zoals ik je eigenlijk altijd wilde, toch?'

'Ja,' zei hij, 'ja.' Zonder te weten waarop hij precies ja zei, hooguit dat hij ja zei tegen dit leven, dit huis, deze vrouw, zijn baan, zijn oudedagsvoorziening.

Ze ging op bed zitten en ze knoopte zijn broek open. Hij zei: 'Wat maakt die pony nou uit, wat heb jij er voor last van?'

Ze trok zijn onderbroek naar beneden, zij kocht zijn onderbroeken, al jaren deed ze dat, hij vertrouwde zijn vrouw, niet alleen als het om onderbroeken ging, maar de Pool wilde niet dat ze hem nu pijpte, hij had geen erectie, hij had wel 'ja' gezegd, dat wel. Het was een 'ja' in het algemeen geweest, een 'ja' waarmee je alle kanten uit kon. Ze nam zijn slappe geslachtsdeel in haar mond en ze deed alsof ze de woorden over de pony niet had gehoord. 'Ik doe het helemaal alleen,' zei hij en langzaam kreeg hij een erectie, want alles functioneerde nog ongeveer zoals het moest. Hij besloot verder over de pony te zwijgen, dit was niet het moment.

Hij trok zijn Wen omhoog, duwde haar zachtjes op het bed en hij ontdeed haar met enige moeite van haar spijkerbroek, hij trok haar onderbroek uit, begon haar benen te likken. De binnenkant van haar dijen.

'Wat ben je daar lang niet geweest,' zei ze.

'Het was een tijd geleden,' zei hij.

'Ga op onderzoek uit,' sommeerde ze hem. 'Onderzoek mij alsof je me voor de eerste keer ziet.'

De Pool werd ongeduldig want eigenlijk wilde hij haar niet onderzoeken maar hij wilde haar ook niet teleurstellen, hij wilde haar behagen, meer dan wat dan ook wilde hij dat en daarom onderzocht hij haar alsof hij de eerste keer tussen haar benen lag en zij zei: 'Vertel me wat je ziet.'

'Hoe bedoel je, wat ik zie?' vroeg hij.

'Wat zie je? Wat zie je, Pool?'

Eigenlijk sprak ze hem alleen met 'Pool' aan als ze hem wilde plagen. Kennelijk wilde ze hem plagen nu hij na zo lange tijd weer tussen haar benen lag. Als ze hem een beetje plaagde hield hij het meest van haar.

Hij keek naar de binnenkant van haar benen en wat daartussen zat, haar geslachtsdeel, dat zij doorgaans haar poesje noemde, voor zover ze over haar geslachtsdeel sprak. En hij zei dat hij haar schaamlippen zag. 'Ik zie ze,' zei hij.

'Speel ermee,' antwoordde ze, 'duw ze opzij.'

De Pool wist eigenlijk niet precies hoe je met schaamlippen moest spelen, toch speelde hij ermee – ook dit hoorde bij de plichten die een goede man moest vervullen.

Vroeger had ze nooit instructies gegeven, nu was de tijd voor instructies aangebroken en daarvan werd hij onzeker. Hij deed de schaamlippen voorzichtig opzij.

'Ga er met je lippen overheen,' zei ze. 'Niet met je tong. Alleen met je lippen.'

Hij ging er met zijn lippen overheen en even dacht hij aan de vrouw van Beckers en aan haar wang. Toen concentreerde hij zich weer op het poesje van zijn eigen vrouw en op het feit dat hij en zijn vrouw geen troost nodig hadden, dat ze gelijk had, andere mensen hadden een kind gekregen met een spierziekte, zij hadden dit gekregen, alleen de pony, die wilde hij toch redden, omdat het in zijn macht lag, desnoods zou hij het stiekem doen.

Hij kuste haar poesje zonder te beschrijven wat hij had gezien, hij wist niet zeker hoe hij de kleur moest omschrijven van het lieve poesje van zijn vrouw. Hij was geen schilder. Roze of rood of bruin of misschien genuanceerder. Ze zei dat hij haar nu ook mocht likken. 'Maar verlies niet te veel speeksel,' zei ze. 'Je verliest altijd zoveel speeksel als je me likt. Hoe komt dat toch?'

'Ik kan er niets aan doen,' antwoordde hij. 'Er zit speeksel in mijn mond en dat komt soms naar buiten.' Weer dacht hij aan eten, aan het zuur dat nog steeds naar boven kwam.

'Het moet niet te nat worden, want dan voel ik niets meer,' zei ze. 'Probeer me maar te likken en te vingeren tegelijkertijd. Dat vind ik lekker.'

Hij likte terwijl hij zijn speeksel probeerde binnen te houden en hij vingerde haar.

'Dit voelt niet goed,' zei ze, 'misschien kun je geen twee dingen tegelijk. Hou maar op met dat vingeren. Dit gaat zo niet.'

'O.'

Zijn stem moest ietwat terneergeslagen hebben geklonken, want ze zei: 'Geeft niet. Jij kunt weer andere dingen. Hier zijn de jongens door naar buiten gekomen. Onze twee jongens.'

'Ja,' zei hij. Ze had gelijk. Hij had Borys geboren zien

worden en hij had niet gedacht aan een intercity naar Amsterdam, geen moment had hij daaraan gedacht. Tegen aanstaande ouders zou hij zeggen: De kansen zijn minimaal maar denk even aan de intercity naar Amsterdam als jullie baby naar buiten komt, denk er voor de zekerheid even aan.

Wen pakte zijn hoofd en drukte het tegen zich aan. Het voelde niet alsof het hoofd iets met hem te maken had, alsof het om zíjn hoofd ging, het kon het hoofd zijn van iedereen, zijn hoofd was een willekeurig hoofd en dat was een bevrijding. Het had niets meer met hem te maken, het lag tussen haar benen en het mocht niet te veel speeksel verliezen. Zoals je een brand moet blussen met een minimale hoeveelheid water.

Ze hijgde. Ze drukte hem tegen zich aan, ze trok aan zijn haren. Als het te nat werd voelde ze niets meer, maar hoe verlies je geen speeksel als je het poesje van je vrouw aan het likken bent en daardoor alles nat wordt, je neus, je mond, je wang, je kin, het laken? Hij deed zijn best maar het leek alsof er overal speeksel was, alsof het bed alleen nog uit speeksel bestond en zijn vrouw drukte zijn hoofd dichter tegen zich aan, alsof ze zijn hoofd naar binnen wilde drukken, alsof het de weg moest afleggen die hun jongen had afgelegd in tegenovergestelde richting. Hun jongens, maar hij dacht even niet aan de jongen beneden, de overgeblevene. En toen kwam ze klaar, ze schokte, ze maakte geluiden, geluiden die uit een andere wereld kwamen, niet meer de wereld van de mensen, ook niet die van de dieren, voor zover mens en dier werkelijk van elkaar verschilden, een heel andere wereld, een volstrekt ander universum, zulke geluiden had hij zijn lieve vrouw nog nooit horen maken en hij concentreerde zich op zijn speeksel dat hij binnen moest zien te houden.

Haar orgasme bevredigde hem, zoals het blussen van een grote brand met overlevenden hem op een eigenaardige manier bevredigde, burgers die gered waren, die tijdig naar buiten waren gedragen of gesleurd.

Hij kwam tussen haar benen vandaan. Hij wilde haar kussen, haar liefkozen, maar ze duwde hem weg. 'Ik hoef mezelf niet te ruiken,' zei ze, nog altijd hijgend, 'ik wil mezelf niet proeven. Je ruikt naar mij, ik proef mezelf als ik je kus.'

Het drong tot hem door dat het hijgen was overgegaan in huilen, dat het misschien al die tijd al huilen was geweest. 'Ga weg,' riep ze.

Hij ging niet weg, hij bleef naast haar zitten en ze huilde alsof er een nieuwe ramp was gebeurd. Alles was nu goed. De oude ramp was een tijd geleden, als je de eerste weken had doorstaan dan zou je de rest ook doorstaan. Ze hadden de ramp achter zich gelaten, er was alleen nog een postscriptum in de vorm van een pony en om haar zou hij zich bekommeren.

'Ik walg van mezelf,' zei ze.

Hij bleef op het bed zitten, naast het hoofd van zijn vrouw. Het huilen ging verder. Was het wel huilen? Of was het een onverstaanbare aanklacht, een woedende reeks van geluiden die de mond van zijn vrouw verliet? Hij zei dat dit niet hoefde, dat er geen reden was van jezelf te walgen, dat ze een geweldige vrouw was, dat ze zijn Wen was. Hij zei niet dat de vrouw van Beckers troost had geboden, hoewel hij dat had willen bespreken, maar dit was niet het moment. De Pool haalde wc-papier uit de badkamer, depte haar tranen en daarna maakte hij een washandje met lauwwarm water vochtig en hij veegde de uitgelopen make-up van haar gezicht. Wen bleef roepen dat ze van zichzelf walgde, dat ze zichzelf niet wilde ruiken en dat ze zichzelf niet wilde proeven en dat hij moest opdonderen, want hij rook naar haar. Ze wilde zichzelf niet ruiken, ze kon zichzelf niet ruiken zonder gek te worden van de geur. Hij donderde niet op, hij zei dat ze zich niet zo moest opwinden, dat ze het ergste achter de rug hadden. De Pool zong een Pools lied voor haar dat zijn vader lang geleden voor hem had gezongen en dat hij voor zijn beide jongens had gezongen. Langzaam werd ze rustiger.

De Pool hielp haar uit bed, ze hadden de rest van hun kleren uitgedaan en naakt liepen ze naar beneden. Hij naakt, zij naakt. Halverwege de trap hoorde hij het al. Hij begreep niet dat ze het boven niet hadden gehoord. Beneden zagen ze hun jongen op de grond liggen. Ook hij huilde, ook hij krijste, maar anders. Zijn stoeltje was omgevallen. Wen tilde hem op. 'Zijn hoofd,' riep ze. 'Zijn hoofdje. Zou hij een hersenschudding hebben?'

Ze liep met hem heen en weer en op tafel stonden nog de restanten van het eten. Ze probeerde het kind te kalmeren en omdat de Pool niet wist wat hij moest doen begon hij de tafel af te ruimen. Hij zei nog wel dat als de jongen niet kotste het misschien niet zo erg was en dat hij niet begreep hoe hij gevallen kon zijn. Had hij misschien geprobeerd uit zijn stoeltje te klimmen? Ze hadden hem ook niet alleen achter moeten laten aan tafel, zo'n jong kind hoort niet alleen aan tafel achter te blijven. Eerst de jongen naar bed, dan het genot. Maar dat laatste zei hij niet en in de woonkamer liep Wen met de jongen heen en weer. Ze vroeg of ze naar het ziekenhuis moesten.

Toen het huilen eindelijk ophield zei de Pool dat dit niet hoefde. Dat het goed was gekomen, dat er een buil zou verschijnen op het achterhoofd van hun overgebleven jongen maar dat was niet erg. Het was een sterke jongen.

Ze gingen naar boven, nog altijd naakt en Wen droeg Jurek in haar armen. Ze brachten hem naar bed. Het jongetje was uitgeput, van het huilen, het krijsen. Hij had zo lang geschreeuwd dat hij helemaal rood aangelopen was toen ze hem vonden. De Pool moest er niet aan denken, niet aan wat er boven was gebeurd en niet aan wat er tegelijkertijd beneden was gebeurd. Het een leek het ander erger te maken.

De jongen viel in slaap en de naakte ouders bleven naast zijn bedje staan, ze bekeken hem vol bewondering. 'Je hebt me lekker gelikt,' zei Wen. 'Dat is het probleem niet.'

Ze kwam dichterbij en streelde zijn wang.

'Ja, was het lekker?' vroeg hij.

'Heel lekker,' zei ze, 'maar misschien moeten we het niet meer doen.' Ze bleef hem strelen, eerst zijn wang, nu zijn borst, zijn harige borst. 'We hebben nog wel seks, maar likken, dat niet meer.'

'Als jij het zegt,' antwoordde hij.

'Ik hou van je, Pool,' zei ze. 'Ik hou heel veel van je. Maar dat likken, daar kan ik niet meer tegen. Ik kan niet meer tegen mijn eigen genot. Misschien dat ik er over een jaar anders over denk. Anderhalf jaar.'

Ze verroerden zich niet, zij had haar hand nog altijd op zijn borst. Ze luisterden naar de ademhaling van hun overgebleven jongen en toen zei de Pool: 'De vrouw van Beckers wil ons troosten.'

Hij hoorde de jongen ademen, hij hoorde zijn vrouw ademen, het leek alsof de ademhaling van zijn jongen overging in die van zijn vrouw en eindelijk zei ze: 'Dat hebben we niet nodig, we zijn sterk.'

'Ja,' zei hij.

'Heb je haar vriendelijk bedankt?' vroeg Wen. 'Of moet ik dat doen?'

'Nee,' zei hij. 'Ik heb haar vriendelijk bedankt.'

Beneden gingen ze op de bank zitten en Wen zei: 'Er zijn denk ik veel mensen die ons willen troosten. Op mijn werk hebben ze het ook al een paar keer aangeboden. Maar ze doen het voor zichzelf. Het zijn net roofvogels, die troosters. Ze willen het vlees van je botten eten.'

De Pool zette de televisie aan, ze keken naar het weerbericht. En Wen zei zonder hem aan te raken, zonder haar blik van de weerman af te wenden: 'Niets kan ons uit elkaar drijven, dat weten we nu zeker.'

# 5

Met de boer probeerde hij het op een akkoordje te gooien, hij stelde voor dat de pony nog een paar maanden respijt kreeg. Zij was het laatste dier op de boerderij. De koeien waren weggehaald, de knecht was vertrokken, maar tegen betaling plus toeslag hoopte hij dat de pony nog even kon blijven.

Hij hoopte vurig dat de boer over onverwacht mededogen beschikte, dat hij het sentiment in de boer wakker kon schudden, hij sloot niet uit dat de boer eigenlijk een sentimenteel mens was en dat hij aan de wereld ook wat goedheid wilde tonen, op z'n minst aan de Pool. Maar het was anders gelopen, de boer had redeneringen opgehangen waarvan de Pool niets begreep maar die zeer beslist klonken en uiteindelijk was de Pool over brandveiligheid begonnen.

Hij vertelde dat hij op een onbewaakt moment naar boven was gegaan en dat hij had gezien hoe de boerin erbij lag, dat het hem niets aanging maar dat hij als brandweerman de plicht had de brandveiligheid in de gaten te houden. Iemand vastbinden op bed ging tegen de basisregels van de brandveiligheid in.

De boer begon te jammeren, niet vanwege een mogelijke brand maar het idee dat zijn vrouw zich vrijelijk door het huis kon bewegen maakte hem kennelijk doodziek. Hij zei: 'Jij weet niet wat ze aanricht, jij weet niet hoe ze is, tegen jou doet ze poeslief, ik heb haar ware karakter leren kennen. Dat ik haar in leven heb gelaten is pure mensllievendheid, alleen al daarvoor kom ik in de hemel.'

De Pool antwoordde dat er wat hem betreft geen hemel was, de mogelijkheid van God hield hij op een kiertje.

Brandveiligheid bestond wel. Hij zei: 'Ik ben bereid te vergeten wat ik heb gezien als u de pony nog een paar maanden gedoogt.'

Eerst snoof de boer verachtelijk, al snel gaf hij toe dat hem dat wel een goede ruil leek. Een pony gedogen was niet veel werk en hij kreeg er nog voor betaald ook. Sterker nog, de boer vroeg een flinke toeslag voor de huur van de stal en dat terwijl de Pool de stal vanaf nu zelf moest uitmesten. De knecht, de dierenknecht was namelijk verdwenen, daarvoor was een 'mensenknecht' gekomen die de boer hielp bij het wassen, die eten meebracht, die boodschappen deed en die ook de vrouw van de boer verzorgde.

'Je zult die knecht wel tegenkomen,' zei de boer, 'hij is lang en blond. En je ziet het niet aan hem maar hij is een Jood. Niet dat ik iets tegen Joden heb, ik heb wel slechte ervaringen met ze. Sluw en cynisch zijn ze. Dat noemen ze ironie maar het is pure sluwheid. Goede mensen zijn cynisch noch ironisch. Alleen je hebt het niet voor het uitkiezen als je een mensenknecht zoekt.'

'O,' zei de Pool.

'Er was hier een veehandelaar,' ging de boer door, 'lang geleden, die was Jood. Hij was anders dan andere veehandelaren. Ik wist dat hij me wilde oplichten, want dat doen Joden, daar kunnen ze verder niets aan doen, dat zit in hun bloed. Daarom heb ik hem opgelicht. Dan was ik in elk geval de eerste. Ik wilde niet de laatste zijn. Ik wilde niet dat ze me uitlachten, de andere boeren.'

Dat begreep de Pool en het drong tot hem door dat alles in het leven van de boer erop was gericht om niet te worden uitgelachen, dat de rest hem niet zoveel kon schelen zolang hij maar niet werd uitgelachen.

Toch kon de Pool zich niet aan de indruk onttrekken dat de boer hem ook oplichtte, terwijl hij geen Jood was, hij was een doodgewone Pool, voorheen christelijk, nu atheïst. Of geloofde de boer dat de Polen het oplichten eveneens in het bloed zat? Maar de Pool had geen kracht om lang met de boer te discussiëren, want hij wist dat hij die discussie zou verliezen. Hij was hier voor de pony.

Om die reden had hij ook niet met zijn vrouw over zijn voornemen gesproken, want zij was sterker, sterker met woorden, sterker met emoties die aan de woorden vastzaten, of beter gezegd die werden opgeroepen door de woorden. Er kwamen woorden uit haar mond en plotseling waren dat emoties en dat maakte de Pool zwak. Daarom begon hij voor het eerst in zijn leven te liegen tegen zijn vrouw, omdat hij een redder was, geen mensenredder, een dierenredder. Het was niet echt liegen, het was verzwijgen. Hij verzweeg waar hij heen ging en hij haalde geld van zijn spaarrekening om het aan de boer te geven voor het in leven laten van de pony. De boer rekte het leven tegen contante betaling en de vrouw van de Pool mocht daar niet achter komen, want ze hadden het niet breed, niet breed genoeg om voor redder te spelen.

Soms vroeg ze waar hij was geweest op zijn vrije dagen. Dan zei hij: 'Ik was met een paar jongens van de C-ploeg op pad.' Een keer zei ze: 'Je ruikt naar paard.' 'Een van de jongens van de C-ploeg ruikt naar paard,' antwoordde hij, 'iedereen die bij hem in de buurt is geweest begint naar paard te ruiken.' Zijn vrouw nam genoegen met dat antwoord.

Toch was het niet zo dat hij daar in die stal volop met de oude, vereenzaamde pony in de weer was. Aangezien hij niet veel wist van paarden en pony's en eigenlijk ook niet de behoefte voelde zich er werkelijk in te verdiepen durfde hij het dier nauwelijks aan te raken. Soms, als hij de stal moest uitmesten, leidde hij haar voorzichtig naar buiten. In het begin had hij haar nog vastgebonden maar ze liep niet weg en daarom bond hij haar niet meer vast. Hij wilde zich niet aan haar opdringen. De Pool respecteerde haar ouderdom en haar eenzaamheid. Dat laatste wilde hij ook niet van haar afpakken. Ook dieren hadden recht op hun eenzaamheid. Veeleer was het zo dat hij een deel van zijn vrije dagen doorbracht in de stal. Dat ze het met elkaar konden vinden was te veel gezegd, ze deelden probleemloos een ruimte, de Pool stond daar gewoon en er waren middagen dat de Pool tegen de pony begon te spreken omdat hij de stilte niet meer verdroeg. Dan zei hij: 'Mijn jongen vond jou geweldig. Je bent oud en zonder tussenkomst van de veearts was je kreupel geweest, vermoedelijk dood, maar mijn jongen vond je hoe dan ook geweldig. Alleen is hij er niet meer. Daarom sta ik nu hier. In zijn plaats.'

Zo bleef hij dan nog een tijdje staan. Ook tegen de pony wist hij niet veel te zeggen. Soms hurkte hij in een hoek zoals hun jongen had gehurkt maar van het hurken kreeg hij pijn in zijn knieën, daarom deed hij dat niet vaak.

Als hij van de boerderij kwam besprenkelde hij zich voorzichtigheidshalve met aftershave, want hij wilde niet dat zijn vrouw nog een keer zou zeggen: 'Je ruikt naar paard.' Dat zei ze ook niet meer. Ze rook het niet meer of ze vond het gewoon geworden: haar man was naar paard gaan ruiken en met die geur kon ze best leven.

Op een middag toen hij naar zijn auto liep kwam hij de mensenknecht tegen. Deze was net zo slungelig als de vorige knecht, lang en mager. Hij had melkwit haar en blauwe ogen. Inderdaad leek hij in niets op een Jood. Meer op een Zweed of een Noor. De Pool hoefde niet naar de mensenknecht toe te lopen, de knecht kwam zelf op hem af: 'Ik zal me even voorstellen,' zei hij, 'ik ben Ruud. Ik zorg hier voor de boer en zijn vrouw, omdat ze allebei de boerderij niet willen verlaten.'

'Ik weet het,' zei de Pool.

'En jij bent de man van de pony?' vervolgde de mensenknecht. 'De boer heeft me over je verteld.'

'Ik ben de man van de pony.'

De mensenknecht glimlachte vriendelijk. 'Hij zal ook

wel over mij hebben verteld. Hij noemt me de mensenknecht, want ik verzorg mensen, moeilijke gevallen of mensen die afgezonderd leven, ver buiten de stad en die via de reguliere kanalen nauwelijks meer verzorgd kunnen worden. Ze moeten natuurlijk wel over middelen beschikken om mij te kunnen betalen, al ben ik niet duur.'

Er viel een stilte.

De Pool wees naar de eerste verdieping. 'Die vrouw ligt daarboven,' zei hij.

'Daar is de slaapkamer,' beaamde de mensenknecht. 'De boer zelf slaapt beneden. Je bent een uur bezig om hem boven te krijgen. Dat is zonde van de tijd, en het geld.'

'Vastgebonden,' zei de Pool. 'Ze ligt daar vastgebonden.'

De mensenknecht knikte. 'Ik weet het,' zei hij, 'ze bonden haar vast, dat was traditie. De knecht en de boer. Jaren heeft ze zo geleefd. Ze had zich helemaal verzoend met haar lot. Ze moest er niet aan denken niet meer vastgebonden te zijn. Het leek haar erger dan sterven. Ik heb lang met haar gepraat en ik heb haar deze week toch losgemaakt. Als verzorger heb je verplichtingen, je houdt rekening met de wensen van de mensen die je komt helpen maar soms moet je ook tegen die wensen ingaan. Niet alles wat mensen willen is goed voor hen. Ze wil eigenlijk de kamer niet uit en dat moet je dan wel respecteren. Je kunt mensen niet dwingen naar buiten te gaan als ze al zo lang niet buiten zijn geweest, zeker geen mensen van die leeftijd. Maar aan dat vastbinden heb ik een eind gemaakt.'

'Ik ben brandweerman,' zei de Pool, 'en ik denk aan brandveiligheid bij dat soort gevallen.'

Weer knikte de mensenknecht. 'Dat begrijp ik. Op hun manier houden ze wel van elkaar, die twee. Zij leeft boven, hij voornamelijk beneden, ze communiceren met elkaar door tegen de muren te kloppen. Ze hebben een heel eigen taal ontwikkeld. Heb je dat nooit gemerkt?'

'Nooit iets van gemerkt,' zei de Pool.

De mensenknecht keek peinzend. Hij leek zich amper te kunnen voorstellen dat de boer ook weleens niet op muren klopte. Toen zei hij: 'We komen elkaar hier vast wel vaker tegen.' Hij wilde doorlopen maar de Pool wilde nog iets weten. 'Een gekke vraag misschien,' zei hij. 'Ruik ik naar paard?'

De mensenknecht bracht zijn neus iets dichter bij de hals van de Pool. 'Nee,' zei hij. 'Naar boerderij misschien. Alles en iedereen ruikt hier naar boerderij. Als ik hier klaar ben met werken spring ik meteen onder de douche. Mijn vriendin noemt me soms liefkozend mijn boertje.'

Toen liep de mensenknecht naar de boerderij. De Pool ging in zijn auto zitten, besprenkelde zich met aftershave die hij in een klein flesje bij zich droeg en reed terug naar de stad. Hij reed langs zijn eigen huis, hij stopte niet, hij reed langs het huis alsof het niet van hem was, hij keek naar de voordeur en hij kon zich goed voorstellen dat een ander dagelijks door die deur naar binnen en buiten ging. Zijn vrouw en zoon woonden er nog, hij niet meer. Hij was verdwenen. De gedachte dat hij niet gemist zou worden kwetste hem niet, die gedachte stelde hem juist gerust. Hij reed langs het naargeestige station van Heerlen en toen kwam hij in de straat waar Beckers woonde. Ook niet de meest opwekkende straat om in te wonen. De Pool parkeerde en liep naar het huis van Beckers. Hij belde aan.

Een kind deed open. Het keek hem nors en ook ietwat slaperig aan. 'Is je papa of mama thuis?' vroeg de Pool. 'Ik ben een collega van je vader.'

Het kind monsterde hem. De Pool had het gevoel dat hij niet werd geloofd, dat het kind dacht: zo zien collega's van mijn vader er niet uit. 'Mama is thuis,' het kind draaide zich om en liep weg. De Pool bleef in de deuropening staan. Het voelde alsof hij iets wilde verkopen waarop niemand zat te wachten. Een encyclopedie bijvoorbeeld. Wie had nu nog een encyclopedie nodig? Zijn vader had een encyclopedie gehad. Meer dan twintig delen. Hij had er nooit in gekeken.

De vrouw van Beckers deed de tussendeur open. Ze droeg een schort. 'Jij,' zei ze.

De Pool kon niet opmaken uit dat woord en uit haar stemgeluid of ze verheugd was over zijn komst of juist geergerd. Ze had niets anders gezegd. Alleen 'jij'.

'Ja,' zei hij, 'ik ben het.'

'Verderop is een café,' zei ze, 'laten we daarheen gaan.'

Ze riep dat ze zo terug was, naar haar kinderen vermoedelijk. Of toch naar haar man? Was Beckers stiekem thuis? Het bleef stil in huis. Als de kinderen speelden deden ze het dit keer in stilte.

Ze trok haar opvallende regenjas aan hoewel het helemaal niet regende en liep met de Pool naar de hoek van de straat waar zich een café bevond. Ze gingen naast de jukebox zitten. Het rook er muf, maar dat vond de Pool niet erg. Hij bestelde koffie en zij vroeg om een biertje. 'Het is benauwd,' zei ze. 'Of ligt dat aan mij? Ik heb de hele dag al dorst.'

De Pool keek om zich heen, hij was hier nog niet eerder geweest.

'Ik doe het nu zelf,' zei hij toen de helft van zijn koffie was opgedronken. De vrouw van Beckers vroeg namelijk niets. Elke keer nadat ze een slok had genomen dacht hij: nu gaat ze iets vragen. Dan keek ze toch weer naar haar bier of naar hem en ze vroeg niets. Daarom begon hij zelf maar te vertellen. 'Ik heb niemand voor de pony gevonden, dus ik doe het.'

Ze fronste haar wenkbrauwen en wierp hem een afkeurende blik toe. Kennelijk vond ook zij dat hij iets deed wat hij beter kon laten. Net als zijn eigen vrouw, al wist die er dan niets van. Hij had zich weleens afgevraagd waarom ze er nooit meer naar vroeg, hij vermoedde dat ze het beest gewoon niet belangrijk genoeg vond. Ze was het vergeten.

'Het is zeker een avontuur?' vroeg de vrouw van Beckers.

Een avontuur.

De uitbater van het café was bezig een tosti te bakken.

'Nee, het is geen avontuur,' zei de Pool uiteindelijk. Het begon ietwat aangebrand te ruiken.

'Waarom doe je het?' vroeg ze. 'Maakt dat het makkelijker?'

Hij schudde zijn hoofd. 'Ik heb het er met mijn vrouw over gehad, dat je ons wilde troosten. Maar ze zei dat we daar geen behoefte aan hadden.'

De vrouw van Beckers nam een slok van haar bier. 'Jullie weten zelf het beste waar jullie behoefte aan hebben,' fluisterde ze en ze leunde een beetje opzij alsof hij haar niet kon verstaan als ze haar mond niet dichter bij zijn oor bracht. 'Jullie weten dat ik het beste met jullie voorheb. Ik bid wel voor jullie. Daar hebben jullie geen last van, daarvoor heb ik jullie toestemming niet nodig.'

De Pool knikte. Dat had hij niet verwacht. Dat er nog werd gebeden. Voor hem was bidden een hobby van mensen van vroeger, toen er nog geen smartphones waren. Ze communiceerden met God omdat er geen spelletjes waren die ze op hun telefoon konden spelen, geen sms'jes die ze konden versturen.

Ze stond op en ging naar het toilet en hij keek naar de uitbater, die de tosti kennelijk voor zichzelf had gebakken, want die was hij nu aan het eten terwijl hij de krant las. Als ze terugkwam van de wc zou de Pool afscheid van de vrouw van Beckers nemen en naar huis rijden. Hij wist zelf niet meer waarom hij bij haar langs was gegaan. Echt alleen om te vertellen dat hij zich had ontfermd over de pony en dat hem dat goed afging? Dat hij naast haar in de stal stond, soms wel twee uur, en dat ze elkaars eenzaamheid respecteerden? Misschien had hij gehoopt dat ze gezegd had: Ik kan ook wel voor dat beest zorgen. Als ik jullie niet kan troosten, dan zal ik de pony troosten.

Hij zou haar niet meer opzoeken, de eerste keer was al een vergissing geweest, de tweede keer een nog grotere. Haar vage beloftes hadden verwachtingen in hem opgeroepen die niet realistisch waren.

De vrouw van Beckers kwam maar niet terug van het toilet en de uitbater was met een sponsje in de weer. Zijn tosti had hij achter de kiezen. Verder was er niemand in dit café, waar de geur van verbrand brood zich nu vermengde met die van schoonmaakmiddel. De Pool stond op. Hij liep in de richting van het toilet, hij moest naar huis, de overgebleven jongen wachtte op hem, hij had dingen te doen. Hij klopte op de deur van het damestoilet. 'Gaat het?' vroeg hij. 'Ik moet er zo vandoor.'

Daarop werd de deur geopend en ze sleurde hem naar binnen, zoals je een kind naar binnen trekt op wie je lang hebt zitten wachten. Boos dat het je zo lang heeft laten wachten maar ook opgelucht dat het nog leeft. Ze sloot de deur. Ze ging op het toilet zitten terwijl ze alles aanhad. Ze was niet aan het plassen, ze zat daar gewoon alsof de wc een stoel was. 'Ik ben voor jullie aan het bidden,' zei ze, harder dan daarnet. 'Dat kan niemand me verbieden.'

Toen stond ze op en ze begon de Pool te zoenen, ze zoende hem op zijn wang en met enige moeite op zijn mond, ze moest hem naar beneden trekken en hij zoende terug. Eerst voorzichtig, toen minder voorzichtig en daarna hield hij op en hij zei: 'Ik heb zo'n zin in je, maar je bent de vrouw van Beckers.'

Hij schrok van wat hij had gezegd. Iets in hem had gesproken, tegen zijn wil in, hij was niet iemand die tegen mensen zei: Ik heb zin in je. Hij was een zwijgzame Pool en hoewel hij wist dat sommige mensen daar moeite mee hadden, had hij in de loop der jaren genoeg mensen ontmoet die de zwijgzaamheid juist prettig vonden omdat er al zoveel gesproken werd op deze wereld.

'Ja,' zei ze, 'dat ben ik. De vrouw van Beckers.' En daarop zoende ze hem weer, ze hield zijn hoofd vast en zoende hem voorzichtig en toch gretig. Soms trok ze haar hoofd terug alsof ze zich op die momenten herinnerde dat ze de vrouw van Beckers was, snel daarna bracht ze haar mond weer naar de zijne. Ze was de vrouw van zijn collega maar ze was ook nog een andere vrouw, een vrouw die op het damestoilet van een ietwat groezelig café stond te zoenen met de Pool.

Met zijn hand ging hij over haar lichaam, over haar rug, tot bij haar billen en toen weer omhoog. Hij dacht niet aan zijn vrouw, niet aan de eerste keer dat hij haar had gezoend, hoewel hij daar best aan had kunnen denken. Want ook toen had hij zin gehad, heel veel zelfs, maar hij had het niet gezegd, hij had alleen gedaan wat mensen doen als ze zin hebben. Hij dacht ook niet aan zijn jongen of aan de stal, hij dacht alleen aan haar, de vrouw van Beckers. Dat ze daar in het damestoilet stond met haar schort nog om. Vaag rook hij het bier dat ze had gedronken, vooral rook hij haar. Hij vond dat ze lekker rook. Hij vond dat ze verrukkelijk rook. Met die gedachte klemde hij zich aan haar vast, met de ontdekking dat de vrouw van Beckers heerlijk rook, zelfs hier op deze plek waar frituurlucht, schoonmaakmiddel en de geur van het riool zich met elkaar vermengden. Was dit wat ze bedoelden met bidden en troost? Hij wilde het haar niet vragen, hij wilde geen antwoorden, geen gesprekken. Hij zoende haar wilder dan zij hem zoende. Toen trok ze haar hoofd weer terug. Ze zei: 'Ik vind het fijn dat je zin in me hebt, ik heb ook zo'n zin in jou, maar ik moet naar huis, de kinderen wachten op me. Ik was aan het koken.'

'Ja,' zei hij en hij slikte overtollig speeksel weg. 'Je was aan het koken.'

Nog een keer zoende hij haar, omdat ze ook zo'n zin had in hem. In de Pool, hoe was het mogelijk? Hij begreep het niet, waarom in hem?

‘Ik moet gaan,’ zei ze. ‘Er staat een boeuf bourguignon op het vuur.’

Ze trok haar kleren recht. Terwijl hij toch zijn handen thuis had gehouden, hij was nergens onder gegaan met zijn handen, ze was de vrouw van Beckers en dat respecteerde hij. ‘Blijf jij even hier wachten,’ zei ze. ‘Dat is beter.’

Ze glipte achteloos naar buiten en hij bleef in het damestoilet achter. Hij telde tot zestig, de uitbater moest denken dat de Pool verstopping had.

Toen kwam hij tevoorschijn. Ze zat aan het tafeltje achter haar bier. Het glas was nu vrijwel leeg, ze bracht het naar haar mond. Met vaste tussenpozen. Ook al was het nu helemaal leeg, ze bleef het naar haar mond brengen.

‘Daar ben je,’ zei ze.

De Pool ging zitten.

‘Het was gezellig,’ antwoordde hij.

‘Ja,’ zei ze.

En hij begreep niet voor wie ze dit toneelstukje opvoerden, want de uitbater was verdiept in de krant.

Ze stonden gelijktijdig op. ‘Mijn auto staat daar,’ zei hij.

Ze liep een stukje met hem mee. ‘Mijn huwelijk is een liefdeloos huwelijk,’ vertelde ze op een toon alsof het haar eigenlijk niet aanging. En meteen daarop zei ze: ‘Even een steentje uit mijn schoen halen.’ Ze zocht iets in haar schoen maar er zat niets. Toen liep ze weer verder. ‘Toch hou ik zielsveel van mijn man, begrijp je dat?’ vroeg ze.

‘Ja,’ zei de Pool. ‘Dat soort dingen begrijp ik.’

‘Jullie zijn vrienden, toch?’

‘We zijn collega’s. We zijn goede collega’s, betere vind je niet, denk ik.’

‘Toen ik jou zag,’ zei ze, ‘toen ik jullie zag, jullie verlies, wilde ik vergeten dat ik getrouwd was. Soms lukt me dat. Kun je je dat voorstellen?’

De Pool schudde zijn hoofd. ‘Dat hoef je helemaal niet te vergeten.’

Ze nam afscheid van hem met een knikje, een hand die even zijn schouder aanraakte. Daarna liep ze terug naar huis. Ze draaide zich niet om, de Pool bleef haar nakijken zoals hij zijn jongen had willen nakijken die laatste ochtend dat hij naar school ging. Hij had zijn jongen bijna nooit nagekeken. Hij had hem gedwongen naar school te gaan toen hij dat niet meer wilde omdat hij in zijn broek poepte. Hij had hem losgerukt van lantaarnpalen en bomen waaraan de jongen zich had vastgeklemd. Nagekeken had de Pool de jongen nooit, hij had andere dingen te doen. En die dag had hij het niet eens kunnen doen, hij was op de kazerne. Nu dacht hij weleens: als ik hem had nagekeken, als ik hem vaker had nagekeken dan had ik iets gezien, dan had ik iets meer begrepen.

De Pool ging naar huis. Zijn vrouw en Jurek lagen in de woonkamer op de grond. Zij op haar rug naast de jongen die rustig met blokken aan het spelen was.

De Pool bukte zich, gaf haar een kus. 'Wat spelen jullie?' vroeg hij.

'Ik was een beetje in slaap gevallen,' antwoordde ze.

Ook de jongen gaf hij een kus, hij aaide hem over zijn hoofd en even wist hij niet meer of hij een vader was of gewoon tamelijk overtuigend voor vader speelde.

'Je ruikt naar tosti,' zei ze.

'Dat kan niet,' antwoordde hij en hij schrok.

'Is niet erg,' mompelde ze. 'Er is niets mis met tosti's.'

Hij ging op de grond zitten en hij speelde samen met haar en met de overgebleven jongen en tussen het spelen door vroeg hij: 'Weet je zeker dat we geen troost nodig hebben?'

'Heel zeker,' zei ze, terwijl ze een trein over houten rails liet rijden. 'We hebben elkaar toch? We hebben hem. We hebben Jurek. We hebben alles wat we nodig hebben.'

'Dat is waar,' zei hij. 'We hebben alles wat we nodig hebben.' En terwijl hij dat zei besloot hij dat hij het haar zou vertellen, van de pony, die avond nog. Dat het niet zo kon doorgaan. Dat hij het haar zou uitleggen. Ze zou het vast begrijpen. Als hij de juiste woorden kon vinden, het juiste moment.

Samen brachten ze de overgebleven jongen naar boven, samen wasten ze hem en samen droogden ze hem af. Bij voorkeur deed Wen dat vóór het eten, zodat hij in zijn pyjama aan tafel kon zitten en ze hem daarna alleen nog hoefde voor te lezen en in slaap te wiegen.

Toen ze daarmee klaar waren, toen Jurek zijn pyjama aanhad, toen hij geruststellend naar babyshampoo rook en zijn woordjes brabbelde, zei de Pool: 'Ik was je nog iets vergeten te zeggen.'

'Wat?' Haar stem klonk scherp. Angstig eigenlijk. Alsof ze allang wist dat hij iets vergeten was te zeggen en ze toch hoopte dat ze zich vergiste. Dat hij alles had gezegd, alles wat er te zeggen viel.

'Niets om van te schrikken,' zei hij.

Het eten kwam die avond uit de magnetron. Eigenlijk hield Wen daar niet van, maar een keer per week, soms een keer in de twee weken gunde ze zich het gemak en hij ging daarin mee. Hij volgde haar, niet omdat hij zo volgzaam was maar omdat hij de meeste conflicten niet de moeite waard vond, dus als zij zei: 'Het eten komt vandaag uit de magnetron,' dan zei hij niet: 'Ik kook wel.' Dan zei hij: 'Oké. Lekker.'

'Er is een ander?' vroeg ze.

'Nee,' zei hij, met Jurek in zijn armen. 'Geen ander. Maar ik heb de pony niet weggedaan. Ze is er nog. Ik ga er een paar keer per week heen.'

'Nee,' zei ze en ze schreeuwde bijna, 'nee, Geniek. Ik had het er niet meer over omdat ik dacht dat ze allang dood was. Dat ze allang in een hamburger zat. Daarom was ik er nooit meer over begonnen.'

'Ze zit niet in een hamburger. Volgens mij zitten er

nooit pony's in hamburgers.'

Ze had hem Geniek genoemd. Zo noemde ze hem bijna nooit meer.

'De gedachte dat jij daar heen gaat... Ik wil het niet,' zei ze. 'Het voelt oneerlijk. Je sluit me buiten. Jij gaat daarheen. Naar die plek waar hij is geweest. Al die weken, maanden, hoelang is het eigenlijk? Ik ben daar nooit geweest. Nooit. Geen een keer ben ik meegegaan om dat beest te zien, om dat beest van hem te bekijken, omdat ik geloofde... Ik vond eigenlijk dat het niets voor jongens was. Ik dacht: het gaat wel over. Ik begreep het niet. En nu ga jij daarheen. En je pakt hem van me af. Je pakt hem nog een keer van me af. Niet dat jij hem de eerste keer van mij hebt afgepakt. Maar dat hij er niet meer is, dat is iets van ons samen en als jij daarheen gaat, naar dat beest, dan is het iets van jou, van jou alleen.'

'Ga dan mee,' zei hij. 'Dan is het van ons. Ik doe niets met haar. Ik sta gewoon in de stal.' Terwijl hij nog altijd de overgebleven jongen vasthield streelde hij even haar arm, om aan te geven dat hij haar niet wilde buitensluiten. Dat ze mee mocht. Dat ze erbij hoorde. Dat het gat van hun samen was.

'Je staat in de stal?' vroeg ze. 'Je staat in de stal zoals koeien in de stal staan?'

'Niet zoals koeien. Onze jongen bracht daar de laatste weken van zijn leven door. We weten dat hij daar het liefste heen ging. En op de een of andere manier stelt het me gerust om daar ook heen te gaan, om daar te staan. Waar hij stond.'

'Dus dat is wat je deed terwijl je mij vertelde dat je met je collega's op pad was, je hebt in een stal gestaan. Ik had het dus toch goed geroken.'

Ze rende naar beneden, naar de keuken, alsof hij haar had opgebiecht dat hij al maanden een minnares had, en hij volgde haar en hij keek toe terwijl ze een magnetronmaaltijd in de magnetron deed. Hij hield de jongen vast en hij wist niet wat hij moest zeggen. Hij wist opeens niet hoe hij het kon uitleggen.

'Mijn man staat in een stal. Onze jongen is onder een trein gekomen en daarom staat mijn man middagen lang in een stal, naast een doodzieke pony die van onze jongen was, omdat hij geen vrienden had. Want dat is de waarheid, Geniek, hij had geen vrienden, niemand wilde zijn vriend zijn en we hebben er niets aan gedaan, we hebben het zo gelaten, we hebben gedacht: het loopt wel los. Zolang hij maar niet in zijn broek poept. En toen hij niet meer in zijn broek poepte waren we opgelucht, we waren reuzetevreden. En nu ga jij daar staan, naast die pony en ik moet dat normaal vinden. Wil jij je eigen zoon worden? Denk je dat het helpt als je op hem gaat lijken? Ga je straks ook in je broek poepen?'

'Nee,' zei hij zacht, 'natuurlijk niet. En het gaat er niet om dat ik hem wil worden, het gaat erom dat ik vind dat ze niet dood moet en ik ga naast haar staan omdat ik dat prettig vind. Misschien had ik het eerder moeten zeggen. Misschien had ik het moeten vertellen, maar ik vóélde wat jij net uitsprak... Dat je het afkeurde. Ik wilde niet dat je het afkeurde. Daarom dacht ik: ik begin er niet over. Dan hoef je niets af te keuren.'

Hij keek naar de magnetron. Kip met rijst. Daarop pakte hij de borden, met de jongen nog altijd op zijn arm, en hij begon de tafel te dekken. Zij bleef achter in de keuken en hij kwam terug om nog wat bestek te pakken en toen ook dat was gebeurd, toen de tafel gedekt was, zei ze: 'Jij vindt het misschien oké om middagen lang in een stal te staan, maar dat komt omdat je met niemand praat. Als je het zou voorleggen aan mensen, als je het voorlegde aan je collega's dan kreeg je te horen dat het niet normaal is. Maar dat doe je niet. Er is geen sla. Ik heb geen zin om sla te maken. Vind je dat erg?'

'Nee,' zei hij.

Ze haalde de magnetronmaaltijd uit de magnetron en verdeelde die over twee borden, daarna warmde ze nog het stamppotje op dat de overgebleven jongen kreeg en uiteindelijk gingen ze de eetkamer in. Hij zette de jongen in zijn stoeltje, pas toen ze allemaal zaten zei hij: 'Je bent ooit verliefd geworden op een zwijgzame Pool. Je wist wie ik was.'

'Ik wist wie je was en je zwijgzaamheid vond ik mysterieus en aantrekkelijk, maar nu word ik er gek van.' Ze prakte haar rijst zonder dat daar reden toe was, ze prakte de rijst alsof de korrels te groot waren. 'En toch,' zei ze toen ze klaar was met prakken, 'het maakt me niet uit, het is niet dat ik weg wil, we groeien naar elkaar toe als twee bomen maar soms zitten je wortels me in de weg.'

De Pool moest hierover nadenken. De wortels, de bomen, het klonk vertrouwd. Langzaam begon hij ook te eten. De kip was een beetje zoet.

'Ik neem je mee,' zei hij. 'De eerstvolgende keer dat ik erheen ga, ga je mee. Ik laat je de boerderij zien, ik weet dat je er niet heen wilde, na zijn dood... Omdat... Omdat je het niet nodig vond. Zoals we ook zijn kamer niet meer wilden opendoen. Zoals we dachten: het is goed. Het kan ons niets schelen wat andere mensen zeggen, we doen het zoals wij denken dat het goed is. En eigenlijk praat ik best veel. Hier in huis ben ik allang geen zwijgzame Pool meer. Ik ben gewoon de Pool.'

Ze at verder en nu was zij het die niets zei en toen haar bord leeg was en het bord van de Pool nog vol lag met kip en rijst zei ze: 'Oké, ik ga mee. Als dat is wat je wil. Maar ik begrijp het niet. Ik zeg het nu al en ik denk niet dat ik het ga begrijpen. Er valt niets meer te veranderen aan het verleden. Al blijf je de rest van je leven in die stal staan. Concentreer je op de zoon die je nog hebt.'

De Pool deed zijn best al wist hij vrij zeker dat hij de kip niet weg zou krijgen. En om te bewijzen dat hij zich concentreerde op de zoon die hij nog had haalde hij de jongen uit zijn stoeltje en hij zei tegen de jongen: 'Ik concentreer me op jou. De Pool concentreert zich op jou.' En hij liep door de eetkamer, eigenlijk vooral als excuus om niet te hoeven eten, maar de jongen lachte en toen moest Wen ook lachen.

'We moeten het afsluiten,' zei Wen, 'dat is wat ik bedoel. Natuurlijk kun je het niet echt afsluiten, we moeten doen alsof, anders word ik hier gek. Ik kan er niet tegen dat ik het gevoel heb dat ik ook tegen hem praat als ik tegen jou praat. Vanaf nu moeten we tegen elkaar zeggen: we waren met z'n vieren, nu zijn we met z'n drieën en dat accepteren we.'

Lopend door de kamer zei de Pool: 'Het is niet afgesloten zolang zij er nog is. Begrijp je dat niet?'

Hij bracht de jongen naar boven. Gelukkig zei zijn vrouw er niets van dat hij de helft van de magnetronmaaltijd had laten staan.

Pas toen ze in bed lagen merkte ze op: 'Je wordt mager.'

'Ik was wat te zwaar,' antwoordde hij.

'Welnee,' antwoordde ze, 'je was gespierd. Je bent gespierd. Dat was geen vet, dat zijn spieren. Je bent een mooie man.'

Hij omhelsde zijn lieve vrouw maar hij kuste haar niet op de mond, hij kon haar niet op de mond kussen, eigenlijk op dezelfde manier zoals hij zijn kip niet had kunnen eten.

# 6

Op de eerstvolgende vrije zaterdag zouden ze erheen gaan. 's Ochtends wachtte hij tot zij iets zou zeggen maar uiteindelijk moest hij vragen: 'Wilde je nog mee?' Het deed hem pijn dat zij er niet over was begonnen. Alsof ze het met tegenzin deed, alleen voor hem, voor de lieve vrede. Ze vroeg: 'Waarheen?' Meteen daarna zei ze: 'O ja, natuurlijk.'

'Ik wil niet dat Jurek meegaat,' voegde ze eraan toe. 'Ik breng hem wel naar de overburen.'

Toen ze de overgebleven jongen bij de overburen had afgeleverd informeerde ze of ze kaplaarzen aan moest. 'Nou ja,' antwoordde de Pool – op een dergelijke vraag had hij niet gerekend – 'we gaan naar een stal. Maar kaplaarzen... Het heeft niet geregend. Nee. Dat hoeft niet.'

'Ik doe toch kaplaarzen aan,' zei ze. 'Voor de zekerheid.' Kennelijk vreesde ze een hoop smerigheid aan te treffen op de boerderij.

Wen ging naar boven en kwam terug met blauwe kaplaarzen met rode en gele bloemen erop getekend. Ook had ze een oude spijkerbroek aangetrokken die ze anders alleen aandeed als ze in de tuin ging werken, wat ze tegenwoordig maar zelden deed. Hij kon zich niet herinneren wanneer hij haar voor het laatst in die oude spijkerbroek had gezien.

Ze maakte zich op voor de spiegel, ze werkte geconcentreerd haar wallen weg. 'Mag ik zo mee?'

'We gaan naar een stal,' antwoordde hij.

'Zie ik er niet goed uit?' vroeg ze.

In de auto zei ze niet veel meer. Ze luisterde naar de radio en af en toe vertelde ze iets over wat ze op de radio hoorde, over de crisis, de banken, ook noemde ze de naam van een zangeres die hij niet kende en dat ze weer eens wilde dansen.

Ze kwamen bij de boerderij en ze wees naar de boer voor het raam. 'Die man staart naar ons.'

'Dat doet hij altijd,' zei de Pool. 'Staren. Hij zit in een rolstoel. Heb ik dat niet verteld?'

'Volgens mij niet,' antwoordde ze. 'Je vertelt bijna nooit iets. Bovendien heb je ook mensen in een rolstoel die niet de hele dag naar buiten zitten te staren.'

Ze liepen naar de stal en de Pool herinnerde zich de veearts, het wonder dat te laat was gekomen, zijn oudste jongen. En hij besefte dat hij niets liever wilde dan samen met zijn vrouw in de stal staan, naast het dier. Daar gewoon staan en kijken naar de lege hokken, de tralies, de drinkbak. Urenlang. Tot ze rustig waren geworden, tot ze weer van elkaar hielden zoals vroeger, tot ze begrepen dat je ook zo kon leven.

'Daar', hij wees naar de enige stal waar nog een levend dier stond. Het laatste levende dier hier, als je de poezen, muizen en insecten niet meerekende.

Ze gingen naar binnen, hij deed het licht aan.

'Zoveel lege hokken,' zei de vrouw van de Pool. En ze keek naar haar kaplaarzen, het waren laarzen die kleuters prachtig vonden.

Ze liepen naar de pony van Borys, langzaam, Wen zette haar voeten voorzichtig neer. 'Het is niet vies,' zei de Pool. 'Het is hier alleen donker.'

'Zo eenzaam,' zei ze toen ze voor het hok stonden. 'Zielig.'

'Ik zorg toch voor haar.' Zielig vond hij het dier namelijk niet, zoals hij uiteindelijk ook hun jongen niet zielig had gevonden. Noodlottig, tragisch, onbegrepen, dat waren woorden die hem te binnen schoten, niet zielig. Hij hield niet van dat woord. 'Ik ga er zo vaak heen als ik kan.'

'Precies,' zei ze, 'en ik zou willen dat je dat niet deed.'

Hij pakte haar hand, maar ze trok hem voorzichtig los.

De Pool opende het hok en zoals gebruikelijk reageerde de pony amper, een kleine beweging met het hoofd. Hij had het gevoel dat hij zijn vrouw voorstelde aan een verloren gewaand familielid.

'Ze is groot,' zei Wen, 'volgens mij zijn pony's kleiner.'

'Je hebt grote en kleine pony's.' Hij merkte dat hij weer als een expert klonk, een man die expertise veinsde die hij niet bezat. Een man die zich nooit voor dieren had geïnteresseerd en die nu deed alsof dieren zijn beste vrienden waren.

'Het ruikt hier naar jou,' zei Wen.

'Hoe bedoel je?'

'Het ruikt zoals jij ruikt.'

'Ik ben hier de laatste tijd veel geweest.'

Ze keek hem aan. 'Ben jij naar dit hok gaan ruiken of is dit hok naar jou gaan ruiken?'

Hij haalde zijn schouders op. Hoewel hij er niet echt zin in had kuste hij zijn lieve vrouw en hij fluisterde in haar oor of ze nu het verschil kon ruiken tussen het hok en haar man. Ze lachte.

'Hier sta ik meestal,' zei de Pool en hij ging naast de pony staan. Om het te laten zien, hoe onschuldig het was wat hij hier deed. Even legde hij zijn hand op het hoofd van de pony. Hij aaide haar niet, ze was geen knuffeldier.

Ze stonden naast elkaar en allebei keken ze naar zijn vrouw, de man en het dier. De blik van Wen ging van de pony naar haar man en terug naar de pony. 'Alsof je jezelf levend begraaft,' mompelde ze.

De Pool schudde zijn hoofd. 'Juist niet, hier is het leven.'

'Niet bij mij? Niet thuis? Hier in deze stal wel?'

Hij gaf de verkeerde antwoorden maar hij wilde niet liegen, want ze was zijn lieve vrouw en dat moest ze blijven. Er bestond geen leven buiten haar, zelfs al stond haar tong hem net zo tegen als de kip uit de magnetronmaaltijd. Nu hij erover nadacht deed haar tong hem aan die kip denken.

'Misschien kunnen we hier samen gaan staan,' zei de Pool. 'Dan zul je het zien. Hoe fijn het is. Gewoon staan. Naast haar. Leven en toch niet leven.'

'Ik heb geen zin om naar de tralies te kijken,' zei zijn vrouw, 'kijk dan, dit oude beest ziet geen zonlicht meer, ziet alleen nog tralies, ziet geen andere dieren meer, ziet alleen jou af en toe. Laat haar afmaken als je van haar houdt, breng haar weg.'

De Pool schudde zijn hoofd. Dit ging de verkeerde kant op. 'Kom dan naast me staan, dan zie je het. Dan voel je het. Soms ga ik met haar naar buiten. Als het weer het toelaat. Dan lopen we een stukje. Wil je dat zien?'

'Nee!' riep ze.

Het geluid van haar stem ging de Pool door merg en been want hij hield van de stilte en hij had het gevoel dat haar geschreeuw de stilte van deze plek ontheiligde. Bovendien vreesde hij de boosheid van zijn vrouw, niet omdat hij bang voor haar was maar omdat die boosheid hem het gevoel gaf dat hij faalde. Soms knielde hij hier in deze stal omdat hij overmand werd door gevoelens – het gevoel niets te zijn behalve het voortdurend tekortschieten – waarmee hij zich geen raad wist.

Ze liep door het hok terwijl hij bleef staan, denkend aan Borys en dan toch weer aan de C-ploeg, zijn vrouw, de vrouw van Beckers, het beest gezelschap houdend dat misschien niet op zijn gezelschap zat te wachten. Hij wilde de eenzaamheid niet van haar afpakken. Hij was niet gekomen om verlichting te brengen want hij wist dat hij dat niet kon. Hooguit kon je zeggen dat hij hier stond uit solidariteit, al zou hij dat zelf nooit zo noemen. Af en toe raakte hij haar respectvol aan, de vereenzaamde, oude vrouw, door de veearts consequent 'meisje' genoemd, een hand op de rug of het hoofd, als er vliegen waren joeg hij ze weg. In uitzonderlijke gevallen krabbelde hij haar en zei hij: 'Onze jongen heeft tegen je gesproken, maar ik heb niets te zeggen.'

Achter zich hoorde hij zijn vrouw door het stro bewegen, hij keek niet om tot ze hem riep. 'Kom eens,' zei ze. 'Heeft hij hier gelopen? Heeft Borys hier gestaan?'

Hij keek om en hij zei: 'Daar hurkte hij.'

De Pool ging achterin, in de donkere hoek staan. 'Dat heb ik je toch verteld,' zei hij. 'Dat hij hier zijn behoefte deed?'

'Ik heb het verdrongen,' zei ze.

'Hij ging volgens mij niet meer naar de mensen-wc. Ik heb het hem nooit durven vragen.'

'Bestaan er dan ook dieren-wc's?' wilde ze weten.

'Hij hield van haar,' zei de Pool. 'In elk geval, dat denk ik. En daarom hou ik nu van haar.'

Ze begon te ijsberen, steeds driftiger alsof ze zelf een gekooid dier was. 'Jij noemt het liefde, maar het is mishandeling. Een wonder, zei je, dat de veearts had verricht, ik zie geen wonder. Ik zie een oud beest dat uit haar lijden verlost moet worden en het is puur egoïsme dat jij dat niet doet. Hoe kun je egoïsme liefde noemen? Hoe kun je je gezin verwaarlozen voor dit beest dat alleen nog op de dood wacht? Een dood die jij haar niet gunt omdat je te laf bent, omdat je denkt dat je het lijden kunt ontlopen, maar je kunt het niet ontlopen. Is dat niet wat onze jongen ons heeft geleerd? Dat je het niet kunt ontlopen?'

Ze beende weg en hij ging achter haar aan. Voor het hok bleef ze staan. 'Ik wil niet meer dat je hier komt,' zei ze. 'Als je bij mij wilt blijven, als je bij ons wilt blijven dan moet je beloven hier niet meer te komen. Dit is een onheilsplek. Ik weet zeker dat het allemaal niet was gebeurd als hij hier niet was gekomen, als hij hier niet heen was gegaan, als een bezetene, elke dag weer. Hij is hier op ideeën gekomen. En als jij hierheen blijft gaan dan kom je ook op die ideeën, daarom zeg ik het heel duidelijk. Als je bij ons wilt blijven dan breng je haar weg. En als je dat hebt gedaan dan zul je zien dat het voor haar ook het beste was. Soms is liefde ook laten inslapen.'

De Pool wist niet wat hij hierop moest antwoorden, hij sloot het hok zoals hij dat minstens drie, vier keer per week deed, altijd met een soort van weemoed, alsof hij hier meer thuishoorde dan bij zijn gezin. Hij antwoordde niet op wat zijn lieve vrouw allemaal had gezegd, hij liep achter haar aan, terug naar de auto, een paar passen liep hij achter haar. Het voelde alsof ook hij zachtjes moest inslapen.

'Heb ik je kunnen overtuigen?' Ze praatte zonder zich om te draaien, ze praatte hard. 'Beloof je het? Dat je hier niet meer komt? Dat het afgelopen is met je bezoeken? Begrijp je het?'

Hij zei ja, maar dat was kennelijk niet voldoende, want ze stond stil, ze draaide zich om en ze vroeg: 'Beloof je het?'

De Pool beloofde het en daarna zei Wen nog dat als ze zich levend in het verleden zouden begraven, met zijn tweeën, als ze zich bleven wentelen in herinneringen Jurek er net zo goed niet kon zijn.

Even wilde de Pool zeggen dat hij zich nergens in wentelde, maar hij slikte zijn opmerking in. Hij moest voor zijn vrouw kiezen, niet voor de pony, niet voor het verleden.

Toen ze bij de auto waren hoorden ze hoe de boer tegen het raam tikte. Eigenlijk wilde de Pool het negeren, maar het tikken hield niet op, het leek alsof de boer met een scherp voorwerp, een schaar of een mes, tegen het raam sloeg. Het kwam hem voor alsof de boer het raam stuk wilde slaan.

'Wat wil hij?' vroeg Wen.

De Pool haalde zijn schouders op. 'Geen idee, hij wil ons vast spreken. Heb ik geen zin in.' Hij maakte aanstalten om in te stappen, maar met een fierheid die hem verraste antwoordde Wen: 'Ik wil hem wel spreken, ik wil hem weleens van dichtbij zien, ik zal hem de waarheid zeggen.'

De boer leek hem iemand met een onwankelbaar geloof in zijn eigen waarheden en weinig tot geen geduld voor die van andere mensen. Maar aangezien hij net beloofd had de pony weg te brengen deed het er misschien niet meer toe welke waarheden ze allemaal aan de boer vertelde. Het ergste wat kon gebeuren was al gebeurd. Al vreesde de Pool dat er nog iets te gebeuren stond. Hij kon zich niet voorstellen dat al het lijden over hem en zijn vrouw was uitgestort. Hij was niet iemand die zich afvroeg: waaraan heb ik dit verdiend? De ramp was geen straf. De pech was betekenisloos en juist dat maakte de pech zo taai, zo ondraaglijk soms, op onvermoede momenten.

Voor hij langer over pech kon nadenken was zijn vrouw al naar het huis gelopen. Alsof ze de weg kende, zo liep ze daar, alsof ze hier vaker was geweest. Ze duwde de deur naar de keuken open. 'Wat een rotzooi,' zei ze. 'Vanbuiten en vanbinnen vervallen.'

De Pool haalde zijn schouders op. 'Het is naar rechts,' zei hij zacht.

Daar zat de boer, hij manoeuvreerde bij het raam vandaan. Het viel de Pool op hoe snel de boer achteruitging, zijn wangen waren ingevallen, zijn lippen waren blauw, hij was dagen, misschien weken niet geschoren. 'Hallo,' zei de Pool. 'We hebben een besluit genomen.' Want de boer deed zijn mond niet open.

De oude man hief zijn hand op. Hij maakte bewegingen met zijn kaak. Zijn tanden leken niet goed in zijn mond te zitten en nu probeerde hij met tong- en kaakbewegingen ze op de juiste plaats te krijgen.

'Dit is mijn vrouw,' zei de Pool.

De boer zwaaide met zijn hand, vermoedelijk om het bezoek duidelijk te maken dat het stil moest zijn, dat het nog niet aan de beurt was om te spreken. Hier sprak je slechts als je gevraagd werd te spreken.

Eindelijk lukte het de boer om iets te zeggen. 'Ik weet

wie ze is,' zei hij licht hijgend. En hij wees op twee knipsels die op de tafel lagen. De rouwadvertentie, discreet en toch weer niet.

'Dus nu is het ook met het eenzame meisje afgelopen,' zei de boer en het klonk alsof het hem speet.

'Welk meisje?' vroeg Wen.

'De pony,' zei de boer, 'het eenzaamste meisje op deze boerderij.' Hij lachte moeizaam, alsof ook het lachen hem pijn deed.

'Leeft u hier alleen?' vroeg Wen nadat de boer was stilgevallen. 'Hebt u geen hulp?'

Het oude tafellaken, voor zover dat woord klopte, was vervangen door iets wat nog meer dan het vorige op een vloerkleed leek.

De boer lachte weer, de vraag leek hem te amuseren. 'Leef ik alleen?' vroeg hij. Toen verhief hij zijn stem. 'Heb ik geen hulp?' riep hij met onvermoede kracht.

De Pool moest denken aan de vrouw die boven in haar kamer lag en dat de mensenknecht hem had verteld dat de boer en zijn vrouw communiceerden door op de muur te kloppen. De oude man begon te hoesten en daarna probeerde hij weer met tong- en kaakbewegingen zijn tanden op de juiste plaats te krijgen. Het bezoek zweeg en de Pool besefte dat er ook een voordeel zat aan de dood die liefde was – dat hij hier niet meer hoefde te komen. Zijn vrouw pakte zijn hand en kneep erin. Ze kon slecht tegen verval, ook menselijk verval.

'Ik heb kinderen,' zei de boer, 'die komen een paar keer per jaar naar mij kijken. U hebt een kind verloren.' Hij tikte met zijn vingers op tafel waar de knipsels lagen. 'U vraagt zich af: waarom komen de kinderen niet vaker naar de oude man kijken? Omdat ze een hekel aan hem hebben. Mensen zijn vreemde wezens. Ik heb de koeien altijd minder vreemd gevonden dan mensen. Soms wordt er een kalfje doodgetrapt, daar maken de koeien geen drama van.'

Wen kneep nu harder in zijn hand en ze zei: 'Mensen zijn geen koeien. Onze jongen is geen doodgetrapt kalfje. We zijn u dankbaar dat hij hier kon komen, dat hij hier iets vond wat hij kennelijk elders niet kon vinden. Maar we hebben de deur naar het verleden gesloten. Wij moeten verder. We hebben nog een zoon. Borys heeft nooit iets over u verteld en ik wilde toch zien wie de boer was waar hij bijna dagelijks heen fietste.'

Ze was welbespraakt, dat kwam ook door de kleuters. Met schreeuwen kwam je niet ver. Het viel hem op dat ze tegen de boer praatte zoals ze ook tegen ouders van kleuters kon praten. Het was haar stem als ze zich eigenlijk ergerde. Ze liet de Pool niet los, ze drukte zijn hand tegen haar zij. Alsof ze aan de boer wilde laten zien: kijk dit is mijn man, niet altijd makkelijk, soms een last, maar ik zal de last blijven dragen.

'Uw zoon,' zei de boer en zijn handen rustten op tafel, op de knipsels. Even dacht de Pool dat die knipsels daar altijd op tafel lagen en dat gaf hem een onbehaaglijk gevoel. 'Uw zoon zag ik bijna nooit, hij ging regelrecht naar de stal en van de stal weer naar huis. Een paar keer is hij hierbinnen geweest. Ik bood hem een snoepje aan, maar hij wilde geen snoepje. Een reepje chocolade wilde hij ook niet. Ik zei: neem een reep jongen, een lekkere reep. Nee. Ik zag het meteen: hij is doodongelukkig. Ik zie aura's, bij dieren en bij mensen. Ik haalde de zieke kalveren er zo tussenuit. Ik zag de kleur van zijn ziekte. Felgeel. Zo fel dat ik moest wegkijken. Mijn vader had het ook. Die werd er gek van. Hij nam het persoonlijk. Dat de mensen ziek zijn. Ik niet. Ik kan er niets aan doen dat ze ziek zijn. Ik heb ze niet ziek gemaakt. Dat wilde ik u vertellen. Dat het zo beter is. Met zo'n aura kun je niet in het leven staan. Ik heb nog geprobeerd te helpen. Ik heb geneeskrachtige handen. Maar het was te laat. Dat wilde ik zeggen. Dat u vrede hebt.'

Wen zei: 'Ik wil niet dat u zo over ons kind praat. De

kleur van zijn ziekte. Zijn aura. Hij was niet ziek. U weet niets over hem.'

De boer lachte weer. Hij rochelde, spoog iets in een zakdoek. 'Hij was niet ziek,' zei hij. 'Dat denken ze altijd. Ze geloven me niet. De mensen willen het niet weten. Ik zie jullie kleuren ook en ik zeg: doe er iets aan voor het te laat is.'

De Pool hoorde hoe een auto het erf op reed. Zijn vrouw bleef hem maar knijpen. Uit liefde. De wanhoop die liefde heet.

'Dat is mijn mensenknecht,' zei de boer. Voor het eerst deze middag klonk de boer angstig. Er viel een stilte. Zijn agressieve vrolijkheid, zijn behoefte anderen te confronteren met waarheden en aura's, het was allemaal verdwenen.

'Uw oren doen het nog goed,' zei de Pool en zijn vrouw krabbelde hem een beetje over zijn achterhoofd zoals je een hond over zijn vacht krabbelt.

'Ja, mijn oren doen het nog goed,' antwoordde de boer. 'Iets moet het toch goed doen. En weet je wat mijn geheim is? Nooit schoonmaken. Gaan je oren kapot van. En nooit naar concerten. Gaan ze ook kapot van. Mijn kinderen wilden me meenemen. Ik heb het geweigerd. Wat door de radio aan muziek dit huis binnenkwam vond ik mooi zat. Mijn oudste is nu doof.'

De Pool hoorde de mensenknecht door de keuken lopen. Toen kwam hij binnen, beter verzorgd dan de dierenknecht maar ook broodmager. Hij had een plastic tas bij zich die hij meteen openmaakte.

'Babi pangang,' waren de eerste woorden van de mensenknecht, 'dat vind je toch lekker?'

De knecht haalde babi pangang en rijst uit de plastic tas en zette de bakken op de kranten en de uitgeknipte rouwadvertentie, een noodlottig ongeval, zo werd het genoemd, zo wilde de Pool het ook noemen.

'Nee,' zei de boer.

Pas daarna richtte de mensenknecht zich tot het bezoek, hij vroeg: 'Alles goed?' Vervolgens richtte hij zich tot Wen: 'Ik kom hier af en toe helpen. 's Ochtends. 's Avonds. Rond etenstijd. Het is nog vroeg, de boer eet vroeg. Meestal kom ik zelf, een enkele keer komt een collega.'

'Ja,' zei de boer. 'Ik eet vroeg. En met tegenzin.'

'Onzin,' zei de mensenknecht. 'Het gaat er steeds beter in.'

De man ging zitten. Hij hing zijn jas over de stoel, haalde de plastic handschoenen uit de tas, handschoenen die de Pool aan het ziekenhuis deden denken.

'De boer noemt me mensenknecht,' zei de mensenknecht, 'en daarom ben ik op het idee gekomen om mezelf ook maar zo te noemen.'

Hij trok de handschoen aan en wurmde twee, drie vingers in de mond van de boer. 'Even kijken of alles nog goed zit,' zei de mensenknecht. 'Anders stikt-ie. Jullie mogen best gaan zitten. Jullie mogen er best bij blijven, het is even een operatie, de boer voederen, maar het is geen geheim.'

'Nee,' zei de Pool. 'We blijven wel staan. We moeten zo weer weg.'

De mensenknecht haalde plastic bestek uit de tas en begon de boer te voeren die tijdens het eten zuchtte en steunde en af en toe ook met zijn hand zwaaide alsof hij weer mensen het zwijgen wilde opleggen, terwijl niemand praatte. Af en toe riep de boer: 'Genoeg.' Maar de mensenknecht antwoordde resoluut: 'Nee, we eten nog even door.' Aan de linkerhand van de mensenknecht zat nog altijd een plastic handschoen.

De Pool begreep niet waarom zijn vrouw geen aanstalten maakte om te gaan. Ze bleef gefascineerd kijken, alsof ze nog nooit had gezien hoe iemand gevoerd werd. 'Hij kan zelf eten,' zei de mensenknecht terwijl hij wat rijst in de mond van de boer stopte, 'maar hij doet het niet, daarom heeft hij me ingehuurd. Beter gezegd, zijn kinderen hebben me ingehuurd, want zij hebben geen tijd. En ze wonen ook niet in de buurt.'

De boer leek wat te willen zeggen, maar de mensenknecht hield zijn hand voor de mond van de boer. 'Anders spuugt hij het uit, dat is zonde.'

Wen leek zich niet los te kunnen maken van dit schouwspel, ze staarde naar de mensenknecht, zo'n schouwspel had ze kennelijk niet eerder gezien.

Met een papieren servetje werd over de mond van de boer gewreven, waardoor hij er nog hulpelozer uitzag dan tijdens het voeren en met terugwerkende kracht kon je bijna niet anders dan de man vergeven dat hij over de aura van hun jongen had gesproken.

'Ik werk buiten de reguliere zorgverlening om,' zei de mensenknecht. 'Ik kom ook bij dementerenden die op maat gesneden verzorging willen. Die konden vaak mijn naam niet onthouden. Martin. Laurens. David. Ik was elke keer weer iemand anders, maar mensenknecht konden ze wel onthouden en daarom ben ik de mensenknecht en niets anders. Ik heb Ruud op mijn visitekaartje doorgestreept.' Terwijl hij de plastic lepel nog in de mond van de boer hield viste hij een visitekaartje uit zijn broekzak en overhandigde die met enige moeite aan Wen.

Ze keken ernaar. 'Mensenknecht', stond op het kaartje. Daaronder een doorgestreepte naam en daar weer onder een e-mailadres en een telefoonnummer.

'Hulp,' zei Ruud de mensenknecht terwijl hij wat vlees in de mond van de boer stopte, 'gaat altijd van boven naar beneden. Jullie hebben hulp nodig en daar komt de hulpverlener, die geeft iets, daarom zijn jullie de mindere van de hulpverlener. Dat vinden veel mensen niet prettig, die willen niet dat er op hen wordt neergekeken door de hulpverlener en in dat gat ben ik gesprongen. Ik maak me klein, de mensenknecht maakt zich piepklein. Kijk maar op me neer, zegt de mensenknecht. Dat is niet erg. Dat mag. Ik ben er om te verzorgen. En dat is voor niemand een pretje. De mensen willen zichzelf verzorgen. Ze zijn geen baby's. Maar dat gaat niet altijd. En ze willen het ook niet echt.'

Hij veegde de mond van de boer af. 'Is het lekker?' vroeg de mensenknecht.

'Nee,' zei de boer.

'Hij vindt weinig meer lekker,' zei de mensenknecht opgewekt en hij stopte wat rijst in de mond van de oude man, 'maar hij wil niet opgeven, is het niet, je wil niet opgeven?'

De mensenknecht wachtte even tot de oude man het eten had doorgeslikt en toen zei de boer: 'Dat zouden ze willen, mijn kinderen, dat ik opgeef. Nooit.'

De mensenknecht knikte. 'Hij denkt dat zijn kinderen hem haten, hij leeft om zijn kinderen dwars te zitten omdat hij denkt dat ze zullen juichen als hij eindelijk doodgaat en hij gunt hun dat gejuich niet, heeft hun vermoedelijk nooit veel gejuich gegund. Maar ze betalen mij veel geld om hem in leven te houden, dat zouden ze niet doen als ze niet van hun vader hielden. Ik word nog niet vergoed door de ziektekostenverzekeringen. Die tijd zal komen, nu is het nog niet zover. Als je arm bent komt de mensenknecht niet voorbij, dat is spijtig maar zo is het. Nog niet, zeg ik er met nadruk achteraan. In de toekomst heeft iedereen zijn eigen mensenknecht. Je leeft toch omdat je het je kinderen niet gunt?'

De boer knikte.

De Pool kon zich nu niet meer bedwingen. 'En straks ga je naar boven?' vroeg hij.

'Zeker,' zei de mensenknecht. 'Dan geef ik mevrouw eten. Soms klopt hij op de muur. Klopt hij één keer dan betekent dat: ik hou van je, twee keer kloppen betekent: ik haat je. Soms haat je je vrouw, soms hou je van haar. Niet?' Even gaf de mensenknecht liefkozend tikjes op de rug van de boer alsof de man een levensgrote baby was die een boertje moest laten.

De boer knikte. Hij manoeuvreerde zijn rolstoel in de richting van de muur achter hem en klopte twee keer hard op de muur.

'Je bent nog niet klaar met eten,' zei de mensenknecht.

De oude man manoeuvreerde zijn rolstoel weer in de richting van de tafel waar de mensenknecht al klaarzat met de lepel, maar de boer duwde de lepel weg. Er kwam nu een piepend geluid uit zijn neus.

'U doet het zo professioneel en liefdevol,' zei Wen. 'Ik heb dat ook weleens anders gezien.'

'We moeten naar huis,' zei de Pool. 'De pony gaat weg, dus je zult ons hier niet meer zien.'

Hij maakte zich los van zijn vrouw en liep om de tafel naar de mensenknecht toe.

Zijn vrouw volgde hem aarzelend. Ze was lief, hij wist het zeker, zijn vrouw was lief en zou dat altijd blijven.

'Jullie hebben mijn nummer,' zei de mensenknecht. 'Als jullie nog iemand weten die van mijn diensten gebruik wil maken? Ik sta niet boven de hulpbehoevenden, diep vanbinnen ben ik ook een hulpbehoevende, als je goed kijkt zijn er alleen hulpbehoevenden. Daarom hebben we mensenknechten nodig.'

'Denkt u,' vroeg Wen, 'dat u mensen ook zou kunnen helpen met leven?'

'Hoe bedoelt u?'

'Dat mensen kunnen zeggen: vandaag leeft de mensenknecht voor me, ik doe het vandaag even niet, ik kan het vandaag niet.'

De mensenknecht schudde zijn hoofd. 'Het blijft hulpverlening, genieten moeten de mensen voorlopig nog zelf doen.'

Terwijl het afscheidsritueel zich voltrok had de boer zich in zijn rolstoel weer van de tafel af gemanoeuvreerd en klopte twee keer hard op de muur.

De mensenknecht onderbrak het afscheidsritueel. Hij

keek vertederd naar de boer. 'Ik vind het zo mooi,' zei hij, 'dat mensen op die leeftijd met zoveel hartstocht communiceren.'

# 7

De eerste slachter die de Pool belde zei dat een pony slachten geen probleem was, dat hij ook paarden deed, dat hij eigenlijk alles deed, alleen geen pluimvee. De Pool kon het dier op een vrijdag- of dinsdagochtend langsbrengen, het liefst voor tien uur. Hij mocht ook al de avond ervoor langskomen, maar dan weer niet te laat. De slachter ging vroeg slapen. Het kostte 120 euro exclusief btw, al hing het er natuurlijk een beetje van af of de Pool nog vlees mee naar huis wilde nemen.

De Pool zei dat hij geen vlees mee naar huis wilde nemen.

'Dan kunnen we het denk ik op 120 euro houden,' antwoordde de slachter, die zich Tim noemde.

Ze maakten een afspraak voor vrijdagochtend en de slachter zei nog dat de Pool zelf voor vervoer moest zorgen. 'Vroeger kwam ik de dieren weleens ophalen,' legde hij uit, 'maar daar begin ik niet meer aan. Ik ben slachter. Geen transportbedrijf.'

De Pool hing op. Hij moest nu alleen nog zo'n ding regelen waarmee het dier vervoerd kon worden. Dat viel tegen. De meeste verhuurbedrijven hadden niets waarin pony's vervoerd konden worden, in elk geval niet op voorraad. Uiteindelijk besloot hij op het internet naar paardenvervoer te zoeken. Er bleek een paardentaxi te bestaan maar die was weer niet in de buurt, wat de paardentaxi kostbaar maakte. Bovendien stond het woord 'paardentaxi' hem tegen. Je nam geen paardentaxi naar de dood. Via de paardentaxi kwam hij bij een particulier terecht die zelf paarden bezat en die de Pool vertelde dat hij een paardencamionette had waarover hij zeer tevreden was, alsmede een trailer en dat hij wel bereid was de camionette of trailer te verhuren. Zeker toen de Pool hem uitlegde waar het voor was. 'Ja,' zei de verhuurder, 'zo'n leven is niets.'

De camionette stond de Pool ook tegen, alleen al vanwege de naam. Hij zei: 'Ik neem de trailer.' Duur was de trailer niet. Het was ook maar voor een dag. 's Ochtends vol heen, aan het eind van de ochtend leeg terug, zo stelde hij het zich voor, hij probeerde het zakelijk te benaderen want anders zou het hem niet lukken, vreesde hij. Voor de zekerheid had hij de trailer de hele dag gehuurd. Hij had ook de hele dag ervoor uitgetrokken, hij wist niet precies hoelang zoiets duurde, je moest rekening houden met tegenslag.

's Ochtends vroeg ging hij weg om de trailer af te halen. Daarvoor had hij al wat extra peentjes en appels gekocht. De man die het verhuurde hielp de Pool om de trailer vast te maken aan zijn auto. 'Niet te hard rijden,' zei hij nog, 'dat ding kan gaan slingeren. Zeker als het waait. En zo'n paard staat nooit helemaal stil.'

De Pool gaf hem bij het afscheid een ferme hand. Hij zei: 'U woont mooi.' Dat was ook zo. De man woonde mooi. Boven op een heuvel, een magnifiek uitzicht. Zeker voor Nederlandse begrippen.

Zijn vrouw had hij niet verteld dat deze vrijdag de pony zou worden weggebracht, dat de opvatting dat de dood liefde was vandaag in praktijk zou worden gebracht. Hij had geen behoefte aan haar medelijden, al was het maar omdat hij vond dat hij haar medelijden niet verdiende. Hij wilde er verder geen woorden aan vuilmaken. Hij bracht een offer.

Hij reed langzaam, voorzichtig als hij nu eenmaal was, de waarschuwingen van de verhuurder negeerde hij niet. Al kon dat langzame rijden er ook mee te maken hebben dat hij het uitstelde, het moment dat hij met de trailer het erf van de boerderij op zou rijden, het moment dat hij het beest uit de stal zou halen in het besef dat het daar nooit meer terugkeerde. De boer zou vast triomfantelijk lachen. Wat hij had voorspeld ging gebeuren en terwijl de Pool zich liet inhalen door een vrachtwagen vroeg hij zich af hoe hij zijn dagen zou vullen als hij niet meer naast dat dier in de stal zou staan. Wat deed hij vroeger? De dagen waren omgevlogen al kon hij zich niet goed herinneren waarmee.

Iets voor halftien reed hij het erf op. Hij was wat laat voor de slachter, maar vanaf hier zou het snel gaan. De boer zat waar hij altijd zat. Dit keer werd er niet tegen het raam getikt.

Langzaam en zorgvuldig liep hij naar de stal, hij keek precies waar hij zijn voeten neerzette. Hij zadelde de pony zo goed en zo kwaad als het ging, veel ervaring had hij daar niet mee. 'We gaan op reis,' zei hij en hij leidde haar naar buiten. Dat zadelen was eigenlijk niet nodig geweest, want hij ging ook nu niet op haar rijden, maar op de een of andere manier vond hij dat ze met haar zadel het slachthuis moest betreden, zo waardig mogelijk. Niet als een oud en vereenzaamd beest maar als een wonder, het wonder dat de veearts in haar had gezien en van haar had gemaakt.

Hij leidde haar naar het erf, zij stapte naast hem, zoals ze dat vaker deed die dagen dat hij met haar was gaan stappen. Soms bleef ze staan of wilde ze aan de andere kant van de Pool lopen. Echt nukkig was ze ook nu niet.

Toen ze eenmaal voor de trailer stonden was er geen beweging in het dier te krijgen. Op advies van de verhuurder had hij wat vers hooi in de trailer gelegd. 'Lok haar met een appeltje, lok haar met een peen als ze moeilijk doet,' had de verhuurder nog gezegd, op de vaderlijke en ook ietwat arrogante wijze van iemand die wist dat hij met een leek te maken had.

Ze deed moeilijk, ze zette zich schrap, er was geen beweging in haar te krijgen, ze deed wat ze nog nooit had gedaan, niet zolang de Pool haar kende althans, ze verzette zich. Nu was het tijd de peen tevoorschijn te halen. Uit zijn auto haalde hij een grote winterpeen, hij ging in de trailer staan en terwijl hij zwaaide met de peen riep hij: 'Kom maar, kom maar meisje, kom maar.'

Maar ze kwam niet. Hoe hard hij ook aan het touw trok, er was geen beweging in haar te krijgen. Zelfs de peen kon haar niet verleiden.

Terwijl hij met de ene hand trok en met de andere hand met de peen zwaaide besefte hij dat de boer naar hem keek. Hij werd uitgelachen, daaraan twijfelde hij niet. Hij faalde, hij was een man die beweerde te houden van een dier dat hij niet eens in een trailer kon krijgen. Hij liet de peen vallen, trok nu met beide handen aan het touw, maar het dier was sterker, het zette zich schrap, onvermoede krachten waren in de oude pony naar boven gekomen. Ze gooide haar voorbenen in de lucht, ze steigerde en dat voor zo'n oud beest. Kwam het wonder nu pas goed tot uitdrukking? Al die tijd had het dier stom en vrijwel onbeweeglijk in de stal gestaan en nu gooide het zichzelf de lucht in alsof het leven hier pas begon, zo vlak voor de dood. Ze weigerde te doen wat de Pool van haar verlangde. En omdat hij er niet aan twijfelde dat de boer hem observeerde, omdat hij meende te weten wat de boer dacht was dit niet meer iets tussen hem en de pony alleen, het was iets tussen hem, de boer en het beest. De Pool moest iets bewijzen aan de oude man in zijn rolstoel. Hij liep de trailer uit, het touw in zijn hand, ging naar de auto, pakte een appeltje.

Hij voerde het oude, eenzame meisje een appel, die ze gretig at. 'Straks krijg je nog een appeltje,' zei hij zacht. 'Daarbinnen zal ik je heel veel appeltjes geven.'

Hij walgde van zichzelf dat dit moest gebeuren. Omdat er nog steeds geen beweging in haar te krijgen was, omdat ze sterker was dan de Pool en omdat hij vreesde haar pijn te zullen doen als hij te hard trok ging hij achter haar staan, hij duwde met twee handen tegen haar achterwerk en het enige resultaat was dat ze hem schopte. Niet hard maar hard genoeg. Het zou wel een blauwe plek worden op zijn bovenbeen. Hij ging naast haar staan, bracht zijn mond naar haar oor, zo dat de boer hem niet kon zien en hij fluisterde: 'Je moet me helpen. De beslissing is al genomen. Verzet is zinloos.' En hij streelde haar voorzichtig terwijl hij aan hun jongen dacht en hij zich niet aan de indruk kon onttrekken dat het hun jongen was die hij de trailer in probeerde te duwen.

Weer liep hij naar de auto, weer probeerde hij het oude, eenzame meisje te verleiden, dit keer met een winterpeen, maar ze liet zich niet verleiden, ze stond stoer en stil en het leek alsof ze wist dat ze zich niet hoefde te bewegen, alsof ze wist dat hij toch wel met die peen naar haar toe kwam.

Ze wilde overal heen alleen niet naar de trailer.

Toen ze drie appels en drie winterpenen ophad begon het tikken op de ruit. Ook dit keer met een scherp voorwerp. De boer tikte als een waanzinnige op het raam, ritmisch alsof hij muziek aan het maken was, met de energie van een jonge maar niet bijzonder talentvolle muzikant, en hoewel de Pool het had willen negeren kon hij zich al snel niet meer op zijn taak concentreren omdat hij alleen het lawaai hoorde dat de boer produceerde.

Hij maakte de pony vast aan een boom en liep naar de boerderij. Toen hij dichterbij kwam zag hij dat de boer met een schaar tegen het raam aan het tikken was.

Daar stond hij weer in de kamer waar hij naar zijn mening al te vaak had gestaan. De boer zei niets, hij reed in zijn rolstoel naar een kast, rukte een lade open en haalde een oude zweep tevoorschijn. Toen zei hij: 'Rij me naar buiten.'

De Pool reed de oude man naar buiten, de boer hield de zweep in zijn hand maar hij zei niets. Pas in de buurt van de pony commandeerde de boer: 'Maak haar los. Jij trekt aan haar. Ik duw haar van achteren. Samen krijgen we haar die trailer in.'

De Pool begon weer aan het touw te trekken, al had hij het gevoel dat hij de grote pony half wurgde. De paar honderd kilo die ze woog waren niet in beweging te krijgen.

Schuin achter haar zat de boer in zijn rolstoel en de Pool begreep nu wat de boer bedoelde met duwen. Vanuit zijn rolstoel sloeg de boer met de zweep op de flanken en op de rug van de pony met een kracht en een energie die de Pool verbaasde. Nog een laatste keer leek de jeugd bezit te hebben genomen van de boer, een razernij die het leven zelf leek te zijn had zich meester gemaakt van de oude man, al het verzet tegen zijn eigen dood bleek geen andere betekenis te hebben dan dat hij bereid was het oude, eenzame meisje dood te slaan.

'Vort,' riep de boer. Hoe harder hij sloeg hoe meer het beest zich verzette en dat verzet bestond uit stilstaan, zich niet verroeren. Het keek naar de Pool, het keek hem aan, het keek hem vragend aan. Niet smekend, vragend, verbaasd. Is dit wat jouw liefde betekent?

'Rustig,' riep de Pool. 'Rustig. Ze hoeft niet dood. Nog niet.'

Hij zag hoe er bloed door de vacht van het beest begon te sijpelen en dat maakte gek genoeg dat ook de krachten van de Pool afnamen.

'Vort,' bleef de boer roepen, 'vort, naar binnen met jou.' En hij bleef slaan, zoals een bokser touwtjespringt, nee zoals een bokser bokst. Hij was zich niet aan het voorbereiden op de wedstrijd, dit was de wedstrijd.

'Trek dan,' riep de boer, 'trek dan, we hebben haar bijna gebroken.'

Niet veel later lukte het de Pool de pony de trailer in te trekken. Hij maakte haar vast, zoals de verhuurder hem had uitgelegd en ging voorzichtig met de rug van zijn hand over haar wonden. Uit zijn zak haalde hij een appel. 'Eet maar,' zei hij. 'Eet maar, meisje.'

Hij had gedacht dat ze zou weigeren, dat ze deze appel niet zou eten, maar ook dit appeltje at ze op. Ze had geen trots. Dieren hebben geen trots en de meeste mensen evenmin. Er waren uitzonderingen, de Pool had niet de illusie dat hij tot die uitzonderingen gerekend moest worden.

Hij ging naar buiten, sloot de trailer, hij zag hoe de pony nog omkeek.

De boer zat op de plek waar hij al die tijd had gezeten. Hij hijgde, de zweep in zijn hand. 'Breng me naar binnen.'

De Pool reed de boer naar binnen. Ze zeiden niets. Binnen in de kamer waar hij at en sliep, waar hij leefde en waar hij ongetwijfeld zou sterven legde de boer de zweep weer in de la. Hij deed het zorgvuldig, bijna plechtig, en de Pool had het gevoel dat het niet de laatste keer zou zijn dat hij de zweep uit de la tevoorschijn haalde.

Naast de kranten op tafel lag de schaar waarmee de boer tegen het raam had getikt. Kennelijk knipte hij nog steeds stukken uit de krant die hem interesseerden. Maar op de tafel waarop alles lag wat de boer nodig leek te hebben lagen nog altijd slechts twee knipsels, een rouwadvertentie en een artikel over ernstige vertragingen op het traject Heerlen-Sittard.

De Pool verliet de boer zonder nog iets te zeggen, zonder verder iets te vragen. Hij liep naar zijn auto, controleerde nog een keer of het dier goed in de trailer stond en reed toen naar de slachter. Voorzichtig en toch gehaast.

Hij was nog nooit bij een slachter geweest. Vanbuiten zag het eruit als een gewone boerderij. Vooralsnog wees weinig op de dood. Er stonden dieren in een stal, allerlei soorten dieren, van elkaar gescheiden, dat wel. De Pool vroeg aan een behoorlijk jonge knecht waar hij de pony kon afleveren. De knecht keek alleen verschrikt om zich heen en liep toen weg.

Daarom ging de Pool zelf op zoek naar de man met wie hij getelefoneerd had. In een bijgebouw dat het midden hield tussen een klein kantoor en een keuken zat een man aan een lange tafel een sigaret te roken. Hij had felle, blauwe ogen en hoewel hij de Pool had waargenomen begroette hij hem niet. Hij keek dwars door de Pool heen. De verte leek hem meer te interesseren dan de man die voor hem stond. Daarom zei de Pool zelf: 'Ik had gebeld.'

'Waarover?' vroeg de man.

'Over mijn pony.'

De man nam een trek van zijn sigaret, blies de rook langzaam uit en zei: 'Dat is waar. Je bent laat.'

'We hadden moeilijkheden,' zei de Pool en hij vroeg zich af of hij moest gaan zitten. Hij had wel al besloten niets te zeggen over de aard van de moeilijkheden, die gingen de slachter niets aan.

'Maakt niet uit,' zei de man. 'Het vlees is niet voor consumptie als ik me niet vergis, dus keuren kunnen we achterwege laten. Waar is het dier?'

'In de trailer,' zei de Pool en hij ging toch maar zitten.

De man gaf hem over de tafel heen een hand. 'Tim.'

Ook de Pool stelde zich voor.

'Koffie?' vroeg Tim.

De Pool knikte.

Tim stond op, liep naar een koffieapparaat, schonk koffie in en zette het op tafel neer. 'Het staat al vanaf vanochtend vroeg maar het is nog prima te drinken. Melk en suiker?'

De Pool schudde zijn hoofd. Hij nam een slok.

'Ik heb nog niet eerder iets voor jou geslacht, dus ik wil je vragen of je nu al kan betalen. Het liefst contant.'

'Dat is goed,' zei de Pool. Hij pakte zijn portemonnee.

'De vrouw die de administratie doet is er vanochtend niet. Ze maakt later een factuur en die stuurt zij dan op.'

'Ik heb geen factuur nodig,' zei de Pool.

‘Ik stuur er toch een’, en Tim stopte het geld in zijn borstzak. ‘Je hebt de schijn tegenwoordig tegen je. Vooral als slachter. Als je eens wist wat voor dreigmails ik krijg. Ze maken me voor nazibeul uit, het blijkt wel dat ze niets van geschiedenis weten.’

De sigaret werd gedoofd. De Pool keek om zich heen. Het was een vredige omgeving hier in deze keuken annex kantoor. Vaag deed het hem een beetje aan zijn brandweerkazerne denken.

‘Kun je het dier zelf uitladen?’ vroeg Tim. ‘Er loopt een jongen rond, die wijst je wel waar je het achter kunt laten.’

‘Die jonge jongen?’ vroeg de Pool.

‘Dat is geen *jonge* jongen. Dat is een dwerg. Kun je het verschil niet zien tussen jong en klein?’

‘Ik zag het niet,’ zei de Pool en omdat hij op zijn eigen manier ook gevat was voegde hij eraan toe: ‘Ik heb weinig ervaring met dwergen.’

Tim stak nog een sigaret op. ‘Ik neem voor dat baantje altijd mensen in dienst met een achterstand, met een beperking, dat stukje sociale verantwoordelijkheid, dat neem ik. Het is een goeie jongen. Bangig, maar wat wil je als je een dwerg bent, en als hij problemen heeft met de grote beesten, de koeien of de paarden, dan komt een van ons hem even helpen. Voor de varkens is zo’n dwerg eigenlijk ideaal. Die zien de dwerg en die denken volgens mij toch een beetje: dat is er eentje van ons.’

De Pool knikte.

‘Ik schrijf mensen met een beperking niet af,’ ging Tim verder, ‘die kunnen bij mij in de hokken werken. En je krijgt er nog subsidie voor ook. Niet veel hoor. Wat ze je met de ene hand geven nemen ze met de andere hand weer van je af.’

De Pool zweeg. Hij staarde naar zijn knokkels en zonder zijn blik van zijn handen af te wenden zei hij: ‘Ik wil er graag bij blijven, ik wil graag bij het dier blijven zo lang als het kan.’

'Bij de pony?'

'Bij het slachten,' zei de Pool. 'Ik wil er graag bij zijn als zij deze wereld verlaat.'

'Ben je zelf slachter?'

De Pool schudde zijn hoofd.

'Heb je weleens geslacht?'

'Nee, ik ben brandweerman.'

'O.' Tim pakte het pakje sigaretten van tafel en stopte het in zijn broekzak. 'Dan ben je vast wel wat gewend. Maar ik kan er niet aan beginnen. Het is hier geen realityshow.'

'Ik wil het graag,' zei de Pool. 'Als het moet betaal ik extra.'

'Voor wat?'

'Om erbij te mogen blijven.'

Tim zuchtte. Hij keek de Pool strak aan met zijn felle, blauwe ogen, de Pool werd er ongemakkelijk van. Zo vreemd was zijn verzoek ook weer niet. Het was niet dat hij zei: ik wil zelf slachten. Hij wilde er gewoon bij blijven.

'Het is hier geen stierengevecht, we hebben geen tribunes waarvandaan je kunt kijken, we zijn een bedrijf, ik werk voor mijn geld. Er valt hier niets te zien. Of ben je van de dierenbescherming of zo?'

'Ik werk voor de brandweer,' herhaalde de Pool.

'Ook niet als hobby? Dieren beschermen en ze eigenlijk de vernieling in helpen, want dat doet de dierenbescherming, ze beweren te helpen maar ze maken de zaak alleen erger. Ik hou van dieren, anders zou ik ze niet slachten. Je kunt slachten en slachten, je kunt een dier de vernieling in helpen of je kunt een dier zachtjes over de drempel heen tillen.'

'Het is niet mijn hobby,' zei de Pool. 'Dat soort hobby's heb ik niet.'

Tim schudde langzaam zijn hoofd. 'Sorry, ik doe het niet. Je kijkt maar op YouTube als je filmpjes wilt zien.'

'Daar gaat het niet om,' zei de Pool en hij wreef met zijn handen over de tafel alsof hij iets wilde schoonvegen, 'ik wil haar graag begeleiden.'

'Begeleiden?' Tim leek nu nog feller te kijken. 'Ben jij er zo een? Dan komen ze hierheen en dan kunnen ze toch geen afscheid nemen. Maar als het dier eenmaal bij mij in de stal staat dan moet het dood, vanwege besmettingsgevaar, linksom of rechtsom. Heb je het al uitgeladen?'

'Ze staat nog in de trailer.'

'Dan kun je haar in theorie nog meenemen. Rij weg voor het te laat is.'

Tim pakte het geld uit zijn borstzak, maar de Pool zei: 'Je hebt me verkeerd begrepen. Ik wil haar niet meenemen. Ze moet... Maar ik wil er graag bij blijven. Ik hou me wel op de achtergrond. Je zult geen last van me hebben.'

De slachter borg het geld weer op. 'Je kunt hierboven blijven wachten. Dan vertel ik je hoe het gegaan is. Ik wil geen pottenkijkers.'

Er kwam een vaal zonnetje door het raam naar binnen, je kon wat heuvels zien. Een huis in de verte, bomen. De Pool begreep dat er maar één manier was waarop hij de slachter kon overhalen, hij moest vertellen wat hij eigenlijk niet wilde vertellen, hij moest medelijden opwekken. Erbarmen. Hij haatte het.

'De pony is van onze jongen geweest,' zei de Pool.

'En die had er genoeg van?'

'Nee, dat niet.'

De Pool wreef weer over de tafel. Hij masseerde zijn knokkels. Had de slachter nu precies gezegd wat er aan de hand was? Zonder het te weten? Borys had er genoeg van gehad, van dit leven.

'Hij kwam onder de trein,' zei de Pool. 'De een zegt gesprongen, ik zeg gevallen. In het begin zei ik nog weleens: hij is geduwd. We hebben nooit een afscheidsbrief gevonden. We hebben ook niet alles doorzocht. Al snel zeiden we: we laten het erbij. We weten genoeg. We weten eigenlijk te veel.'

De slachter knikte.

'Dus daarom...' zei de Pool.

Tim inhaleerde en de Pool keek naar de rook. En toen hij daar genoeg van had staarde hij weer uit het raam en bekeek het landschap dat hij zo goed kende omdat hij een groot gedeelte van zijn jeugd in dit landschap had doorgebracht, zonder dat hij zich er ooit mee had vereenzelvigd. Hij wist niet goed waarmee hij zich wel had vereenzelvigd, met de brandweer, met zijn gezin en de laatste weken met de pony.

'Doe maar wat je doen moet,' zei Tim. 'Ik zal het de mannen beneden uitleggen. Blijf maar bij dat dier. Als je het nodig hebt.' Hij duwde zijn stoel naar achteren, ging naar beneden en de Pool volgde hem. Hij wist dat hij de pony nu moest gaan uitladen. Hij zag ertegen op, niet alleen om wat komen zou, ook omdat hij vreesde dat het weer een gevecht werd, het uitladen. Hij zag de boer voor zich met zijn zweep.

De slachter verdween in een ruimte waar ongetwijfeld geslacht werd en de Pool maakte de pony los. Uit de trailer halen bleek geen probleem. Ze kwam er vanzelf uit, hij hoefde vrijwel niets te doen. Hij zwaaide wat met een winterpeen, zelfs dat bleek amper nodig. Hij leidde haar in de richting van de ruimte die hem nog altijd erg aan een boerderij deed denken.

Daar liep de knecht weer, een jonge dwerg dus. De Pool was niet gek, deze dwerg was jong. In zijn ene hand had de Pool de pony vast aan een touw, in zijn andere hand hield hij een plastic zak met peentjes en appels.

De dwerg zei: 'Ze zijn bijna klaar met de varkens. Geef maar aan mij.'

'Ik wil er graag bij blijven,' antwoordde de Pool. 'Het mocht van Tim.'

De jonge dwerg haalde zijn schouders op maar hij deed verder niets, hij stond stil en keek recht voor zich uit. Hoewel dat misschien neerbuigend was, al was het zo niet bedoeld, legde de Pool zijn hand op het hoofd van de dwerg en ging tegelijkertijd een beetje door zijn knieën. 'Heb je een plekje waar we even samen kunnen zijn?'

'Wij?' vroeg de dwerg. 'Ik heb een vriendin. Waar zie je me voor aan?'

De Pool haalde zijn hand van het hoofd van de dwerg – de dwerg had een warm hoofd, alsof hij koorts had – en hij ging door zijn hurken. Nu was hij op ooghoogte met de jongeman en nu vielen hem de mooie ogen op, heldere ogen had de jonge knecht. De Pool had medelijden met hem want kleine mensen hebben het niet makkelijk. Hij glimlachte, zoals hij ook weleens deed als ze met de brandweer bij mensen thuiskwamen die niet goed waren, overstuur, of verwaarloosd, een glimlach kon wonderen doen. Hij had weleens tegen de jonge gasten gezegd: 'Een glimlach kost niets en er is nog nooit iemand aan doodgegaan.' Hijzelf had het moeten leren van een ploegchef. 'Ik blijf bij de pony,' zei de Pool, 'om onze jongen te eren, in zijn naam zeg maar. Ik heb het niet over jou maar over de pony.'

De dwerg zei: 'Als hij dat goedvindt. De paarden zijn als laatste aan de beurt.' En toen legde de Pool het voor de zekerheid nog een keer uit, gehurkt, dat hij graag samen met het dier wilde wachten. Hij zei niet waarop hij wilde wachten, dat was wel duidelijk want op deze plek was er slechts één ding waarop je kon wachten.

De jonge dwerg leek het nu eindelijk te begrijpen, hij pakte de hand van de Pool en trok hem mee naar achteren, dieper de stal in die dus eigenlijk meer wachtkamer was dan stal, alsof de Pool ook een dier was. De dwerg sleurde Pool en pony mee, maar misschien begreep hij het sleuren van de knecht verkeerd, misschien was het onschuldig en zag de dwerg toch een vriend in hem, een man die een vriend zou kunnen worden als hij langer had kunnen blijven. Een goed mens, een soortgenoot.

Er waren varkens, biggetjes, lammeren, koeien, drie geiten en helemaal achteraan stond nog een paard. Het paard was onrustig en toen hij merkte dat de dwerg hem naast dat paard wilde zetten zei hij dat hij daar liever niet met de pony wilde staan, want hij vreesde toch vertrapt te worden, of platgedrukt tegen een muur. Was er niet een plekje waar ze afgezonderd konden zijn, zonder andere dieren, niet privé, gewoon afgezonderd? Uiteindelijk begreep de dwerg hem, hij zei: 'Kijk daar.' Hij wees op een vierkant tussen wat koeien en schapen in. Afgescheiden en leeg. De dwerg leidde de Pool, en de Pool leidde nu de pony en terwijl ze elkaar zo leidden zei de dwerg nog wijzend op de koeien: 'Maak je geen zorgen, dat zijn geen stieren. Dit zijn rustige koeien.' En toen wees de dwerg op de wonden op de rug van de pony en hij vroeg: 'Wat hebben jullie met haar gedaan?' Maar hij wachtte niet op antwoord.

Daar stonden ze, hij en het overblijfsel van hun jongen, ingeklemd tussen allerlei andere dieren, slordig afgescheiden door hekken die verplaatst konden worden, afhankelijk natuurlijk van het aanbod. Zoveel begreep de Pool. Er waren dagen dat er meer geiten of lammeren waren dan vandaag. Elke dag was anders, elke dag was een verrassing.

Uit zijn plastic zak haalde hij een peen en voerde die aan de pony. Zelf at hij er ook een want hij had trek en ander eten had hij niet bij zich. 'Neem nog een appeltje,' zei hij tegen de pony en hij haalde een appel uit de plastic zak, terwijl hij zag hoe de jonge dwerg wat varkens duwde naar een soort sluis die ongetwijfeld naar de slachterij leidde. De Pool besefte dat het vreemd was op deze plek tegen het dier te praten.

Verder hoopte hij dat de pony honger had. De zak zat nog vol met appels en penen, hij wilde dat het dier genoot van zijn laatste uren op aarde. Wat voor genot was er anders voor eenzame en oude meisjes zoals zij? Eten, misschien, gekriebeld worden maar echt goed kriebelen had hij nooit gedurfd.

Het knechtje kwam weer naar hen toe. 'Niet voeren,' zei hij. 'Dat is niet goed. Ze moeten nu niets meer eten.' De dwerg keek nog eens naar het dier. En toen zei hij: 'Haal dat zadel eraf. Waarom heb je haar gezadeld?'

Nu was het de Pool die niets zei, hij begon het dier af te zadelen terwijl hij fluisterde: 'We mogen niet meer eten. Net als voor de operatie.'

Hij legde het zadel op het spaarzame stro op de grond en nog altijd hield hij de plastic zak in zijn hand. De Pool vond het ongepast zelf een appel te eten nu hij wist dat de pony niets meer mocht eten. Dat ging niet, je kon niet zelf gaan eten als de ander moest vasten. Hij keek naar de dieren die werden weggehaald en af en toe kriebelde hij het dier naast zich, want veel anders was er nu niet meer te doen, dit was het enige wat hij kon doen om het levensgeluk van het dier te vergroten tijdens de laatste uren dat het op aarde was.

Hij was blij dat zijn vrouw hier niet bij was, dat niemand hierbij was. 'Ik blijf tot het eind bij je,' zei hij tegen het dier. 'Ik ben brandweerman. Ik zou je nu wat moeten voorlezen uit de bijbel maar ik heb geen bijbel bij me.'

De varkens en de biggen waren verdwenen. Het werd leger om hem heen. De koeien waren onrustig geworden, het paard was nog steeds opgefokt en de Pool had het gevoel dat hij zijn taken eindelijk naar behoren vervulde, hij was bijna gelukkig. Morgen had hij weer dienst, om zeven uur.

De dwerg kwam naar hem toe. 'Tim heeft gezegd dat we die pony wel tussendoor kunnen doen. Kom maar mee.'

De afscheiding ging open en hij volgde de dwerg met het beest naar de sluis. Er stond een koe voor hem. En tussen hem en de koe was ook een soort afscheiding aangebracht die hem deed denken aan het beurtbalkje in de supermarkt. Hij was de volgende klant.

Hij wachtte. Nu de dood zo dichtbij was zei hij niets meer tegen het dier, zijn hand rustte op de rug van het beest omdat hij wilde aangeven dat hij er voor haar was.

Er klonk een geluid alsof er geheid werd uit de ruimte aan de andere kant en de Pool keek om zich heen. De dwerg was nu nergens meer te bekennen en merkwaardig genoeg moest hij denken aan de mensen die hij had zien sterven tijdens zijn jaren bij de brandweer. Een enkele keer in zijn armen, als het gebeurde kwam het meestal omdat ze te laat waren gekomen, omdat de rookontwikkeling te snel was gegaan, de brand om zich heen had gegrepen.

'Ja,' hoorde hij roepen en nu kwam de dwerg tevoorschijn en begon met een soort draagbaar hek van achteren tegen de pony aan te duwen. De Pool hielp mee. Hij trok aan de pony, zonder haar pijn te willen doen. Ze gingen nu door een plastic strokengordijn dat de overgang van de ene ruimte naar de andere markeerde. Anders dan in de stallen was het in de volgende ruimte, de laatste ruimte, felverlicht. De Pool moest wennen aan het licht. Hij zag de net geslachte beesten hangen, de geur hier deed hem vaag aan een kraamafdeling denken. Zoetig. Verder was het erg warm.

Toen zag hij Tim in een blauwe overall. Aan de andere kant van de afscheiding, er was namelijk nog een hek dat het dier van de slachter scheidde, donkerblauw geschilderd. Ze stonden in een kooi die vanboven open was, hij en het dier.

'Wat doe je hier?' vroeg Tim.

Er waren ook andere mannen en ze keken allemaal naar hem. Ze waren opgehouden met werken. De radio stond aan, hij herkende het nummer, hij had het mee kunnen neuriën.

'Je zei toch dat ik erbij mocht blijven?' zei de Pool en even schaamde hij zich dat hij hier stond want het was beschamend om dood te gaan. Het was beschamend om bij de stervenden te zijn, om hun einde te bekijken. De Pool kwam amper boven de radio uit, zo hard stond de muziek. Tot hier was hij gekomen en nu zou hij ook de laatste minuten met dit beest delen.

Ze bleven naar hem kijken, de mannen, alsof ze zoiets nog nooit hadden gezien, terwijl hij toch een man onder de mannen was, altijd geweest ook. Hij had zich niet hoeven aan te passen, hij was aangepast ter wereld gekomen.

'Niet tot hier,' riep Tim. 'Wil je soms ook geslacht worden?'

Enkele mannen begonnen te lachen. Ze vonden het grappig en hij begreep dat. Ze hadden nog nooit een mens geslacht en nu was er een per ongeluk tussen de dieren beland. Ondanks het gelach wist hij nog steeds zeker dat hij voet bij stuk zou houden, al wist hij ook dat hij het niet kon uitleggen, hij vertrouwde op de goedhartigheid van de slachter, die zou hem ook wel die laatste minuten gunnen. Het was een aardig verhaal 's avonds bij de koffie of het bier. De brandweerman die zijn pony niet alleen kon laten. Tot op het laatste moment niet. Een hardnekkige klant.

'Ik blijf erbij,' zei de Pool zonder de pony los te laten. 'Onze jongen had het zo gewild.'

Een leugen. Hij wist niet wat de jongen had gewild, de jongen had er niet meer willen zijn maar zelfs dat wist hij niet zeker.

Tim kwam nu naar hem toe. De pony en hij stonden net iets hoger dan Tim, zodat hij een beetje naar boven moest kijken en dat gaf de Pool toch een gevoel van autoriteit. Hij stond nu wel op de plek waar de dieren stonden, de seconden, de minuten voor ze verlost werden, maar het was een plek die niet geheel ontdaan was van autoriteit. Het was een heilige plek want alleen de dood maakte alles heilig, zonder dood was er niets heilig. Het eeuwige leven was de grote ontheiliging.

‘We kunnen niet alles doen wat jouw jongen heeft gewild, straks had die jongen van jou gewild dat je met een paashaas de wereld rondvloog, zou je dat ook doen?’

‘Ik doe niemand kwaad,’ zei de Pool beslist.

Tim werd nu kwaad. ‘We schieten straks iets door haar kop, dan is ze hersendood, dan valt ze neer, als ze op jou valt hebben we een probleem.’

‘Ze valt niet op mij,’ zei de Pool. ‘Ik duw haar wel de andere kant op.’

‘Het is tegen alle voorschriften in,’ zei Tim.

‘Soms moet je tegen de voorschriften ingaan.’ De Pool zag hoe de slachter aan het twijfelen was gebracht.

‘Dit kost me te veel tijd,’ zei Tim na een korte pauze. ‘Blijf erbij. Als je zo nodig moet. Maar als ze op je valt, als ze je bezeert is het jouw probleem. En je betaalt me straks honderd euro extra.’

‘Dat is goed,’ zei de Pool. Zijn vrouw, zijn lieve vrouw zou hem vervloeken als ze het te weten kwam maar dat deed er niet toe. Ze zou hier nooit achter komen.

De pony werd van achteren nog iets naar voren geduwd tot hij niet meer verder kon. Een man met melkwit haar klom op een verhoging, hij had iets wat op een pistool leek in zijn hand, anders dan andere pistolen en richtte het op het hoofd van de pony.

‘Als hij straks schiet,’ zei Tim, ‘moet je haar meteen van je af duwen. Het hek aan haar andere kant gaat open en dan rolt ze naar beneden.’

‘Dat is goed,’ zei de Pool en zijn hand bleef op de rug van de pony rusten terwijl zijn spieren zich spanden. Ook de pony werd nu onrustig, zij bewoog, zij duwde de Pool tegen de muur, de Pool duwde terug en de man met het melkwitte haar en het grote pistool in zijn hand bewoog rustig en geconcentreerd met de pony mee, wachtend op het juiste moment, om in het midden, iets boven de ogen te kunnen schieten, want daarop mikte hij, zoveel had de

Pool gezien. Zoveel had de Pool begrepen. Daar gebeurde het, tussen de ogen.

Niet eerder was de pony zo onrustig geweest. Zou ze het ruiken? Zou ze iets weten? Een voorkennis die dieren misschien toch hadden, of was dat de menselijke verbeelding? Was ze gewoon zo opgewonden omdat ze in een te kleine ruimte stond en ze geen kant meer op kon? Was het gebrek aan bewegingsvrijheid dat het oude, eenzame meisje zo nerveus maakte? Hoe dan ook, de Pool bleef rustig, met zijn hand op haar rug probeerde hij het beest te kalmeren, hij durfde alleen niets te fluisteren, niets te zeggen, hier werd gezwegen en hij dacht aan zijn jongen, hun jongen, die hij betrapt had in de stal terwijl hij met het dier praatte. Hij was nu bijna gelukkig, het onomkeerbare van de situatie stelde hem gerust, er was niets meer aan te doen, tot hier waren ze gekomen, met z'n tweeën, de rest ging vanzelf.

Toen klonk de knal. Bijna op hetzelfde moment zakte de pony door haar poten. Met alle kracht duwde de Pool het dier van zich af – door haar zo van zich af te duwen had hij even het gevoel dat hij het was die haar vermoordde – het hek ging omhoog en zo gleed de pony uit het hok op de grond.

Daar werd ze aan haar twee achterpoten razendsnel omhoog getakeld. Een jongeman sneed haar halsslagader door en het bloed gutste eruit terwijl de Pool stokstijf was blijven staan en een volstrekt krankzinnige gedachte zich meester van hem maakte: als er geen God was wilde hij niet meer op deze wereld blijven.

Er waren wat slachters die naar hem keken en naar hem wezen. Zoals hij daar stond, verdwaald, niet zozeer verloren, verdwaald tussen dieren waarbij hij niet hoorde. Ze lachten, de slachters, misschien lachten ze hem niet uit, dat wist hij niet zeker, ze lachten wel en ze zeiden ook wat tegen hem, maar hij kon hen niet verstaan, de muziek stond te hard, de machines maakten te veel lawaai.

Toen kwam de dwerg, hij glipte door de spijlen heen – nu begreep de Pool beter waarom Tim hem had aangenomen – en de dwerg pakte hem bij zijn hand en begeleidde hem naar buiten. In zijn ooghoeken zag hij nog hoe de pony in tweeën werd gesneden. Hij wist dat hij Tim honderd euro verschuldigd was, hij concentreerde zich daarop, op de honderd euro die hij moest betalen. Alsof het iets was waarvoor je moest oefenen omdat je het anders niet voor elkaar kreeg.

In de stallen annex wachtruimte lag nog een plastic tas met penen, appeltjes en het zadel lag er ook nog. Hij liet ze daar liggen. Voor de eerlijke vinder.

# IV

## *Franse troost*

## 1

Van de slachter reed hij naar Beckers. Alsof hij werd geroepen. Hij kon zich maar één persoon voorstellen aan wie hij wilde vertellen wat hij net had gezien, wat hij had meegemaakt. Hij hoefde niet bang te zijn dat Beckers thuis was, Beckers was op zijn vrije dagen meestal aan het klussen. Geld, of beter gezegd de angst het niet meer te hebben speelde een belangrijke rol in zijn leven.

De Pool parkeerde om de hoek, in de straat waar hij al eerder had geparkeerd. Hij liep naar het huis alsof hij daar verwacht werd, alsof hij er al woonde.

De vrouw van Beckers deed open. 'Het komt niet uit,' zei ze na een korte stilte en ze keek naar beneden, naar zijn gympen. 'Ik zit hier met twee vriendinnen.'

De Pool probeerde haar met zijn ogen te lokken, hij wilde dat zij hem aankeek en niet naar zijn schoenen staarde en hij antwoordde: 'Het is zover.'

'Wat is zover?' Ze leek geschrokken.

'Ik kan getroost worden. Ik ben er klaar voor.'

Ze keek bedenkelijk. De vrouw van Beckers had kennelijk van alles verwacht maar niet dit. 'Zo werkt het niet,' zei ze zacht, 'ik bood het aan en toen wilde je er niets van weten. Troost kun je niet bestellen.'

Was het aanbod verstreken? Kwam hij te laat? Had de troost een houdbaarheidsdatum?

'Ruik je het?' vroeg hij uiteindelijk en hij bracht zijn hoofd dichter bij dat van de vrouw van Beckers, die nog altijd in de deuropening stond.

'Wat moet ik ruiken?'

'Bloed.'

'Van wie?' Ze klonk geschrokken. Zag ze in hem een

moordenaar? Een man die niet tijdig getroost was en toen zijn conclusies had getrokken? – Geen troost? Dan maar bloed.

'Van het beest. Het is geslacht.'

'Ik ruik niets,' zei ze. 'Ik zie wel dat er bloed op je gympen zit, maar ik ben met mijn vriendinnen aan het kletsen. Kun je morgen komen?'

Hij keek nog eens goed. Er zat inderdaad een grote vlek op zijn witte gympen waaraan nog wat stro kleefde. 'Morgen heeft de C-ploeg dienst,' zei hij.

'Overmorgen?'

'Is goed,' mompelde hij.

Hij liep naar zijn auto, hij reed naar zijn huis en trommelde op het stuur alsof hij naar marsmuziek luisterde.

Zijn vrouw was op de kleuterschool, de overgebleven jongen zat op het kinderdagverblijf en in het hoofd van de Pool speelde marsmuziek. Hij zette koffie. Eigenlijk wilde hij een biertje maar omdat hij zich dat niet toestond nam hij genoegen met koffie.

Wandelend door het huis dronk hij zijn koffie, in de badkamer trok hij zich staand naast de wc af. Hij concentreerde zich op de vrouw van Beckers, merkwaardig genoeg had de vrouw van Beckers in zijn fantasie het hoofd van Tim. Op haar ietwat voluptueuze lichaam zat het hoofd van de slachter en hoe hij ook zijn best deed dat hoofd te verwijderen van het lichaam waarop het niet hoorde, het kwam telkens terug.

Morgenochtend, zeven uur in de kazerne. Dan begon het gewone, het nieuwe leven. Nieuw, omdat hij had erkend dat hij troost nodig had, hij had het uitgesproken, hij was geen slachtoffer, verre van, en toch had hij behoefte aan troost. Hij was iets gaan missen wat hij vroeger nooit had gemist.

Hij kon het bloed zelf nog ruiken, de vrouw van Beckers had een slechte neus. Hij besprenkelde zich met aftershave en bleef door het huis wandelen. In zijn telefoon zocht hij het nummer van Beckers, hij vond alleen een mobiel nummer. Dat had hij niet nodig, hij wilde niet Beckers zelf bellen, hij wilde de vrouw van Beckers bellen. Misschien hadden ze een vaste lijn maar hij had niet het geduld om ernaar te zoeken. Hij dronk nog een halve kop koffie, opende even de kamer van hun jongen. Zomaar, iets wat hij al die tijd na die ene avond niet had gedaan. Nu deed hij het alsof het de gewoonste zaak van de wereld was. Niets was veranderd, hij ging niet naar binnen, dat was een stap te ver. Hij schrok er zelf van hoe verstild en toch vers alles erbij lag. Het onopgemaakte bed, de boeken, de oude knuffels, de kleren op de grond. Alsof hij er net nog had geslapen, de jongen. Er lag wat stof maar daar keek je overheen. Hier in deze kamer stond de tijd stil.

Achter in de klerenkast vond hij een oude bijbel die hij als kind had gekregen. 'Voor Geniek', had zijn vader erin geschreven, 'om van te leren, om je te begeleiden op je levenspad.' Hij bladerde erin, las een paar zinnen hardop voor: 'Mensenkind, ga naar binnen, sluit je op in je huis. Je wordt er met touwen vastgebonden, zodat je niet meer naar buiten kunt gaan om je tussen de mensen te begeven. Ik zal ervoor zorgen dat je tong aan je gehemelte vastkleeft, zodat je stom zult zijn. Je mag hen niet meer waarschuwen, want ze zijn hoe dan ook opstandig.' En toen liep hij naar zijn auto.

Aan de bijbel had je ook weinig, dat wist de Pool nu. Bovendien wilde hij de mensen niet waarschuwen en waartegen dan wel? De tong die aan het gehemelte bleef kleven leek hem ook geen pretje.

Hij moest door, zijn vrouw had het gezegd, wat niet veranderd kon worden moest worden geaccepteerd. Hij reed terug naar Beckers en belde aan. Twee keer moest hij bellen voor ze opendeed. Ze keek minder verbaasd dan daarnet maar van blijdschap was nog geen sprake, terwijl hij het toch was, de Pool die ze wilde troosten. 'Ik ben het,' had hij willen schreeuwen, ‘ik ben het. Zie je het niet?’

Ze kon best wat blijer zijn, ze had zich over hem willen ontfermen en nu was hij beschikbaar. De Pool was een beetje licht in zijn hoofd, vermoedelijk omdat hij vanaf vanochtend op één winterpeen en koffie had geleefd.

‘Ik heb je toch gezegd dat ik hier met vriendinnen zit,’ zei ze.

‘Ja, dat heb je gezegd.’

Hij ging de vestibule in, zij sloot de deur en toch kon hij de vrouwen nog horen praten, waarover ze spraken verstond hij niet maar hun stemmen waren goed hoorbaar. Blije, hoge, ietwat lacherige stemmen. De Pool moest zich een beetje bukken maar hij was het gewend, zijn lengte dwong hem daar dagelijks toe, hij ging bukkend door het leven en nu bukte hij zich om de troost te krijgen waarnaar hij verlangde.

‘Ik heb wat in de bijbel zitten lezen,’ zei hij en daarop werd het hem te veel, hij pakte het hoofd van de vrouw van Beckers zacht vast, duwde zijn mond op die van haar, kuste, zoende, speelde met haar tong, nee het was geen spelen, het was vechten. Het was een gevecht tussen twee tongen, een zwaardgevecht. Hij herinnerde zich hoe hij met Borys alle *Star Wars*-films had gekeken.

‘Jij,’ zei hij. ‘Jij.’

Ze duwde hem van zich af, lachend alsof het een grap was. Zijn komst, zijn zoen. ‘Wat doe je?’ vroeg ze. ‘Waar ben je in godsnaam mee bezig?’

‘Wat doe jij?’

‘Ik had geen keus, je overviel me.’ Ze veegde haar mond af.

Hij legde zijn hand op haar schouder. Ze week niet terug, er was ook geen ruimte om terug te wijken. ‘Je bent me aan het troosten,’ zei hij zacht.

‘Lust is geen troost,’ antwoordde de vrouw van Beckers. ‘Dit is lust, ordinaire lust.’

'Vergeef me.' Ordinaire lust klonk erg. Erger dan gewone lust en hij zou niet eens kunnen zeggen waar de gewone lust ophield en de ordinaire lust begon, al had hij wel zo zijn vermoedens. 'Ik moet je spreken.'

'Spreken?'

'Spreken.'

'Later. Misschien kunnen we een wandelingetje maken, kom me later vanmiddag maar halen. Ik moet nu naar mijn vriendinnen.' En hij hoorde hen weer lachen. Ze riepen haar naam, dat kon hij verstaan, lachend, alsof ze blij waren dat ze er zo weer bij was.

Hij pakte haar hand. Een koude hand. 'Koud,' zei hij.

'Een vrouwenkwaaltje,' merkte ze lachend op. Toen duwde ze hem de deur uit. Hij was een reus, de Pool, maar de vrouw van Beckers wist wat duwen was.

Daarop reed hij weer naar huis, hij ging in de woonkamer zitten. Bij de buurman werd vioolgespeeld. Een dergelijk geluid had hij niet eerder uit dat huis gehoord. Ze waren daar kennelijk recentelijk begonnen met vioolspelen. Of was het cello? Hij wist het niet zeker. Zittend aan de eettafel begon de Pool na te denken over ordinaire lust en andere lust, de minder ordinaire soort. Zou het verschil tussen die twee net zoiets zijn als het verschil tussen de cello en de viool?

Hij moest de vrouw van Beckers straks vertellen waarom hij troost nodig had, waarom hij haar aanbod niet meer wilde afwijzen, zolang het nog geldig was. Het enige wat hem te binnen schoot, als hij zich voorstelde hoe hij het haar zou uitleggen, hoe hij alles zou verklaren, was dat hij niet misselijk werd als hij haar zoende, dat hij niet moest kokhalzen als hij zijn tong in haar mond duwde, al begreep hij dat de vrouw van Beckers niet op dergelijke openbaringen zat te wachten. De echte troost was de verboden troost. Dat zou zij begrijpen.

Hij wachtte tot het later werd, tot hij naar haar toe mocht, zoals de hongerigen wachten tot de gaarkeukens opengaan. Hij deed niet veel. Voor hij zich klaarmaakte om voor de derde keer die dag naar de vrouw van Beckers te gaan zocht hij in de schuur nog naar iets om zijn schoen mee schoon te vegen, maar het enige wat hij vond was een voorraadje winterpenen. Achteloos begon hij er aan een te knagen, die gymp zou hij later wel schoonmaken. Het restant penen legde hij in de keuken op het aanrecht, daar kon Wen vanavond sap van maken. Even dacht hij aan de jonge dwerg die met alle kracht die hij in zich had de pony had bedwongen.

Dit keer verwachtte de vrouw van Beckers hem wel. Ze stond al klaar met haar jas aan. 'We gaan een stukje lopen.' Ze wilde de deur dichtdoen en toen vroeg ze: 'Denk je dat we een paraplu nodig hebben?'

'Nee,' zei hij.

Ze liepen naast elkaar zonder iets te zeggen, niet zoals een man en een vrouw lopen, niet zoals mensen lopen die moeten bespreken wat het verschil is tussen ordinaire lust en troost, meer zoals arbeiders lopen die naar de fabriek gaan. Gehaast en toch met iets van tegenzin.

Tijdens het lopen zocht de Pool naar woorden maar hij kwam er niet uit, hij kwam steeds terug op die ene mededeling dat hij niet misselijk werd als hij haar zoende, dat hij van zijn lieve vrouw hield, boven alles, maar dat hij misselijk van haar werd, dat hij het vreselijk vond maar dat het zo was. En toch zei hij dat niet en in het park gingen ze op een bankje zitten hoewel het daar eigenlijk te koud voor was en nog steeds zwegen ze.

Tot de vrouw van Beckers zei: 'Toen ik negentien was ging ik met mijn beste vriendin naar Zuid-Frankrijk. Ik had er lang voor gespaard. Een van de eerste dagen daar zaten we in een café en toen kwam er een Fransman op me af, hij wees naar me en hij zei: "Jij wordt mijn vrouw." Zomaar uit het niets. Ik sprak slecht Frans maar dat verstond ik. Hij was ouder, toch kregen we wat, een vakantieliefde, een eerste liefde, ik weet niet hoe je die dingen noemen moet, en op het eind van de reis toen mijn vriendin en ik weer naar huis moesten zei hij: "Haal je spullen op in Nederland en kom de volgende dag weer hierheen." Ik zei alleen: "Ik kom zo snel mogelijk." Maar toen ik thuis was durfde ik niet. Ik belde dat ik zou komen, dat ik nog wat tijd nodig had. En zo gingen eerst dagen en toen weken voorbij. Op een gegeven moment belde hij op en hij zei: "Ik weet dat je niet meer komt." Maar in mijn dromen zie ik hem nog. Gek genoeg durf ik het ook in de droom niet. Nooit ga ik erheen. Ik was bang, ik sprak de taal amper, ik zag me daar al zitten aan de Côte d'Azur, ik was zo jong. Ik was bang bedrogen te worden, bang naïef te zijn. En op een gegeven moment ging ik terug naar de jongen die ik al kende van de lagere school, Beckers.'

Er was niemand in het park. De Pool keek naar de kiezelsteentjes rondom het bankje. Waarom vertelde ze hem dit? Wilde ze hem vertellen dat ze ongelukkig was? Dat zij troost had aangeboden omdat zij het was die getroost moest worden? Of bedoelde ze dat er een overeenkomst was tussen de Fransman wiens aanbod ze had geweigerd en zijn jongen?

Hij zei ietwat aarzelend: 'Ik heb haar geslacht. Dat wilde ik je eigenlijk vertellen.' De Pool had nooit tegen iemand gezegd: 'Jij wordt mijn vrouw.' Hij had zijn vrouw ten huwelijk gevraagd, maar pas toen hij zeker wist dat ze ja zou zeggen. Van jongs af had hij geleerd dat je risico's moest vermijden omdat het leven al risicovol genoeg was. Wel had hij een offer gebracht voor zijn huwelijk, hij had een pony geslacht.

'Het is beter zo. Of moet ik nu medelijden met je hebben?' Ze keek strak voor zich uit en hij wroette met zijn gympen in de kiezelsteentjes. Het klonk alsof zij die troost had geboden een hekel had aan medelijden. Zo zag ze hem nu dus: iemand die medelijden opeiste. Het klonk vreselijk. Zo iemand wilde hij niet zijn.

'Kijk,' ze boog haar hoofd naar hem toe, 'ik word al grijs.'

'Ik zie niets,' zei hij naar waarheid. Hij bleef naar haar hoofd staren, naar haar haren, en met een vinger, de wijsvinger van zijn rechterhand ging hij langzaam over haar hoofdhuid alsof hij een route wilde uittekenen, de route van Zuid-Limburg naar de Côte d'Azur en terug, en toen ging ze weer normaal zitten. Ze pakte zijn hand en ze zei dat de zijne nu koud was en zijn hand speelde met haar hand, in het park, op het bankje, terwijl het eigenlijk te kil was om op dat bankje te zitten en met zijn andere hand ging hij over haar rug, onder haar blouse, om warm te worden – was dat het waarnaar hij verlangde? Warm worden? – en even drukte hij weer zijn mond op die van haar. Ze liet hem begaan. Toen pakte ze met beide handen zijn gezicht vast en ze fluisterde: 'Je bent zo vertrouwd.'

'Vertrouwd?' vroeg hij. 'Vertrouwd of getrouwd?'

'Vertrouwd. Alsof ik je ken. Alsof ik weet wie je bent.'

'Iedereen hier weet wie ik ben.'

Ze pakte zijn hand weer, ze keek peinzend en toen zei ze zacht in zijn oor: 'Jij verlangt niet meer van deze wereld dan ordinaire lust, dat is alles wat je ervan kent, dat is alles wat je ervan begrijpt.'

Het voelde als een beschuldiging, een oordeel waaraan hij zich moest onttrekken. Hij schudde zijn hoofd, echt ontkennen durfde hij niet.

'Wat verlang je dan van mij?' vroeg de vrouw van Beckers. 'Wat verlang je van mij?'

Nu moest hij het zeggen. Maar hij had het al gezegd. Ze had het aangeboden en nu moest hij haar aanbod toelichten? Moest hij herhalen wat zijzelf meerdere malen had gezegd?

'Je hebt me iets aangeboden,' zei hij, 'je wilde mij en

mijn vrouw iets geven. Mijn vrouw wilde het niet hebben, ze had het niet nodig, maar ik heb er lang over nagedacht en ik wil het toch wel hebben, dus geef het maar.' En nu was hij het die haar hoofd pakte en hij keek nog eens goed en hij zei: 'Ik zie echt geen grijze haren.'

Ze rukte zich los. 'Je kijkt niet goed. Ik heb lang gedacht dat hij zou komen, want na mijn derde kind was ik er klaar voor. Het klinkt raar, het klinkt misschien vreselijk, alsof ik een slechte moeder ben. Na die geboorte wist ik het zeker: kinderen of geen kinderen, ik ben klaar voor de Fransman. Hij komt me wel halen. Maar hij kwam niet. Hij wist waar ik woonde want ik stuur hem ieder jaar met kerst een kaartje. Ik hoopte dat hij op me bleef wachten, ook al had hij zelf kinderen, ook al had hij een gezin, hij zou blijven wachten, maar hij kwam niet en nu weet ik zeker dat hij niet meer komt, ik word al grijs.'

De Pool steunde met zijn ellebogen op zijn bovenbenen en hield zijn hoofd vast. 'Neem me niet kwalijk,' zei hij, 'wat heeft dit met mij en mijn jongen te maken?'

'Niets,' zei ze. 'En alles. Als ik aan jou denk dan denk ik vaak ook aan hem en in het begin geloofde ik echt dat ik iets voor jullie kon doen, voor je vrouw en jou, maar na dat gesprek in het café besefte ik dat ik het niet kan. Dat ik jullie niets te bieden heb. Ik vind het vreselijk maar jullie moeten het zelf doen, zoals ik het ook zelf moet doen.'

Ze leek nog iets te willen zeggen, er kwam nog wat geluid uit haar mond, onduidelijk geluid, en de Pool wilde opstaan en naar zijn vrouw gaan maar hij zei: 'Ik heb erover nagedacht, ordinaire lust en gewone, alledaagse, beschaafde lust verhouden zich tot elkaar als de cello en de viool. Ze vullen elkaar aan.'

'O,' zei ze. 'O. Dat soort uitspraken had ik niet van jou verwacht.'

'Nee?' vroeg hij.

Toen kon de Pool zich niet meer inhouden omdat hij

begreep dat het verhaal over de Fransman die had gezegd: 'Jij wordt mijn vrouw' ging over gemiste kansen, omdat hij meende dat ze het hem daarom had verteld, om hem een les te leren en als hij nu opstond zonder haar nog een keer te hebben gezoend dan was dat een gemiste kans. Het waren de gemiste kansen die je achtervolgden, zoals de gemiste kans dat hij zijn jongen, hun jongen, nooit had uitgezwaaid, hem nooit had nageroepen als hij zich klaarmaakte om naar school te fietsen. Al was het maar: 'Fiets voorzichtig.' Of: 'Ik hou van je.' Hij had hem alleen losgerukt van bomen en lantaarnpalen. Dat wel. Hij vernietigde het vertrouwen van zijn vrouw door hier te zitten, door te voelen wat hij voelde, maar ze wist het niet en hij kon alleen aan de gemiste kans denken en dat hij niets aan zijn gevoelens kon doen. Hij was onschuldig. Hij pakte het hoofd van de vrouw van Beckers weer vast en hij zoende en zij zoende en zo zaten ze in het park als twee tieners. Hij wist maar één ding, dat hij haar niet wilde loslaten. Tot ze zei: 'De kinderen komen zo thuis. Een cello en een viool, hoe kom je daar nu weer bij? Denk je dat je me bespeelt?'

De Pool schudde zijn hoofd. 'Nee, dat niet. Ik weet niet hoe ik erbij kwam.'

Ze liepen terug en ze zei: 'Ga maar niet helemaal mee tot aan de voordeur.' Hij antwoordde: 'Nee, beter van niet,' terwijl hij dacht aan wat ze had gezegd, dat hij zo vertrouwd was en hij hoopte dat ze het nog een keer zou zeggen, hoewel hij niet precies wist wat ze ermee bedoelde maar het troostte hem, dat ze dat zei, dat ze dat meende, dat ze dat voelde, en daarom wilde hij dat ze het nog een keer zou voelen, dat ze het bleef zeggen, dat hij zo vertrouwd was, hij de zwijgzame Pool, vertrouwd. Maar omdat ze nu over straat liepen waar meer mensen waren dan in het koude park durfde hij haar niet nog een keer vast te pakken en hij liep op gepaste afstand naast haar, alsof hij de klusjesman was en zij de cliënt, tot ze zei: 'Hier moet je afslaan.'

Hij sloeg af voordat hij had kunnen vragen wanneer ze elkaar weer zagen. Ze moesten verder praten over het verschil tussen lust en ordinaire lust, over de cello en de viool, had hij willen zeggen, hoewel hij niets van cello noch viool wist en eigenlijk wist hij niet veel te zeggen maar voor haar zou hij zijn best doen. Hij zou haar alles vertellen, zoals zijn zoon alles aan de pony had verteld. De Pool keek nog eens om, ze was al ver weg.

Thuis bladerde hij nog een paar keer in de bijbel die hij als kind van zijn vader had gekregen. Nee, de Bijbel was geen troost.

# 2

Die middag, voor hij Jurek van de crèche zou halen timmerde hij een paar keer met zijn vuisten op de muur, zoals voetballers die zich niet kunnen beheersen op de muren van de kleedkamers slaan als ze hebben verloren. Hij dacht aan zijn vrouw, zonder wie hij niet wenste te leven, en hij schaamde zich dat hij de vrouw van Beckers liever kuste dan zijn echtgenote. De schaamte was vreselijk, hij voelde zich onrein. Met dat gevoel haalde hij de overgebleven jongen op van het kinderdagverblijf en hij knuffelde de jongen, hij speelde met autootjes in de woonkamer opdat zijn vrouw zou zien dat hij niet in het verleden leefde maar in het nu. En liggend op de grond met een autootje in zijn hand zei hij: 'Jij bent de liefste jongen die ik ken.' En hij drukte de jongen, die hem niet-begrijpend aankeek, tegen zich aan. Jurek wist niet waar zijn vader bang voor was, hij kon dat niet weten.

Toen zijn vrouw thuiskwam zag ze hem zo, spelend op de grond met Jurek. Ze begroette haar zoon en haar man en deed haar jas uit. Ze kwam er niet bij zitten, ze liep door naar de keuken. Hij ging kijken wat ze daar aan het doen was, ze duwde penen door de sapcentrifuge. 'Wil je ook wat sap?' vroeg ze. 'Je hebt zoveel winterpenen in huis gehaald. Ik maak er sap van.'

'Nee, niet nu,' zei hij.

En hij besefte dat hij niet moest wachten, dat hij het nu moest doen. Hij pakte zijn vrouw vast, dwong haar het net uitgeperste wortelsap op het aanrecht te zetten, kuste haar. Net zoals hij eerder op de dag zijn mond op die van de vrouw van Beckers had gedrukt maar ook zij duwde hem van zich af. 'Wat bezielt je?'

'Niets. Ik verlang naar je.'

Geloofde ze hem? Niet echt kennelijk, want ze zei: 'Opeens? Zomaar? Ik heb daar de afgelopen tijd weinig van gemerkt.'

'Verlangen komt toch altijd zomaar?'

'Nee, verlangen is er niet zomaar. Zo werkt dat niet.' Ze pakte haar wortelsap weer op. 'Kijk jij even wat hij aan het doen is? Het is zo stil.'

De Pool ging kijken en hij kwam meteen weer terug. 'Hij is gewoon aan het spelen.' Hij wist dat hij het nu moest doen, na het avondeten zou hij de kracht er niet meer voor hebben, hij zou moe zijn, na het avondeten bekroop hem de laatste tijd een lichte wanhoop. Zijn vrouw had gezegd dat die wanhoop logisch was. 'Ons gezin is kleiner geworden, daar moeten we aan wennen.'

Zijn lieve vrouw droeg een trui, hij probeerde haar trui uit te trekken alsof ze een etalagepop was en hij een verkoper in opleiding die niet eerder etalagepoppen van hun kleding had ontdaan.

'Waar ben je mee bezig?' vroeg ze terwijl hij aan haar trui rukte. Voorzichtig, want hij wilde niets kapotmaken. Hij moest het nu doen. Als hij zijn vrouw begeerde dan kon hij de vrouw van Beckers verdrijven. En de Pool moest haar verdrijven zoals hij de pony had verdreven, zoals hij hun jongen, nee de gedachten aan hun jongen zou verdrijven. De trui was uit. Ze stond daar in haar beha voor hem, een lichtroze beha. Hij sloot zijn ogen en hij zoende haar en hij begon te bidden, niet tot een god, tot zichzelf, tot zijn begeerte. Kom terug, begeerte, bad hij, kom terug, heerlijke begeerte, neem bezit van me, overman me zoals je me ooit, lang geleden hebt overmand. Zij is mijn vrouw. Ik moet mijn mannelijke plichten doen.

En hij leek haar overtuigend te hebben gezoend, zijn vrouw, want ze deed haar beha zelf uit. Ze legde de beha op het aanrecht, naast de laatste winterpenen, de overblijfselen van de pony. En ze zei: ‘Neem me hier. Doe het hier. Het is goed voor je.’

Voor hem? Was het goed voor hem? Deed zij dit voor hem? Seks als een griepprik. Doe het omdat het goed voor je is en wacht er niet te lang mee.

‘Het is goed voor ons,’ zei ze alsof ze zijn gedachten had geraden. ‘Dit hebben we te lang niet gedaan.’

‘Ik zet de jongen voor de zekerheid even in de box,’ zei hij. In de woonkamer pakte hij de overgebleven jongen voorzichtig op en zette hem in de box. De jongen begon te huilen. ‘Ik ben zo terug,’ zei de Pool, ‘we zijn zo terug, lieve jongen. Mama en papa moeten even iets doen.’

In de keuken stond Wen topless op hem te wachten. ‘Laat hem maar huilen,’ zei ze. ‘We moeten hem niet te veel verwennen. Dat is niet goed voor hem. We moeten niet gaan overcompenseren.’ De Pool knoopte zijn overhemd open, gooide het op de wasmachine, maakte zijn gympen los, deed ze uit. Op de achtergrond hoorde hij zijn jongen huilen en zijn vrouw wachtte geleund tegen het aanrecht op de begeerte van de Pool.

Hij bukte zich voor zijn vrouw om zijn sokken uit te doen, pas daarna ontdeed hij zich van spijkerbroek en onderbroek. Naakt stond hij nu voor zijn vrouw, hij keek naar de sapcentrifuge en Wen zei: ‘Je bent slap.’

‘Ik word zo stijf,’ antwoordde hij.

‘Moet ik het doen?’

‘Nee. Ik doe het zelf.’

In de woonkamer huilde Jurek. De Pool begon zich af te trekken, staand voor zijn vrouw, zijn rug een beetje gekromd en hij keek haar in de ogen. Hij staarde haar in de ogen, die hij zo goed kende, die hij jaren had gezien bij het wakker worden en waarover hij nooit had nagedacht want zo was hij niet. Lang geleden had iemand gevraagd: ‘Wat voor kleur ogen heeft je vrouw?’ En hij moest erkennen dat hij het niet precies wist, iets tussen grijs en bruin in, misschien met wat groen erdoor. 'Ik moet nog eens goed kijken,' had hij geantwoord.

'Het lukt niet,' zei ze.

'Jawel,' hij trok zichzelf nog fanatieker af – was seks niet bij uitstek een bezigheid voor fanatici? Voor de fanaticus in de mens? – maar het wilde inderdaad niet lukken. Ze wachtte nog even, hij zag haar wachten, in haar blik zag hij hopeloosheid, verslagenheid. Alsof het zijn slappe geslachtsdeel was dat ervoor had gezorgd dat hun jongen onder de intercity naar Amsterdam was gekomen. In opperste nood dacht hij aan de vrouw van Beckers, hoe ze naast hem zat, hoe ze zei dat hij zo vertrouwd was, maar zelfs dat wilde niet helpen, tot zijn vrouw hem een klein zetje gaf, ze duwde hem van zich af en zei: 'Hou maar op. Dit heeft geen zin.'

'Het komt zo,' antwoordde de Pool.

Even leek zijn vrouw medelijden met hem te hebben, het medelijden dat hij verachtte omdat troost iets anders was dan medelijden, iets volstrekt anders, en ze vroeg: 'Zal ik tegen je aan rijden met mijn billen?' Ze zei het met een stem die hij van haar kende en die hij lang niet had gehoord, de stem van de geilheid, de stem van de opwinding of van de gespeelde opwinding, dat wist je nooit zeker. Zijn vrouw die haar ondeugende stem opzette, of misschien was het geen opzetten, het kon goed zijn dat zij werkelijk werd overvallen door iets wat de vrouw van Beckers ordinaire lust had genoemd.

Ze draaide zich om en ze duwde met haar in een spijkerbroek gestoken billen tegen zijn slappe geslachtsdeel en hij duwde tegen haar billen, hij duwde uit alle macht tegen haar billen, tegen de bilspleet, hij moest een beetje door zijn knieën gaan, anders zou hij tegen haar onderrug aan duwen en dat was niet de bedoeling. Vroeger hadden ze dit vaker gedaan, vrijen met kleren aan, in de auto, tussendoor in de kazerne, als ze even langskwam. Later was het niet meer nodig geweest. Ze hadden alle tijd en plaats om te vrijen zonder kleren aan. Er was ruimte voor naaktheid. Of was het niet de tijd en de plaats geweest? Was dat het begin geweest van het einde, toen ze voor gezinnetje gingen spelen? Was hun zoon gestorven uit gebrek aan liefde? Omdat de Pool niet genoeg van zijn lieve vrouw had gehouden en ook niet van hun jongen?

Ze hield zich vast aan het aanrecht en hij wilde vragen of zij geen troost nodig had, of ze dat zeker wist, of ze het niet toch wilde overwegen. Waren ze niet te stoer geweest, hooghartig bijna in hun ongenaakbaarheid? Was het niet arrogant te denken dat zij konden wat andere mensen niet of zoveel moeilijker konden, over het verlies van een kind heen stappen alsof het niet meer was dan een geliefd parasolletje dat ze waren kwijtgeraakt? Zijn vrouw had hem weleens verteld dat ze een parasolletje had gehad als kind en dat ze dat op een vakantie in Griekenland was kwijtgeraakt. Ze was ontroostbaar geweest, dagenlang. Ze had een nieuw parasolletje gekregen maar het was niet hetzelfde. Toen ze elkaar net kenden had dat verhaal veel indruk op hem gemaakt. Hij zag zijn vrouw, zijn geile, fijne vrouw, als kind, als ontroostbaar kind en hij had een parasolletje voor haar gekocht. Ze had hem uitgelachen, vriendelijk maar toch. 'Mallerd,' had ze gezegd. Of was het een ander woord geweest, een soortgelijk woord in elk geval. 'Ik ben daar toch allang overheen.'

Terwijl zij haar billen tegen zijn slappe geslachtsdeel duwde dacht hij aan dat parasolletje. Ze was er allang overheen en zo hadden ze ook over hun jongen moeten heen komen. De ontroostbaarheid is voorbehouden aan kinderen en al snel kunnen zelfs zij zich niet herinneren waarom ze ontroostbaar zijn geweest. Zo moet ook de rouw werken. Waarom was dit anders, deze rouw? Hij trok zijn vrouw zachtjes aan haar halflange haren.

'Het is de spijkerbroek,' zei hij met schorre stem. Hij

was niet buiten adem maar het was vermoeiend, het langdurige aftrekken. 'Misschien kun je je broek uitdoen?'

Ze draaide zich om en keek hem liefdevol aan. Medelijden was het niet, het was liefde. Geen geilheid, geen opwinding, hij zag het in haar blik. Ze hoorden bij elkaar.

Wen nam nog een slokje wortelsap. Nu was het glas leeg en ze deed haar broek uit terwijl ze hem een knipoog gaf, alsof ze wilde zeggen dat het een geheim moest blijven tussen haar en hem dat zij in de keuken haar spijkerbroek uitdeed, terwijl ze eigenlijk voor het avondeten had moeten zorgen, zich om de overgebleven jongen had moeten bekommeren. Deze frivoliteit misstond ouders, dit was niet het uur van de speelsheid.

Ze stond voor hem in haar string. Ook roze, ander roze dan de beha. Ze draaide zich weer om. 'Vind je dit lekker?' vroeg hij. 'We kunnen het ook later doen.' De aarzeling had hem overvallen, misschien was later toch beter. Misschien was dit niet het goede moment. Misschien vond ze het echt niet lekker. 'Nee,' zei ze, 'je bent mijn man. Het is belangrijk dat wij dit blijven doen. Als we bij elkaar willen blijven.'

'Ja,' zei hij, 'als wij bij elkaar willen blijven. Dan moeten we dit doen.' En hij stootte tegen haar billen, hij zag een blauwe plek op haar rechterbil, ze moest zich hebben bezeerd.

'In godsnaam, neem me,' zei ze. Daar was haar stem weer, de stem van de gespeelde opwinding, hij twijfelde er niet aan, ze veinsde geilheid omdat ze vond dat het erbij hoorde. Ze was te jong om nooit meer geil te zijn, daarom deed ze alsof.

En hij probeerde zijn slappe geslachtsdeel in haar geslachtsdeel te frummelen, dan moest het maar zo. Frummelen, waarom niet? Zo begon de menselijke seksualiteit, frummelend, zo kon die ook eindigen, als dit het einde was. Zeker wist je dat natuurlijk niet. Maar het frummelen leverde niets op. Ze keek om en ze vroeg wat hij aan het doen was, of hij zelf wel wist waarmee hij bezig was. Er klonk teleurstelling in haar stem. Bitterheid.

'Ik wil je,' zei hij. Het minste wat hij kon doen was dat zeggen. Als hij het niet kon doen dan kon hij het zeggen. Hij was altijd een doener geweest. Een man was een doener, nu werd hij een prater omdat hij het niet kon. De praters waren mensen die iets niet konden doen en die daarom praatten om te verbergen dat ze het niet konden. De Pool schraapte zijn keel. 'Ik wil je hard neuken. Ik wil je zo hard neuken zoals je nog nooit geneukt bent.'

'Doe het dan.' Aan haar stem hoorde hij dat zijn woorden haar hadden opgewonden maar zijn geslachtsdeel was onveranderd. Weer concentreerde hij zich op de vrouw van Beckers hoewel hij het zondig vond. Het hielp niet.

Ze draaide zich om. 'Hou op,' zei ze, 'je wilt me niet echt. Doe dan ook niet alsof je me wil.' Ze griste haar beha van het aanrecht en deed hem weer om maar voor ze haar trui kon aantrekken barstte ze in huilen uit en hij zei, zonder op te geven, zich aftrekkend: 'Onze overgebleven jongen huilt en nu huil jij ook. Dat is veel. Hoe kan ik zo geil worden? Ik doe mijn best, ik doe godverdomme mijn best.'

'Misschien moet je iets slikken,' zei ze, 'of misschien moeten we geen seks meer hebben, misschien moeten we gewoon onze jongen opvoeden. En het daarbij laten.' Ze huilde nog steeds en hij hield niet op zich af te trekken want hij was een man van eer, een man die zijn belofte nakwam, een man die begeerte kon afdwingen als het moest.

'Maar dat is toch niet genoeg?' zei hij terwijl hij doorging. 'Samen een kind opvoeden is toch niet genoeg? We zijn geen kinderdagverblijf, we zijn toch man en vrouw?'

Ze haalde haar schouders op en even meende hij dat er vooruitgang in zat, dat er iets hard aan het worden was. Zij keek en hij zag haar blik en meteen daarop besefte hij dat het een illusie was. Er werd niets hard, alleen zijn woorden, die waren hard, zijn kaakspieren, zijn hoofd.

'Nee,' zei ze, 'we zijn geen kinderdagverblijf, maar als jij me niet meer kan neuken dan moeten we misschien ophouden met die belachelijke pogingen, want hier worden we allebei niet gelukkig van.'

Hij streelde zijn vrouw met zijn vrije hand terwijl hij doorging en zag dat het een beetje begon te bloeden, zijn pik was aan het bloeden, hij had de huid kapotgetrokken. 'Kijk dan,' zei ze, 'hoe je daar staat. Kijk dan naar jezelf. Moet dit een echtgenoot voorstellen?'

De Pool begreep dat hij iets moest doen maar hij wist niet wat. Hij hield op en keek naar zijn slappe geslacht. Het bloed dat aan zijn rechterhand zat veegde hij af aan een theedoek.

'Doe dit nou niet,' zei ze. 'Bloed gaat er zo moeilijk uit. Pak gewoon een wc-papiertje.'

'We kopen wel een nieuwe theedoek.'

Hij was geen vader, wat was dan wel een vader? Iemand die de moeder van zijn kinderen hard neukte? Iemand die zijn zoon uitzwaaide als hij naar school fietste? Hij had een pony voor hem gekocht, hij had ervoor gezorgd dat de jongen niet meer op school in zijn broek poepte, was dat niet ook wat vaders behoorden te doen?

Hij draaide zijn vrouw om. Zijn geslacht mocht slap zijn, zijn armen waren het niet. De Pool pakte een overgebleven winterpeen van het aanrecht, de kleinste die hij kon vinden, duwde haar string een beetje opzij en stootte de winterpeen in haar.

'Wat doe je?' vroeg ze. 'Waar ben je mee bezig?'

Hij haalde de winterpeen uit haar en stootte hem opnieuw in haar vagina. In het geslachtsdeel dat hij eigenlijk altijd onbenoemd had gelaten want hij hield niet van vieze woorden.

'Die waren voor de pony bedoeld,' zei hij, 'maar de pony kan ze niet meer eten en daarom neuk ik je nu met wat de pony heeft laten staan, het beest is namelijk geslacht.'

'Wanneer?' Ze hijgde. Of het uit genot was of uit verdriet of uit woede wist hij niet zeker, ze hijgde.

Steeds sneller bewoog hij de peen in haar. 'Vandaag.' Met zijn linkerhand hield hij haar nek vast, met zijn rechterhand bewoog hij de peen in zijn vrouw en vanuit de woonkamer hoorde hij het gejengel van de overgebleven jongen. 'We moeten ons om de jongen bekommeren,' zei hij. 'Hoor je niet hoe hij ons nodig heeft? We moeten minder aan onze eigen lusten denken en meer aan Jurek.' Hij haalde de winterpeen uit de kut van zijn vrouw en stopte hem in haar kont. Ze gilde, anders dan ze normaal gilde, ze gilde hoe dan ook niet veel. 'O fuck,' zei ze. Wat ze anders nooit zei. Van dat gegil schrok hij. Daarom verslapte zijn linkerhand waarmee hij haar nek vastgeklemd hield. Ze ontsnapte aan zijn greep, pakte de sapcentrifuge met twee handen vast en voor hij begreep wat ze van plan was had ze hem met de sapcentrifuge op het voorhoofd geslagen.

Hij wankelde en viel tegen de muur. Hij hield zich vast aan de muur en de wasmachine. Met zijn hand ging hij over zijn voorhoofd. Er zat bloed op zijn hand. In zijn andere hand hield hij nog altijd de winterpeen vast.

'Ben je gek geworden?' vroeg hij. 'Moet ik dood?'

'Jij stopte opeens zo'n groot ding in mijn kont.'

Wen had de sapcentrifuge in haar handen en ze keek hem aan vol razernij die misschien lust was maar waarschijnlijker gewoon razernij. Het ging door hem heen dat ze hem echt dood wilde hebben. Omdat hij geen goede echtgenoot was, omdat hij wel over hard neuken kon praten maar het niet meer kon doen, omdat de lust hem verlaten had. Omdat hun zoon voor de trein was gesprongen. Omdat liefde en dood hetzelfde konden zijn.

'Waar was je mee bezig?' vroeg ze nu iets kalmer. 'Wat was je aan het doen?' Ze zette de sapcentrifuge weer op het aanrecht, hij zag tranen in haar ogen. Nieuwe tranen.

Hij pakte de theedoek en drukte die tegen zijn voorhoofd. 'Ik deed wat een man behoort te doen. Ik neukte je.' De theedoek gleed uit zijn hand op de grond. Onder het bloed. Die konden ze inderdaad beter weggooien.

'Met een winterpeen,' riep ze. 'Omdat je slap bent.' En ze tikte met haar wijsvinger tegen zijn pik. Het voelde onaangenaam.

'Waarmee is onbelangrijk.' De Pool ging naar de woonkamer, kalmeerde de jongen en liep terug naar de keuken. Zijn vrouw bestudeerde de sapcentrifuge. Ze zag er verward uit. Was hij als brandweerman dit huis binnengekomen dan zou hij hebben doorgegeven dat er een verwarde vrouw met een sapcentrifuge in de keuken stond. Hij begreep het. Ze voelde zich afgewezen. Zijn pik wees haar af maar zo was het niet bedoeld.

Er zat niets anders op dan van haar te houden. Het feit dat ze hem met een sapcentrifuge op het hoofd had geslagen deed daar niets aan af. Ze wilde kennelijk niet met een winterpeen geneukt worden terwijl het hem beter had geleken dan niets.

'Je bloedt.' Ze zette de sapcentrifuge in de gootsteen en ze wees op de druppels op de grond. 'Kijk dan,' zei ze.

Hij ging naar boven en bestudeerde zijn wond in de spiegel. Het zag er niet uit alsof het gehecht moest worden. Hij plakte een pleister op de wond, dat zou het bloeden stelpen.

Toen ging hij weer naar beneden.

Er lagen nog wat winterpenen op het aanrecht. 'Ik zal meer wortelsap maken.' Toen hij de winterpenen door de centrifuge probeerde te halen merkte hij dat de machine niet meer werkte. 'Je hebt hem kapotgemaakt,' zei hij.

Zonder spijkerbroek liep ze nog altijd door de keuken. En hij was naakt, hij pakte het overhemd van de wasmachine.

'Wacht.' Hij fatsoeneerde van achteren haar string. 'Je bent mooi,' verklaarde hij.

Objectief gezien was ze mooi. Nog altijd mooi. Haar haren, haar neus, haar ogen, haar lichaam. Mensen schatten haar ook jonger. Iets meisjesachtigs had ze altijd behouden. Ze wekte de indruk nog altijd met vriendinnen op straat te kunnen hinkelen. Toch had de lust hem verlaten.

'Het spijt me,' zei ze, 'van die sapcentrifuge.'

'Geeft niet, we kopen wel een nieuwe.'

'Het bloedt nog steeds. Het komt erdoorheen.'

'Ik doe er zo nog een gaasje op.'

De Pool pakte de sapcentrifuge en gooide die in de vuilnisbak. 'Zo duur zijn die dingen niet.' Hij bleef bij de vuilnisbak staan, starend naar de sapcentrifuge. 'We moeten bij elkaar blijven,' zei hij. 'Voor onze jongens.'

'Ja,' zei ze, 'voor onze jongens.'

# 3

Ze speelden een partijtje volleybal en pas bij het douchen erna vroeg de ploegchef of de Pool soms ruzie had gemaakt in het café. 'Nee,' zei de Pool met een stijfheid die hijzelf ongemakkelijk vond, 'ik heb me gestoten in de keuken.' Hij merkte dat de pleister door het water half los was gaan zitten en rukte hem geïrriteerd van zijn voorhoofd alsof het allemaal de schuld van de pleister was.

Verder zei niemand iets, dus de Pool hoefde niets meer uit te leggen, niet hoe hij zich had gestoten, niet of zijn vrouw erbij was geweest. De mannen maakten geen grappen over de wond op zijn voorhoofd omdat er die dag veel andere dingen waren waarover ze grappen konden maken en vooral omdat ze vonden dat ze hem moesten ontzien. Vooralsnog was de Pool een man die ontzien moest worden. En hoewel niemand mocht denken dat ze bij de brandweer zaten te kaarten tot er weer een brand uitbrak – een vooroordeel waarmee ook de Pool regelmatig te kampen had – bestond het werk natuurlijk voor een deel uit wachten. Die tijd vulden de mannen met grappen omdat ze vanbinnen verdrietig en onrustig werden van al dat wachten op andermans ellende.

Na de lunch deden ze een blindloopoefening. De Pool had die oefening talloze malen gedaan. Je moest met een fles ademlucht op de tast een oefenruimte in, een gefingeerde woning of kantoorruimte, en op de tast moest je die ruimte ook weer verlaten. Soms kreeg je de taak na te gaan of er zich nog mensen in de ruimte bevonden. De oefening was routine, net als de partijtjes volleybal dat waren, al moest je geconcentreerd blijven, daarvoor was die oefening ook bedoeld, om ervoor te zorgen dat je scherp bleef, dat je niet overmoedig werd, dat je je niet onkwetsbaar waande. Deze mannen waanden zich graag onkwetsbaar, tot ze het verval niet langer konden ontkennen en tegen die tijd kregen ze meestal een administratieve functie of ze gingen met pensioen.

De Pool was als laatste aan de beurt en toen hij het masker opzette merkte hij dat hij toch hard was geslagen met de sapcentrifuge, ze had zich niet ingehouden, zijn lieve vrouw, het masker drukte pijnlijk op de wond maar dat was niet erg, hij nam zijn vrouw niets kwalijk. Nooit zou hij haar iets kwalijk nemen. Hij kon zich dat niet voorstellen. Als mensen het hadden over onvoorwaardelijke liefde dan hadden ze het daarover, dat ze elkaar nooit iets kwalijk namen.

De fles met ademlucht hing op zijn rug, Beckers stond naast hem. Hij kon hem niet meer zien, hij wist dat het Beckers was, dat voelde hij. Als je zo lang samen optrekt, als je zoveel tijd samen doorbrengt, dan weet je bijna alles van elkaar, dan ben je als man en vrouw.

De oefenruimte was dit keer een trappenhuis. Hij moest twee trappen omhoog. Met de rug van zijn hand hield hij contact met de muur, altijd met de rug van je hand voelen om verbrandingsgevaar te voorkomen, anders bestaat het gevaar dat je iets vastgrijpt wat je niet moet vastgrijpen. Op de tweede verdieping bevond zich de gefingeerde woning. Hij maakte een rondje door de woning en ging toen weer het trappenhuis in, de trap af. Hij hoorde zichzelf ademen zoals je ademt als je een masker op hebt, alsof je de lucht door een rietje opzuigt. De blindloopoefening was zijn favoriete oefening al wist hij zelf niet waarom. Het blindlopen, de routine maakte hem op een vreemde manier rustig. Was hij niet daarom brandweerman geworden? Om de dichte rook in te gaan en te zien of zich nog een levend wezen in de rook bevond, om te zien waar niets te zien was, om te gaan waar verder niemand ging?

De Pool bleef altijd rustig, hoewel je gebouwen en fabriekshallen moest binnengaan die de gewone burger juist had moeten verlaten. Je liep niet weg voor de brand, je ging erin. Al zei de ploegchef weleens: 'Het is de bedoeling dat we met z'n allen terugkeren naar de kazerne.'

Toen hij dit keer naar beneden liep, tastend, behoedzaam, zich concentrerend op de herkenningspunten die hij had onthouden, een loszittende steen, een leuning die was afgebroken, raakte hij in paniek. Hij had het gevoel dat de toevoer van de ademlucht haperde, dat hij stikte. Nooit was hij bang geweest te stikken, nooit was hij in paniek geraakt, hij gaf te weinig om zijn eigen leven, en nu werd hij overvallen door de sensatie te stikken. Hij wist dat paniek schadelijk was. Wie in paniek raakte verbruikte nog meer ademlucht, hij kon er niets aan doen, de paniek was sterker dan de Pool. Er was geen twijfel over mogelijk, hij was bezig te stikken.

Misschien verbeeldde hij het zich maar het kon ook zijn dat de toevoer daadwerkelijk haperde, dat gebeurde weleens. Niet vaak, soms liet de techniek de brandweerman in de steek, daarom controleerden ze alles eindeloos.

'Laten we de oefening afbreken,' zei de Pool zo rustig en kalm mogelijk. Hij sjorde aan zijn masker maar het lukte hem niet het af te krijgen. Ze moesten hem gehoord hebben, al kwam er geen reactie op zijn bericht.

Het gewicht van de fles op zijn rug voelde zwaarder dan anders. Het duizelde hem. De Pool hield zich vast, hij was niet meer in staat te bewegen. 'Laten we de oefening afbreken,' zei hij nog een keer door de portofoon en hij zag de vrouw van Beckers voor zich, zoals ze was op haar achttiende, het was alsof hij haar had gekend, alsof hij erbij was geweest toen de Fransman daar in dat café aan de Côte d'Azur naar haar had gewezen en had gezegd: 'Jij wordt mijn vrouw.' Het kwam hem voor dat hij die Fransman was, dat hij in een ander leven Fransman was geweest.

Hij hoorde discomuziek, hij voelde zich steeds duizeliger worden. Waarom kreeg hij het masker niet af?

Het was niet de bedoeling dat je het masker afzette in een brandend gebouw maar dit was geen brandend gebouw, dit was niet het leven zelf, dit was oefenen voor het leven.

'We breken de oefening af,' zei hij en hij hoorde zijn eigen, vervormde stem. Hij was bang dat hij zou zeggen: 'Ik verlang naar de vrouw van Beckers, ik kan er niets aan doen.' En daar had hij het al gezegd. Hij had zich verraden. Ongelooflijk, als de eerste de beste idioot. Als een schooljongen. Dat kwam ook omdat hij bezig was te stikken, omdat hij duizelig was, omdat hij zich niet meer staande kon houden. Hij had geen controle meer over wat er allemaal uit kwam.

Waar bleven ze? Waarom kwamen ze niet? Ze moesten vlak bij hem zijn. Het was geen doodsangst die hem overviel, althans hij was niet bang dood te gaan maar hij dacht aan de nederlaag die dit zou zijn, sterven tijdens een oefening, alsof je in de badkuip uitgleed en je nek brak. Wat een laffe dood.

Toen kwamen ze. Ze hielpen hem het masker af te doen.

'Waar waren jullie?' Hij merkte hoe hij hijgde, hoe samengeknepen zijn stem klonk. Ze keken hem aan, de mannen, verbaasd, ook ietwat ongerust. Alsof ze het niet konden geloven dat hij faalde, de Pool die nooit faalde, die weinig zei maar die ook nooit faalde. Die deed wat hij doen moest. Een harde werker. Een teamspeler. Hij was getest.

'Ik kreeg geen lucht meer,' zei hij, 'en het masker ging niet af.'

De ploegchef pakte hem bijna teder bij de bovenarm. 'We hadden een technisch probleem,' zei hij, 'we gaan kijken wat er aan de hand was. Ga even zitten.'

De Pool ging op de trap zitten. De oefening werd voor beëindigd verklaard. Een man die Haas werd genoemd zei:

‘Heb ik ook een keer gehad. Als de paniek eenmaal toeslaat is er weinig meer aan te doen.’

‘Het was geen paniek,’ zei de Pool. ‘Ik kreeg geen lucht meer. En mijn masker ging ook niet af.’

‘Dat is de paniek,’ zei de man die Haas werd genoemd, met een kalmte die de Pool vervelend vond.

Toen stond de Pool op, hij ontdeed zich van zijn pak en Haas bleef bij hem alsof hij met hem te doen had, alsof hij de opdracht had gekregen de Pool in de gaten te houden.

Ze gingen naar het woongedeelte van de kazerne. In de keuken waste de Pool zijn handen.

‘Jij kookt vandaag toch?’ vroeg Haas.

‘Ja,’ zei hij, ‘ik kook vandaag.’ De Pool wilde weten of ze hadden gehoord wat hij had gezegd, in dat moment van paniek, die seconden dat hij geloofde dat hij zou sterven. Zouden ze besloten hebben hem te laten sterven, de mannen van de C-ploeg, omdat ze het al wisten voor hij het had uitgesproken? Dat hij begeerde wat hem niet toekwam, dat hij verlangde waarnaar hij niet mocht verlangen en dat de Pool daarom dood moest? Zouden ze nu over hem aan het vergaderen zijn? Waren ze nu met z’n allen bij elkaar om te overleggen wat ze met hem moesten doen? Met de collega die bij nader inzien geen teamspeler bleek te zijn.

Toen zag hij een paar mannen van de C-ploeg aan de tafel zitten waar ze zo gingen eten en hij besefte dat ze niet over hem aan het praten waren. Ze keken hem gewoon aan, alsof er niets was gebeurd. Alsof ze niets hadden gehoord. Alsof hij niets had gezegd.

‘Je kunt alvast beginnen met koken,’ zei Haas. En dat deed de Pool. Dat deed hij met plezier en met toewijding, zoals hij vroeger had geneukt zo kookte hij in de kazerne. Tegen de tijd dat hij klaar zou zijn met koken was het etenstijd. Ze aten vroeg, liefst precies om vijf uur. De mannen hielden van regelmaat.

Als groente waren er sperzieboontjes. Hij probeerde niet aan de vrouw van Beckers te denken maar aan het partijtje volleybal dat ze die ochtend hadden gespeeld. Het team van de Pool had gewonnen. Fanatiek was hij er niet in, de andere mannen waren fanatieker, alleen al uit sportiviteit veinsde hij fanatisme.

Beckers had aangeboden te helpen met het koken. Hij stond naast hem en schoof de sperzieboontjes in een pan met kokend water. En tussen het frituren van de patat en het bakken van de hamburgers sneed de Pool tomaten. Ze waren die dag, voor het volleyballen, één keer uitgerukt. Alarm in een winkelcentrum, loos alarm.

Terwijl hij met de tomaten bezig was keek de Pool naar Beckers en hij moest weer aan de vrouw van Beckers denken. Hij dacht eraan dat hij kon zeggen: Jouw vrouw wacht op een Fransman. Vanaf het moment dat jullie derde kind is geboren is ze begonnen met wachten. Zoiets zou hij nooit zeggen, maar juist daarom was hij bang dat hij het deed, hij was bang dat hij vanaf nu alleen nog zei wat hij eigenlijk niet zeggen mocht.

Het was alsof Beckers voelde dat er aan hem werd gedacht, dat er naar hem werd gekeken, want hij vroeg: 'Hoe is het eigenlijk met dat paard afgelopen?' Nooit meer was hij over het paard begonnen en nu opeens terwijl hij met de patat bezig was moest hij kennelijk weer aan dat paard denken.

'Pony,' zei de Pool.

'Pony, paard, wat is het verschil.' Beckers stopte een boontje in zijn mond. 'Hoe is het met de pony afgelopen?'

De Pool haalde een vinger over zijn keel en Beckers zei: 'Beter zo.'

Toen goot Beckers de boontjes af en hij riep: 'De tafel kan gedekt.' De andere mannen begonnen de tafel te dekken, de Pool had willen zeggen, zo tussen neus en lippen door: Ik verlang naar je vrouw, Beckers. Sinds onze jongen er niet meer is verlang ik nergens meer naar maar nu verlang ik naar je vrouw, Beckers. Ik kan aan niets anders meer denken, ik kan er niets aan doen.

Het leek hem een opluchting dat te kunnen zeggen, hoewel hij niet zeker wist of hij er echt niets aan kon doen maar hij vreesde de reacties; als het eenmaal was gezegd was er geen weg terug. Dan was de Pool die hij was geweest voorgoed verdwenen, de Pool die bekendstond als een goede collega, een lange en betrouwbare man, de teamspeler, die was er dan niet meer. En het zou zijn alsof die er nooit was geweest. Ze zouden over hem praten als over een rat, eentje die begeerde wat hem niet toekwam, die verlangde wat van iemand anders was. De mannen zouden het niet licht opnemen, ze hielden niet van verraad.

De borden kwamen langs en de Pool legde hamburgers op de borden en toen gingen ze zitten en de Pool deed zijn best niet meer aan de vrouw van Beckers te denken, want het waren de gedachten die je gek maakten. Dat lukte pas toen een van de mannen op de krant wees die op tafel lag en zei: 'Het wordt steeds erger met die buitenlanders.'

De collega die Haas werd genoemd, vanwege zijn oren, zei: 'Straks hebben ze biologische wapens. Dan kunnen we het helemaal vergeten. Dan zijn het niet meer twintig of dertig doden, dan zijn het duizenden.'

De Pool zei: 'We hadden ze nooit binnen moeten laten.'

Even viel er een stilte, ze keken naar hem, de mannen van de C-ploeg, en even bekroop de Pool het eigenaardige gevoel dat ze het wisten. Dat ze toch hadden gehoord wat hij in paniek had gezegd tijdens de blindloopoefening. Hij at zijn sperzieboontjes met lichte tegenzin tot de ploegchef zei: 'Het was weer lekker, Pool. Patat bakken kan je. Ja, daar zijn die Polen goed in.'

Na het eten gingen ze in de luie stoelen voor de televisie zitten. Twee mannen wasten af. De Pool had al geholpen het fornuis schoon te maken en nu ging ook hij voor de televisie zitten om naar een film te kijken waarop hij zich niet kon concentreren. Nu en dan viel hij in slaap, als hij wakker was dwaalden zijn gedachten af.

Halverwege vertrok hij naar zijn kamer, hij ging op zijn bed liggen en belde zijn vrouw om te vragen of alles rustig was. Ze zei dat hun jongen sliep en dat ze wat aan het breien was, dat ze voor het eerst sinds jaren weer zin had gekregen om te breien.

'Wat ben je aan het breien?' vroeg hij.

'Ik ben een sjaal voor je aan het breien.'

'Dat is lief.' Hij wilde nog niet ophangen maar hij wist niet wat hij verder moest zeggen. Waarom ze was begonnen met breien? Hij vond het niets voor zijn vrouw om te gaan breien.

'Goede dienst,' zei ze, 'tot morgenochtend.'

'Slaap lekker,' antwoordde hij.

Toen verbrak ze de verbinding. En hij staarde naar het plafond, zag een spinnenweb, geen spin, en bleef op bed liggen.

De ploegchef klopte op de deur, kwam binnen en vroeg: 'Alles goed?'

De Pool knikte.

'Zijn jullie er weer een beetje bovenop?' Hij deed een paar passen in de richting van het bed. En toen zag hij kennelijk ook het spinnenweb. 'Zo, ze mogen het plafond ook weleens schoonmaken.'

'Alles gaat zijn gangetje,' zei de Pool.

'Mooi. We zijn nog aan het kijken wat er precies misging tijdens jouw blindloopoefening.' De ploegchef legde een hand op de schouder van de Pool en de Pool had weer verboden gedachten, hij zei alleen: 'Oké.' De ploegchef ging weg en de Pool luisterde naar zijn voetstappen op de gang die hem op de een of andere manier geruststellend voorkwamen.

Aan het eind van de avond moesten ze uitrukken. Een

verwarde man had in zijn woonkamer met kranten geprobeerd een tafel in brand te steken. De politie was erbij gehaald en was tot de conclusie gekomen dat de man niet alleen kon blijven. Daar was de ploegchef het mee eens geweest. 'Anders staan we hier morgenochtend weer,' zei hij.

De rest van de nacht was het rustig maar de Pool, die anders op de kazerne prima kon slapen, sliep deze nacht slecht. Steeds weer schrok hij wakker. In zijn dromen leek het alsof iedereen alles wist. In zijn dromen was hij vanuit de kazerne met de vrouw van Beckers aan het telefoneren en zei hij: 'Ik moet nu ophangen, want je man komt eraan.'

's Ochtends vroeg ruimde hij zijn kamer op, pakte zijn tas, wachtte op de aflossing en liep toen naar de parkeerplaats.

Thuis was zijn vrouw bezig het kind klaar te maken voor het kinderdagverblijf. Ze zei: 'Ik heb gisteren meteen een nieuwe sapcentrifuge gekocht.' En ze liet hem trots het exemplaar zien dat op het aanrecht stond. Groter dan de vorige, een reusachtig ding eigenlijk.

'Hier kun je me zeker mee doodslaan,' merkte de Pool luchtig op.

Ze moest lachen. 'Was in de aanbieding.'

Hij ging in de woonkamer naast Jurek zitten die aan tafel in zijn stoeltje zat en hielp hem met het eten van zijn boterham. 'Tatoe, tatoe,' zei Jurek en dat betekende brandweer of brandweerauto. 'Ja,' zei de Pool, 'daar kom ik net vandaan.' En daarna fluisterde hij: 'Ik ben geen man die troost nodig heeft. Ik heb me vergist. Ik heb alleen jou en je moeder nodig.'

De overgebleven jongen moest lachen en toen kwam de vrouw van de Pool binnen en ze pakte haar fototoestel en maakte een foto. 'Vader en zoon,' zei ze. 'Dat is mooi. Zoals jullie daar zitten.'

De vrouw ging weg met het kind en de Pool bleef aan tafel zitten, zoals mannen zitten die na enige aarzeling toch tot de conclusie zijn gekomen dat ze geen troost nodig hebben. Daarna ging hij naar de keuken en bekeek de nieuwe sapcentrifuge. Hier konden ze de komende jaren duizenden appels en wortels mee uitpersen. Dit was een degelijk ding. Nee, aan vers uitgeperst sap zouden ze geen gebrek hebben.

# 4

Na een dutje trok hij zich in de keuken af om zeker te weten dat alles nog functioneerde. Daarna dweilde hij de vloer die toch nodig gedweild moest worden en toen reed hij naar het huis van Beckers. Halverwege stopte hij bij een bloemenwinkel.

‘Ik heb een bosje bloemen nodig,’ zei hij.

‘Wat voor bloemen?’ vroeg de verkoopster. ‘Is het voor een speciale gelegenheid?’

‘Ik ga bij iemand op visite. Gewone bloemen.’

‘Rozen misschien? Rozen zijn gewoon en toch speciaal.’

De Pool schudde zijn hoofd. Voor zijn vrouw kocht hij op haar verjaardag altijd rozen.

‘Ik heb mooie zonnebloemen,’ zei de verkoopster.

‘Oké.’ Zonnebloemen leken hem prima. En met de zonnebloemen ging hij naar het huis van Beckers, waar niemand opendeed. Hij belde drie keer aan en bleef nog even wachten om te kijken of ze misschien weg was gegaan voor een boodschap. Na vijf minuten gaf hij het op. Hij ging terug naar huis, zette de zonnebloemen in een vaas en repareerde een keukenkastje dat hij al een tijd geleden zou hebben gerepareerd.

Na de lunch – de eetlust was niet teruggekeerd, maar twee boterhammen kreeg hij wel naar binnen – werkte hij voor het eerst sinds maanden in de tuin en vermoedelijk kwam het daardoor dat hij de bel niet hoorde. Pas toen hij in de keuken stond om wat water te drinken hoorde hij hoe er werd gebeld.

Daar stond ze, met een paraplu in haar hand. ‘Ik sta hier al een tijd,’ zei de vrouw van Beckers.

‘Ik was in de tuin bezig.’

Ze keek hem aan alsof ze hem niet geloofde. Dacht ze dat hij dergelijke werkzaamheden aan zijn vrouw overliet?

'Ik wil liever niet meer dat je komt,' zei ze. 'Het is niet goed.'

Hij veegde zijn handen af aan zijn broek, hoewel hij geen oude broek had aangedaan om in de tuin te werken. Alle oude broeken waren weggegeven aan het Leger des Heils. Zijn vrouw had geprobeerd op te ruimen.

'Voor wie is het niet goed?'

'Voor jou niet, voor mij niet.'

'Kom binnen,' zei hij. 'Ik begrijp het niet.'

Ze lachte. 'Het blijft een verleidelijk aanbod,' zei ze, 'ook al is het niet goed.' Ze kwam binnen met de opgevouwen paraplu in haar hand. Hij leidde haar verder het huis in en terwijl hij haar naar de eettafel voerde schoof hij met zijn voet Jureks speelgoed opzij. Ze ging zitten, hij kwam terug met de zonnebloemen en zette die voor haar neer. 'Ik heb het papier nog bewaard,' zei hij. 'Voor jou.'

'Dat had je niet moeten doen,' antwoordde ze.

Hij nam plaats tegenover haar. 'Ik was in de tuin bezig,' herhaalde hij, 'daarom zijn mijn handen vies.'

Ze keek naar zijn handen en toen naar de tuin. 'Wil je iets over hem vertellen?' vroeg ze. 'Over je oudste zoon? Je hebt het altijd maar over die pony, nooit over je zoon.'

Ze had de paraplu nog altijd vast alsof ze niet wist wat ze ermee moest. 'Geef maar hier,' zei hij. En hij bracht de paraplu naar de paraplustandaard in de gang. Daarna ging hij weer naast haar zitten. 'Ik heb niet zoveel over hem te vertellen. Hij is er niet meer.' Hij voegde eraan toe: 'Je hebt gelijk. We moeten hiermee ophouden. Ik heb geen troost nodig. Ik zat in de bijbel te lezen en ik besefte dat je daar ook niets aan hebt. Mooie woorden zijn geen troost. Je moet door. Dat is troost. En jij hebt jouw leven, jij hebt de Fransman. Als we elkaar weer zien, als dat ooit zal gebeuren, dan zal het zijn zoals het vroeger was toen we elkaar niet kenden.'

'Ja, zo zal het zijn.' Ze knikte een paar keer alsof ze zich voorstelde hoe het zou zijn als ze elkaar weer zagen. Uiteindelijk vroeg ze: 'Heb je een biertje voor me? Of is dat te veel gevraagd?'

'Nee hoor.'

De Pool ging naar de keuken en kwam terug met bier en omdat zij dronk nam hij er ook een. Hij wees naar de tuin: 'Ik heb wat onkruid weggehaald.'

'Bij ons zorgt mijn man ook voor de tuin.'

Hij moest aan Beckers denken. Zijn collega, zijn vriend, Beckers was net als hij een teamspeler. Anderen waren afgevallen, die hadden last van hoogtevrees of ze waren geen teamspeler. Beckers en hij waren overgebleven.

Ze nam een slok en ze zei meer tegen zichzelf dan tegen de Pool: 'Ik ben niet de moeder die ik zou willen zijn maar dit biertje heb ik verdiend. Ik geloofde dat ik je kon troosten. Een vergissing. Sorry dat ik je met die vergissing heb opgezadeld.'

De Pool keek naar zijn tuin.

'Wat ik je wilde vragen,' zei de vrouw van Beckers en ze legde haar hand op de zijne, 'ook als we vrienden worden: gebruik me niet om je leegte mee te vullen of om je eenzaamheid mee te verdrijven. Be gentle with me.'

'Be wat?'

'Be gentle with me.'

'Wat bedoel je?'

'Dat je gentle met me moet zijn.'

'O,' zei de Pool en hij begreep nog steeds niet waarom ze dat in het Engels had gezegd, daarom vroeg hij het.

'Ik wacht op de Fransman,' legde ze uit, 'ook al denk ik dat hij niet meer komt, maar ik heb de hoop niet opgegeven. Het lukte me niet om de hoop op te geven. En als hij komt zal ik Engels met hem spreken, dan zal ik hem alles in het Engels vertellen. Ik zal tegen hem zeggen: be gentle with me.'

'Die man spreekt toch Frans?'

'Ja maar ik niet,' zei de vrouw van Beckers.

Hij zette het bierglas op tafel en hij begreep niet waar het verlangen vandaan kwam. Het was een dagdroom, nee een vergrijp waaraan een man van zijn leeftijd in zijn omstandigheden zich niet schuldig zou mogen maken.

'En waarom zeg je dat nu tegen mij?'

Zittend deed ze haar regenjas uit en hing hem over de stoel naast haar. 'Zomaar,' zei ze.

'Je hebt mij en mijn vrouw troost aangeboden, maar eigenlijk zit je er zelf om verlegen.' Het klonk verwijtend. Zo was het niet bedoeld.

'Verlegen?' Ze schudde haar hoofd. 'Nee, ik wilde gewoon zeggen: gebruik me niet. Gebruik me niet verkeerd, gebruik me op een goede manier.' Ze haalde haar hand door haar lange bruine haren.

Mensen moesten elkaar niet gebruiken, dat was niet netjes, en ze moesten niemand verraden. Alleen hun eigen verlangens mochten ze verraden, moesten ze verraden. Hij pakte haar hand en hij nam haar mee naar boven en pas in de slaapkamer bevroor hij. Uiteindelijk was zij het die vroeg: 'Is dit jullie slaapkamer?'

'Ja.'

'Maakt je vrouw de bedden nooit op?'

'Soms wel. Soms niet.'

'Ik maak ze elke dag op.' Ze deed haar schoenen uit en ging op het bed zitten. 'Dus hier had ik jullie kunnen troosten?' Ze zat aan de kant waar zijn vrouw altijd sliep en ze deed haar blouse uit. 'Het spijt me,' zei ze, 'ik kan het niet helpen.' Ze voegde eraan toe: 'Deze beha zal ik dragen als hij me komt halen.'

'O,' zei de Pool.

Ze stond op. 'Laat mij zijn kamer zien. Waar heeft die

jongen geleefd?' Nog voor hij iets kon zeggen ging ze de slaapkamer uit en liep op de kamer van Borys af. De Pool drukte haar tegen de deur van Borys en zoende haar. Hij proefde de wat muffe smaak van oud bier en niet meer helemaal fris speeksel, maar voor hem was het de lekkerste smaak van de wereld en toen hij klaar was met zoenen zei hij: 'Ik wil je neuken.'

Ze keek hem misprijzend aan. 'Is dat alles wat je je kan voorstellen bij troost? Wat ben je toch een ordinaire man.' Ze ging terug naar de slaapkamer en daar deed ze zittend op het echtelijk bed ook haar beha uit. 'Kijk,' zei ze, 'ik ben grijs aan het worden, maar mijn borsten hangen niet. Dat zal ik ook zeggen als hij komt: "I'm getting grey hair, but take a look at my breasts."'

De Pool ging naast haar op het bed zitten aan de kant waar zijn vrouw altijd lag, zijn lieve vrouw die de bedden alleen heel soms opmaakte.

Als de vrouw van Beckers in hem een ordinaire man zag die het verschil niet kende tussen neuken en troost, dan was dat ook goed. 'Doe je beha weer aan,' zei hij zonder naar haar te kijken. 'Toen ik in de stal stond naast dat beest, dat we hebben gedood uit liefde, toen heb ik me met alles verzoend, niet alleen met zijn dood, ook met mijn eigen leven.'

Hij wilde nog meer zeggen maar dit was genoeg en daarna keek hij naar haar en zij zat daar nog steeds met haar blote borsten en het waren niet de borsten, wel hoe ze hem aankeek, ze keek hem zo aan dat hij de behoefte voelde te zeggen dat hij niet de Fransman was, alleen een collega van haar man. Haar blik maakte hem zwak. Haar blik doodde de teamspeler in hem.

'Jij bent naar mij toe gekomen,' zei ze. 'Het is geen toeval.' De vrouw van Beckers bestudeerde haar borsten. 'Ik zal hem ook de rest laten zien als hij me komt halen. Hij heeft altijd gezegd dat hij me komt halen en ik geloof niet dat hij zijn belofte is vergeten.'

En toen stond ze op, ze deed haar rok uit en ze trok haar onderbroek uit, een simpele zwarte onderbroek. De Pool durfde nu helemaal niet meer te kijken want hij had na zijn vrouw nooit een andere vrouw naakt gezien. Hij had weleens porno gekeken, daarbij had hij zich altijd onbehaaglijk gevoeld, beschaamd. Iets in hem had hem verteld dat hij de straf voor dergelijke activiteiten niet zou kunnen ontlopen.

Hij was een man die vergeten was dat je verliefd kon worden, hij wilde niet naar haar benen kijken of naar haar kruis en dat deed hij dus ook niet, hij keek haar recht in de ogen en hij zei: 'Je kijkt me zo liefdevol aan.'

'Je herkent het dus,' zei ze.

'Hoe bedoel je?'

'Je ziet het.'

'Wat?'

'Je herkent liefde.'

De Pool schudde zijn hoofd. 'Ik weet niet wat ik herken.'

Ze ging op bed liggen en daarom dacht de Pool dat zij naar hem verlangde, dat zij was gekomen omdat ze naar zijn lichaam verlangde, naar zijn ordinaire lust, de ordinaire lust van een brandweerman, vulgaire begeerte waarvoor hij zich schaamde, vooral omdat die hem in de steek liet, omdat er zo vaak niets over was van die begeerte, alleen een vage herinnering, een echo.

Nooit had hij nagedacht over de vraag hoe hij moest leven, omdat het hem vanzelfsprekend was voorgekomen, omdat hij intuïtief wel wist hoe dat moest. In het bijzijn van de vrouw van Beckers besefte hij dat er andere levens mogelijk waren met andere opvattingen en andere gewoontes en daarom kleedde hij zich uit. Zijn trui, zijn schoenen, zijn sokken, zijn broek waaraan hij zijn handen had afgeveegd en tot slot zijn onderbroek, alsof hij ging douchen met de mannen in de kazerne.

Hij stond daar naast het bed, aarzelend, licht opgewonden en hij vroeg zich af wat hij van haar verwachtte, wat hij van haar wilde, of het iets wezenlijks anders was dan wat hij van de pony had gewild, waar hij alleen maar naast in de stal had gestaan, die hij had geroken, die hij niet bijzonder veel had aangeraakt. Haar gezelschap was genoeg geweest.

Ze ging met haar hand over zijn bovenbeen en toen pakte ze zijn geslachtsdeel, zijn slappe geslachtsdeel en ze speelde ermee. De Pool wilde van alles zeggen, hij durfde niet, hij liet haar begaan.

'Je denkt dat je hebt gefaald als vader,' zei hij uiteindelijk, 'en het is te laat om er iets aan te doen.' En zij bleef met zijn geslachtsdeel spelen terwijl hij begreep dat zijn huwelijk bestond uit een dode jongen, dat het een dode jongen was die hem aan zijn vrouw bond, de dode kleurde zijn leven, zijn liefde, zijn verlangen.

Toen hij eindelijk stijf was wilde hij op de vrouw van Beckers gaan liggen maar ze zei: 'Nee, dat mag niet. Dat mogen alleen de Fransman en mijn echtgenoot. Dat begrijp je toch wel?'

'Dat begrijp ik niet,' antwoordde hij. 'Ik wil je neuken. Jij wilde dat toch ook? Waarom zou je anders met mijn pik spelen?'

Ze schudde haar hoofd. 'Dat gaat niet. Dat mag niet. Misschien later, voorlopig niet.'

Hij ging naast haar zitten en zij kriebelde hem over zijn rug. Zo wachtte hij wat er ging gebeuren en op een gegeven moment had hij het gevoel dat hij zo lang naast haar had gezeten dat zijn vrouw bijna thuis kon komen. Even voelde het alsof zijn slaapkamer veranderd was in de stal, waar hij soms ook de tijd was vergeten, waar hij zijn vrouw was vergeten.

'Ik kan jou wel neuken,' zei de vrouw van Beckers. 'Je mag alleen mij niet neuken, dat mag alleen de Fransman, maar als het je helpt, als het je troost, kan ik jou wel...'

'Hoe bedoel je?' Hij ging verzitten zodat hij haar gezicht kon zien en toen begreep hij weer waarom hij naar haar verlangde. Omdat ze hem zo liefdevol aankeek, zo vol bewondering, ja dat was het woord, ze keek hem aan alsof ze hem bewonderde terwijl er niets aan hem te bewonderen viel. Hij was niet uitzonderlijk, hij had nooit naar uitzonderlijkheid gestreefd, het goede was voor hem het onopvallende.

'Zoals ik het zeg', ze bleef hem aankijken met alle liefde van de wereld, 'ik kan je neuken. Heb je een dildo?'

'Nee.'

'Heeft je vrouw geen dildo?'

'Nee.' Hij bloosde, het woord deed hem blozen, hij voelde hoe hij rood werd. De Pool kon zich niet herinneren dat hij tegenover zijn vrouw ooit dat woord in de mond had genomen of zij tegenover hem. 'En als ze er een had dan weet ik niet of zij zou willen dat jij mij met haar dildo neukte.' Hij zei het zo hard, zo kil, om te verbergen dat hij wist hoe rood hij was geworden.

'Wat zou je vrouw dan willen?'

Daar moest hij even over nadenken en toen zei hij: 'Ik denk dat ze zou willen dat je ons met rust liet.'

'O.' De vrouw van Beckers klonk oprecht teleurgesteld. 'Ze wil alleen dat ik jullie met rust laat? Meer niet?'

'Ja.' Hij keek haar in de ogen, de vrouw van Beckers, die wachtte op haar Fransman, en ook al wist hij niet veel, hij wist genoeg, hij wist namelijk dat die Fransman niet zou komen, zoals de doden niet zouden opstaan uit hun graven, zelfs niet als Jezus terugkeerde op aarde, wat hij hoe dan ook niet geloofde, maar dan nog zouden de doden niet opstaan uit hun graven.

'We hebben beneden nog wel wat winterpenen voor de pony,' zei hij meer tegen zichzelf dan tegen haar. 'Ik had een flinke voorraad gekocht, die is nog niet helemaal door de sapcentrifuge.' En daaraan voegde hij toe: 'Maar dat is toch idioot. Je gaat me toch niet neuken met een winterpeen? Dat is toch geen liefde?'

'Nee,' zei ze, 'dat is geen liefde maar wat jij met mij wilde doen was ook geen liefde.'

Daar moest hij over nadenken en toen zei hij: 'Het was verlangen. En jij bent ermee begonnen, als jij geen troost had aangeboden was ik nooit naar je gaan verlangen.'

Hij ging naar beneden, naakt, en daar lagen ze nog, de winterpenen die hij had gekocht voor het beest van de dode jongen, het beest dat nu zelf dood was, de winterpenen die zijn vrouw nog niet door de sapcentrifuge had gehaald. Ze lagen naast de aardappelen. Hij pakte er twee, ging ermee naar boven en hij besefte dat ze zich moesten haasten. 'Hier.' De Pool drukte de penen in haar hand alsof hij niet meer was dan een groenteboer.

Hij ging op zijn buik liggen naast de vrouw van Beckers.

'Ik weet niet of je ze kan hebben.' Ze wreef met een van de penen over zijn rug en zijn billen en hij sloot zijn ogen. Even dacht hij aan zijn jongen, de dode jongen was overal, en hij vroeg of ze echt geloofde dat de Fransman nog zou komen terwijl ze met de winterpeen over zijn onderrug bewoog. De vrouw van Beckers antwoordde dat ze de hoop niet had opgegeven omdat ze hem elk jaar een zelfgemaakt kerstkaartje stuurde en toen begon ze voorzichtig met de winterpeen tegen zijn anus aan te duwen. Ze zei dat ze de winterpeen vochtig moest maken en dat ze de peen daarom in haar mond moest nemen, of de Pool daar bezwaar tegen had en hij zei zonder naar haar te kijken dat hij dat prima vond, dat hij zich in haar handen bevond, in haar liefdevolle handen en dat zij wel zou weten wat goed was. Goed voor hem, goed voor haar, goed voor de troost. En toen voelde hij hoe ze met haar vingers over zijn bilspleet wreef en hij zag zijn jongen voor zich terwijl zij nog aan het prevelen was. Ze prevelde dat je voorzichtig moest zijn maar dat als je te voorzichtig was er nooit iets gebeurde, je kon ook te voorzichtig zijn, misschien maakte je wel iets kapot vanbinnen, maar je kon niet door het leven gaan zonder dingen vanbinnen kapot te maken. De Fransman had ook van alles vanbinnen kapotgemaakt omdat hij zoveel van haar hield, fluisterde ze, zoveel, met zoveel overgave, en de Pool lag op zijn echtelijk bed en hij wachtte af en zij zei dat ze de winterpeen nu vochtig ging maken. Ze likte aan de winterpeen en vervolgens voelde hij hoe ze de winterpeen in zijn anus dreef en hij moest zich inhouden om niet te schreeuwen want dit was geen genot, dit was geen troost, dit was pijn en hij kon zich niet voorstellen dat troost pijn kon zijn.

'Ja,' zei de vrouw van Beckers, 'ik heb de hoop niet opgegeven, ik heb het geprobeerd maar ik weet niet hoe dat moet. Weet jij hoe dat moet?'

Langzaam haalde ze de winterpeen weer uit zijn anus en hij herinnerde zich hoe hij een paar jaar geleden een soort kijkoperatie had gehad omdat hij voortdurend buikpijn had, maar het was niets. De pijn moest vanzelf weggaan zei de dokter, misschien minder snel eten, en de pijn was inderdaad weggegaan. Hij was ook minder snel gaan eten want de Pool was geen man die de autoriteiten wantrouwde, hij was een man die de adviezen van de autoriteiten met een instinctieve gehoorzaamheid opvolgde.

Hij lag op zijn buik, wachtte wat komen zou en hij hoorde de vrouw van Beckers ademen. Hij deed zijn ogen dicht en hij zei: 'Ik hou van je, ik weet dat het onbetamelijk is, dat het niet mag, ik kan er niets aan doen, ik moet ermee ophouden.'

'Nee,' zei ze, 'jij mag niet van me houden. Dat kun je ook helemaal niet. Wie denk je dat je bent dat jij van mij kunt houden? Denk je dat jij een Fransman bent? Weet je hoe je de hoop moet opgeven, weet je dat misschien?' En opnieuw dreef ze de winterpeen in zijn anus, met nog meer kracht dan de eerste keer, en hij had het gevoel dat hij werd opengescheurd, dat hij uitscheurde. Hij vroeg zich af of dit op bevallen leek.

De Pool beet op zijn lippen. De angst dat zijn vrouw thuis zou komen overviel hem en hij wilde weten hoe laat het was, de vrouw van Beckers antwoordde niet, ze haalde alleen de peen uit zijn anus en wachtte een paar seconden. Hij kon alleen herhalen dat hij wilde weten hoe laat het was en nog een keer sloeg ze de winterpeen in zijn anus, ze sloeg de peen erin zoals ze een spijker in de muur sloeg, als ze dat ooit al deed. Klusjes liet ze natuurlijk aan Beckers over.

'Ben je genoeg getroost?' vroeg ze.

'Ja,' zei hij. 'Genoeg, voor vandaag genoeg. Als dit troost was dan is het genoeg voor vandaag.'

Ze haalde de peen uit hem en wierp hem achteloos op de grond en toen kleedde ze zich aan en ook hij kleedde zich snel aan en de vrouw van Beckers zei dat ze dit niet voor haar plezier deed, dat ze met hem te doen had. En ze vertelde nog dat de Fransman gestudeerd had, wat wist ze niet meer precies. Als ze ooit bij hem was zou ze over andere dingen praten dan ze met haar man besprak en tot die tijd troostte ze de Pool. Omdat hij zijn lot niet had verdiend. Dat zei ze met een glimlachje alsof ze precies wist welk lot hij wel had verdiend. En daarna vroeg ze: 'Heb je bodylotion?'

'Wat?'

'Bodylotion of iets om make-up mee te verwijderen, ik ben bang dat het wat is uitgelopen.'

De Pool nam haar mee naar de badkamer en gaf haar de bodylotion van zijn vrouw en in de badkamer verwijderde ze de make-up, die inderdaad was uitgelopen, van haar gezicht, alsof ze had gehuild terwijl ze de winterpeen in de Pool dreef.

Ze namen afscheid in de gang beneden. Ze gaf hem een kusje op zijn wang en ze zei: 'We leren elkaar steeds beter kennen en ik hoop dat je geen verkeerde conclusies over me trekt. Ik ben geen vrouw die haar kinderen in de steek laat. Ik ben een vrouw die hoopt. Die het hopen niet kan laten.'

Hij knikte en hij wilde nog zeggen dat hij begreep dat ze op de Fransman hoopte maar of hij haar toch mocht vragen, nu ze zo intiem waren geweest, nu zij een winterpeen in zijn anus had gedreven wat tot nu toe niemand had gedaan, wat hem betreft was ze de enige die dat deed en als hij eerlijk was wist hij ook niet of het voor herhaling vatbaar was, maar nu ze dat achter de rug hadden wilde hij weten of ze ook niet een beetje op hem hoopte, al was het als tweede keus, op hem, de lange, stille Pool, plan B.

Maar ze glipte de deur uit, ze zwaaide nog even en toen fatsoeneerde hij het bed en hij bestudeerde wat vlekken en hij vertrouwde erop dat zijn vrouw die niet zou zien want ze was geen schoonheidsmaniak. Een peen vond hij op de grond, de andere lag naast het hoofdkussen.

Voor de zekerheid veegde hij beide penen af aan een handdoek en legde ze toen tussen de andere winterpenen in de keuken naast de aardappelen, daarna gooide hij de bierflesjes weg en waste het glas af waaruit de vrouw van Beckers had gedronken. Tot slot ging hij weer in de tuin werken. Terwijl hij bezig was met het onkruid merkte hij dat er wat uit zijn anus liep. De Pool ging naar de badkamer, hij keek in zijn onderbroek, deed een nieuwe onderbroek aan en om ongelukken te voorkomen zocht hij in het medicijnkastje naar tampons van zijn vrouw. Hij aarzelde even want er lagen kleine en grotere tampons, uiteindelijk duwde hij de grotere tampon in zijn anus. Toen voelde hij zich opgelucht.

Eerst ging hij weer in de tuin werken maar hij kon zich niet meer op het onkruid concentreren en daarom liep hij al snel rusteloos door het huis terwijl hij voelde hoe de tampon in zijn anus stak, om ongelukken te voorkomen.

Soms moest je iets kleins kapotmaken, de eigen anus bijvoorbeeld, om ergere pijn te voorkomen. In kleermakerszit ging hij voor de kamer van de dode jongen zitten en hij zong een lied dat hij zich herinnerde uit zijn jeugd. Terwijl hij daar nog mee bezig was hoorde hij zijn vrouw thuiskomen en hij hield abrupt op met zingen. Hij haastte zich naar beneden en zij vroeg of hij even de jongen van de crèche kon halen want zij moest dringend met een moeder telefoneren. Dat was natuurlijk geen probleem. Hij haalde de jongen van de crèche, met de tampon in zijn anus, en hij vroeg zich af of hij die moest vernieuwen of dat het gevaar dat er iets uit liep inmiddels geweken was. Met de overgebleven jongen in zijn armen liep hij naar huis.

Daar vroeg zijn vrouw: 'Heb je aan mijn bodylotion gezeten?'

'Ja,' zei hij. 'Dat vind je toch niet erg?'

'Wat moest je met mijn bodylotion?'

'Ik moest iets invetten. Mijn huid. Die was droog. Ik werkte in de tuin. Toen heb ik mijn huid ingevet.'

'O,' zei ze, 'maar daar kun je beter ander spul voor gebruiken, als het echt droog is, ik zal je vanavond insmeren.'

Ze gingen naar beneden en in de keuken vertelde ze dat ze verse gember had gekocht en ze haalde appels, winterpenen en gember door de sapcentrifuge met een passie alsof dit haar leven was. Hij stond naast haar met het kind op zijn arm en ze zette een glas wortel-appel-gembersap voor hem neer. 'We moeten gezond blijven. Dat is het belangrijkste.'

Hij dronk het sap van zijn vrouw, de liefste vrouw van de wereld, de enige van wie hij mocht houden, de enige van wie hij echt wilde houden als puntje bij paaltje kwam. En hij beaamde wat ze had gezegd, hij liet niets van het vers uitgeperste sap staan en hij herhaalde dat gezond blijven het belangrijkste was, dat het daarop neerkwam. De rest was bijzaak.

# 5

Het was in de zevende maand nadat de intercity naar Amsterdam de jongen had meegenomen dat de Pool begreep dat hij een dubbelleven aan het leiden was, dat het niet langer ontkend kon worden. Ook al had hij de vrouw van Beckers nooit gepenetreerd – ze had herhaaldelijk verklaard dat ze monogaam was en dat ze dat zou blijven tot de Fransman haar kwam halen – zij had hem wel gepenetreerd, niet alleen met winterpenen, met allerlei voorwerpen, ze was inventief en ze beweerde: 'Hoe groter het voorwerp, hoe groter de troost.' Daaraan had ze een keer toegevoegd: 'Eigenlijk had ik kunstenares willen worden, maar dat lieten mijn ouders niet toe. Ze waren keurig en ik moest en zou ook keurig worden.'

Het was voor de Pool vanzelfsprekend dat de mensen keurig waren en dat ze dat ook wilden blijven. Wat was het alternatief? Het verbaasde hem dat kunstenaars zich kennelijk aan die basisbehoefte onttrokken. Hij was weleens in een museum geweest, op vakantie een paar keer, en dat vond hij een keurige plek, misschien wel de keurigste plek waar hij was geweest sinds hij niet meer in de kerk kwam. Maar omdat hij vreesde zijn domheid te laten blijken, of beter gezegd te onderstrepen, vroeg hij niet verder. Hij lag zwijgend op het bed terwijl zij met hem bezig was. Soms deed het hem aan acupunctuur denken, terwijl hij daar lag stelde hij zich ook weleens God voor die de gedaante had aangenomen van de vrouw van Beckers. Zo werd hij bewerkt, ja zo voelde het, dat hij bewerkt werd, en het kwam hem aannemelijk voor dat God zelf ook wachtte op een Fransman die in de buurt van Nice woonde. God woonde in alle mensen, in sommige mensen iets meer dan in andere en God leek het meest in de vrouw van Beckers te wonen. Zijn liefde voor God was een verboden liefde.

Door de vrouw van Beckers had hij begrepen dat de mens net als het land bewerkt moest worden.

Ze had hem alles laten zien, de jurk, de jas, de schoenen die ze zou dragen als ze werd opgehaald door de Fransman. Ze was voorbereid.

Meestal wilde hij niet weten wat de vrouw van Beckers in hem duwde, hij nam het voor lief omdat hij naar haar gezelschap verlangde, naar haar aanwezigheid, en omdat hij diep vanbinnen geloofde wat ze zei, dat dit troost was, dat dit de enige troost was die de mensen elkaar te bieden hadden. En als het pijn deed dacht hij: vergeleken met meegesleurd worden door de intercity naar Amsterdam was dit niets, niet veel in elk geval. Eén keer had hij het niet kunnen laten, hij had omgekeken terwijl hij op zijn buik op zijn echtelijk bed lag en toen had hij gezien hoe ze de hak van een schoen waarop ze met de Fransman naar de Côte d'Azur wilde reizen in hem dreef en daarna was hij een beetje misselijk geworden. Ze had een condoom om de hak gewikkeld en toen hij informeerde wat dat te betekenen had zei ze: 'Ja, we moeten het voorzichtig en veilig doen, anders is het geen liefde.'

Ze smeerde hem ook altijd eerst in met de nachtcrème van zijn vrouw, tussen zijn billen, want veiligheid en behoedzaamheid gingen aan de troost en de liefde vooraf.

De Pool overdacht haar woorden en uiteindelijk zei hij, met de hak van haar lievelingsschoen half in zijn lichaam: 'Maar dit was toch geen liefde? Dit was ordinaire lust.'

'Nee,' zei ze, 'ik heb me vergist, als het troost is, is het liefde. Alle troost is liefde.'

Dat vond de Pool nou echt een opmerking voor God en hij merkte dat hij de pijn pas goed voelde als hij zag wat ze in hem stopte. Even vroeg hij zich af wat ze nog meer in hem zou stoppen, of er niet een grens was wat er in hem kon verdwijnen. Als dit troost was dan was troost gevaarlijk. Of was dit de kunst die ze had willen maken en waar haar ouders een stokje voor hadden gestoken? Nou ja, gevaarlijk, hij zou er niet aan doodgaan, ook als er vanbinnen van alles kapot was gemaakt dan zou het wel herstellen. De troost zou niet eindeloos door hoeven te gaan. Op een dag zou de Fransman de vrouw van Beckers allicht ophalen of ze zou er zelf heen gaan en blijven hangen aan een andere Fransman en dan zou het hoe dan ook afgelopen zijn. Dan zat ze ergens aan de Middellandse Zee, dan zou ze hem en zijn erbarmelijke behoefte aan troost zijn vergeten. Ja, erbarmelijk was zijn behoefte aan troost.

Het was kort nadat hij was gepenetreerd met de lievelingsschoen van de vrouw van Beckers – schoenen van een duur Frans merk, al waren ze dan in de uitverkoop gekocht – dat de vrouw van de Pool vroeg wat hij toch met haar tampons deed. Omdat hij daar niet echt een goed antwoord op kon geven, omdat hem dat niet lukte, omdat de beleefdheidsleugentjes die uit zijn mond kwamen hem zelf in verwarring brachten besefte hij dat het dubbelleven niet langer ontkend kon worden. En toen hij dat begreep wilde hij er meteen een eind aan maken. Aan dat dubbelleven. Eén leven was genoeg, eigenlijk al te veel, twee was echt overdreven. Hoe langer het duurde hoe groter de kans dat Wen erachter zou komen en hij wilde haar niet nog meer belasten.

De Pool had gezegd dat hij last had van diarree en om tijdens oefeningen niet voor al te veel problemen te zorgen, zo vertelde hij, stopte hij er nu en dan een tampon in en zijn lieve vrouw ging daar serieus op in – ze was niet alleen lief, ze was ook ernstig, op hun eerste date had ze gezegd: 'Ik heb geen gevoel voor humor', en daarop had de Pool geantwoord: 'Ik ook niet, totaal niet zelfs...' – en ze pakte zijn hoofd en zei: 'Lieverd, hoe kom je aan die diarree?'

Zijn vrouw zei bijna bezorgd dat een tampon niet hielp

tegen darmproblemen en daarop antwoordde hij, overigens geheel naar waarheid, dat er soms ook bloed naar buiten kwam. 'Dan moet je naar de dokter,' zei ze met iets wat leek op een snik in haar stem. 'Bloed is geen goed teken. Weet je zeker dat het bloed is en niet dat je rode bieten hebt gegeten of zoiets?'

Hij zei dat hij heel zeker wist dat het bloed was omdat ze slechts zelden rode bieten aten, thuis, en op de kazerne aten ze al helemaal nooit rode bieten want de mannen hielden niet van rode bieten, en zijn vrouw streelde hem, Wen, de liefste, de enige en toch ook weer niet, ze zei: 'Laat je maar eens helemaal onderzoeken, een tampon is geen oplossing. Een check-up, dat is wat je nodig hebt. Als je wil ga ik wel met je mee.'

Het was nog lente maar de temperaturen waren al zomers, de hitte hing over het hele land en in het zuiden van Limburg concentreerde de hitte zich, daar werden de hoogste temperaturen gemeten, het weer ging gepaard met onweersbuien die nauwelijks voor verkoeling zorgden. De avonden waren lang, de overgebleven jongen sliep al een tijdje en toch bleef het nog volop licht alsof er geen einde kwam aan de dag, alsof er geen nacht meer was, alsof de nacht aan het verdwijnen was, en die avond, die hete avond die gevuld was met onweersbuien, die avond dat Wen had gevraagd wat hij toch met haar tampons deed zei ze: 'Ik heb een dvd gekocht.'

'O,' antwoordde de Pool.

'Een sensuele dvd.'

'O,' zei de Pool en hij ging snel naar de wc om de tampon uit zijn anus te halen want hij had een voorgevoel.

'Ik denk dat we hier wat van kunnen leren.' De vrouw van de Pool stopte de dvd in de dvd-speler en ze gingen op de bank voor de tv zitten.

Een jongedame verscheen in beeld, ze sprak Engels.

'Zij is een seksuologe,' zei Wen.

‘Er zit geen ondertiteling bij,’ merkte de Pool op.

‘Nee,’ zei zijn lieve vrouw. ‘Dat geeft niet. Je verstaat het toch wel?’ Hij luisterde even en schudde zijn hoofd. ‘Ik versta de helft niet. Ze spreekt ingewikkeld Engels.’

‘Er komt ook beeld bij,’ zei de vrouw van de Pool. ‘Dat hoef je niet te verstaan. Wil je een biertje?’

Hij knikte.

De vrouw van de Pool haalde een biertje en voor zichzelf schonk ze een glas rosé in. Buiten onweerde het en in zijn huiskamer keek de Pool naar een seksuologe die hij voor de helft kon verstaan.

‘Ze zegt dat we *quirky* moeten zijn,’ zei hij. ‘Weet jij wat ze daar precies mee bedoelt?’

‘Nee,’ zei Wen, ‘niet precies, maar we kunnen het opzoeken.’

‘Quirky,’ herhaalde hij, ‘quirky, quirky, quirky,’ alsof een vogel aan het tsjilpen is.’

‘Stil,’ zei ze. ‘We moeten luisteren.’ De Pool wist nog altijd niet wat quirky betekende.

Ze dronken hun bier en hun rosé, de Pool dacht aan de vrouw van Beckers toen er een vagina in beeld kwam. ‘Kijk,’ zei Wen. ‘Teder, zachtjes, zo moeten we dat doen.’

‘We hebben nooit meer seks,’ zei hij fluisterend. Hij wist niet of hij dit wel kon uitspreken. Als je het niet uitsprak dan leek het misschien of zijn verlangen niet was gestorven en hij telde de seconden tussen de bliksem en de donder. ‘Dat is hier vlakbij,’ fluisterde hij nog steeds.

‘We gaan weer seks hebben,’ zei zijn lieve vrouw. ‘We gaan weer heel veel seks hebben. Want we zijn man en vrouw. Je verlangt toch naar me?’

Daarop keek ze hem aan met zulke treurige ogen, alsof de dood van zijn verlangen eigenlijk net zo erg was als de dood van hun jongen, alsof de dood van hun jongen en van zijn verlangen in elkaar overliepen. Jongen, verlangen en dood waren één ding geworden in dit gezin, één amorfe massa en de treurnis in haar ogen was hem te veel, greep hem aan, deed hem aan de pony denken, daarom zei hij: 'Jazeker.'

'Ik wist het,' zei ze getergd, 'en we gaan het vanaf nu heel lief en teder doen. Daar kan zij ons bij helpen.' Ze wees op de seksuologe die de Pool deed denken aan een aardrijkskundelerares die hij op de middelbare school had gehad, een aardige vrouw trouwens. Ze had hem na de dood van zijn moeder vaak na de les apart genomen en een praatje gemaakt dat ongemakkelijk was geweest en dat hij toch prettig had gevonden.

'We hebben twee kinderen op de wereld gezet,' zei hij, 'zonder naar een dvd te kijken en nu moeten we opeens naar een dvd kijken. Ik vind het prima hoor, maar moet dit echt?' Er kwam een levensgrote vagina in beeld die werd bewerkt door twee vingers.

'Kijk,' zei Wen, 'zo doe je dat.'

'Ik heb grote vingers,' zei de Pool, 'en dat zijn kleine vingertjes.'

'Ook mensen met grote vingers kunnen teder zijn.' En ze vroeg: 'Word je opgewonden van die vagina?'

Hij keek nog eens naar het scherm. 'Eigenlijk niet, het is een beetje overbelicht, er staat tl-licht op de vagina, je ziet alles, je ziet te veel, ik ben geen gynaecoloog.' Hij dronk zijn bier, het onweer dreef over, de warmte hing nog in hun woonkamer en de Pool vroeg: 'Deden we het niet teder?'

'Je deed het een beetje ruw als ik eerlijk ben. Je sloeg mijn benen over, je vergat dat ik benen had. Je ging direct naar mijn poesje. Ik heb er heel lang niets van gezegd omdat ik erop vertrouwde dat de tederheid wel terug zou komen, toen ging onze jongen dood en toen wist ik dat de tederheid... Nou ja, dat de tederheid niet vanzelf terug zou komen en ik vroeg me opeens af of die er ooit wel echt was geweest. Of ik die tederheid niet verzonnen had. En het gaat er ook niet om kinderen op de wereld te zetten. We zetten geen kinderen meer op de wereld. Dat is voorbij. We hebben nu seks omdat we man en vrouw zijn, omdat we van elkaar moeten genieten.'

Hij dronk zijn bier, hij keek naar het scherm, hij dacht aan de vrouw van Beckers en hij zei: 'Ja, we moeten van elkaar genieten. Maar we kunnen toch ook nog een kind op de wereld zetten? Om onze jongen te vervangen.'

Ze zette haar glas wijn op de lage tafel. 'Nee, onze jongen is niet vervangbaar. Kinderen zijn niet vervangbaar.'

Hij veegde met de rug van zijn hand over zijn mond. 'We kunnen toch doen alsof?'

Wen schudde resoluut haar hoofd. 'Er komen geen kinderen meer. We gaan niets vervangen. Er valt niets te vervangen. Ik ben te oud en zelfs als ik niet te oud was geweest...'

Dat was duidelijk. Hij leunde achterover op de bank. Dit onderwerp was afgehandeld. De mensen waren onvervangbaar.

'Dus nu gaan we van elkaar genieten?'

'Ja,' zei ze.

'Dat doen we toch?' merkte hij vragend op alsof hij zelf twijfelde, alsof hij zonder het te weten zijn lieve vrouw de hersens uit haar hoofd had geneukt de laatste weken.

'Nee, dat doen we niet. Eerst sloeg je mijn benen over, je vergat dat ik benen heb en uiteindelijk vergat je dat ik een kut heb.'

'Ben ik dat echt vergeten?' Dat leek hem stug. Hij ging naar de keuken, haalde nog een biertje en op de dvd werd de vagina nu bewerkt met een tong. De Pool vroeg zich af of het de vagina was van de seksuologe of van een model.

'Wil je nog wat rosé?'

'Ik haal zelf wel.' Toen haar glas was gevuld ging ze weer naast hem zitten en ze fluisterde in zijn oor dat mensen soms dingen vergeten, heel voor de hand liggende dingen, bijvoorbeeld om de deur op slot te doen, dat je mensen er best aan mocht herinneren, aan die voor de hand liggende dingen en ze fluisterde: 'Ik wil je eraan herinneren dat ik een kut heb.' Vervolgens likte ze zijn oor. 'Andere vrouwen gaan scheiden als hun man dat soort dingen vergeet, ik herinner je eraan.' Ze wees op het scherm. 'Kijk, de tong draait achtjes.'

'Heb je de dvd al eens bekeken?'

Ze knikte. 'Ik moet toch weten wat ik je voorzet.'

Hij telde de seconden tussen de bliksem en de donder en hij zei: 'Het onweer komt weer dichterbij.'

Ze nam een grote slok wijn. Het leek alsof ze haar mond spoelde met de rosé alsof het mondwater was en de Pool begreep dat zijn dubbelleven moest ophouden, het kon zo niet door blijven gaan. Hij moest alles vertellen aan zijn lieve vrouw, ze zou hem begrijpen. Een vrouw die bereid was haar man aan het feit te herinneren dat ze een vagina had zou ook begrijpen dat hij troost en ordinaire lust door elkaar had gehaald.

'Kijk,' zei ze, 'je moet niet te veel druk geven met de tong, je moet zachtjes cirkelen maar je mag af en toe wel teder in een schaamlip bijten.'

'Is dat wat ze zegt?' vroeg hij.

'Ja, dat is wat ze zegt.'

'Dat ik teder in een schaamlip moet bijten?'

'Stil nou,' zei zijn lieve vrouw, 'ze heeft meer interessante dingen te zeggen.'

Hij luisterde, maar hij verstond er eigenlijk niets van.

'Gaf ik te veel druk met mijn tong?' vroeg hij na een tijdje.

'Een beetje. Het is niet dat je een biefstuk moet platslaan. En je hebt ook gewoon een erg grote tong.'

Ze kriebelde hem in zijn nek.

'We hebben toch al heel lang... Ik heb toch al heel lang mijn tong niet gebruikt. In elk geval niet op die manier. Dat wilde je niet meer.'

'Nee, dat wilde ik niet meer,' en ze zuchtte een beetje overdreven alsof ze vond dat die zucht nodig was. 'Dat hoorde bij een ander leven.'

'Een leven voor de dood.'

'Ja, voor de dood, ons seksleven was voor de dood, nu moeten we ons seksleven nieuw leven inblazen. Nu moeten we aan het seksleven na de dood beginnen.'

Hij dronk zijn bier, luisterde naar de regen en hij was vastbesloten niet meer van de vrouw van Beckers te houden en niet meer naar haar te verlangen. Het moest ophouden, het zou ophouden. De Pool voelde zich zo zeker, zo sterk dat hij meende dat hij nooit van de vrouw van Beckers had gehouden, dat hij nooit naar haar had verlangd en dat hij nooit God in haar had herkend.

'Ben je er klaar voor?' vroeg zijn lieve vrouw.

'Waarvoor?'

'Om het te proberen? Laten we het nog een kans geven.' Ze nam opnieuw een slok rosé. Hij zag hoe iemand met een paraplu door de straat rende. Het regende veel te hard voor een paraplu. De man werd drijfnat.

'Met mijn tong?' vroeg hij.

Ze knikte, ze ging voor hem staan, ze deed haar rok omhoog.

'Je hebt geen onderbroek aan,' zei hij.

'Ik wilde voorbereid zijn. Maar je moet niet bij mijn kut beginnen. Begin bij mijn knie, begin bij mijn bovenbeen.'

De Pool nam nog een slok bier en toen begon hij de knie van zijn lieve vrouw te likken. Op de achtergrond praatte de seksuologe nog altijd door en opnieuw besefte hij hoe weinig hij van haar Engels verstond. Ze praatte ook best snel, alsof ze te veel te vertellen had voor één dvd. 'Is dit misschien Schots Engels?' vroeg hij.

'Probeer je te verliezen in je opwinding,' zei zijn vrouw en hij beloofde dat hij dat nu zou doen, dat hij zich niet meer zou afvragen wat ze daar aan het spreken was, Iers

Engels, Schots Engels, Australisch Engels of helemaal geen Engels misschien.

Hij likte de knie van zijn vrouw, ging toen langzaam omhoog en vervolgens liet ze hem zien wat ze op de dvd aan het doen waren, ze duwde zijn hoofd zachtjes onder haar benen door in de richting van het televisiescherm. 'Kijk maar.' Ze mompelde: 'Je kunt je tong en vingers tegelijkertijd gebruiken, zie je dat?'

Het was geen comfortabele houding om naar een scherm te kijken waarop een vagina in close-up werd bewerkt door een mooie tong, dat moest gezegd, de tong was mooi, die zag er gezond uit, die tong, geen aanslag.

'Zal ik mijn handen wassen?' vroeg de Pool want hij vond het niet netjes om met zijn vieze vingers de vagina van zijn lieve vrouw binnen te gaan, hij voelde zich zo vies maar zij zei dat dit niet hoefde, dat hij schoon was, schoon genoeg voor haar en hij ging met zijn tong over haar bovenbenen en toen hij bijna bij haar vagina was aangekomen zei hij: 'Ik dacht echt dat je dit niet meer wilde.'

'Dat was toen.'

Hij likte nog een beetje verder, zonder haar vagina aan te raken en daarna zei hij: 'Ik moet je wat vertellen.'

'Niet nu,' zei ze, 'ga er met twee vingers zachtjes overheen alsof je vingers penselen zijn.'

'Ja.' En hij ging met zijn vingers over haar vagina alsof die vingers penselen waren en zij zei: 'Je werd steeds ruiger en ruwer. Nu gaan we terug naar wie je was.'

De vrouw van de dvd was nog altijd aan het woord en hij hoorde nu ook een andere vrouwenstem, het leek alsof de seksuologe iemand aan het interviewen was.

'Weet je nog dat we het over troost hebben gehad?' vroeg hij.

'Laten we het daar nu niet over hebben. Merk je hoe nat je me maakt? Je maakt me drijfnat en toch heb ik een strak kutje. Zelfs na twee kinderen.'

'Strak,' herhaalde hij. Zo had ze nooit tegen hem gepraat. Het moest door de dvd komen of door iets anders, door de dood. Ze was de dingen gaan benoemen. Het poesje was kutje geworden.

'En nu weer je tong,' zei ze, 'draai achtjes met je tong, doe alsof je aan het schaatsen bent met je tong en je het ijs niet al te veel pijn wilt doen met je ijzers.'

En hij deed alsof zijn tong een schaats was waarmee hij zijn vrouw niet te veel pijn wilde doen, want zij was het ijs en hij was de schaatser, en toen hij even op adem moest komen zei hij: 'Ik heb de laatste tijd veel contact met de vrouw van Beckers.'

'Oké,' zei ze en ze duwde hem weer tegen zich aan. 'Heel goed, want je bent altijd zo'n loner geweest, altijd zo op jezelf. Weet je nog dat je een tijd een pony als beste vriend had?'

Hij hield op met likken. 'Niet een pony, zijn pony. En het was niet dat de pony mijn beste vriend was, daar kwam ik tot rust.'

Ze knikte en hij pakte de afstandsbediening en zette de dvd stop. 'Ik kan me niet concentreren.'

'We kijken er toch nog een andere keer samen naar?' vroeg ze.

'Zeker.' En hij cirkelde met zijn tong zoals hij op de dvd had gezien. Alles was zo groot aan hem, zo weinig verfijnd maar dit was wie hij was.

'Doe je het zoals je op de dvd hebt gezien?'

'Ik draai achtjes.' En hij pakte haar billen en duwde zijn gezicht met toewijding in haar schaamstreek. Hij duwde zijn tong in haar. Hij probeerde het zo te doen dat het niet zou lijken alsof hij met zijn tong een biefstuk aan het platslaan was. Zijn vrouw zei: 'Dit is goed, dit is lekker, je maakt me geil, maar wanneer ben jij voor het laatst geil geweest?'

'Nu.'

'Ik bedoel echt geil, dat je jezelf niet kon helpen. Het is geen huiswerk.'

'Ben ik niet geil genoeg? Ik heb een erectie.'

Het was waar, hij had een erectie gekregen en hij herinnerde zich de jaren voor hun jongen was meegenomen door de intercity naar Amsterdam. Het was niet zo dat zijn verlangen daarna langzaam was uitgedoofd. Het verlangen was al eerder aan verval onderhevig geweest en misschien was dat ook niet zo erg. Er was meer dan verlangen. Alleen zijn lieve vrouw meende dat waar het verlangen verdwenen was de dood al was begonnen, maar zo zaten de dingen niet in elkaar. En terwijl hij achtjes draaide met zijn tong besloot hij dat hij het nu moest zeggen, dat dit het moment was, dat uitstel het alleen erger zou maken. Als hij geen vreemde wilde worden voor zijn vrouw moest ze weten wie hij was en wie hij was geweest, en dit was wie hij was geweest: een man die van de vrouw van Beckers had gehouden maar die ermee was gestopt, met moeite weliswaar, omdat hij besefte dat die gevoelens vergissingen waren. Onbetamelijkheden.

Hij haalde zijn hoofd uit het kruis van zijn vrouw en hij zei: 'Je smaakt zo lekker.' En dat meende hij, ze smaakte vertrouwd, ze smaakte naar de aarde, naar zijn jeugd toen hij buiten speelde en in de aarde wroette.

'Ik heb van de vrouw van Beckers gehouden,' zei hij.

Eerst leek ze hem niet te verstaan want ze duwde zijn gezicht alleen dichter tegen haar kruis en ze zei: 'Dat is fijn wat je doet. Dit is fijn.'

Ze ademde zwaar. Het was prettig om zijn lieve vrouw te zien, nee te horen genieten. Als ze het niet had verstaan was het ook goed. Dan had hij het gezegd. Dat was het belangrijkste.

Maar toen duwde ze zijn hoofd van zich af en ze vroeg: 'Je hebt van wie gehouden?'

'Van de vrouw van Beckers.'

'Waarom dat? Waar kwam dat opeens vandaan?' En ze duwde zijn hoofd weer tegen zich aan en hij likte zoals hij op de dvd had gezien, hij had het gevoel dat hij het echt goed deed. Voor het eerst sinds zijn jeugd, sinds de ziekte van zijn moeder bad hij tot God. Likkend, zoals ze op de dvd hadden voorgedaan.

God geef mij geilheid, bad hij in stilte, geef mij geilheid, geen erectie, die heb ik al, geilheid zodat ik mezelf niet helpen kan. Geef mij dat, God, want anders ben ik een dode onder de levenden.

En meteen daarna vroeg hij zich af of je God wel kon vragen om geilheid. Was dat geen belediging voor God? Deelde hij wel geilheid uit? Maar als hij de dood en genezing verdeelde kon hij zich toch ook bekommeren om de menselijke opwinding, om de onbetamelijke menselijke opwinding?

'Waarom?' ze duwde zijn hoofd weer van zich af, 'waarom heb je van die vrouw gehouden?'

'Ik kon het niet helpen,' zei hij. 'Het gebeurde.'

'Het gebeurde? Zulke dingen gebeuren niet. Zulke dingen laat je gebeuren. En ze denkt dat ze heel wat is. Met haar jurkjes en haar schoentjes en haar gekamde en gekrulde haartjes, maar ze is gewoon een vrouw van een brandweerman. Meer niet.'

Zijn liefste hield niet van de vrouw van Beckers, dat was duidelijk, ze doorzag haar en hij had nog niets verteld.

'Ja,' zei hij, 'dat is ze.'

En daarop duwde zijn lieve vrouw zijn hoofd weer naar zich toe, in haar schaamstreek, in haar zorgvuldig bijgewerkte schaamhaar. En hij likte en hij bad, hij bad en hij likte. De Pool deed wat hij de tong en de vingers op de dvd had zien doen – was het eigenlijk de tong van een vrouw of een man geweest? – tot hij eindelijk overmand werd door iets wat geilheid kon worden genoemd. Er kwam lust in hem boven. Hij zoog zich vast aan een van haar schaamlippen en dwars door het harde geluid van de regen hoorde hij zijn lieve vrouw zwaar ademen, ze hijgde nooit echt, ze ademde alleen zwaar en terwijl hij naar haar luisterde besefte hij dat de lust haat was. De lust die hem had overmand was afschuw. Moordlust.

En hij dankte God dat hij de erbarmelijke gebeden van de erbarmelijke Pool had verhoord en hem geilheid had gegeven, al was de geilheid dan moordlust.

Hij kon haar wel vermoorden omdat ze hem geen nieuw kind wilde geven, omdat ze hun jongen niet wilde vervangen, terwijl leven toch vervangen was, alles vervangen, alles voortdurend vervangen. En doodgaan was niets meer vervangen.

'Wel teder blijven schatje,' zei ze, en hij zat nog op de bank en zij hurkte nu, zijn kleine lieve vrouw. Zij hurkte voor hem neer zodat hij haar niet meer kon likken en toch bleef hij God danken voor de geilheid die hem op het laatste moment, op het nippertje was gestuurd.

'Wat is er met de vrouw van Beckers gebeurd?'

Hij veegde zijn mond af en ook zij deed dat, ze veegde zijn mond af, ze pulkte een haar bij zijn lippen vandaan. 'Een haar van mij,' zei ze.

'Niets,' zei hij.

'Niets?'

'Niet veel.'

'Dat is wat er gebeurd is?'

'Ja,' zei hij.

'Je hebt van haar gehouden.'

'Ik heb van haar gehouden. Meer is er niet gebeurd. Maar ik ben nu geil. Laten we van elkaar genieten. Zoals je zei.'

'Nee. Straks. Van hoeveel mensen hou je eigenlijk?'

'Van jou, van onze jongens.'

'Waarom hield je van haar? Ze is zo vreselijk aanstellerig. Zo gemaakt. Zo onecht.'

'Waarom ik van haar hield, dat is een moeilijke vraag.' Hij voelde hoe de lust hem dreigde te verlaten. 'Omdat ze zo aanstellerig is misschien.' Zo warm en zo koud tegelijk in haar aanstellerigheid, had hij nog willen zeggen.

'Kun je gewoon uitleggen waarom je van haar hield? Kun je het uitleggen? Kun je me dat vertellen?'

Ze wilde het weten omdat ze hem wilde straffen. Ze wilde hem straffen voor zijn liefde, de liefde van de Pool was liefde waarvoor je gestraft moest worden en daarom zou hij er ook mee ophouden, voor eens en voor altijd.

'Omdat ze me troostte?'

Ze fronste haar wenkbrauwen. 'Is dat een vraag?'

'Ja.'

'Hoe heeft ze jou getroost?'

Hij keek zijn vrouw recht in de ogen en hij dacht: dit zijn de ogen van een vreemde. Ik ken deze vrouw niet. Dit is niet de moeder van mijn kinderen. 'Met voorwerpen.'

'Met voorwerpen?'

'Ja.'

'Voorwerpen?' Ze schreeuwde. Het woord beviel haar niet. Het maakte haar woedend, terwijl het zo'n gewoon, zo'n neutraal woord was. 'Wat voor voorwerpen?'

'Haar schoenen bijvoorbeeld.'

'Haar schoenen? Ben je ziek? Hallucineer je?' De vrouw van de Pool schudde haar man aan zijn schouders, maar zonder hem pijn te doen.

'Nee ik hallucineer niet. En ik ben nog steeds geil. Laten we iets doen. Dat wilde je toch? Je wilde iets met mijn geilheid doen. Ik wil er iets mee doen. Ik zal je likken.'

Ze kneep met een hand in zijn wang. 'Wat heeft ze met haar schoenen gedaan?'

Hij wist niet zeker of hij het moest zeggen, maar volledige openheid was vermoedelijk het beste, dan hoefde ze er niet over te piekeren, dan hoefde ze zich niet af te vragen wat er nu precies met die schoenen was gebeurd.

'Ze heeft de hak van haar schoen in mijn kont gestopt. Wat maakt het uit? Het duurde niet lang.'

De lieve vrouw van de Pool ging naast hem zitten op

de bank en begon te huilen, zachtjes, onhoorbaar, toch zag hij het, toch voelde hij het en hij sloeg een arm om haar heen maar ze haalde de arm weg. Ze zaten daar tot de Pool vroeg: 'Zal ik de dvd-speler weer aanzetten?'

Ze stond op, hij meende dat ze de dvd-speler weer wilde aanzetten, hoewel ze daarvoor ook een afstandsbediening hadden maar misschien wist ze niet waar ze die had neergelegd. Zijn vrouw haalde de dvd uit de speler en staand voor de televisie knakte ze die tussen haar handen, probeerde ze de dvd te verpulveren alsof het allemaal de schuld van het schijfje was, alsof het aan de seksuoloog lag, alsof hun jongen door de intercity naar Amsterdam was meegenomen omdat de seksuoloog had gefaald. 'Laat maar,' zei ze toen de dvd in stukken op de grond lag. 'Laat maar.' En de Pool, die God had gesmeekt om geilheid, om het vuur waarnaar zij zo verlangde, begreep dat hij iets moest doen. Dit kon hij niet laten passeren, hierop kon hij niet reageren met woorden als 'doe rustig,' of 'stel je niet zo aan'.

Hij stond op en zei: 'Het is voorbij.'

'Tussen ons?' vroeg Wen.

'Nee, tussen mij en de vrouw van Beckers. Er is nooit iets tussen ons geweest dus waarschijnlijk is "voorbij" niet het goede woord. Ze zal niets meer in me stoppen.'

'Jezus,' zei ze, 'is dat wat je wilde? Is dat waarnaar je verlangde? En durfde je het niet te zeggen? Durfde je het mij niet te vertellen? Al die jaren dat we samen zijn. Ik walg van je. Ik kan me niet voorstellen dat ik ooit nog door jou aangeraakt wil worden. Ze moest dingen in je stoppen en dat noem je troost? Ontheilig onze jongen niet. Jouw troost is... Jouw troost is geen troost. Jouw troost is een vloek. Jouw manier van rouwen is een vloek.'

Hij wilde haar tegen zich aan drukken maar hij durfde niet, hij kon het ook niet.

'Ik rouw niet. Ik bedoel, rouwen is iets anders en troost

misschien ook.' Hij probeerde zijn vrouw aan te kijken met alle liefde die hij voor haar voelde. Hij hoopte dat ze het zag, dat ze het kon zien in zijn ogen, in zijn handen, in zijn tong, in de manier waarop hij met zijn tong over zijn lippen ging.

De Pool deed een paar stappen in de richting van de dvd die in stukken op de grond lag. Hij raapte de stukken op en het voelde alsof hij zijn lieve vrouw opraapte, alsof zij niet meer was dan de dvd die ze tussen haar handen had geknakt.

'Ik wilde het niet,' zei hij. 'Het was haar idee.'

'Zij wilde het? Lafaard. Is dat ook waarom je tampons nodig had? Is dat de reden dat je al wekenlang stiekem mijn tampons gebruikt?'

Hij keek naar de kapotte dvd. Moesten de details benoemd worden? Mocht echt niets onbenoemd blijven? Hij had een paar dingen verteld, moest hij nu alles vertellen, echt alles? Moest hij vertellen dat ze had gezegd: 'We moeten het wel voorzichtig en veilig doen, anders is het geen liefde'? En op dat moment besefte hij dat dit de grote leugen was, de grote leugen van de volwassenen, dat het pas liefde mocht heten als het veilig en voorzichtig werd gedaan, terwijl hij meende dat als de liefde iets was dan toch zeker iets onveiligs en iets onvoorzichtigs.

'Ja,' zei hij na een tijdje, 'als je het eerlijk wil weten, ja. Daarom die tampons. Ze stopte er alleen dingen in die er niet in pasten want als het erin paste was het geen troost. Daarom kwam er ook van alles uit. Maar nu zal dat niet meer gebeuren. Ze gaat er niets meer in stoppen. Ik heb jouw tampons niet meer nodig.'

Ze keek hem aan met grote koude ogen en hij kende die blik, ze zou hem een klap willen geven. Ze dacht dat hij haar was vergeten, dat hij haar achteloos opzij had geschoven maar het was gebeurd omdat hem troost was aangeboden en hij uit wanhoop die troost had geaccepteerd.

'Ik walg van je,' zei ze zakelijk, 'ik heb spijt dat ik ooit kinderen met je heb gemaakt.'

In haar ogen zag hij geen agressie meer maar verdriet en hij besefte dat hij haar alleen kon troosten als hij haar nu zou neuken, ter plekke, zonder aarzeling, als iemand die niet anders kon, als een gek, een man die niet het verlangen kent een goede man te zijn, een man die eigenlijk alleen maar één verlangen kent, zijn lieve vrouw te nemen, en daarom smeekte hij God opnieuw om geilheid.

Hij deed een poging haar handen te pakken maar ze sloeg zijn handen weg alsof het grote bromvliegen waren. 'Ik wil het uitleggen,' zei hij kijkend naar zijn grote handen. 'Ik was in de war, ik wist het verschil niet tussen ordinaire lust en troost. Die verwarring is over, ik weet het weer. Ik heb het verschil nu begrepen.'

'Je weet wat weer?'

'Het verschil.'

En opnieuw dacht hij aan God, die hem moordlust had gestuurd, hij zou er niet aan toegeven. Nooit. Hij was een goede man, een zorgzame man, ze konden hem op de proef stellen, de mensen, God, hij zou blijven wie hij was, een goede en zorgzame man. Al moest hij daarvoor zich van alles en iedereen losmaken, al moest hij zichzelf levend begraven, hij zou een goede man blijven.

'Ik wil je niet meer,' zei ze, 'ik weet niet waarom ik jou ooit heb gewild. Ik heb jou nooit gewild denk ik. Ik was bang, ik dacht dat het liefde was maar ik was gewoon bang, ik dacht: deze wil me, daarom neem ik die maar. Nu weet je alles. Ik heb je nooit bedrogen. Ik heb je ook nooit echt gewild. Nooit. Soms maakte ik het mezelf wijs, soms geloofde ik erin.'

Ze ging de kamer uit, hij hoorde haar de trap op rennen en met de stukken dvd in zijn hand ging hij haar achterna. Ze had de deur van de kamer van de verdwenen jongen opengerukt, ze was op zijn bed gaan liggen, op zijn kleine jongensbed, ze had haar gezicht in de kussens gestopt.

En hij hurkte naast haar neer, naast het bed. Zo had hij eerder gehurkt, als hun jongen niet naar school wilde, als hij weigerde op te staan, als hij zich dreigde te verstoppen of dat ook echt deed, onder het bed, in de kast. Hij zei zo zacht en rustig mogelijk: 'Dit zouden we toch niet doen, we zouden deze kamer niet opendoen. Dit is jouw bed niet. Dit is zijn bed.'

'Laat me met rust,' zei ze.

Hij streelde haar rug, ze kroop in de hoek tegen de muur aan, ze pakte een knuffel van de verdwenen jongen en hield die vast. Ze beschermde haar lichaam met de knuffel van de verdwenen jongen tegen de handen van de Pool die haar wilde troosten.

'Dit is niet jouw bed, dit is het bed van onze jongen. Kom eraf. We hebben ons eigen bed.' Hij wilde haar vastpakken maar dat liet ze niet toe, ze sloeg hem met de knuffel en hoe meer ze hem sloeg hoe meer hij hun jongen rook en uiteindelijk ging hij naast haar liggen op het bed van hun jongen. Nog altijd had hij stukken van de dvd in zijn hand en hij zei dat ze echt beter van het bed kon komen, dat ze naar hun eigen bed moesten gaan. Maar ze verroerde zich niet en ze zei ook niets. Ze bleef daar liggen en hij herinnerde zich dat ze geen onderbroek aanhad en dat hij haar zou kunnen troosten als hij zich overmand door geilheid op haar stortte. Dat wist hij zeker, dat dit haar zou troosten. Er was slechts één ding dat haar zou kunnen overtuigen van zijn liefde, dat haar woede de mond kon snoeren. Nu was hij niet door geilheid overmand, misschien kon hij doen alsof. Misschien kon hij toch nog overmand worden, zomaar geheel tegen alle verwachtingen in, God kon hem nog eens geilheid sturen en hij begon weer te bidden, zo zacht dat ze hem niet kon horen.

Hij streelde haar been zoals ze hem eerder op de avond had opgedragen toen het zo regende en hij naar de donder had geluisterd en ze liet hem begaan. Ze sloeg hem niet meer, niet met haar handen, niet met de knuffel van hun jongen, ze liet hem haar been strelen en hij ging steeds hoger terwijl hij in zijn ene hand nog altijd de kapotte dvd hield en hij onhoorbaar tot God bad om de geilheid, ook al leek die op moordlust.

'Ik voel zoveel walging voor je,' zei ze met haar hoofd in het kussen en toch was het duidelijk hoorbaar. 'Omdat je het nooit hebt gezegd. Omdat je nooit je verlangens hebt uitgesproken. Nooit. Al die jaren.'

Hij pakte haar nek, duwde haar gezicht dieper in het kussen van hun jongen. 'Begrijp je het dan nog niet,' siste hij in haar oor, 'ik heb geen verlangens. Mijn enige verlangen is om een goede man te zijn. Dat is mijn verlangen. Ik heb geen verlangens.'

En daarna ging hij weer door met het strelen van haar been met zijn rechterhand en in zijn linkerhand hield hij de stukken van de dvd vast alsof hij verloren zou zijn als hij die stukken zou loslaten. Hij bewerkte het geslachtsdeel van zijn vrouw met de tederheid waarop de seksuoloog in de vertaling van zijn vrouw hem had gewezen en hij bad tot God om tederheid en geilheid.

'Ik had zo gedacht...' zei zijn lieve vrouw met haar gezicht in het kussen.

'Wat?' vroeg hij terwijl hij niet ophield haar te strelen, haar te bewerken.

Even zweeg ze, toen tilde ze haar hoofd een beetje op en ze zei: 'Dat als we samen naar die dvd zouden kijken het dan allemaal goed kwam, ik had het zo gehoopt maar niets komt goed. Jij wil mij niet. Jij wil iemand anders.'

'Nee,' zei hij terwijl hij in gedachten doorging met bidden, 'ik wil jou, alleen jou, alleen soms zijn er afleidingen, stoorzenders. Verwarde mensen die troost aanbieden terwijl ze dat zelf nodig hebben. Daarom moet je oppassen voor de mensen die troost aanbieden want ze hebben het zelf zo hard nodig, maar dat wist ik niet.'

Wat hij zei was een gebed. Wat hij dacht was een gebed.

En ze zuchtte, ze liet hem begaan, in het bed van hun jongen vingerde hij zijn vrouw alsof zijn vingers penselen waren en haar geslachtsdeel een delicaat doek dat met uiterste behoedzaamheid beschilderd diende te worden.

'Niets komt goed,' herhaalde ze.

'We hebben nog een jongen,' reageerde hij strelend en denkend aan de seksuoloog, 'alles komt goed, alleen omdat hij er is.'

'Hou op,' riep ze in het kussen, 'hou op altijd over onze jongen te beginnen. Wil je me of wil je me niet? Dat wil ik weten.'

'Ik wil je,' en hij legde de vijf stukken van de dvd op het bed, het kleine bed, dat eigenlijk te klein was voor twee volwassenen van wie er een zelfs een soort reus was. Hij stond op, deed zijn sokken en zijn broek uit in de kamer van hun jongen, en hij zag de schriften van hun jongen, het huiswerk waaraan hij had gewerkt, hier lagen zijn geheimen, en toen was de Pool naakt.

Hij keerde zijn vrouw voorzichtig om en hij knoopte haar blouse open, geconcentreerd en voorzichtig. 'We kopen een nieuwe dvd, we gaan er samen naar kijken. Ik ga dingen leren waarvan ik niet wist dat ik ze kon leren.'

'Laat maar, het was misschien ook geen goed idee.'

'Geef niet op, geef niet op.' Hij hielp haar uit haar blouse alsof ze in het ziekenhuis waren en hij wilde haar beha ook uitdoen maar ze deed het zelf. Hij legde de beha op het nachtkastje van hun oudste jongen, voorzichtig, want hij wilde niets verplaatsen, alles moest blijven zoals het was.

Ze ging weer op haar buik liggen en de Pool schoof de rok van zijn lieve vrouw voorzichtig omhoog en hij manoeuvreerde zichzelf tussen haar benen. De Pool had een erectie en hij voelde de moordlust weer opkomen, de moordlust die geilheid heette. God had zijn gebeden verhoord. Geconcentreerd bewoog hij met zijn stijve geslachtsdeel over haar geslachtsdeel. 'Ik wil ook best een schoen in je stoppen,' zei ze met luide, ja zelfs ietwat schelle stem. 'Als dat is wat je wil moet je het zeggen. Schoenen zat.'

'Nee,' zei hij, 'dat hoeft echt niet.'

Ze kneep in het kussen en hij bewoog zijn geslachtsdeel over dat van haar tot hij meende dat hij het geslachtsdeel in haar kon stoppen.

'Wat heeft ze eigenlijk nog meer in je gestopt? Een winterpeen? Een bierfles? Een afstandsbediening? Wat voor voorwerpen stoppen mensen tegenwoordig in elkaar?'

'Ik weet het niet, ik weet het echt niet. Voorwerpen, dat is alles wat ik weet. Ik keek niet. Ik lag zoals jij nu ligt. Ik had mijn ogen dicht, ik werd getroost, dat was genoeg.'

'Maar wij hebben hier ook voorwerpen in huis. Ik wil het best doen. Als dat is wat je wilt, wil ik het best doen. Ik ben bereid elk voorwerp dat we hier in huis hebben in je kont te stoppen. Echt, ik doe het. Als dat is hoe je wilt rouwen, als dat is wat je sterker maakt. Ik doe het.' Ze praatte hard, het leek bijna op schreeuwen.

'Niet nodig,' en hij neukte zijn lieve vrouw, met de blinde begeerte van de moordzucht. Ze begon iets zwaarder te ademen. 'We liggen in zijn bed,' zei hij. 'Daar gaat het om. We liggen in zijn bed. Dat is toch wat je wilde? Je wilde het in zijn bed doen. Je wilde het in deze kamer doen. Je wilde laten zien dat je...'

'Ja, ik wilde het hier doen,' zei ze. 'En nu je mond houden. Neem me.' En hij neukte verder, elke stoot bracht hem dichter bij God.

Hij concentreerde zich op zijn orgasme, hij probeerde de jongen en zijn kamer en zijn schriften te vergeten, hij probeerde alles te vergeten, hij wilde dat er alleen nog maar dit was, deze poging tot genot, deze erbarmelijke vleselijkheid. Het was een woord dat niet meer uit zijn hoofd ging sinds hij de pony naar het mes had geleid. Erbarmelijk was hij, erbarmelijk waren de verlangens die hij niet had en terwijl hij neukte greep hij haar billen zoals hij vroeger had gedaan, zoals hij zou blijven doen, omdat ze man en vrouw waren.

En toen kwam ze klaar, hij hoorde het aan haar ademhaling, aan de geluiden die ze maakte, geluiden die niets meer met hem of haar te maken hadden, geluiden uit de stal waren het, geluiden van het dier, en daarna overwoog hij te doen alsof hij ook klaarkwam maar hij wist dat ze het zou controleren want ze was niet lichtgelovig, ze zou controleren of er sperma uit haar vagina droop.

Daarom neukte hij verder, denkend aan zijn vrouw met een ander en pas zo, toen hij haar in zijn fantasie had verloren, kwam hij klaar.

Hij ging naast haar liggen op het te kleine bed van de verdwenen jongen, met zijn hoofd op zijn knuffel en alles leek nu goed. Hij had bewezen dat hij van zijn vrouw hield, dat de vrouw van Beckers niet meer was dan een verkeerde afslag die hij had genomen, al gloeide er nog wat na van die afslag, diep in hem.

'Ik wil niet dat je haar ooit nog ziet,' zei ze met haar gezicht naar hem toe gekeerd, 'de vrouw van Beckers. Je mag haar nooit meer zien. Voor jou is ze dood. En je weet niet waar ze is begraven.'

'Ze is dood,' herhaalde hij. En hij schrok van die woorden.

Alles moest dood in dit gezin en alles ging dood, want hier was de dood liefde.

'En je weet niet waar ze is begraven.'

'Ik weet niet waar ze is begraven.'

'Zo dood als de pony,' zei zijn vrouw.

'Ik moest haar slachten voor de liefde.'

'Ja,' zei zijn lieve vrouw. 'Je moest haar slachten voor de liefde.'

Er moest wel veel voor de liefde worden geslacht.

'Beloof je het?' vroeg ze.

Hij keek haar aan, hij perste de geloofwaardigheid uit zijn ogen en hij meende het, hij was geen leugenaar. 'Ja.'

'Anders ben ik vertrokken. Als je haar blijft zien. Want als je haar blijft zien dan blijft ze je troosten en ik kan niet leven met haar troost. Ik wil er niet mee leven.'

'Ik begrijp het.' Hij keek naar het plafond.

Ze streelde hem over zijn hoofd, ze veegde een schilfer van zijn voorhoofd en ze zei: 'Als ik voorwerpen in je moet stoppen dan moet je het zeggen. Als dat bij onze liefde hoort dan doe ik het. Ik doe het graag. Maar ík doe het, niet dat wijf van die Beckers.' Ze hield even op met strelen. 'Is dat duidelijk? Ik moet mijn grenzen stellen anders ga jij over al mijn grenzen heen.'

'Ja,' zei hij, 'dat is heel duidelijk. Mensen hebben grenzen, net als dieren eigenlijk. Maar er hoeven geen voorwerpen in me te worden gestopt. Het was een verkeerde afslag die ik nam.'

Naar dat plafond had hun jongen dus gekeken als hij in bed lag en de slaap niet kon vatten. Er was niet veel aan te zien, het was een gewoon plafond. Hooguit kon je zeggen dat het wel wat verf nodig had.

'Een verkeerde afslag,' zei ze en haar stem klonk zo lief, zo teder, 'loop je daarom met tampons in je kont? Het was toch troost? Kan troost een verkeerde afslag zijn? Maar als het een afslag was die je niet had moeten nemen vind ik het ook prima. Ga toch naar een dokter. Zo'n tampon is niets.'

'Nee liefste,' antwoordde hij, 'ik laat nu alles genezen en dan heb ik ook geen tampons meer nodig. Dan is het klaar.'

Ze knikte, ze zei niets meer. Misschien dacht ze aan haar schoenen met hoge hakken, schoenen die ze alleen droeg op uitzonderlijke gelegenheden en vond ze het jammer dat ze die niet in hem had kunnen stoppen.

'Zullen we hier blijven liggen?' vroeg ze toen hij bijna overmand was door de slaap, toen zijn ogen waren dicht-gevallen en hij opschrok van haar woorden die hij niet meer had verwacht.

'We hebben onze tanden niet gepoetst.'

'Maakt niet uit, we kunnen ook weleens een keertje onze tanden niet poetsen.'

Dat was ook zo, daarom stond hij op en deed het licht uit in de kamer van de verdwenen jongen. Hij vroeg of hij ook de gordijnen dicht moest doen, dat hoefde niet. Zo ging hij naast haar liggen. Ongepoetst en ongewassen waren ze, onvoorbereid op de nacht. Hij vreesde dat hij niet zou kunnen slapen maar hij viel toch in slaap, in het bed van hun verdwenen jongen.

De Pool sliep onrustig. Elke keer als hij zich omdraaide had hij het gevoel dat hij zijn vrouw schopte of tegen de muur drukte. En zijn eigen voeten hingen uit het bed. De Pool had altijd geloofd dat hij overal kon slapen en dat was ook zo, hij sliep maar wel onrustig.

's Ochtends vroeg, nog voor zijn vrouw wakker was, nog voor de overgebleven jongen wakker was ging hij aan de eettafel zitten en schreef een brief. De eerste brief die hij in jaren had geschreven.

'Aan de vrouw van Beckers,' schreef hij. 'Ik heb me vergist. Ik heb nooit van je gehouden. Je had gelijk. Wat ik aanzag voor troost was ordinaire lust. Ik kan je niet meer zien, anders verval ik in herhalingen. Ondanks alles. Je bent dood voor me. Neem me niet kwalijk. Niettemin dank voor alles. Ik zal het nooit vergeten. De Fransman zal komen om je te halen en je wachtte op de Fransman, niet op mij. Ik zal bidden dat de Fransman je komt halen. Ik ben niet gelovig maar ik ben sinds kort begonnen met bidden. Want als we elkaar blijven zien gaat het door en het moet ophouden. Ik zal je niet vergeten. Maar jij hebt Beckers en je drie dochters, ik heb één zoon en een lieve vrouw. En jij hebt bovendien je Fransman. Hij zal je komen halen. Hartelijke groet.'

Toen wachtte hij even want hij wist niet hoe hij de brief moest ondertekenen, uiteindelijk besloot hij gewoon af te sluiten met 'de Pool'. Dat was het beste. Dat was wie hij was.

Hij zocht een enveloppe, vond die niet en besloot er later een te kopen want hij kon de brief niet zo door de brievenbus duwen. Dat ging niet.

Maar eerst haalde hij de overgebleven jongen uit bed en hij bracht hem naar de kamer van zijn broertje waar de lieve vrouw van de Pool nog lag te slapen in een bed dat ook te klein voor haar was.

'Daar ligt mama,' zei hij tegen de jongen. 'Ze ligt vandaag in een ander bed.'

En met de jongen in zijn arm kriebelde hij zijn vrouw zachtjes in haar nek zodat ze wakker zou worden. De jongen lachte, hij keek nieuwsgierig. En toen de moeder van de jongen haar ogen opende zei de Pool lieve woordjes tegen haar, zo ongeveer alle lieve woorden die hij kende.

Het was vroeg, hij moest zo naar de kazerne en samen kleedden ze hun jongen aan. De Pool vroeg of het erg was dat hij haar zo vroeg wakker had gemaakt maar ze zei dat dit niet erg was, dat ze nog wat zou spelen met de jongen, dat het prima was, dat ze toch genoeg had geslapen. En de Pool zei: 'We moeten daar maar niet meer komen.'

'We doen de deur weer dicht,' zei zijn vrouw en ze begon te neuriën terwijl ze naar beneden liep.

Hij ging de kamer van de verdwenen jongen in, pakte de stukken van de dvd en gooide die in de keuken in de afvalbak. En in de woonkamer zong zijn vrouw liederen over de liefde.

# 6

Bij het volleyballen die ochtend botste Beckers hard met de Pool. Beckers sprong bij het net toen hij een bal probeerde te blokkeren en klapte met zijn hoofd tegen dat van de Pool. Een kopstoot was het geweest, alsof Beckers niet de bal wilde blokkeren maar het hoofd van zijn collega. Of was het een vuist geweest die hem boven het oog raakte, die hem naar adem deed happen en hem het gevoel gaf dat zijn lichaam alleen nog bestond uit een paar vierkante centimeter boven zijn rechteroog? De vuist of het hoofd van Beckers, het effect was hetzelfde. De Pool bleef bij het net op de grond liggen. Hij was duizelig.

'Jezus, sorry,' zei Beckers en hij probeerde zijn vriend de Pool overeind te helpen, al had hij die vriend zelf tegen de vlakte gewerkt. In zijn korte, zwarte gymbroek stond Beckers over de Pool gebogen. Was Beckers een vriend? Ja, de mannen van de C-ploeg waren zijn vrienden. Wat er ook tussen de vrouw van Beckers en de Pool was voorgevallen, het stond buiten hun vriendschap, het was in een andere wereld gebeurd, een parallelluniversum.

'Sorry, ik dacht dat die bal voor mij was. Gaat het?' vroeg Beckers en hij leek steeds meer te schrikken van wat hij had aangericht.

'Laat me maar,' antwoordde de Pool, 'komt wel goed.' Hij kroop als een hond naar de kant want hij kon even niet opstaan. Hij voelde zich steeds duizeliger worden, en verslagen, ook dat. Niet eerder had hij zich zo verslagen gevoeld. Dat hij met zijn lieve vrouw in het bed van de verdwenen jongen de liefde had bedreven, dat had hem verward. De troost van de vrouw van Beckers was verwarrende troost geweest. Maar misschien was alle ware troost verwarrend. Verslagen had hij zich nooit echt gevoeld, niet toen zijn vader het verlies van zijn vrouw verwerkte door zich af te sluiten van zijn vorige leven en een volstrekt nieuw leven te beginnen. Niet toen hij zijn oudste jongen van de rails krabde. Hij had aan de overgebleven jongen gedacht, toen al, toen hij op de rails stond en hij had zich voorgenomen zich niet te laten verslaan want op dat voornemen kwam het leven neer. Nu voelde hij zich verslagen. De kopstoot had hem verslagen. De vuistslag. Beckers zelf had hem verslagen.

Hij wreef voorzichtig over zijn voorhoofd en veegde zijn hand toen af aan zijn broek. Het was geen zweet dat daar op zijn voorhoofd zat, het was bloed.

De ploegchef kwam naar hem toe. De Pool lag aan de kant van de sportzaal op de grond. 'Je ziet wit,' zei de ploegchef. 'Hij heeft je flink geraakt.' Er verscheen een glimlachje op het gezicht van de ploegchef, die anders zelden glimlachte.

'Volgens mij raakte hij me met zijn hoofd,' zei de Pool moeizaam. 'Volgens mij gaf hij me per ongeluk een kopstoot.'

'Met zijn hand,' zei de ploegchef. 'Het was jouw bal ook niet. Wat deed je daar? Je had hem moeten laten gaan. Nou ja. Kan gebeuren.'

De mannen haalden een zak ijs en drukten dat op het hoofd van de Pool. Hij hield zijn ogen gesloten, hij kon niet zien welke mannen met hem bezig waren, hij hoorde alleen de ploegchef zeggen dat hij goed en rustig moest blijven ademen en dat deed hij dus ook. Rustig ademde hij en hij vroeg zich af of het er zo aan toeging als je verslagen werd, of het er zo uitzag. Zo alledaags, zo gewoon. Tijdens een partijtje volleybal om de conditie op peil te houden.

'Het is daar boven je oog wat gezwollen,' zei de ploegchef. 'Hoe voel je je? Moet er iemand naar kijken?'

De Pool schudde zijn hoofd, hij opende zijn ogen, stond

moeizaam op en wankelde naar de wc. Daar kotste hij. Toen liep hij moeizaam naar de slaapruimte en ging op bed liggen. Het kotsen had opgelucht, het gevoel verslagen te zijn was niet weggegaan. Jaren ging je door het leven met het idee dat wat er ook gebeurde je er wel uit zou komen, een druppeltje onoverwinnelijkheid had ondanks alles in de Pool gezeten. Nu was dat weg. Verdwenen. Zo laat pas. Hij had het langer volgehouden dan zijn vader.

De mannen waren achter hem aan gekomen met de zak ijs. Ze drukten de zak weer op zijn voorhoofd en ze zeiden dat hij zo maar even moest blijven liggen.

'En als we moeten uitrukken?' vroeg de Pool, meer mompelend dan vragend. Alsof hij droomde. Alsof ze in een droom om zijn bed stonden en hem in die droom verzorgden.

'Geen probleem,' antwoordde de ploegchef. 'Als het groot alarm is vraag ik er wel wat jongens van een andere kazerne bij.' Met die woorden lieten de mannen de Pool alleen in zijn kamer. En hij lag daar, wakend, dan weer slapend, bezig zijn herinneringen te ordenen. Zijn nieuwe leven te ordenen, het leven van de verslagene. Maar hij zou het geheimhouden. Niemand zou het te weten komen.

Bij de lunch ging het al iets beter, al had hij geen eetlust maar dat was niets nieuws en toen ze boodschappen gingen doen was de Pool weer van de partij. Als ze moesten uitrukken zou hij er ook bij zijn. Hij was niet alleen een goede, ook een sterke man. Verslagen en toch sterk. De ploegchef vroeg nog eens of het echt wel ging, of alles oké was. 'Er hoeft niemand naar me te kijken,' antwoordde de Pool. 'Het gaat. Het zal hooguit een buil worden. Ik heb een stevig hoofd.'

In de supermarkt kocht hij snel wat enveloppen. En bij het avondeten voelde hij zich beter. Hij had nog wel hoofdpijn en er zat inderdaad een bult op zijn kop. Het bloeden was gestopt, er hoefde niets gehecht te worden. De mannen spraken over vluchtelingen en wat er allemaal van hardwerkende en welwillende burgers werd afgepikt, vooral door hordes islamieten, terwijl de Pool zachtjes aan zijn voorhoofd voelde. Er werd te veel van de mannen afgepikt, de politici, die zakkenvullers deden alles voor de vluchtelingen en niets voor de eigen burgers, zeiden de mannen, maar ze moesten branden blussen en auto's openknippen en nu en dan ook katten uit bomen redden dus lang konden ze er niet bij stilstaan. Bij het afwassen merkte Beckers op: 'Straks zijn we vreemdelingen in eigen land.'

De Pool knikte. Stiekem waren ze dat al, vreemdelingen in eigen land, althans zo voelde de Pool zich. Er was een tijd dat dit anders was geweest. Dat de aarde van hen was maar die tijd was voorbij, al konden ze zich nog goed herinneren dat het anders, beter was geweest. En toen spraken de mannen weer over vreemdelingen en vluchtelingen, Arabieren en Afrikanen, terwijl ze aan het afwassen waren. 'Ze komen voor onze vrouwen en voor ons geld,' zei Beckers. 'In onze cultuur hebben ze geen interesse.'

De ploegchef vulde aan: 'Zero interesse in onze cultuur maar de politici kan het niets schelen.' En de Pool zag de vrouwen van zijn collega's voor zich, vrouwen voor wie de Arabieren en Afrikanen waren gekomen, vooral de vrouw van Beckers natuurlijk. Op cultuur kon hij zich even niet concentreren, daarvoor deed zijn hoofd te veel pijn.

En met herinneringen aan een tijd dat ze onder elkaar waren, zonder vreemdelingen die op hun vrouwen aasden, zonder akelige toekomstvisioenen sloten ze de avond af en Beckers zei nog dat hij bang was voor zijn dochters. Als hij naar hen keek dan vreesde hij de toekomst, dan vreesde hij wat er met zijn meisjes zou gebeuren.

En toen zei hij: 'Misschien is dat raar om tegen jou te zeggen, met het kind dat je hebt verloren.'

De Pool antwoordde: 'Niets is raar.' Hij had geen akelige toekomstvisioenen nodig, hij liet alles op zich afkomen, hoewel sommige mensen zouden zeggen dat hijzelf midden in een akelig toekomstvisioen terecht was gekomen, al zag hij dat niet zo. Het deed pijn maar het was uit te houden in de toekomst. En toen ze naar bed gingen zei Beckers bij de wastafels: 'Gaat het? Ik was te fanatiek, ik wilde dat potje per se winnen.'

'Geeft niet.' De Pool raakte even de rug van Beckers aan. Zoals vrienden dat bij elkaar doen, collega's die vrienden zijn geworden. Intimi. 'Ik ben blij dat ik mijn tanden nog heb.'

Beckers knikte en toen ging hij verder over zijn dochters terwijl ze bij de wastafels stonden en in het helse licht naar de spiegels staarden en het ontging de Pool niet dat de inhammen van Beckers steeds dieper werden, zijn rimpels steeds talrijker en hoewel Beckers nog aan het spreken was over de akelige toekomst die zijn dochters te wachten stond als ze niets deden poetste de Pool zijn tanden. 'Ik zie voor me wat die Arabieren straks met mijn dochter gaan doen. Ik zie het bijna elke dag voor me, met de gruwelijkste details en die willen dan niet uit je hoofd,' zei Beckers.

De Pool haalde de tandenborstel uit zijn mond en zei: 'Ja, dat is vreselijk. Al die details. Gelukkig zijn ze nog niet hier.'

'Je kijkt niet goed,' zei Beckers, 'hier in het centrum van Heerlen zijn ze er al, de Arabieren. Daarom gaan we verhuizen, we willen naar een dorp. Want in de dorpen zitten ze nog niet.'

'Gaan jullie verhuizen?' vroeg de Pool.

'We zijn ermee bezig,' zei Beckers, 'voor de veiligheid van het gezin.'

En de Pool kon alleen denken: ze gaan verhuizen. Alsof de vrouw van Beckers weet dat ze al dood is en hij de plek waar ze begraven zou worden niet mocht kennen.

De volgende dag gooide de Pool de brief die voor de vrouw van Beckers bestemd was weg. 'Mevrouw Beckers,' had hij op de enveloppe geschreven, dat leek hem voldoende, nu vond hij de brief onbeholpen. Hij moest een nieuwe brief schrijven, eentje die beter was, die recht deed aan de krankzinnige gevoelens die hij kortstondig had gehad en nog voor het avond was belde ze maar hij nam niet op. Op zijn voicemail had ze ingesproken: 'Ik wil je zien.'

Hij verwijderde het bericht. De dagen daarop bleef ze bellen en bleef ze berichten inspreken en vier dagen later stond ze zelfs voor zijn deur maar hij deed niet open. Hij zag haar staan en hij verstopte zich. Eerst in de keuken en toen ze bleef bellen rende hij naar boven en ging op bed liggen. Ze bleef aanbellen en hij lag op het echtelijk bed met zijn vingers in zijn oren en hij bad.

'Is dat wat ik verdiend heb?' sprak ze later in op zijn voicemail. 'Omdat ik mij voor jou heb geopend?' Hij verwijderde ook dit bericht. Als hij dat niet deed, zo vreesde hij, zou hij er steeds weer naar luisteren. Dan zou hij zwak worden en dat mocht niet gebeuren.

Een keer nam hij op omdat ze niet ophield, omdat ze zijn stilte weigerde te accepteren. Letterlijk had ze gezegd: 'Zo makkelijk kom je niet van me af.'

Was dat hoe de verdrijving uit het paradijs in zijn werk ging? Je werd verleid van de verboden vrucht te eten, vervolgens werd je gestraft met verdrijving en toch kwam je er niet vanaf, niet van degene die je verleidde, niet van de vrucht waarvan je hebt gegeten.

Waren radicalere maatregelen nodig? Om de verleidster het verleiden onmogelijk te maken? Hun jongen had radicale maatregelen genomen. Daarom nam de Pool de telefoon op, om duidelijk te maken dat ze echt van elkaar af moesten komen. Hij zei snel voor zij iets had kunnen zeggen: 'Je bent dood en ik weet niet waar je begraven ligt, ook dat is liefde.' Toen hing hij op. Hij zou nog een brief schrijven, een goede brief.

Pas later kwam hij op het idee haar nummer te blokkeren. Je moest hard zijn als je de liefde wilde redden, hard en duidelijk en onverbiddelijk.

Ze was inventief, de vrouw van Beckers, ze belde met andere nummers, steeds weer met andere nummers. Aanvankelijk had ze gesmeekt en gevleid. Het vleien was langzaam een aanval geworden. 'Je bent erger dan de Fransman,' sprak ze in op zijn voicemail, 'de Fransman had tenminste stijl. Jij bent een miezerige, kleine Pool. Zonder stijl. Jij bent niets. Ik heb me in je vergist.'

Hij verwijderde alle berichten en hoe sterker hij werd hoe meer hij bad en hoe meer hij bad hoe meer hij de vrouw van Beckers zag. Hij zag haar overal. In de auto van een spookrijder, één dode, één zwaargewonde. In de eigenaresse van een kledingwinkel na afloop van een brandje, geen gewonden, alleen materiële schade. In de keuken van een restaurant, één lichtgewonde. En overal sprak ze hem aan op zijn miezerigheid. Overal zei ze tegen hem: 'Jij hebt niets te bieden. En jij bent niets. Onaardig en slecht ben je.' Maar ze zei het met veel liefde. Met zo verschrikkelijk veel liefde. Ze zei het om hem te redden, dat was duidelijk.

Een enkele keer keek ze alleen naar hem maar wat ze wilde zeggen zag hij in haar ogen. Ze nam de gedaantes aan van de meest uiteenlopende personen. Het ene moment liep ze door de supermarkt en kneep ze in avocado's, het volgende moment fietste ze alweer over straat met een grote blauwe boodschappentas aan het stuur. Ze zat in een rolstoel en in een stadsbus, ze had alle leeftijden, van begin twintig tot eind zestig. Hoe meer hij haar zag, hoe minder hij zich kon concentreren. Hij was niet zozeer een vreemdeling in eigen land, hij was een vreemdeling in eigen huis want hij zag dingen die zijn vrouw en kind niet zagen, hij hoorde stemmen die zijn vrouw en kind niet hoorden, al was het omdat hij wist wat er op zijn voicemail was ingesproken en zij niet.

Hij ging naar een sekswinkel en hij zei tegen de man achter de toonbank, een oudere kerel zonder haar – toch had hij ook in hem een kort moment de vrouw van Beckers herkend: 'Ik zoek een voorlichtings-dvd.'

De man schraapte zijn keel, wreef met een hand over zijn kale hoofd en zei: 'Je bedoelt seks in de schoolbanken?'

'Nee, dat bedoel ik niet,' zei de Pool. 'Ik bedoel hoe je het kunt leren, hoe je er beter in kunt worden.'

'In wat?'

De Pool meende even dat hij in de maling werd genomen maar de man bleef hem vriendelijk aankijken en daaruit maakte hij op dat er geen sprake was van in de maling te worden genomen. 'In seks. Hoe de seks beter kan worden. Teder. Meer tederheid. Opwindender. De techniek. Zeg maar.' De Pool nam zijn ene hand in de andere en drukte op de knokkels.

'Voor wie is het?' vroeg de kale man.

'Voor mijn vrouw en mij.'

'O, de techniek,' mompelde de oude man, 'de techniek.'

Hij ging naar achteren, bleef een paar minuten weg en kwam terug met een dvd die hij op de toonbank gooide alsof de Pool hem had beledigd. 'Ik had niet verwacht,' zei de man, 'dat ik deze ooit nog zou verkopen. Maar mijn vrouw zegt altijd: doe die voorraden nou niet weg, er is altijd wel iemand die het wil hebben. Je hebt altijd verzamelaars. Je kunt het zo gek niet bedenken of er is een verzamelaar die het wil hebben. Nou, ze heeft gelijk.'

De Pool bekeek de dvd.

'Techniek,' zei de man. 'Dit gaat over techniek.'

De Pool vroeg zich af of zijn vrouw hier tevreden mee zou zijn maar toen hij las wat erop stond – dat het seksleven weer een feest kon worden – besloot hij dat dit inderdaad in de buurt kwam waarop zijn vrouw en hij zaten te wachten. 'Kunt u het inpakken?'

De man schudde zijn hoofd. 'We hebben geen cadeaupapier. Ik kan je wel een plastic tasje geven.'

Met een plastic tasje in zijn hand reed de Pool naar een warenhuis waar hij cadeaupapier kocht – neutraal cadeaupapier, blauw met wat gouden sterretjes – en aan de keukentafel pakte hij de dvd in die beloofde dat het seksleven weer een feest kon worden. Niemand hoefde te wanhopen. Je kwam niet van de mensen af of je moest radicale maatregelen nemen maar er was de redding van de techniek.

'Ze is dood en begraven,' zei hij die avond tegen zijn vrouw, 'ik heb mijn woord gehouden. Geen idee waar. Een zeemansgraf.' Daarop kriebelde ze hem over zijn nek, zijn lieve vrouw, uit dankbaarheid, ongetwijfeld uit dankbaarheid.

'Nu is alles goed,' zei de lieve vrouw van de Pool. 'Het verdriet is er altijd maar jij bent er ook altijd.'

Zij waren er altijd, het verdriet en de Pool. Hij kon zich niet aan de indruk onttrekken dat hij, de Pool, het verdriet was en eigenlijk had hij dat niet willen zijn maar de dvd beloofde dat niemand hoefde te wanhopen.

Hij pakte de dvd en zei: 'Ik heb een cadeautje voor je.'

Ze nam het cadeautje aan, ze lachte, vroeg: 'Heb je dat zelf ingepakt? Ik kan zien dat je het zelf hebt ingepakt.'

Ze scheurde het cadeaupapier van de dvd. Ze keek ernaar, de lach verdween, ze draaide de dvd-hoes om, begon te lezen. Over het feest dat voor iedereen binnen handbereik lag, zelfs voor mensen die al jaren wanhoopten. Ze zei met een klein en eigenlijk ietwat triest glimlachje: 'Dat hoeft niet. We kunnen het toch ook zonder.'

'Omdat je die andere kapot had gemaakt, weet je nog...'

'Het is lief,' zei ze. 'Het is zo lief. Jij bent zo lief. Maar het was misschien ook niet zo'n goed idee van mij.'

Ze legde de dvd op tafel en daarna ging ze naar de keuken. Ze perste wortel, appel en gember. De nieuwe sapcentrifuge vervulde een belangrijke rol in dit huishouden. En toen gingen ze slapen. Teder en toch weemoedig lagen ze naast elkaar, de overgebleven jongen sliep in zijn kamer. Ze waren nog naar hem gaan kijken, hij ademde rustig.

Pas na een week of drie hielden de berichten van de vrouw van Beckers op. De boutades, de smeekbedes, verhalen over pijn die hij haar had aangedaan, die zaten er ook tussen, de zakelijke berichten waarin ze stelde dat ze het besluit van hem respecteerde maar dat ze het op een goede manier wilde afsluiten. Hij had nergens meer op gereageerd, elk bericht van haar had hij verwijderd. Een tijd had hij gedacht dat hij nog een brief zou schrijven tot hij besefte dat die brief er niet van kwam. Dat de stilte misschien beter was. Eerlijker, vooral dat.

En toen ze ophield hem lastig te vallen, toen hij duidelijk had gemaakt dat hij aan haar kon en zou ontkomen, pas toen werd de vrouw van Beckers goed levend. Ze scharrelde door zijn huis en door zijn dromen, ze volgde hem in de kazerne, ze deed mee aan oefeningen, ze strak branden aan en hielp die blussen. Ze stond in zijn woonkamer, ze lag in zijn bed, maakte maaltijden klaar in zijn keuken en at mee als hij met vrouw en kind aan tafel zat.

Hij bad tot God om de vrouw van Beckers, die hij op verzoek van zijn vrouw dood had verklaard – en het was ook beter zo, dood waren de mensen eigenlijk prima te verdragen – te laten verdwijnen. Dit keer verhoorde God zijn gebeden niet. In plaats van doder werd de vrouw van Beckers slechts levendiger, misschien omdat God meer in haar woonde dan in andere mensen.

De hoofdpijn die hij aan de botsing met Beckers had overgehouden verdween eindelijk, de bult verdween niet en zij ook niet, ze bleef steeds hetzelfde tegen hem zeggen: Jij hebt niets te bieden. En jij bent niets.

En op een middag, zijn vrouw was nog niet thuis, besloot hij te gaan wandelen. Hij liet een briefje voor haar achter dat hij op de eettafel legde. 'Welkom thuis lieverd,' schreef hij, 'ze is dood en begraven, dat wijf van een Beckers, ik weet niet waar. Toch kom ik haar steeds weer tegen. Ik ga even in de heuvels wandelen om mijn hoofd leeg te maken. Reken niet op me voor het eten. Tot later, de Pool.'

Toen vertrok hij.

Hij liep de straat uit, de stad uit, de heuvels in. De zon scheen, het was een warme dag geweest, een van de laatste echt warme dagen van het jaar vermoedelijk, maar in de bossen tussen de bomen hing een aangename koelte. Vroeger, lang geleden, had hij hier gerend. Toen hij last kreeg van zijn knieën was hij met het rennen gestopt. Nu hij hier liep besefte hij wat hij had gemist, de schoonheid van de heuvels. Zo bewoonbaar en toch zo leeg, zo ontdaan van mensen. Hij zou het vaker moeten doen, wandelen. Na ruim twee uur gelopen te hebben besefte hij dat hij drinken had moeten meenemen maar hij was getraind op noodsituaties, hij zou het volhouden. Bovendien had hij een doel.

De Pool wandelde verder, kwam langs paarden, even meende hij de pony te zien of althans een dier dat erg op de pony van hun jongen leek. Hij bleef staan om naar het beest te kijken, het reageerde niet op zijn aanwezigheid. Hij riep het dier, probeerde het te lokken met geluiden en kooswoorden, maar het kwam niet en toen liep de Pool verder, op een eigenaardige manier teleurgesteld, tot hij eindelijk zijn bestemming bereikte. Het schemerde al maar de warmte was nog niet verdwenen. De Pool zweette.

Er hing een ouderwetse bel. Twee keer moest hij bellen. Eindelijk werd er opengedaan. Hij besefte dat hij verlegen voor deze grote oude deur stond maar zijn verlegenheid, zijn nietigheid waren geen raadsel voor hem. Ze waren er. Ze hoorden bij de verslagene die hij in het geheim was. Als hij al een dubbelleven had, als er al iets van het oude dubbelleven was overgebleven dan was het dit, dat hij een geheime verslagene was. De woorden van de vrouw van Beckers schalden in hem.

De man die de poort opendeed en voor hem stond had

een gezicht zoals veel mensen in deze omgeving. Zijn ogen waren bruin, zijn haar was vlassig, rechts van zijn neus zat een grote moedervlek en hij liep op sandalen. Vermoedelijk was de man een jaar of vijftig, misschien iets ouder.

Toen de Pool, die uit verlegenheid naar beneden keek, de voeten van de man beter zag constateerde hij dat er merkwaardige knobbels op de tenen groeiden. Het zag er behoorlijk gruwelijk uit. De tenen van de man waren misvormd, vrijwel alle tenen. Vooral de grote tenen.

'Wat kan ik voor u doen?' vroeg de man.

'Ik wil hier blijven.' Het spreken viel de Pool moeilijk omdat hij zo uitgedroogd was. Het leek alsof er spinnenwebben in zijn mond zaten en het web van de spinnetjes sterker was dan zijn kaken.

'De gastenverblijven zitten vol,' zei de man rustig en routineus, alsof hij het deze dag al twintig keer had gezegd. 'Volgende week hebben we weer plaats. Ik kan een reservering aannemen.'

'Ik kom niet voor de gastenverblijven. Ik wil toetreden.'

Er viel een stilte. De Pool hoorde vogels. Hij kuchte. Had hij het anders moeten zeggen? Andere woorden moeten gebruiken? Betere woorden?

'Dat is een grote beslissing,' zei de man bedachtzaam, 'die zou niemand intuïtief moeten nemen. Niet zomaar. Op een avond zoals deze. Zo'n mooie avond.' De man keek naar de hemel, hij wees naar de bomen, het gras. Alles bloeide nog. Het was inderdaad een mooie avond.

'Ik heb er lang over nagedacht,' zei de Pool. 'Ik kom hier niet onvoorbereid. Ik ben een eenvoudige man maar ik...' Hij maakte zijn zin niet af, hij keek naar de man, hij keek hem recht aan in de hoop dat deze man voor hem zou gaan praten. Dat hij de woorden uitsprak die de Pool niet kon vinden. Bidden had niet geholpen. God had hem geilheid gegeven, geen woorden.

De man keek alleen, vol verwachting leek het, en eindelijk zei hij: 'Het is laat, voor ons is het zelfs erg laat. De dag begint vroeg hier en de nacht ook maar kom even binnen. Wij sturen niemand weg. U wilt vast praten. Terwijl u zwijgend vermoedelijk dichter bij Hem komt. Wist u dat? Wij vragen niemand om te spreken, als mensen het niet kunnen laten dan luisteren wij.'

'Ik zwijg graag, zwijgen is mijn specialiteit.' De Pool liep door de poort achter de man aan, ze gingen meteen links en kwamen in een klein donker kamertje met een houten bureau. In een kast stonden twee ordners en enkele boeken. De Pool kon niet zien wat voor boeken.

Ze gingen zitten, tegenover elkaar. De Pool had dorst maar hij durfde niet om water te vragen. De dorst hoorde bij hem, hij was hier ook gekomen om de dorst te overwinnen.

'Ja ja,' zei de man, 'de zwijgers, ik heb ze hier vaker gehad. De mensen komen hier om de meest uiteenlopende redenen. Uit alle lagen van de bevolking komen ze naar ons toe. Niet alle redenen zijn goede redenen, dat zeg ik u meteen. Sommige mensen willen...' hij liet zijn stem dalen, 'monnikje spelen. Ze voelen zich aangetrokken tot het uniform. Dat is echter niet waarom ze hierheen moeten komen. Ze houden het hier dan ook niet lang vol. Het is het uniform dat trekt.' Hij glimlachte weemoedig alsof hij de aantrekkingskracht van het uniform begreep maar er toch boven stond.

'Ik ben brandweerman,' zei de Pool. 'Ik heb al een uniform.'

'Zolang ik hier ben is er nooit brand geweest. In de oorlog zaten hier de Duitsers en er zijn Engelse vliegtuigen neergeschoten. Maar brand, nee. Ik betwijfel of de brandweer overal mag komen. Een deel hier is niet voor iedereen toegankelijk, dat noemen we "het slot". De abt is ook praktisch. Hij wijst ons de weg. Iemand moet ons de weg wijzen, iemand moet ons vertellen waarheen we moeten gaan. Ook bij brand.'

De Pool knikte. Toen zei hij: 'Ik wil Hem ter verantwoording roepen, daarom ben ik gekomen en waar kan dat beter dan hier? Ik kan de mensen niet ter verantwoording roepen, de mensen zijn... Ik daag jullie God uit, als Hij van de mensen houdt, als Hij van mij houdt dan moet Hij dat maar eens laten zien, dan moet Hij...' De Pool maakte ook deze zin niet af, hij legde zijn handen op de houten tafel. De vader van de Pool hield veel van massief hout.

'Pas hier, na een tijd,' zei de man peinzend, alsof hij het nog nooit eerder had gezegd, wat toch niet het geval kon zijn, er moesten toch tientallen mensen hier zijn verschenen zoals de Pool en al die mensen zouden toch aan dezelfde tafel hebben gezeten, aan deze tafel, ze zouden vast dezelfde behoeftes hebben gehad, dezelfde vragen hebben gesteld, dezelfde erbarmelijkheid tentoon hebben gespreid. 'Pas hier heb ik ontdekt wat liefde is. Dat duurt even. Het heeft mij jaren gekost. God houdt van ons, je kunt Hem en Zijn liefde niet uitdagen. Dat is absurd. Je kunt het alleen ondergaan.'

De Pool bleef zwijgen want hij wist hier niets op te zeggen. Het zou ook kunnen omdat hij de vrouw van Beckers zag, dit keer als non. Ze wachtte merkwaardig genoeg nog steeds op de Fransman. Ze liep op de schoenen die ze speciaal voor hem in de uitverkoop had aangeschaft. Ze was betoverend.

'Je lichaam,' ging de man verder, 'mijn lichaam is niet meer van mij, het is van Hem. Hij bepaalt wat ermee gebeurt. Dat is een proces. Ook dat duurt even. De overgave heeft tijd nodig. De overgave vereist ook een offer maar na een tijd voelt het niet meer als offer. De mensen vragen nog wel: is het een offer? Nee, zeg ik, nee. Een bevrijding. U ziet een offer, ik zie bevrijding. Hier loopt iemand rond, een monnik, je hoeft alleen maar naar hem te kijken en je ziet wat liefde is. De blik van die man is zoiets ongelooflijks. Zo zacht. Zijn ogen. Zijn woorden. Als hij praat. Hij praat ook niet veel. Zijn lippen, zo teder.'

Er viel weer een stilte en de man tegenover de Pool veegde wat van tafel maar de Pool kon niet zien wat.

'Mijn lichaam is nooit van mij geweest,' zei de Pool. 'Ik heb geen idee van wie het is. Het zal wel van de maatschappij zijn, als brandweerman is je lichaam van de maatschappij. Het is natuurlijk de bedoeling dat je levend het brandende gebouw weer uit gaat, je gaat er levend in, je moet er weer levend uit. We gaan met z'n allen terug naar de kazerne. Dat is de bedoeling. Daar doen we alles aan. Dat staat voorop, zegt de ploegchef. Die zekerheid heb ik niet meer. Wat voor mij vooropstaat weet ik niet meer.'

De man knikte. Zijn vriendelijke ogen gingen door de ruimte, keken de Pool steeds wel even aan maar niet lang, nooit lang.

'Ik wilde een goede man zijn,' zei de Pool uiteindelijk. Want iemand moest hier toch praten? Dan zou hij het doen. Het was niet zijn specialiteit maar als het moest dan kon hij het wel. 'Dat is geen verlangen. Dat is iets anders. Ik ben tot de conclusie gekomen dat ik geen goede man ben. Geen goede vader. De vrouw van Beckers, u weet niet wie dat is, dat doet er ook niet toe, de vrouw van Beckers, dat moet volstaan, heeft mij doorzien. Zij heeft gezegd, de vrouw van Beckers, jij bent niets en je hebt niets te bieden. Dat is het voornaamste wat u over mij moet weten. En dat ik dus geen verlangens meer heb. Of misschien toch...'

De vogels waren te horen. Wat maakten ze veel lawaai, de vogels.

'U had het over uitdagen,' zei de man. 'Misschien moet u nadenken over dankbaarheid. Hoe zou die uitdaging eruit moeten zien? Onze sterfelijkheid is een detail. De sterfelijkheid zit de mensen zo in de weg. Maar het is een detail. De mensen kijken door het rietje van de sterfelijkheid naar het bestaan, geen wonder dat ze in de war raken.'

'Een detail?' vroeg de Pool.

'Onze sterfelijkheid. Wat wij aanzien voor sterfelijkheid. Ons lichaam. Het sterfelijke lichaam. We staren ons er blind op, we staren ons blind op dit leven.'

'De dood is een detail?' informeerde de Pool want hij vreesde het verkeerd te hebben begrepen en dan zou hij hier nooit worden toegelaten.

'De dood niet. Onze sterfelijkheid wel. Dat zijn twee verschillende dingen.'

'Ik begrijp het verschil tussen de sterfelijkheid en de dood niet. Waar sterfelijkheid is is de dood en waar de dood is is sterfelijkheid.'

De man knikte. 'Wij lezen hier heel veel maar we lezen altijd hetzelfde. Als we het boek uit hebben beginnen we opnieuw. En langzaam worden dingen duidelijk. Wat ik u wilde zeggen is: iedereen kan over dankbaarheid nadenken. Dat kan iedereen. Liefde begint met dankbaarheid. Zonder dankbaarheid zal de liefde ons altijd vreemd blijven.'

'Ik ben niet gekomen voor dankbaarheid.'

'De mensen komen hier voor dankbaarheid. Ze noemen het soms anders hoor. Ze geven er andere namen aan, de gekste namen, maar wij die hier wonen, wij die hier thuishoren, wij weten het, wij zien het, wij voelen het, ze komen voor de liefde die dankbaarheid is.'

'Nee dank u.'

'Niet iedereen die hier komt weet waarvoor hij komt. Dat moeten de bezoekers zelf ontdekken. Of ze weten het wel, onze gasten, de nieuwelingen, ze durven het alleen nog niet te zeggen.'

'Ik kom niet voor liefde. Ik heb liefde gekend. Te veel misschien wel.'

De man haalde zijn schouders op. 'U mag het woord onprettig vinden. U mag mijn overtuigingen onprettig vinden. Maar u bent hier gekomen. Wij hebben u niet geroepen. U hebt hier aangebeld. Wij vragen niet veel van onze gasten. Dat ze de stilte die om tien uur 's avonds begint respecteren. Dat ze één dienst per etmaal bijwonen.'

'Ik wil geen gast zijn. Daarvoor ben ik niet gekomen. Ik heb mijn situatie uitgelegd.' De Pool keek naar de tafel, hij vroeg zich af of ze die zelf hadden gemaakt en eindelijk zei de man: 'Ik raad u aan nu naar huis te gaan en als u over twee weken hetzelfde voelt als vandaag dan komt u nog eens terug. Dan is er vermoedelijk ook plaats in de gastenverblijven. Er is verlossing. Uw vermoeden is juist, als dat uw vermoeden is, maar als je hier lang bent dan ontdek je dat verlossing zoiets kleins is. Je ziet de verlossing zo makkelijk over het hoofd.' Hij liet met zijn vingers zien hoe klein, zo klein als een piepklein spinnetje.

Langzaam stond de Pool op en even geloofde hij echt dat hij nu weer naar huis zou gaan. Voor wandelen was het waarschijnlijk te laat, de duisternis zou hem overvallen. Hier in de buurt was vast wel een bushalte.

Maar terwijl hij daar stond, nog voor hij een stap had gezet besefte hij al dat het onmogelijk was, dat het hem fysiek onmogelijk was naar huis terug te keren, dat het onverstandig was, zelfs gevaarlijk. Er was geen thuis meer, voor zover het er ooit was geweest en hij liep om de tafel heen, niet naar de uitgang, naar de man. De zittende man. Hij ging naast hem staan en legde zijn handen, zijn grote handen om de keel van de man en de man verweerde zich niet, hij bleef zitten alsof niets in hem zich wilde verweren tegen de grote handen van de Pool, alsof de Pool zo het leven uit zijn tere lichaam mocht knijpen. Alsof dat zelfs goed was. De Pool zei zacht: 'U begrijpt het niet. Ik kan niet voor mezelf instaan, daarom ben ik gekomen. Ik heb om geilheid gesmeekt en ik heb moordlust gekregen.'

Hij liet de man los, deed een paar stappen naar achteren, leunde tegen de muur, de koude stenen muur. Nu had hij het verpest. Ze zouden hem niet toelaten. Hij had zich laten kennen als de eerste de beste schoft.

De man wreef even over zijn hals. Verbaasd leek hij niet te zijn. Misschien hadden ze hem vaker geprobeerd te wurgen. Hij draaide zijn hoofd naar de Pool, ging iets verzitten en zei: 'Geilheid? Daar moet u ook niet om vragen. Het gaat mij niets aan wat mensen vragen, ze mogen alles vragen, maar Hij is geen uitdeler. Hij deelt niets uit. Als u het mij persoonlijk vroeg zou ik zeggen: Hij heeft niets om uit te delen. En waarom vraagt u ook om geilheid? Wat moet u ermee? Als u erom moet vragen gelooft u er zelf toch niet in. Misschien bent u beter af zonder.'

Even leek het alsof de man pretoogjes had, al kon dat verbeelding zijn. De Pool stond nog altijd tegen de muur geleund. Hij kon niet naar huis, hij wist niet waar hij heen moest als dit gesprek beëindigd werd, waar hij heen kon, hoe hij de nacht zou doorbrengen.

'Ze zeggen dat Hij liefde is,' zei de Pool. 'Ik heb daar weinig van gemerkt.'

De man keek de Pool verbaasd aan. 'Dat u niet voor uzelf kunt instaan dat is als ik zo vrij mag zijn een goed teken. Bij het besef dat wij niet voor onszelf in kunnen staan, daar begint het inzicht.'

De Pool bleef tegen de muur leunen. Meer dan anders was hij zich bewust van zijn lengte en zijn verlegenheid. Hij had het leven uit de man kunnen knijpen, hij had het gekund. Het was niet moeilijk geweest. 'Ik ben aan de liefde ontkomen,' zei de Pool met een kalmte die hem zelf verbaasde, met een gemak dat hij niet van zichzelf kende, 'en anderen zijn aan mijn liefde ontkomen. Mijn jongen bijvoorbeeld, onze jongen. Wat ik nu zoek is de liefde waaraan je níét kunt ontkomen.'

De man ondersteunde zijn hoofd met een hand. Hij bleef zo zitten, met zijn hoofd tegen zijn linkerhand. De

Pool had het gevoel dat hij vergeten was, dat de ander niet meer wist dat hij, de Pool, hier ook was, maar uiteindelijk zei de zittende man: 'Zelfs als u een hond was zou ik u nu niet wegsturen.'

*Een brief*

**INTERMEZZO**

Waarde Abt,

Ten einde raad schrijf ik u, omdat u mij niet wilt spreken, zelfs niet door de telefoon. Terwijl ik weet dat u een telefoon hebt. En u zou mij kunnen zien, u moet mij hebben gezien, want ik ben vaak bij u geweest. Minstens één keer per week sta ik voor uw deur. Ik zie u wel maar u ziet mij niet, ik wenk u maar u doet alsof u mijn wenken niet ziet, daarom neem ik mijn toevlucht tot deze brief. Met tegenzin. Want ik had dit graag, zo vreselijk graag, recht in uw gezicht gezegd.

Een vriend helpt mij met deze brief, want ik ben niet zo'n schrijver, ik ben meer een prater, maar u wilde niet met mij praten. Nu moet ik schrijven en daarom heb ik de hulp gezocht van een goede bekende. Omdat ik zeker wil zijn dat u mij begrijpt, omdat ik mij geen vergissingen kan permitteren.

Leest u alstublieft zorgvuldig. Ik kan alles nader verklaren, als dat nodig is. Mijn hoop is dat u mij zult uitnodigen voor een gesprek nadat u deze brief hebt gelezen.

Meer dan een halfjaar zit mijn man nu bij u, mijn man die niet alleen mijn man is maar ook de vader van Jurek, mijn enige jongen. Mijn laatste jongen. Zeker een keer per week ben ik naar de dienst gegaan met mijn jongen, met onze jongen, om hem zijn vader te laten zien, opdat hij hem niet vergeet. Maar ook mijn man doet alsof hij ons niet ziet. Net als u. Hij zingt wel maar hij zingt niet voor ons en wij horen hem praten maar hij praat niet tegen ons. Hij kijkt weleens onze kant uit, maar dan kijkt hij recht door ons heen. En na afloop zeg ik tegen mijn jongen: 'Dat was papa. Heb je papa gezien?'

Onze jongen kijkt dan treurig, intens verdrietig. Hij zegt in zijn brabbeltaaltje dat hij niet begrijpt waarom papa niets heeft gezegd. 'Papa nou?' vraagt hij.

Die vraag wil ik u ook stellen: waar is hij?

Hij zit daar achter het gedeelte dat Het Slot heet en waar wij gewone mensen niet mogen komen. Wij leken. Wij burgers. Hij zit daar achter Het Slot, onzichtbaar voor ons.

De laatste tijd zien we hem helemaal niet meer, niet eens bij de dienst. We nemen plaats op de banken en we wachten, maar we zien hem niet.

De broeder die verantwoordelijk is voor de gasten en die me altijd vriendelijk te woord heeft gestaan zegt dat mensen een vrije wil hebben. Dat dit de genade van god is, dat de vrije wil niet absoluut is maar een cadeautje.

Een cadeautje. Wat een vreselijke cadeaus geeft god ons.

Ze kunnen komen en gaan, zegt de broeder die met de gasten mag spreken. Niemand hoeft te blijven, zeker in het begin niet. Maar ik zeg u, mijn man, de vader van mijn jongen, heeft geen vrije wil meer want als hij die had zat hij niet bij u, zonder ons iets te laten weten, zonder mijn jongen die zijn jongen is te erkennen. Hij heeft ons afgezworen en u kunt zich niet voorstellen hoeveel pijn dat doet.

Ik had gedacht dat ik alles aan zou kunnen na wat ons is overkomen maar dit is me te veel.

Als u de pijn kon voelen die ik voel, die mijn jongen voelt, onze jongen, dan zou u mijn man niet meer tolereren in uw gemeente. Dan zou u hem de deur wijzen. Dan zou u tegen hem zeggen: god wil jouw liefde niet.

Want volgens die broeder die met mij spreekt gaat het allemaal over liefde. Liefde, liefde en nog eens liefde. Ik kan het woord niet meer horen. Want heeft mijn jongen geen vader nodig? Is dat niet ook liefde?

De broeder die met mij spreekt, die mij aanhoort, nooit zegt hij 'nu moet u gaan', heeft mij verteld dat mijn man nu naar de naam Malechias luistert – maar hij heet geen

Malechias, ik weiger zijn nieuwe naam te erkennen, ik zal hem nooit Malechias noemen. En deze Malechias is een kluizenaar geworden en heeft zijn intrek genomen in een kippenhok. Dat we hem daarom niet meer zien bij de dienst, de laatste weken, omdat hij niet meer naar de dienst gaat. Hij komt alleen nog naar de keuken, zegt de broeder, en dan haalt hij het eten op in een pannetje en dan eet hij dat in het kippenhok op. En de volgende dag wast hij het vieze pannetje af en haalt dan in het schone pannetje weer eten en dat eet hij op in het kippenhok waar tegenwoordig geen kippen meer zitten, alleen hij, mijn man. En de broeder, die zo langzamerhand een vriend van me is geworden, zegt dat mijn man met helemaal niemand meer praat, dat zelfs de kippen hem zouden storen in zijn zoektocht naar eenzaamheid. Alleen god kan hij eigenlijk nog verdragen, mijn man. Dus we moeten het niet persoonlijk nemen. Zegt hij.

Dat hij daarom een kluizenaar is geworden, om dichter bij de liefde te zijn en vandaar het kippenhok.

'Het was geen vlucht,' zegt die broeder, 'want dan had de abt het niet toegestaan, we zijn niet zen, de stilte is geen doel. Het spreken kan ons ook dichter tot Hem brengen, als het maar geen spreken is om de stilte te vullen. Maar in de stilte kun je soms het "ja" van God horen en in de stilte hoort uw man een oorverdovend "ja" van God.'

Ik krijg die zinnen niet uit mijn hoofd. Ik maal. Ik heb nachtmerries.

Waarom hoort hij ons niet, mijn man?

De broeder zegt dat het een enkele keer vaker voorkomt dat een monnik zich afzondert van zijn broeders, dat er een paar jaar geleden een monnik was die zijn intrek had genomen in een leegstaande wasruimte en dat ook hij geen woord meer heeft gezegd, geen dienst meer heeft bijgewoond, hij was een en al liefde, hij woonde tussen de oude wasmachines. En de broeder zei: 'God is overal maar soms vinden mensen Hem op een specifieke plek.'

'In de leegstaande wasruimte?' vroeg ik.

'Ja,' zei de broeder. 'Ook daar.'

Met een vrouw had ik vrede gehad. Dan was ik verdrietig geweest, maar ik was verder gegaan. Wij waren verder gegaan. Met een kippenhok kan ik geen vrede hebben. Het lukt me niet. Begrijpt u dat?

Daarom blijven we naar de diensten komen om een glimp van hem op te vangen. Omdat we de hoop niet opgeven. Omdat ik tegen mijn jongen zeg: 'Misschien komt papa vandaag uit het kippenhok. Hij weet toch dat wij blijven komen, hij weet toch dat we daar zitten, in de kerk, om naar hem te kijken, om naar hem te luisteren, om zijn stem te horen, om te zien hoe hij zijn liefde verspilt? Misschien komt hij vandaag voor ons uit het kippenhok.' Dat zeg ik tegen mijn jongen.

Het spijt me dat ik het moet schrijven maar hij verspilt zijn liefde. Het is een grote verspilling wat daar gebeurt, als het al liefde is.

U zult dit misschien beledigend vinden. Ik ben niet gelovig maar ik wil niemand beledigen. De broeder zegt dat liefde nooit verspild is. Ik kan u alleen overtuigen als ik niet tegen u lieg. De broeder zegt ook: 'Onze vader-abt kan niet met u spreken.' Terwijl ik zo gesmeekt heb: 'Laat mij met de abt spreken, mijn man heeft mij nodig, hij is in de war.'

Ik zei tegen hem: 'Wij mensen zijn toch niet gemaakt om in kippenhokken te leven? En hij is zo groot, mijn man, hoe past hij in het hok? Hij moet daar dubbelgevouwen leven. Dat is toch geen leven?'

's Avonds in bed, in het lege bed, probeer ik me voor te stellen hoe mijn man in het kippenhok leeft. Het is afschuwelijk. Nooit heb ik hem gemist, nu mis ik hem. Wie heeft al die jaren naast me gelegen? Wie was dat? Was hij al met zijn gedachten in het kippenhok terwijl hij naast me lag?

Nooit heeft mijn man zich om uw god bekommerd, nooit heeft hij uw god genoemd, nooit heeft hij zich druk gemaakt om dergelijke aangelegenheden, ook niet toen onze oudste jongen om het leven is gekomen. Er kwam geen god aan te pas. Het is maar dat u het weet.

Waarde abt, ik heb gehoord dat u mensen uit uw klooster kunt verwijderen, dat u mensen in de ban kunt doen. Doet u mijn man in de ban. Ik smeek het u. Ik haat het om te smeken, maar nu moet het toch gebeuren. Ik ben van niets meer vies.

Als u de moeite neemt om bij ons aan te bellen, dan ziet u hoe wij langzaam kapotgaan.

Mijn man en ik zijn indertijd niet kapotgegaan, wij zijn sterk gebleven, wij zijn bij elkaar gebleven, na de dood van Borys, onze oudste, maar nu mijn man besloten heeft ons af te zweren, voor god mag weten wat, gaan wij kapot want ik begrijp het niet. En ik wil het niet begrijpen. Ik heb er geen vrede mee.

Als het een vrouw was geweest, had ik naar die vrouw kunnen gaan en ik had kunnen zeggen: 'Jij bent het dus.' En ik had tegen mezelf kunnen zeggen: Ze is mooier. Ze ruikt lekkerder. Ze heeft geen verdriet. Ik begrijp het. Of: Wat een lelijk kreng, wat een belediging dat hij me daarvoor verlaat.

Maar het kippenhok begrijp ik niet.

De broeder zegt dat hij een beetje gebukt loopt, anders dan anders, alsof het kippenhok altijd om hem heen zit. Dat het celibaat een voorwaarde is voor de eenwording met god. Is dat liefde? Dat een mens leeft alsof er een kippenhok om hem heen zit?

De broeder zegt: 'Het celibaat is een snelweg naar God, maar soms gebeuren er ongelukken op die snelweg, zoals op elke snelweg.'

Aan wat voor ongelukken moet ik denken? En als iemand dan al naar god moet, waarom via de snelweg als daar kennelijk zo veel ongelukken gebeuren?

Natuurlijk vraag ik me af of ik hem genoeg liefde heb gegeven, of ik hem zonder het te willen heb weggejaagd. Dat vraag ik me af, dat knaagt aan me, maar hoeveel liefde kun je een ander mens geven? Hoeveel liefde moet je een ander mens precies geven om ervoor te zorgen dat hij zich niet van je afkeert? En wat als hij die liefde niet wil, als de liefde hem alleen ergert, hem in de weg zit?

Stuurt u hem weg, mijn man. De broeder die mijn vragen beantwoordt zegt: 'Er zijn geheimen, ik kan u niet alles vertellen. Dit is een plek van de liefde.'

Vriendinnen zeggen: er zijn toch andere mannen. Zeker, die zijn er. Er zijn zoveel mannen.

Maar het is niet te verkroppen. Ik wil het niet verkroppen, en daarom wil ik geen andere man.

Niemand verdient het de rest van zijn leven in een kippenhok door te brengen, niemand verdient het te geloven dat dat hok een hok van de liefde is. Ik smeek u.

Hoogachtend,

Wen, de vrouw van de man in het kippenhok, de moeder van zijn zoon Jurek

# V

## *Terugkeer*

# 1

Ze deed open en aan haar gezicht zag hij dat ze schrok. Het was geen blijdschap die hij in haar ogen zag, eerder afgrijzen en dat had hij niet verwacht. Ze zei niets, ze staarde hem aan.

Hoe moest hij zich gedragen? Was zij nog zijn vrouw? Was dit zijn huis? Zou hij haar kussen? Een hand geven? Hij wist het niet zeker, al had hij vermoedens. Eindelijk deed zij iets. Ze pakte zijn hand en hield die vast alsof de hand een uit het nest gevallen vogeltje was. 'Ben je komen lopen?' vroeg ze.

'Ja,' zei hij.

'Zo droog is je hand. Zo ruw.' Zachtjes masseerde ze de hand. Toen keek ze naar zijn blote voeten. Nog altijd had ze niet gezegd dat hij binnen moest komen, waardoor hij het gevoel kreeg dat er een ander was. Er zat een andere man in zijn stoel. Er sliep een andere man in zijn bed. Als dat zo was zou hij weer weggaan. Niet terug naar het klooster, die poort was gesloten. Hij zou een flatje huren of tijdelijk in een vakantiehuisje gaan zitten. Hij kende gescheiden mannen die in een vakantiehuisje hun intrek hadden genomen en nooit meer waren weggegaan.

'Heb je een glas water voor me?' vroeg hij.

Vriendelijk maar toch ook streng trok ze hem naar binnen, zoals je een kind naar binnen trekt dat te lang buiten heeft gespeeld. Ze liet zijn hand los en sloot de deur. Daarna ging ze weg, ze liet hem staan in de vestibule en hij hoorde haar roepen: 'Papa is er. Papa is terug.' Haar stem verried meer opwinding dan haar gezicht.

Met de jongen op haar arm kwam ze naar hem toe. Het kind wendde zich van hem af. De Pool moest zijn veranderd, zijn toch al spaarzame haren waren nog spaarzamer geworden, de blik in zijn ogen was anders, hij had het zelf gezien, alsof hij terugkwam uit een oorlog zo keerde hij terug van de liefde van God. Alles aan hem was veranderd. Toen hij definitief had besloten God alleen te laten en terug te gaan naar zijn vrouw had hij goed in de spiegel gekeken.

Wen wilde de jongen aan hem geven, het kind begon te huilen, trappelde in de lucht. Daarop zette ze de jongen op de grond en hij snelde weg op zijn kleine beentjes. De Pool keek hem na, hij besefte dat hij van zijn overgebleven jongen hield. Het was geen gelukzalig gevoel. Voor de Pool was liefde onlosmakelijk verbonden met falen, waar liefde was faalde je en waar je faalde was soms ook liefde, alleen de pijnlijke tederheid van de Eeuwige groeide boven het falen uit.

'Het is je baard,' zei ze verontschuldigend. 'Hij is er niet aan gewend.'

Hij voelde aan zijn baard. 'Ik zal me scheren.' Hij besefte dat hij ontroering miste. Hij had zich er zo op verheugd, hij had ernaar uitgekeken, nu het eindelijk zover was voelde hij te weinig. Weer te weinig.

'Blijf je dan?' vroeg ze. 'Blijf je?' Nog altijd had ze niet gezegd: Kom verder. Omhelsd had ze hem ook niet. Ze bleven in de hal staan en een glas water had ze hem ook niet gegeven.

'Ja,' zei hij een beetje aarzelend, alsof hij niet wist of dat de bedoeling was: blijven, zijn taken hervatten, doen alsof er niets was gebeurd. 'Ja, ik blijf. Ik ben er weer.' Hij dacht: als het moet kan ik ook weggaan. Ik heb mijn plaats verspeeld. Ze had hem ingeruild. Dit vermoeden deed pijn al was er ook opluchting, zijn liefde voor God had haar geen kwaad gedaan, ze had vervanging voor de Pool gevonden. Hij wist nu wat hem te doen stond en bijna had hij dat ook gezegd: een goede man zet een stapje opzij als dat nodig is.

'Je stinkt,' zei ze.
'Ik ruik het niet.'
'Wanneer heb je voor het laatst gedoucht?'
'Ik waste me als het nodig was.'
'Heb je me nooit gezien? Ik ben zo vaak naar je toe gekomen, ik heb er zo vaak gezeten, met Jurek, onze jongen, jouw jongen, je hebt niet eens naar ons geknikt. Zelfs dat niet. We bestonden niet voor je. Wilde je ons niet zien?'
'Ik was bang.'
'Bang? Waarvoor?'
Hij leunde met een hand tegen de muur. 'Dat ik jullie iets zou aandoen.'
'Ons iets zou aandoen?' Ze haalde haar hand door haar haren, ze leek zich op te winden. 'Waarom zou je ons nog iets aandoen? Door weg te gaan heb je ons al genoeg aangedaan.'
'Heb je wat water voor me?'
Ze nam hem mee naar de keuken. De jongen zat op de grond met een brandweerauto te spelen en zijn moeder zei: 'Hij is er weer. Papa, lieverd. Dat is papa.' Haar stem sloeg over maar de jongen keurde hem geen blik waardig, hij speelde stug, bijna trots door met zijn auto.
'Hij kan nu lopen,' zei ze. 'Heb je het gezien? Hij was zo trots toen hij begon te lopen. Toen hij zijn eerste stapjes zette. Kijk.' Ze liet hem een foto zien die met een magneet aan de koelkast bevestigd was.
'Mooi,' antwoordde de Pool. 'Trots inderdaad.' Hij zou de jongen wel willen oppakken, hem aanraken, hem knuffelen, hem vertellen dat ook hij trots was dat Jurek nu kon lopen, maar hij durfde het niet. Hij wilde zich niet opdringen. De vader was ervandoor gegaan, hij zou wachten tot de jongen hem weer had geaccepteerd. Hij moest geduld hebben.
De Pool keek rond. Er was niet veel veranderd in de keuken en toch kon hij zich slechts met moeite herinneren

dat hij hier had gewoond, alsof het een ander was geweest die hier voor vader had gespeeld. Een andere man was hier met de sapcentrifuge op zijn hoofd geslagen.

'Kom ik eigenlijk gelegen?' vroeg hij.

'Natuurlijk,' zei ze. 'Natuurlijk kom je gelegen. Jij komt altijd gelegen. Jij bent toch mijn man? Wij horen toch bij elkaar?'

Ja, dat was hij, haar man, ze waren niet gescheiden. Desondanks wist hij het niet zeker.

Hij leunde tegen het aanrecht. 'Je hebt op me gewacht? Er is geen ander? Ik zou het begrijpen hoor. Ik heb jullie in de steek gelaten.'

'Er is geen ander,' ze klonk resoluut, 'wat denk je dat ik heb gedaan, wat wij hebben gedaan? We hebben op je gewacht. Wat hadden we moeten doen? Welke keus liet je ons? Hadden we je moeten vergeten? Hadden we moeten doen alsof je er nooit was geweest?'

Eindelijk omhelsde ze hem. Het voelde goed en tegelijkertijd bedenkelijk. Vergeleken met zijn fantasieën over de omhelzing kon de omhelzing zelf alleen tegenvallen. Hij vroeg zich af waarom hij geen wroeging voelde. Waar was de wroeging? Waar bleef ze? Hij was teruggekomen om een schuld in te lossen, de schuld was sterker gebleken dan de liefde van God. Voor hij verder over liefde en schuld kon nadenken liet zijn vrouw hem weer los. 'Je stinkt echt enorm, je moet in bad. Het is niet te harden. Heeft daar niemand iets van de stank gezegd?'

Hij schudde zijn hoofd.

'Hoe je er ook uitziet. Zo verwaarloosd. Zo...' Ze wendde zich tot hun jongen en ze zei: 'Kom, we gaan papa wassen.' Alsof de vader alleen een extra kind was, een verloren zoon.

Zijn vrouw pakte zijn hand en leidde hem de trap op. 'Ik had eigenlijk de hoop opgegeven. Je had je intrek genomen in een kippenhok, vertelden ze in het klooster.'

Hij knikte in gedachten verzonken en hij zag nog net dat de jongen achter hen aan de trap op kwam geklauterd.

In de badkamer begon ze aan zijn pij te trekken. 'Mijn god, had je niet je eigen kleren kunnen aandoen voor je hier kwam?'

'Ik had niets meer.'

'Je had niets meer?'

'Nee, niets.'

'En je huissleutels?'

'Heb ik ook niet meer.'

'Ik heb nog wel reservesleutels. Dit is toch jouw huis?' Het klonk alsof ze het zelf nu ook niet meer zeker wist. Van wie was dit huis? Van wie was deze man die eerder verloren zoon dan echtgenoot was? Ze vroeg aan haar jongen: 'Ben je blij dat papa er weer is?'

De jongen stond bij de deur van de badkamer. Zijn blijdschap deed aan vrees denken, aan een angstig, noodlottig vermoeden.

Eindelijk lukte het haar hem de pij en een wollen hemd dat hij daaronder droeg uit te trekken. Toen stond hij voor haar in zijn ondergoed. Verlegen was hij niet, wel onwennig. Alsof hij voor het eerst weer naakt voor haar stond, alsof haar ogen hem de allereerste keer aftastten.

'Deze onderbroek ken ik niet,' zei ze. En toen: 'Wat is er met je bovenlijf gebeurd? Al die wonden... Ik zie zelfs pus.'

'Ja, ach, pus. Dat gaat zo weer weg.' Even streelde hij haar haren. Ze had ze iets korter geknipt.

'Hoelang heb je erover gedaan?' vroeg ze. 'Ben je komen lopen?'

'Ik heb onderweg uitgerust. Ik ben lopend naar... ik ben er lopend heen gegaan, ik wilde ook lopend bij Hem vandaan.'

Ze kamde met haar vingers zijn baard alsof ze de klitten eruit wilde halen en hij zei nog een keer: 'Ik zal me scheren.'

Toen draaide ze hem teder om. 'Jezus, wat hebben ze met je gedaan?' Ze voelde voorzichtig over zijn rug. 'Met wat hebben ze je bewerkt? Met gloeiende stangen?' In de deuropening stond de jongen en hij zag alles.

De vader ging op de rand van de badkuip zitten en hij zei rustig: 'Er bestaat liefde die niet van deze wereld is.' Meteen veerde hij weer op, ging naar de wastafel, dronk wat water, de dorst was niet te harden. En zij stond achter hem en voelde zachtjes aan zijn rug. Ze vroeg: 'Heeft er een dokter naar gekeken? Wat hebben ze in godsnaam met je gedaan?' Ze ging met de rug van haar hand teder over zijn lichaam, zijn schouders, zijn onderrug en hij dronk nog meer water. Hij had zo'n dorst.

'Je nek,' zei ze, 'je nek zit scheef lijkt het. Is dat ook van het kippenhok?' Het klonk alsof ze boos was op het kippenhok.

Hij schudde zijn hoofd en ging weer op de rand van de badkuip zitten. 'Je hebt zijn deur toch nooit opengedaan?' vroeg hij. 'De kamer van onze jongen, daar ben je toch nooit geweest?'

'Nee,' ze liet het bad vollopen, 'daar zijn we nooit geweest. Daar hadden we niets te zoeken.'

Hij zag hoe ze naar Jurek keek die bij de deur stond als een nieuwsgierig en ook angstig diertje. 'Het is echt je baard,' zei ze, 'hij herkent je niet door de baard.' Met haar hand voelde ze of het water de juiste temperatuur had. Ze deed er douchegel en badzout in en zei: 'Trek je onderbroek uit, dan zullen we je wassen. Daarna zal ik eten voor je maken. Je zult wel honger hebben.' En opnieuw leek ze bevangen te worden door onzekerheid: 'Je blijft toch?'

Hij knikte. 'De honger valt mee.' Hij stond op, deed zijn onderbroek uit en stapte in bad.

'Jezus, je billen, wat hebben ze daarmee gedaan? Ben je in prikkeldraad gaan zitten?'

Langzaam liet hij zich in het water zakken, het warme

water deed hem pijn en weer mompelde hij: 'Er is een liefde die niet van deze wereld is.'

'Nee, dat is geen liefde, dat is een pak slaag.' Ze pakte een washandje en begon de Pool voorzichtig te wassen, desondanks kon hij af en toe niet verhullen dat de washand hem pijn deed. 'Die wondjes,' zei ze. 'Wat is dat toch? Is het eczeem? Heb je jezelf gekrabd?'

Hij sloot zijn ogen. 'Ik heb mezelf gekrabd,' zei hij, 'ik had last van jeuk, zij hebben me ook gekrabd, bewerkt... Wat wij onder liefde verstaan, onze strelingen... onze tederheid... dat is geen liefde, dat is... commercie. Tijdverdrijf. Grappenmakerij. Frivoliteit. God heeft ons lief met het zwaard, het vuur, de zweep en het prikkeldraad. Zijn vertegenwoordigers op aarde, zij weten hoe het moet...' Nu opende de Pool zijn ogen en hij zag de gefronste blik van Wen.

'Nou ja,' reageerde ze, 'ik volg je niet helemaal. Je zult ook wel moe zijn. Het moet voor jou ook verwarrend zijn. Leg het later een keer aan me uit. Als je rustig bent.' Ze krabde aan een korstje op zijn arm. 'We hoopten zo op een teken als we daar zaten, op één enkel teken maar je hebt ons nooit gezien.'

Hij probeerde zich te ontspannen in het water en zij ging met een washandje over zijn armen, alsof ze zelf niet meer wist hoe ze hem moest wassen zonder hem pijn te doen. Ook waste ze zijn voeten. Vooral daar was ze even mee bezig. 'Wat een eelt. Dat moet je er later afschrapen. Van dat prikkeldraad en het zwaard moet ik echt niets hebben. Sorry. Ik kan er niet tegen.'

'Nee, de mensen zijn er niet klaar voor.' Hij haalde diep adem, hij voelde zijn ribben, zijn buikspieren. 'Heb je contact gehad met de brandweer?' vroeg hij.

'In het begin wel. De Beckers zijn verhuisd.' Ze waste zijn oksels en zijn gezicht en nog een keer probeerde ze de viezigheid tussen zijn tenen weg te halen. 'Je bent zo verschrikkelijk vies. Ik heb nog nooit iemand gezien die zo vies is als jij. De geur ook die om je heen hing. Financieel was het niet makkelijk. Ik heb moeten praten als Brugman. Als-ie ziek is is-ie thuis, zeiden ze bij de gemeente. Maar je was niet thuis. Je was in het klooster.'

'Ik was ook niet ziek.'

'Nou, ik heb mijn uiterste best gedaan iedereen ervan te overtuigen dat je wel ziek was, dus ik zou dat nu niet gaan ontkennen en als ik zo naar je lichaam kijk ziet het er ook behoorlijk ziek uit.'

Jurek kwam iets dichterbij. 'Dit is papa,' zei Wen, 'kun je je papa nog herinneren? Zeg eens iets tegen papa.'

Met half toegeknepen ogen, vanwege het water dat over zijn gezicht droop, glimlachte de Pool naar de jongen, hij stak zelfs een hand uit, die de jongen ontweek.

'Hij was zo gewend met me alleen te zijn.' Ze verdween, de jongen ging achter haar aan en ze kwam terug met een grote, blauwe handdoek. Een handdoek die hij niet kende.

'Nieuw?' vroeg hij.

'Ja, ik heb nieuwe handdoeken gekocht. Stap er maar uit. Je bent een tijd weg geweest, het was niet een weekje. Ik heb hier veel vernieuwd.'

Hij deed wat hem was opgedragen. 'Een jaar,' zei hij. 'Bijna een jaar.'

Ze droogde hem af alsof ze zijn moeder was. 'Weet je eigenlijk hoe wij het hier hebben gehad? Hoe wij hier hebben moeten leven. Terwijl jij... met jouw liefde bezig was.'

'Nee,' antwoordde hij en dat was de waarheid. Hij wist het niet, hij was elders geweest met zijn gedachten, zijn gebeden, zijn lichaam.

Ze bleef hem afdrogen, steeds hardhandiger, alsof ze hem pijn wilde doen, alsof ze hem wilde laten zien dat zij hem ook pijn kon doen, dat hij daarvoor echt niet naar het klooster had gehoeven. Hij wilde zeggen dat hij daar niet ordinaire pijn had ontvangen, dat de liefde die pijnigt iets radicaal anders is. Hij durfde het niet te zeggen. Beter zo min mogelijk uitleggen.

'Je moet niet bang zijn,' zei ze tegen Jurek, 'dit is geen vreemde meneer. Dit is papa.'

Hij keek in de spiegel terwijl ze hem afdroogde. 'Ik zal me weer melden bij de brandweer, ik moet aan het werk.'

Daarop zei ze niets, ze pakte alleen een onderbroek, eentje van vroeger, een blauwe, als een kleine jongen stapte hij erin. 'Zo,' zei ze, 'ik zal je rug en je billen insmeren met wat vette zalf, ik denk dat het toch goed is als een dokter ernaar kijkt.'

Ze smeerde hem in en hij kon zich niet aan de indruk onttrekken dat hij een vreemde voor haar was, dat hij altijd een vreemde was geweest, al smeerde ze hem nu liefdevol in, al behandelde ze zijn wonden. Dat deden verpleegkundigen ook. Ze stonden voor de spiegel en toen draaide ze hem om, ze pakte een nagelschaartje en zei: 'Als die baard weg is dan weet hij weer wie je bent.'

'Hij zal wel boos zijn,' zei de Pool. 'Dat begrijp ik. Het heeft tijd nodig. Ik heb hem verwaarloosd. Ik heb veel mensen verwaarloosd.'

'Je bent er weer, daar gaat het nu om.'

Hij ging op de rand van de badkuip zitten en met het schaartje knipte ze zijn baard. 'Dat die baard zo lang kan worden.' Ze leek in gedachten verzonken. 'In het begin hebben mensen naar je gevraagd. Collega's zijn langs geweest maar toen bekend werd dat je in een kippenhok woonde, ja toen werden mensen argwanend. Ik had je ziekgemeld. Er zijn hier allerlei mensen geweest, bedrijfsartsen, ambtenaren, die wilden van alles weten en toen ik ze vertelde dat je in een kippenhok woonde – ze wisten het stiekem allang, iedereen wist het, dat soort dingen blijven niet geheim – toen heb ik hemel en aarde bewogen, ik heb Borys erbij gehaald en toen zeiden ze: ja we houden het op ziek, tijdelijk arbeidsongeschikt. Zij mochten ook niet naar binnen bij het klooster. De abt hield iedereen bij je vandaan, zelfs de bedrijfsartsen.'

Ze bleef knippen.

'Onze vader-abt is een wijs man.' Hij zuchtte. Was hij teruggekomen om zich te verantwoorden? Om verhalen te vertellen over gebeurtenissen die hij zelf niet begreep? Hij keek naar de haartjes die op de grond vielen. 'Vind je het fijn dat ik er weer ben?' vroeg hij.

'Wij hebben zo op je gewacht. Wat denk je zelf?' Hij keek naar de jongen die nu met een grote brandweerwagen in de deuropening van de badkamer stond. 'Ik zal even moeten wennen,' ging ze verder. 'Ik weet niet wie ik heb teruggekregen.'

'Ik lijk op de oude Pool.'

'De rest moet je scheren.' Ze borg het nagelschaartje op en ging voor hem staan met haar armen over elkaar. 'Ik heb zo vaak nagedacht dat ik bang werd dat ik ging malen. Wat zoekt hij daar, vroeg ik me steeds weer af. Straft hij ons? Straft hij mij? Je hoeft het me nu niet te vertellen, ooit wil ik het weten, zodat ik er vrede mee kan hebben.'

Hij ging voor de spiegel staan, ze gaf hem een scheermesje. 'Het klinkt raar,' zei hij, 'maar ik kon hier niet meer blijven, ik ben daarheen gegaan om weer levend te worden. God is niet anders dan het leven en ik was niet meer levend.'

'Levend?' Ze bukte zich en zei tegen het kind: 'Omdat papa zoveel van je houdt is hij teruggekomen.' Ze bleven naar hem staan kijken terwijl hij zijn gezicht inzeepte, zijn vrouw en zijn zoon, en hij meende te zien wat zij zagen, dat hij oud was geworden. Het is de liefde die oud maakt, overwoog hij, de liefde die niet van deze wereld is. En toen zijn gezicht was ingezeept begon hij zich te scheren, langzaam en grondig. Hij had het zo lang niet gedaan dat hij een nieuw scheermesje nodig had, hij zeepte zich nog een keer in en herhaalde het proces. 'Het zijn stugge haren.'

Wen zei: 'Ik moet het nu toch weten. Wat heb je daar gedaan? Ben je weer gaan leven? Was je bij mij niet levend genoeg? Heeft het geholpen?'

Hij keek opzij. Ze klonk zo boos, zo vol verwijten. Altijd falen, wat je ook deed, overal faalde je. Hij herhaalde: 'Ik was bang dat ik jullie iets zou aandoen. Dat ook. Ik wilde even niet meer onder de mensen zijn.'

'Jij zou ons toch nooit iets aandoen.' Met een handdoek verwijderde ze het scheerschuim van zijn gezicht en toen tilde ze de jongen op en drukte hem tegen zich aan. De jongen bleef zwijgen, zijn gezichtsuitdrukking was neutraal.

'Ik zal iets voor je in de pan gooien.' Ze zette de jongen op de grond, hij liep achter haar aan naar de slaapkamer en daar haalde ze kleren uit de kast, die precies op dezelfde plek hingen waar ze een jaar geleden ook hadden gehangen. Toen hij in zijn spijkerbroek stapte zei ze: 'Je bent afgevallen. Ik zal ervoor zorgen dat je weer aankomt.'

'Ik eet geen vlees.'

Ze bleef staan. 'Sinds wanneer?'

Hij haalde zijn schouders op, trok de riem strakker zodat zijn broek niet zou afzakken.

Ze gingen naar beneden, het kind, zijn vrouw en hij en in de keuken vroeg ze: 'Wat zal ik voor je maken? Je hield altijd zo van vlees.' Ze streelde zijn wang. 'Zacht,' zei ze. 'Die baard was niets. Die stond je ook niet, hij maakte je zo oud. Zo treurig, je bent geen treurige man. Nooit geweest. Je bent een stille man. Wat zal ik voor je maken?'

'Wat niet te veel moeite is. Ik eet ook geen vis.'

'Dan maak ik pasta.' Hij bekeek de tuin. 'Heb je ons gemist?' vroeg ze. 'Waren wij in je gedachten? Wat voelde je als je aan ons dacht?'

Zonder zich om te draaien antwoordde hij: 'Jullie waren in mijn gedachten ja. Dat is wat ik voelde.'

Ze begon met koken en het kind zat stil met de brandweerwagen op de grond. 'De tuin,' zei hij, 'die staat er mooi bij.'

Ze knikte, ze sneed champignons en ze merkte op: 'Nou ja, alles staat in bloei. Ik maak spaghetti met romige champignonsaus.' Hij antwoordde, kijkend naar de tuin: 'Ik hou van jullie, ik ben niet gemaakt voor de liefde maar ik geef niet op.'

Ze kookte de spaghetti, bereidde romige champignonsaus in een pannetje en kondigde tevens een wat ze noemde 'simpele salade' aan, terwijl de jongen zo lief met zijn brandweerwagen op de grond zat. Zo stil, zo braaf.

Na een tijdje, toen ze de spaghetti had afgegoten in een zeef in de gootsteen, draaide ze zich abrupt om en zei: 'Hou me vast.'

Hij hield haar vast.

'Je ruikt nu veel beter.' En ze vroeg: 'Hou je nog wel van míjn vlees?'

Even herinnerde hij zich het kippenhok, toen fluisterde hij in haar oor: 'Ja, nu weet ik jouw vlees pas goed te appreciëren.'

'Het is weer van jou,' fluisterde ze, alsof de jongen dit inderdaad niet mocht horen, alsof hij alles mocht horen alleen dit niet. 'Je hebt dat kippenhok achter je gelaten, is het niet?'

Hij zweeg.

'Ik heb zin in je,' zei ze nog steeds fluisterend, 'we gaan ons niet levend begraven. Je bent niet meer in het kippenhok, lieverd. Je bent hier bij mij. Bij mijn vlees.'

'Het kippenhok,' zei hij. 'Ja, dat is voorbij.'

'Je bent klaar met die god van jou. Die is voorbij.'

'Ik heb me losgerukt,' zei de Pool.

Ze verdeelde de spaghetti over de borden. Een klein bordje voor de jongen. Een kinderbordje, met aapjes erop. Ook dat bord was nieuw.

'Wil je wat champignonsaus erbij? Of alleen boter en kaas?' vroeg ze aan de jongen.

'Boter kaas,' zei de jongen, 'lekker kaas.' Hij had nog altijd geen woord met de Pool gewisseld.

Zijn vrouw deed wat boter en geraspte kaas op de spaghetti in het kinderbordje en het drong tot de Pool door dat zijn terugkeer net zo intuïtief was geweest als zijn vertrek maar hij zou gehoor geven aan zijn intuïtie zoals hij dat ook toen had gedaan.

Ze aten in stilte. Pas toen ze klaar was, toen haar bord helemaal leeg was, zei zij: 'Ik zou toch graag weten hoe je aan die wonden komt. Ik bedoel, je bent mijn man. De vader van mijn kind. Mijn kinderen.'

Hij keek naar zijn eten. 'Hoe groter de liefde, hoe groter de wond.'

'O,' ze keek naar zijn bord, 'heb je geen honger?'

'Ik ben niet meer gewend zoveel te eten.'

Ze begon met het opstapelen van de borden. 'Was onze liefde niet genoeg? Heb ik je te weinig wonden gegeven?'

Hij aarzelde, veegde met het papieren servet over zijn mond. 'Onze liefde was van deze wereld.'

Hij bracht de slabak naar de keuken. 'Ik breng hem naar bed,' zei zij, 'ik ga zijn tanden poetsen en hem voorlezen. Wacht eventjes hier. Hij moet nog aan je wennen, het is een grote omschakeling voor zo'n jongen.'

En hij wachtte in de keuken terwijl Jurek werd voorgelezen, zijn Jurek. Hij ging niet zitten, bleef staan, bladerde wat door een krant van twee dagen geleden. Toen hij onrustig werd ging hij naar de gang, hij hoorde zijn vrouw boven voorlezen en eindelijk kwam ze de trap af. Ze ging bij hem staan. 'Hij slaapt,' zei ze. 'Ik ben zo blij dat jij er weer bent. Ben jij ook blij? Ik ben onzeker geworden. Ik weet niet meer wat ik zie. Zie ik blijdschap of juist niet?'

Hij knikte. 'Ik ben nooit zo goed geweest in blijdschap. Maar ik ben teruggekomen, daar gaat het om. Vind je niet?'

Ze gooide de overgebleven sla in de afvalbak. 'Waarom dan? Miste je ons? Miste je ons zoals wij jou misten?'

Hij dacht na. 'Ik hoorde jullie stemmen. Tijdens het bidden en het werken. En werken is bidden, bidden is werken.'

'O,' zei ze weer. Als hij iets probeerde uit te leggen van wat hij daar had meegemaakt zei ze voornamelijk: 'O.'

'Ik hoorde eigenlijk vooral jouw stem en toen wist ik dat ik bij jullie hoorde, na een tijd twijfelde ik er niet meer aan. Dat ik daar weg moest, dat ik daar niet op mijn plaats was. Dat ik me moest losrukken.'

'Wat hoorde je dan?'

'Je praatte.'

'En wat zei ik?'

Hij ging met zijn hand over zijn hoofdhuid. 'Dat het mijn schuld was.'

'Wat?'

'Hoe jij eraan toe was.'

'En daarom ben je teruggekomen?'

'Ja. Je zei dat ik je kwelde.' Hij was even stil, zocht naar woorden. 'Onze vader-abt zei dat we God niet kunnen vervangen maar dat we ook weer niet te bescheiden moeten zijn en op een gegeven moment begreep ik dat ik te bescheiden was geweest, daar in dat kippenhok. En toen begon ik jouw stem te horen.' Hij aarzelde even. 'Er is geen verschil tussen het hemelse en het aardse, de ziel en het lichaam, dat zijn valse aannames.'

'Aannames?'

'Ja. Als de ziel lijdt, lijdt het lichaam.'

'O,' zei ze, 'ik kan die abt van jou niet uitstaan, weet je dat? Ik spuug op hem.' En ze zoende hem alsof ze op de abt spoog door haar man te zoenen. Eindelijk zoende ze hem.

Het beviel hem matig dat ze op alles spoog waarvan hij hield, de pony, de vrouw van Beckers, de abt. Misschien was ook dat liefde, dat je spoog op de zaken waarvan je echtgenoot hield omdat je al zijn liefde voor jou alleen wilde. Terwijl hij juist twijfelde aan die liefde.

Ze nam hem mee naar boven. 'Ik had je niet verwacht, anders had ik me mooi voor je aangekleed. Ik heb mijn benen niet geschoren maar dat maakt jou niets uit, toch? Ik ben eigenlijk altijd klaar voor je. Ik heb onze jongen nooit laten blijken... Hij heeft niets gemerkt van mijn wanhoop. Ik heb zo vaak gemasturbeerd en aan je gedacht. Hoe je mij nam.' Ze zoende hem weer. Hij zoende terug. Hij was dat niet meer gewend om zo te zoenen, hij had het zwaard en het prikkeldraad leren kennen, maar hij had zich losgerukt. Hij was de man die zich had losgerukt.

'Vroeger deed je dat nooit, vroeger miste je me nooit.'

'Nee,' zei ze, 'maar vroeger was je er. Ik dacht: als ik vaak genoeg masturbeer en aan je denk dan kom je terug, dan merk je dat ik je nodig heb. Ik riep je terwijl ik masturbeerde.' Ze ging met haar handen over zijn buik, zijn borst.

'Ik had mijn lichaam aan de Heer gegeven. Ik hoorde in het begin niets anders dan de stem van God. Daarom ben ik ook in dat kippenhok gaan wonen. Ik was Malechias. Wat riep je dan?'

Ze ging op het bed liggen met haar kleren en schoenen aan. 'Zo lag ik,' zei ze. En dan riep ik: "Pool, kom terug. Kom terug, Pool, alsjeblieft, kom terug."' Ze bleef even liggen, keek hem aan, hoe hij daar stond, in kleren die hem niet meer helemaal pasten. Hij vroeg zich af wat ze zag. Kon je aan hem zien wat hij had meegemaakt? Dat hij iets had leren kennen waarover hij niet kon spreken? Nu niet althans, misschien nooit.

Ze stond op, drukte hem tegen de kast. 'Ik dacht,' zei ze, 'als ik vaak genoeg masturbeer dan drijven we hem uit, die god van je, ik dacht zelfs aan de winterpeen. Ik wist dat ik ondankbaar was geweest, ik had blij moeten zijn met de winterpeen die je in me stopte.'

'De winterpeen,' mompelde hij. 'Dat is lang geleden.'

Ze streelde over zijn gladde wang, hij voelde hoe de huid nog prikte. 'Wat moet er van ons worden?' vroeg ze.

‘Wat moet er nu van ons worden, lieve Pool?’

Hij liet zich strelen, hij had haar tegen zich aan willen drukken, hij durfde nog niet, hij kon het nog niet.

‘Ik weet niet. We zijn sterk.’

‘Dit,’ zei ze, ‘dit moet er van ons worden.’ Ze begon zich uit te kleden. ‘Ik denk, hoe raar dat ook klinkt, dat ik hem heb uitgedreven, jouw god, door hier elke dag te masturberen. Ik heb geen dag overgeslagen, ook als ik niet in de stemming was, zo heb ik je geroepen en daarom heeft onze jongen nu weer een vader. Ik heb hem uitgedreven, die god van je.’

Hij stond daar, aarzelend, op zijn sokken, schoenen had hij nog niet aangetrokken en hij wist niet wat hij moest doen. Na al die maanden moest hij weer wennen aan liefde die wél van deze wereld was, de dagelijkse liefde die gepaard ging met tanden poetsen en een wekker in plaats van het beieren van de klokken, de dagelijkse liefde die gepaard ging met zijn lieve vrouw.

‘De broeder die ons te woord stond vertelde dat er diverse wegen zijn naar God, dat het celibaat slechts een snelweg is en dat er weleens ongelukken op die snelweg gebeuren. Zijn er ongelukken gebeurd? Heb jij een ongeluk gehad op die snelweg, lieve Pool?’

Ze had alleen nog haar panty en haar beha aan, haar schoenen. Ze ging door de knieën en knoopte zijn broek open alsof ze het ongeluk dat hij op de snelweg had gehad wilde onderzoeken. Ze wilde het bekijken, ze wilde het bestuderen.

‘Ik kan me van ongelukken niets herinneren,’ antwoordde hij, ‘maar God heeft me aangeraakt, als je dat bedoelt. Dat wel. Dat mag je een ongeluk noemen.’

‘O,’ ze giechelde ongemakkelijk terwijl ze met zijn ballen speelde. ‘Ik vind god onnozel.’

‘Misschien is Hij dat.’ Hij voelde dat hij een erectie kreeg, dat hij zin had om zijn vrouw te nemen, hard en meedogenloos, zoals God dat kon zijn.

Vervolgens nam ze zijn geslachtsdeel in haar mond. Ze pijpte hem met een overgave en een fanatisme die hem bijna pijn deden. Nog even dacht hij aan de andere liefde, aan visioenen, aan de psalmen, aan de zachtaardige abt die hem het bloed had laten drinken en hem het vlees liet eten. Ze haalde zijn geslachtsdeel uit haar mond en vroeg of god dat ook weleens bij hem had gedaan, of hij hem zo had verwend, die god van hem met zijn liefde die niet van deze wereld was, en hij zei dat dit niet het geval was, dat had hij niet gedaan. 'Dit zal hem dan wel jaloers maken,' zei ze, 'dat ik nu je ballen en je pik lik. Wat moet die god van je nu nijdig zijn, wat zal hij zich afgewezen voelen. Vernederd.'

'Het is aan ons om God te verwennen,' zei hij, leunend tegen de klerenkast, 'God wil verwend worden.' Ze likte verder en hij vroeg zich af of zijn vrouw gelijk had, of dit God jaloers zou maken. Zou God jaloers zijn? In de pijn kon de goddelijke extase zich openbaren, zoveel had hij geleerd maar over jaloezie was hij weinig te weten gekomen.

Toen stond ze op. Er zat speeksel om haar mond, een haartje zag hij, van hem vermoedelijk. 'Je smaakt anders,' zei ze. 'Dat geeft niets.' Ze verwijderde het haartje.

Ze draaide zich om en trok haar onderbroek uit. 'Weet je nog?' vroeg ze, 'van die winterpeen? Weet je dat nog?'

'Ja. Dat weet ik nog.'

'Neem me daar.'

Hij aarzelde, ze moest hem hebben zien aarzelen. Ze zei: 'Neem me in mijn onvruchtbare plek.'

'Je onvruchtbare plek?'

'Ik wil dat je mijn onvruchtbare plek uitwoont.'

'Ik vind je vruchtbare plek ook prima. Ik heb daar nooit problemen mee gehad.'

Ze pakte zijn hoofd. 'Ik wil dat je de stront uit me neukt. Zo laten we hem zien dat wij hier alles met elkaar doen, alles, wat we maar willen en dat hij niets met jou heeft gedaan, niets, en dat hij niets met jou zal doen. Ik heb gewonnen, ik heb van die god van jou gewonnen, hij krijgt jou nooit meer te pakken. Ik heb hem klein gekregen. Zoals andere mensen een hondenallergie hebben of een kattenallergie, zo ben ik allergisch voor god. En geloof me, vanaf vandaag is hij allergisch voor mij.'

Zei ze dat om hem op te winden? Of meende ze het? 'Je hoeft niet te laten zien dat we hier alles met elkaar doen, dat je gewonnen hebt. Het is voorbij, ik ben weer terug.'

Ze ging tegen de kast staan, de klerenkast waarin hun kleren waren opgeborgen, waarin ook de zijne nog hingen, de kleren van een dode die was opgestaan, waarin haar enige cocktailjurk hing die ze ooit had gekocht voor een feest dat haar uiteindelijk was tegengevallen. 'Doe het,' drong ze aan.

'Ik wil je geen pijn doen.' Met zijn broek op de knieën stond hij in zijn oude slaapkamer. Als dit bij zijn terugkeer hoorde, als hij dit moest doen om weer te worden opgenomen in het gezin dan was hij daartoe bereid. Al was de overgang groot. Het gevoel dat hij een dienst miste bekroop hem, het bidden, het knielen, het zat nog als een reflex in hem.

'Laat zien dat we van die sukkelige god van jou gewonnen hebben,' zei ze. 'Wrijf je pik over mijn kont en steek hem dan in één keer naar binnen. Ik kan ook wel wat pijn hebben. Ik ben echt niet kleinzielig.'

Hij wilde zeggen dat God, wat je verder van hem mocht denken, toch niet iemand was van wie je kon winnen en zeker niet door je pik in de kont van je echtgenote te steken, al was dat volstrekt normaal in deze tijd, alleen hij had weinig meer dan een winterpeen in haar kont gestoken maar dat kwam doordat de Pool een verlegen man was die jarenlang tevreden was geweest met haar vagina en haar mond, tot het noodlottige ongeluk van hun oudste jongen. Tevreden, dat was het woord. Misschien was die tevredenheid oppervlakkig, op een eigenaardige manier zondig, dat moest dan zo zijn. Hij had niets gemist, al die jaren, en hij had dus ook niets gezocht. Het zoeken had hem verrast, net als het einde van de zoektocht.

Hij ging achter zijn wettige echtgenote staan en deed wat van hem verwacht werd, met passie, met opwinding waar hij niet meer om hoefde te smeken. 'Vind je dit lekker?' vroeg ze halverwege, 'vind je dit net zo lekker als ik? Ik voel hoe geil je bent. Nu je in me zit, nu je me neemt in het gat dat alleen voor jou is, in de uitgang die helemaal van jou is, van niemand anders, nu blijft er niets over van dat jaar dat je weg was, niets, het is alsof je niet bent weg geweest.'

'Dit is mijn uitgang,' zei hij en hij neukte haar alsof geslachtsgemeenschap het betere visioen was.

'Ik wil dat je sperma uit mijn kont druipt.' Hij deed zijn uiterste best. Zoals hij dat in het kippenhok had gedaan, zo deed hij ook hier zijn best.

# 2

Hij liep naar de kazerne, hij wilde niet met de auto, hij wilde de kazerne langzaam naderen. Hij verheugde zich op zijn vrienden, op de rituelen, de stemmen, ook dit zou een soort thuiskomst zijn. Ze zouden veel vragen hebben, zijn vrienden, ze zouden hem vreemd vinden, hij kende hun opvattingen, uiteindelijk zou blijdschap overheersen. Zo liep hij door de stad, die hem minder lelijk voorkwam dan vroeger, als je in het kippenhok had geleefd dan veranderden je opvattingen over mooi en lelijk, wat mooi was werd lelijk, wat lelijk was werd mooi, liefde werd kitsch, pijn werd tederheid.

Eindelijk zaten ze in de kamer van de ploegchef. De C-ploeg was weer compleet. Dat had de ploegchef als eerste gezegd toen de Pool binnenkwam en ze hem met z'n allen hadden verwelkomd. Niet als een verloren zoon maar ook weer niet als een verschoppeling. En precies zo voelde de Pool het, ze waren weer compleet. De mannen zagen er nog net zo uit als op de dag dat hij hen had verlaten – ja, ook hen had hij verlaten – ze hadden hem op dezelfde manier op zijn schouders geklopt als vroeger, ze roken hetzelfde, ze mompelden dezelfde begroeting. En nu zaten ze in de kamer van de ploegchef met z'n allen zoals ze daar wel vaker zaten als er iets te bespreken viel. Toch had hij het gevoel dat er iets veranderd was, iets wat nauwelijks te benoemen was maar wat hij desondanks merkte. Er hing iets in de lucht.

Ze dronken hun koffie en ze bekeken hem zonder iets te zeggen. Misschien was dat wat er was veranderd, ze bekeken hem alsof ze hem niet eerder hadden gezien.

'Natuurlijk ben je weer welkom,' zei de ploegchef toen

ze hun koffie op hadden. 'We hebben tijdelijk vervanging gezocht, tijdelijk want we hebben altijd tegen elkaar gezegd: de Pool komt terug.'

De mannen knikten.

Het was goed om dat te horen. Ze waren hem niet vergeten, ze hadden hem niet afgeschreven. Ook hier hadden ze op de lange, zwijgzame Pool gewacht. Het verwarmde zijn hart. Ook deze mannen, deze familieleden hadden op hem gewacht, hadden hem gemist, hij kon niet ongemerkt verdwijnen.

'Al duurde het op een gegeven moment wel lang,' zei de ploegchef. De mannen knikten opnieuw. Beckers voegde eraan toe: 'Een eeuwigheid.'

Er werd een tweede kop ingeschonken en ze dronken hun koffie, een enkeling dronk thee en ze keken hem aan alsof ze verwachtten dat hij nu iets ging zeggen. Iets over de eeuwigheid, zijn verdwijning die geen verdwijning meer was, over blijdschap misschien, blijdschap dat hij weer bij hen was.

Een eeuwigheid, had het echt een eeuwigheid geduurd? Daar in het klooster was elk gevoel voor tijd hem ontglipt. De dagen leken op elkaar en op een gegeven moment had hij het idee dat de dagen altijd al op elkaar hadden geleken. De seizoenen, de weken. Zomer. Winter. De weekenden. Wat was het verschil?

Zijn vrouw had gezegd: 'We moeten veel genieten en ook toen jij er niet was, toen we langzaam bezig waren kapot te gaan probeerde ik toch tussendoor te genieten.'

Het ene genot werd afgewisseld door het andere, tussendoor ging je kapot en vanaf daar, vanaf die andere plek had het geleken alsof het ene genot niet meer van het andere te scheiden was. Alles was genieten, ook lijden was genieten als je er op een bepaalde manier naar keek. De juiste manier.

'We begrijpen natuurlijk dat er iets aan vooraf is gegaan,' zei de ploegchef. 'Je bent niet zomaar verdwenen, je hebt heel wat voor je kiezen gekregen.'

De Pool speelde met zijn lege bekertje en hij zei: 'Ik ben er weer, daar gaat het om. Ik wil me helemaal voor de ploeg inzetten, zoals vroeger. Ik zal me nog meer inzetten.'

De ploegchef knikte. 'We hoorden dat je op een gegeven moment in een...' hij kuchte, zijn tong gleed over zijn lippen, 'in een kippenhok bent gaan wonen.'

Ze keken hem allemaal aan. Dus daar ging het om. Dat was de reden van deze bijeenkomst. Ze vertrouwden het niet. Een collega die zijn intrek nam in een kippenhok, dat was niet zoals het hoorde. Kon je op zo iemand nog rekenen als je met z'n allen een brandend huis in moest? Is iemand die in een kippenhok heeft gewoond nog wel een teamspeler? Hij moest bewijzen dat hij nog steeds een teamspeler was en dat zou hem ook lukken.

'Ja,' zei de Pool na een korte pauze. 'Maar er waren geen kippen meer. Er woonde verder niemand. Alleen ik. Het was eigenlijk een soort leegstaande woning.'

'Een woning?' reageerde Beckers. 'Ja voor Afrikanen, toch niet voor jou.'

'We vroegen ons af...' De ploegchef raapte iets van de grond op, een pen en toen hij de pen bijna plechtig op tafel had gelegd vervolgde hij: 'We vroegen ons af wat je daar zocht. In die leegstaande woning zal ik maar zeggen.'

Beckers nam het over: 'We praten hier met meel in ons mond, ik zal het dan maar even melden: dat vonden we niet normaal. Kijk, dat je rust zoekt in een klooster om tot jezelf te komen, dat konden we begrijpen, alleen dat kippenhok, daar konden we niet bij. We vonden het raar, extremistisch eigenlijk.'

De ploegchef tikte zachtjes en ritmisch met een vinger op tafel en hij zei: 'Het is goed om dit onderwerp uit de weg te ruimen, dat we het daar later niet meer over hoeven te hebben. We zijn een team en dat moeten we ook blijven, dus misschien kun je ons vertellen wat je daar zocht, wat je daar hebt uitgespookt. In dat kippenhok. Dan weten we dat. Dan kunnen we zeggen: o dat was het. En dan gaan we over tot de orde van de dag.'

Ze keken allemaal naar de Pool alsof ze nu het geheim gingen horen waarop ze al hun hele leven hadden gewacht.

'Tsja,' zei de Pool, 'ik kan daar eigenlijk weinig over vertellen. Ik kon de mensen even... moeilijk verdragen.'

'Moeilijk verdragen?' vroeg Beckers.

'Ik wilde alleen zijn en toen... hoe zal ik het zeggen, het kippenhok kwam vrij.'

'Het kwam vrij...' herhaalde de man die Haas werd genoemd.

De Pool herinnerde zich zijn dagen, zijn weken in het kippenhok, het waren schimmige herinneringen. Hij zag het hok niet meer scherp voor zich en hij kon zich amper herinneren wat hem precies had bewogen om daar zijn intrek te nemen. Het kluizenaarschap had hem een oplossing geleken. Hij had de liefde gezocht waaraan je niet kon ontkomen en die had hij gevonden, hij had nooit geweten hoeveel pijn die liefde kon doen tot hij haar op zijn lichaam had voelen branden, toen wist hij het. Van 't een kwam 't ander, de liefde had hem naar het kippenhok gelokt, de liefde die ervoor zorgde dat je elke wond wel wilde omarmen, elke pijn zingend tegemoet ging, elke dood als een geschenk wilde aanvaarden, al zou hij daarover niet spreken.

Fransen, die bijna met pensioen zou gaan, zei: 'We zeiden tegen elkaar: hij is toch nooit extreem geweest? De Pool is een Pool, maar extreem? Dat zeiden we tegen elkaar. Zo kenden we je niet. Vandaag een kippenhok, morgen een... We zeiden tegen elkaar: hij lijkt wel zo'n moslimfundamentalist.'

'Een moslimfundamentalist?' vroeg de Pool.

Beckers vulde aan: 'Ja, extremistisch, islamitisch, fundamentalistisch, hoe je het wil noemen. We werden bang van jou en je kippenhok en tegelijkertijd zagen we er ook een carnavalsgrap in. Tot we met je vrouw spraken. Toen begrepen we dat het geen grap was. Toen zeiden we: jezus. Holy shit. Hij is van het padje af. Onze Pool.'

De ploegchef onderbrak Beckers. 'Hoe woonde je daar eigenlijk? Kun je ons dat vertellen? Dat we ons er een voorstelling van kunnen maken. Zullen we daarmee beginnen? Dat we het beter begrijpen. Is zo'n hok voor menselijke bewoning geschikt? Had je er een matras neergelegd?'

Daarop veegde de Pool met zijn handen over zijn broek en hij dacht aan zijn vrouw die hem had bezworen dat hij naar de dokter moest. Hij besefte dat ze zijn wonden ook hier zouden zien bij het douchen, ze zouden er commentaar op leveren. Dat was niet erg. Ook niet als ze grapjes maakten, hij kon ertegen. Het was ongetwijfeld goed bedoeld, die grapjes. Een beetje plagen, een beetje pesten. Mannen onder elkaar. Jongens. Geintje.

'De kippen waren geruimd,' zei de Pool, 'ze hebben daar beesten, van de kippen wilden ze af en toen had ik een ingeving. Ik zei tegen de abt... Ik sprak met de abt... Ik had gedachten... Ik hoorde wat ze tegen me zeiden. Ik zei: ik ga wel daar wonen. Ik trek daar wel in. Het staat toch leeg. De mensen zijn me te veel. Zei ik tegen de abt. De wereld is me te veel. Maar een matras, nee. Ik lag gewoon waarop de kippen hadden gelegen. Een beetje stro.'

'We kunnen je niet volgen,' zei Beckers, 'misschien moeten we het ook niet willen begrijpen. Wilde je boetedoen? Was dat het? Voelde je je ergens schuldig over?'

De Pool bleef over zijn broek wrijven. 'Het kippenhok gaf me rust, ik voelde me er thuis, je hebt niet zoveel nodig. De mensen...' Hij zag hoe de mannen hem aanstaarden, alsof hij een levensgrote kip was, een circusattractie die vandaag op de brandweerkazerne was beland. Morgen zou hij weer ergens anders staan. Dit kwam niet meer goed. Hij zag het aan hun blikken. De ploegchef schudde langzaam zijn hoofd en de Pool voelde hoe zijn collega's hem zwijgend afkeurden, ze deden het bijna tegen hun zin in. Ze konden niet anders.

'Het is voorbij,' zei de Pool toen gauw. 'Ik was in de war. Ik zou het nu niet meer doen.' Dat was het beste om te zeggen. Mensen mochten heus in de war zijn, als het maar niet te lang duurde. En als ze na afloop sorry zeiden, dan was het goed. Hij was in de war geweest, de verwarring was over. Daar moest het bij blijven.

'Had je gedronken?' vroeg Beckers.

'Toen ik in de war was? Nee,' zei de Pool.

'Drugs gebruikt?' wilde Fransen weten.

De Pool schudde zijn hoofd. Hij plette zijn lege bekertje tot het een plat cirkelvormig voorwerp was geworden.

'Heb je het met mannen gedaan?' vroeg Fransen. 'Was dat kippenhok een plek waar je het met mannen deed? Je kan het aan ons zeggen. Ik bedoel, het is niet aan mij besteed, de herenliefde, maar ik heb er ook niets op tegen. Iedereen moet zelf weten hoe hij aan zijn gerief komt, zolang ze maar van kinderen afblijven.'

'Wil je nog wat koffie?' vroeg de ploegchef, die de onderwerpen homoseksualiteit en pedofilie kennelijk wilde vermijden.

'Is de vaselinepot eraan te pas gekomen?' wilde Beckers toch weten. 'Is dat het?'

De Pool knikte dankbaar. 'Nog wat koffie,' zei hij. 'Graag en nee ik heb het niet met mannen gedaan. Ik heb de liefde leren kennen...'

Dat laatste had hij niet moeten zeggen, gelukkig hadden ze hem niet gehoord of ze deden alsof. Hij kreeg een nieuw kopje en Fransen wilde weten of de Pool echt niet meer in de Heer was.

'Nee, zeker niet,' zei de Pool. 'Nooit geweest ook. De Heer was in mij, ik was niet in de Heer.'

'Gelukkig,' zei Fransen, die de Pool amper had laten uitpraten. 'Ik heb een oom die in de Heer is. Daar valt niet mee te praten, er komt alleen wartaal uit die man. We zijn hier bij de brandweer, we redden lichamen, geen zielen. Punt.'

De ploegchef tikte met zijn rechterhand op tafel. 'We kennen je al zo lang,' zei hij, 'dat geeft voor mij de doorslag. Vanaf volgende week rooster ik je weer in en dan kijken we waar het schip strandt. Dat kippenhok vergeten we. Hebben we het niet meer over. Je was in de war. Overkomt de beste. Nu zit je weer in de C-ploeg. Je bent weer een van ons.'

'Dank je,' zei de Pool zachtjes en hij merkte hoe deze woorden hem ontroerden, hij moest er bijna van huilen. Om dat te verbergen deed hij alsof hij moest hoesten.

De ploegchef stond op en een voor een stonden ook de andere mannen op. Fransen bleef als laatste zitten. Hij streelde zijn snor zoals hij dat al jaren deed sinds hij op een dag besloten had om een snor te laten staan en een voor een gaf de Pool zijn mannen een hand. Tegen Beckers zei hij: 'Ik heb gehoord dat jullie verhuisd zijn.'

'Klopt,' zei Beckers, 'we wonen nu in Wahlwiller. Meer ruimte, vooral voor de meisjes is dat fijn. Geen Arabieren om ons heen. Scheelt ook. In heel Wahlwiller is geen Arabier te bekennen en negers zie je er ook niet.'

De Pool knikte en daarop gaf hij Fransen nog een hand. Ze keken allemaal vriendelijk naar hem en toch kon hij zich niet aan de indruk onttrekken dat hij geen collega meer was, dat hij een vijand was geworden, iemand die ze moesten zien weg te werken.

'Ik laat je weten wanneer ik je precies inrooster,' riep de ploegchef hem na. Met het bekertje koffie liep de Pool naar buiten. Hij moest wennen aan de mensen, aan hun beslommeringen, aan de echte wereld die op een eigenaardige manier ijl was geworden sinds hij in het kippenhok had gelegen. Het was geen wonen geweest wat hij daar had gedaan, hij had daar gelegen. Hij had liggend geleefd.

De Pool liep door de stad. De lelijkste stad van Nederland volgens zijn vrouw maar het was een geruststellende lelijkheid, het lelijke was bijna mooi geworden. Hier was hij thuis, in deze lelijkheid was je thuis, in deze koopgeul, en als je een halfuur flink doorliep was je in de heuvels en dan was er van de lelijkheid niets te merken, dan was je alleen met de natuur die nergens anders mooier was. Hij deed zijn best om naar de mensen te glimlachen en zonder dat hij dat had bedacht, zonder dat hij echt het besluit had genomen daarheen te gaan, liep hij naar de woning waar de Beckers hadden gewoond. Hij hoefde niet bang te zijn de vrouw van Beckers tegen te komen, ze woonde nu in een dorp waar de Arabieren nog niet heen waren getrokken. Hij wilde de woning zien. Iets in hem trok hem naar die woning zoals pelgrims naar heilige plekken werden gedwongen.

Er hing andere vitrage, een soort kindergordijnen, op het naambordje bij de deur stond nu: 'Fam. Schwabe'. Even speelde hij met de gedachte aan te bellen, toen besloot hij door te lopen, wat moest hij zeggen tegen de familie Schwabe?

Een buurvrouw, met een tas in haar hand stond ze in het belendende voortuintje, riep: 'Ze zijn verhuisd, de Beckers. Ze wonen hier niet meer.'

Ze staarde hem aan, ze leek hem te herkennen. Ze deed een pas in zijn richting. 'Jij bent het,' zei ze.

'Wie?' vroeg de Pool.

'Jij bent toch de man die naar het klooster is gegaan?'

'Ja,' zei de Pool.

'Er is veel over je gesproken. Je bent over de tong gegaan. Vreselijk, wat er allemaal gebeurd is.' Ze zette nog een stap in zijn richting, ze stond nu bij de heg, ze kon niet verder. 'Is het waar wat ze zeggen?'

‘Ik denk van niet.’ Hij knikte vriendelijk en liep verder.

Er was veel over hem gesproken. Zo ging dat. Nu hij weer terug was en zijn werk en zijn vaderlijke plichten zou hervatten gingen ze hopelijk snel over andere mensen spreken. Ze zouden hem vergeten en dat was goed. Het onopvallende bestaan was zijn bestaan.

Op het kinderdagverblijf werkte een nieuwe dame die hem verwelkomde met de argwaan die bij de wereld van het kind en het kinderdagverblijf hoort.

‘Ik kom voor Jurek,’ zei hij. ‘Ik kom hem wat eerder halen. Ik heb een dagje vrij.’ Hij wees hem aan.

‘Bent u zijn oom?’ vroeg de nieuwe dame.

‘Ik ben zijn vader,’ zei de Pool trots.

De dame vroeg aan Jurek: ‘Is dat je papa?’

De jongen keek hem alleen aan. Hij zei geen boe of bah. Een blik van herkenning was niet op zijn gezicht af te lezen. Daarop vroeg de nieuwe dame of de Pool zich kon legitimeren en hij antwoordde dat hij dat best wilde doen maar dat ze het even aan haar collega moest vragen. ‘Zetta weet nog wie ik ben.’

De nieuwe dame antwoordde: ‘Zetta is met zwangerschapsverlof.’

‘O,’ zei de Pool, ‘o, dat is me ontgaan. Sorry.’ En daarop ging hij door zijn knieën en zei tegen zijn zoon: ‘Herken je me dan niet meer? Ik ben je papa. Doe niet zo gek, mallerd. Ik ben je vader. Ik ben papa. Ik hou zo veel van je.’

Het was warm hier, een warmte die hem deed denken aan sommige avonden in het kippenhok als de zon de hele dag op het dak had geschenen. Hij had daar gelegen, leven en dood waren niet meer van elkaar te onderscheiden, de eeuwigheid had op het deurtje van het kippenhok geklopt, dood en leven vermengd tot één grote hallucinerende cocktail.

De Pool stond op en keek de nieuwe dame aan, een meisje eigenlijk nog dat hem nauwlettend in de gaten hield. Meer een bewaakster in een gevangenis dan een medewerkster van een kinderdagverblijf. 'Ik was een tijd op reis,' zei de Pool en hij stond op om haar beter aan te kunnen kijken, met meer overtuiging te kunnen spreken. 'Het kind heeft zijn papa moeten missen.'

Er werd veel over hem gesproken in het stadje maar misschien niet op het kinderdagverblijf. Het leek hem ongepast in een kinderdagverblijf het woord 'kippenhok' in zijn mond te nemen.

Weer ging hij door zijn knieën en hij strekte zijn handen uit naar Jurek die met blokken aan het spelen was, maar het kind kwam niet naar hem toe. Het bestudeerde hem zoals de mannen op de kazerne hem hadden bestudeerd, alsof ook het kind niet kon wennen aan de gedachte dat zijn papa zijn intrek had genomen in een hok. Tijdelijk, en toch, het was een smet waarvan de Pool kennelijk niet afkwam.

Van achter kwam Tess en die herkende hem, al hield ze zich een beetje op afstand. 'Ja, dat is de vader van Jurek,' zei Tess. En tegen de Pool zei ze: 'Goed dat je er weer bent, hij is groot geworden, niet?'

Aan haar stem hoorde hij dat ook zij op de hoogte was. Hij tilde Jurek op die gelukkig niet ging huilen. Tess reikte hem de jas van Jurek aan en een rugzakje. 'Ik help hem wel even in zijn jasje.' Ze nam de jongen van hem over. Hij lachte naar haar en toch voelde het, meer nog dan vroeger, alsof hij vader aan het spelen was.

Terwijl ze met Jurek bezig was zei de nieuwe dame: 'We moeten voorzichtig zijn. Sorry.'

'Ja,' zei de Pool. 'We moeten voorzichtig zijn.'

Jurek had nu zijn jasje aan. 'Dag Jurek,' zei Tess, 'ga je lekker met papa mee? Ga je fijn naar huis? Zien we je morgen weer?'

'Hij gaat lekker met papa mee,' zei de Pool. Hij tilde Jurek op die niet tegenstribbelde. 'Tot morgen Jurek,' riep

Tess. Jurek zwaaide nog een beetje halfslachtig naar Tess en zo liep de Pool met zijn zoon het kinderdagverblijf uit. Toch had hij zelf het gevoel dat hij aan een ontvoering bezig was.

Het was gaan waaien. Hij drukte de jongen stevig tegen zich aan. 'Ik weet dat je zelf kunt lopen,' zei hij zacht, 'maar laten we snel naar huis gaan. Voor het gaat regenen.' En voor het eerst sinds zijn terugkeer zag hij warmte in de ogen van de overgebleven jongen. Herkenning. Misschien iets van liefde, dat wist hij niet zeker. Het was ook een groot woord, te groot voor deze kleine, overgebleven jongen.

Hij wilde de straat oversteken maar merkte hoe een man hem aanstaarde. Vast weer iemand die over hem had gesproken. Hij had toch niet in de krant gestaan? Hoe zouden ze hem herkennen? Zouden de mensen foto's van hem aan elkaar hebben laten zien? Dit is hem. Die gast woont in een kippenhok. Hadden ze gelachen? Of net als zijn collega's van ontzetting hun hoofd geschud? Hij vermoedde dat zijn collega's ook hadden gelachen, ze hadden gelachen om de Pool, de bevrijdende lach van de minachting. Het was niet erg. Vroeger zou hij ook om zichzelf hebben gelachen.

'Weet je niet meer wie ik ben?' vroeg de man.

De Pool schudde zijn hoofd.

'De mensenknecht,' zei de man. 'We hebben elkaar bij de boer ontmoet.'

'O ja.'

De man zag er anders uit dan toen. Stads, bijna deftig. 'Ik heb slecht nieuws voor je,' zei hij.

'O.' De Pool klemde Jurek steviger tegen zich aan.

'De boer leeft niet meer.'

'Gecondoleerd.' De Pool wilde doorlopen maar de mensenknecht had nog iets te zeggen. 'Zijn vrouw is ook dood. Binnen tien dagen was het gebeurd. Ze wilde niet meer eten. En de kinderen zeiden: "Laat haar met rust. Dwing haar niet." Ze zei: "Ik heb hem nooit gemogen. Vanaf dag één niet. Maar zonder hem is er ook niets aan." Mooi niet? Hoe krachtig de liefde kan zijn. Hoe onoverwinnelijk. Ja, het gaf me veel hoop en moed.'

'Ach,' zei de Pool, 'mooi.' Hij deed weer een poging over te steken, de man hield hem tegen. 'Wacht even. Mag ik je mijn nieuwe visitekaartje geven? We zijn gegroeid. Er zijn nu bijna twintig man in dienst. Ik heet niet meer de mensenknecht, veel klanten hadden toch bezwaar tegen het woord knecht. Vonden ze niet meer van deze tijd. Ik noem mezelf nu het menselijk verlengstuk. Hulp is een extra arm, een extra been, een extra hand, oftewel verlengstuk. Ik ben het verlengstuk van de ander. Wij zijn het verlengstuk van de ander, want we zijn gegroeid.'

Hij haalde een visitekaartje tevoorschijn en gaf het aan de Pool die het aannam en er beleefdheidshalve een blik op wierp. Er stond: HET MENSELIJK VERLENGSTUK B.V. RESPECTVOLLE ZORG OP MAAT GESNEDEN. VOOR IEDEREEN. JONG & OUD. In kleine letters eronder: Zorg op krediet mogelijk.

De Pool stopte het kaartje in zijn zak en daarna streelde hij Jurek over zijn hoofd.

'We worden nog altijd niet vergoed,' zei de man, 'de officiële instanties werken ons tegen maar dat is een kwestie van tijd. Daarom werken we op krediet. Ideaal voor de kleine man. De oude zorg is namelijk niet meer van nu. De mensen willen geen baas die voor hen zorgt, ze willen een verlengstuk. Wij kijken op naar onze cliënten. De zorg die wij bieden is een fantasie die werkelijkheid is geworden. Natuurlijk zijn er mensen die zeggen: ja het liefst had ik geen zorg nodig gehad. Het liefst had ik zelf naar de wc gekund. Die tijd is voorbij. De tijd dat we alles alleen kunnen. We kunnen niets meer alleen. Niet eens naar de wc. Die tijd is aangebroken. En daarop moet je inspelen. Ik heb een jonge Afghaan in dienst. Die begrijpt het. Hij is jong, eenentwintig, maar hij voelt wat de cliënt nodig heeft. Hij knielt voor de cliënt. Niet om zich te vernederen, om de hulpbehoevende op zijn gemak te stellen. Als je iemands billen moet afvegen dan moet diegene je vertrouwen, anders kun je het net zo goed door een robot laten doen. De hulpbehoevende moet voelen dat daar iemand staat die met net zoveel liefde zijn billen afveegt als vroeger zijn papa of mama dat deed. We zijn allemaal hulpbehoevend, de een alleen iets meer dan de ander. Dat is het motto van Het Menselijk Verlengstuk b.v. De eindtijd nadert en dan moet je je gezondheidszorg daarop aanpassen. In de toekomst gaan mensen niet meer op vakantie, ze gaan niet meer skiën of parachutespringen. Ze gaan zorg inkopen omdat ze dat nodig hebben én omdat ze het lekker vinden. Ze zullen er steeds vroeger mee beginnen. Er zal uiteindelijk geen verschil meer zijn tussen zorg en liefde. Ik zeg dit niet om reclame te maken voor het bedrijf.'

'Ik moet echt naar huis,' onderbrak de Pool. 'Er wachten mensen op mij.'

'Ik zeg dit,' ging de man verder, 'omdat ik in jou een verlengstuk zie. Jij begrijpt het. Open je ogen, zeg ik tegen onze mensen, de wereld is een ziekenhuis. In de toekomst zullen wij allemaal elkaars billen afvegen. Dat is het paradijs. Als er al een paradijs mogelijk is.'

'Er wacht iemand op me,' zei de Pool nu nadrukkelijk, 'als ik werk nodig heb zal ik je bellen. Ik ben brandweerman en dat wil ik nog een tijdje blijven.'

Het menselijk verlengstuk legde een hand op de schouder van de Pool en het voelde inderdaad als een zorgzame hand, dwingend doch zorgzaam. 'Ik laat nu een proefballonnetje op in Aken. Kijken hoe het daar gaat. Ik denk dat ze daar openstaan voor mijn ideeën. Ze kunnen het niet meer alleen, de mensen, ze zijn verloren. En het menselijk verlengstuk zegt: dat geeft niet. We gaan nu even de praktische zorg op ons nemen. Dat is niet alles, maar het is heel wat. Als je niet meer kunt of wilt eten, als je je vork niet meer naar je mond kunt brengen dan is het fijn dat iemand je liefdevol komt voeren in plaats van het eten in je mond te proppen. Als je niet meer de deur uit kunt dan gaan wij een stukje met je wandelen. We zijn niet goedkoop, dat geef ik toe. Wat is belangrijker? Goede zorg in de toekomst of restaurantbezoek vandaag waarvan je je de volgende dag niets meer kunt herinneren. Wat denk jij? Zijn ze ook in Duitsland klaar voor mijn ideeën?'

'Ik denk het. Tot ziens.' De Pool groette nu echt heel resoluut en vervolgde zijn weg naar huis. Toen hij ver genoeg verwijderd was van de man begon hij tegen Jurek te spreken. 'Ik zal mijn mond opendoen,' zei hij zachtjes in het oor van de jongen, 'ik sta bekend als de zwijgzame Pool maar het wordt tijd dat ik een beetje ga spreken. Ik ben je vader. Je hoeft niet te doen alsof je me niet kent. Jij mag me herkennen. Jij bent de overgebleven jongen. Wij zullen elkaar gezelschap houden. Dat klinkt raar maar dat is toch waar het vaderschap op neerkomt? Dat jij je kind gezelschap houdt. En je kind jou. Opvoeden, ik weet het niet. We hebben je broer opgevoed. Je lieve, grote broer. Het schijnt hem niet goed bekomen te zijn, onze opvoeding.'

De jongen zei niets terug. Hij keek zijn vader wel aan en in die blik zag de Pool alles wat hij nodig had, alles wat hij van de jongen verwachtte.

Toen zijn vrouw thuiskwam was hij met de jongen aan het spelen. Hij vroeg hoe ze het had gehad. Ze vertelde niet veel. Vroeger toen ze elkaar net kenden wist hij de namen van al haar kleuters uit z'n hoofd. Hij wist van al hun eigenaardigheden. Er kwamen nieuwe kleuters en geleidelijk leerde hij de namen van haar leerlingen niet meer uit zijn hoofd. Het was geen beslissing, dat was gewoon hoe het ging. Zij vertelde steeds minder en hij vroeg steeds minder. Je kon niet alles van elkaar bijhouden. Er was te veel informatie. Je hoefde niet alles te weten.

Ze ging naast hem zitten, in kleermakerszit, zonder

haar jas uit te doen. 'Hoe was dat?' vroeg ze, 'toen je in dat kippenhok zat. Dat je opeens besloot terug te komen? Hoe was dat? Ik probeer het me voor te stellen. Het laat me niet los.'

Eerst zei hij niets want hij had zich voorgenomen niet meer over het kippenhok te spreken. Hij wist niet meer zeker of het hok een visioen was of dat visoenen hem naar het hok hadden gedreven. Daar had hij de geweldige en gewelddadige macht van de liefde ontdekt. Maar omdat ze hem indringend bleef aankijken zei hij: 'Ja, hoe was dat? Eerst riep God me en toen riepen jullie me. Dat is toch leven,' hij probeerde zijn vrouw te kussen, 'dat er steeds weer iemand is die je roept?'

# VI

## *Het tiende jaar*

# 1

Hij was naar de stervende vrouw van Beckers gegaan om afscheid te nemen, om echt afscheid te nemen, omdat de brief nooit verstuurd was, omdat hij zijn zwijgen nooit had verklaard, omdat hij had gedacht en gehoopt dat stilte genoeg zou zijn. Er was getroost, lang geleden, onbeholpen en misschien op een manier zoals mensen niet getroost moeten worden maar de troost was nooit afgesloten. Nooit was klip-en-klaar gezegd: we zijn klaar met de troost, hij is niet meer nodig.

Toen hij thuiskwam stond zijn vrouw op hem te wachten. Ze stond in de gang met haar jas aan.

'Wat doe je hier?' vroeg hij. 'Je zou toch naar dat feest gaan?'

'Heb ik laten zitten.'

'Ik dacht dat het belangrijk was.'

'Was het ook.'

'Waarom heb je het dan laten zitten?'

'Om met jou te praten.'

Ze wist het, hij zag het aan haar gezicht. Ze moest het hebben geroken, de geur van het ziekenhuis, de geur van de dood, sterker dan die van de bossen. Ze keek hem aan, ze ging voor hem staan als een douanier die een passagier moest controleren. Ze had talloze rimpeltjes om haar ogen, ze was zo anders dan vroeger toen ze nog met z'n vieren waren. Zijn vrouw was zekerder van zichzelf, ze was een autoriteit geworden. Hij merkte het aan haar verhalen over de dikwijls veeleisende ouders van de kleuters, vroeger liet ze zich weleens intimideren door ouders, nu maakte ze korte metten met hen. De veeleisende ouder had tegenover Wen niets meer te vertellen. Ze duldde nog tegenspraak maar eigenlijk alleen omdat de beleefdheid dat vereiste.

Zo stond ze daar voor hem, nog altijd had ze haar jas niet uitgedaan, ze monsterde hem en hij zei: 'Ik heb een flink eind gewandeld. Tot bij Epen, iets voor de grens en toen weer terug.'

'Je bent een frisse neus gaan halen.'

'Nou ja, frisse neus.'

Ze schudde meewarig haar hoofd.

'Ik was ook in het ziekenhuis,' zei hij zachtjes, bijna als een kind, 'ik heb even dag gezegd.'

'Dag gezegd?' vroeg ze. 'Ik heb je gewaarschuwd. We hebben het er vanochtend uitvoerig over gehad. We hebben genoeg meegemaakt. Ik ben er klaar mee. Ik ben er helemaal klaar mee.' Ze draaide zich om, beende weg en hij liep achter haar aan door het huis.

Op de bank in de woonkamer zat Jurek met zijn moeders telefoon in de hand, koptelefoon op zijn hoofd. Hij keek niet op. De Pool kon zich niet voorstellen dat zijn vrouw na al die jaren nog zou weggaan. Het was zoals sommige stellen wachten op een kind. Op een gegeven moment weten ze dat het er niet meer van komt. Nu nog weggaan was dwaasheid. Die kans had ze gehad, ze had hem voorbij laten gaan en hij ook, voor zover hij dat echt had gewild, weggaan.

Ze ging de trap op, eigenlijk heel kalm, en hij ging erachteraan, zonder iets te vragen. Boven in de slaapkamer pakte ze een koffer uit de kast, ze waren er van de zomer mee naar Italië geweest. Hij was nieuw, speciaal aangeschaft voor de Italiëreis. Roze. Ze had een roze koffer gewild. 'Lekker opvallend,' had ze gezegd, 'bovendien was hij in de uitverkoop.' Het was een fijne vakantie geweest, ontspannen, ontspannener dan ooit eigenlijk. Een huisje in de buurt van het Comomeer, daar hadden ze twee weken gezeten. De locatie viel aanvankelijk tegen, het Comomeer was verder weg dan ze hadden gedacht maar ze wenden aan de afstand en de bergen om het meer waren mooi. Misschien wist ze het toen al. Had ze gedacht: als het echt goed herfst is, zo eind november dan ga ik. Nog een paar maanden. Waarom had ze gewacht tot eind november? Had ze op een teken gewacht? Een ingeving?

Ze deed de koffer open. De Pool vond dat de koffer naar Italië rook, naar de zomer. Jurek had in een hangmat gelegen alsof zijn leven ervan afhing, de Pool had geprobeerd te lezen. Zijn vrouw had hem een boek aanbevolen maar hij viel steeds in slaap en uiteindelijk gaf hij het op en hij concentreerde zich op zijn sudoku-boekje.

'Ik wil niet hysterisch doen,' zei ze, 'maar dit is de druppel. We hadden een afspraak. Ik wil geen spoken meer uit het verleden en jij blijft ze meeslepen en precies de vrouw van Beckers wil ik er niet bij hebben. Die was al dood. Die was al eens gestorven. Het is een gepasseerd station. Ik ben moe. Ik ben doodmoe.'

Hij keek haar verbaasd aan. 'Is dit het begin van een migraineaanval?' opperde hij.

'Nee, dit is niet het begin van een migraineaanval. Dit is helemaal geen migraine. En ook geen gewone koppijn. Dit gaat om jou.'

Eigenlijk kon hij zich niet voorstellen dat het zo zou eindigen na alles wat er was gebeurd. Op een gegeven moment ga je niet meer weg zoals je op een gegeven moment niet meer gaat leren diepzeeduiken. Ze deed alsof ze wegging, dacht de Pool, omdat ze wilde voelen dat hij nog altijd om haar gaf. Dat was het. Een test. Het was te harmonieus geworden, ze zocht spanning, maar diep vanbinnen wist hij dat zijn eigen geruststellingen niet klopten.

'In feite ben jij zelf een spook uit het verleden.' Ze pakte met een hand zijn bovenarm vast en ze zei: 'Geef het toe. Geef het eindelijk toe. We houden niet meer van elkaar, misschien hebben we nooit van elkaar gehouden. Dat kan.

We hebben samen iets meegemaakt, dat is niet hetzelfde als houden van.'

'We hebben een kind verloren,' zei de Pool, 'op een eigenaardige manier verloren. Zo hoor je geen kind te verliezen. Dat is een decennium geleden. En we hebben nog een zoon, die zit beneden op de bank.'

'Ja, die zit beneden op de bank.' Ze pakte een stapeltje ondergoed. 'Het is niet dat ik je niet mag, het is niet dat we elkaar nooit meer zullen zien. En je hebt gelijk, we hebben nog een kind samen. Maar dít wil ik niet meer.' Ze deed een spijkerbroek in de koffer en een rok die hij haar al jaren niet had zien dragen, waarvan hij het bestaan was vergeten.

'Waar ga je heen?' vroeg hij. 'En wat precies wil je niet meer?'

'Ik ga naar een vriendin.'

'Wie, als ik vragen mag?'

'Magda.'

'Magda, ik wist niet dat jullie zo close waren. Magda. En de jongen?'

'De jongen,' zei ze, 'Jurek. Dat bedoel ik, is dat alles wat wij samen hebben? De jongen. Is er niet meer dan dat? De jongen, de jongen. Ben ik een wormvormig aanhangsel van Jurek?'

Ze pakte een vest, bekeek het en legde het weer terug in de kast. 'Ik ben niet weg, het is niet dat ik nu opeens verdwenen ben. Ik ga weg uit dit huis. Ik ga bij jou weg maar we blijven aan elkaar verbonden, samen hebben we inderdaad Jurek. De helft van de tijd kan hij bij mij wonen, de andere helft bij jou, daar komen we wel uit.' Ze klonk ontspannen, het klonk alsof ze al een tijd had zitten oefenen om dit te kunnen zeggen. Het was geen opwelling, geen spontane actie. Misschien had ze het met Magda besproken en had Magda gezegd: 'Ga weg, je verdient beter.'

Hij voelde niet de behoefte zich te verzetten en dat verbaasde hem het meest. Hij had geen zin te roepen: Wat maakt het nou uit of ik zo'n stervende vrouw nog een bloemetje breng. Wen zou wel terugkomen, dit was slechts een opwelling waarvan ze morgen alweer spijt had. 'Vind je me oud geworden?' vroeg hij.

'Nee,' zei ze, terwijl ze een zomerjurk inpakte, aan het eind van de herfst, een zomerjurk, 'je ziet er prima uit. Ik wil dat je één ding weet: ik ben al die jaren monogaam geweest. Ik ben een monogame vrouw. Je kijkt naar een monogame vrouw.'

Hij keek naar haar koffer, die was nu voor de helft vol. 'Dat is fijn. Monogaam. Geen bedrog.' Even zag hij de vrouw van Beckers in het ziekenhuis voor zich, meer dood dan levend. Het leek hem beter verder over monogamie te zwijgen.

'Zonde,' zei hij, en hij wees op de groene jurk onder haar jas, 'die had je speciaal voor het feest laten stomen en nu heeft niemand je in die jurk gezien. Hij staat je zo goed.'

Ze knikte. 'Ik ben wel verliefd,' zei ze. 'Dat je dat weet. Op een andere man.'

'O.' De Pool ging op het bed zitten. Verliefd, dat had hij niet gedacht. Wen kwam naast hem zitten, haar ogen waren vochtig, ze sloeg een arm om haar man heen, de vader van haar kind. 'Ik wilde zo graag nog eens verliefd worden,' zei ze, 'begrijp je dat? Ik wilde het zo graag. Straks ga ik dood en ben ik nooit meer verliefd geweest. En toen gebeurde het. Het overviel me. Maar ik ben monogaam gebleven. Ik wil dat je dat weet. Een kus op het station. Meer niet.'

De Pool knikte. 'Welk station?' vroeg hij.

'Heerlen.'

Ze liet hem niet los. 'Begrijp je het? Ik bedoel, wij zijn toch... wij zijn een beetje dood. We hebben niets tegen elkaar te zeggen. We leven langs elkaar heen. We delen een huis, een badkamer.'

‘Je had opnieuw verliefd op mij kunnen worden,’ zei de Pool, ‘of is dat te veel gevraagd?’

‘Opnieuw verliefd worden? Denk je dat dit kan? Ben jij ooit op iemand opnieuw verliefd geworden? In welke wereld leef jij? Kun je je voorstellen dat je opnieuw verliefd wordt op die god van je?’

‘Nee, maar op Hem ben ik ook nooit verliefd geweest.’

‘Ik heb mijn best gedaan,’ ging ze verder. ‘Ik heb gewerkt, ik heb hard gewerkt, ze zeggen altijd dat relaties werk zijn, dat liefde hard werken is, nou ik heb niet stilgezeten. Dat gebrek aan seks, dat kan het toch niet zijn.’

‘Gebrek?’

Ze ging weg. Vergeleken met Borys viel dit mee. Zolang mensen niet onder de trein sprongen viel eigenlijk alles mee.

‘Ik zal van je blijven houden,’ zei ze, ‘ik wil alleen niet langzaam verder sterven. Het is misschien hard wat ik zeg maar alles om jou heen gaat dood.’

Hij wilde zich wel verdedigen, hij wist niet hoe, alles wat hij kon zeggen kwam hem futiel voor. Ze was verliefd, monogaam en verliefd. Wat kon hij daar tegenoverstellen? Hij had net afscheid genomen van de vrouw van Beckers.

‘Op wie ben je eigenlijk verliefd?’ vroeg hij.

‘Wat doet het ertoe. Wil je met hem vechten?’ Ze lachte, vrolijk klonk het niet.

‘Integendeel, ik wil er alles aan doen om ervoor te zorgen dat je een goed leven hebt.’

‘Wat zal ik nog meer meenemen?’ vroeg ze en ze stond op. Alsof hij haar moest helpen met inpakken, alsof het een reisje was van een paar dagen.

‘Geen idee. Fijn dat je al die tijd monogaam bent geweest maar wat deed je dan met die man... die man op wie je verliefd bent? Wat doe je precies als je verliefd bent en toch monogaam? Misschien een domme vraag.’

Ze zuchtte alsof ze dat inderdaad een domme vraag

vond. ‘We schrijven elkaar brieven. Heb je daar niets van gemerkt?’

Hij schudde zijn hoofd. ‘Nee, niets van gemerkt. Waar hadden jullie het over?’

‘Over astrologie, hij doet aan astrologie in zijn vrije tijd.’

‘Jij gelooft niet in astrologie.’

‘Nee maar ik ben verliefd. Dan is alles prachtig. Alles. Dat weet je toch. Ik ben geen bakvis, ik denk wel over de dingen na. Het is heerlijk om alles prachtig te vinden, zelfs astrologie.’

‘Ja,’ zei de Pool. ‘Dat is heerlijk. Astrologie is ook fascinerend.’ Hij zou boos kunnen worden maar als hij iets niet wilde was het woede. Hij was boos geweest toen hij het kippenhok in ging, zijn verlangen was woede geweest. Die woede was overwonnen. Nooit meer woede, dat was zijn devies.

‘Ik heb hem niet aangeraakt. Ik dacht: als ik hem aanraak is het voorbij. Ik wilde ons nog een kans geven.’

‘Wat lief. Ik heb dus een kans gemist?’ Even voelde de Pool een diepe treurnis, zo moest je je voelen als je wist dat je doodging. Dit was het dus. Opluchting en treurnis, brokstukken van anekdotes, een kleine waslijst aan gemiste kansen, een soort gebed. Treurnis om niet geleefde levens.

Ze deed de koffer dicht. ‘Weet je, toen je vanochtend zei dat je naar de vrouw van Beckers wilde, dat je in het ziekenhuis afscheid van haar wilde nemen, toen wist ik dat het verleden nooit voorbij zal zijn. Dat jij het achter je aan sleept en ik kan daar niet meer tegen. Het is niet dat we niets geprobeerd hebben, relatietherapie, reisjes, samen zwemmen, weet ik wat. En ik heb ook gedacht: moeten we die kamer niet leegmaken? Misschien moeten we alles wat van hem is geweest weggooien zonder er nog naar te kijken.’ Ze pakte zijn hand en liet die weer los. ‘Ik heb geen spijt,’ vervolgde ze, ‘jij blijft de vader van mijn kinderen.

Als ik hier blijf dan voelt het alsof ik het leven uitzit. Wachten tot Jurek het huis uit is, wachten op een verzorgingsflat. Kleinkinderen misschien? Nee.' Ze zette de koffer overeind.

'Wil je geen kleinkinderen?'

'Dat bedoel ik niet.'

'Wat moeten we Jurek vertellen?' vroeg hij.

Ze haalde haar schouders op. 'Ik ga zo naar beneden, ik spreek wel met hem.' De Pool bleef op bed zitten. Hij werd verlaten, zijn vrouw, de moeder van zijn kinderen ging weg. Eigenlijk om dezelfde reden als waarom zijn vader ooit alle contact met hem had verbroken, hij rook naar de dood, hij sleepte een verleden achter zich aan waaraan de mensen niet herinnerd wilden worden. En hij deed het niet expres.

'Ik heb mezelf verloren,' zei ze. 'Ik ben mezelf kwijtgeraakt, dat is wat ik bedoel. Ik heb alleen functies. Juf. Moeder. Van een levende jongen. Moeder van een dode jongen. Vrouw van een brandweerman. Wie ben ik echt? Ik weet niet meer wie ik ben. Het lijkt alsof wij pech aantrekken, alsof dat het enige is wat wij nog zijn, pechmagneten.'

'Pechmagneten? Hebben we alleen pech gehad? Is dit gezin niets dan een verzameling pechvogels?'

Eerst schudde ze haar hoofd en toen knikte ze. 'Ik had iets anders gewild.'

'Iets anders?' Hij moest weer aan de vrouw van Beckers denken en de Fransman. Was ze tot het eind blijven hopen? Had ze hem nog eens gebeld? Was hij toch gekomen maar had ze gezegd: Nee, nu hoeft het niet meer. Te laat. Sorry.

'Ik weet echt niet meer wie ik ben,' zei Wen. Hij merkte dat ze huilde.

Hij was Pool en brandweerman. Dat was genoeg. Wat moest je meer over jezelf weten? Iedereen moest tegenwoordig grote dingen doen, verre reizen maken, zichzelf overstijgen. Het kleine leven mocht niet meer bestaan, voor dat leven was geen plaats meer. Hij vond het kleine, alledaagse, onopvallende prima.

'Wat wil jij dan?' vroeg ze. 'Ik heb het je zo vaak gevraagd. Wat wil jíj?'

'Ja, dat heb je vaak gevraagd. Ik heb altijd hetzelfde geantwoord, ik wil een goede vader zijn en een goede echtgenoot en op de kazerne wil ik een goede brandweerman zijn. Waren mijn antwoorden saai?'

'Saai, dat was het probleem niet. Met saaiheid valt te leven. Jouw saaiheid is doods.' Ze liep naar de deur. 'Ik ga het aan Jurek vertellen.'

Hij liep mee naar de overloop en keek hoe Wen met iets van aarzeling de trap afliep. Even later hoorde hij ze beneden praten. Omdat het lang duurde ging hij ten slotte naar de badkamer en poetste zijn tanden. Hij had een vieze smaak in zijn mond. Weer dacht hij aan hun laatste vakantie. De laatste keer seks, de laatste zoen, het laatste ontbijt.

De overgebleven jongen had willen snorkelen daar in Italië, ze waren drie keer naar het meer gereden, anderhalf uur rijden, maar dat had Jurek niet genoeg gevonden. Alleen snorkelen in zee kon hem gelukkig maken.

'Volgend jaar gaan we naar zee,' had de Pool gezegd en de jongen lag op zijn hangmat met de snorkel op zijn buik en staarde naar de lucht. Hij wilde de hele dag snorkelen, hij wilde vooral wat niet kon. Misschien had hij dat van zijn moeder, die wilde ook vooral wat niet kon. Alleen toen nog niet, daar boven het Meer van Como, toen leek het alsof ze tevreden was. Toen had ze gezwegen over laatste kansen en de dood, over monogamie en verliefdheid. Zij las en de Pool loste sudoku's op. Alles leek harmonieus. Had hij iets moeten missen? Wat miste Wen wat hij niet miste? Moest je snel verliefd worden voor je doodging?

Er was een tijd dat hij iemand had gemist, het was hem slecht bekomen.

Toen hij klaar was in de badkamer hoorde hij zijn vrouw beneden nog steeds praten. Zij was meer aan het woord dan de jongen. Dat verbaasde hem niet, ze had iets uit te leggen.

De Pool ging op bed liggen. Hij wachtte zonder veel na te denken over de rest van zijn leven. Die rest zou vanzelf komen. Hij maakte zich geen zorgen omdat hij de man er niet naar was zich nog zorgen te maken.

Eindelijk kwam zijn vrouw naar boven. Ja, ze ging weg, al bleef ze zijn lieve vrouw. Dat zou ze ook altijd blijven. Een goede man doet een stapje opzij als dat nodig is. 'En?' vroeg hij.

Ze haalde haar schouders op. 'Hij wil met me mee, ik heb gezegd dat dit niet kan. Zo groot woont Magda niet. Dat hij voorlopig bij jou moet blijven, heb ik gezegd. Dat we niet boos op elkaar zijn. Alleen op elkaar uitgekeken.'

'Op elkaar uitgekeken,' herhaalde de Pool.

'Over de verliefdheid heb ik gezwegen.'

'Dat is beter,' zei de Pool. 'Heeft Magda eigenlijk een man en kinderen?'

'Nee, daar houdt ze niet van.'

Dat kwam voor, sommige mensen hielden niet van mannen en kinderen. Hoewel je van een kleuterjuffrouw zou verwachten dat ze van kinderen hield, maar misschien was dat een naïeve gedachte.

'Jurek zei niet veel,' vervolgde Wen. 'Hij zei "best" toen hij begreep dat hij echt niet mee kon. Dat is weinig als je ouders uit elkaar gaan, vind je niet? Maar jij zegt ook niet veel. Jullie lijken op elkaar. Alles is best. Alles is altijd best.'

'Van de zomer wist Jurek wat hij wilde: snorkelen. Toen was niet alles best.'

'Ik ga. Er is nog wat soep van gisteren. Dat kun je opwarmen. En sla, een maaltijdsalade.' Ze klonk nu zakelijk, alsof ze een huisarts was die een bezoek aan de patiënt had afgelegd en weer verderging. Het zou goed komen. Eerst even aanzien vóór de specialist moest worden gebeld. Er wachtten andere patiënten.

'Ga je nu naar Magda?' vroeg hij. 'Of ga je toch naar die man?'

Zij pakte haar koffer en ging de trap af.

'Laat mij maar dragen.' Hij nam de koffer van haar over.

Wen ging nog de woonkamer in en kuste Jurek op zijn hoofd. Even meende de Pool een emotie in Jureks blik te zien. Angst. Of afschuw. Of allebei tegelijk. Toen liep hij met zijn lieve vrouw naar haar auto, hij droeg haar koffer, alsof ze een paar dagen met wat vriendinnen op vakantie zou gaan. Even uitblazen.

Voor haar auto bleef hij aarzelend staan, een moment verwachtte hij dat ze zich nog zou bedenken.

'Nee, ik ga nu niet naar die man,' zei ze, 'waar zie je me voor aan? Ik ben geen sloerie die van de ene man naar de volgende gaat. Zo zit ik niet in elkaar. Ik ga naar Magda. Daar ga ik op de bank slapen.'

Hij deed haar koffer in de kofferbak. 'Weet je,' zei hij, 'van mij hoef je niet weg. Verliefd of niet verliefd. Ik... Je mag hier blijven. Ook al ben je verliefd op een ander. Ik zal je niet storen in je verliefdheid. Ik doe een stapje opzij, ik wil graag een stapje opzij doen als ik je daarmee gelukkig maak.' Hij krabde aan zijn baardstoppels. En op dat moment begreep hij waarom zijn leven nu niet instortte. Omdat het al was ingestort. Twee keer instorten ging niet. Zij kende de ruïne door en door, was niet ongevoelig voor de schoonheid ervan maar wilde de ruïne nu toch verlaten.

Alleen kon ze de Pool niet echt verlaten, zelfs al zou ze al het contact met hem verbreken dan nog zou ze nooit echt weggaan. Het verleden zat als een strop om hun beider nekken, het zat in hun bloed, in hun DNA. In hun stemmen en in hun huid, in hun tong. Daarom kon hij zo rustig blijven, zo kalm, daarom schreeuwde hij niet. Ze zou er altijd zijn, zoals de dode er altijd was.

'Ik weet het.' Ze nam zijn gezicht in haar handen. 'Je hebt je hele leven niets anders gedaan dan stapjes opzij zetten en daarvan werd ik doodongelukkig. Het spijt me,' fluisterde ze en ze kuste hem. Toen ging ze in de auto zitten.

'Tot ziens, lieverd,' riep hij, want andere woorden schoten hem niet te binnen.

De Pool ging naar de keuken. Er stond inderdaad nog soep in de koelkast. De maaltijdsalade liet hij staan. Misschien moest hij met zijn jongen over huiswerk praten. Zijn vrouw had onlangs gezegd: 'Pubers kunnen veel maar ze kunnen hun leven niet organiseren. Dat kunnen ze echt niet. Ze hebben daar hulp bij nodig.'

Er lagen wat tomaten op het aanrecht. Hij sneed een tomaat in tweeën, strooide peper en zout op de helften en at die met een schijfje ui geconcentreerd op. De Pool pakte een spiegeltje dat naast de tomaten lag, het kwam uit het make-upetui van Wen, ze moest het per ongeluk daar hebben laten liggen, die ochtend voor ze naar school ging. Hij bekeek zichzelf in de spiegel en wat hij zag beviel hem matig. Hoe kon je niet meer weten wie je was?

In de woonkamer ging hij voorzichtig naast Jurek op de bank zitten. Niet te dichtbij want hij respecteerde grenzen. Ze zaten een tijdje zwijgend naast elkaar. De jongen bekeek nu een serie op tv en de Pool keek mee. Toen de serie was afgelopen zei Jurek: 'Je hebt haar weggepest.'

'Ik? Nee,' zei de Pool. 'Hoe kom je daarbij?' Hij had zich ingesteld op verwijten, alleen niet meteen, niet zo direct.

'Het is je gelukt,' zei de prepuber.

Overal waren verwijten. Je moest ermee leren omgaan, eerst rustig luisteren, dan de verwijten weerleggen, de burger geruststellen, kalmeren – als niet de burger dan wel je eigen zoon. 'Ik heb haar niet weggepest,' zei de Pool. 'Ze wist niet meer wie ze was. Dat is iets anders. Wat wil je eten? Er is nog soep van gisteren.'

De prepuber stond op. Zijn blik was ondoorgrondelijk, je zou bijna zeggen: koud. De Pool wist dat het geen kilte was, het was iets anders, zelfbescherming, zo kon je het noemen. 'Ik denk dat ze niet terugkomt,' zei hij meer tegen zichzelf dan tegen de jongen, 'over een tijdje zul je de helft van de maand bij haar zijn en de andere helft bij mij. Het zal niet erg zijn. We zijn niet boos op elkaar. We houden van elkaar maar ze weet niet meer wie ze is.'

De prepuber bleef naar zijn vader staan kijken. 'Je stinkt naar ui.' Hij ging de kamer niet uit, hij stond naar zijn vader te kijken, zijn Jurek, die ooit brandweerman had willen worden. Zijn kijken was een uitdaging. Een beschuldiging, ook dat. Toen Jurek klein was had de Pool verteld over de slang, de wagens, de oefeningen, ademlucht, de brand die geblust moest worden. Nu wilde de jongen geen brandweerman meer worden, hij zag in de brandweer alleen een organisatie die wilde blussen wat niet geblust had mogen worden, wat hem betreft mocht half Heerlen in de fik opgaan en zelfs als Aken eraan ging zou hij er niet wakker van liggen. De minachting die de jongen de laatste weken tentoonspreidde zou wel bij de puberteit horen, aangenaam was het niet. Geminacht worden in de eigen woonkamer is niet comfortabel.

'Heb je veel huiswerk voor morgen?' vroeg de Pool.

'Al gedaan.'

'Voor wat?'

'Weet ik niet meer.'

'Je hebt het al gedaan maar je weet niet meer voor wat?'

'Ja.'

'Hoe kan dat?'

'Ik onthou alleen dingen die ik moet onthouden.'

'Huiswerk is toch dat je dingen moet onthouden? Dat je dingen uit je hoofd leert?'

'Dat was vroeger. Je loopt achter. Omdat je uit Polen komt denk ik.'

'Zullen we zo gaan eten?'

Jurek ging voor hem staan. Het zag ernaar uit dat hij groter zou worden dan zijn vader. 'Waarom heb je haar weggepest?' De zoon nam de rol van inquisiteur op zich. Hij wilde de waarheid weten en hij zou die uit zijn vader trekken.

'Dat heb ik niet gedaan. Ik heb...' Hij wilde zeggen dat hij geprobeerd had een goede echtgenoot te zijn maar dat was misschien ook niet waar. Hij was banger geweest Jurek te verliezen dan zijn vrouw, zijn vrouw was veilig, om haar hoefde hij zich niet zoveel zorgen te maken. Nooit had hij gedacht dat Wen een vrouw was die niet meer wist wie ze was, die tegen hem zou zeggen: 'Ik heb mezelf verloren.'

'Ik zal de soep opwarmen.' Hij stond op, bekeek de overgebleven jongen die midden in de kamer was blijven staan, bekeek hem goed. Er kwam geen reactie. Hij strekte zijn hand uit om Jurek te strelen. De jongen deinsde terug. 'Blijf van me af, tyfushond.'

'Zo spreek je niet tegen me.' De Pool wilde zijn zoon een klap geven maar hij deed het niet. Opvoeden maakte hem bang. Als brandweerman wist hij hoe je fouten kon voorkomen, als opvoeder niet. De moderne ouders accepteerden veel en ze waren moderne ouders geweest, hij en zijn vrouw. Het kind had emoties, het kind moest die emoties luchten. 'Grenzen stellen en perspectief bieden, dat is opvoeden,' had zijn lieve vrouw altijd gezegd. Wat voor perspectief moest hij bieden? En aan grenzen stellen had hij een hekel gekregen. Altijd als hij dacht aan grenzen stellen zag hij Borys die zich vastklampte aan lantaarnpalen en bomen omdat hij niet naar school wilde.

Hij liep naar de keuken in de hoop dat de jongen achter hem aan zou komen. Dat deed Jurek niet. De Pool warmde mosterdsoep op en terwijl de soep warm werd ging hij terug naar de woonkamer om te kijken wat zijn zoon aan het doen was. Die stond nog steeds stokstijf midden in de kamer.

‘We moeten het met elkaar doen,’ zei de Pool en hij strekte opnieuw een hand uit. Nu reageerde de jongen niet. Hij kwam dichterbij, de Pool. Hij strekte beiden armen naar de overgebleven jongen uit en de jongen liet het toe, hij liet zich omhelzen door zijn vader.

‘We moeten het nu met elkaar doen,’ herhaalde de Pool. ‘Jij en ik. We moeten het met elkaar doen.’

‘Ja,’ antwoordde Jurek bedachtzaam. ‘We moeten het met elkaar doen.’ Het klonk liefdevol en toch ook uitdagend, alsof Jurek al wist dat hij sterker was dan zijn vader.

## 2

De vrouw van Beckers stierf eindelijk echt. Ze was nu niet alleen dood voor de Pool, ze was voor iedereen dood, ook voor haar eigen man en voor de Fransman die haar nooit had opgehaald. En hoewel de Pool dat even een opluchting had geleken, dat ze dood was voor iedereen, viel haar echte dood hem toch tegen. Van opluchting was geen sprake. Hij kon zich nog goed herinneren dat zijn leven, hoe kortstondig ook, om de vrouw van Beckers had gedraaid en om de belofte van troost die ze had gedaan. Tien jaar lag er tussen de ene en de andere dood, maar het leek niets. Het was meer dat met het echte sterven van de vrouw van Beckers de liefde, voor zover die iets anders was dan een plicht die hij met graagte vervulde, voor altijd uit zijn leven verdwenen leek te zijn.

De Pool ging naar de begrafenis omdat alle mannen van de C-ploeg erheen gingen en hij wist zich geen houding te geven, want hij was onzeker over zijn positie. Hoe stond hij daar? Als brandweerman of toch als vriend van de dode? Ten slotte leek het hem het beste om daar te staan als een lid van de C-ploeg, als een van de mannen. En hij deed zijn best tijdens de toespraken niet aan de Fransman te denken, al kon hij het niet nalaten om zich heen te kijken om te zien of die er niet toch stiekem zat.

Zijn Wen kwam evenmin terug. De verliefdheid bleek duurzaam, al sprak ze er weinig over tijdens de spaarzame keren dat ze hem belde en hij wilde er niet naar vragen. Vooral wilde hij niet de indruk wekken dat hij jaloers of gekwetst was. Als de liefde van God – die hij achter zich had gelaten, daar niet van – hem iets had geleerd was het dit: hoe dieper de wond hoe groter de liefde.

'Dat wil jij toch ook niet?' zei Wen via de telefoon. 'Dat we het nog een keer proberen terwijl we weten hoe dat afloopt.'

Hij was te trots om aan te dringen, te bang, ook dat. Daarom zei hij: 'Nee, dat wil ik ook niet.' De scheiding was zo definitief als de dood.

Ze was heel vriendelijk, bijna lief, maar als er nog twijfel had bestaan dan had die haar verlaten. Alle twijfel had haar verlaten en dat maakte haar gelukkiger. De Pool hoorde het aan, zonder paniek, hooguit met het onbestemde gevoel dat het leven een teleurstellende aangelegenheid kon zijn. Ze hadden een paar teleurstellende jaren achter zich, toch waren er ook gelukkige maanden en jaren geweest.

Bij het volgende telefoongesprek vroeg Wen of ze de scheiding zonder een advocaat konden regelen, gewoon met een mediator, een vriendelijke scheiding. Ze hielden immers van elkaar?

Een vriendelijke scheiding, dat leek de Pool wel wat. Hij wilde niet scheiden, het had van hem niet gehoeven maar hij wilde zich er ook niet tegen verweren, omdat hij wist dat het zinloos was. En ja, hij hield van haar. Er was pijn, al was hij zo aan pijn gewend geraakt dat hij die nauwelijks opmerkte. De pijn – een 5,5 op een schaal van 10 – was zijn vriend.

Een week later ging hij met zijn Wen die eigenlijk zijn Wen niet meer was naar het café waar hij ooit met de vrouw van Beckers had gezeten. Hij had voorgesteld niet uitsluitend te bellen, elkaar ook te zien, dat maakte het makkelijker. Toen ze daar in dat café zaten vroeg hij nog een keer, omdat ze van elkaar hielden, of Wen nu weer wist wie ze was. Dat soort dingen mocht hij wel vragen. Ze zei niets en hij drong aan. Hij wilde een antwoord want daarom was ze weggegaan, omdat ze niet meer wist wie ze was. Nu moest ze het zeggen, wie ze was. Hij pakte haar hand, hij merkte dat haar dat ongemakkelijk maakte en toen trok hij zijn hand weer terug.

'Het zal nog een tijd duren,' zei ze. 'Ik weet het nog steeds niet precies. En hoe gaat het met jou?'

'Het gaat.' De Pool roerde in zijn koffie. 'Het gaat. Ik mis je en het is niet makkelijk met de jongen, dat heeft tijd nodig.'

Jurek, de overgeblevene, zat met zijn vader in een te groot huis en beperkte gesprekken tot een minimum. Opgroeien was niet makkelijk, niet voor degene die het moest doen en niet voor de mensen die in de buurt waren. Een scheiding maakte het niet beter. De overgebleven jongen wilde niet gestoord worden in de bezigheid die mensen soms zo vanzelfsprekend 'groter worden' noemden. Hij deed het alleen, hij wilde het alleen blijven doen.

'Het huis is leeg... Je bent toch nog weggegaan.' Het klonk als een verwijt en zo wilde de Pool het niet laten klinken. Er was een nieuwe situatie ontstaan, daaraan moesten ze wennen. Ze had altijd gezegd: spreek over je gevoelens. En hij had nooit begrepen waarom je over gevoelens moest spreken. Je had ze, was dat niet genoeg? En nu hij erover had gesproken, om haar een plezier te doen, merkte hij meteen welke misverstanden dat spreken kon oproepen.

'Ik ben niet tóch nóg weggegaan. Het heeft niets te maken met wat er is gebeurd, lang geleden. Daar zijn we overheen, niet?'

'Ja, daar zijn we overheen.' De Pool wilde nog iets zeggen, weer haar hand pakken, niet om haar de liefde te verklaren maar om zijn genegenheid te laten blijken. Zijn betrokkenheid, om te laten zien dat hij een goede ex kon zijn.

'Ik moet zo weer gaan,' zei ze. 'Ik ga naar het theater. We moeten ook aan Jurek denken. Mist hij me?'

'Hij zegt weinig,' zei de Pool.

'Als ik hem bel dan moet ik elk woord uit hem trekken.'

'Ja, wat wil je. Jij bent weggegaan. Hij voelt zich afgewezen.'

'Hij hoeft me niet te missen. Dat vraag ik niet. Ik heb jullie verlaten. Hij mag best boos zijn.' Toch klonk zijn vrouw teleurgesteld. Niet gemist worden is gruwelijk voor hen die zich geliefd willen wanen.

Zoals de Janowski's eerst probeerden te leven alsof ze nooit een jongen hadden gehad die onder de trein was gekomen, zo probeerden vader en zoon nu te leven alsof er nooit een moeder was geweest, alsof ze altijd al voorbestemd waren met z'n tweeën opgescheept te zitten.

'Wat ga je eigenlijk zien in het theater?' vroeg de Pool.

'Cabaret. De cabaretier die van die harde grappen maakt. Ik ben wel toe aan een paar harde grappen.'

De Pool vroeg om de rekening.

'Straks,' zei ze, 'als alles is geregeld dan is hij twee weken bij mij, twee weken bij jou. Dan zal hij wel spraakzamer worden. Als ze ouder worden gaan ze weer praten. En jij komt er ook vast bovenop.'

'Men heeft mijn zoon van mij afgenomen, Borys. En jij bent van mij afgenomen,' zei de Pool. 'Maar ik kijk naar wat ik heb. Jurek. Een huis, werk. Voeten, handen, benen, armen, ogen, ik heb heel veel. Zo zie ik het. Ik ben een gezegend mens.'

Wen betaalde de rekening. Hij wilde het doen maar ze was hem voor.

'Jij moet nu ook aan een nieuw leven beginnen,' zei Wen toen ze buiten stonden en hij zich vernederd voelde omdat ze de rekening had betaald. Zelfs dat gunde ze hem niet, zelfs die kleine geste weigerde ze aan te nemen. 'Het is belangrijk dat je dat gaat doen.'

Even voelde hij de aanvechting te zeggen dat ze zich niet met zijn leven moest bemoeien. Dat zei hij niet, hij mompelde alleen: 'Ik kijk wel.'

Terwijl hij driftig naar huis liep besloot de Pool dat ze gelijk had. Hij moest een nieuw leven opbouwen. Het oude was voorbij, het nieuwe moest beginnen, de andere mogelijkheid was sterven en daar was hij te jong voor.

Toen hij die avond aan tafel zat, hij had wat eten gehaald bij de Thai, kippensoep voor de jongen, groenteloempia's en een vegetarische curry voor zichzelf, zei hij tegen Jurek: 'Mama komt niet terug. Ik weet het nu zeker.'

'O.'

'Ik bedoel, je zult haar vaak zien maar niet in dit huis.'

'Wist ik al.'

'Wat vind je daarvan?'

'Best,' zei de overgebleven jongen. 'Je hebt haar weggepest. Zei ik toch.'

'Best?' De Pool verhief zijn stem. 'Je moeder gaat weg en jij vindt alles best. Niets kan je wat schelen. Dat maakt me razend.'

'Als je moet uitrazen dan moet je dat doen,' zei Jurek.

De Pool ademde een paar keer diep in. Toen zei hij: 'Ik denk dat ik een vrouw ga zoeken.'

'Je gaat wat?' De jongen smulde van zijn Thaise kippensoep. Hij at graag vlees, het liefst uitsluitend. Ook over het eten zei hij weinig, het opgroeien had hem nors en nukkig gemaakt maar van bepaalde gerechten kon hij hoor- en zichtbaar genieten en dat was eveneens een soort liefde, genieten van het eten.

'Ik ga een vrouw zoeken,' herhaalde de Pool langzaam en nadrukkelijk. Jurek had recht op openheid, op eerlijkheid.

'Good luck, man.'

'Mama is het daarmee eens, ze vindt het een goed idee.'

'Ze is het daarmee eens?' Jurek keek hem aan alsof hij zich dat niet kon voorstellen. Alsof hij zich totaal niet kon voorstellen dat ze zoiets had gezegd.

'Ze is het niet alleen daarmee eens,' herhaalde de Pool. 'Ze heeft het zelf voorgesteld.' Letterlijk had ze het weliswaar niet zo gezegd maar wat kon ze met dat nieuwe leven anders bedoelen dan een nieuwe vrouw? Nieuwe kinderen waren uitgesloten, een nieuwe vrouw lag voor de hand nu de oude ervandoor was gegaan.

'Misschien moet jij haar vragen of zij voor je gaat zoeken?' De jongen lachte even en concentreerde zich toen weer op zijn Thaise kippensoep.

'En wat vind jij ervan?' vroeg de Pool.

'Kan me niets schelen.'

'Weet je dat zeker?'

De overgebleven jongen knikte. 'Ik vind het best.'

De razernij had de Pool verlaten. Hij had zich verzoend met Jurek en zijn pubertaire gelatenheid. Al kon hij zich soms niet aan de indruk onttrekken dat de gelatenheid van Jurek een vorm van niet-leven was, dat ook zijn jongste jongen eigenlijk niet wilde leven. Na de soep en de loempia's was er nog de curry. Ze deelden een bakje met z'n tweeën en voor de zekerheid herhaalde hij wat zijn ex in het café had gezegd. Dat er een regeling zou komen voor Jurek en dat de Pool een nieuwe liefde ging zoeken. Hij vond het belangrijk om dat woord te gebruiken, liefde. 'Ze komt hier niet meteen wonen,' zei hij nog, lepelend in de restanten curry. 'Maar ik ga wel zoeken.'

'Je gaat zoeken? Zoeken? Doe wat je niet laten kan. Ik geef je niet veel kans, man. Misschien kun je homo worden.' En toen zette de overgebleven jongen zijn koptelefoon op maar dat mocht niet van de Pool. Niet tijdens het eten. Tijdens het eten werd er niet naar muziek geluisterd via een koptelefoon, al was het dan eten uit een bakje. De jongen gehoorzaamde, iets aan autoriteit had de Pool nog. Toen ook de curry op was zette hij het bestek en de borden in de afwasmachine en vroeg zich vervolgens af waar hij het beste een vrouw kon zoeken. De vorige had hij niet echt gezocht, hij was erover gestruikeld. Ze had zich aangediend, hij had zich opengesteld. Hoe het precies was gegaan wist hij nauwelijks meer. Wat hij had gedaan en gezegd, hoe hij haar voor zich had gewonnen.

Nu was hij oud, nou ja oud, hij was nog fit, goed verzorgd, kaal maar goed verzorgd, een man op de helft van zijn leven, nog wel zeer bruikbaar, op velerlei manieren. Ja, een zeer bruikbare Pool was hij en dat zou hij tijdens het zoeken ook niet onder stoelen of banken steken. Jurek had ongelijk, hij zou in zijn missie slagen. Hij moest wel actief gaan zoeken. Het ging niet meer vanzelf, voor zover het ooit vanzelf was gegaan. De Pool kon informeren bij collega's hoe zij dat hadden gedaan na de scheiding, alleen schaamde hij zich daarvoor. Er zaten twee gescheiden mannen in de C-ploeg, die hadden allebei nu een vriendin en in de andere ploegen zaten meer gescheiden mannen. Hij had op de kazerne nog niet verteld dat zijn vrouw ervandoor was. Hij stelde het steeds weer uit. Dat ze niet meer wist wie ze was zou hij achterwege laten. Op dergelijke informatie zaten de mannen van de C-ploeg niet te wachten. Zij wisten namelijk wie ze waren en ze konden zich niet voorstellen dat er mensen waren die dat niet wisten.

# 3

Er zaten negen weken en vier dagen tussen de middag dat Wen had gezegd dat hij aan een nieuw leven moest beginnen en het moment dat de Pool zich inschreef bij een datingsite. Hij had het steeds weer uitgesteld, had getwijfeld, zich verzoend met eenzaamheid (de derde week), veel in de Bijbel gelezen (de vierde week) en hij had zich in een massagesalon laten masseren door een Chinese dame (de vijfde week) maar toen ze aan de *happy ending* wilde beginnen was hij in paniek geraakt. 'Zo groot, zo vreselijk groot,' had de Chinese dame gezegd en de Pool had gereageerd: 'Ik ben gewoon een lange man, voor mijn lengte is dit heel normaal. Zelfs een beetje klein.' Daarna had de lust hem verlaten, hij had betaald en was naar huis gereden.

De zesde week had hij geprobeerd veel met Jurek op te trekken, de zevende week was hij in z'n eentje in een bar wat gaan drinken, daar had hij ruzie gekregen met een aangeschoten Fransman, wat hem verbaasde want hij was er de man niet naar om ruzie te zoeken in het café en hij sprak geen Frans. De achtste week schreef hij een lange en gevoelige brief aan Wen die hij daarna verbrandde en de negende week meldde hij zich eindelijk aan bij een datingsite.

Hij omschreef zichzelf als 'lang, betrouwbaar en geestig. Kinderen geen bezwaar'. Weliswaar vond de Pool zichzelf niet geestig maar humor en betrouwbaarheid hoorden nu eenmaal bij de zoektocht naar de liefde. Betrouwbaar was hij, dus het was slechts een halve leugen. Onder hobby's had hij gezet: lezen, films en de natuur. Ook dat was niet helemaal waar. Lezen deed hij niet, hooguit de krant, naar de film ging hij zelden, twee keer per jaar was al veel, maar van de natuur kon hij genieten. Meer nog dan vroeger. Sinds hij in het kippenhok had gewoond had hij een speciale band met de natuur, de bomen, de planten, het mos, niet dat hij wist hoe alles heette. Je hoefde de namen van de bomen niet te kennen om er toch van te kunnen houden. Hij wandelde graag door de heuvels, in elk jaargetijde, en hij keek met verwondering naar wat leefde en niet bij de wereld van de mensen hoorde. Verwondering was voor hem een teken van schoonheid. Vroeger had hij Jurek weleens meegenomen maar die wilde nu niet meer wandelen. De heuvels lieten Jurek koud.

Bewust had de Pool zijn beroep niet vermeld in zijn profiel, hij had weinig behoefte over zijn werk te praten. Brandweerman was nu eenmaal een beroep waar iedereen ideeën, opinies en fantasieën over had. En verder zou hij zich aanpassen aan de eisen en wensen van de nieuwe partner, voor zover er in relaties een wezenlijk verschil bestond tussen wensen en eisen.

Vrij snel had hij per e-mail contact met een stuk of zes vrouwen. Vooral dat 'kinderen geen bezwaar' sloeg aan.

Aan het beantwoorden van de e-mails beleefde hij weinig plezier. Een keer viel hij in slaap terwijl hij aan het typen was. Het zoeken was nog maar net begonnen en het maakte hem nu al moe en nerveus.

Hij dronk een biertje met een weduwe van zijn leeftijd in de lobby van een hotel aan de rand van Heerlen. Ze had twee kinderen in de puberteit. Haar man was bij het sporten omgekomen. De Pool vond het ongepast om te vragen bij welke sport. Als ze dat had willen zeggen had ze de sport zelf wel genoemd. Toch liet het hem niet los. Terwijl zij allang over iets anders praatte bleef hij aan haar man denken. Een lawine tijdens het skiën? Een hartinfarct tijdens een marathon? Toen hij vroeg of ze nog iets wilde drinken zei ze: 'Nee, ik moet naar mijn kinderen en ik zeg het maar meteen want als je dit doet kun je beter eerlijk zijn: ik had iets sprankelenders verwacht.'

De Pool vond haar ook niet bijzonder sprankelend maar moest een weduwe sprankelend zijn? Hij had zich niet bepaald op iets sprankelends voorbereid. Hij wist eigenlijk niet waarop hij zich dan wel had voorbereid. Zelfs jonge mensen vond hij lang niet allemaal sprankelend. Als hij naar zijn jongste zoon keek kon hij weinig sprankelends aan de jongen ontdekken en de zeldzame keren dat hij wat vriendjes en zelfs vriendinnetjes te zien kreeg, was het vooral hun gedesillusioneerde levenshouding die hem trof.

'Hoe bedoel je, sprankelend?' vroeg de Pool.

'Mijn man was sprankelend,' zei ze enthousiast.

Maar die man was dood. Het speet hem dat hij niet aan haar verwachtingen voldeed want al voelde hij niets bij haar, niet eens afkeer – dat was nog íéts geweest – hooguit een dof soort medelijden, hij wilde toch graag aan haar verwachtingen voldoen. 'Ik ben eigenlijk nooit anders geweest dan dit,' zei de Pool. 'Dit is wie ik ben. Ik ben een bruikbare man.'

Ze keek hem glimlachend, bijna uitnodigend aan, alsof ze dacht dat hij een grapje maakte. Daarna betrok haar gezicht. 'Zullen we het dan hierbij laten?' De Pool ging akkoord, al kon hij zich nog altijd niet onttrekken aan een gevoel van falen toen hij naar huis reed. Daarna had hij nog een ontmoeting met een vrouw die twaalf jaar ouder was dan hij. Geen weduwe, wel gescheiden, twee keer zelfs. Ze had een kind dat het huis uit was maar weer was teruggekomen na wat zij noemde 'een zoektocht' en ze wilde nu iemand om, zoals ze had geschreven, 'het avontuur van het leven te kunnen delen'.

'Ik heb een zoon die nog lang niet het huis uit is en ik heb een vaste baan,' zei de Pool. 'Aan wat voor avontuur denk je?' Hij vreesde dat hij voortdurend met haar op reis zou moeten en dat bleek niet verkeerd gedacht. Ze hield ook van muziek, vertelde ze. Van concerten. Kamermuziek. Ze noemde componisten van wie de Pool weleens had gehoord maar daar was het meeste mee gezegd. Gek genoeg zag ze hem ondanks zijn afwerende gebaren en zijn korte antwoorden wel zitten. 'Ik vind lengte belangrijk,' zei ze, 'ik wil geen partner die kleiner is dan ik. Zelf ben ik niet de kleinste, dus dan heb je niet veel keus.'

De Pool had genoeg gehoord, al was zijn lengte een pre. Omdat hij niet het type was om te zeggen dat ze het hier maar bij moesten laten zocht hij naar een diplomatieke uitweg. Die vond hij niet, er bleven alleen beleefdheidsleugentjes over.

Zo gingen weken voorbij. De vrouw van Beckers werd doder, Beckers zelf werd niet echt levendiger. Hij moest nu niet denken aan een nieuwe vrouw, had hij tijdens een oefening verklaard. De Pool probeerde zijn jongen op te voeden en te verzorgen, alsof hij altijd had geweten dat zijn lieve vrouw zou verdwijnen omdat ze niet meer wist wie ze was.

Een derde vrouw die had gereageerd via de datingsite zegde een paar keer af en toen had de Pool er genoeg van. Hij wilde aan een nieuw leven beginnen, alleen niet op deze manier. Hij zou andere wegen bewandelen, betere strategieën uitdenken. Misschien toch gewoon in een bar gaan zitten maar dan zonder ruzie te maken met dronken buitenlanders.

De vrouwen die hij had ontmoet leken niet het nieuwe leven in te willen duiken zoals hij dat wilde, ze wilden gewoon het oude voortzetten, hooguit met een nieuwe man.

De spot van Jurek ('Heb je al een vrouw gevonden of geef je het op?') had plaatsgemaakt voor zakelijke mededelingen. 'Kun je de vuilniszak buiten zetten, het stinkt in de keuken,' zei hij bijvoorbeeld. Dan antwoordde de Pool: 'Doe het zelf.' De angst tot opvoeding over te gaan betekende niet dat er helemaal geen grenzen konden worden gesteld. Hij vroeg ook naar cijfers, naar proefwerken, naar school, dat was opvoeding die de Pool aandurfde na het echec in het verleden en zelfs dat deed hij met tegenzin. Altijd had hij het gevoel dat hij te veel of juist te weinig verwachtte, daarom gaf hij zo min mogelijk commentaar op de cijfers.

Na een tijd begon Jurek lievere dingen te zeggen, zoals: 'Ik blijf bij een vriend eten. Vind je dat goed?' En dan voegde hij eraan toe: 'Jij eet toch wel zonder mij? Of ga je vasten?' Alsof de jongen wist dat de Pool niet voor zichzelf kookte als hij alleen thuis was. Ontroerend vond de Pool dat, de zorgzaamheid, de oplettendheid. Het emotioneerde hem.

Een heel enkele keer liet Jurek het toe dat de Pool naderbij kwam, dat de vader over het hoofd van de zoon aaide, dat een schouder werd vastgepakt, dat er gestoeid werd in de voortuin. Er was lichamelijk contact en daarin zat meer liefde dan in de nog altijd moeizame gesprekken. Aan die momenten hield de Pool zich vast, daaruit putte hij moed.

De mediator, die de scheiding snel en goed zou regelen, zo had ze telefonisch aangekondigd, was een dame met grijs haar en een Franse naam. De Pool verdacht haar ervan de mensen te haten, vooral haar klanten en verder iedereen die geen Franse naam had, maar ondanks de vriendelijke minachting die ze uitstraalde deed ze haar werk grondig. Ze glimlachte veel, dat gaat goed samen met minachting. Wen en de Pool werden het eens, de mediator merkte nog op dat ze het niet vaak had meegemaakt dat haar cliënten zo snel een akkoord bereikten. De Pool vatte het op als een compliment, terwijl zijn ex en hij in het kantoortje van de mediator zaten en probeerden beleefd te blijven alsof leven niets anders was dan een kwestie van beleefdheid.

Toch voelde het ook alsof ze gestraft werden voor onheus gedrag, mensen die het zo goed met elkaar konden vinden moesten bij elkaar blijven. Hij zei tegen de mediator: 'We houden ondanks alles van elkaar.' Zijn lieve ex reageerde niet.

Toen de scheiding helemaal voltooid was – er waren tranen gelaten, dat hoorde erbij – en ze op de stoep van de mediator stonden zei Wen: 'Ik wil je nog vertellen dat ik ben ingetrokken bij de man op wie ik verliefd ben.'

De Pool keek naar de lucht. Hij herinnerde zich de dode jongen, de lantaarnpalen die Borys omhelsd had omdat hij niet naar school wilde. 'Wat snel,' zei hij.

'Ja, ik kon niet eeuwig bij Magda op de bank blijven slapen. Zij heeft ook wat ruimte nodig.'

'Gastvrijheid heeft zijn grenzen.' De Pool pulkte aan een velletje bij zijn nagelriem.

'Heb jij al iemand ontmoet?'

'Ik? Nee. Nog niet.'

'Je hebt het wel geprobeerd? Neem ik aan? Je hebt toch je best gedaan? Je weet dat ik niet terugkom?' Ze vreesde kennelijk dat hij nog altijd hoopte op haar terugkeer maar dat was niet zo.

'Mijn best gedaan, mijn best gedaan, jezus, het is geen examen. Ik kijk rond. Ik maak hier en daar een praatje.' Over de datingsite zweeg hij. Het was allang geen schande meer maar toch.

'Hoe langer je wacht, hoe moeilijker het wordt. Vind je het leuk als ik je aan iemand voorstel?'

Ze liepen een stukje op, hij naar zijn auto, zij naar die van haar. Tussen de twee auto's bleven ze staan. Onhandig, alsof ze een eerste date hadden.

'Meen je dat?' vroeg hij, bijna kwaad.

'Ik kom weleens mensen tegen. Je bent de vader van mijn kind. Kinderen. Ik wil dat het je goed gaat.' Het klonk verontschuldigend.

'Ik heb je hulp niet nodig,' zei hij hard. 'Ik heb je troost niet nodig.' Hij zocht naar zijn autosleutel. Wen was blijven staan. 'Woon je eigenlijk mooi?' vroeg hij.

'Een flatje. Leuk uitzicht. Wil je hem ontmoeten?'

'Die man? Hij is met astrologie bezig toch?'

'Niet de hele tijd, Geniek. Hij is geen astroloog. Het is zijn hobby. Het is misschien goed voor Jurek als je hem ontmoet.' Ze pakte de Pool teder bij zijn arm. 'Ik wil graag dat jij hem ontmoet voor Jurek hem ontmoet. Ik denk dat jullie zelfs vrienden kunnen worden. Volgens mij ken je hem. En je bent nog altijd een heel aantrekkelijke man, er zijn best wat vriendinnen van me die zeggen: die Pool van jou die mocht er best wezen.'

Hoewel hij ertegen opzag zei de Pool: 'Prima, ik ga die astroloog ontmoeten.' Hij wilde nu eenmaal een goede ex zijn en daar hoorden dergelijke ontmoetingen bij. In noodgevallen konden ze het altijd nog over sterrenbeelden hebben. Hij kon zich niet voorstellen dat vriendinnen van Wen over hem zouden zeggen dat hij er goed uitzag. Wen bedoelde het goed, ze wilde hem opvrolijken.

'Het hoeft niet lang te duren,' zei ze. 'Gewoon, dat je weet wie het is. Jurek zal wel met verhalen thuiskomen als hij bij ons is geweest.'

'Jurek is niet zo'n prater, dat weet je net zo goed als ik.'

'Zullen we over een paar dagen in een café afspreken? Een café, dat is neutraal terrein, vind je niet?'

De Pool wist niet of ze neutraal terrein nodig hadden maar hij had er ook niets op tegen. Toch werd hij weer even overmand door het gevoel dat hij bij Wen had willen blijven, onvolmaakt als ze waren. Het onvolmaakte huwelijk was hem al met al prima bevallen. Even vreesde hij dat hij een terugval zou krijgen, dat hij weer naar het kippenhok zou gaan verlangen. Hij moest zich concentreren op praktische zaken, het huishouden, de opvoeding, een nieuwe liefde.

Een paar dagen later zat de Pool in het hem zo bekende café, zekerheidshalve was hij te vroeg gekomen. Toen hij twee koffie had gedronken bestelde hij bier. De krant die anders altijd op de bar lag was dit keer nergens te vinden. Wen was te laat zodat de Pool een halfuur moest wachten. Hij was nerveuzer dan tijdens de dates die hij achter zich had, al was er niets uit voortgekomen, geen liefde, geen seks.

Tussendoor borrelden gedachten aan de vrouw van Beckers op, hoe hij hier met haar had gezeten, aan hetzelfde tafeltje. Hoe ze hem had aangekeken en hem troost had toegezegd. Er was weinig veranderd in dit café. Dezelfde man werkte er nog.

Toen Wen eindelijk verscheen begreep hij eerst niet dat de man die achter haar het café in kwam bij haar hoorde, Het Menselijk Verlengstuk. Pas toen Wen zei: ‘Dit is hem nou’, en ze de man naar voren duwde besefte de Pool dat ’t het verlengstuk was dat haar hart sneller had doen kloppen.

Hij schudde de man de hand en hij vroeg zich af wat zijn naam ook alweer was, je kon moeilijk Verlengstuk zeggen tegen een mens. Hij was vermagerd, de man. Hij was niet meer de zelfverzekerde hulpverlener van een decennium geleden. Hij had iets verslagens over zich. Iets gebrokens.

De man sloeg de Pool joviaal op de schouder en daarop omhelsde de Pool het verlengstuk onhandig. Hij drukte de vriend van zijn vrouw tegen zich aan, hij drukte hem bijna fijn om zijn goede bedoelingen te laten blijken.

Ze gingen zitten, Wen begon met praten en hield er vervolgens niet meer mee op, ze ratelde, ze zei zoveel dat de Pool nauwelijks kon onthouden wat ze te berde bracht, over de kleuterschool, over zorg, ouders, deze tijd, over vrouw-zijn, hij kon het allemaal niet bijhouden, hij maakte uit haar geratel in elk geval op dat ook zij behoorlijk zenuwachtig was. Tot hij haar onderbrak met de vraag: ‘Wat willen jullie drinken?’

‘Koffie,’ zei ze en het verlengstuk wilde hetzelfde. De

Pool zat al aan het bier dus daar hield hij het bij.

'Dat had ik niet gedacht,' zei hij toen iedereen zijn bestelling had gekregen. 'Het Menselijk Verlengstuk.'

'Ruud,' antwoordde de man, 'zeg toch gewoon Ruud! Ik wist dat we elkaar nog eens zouden tegenkomen zij het niet op deze manier. Niet zo.' Nu hij het woord had genomen kwam het menselijk verlengstuk al minder verslagen over dan daarnet.

'Hoe hebben jullie elkaar ontmoet?' Dat wilde de Pool wel weten.

'Via mijn bedrijf,' zei Ruud, 'ik was aan het uitbreiden. Ik begon met bejaarden, dat weet je en dat was een succes. Er zijn zoveel bejaarden en er komen er steeds meer bij. Wie wil dood als je de zorg van een menselijk verlengstuk kunt krijgen? Het was een succes. Van Venlo tot Maastricht liepen er menselijke verlengstukken rond en net over de grens, Mönchengladbach, Aken, daar liepen ze ook. Geleidelijk kwam ik erachter dat het niet alleen bejaarden waren die behoefte hadden aan zo'n verlengstuk. Er is zoveel zorg nodig.' Bij deze woorden keek hij de Pool indringend aan, hij liet een stilte vallen maar de Pool zei niets.

'Als mensen eenmaal de juiste zorg hebben gehad,' ging het verlengstuk verder, 'dan willen ze niet meer zonder.' Het verlengstuk sprak, zelf kon hij stil zijn. Hij hoefde alleen te luisteren. Dat vond de Pool bijzonder aangenaam.

'De verbinding, daar gaat het om, waar vind je die nog?'

'De verbinding?' De Pool nam een grote slok bier.

'De verbinding tussen mensen,' legde het verlengstuk uit. 'Een jaar of wat geleden kwam ik erachter dat ik niet alleen zorg moest aanbieden, ook verbinding. Iedereen die zorg nodig heeft wil verbinding, er zijn mensen die geen zorg nodig hebben en toch snakken naar verbinding. En voor hen richtte ik die tweede tak van mijn bedrijfje op. De tak die verbinding aanbood aan mensen die zich verder nog zelf konden aankleden maar die iets fundamenteels misten.' Daarbij keek de voormalige mensenknecht naar Wen waaruit de Pool opmaakte dat zijn vrouw kennelijk iets fundamenteels had gemist.

'Ah,' zei de Pool terwijl zijn ex bezig was iets te zoeken in haar tas.

'We groeiden te snel,' vervolgde het verlengstuk. 'Ik nam mensen in dienst die het niet in zich hadden.'

'Hoe heb je nou mijn vrouw ontmoet?' vroeg de Pool.

'Ja, ja.' Ruud klonk geïrriteerd. 'Dat komt zo. Ik vertel het even chronologisch. Dat zeg ik ook altijd bij intakegesprekken, hou het chronologisch. Je hebt toch geen haast?'

'Nee,' zei de Pool.

Het menselijk verlengstuk nam een slok koffie. 'Ik ging zelf weer werken als verlengstuk om te weten wat er leefde. Om te zien waar het misging. Er waren mensen in dienst gekomen die geen kaas hadden gegeten van op maat gesneden zorg en verbinding. Die dachten: werken als verlengstuk is zoiets als werken in de horeca. Je smijt wat eten op tafel en als je erbij lacht krijg je een fooi op de koop toe. Nee, zo werkt het niet.' De man begon zich op te winden bij de gedachte aan onkundige werknemers. Hij staarde even geërgerd voor zich uit en toen hervatte hij zijn verhaal. 'Ik ben verbinder bij uitstek, ik zeg het eerlijk, ik ben begonnen met zorg maar verbinden is wat ik echt kan.'

'Ja. Dat is mooi.' Het glas van de Pool was nu leeg. 'En zo heb je mijn vrouw ontmoet?' Hij wilde graag weten hoe het menselijk verlengstuk op Wendela was gestoten. Niet uit jaloezie. Hij was gekwetst, dat was normaal, niet bovenmatig jaloers. En gekwetst worden hoorde bij het leven.

'Zo ongeveer,' zei de man. 'Ze zocht werk als verbinder.'

'Je zocht werk?' De Pool keek naar de vrouw die nog altijd voelde als zijn lieve vrouw, ook al was ze dan niet meer bij hem en woonde ze nu samen met de voormalige mensenknecht. 'Ja,' zei Wen.

'Je had toch werk?'

'Ik zocht ander werk, ik wilde me oriënteren.'

De Pool knikte.

'Ze kwam voor een kennismakingsgesprek,' zei de verbinder, 'en toen herinnerde ik me haar weer. Ik vroeg: hoe is het met je man. En vervolgens zei ze, ja, vervolgens zei ze hoe het was. Ze zei precies hoe het was.'

Onder het lege glas bier lag een viltje en de Pool begon ermee te spelen. Ze had precies gezegd hoe het was. Hij had dat verhaal wel willen horen. Daarop vroeg hij: 'Wat doet een verbinder precies?'

'Goede vraag,' zei de voormalige mensenknecht, 'dat is een ingewikkeld verhaal.' Meteen had de Pool spijt dat hij die vraag had gesteld.

'Een verbinder...' er viel weer een stilte, 'een verbinder verbindt. Hij verbindt zich met de ander. Ik verbind me met iedereen, ik kan het niet helpen, ik heb die gave. Ik verbind me bijvoorbeeld nu met jou. Voel je dat?'

De Pool keek hem aan.

'Je moet het tijd geven,' zei de voormalige mensenknecht. 'Je moet je ervoor openstellen. Sommige mensen kunnen zich er niet voor openstellen en dan komt de professionele verbinder van pas. Die heeft geduld. Die zoekt een opening. In ieder menselijk harnas zit een opening, ook in het jouwe.'

Dat vond de Pool niet prettig om te horen. Hij had niet het idee dat hij een harnas aanhad en als er al een harnas om hem heen zat was het niet aan de nieuwe vriend van zijn vrouw om naar openingen te zoeken. Hij keek om zich heen. Een vrouw met een hoedje was binnengekomen, ze had een puzzelboekje uit haar tas gehaald. Straks moest hij nog naar de supermarkt voor morgenochtend, de yoghurt en de muesli waren op. Als hij iets had geleerd was het dit: opvoeding was niet verbinden, opvoeden was het ontbijt klaarzetten met onverstoorbare kalmte.

'Dus zo hebben jullie elkaar ontmoet,' zei de Pool in de

hoop het gesprek op die manier langzaam te beëindigen. Even voelde hij de aanvechting om te zeggen: Wen, had hij niet gewoon je minnaar kunnen worden, waarom meteen scheiden? Had het eerst een tijdje met twee mannen geprobeerd.

De voormalige mensenknecht knikte. 'We hebben elkaar geschreven. Brieven. Echte, ouderwetse brieven. Omdat ik je vrouw, ik noem haar jouw vrouw want op een bepaalde manier is ze jouw vrouw en zal ze altijd jouw vrouw blijven, jullie hebben een dood kind en een levend kind, niets verbindt zo als een dood kind, dat respecteer ik, maar omdat jouw vrouw wel verbinder wilde worden heb ik gezegd: weet wat je doet. Nu heb je genoeg van de kleuterschool, straks verlang je nog naar de kleuters en dan is het te laat. Het is geen makkelijk beroep.'

De Pool staarde naar zijn vrouw, zijn ex en hij zei: 'Ik wist niet dat je er genoeg van had, van de kleuterschool.'

Ze haalde haar schouders op. 'Het was ook niet dat ik er genoeg van had. Maar als ik nog eens iets anders wilde dan moest ik niet te lang wachten.'

'Dat is zo,' zei de Pool. 'Als je iets anders wilt moet je niet te lang wachten.' Er viel een stilte en daarna vroeg de Pool aan de nieuwe vriend van zijn vrouw: 'Jij doet aan astrologie, niet?'

'Mag geen naam hebben,' zei de man, 'een hobby, als je een keer bij ons komt eten zal ik je informatie over jezelf geven. Daar kun je je voordeel mee doen. Kreeft, toch?'

Toen zeiden ze niets meer, de voormalige mensenknecht, de Pool en ook de vrouw die tussen hen in zat niet, tot het de voormalige mensenknecht was die opmerkte: 'Als je zoon bij ons is dan zal ik me terughoudend opstellen, dat is wat je moet weten. Ik kan jou niet vervangen. Ik wíl jou niet vervangen. Je moet de kinderen naar je toe laten komen. Vertrouwen win je niet door je aan hen op te dringen. Ik zal je zoon laten komen, ik zal rustig afwachten tot hij naar me toe komt. Als hij niet komt is het ook goed.'

'Ja,' zei de Pool, 'fijn.' Toen stonden ze op en de twee mannen omhelsden elkaar. Vervolgens omhelsde de Pool zijn ex, hij drukte haar tegen zich aan. 'Ik moet nog naar de supermarkt,' zei hij. 'Weet je wat ik onlangs vond? De sjaal die je voor me gebreid hebt. Toen je opeens ging breien.'

'Mijn spulletjes,' zei ze, 'mijn spulletjes zijn nog bij jou. Moet ik die ophalen? Heeft dat haast? Mogen die nog even daar blijven?'

'Je spulletjes. Nee, dat heeft geen haast. Het is een mooie sjaal geworden. Als het koud is doe ik hem om.'

'Ik leef nog even uit koffers, die spullen van mij staan niet in de weg, toch? Zodra Ruud en ik groter wonen komen we ze ophalen.'

Ze gingen naar buiten en op straat zei de voormalige mensenknecht nog dat de Pool altijd welkom was maar hij begreep dat dingen tijd nodig hadden. De Pool moest zelf aangeven als de tijd was aangebroken, de tijd van vriendschap, de tijd van nabijheid en verbinding.

'Dat zal ik doen,' riep de Pool iets te joviaal. Daarop liep hij naar de supermarkt en hoewel een mandje groot genoeg was nam hij een karretje en duwde dit eerst langs de groente, ook al had hij geen groente nodig, en toen langs de zuivel. Hij legde twee pakken yoghurt in het karretje en nam een pak muesli uit het schap. Het nieuwe leven was begonnen. Zijn lieve ex was er al mee begonnen. Of ze gelukkig was kon hij niet met zekerheid zeggen, misschien ging het daar niet om.

Hij vroeg zich af hoe zijn nieuwe leven eruit zou zien. Zoals zijn vader dat had gedaan? Naar een andere stad vertrekken en korte metten maken met het verleden, nee dat was niets voor hem.

Bij het prikbord waar mensen gratis advertenties konden ophangen bleef hij staan. Zijn oog bleef hangen aan een advertentie: 'Zoekt u ware liefde? Bent u romantisch aangelegd? Bent u ontevreden over uw leven? Kijk eens verder dan uw neus lang is.' Hij deed een stap dichterbij om de advertentie beter te bestuderen. 'In Rusland, Oekraïne, China, Peru of Brazilië wacht uw partner vol ongeduld op u,' las hij. 'Wij brengen u in contact met ware en duurzame liefde.'

Hij maakte een foto van de advertentie en toen hij merkte dat er iemand naar hem stond te kijken liep hij beschaamd de supermarkt uit.

## 4

Op een middag toen Jurek weer eens terugkwam van zijn moeder en het menselijk verlengstuk en de jongen op de vraag hoe hij het daar had gehad niet meer zei dan 'oké' – zoals alle voorgaande keren – besloot de Pool dat het tijd was om actie te ondernemen. Hij kon niet blijven wachten op een teken. Er was genoeg gewacht. Straks zou Jurek het huis uit zijn, hij zou gaan studeren of werken en dan was de Pool alleen. Het vooruitzicht vond hij niet eens onaantrekkelijk maar hij was bang voor wat de mensen zouden zeggen. Hij wilde niet eindigen als een eenzame, oude man. Behoeftig en van god en iedereen verlaten. Zo'n man van wie je niet met zekerheid kon zeggen of hij de mensen had verstoten of de mensen hem. Het soort dat hij als brandweerman al te goed kende. Ze waren vaak niet heel oud geweest maar kennelijk wel vereenzaamd want ze lagen al een tijdje weg te rotten, zo lang dat de buren over stank begonnen te klagen. Een keer waren ze bij een man geweest met allemaal vogeltjes, die waren doodgedaan in hun kooitjes. Van de dorst en de honger. De dode man stonk niet eens zo, het waren de vogeltjes die vreselijk stonken. Het was hun lucht die niet te harden was. Nee, zo iemand wilde de Pool niet worden, een man met vogeltjes om zich heen in plaats van mensen, en daarom besloot hij nog die dag te bellen met het bedrijf waarvan hij de advertentie had zien hangen in de supermarkt.

Hij ging naar boven, naar de slaapkamer waar de spulletjes van zijn vrouw nog steeds niet waren verdwenen. Ze stelde het telkens uit. Hij was gewend geraakt aan haar spulletjes die door haar afwezigheid des te aanweziger waren. Een goed alternatief voor de mens: zijn spulletjes, zijn lieve spulletjes.

Het bedrijf heette Liefde over de Grens. Zittend op het bed belde hij, een tikkeltje zenuwachtig, dat wel. Hij had nog nooit met dergelijke bedrijven gebeld.

Hij hoorde een mannenstem: 'Hallo.'

'Is dit Liefde over de Grens?' vroeg de Pool voor de zekerheid. Hij had iets zakelijkers verwacht, nu had hij het gevoel dat hij gewoon naar iemands huis belde, naar een privépersoon.

'Zeker,' zei de man en zijn stem klonk meteen anders. 'Dit is Paul van Liefde over de Grens. Wat kan ik voor je doen?'

De Pool bekeek zijn rechterhand. Aan handen kon je de leeftijd van mensen aflezen maar zijn hand was best oké. Hij kon nu ophangen, dan zou er misschien nooit een nieuw leven beginnen. 'Ik zag jullie advertentie in de supermarkt.'

'Ja,' zei Paul. 'Waarmee kan ik je helpen? Wat zoek je?'

'Hoe bedoel je?'

'Een Chineesje?'

'Een wat?'

'Zoek je een Chinese partner?'

'Nee, hoezo?'

'Over twee weken hebben we onze grote Chinareis gepland. Het slaagpercentage ligt hoog in China, bijna iedere man vindt daar iets van zijn gading.'

De Pool bestudeerde zijn nagels.

'Ben je daar nog?' vroeg Paul.

'Ik spreek geen Chinees.'

'Dat geeft helemaal niets. We hebben uitstekende vertalers en als jouw Chinese dame eenmaal in Nederland is spreekt ze binnen de kortste keren Nederlands. Daar komt bij dat de taal van de liefde internationaal is, daar heb je helemaal geen Chinees voor nodig. Is dit je eerste partner of ben je al eens samen geweest met... Met iemand?' Paul klonk nu eerder aarzelend, niet meer overrompelend.

'Ik ben getrouwd. Geweest.'

'Juist. Ja. En nu gescheiden?'

'Ja.' De Pool ging verzitten. Hij keek naar de spulletjes. Zelfs haar wekker stond er nog. Ze gebruikte nu vast de wekker van het menselijk verlengstuk. De man die wist dat de wereld zou uitmonden in zorg en verbinding.

'Wat voor type was je ex? Is het handig om iets soortgelijks te zoeken of wil je liever iets anders, iets totaal anders?'

'Type?'

'Blondine? Brunette?'

'Blondine.'

'Blondine. Zullen we het dan in die richting zoeken?' vroeg Paul.

'Dat is goed,' zei de Pool.

'Oekraïne. Daar vind je beslist wat je zoekt. Hoe heet je eigenlijk?'

De Pool noemde zijn naam.

'Oekraïne,' zei Paul van Liefde over de Grens zonder verder op de naam van de Pool in te gaan. 'Dat is het voor jou. Over vijf weken hebben we weer een reis naar Kiev. Ook een hoog slagingspercentage daar. Zelfs de meest cynische man moet toegeven dat Oekraïne iets met je doet. Wat is je beroep?'

'Doet dat ertoe?' De Pool wilde graag anoniem blijven. Niet iedereen hoefde te weten dat hij liefde over de grens zocht. Het was beschamend. Het viel buiten het bestek van wat normaal heette, hoewel ze vroeger een brandweerman op de kazerne hadden gehad die thuis met een Thais vrouwtje zat maar dat was een rare brandweerman. Hij had niet lekker in de groep gelegen. Geen teamspeler. Binnen een paar jaar was hij verdwenen. Naar Thailand met zijn vrouw. Hij zou daar iets in de export zijn gaan doen. Nooit meer iets van de man gehoord. Zelfs geen kaartje.

'Je zult je partner naar Nederland moeten halen,' zei de

man van Liefde over de Grens. 'Of zit je in België?'

'Ik zit in Nederland.'

'Juist, wij opereren in Nederland en België, soms ook een beetje in Duitsland. Het is wel zaak dat je boven het minimumloon verdient, anders wordt het moeilijk je partner naar Nederland te halen. Zit je boven het minimumloon?'

'Ik ben brandweerman,' zei de Pool toen toch maar.

'Mooi,' zei Paul. 'Een ambtenaar. Dat moet lukken. Wij geven niet op. Dat je dat weet. Wij geven nooit op. Hoe moeilijker de man is hoe meer er ons aan gelegen is hem te helpen. Niemand is onbemiddelbaar, op elk potje past een dekseltje. En ik zal er persoonlijk voor zorgen dat er ook op jouw potje binnenkort een dekseltje past. Kun je je naam nog een keer noemen?'

De Pool dacht even na. 'Iedereen noemt me de Pool,' zei hij.

'Ik heb echt je naam even nodig.'

'Geniek.' Hij spelde het. En daarna gaf hij zijn e-mailadres. Alle informatie zou hem worden toegestuurd. Paul vroeg nog of hij de dagen dat de grote Oekraïnereis was gepland alvast wilde vrijhouden en de Pool wist niet wat hij moest zeggen want hij was nog niet helemaal van Oekraïne overtuigd. Hij was van plan aan een nieuw leven te beginnen maar nu het zo dichtbij kwam klonk Oekraïne erg ver weg, erg nieuw. Te nieuw misschien.

De informatie kwam, de Pool vulde de formulieren in en stuurde alles terug per e-mail. Al had hij op veel vragen geen goed antwoord geweten. Hij wist niet wat hij zocht. Liefde vermoedelijk, zelfs daar was hij niet zeker van. Wat was liefde in de praktijk? Aanspraak die op je werd gemaakt, de versmelting, waar hij als hij eerlijk was tegen opzag. Weer versmelten. En dan? Hoe vaak kon een mens versmelten? Bovendien had hij de ervaring dat alles waarmee hij versmolt doodging of de benen nam. Even herinnerde hij zich zijn moeder, weinig stond hem nog van haar bij. Een gat was zij, een gemis, zij die er niet was, de mensen eindigden als gaten in het geheugen van de ander. Een plastic zak met perziken die ze hem op een zomerse dag had gegeven, dat stond hem nog bij. Die perziken, de smaak ervan, die herinnerde hij zich beter dan zijn moeder. En zo was ook zijn vader een gat geworden, net als zijn oudste. De Pool was een man zonder verleden en hij besloot dat juist dat soort mannen een toekomst nodig hadden. De liefde had hij leren kennen, lang geleden, bij de Grote Vader, nu wilde hij minder ambitieus te werk gaan: gezelschap was al goed.

Hij deed zijn best, hij vulde alles in wat ze van hem wilden weten, van zijn verlangens en zijn wensen, hij sloeg geen vraag over, want hij had een toekomst nodig. Ze vroegen ook naar zijn gezondheid en een eventuele kinderwens en aan het eind las hij alles nog een keer door en stuurde de formulieren per e-mail aan Liefde over de Grens.

Na nog geen twee dagen kreeg hij bericht dat zijn inschrijving was geaccepteerd, dat hij was ingeschreven voor de grote Oekraïne-Liefdesreis. Er zouden tussen de 15 en 25 mannen meegaan, werd hem meegedeeld, maar meneer Janowski hoefde zich geen zorgen te maken, er was zeer veel aandacht voor elke individuele deelnemer en zijn specifieke wensen. Het geld moest binnen tien dagen worden overgemaakt.

De Pool maakte zich toch een beetje zorgen, al wist hij niet waarover. De reis en Oekraïne waren abstract geweest en nu het zo dichtbij kwam werden Oekraïne en liefde akelig concreet, en duur, ook dat. Om te beginnen moest hij het aan Jurek vertellen.

'Ik ga naar Kiev,' zei hij die avond. Ze stonden allebei in de badkamer. Jurek zei niets, daarom voegde de Pool eraan toe: 'Niet lang. Een paar dagen.'

'Waarnaartoe?'

'Kiev, Oekraïne.'

'Wat ga je daar doen?'

'Wat ik daar ga doen?' De Pool hing een handdoek recht. Hij besloot het zo eerlijk mogelijk te zeggen. 'Ik ga liefde zoeken. Gezelschap. Iemand om mee oud te worden.'

'Liefde?'

'Ja. Een vrouw.'

'In Kiev?'

'Ja,' zei de Pool.

'Waarom?'

'Omdat ik dacht...' zei de Pool. 'Omdat ik meega met een reis.'

'Een reis?'

'We gaan met een paar mensen op reis, we gaan de liefde zoeken.'

'Met z'n allen?'

'Nee, ieder voor zich.'

'Is dat normaal?'

'Wat?'

Jurek had zijn tanden gepoetst en hij was nu bezig met een mee-eter op zijn neus.

'Ja, best normaal,' zei de Pool. 'Je kunt alleen zoeken of je kunt online zoeken of je kunt met een paar mensen op reis gaan. Iedereen zoekt op zijn eigen manier naar de liefde. Er zijn steeds meer mensen die dat over de grens doen. Bij jou in de klas zitten toch ook kinderen met een buitenlandse ouder?'

De overgebleven jongen keek even nadenkend naar zijn vader, concentreerde zich toen weer op zijn neus en zei: 'Ja, maar die hebben toevallig iemand ontmoet op de camping of zo. Die zijn niet helemaal ergens heen gegaan om liefde te vinden. Dat is niet normaal.'

'Nou ja,' zei de Pool na een korte pauze, 'ik doe dat dus wel.'

'Kiev?' vroeg de jongen. 'Waarom Kiev?'

De Pool was nog steeds met de handdoeken in de weer. Eerlijk gezegd wist hij niet precies waarom het Kiev was geworden. 'Ik heb hier gezocht maar het leek me beter om het elders te proberen. Ik kan hier geen goede vrouw vinden.'

'Onzin,' zei de jongen met zijn gezicht onder de kraan. 'Er zijn hier genoeg vrouwen. Ze willen je niet hebben, is dat het? De chickies, ze moeten je niet. Dat is het hè?'

De Pool schudde zijn hoofd. 'Ze willen me best hebben. Ik heb een vrouw ontmoet die me wilde hebben, ze wilde met me op reis. Dat ging niet. Ik heb jou, ik heb mijn werk. Ik kan niet langdurig op reis.'

De overgebleven jongen begon zijn gezicht droog te wrijven en bestudeerde zijn neus daarna weer in de spiegel. Het was de Pool duidelijk dat Kiev de jongen niet beviel maar wat wist hij eigenlijk van Kiev? Had de Pool zich dan moeten inschrijven voor de grote Chinareis? Alleen al de lange vliegreis had hem afgeschrikt.

Ook hij bekeek zichzelf in de spiegel en hij stelde zich voor wat de vrouwen in Kiev zouden zien als ze naar hem keken. 'Ik wil een nieuw leven beginnen en daar hoort een vrouw bij,' zei hij meer tegen zichzelf dan tegen de overgebleven jongen. 'Kiev. Berlijn. Maastricht. Wat maakt het uit? Je hoeft niet bang te zijn, ze zal nooit tussen ons in komen te staan. Ik wil gewoon iets anders.'

Zijn jongen keek nog misprijzender dan daarnet. De Pool moest het beter uitleggen. 'Kiev is een goede stad voor de liefde. Zelfs de meeste cynische man vindt daar wel iets. En ik ben geen cynische man. Sinds je moeder is weggegaan ontbreekt er iets... Ik ga een nieuw leven beginnen zoals jouw moeder dat is begonnen, van wie ik nog veel hou maar we konden niet samen...' Hij praatte het bedrijf na, hij praatte zijn ex na, hij had geen idee hoe hij het anders aan zijn overgebleven jongen kon vertellen. 'Jij bent dan bij mama,' zei hij tegen de overgebleven jongen. 'Jij hebt nergens last van. Als ik in Kiev ben.'

'Hmm,' zei de jongen en hij knipte met een nagelschaartje een haartje bij zijn linker wenkbrauw weg. 'En dan kom je terug?' vroeg hij, 'dan sta je hier in de badkamer met een wildvreemd wijf uit Kiev? Nou, dan ga ik bij vrienden wonen. Of bij mama. Al kan ik die verhalen van haar Ruud ook niet meer horen.'

'Nee,' zei de Pool. 'Je hoeft niet bang te zijn. Dat "wijf" komt niet meteen hier. Je wordt verliefd, dan ga je elkaar schrijven en op een dag staat ze hier voor de deur met twee of drie koffers, zo stel ik het me voor. Die dag is nog ver weg. En misschien lukt het ook niet in Kiev. En jij staat op nummer één.'

De jongen was klaar met het bestuderen van zijn gezicht. 'Ik weet het niet,' zei hij, 'van mij had het niet gehoeven. Het is prima zo. Ik bedoel, zonder mama, jij en ik.' De jongen wilde weggaan, toch zei de Pool: 'Ik kan niet alleen blijven. Het lijkt ver weg, maar straks ben je het huis uit en dan...'

De jongen haalde zijn schouders op. 'Je kunt prima alleen blijven, je bent altijd alleen geweest en je hebt mama. Die komt heus wel langs als ik het huis uit ben. En ik zal heus ook niet doen alsof ik niet weet wie je bent.'

'Nee, ik heb mama niet meer. Mama heeft iemand anders. Mama wist niet meer wie ze was, ik geloof dat ze dat nu weer weet, jij ziet haar vaker dan ik.'

'Ja,' zei de jongen, 'ze weet het weer. Kun je me even alleen laten? Ik wil naar de wc.'

De Pool bleef door het huis drentelen. Hij had alvast drie dagen vrij gevraagd voor de Oekraïnereis – de liefde was wel wat vrije dagen waard – en hij had uiteindelijk op de kazerne verteld over de scheiding. De mannen van de C-ploeg hadden er goed op gereageerd. Ze vonden zo'n scheiding geen bewijs voor falen, het woord 'mislukking' was niet over hun lippen gekomen. De nieuwe liefde bezorgde hem hoofdpijn, moest hij bekennen. Om te beginnen omdat hij zich niets bij die stad en dat land kon voorstellen maar ook omdat hij opzag tegen de ontmoeting. Wat zeg je tegen je nieuwe liefde? Moest je meteen over jezelf vertellen?

De volgende middag belde hij zijn ex. Ze vroeg hoe het ging en toen ze de wederzijdse formaliteiten hadden afgewerkt wilde ze weten waarom hij belde, of er niet toch iets was. Ze klonk liefdevol, ongerust zelfs.

'Ik ga naar Kiev,' zei hij. 'Eind van de maand.'

'O.'

'Ik ga er een paar dagen tussenuit. Ik heb vrij genomen, Jurek is dan bij jou dus hij zal nergens last van hebben.'

'Wat ga je daar doen?'

De Pool speelde met een tandenstoker en zei toen dat hij daar verliefd ging worden. Hij had niet het idee dat hij zomaar iets zei, dat hij iets verzon. Hij voelde ineens dat hij in Kiev verliefd zou worden. Bij een nieuw leven hoorde verliefdheid. Eerst verliefdheid dan het nieuwe leven. Als het alleen om gezelschap ging had hij lid kunnen worden van een eetclubje.

'Verliefd?' vroeg zijn ex. 'Maak je een grapje?' Ze klonk niet alleen sceptisch, ze klonk ongerust.

'Nee. Geen grapje. Soms heb je een gevoel, ken je dat niet?'

Ze zei niets terwijl hij precies deed wat ze van hem verwachtte, al had ze vermoedelijk geen rekening met Kiev gehouden. 'Ik wilde je het vertellen zodat je het niet van de jongen hoort,' zei hij.

Ze zuchtte. Of leek dat zo? 'Ik vind het een vreemd verhaal. Je bent toch niet in handen van een oplichtster gevallen? Is het daar trouwens geen oorlog?'

Oorlog, daar had hij niet aan gedacht. Was daar oorlog?

'Ik geloof dat die alweer voorbij is.'

'Je stort je niet in iets waar je later spijt van krijgt?' vroeg ze.

'Spijt? Nee. Ik volg je advies op.'

'Mijn advies?'

'Ja, een nieuw leven. Een nieuwe liefde.'

Ze zuchtte opnieuw leek het. 'Ik had het niet over... ik had het over... Ja, god, ik had het over levensvreugde. Ik had het gewoon... Ik had het over gewone dingen. Over vreugde.'

Over gewone dingen? Over vreugde? Niet over een vrouw? Lekker wandelen, een biertje op een zomerse avond, had ze dat bedoeld? Maar met wie dan? Alleen? 'Gewone dingen,' zei de Pool. 'Daar heb ik het ook over. Gewone dingen. Ik denk dat ik die in Kiev ga vinden. Kiev is gewoon.' Hij merkte dat hij zich begon op te winden. 'Waarom zou je levensvreugde niet in Kiev mogen vinden? Waarom zou je die alleen om de hoek mogen tegenkomen?'

'Jij moet doen waarvan je denkt dat het goed voor je is. Het is jouw leven, Geniek. Het is helemaal van jou. Het is altijd van jou geweest, al wilde je dat niet weten. Heb je wel af en toe seks?'

De Pool stak de tandenstoker in zijn mond en probeerde iets tussen zijn voortanden te verwijderen. 'Niet bovenmatig,' zei hij met de tandenstoker in zijn mond.

'Ik zeg het eerlijk, het liefst zou ik willen dat je nooit meer met iemand naar bed zou gaan, dat je altijd naar mij zou blijven verlangen, maar dat is egoïstisch en dat ben ik niet. Je moet wel blijven neuken, Geniek. Anders word je zo'n... Zo'n, nou ja je weet wel, desnoods pik je iemand op die je helemaal niet aantrekkelijk vindt.'

'Desnoods zal ik dat doen,' zei de Pool. Ze spraken nog wat over Jurek en zijn ex zei dat de Pool maar moest langskomen om te eten als hij terug was uit Kiev, dat het dan wel zou kunnen. Hij antwoordde dat hij na Kiev zou komen eten en het huis zou zien waar zijn ex met de voormalige mensenknecht woonde. 'Een flatje,' antwoordde ze, 'we wonen gewoon in een flatje. We zoeken iets groters.'

Toen het telefoongesprek was beëindigd ging hij achter

zijn laptop zitten en nam de instructies van Liefde over de Grens nog eens door. De instructies begonnen met de zin: 'Iedereen zoekt liefde, maar sommige mensen maken er echt werk van.' De Pool had het gevoel dat hij een van de mensen was die er echt werk van maakten omdat hij helemaal naar Kiev ging. De liefde mocht wat kosten.

Hij had de adviezen al eens gelezen, nu nam hij ze zekerheidshalve voor de derde keer door en maakte aantekeningen in een notitieboekje dat hij speciaal voor de reis had aangeschaft. Hij was bang dingen te vergeten.

'De dames in Oekraïne houden van hoffelijkheid,' las hij. 'Een bloemetje doet wonderen.' En ook: 'Een dame als eerste door een deur laten gaan en haar in haar mantel helpen wordt in Oekraïne buitengewoon op prijs gesteld.'

Verder stond er hoe je je het beste kon voorbereiden op de liefdesreis. 'Neem de dagen voor de reis genoeg rust. De liefdesreizen van Liefde over de Grens zijn intensief want wij willen niet dat je met lege handen thuiskomt.' En dat je geen grote cadeaus voor de toekomstige geliefde moest meenemen, dat de dames het wel leuk zouden vinden als je een souvenir meenam dat typerend was voor de regio of de stad waar 'jij die de liefde zoekt woont'.

In zijn boekje schreef hij: 'Souvenirs meenemen uit eigen regio.' Hij had geen flauw benul welke souvenirs hij kon aanschaffen tot hij op het idee kwam wat vlaaien mee naar Kiev te nemen. Met een vlaai deed je altijd iedereen een plezier en vlaaien hadden ze daar vast niet.

## 5

De dag voor zijn vertrek ging hij naar de bakker die bekendstond als de beste in Heerlen en hij zei dat hij drie vlaaien nodig had om mee te nemen naar Kiev.

'Kiev?' vroeg het meisje achter de toonbank.

'Oekraïne.'

'Dat is ver weg,' merkte ze op.

'Blijven ze lang goed?' vroeg de Pool.

'Wanneer worden ze gegeten?'

'Over een paar dagen.' De reis zou vijf dagen duren en in de instructies stond dat je niet je hart moest verliezen aan de eerste de beste dame die je tegenkwam. Dat zou onverstandig zijn. 'Geef je ogen goed de kost,' stond er. 'Neem een weloverwogen besluit.'

De Pool zou zijn ogen goed de kost geven. Hij wilde drie vlaaien meenemen omdat hij geen idee had wanneer hij verliefd zou worden, of het al op de eerste dag gebeurde of pas vlak voor zijn vertrek. Of de eerste dame de juiste zou blijken te zijn, of dat hij pas bij nummer drie ontdekte wat op de website van Liefde over de Grens 'het geheimzinnige' werd genoemd. 'Mensen die verliefd worden doen wat mensen die verliefd worden doen,' stond er. 'Het is wat wij "het geheimzinnige" noemen.' De Pool had die zinnen al zeker vijf keer gelezen om zich ervan te vergewissen dat hij het bedrijf goed begreep. Tot nu toe had hij liefde niet in verband gebracht met het geheimzinnige. Weinig zou hij daarmee in verband willen brengen, zelfs de maanden die hij in een kippenhok had doorgebracht zou hij niet onder het geheimzinnige willen rangschikken.

Terwijl hij wachtte tot de vlaaien waren ingepakt vond hij dat hij een goede keus had gemaakt. Mocht hij de eerste twee vlaaien hebben weggegeven aan dames die bij nader inzien niet de juiste geheimzinnigheid over hem hadden kunnen uitstorten en hij niet over hen, dan hoefde hij bij nummer drie niet met lege handen aan te komen.

'Ik zal wat folie om de doos heen doen, dan komt er geen lucht bij,' zei het meisje. 'Dan blijven ze langer goed. Een verse vlaai is natuurlijk een verse vlaai maar onze vlaaien kunnen prima na een paar dagen gegeten worden. Desnoods warm je ze even op.'

Dat opwarmen leek hem onmogelijk. Hij had naam en adres van het hotel doorgekregen (vier sterren) en kon zich niet voorstellen dat op zo'n hotelkamer iets kon worden opgewarmd, met folie zou het goed komen. Het ging ook om de geste.

Toen hij naar huis liep met de goed ingepakte dozen in een speciale tas – hij had voor een kersen-, een abrikozen- en een appelvlaai gekozen – vroeg hij zich even af of dit geen kinderachtig souvenir was. Een vlaai, was dat mannelijk genoeg? Niet dat hij aan zijn mannelijkheid twijfelde maar bij de adviezen stond dat mannelijkheid in Oekraïne nog hogelijk werd gewaardeerd en dat de deelnemers dat vooral niet moesten verwarren met agressiviteit. 'Blijf te allen tijden een gentleman,' was een ander advies dat Liefde over de Grens de cliënten op het hart drukte.

Hij zou het blijven, hij zou er desnoods een worden mocht blijken dat hij toch geen gentleman was. Tot nu toe had hij zich nooit zo bekommerd om het in jassen helpen van dames maar bij een nieuw leven hoorden nieuwe gewoontes.

Jurek was al bij zijn moeder en het menselijk verlengstuk en de Pool bracht de avond door met het zorgvuldig inpakken van een kleine koffer die hij voor deze reis had gekocht. Een nieuw leven, een nieuwe koffer.

Het bureau had de reizigers nog kledingadviezen gegeven. 'Het is geen jasje-dasje in Oekraïne, met een goed zittend pak maak je echter altijd indruk. Neem iets mee voor alle gelegenheden, ook wat regenkleding en wat warms.' De Pool had nauwelijks pakken, zijn trouwpak ja, maar het zinde hem niet verliefd te worden in zijn oude trouwpak, voor zover het hem überhaupt nog paste, daarom had hij een jasje bij een kledingzaak in het centrum gekocht. De verkoper had gezegd dat het gekleed was, 'niet te' en dat het prima op een spijkerbroek ging. 'Of anders een strakke zwarte broek.' Voor de zekerheid schafte de Pool nog een overhemd aan dat goed bij het jasje paste. Een bloemetjesoverhemd. Normaal droeg de Pool dat soort overhemden niet maar de verkoper had gezegd: 'Jij kan het hebben. Het maakt je jong. Je ziet er modieus in uit.' Modieus, zo wilde de Pool best overkomen in Oekraïne.

Toen hij die avond zichzelf in zijn net aangeschafte jasje en bloemetjesoverhemd voor de spiegel bekeek moest hij toegeven dat hij eruitzag als iemand die klaar was voor de liefde, van top tot teen gereed voor hartstocht. Dit was niet meer de oude Pool, dit was inderdaad de nieuwe, al waren zijn schoenen dan wat oud en afgetrapt, maar zittend op de keukenvloer poetste hij zijn schoenen en toen zag je er niets meer van. Een gentleman liep in goed gepoetste schoenen rond.

In een kiosk had hij een mueslireep en een thriller gekocht. Mocht hij zich vervelen in het vliegtuig had hij iets bij zich om te lezen. Ook had hij bij zijn bank geïnformeerd of hij kon pinnen in Kiev en dat kon. Een mevrouw van de bank zei dat zijn pas was vrijgegeven voor gebruik in Oekraïne.

Hij was klaar voor de reis.

De Pool vroeg zich alleen nog af of hij een pet moest opzetten. De dames in Oekraïne hoefden niet meteen te zien dat hij vrijwel kaal was en als het kouder bleek te zijn dan voorspeld had hij iets op zijn hoofd. Een pet, besloot de Pool, hij zou met pet Oekraïne betreden.

Toen kon hij slapen maar de slaap wilde niet komen. Bij een nieuw leven hoorde afscheid van het oude en liggend in bed drong het tot hem door dat hij niet goed wist waarvan hij afscheid ging nemen. Hij stond weer op, deed het licht aan. Hier en daar trok hij kasten open, overal lagen en hingen nog de spulletjes van zijn ex. De meeste van haar kleren had ze niet meegenomen. Had ze alles nieuw gekocht? Hij betastte haar garderobe, begerig en toch aarzelend, alsof het heiligschennis was. Alsof dat nu niet meer mocht. De Pool rook eraan, hij rook alleen lavendel. Zijn ex legde graag lavendelzakjes in klerenkasten. Toen dwaalde hij verder door het huis op zoek naar resten van het oude leven dat nu spoedig zou eindigen.

De volgende ochtend zouden de deelnemers elkaar ontmoeten in de vertrekhal van het vliegveld van Düsseldorf. Paul, die deze reis hoogstpersoonlijk leidde, zou te herkennen zijn aan zijn groene paraplu, zo hadden de deelnemers per e-mail doorgekregen. Men moest goed uitgerust op reis gaan, men moest fit aan de liefdesreis beginnen maar de Pool deed die nacht geen oog dicht. Hij lag te woelen, hij meende een mug te horen, hij stond voor de deur van de kamer van de verdwenen jongen, deed een poging zich af te trekken en dwaalde daarna toch weer door het huis alsof het niet van hem was, alsof het oude leven al niet meer van hem was. Hij moest beginnen met leven, hoewel het hem tegelijkertijd onrechtvaardig leek te doen alsof hij al die jaren niet geleefd had, dat zijn vrouw en kinderen met een levend lijk opgescheept hadden gezeten. Nee, dat kon niet het geval zijn. Een levend lijk, dat was hij niet geweest.

De Pool arriveerde drie kwartier te vroeg op het vliegveld van Düsseldorf en nergens zag hij een man met een groene paraplu. Hij overwoog koffie te gaan drinken maar deed dat toch niet. Het was het beste rustig in de vertrekhal te blijven staan tot de man met de groene paraplu zou arriveren. Af en toe zag hij mannen alleen door de vertrekhal slenteren en hij vermoedde dat ook zij bij de liefdesreis hoorden. Dat zij naar Kiev gingen om het nieuwe leven te laten beginnen, om de liefde te vinden die hun tot dan toe door de neus was geboord.

Ze verdwenen weer, ze losten op in de massa en toen hij eindelijk een man met een groene paraplu zag waren zijn gedachten meer bij Jurek dan bij de liefdesreis en de andere deelnemers. Hij hoopte dat hij terug zou komen met een vrouw die Jurek beviel. Ze hoefde geen stiefmoeder te worden, als ze maar goed met de jongen kon opschieten. Dat was alles. Hij had zich voorgenomen vrijwel meteen tegen de dames in Oekraïne te zeggen dat er een jongen aan hem vastzat en dat als ze niet tegen kinderen konden het niets werd tussen hen.

'Geniek?' vroeg de man met de groene paraplu.

Ze hadden een foto van zichzelf moeten opsturen, dus de man met de paraplu wist hoe de deelnemers eruitzagen. 'Iedereen noemt me de Pool,' zei de Pool zoals hij aan de telefoon al had gemeld en hij voegde er voor de zekerheid aan toe hoe zijn naam moest worden uitgesproken.

De man zei dat hij Paul was hoewel de Pool dat natuurlijk allang wist en hij voelde hoe Pauls vochtige hand de zijne vastpakte en even flink schudde. Zou Paul ook zenuwachtig zijn of had hij altijd vochtige handen? Ze stonden zwijgend tegenover elkaar en de Pool merkte dat de reisleider hem kritisch opnam, onderzoekend. Paul zelf zag er anders uit dan de Pool had verwacht, kleiner en ietwat gezet. Zijn haar leek geverfd.

'Je bent vroeg,' zei Paul toen hij een tijdje om zich heen had gekeken. Hij had weinig zin in een gesprek want na die opmerking kwam er geen woord meer uit de reisleider en de Pool vroeg zich af of het aan hem was allemaal vragen te stellen. Nieuwsgierig was hij wel. Hoe gingen ze de dames precies ontmoeten? In algemene bewoordingen was daar informatie over gestuurd maar de Pool wilde graag concretere informatie. Wat ging er gebeuren daar in Kiev, dat wilde hij weten, hij durfde het niet te vragen. Ten slotte was het Paul die vroeg: 'Heb je er zin in?'

'Zeker,' zei de Pool.

De reisleider knikte tevreden. Hij had natuurlijk geen behoefte aan deelnemers die de hoop bij voorbaat opgaven, de reisleider wilde enthousiastelingen om zich heen. 'Het is mijn negende keer naar Oekraïne,' vertelde hij. 'Het is een van mijn favoriete bestemmingen. Je zult van het land en zijn vrouwen gaan houden. China is ook fijn, wel ingrijpend.'

'Ja.' Dat China ingrijpend was kwam de Pool niet onlogisch voor. Hij vond Oekraïne al ingrijpend. Alleen wilde hij niet van het land en zijn vrouwen houden, hij wilde van één vrouw houden, het land kon hem gestolen worden. Toen begon Paul te vertellen hoe hij zijn eigen vrouw in Rusland had ontmoet en hoe hij daar één keer per jaar naartoe ging, met de auto, en hoe avontuurlijk dat was en wat hij allemaal voor zijn schoonouders uit Nederland moest meenemen tegenwoordig. Eerst waren ze eenkennig en nationalistisch geweest maar na een paar jaar hadden ze de stroopwafel ontdekt en tegelijkertijd met de stroopwafel waren ze van Nederland en hun schoonzoon gaan houden. Sindsdien stopte hij iedere zomer de achterbak vol met stroopwafels.

Bij het woord 'stroopwafel' veerde de Pool op, omdat het hem deed beseffen dat de drie vlaaien die hij bij zich had nog zo gek niet waren. Hij had het goede souvenir uitgezocht. Even later kwam er een oudere man met een stok bij hen staan die ook een deelnemer bleek te zijn en die Paul kennelijk goed kende. Ze omhelsden elkaar in elk geval en toen de man met de stok zich eindelijk tot de Pool wendde vroeg hij: 'De hoeveelste keer is dit voor jou?'

'De eerste keer.'

De man met de stok, die zich voorstelde als John, zei dat het al de zevende keer was dat hij meeging. Hij leek er trots op te zijn. Een veteraan, een man die alles wist van het land en zijn inwoners. De Pool voelde een lichte wanhoop in zich opkomen. Als deze man al zeven keer was meegegaan zonder te hebben gevonden wat hij zocht, hoe vaak zou de Pool dan mee moeten? Hij had er zo op gerekend dat het de eerste keer, in die vijf dagen zou lukken. Misschien was dat naïef maar zeiden experts niet altijd dat verliefd worden een beslissing was, iets waarvoor je je moest openstellen? Ze waren nog niet eens opgestegen en hij stond er nu al voor open.

'Heb je nooit gevonden wat je zocht in Oekraïne?' vroeg de Pool voorzichtig terwijl Paul een andere liefdesreisdeelnemer verwelkomde.

'Ach,' zei John, die met één voet op de drempel van het bejaardentehuis leek te staan. 'Je vindt altijd wat, het houdt nooit stand. Niet in mijn geval. Een paar weken, een paar maanden. Eentje heb ik er hierheen gehaald. Dat doe ik nooit meer. Het vrouwtje was net in mijn huis of ze dacht de baas over me te spelen. Dat moet je bij mij niet doen.'

De Pool knikte begripvol en hij zag dat een man in een grijs trainingsjack zich bij de groep had gevoegd. Het vrouwtje dat de baas kwam spelen klonk hem niet zo prettig in de oren. Aan de andere kant kon het de Pool niet zoveel schelen als er thuis iemand was die de baas wilde spelen, als ze het maar deed uit liefde. Ook op de kazerne had hij nooit bevelvoerder willen worden. Tijdens een functioneringsgesprek was hem eens gevraagd of hij verantwoordelijkheid meed, of hij daaraan een hekel had. Hij zei dat dit niet het geval was, integendeel. Verantwoordelijkheid vond hij prima, anderen bevelen geven, dat lag hem niet. Hij was liever degene die het bevel ontving, die het uitvoerde dan degene die het gaf. 'Je bent dus meer een uitvoerder,' had de ploegchef geconcludeerd. De Pool had geknikt. Een uitvoerder, dat was hij. Misschien was dat niet mannelijk, uitvoerder zijn. Hij zou zich in Oekraïne hoe dan ook mannelijk voordoen. Hopelijk was zijn lengte al mannelijk genoeg.

Langzamerhand werd het drukker rondom de man met de groene paraplu. De meeste deelnemers waren ouder dan hij had verwacht. Er was een man in pak en verder een wat jongere man zonder jas die een blouse met felle kleuren droeg en een rugzak. Nog een man in een trainingspak. Er werd ook Duits gesproken. Hij hoorde minstens drie mannen Duits spreken. Het drong tot hem door dat dit zijn concurrenten waren. Hij had gedacht gelijkgestemden te vinden maar als hij naar deze mannen keek kon hij zich niet voorstellen dat zij gelijkgestemden waren of dat zouden worden, ergens halverwege de reis. Concurrenten, dat was de correcte omschrijving. Hij kon amper geloven dat de vrouw op wie hij verliefd werd in Kiev oog zou hebben voor deze mannen. Ze waren te verschillend, de mannen en hij.

'We gaan inchecken,' riep Paul. Hij was herder, coach en reisleider ineen en hij ging zoals dat hoort voorop alsof hijzelf een nieuw leven in Oekraïne zocht.

De Pool telde twaalf deelnemers plus Paul. Er was ook een Chinees bij, althans een man die eruitzag als een Chinees. Hij had een donkerrode regenjas aan met een capuchon. Het zag er wat potsierlijk uit vond de Pool maar misschien was het mode. Ze liepen naar de incheckbalie, sommigen aarzelend en met iets wat op tegenzin leek, anderen met een enthousiasme dat de Pool eigenlijk tegenstond, alsof ze van plan waren meteen al op de eerste de beste grondstewardess verliefd te worden. Hij stond in het midden van de rij, hij wilde namelijk niet bij de enthousiastelingen horen die naar voren stormden alsof ze zich niet in konden houden maar ook niet bij hen die met tegenzin naar de incheckbalie schuifelden alsof ze naar de slachtbank gingen. Iedereen had wel een koffer of tas bij zich die moest worden ingecheckt. Alleen de jongen die geen jas aanhad kondigde aan dat zijn rugzak handbagage was. Hij had al een instapkaart, hij stond niet in de rij. Hij was met zijn telefoon bezig.

Van sommige deelnemers schudde de Pool de hand in de rij voor het inchecken. Een beetje onhandig zoals je op verjaardagen verre familieleden de hand schudt van wie je niet meer zeker weet of je ze ooit al eens ontmoet hebt. Een echt gesprek had hij nog niet aangeknoopt. Ze waren hier niet voor elkaar, ze waren hier voor het nieuwe leven, al zou het aardig zijn geweest als ze elkaar begrepen, als ze elkaar ondanks alles een beetje zouden ondersteunen daar in Kiev. Daarop had hij gehoopt, een saamhorigheid, een verwantschap, intuïtief wist hij nu dat dit niet het geval was. Hij stond er alleen voor, misschien beter ook. Je werd niet met z'n allen verliefd, je werd moederziel alleen verliefd.

Een man met nieuwe witte gympen stond achter de Pool en begon een gesprek met hem in het Duits. Die taal beheerste de Pool redelijk en hij gaf vriendelijke antwoorden op de vragen van de man die uit Recklinghausen bleek te komen en die net als de Pool nog nooit aan een georganiseerde liefdesreis had deelgenomen.

'Du auch nicht,' zei de man uit Recklinghausen met een tevredenheid die de Pool geruststelde, 'dann brauchen wir uns ja nicht zu schämen. Wir sind neu hier.'

'Nein, nein,' zei de Pool en ze schoven weer een halve meter op.

De man uit Recklinghausen bleek schilder te zijn, binnenhuisschilder, hij had een tijd in de bouw gewerkt maar schilderen beviel hem beter. Zeker in de winter. Buiten was het niets gedaan in de winter, binnen was het aangenamer. Hij schilderde graag al was er tegenwoordig veel concurrentie uit het oosten, mannen die voor een habbekrats schilderden zonder dat echt te kunnen. Polen, Tsjechen, Roemenen, Hongaren. Schilderen konden ze niet. 'Und was machst du?' vroeg de man uit Recklinghausen toen de Pool bijna aan de beurt was.

'Feuerwehrmann,' zei de Pool.

'Na so was,' zei de man uit Recklinghausen en de Pool pakte zijn paspoort, hij was zo ongeveer aan de beurt.

'Bei der Feuerwehr gibt es doch sicher kein Ausländer, oder?'

Alleen de Chinees in zijn donkerrode jas stond nog voor de Pool, hij voerde een discussie met de grondstewardess. Waar ze het over hadden was onduidelijk. De Pool zei dat hij het prima naar zijn zin had bij de brandweer, al kwam er een grote reorganisatie aan waar niemand op zat te wachten. De 24-uursdienst zou worden afgeschaft, dus niet meer één etmaal werken, twee etmalen vrij, de kazerne mocht geen eilandje meer zijn, het zou er niet beter op worden, zoveel was zeker. Ze hadden het regelmatig over efficiency, de Pool wist wat ze daarmee bedoelden: inkrimpen.

De man uit Recklinghausen ging er totaal niet op in. 'Hey du,' hij raakte de bovenarm van de Pool bijna teder aan, 'ich bin Tom, und du?'

Het leek de Pool ongepast te zeggen dat iedereen hem de Pool noemde, daarom gaf hij de naam die hij eigenlijk nauwelijks meer gebruikte. De verdwenen naam.

'Bist du Pole?' vroeg de man uit Recklinghausen en de Pool antwoordde dat hij Nederlander was maar dat zijn vader in Polen was geboren en zijn moeder in Duitsland, in de Eifel, en dat hij met de familie van zijn ouders geen contact meer had.

'Du solltest das nicht persönlich nehmen, das, was ich da über die Polen gesagt habe,' zei de man uit Recklinghausen. 'Dort in Polen gibt es auch ganz anständige Leute, die noch wissen wie man eine Wand streicht.'

'Ja,' zei de Pool, al moest hij toegeven dat hij zelf nauwelijks Polen kende en al helemaal geen Polen die wisten hoe je een muur schilderde.

Hij checkte in, voerde een zakelijk gesprek met de grondstewardess dat toch gelardeerd was met onderdrukte begeerte ('Ich wünsch Ihnen noch einen sehr schönen Tag,' zei hij schalks), vooruitlopend op Oekraïne als het ware, hij kon beter nu al met begeren beginnen. Vervolgens keek hij zijn koffer ietwat bezorgd na en bestudeerde zijn instapkaarten. Ze zouden overstappen in Wenen.

Hij ging achter de mannen aan, met in zijn ene hand de tas met de thriller en de mueslireep en in zijn andere hand de taartentas met de vlaaien.

De man uit Recklinghausen was achter hem aan komen lopen en tikte de Pool op de schouder. 'Hey du,' de man vroeg of de Pool nog wat wilde kopen op het vliegveld. Of hij nog belastingvrij ging winkelen. Drank was goedkoop in Oekraïne had hij gehoord maar ze dronken daar beslist alleen wodka en hij, Tom, was dol op rum. Rum met cola, met bananensap, mangosap, sinaasappelsap, aalbessensap. Als er maar rum in zat. Daarom was hij van plan taxfree wat rum te kopen. Dat kon hij dan aanbieden aan de dames. Hij voegde er nog aan toe dat vrouwen van rum hielden, met rum zat je bij de meisjes altijd goed.

Rum als souvenir uit Recklinghausen, de Pool vond het merkwaardig, toch volgde hij de man naar de taxfreeshop en om niet uit de toon te vallen kocht hij een klein flesje. Het kon misschien geen kwaad wat rum bij je te hebben in Oekraïne, je wist inderdaad nooit wie je er een plezier mee zou doen.

Hij stopte het flesje in zijn plastic tas. Tom had twee grote flessen bij zich. Ze liepen naar de gate en daar zaten de mannen die de liefde gingen zoeken al in een groepje. Ze praatten alsof ze elkaar al jaren kenden. Alleen de Chinees was iets in een boekje aan het schrijven. De man uit Recklinghausen plofte naast de Pool neer en begon over

Borussia Dortmund te vertellen. Dat hij weliswaar een binnenhuisschilder was maar dat hij leefde voor Borussia en dat hij twee seizoenkaarten had, hoewel dat lang niet makkelijk was, om zo'n seizoenkaart te bemachtigen, de tweede was voor zijn vriendin. Die had hij nu niet dus nam hij steeds andere vrouwen mee en soms ook vrienden, maar omdat hij had besloten dat de tijd rijp was voor een vaste relatie had hij voor haar alvast een seizoenkaart bemachtigd, anders moest je er jaren op wachten. Een vrouw die niet mee wilde naar Borussia hoefde het bij hem niet te proberen. De Pool werd niets gevraagd, hij hoefde alleen te luisteren. Het maakte hem rustig.

Ze gingen boarden en de man uit Recklinghausen bleek in het vliegtuig in de rij achter de Pool te zitten. Hij boog zich voorover en praatte verder alsof hij al maanden niet had gepraat en hij nu de mogelijkheid zich voordeed er flink gebruik van wenste te maken. 'Wenn die Borussen gewonnen haben, dann ficke ich,' fluisterde hij in het oor van de Pool, 'aber wenn die verloren haben oder wenn das Spiel unentschieden ausgegangen ist, dann wird nicht gefickt, da bin ich ganz hart. Gefickt wird nur bei einem Sieg.'

'Und wo fickst du?' vroeg de Pool. Een betere vraag schoot hem niet te binnen.

'Im Club,' zei de man uit Recklinghausen. Daarna ontspande hij zich, hij hield op in het oor van de Pool te fluisteren. Ook de Pool ontspande zich nu, hij was niet zo dol op voetbal. Hij pakte zijn thriller en las een halve bladzijde. De stoel naast hem was leeg en daarnaast zat een man met wit haar die bij de groep hoorde en die een rol pepermuntjes bij zich had. Telkens stopte hij een nieuw pepermuntje in zijn mond en toen de stewardessen klaar waren met de veiligheidsinstructies wendde de man met het witte haar zich tot de Pool. 'Ik ben Lucas,' zei hij. 'Jij maakt ook deel uit van onze groep?'

De Pool beaamde dat, hij had het gevoel dat ze met z'n

allen stiekem lid waren van een geheim genootschap.

Lucas vertelde dat hij gepensioneerd huisarts was. Zijn vrouw was zes jaar geleden overleden en hij wilde nu langzamerhand toch een nieuwe partner vinden. 'Het is via natuurlijke weg niet gelukt,' zei Lucas en hij klonk een beetje verdrietig. 'Ik heb vriendinnen gehad maar ze wilden altijd te veel of te weinig en een van mijn patiënten was mee geweest op zo'n liefdesreis, die vertelde daar enthousiast over, Liefde over de Grens, en toen zei ik tegen mezelf: waarom niet? Voel ik me daar soms te goed voor? Waarom zou een huisarts niet een handje geholpen mogen worden bij de zoektocht naar de liefde?'

De Pool knikte en kreeg een pepermuntje in zijn hand gedrukt. Lucas moest flink rochelen en toen hij daarmee klaar was vertelde hij vrolijk dat hij niet verwachtte nog een grote liefde tegen te komen daar in Kiev, dat eigenlijk niemand dat zou mogen verwachten op zijn leeftijd en al helemaal niet in Kiev, maar hij hoopte iemand te vinden om samen mee te sterven. Ze waren intussen aan het taxien. 'Samen oud worden is onzin,' zei Lucas, 'ik ben al oud, ik ben alleen oud geworden, nou ja officieel met mijn overleden vrouw maar feitelijk heb ik het alleen gedaan.'

Terwijl hij zijn plastic tassen zachtjes tussen zijn knieën geklemd hield dacht de Pool aan zijn lieve ex en hij hoorde nog de gepensioneerde huisarts vertellen dat seks gezond was, ook op zijn leeftijd. 'Houd er niet mee op,' zei de man, 'al gaat het moeilijk. Het is net als wandelen. Een beetje bewegen is altijd beter dan niet bewegen. Tegen de ouderen in mijn praktijk heb ik altijd gezegd: "Dan maak je maar zin." Leg desnoods een vies blaadje naast je hoofdkussen. Hulpmiddelen zijn toegestaan.' En daarop bood de gepensioneerde huisarts de Pool opnieuw een pepermuntje aan. Vervolgens zei hij nog: 'Ja mijn vrouw was alcoholist. Ik kocht de drank voor haar want op een gegeven moment kon ze met goed fatsoen niet meer over straat. Iedereen mag daar het zijne van denken, ik noem het naastenliefde.'

Toen zei de captain dat ze nummer twee waren om op te stijgen en de gepensioneerde huisarts stopte het laatste pepermuntje in zijn mond. Hij hield op met praten, sloot zijn ogen en ook de Pool deed zijn ogen dicht. Tot nu toe had niemand hem een vraag gesteld, alleen hoe hij heette en of hij al eerder op zo'n reis mee was geweest. De Pool was kennelijk geen man om vragen aan te stellen, alsof de mensen voelden dat hij niets te vertellen had. Wie iets over zichzelf kwijt wil neemt het woord wel, al stond in de instructies van het bedrijf dat de dames in Oekraïne het prettig vonden als de heren ook wat over zichzelf konden mededelen. 'Maak van je hart geen moordkuil,' had hij gelezen, 'maar wees niet te direct. Wie na vijf minuten al zegt: "I love you", moet er niet op rekenen serieus te worden genomen.' Verder werd aangeraden een jeugdfoto mee te nemen. Dat had de Pool gedaan, een wat verkleurde foto uit zijn jeugd. De Pool als zesjarige, zijn moeder leefde toen nog.

Niet veel later hingen ze in de lucht. Het vliegtuig schudde heen en weer. De Pool vond dat niet prettig, de liefdesreis had hem nu al uitgeput.

Vlak voor ze gingen landen in Wenen wendde hij zich tot Lucas die voor zich uit zat te staren met een tijdschrift op zijn schoot. 'Wat heb jij eigenlijk meegenomen?' vroeg de Pool.

'Hoe bedoel je?'

'Als souvenir uit je regio.'

De gepensioneerde huisarts schudde zijn hoofd. 'Ik ben te oud voor die onzin,' zei hij. Het klonk bijna boos.

Lang had de Pool gedacht dat het slagen van zijn missie afhing van de souvenirs die in de taartentas zaten, nu troostte hij zich met de gedachte dat hij die vlaaien altijd in Kiev nog kon weggooien. Of zelf opeten, als het niet het juiste cadeau bleek te zijn. Nee, de liefde hing niet van souvenirs af.

# 6

Op het vliegveld van Wenen gingen de meeste liefdesreizigers weer taxfree inkopen doen maar de Pool deed daar niet aan mee. Hij zat op een stoel bij de gate te wachten op het vliegtuig naar Kiev, met de thriller op zijn schoot. Op de een of andere manier kwam hij er niet toe het boek te openen. Toen hij opstond om zijn benen te strekken zag hij de Chinees komen aanlopen. 'Hi,' zei de man, 'ik ben Han en jij?'

De Pool noemde zijn naam en hij voegde eraan toe dat iedereen hem de Pool noemde. Han vertelde dat hij uit Zaandam kwam, zijn moeder was geboren in Maleisië, zijn vader had nog in Nederlands-Indië gewoond. Chinees was hij dus niet. Hij vroeg aan de Pool of hij daar weleens was geweest.

'Maleisië, Indonesië, nee,' zei de Pool. 'Nooit.'

'Ik bedoelde Zaandam,' antwoordde Han en het klonk verlegen, 'ik had het over Zaandam.'

'Nee,' zei de Pool na een paar seconden bedenktijd, 'daar ben ik ook nooit geweest.' Han bleef zwijgend staan, met zijn donkerrode regenjas over zijn arm en toen zei hij: 'We zijn een soort astronauten. Astronauten zoeken leven op Mars, wij zoeken liefde in Kiev.'

'Ja,' zei de Pool. Een astronaut voelde hij zich niet, al begreep hij wat Han bedoelde. Het had iets buitenaards, deze reis. Toch hoopte hij dat Kiev minder onbewoonbaar was dan Mars. Op de een of andere manier had hij meer sympathie voor deze Han dan voor de man uit Recklinghausen die opnieuw op zoek was gegaan naar rum. Hij kon zich voorstellen dat Han en hij in Kiev samen verliefd werden, niet op elkaar, ieder op een andere vrouw natuurlijk, en dat ze dan in de lobby van het hotel elkaar verhalen zouden vertellen over hun prille liefde. Zo kon het gaan. Hij zou iets delen met Han, zijn liefde, zijn nieuwe liefde. Dat vooruitzicht stemde de Pool gelukkig.

Han ging eindelijk zitten. De Pool opende zijn boek, las een paar zinnen maar hij was onrustig, hij kon zich niet concentreren. Of Han kinderen had, wilde de Pool weten. Han antwoordde dat hij bij zijn moeder woonde en kinderen van hem niet zo nodig hoefden. Hij was al zes keer op een liefdesreis geweest. 'Ik heb aardig wat ervaring. Ze hebben me zelfs korting gegeven. Ik ben twee keer naar Rusland geweest, een keer naar China, een keer naar Peru, een keer naar Oekraïne en een keer naar Costa Rica, daar gaan ze tegenwoordig niet meer heen.'

'En hoe was het?' vroeg de Pool.

Han bracht zijn mond dicht bij het oor van de Pool. 'Je zult het wel gemerkt hebben,' fluisterde hij, 'de meeste mannen die op zo'n reis meegaan zijn niet helemaal normaal.' Han keek om zich heen alsof de mensen niet mochten horen wat hij had gezegd. 'Zeg maar gerust knettergek. Vertel het niet aan Paul dat ik dit heb gezegd, die kan nijdig worden als hij het gevoel heeft dat deelnemers de boel saboteren, van mij heb je het niet. Vooral die reis naar Peru, dat was niet oké.'

De Pool knikte en hij vroeg: 'Wat gebeurde daar dan allemaal?'

'Ik wil het er eigenlijk niet over hebben,' zei Han, 'het was... Het was excessief. De politie kwam eraan te pas. Dat heb ik nergens anders meegemaakt. Deelnemers verloren zichzelf. Twee jongens zijn naar huis gestuurd. Ik wil er verder niet over spreken. Ben jij al eens mee geweest?'

'Nog nooit,' zei de Pool.

Han knikte. Hij moest iets hebben gezien in de ogen van de brandweerman. Een ongerustheid, een beginnende teleurstelling. 'Het zal dit keer meevallen,' zei hij. 'In Kiev is volgens mij alles goed georganiseerd.'

Toen stond Han op en liep weg, de Pool bleef achter, door het raam kon hij het vliegtuig al zien staan. Hij vroeg zich af waarom zoveel deelnemers zo vaak op zo'n liefdesreis mee waren geweest en waarom Han, die kennelijk niet te spreken was over Liefde over de Grens, toch bleef meegaan. Ook vroeg hij zich af hoe het kwam dat de deelnemers in Peru zich hadden verloren. Dat zou hem niet overkomen, verliefd worden was iets anders dan je verliezen. De Pool sloeg het boek weer open maar hij merkte dat hij steeds weer om zich heen gluurde om te kijken of hij deelnemers aan de liefdesreis zag, deelnemers die volgens Han in de meeste gevallen knettergek waren. Hij gluurde om te kijken of hij de mannen kon betrappen op hun abnormaliteit. De gepensioneerde huisarts had de Pool normaal geleken. Hij had eigenlijk precies verwoord wat de Pool dacht: waarom zou je niet een handje geholpen mogen worden bij de zoektocht naar de liefde? Er was veel normaal, dat was geruststellend.

In de aankomsthal van het vliegveld van Kiev verzamelde Paul de mannen om zich heen. 'We hebben een paar jongens uit Duitsland bij ons,' zei hij, 'ik zal dus afwisselend Nederlands en Duits spreken. Het is een beetje raar als het nu opeens allemaal in het Engels moet. Ik wil onze Duitse vrienden vragen mij te onderbreken als ze iets niet begrijpen en anders neem ik ze na afloop nog even apart.' De Duitsers knikten, ze konden het Nederlands kennelijk aardig volgen.

'We zijn er, mannen,' zei Paul plechtig. 'Dit is Kiev. We zijn allemaal goed door de douane gekomen. We gaan nu in een bus naar het hotel en daar krijgen jullie de tijd om je op te frissen. Maar ik wil binnen een uur na aankomst iedereen verzamelen om het programma van de komende dagen door te nemen. Dit is waar het gaat gebeuren, mannen. Hebben jullie er zin in?'

De man uit Recklinghausen riep: 'Ja.' Veel andere mannen knikten gewoon en ook de Pool knikte, minstens de helft stond er bedremmeld bij. Ze leken meer op een stel bannelingen dan op heren die behoorlijk wat geld hadden betaald om de liefde te vinden. De Pool had zijn spaargeld moeten aanspreken om de reis te kunnen bekostigen en hij vermoedde dat ook het spaargeld van de andere deelnemers flink was geslonken.

Paul informeerde bij de liefdesreizigers of er nog vragen waren en een van de Duitse mannen zei dat hij dieetwensen had doorgegeven, dat hij daar verder niets meer over had gehoord en dat hij zich nu zorgen maakte, hij had een ernstige glutenallergie en hij wilde er zeker van zijn dat die glutenallergie serieus werd genomen. Paul antwoordde dat hij zich geen zorgen hoefde te maken, dat hij zeker niet de eerste man met een glutenallergie was die op een liefdesreis meeging. Er zou met hem en zijn dieetwensen rekening worden gehouden. Er waren nog meer mensen met dieetwensen en alles stond genoteerd. Niemand hoefde daar bezorgd over te zijn, alles was erop gericht en alles was eraan gedaan om ervoor te zorgen dat de mannen zich konden richten op hun belangrijkste taak: het vinden van een partner, het vinden van ware liefde.

Toen Paul was uitgesproken applaudisseerden een paar mannen. Ook de Pool deed dat. De liefde verdiende applaus. Daarna werden ze naar een bus gebracht. Er kwam niemand naast de Pool zitten, de meeste mannen zaten alleen. Dat vond de Pool prettig; hij was geen uitzondering, geen zwart schaap. Alleen Paul had iemand naast zich.

Het hotel was een groot flatgebouw dat hem deed denken aan flats aan de rand van Heerlen waarover zijn ex had gezegd dat als je daar lang woonde je vanzelf op een bepaald moment naar beneden zou springen. Deze flat was nog mistroostiger al had de Pool goede hoop dat de kamers meevielen.

In de lobby, waar ze even moesten wachten voor ze konden inchecken, keek de Pool om zich heen om te zien hoe het met de brandveiligheid gesteld was. Matig. Hij was nu een gentleman maar hij bleef een brandweerman.

Hij zag vrouwen die duidelijk anders waren gekleed dan vrouwen in Nederland, verzorgder, vrouwelijker, uitdagender, alleen was het te vroeg om verliefd te worden. De Pool wilde eerst de bijeenkomst afwachten waar goed zou worden uitgelegd wat er de komende dagen allemaal te gebeuren stond.

Hij kreeg een kamer op de elfde verdieping, een tweepersoonskamer. In de minibar lagen twee condooms. Het uitzicht was niet veelbelovend. Groot en grijs was de stad, het regende. De Pool opende zijn koffer en legde zijn kleren in de kast.

De vlaaien leken de reis goed doorstaan te hebben. Ze pasten niet in de minibar, hij gaf ze een plaatsje onder in de klerenkast. De rum zette hij ernaast. De kamer voldeed aan zijn verwachtingen, als het moest kon hij hier een nieuwe liefde ontvangen.

Toen vroeg hij zich af of hij zijn jasje met bloemetjesblouse nu al zou aantrekken of er nog even mee zou wachten. Hij besloot dat 't het beste was om meteen al bij de openingsbijeenkomst een goede indruk te maken. Hij kleedde zich uit, trok blouse en colbert aan, schreef aan Jurek een appje dat hij goed was aangekomen in Kiev, ook nog een berichtje aan zijn ex, en deed voor de spiegel aftershave op. Tot slot twijfelde hij of hij zijn pet moest ophouden. Hij bekeek zichzelf met en zonder pet en besloot hem af te zetten. IJdel was hij nooit geweest maar een eerste indruk kon veel verpesten. Dat wist hij, daarvoor had hij geen instructies van Liefde over de Grens nodig. De afwezigheid van hoofdhaar, op wat stekeltjes na, kon hij eigenlijk best goed hebben.

Toen hij besloten had de vrouwen van Kiev vrijwel kaal

tegemoet te treden bladerde hij nog even in het informatiepakket dat hij bij het inchecken had gekregen. De bijeenkomst zou in de Mozartzaal op de tweede verdieping plaatsvinden. Het was wat vroeg maar hij hield het op zijn kamer niet uit, hij ging naar de tweede verdieping waar hij een Beethovenzaal zag en een Vivaldizaal, geen Mozartzaal. Hij vroeg het aan een dame die een karretje met etenswaren voor zich uit duwde. Ze verstond hem eerst niet en toen zei hij nog eens luid en duidelijk: 'Mozart.' En daarna nog een keer: 'Mo-zart.' Toen begreep ze hem. 'Around the corner,' zei ze.

De Mozartzaal bleek geen echte zaal te zijn, meer een grote kamer waar een stuk of twintig stoelen stonden en twee tafels met daarachter nog eens vijf stoelen. Op een van de tafels stond een vaasje met bloemen. De Pool voelde er even aan. Plastic, toch smaakvol gedaan.

Hij ging op de derde rij zitten. Hij was opgewonden, zoals hij zich vaag herinnerde van de eerste dag op de middelbare school. Het leven zou gaan beginnen, het echte leven.

De mannen druppelden binnen. Han ging naast de Pool zitten. Hij wist het nu vrijwel zeker: Han kon een vriend worden. De jongen die geen bagage had ingecheckt ging aan de andere kant van de Pool zitten en vertelde dat hij verpleegkundige was in een kinderziekenhuis. 'Ik verwacht veel van deze reis,' zei hij. ' 'Liefde, daar gaat het toch om in het leven?'

Het was waar, het ging om liefde in het leven, al had de Pool een paar jaar geleden niet gedacht dat zij tot hem zou komen in Kiev maar het was misschien waar wat de mensen zeiden, dat je haar kon vinden op de meest onverwachte plaatsen. Een kippenhok was een merkwaardige plaats om liefde te vinden.

De Pool zag dat John ook een bloemetjesblouse had aangetrokken, zonder jasje. Hij vergeleek zichzelf met John en concludeerde dat hij er goed uitzag. Hij had zich getransformeerd tot gentleman, de zwijgzame Pool die hij ooit was geweest was niet verdwenen, er was een gentleman uit hem tevoorschijn gekomen. In de binnenzak van zijn jasje had hij zijn jeugdfoto gestoken, voor het geval er al de eerste avond ontmoetingen zouden plaatsvinden.

Paul kwam binnen met een groepje vrouwen achter zich aan en een jongen. Twee vrouwen en de jongen gingen naast Paul zitten. De andere bleven aan weerszijden van de stoelen staan. Iedereen was er, behalve de man uit Recklinghausen maar er werd niet op hem gewacht. De deur werd gesloten. Wie nu nog binnenkwam zou te laat komen en de Pool had medelijden met de man uit Recklinghausen. Hij zou zoveel missen. En hij had ervoor betaald.

Paul nam de microfoon in zijn hand. De geluidsinstallatie piepte. 'Mannen,' zei Paul, 'dit is de lokale staf van Liefde over de Grens, aan wie ik jullie nu wil voorstellen. Dit zijn de mensen die jullie gaan begeleiden op jullie zoektocht die voor veel mannen en vrouwen, misschien wel voor alle mannen en vrouwen de belangrijkste in hun leven is. Deze vrouwen zijn jullie vertalers en deze jongeman is de coördinator. Hij spreekt geen Nederlands, wel Engels en een beetje Duits. Hij kan jullie helpen met al jullie vragen, bijvoorbeeld: 'Ik ben verliefd geworden en ik heb bloemen nodig. Waar vind ik in Kiev mooie bloemen?'

Paul wendde zich nu tot de jongeman en zei: 'Wo kann man in Kiev schöne Blumen kaufen, das weisst du, oder?'

De jongeman knikte. 'Das weiss ich ganz genau,' zei hij langzaam en met een zekere trots. Het was de Pool niet duidelijk of hij trots was op het feit dat hij een beetje Duits sprak of trots op het feit dat hij wist waar je mooie bloemen kon krijgen in Kiev.

'Morgenmiddag,' zei Paul, 'na lunchtijd zal de eerste ontmoeting plaatsvinden. 's Ochtends kunnen jullie dan nog een beetje aan sightseeing doen. Er hebben zich ruim zestig vrouwen aangemeld, of beter gezegd, er zijn zestig vrouwen door de ballotage gekomen en dat is een record. Onze ballotage is streng. Het is een hoop, zestig vrouwen. Bereid je erop voor. Morgen zullen jullie met hen kennismaken en misschien zit daar al degene tussen met wie jullie oud gaan worden...'

Paul liet een stilte vallen en iemand riep – de Pool kon niet zien wie: 'Ik wil niet oud worden.' Waarop de gepensioneerde huisarts terugriep: 'Ik ben al oud en jij zult ook oud worden, wen er maar aan.'

'Mannen,' zei Paul, 'oud of jong, groot of klein, iedereen wil liefde en hier in Kiev zijn mensen, zijn vrouwen die hetzelfde willen wat jullie willen, vrouwen die snakken naar liefde. Niet alle vrouwen spreken Engels. Sommige een beetje, sommige heel goed, andere helemaal niet. Daarom hebben we onze vertalers, onze uitstekende en behulpzame vertalers die jullie zullen begeleiden op je zoektocht want de taal van de liefde mag dan internationaal zijn, soms heb je ondertiteling nodig.' Gelach steeg op. 'Zo,' zei Paul, 'en voor ik verderga met wat algemene informatie en voordat de vertalers meer over zichzelf zullen vertellen denk ik dat het goed is dat we een voorstelrondje doen. Wie wil er beginnen? Sta even op als je jezelf voorstelt, dan kunnen we je goed zien.'

Lucas begon. Hij vertelde wat hij al in het vliegtuig had verteld, alleen dat zijn vrouw alcoholiste was en dat hij voor haar altijd de drank had gekocht liet hij achterwege. Toen kwam een Duitser die in de reclame zat. Daarna een fysiotherapeut, gescheiden, kinderen het huis uit. Vervolgens een veteraan die Richard heette maar door iedereen Rich werd genoemd, hij vertelde dat hij twee keer in Afghanistan was geweest en dat de Afghanen daar niets aan hadden gehad, dat hij zelf nu chronische rugpijn had en dat Afghanistan hem ook zijn huwelijk had gekost. 'Dank je,' zei Paul maar de veteraan ging niet zitten. Hij zei: 'Ik heb drie kinderen, ik mag ze niet meer zien. Veel mensen weten niet dat de Kinderbescherming in Nederland erger is dan de taliban...'

'Dank je Rich,' zei Paul. 'Dit is voor nu voldoende.'

'Ik ben nog niet klaar,' zei de veteraan. 'Veel mensen weten niet dat er een fascistische organisatie bestaat die zich Kinderbescherming noemt...' Hij praatte hard en gehaast. Het was duidelijk dat de Kinderbescherming voor hem een emotionele aangelegenheid was. De andere mannen staarden voor zich uit, niemand durfde de veteraan aan te kijken. Ook Lucas bestudeerde zijn nagels.

'Dit is echt voor nu genoeg,' zei Paul met luide stem. 'Je hebt straks alle tijd om te vertellen wat je kwijt wil.' Mokkend ging de veteraan zitten. Hij zei nog: 'Ik denk dat het goed is dat deze mannen hier voor ze aan kinderen beginnen weten wat voor organisatie de Kinderbescherming is.'

En toen was de Pool aan de beurt. Hij hield het kort, zo kort mogelijk. Het was vermoedelijk daarom dat er een vrij lange stilte viel nadat hij was uitgesproken. Daarna kwam de verpleegkundige en die zei wat hij al aan de Pool had verteld, dat het om liefde draaide in het leven en dat hij daarom zo blij was hier te zijn.

Vervolgens kwam Han. Hij had zijn donkerrode regenjas aan alsof het in de Mozartzaal elk moment zou kunnen gaan regenen. 'Dit is mijn zevende keer,' zei hij. 'Ik heb er zin in. Mijn moeder heeft gezegd dat ik niet zonder vrouw moet terugkomen dus ik wil jullie vragen mij een beetje te helpen. Als jullie iemand zien van wie jullie denken: zij is iets voor Han, geef me dan een seintje.'

De mannen lachten, alleen de Pool lachte niet. Hij zou zijn best doen en als hij iemand tegenkwam die iets voor Han was zou hij hem dat meteen laten weten, al had hij geen idee wat voor type Han zocht. Hij moest het later nog eens vragen. 'Bedankt, Han,' zei Paul.

Op dat moment ging de deur open, daar stond de man

uit Recklinghausen. Hij had een ander trainingspak aan, zijn haren staken alle kanten uit alsof hij urenlang op bed had gelegen en toen was opgesprongen en naar de Mozartzaal was gerend. Even bleef hij stil in de deuropening staan, hij mompelde iets van 'Verzeihung' en ging achter de Pool zitten. 'Die Borussen spielen, das kann man doch nicht verpassen. Ich bin dann doch gegangen, denn das Spiel war Mist. Die Borussen werden das heute nicht schaffen,' fluisterde hij in het oor van de Pool. De man uit Recklinghausen rook naar drank en hij kreeg meteen het woord. Hij vertelde dat hij huisschilder was, dat hij met zijn ouders een paar keer naar Zeeland was geweest en daarom een paar woorden Nederlands sprak. Over rum, Borussia Dortmund en de liefde zweeg hij. Nadat hij eindelijk was uitgesproken zonk hij neer op de stoel naast de Pool. De man zag er radeloos en uitgeput uit.

Nu stelden de vertalers zich voor aan het gezelschap. Het Engels van sommige vertalers kon hij uitstekend verstaan, van het Engels van andere begreep hij weinig. Minstens twee van de vertaalsters troffen hem. Hun haar, hun ogen, de manier waarop ze zich voorstelden aan het publiek.

Paul zei: 'Ik zeg dit maar één keer, jullie mogen ook verliefd worden op de vertaalsters.' In de Mozartzaal ging gejuich op.

Die avond aten de mannen met de vertaalsters in een typisch Oekraïens restaurant – er stond bijna niets vegetarisch op de menukaart, daarom bestelde de Pool bietensoep, waar toch stukjes vlees in bleken te drijven. Noodgedwongen dronk hij de soep en liet het vlees zoveel mogelijk liggen. Hij zat ingeklemd tussen de man uit Recklinghausen en de gepensioneerde huisarts die om de beurt op hem in spraken, zodat het hem onmogelijk werd gemaakt het woord te richten tot de vertaalster die tegenover hem zat en tegen wie hij graag wat had willen zeggen. Even vroeg hij zich zelfs af of deze twee mannen wel voor de liefde naar Kiev waren gekomen of alleen om eens ongestoord te kunnen praten.

Pas bij het verlaten van het restaurant lukte het de Pool een paar woorden tegen de vertaalster te zeggen en hij slaagde er zelfs in de jeugdfoto uit zijn binnenzak te vissen en die aan haar te laten zien. Ze wierp er een gehaaste blik op.

'Six years old,' zei de Pool.

'How cute,' mompelde ze. 'So cute.'

# 7

De eerste bijeenkomst met dames in het centrum van de stad was wat de Pool betrof geen groot succes. Hij had met vijf vrouwen gepraat, voor zijn doen intensief, bij niemand was een vonk overgesprongen. Hij had de vrouwen niet begrepen of hij leek hen te vervelen en de dame die interesse in hem toonde vond hij te materialistisch. Ze had zeker tien minuten over wisselkoersen gepraat en hij kon veel hebben maar wisselkoersen interesseerden hem echt niet.

De tweede bijeenkomst met de dames uit Kiev zou plaatsvinden in een buitenwijk van de stad. Ze gingen met z'n allen met de metro naar de buitenwijk en in de metro was de Pool ondanks zijn goede voornemens somber geworden. Hij vond dat de mensen er treurig uitzagen met hun mutsen en hun winterjassen, hun peinzende blikken, hun door het weer, drank en sigaretten aangetaste huid. Even vroeg hij zich af of hij in een stad als Kiev wel liefde zou kunnen vinden die deze naam verdiende. Seks vond je overal, desnoods im Club, dat was het probleem niet. Zij die om die reden waren meegegaan zouden beslist bevredigd terugkomen, maar de pure, lichamelijke bevrediging was hem te kil, te pragmatisch.

De Pool droeg ook nu zijn nieuwe colbertje met de bloemetjesblouse. Zo koud was het niet en hij vond dat je een nieuwe outfit een paar dagen achter elkaar aan mocht hebben. Hij bestudeerde zijn buren in het metrostel, hun treurnis was diep en ondoorgrondelijk. Nu wist hij dat mensen in metro's altijd treurig keken, zelfs in Parijs, maar het was niet voor niets dat hij zo min mogelijk met het openbaar vervoer reisde. Hij wilde liever niet met andermans zwaarmoedigheid worden geconfronteerd.

In het metrostation waar ze uitstapten werden veel bloemen verkocht. Hij zag een oudere vrouw op een kleedje zitten met foto's van een jongen voor zich uitgestald. Er stond een tekst bij in het Russisch. Hij vermoedde dat het haar zoon was en dat ze aan het bedelen was, al zag hij geen bekertje met kleingeld. Omdat hij hoopte dat het hem geluk bracht legde hij een bankbiljet op het kleedje en liep toen snel verder.

De Pool overwoog bloemen te kopen, voor het geval dat en hij had niet voor niets geld uit de muur getrokken, maar omdat geen van de andere mannen interesse toonden in bloemen zag hij van het plan af. Hij wilde niet als enige met rozen of anjers op de bijeenkomst verschijnen. Hij wilde geen buitenbeentje zijn. Als mensen hem nu zouden vragen: Heb je behalve liefde nog iets nodig, verlang je verder iets, dan had hij geantwoord: Ik wil geen buitenbeentje zijn.

Ze liepen door een park met daaromheen flatgebouwen die hem troosteloos voorkwamen. Hoe kon er liefde zonder hoop zijn? Gisteren had een vertaalster tegen hem gezegd dat dit het nieuwe Kiev was, vol idealisten en jonge mensen die de oligarchen zouden verdrijven, hip zou het hier worden, het nieuwe Berlijn, het was slechts een kwestie van tijd. Maar als dit het nieuwe, hoopvolle Kiev was, hoe had het oude er dan in hemelsnaam uitgezien?

De mannen van de liefdesreis zwaaiden met hun armen, ze liepen in een rij alsof ze een schooluitstapje aan het maken waren of soldaten waren die vol levenslust op hun noodlot afliepen. Zo marcheerden zij naar de liefde.

Na een tijdje stonden ze voor het zalencomplex. De mannen die in de metro nog gelachen hadden en grappen hadden gemaakt, zoals mannen dat doen als ze met z'n allen op reis zijn, keken nu verslagen. Op hetzelfde moment dat deze mannen op zoek gingen naar de ware vond in een andere zaal een bijeenkomst plaats van gehandicapte sporters. Even was er verwarring waar de mannen moesten zijn en toen ze de rolstoelen zagen en de eenbenigen begonnen ze te morren. Lucas zei: 'Het klinkt misschien hard maar gehandicapten kunnen we thuis ook krijgen.' De andere mannen beaamden dat. Voor eenbenigen waren ze niet naar Kiev afgereisd, die waren ook in de Randstad, Zuid-Limburg, en op de Waddeneilanden volop in de aanbieding.

Gelukkig riep Paul: 'Jongens, we moeten hiernaast zijn. Wees niet bang. Onze vrouwen hebben al hun ledematen nog.'

Net als de dag ervoor sprak Paul de mannen toe voor ze de zaal binnengingen, zoals een voetbaltrainer zijn elftal toespreekt dat al een paar maanden alleen verliezen heeft geleden. 'Wees van jezelf overtuigd,' zei hij. 'Hier begint het. Jullie verdienen het. Jullie zijn de liefde van deze dames waard. Jullie moeten er alleen zelf in geloven. Geloven jullie dat je de liefde van deze dames waard bent?'

'Ja,' riepen de meeste mannen, ze geloofden het, al waren er weer een paar bij die niets riepen en naar hun schoenen staarden.

Paul voegde er nog aan toe dat ze hier in een arme buurt waren. 'Dit is niet de buurt waar de dure winkels zijn, waar je de modieuze restaurantjes en de hippe cafeetjes vindt. Denk eraan, hoe armer de mensen hoe groter hun verlangen. Vergeet dat niet als jullie straks naar binnen gaan.'

Net voor de deuren van het zaaltje opengingen begon de veteraan opnieuw over de Kinderbescherming. De mannen lieten Rich uitrazen, ze waren het inmiddels gewend, vervolgens stapten ze als overwinnaars naar binnen en aan grote ronde tafels, waarop kaarsen stonden, zaten dames die champagne dronken of wat er in de achterstandswijken van Kiev voor champagne doorging. Op de tafels stonden ook koekjes en de vertaalsters liepen rond, klaar om bij te springen, altijd gereed om een woordje te vertalen waar dat nodig mocht zijn. Om liefdesverklaringen naar het Oekraïens of Russisch over te brengen.

De Pool liep naar de eerste de beste tafel waar nog geen man heen was gegaan en daar zat een vrouw met een blauwe jurk die zijn aandacht trok, hij was zo mooi blauw. Hij ging naast haar zitten en vroeg hoe ze heette en wat ze deed. Ze zei dat ze 'bookkeeper' was – haar naam had hij niet verstaan – 'and you?' wilde ze weten.

Hij zei dat hij Geniek heette en dat hij 'fireman' was. zij antwoordde: 'I love firemen.'

En hij vroeg: 'Could you love this fireman? I know it's early, but could you love this fireman?' Wat was hem overkomen, welke emotie had hem te pakken gekregen dat hij nu al dit soort vragen durfde te stellen? Maar hij was in Kiev en hij praatte niet in zijn eigen taal, de Pool had helemaal geen eigen taal, stilte was zijn taal. Hier durfde hij meer dan thuis, de schaamte was terzijde geschoven.

Zij antwoordde: 'Maybe.'

Toen ze dat had geantwoord, toen ze 'misschien' had gezegd en hem had aangekeken op zo'n manier dat het helemaal geen misschien leek maar dat ze eigenlijk stiekem al een beetje van hem hield, toen was het gebeurd. Of daarvoor al. Door haar blauwe jurk. Haar blik. Hij wist niet hoe ze heette en waar ze vandaan kwam maar hij dacht: met deze vrouw ga ik oud worden. En voor ik oud word ga ik met haar leven. Ik ga leven. Dit is ze, hier begint het nieuwe leven.

Daarop nam hij een koekje van de schaal. Hij had gesproken, nu wist hij niets meer te zeggen. Hij zat naast haar en hij wilde daar eigenlijk alleen maar blijven zitten en haar hand vasthouden. Hij had geen tekst meer, hij was weer de zwijgzame Pool die hij altijd was geweest. Gelukkig schoot hem bijtijds te binnen dat hij een jeugdfoto in zijn binnenzak had en die liet hij haar zien. Ze bekeek hem aandachtig, en toen vroeg ze: 'This is your child?'

'No, this is me.'
'You are handsome.'
'Thank you,' zei hij.
En toen was het weer stil, ze gaf hem de foto terug, hij borg die op en hij informeerde bij haar of zij ook foto's had van vroeger, van toen ze een kind was. Uit haar tas haalde ze een portemonnee, een klein zwart portemonneetje en uit dat portemonneetje kwam een pasfoto tevoorschijn. 'Me,' zei ze, 'ten years old.'
Hij bekeek de foto en hij zag een engeltje. Ze had wat sproeten en haar tanden stonden scheef, dat maakte de engel alleen engelachtiger.
'You have not changed.' Hij meende het. Ze was nauwelijks veranderd. Ze lachte en hij vroeg zich af of hij naar een andere tafel moest maar hij wilde niet weg bij de vrouw in het blauw. Toen bedacht hij dat het lomp was geweest om te zeggen dat ze niet was veranderd en hij merkte op: 'Your teeth have changed.'
Ze knikte. 'Yes, my teeth have changed.' En ze lachte met wijd open mond alsof ze wilde laten zien hoeveel haar tanden waren veranderd, dat er een klein wonder in haar mond had plaatsgevonden.
Hij bleef gewoon zitten alsof hij thuis was en af en toe nam hij een koekje. Dan had hij iets te doen. Hij glimlachte naar de dames aan de andere tafels die van hun Oekraïense champagne nipten maar in hen was hij niet geïnteresseerd. Geniek wilde de vrouw in het blauw meenemen naar Nederland, zoals ze was, met haar halfscheve tanden want helemaal recht waren ze niet geworden, met haar jurk en de vage geur van sigarettenrook die om haar haren hing maar hij kon haar moeilijk optillen en wegdragen, al zou ze het misschien hebben begrepen aangezien hij al had verteld dat hij brandweerman was. Ja, hij wilde haar meenemen zonder er nog veel woorden vuil aan te maken.
Uiteindelijk vroeg hij of ze iets wilde eten met hem. Hij

herhaalde de vraag voor de zekerheid, mocht ze hem verkeerd verstaan hebben.

'Now?' vroeg ze.

En hij antwoordde: 'Now.'

Ze dacht even na en zei toen dat ze wel wat wilde eten en drinken.

'Do you know a nice restaurant?' vroeg hij.

Ze boog zich naar het meisje dat links van haar zat en toen boog ze zich weer naar de Pool en ze zei in zijn oor: 'Can my friend come also?'

Ze moest hard praten want de muziek was steeds harder gaan spelen. De mensen moesten worden opgezweept. Zo begon de liefde en zo eindigde die meestal ook, wist de Pool uit ervaring: opzwepend.

De Pool was eerst teleurgesteld, hij wilde met haar alleen zijn, toch zei hij dat het goed was. Hij wilde zeggen dat haar vrienden zijn vrienden waren en hoe meer zielen hoe meer vreugd maar de juiste woorden schoten hem niet te binnen in het Engels. Toen vroeg ze of ze nu al zouden gaan want ze hadden best honger, haar vriendin en zij, en van die koekjes werd je dik, ze wilden iets hartigs eten. Zoveel begreep hij althans van wat ze zei want ze mengde door het Engels nog wat Russisch of Oekraïens, die twee talen kon hij niet uit elkaar houden. Hij stond op en verliet de zaal, met achter zich de twee dames. Hij voelde zich een winnaar. Alle vernederingen en nederlagen hadden hem verlaten, alle nederlagen hadden alleen maar plaatsgevonden om deze overwinning mogelijk te maken. Hij keek nog eens om naar de andere mannen maar ze hadden geen oog voor hem. Niemand leek hem te zien.

Buiten de zaal begonnen de vrouwen snel te lopen, ze liepen door het zalencomplex langs de gehandicapten en even later stonden ze op straat, in het ongenadige licht van de troosteloze wijk maar hij vond haar nog steeds prachtig, zijn toekomstige vrouw, met de halfscheve tanden, minder scheef dan vroeger, en de naar sigaretten ruikende haren. Ze droeg nu een leren jasje over haar blauwe jurk en hij vroeg of ze het niet koud had. Ze zei van niet en daarna stelde hij zich eindelijk voor aan de vriendin van zijn toekomstige vrouw. Zij heette Dana en hij deed zijn best de gentleman te zijn die Liefde over de Grens van hem had willen maken want hij wist hoe belangrijk vriendinnen van je toekomstige vrouw waren.

De buurt leek steeds minder troosteloos en de Pool vroeg nog een keer: 'Do you know a nice restaurant?' De dames knikten en vervolgens liepen ze nog sneller terwijl ze met elkaar in het Russisch of Oekraïens aan het praten waren. Af en toe keek de vrouw in de blauwe jurk hem aan en dan wist hij weer dat hij zich niets wijsmaakte, dat zijn prille gevoelens werden beantwoord. En waarom zouden zijn gevoelens niet worden beantwoord? Hij was bruikbaar, ook voor hen die liefde zochten.

Het restaurant leek op een nachtclub. De vrouwen gingen aan een tafel zitten in het halfdonker en hij vroeg voor de zekerheid of dit echt een restaurant was. Ze zei dat je hier prima kon eten, dus dat het een restaurant was, zijn toekomstige vrouw. Daarna bestelde ze een fles wodka en een fles sinaasappelsap en ze vroeg wat hij bij de wodka wilde drinken. 'Water,' zei hij.

Er kwam een fles water op tafel. Vervolgens verschenen er augurken en iets anders wat ingemaakte watermeloen bleek te zijn. Nog een keer vroeg hij of er iets gegeten ging worden, want alleen ingemaakte watermeloen en augurken vond hij wat mager, gezien de gentleman die hij nu was. Hij moest voor haar zorgen, hij moest zich over haar ontfermen. Als hij nog op de wereld was dan was dat omdat hij een taak had, namelijk zich ontfermen over deze en gene, zijn overgebleven jongen en nu dus deze vrouw uit Kiev. Meteen daarna biechtte hij aan zijn toekomstige vrouw op dat hij eigenlijk niet goed had verstaan hoe ze heette en of ze nog een keer haar naam wilde zeggen, of ze dat niet erg vond.

Ze schudde van nee en toen zei ze haar naam en ze lachte en door die lach verstond hij haar weer niet. Daarna schreef ze het in een notitieboekje dat uit haar tasje kwam, ze scheurde de pagina uit het boekje en gaf het aan de Pool. Ze bleek Yulia te heten maar ze sprak het anders uit, als Joelia.

Daarop zei zij dat zij ook niet goed had verstaan hoe hij heette en hij schreef zijn naam op en hij sprak hem uit. Ze vroeg of hij van dansen hield.

'Nee, ik hou niet van dansen.'

Met dat antwoord namen zij en Dana geen genoegen. Ze dronken meer wodka en aten watermeloen, ze legden uit dat hij daarvan ook beslist moest eten en toen sleurden ze hem de dansvloer op. Hij liet zich meesleuren, gewillig was hij, een gewillige Pool. Had hij ooit iets anders willen zijn?

Ze dansten met z'n drieën en hij zei in het oor van zijn toekomstige vrouw dat hij van haar hield. Hij zei dat hij haar mee wilde nemen naar de plek waar hij woonde, naar Heerlen. 'Do you know Heerlen?' riep hij in haar oor om de muziek te overstemmen.

'No,' riep ze terug, 'I don't know.'

'Do you know the Netherlands?' riep hij weer.

En zij riep terug: 'No.'

En hij: 'But you have heard of the Netherlands?'

'Yes,' riep ze.

Ze gingen aan tafel zitten en ze vroeg of het mooi was waar hij woonde. De Pool moest even nadenken, toen zei hij: 'Small mountains, tiny mountains. The rest of the Netherlands is flat. Below sea level.'

En Yulia vroeg: 'And you are fireman?'

'Yes,' zei hij met een zekere trots en hij meende een glinstering in hun ogen te zien. 'Fireman. Are we going to eat?'

Hij had nu echt trek. Nederlagen ontnamen je de eetlust, van overwinningen werd je hongerig.

Yulia vroeg de kaart en Dana keek hem glimlachend aan en ze vroeg aan de Pool: 'You have wife?'

'Ex-wife.'

Dana knikte – er waren natuurlijk ook mannen die in Oekraïne naar liefde zochten terwijl thuis vrouw en kinderen op hen wachtten – en Yulia bestelde eindelijk iets. Ze had gezegd dat ze wist wat lekker was en hij had geantwoord dat alles goed was.

De kelner was een jongen in een zwarte spijkerbroek en een witte blouse, met tatoeages op allebei zijn armen en ook nog op al zijn vingers. Ze dronken wodka en af en toe praatte Yulia met haar vriendin, maar de Pool deed geen moeite zich erin te mengen. Het was goed zo. Het voelde vertrouwd, alsof hij al jaren met haar en Dana op stap ging. Het bestelde eten bleek een berg lamsvlees te zijn; er kwam een schaal met een overvloed aan lamskarbonades op tafel en daarna meer lamsvlees en brood en rijst.

'You eat everything?' vroeg Yulia.

'Yes,' zei de Pool. 'Everything.' Het was niet het moment om te zeggen dat hij vegetariër was. Hij zou vlees eten, een gentleman moest beleefd zijn. Later legde hij het wel uit, dat vlees en vis voor hem niet meer hoefde, hij zou alles vertellen, nee, niet alles, het meeste.

Ze aten alsof ze uitgehongerd waren, misschien waren ze dat, en toch bleven ze keurig. Ze dronken meer wodka met sinaasappelsap of water, ze raakten aangeschoten maar ze bleven keurig. De Pool at nauwelijks – hij was de smaak van vlees ontwend en vreesde dat zijn maag zoveel lamsvlees niet meer zou verdragen. Nadat hij wat aan een karbonade had geknaagd vroeg hij waar ze woonde, zijn toekomstige vrouw.

'Here,' zei ze. 'In the city.'

'Alone?'

'No, with father,' zei ze.

'And mother?'

'Dead.'

'Ah,' zei de Pool. 'Sorry. Long time ago?'

'Five years ago.'

Hij pakte haar hand. De dood verdreef de laatste schaamte, dankzij de dood kwam het beest, de lust, een klein beetje naar buiten en met haar hand in de zijne vroeg hij of hij haar vader kon ontmoeten. Hij zei dat hij graag wilde zien waar ze woonde, waar ze was opgegroeid, en hij had iets voor haar meegebracht. Uit zijn regio, de plek waar hij vandaan kwam. Een kleinigheid. Een souvenir.

Ze leek hem niet te begrijpen. Ze dronk haar glas leeg, nam een augurkje en hield het augurkje tussen haar half-scheve tanden geklemd terwijl ze hem aanstaarde. Door dat augurkje tussen haar tanden werd hij alleen maar verliefder en hij zei: 'I have a gift for you and your father.'

Ze bleef hem aankijken terwijl ze het augurkje verorberde. 'Now?' vroeg ze, en daarna trok ze haar hand uit de zijne om nog een stukje watermeloen in haar mond te stoppen.

'No,' antwoordde hij, 'not now. In my hotel. Can I come to your place with the gift for you and your father?'

Ze keek naar Dana en ze bespraken iets in het Russisch of Oekraïens en de Pool stopte ook een augurkje in zijn mond terwijl hij het oordeel van Yulia en haar vriendin afwachtte. Toen ze was uitgesproken stopte Yulia na alle augurken, lamskarbonaadjes en ingelegde watermeloen een kauwgumpje in haar mond en ze zei: 'You can come tomorrow to my place.'

Meer hoefde de Pool niet te weten. Ze vond hem echt leuk. Jurek had ongelijk, de chickies zagen hem nog staan.

'What time?' vroeg de Pool.

'Afternoon, late afternoon. Five. Is that okay for you?' Ze pakte een pen uit haar tasje, ze schreef een adres op, gaf het papiertje aan de Pool en hij bestudeerde het met de devotie van een heilige. Vervolgens pakte hij haar pen en schreef op een servetje zijn telefoonnummer en de naam van zijn hotel, voor het geval dat. Daarop zei hij: 'You must know I have a son.'

'A son?'

'Yes,' zei hij.

'One son?'

De Pool knikte. 'There were two sons, but one is gone.'

'Okay,' zei Yulia. 'Let's go.'

Ze had hem vermoedelijk niet begrepen, hij zou het later uitleggen. Misschien moest hij er niet te veel aandacht aan besteden, het ging om de zoon die er nog was. Hij betaalde de rekening want hij was een gentleman – het was goed dat hij flink gepind had, het lamsvlees bleek peperduur – en daarna gingen ze naar buiten.

Het was donker en het miezerde maar het nieuwe leven van de Pool was begonnen. Bovendien zou hij hier over een paar dagen weggaan en hij zou haar meenemen. Natuurlijk niet meteen, hij wist dat zoiets tijd kostte. Zo liepen ze samen naar de metro, daar vroeg Yulia of hij een muntje had en toen hij dat niet bleek te hebben kochten ze er een voor hem. Dat vatte hij op als een teken van liefde of op z'n minst genegenheid, waarom onderscheid maken tussen die twee? Overal waren tekens. Je moest ze alleen herkennen. En hij gaf zowel Dana als Yulia twee kussen, op elke wang een en hij zei: 'I'll see you tomorrow.' Hij bleef de dames nakijken, hij hoopte dat ze zich nog een keer zouden omdraaien maar dat gebeurde niet, ze werden opgenomen in de mensenmassa en uiteindelijk werd ook hij opgenomen in de mensenmassa. Hij zat weer in de metro tussen passagiers in winterjassen die voor zich uit staarden of naar hun telefoon staarden, nu deerde het hem niet. Hij stapte bij een verkeerde halte uit en dwaalde een uur door de koude stad. Ook dat deerde hem niet. In de lobby kwam hij de man uit Recklinghausen tegen die zei: 'Du, hey du, trink was mit mir in der Bar. Ich sitze dort mit drei herrlichen Frauen, die wissen hier noch was Freude macht. Die Kultur ist hier noch nicht ganz so versaut wie bei uns.'

De Pool zei dat hij moe was en naar zijn kamer wilde en daar stuurde hij, zittend op het bed, een appje naar zijn ex dat zijn nieuwe leven was begonnen.

Toen kleedde hij zich uit en nam een bad. In bad besefte hij dat hij geen telefoonnummer had van zijn toekomstige vrouw, al had hij haar adres. Het zou goed komen. Hij trok zich succesvol af maar nog groter dan het beest was de verliefdheid.

Eenmaal uit bad liep hij in zijn ochtendjas naar de klerenkast om te controleren of de vlaaien er nog waren. Het was niet dat hij de kamermeisjes niet vertrouwde, alleen wist je nooit of ze niet per ongeluk door razende honger waren overvallen. Alles lag er nog precies zo bij als hij het had achtergelaten, inclusief de rum. Hij opende het flesje en nam een paar slokken.

Pas toen zag hij dat zijn ex hem had teruggeschreven. 'Hoe gaat het in Kiev?' wilde ze weten. 'Ruud zegt dat het voor de Kreeft een uitstekende maand voor de liefde is. Doe daar je voordeel mee, lieverd.'

Hoewel de Pool weinig van astrologie moest hebben hechtte hij toch waarde aan dit astrologische inzicht. Soms hadden astrologen ondanks zichzelf gelijk. En zittend op bed dronk hij met kleine, voorzichtige slokjes de rum. Hij genoot.

# 8

De Pool werd vroeg wakker, ongeveer zoals hij lang geleden wakker was geworden op zijn verjaardag, ongeduldig, vol verwachting en toch ook met een zweem van angst, dat de cadeautjes zouden tegenvallen, dat hij niet zou krijgen wat hij had gevraagd.

Hij pakte zijn telefoon, stiekem hoopte hij dat Yulia hem een berichtje had gestuurd. Toen dat niet zo bleek te zijn schreef hij aan zijn lieve ex: 'Kreeft heeft liefde gevonden x.' Hij had last van lichte hoofdpijn, van een kater was geen sprake. Voor een kater was hij te gelukkig en vervuld van dat besef bleef hij nog even liggen tot hij vond dat hij lui genoeg was geweest. Hij kleedde zich aan, weer de bloemetjesblouse was misschien overdreven, hij trok wel zijn nieuwe colbertje aan, dat kon prima, dat zou niemand opvallen, met daaronder nu een gewoon wit overhemd. Hij besloot niet naar de ontmoeting met dames uit Kiev te gaan die deze middag op het programma stond. Hij had de juiste dame uit Kiev ontmoet, waarom zou hij er nog meer willen ontmoeten?

Toen hij zijn hotelkamer verliet om beneden te ontbijten zag hij Han op de gang rondlopen in een witte linnen broek, alsof het hartje zomer was. 'Wat ben je aan het doen?' vroeg de Pool.

'Ik ben aan het oefenen,' zei Han. 'Ik heb straks een date. Ik heb een paar zinnen uit mijn hoofd geleerd, in het Russisch, maar ik vergeet ze steeds weer.'

'Wat voor zinnen?'

'Een vertaalster heeft ze fonetisch voor me opgeschreven. Ik zal altijd van je blijven houden. Ik zal je nooit slaan. Dat soort zinnen.' Han deed een paar stappen in de richting van de Pool en zei zachtjes: 'De vorige keer dat ik hier was had ik een date en we zaten te praten. Op een gegeven moment vroeg ze: "Ga je me slaan? Want mannen die slaan hebben we hier genoeg." Ik zei, "Nooit. Alleen mijn moeder slaat weleens."'

Hij lachte alsof het een grapje was maar de Pool kon er niet om lachen. Hij rook de aftershave van Han, een niet zo aangename geur. 'Ik weet niet of jij al een date hebt,' zei Han en nog steeds praatte hij alsof hij geheimen aan het vertellen was. 'Je kunt het beste meteen al zeggen dat je niet zult slaan, ook niet als je veel gedronken hebt, dan heb je zoveel gewonnen.'

'Ik zal het onthouden.' De Pool liep naar de lift. Han ging een vriend worden. Als Yulia naar Nederland was gekomen zou hij met haar naar Zaandam reizen om de nieuwe vriend op te zoeken. Toen hij zich omdraaide zag hij Han weer door de gang ijsberen in zijn fladderende linnen broek.

Beneden aan het ontbijt zat als enige van de mannen John, de liefdesveteraan. De Pool ging niet naast hem zitten, hij pakte wat roerei, yoghurt en een sneetje bruinbrood en koos een tafeltje voor zich alleen. Daar at hij geconcentreerd en toch ietwat gehaast zijn ontbijt, de lichte hoofdpijn was erger geworden, maar het enthousiasme dat in hem was ontwaakt, de herboren hartstocht en een verlangen dat hij al heel lang niet zo had gevoeld, misschien wel nooit, waren zoveel sterker dan dat beetje hoofdpijn. Toen hij klaar was met ontbijten stuurde hij een bericht aan Jurek. Dat alles goed ging in Kiev en dat hij zijn zoon miste. Hij overwoog nog te schrijven dat hij een chickie had gevonden, tegenover zijn zoon vond hij dat toch wat voorbarig. Er kwam vrijwel meteen een berichtje terug, iets over sexting. En meteen daarna: 'Sorry, niet voor jou.'

De Pool wist niet hoe hij hierop moest reageren. Het was beter hierover een gesprek te beginnen. Dat zou hij doen als hij terug was, nu waren er andere zaken die zijn aandacht opeisten. Bovendien wilde hij zich eerst even goed in sexting verdiepen voor hij Jurek daarop zou aanspreken.

Lucas kwam de ontbijtzaal binnen en snelde op de Pool af. 'Heb je beet?' vroeg de gepensioneerde huisarts. 'Heeft de visser een visje gevangen? Twee visjes dacht ik te zien.'

'Ik heb iemand leren kennen,' zei de Pool voorzichtig. 'En jij?'

'Man,' zei de huisarts, 'ik heb zoveel vrouwen leren kennen. Op één dag meer dan in heel mijn leven in Nederland. Ja, in mijn praktijk heb ik vrouwen ontmoet maar ik heb de grens nooit overschreden. Oekraïne is een paradijs. Ik heb spijt dat ik het niet eerder heb beseft. Hier in Kiev heb ik nu al dingen meegemaakt die ik al die jaren tijdens mijn huwelijk nooit heb meegemaakt en eigenlijk ook niet in de jaren erna. Of de vrouw erbij zit in wier armen ik zal sterven, dat weet ik nog niet, ik heb eigenlijk helemaal geen zin meer om te sterven.'

De gepensioneerde huisarts liet zijn stem dalen: 'Wij in het Westen, wij lopen op onze laatste poten. Ik zag het aan mijn vrouw, ik zag het aan mijn patiënten, ze wilden niet dood hoor, ze wilden best leven en gezond blijven maar van levenslust was geen sprake meer. Sommige van mijn patiënten genazen met tegenzin. Ze wilden er niets voor doen. Alle moeite moest van de arts komen. Ja, wat kun je dan verwachten?'

De Pool had daar geen antwoord op. Hij zei: 'Je bent ook veel te jong om dood te gaan,' en meteen daarna stond hij op, want hij had Paul gezien. Hij liep op hem af, anders dan hiervoor. Als een echte gentleman. 'Paul,' zei de Pool, 'ik kom vanmiddag niet naar de ontmoeting met de dames want ik heb een date.'

'Mooi,' zei Paul, die een bord vol met kaas en worst voor zich had. Daarnaast lagen vier sneetjes toast op een servetje. ‘Heb je het een beetje naar je zin? Heb je een vertaalster nodig?’

‘Nee,’ zei de Pool. ‘Ze spreekt prima Engels.’

Paul veegde zijn mond af. ‘Je kan hier zoveel eten als je wil,’ merkte hij op. ‘Neem het ervan. Het is zonde om er geen gebruik van te maken, je hebt ervoor betaald.’

‘Ja, dat is zonde.’ De Pool was een beetje teleurgesteld over het gebrek aan enthousiasme van Paul maar die man was natuurlijk door alle liefdesreizen afgestompt. Op zijn kamer ging hij op bed liggen en probeerde weer de thriller te lezen, het verhaal boeide hem nog steeds niet. Hij ging voor het raam staan en keek naar de regen.

Een kamermeisje kwam binnen om zijn bed op te maken waarbij ze zich schichtig door de kamer bewoog alsof hij een bruut was. Vlak voor ze wegging legde ze nog chocolaatjes op de hoofdkussens.

Toen had hij nog zeker drie uur te gaan. Hij keek op zijn telefoon. Noch zijn overgebleven jongen, noch zijn ex liet iets horen.

Hij trok zijn kleren uit, zette het alarm en ging weer op bed liggen. Hoewel hij niet moe was viel hij in slaap en toen hij wakker werd regende het niet meer. Het was overbodig maar hij schoor zich nog een keer. Hij depte een wondje met wc-papier en daarna neuriede hij een lied dat hij zich herinnerde uit zijn jeugd. De tekst wist hij niet meer, de melodie stond hem nog goed bij. Met een gevoel van opwinding, geen seksuele opwinding, de opwinding van een kind, kleedde hij zich weer aan. Het witte overhemd stond hem niet zo goed als de bloemetjesblouse, hij vond dat het hem wat ernstig maakte, somber, maar een zekere ernst paste bij deze situatie, hij zou de vader van zijn toekomstige vrouw leren kennen. Dat was niet iets om grapjes over te maken hoewel hij met zijn vorige schoonfamilie weinig tot geen contact had gehad, dat kwam doordat zijn ex met haar ouders nauwelijks contact onderhield.

Zekerheidshalve zette hij zijn pet op. Die pet gaf hem toch iets jeugdigs.

Toen ging hij voor de klerenkast staan en hij vroeg zich af of hij alle drie de vlaaien zou meenemen of slechts een. Hij had gerekend op één vlaai per vrouw, nu voelde het als verraad om twee vlaaien achter te houden voor het geval dat. Hij had zijn toekomstige vrouw ontmoet.

Hij griste de drie vlaaien uit de kast en liep naar beneden. Bij de receptie vroeg hij in zijn beste Engels of ze hem wilde helpen met een taxi. Hij liet het adres aan de receptioniste zien, die het op haar beurt weer aan een collega liet zien die het papiertje doorgaf aan de manager en het was de manager die ten slotte zei: 'We will arrange a car for you.'

Een meneer van de receptie begeleidde de Pool naar buiten en daar werd hij in een taxi geholpen. Geen gewone taxi, een soort hoteltaxi vermoedelijk. De manager zei nog wat de rit zou kosten, een hoop geld, bijna net zoveel als het eten de dag ervoor maar omgerekend in euro's viel het allemaal mee. En als het nieuwe leven begon dan keek je niet op tien of twintig euro meer.

De Pool zat op de achterbank, de vlaaien hield hij op zijn schoot alsof het zijn kinderen waren. Hij zag de veteraan met twee vrouwen het hotel uit komen.

Er waren veel files in Kiev. Hoe ver ze ook oostwaarts gingen, de files bleven hen achtervolgen. Ze reden en ze reden, eerst door het centrum, toen kwamen ze in buitenwijken terecht en vervolgens in buitenwijken van buitenwijken en nog altijd waren ze er niet. Hoe langer de reis duurde, hoe groter de angst van de Pool dat er niemand zou opendoen, dat hij voor een gesloten deur zou staan, of dat alleen de vader thuis was en dat die zou zeggen: Mijn dochter is vanochtend vroeg vertrokken voor een wereldreis van een halfjaar, het spijt me.

'Is this still Kiev?' vroeg de Pool.

'Kiev,' zei de chauffeur.

Omdat er verder geen geluid uit de man kwam hield de Pool ook zijn mond. Hij was ruim op tijd vertrokken, hij zou niet te laat bij zijn nieuwe vrouw verschijnen. Hij vroeg zich wel af hoe hij terug moest komen. Als ze al thuis was, Yulia. Hij kon er niet blijven slapen. Dat gaf geen pas al had hij voor de zekerheid zijn beste onderbroek aangetrokken. Het nieuwe leven zou verrassingen voor hem in petto hebben. Daaraan twijfelde hij niet.

Na een reis van ruim een uur kwamen ze terecht bij een reeks hoge flatgebouwen die de Pool opnieuw weemoedig stemden. Je zou hier maar wonen. Ja, hij zou zijn toekomstige vrouw redden uit deze architectuur. Heerlen mocht de lelijkste stad van Nederland zijn, als hij dit zo zag kon het nog erger. Als ze gered wilde worden had ze haar redder gevonden.

'Our Manhattan.' De chauffeur wees op de flats.

Ze stopten bij een van de flatgebouwen. Kinderen speelden met een kat en een vrouw met een boodschappentas was stil blijven staan om te kijken wie er uit de auto kwam. De Pool betaalde, wat nog even duurde omdat er een discussie ontstond over de fooi, een discussie die de Pool uiteindelijk in zijn voordeel beslechtte. Hij was een gentleman maar hij was niet gek. Fooien werden vrijwillig gegeven en niet afgedwongen. Meer dan tien procent fooi was overdreven. De chauffeur begon te schelden op Europa, Amerika en Afrika in het algemeen en de Pool in het bijzonder. Daar was de Pool hard in, schelden leverde niet meer fooi op.

De weg was modderig. Hij liep op het flatgebouw af, nagestaard door de vrouw met de boodschappentassen. Hij keek op het papiertje naar het huisnummer en toen hij voor het flatgebouw stond zocht hij dat nummer maar hij zag alleen namen, geen nummers, en de namen kon hij niet lezen. Hij voelde zich weer moedeloos worden. Het nieuwe leven was zo broos, de hartstocht kon zo makkelijk ontsnappen.

Gelukkig kwam de vrouw met de boodschappen zijn kant uit. Met de vlaaien in zijn arm probeerde hij haar liefdevol aan te kijken, hij wist dat je als buitenlander altijd extra je best moest doen en hij zei in zijn beste Engels: 'Could you please help me? I'm looking for this family.'

Hij overhandigde haar het papiertje dat ze aannam nadat ze de boodschappentassen op de grond had gezet. Ze bekeek het papiertje langdurig en toen wees ze op een ander flatgebouw. 'Over there?' vroeg hij. Ze knikte en gaf hem een duwtje in de richting van het andere flatgebouw. Vervolgens pakte ze uit haar boodschappentas een klein Oekraïens vlaggetje en begon daarmee te zwaaien.

Hij liep in de richting van het flatgebouw dat ze hem had aangewezen en toen hij zich omdraaide was ze nog altijd bezig met haar vlaggetje te zwaaien. Ze riep ook iets wat hij niet verstond. Ondanks de drie vlaaien in zijn arm lukte het hem te salueren. Dat leek hem gepast aangezien hij vermoedde dat de oudere dame een soldate was, of een vrouw van een soldaat, iemand die voor haar land had gevochten, thuis of aan het front, en die te allen tijde bereid was dat weer te doen. Ze zou blijven vechten, tot haar laatste snik. Die indruk had ze gewekt. Het was een instelling die hem beviel. Hij wilde best salueren voor de strijders, zeker als ze hem de weg hadden gewezen.

Het flatgebouw dat ze hem had aangewezen had wel huisnummers bij de ingang. Hij vermoedde, afgaand op het nummer, dat zijn toekomstige vrouw op de achtste verdieping woonde en hij nam de lift, liep over de galerij naar de woning waarvan hij meende dat zij daar met haar vader woonde. De deur had een nummer dat overeenkwam met het nummer op zijn papiertje. Als dit het goede flatgebouw was dan zou dit de goede woning moeten zijn. Achter deze deur moesten zijn toekomstige vrouw en haar vader schuilgaan. Hij wachtte even voor hij aanbelde, hij bekeek zijn spiegelbeeld in de ruit, het was goed dat hij een petje had opgezet, het gaf hem echt iets jeugdigs. Toen draaide hij zich om, het uitzicht bleef grauw, al kon dat komen door het weer. Hij vroeg zich af hoeveel mensen hier naar beneden waren gesprongen en meteen daarna belde hij aan.

Ze deed zelf open. Ze was gewoon thuis, zijn toekomstige vrouw. Ze liep in een spijkerbroek, droeg roze pantoffels en had een donkerblauwe trui aan, ze was nog steeds prachtig.

'I'm so glad you are here,' zei de Pool.

En zij antwoordde enigszins verbaasd: 'But I live here.'

Hij deed zijn colbertje uit dat ze aannam en in een andere kamer opborg. Zijn pet liet hij op en de drie vlaaien hield hij stevig vast. Hij wachtte op het juiste moment om die aan het gezin te overhandigen.

In een eenvoudig ingerichte woonkamer zat een man op een leren bank. Er waren twee zwarte leren fauteuils en op een van de fauteuils mocht de Pool plaatsnemen. Hij gaf de vader een hand en stelde zich voor. Yulia vroeg wat hij wilde drinken, thee, koffie, iets sterkers. Hij koos voor de thee hoewel hij al had gezien dat de vader bezig was met iets sterkers.

'Who are you?' vroeg de vader toen de Pool op de zwarte fauteuil had plaatsgenomen.

Hij had zich net voorgesteld maar hij wilde het best nog eens doen. 'I'm Geniek. A fireman from the Netherlands. A fireman from Heerlen. My father was born in Poland. My mother was born in Germany. I'm born in the Netherlands. I speak a little bit Polish.'

'Father doesn't see well,' zei Yulia die terug was uit de keuken waar hij haar had horen rommelen. 'Accident at work. He sees half of what we see.'

'Ah,' zei de Pool. 'I'm sorry.'

'Why?' vroeg de vader.

'That you don't see well. Sorry for the accident at work.'

'That's not your business.' De vader leunde achterover. Hij had grijs haar en een stevige kaaklijn, hij zag er een beetje uit als een bokser, in elk geval als iemand die zwaar fysiek werk had verricht. Ook de Pool werkte met zijn handen, dat was in zijn voordeel misschien. Hij zat daar nog altijd met de vlaaien op zijn schoot en wachtte tot Yulia die weer in de keuken was verdwenen zou terugkeren want het leek hem beter het gesprek te hervatten in haar aanwezigheid.

Toen ze terug was en hij zijn thee had, zij dronk ook thee, de vader nam af en toe een slok van zijn sterkedrank, zei de Pool: 'I brought you something from my country, sir. From my region. We call it vlaai, sir.' Yulia zat naast hem, hij had een arm om haar heen willen slaan. Hij had haar teder willen aanraken. Het was nog te vroeg daarvoor.

Er viel een stilte. De vader zei iets in het Russisch en meteen daarna zei hij: 'I don't understand. Why are you here?'

De Pool kuchte. 'I'm a friend of your daughter. I brought you vlaai. It's something to eat. It's sweet. It comes in different tastes, apple, cherry, peach.' Hij kon even niet op het Engelse woord voor abrikoos komen. 'It tastes good.'

De Pool stond op om de drie vlaaien aan Yulia te overhandigen, maar omdat zij niet opkeek ging hij weer zitten en zo bleef hij daar zitten met de drie vlaaien op zijn schoot. Hij vond zijn toekomstige vrouw zo mooi en al rook het in dit huis wat bedompt, zij rook heerlijk.

Op dat moment kreeg de vader een hoestaanval die hij onderdrukte door wat te drinken en toen zei hij: 'You want to fuck my daughter, you want to fuck my family, you want to fuck my country, you are a foreigner.'

De Pool knikte. Er zat zo te horen veel woede in zijn toekomstige schoonvader maar dat deed er niet toe. De toekomstige schoonvader had een ongeluk op zijn werk gehad waardoor hij weinig kon zien, dan mocht je boos zijn. Woede was begrijpelijk, er was veel tegenslag en op de tegenslag volgde doorgaans de woede, en dan had je nog mensen zonder tegenslag die preventief boos waren. Als je halfblind was mocht je als vader best aan de man vragen die met je dochter wilde trouwen: Ben je hier gekomen om haar te neuken of heb je meer in de aanbieding?

'Yes,' zei de Pool, 'yes, I'm a foreigner, but I don't want to fuck your daughter, sir, or your country or your family. My intentions are good. I brought you a gift.' De man had iets tegen buitenlanders en ook dat begreep de Pool. Hij stond op en knielde met de drie vlaaien voor de halfblinde man. De eerste doos met vlaai, een kersenvlaai, opende hij nog altijd knielend voor de halfblinde en hij zei: 'You can smell it. This comes from our region. Limburg. We call it vlaai.'

De man zei: 'I don't smell anything.'

Waarop de Pool zich tot zijn toekomstige vrouw wendde. 'Do you have a knife?' Waar niet geroken kon worden daar moest worden geproefd. Ze nam hem mee, hij stalde de vlaaien uit op het aanrecht in de kleine keuken, kreeg een broodmes in zijn handen gedrukt en hij sneed de appelvlaai in zes stukken, het leek hem veilig met appelvlaai te beginnen. 'I hope you are hungry,' zei hij en zij antwoordde: 'Daddy is a good man. He suffered a lot. He doesn't like most people. But he is a decent man and a good father.'

Hij keek haar aan met al het medeleven dat hij in zich had, hij perste het uit zijn ogen, uit zijn ziel. Hoewel hij eigenlijk niet meer aan lijden had willen denken. Daar was genoeg aan gedacht. Het nieuwe leven zou niet zonder zijn, dat was niet realistisch, maar wel met minder lijden. Als dat niet zo was waarom moest het dan nieuw worden genoemd? Genoeg lijden, weg met het lijden. Ze pakte wat bordjes waarop hij stukken vlaai legde. Hij nam haar rechterhand in zijn hand en hij verklaarde dat hij van haar hield. Of ze hem wilde vergeven. 'Forgive me,' zei hij. 'Forgive me.' Want als hij één ding had geleerd in het kippenhok was het de liefde te wantrouwen, als hij één ding aan het kippenhok had overgehouden was het de alles overwoekerende onzekerheid of je de mensen überhaupt kon opzadelen met je liefde. Of je dat niet moest laten. Toen had hij gedacht dat hij met zijn liefde, zijn afschuwelijke liefde, alleen bij God terechtkon. Nu was hij in Kiev, daarom had hij deze reis ondernomen, om ondanks alles de mensen op te zadelen met zijn liefde, met die gruwelijke liefde van hem, al waren het de mensen in Kiev. Nee, niet de mensen. Eén mens. Eén Yulia. En deze Yulia had zich niet zonder reden aangemeld bij Liefde over de Grens, zij wilde kennelijk met iets worden opgezadeld. Hij zou beminnen en tegelijkertijd om vergiffenis vragen voor zijn liefde, hij zou liefde geven en om vergiffenis vragen, niet aan God maar aan de mensen, aan één mens.

Ze ging naar binnen met de bordjes. De Pool volgde haar, hij ging in zijn fauteuil zitten en de halfblinde man nam een paar happen van de vlaai. Daarop zette hij het bordje op de tafel en hij zei luid en duidelijk: 'No.' En toen nog eens: 'No.'

'No?' vroeg de Pool.

'No, this is not for us.'

'You don't like it?'

'No,' zei de halfblinde man, 'it's dry and old and no taste whatsoever. Maybe you like this, in your country you eat this, maybe you Polish people eat this shit, but this is not what we eat here. We don't eat shit here.'

'I'm not Polish, I'm from the Netherlands. My father was from Poland.'

'Daddy is a very honest man,' zei Yulia, 'he is one of the more honest men in Ukraine.'

'This is for pigs,' zei de oude man met iets wat op levenslust begon te lijken.

'Ah,' zei de Pool en hij at zijn vlaai stug op. De vlaai was inderdaad aan de droge kant, toch een beetje oud geworden maar nog altijd goed eetbaar en gelukkig at Yulia ook haar vlaai. Toen hij klaar was met eten ging de Pool staan en hij zei: 'I'm not a good speaker. I'm a fireman. My father was a humble man. Still alive. My mother came from Rhineland, Germany. A humble woman. Dead.'

'She died because of you,' zei de oude man. 'Mothers die because of their sons. Fathers die because of their daughters.'

De Pool was vastbesloten zich niets meer aan te trekken van alles wat de vader van Yulia verder nog te zeggen had. Hij vervolgde: 'I had two sons. Now I have only one son. I want to marry your daughter. I ask you, could you allow me to be with your daughter? Could you think of me as the husband of your daughter? Could you forgive me if I become your daughter's husband?'

De halfblinde man nam een slok, veegde zijn mond af en keek naar zijn dochter. Toen zei hij: 'The Russians fucked us. The Germans fucked us. The Americans fucked us. Now you come and you want to fuck us again. We are here where we live, where we belong, and other people fuck us, again and again and again. Leave us alone, go and fuck somebody else.'

De Pool keek naar Yulia en zij zei opnieuw dat haar vader zo'n eerlijke man was, haar ogen stonden nu wel treurig. Ze zei dat hij niet kon liegen en de Pool had de handen van de halfblinde man willen pakken om zijn pogingen tot het vragen van vergiffenis kracht bij te zetten maar dat deed hij niet, dat durfde hij niet. Hij zette een paar stappen in de richting van de halfblinde. Hij knielde neer alsof hij de vader zelf ten huwelijk ging vragen en hij zei: 'Forgive me, forgive me sir. I ask you for forgiveness, because foreigners fucked your country. I'm not here to fuck your country, sir. I'm here to marry your daughter.'

'I have only one daughter,' antwoordde de man, 'and one son.'

De Pool herinnerde zich zijn eigen vader, zijn ex, de overgebleven jongen en toen vroeg hij de halfblinde vader of hij toestemming wilde geven dat Yulia naar Nederland kwam. Dan konden ze uitproberen of het wat was. Het was aan de vroege kant, zei hij. Hij wist het, zei hij. 'It's early,' zei de Pool. Maar waarop wachten, vroeg hij. Waarop? Over twee dagen ging hij alweer weg, dan vlogen ze terug naar Düsseldorf.

Hij wendde zich nu tot Yulia en hij werd overweldigd door het verleden. Het verleden waarvan hij nu afscheid nam, hier in deze buitenwijk van een buitenwijk in Kiev nam hij afscheid van zijn verleden. Van zijn verdwenen jongen, van de pony van de jongen, de boer, het kippenhok, zijn ex, hij nam er afscheid van, ze trokken aan zijn oog voorbij en hij moest zich vasthouden omdat het verleden hem duizelig maakte.

'Come and visit me,' zei hij. 'If you don't like it, you go back. Geen man overboord. If you like it, we stay together.'

'I can try,' zei ze aarzelend. 'I can try.'

De halfblinde moest weer hoesten en toen vroeg hij: 'So you had a wife? She left you because you fucked her over, again and again and again? You gave her this shit to eat?'

'No,' zei de Pool, 'we divorced because the love was over.' Hij keek naar het plafond alsof de liefde daardoorheen naar buiten was gevlogen. Hij zag vochtplekken. 'The love was gone, but the child remains. The child will always be there. The child is stronger than love.' Daarna keek hij naar Yulia, naar haar pantoffels, haar trui en hij wist niet wat hij verder moest zeggen.

De halfblinde vader opende zijn mond, het leek alsof hij wilde schreeuwen, toen verwijderde hij met zijn vinger iets wat tussen zijn tanden zat. Daarna zei hij, gelaten, bijna verdrietig, liefdevol eigenlijk: 'My daughter is adult. Only one daughter. But she is adult. Don't ask me. Ask her. I don't like foreigners, I don't trust foreigners. But what can I do? What can we do?'

Daarna stond de oude man op en hij verdween naar wat vermoedelijk zijn slaapkamer was en ook Yulia ging weg. Ze kwam terug met de twee vlaaien, zachtjes zei ze: 'Take this with you. This is not for us.'

De Pool knikte, het was gewoon een aardigheidje geweest, het cadeau uit de eigen regio, en hij antwoordde: 'I'd like to take you with me.'

Waarop zij fluisterde: 'Yes, later. Maybe. If you send me ticket, I'll come.'

Het sturen van een ticket, over dergelijke praktische zaken had de Pool nog helemaal niet nagedacht, Yulia kennelijk wel. Hoe dan ook begreep hij dat het tijd was om terug te keren naar zijn hotel. Toch iets vroeger dan hij had gedacht, het was allemaal snel verlopen. De sensatie van verlies, van verliezen en verloren zijn maakte zich van hem meester maar er was nog niets definitief verloren. Ze was bereid naar Nederland te komen als hij haar een ticket stuurde. Hij zou zijn toekomstige schoonvader uiteindelijk mild stemmen. Hij zou zijn liefde winnen, met geduld en doorzettingsvermogen en niet-aflatende vriendelijkheid.

'Before I leave,' vroeg hij, 'do I see you?'

'Tomorrow,' zei ze zacht alsof het een geheim was, 'tomorrow in your hotel. I bring friend. Okay? Three? Afternoon?'

'Yes,' zei de Pool, 'yes. Tomorrow. Afternoon. I wait for you in the lobby. I wait for you. I miss you. You know my hotel?'

'Yes, I know your hotel. You always stay in the same hotel.' Hij was kennelijk niet de eerste man van Liefde over de Grens in haar leven, dat was niet erg, hij was de ware. En daarop kuste hij haar hand. Zoals hij altijd een goede brandweerman was geweest was hij nu een goede gentleman geworden. Hij pakte de twee overgebleven vlaaien, ze reikte hem zijn colbertje aan en hij verliet de woning.

Op de galerij bleef hij staan, op haar pantoffels begeleidde ze hem naar buiten. Er viel natte sneeuw. 'Aren't you cold?' vroeg ze.

'No, no, I'm fine.' Ondanks de twee vlaaien in zijn armen lukte het hem haar hand te grijpen. 'Because of you,' zei hij. 'Because of you I want to live.'

Ze knikte en ze zei: 'Send me ticket. I will love you. See you tomorrow.' Haar woorden hadden in de oren van een buitenstaander misschien kil geklonken, wie wilde niet dat hem een ticket werd gestuurd, dat besefte de Pool, dat andere mensen kilte zouden ontwaren waar hij op iets heel anders was gestoten, hij kon ook haar ogen zien en wie haar ogen zag wist dat haar woorden niet kil bedoeld waren, dat zij niet in staat was tot kilheid.

Hij nam de lift naar beneden en vanaf daar keek hij even naar boven om te zien of ze nog op de galerij stond, hij zag alleen twee jongens die iets naar hem riepen, hij kon niet verstaan wat.

Hij liep over het modderige pad en nog een keer draaide hij zich om. Toen zag hij haar, ze stond op de galerij en ze zwaaide naar hem. Hij zwaaide terug en hij riep haar naam met de twee vlaaien onder zijn arm. Ze hoefden nu niet meer heel te blijven, de vlaaien. Hij zou ze toch niet meer weggeven en zo zwaaide hij naar haar en hij riep haar naam met alle levenslust die hij in zich had. Tot ze naar binnen ging, toen hield hij op met roepen. En hij liep verder, hij dwaalde door de buitenwijk van de buitenwijk op zoek naar een metrohalte, een taxi of welke vorm van vervoer dan ook. Het was goed dat hij een pet op had, de natte sneeuw bleef vallen.

Bij een grotere weg vroeg hij een mevrouw naar het hotel, ze begreep hem niet. Hij liet haar het visitekaartje van het hotel zien, ze wist het niet. Hij was verdwaald. 'City center?' vroeg hij.

Ze knikte. Die woorden kwamen de mevrouw bekend voor, die woorden leek ze te begrijpen. Ze nam hem mee naar iets wat kennelijk een bushalte was en daar kwam hij op het idee haar uit dankbaarheid voor de hulp een van zijn twee vlaaien aan te bieden maar dat geschenk sloeg ze resoluut af.

Na een minuut of vijf arriveerde de bus, meer een groot uitgevallen bestelwagen dan een bus. De vrouw moest zijn richting uit, ze stapte samen met hem in, hielp hem met betalen.

Ze reden door de buitenwijken, de natte sneeuw bleef maar vallen en af en toe vroeg de Pool: 'City center?'

De dame knikte, gebaarde dat hij moest blijven zitten en terwijl hij daar zat dacht hij aan de liefde, dat het zo wonderbaarlijk was dat hij in deze stad de liefde had gevonden. Misschien had het menselijk verlengstuk gelijk, dit was de maand van de liefde voor Kreeften.

Toen de dame hem na een kleine drie kwartier het busje uit duwde met de woorden 'city center' herkende de Pool niets. Hij wist niet eens zeker of hij nog in Kiev was. Maar hij was niet alleen verliefd, hij was oplossingsgericht, daarom liet hij aan diverse voorbijgangers het visitekaartje van het hotel zien. Tot een meneer met een hoed zich over hem ontfermde. De man met de hoed sprak zelfs behoorlijk goed Engels, beter nog dan de Pool. Hij vertelde dat het een halfuurtje lopen was, misschien twintig minuten als er snel werd gewandeld.

'I walk fast,' zei de Pool met het enthousiasme van de verliefde.

Zo liep hij naar zijn hotel door de natte sneeuw. Razendsnel en verliefd. Toen hij bij het hotel aankwam was het aardedonker en pas op zijn kamer merkte hij hoe nat hij was geworden en hoe koud hij het had. Hij nam een bad, trok een ochtendjas aan die in de badkamer hing en besefte dat hij nu eigenlijk moest eten. Hij had geen zin om naar buiten te gaan. Wat had hij nog in Kiev te zoeken nu hij gevonden had waarop hij nauwelijks had durven hopen?

Gelukkig had hij de vlaaien. De eerste doos die hij opende bleek de abrikozenvlaai te bevatten en die at hij zittend aan zijn bureau gedachteloos en toch verliefd half op. Hij dronk wat water uit een flesje, het kraanwater hier vertrouwde hij niet, en hoewel hij eigenlijk geen honger had opende hij de tweede doos. Ook de kersenvlaai at hij gedachteloos voor de helft op. Daarna nam hij nog een paar slokken rum om het leven te vieren.

Vervolgens ging hij in bed liggen. Er was een berichtje van Wen. 'Lieve Kreeft,' had ze geschreven, 'wij wensen je veel geluk. We missen je wel een beetje, Jurek en ik.'

De Pool had geen zin hierop te antwoorden, hij dacht aan Yulia. Verder had hij buikpijn maar daar maakte hij zich geen zorgen over. Hij had Yulia, zij had hem, het leven was net zo bekoorlijk als zijn nieuwe vrouw. Juist vanwege haar kleine onvolmaaktheden (haar voortanden) hield hij van haar en hij vertrouwde erop dat zijn onvolmaaktheden en tekortkomingen genade zouden vinden in haar ogen.

# 9

Hij werd wakker met een vieze smaak in zijn mond. Op weg naar de badkamer zag hij dat er een papier onder de deur was geschoven. 'Aan de deelnemers van de liefdesreis van Liefde over de Grens,' stond erop. 'Om tien uur is er een extra bijeenkomst in de Mozartzaal op de eerste verdieping van het hotel. Wij verzoeken iedereen daar stipt op tijd aanwezig te zijn.' Daaronder stond dezelfde tekst nog eens in het Duits.

Hij moest opschieten. Eigenlijk had de Pool willen ontbijten maar hij deed er lang over om te douchen en zich te scheren en bovendien had hij nog buikpijn. Hij zou later theedrinken. Die souvenirs uit de eigen regio waren hem in ieder geval niet goed bekomen.

Het nieuwe colbertje liet hij dit keer achterwege. Hij deed een trui aan en om klokslag tien uur meldde hij zich in de Mozartzaal. Paul zat achter een tafel, er waren twee vertaalsters en de jongeman die Liefde over de Grens in Kiev vertegenwoordigde, hij had een beteuterd gezicht. De mannen op zoek naar de liefde waren er ook, in afwachting van wat komen zou. De man uit Recklinghausen knikte hem toe, net als Lucas. De andere mannen negeerden hem. Even moest de Pool denken aan zijn tijd in het kippenhok, deze mannen waren voornamelijk gevallen engelen maar hij had zijn val kunnen breken, dankzij Yulia. Genade was hem in Kiev ten deel gevallen. Pure genade.

Eindelijk nam Paul het woord. 'Mannen,' zei hij, 'wij zijn naar Kiev gegaan om de liefde te vinden. Een enkeling zal een andere agenda hebben gehad, een enkeling zal hierheen zijn gereisd voor liefdeloze seks, daar gaat het nu niet om. Sommigen van jullie hebben al wat liefde gevonden want dat kan ook op de eerste dag gebeuren, anderen hebben vorderingen gemaakt, misschien wacht iemand nog op de eerste klik. De belangrijkste zoektocht in ons leven mag best even duren. Han heeft de zoektocht gestaakt. Dat wilde ik jullie vertellen. Hij heeft besloten niet meer naar liefde te willen zoeken. Hij is eruit gestapt. Natuurlijk voelen wij...' Paul nam een grote slok water. De Pool keek naar de andere mannen en hij had het idee dat ze er schuldbewust bij zaten maar dat kon verbeelding zijn en zat hij er zelf zo bij. Het was hem niet eens opgevallen dat Han er niet was. Was dat de schuld die hij bij zichzelf bespeurde? De afwezigheid van Han die hem was ontgaan?

Nu boog de gepensioneerde huisarts zich naar de Pool toe. 'Wist je het nog niet?' fluisterde hij. 'Een overdosis slaaptabletten. Hij schijnt het al eerder geprobeerd te hebben. Het kamermeisje heeft hem gisteravond laat gevonden omdat hij de kraan in de badkamer open had laten staan. Geen afscheidsbrief, niets. Hij lag daar in bad. Met zijn regenjas aan. Fuck de liefde.'

Lucas schudde zijn hoofd. De Pool vond dat hij naar drank rook. Kiev liet de mannen niet onberoerd. En hij zag Han voor zich, in zijn donkerrode regenjas, liggend in bad, de doosjes van de slaaptabletten naast hem.

Paul hoestte een paar keer. Hij veegde met de rug van zijn hand over zijn mond. 'Wij hebben ons natuurlijk als organisatie afgevraagd of wij fouten hebben gemaakt,' zei hij een beetje schor. 'Of wij de deelnemers beter hadden moeten begeleiden, maar zoiets kan overal gebeuren. En Han was...' hij nam weer een slok water, 'een uitstekende klant. Han was...' Paul keek rond alsof hij steun zocht bij de mannen, 'een van onze beste klanten. Hij was al zo vaak mee geweest maar hij gaf niet op. Hij bleef optimistisch. Overal meende hij liefde te zien. Zo moeten wij hem ons ook herinneren, als iemand die overal liefde zag. Hij was ervan overtuigd dat het hem dit keer ging lukken. Gistermiddag zei hij nog tegen mij: "Ik denk dat ik dit keer raak heb geschoten." Hij was zo blij.'

Paul boog het hoofd, de Pool had het gevoel dat hun reisleider oprecht geëmotioneerd was, wat hem verbaasde want hij had het idee dat het werk Paul gevoelloos had gemaakt. Een overdosis liefde als het ware. Te veel verlangen van zoekende mannen.

'Het is voor zijn moeder een vreselijke klap,' vervolgde Paul, 'het is voor ons een klap.'

Niemand keek naar Paul en Paul zelf leek niet meer te weten wat hij moest zeggen maar hij durfde kennelijk geen eind aan de bijeenkomst te maken. 'We hebben ons natuurlijk afgevraagd: moeten wij deze liefdesreis annuleren na dit... na dit ongeluk? In overleg met de directie is besloten dat dit fout zou zijn. De liefde is onze missie. Han had vast niet gewild dat wij nu zouden stoppen. Wij blijven zoeken naar de liefde, wij geven niet op. Dat wilde ik zeggen. Natuurlijk ken ik de verhalen: Liefde over de Grens, dat is het afvoerputje van de liefde, wie nergens meer terechtkan die gaat daarheen. Klinkklare onzin, mannen. Kijk om je heen, kijk elkaar aan.'

Paul zweette zichtbaar, het leek alsof hij de hele nacht niet had geslapen, alsof hij de hele nacht had gedronken en enkele van de mannen keken elkaar aan. De Pool staarde recht in het gezicht van de man uit Recklinghausen.

'Zijn wij hier met z'n allen het afvoerputje van de liefde?' Pauls stem sloeg over. 'Nee, wij zijn gelukszoekers, vrienden van de liefde, dat is wat wij zijn, vrienden van de liefde. Laten we aan Han denken, laten we...' Paul keek naar de vertaalsters, misschien in de hoop dat zij ook nog iets zeiden.

'Vanochtend heb ik met Hans moeder gesproken. Ik heb haar verteld dat zij een fantastische zoon had. Dat zij trots op hem kan zijn. Een ware vriend van de liefde.' Paul kuchte. 'Ik stel voor dat we nu gaan staan en twee minuten stil zijn om Han te gedenken. Steh auf, bitte, jetzt wird an Han gedacht.'

De mannen stonden op. Het lukte de Pool alleen niet om aan Han te denken, hij was weer vol van de verdwenen jongen, en van Yulia.

De twee minuten leken eindeloos en hij hoorde de mannen naast zich schuifelen, hij hoorde een vrouw praten op de gang. Tussendoor zag hij Han in zijn donkerrode regenjas in de badkuip liggen. En ook zijn verdwenen jongen zag de Pool. Zijn gezicht was vervaagd maar zijn kleren, zijn schoenen, bepaalde details, die zag hij nauwkeurig voor zich.

Nadat de twee minuten voorbij waren zei Paul: 'Dit was het. Dank jullie wel. Om halfdrie verzamelen we in de lobby en dan gaan we per bus naar de volgende ontmoeting met dames uit Kiev en omstreken. Het belooft iets moois te worden.'

Toen verlieten ze de Mozartzaal, zonder nog veel te zeggen. Hier en daar werd gefluisterd. In de lift stond de Pool alleen met de veteraan. Ze zwegen. Vlak voor de Pool wilde uitstappen zei Rich: 'Ik heb die klootzakken van de Kinderbescherming gezegd: "Als jullie zo doorgaan verhang ik mezelf. Is dat wat jullie willen?" Dat heb ik ze gezegd.'

'Ja,' zei de Pool. 'Dat begrijp ik.' Toen stapte hij uit. Hij draaide zich nog even om en keek naar de veteraan alsof hij zich ervan wilde vergewissen dat deze zich niet vanmiddag zou opknopen. Daar zag het gelukkig niet naar uit. De veteraan straalde strijdlust uit. Hij balde zijn linkervuist, stak die omhoog en riep: 'Seks hoeft van mij niet zo nodig, maar voor een blowjob mogen ze me altijd wakker maken.' Toen gingen de liftdeuren dicht.

De Pool ging weer op bed liggen. Hij wilde een berichtje aan zijn ex en Jurek sturen. Er schoot hem niets te binnen, hij vond de juiste woorden niet. Het leek hem vreemd het voorval met Han te verzwijgen maar hij wist niet hoe hij erover moest vertellen. Een voorval was misschien niet het juiste woord.

Hij stond op en sloeg een paar keer met zijn vuist tegen de muur, hij wierp de afstandsbediening door de kamer. Hij haatte Han. Juist nu de verliefdheid was opgebloeid, juist nu het nieuwe leven was begonnen en genade hem ten deel was gevallen moest Han hem herinneren aan het verleden dat zo goed, zo hermetisch was afgesloten, moest Han de wanhoop in de Pool weer wakker kussen. Juist Han, die een vriend had kunnen worden. 'Ik heb geen behoefte aan troost,' zei de Pool zachtjes, 'want zij die behoefte hebben aan troost kunnen geen liefde geven.'

Hij wachtte op de namiddag zoals men wacht op een geliefde en in dit geval vielen geliefde en namiddag keurig samen. De lunch sloeg hij over, uit de minibar had hij een zakje chips gehaald. Zelfs dat at hij niet op. Daarna trok hij toch zijn bloemetjesblouse aan, de blouse stonk een beetje naar zweet, voor Yulia en voor Han.

Hij ging in de lobby zitten. Nu al, terwijl hij haar nauwelijks kende, voelde hij zich verloren zonder Yulia.

Ze verscheen met haar vriendin en hij stelde voor in het hotel wat te gaan drinken maar ze zei dat ze liever ergens anders heen wilde. Ze liepen door de straten van Kiev. Er viel geen natte sneeuw, maar het was koud. De Pool voelde het niet echt, de kou drong niet tot hem door. Yulia was er, zijn Yulia. Ze gingen een café binnen waar taartjes in de etalage stonden, Yulia en haar vriendin kozen een taartje uit en ook de Pool nam er een hoewel hij meer zin had in iets hartigs.

Toen zei hij: 'Han killed himself.'

'Who is Han?'

'One of our group. A young man. Red raincoat? You must have seen him.'

'Yes. Maybe,' Yulia keek naar haar vriendin. Ze zeiden iets tegen elkaar en daarna zei Yulia: 'I don't remember him, I'm sorry.'

De Pool roerde in zijn koffie. Hij keek zijn toekomstige echtgenote liefdevol aan en hij zei: 'My son killed himself.'

'Your son?'

'My other son,' zei de Pool.

'That's awful.' Yulia pakte zijn hand en masseerde die. Dat voelde goed.

'Yes,' zei de Pool, 'pretty awful.' Hij nam een hapje van zijn taart maar kon zich alleen concentreren op de hand, de massage. De liefde.

'If you send me ticket I come to Holland.'

Hij keek Yulia recht in de ogen en zei: 'I live in Heerlen. Do you know where that is?'

'No,' zei ze, 'no.'

'Not far from Germany. Do you want to live with me in Heerlen?'

'If you send me ticket I come and I'll see.'

Even vroeg de Pool zich af hoeveel tickets er al naar Yulia waren gestuurd. Omdat hij zijn nieuwsgierigheid niet kon bedwingen vroeg hij of ze al vaak in het buitenland was geweest.

'Only Russia. I speak Russian, my heart is Russian, my soul is Ukrainian.'

'I see,' zei de Pool. 'I see.' Toen pakte hij haar hand en verklaarde alsof het een geloofsbelijdenis was: 'I'll send you a ticket. And later I'll send a ticket for your daddy too.'

# VII

## *Je had erbij moeten zijn*

## 1

Met moeite had de Pool Jurek ervan kunnen overtuigen mee te komen naar Schiphol. Zelf had hij een spandoek gemaakt, tijdens een weekenddienst op de kazerne, waarop in grote rode letters stond: WELCOME HOME, YULIA.

Jurek had gezegd: 'Ze komt helemaal niet thuis, man. Ze woont in Kiev. Dat chickie komt gewoon op bezoek.'

Het was een gevecht geweest maar de Pool had gewonnen, ze zouden Yulia samen verwelkomen. En de discussie over waar Yulia thuis was had hij verder geprobeerd te vermijden.

Al had hij in de auto nog wel uitgelegd dat Kiev voor Yulia niet meer zou zijn dan een omweg naar haar werkelijke huis in Heerlen. Hoe meer hij dergelijke dingen verkondigde, hoe meer hij erin begon te geloven. Onderweg had hij 27 rode rozen gekocht want ze was 27, had ze hem een paar weken geleden per sms laten weten toen hij eindelijk naar haar leeftijd durfde te vragen. Zo was hij de aankomsthal binnengelopen, met spandoek, zoon en rozen. Een gelukkig man.

Hij had zich voor de uitgang waar ze doorheen moest komen geposteerd met het spandoek in zijn rechter- en de rozen in zijn linkerhand. Jurek had de andere kant van het spandoek moeten vasthouden. Met tegenzin deed hij het, je kon het aflezen aan zijn gezicht. Eerst had hij geweigerd maar de vader had hem op weinig subtiele wijze weten over te halen. De Pool had gezegd: 'Als je dit voor me doet dan koop ik een nieuwe telefoon voor je. Jij mag kiezen welke.' Dat had de jongen overtuigd, voor een nieuwe telefoon deed hij veel.

Daar stonden vader en zoon, met het grote spandoek

waarop Yulia welkom werd geheten. De vader half knielend. 'Moet dat echt?' vroeg de zoon. De Pool antwoordde: 'Ik ga voor haar op mijn knieën omdat ik een gentleman ben, omdat ik wil dat ze weet dat ik er een ben. Zo verwelkomt een gentleman zijn geliefde.'

'Alsjeblieft papa, ze zullen je uitlachen. Al die mensen.' De jongen wees op de andere mensen die in de aankomsthal aan het wachten waren.

De Pool pakte de arm van de jongen beet. 'Dat kan me niets schelen, of ze me uitlachen of niet. Denk je dat ik nooit heb gemerkt dat ze me altijd al hebben uitgelachen? Denk je dat ik gek ben? Ga zo staan dat ze het spandoek goed kan zien als ze naar buiten komt.'

Daarop had de jongen niets meer te zeggen. En zo wachtten ze daar, de een stond, de ander knielde half, alsof hij een gelovige was die niet zeker wist of hij moest bidden of niet.

Het duurde en het duurde. Ze zagen allerlei passagiers naar buiten komen maar Yulia zat er niet bij. Af en toe riep de jongen: 'Laten we hiermee ophouden, pap. Ik krijg pijn in mijn arm.'

De Pool gaf niet op, ook niet toen er al een hoop passagiers uit Kiev – hij zag het aan hun gezichten, hun koffers en voor de zekerheid had hij het nog gevraagd – langs waren gekomen.

'Ze komt niet meer,' riep Jurek, 'misschien komt ze morgen.'

'Nee,' hield de Pool vol, 'ze heeft me een berichtje gestuurd toen ze aan boord ging. Ze komt vandaag, ik weet het zeker.'

Half knielend bleef hij zitten, ook toen het ernaar uitzag dat de meeste passagiers uit Kiev naar buiten waren gekomen, hij verroerde zich niet. Hij bleef zitten zoals hij zat, een knie op de grond, het spandoek in de rechter-, de rozen in de linkerhand. De blikken van de mensen deerden hem niet. Hij wist niet eens zeker of ze naar hem keken. Er hadden hier vast vaker mensen met spandoeken en rozen gestaan. Misschien niet met een knie op de grond maar wat maakte dat uit? Alles in zijn leven had hem naar deze vasthoudendheid toe gedreven, alles in zijn leven had hem geleerd dat hij niet moest loslaten en dat deed hij dan ook niet. Niet nu. Als hij had willen loslaten had hij het eerder moeten doen.

Daar verscheen ze. Ze droeg een mantel, beige, had een middelgrote blauwe koffer bij zich en ze liep op hoge hakken. Ze zag eruit, vond de Pool, als een filmster en dat versterkte zijn overtuiging dat het goed was dat hij daar knielend zat. Hij riep haar naam, hij riep nog een keer harder. Ze keek voor zich uit, ze keek niet naar beneden terwijl hij zich juist klein voor haar had gemaakt, de grote Pool maakte zich klein voor zijn toekomstige vrouw, want dat was naar zijn idee wat de gentleman deed, die maakte zich klein voor de ander en al helemaal voor zijn eigen vrouw.

Eindelijk zag ze hem. Ze keek verbaasd alsof ze iemand anders had verwacht terwijl hij toch af en toe selfies had gestuurd om het wachten minder lang te laten duren. Ze kwam naar hem toe en zonder overeind te komen drukte hij haar de rozen in de hand. 'For you,' zei hij, 'for my future wife.'

Pas toen kwam hij overeind en hij omhelsde haar, drukte een kus op haar wang. Hij had een paar weken geleden een app op zijn telefoon geïnstalleerd om beter Engels te leren en stiekem hoopte hij dat Yulia het zou merken. Hij had het voor haar gedaan.

'You are so sweet,' zei ze met de rozen in haar hand. Ze stond er een beetje verlegen en ongemakkelijk bij. Ze glimlachte, een bevroren glimlach.

Daarna kwam Jurek bij hen staan alsof hij er eigenlijk niet bij hoorde, alsof hij op iemand anders had staan wachten en de Pool zei: 'This is my son, Jurek.'

'I know,' zei ze, 'I know.'

'Hi,' zei Jurek bijna onverstaanbaar.

Uit haar handtas haalde ze een cadeautje dat in kerstcadeaupapier zat en ze gaf het aan de jongen. 'It's just chocolates,' zei ze, 'but good chocolates from my country.' De Pool keek naar Jurek en wachtte tot hij zou bedanken maar de jongen zei niets. Geen woord.

Daarna liepen ze naar de parkeergarage, Yulia glimlachte nog steeds en de Pool begon zich zorgen te maken of zij het spandoek echt had gezien. 'Het ging allemaal zo haastig,' fluisterde hij tegen Jurek, 'ze heeft het misschien niet opgemerkt?' Voor de zekerheid vouwde hij het grote spandoek in de parkeergarage voor zijn auto samen met zijn jongen nog een keer uit. De Pool zei dat hij dit op de kazerne voor haar had gemaakt en dat ze wat hem betreft thuis was gekomen.

'I saw it,' zei Yulia. 'You are sweet. Welcome home, so sweet.' Toen was de Pool gerustgesteld, hij legde het spandoek en haar koffer in de achterbak.

In de auto vroeg hij of het warm genoeg was en hoe het weer eigenlijk was in Kiev. 'Cold.' Ze keek naar buiten en vroeg: 'So this is Holland?' Klonk ze verontrust? Of leek het alleen zo?

'In the rain,' zei de Pool. 'Holland in the rain. Where we live, there are hills. Little hills but we don't need big hills.' Hij lachte, zij lachte niet mee.

De overgebleven jongen zat op de achterbank, hij had een koptelefoon op. Nu ze er was, nu ze er eindelijk was, leek het alsof hun gespreksstof in alle berichten die ze hadden uitgewisseld was opgebruikt. Of was het eerder zo dat er zoveel gespreksstof was dat ze niet wisten waar ze moesten beginnen?

Ze stopten bij een benzinestation en de Pool vroeg of ze honger had. 'No.' Ze had al gegeten in het vliegtuig. Lekker was het niet, wel vullend. Zo begreep hij het althans en hij zei: 'Tonight we go to a restaurant, you tell me what you like. We have something to celebrate.'

Ze zei dat ze dat zou doen, dat ze hem zou vertellen waar ze van hield en de Pool wachtte in spanning af maar er kwam niets meer. Ze had hem eens een appje gestuurd met de tekst: 'I love sushi.' Nu zei ze niets over sushi. Nu zweeg ze erover.

Ze reden door naar het huis van de Pool. Het was stil in de auto. Het was geen naargeestig zwijgen, het was een opgewekt, een vertrouwd zwijgen. Zwijgend stonden ze ten slotte voor de deur van het huis. Het oude huis midden in het nieuwe leven, zo voelde het. 'My house,' zei de Pool met gepaste trots na een tijdje.

'So this is where you live,' mompelde ze. De Pool vroeg zich af of ze iets anders had verwacht of dat ze juist aangenaam verrast was.

'I'm a fireman, you know that. This is what you get with a fireman's salary. The front garden is small, but in the back it's nice. In summertime you can sit there.'

Ze gingen naar binnen en ze liep zo licht door de woonkamer, zo vederlicht liep ze daar rond, alsof ze zich had losgemaakt van de wereld. Ze bekeek alles en ze raakte ook hier en daar iets aan, een muur, een snuisterij, een stoel. 'Where is my room?' vroeg ze.

De Pool zei: 'You stay in my room, but if that makes you uncomfortable I can sleep on the couch. You tell me what you like.'

'No,' zei ze. 'That's fine. Your room is fine.'

Ze gingen naar boven. De jongen bleef op de bank met zijn telefoon en de Pool ontfermde zich over Yulia's koffer die hij in de goed opgeruimde slaapkamer stalde.

Yulia opende een kast. Ze haalde er een jurk uit. 'What's this?'

'My ex-wife's dress, she still has a few clothes here. I don't want to throw them away. She will come and pick them up one day. She is... verstrooid, how do you say that? Verstrooid? Busy. She is very busy.'

Yulia ging op het bed zitten. Het leek alsof ze het matras uitprobeerde.

De Pool opende een andere kast en zei dat dit voor haar was, voor Yulia. 'Empty, for you. Totally empty.'

Hij liet haar de badkamer zien, ze raakte het douchegordijn even aan en rook aan een flesje aftershave. Daarna toonde hij haar de kamer van Jurek. 'A teenager, you know teenagers, a mess. Always a mess.' Ze wees op een poster van een of andere rapper aan de muur. 'Handsome guy.'

Toen liepen ze weer in de richting van de trap maar voor de Pool naar beneden kon gaan wees ze op de deur van de kamer van de verdwenen jongen. 'What's that?'

De Pool liep naar de deur. Hij legde zijn hand op de klink. 'The dead boy's room.'

'Can I see it?'

'You want to see it?' Ze bevestigde dat ze de kamer wilde zien. 'Okay, but there is nothing to see. Nothing. Just a room.' En hij opende de deur.

Ze ging naar binnen, raakte het bed aan, opende een kast, voelde aan een jas, pakte een schoen op. 'So fresh,' reageerde ze. 'So fresh. Is he really dead?'

'I cannot throw the things away.' De Pool voelde zich beschaamd. Een man die ruim tien jaar na dato de spulletjes van zijn dode kind nog altijd niet kon weggooien, dat moest wel een zwakke man zijn. 'It hurts. It's better like this. It's a long time ago but better like this.'

'Beautiful room, beautiful light.' Ze keek naar een foto die gemaakt was op school en op zijn bureau zwierf. Vergeeld maar toch nog herkenbaar. Hij was het. De jongen. 'Beautiful boy. He looks like you.'

'Not really,' weerlegde de Pool. 'He looks like himself. He is totally unique.'

Ze gingen naar buiten. Hij sloot de deur zorgvuldig

en ze volgde hem naar beneden. Hij vroeg of ze iets wilde drinken, iets sterks of wijn of bier, koffie was er ook. Thee, ze wilde thee. Hij zette thee en voor zichzelf schonk hij een biertje in. Zo zaten ze aan tafel en hij benadrukte dat ze dadelijk naar een restaurant zouden gaan, maar als ze honger had kon hij haar nu al iets geven. Welk eten ze lekker vond, vroeg hij nog een keer. Ze zei dat ze elk eten lekker vond en daarop besloot hij dat ze Frans gingen eten. Een collega had hem een klein Frans restaurant aanbevolen waar hij nog nooit was geweest. Daar zou hij heen gaan, hij vond Frans eten wel passen bij de gentleman die hij graag wilde zijn en bij Yulia, elegante Yulia.

Terwijl ze haar thee dronk, wat onwennig, ze was er ook nog niet zo lang, zei hij wat hij allang had voorbereid. Wat hij in gedachten al twintig of dertig keer had gezegd. Dat dit haar huis was, dat ze zich thuis moest voelen, dat hij zijn leven met haar wilde delen, dat hij haar man wilde zijn. Ja, hij kon best alleen zijn maar sinds hij haar had ontmoet wilde hij bij haar zijn. Hoewel hij in gedachten veel langer had gesproken en allerlei dingen nog had willen zeggen liet hij het hierbij.

'I realize,' zei hij toen nog, 'that you are much younger. You are twenty-seven. But...'

'No,' zei ze, 'age is not a problem. I hope this will work out. You are a sweet man. Maybe language is a problem? Maybe?'

'No. Language is never a problem. Language is just language. The people talk too much.'

'Netherlands people?'

'No people in general. Human beings. They talk all the time.'

Daarna liet hij haar de achtertuin zien en toen het avond was kleedde hij zich om. Hij deed toch weer de bloemetjesblouse en het colbert aan, misschien was ze die vergeten, en hij vroeg of ze nog wilde douchen.

Ze wilde zich opfrissen. Hij begeleidde haar naar de badkamer en liet haar daar alleen. Ze moest wennen.

Tegen de jongen zei hij: 'We gaan Frans eten. Doe iets netjes aan. Voor Yulia.'

'Uitslover.' Jurek ging naar boven en kwam terug in een trainingsjack.

'Noem je dat netjes?' vroeg de Pool.

'Het is gewassen,' zei Jurek, 'dat is toch netjes? Ik stink niet.'

'Je stinkt naar haargel.'

Yulia kwam naar beneden, ze rook zoet en toen zei de Pool dat hij gereserveerd had in een aardig Frans restaurant voor hun drietjes en hij betrapte zich weer op het geluk, het Oekraïense geluk, zo moest het worden genoemd.

Ze reden naar het centrum. Hij liet haar het plein met de cafés zien, de winkelstraat die leek op andere winkelstraten maar dat was geruststellend. Niets was vreemd hier. Wie Heerlen had gezien kende heel Nederland. 'The city is not very nice,' zei de Pool, 'but the nature is nice, around the city. Do you think our city is ugly?'

'Small,' ze. 'Small city. Not ugly.'

Ze gingen het Franse restaurant in. Het was klein, piepklein, de mensen zaten op elkaar en omdat het zo klein was voelde de Pool zich groter dan anders. Hij nam de jas aan van Yulia en hoewel het een goed restaurant scheen te zijn moest je zelf je jas ophangen. Dat deed de Pool overigens graag. Toch zei hij voor de zekerheid: 'This is a very good restaurant.'

'Yes,' zei Yulia. 'I know.'

Ze gingen zitten en de Pool bestelde een fles rode wijn. 'Zoek iets lekkers uit,' zei hij de tegen serveerster, die tevens eigenaresse van dit restaurant bleek te zijn. 'Maar ik eet geen vlees,' voegde hij er haastig aan toe.

'Ik noteer eerst wat u wilt drinken,' zei ze afgemeten.

De wijn kwam, de Pool proefde. Hij vond hem heerlijk

smaken. Ze toostten. Hij keek Yulia diep in de ogen en zei: 'To our new life.'

De eigenaresse kwam vertellen dat er buiten het menu verse slakken waren. Escargots.

'Do you like those escargots?' vroeg de Pool.

En Yulia zei: 'I don't know.'

Jurek zei: 'Snails. Dat heet snails, papa.'

'Do you like snails?'

'Snakes?' vroeg ze.

Jurek moest lachen, hij schaterde maar toen legde hij het aan Yulia uit want hij was lief, moeilijk maar lief, net als zijn broer. 'You find snails in the garden.'

Yulia knikte, het was vreesde de Pool een knikje uit beleefdheid. Nu de wijn was geproefd zei hij voor de zekerheid nog een keer: 'Ik eet geen vlees.'

'En vis?' vroeg de eigenaresse.

'Nee, eigenlijk ook niet.'

'We zijn een Frans restaurant. Ik zal kijken wat de keuken voor u kan doen.'

'Er zijn in Frankrijk toch ook vegetariërs,' zei hij gevat.

Ze schudde haar hoofd. 'Geen vis, geen vlees, geen zuivel, echte Fransen doen daar niet aan.'

De Pool lette niet op de prijs want hij vond dat dit niet paste bij een gentleman. Dat krenterige gedoe moest maar eens afgelopen zijn. 'Order what you want,' spoorde hij Yulia aan. 'This is the most beautiful day in my life.'

Omdat de wijn zo heerlijk was en omdat de liefde, vooral de prille liefde overmoedig maakte overtuigde hij Yulia ervan de slakken te bestellen. En daarna biefstuk met patat. Hij zei dat hij in plaats van de biefstuk een ei wilde. 'Gewoon een lekker spiegelei,' zei hij tegen de eigenaresse, die antwoordde: 'We zijn geen eetcafé maar als u een spiegelei wilt kan de chef de cuisine er misschien een voor u maken.'

'Een spiegelei met spinazie,' zei de Pool.

Jurek zei: 'Ik wil weleens slakken proberen.'

Yulia keek de jongen aan en zei: 'You look so adultlike.'

'Yes,' zei de Pool, 'he is very wise for his age. He is big.' Hij dronk de meeste wijn, want behalve de overmoed waren de restanten van het ongemak ook nog aanwezig.

Toen de slakken kwamen zei Yulia: 'Oh, now I know.' Ze at slechts twee slakken en Jurek bleek bij nader inzien eveneens niet bijzonder gesteld op slakken en zo zat de Pool met een stuk of dertien slakken opgescheept. Hij vroeg zich af of de gentleman-vegetariër de restjes moest opeten, al bestonden de restjes uit slakken. Hij deed het voor de zekerheid toch, restjes mocht je als vegetariër altijd eten. De slakken smaakten vooral naar knoflookboter.

Het hoofdgerecht kwam en hij kreeg een bord met groente, een spiegelei en frietjes. 'You don't eat meat?' vroeg Yulia.

'No. I told you, no?'

'But you eat those little things? And in Kiev you ate meat?'

'Sometimes. Only sometimes. With nice people. With very nice and special people.'

'Special?' Ook van de steak liet Yulia de helft staan. Ze bleek een kleine eter te zijn, alleen het toetje, crème brûlée, at ze wel helemaal en razendsnel op.

'How is your brother?' wilde hij weten, want converseren hoorde ondanks al zijn bezwaren bij de gentleman die hij was geworden en bij de liefde.

'I don't want to talk about him.'

De Pool liet dessertwijn aanrukken maar halverwege bedacht hij dat hij nog moest rijden en hij gaf het restant aan zijn nieuwe vrouw die het gretig achteroversloeg. De dessertwijn beviel haar uitstekend. Als zij gelukkig was, was hij dat ook.

De Pool vroeg om de rekening hoewel het nog niet laat was, ze hadden nog even kunnen blijven zitten maar hij verlangde ernaar alleen te zijn met zijn nieuwe vrouw. De rekening kwam. Hij had zich voorbereid op een gepeperde rekening, maar de prijs van de drank voelde toch als een draai om zijn oren. Hij betaalde niettemin met de souplesse van de gentleman-vegetariër en daarna reden ze naar huis. Jurek ging gamen en de Pool vroeg aan zijn nieuwe vrouw of ze moe was.

'A bit,' zei ze.

Hij nam haar mee naar de slaapkamer. 'Can I take a shower?' vroeg ze.

'Yes of course,' zei de Pool.

'Do you have a towel?' Hij zei dat er in de badkamer al een handdoek voor haar klaarlag, hij had nieuwe gekocht. De oude waren verwassen.

Ze ging naar de badkamer. Het duurde even voor hij de douche hoorde en hij vroeg zich af wat ze daar allemaal aan het doen was. Misschien verwijderde ze make-up van haar gezicht en op dat moment kwam de gedachte in hem op dat ze daar in haar eentje aan het huilen was. Zittend op de rand van de badkuip, radeloos. Verloren. Ze miste Kiev, haar vrienden, haar vader die een hekel had aan buitenlanders maar die zijn dochter niet kon tegenhouden. Hij zag de man weer voor zich, boos en toch onschuldig.

De Pool bleef op bed zitten, wachtend op de terugkeer van zijn nieuwe vrouw. Hij verdreef de gedachten dat ze daar helemaal alleen aan het huilen was. Ze was gewoon met lichamelijke verzorging bezig. Het duurde lang maar ze wilde na zo'n lange reis haar lichaam natuurlijk goed verzorgen. Alles moest worden schoongemaakt.

Eindelijk kwam ze terug. Ze had een handdoek omgeslagen en ging aan haar kant van het bed onder de dekens liggen met de handdoek nog om zich heen. De kant waar zijn ex altijd had gelegen.

De Pool wilde iets zeggen. Iets wat al eerder in hem was opgekomen, al die tijd dat hij had gewacht op de komst van

Yulia. Hier werd niet geleefd, wilde hij zeggen. Hier vergaten we te leven. Het nieuwe leven is het leven zelf. Nu gaan we leven. Omdat jij er bent, Yulia, nu gaan we leven. We vergaten het, we durfden niet, we zagen ertegenop. Hier werd niet geleefd, hier werd langzaam gestorven.

In het Engels kwam het er minder goed uit, hij probeerde het toch. 'We didn't live here.'

'No?' vroeg ze.

'No.' Hij voelde een onverwachte woede in zich opkomen. Het was als een golf die hem overspoelde, die hem meenam. Een heel leven aan opgespaarde woede kwam in hem omhoog, verstikte hem, verbrijzelde hem. Hij voelde zich tegen de muur geworpen.

'No,' riep hij, 'we forgot to live. We couldn't live.' Hij zag dat ze schrok van zijn stem, zijn zware stem. Alsof het haar fout was, alsof zij ter verantwoording moest worden geroepen voor het onvermogen van andere mensen. Hij zag meteen in hoe onrechtvaardig dat was en hij corrigeerde zichzelf, hij legde een hand op de deken en met zijn gebruikelijke, zachte, bijna fluisterende stem zei hij dat hij zo blij was dat zij er was, omdat zij het leven vertegenwoordigde.

'O.' Ze schudde haar hoofd wat hij opvatte als een teken van medeleven en bescheidenheid. Ze wilde natuurlijk niet in haar eentje het leven vertegenwoordigen.

De Pool kleedde zich uit, zijn onderbroek hield hij aan en ook hij ging onder de deken liggen. Hij kroop tegen haar aan. Tegelijkertijd met de woede had hij een kort moment van intense lust gevoeld, de behoefte de handdoek van haar af te rukken maar nu was hij weer zichzelf, niet meer woedend, ook niet meer opgewonden en hij streelde haar door handdoek en deken heen. 'Are you sad?' vroeg hij.

Ze schudde haar hoofd.

'You can tell me everything.'

Ze zei dat ze niet verdrietig was en hij kroop nog dichter tegen haar aan waarop zij verder van hem weg schoof. Alsof ze het bed uit wilde kruipen, alsof ze naar Kiev terug wilde kruipen.

'No, I'm not sad.' Daarna draaide ze zich naar hem om. 'But it's our first night. By the way, I stopped smoking.'

'Great.' De Pool snuffelde aan haar haren. 'Yes, I can smell it. You quit smoking.'

Toen was ze weer stil. De eerste nacht, het was hun eerste nacht. Al voelde het niet zo, het voelde vertrouwd. Hij had naar dit moment uitgekeken, hij had het in gedachten al zo vaak beleefd dat het voelde als de twintigste, de dertigste nacht.

'Maybe we should wait a bit,' zei ze aarzelend, maar in haar mooie ogen meende hij verlangen te zien.

'Of course. We can wait. As long as you want. No hurry.' De Pool zei dat hij helemaal geen haast had, dat het erom ging dat ze hier was. Dat ze moest wennen, dat hij dat begreep, dat hij alles begreep, dat hij alles wilde begrijpen. Was hij te haastig geweest? Was hij ongeduldig geweest? En zij zei: 'There are so many things I want to tell you but language is a problem.'

De Pool herhaalde dat taal nooit een probleem zou zijn, dat ze daar niet bang voor hoefde te zijn. 'I remained silent much of my life. I like to remain silent.' En hij sprak haar naam uit, 'Yulia', alsof het noemen van die naam haar nader tot hem zou brengen. Alleen al het noemen van die naam was nabijheid, genoeg voor nu. En later, dat zou hij wel zien.

Ze bleef daar liggen en hij zei niets meer, hij voegde de daad bij het woord, hij deed wat hij al zijn hele leven had gedaan. Toen begon ze opeens te huilen. De Pool wist niet hoe hij moest reageren, vooral omdat hij niet zeker wist waarom ze huilde. Maakte hij haar aan het huilen? Was zijn aanwezigheid niet wat ze ervan had verwacht? Zou hij ook haar, zelfs haar aan de dood doen denken? Hij wist niet wat hij moest doen. Moest hij haar aanraken? Mocht hij haar aanraken? Wat hij wist van troost waren de vrouw van Beckers en het kippenhok. Troost was niet altijd even heilzaam, niet alle mensen konden ertegen. Hij wilde gewoon een goede gentleman zijn maar als het aankwam op troosten liet de intuïtie hem in de steek. Moest hij haar vragen stellen? Waarom huil je? Was zijn jongen daarom verdwenen, omdat hij die zo graag een goede vader wilde zijn niet wist hoe je moest troosten? Het was begrijpelijk dat je op de vlucht sloeg voor andermans verdriet. Na enige aarzeling legde hij een hand op de deken en met zijn andere hand pakte hij onder de deken haar hand. En hij vroeg of ze Kiev miste, of ze haar vader en haar vrienden miste. Op die vragen zei ze 'yes'. Het huilen stopte niet. Hij was geen vervanging, hij kon wat zij miste niet vervangen en al wist hij dat hij het niet persoonlijk moest nemen, hij deed het toch.

Toen durfde hij de vraag te stellen die hij niet had willen stellen omdat het een vraag was die hem onrustig maakte, die hem angstig maakte. Hij zou bijna zeggen die hem kapotmaakte, hij stelde hem toch want zelfs als het antwoord kwam dat hij vreesde dan zou hij daarmee kunnen leven, hij was feitelijk al verslagen. Hij kon met elk antwoord leven. Er was maar één echte onoverwinnelijkheid, dat had hij geleerd in het kippenhok: volledig verslagen zijn. 'Do you want to go back home?' vroeg hij.

Hij vreesde het antwoord maar hij zou alles overleven.

Dit was een thuis, ook voor haar, al moest het nog groeien, het thuis, als een plant moest het groeien, als een wingerd moest het huis zich om haar heen slingeren. Maar er was nog een ander thuis. Hij had het willen ontkennen, hij had er niet aan willen denken en nog voor de eerste nacht goed en wel was begonnen drong het andere huis zich aan hem op. Daarover hadden ze niets verteld bij Liefde over de Grens, dat zij die liefde en een beter leven in het

Westen zochten heimwee konden hebben, dat ze overvallen konden worden door een verlangen naar het land van herkomst, al leek de toekomst daar niet rooskleurig, al zag hij, denkend aan haar stad, de grijze, vochtige flat voor zich waar ze met haar halfblinde en woedende vader woonde, in een buitenwijk van een buitenwijk van Kiev.

Zij kneep in zijn hand, ze liet de hand niet los. Ze zei: 'I'll stay here. I'm not going back now, but can I sleep in the dead boy's room?'

Hij keek haar aan, recht in haar betraande gezicht. Hij veegde het droog met de rug van zijn hand, zijn andere hand, de hand die zij niet vasthield en hij vroeg: 'Are you sure?'

Ze knikte. Daarop zei hij dat ze altijd samen op vakantie konden naar Oekraïne, om haar vader te bezoeken, haar vrienden. De deur naar Oekraïne was niet dicht. Yulia lag stil naast hem. Het leek alsof ze niet had gehoord wat hij had gezegd.

'I won't touch you,' zei hij. 'I'm not that kind of man.' Hij wilde nog meer zeggen, dat de woede hem verlaten had en dat dit goed was. De lust was een zeldzaamheid geworden in zijn leven maar hij kon zijn mannelijke plicht doen, daarvoor hoefde ze niet te vrezen want hij was een gentleman. Als ze klaar was voor de lust dan zou hij zijn plicht doen. Wachten was geen probleem. Dat zei hij allemaal niet. Ze lagen daar hand in hand in het echtelijk bed en hij had daar zo de hele nacht kunnen blijven liggen. Dit was genoeg. Meer was niet nodig. Niet nu, misschien nooit.

Het was Yulia die de stilte verbrak. 'I know, you are not that kind of man. But I'd like to be alone. I'd like to be in the dead boy's room. I'm sorry.'

Toen stond hij op. Hij wist wat hij moest doen. In zijn onderbroek liep hij naar de kamer van de verdwenen jongen.

Het was niet laat. De overgebleven jongen was nog op. Uit de woonkamer kwam geluid, hij zat daar nog te gamen.

Straks als Yulia sliep, als ze alleen sliep zoals ze wenste, zou hij Jurek naar bed sturen.

Yulia kwam achter hem aan, met de handdoek om zich heen, en even was er toch een echo van lust, de herinnering aan lust, maar de kamer van de verdwenen jongen, de dood, was sterker.

Hij opende de deur, hij sloeg de deken van het bed terug. 'It's a small bed.'

'I'm not a big woman.' Ze stond naast hem. Ze aarzelde, met haar prachtige ogen en haar halfscheve tanden, ze aarzelde en hij kon zich voorstellen dat ze nu niet meer zeker wist of ze in dit kinderbed moest liggen. Wie wilde daar liggen? Wie wilde slapen met de gedachte aan het dode kind? 'I hope you don't mind,' zei ze en ze hield de handdoek voor de zekerheid vast alsof dat haar laatste houvast was. Alleen nog de handdoek, verder niets, alleen nog die.

'No,' zei hij. Dit huis was haar huis, ook de kamer van de verdwenen jongen was haar kamer. Hij zei dat ze daar best mocht gaan liggen, dat het goed was, dat ze niet bang hoefde te zijn, dat hij haar morgen wakker zou maken. Hij zei nog dat hij naar haar zou verlangen vanuit zijn eigen bed maar dat zei hij in het Nederlands. Daarop kroop ze in het bed van de verdwenen jongen.

'It's strange,' zei ze.

Hij knikte.

'He feels so alive.'

'We keep him alive,' zei de Pool.

'He is a ghost.'

'No, he is not a ghost. He is our son.' Hij knielde naast het bed zoals hij vroeger ook had geknield, vanavond werd er niets voorgelezen. Wij. Hij had 'we' gezegd maar zijn ex had de strijd opgegeven. Zijn ex wilde leven. Hoe kon je leven zonder de doden te verraden? Hij ging opnieuw leven, zonder de dode jongen te verraden, hij was anders. Niet beter, anders.

De Pool legde zijn handen op de deken. 'We belong together.'

'You are a strange man,' was haar antwoord. Hij slikte een paar keer overtollig speeksel weg, daarna zei hij nog dat dit klopte, dat hij dat wel wist, gewoon en toch vreemd, in de ogen van anderen althans, ook daarom zweeg hij, om aan het oordeel van anderen te ontsnappen. Dat wilde hij zeggen maar dat zei hij niet meer.

Sinds hij zijn intrek in het kippenhok had genomen keken de mensen anders naar hem en daarom keek hij anders naar de mensen. Ze waren vreemden voor elkaar geworden, de mensen en hij, niet zo vreemd dat de mensen zich zorgen hoefden te maken. Hij hoorde bij hen, de Pool was een van hen, maar toch.

Knielend naast haar bed, met een hand op de kinderdeken fluisterde hij dat ze moest gaan slapen, dat ze hier lekker zou slapen. Dat hij, voor zover de Pool wist, het kind, Borys, hier ook altijd lekker had geslapen. Toen had hij niets meer te zeggen. Hij werd overvallen door moeheid, hij was uitgeput, wilde zelf slapen. De Pool zei nog dat Yulia altijd naar hem toe kon komen, zelfs midden in de nacht. Ze mocht hem wakker maken. Als ze bang was. Als ze heimwee had. Als ze dorst had. En hij vroeg nog of ze bij elkaar hoorden. Of dat zo was?

Ze antwoordde dat dit zo was en ze voegde eraan toe terwijl ze in zijn arm kneep dat ze hem zo veel te vertellen had, zo veel, maar dat dit niet ging omdat taal een probleem was. Dit keer had hij niet de kracht daar tegenin te gaan en dwars door al het verlangen en de hoop, door alle liefde waaraan hij niet twijfelde, waaraan hij geen moment zou twijfelen, zag hij een vreemde vrouw in het bed van zijn dode jongen liggen.

## 2

De Pool wachtte tot Yulia zou zeggen dat ze niet meer in het bed van de dode jongen hoefde te slapen. Dat ze gewend was, gewend aan de Pool, gewend aan het huis, gewend aan Jurek, dat nu het moment was aangebroken dat ze bij hem kon liggen. Hij had geduld.

Ze was bang alleen de straat op te gaan, al zei ze daar niets over. Hij merkte het, ze ging gewoon niet alleen de straat op, de dagen dat hij dienst had bleef ze thuis en nadat hij dit een keer of drie had aangezien vroeg hij Jurek of hij zich een beetje wilde bekommeren om Yulia. 'Ze is niet je moeder,' zei de Pool, 'dat weet ik. Vraag haar wat ze nodig heeft. Help haar een beetje. Alsjeblieft. Je bent toch een lieve jongen.'

'Het komt gewoon doordat je haar niet verstaat,' antwoordde Jurek. 'Ze is hier ongelukkig, iedereen zou hier ongelukkig zijn. Ik wil hier weg en ik ga hier ook weg zodra ik klaar ben met school.'

De Pool verzoende zich met dit antwoord door aan de puberteit te denken. Wat kon je van een puber anders verwachten? Dwars door het pantser heen zag hij de zachtheid van zijn overgebleven zoon.

'Doe het nou maar,' zei hij. 'Help haar een beetje.' De opmerking van de jongen over het ongelukkig zijn probeerde hij te negeren. Je moest niet op alle provocaties van pubers ingaan. Natuurlijk wilde Jurek weg, pubers willen altijd weg, gezonde pubers althans.

Jurek zei eerst dat hij er geen zin in had, dat hij betere dingen had te doen, dat hij zich niet hoefde te bekommeren om een chickie dat in Kiev thuishoorde en dat onder valse voorwendselen naar Heerlen was gelokt, terwijl er helemaal niemand naar Heerlen gelokt moest worden. Toen zei de Pool: 'Ik heb haar niet gelokt, de liefde heeft haar gelokt. Nu is het genoeg geweest.'

Uiteindelijk ging Jurek toch een keer met Yulia naar buiten. Hij had er niet veel over willen vertellen. Het leek erop dat ze elkaar aardig begonnen te vinden, op z'n minst accepteerden ze elkaar. Misschien omdat ze iets gemeen hadden, ze waren overgeleverd aan de Pool. Had Yulia echt voor hem gekozen, zoals hij beweerde, zoals hij wilde denken? Of was hij toch het noodlot in vermomming geweest? Hij had haar gezien, hij had haar gekozen, zij had zich laten kiezen.

Hij deed zijn best zijn nieuwe vrouw zich zoveel mogelijk thuis te laten voelen. De Pool haalde het eten in huis dat Yulia lekker vond. Soep, ze was dol op soep. Kippensoep, tomatensoep, bietensoep, linzensoep, runderbouillon. Ze aten soep alsof er geen ander voedsel was, tot Yulia verklaarde dat een stukje lamsvlees wat haar betreft ook prima was. Hij had een lerares voor haar gevonden, een gepensioneerde lerares Nederlands die nu lesgaf aan buitenlanders. Hij wist eigenlijk niet zeker of ze gepensioneerd was of overspannen, ze gaf hoe dan ook geen les meer aan pubers, alleen nog aan volwassen buitenlanders. En dat was Yulia, een volwassen buitenlander. Ze ging erheen en vond het leuk. In elk geval, dat zei ze. 'Leuk,' zei ze. 'Ja leuk.' Ze leerde wat woordjes die ze te pas en te onpas door haar conversatie strooide en al zei ze nog minstens één keer per dag dat taal een probleem was, de Pool ging daar steevast tegenin. Als iets geen probleem was dan was het taal.

Jurek en Yulia speelden nu steeds vaker samen spelletjes op de computer, spelletjes die de Pool nooit had willen spelen, waarvoor hij geen geduld had, die hij niet begreep. Je had er geen taal voor nodig, dat was waar.

En na een week of vijf zei Yulia: 'I can sleep in your room.' Ze hadden linzensoep gegeten, Thaise linzensoep.

Ze zat spelletjes op de computer te spelen met Jurek en de Pool zat tegenover hen en hij dronk wat thee. Hij kon tv-kijken, hij kon een krant lezen maar hij keek naar Yulia, dat was voldoende voor hem. Hij was, dat wist hij nu zeker, niet alleen een zwijgende Pool, ook een vreemde Pool. Hij zag het in de blik van zijn jongen, in zijn liefdevolle spot, in zijn net niet onderdrukte schaamte. Waarom hij vreemd was wist hij niet, alleen dat hij het was. Hij had zich erbij neergelegd, bij de vreemdheid. Daarom zat hij rustig naar zijn nieuwe vrouw te kijken, bijna gelukkig. 'You trust me?' vroeg hij.

Hij had al die tijd gedacht dat het gebrek aan vertrouwen was dat ze nog niet bij hem was gaan liggen, dat ze in de kamer van de dode jongen bleef waar ze naar eigen zeggen sliep als een baby.

'I've always trusted you, but I was not ready.'

Dat kon de Pool begrijpen, ze was nog niet klaar geweest om die stap te zetten, de stap uit Kiev naar zijn slaapkamer. Nu was ze zover, ze was definitief aangekomen in Heerlen. Hij was er ook klaar voor, klaar om met haar in een bed te liggen, klaar om met haar te doen wat, zoals volgens Liefde over de Grens, verliefde mensen nu eenmaal met elkaar doen. Dat was hij namelijk, een verliefde Pool, meer nog dan een vreemde Pool. Hij vroeg zich af of ze nu al naar boven moesten gaan of dat ze moesten wachten, ze was nog zo druk bezig met het computerspelletje. Ze ging erin op, net als Jurek. Tot hij tegen de jongen zei: 'Nu moet je naar bed. Heb je al je huiswerk gemaakt?'

De jongen mompelde iets onverstaanbaars en de Pool ging er maar van uit dat het 'ja' was. Bovendien was dit niet het moment om in discussie te treden met Jurek, dit was het moment dat Yulia verhuisde van de kamer van de dode jongen naar de slaapkamer van de Pool. Het grote moment.

Het spel werd afgesloten. 'Wat spelen jullie eigenlijk?'

Het antwoord op die vraag was ook onverstaanbaar en dat vond de Pool prima. De vraag was belangrijker dan het antwoord. Het was geen verhoor, een gesprek met je eigen kind.

Eerst ging de jongen naar boven en vervolgens bracht de Pool de theekopjes naar de keuken en Yulia riep hem na: 'It's funny, your son is closer to me agewise than you.'

De Pool keerde terug uit de keuken. Hij was op de een of andere manier zenuwachtig, veel zenuwachtiger dan toen hij haar had afgehaald en hij knielend met het spandoek op haar had gewacht in de aankomsthal.

'Yes,' zei de Pool, 'funny.' Daaraan voegde hij toe dat het goed was dat ze aansluiting had gevonden bij Jurek, althans zo ongeveer zei hij dat in het Engels en ze antwoordde: 'Ja, goed.' Want de lessen Nederlands zetten nog geen echte zoden aan de dijk.

Ze gingen de trap op, zij voor, hij erachteraan en hij legde even een hand op haar billen, meer om haar een duwtje te geven dan dat de lust hem voortdreef.

Toen stonden ze voor de deur van de dode jongen. Ze aarzelde. 'I get my T-shirt.' Ze ging naar binnen en pakte haar T-shirt van het bed. Ze sloot de deur van de kamer zorgvuldig en even later stonden ze naast elkaar in de badkamer hun tanden te poetsen.

Hij spoelde zijn mond en zij waste haar gezicht met een handdoekje. Ze zei: 'You have nice teeth.'

'Thanks.'

'Clean.'

'Yes,' zei de Pool. 'I'm careful with my teeth, I'm careful with my body. For a fireman that's important.'

Ze knikte en de Pool ging alvast vooruit naar de slaapkamer. Hij kleedde zich uit, hij wreef over zijn vrijwel kale hoofd, hij moest aan zijn ex denken. Sinds de nieuwe vrouw naar de stad was gekomen was zij steeds stiller geworden. Hij had al gevraagd of ze Yulia niet wilde ontmoeten maar ze had geantwoord: 'Nee, dat is nog te vroeg.'

Yulia kwam uit de badkamer. Ze had geen handdoek omgeslagen. Ze droeg een fraaie rode onderbroek en een bijpassende beha. Ze ging naast hem liggen zoals je naast je partner gaat liggen. Hij keek naar het plafond omdat hij niet naar zijn nieuwe vrouw durfde te kijken, bang als hij was dat hij overmand zou worden door iets wat zoveel sterker was dan hij, door iets wat haar pijn kon doen. Zonder haar aan te kijken kroop zijn hand over laken en dekbed naar haar arm. Hij pakte haar arm en hij moest aan het kippenhok denken waar hij de liefde van God had ontdekt. Het was niet de bedoeling dat je de liefde van God overleefde. Hij was eraan ontsnapt maar of dat een prestatie was of een nederlaag wist hij niet zeker. Misschien was het in het algemeen niet de bedoeling dat je liefde overleefde, ook daarom durfde hij zijn nieuwe vrouw niet aan te kijken.

Hij voelde haar warme arm, verder dan dat durfde hij niet te gaan. Hij bleef naar het plafond staren en waar zij naar keek wist hij niet. Het was goed zo, alles was goed. Ze was aan hem gewend, dat ze nu naast hem kwam liggen was een teken dat ze zou blijven, dat ze Kiev en de troosteloze flat waar haar vader woonde zou afzweren.

'You can do with me what you did with your ex-wife. I'm ready,' zei ze.

Dat was liefde, dat hij met haar zou doen wat hij met zijn ex had gedaan, als hij nog maar wist wat hij met zijn ex had gedaan. De herinneringen waren vervaagd. Het gevoel was gebleven, een vage sensatie van gemis, een idee van onbegrip en bovenal de dood. Als hij aan zijn ex dacht dan dacht hij aan de locomotief waarvan hij zijn jongen had afgekrabd, zijn ex was een locomotief waarvan hij nooit zou loskomen.

Hij liet Yulia's arm los en begon haar te zoenen, onverwacht, zelfs voor hem onverwacht. Hij proefde haar tandpasta, hij rook haar gezichtscrème en hij begreep zelf niet waarom hij zo lang had gewacht, waarop hij had gewacht. Op haar maar waarop had zij gewacht? Hij durfde niet verder te gaan dan haar gezicht, hij hield zich in, hij kon niet anders.

Ze duwde hem van zich af en ze zei: 'Don't be polite. I know you are not polite.'

Hij vroeg wat ze bedoelde en ze antwoordde: 'You are like other men. I know you are like other men.'

Vreemd genoeg klonk dit als een geruststelling, hij was gewoon zoals andere mannen. Niet vreemd, niet merkwaardig, zoals de anderen. Hij ontdeed haar van de beha, hij kuste haar borsten. Niet eerder had hij die borsten zo goed gezien, een glimp had hij weleens opgevangen in de badkamer. De borsten verrukten hem zoals de vaststelling dat hij was zoals andere mannen hem had verrukt.

Haar borsten waren prachtig, zo anders dan die van zijn ex, zonder dat hij kon uitleggen waarin het verschil zat. Hij was geen expert, hij was niet iemand die zich vergaapte aan andermans naaktheid, hooguit zag hij de naaktheid van de mannen van de C-ploeg. Met hun naaktheid werd hij geconfronteerd, van vergapen was geen sprake.

Even speelde hij met de tepels van Yulia maar hij vreesde haar pijn te doen, zoals hij vreesde de mensen pijn te doen.

'Do with me what you did with your ex-wife,' zei ze weer en ze keek hem aan alsof ze geen ander verlangen kende dan dit, dat er met haar werd gedaan wat ook met de ex van de Pool was gedaan, alsof ze iets tekortkwam als haar niet precies dezelfde behandeling ten deel zou vallen. De ex die ze nooit had ontmoet, de ex die geen trek had in een ontmoeting, die nu met een man leefde die geloofde dat de mensen geen andere behoefte hadden dan verzorging.

De Pool zei tegen Yulia dat hij betere dingen met haar wilde doen, 'better things', maar ze wilde geen betere dingen, ze wilde precies hetzelfde. 'I will be your wife?' vroeg ze alsof alleen dat impliceerde dat haar dezelfde behandeling ten deel moest vallen. Goed of slecht, dat deed er niet toe, hetzelfde moest het zijn.

'I couldn't make love to my wife anymore,' zei hij uiteindelijk. 'That's the story. Not often. Not really love.' Daarmee was voldoende gezegd, meende hij, voldoende verklaard. Dat hetzelfde geen oplossing zou bieden, dat hetzelfde een doodlopende weg was. Anders moest het, volstrekt anders.

'O.' Ze keek hem aan, verlegen en uitdagend tegelijk. Hij dacht eraan hoe ze al die nachten in het bed van de dode jongen had gelegen, het bed dat nu naar haar zou ruiken.

Daarop pakte ze zijn pik en begon die te masseren, te rollen, alsof er ook in haar lust woonde en hij trok haar onderbroek uit, niet meer angstig en beleefd. Het moest anders. Hij betastte haar geslachtsdeel en herinnerde zich de instructievideo's die zijn ex hem had laten zien, dat hij nu achtjes moest draaien met twee of drie vingers en terwijl hij achtjes draaide met twee en daarna met drie vingers over haar vrijwel volledig geschoren geslachtsdeel dreigde de lust toch nog even te verdwijnen. Het voelde alsof hij bezig was met een oefening in de kazerne, maar de lust kwam terug zoals God was teruggekomen, in het kippenhok. God had hem verlaten en was teruggekomen. Ze leken op elkaar, de lust en God, ze kwamen en ze gingen maar bijna nooit op het juiste moment. Wispelturig waren ze, onberekenbare meesters.

Langzaam ging hij bij haar naar binnen en hij zei: 'I like a bit of hair. You don't have to shave yourself completely.'

'What do you mean?'

'Your hair. Downstairs. Without hair is so empty.'

'Okay,' zei ze, 'language is a problem, but now you can do with me what you did with ex-wife.'

'I can fuck you?' vroeg hij. Het woord wond hem onverwacht op, alsof alle ge- en verboden in dat woord werden samengebald, alsof overtreding en inkeer in één woord werden bekrachtigd.

'Yes,' zei ze, 'fuck me. Please. Fuck me. You are not a silent man. You talk all the time.'

'You changed me.' Daarop begon hij haar te neuken met alle hoop en liefde die hij in zich had en uiteindelijk met de lust die op God leek en die misschien wel God was en toen hij was klaargekomen durfde hij niet te vragen of zij was klaargekomen maar hij deed het na een tijdje toch.

'Not for now,' zei ze.

'Shall I do something?'

'No. Just hold me a bit.'

Hij hield haar vast en zij vroeg: 'Can I stay here?'

De Pool antwoordde dat ze vanzelfsprekend hier kon blijven, dat ze zijn vrouw was, dat ze hier altijd mocht blijven. In dit bed dat haar bed was. In dit huis dat haar huis was.

'You don't know me,' zei ze.

'That's better,' antwoordde hij. 'Much better. We don't have to know each other, we have to love each other. The more we know, the more difficult it is.'

Hij wachtte tot ze in slaap was gevallen. Het duurde lang. Ze wierp zich van de ene zij op de andere, ze hield hem vast, liet hem weer los. Pas toen haar ademhaling rustig werd kon de Pool ook slapen.

# 3

Zo werden ze man en vrouw, ze deden wat verliefde mensen met elkaar doen, wat stelletjes dikwijls met elkaar blijven doen, ook als ze niet meer op elkaar verliefd zijn: ze maakten liefdevol gebruik van elkaars geslachtsdeel. Als de Pool thuis sliep ging hij met haar naar bed, bleef hij op de kazerne slapen dan belde hij haar 's avonds op, hoewel met name tijdens die telefoongesprekken de stiltes hem opvielen. Stiltes die hij probeerde op te vullen door te gaan neuriën en een enkele keer neuriede Yulia terug. Dan wist hij dat hij haar had bereikt, dat het goed met haar ging.

Sliep hij thuis dan wilde Yulia pas in slaap vallen als er was gevreeën, alsof de afwezigheid van seks nu ze naast hem lag diepe onzekerheid in haar losmaakte. Een ander soort stilte die zij ondraaglijk vond. Ze eiste het op, het vrijen. Ze liet hem niet slapen tot het was gebeurd, ze pakte zijn piemel en speelde ermee tot de slaap uit zijn lichaam was verdwenen. Ze ging op hem liggen en ze zei: 'I'm here. Do you understand me?' En hij antwoordde: 'Yes, I understand.' Dan deed hij alsnog zijn plicht hoewel het meer was dan dat. Plicht klonk zo kil, alsof het werk was, het vrijen, het houden van. Nee, zo was het niet. Er was liefde. Hij zei het tegen zichzelf, hij zei het tegen haar, hij zei het tegen de mannen van de C-ploeg, hij zei het tegen de caissière in de supermarkt en tegen het meisje in het Japanse restaurant want Yulia hield nog altijd veel van sushi. Hij zei het tegen iedereen die maar luisteren wilde.

En zij, de nieuwe vrouw ging naar Nederlandse les, ze gamede met de overgebleven jongen, ze liep door de straten van Heerlen, ze keek naar de huizen, ze ging de honden van de stad uit de weg want van honden moest ze niets hebben. Soms gingen ze samen boodschappen doen, een enkele keer ging ze alleen boodschappen doen hoewel ze dat eng leek te vinden. Ze liepen door de winkelstraat, ze wandelden door de heuvels maar van lange wandelingen hield ze niet en daarom bereikten ze niet het dorp waarheen hij had willen wandelen. 'Mooi?' Hij wees op de heuvels, de weilanden, de bomen, windmolens in de verte. Als dit niet mooi was, wat dan wel?

Hij moedigde haar aan meer alleen te doen, minder afhankelijk van hem te zijn. Ook als hij haar een papiertje meegaf waarop precies stond wat ze nodig hadden van de supermarkt en hij de uitspraak met haar oefende merkte hij dat ze de angst voor het vreemde nog niet had overwonnen. Het had tijd nodig. Ze vond de mensen eng. Althans de mensen in deze stad die ze niet kon verstaan. Desondanks worstelde ze zich door de mensenmassa. Hij ging haar weleens zoeken als hij vond dat ze te lang wegbleef en dan zag hij haar lopen in het centrum door de winkelstraat met de boodschappen. 'Are you lost?' vroeg hij.

Dan antwoordde ze dat ze niet verdwaald was maar gewoon langzaam naar huis aan het wandelen was. Dat ze dingen aan het bekijken was. Vervolgens wees ze op een mus alsof er geen mussen waren in Kiev.

'Oké,' zei hij en daarna nam hij haar bij de arm, hij geloofde haar niet. Hij vreesde dat ze wél verdwaald was en dat ze op een dag niet zou thuiskomen als hij haar niet tijdig ging zoeken, dat ze op een dag door de heuvels zou wandelen en kwijt zou raken, zou verdwijnen, dat was wat hij vreesde en de vrees was groter dan de lust.

Een keer per week belde ze met haar vader en steeds weer bekroop hem het gevoel dat ze ruziemaakte met de man. Hoe ze met hem praatte, hoe ze soms minutenlang zweeg alsof de vader in Kiev een tirade aan het houden was die ze alleen kon aanhoren, die ze niet durfde te onderbreken. Misschien was dat hoe ze altijd al had gepraat met de oude man in de vochtige flat: hij sprak, zij luisterde. De Pool stelde zich voor dat hij haar verwijten maakte, verwijten die eigenlijk voor hem bedoeld waren. Waarom ben je niet hier gebleven, Yulia? Wat heb je te zoeken bij die oude Pool? Hij houdt niet van je, hij viert zijn lusten op je bot. De Pool kon het de man horen zeggen, in het Oekraïens dan. Later als ze hier gewend was, zo fantaseerde hij, zou hij naar Kiev reizen, samen zouden ze naar Kiev reizen, als man en vrouw, en hij zou ook de liefde van zijn nieuwe schoonvader winnen. Hij zou hem vertellen dat hij geen oude Pool was die zijn lusten botvierde op een jonge vrouw uit Kiev. Hij zou de verliefdheid beschrijven, het zoeken en het vinden. Het leven, het opleven. Wat hij in haar zag toen hij haar de eerste keer tussen alle andere vrouwen had waargenomen: de vreugde. Hoe hij haar had afgehaald van Schiphol. Hoe ze was thuisgekomen. Bij hem, de Pool. Het spandoek dat ergens in huis lag zou hij meenemen naar Kiev als souvenir. Hij zou het woord 'genade' opzoeken in het Oekraïens.

In feite wilde hij de liefde van iedereen winnen, van zijn ex, zijn vrienden oftewel de mannen van de C-ploeg want veel meer vrienden had hij niet, van Jurek. Alleen de liefde van zijn eigen vader wilde hij niet meer winnen, daar viel namelijk niets te winnen. Dat was voorbij. De liefde van de verdwenen jongen, die hoefde hij ook niet, van de doden kon je niets verlangen. Je moest hen met rust laten. Je moest hen alleen laten, hoe moeilijk dat ook was.

Af en toe huilde Yulia. Hij vond haar een keer huilend in de keuken, een andere keer zat ze huilend op de wc, op een dinsdagmiddag trof hij haar huilend aan in de tuin. Die keer dat ze in de tuin stond te huilen zei hij: 'You are not happy.' Hij kon er niet meer omheen. Ze huilde te vaak. Ze schudde haar hoofd. 'You cry,' zei hij en hij zocht naar het woord 'heimwee' in het Engels maar hij vond het niet.

'Sometimes I'm happy.'

Hij wilde haar vasthouden, hij greep slechts haar hand. 'How can I make you happy?'

'It's okay. I'm okay. It's just so confusing.'

'What?'

'You, the city, the language, everything.'

Daarna gingen ze naar binnen, hand in hand en hij dacht: ze heeft een eigen ruimte nodig. Waar ze kan werken, waar ze Nederlands kan leren, waar ze zich kan ontwikkelen en vooral waar ze ongestoord kan huilen. Hij begreep dat ze recht had op haar tranen. Juist zij die uit Kiev kwam had daar recht op, zij die vader, stad en vriendinnen achter zich had gelaten, die gekozen had de vrouw te worden van een man die ze nauwelijks kende. Hij moest ruimte voor haar maken. Ze huilde op straat en in de wc omdat ze geen ruimte had waar ze kon huilen. In de slaapkamer stond nog altijd haar koffer, naast het bed waarin hij al die jaren met zijn ex had gelegen. Een nieuw bed was duur, een nieuw bed was overdreven, het oude voldeed nog prima en daarnaast bleef Yulia's koffer maar staan, of beter gezegd: liggen. Hij had al een paar keer gevraagd of hij die koffer niet moest opbergen maar dat wilde ze niet. Weliswaar had ze de meeste spullen uit de koffer in de kast gelegd die hij voor haar had leeggemaakt, toch stond ze nog regelmatig over de koffer gebogen. Bepaalde spulletjes had ze er niet uit gehaald, wat boekjes, lingerie die ze om de een of andere reden liever in haar koffer bewaarde dan bij hem in de kast. Ook dat weet hij aan het feit dat ze geen eigen ruimte had, eentje die helemaal van haar was en van niemand anders.

Hij moest de kamer van de dode jongen ontruimen, er was geen andere mogelijkheid, hij moest daarvan de kamer van de nieuwe vrouw maken. Al die jaren had hij het vermeden, het was een van de redenen geweest om dit huis niet te verlaten na de scheiding, als hij het huis verkocht zou hij de dode jongen nog een keer doden, maar nu was het genoeg geweest. De nieuwe vrouw was er en zij had ruimte nodig. De doden hadden geen ruimte nodig, die lagen in hun graf.

Eeuwig kon dit niet duren, er zat een houdbaarheidsdatum aan het in leven houden. Er was een nieuwe vrouw, die de dode jongen nooit had gekend. Moest de Pool van haar verwachten dat zij tussen zijn spullen huisde en tussen zijn spullen huilde om een verdriet dat hij maar half begreep – wat wist hij van heimwee? – en dat volgens haar een taalprobleem was? Dat was te veel gevraagd. Hij kon haar niet opzadelen met het verleden.

Hij piekerde over Yulia, hoe hij met haar wilde leven, terwijl hij pannenkoeken aan het bakken was want die had ze nog niet gegeten, typisch Nederlandse pannenkoeken. En terwijl hij die aan het bakken was verdween de laatste twijfel, ja, er moest een eind aan komen, aan de angst, de ontkenning, de vermijding. Aan het eren van de dode, die niets aan die eer had. Zij was er, hij moest haar eren, Yulia moest worden geëerd. Hij sloeg met een theedoek op het aanrecht omdat hij een beslissing had genomen. Op de koelkast hing nog altijd de foto van Jurek van toen hij net had leren lopen en de Pool besefte dat er een foto van Yulia op de koelkast moest komen, ook dat zou helpen.

Toen de pannenkoeken waren gebakken en zij hem vertelde dat ze dit soort dingen ook in Kiev hadden zei hij: 'I will turn the dead boy's room into your room, a room for you alone.'

Jurek was in de woonkamer aan het gamen. In de ogen van Yulia zag hij vreugde maar niet lang, meteen daarna keek ze weer ernstig. Al vanaf het eerste moment dat hij haar zag had ze ernstig gekeken alsof ze wist dat de liefde geen grap was. 'So I have to sleep there again?'

'No, no,' zei hij. 'You sleep with me. But you live there. When you want. It will be your room.'

Ze knikte en met z'n drieën aten ze aan de eettafel de pannenkoeken, met suiker, met kaas en Yulia en Jurek met spek. Na het eten ging ze samen met de overgebleven jongen op de computer. Ze sprak niet meer over de kamer van de dode jongen, niet die avond toen ze vreeën en hij onverwacht het verlangen voelde dat hem altijd weer ongemakkelijk maakte en ook niet de ochtend erna. Voor de zekerheid vroeg hij haar of alles oké was en ze antwoordde: 'Yes, yes.'

Op zijn vrije dag belde hij vroeg in de ochtend Wen. 'Ik wil je niet storen,' zei hij, 'maar ik wil even iets overleggen. Ik wil de kamer van de verdwenen jongen leeghalen. Wat vind jij daarvan? Sorry als ik je hiermee overval.'

Stilte.

'Wen?'

'Ja.'

'Wat vind je ervan?'

'Het werd tijd, Geniek. Het werd tijd. Eens moest het gebeuren. Maar je overvalt me wel een beetje, inderdaad.'

'Sorry.'

'Geeft niet.'

'Wil je dat ik het niet doe?'

Stilte. 'Nee, doe maar wel.'

'Wil je nog iets hebben? Zal ik wachten met leeghalen tot jij... Moet ik iets bewaren voor jou?'

'Bewaar je iets voor jezelf?'

Nu was hij het die stil was. 'Nee. We hebben de foto's.'

'Ja, die hebben we. Ik hoef verder ook niets. Het is te lang geleden. Het is goed zo. Geloof me. Het is goed zo. Wat ga je eigenlijk met die kamer doen?'

'Het wordt Yulia's kamer.'

'O,' zei ze, 'Yulia's kamer. Zij gaat hem dus vervangen. Yulia gaat Borys vervangen.'

'Nee, Yulia heeft jou vervangen. Wacht, niet vervangen. Waarom moest je over vervangen beginnen? Nu zit dat woord in mijn hoofd. Ze gaat in zijn kamer wonen. Wil je haar nu eens ontmoeten? Zullen we een keer langskomen?'

'Na de verhuizing. Dat heb ik je nog niet verteld. We hebben eindelijk iets gevonden. In Eys.'

'Eys. Mooie omgeving. Niet ver van Wahlwiller. Grappig.'

'Nee, ook niet ver van Heerlen. Als we verhuisd zijn, als alles achter de rug is dan kom ik mijn spulletjes ophalen, mijn lieve spulletjes. En is met jou alles goed? Spreek je al Oekraïens?'

'Ik ben verliefd,' zei de Pool langzaam. 'Het leven is begonnen.'

Even bleef het stil aan de andere kant van de lijn. 'Dat is mooi.'

'Ik ben gewoon vergeten te leven. Je moet sterk zijn om te leven. Ik was niet sterk genoeg.'

'En nu wel?'

'Ja,' zei hij, 'nu wel.'

'Wat jammer, wat ontzettend jammer dat je bij mij niet sterk genoeg was om te leven.'

'Ja,' zei de Pool. 'Jammer. Ontzettend jammer.' Toen hingen ze op.

Diezelfde dag haalde de Pool de kamer van de jongen leeg. Alles. Het bureau, het bed, de lakens, de knuffels, de voetbalplaatjes, de posters, de boeken, de spelletjes, de schoenen. Slechts bij één paar schoenen aarzelde hij, het waren babyschoentjes. Hij legde ze onder in de klerenkast in zijn slaapkamer maar verder was hij meedogenloos. Ja, zo voelde het, meedogenloos. Het verleden opruimen was meedogenloze arbeid.

En toen besefte hij: ik moet iets bewaren voor Jurek, ik moet iets voor hem opzijleggen. Hij pakte een lege schoenendoos, deed daar de babyschoentjes in, een schrift, een willekeurig stripalbum, twee voetbalplaatjes, een knuffel (een muis), een T-shirt, een klassenfoto, een autootje dat hij achter in de kast vond, een opstel, een paar stukjes Lego, één sok, een joystick die bij een computerspel hoorde, even aarzelde hij en toen deed hij er toch nog een gymbroek bij. Daarna deed hij de schoenendoos dicht en hij schreef er 'Borys' op. Als het moment daar was, als Jurek er rijp voor was zou hij de schoenendoos aan hem geven en hij zou zeggen: Dit was je broertje. Dit kun je bewaren als aandenken.

De rest moest weg. Hij werkte als een bezetene. Wat verbrand kon worden werd verbrand in de tuin alsof het een barbecue was, een barbecue in de winter. Hij maakte een klein en beheersbaar vuur in de tuin maar niet om vlees te roosteren, om het verleden op te ruimen, om er afscheid van te nemen, om te verklaren dat het verleden was. Wat niet verbrand kon worden ging mee met het vuil. Hij hakte het in stukjes en Yulia vroeg toen ze thuiskwam van Nederlandse les wat hij aan het doen was.

'I am making space for you.'

Jurek kwam uit school. 'Wat ben je aan het doen?' wilde ook hij weten. 'Wat de fuck is hier aan de hand?'

'Ik maak ruimte voor Yulia,' antwoordde de Pool.

De overgebleven jongen rende naar boven, de Pool ging achter hem aan en de jongen keek naar de kamer die nu leeg was, onttakeld, alsof er verbouwd zou worden, alsof deze kamer opgeleverd werd aan een nieuwe huurder. De jongen zei dat het niet nodig was geweest, dat het beter was geweest alles zo te laten. 'Waarom?' vroeg hij aan zijn vader. 'Waarom heb je dit gedaan?'

'Het is zo lang geleden, het is zo verschrikkelijk lang geleden en Yulia is er nu.'

'Het is wel mijn broer. Had het dan eerder gedaan. Had het godverdomme eerder gedaan. Waarom nu?'

De Pool was vastberaden. 'Je broer heeft geen eigen kamer meer nodig. En ik heb dingen voor je bewaard. Die zal ik je ooit geven.'

Alleen het papiertje waarop stond: 'Ik heb geen vrienden. Ik zal nooit vrienden hebben. Ik heb nooit vrienden gehad', had hij niet in de schoenendoos gedaan. Dat had hij in de lade van zijn nachtkastje gelegd. In de rest van de schriften had hij niet gekeken en ook nu, voor hij ze verbrandde, bladerde hij er niet in. Wat had hij eraan? Inzicht zou niet meer helpen, inzicht had nooit geholpen en nu kwam het helemaal te laat. Wat ze nu nog niet wisten zouden ze nooit weten.

De Pool werkte de rest van de dag verder. Hij had niets gegeten, hij had geen honger. Yulia wilde hem helpen, hij antwoordde: 'Let me do this.' Ze wilde hem kussen, ze vroeg of hij dit voor haar deed. Hij zei: 'For us.' Hij voegde eraan toe: 'Voor ons. Wij. Samen. Jij. Ik.'

Het vuur in de tuin was schitterend. Alles brandde, de lakens en de schriften, het in stukken gehakte bureau. De kleren en de voetbalplaatjes. Het was een prachtig vuur. Toen alles wat kon branden brandde stond hij er samen met Yulia naar te kijken. Hij sloeg zijn arm om haar heen, om de kleine, jonge vrouw. Klein vergeleken bij hem.

Hij zei dat dit het was, dat het werk erop zat. Ze antwoordde eerst niet, ze keek naar het vuur en pas later vroeg ze: 'So now the dead boy's room is my room?'

'I will paint it first,' zei hij, 'and then you can work there and cry. If you need to cry you don't have to go to the toilet anymore. You go there and you cry.'

'But I don't want to cry.'

'No. But if you have to cry you have your own space now. What do you want to do?'

Ze keek hem even aan alsof hij haar moest helpen met het vinden van de juiste woorden, hij, de zwijgzame Pool. 'I want to be creative.'

'Oké,' zei de Pool, 'creative, good', en ze gingen naar binnen.

Die avond aten ze in een Japans restaurant want Yulia had weer zin in sushi. Ze dempte de heimwee met sushi en sashimi. Voor zichzelf had de Pool groente-tempura besteld, voor Jurek iets met rundvlees en daarna, tussen het hoofd- en nagerecht (groene thee-ijs), neuriede hij en Yulia neuriede terug tot de andere gasten naar hen keken, want geneurie waren ze niet gewend in een Japans restaurant en Jurek zei: 'Kun je hier alsjeblieft mee ophouden, papa, we zitten wel in een Japans restaurant.' Ze dronken sake, de Pool meer dan Yulia. En hij neuriede nog even door, want hij moest tegenover Yulia laten zien wie de baas was.

Ze reden naar huis en in de auto neuriede hij niet meer. Hij ging naar boven, hij ging de kamer van de verdwenen jongen stofzuigen zodat er binnenkort geverfd kon worden. Het liet hem niet los, hoe eerder het achter de rug was hoe beter. Hij maakte alles schoon, er lagen nog wat snippers die hij weggooide, oud papier. Ergens in een hoek vond hij een sok die hij niet eerder had gezien, hij stuitte op vochtvlekken maar hier was ook nooit geverfd. Deze kamer hadden ze niet aangeroerd, hier had de verrotting zijn gang kunnen gaan. Toen de kamer klaar was om verder onder handen genomen te worden, klaar om na een kleine renovatie in gebruik te worden genomen door de nieuwe vrouw ging hij naar beneden. Op de bank zaten Yulia en zijn overgebleven jongen. Ze keken naar een filmpje op de telefoon van de jongen en hij had het idee dat Yulia de jongen kuste. Niet op zijn mond, dat niet, wel zoals de ene geliefde de andere kust. Op zijn wang. Ze streelde hem door zijn haar. Hij bleef kijken naar dit tafereel, naar Yulia en zijn zoon. Tevreden was hij, misschien zelfs gelukkig. Dit was het huiselijke geluk, dit was integratie. De nieuwe vrouw had het oude kind geaccepteerd. Ze merkten hem niet op, ze keken geconcentreerd naar een filmpje dat de jongen haar op zijn telefoon liet zien.

De Pool bleef er nog even naar kijken, staand op de drempel van de woonkamer, bijna alsof hij ze niet mocht storen, alsof hem dit niets aanging. Vertederd en toch ook weer niet. Hij ging theezetten in de keuken en daar vroeg hij zich af of de nieuwe vrouw niet hém moest strelen. Ze vree met hem. Ze gaf zich aan hem maar wanneer streelde ze hem zoals ze de jongen net had gestreeld? Hij kon zich niet aan de indruk onttrekken dat ze liever de jongen streelde dan hem. De Pool wist dat het niet zo was want zij was zijn nieuwe vrouw en de jongen was een kind, toch was de gedachte hardnekkig. Een vreselijk hardnekkige gedachte.

Met z'n drieën dronken ze vervolgens thee. Dat wil zeggen, Yulia en de jongen hingen op de bank en waren bezig met spelletjes en hij zat op een stoel ernaar te kijken. De Pool zei niets. Hij was tevreden en gelukkig. Zeker, er knaagde iets maar er knaagt altijd iets. Als er niets meer knaagt ben je dood. Hij keek naar de hand van Yulia op de rug van zijn overgebleven jongen. Had hij de verdwenen jongen verkeerd gestreeld, vroeg hij zich af. Kon je mensen op de verkeerde manier strelen? Had zijn ex hem daarom ooit de dvd laten zien, omdat hij iedereen op de verkeerde manier streelde?

Tot ze naar boven gingen, Yulia voorop en hij achter haar aan. Yulia glipte de badkamer in en toen ze eindelijk naar de slaapkamer kwam, ze deed er altijd zo lang over om zich klaar te maken voor de nacht, stelde hij de vraag die eerder de avond in hem was opgekomen. De knagende vraag. Als hij het in het Nederlands had kunnen vragen had hij het anders gevraagd, sympathieker, misschien ook ietwat omslachtiger, maar in het Engels lukte hem dat niet: 'Do you love my son?' vroeg hij.

'Yes, I believe so.'

Ze ging aan haar kant van het bed liggen. Ze droeg een nachthemd dat haar sprookjesachtige verschijning benadrukte. Voor de Pool was ze sprookjesachtig en dat zou ze altijd blijven.

'Do you love him more than you love me?'

'No.' Ze keek de Pool verbaasd aan. Deze vraag had ze kennelijk niet verwacht.

'Forgive me, but do you love me?'

'Why? Of course.'

'You never say you love me.' Het klonk verwijtend en zo had hij het niet bedoeld.

'I say, you are sweet.'

'Yes,' zei hij. 'Yes, sweet, I'm sweet, I do sweet things, but that's not the same.'

'I left everything for you. Everything. I'm here. I'm ashamed. I don't speak your language. I don't understand your jokes. I'm ashamed. I'm not sure if I love your son. I'm ashamed. I cry. I'm ashamed. How can you ask me this question? You don't feel it? How can you ask me this stupid question?'

'I don't make jokes. And I'm not sure what I feel, what I should feel.'

Ze wendde zich van hem af. Ze huilde, hij hoorde het niet maar hij wist dat ze aan het huilen was. Hij pakte haar arm. Liefdevol, bezorgd en desondanks met een zeker verlangen. Hij zei dat ze zich niet hoefde te schamen, dat hij toch niets aan zijn gedachten kon doen. 'I can't help it, I see what I see.'

Ze draaide zich naar hem om. Of dat een goed teken was? In elk geval stopte het huilen. Hij moest het weten omdat het knaagde, hij moest het vragen omdat de gedachtes bleven komen. Ze houdt van het kind en niet van mij. Maar waarom moest er ook van hem worden gehouden, waarom moest er van de mensen worden gehouden? Was het niet genoeg dat hij van haar hield? Dat hij het vuur van de liefde elke dag bluste? Onvermoeibaar, soms met ternauwernood overwonnen tegenzin maar hij deed het.

'Do you want to make love to my son?' vroeg hij.

Ze keek hem aan met de ogen die hij had gezien in Kiev in een donker lokaal tussen allemaal andere ogen die staarden naar mannen uit Nederland en Duitsland, mannen die liefde over de grens zochten. Hij was op haar ogen gevallen. En op haar tanden. Tanden en ogen. Ogen en tanden.

'No,' antwoordde ze. 'No. Of course not. He is too young.'

'But maybe I'm too old?'

'No,' herhaalde ze.

Hij was niet overtuigd. De Pool wilde graag overtuigd zijn maar het lukte hem niet. Even bleef hij liggen, aarzelend of hij nog iets moest zeggen, toen ging hij naar de badkamer, poetste zijn tanden, waste zijn gezicht grondig, bekeek zichzelf in de spiegel en masseerde voor hij het licht uitdeed nog even zijn linkerschouder. Iets deed pijn, hij wist niet wat.

Toen hij terugkwam lag ze naakt op bed, boven op de dekens en ze zei: 'I love you.' De Pool kon het niet helpen, hij dacht: ze denkt nu aan mijn overgebleven jongen. Ze denkt aan hem. Van wie houdt ze eigenlijk?

Ze wenkte dat hij naderbij moest komen, ze sloeg haar armen om hem heen en ze zei nog een keer dat ze van hem hield, van de Pool en ook van zijn zoon. Was hij daar niet blij om? 'He is so shy,' zei ze. De Pool beaamde het. Dat hij blij was en dat de overgebleven jongen verlegen was, al wilde hij daar nog aan toevoegen: Hij kan ook hondsbrutaal zijn, hoor. Van die opmerking kwam het niet meer. Ze kuste hem en hij kuste terug, met de gretigheid die hem zelden overviel, met de gretigheid van de dood. Hij trok zijn onderbroek uit en hij streelde haar lichaam. Haar hele lichaam, haar buik, haar schouders, haar benen, haar knieen, haar voeten, alsof hij alles opnieuw moest ontdekken, alsof alles voor de eerste keer moest worden gestreeld.

'Your body is not old,' zei ze. 'You have a young body.'

'Yes,' zei hij, al vroeg hij zich meteen af wat dan wel oud was, zijn hoofd, zijn manier van doen? 'You will be his friend,' zei hij zachtjes terwijl hij met zijn vingers over haar vagina ging zoals hij het op de dvd van zijn ex had gezien. 'You will be the best friend of my son.'

'Yes.'

'You will teach him to be less shy. To be a good man.'

'Yes,' zei ze. 'We will be family. I will stay here. I'm not going back. I will cry but I'm not going back.'

'You make me happy.' Hij zei het maar hij voelde het niet, zelf begreep hij niet waarom. Misschien was zeggen genoeg. Voelen was niet nodig, als je het zei kwam het voelen vanzelf. Daarop ging hij bij haar naar binnen, ze moest hem een beetje helpen, hij merkte hoe haar hand zijn geslachtsdeel vastpakte en hoe ze die hand wegtrok toen hij goed en wel in haar zat.

Terwijl hij in haar stootte, verdoofd door de opwinding, door de sake, door de knagende gedachten, meende hij dat zij ook nu aan zijn kind dacht. Hij wist het niet zeker want hij durfde het niet te vragen, zelfs als hij het vroeg was het nog niet zeker dat hij een eerlijk antwoord kreeg, maar hij voelde het. Ze lagen daar met een derde, met het overgebleven kind en terwijl hij in haar zat vroeg hij of ze zelf een kind wilde, een eigen kind.

De lust werd weer een huisdier, het huisdier blafte, bijten deed het niet. 'Maybe later,' zei ze. 'If I have my papers. If we still love each other.'

Hij knikte. Hij hervatte de arbeid van het genot. En terwijl hij zich overgaf aan de arbeid kon hij het toch niet laten te vragen: 'Do you want to fuck my son?' De vraag ontsnapte hem. Dit had hij niet moeten vragen, hij wist het, niet dit, niet deze vraag, maar hij zag ze weer voor zich, hoe ze daar op de bank hadden gehangen. Zo vanzelfsprekend, hij kon zich even niet voorstellen ooit zo met zijn nieuwe vrouw op de bank te hangen. Er was een band ontstaan tussen de jongen en Yulia waar hij nooit tussen zou komen, zo voelde het, en hoewel hij blij moest zijn, blij voor zijn zoon, blij voor zichzelf, blij voor Yulia, lukte de blijdschap hem niet. Hij deed zijn best maar er kwam geen blijdschap, alleen angst en verdriet kwamen.

Ze duwde haar bekken omhoog, ze drukte haar onderlijf tegen het zijne aan. 'No,' zei ze, 'you. I want to fuck yóú.'

'Are you sure?' vroeg hij.

'What am I doing? What do you think I'm doing?'

De jongen was er, die stond tussen hen in. Ze waren te weinig alleen. 'Tomorrow,' zei hij, 'tomorrow, he is going to his mother and then we will be two weeks alone.'

'You should come,' antwoordde ze. 'It takes so long. Come. I want you. Come in me. Don't wait.'

'How can I come if you talk like this?' De opmerking was onterecht. Ze had niets verkeerds gezegd, zijn gedachten waren verkeerd, zijn denken was verkeerd.

'I told you, language is a problem,' zei ze.

Hij zoende haar met alle hartstocht die hij in zich kon vinden. Even waren er nog de beelden van zijn nieuwe vrouw met de overgebleven jongen op de bank. Toen concentreerde hij zich, toen verloor hij zich. Hij hield van Yulia, andere gevoelens zou hij zichzelf niet meer toestaan, andere gevoelens zou hij de nek omdraaien.

# 4

De mannen van de C-ploeg hadden besloten een kerstfeest te organiseren voor henzelf en voor hun partners. Ze waren nu eenmaal anders dan andere ploegen, beter en hechter. Ze wilden een eigen feestje. Ook omdat ze goed waren in feestjes, omdat je elke gelegenheid dat er iets te vieren viel moest aangrijpen.

De Pool vertelde Yulia erover, eerst wilde ze niet mee maar hij drong aan, hij zei dat alle mannen of bijna alle mannen hun partner meenamen, het was niet fijn alleen naar zo'n kerstfeest te moeten.

Ze was weleens op de kazerne geweest en hij had haar voorgesteld aan de andere mannen, toch had hij het gevoel dat ze haar nog niet echt hadden leren kennen. Ze moesten haar goed leren kennen. Zijn nieuwe vrouw was geen trofee maar hij was trots op haar. Dat ze bij hem was, dat ze voor hem Kiev had verlaten, dat hij een nieuwe vrouw had, met zulke lieve ogen, met zo'n mooie ziel, dat wilde hij laten zien. Dat er genade bestond.

Hij wilde naast haar staan op het feest van de C-ploeg, hij wilde bewijzen dat het allemaal goed was gekomen. 'I'm proud of you,' zei hij. 'I want to show you to the world. You are not my secret.'

'No,' zei ze, 'I'm not your secret.' Daaruit begreep hij dat ze toch mee wilde, dat ze zijn kerstfeest zou vieren, het kerstfeest van de C-ploeg.

Hoewel het koud was die decemberdag dat het feest werd gevierd besloot de Pool de bloemetjesblouse aan te doen die hij gekocht had om een gentleman in Kiev te zijn. Ook het jasje dat erbij hoorde trok hij aan. Een overjas liet hij achterwege. De nieuwe Pool zou zich in vol ornaat, als de gentleman die hij dan toch nog was geworden aan de mannen van de C-ploeg tonen. Ze gingen er met een taxi heen, met een taxi zou hij zijn nieuwe vrouw en zichzelf weer naar huis laten rijden als het allemaal achter de rug was.

Voor Yulia had hij speciaal voor deze avond een jurk gekocht. Een nieuwe, blauwe jurk, zeeblauw, want zeeblauw stond haar uitstekend. Ze was er blij mee, had ze in de winkel gezegd. Ze had hem een paar keer bedankt, verder zag hij niet veel aan haar, hij kon niet goed opmaken wat ze dacht of wat ze voelde. Ze had hem een keer gevraagd of hij iets wist van de politiek in Oekraïne en daarop had hij ontkennend geantwoord. Yulia had geprobeerd hem het een en ander uit te leggen maar hij was in de war geraakt van alle namen die op elkaar leken. Met zijn ex had hij nooit over politiek gepraat, daar werd je namelijk niet gelukkig van, praten over politiek. Alsof ze dat voelde, zijn Yulia, kroop ze na het eten steeds vaker zwijgend tegen hem aan. Ze gaf de taal niet meer de schuld, ze deed geen poging meer het onzegbare toch te zeggen. Ze hingen samen op de bank zoals Yulia daar had gehangen met de jongen, dan streelde ze hem en hoezeer de Pool van deze momenten genoot, hij had toch het gevoel dat ze hem streelde zoals je een huisdier aait.

Yulia maakte zich op in de badkamer. Hij was al klaar, Jurek was bij zijn moeder, hij had die avond ook een feest, op school. De Pool liep rusteloos door het huis, denkend aan Jurek, in afwachting van het feest, in afwachting van zijn collega's, zijn vrienden, de genade die hij zou kunnen tonen, de genade die liefde was.

De kamer van de dode jongen was langzaam Yulia's kamer geworden. Er was een nieuw bureau neergezet waar ze haar huiswerk voor Nederlandse les maakte en haar koffer stond er. Een goedkope kast had hij tweedehands op de kop getikt, die moest alleen nog worden geverfd. Soms opende hij de deur van de kamer en was nog altijd verbaasd dat de spullen van de dode jongen er niet meer waren. Het had even geduurd, het had misschien lang geduurd zouden mensen zeggen, maar uiteindelijk was hij toch geruisloos verdwenen, Borys was er niet meer.

Yulia was wel een uur bezig met haar haren en haar gezicht. De Pool werd er zenuwachtig van. Wat deed ze daar toch? Ze moesten weg. Hij klopte op de badkamerdeur en hij riep: 'It's just a couple of firemen. Don't overdo it.'

'But they are your friends,' riep ze terug.

Hij ging naar binnen en voor de spiegel stond Yulia haar haren te vlechten in allemaal kleine vlechtjes. Ze had alleen haar ondergoed aan.

'Yes.' Hij kuste haar schouders, ze was frêle. 'They are my friends. But you are beautiful enough,' fluisterde hij in haar oor.

Ze glimlachte, ze geloofde hem niet of ze vond dat hij zich bemoeide met zaken die hem niets aangingen. Onverstoorbaar ging ze verder met vlechten en de Pool liep weer door het huis, dwaalde door de kamers en neuriede een lied.

Toen de taxi kwam was ze nog steeds bezig met haar haren, nu werd de Pool echt zenuwachtig, hij wilde de chauffeur niet laten wachten. 'Yulia,' riep hij. 'Yulia. Verdomme. We have to go.'

Ze zag er stralend uit toen ze eindelijk uit de badkamer kwam, ze kon zo op tv, hij werd er onbehaaglijk van. Alsof hij dit niet verdiende, hij voelde zich klein en kaal bij deze overdaad aan jeugd en schoonheid. Klein was hij niet maar wel kaal. Voor hij naar buiten ging griste hij zijn pet van de kapstok en zette die op. Hand in hand liepen ze naar de taxi en hij zei in het Nederlands dat ze er prachtig uitzag, want dat verstond ze inmiddels. Kleine dingen verstond ze prima, het zou niet lang meer duren en dan sprak ze Nederlands, dan was ze een Nederlandse van Oekraïense afkomst met een Russisch hart.

In de auto ze: 'I'm so nervous. Do you think they will like me? Your friends. They will like me?'

De Pool antwoordde dat ze zich geen zorgen hoefde te maken, dat de mannen van de C-ploeg haar zouden waarderen, het waren prima mannen, Wen hadden ze ook altijd geaccepteerd en meer dan dat, en hij bleef haar hand vasthouden om haar zorgen weg te nemen. Omdat hij van haar hield, omdat hij eindelijk leefde.

Het feest vond plaats in de oefenruimte. Er was muziek, er was een rookmachine. Nelemans had zijn gitaar bij zich, hij zong een vrolijk lied over het leven van een eenzame brandweerman. Ook de eenzaamheid kon vrolijk zijn. Een zelfgemaakt lied natuurlijk, dat deed hij nu eenmaal. Daarvoor leefde hij, voor het zingen.

De ploegchef kwam op de Pool af. 'Dit is mijn nieuwe vrouw, dit is Yulia,' zei de Pool voor de ploegchef iets had kunnen zeggen. De ploegchef schudde haar de hand, glimlachte en hij zei tegen de Pool: 'De catering is de vegetarische hapjes vergeten. Vind je dat erg?'

'Nee,' zei de Pool. 'Helemaal niet. Ik heb al gegeten.'

'Ja, jij bent de enige vegetariër hier,' zei de ploegchef. 'We houden rekening met de minderheid.'

De Pool knikte vriendelijk en hij liep verder, zijn hand omklemde nog altijd Yulia's hand. Ze waren samen. De mannen zouden het zien, de mannen zouden het begrijpen. Ze zouden zien wat hij in Kiev had gezien.

Beckers overhandigde Yulia en hem wat glühwein, Beckers lachte en hij zei: 'Heeft Nelemans gemaakt. Maakt ook glühwein, onze Nelemans. Zingt niet alleen. Maakt ook glühwein.' Beckers moest onbedaarlijk lachen, de Pool lachte mee en Yulia lachte verlegen voor zich uit.

De meeste mannen waren toch zonder partner gekomen maar ze waren er allemaal. De C-ploeg was compleet.

Ze dronken en ze aten en de Pool zei tegen zijn nieuwe vrouw dat ze zoveel van de hapjes mocht nemen als ze wilde, dat hij zelf thuis genoeg had gegeten. Ze stopte een bitterbal in haar mond en haalde die er weer uit omdat hij te heet was. 'I'm making a fool of myself,' zei ze met een aangebeten bitterbal in haar hand.

De Pool stelde haar gerust en hij verwijderde restjes bitterbal van haar lippen. 'It's charming, everything you do is charming.' Zo groeide hij weer een beetje in de rol van de man die hij wilde zijn, hij voelde zich minder klein en onbeduidend naast haar. Nelemans zong verder. Nu een lied dat niet ging over een brandweerman maar over een bergbeklimmer en zijn vrouw. Toen Nelemans was uitgezongen verdween hij met zijn gitaar achter een geïmproviseerde bar alsof naast het zingen de bardienst zijn leven was. 'De bar is open,' riep Nelemans, de mannen lachten en ook de Pool lachte want het was feest, dan hoorde je te lachen. Yulia vroeg of er wodka was of een cocktail want de glühwein vond ze niet te drinken. Cocktails raadde hij haar af. Die kon ze hier beter niet drinken, er was wodka in overvloed. Daar hield ze toch van? De mannen hadden allemaal wat in de pot gelegd, ze waren niet zuinig geweest, er was whisky, rum en wodka, er was van alles. Er was een overdaad aan drank, de mannen waren als het ging om dit soort feestjes niet gierig. Met hun drankjes in de hand liepen ze door de oefenruimte, Yulia en hij, de trappen omhoog en de trappen weer omlaag. 'This is where we exercise,' vertelde de Pool. 'This is where we prepare for the fire.'

Yulia knikte alsof het haar interesseerde, de Pool wist dat het niet haar leven was, dit was zijn leven. Toch wilde hij haar iets van zijn leven laten zien omdat hij dankzij haar weer leefde.

'But in reality it's different,' zei de Pool. 'It's always different.' Als ze niet allebei een glas in hun hand hadden gehad had hij haar tegen zich aan gedrukt. 'Kom, we gaan weer naar beneden.' Hij vertelde nog dat ze hier soms liepen met ademlucht op je rug zoals je liep als je een brandend gebouw in moest. Hij wist niet of ze hem begreep. 'A building on fire,' zei hij. 'We enter the building. We have to.' Ze knikte.

Het liep tegen elven en de mannen van de A-ploeg die dienst had kwamen even kijken en kort daarop hield de chef van de C-ploeg een korte toespraak, dat hij trots was op zijn mannen, dat er veel was gebeurd, dat er veranderingen op komst waren bij de brandweer, veranderingen waarop ze niet allemaal zaten te wachten maar dat ze bij elkaar zouden blijven, wat er ook gebeurde, welke beslissingen in Den Haag ook werden genomen, deze mannen waren onafscheidelijk. Ze waren al zo lang bij elkaar. Ze zouden elkaar nooit in de steek laten.

Er werd geapplaudisseerd en de discomuziek ging weer aan. Nelemans klapte in zijn handen en beneden in het trappenhuis waar ze normaal gesproken het blindlopen deden werd nu gedanst. De drank had de mannen verlost van hun schaamte, van hun behoedzaamheid, hun verlegenheid. Ze dansten alsof ze nooit iets anders hadden gedaan, alsof ze het eeuwige leven hadden. Dwars door de rook, tussen de dansende mannen door, tussen de drinkende mannen door, dwaalde de Pool met zijn nieuwe vrouw. Steeds weer drukte iemand hem een glas in de hand. Overal was drank en overal waren handen die drank aanboden. 'Wees vrolijk, man,' zei Nelemans.

'Ik bén vrolijk,' antwoordde de Pool. 'Ik ben heel vrolijk.'

Ze bleven dansen, de mannen van de C-ploeg, die anders nooit dansten, de Pool had ze in elk geval nog nooit zien dansen, maar deze avond dansten ze en sommigen deden het zelfs goed, alsof ze het stiekem al jaren hadden gedaan. Beckers danste als een bezetene, alleen de Pool beperkte zich tot toekijken, dat was genoeg voor hem, leunend tegen de muur met een glas in zijn hand en de pet op zijn hoofd. Het leven was begonnen. Je kon er ook naar kijken.

'Dance,' zei Yulia uiteindelijk.

'Nee,' zei de Pool.

'Why not?'

'It's not for me. You dance.' Hij streelde eerst haar oorlelletje en toen de rest van haar oor. Hij was ontspannen.

Dat deed Yulia, ze ging zelf dansen. En terwijl ze danste keek ze naar hem en hij keek naar haar en de Pool besefte dat hij gelukkig was, dat dit het geluk was, dat dit het goede leven was, niets anders dan dit, niet meer dan dit en toen kwam de zwetende Beckers naar hem toe en hij zei: 'Ik moet nog even niet aan een nieuwe vrouw denken. Het blijft vers. Misschien ooit. Niet nu.'

'Ja,' zei de Pool.

'Jij wel hè, jij hebt aan een nieuwe vrouw gedacht.'

'Ja.' De Pool keek weer naar Yulia die aan het dansen was en naar zijn collega's die om haar heen dansten. Goede mannen, mannen die ooit tegen hem hadden gezegd: we slepen je erdoorheen. Mannen die zijn huis hadden geverfd, mannen met wie hij op de foto was gegaan in dat pas geverfde huis. Op hun manier hadden ze dat gedaan, ze hadden hem erdoorheen gesleept.

'Je moest er helemaal voor naar Kiev,' zei Beckers, 'voor je nieuwe vrouw. Kiev, is het mooi daar?' Beckers haalde zonder op antwoord te wachten wat te drinken voor hun tweeën en hij zei: 'Proost, man. Wij zijn de nieuwe negers. Je mag het niet zeggen maar ik ben niet gek. Als ik in de spiegel kijk dan zie ik een neger. Wij blanke mannen, wij zijn straks een minderheid in eigen land. Ze pakken alles van ons af.'

'Ja,' zei de Pool. 'Zo gaat dat. Minderheden worden meerderheden en omgekeerd.'

'Proost,' zei Beckers weer en de andere mannen dansten

verder en uitbundiger alsof het dansen een parodie moest zijn, een parodie en toch serieus. De Pool zag zijn nieuwe vrouw niet meer, de rookmachine stond te loeien en de discobol bleef draaien terwijl Beckers praatte, aan één stuk door, over nieuwe en oude minderheden. Het was toch een feest? Dan had je het niet over minderheden. Was er echt niets leukers om over te spreken? 'Zwarte Piet is een klein dingetje,' zei Beckers. 'Die strijd hebben we verloren. Het gaat om meer. Het gaat om respect. Ze respecteren ons niet meer, we hebben dit land opgebouwd maar respect ho maar. Als er brand was in een asielzoekerscentrum zou ik natuurlijk blussen, alleen zou ik het rustig aan doen, ik zou het heel rustig aan doen, ik zeg het eerlijk, voor die mensen ga ik niet mijn leven wagen want zij doen het ook niet voor mij. Zo is het toch, zij doen het ook niet voor ons. Sterker nog, ze haten ons.'

Beckers nam een grote slok. 'Ben je gelukkig?' vroeg hij aan de Pool. 'Ben je nu gelukkig?'

'Ja,' antwoordde de Pool.

'Goed zo,' zei Beckers, 'dat is belangrijk,' en hij praatte verder over de toekomst, de Europeanen, de brandweer, de kinderen die een toekomst moesten hebben en toen ging hij weer wat te drinken halen. Voor hem en de Pool.

De Pool wist niet meer wat hij moest zeggen daarom zei hij: 'Ik ga pissen.'

Gewoontegetrouw liep hij naar het andere gedeelte van de kazerne, waar de mannen van de A-ploeg nog wat voor de tv hingen. Ze keken naar hem, ze zeiden niets. Hij plaste en met zijn rechterhand leunde hij tegen de muur. Als ze nou wat vegetarische hapjes hadden gehad was het minder erg geweest. Frituurolie legde altijd een bodem in je maag, een bodem waarop je heel wat alcohol kwijt kon. Hij voelde zich aangeschoten en hij kon zich de kater van de volgende dag al voorstellen, maar dat was niet erg want hier was het feest en hier was het leven.

Langzaam liep hij terug naar de oefenruimte. Alleen de man die Haas werd genoemd stond er. Hij had wel zijn vrouw bij zich, een wat gezette dame uit Luik die Nederlands sprak met een accent waarover iedereen altijd moest lachen en die misschien daarom besloten had zo min mogelijk te zeggen.

'Haas,' zei de Pool. 'Waar zijn onze vrienden? Is het feest afgelopen?'

'Nee,' zei Haas. 'Het feest is nog niet afgelopen.' Hij legde zijn hand op de schouder van de Pool en hij vroeg: 'Hoe is het?'

'Hoe is wat?'

'Hoe is het met jou?'

'Met mij,' zei de Pool langzaam. 'Met mij is het goed.'

'Onze oudste dochter,' zei Haas, 'die wil geen vlees meer eten.'

'O.'

'Ze eet nog wel vis.'

'Oké.'

'Jij bent de eerste vegetarische brandweerman die ik ken,' zei Haas. 'Jij eet ook geen vis toch?'

'Nee,' zei de Pool.

Haas knikte. 'Al die vleeshaters willen hardwerkende carnivoren een rotgevoel geven, niet? Als ik naar mijn dochter kijk dan denk ik: ze wil me buitensluiten.'

Daarop had de Pool geen antwoord, hij wist ook niet zo goed wat Haas bedoelde. Hij liep door de oefenruimte om Yulia te zoeken. Hij ging de trap op, misschien was ze naar boven gegaan. De toren op. Je had vandaar een mooi uitzicht, over de stad, de heuvels, Aken kon je zien liggen, met een beetje geluk. De heuvels, de dorpen. Vanavond niet. Het miezerde. Toch liep hij steeds verder de trap omhoog, een route die hij vaak had afgelegd met een fles ademlucht op zijn rug. Nu hoefde hij geen gewicht met zich mee te slepen, behalve zijn eigen lichaam maar door de drank kostte het hem meer moeite dan hij had gedacht. 'Yulia,' riep hij en hij gebruikte zijn mobieltje als zaklantaarn.

Hij kwam Beckers en Nelemans en de ploegchef tegen. Ze liepen naar beneden.

'Is het feest afgelopen?' vroeg de Pool.

'Bijna,' zei Nelemans. 'We zijn zo ongeveer door de drank heen.'

'Hebben jullie Yulia gezien?' wilde de Pool weten.

'Boven,' antwoordde de ploegchef.

De Pool liep verder, nu en dan riep hij haar naam maar het enige wat hij hoorde was de muziek van beneden en hij herinnerde zich dat hij haar soms moest gaan zoeken toen ze hier net was en dat hij haar dan in het centrum van de stad vond met haar boodschappentas. Hoe ongerust hij kon zijn als hij haar niet meteen vond. Dat hij vreesde dat ze zou verdwijnen, dat ze zou oplossen, dat hij aan haar vader moest schrijven dat Yulia weg was maar dat hij ervan overtuigd was dat ze vroeg of laat weer zou opduiken. Dat de vader niet bang hoefde te zijn, daar in Kiev. Hoe Yulia hem verdwaasd kon aankijken als hij haar gevonden had, alsof ze zelf niet meer wist wie hij was, alsof ze niet meer wist wat ze hier deed. En dat de Pool dan besefte dat hij niet zonder haar wilde leven, zoals hij ooit niet zonder God had willen leven. De afwezigheid van mensen en dingen was gruwelijker dan de dood.

Tot hij eindelijk boven aankwam, helemaal boven, vanwaar je op heldere dagen Aken kon zien liggen, hij was hier vaak geweest, je kon hier de wind zo goed voelen en in de zomer als het beneden zinderde van de hitte was het hier aangenaam koel, ja, dan stond hij hier weleens om uit te waaien, om zichzelf te vergeten, om één te worden met de vogels en het uitzicht, hoewel het eigenlijk niet mocht omdat je gereed moest zijn om uit te rukken. Maar hij was zo beneden, hij kende de weg.

Toen hoefde hij niet meer over de afwezigheid van Yulia te denken want hij zag haar. Ze lag op de grond, alsof ze sliep, alsof ze niet had kunnen wachten tot ze thuis in bed lag en dacht: ik ga hier een dutje doen. Hij bukte zich, hij richtte zijn mobieltje op haar gezicht. Alle make-up was uitgelopen. Haar zorgvuldig gevlochten haar was niet meer gevlochten. Ze zag eruit alsof ze ternauwernood een brand had overleefd. Hij had het gevoel dat hij geen adem meer kreeg, dat hij in de rook stond.

'What happened?' De Pool bukte zich, veegde haren uit haar gezicht en toen zag hij de wond boven Yulia's rechteroog. Ze moest met haar gezicht tegen de stenen zijn gestoten. Er zat opgedroogd bloed boven haar rechteroog.

'Yulia,' zei de Pool. 'Yulia.'

Ze zweeg en keek hem aan alsof ze echt niet meer wist wie hij was, zoals ze soms kon kijken als hij haar in de stad vond met haar boodschappen. Verdwaasd. Dan leek ze alles te zijn vergeten. Wie ze was, waar ze vandaan kwam, wat ze hier deed, van wie ze hield. Dan moest hij zeggen: 'You are Yulia from Kiev, you are my future wife.' En dan nam hij haar mee naar huis. Soms reed hij met de auto naar de heuvels en gingen ze ergens wat drinken en dan zei hij: 'We hebben het goed hier, niet?'

Dit was anders, dit was niet het centrum van de stad, ze had geen boodschappentas bij zich, ze lag op de grond boven in de toren.

'Yulia,' zei hij, 'zeg iets. Zeg iets. Yulia.' Hij dacht: als ik haar naam noem, als ik haar naam blijf noemen dan weet ze alles weer.

Ze bleef zwijgen, ze keek hem aan met haar betraande ogen, ze gaf geen blijk van herkenning. 'Yulia,' zei de Pool. 'It's me.' Hij veegde haar gezicht schoon, eerst met de rug van zijn hand en toen met zijn zakdoek maar hoe hij ook veegde, het werd alleen viezer.

'Je moet iets zeggen. Wat is er gebeurd? Ik weet dat toch niet. Ik kan dat toch niet weten.' En hij zag dat ze geen schoenen meer aanhad en dat haar panty was gescheurd en haar jurk. Ze moest zijn gevallen. Ze was gevallen. Uitgegleden. Misschien door de drank, ze had vast te veel gedronken. Hij had haar niet moeten meenemen. Hij had moeten wachten, volgend jaar was beter geweest. Volgend jaar zouden ze vast weer een feest organiseren. Ze was er nog niet klaar voor geweest, voor het feest, voor de mannen van de C-ploeg.

'Waar zijn je schoenen?' vroeg hij. 'Your shoes. En je jurk. Helemaal kapot. Helemaal gescheurd. Zo'n mooie jurk. Zo'n nieuwe jurk.' De Pool herinnerde zich hoe ze de jurk hadden gekocht, een merkwaardig verdriet overviel hem. Verdriet om een jurk, dat was merkwaardig verdriet.

Hij vond haar schoenen maar hij liet ze liggen. Die schoenen deden er niet meer toe. De Pool tilde haar op. Zijn nieuwe vrouw tilde hij op alsof het hun huwelijksfeest was en hij haar naar de slaapkamer bracht. Het feest was voorbij, eindelijk begon de nacht, de rest van het leven waar bruid en bruidegom zo naar uit hadden gezien. Het was een ander huwelijksfeest dan hij zich had voorgesteld, volstrekt anders en toch een bruiloft, hun bruiloft. Er zou geen andere komen. De Pool voelde het, de Pool wist het. Hij zou haar naar huis brengen zoals dat van een bruidegom werd verwacht. Maar eerst moesten ze de trap af en dat kostte hem meer moeite dan hij had verwacht, ongetwijfeld vanwege de glühwein en de andere drankjes die ze hem in zijn handen hadden gedrukt. Ze waren royaal, de mannen van de C-ploeg. Wankelend ging hij naar beneden hoewel hij hierop was getraind. Hij kon het blind met een fles ademlucht op zijn rug en hij had nu geen ademlucht nodig. Er was geen brand, hij kon zelf ademen, geen rook, geen brand, er was alleen Yulia, die niets zei, Yulia en haar nieuwe jurk, die nu al kapot was. Langzaam ging hij de trap af. Het was een oefening, dat was wat hij tegen zichzelf zei, het was gewoon een oefening. Een oefening voor de liefde.

Hij had zijn hele leven geoefend voor de liefde en dit was het laatste examen dat hij nog moest afleggen, dan was hij er klaar voor.

Verder ging hij naar beneden, trede voor trede, voorzichtig, neuriënd. Hij zei nu niets meer, hij vroeg niets meer. Hij hield haar trillende lichaam vast en gek genoeg dacht hij aan het appartement in Kiev en aan haar vader. Even kon hij zich niet meer voorstellen dat hij daar ooit weer heen zou gaan om de vader van Yulia te charmeren. Even meende hij dat Kiev voorgoed tot het verleden behoorde en hij neuriede, alsof dat het enige was wat hij nog te zeggen had.

Beneden zaten de mannen. De discomuziek stond uit. Nelemans speelde op zijn gitaar en zong een zelfgemaakt lied, het ging weer over de eenzame brandweerman die vrolijk bleef maar toen hij de Pool zag met de nieuwe vrouw in zijn armen hield Nelemans op met spelen. Hij zette de gitaar tegen de muur.

Ze keken naar hem, de mannen van de C-ploeg, ze staarden naar hem en naar de nieuwe vrouw in zijn armen en de Pool wist niet waar hij heen moest. Hij begreep alles maar hij wist niet waar hij nu heen moest en wat hij moest zeggen. Neuriën deed hij ook al niet meer. Hij stond daar voor zijn vrienden, zijn collega's, de mannen met wie hij een leven had gedeeld. Uiteindelijk was het Nelemans die naar hem toe kwam en die zei: 'Het was een geintje.'

De Pool had het gevoel dat het nu nog stiller was dan daarnet, dat hij zichzelf hoorde ademen.

'Zeg jij nou ook gewoon hoe het is,' zei Nelemans, 'het was een geintje.'

De Pool zweeg en weer was het Nelemans die zei: 'Ze wilde het zelf.' Beckers kwam naast Nelemans staan en hij zei: 'Dit is wat ze wilde. Geloof me. Ze wilde het. We hebben het haar nog gevraagd. Is dit wat je wil, vroegen we. Ze knikte. Dat is wat ze wilde. Wie zijn wij om dan nee te zeggen?'

'Ze vroeg erom,' vulde Nelemans hem aan. 'Het was kennelijk lang niet meer gebeurd. Ja, dat is wat ze wilde.' Ze lachten nu besmuikt, de mannen van de C-ploeg. Ze lachten zoals ze na geintjes lachten. Ze waren een hechte ploeg met een bijzonder gevoel voor humor.

'Je moet niet zo schijnheilig kijken en je moet nu zeker niet schijnheilig gaan doen,' zei Beckers, 'alsof ik niet weet wat je met mijn vrouw hebt uitgespookt. We vergeten niets.' Haas en zijn vrouw waren er niet meer. Er waren nog maar een paar mannen over, ze keken naar hem in de groezelige sfeerverlichting die Nelemans hier had opgehangen, ze keken naar hem alsof hij een dier in een kooi was. De discobal draaide nog rond en de Pool begreep dat Beckers de waarheid had gesproken, de mannen van de C-ploeg vergaten niets. Nu was het de ploegchef die naar hem toe kwam en hij zei: 'Doe niet zo moeilijk. Jij bent vegetarisch. Jij bent een Pool. Je bent een vegetarische Pool. En je hebt in een kippenhok gewoond. Laat zien dat je bij ons hoort. Laat fucking zien dat je een van ons bent. Dit was een geintje, zij zelf vond het ook een geintje.'

De Pool zei niets. Hij keek naar zijn ploegchef, hij had niets te zeggen.

'Nou ja,' zei de ploegchef, 'ze zijn daar in Oekraïne vast wel wat gewend, geloof me.' De Pool staarde naar zijn ploegchef en het viel hem nu pas op dat hij een beetje grijs aan het worden was, ondanks het discolicht meende hij de grijze haren te kunnen zien. Pas toen de ploegchef zijn hand op de schouder van de Pool legde moest de Pool weer aan zijn nieuwe vrouw denken die hij nog altijd in zijn armen had, die hij naar huis moest brengen. En hij wist dat hij hier niet meer zou terugkomen, dat ze dood waren, de mannen van de C-ploeg, zijn mannen, zijn vrienden, ook zij waren nu dood, zo dood als de vrouw van Beckers was geweest, doder nog dan de vrouw van Beckers was geweest.

Nelemans zei nog: 'Je had erbij moeten zijn, daarboven.

Je had erbij moeten zijn. Het was een feestje.'

De Pool keek zijn ploegchef aan alsof er nog iets zou komen. Een dienstmededeling. De hand van de ploegchef rustte niet voor niets op de schouder van de Pool, er kwam nog iets. Hij voelde het gewicht van Yulia op zijn armen drukken, op zijn rug, maar het was een oefening, hij mocht haar niet neerzetten.

'Jij bent een Pool,' zei de ploegchef zachtjes. 'Een matennaaier ben je niet, toch? Jij bent geen matennaaier, Janowski. Dat is het enige wat ik nu even van je wil weten.'

'Nee,' zei de Pool. 'Ik ben geen matennaaier.' Daarop haalde de ploegchef de hand van de schouder van de Pool.

'Vroeger was dit normaal. We zijn een beetje doorgeslagen in wat allemaal niet meer mag.' In de stem van de ploegchef hoorde de Pool een aarzeling, een poging tot toenadering. Het was niet zo bedoeld. Dat probeerde de ploegchef te zeggen en zo zou de Pool ook weggaan, in de overtuiging dat hij ondanks alles bij de mannen van de C-ploeg hoorde, al was de C-ploeg nu dan verleden tijd.

Hij liep naar buiten met Yulia in zijn armen want dat hoorde bij de oefening, dat hij met haar naar huis zou lopen. Het was een lange weg maar hij zou zijn taak volbrengen. Het was het laatste examen, de uiteindelijke beproeving. 'We gaan,' zei hij tegen Yulia toen hij buiten voor de kazerne stond. 'Ik heb geen jas bij me maar ik zal snel lopen. Zo snel als het gaat. Dat je het niet te koud krijgt.'

De Pool liep snel, zo snel als hij kon. Soms moest hij bij een lantaarnpaal blijven staan om het gewicht anders te verdelen. Onderweg kwam hij mensen tegen die naar hem keken. Een enkeling riep zelfs iets, aangeschoten waren de mensen, vermoedelijk ook een feestje, overal waren feesten en borrels. Dat zei hij tegen Yulia: 'They are drunk.'

De Pool zelf was niet meer aangeschoten, hij was broodnuchter. 'We zijn er bijna,' zei hij tegen Yulia maar nog altijd zweeg ze en hij had het gevoel dat ze nooit meer zou spreken. Hij die altijd had gemeend dat spreken overschat was vond dat moeilijk, hij die zo naar de stilte had verlangd miste het spreken nu al, nu het plotseling was afgelopen. Af en toe moest er iets worden gezegd, al was het onbeduidend. Ze mocht ook zingen. Neurie dan, wilde hij zeggen. Neurie, Yulia. Hij zweeg. En opnieuw bleef hij staan, leunend tegen een boom dit keer, om het gewicht van zijn nieuwe vrouw anders over zijn armen te verdelen. Ze bibberde van de kou. 'Ja,' zei hij, 'ik had een taxi willen nemen maar het is anders gelopen dan we hadden verwacht, niet? Het ging anders.'

Hij moest haar neerzetten en dat deed hij, het moest, hij hield haar niet meer. Ze bleef staan en ze staarde voor zich uit. Een paar keer riep hij haar maar hoewel ze vlak naast hem stond reageerde ze niet op zijn geroep. Ze was er niet. Hij tilde haar weer op. Eigenlijk was ze niet heel zwaar, ze was een kleine vrouw, een kleine, frêle vrouw.

Hij liep door zonder nog aan de C-ploeg te denken of aan zichzelf en zijn nieuwe vrouw, alleen nog aan het lopen dacht hij, aan zijn spieren, het lichaam dat hij in zijn armen hield, hij wist dat dit het lichaam van zijn nieuwe vrouw was maar zo voelde het niet meer. Het kon het lichaam zijn van iedereen die hij had gered.

Thuis legde hij Yulia op de bank, hij bedekte haar met dekens die hij van boven haalde. Eerst een, toen twee en ten slotte een derde uit de kamer van de overgebleven jongen want het bibberen hield niet op. De Pool had geen idee hoe laat het was, hij zette thee. 'Drink,' zei hij tegen Yulia. 'Drink.'

Ze nam kleine slokjes van de hete thee en het bibberen leek minder te worden. Hij zat naast haar op de grond en ze zwegen, de Pool en zijn vrouw. Hij had geen idee hoelang ze daar hadden gezeten tot ze vroeg: 'A gaintje, what's that?'

'Een geintje,' zei de Pool. 'Gein-tje. Een geintje. That's, how can I explain it. A joke. A little joke.'

'A joke. So I am a joke?'

'No. Not for me.'

'Where were you, where were you all the time? I called you.'

'I was downstairs, I was talking to Beckers, I was talking to Haas, I was peeing.'

'You were peeing. Yes, that's important.'

'I was looking for you.'

'Are you going to the police?'

De Pool stond op, hij begon te ijsberen door de kamer. 'Yes,' zei hij, 'we can go to the police. Tomorrow. They will call me a matennaaier, but that's fine.'

'What's matnaler?' vroeg ze.

'Maten-naaier. Betrayer. That's a betrayer. They were my friends. They were my family. They were my men.' Hij zei: 'Wat er vanavond is gebeurd dat is slecht, dat wil ik niet goedpraten maar in wezen zijn zij goede mannen, Yulia. Geloof me, ik was een van hen. Ik ben altijd een van hen geweest. Toen Borys stierf toen zeiden ze: we slepen je erdoorheen. Ik hoorde bij de C-ploeg, meer dan waar dan ook bij. Ze waren mijn familie.'

Ze was even stil en hij zag hoe ze naar hem keek. 'What's a matennaaier? I don't understand.'

De Pool hurkte bij haar neer. 'Difficult to explain. A betrayer. That's a matennaaier. I love you. Do you need a doctor? Do you want to take a shower? What do you want?'

'I don't know.'

Hij streelde haar been.

'So I am a joke?' vroeg ze weer. 'A gaintje. Are you going to take revenge for the joke, for the gaintje?'

'No,' zei hij na een korte aarzeling. 'I don't believe in revenge. No, that's not good, revenge. My men. They like jokes. Sometimes they are too... Too aggressive in their jokes. Just too aggressive, they don't know where to stop.'

Ze was even stil en zei: 'Language is not a problem. You are not a man, that is the problem.'

Hij ging naast haar op de bank zitten. Hij veegde over zijn voorhoofd maar er was geen zweet. 'I'm not a man. You are right. I'm not a man. But we can solve this. We can solve this. What do you want besides revenge? Tell me what you want, anything. It sounds strange but I want to give my life for you. They were my friends, you understand.' Hij pakte haar handen, haar koude handen, hij hield ze vast, hij wreef ze warm en nog een keer vroeg hij wat ze wilde, wat ze dan wilde, wat ze in godsnaam wilde, dat ze dat moest zeggen, dat haar wensen zijn wensen waren, haar verlangens zijn verlangens, tot ze zei: 'I want to die. I want to die in my own country.'

Toen begon de Pool weer te ijsberen, hij liep rondjes door de woonkamer tot het licht werd. Hij zei: 'Dat denk je nu, straks denk je er heel anders over. Nu denk je dat. Straks zie je het anders.'

Ook zei hij: 'Niet sterven. Doe maar niet. De dood komt vanzelf, die hoef je niet te ontbieden.'

Zo sprak hij, zo bleef hij spreken tot hij merkte dat hij weer geroepen werd. Het was zover. Sterker dan de vorige keer dat hij de stem had gehoord die hem maande, die hem riep, die hem lokte. Hij doorzag alles, hij begreep alles. Nu wist hij voor welke liefde hij zijn laatste examen had afgelegd.

De Pool ging naar boven en daar belde hij zijn ex maar ze nam niet op. 'Je moet onmiddellijk komen,' sprak hij in. 'Je moet je bekommeren om Yulia, ze ligt hier op de bank. Er is iets gebeurd. Kom je? Wil je dat alsjeblieft voor me doen?'

Toen hij weer naar beneden ging zag hij dat Yulia sliep. Hij ging naast haar zitten en toen ze haar ogen opende pakte hij teder haar handen vast, wetend dat hij ze misschien nooit meer zou kunnen vastpakken. 'Everybody has secrets,' zei hij. 'You are right. There's no language for secrets. They die with you. They die with us. But that's good. You don't know my secrets, I don't know your secrets. The secrets of the boy. We don't know them. And that's good. Better. Much better.'

Hij ademde diep in. 'Het is beter zo. Wat zouden we weten als we het wisten?' zei hij. 'Niets. We zouden nog steeds niets weten.'

Ze keek hem aan, niet eens bijzonder treurig meer, gelaten, boven haar oog zat nog altijd opgedroogd bloed. Het was ook dik daar, opgezwollen.

De Pool stond op.

'Where are you going?' vroeg ze.

'I'm going, my God is calling me. I can't help it. But my ex will be here soon. Together with het menselijk verlengstuk. Human... Human. Extension. They will take care of you. Better than I can. I cannot.'

'I understand. Not a man. You are going. Now?'

Hij knielde naast haar neer en hij zei: 'I'm sorry but He is calling me. I'm not a man indeed and you want to... You want to go. You want to go back. He needs me, so much more than you need me.'

Ze knikte en ze zei: 'He needs you more and I want to die anyway.'

Hij wachtte even of het zou verdwijnen, de lokroep, de stemmen die hem maanden te gaan. Maar ze verdwenen niet, ze werden luider.

'I can't help it. It's stronger. Stronger than everything.' En hij streelde haar waar hij kon maar haar intieme delen raakte hij niet aan. De Pool zei nog dat hij zo veel van haar hield, zo vreselijk veel, meer dan ze zich kon voorstellen, meer dan hij zich ooit had kunnen voorstellen maar dat het sterker was. Het. 'Het' zei hij. En zij zei niets meer. Hij streelde en hij streelde tot hij merkte dat ze rustig was geworden, dat ze sliep.

Toen ging hij. Het huis verliet hij zoals je een huis verlaat dat op instorten staat. Hij liep in de richting van de liefde die niet van deze wereld was.

Soms hield hij zich nog vast aan een boom of een lantaarnpaal. Er waren tegenstrijdige verlangens in hem. Iets in hem wilde er niet heen, iets in hem stribbelde tegen, iets in hem wilde terug naar Yulia, terug naar de overgebleven jongen, naar de liefde van deze wereld, elke keer rukte hij zich los, want de lokroep van de liefde die niet van deze wereld was, die lokroep was veel sterker. De onverdraaglijke liefde, de liefde die ervoor zorgde dat je jezelf nooit meer hoefde te redden. Dat je niemand meer hoefde te redden.

Hij rukte zich los van takken, boomstammen en lantaarnpalen. Steeds weer klemde hij zich vast en steeds weer rukte hij zich los. Hij verstopte zich in struiken, onder banken en in portieken, maar steeds weer werd hij gevonden en telkens werd hij geroepen. Zou zijn oudste jongen ook zo geroepen zijn?

Hij dwaalde door het bos tot hij uitgeput tegen een boom moest leunen. Hij keek naar de bladeren op de grond. Hij meende mieren te zien, allemaal mieren. Het krioelde ervan. Overal mieren.

Toen herinnerde hij zich de schoenendoos die hij voor de overgebleven jongen had gemaakt. Jurek wist niet waar die stond. Hij moest hem aan Jurek geven, vandaag nog, de schoenendoos met de restanten van Borys, het samengevatte leven, het leven dat in één schoenendoos paste.

Eerst de schoenendoos, dan de rest. Voor hij terugkeerde naar zijn plek in het hok moest dat gebeuren.

De levenden riepen hem nu, zo krachtig, zo jammerlijk, zo hartverscheurend. Yulia, zijn jongen, zijn ex, zelfs het menselijk verlengstuk riep hem, ze waren onvermoeibaar, de levenden, onvermoeibaar en ontroostbaar. Hij moest omdraaien, hij moest terug.

Kijkend naar de mieren scheurde hij zijn bloemetjesblouse van zijn lijf. De Pool knielde en hij fluisterde: ‘Doe met me wat u wilt, Vader. En ik weet wat U wilt, ik weet precies wat U wilt. U bent namelijk net zo’n smeerlap als ik. We kunnen elkaar niet ontkomen, God. We zijn voor elkaar gemaakt. Het kippenhok is overal.’

# Dankwoord

Dank aan Richard Brand en Ton Keulen voor hun introductie in de wereld van de brandweer.

Dank aan broeder Johannes en de abt van Abdij Lilbosch.

Dank aan Karel Lesman.

Dank aan Andrea Prins.

Speciale dank aan Fedja en Janne.